ORGANIZATIONS
BEHAVIOR · STRUCTURE · PROCESSES

ORGANIZATIONS
BEHAVIOR · STRUCTURE · PROCESSES

James L. Gibson
Professor of Business Administration
University of Kentucky

John M. Ivancevich
Hugh Roy and Lillie Cranz Cullen Chair
and Professor of Organizational
Behavior and Management
University of Houston

James H. Donnelly, Jr.
Professor of Business Administration
University of Kentucky

1985   Fifth Edition
BUSINESS PUBLICATIONS, INC.   Plano, Texas   75075

This textbook is accompanied by a Student Workbook/Study Guide, published by Business Publications, Inc. and available through your college bookstore. The Study Guide is designed to enhance your learning experience in this course by offering additional supplementary material and review questions for self-examination or extra credit work. If the bookstore does not have the Study Guide in stock, please ask your bookstore manager to order a copy for you.

ISBN 0-256-03265-3

Library of Congress Catalog Card No. 84–71427

Printed in the United States of America

5 6 7 8 9 0 K 2 1 0 9 8 7 6

Preface

Objectives of This Edition

The objective of the fifth edition of *Organizations: Behavior, Structure, Processes* is to present a realistic, relevant, and thorough view of people working in organizations. The text accomplishes this objective by providing theories, research results, and applications that apply to people in organizations. Realism, relevance, and thoroughness are the targets around which the chapters, cases, and exercises are developed. Over the history of *Organizations: Behavior, Structure, and Processes,* the student and instructor feedback that we have received indicates that we have accomplished what we intended.

A theme that is introduced early and carried throughout the book is that the effective management of organizational behavior requires an understanding of theory, research, and practice. Given this theme, our task was to interpret organizational behavior theory and research so that students could comprehend the three characteristics common to all organizations—behavior, structure, processes—as affected by actions of managers. Accordingly, we have illustrated how organizational behavior theory leads to research and how both theory and research provide the basic foundation for practical applications in business firms, hospitals, educational institutions, and governmental agencies.

New Material in This Edition

The fifth edition includes important new subject matter as well as additional learning approaches.

First, *power and politics* are the subjects of a new chapter written for this edition (Chapter 10). Power and politics are two topics that deserved more intensive treatment than they were given in previous editions. The new chapter is based on the most recent theory, research, and application available in the literature. To make room for the new chapter, several chapters were combined into a single chapter.

Second, material in existing chapters was updated. Material on

*expectancy theory, creativity and innovation, punishment, social sup-
port, ERG theory, rewards, groupthink, organizational culture, social
support networks, attribution approaches to leadership, quality of work-
life, socialization, the MAPS approach to organizational design,* and
other topics was added or expanded in appropriate chapters. In all
cases, the new material complements existing material. A listing of
additional references at the end of each chapter provides current
sources for readers who desire more in-depth discussions of these and
other topics.

Third, experiential exercises were introduced in the third edition.
Positive reaction to these exercises in the last two editions has encouraged us to increase the number of experiential exercises in this edition
to *14.* We have also retained the most requested and popular end-
of-chapter cases that were included in the previous edition and added
several new ones, for a total of *18.* Each case has been written to
emphasize a particular issue or managerial technique. The cases cover
a variety of different types and sizes of organizations and include problems of all levels of management. Feedback on the longer cases included in Appendix B was very positive, and two of these cases have
been retained in this edition. "Hovey and Beard Company" and "A
Collapse of Shelving and Its Unusual Aftermath" have been added
to the cases in Appendix B.

Fourth, the "Organizations: Close-Ups" have been enthusiastically
received by students and instructors. The Close-Ups report actual applications of the concepts and theories presented in the chapter. They
appear at the *exact* point in the text discussion where the concept
or theory is being discussed. They were extremely well received in
classroom testing. Most of the chapters in this edition contain three
Close-Ups. Through the identification of actual managerial applications of text materials, the gap between the classroom and the real
world can hopefully be narrowed.

Fifth, we have added a number of self-report questionnaires for
the reader to complete. These are used to get the reader involved
and to have him or her take a close look at personal style, attitudes,
and behavior patterns. Norms and averages are provided so that the
reader can make comparisons.

Sixth, the supplements for the text are thorough and should be
secured from the publisher. The student and instructor were both
considered in preparing these supplements, which add to the student's
understanding and the instructor's ability to teach an exciting course.
We feel that the Instructor's Manual, Lecture Resource Manual,
Transparencies, Test Bank, Computerized Test Service, and Readings
in Organizations are excellent for both in-class and out-of-class assignments.

In addition to the practical relevance that the experiential exercises, cases, Close-Ups, and self-report questionnaires contribute, the text discussion itself carries out our intention to interpret the practical significance of theory and research. Of course, many issues in organizational behavior are unresolved and alternative theories compete. In these instances, issues are presented and readers are encouraged to consider the relative strengths of each. Whenever appropriate, we acknowledge the tenuousness of both contemporary theory and practice.

To heighten reader interest and to highlight the contingency nature of much of the subject matter, each chapter begins by introducing an appropriate "Organizational Issue for Debate." The Organizational Issues for Debate are short presentations of arguments for and arguments against a popular principle, theory, or application. Some of the issues are new, and others have been retained and expanded from the previous edition.

Framework of This Edition

The sequence in which the content of the book is organized is based on the three characteristics cited above as common to all organizations: *behavior, structure, and processes.* This order of presentation has been followed in response to the requests of numerous adopters, who found it easier to discuss the material on human behavior first, followed by the material on structure and processes. It should be mentioned, however, that in this edition each of the major parts has been written as a self-contained unit and can be presented in whatever sequence the instructor prefers.

The text is presented in six major parts:

Part One, Introduction, consists of two chapters that together introduce the subject matter. Chapter 1 presents the significance of organizations as a means by which societies produce and distribute goods and services and introduces the reader to the format and rationale for the book. Chapter 2 develops important ideas concerning the roles of management in achieving effective individual, group, and organizational performance.

Part Two, Behavior within Organizations: The Individual, includes five chapters that focus on *individual behavior in organizations.* Separate chapters are devoted to individual characteristics and differences (Chapter 3); content and process motivation theories and applications (Chapters 4 and 5); rewards, punishment, and discipline (Chapter 6); and individual stress (Chapter 7).

Part Three, Behavior within Organizations: Groups and Interpersonal Influence, focuses on *group behavior and interpersonal influence in organizations.* It consists of four chapters that focus on group behavior (Chapter 8), intergroup behavior (Chapter 9), power and politics (Chapter 10), and leadership (Chapter 11).

Part Four, The Structure of Organizations, includes three chapters that focus on the *structure of organizations.* Separate chapters are devoted to the anatomy of organizations (Chapter 12), job design (Chapter 13), and organizational design (Chapter 14). The latter two follow a micro (job design)–macro (organizational design) sequence.

Part Five, The Processes of Organizations, includes four chapters dealing with *organizational processes.* Chapters 15 and 16, which deal with communications and decision making, begin this part. The rationale is that these two organizational processes are fundamental to the processes of performance evaluation (Chapter 17) and socialization and careers (Chapter 18).

Part Six, Developing Organizational Effectiveness, focuses on *developing organizational effectiveness.* It is a two-chapter sequence that presents the theory of organizational development in the context of an integrated model and then describes and evaluates the more widely used OD techniques.

The book concludes with a short epilogue (Chapter 21), and two appendixes. Appendix A is Procedures and Techniques for Studying *Organizations: Behavior, Structure, Processes.* New in this Appendix is a discussion of qualitative research methods. Some of the material for Appendix A was in Chapter 1 of the previous edition. We believe that it is now convenient for the reader to examine research procedures and techniques on organizational behavior by referring directly to the Appendix A material. Appendix B contains four comprehensive cases that can be used to integrate text materials.

Contributors to This Edition

The authors wish to acknowledge the contributions of reviewers of previous editions whose suggestions are reflected throughout the present edition. For this edition, we are expecially indebted to John L. Berton, Louisiana State University at Shreveport; Gerald Biberman, University of Scranton; Richard S. Blackburn, University of North Carolina, Chapel Hill; Carmen Caruana, St. John's University; Dick Daft, Texas A&M University; Sara M. Freedman, University of Houston; Cynthia V. Fukami, State University of New York at Buffalo; Arthur G. Jago, University of Houston; Richard E. Kopelman, Baruch College–The City University of New York; Mitchell McCorcle, Case Western Reserve University; Samuel Rabinowitz, New York University; Arnon E. Reichers, The Ohio State University; and Robert Zawacki, University of Colorado at Colorado Springs.

A special thank-you is due the Fellows at Harvard Business School, Margaret Fenn of the University of Washington, and Charles Langdon of the University of New Orleans, who permitted us to use cases. We also wish to thank Vic Vroom of Yale University and Art Jago of the University of Houston for permitting us to use their creative ideas and cases to develop a part of our leadership presentation.

Finally, Richard Furst, Dean of the College of Business and Economics, University of Kentucky, and A. Benton Cocanougher, Dean of the College of Business Administration, University of Houston, provided much support for our efforts. Judy Holladay and Karen Lytwyn provided immeasurable assistance in preparing the manuscript.

James L. Gibson
John M. Ivancevich
James H. Donnelly, Jr.

Contents

ORGANIZATIONS
BEHAVIOR · STRUCTURE · PROCESSES

INTRODUCTION

Chapter 1

After completing Chapter 1, you should be able to:

Define the field of organizational behavior.

Describe the role of organizations in our society.

Discuss the authors' assumptions concerning organizational behavior.

Compare the elements of the model for managing organizations (Figure 1–2).

Identify the major characteristics of the field of organizational behavior.

The Study of Organizations

Organizations permeate all levels of our lives. We come into contact with many of them daily. In fact, most of us probably spend most of our lives in—or affected by—organizations. We expend sizable amounts of our time as members of work, school, social, civic, and church organizations. Or we are involved as employees, students, clients, patients, and citizens of organizations.

At some times, these organizations appear to be efficiently run and responsive to our needs, and at other times they are extremely frustrating and irritating. We may even think they are harassing us. Such personal experiences in or with organizations may have already helped form our sense of what it means to be "organized."

While your attitudes about organizations may be positive or negative, what you understand about them so far can provide a good foundation for examining organizations in a more systematic manner.

Organizations exist for one reason: They can accomplish things that we cannot accomplish individually. Thus, whether the goal is to make a profit, provide education, foster religion, improve health care, put a man or woman on the moon, get a candidate elected, or build a new football stadium, organizations get the job done. **Organizations** are characterized by their *goal-directed behavior.* They pursue goals and objectives that can be achieved more efficiently and effectively by the concerted action of individuals *and* groups. *The purpose of this book is to help you learn how to manage individuals and groups as resources of organizations.*

Organizations are essential to the way our society operates. In industry, education, health care, and defense, organizations have created impressive gains for our standard of living and our worldwide image. The size of the organizations with which you deal daily should illustrate the tremendous political, economic, and social powers they separately possess. For example, your college has much economic, political, and social power in its community. If a large firm announced that it was closing its plant in your community, the resulting impact might be devastating economically. On the other hand, if IBM announced that it was opening a plant in your community, the impact would probably be very positive.

Organizations are, however, much more than means for providing goods and services.[1] They create the settings in which most of us spend our lives. In this respect, they have profound influence on our behavior. However, because large-scale organizations have developed only in recent times, we are just now beginning to recognize the necessity

organizations
Entities that enable society to pursue accomplishments that cannot be achieved by individuals acting alone.

---

[1] See L. F. Urwick, "That Word Organization," *Academy of Management Review,* January 1976, pp. 89–91.

for studying them. Researchers have just begun the process of developing ways to study the behavior of people in organizations.

THE IMPORTANCE OF STUDYING ORGANIZATIONAL BEHAVIOR

Why do employees behave as they do in organizations? Why is one individual or group more productive than another? Why do managers continually seek ways to design jobs and delegate authority? These and similar questions are important to the relatively new field of study known as **organizational behavior.** Understanding the behavior of people in organizations has become increasingly important as management concerns—such as employee productivity, the quality of work life, job stress, and career progression—continue to make front-page news.

organizational behavior
The study of individuals and groups within organizational settings.

The field of organizational behavior can be defined as:

> The study of human behavior, attitudes, and performance within an organizational setting; drawing on theory, methods, and principles from such disciplines as psychology, sociology, and cultural anthropology to learn about *individual* perceptions, values, learning capacities, and actions while working in *groups* and within the total *organization;* analyzing the external environment's effect on the organization and its human resources, missions, objectives, and strategies.

This view of organizational behavior illustrates a number of points. First, organizational behavior is a *way of thinking*. Behavior is viewed as operating at individual, group, and organizational levels. This approach suggests that when studying organizational behavior, we must identify clearly the level of analysis being used—individual, group, and/or organizational. Second, organizational behavior is an *interdisciplinary field*. This means that it utilizes principles, models, theories, and methods from existing disciplines. The study of organizational behavior is not a discipline or a generally accepted science with an established theoretical foundation. It is a field that only now is beginning to grow and develop in stature and impact. Third, there is a distinctly *humanistic orientation* within organizational behavior. People and their attitudes, perceptions, learning capacities, feelings, and goals are of major importance. Fourth, the field of organizational behavior is *performance-oriented*. Why is performance low or high? How can performance be improved? Can training enhance on-the-job performance? These are important issues facing practicing managers. Fifth, the *external environment* is seen as having significant impact on organizational behavior. Sixth, since the field of organizational behavior relies heavily on recognized disciplines, the role of the *scientific method* is deemed important in studying variables and relationships. Finally

FIGURE 1–1

Major Characteristics of the Field of Organizational Behavior

Characteristic	Focal Point
Three levels of analysis	Individuals, groups, and the organization are equally important in studying and understanding behavior in organizations.
Interdisciplinary nature	Principles, concepts, and models from the behavioral sciences—psychology, sociology, and cultural anthropology—are utilized.
Humanistic orientation	The importance of attitudes and perceptions in understanding behavior within organizations is stressed.
Performance orientation	Continual emphasis is placed on a search for ways to improve, sustain, and encourage effective performance.
Recognition of external environmental forces	The identification and continual monitoring of external environmental forces are important for improving organizational behavior.
Use of the scientific method	Whenever possible, scientific methods are used to supplement experience and intuition.
Application orientation	Knowledge developed in the field of organizational behavior must be useful to practicing managers when they confront individual, group, and organizational problems.

the field has a distinctive *applications orientation;* it is concerned with providing useful answers to questions which arise in the context of managing organizations. Figure 1–1 summarizes the main characteristics of the field of organizational behavior.

To help you learn how to manage individuals and groups as resources of organizations, this book focuses on the behavior of *individuals, groups,* and *organizations.* Developing the model presented in this book required the use of several assumptions. These assumptions are explained briefly in the following paragraphs, which precede the model.[2]

Organizational Behavior Follows Principles of Human Behavior

The effectiveness of any organization is influenced greatly by human behavior. People are a resource common to all organizations. There is no such thing as a "peopleless" organization.

---

[2] See Andrew Dubrin, *Fundamentals of Organizational Behavior* (New York: Pergamon Press, 1978), chap. 1; and James R. Meindl, "The Abundance of Solutions: Some Thoughts for Theoretical and Practical Solution Seekers," *Administrative Science Quarterly,* December 1982, pp. 670–85.

One important principle of psychology is that each person is different. Each person has unique perceptions, personalities, and life experiences; different capabilities for learning and stress; and different attitudes, beliefs, and aspiration levels. To be effective, managers of organizations must view each employee or member as a unique embodiment of all these behavioral factors.

Organizations as Social Systems

The relationships among individuals and groups in organizations create expectations for the behavior of individuals. These expectations result in certain roles that must be performed. Some people must perform the role of leader, while others play the role of follower. Middle managers must perform both roles because they have both a superior and subordinates. Organizations have systems of authority, status, and power, and people in organizations have varying needs from each system. Groups in organizations also have a powerful impact on individual behavior and on organizational performance.

Many Factors Shape Organizational Behavior

Our behavior in any situation involves the interaction of our personal characteristics and the characteristics of the situation. Thus, identifying all of the factors is time-consuming and difficult; frequently, it is impossible.

contingency approach
An approach to management that believes there is no one best way to manage in every situation but that managers must find different ways that fit different situations.

To help us identify the important managerial factors in organizational behavior, however, we use the **contingency** (or *situational*) **approach.** The basic idea of the contingency approach is that there is no one best way to manage. A method that is very effective in one situation may not even work in others. The contingency approach has grown in popularity over the last two decades because research has shown that, given certain characteristics of a job and certain characteristics of the people doing the job, some management practices work better than others. Thus, when facing a problem, a manager using the contingency approach does not assume that a particular approach will work. Instead, he or she diagnoses the characteristics of the individuals and groups involved, the organizational structure, and his or her own leadership style before deciding on a solution.

How Structure and Process Affect Organizational Behavior

structure
A blueprint of the organization that

An organization's **structure** is the formal pattern of how its people and jobs are grouped. Structure is often illustrated by an organization chart. **Process** refers to activities that give life to the organization

indicates how people and jobs are grouped together. Structure is illustrated by the organization chart.

processes
Those activities that breathe life into the organization structure. Common processes are communication, performance evaluation, decision making, socialization, and career development.

chart. Communication, decision making, performance evaluation, socialization, and career development are processes in organizations. Sometimes, understanding process problems such as breakdowns in communication and decision making or a poorly constructed performance evaluation system will result in a more accurate understanding of organizational behavior than will simply examining structural arrangements.

Effective managers know what to look for in a work situation and how to understand what they find. Therefore, managers must develop diagnostic and action abilities. They must be trained to identify conditions symptomatic of a problem requiring further attention. A manager's problem indicators include declining profits, declining quantity/ or quality of work, increases in absenteeism or lateness, and negative employee attitudes. Each of these problems is an issue of organizational behavior.

A MODEL FOR MANAGING ORGANIZATIONS: BEHAVIOR, STRUCTURE, PROCESSES

A model for understanding organizational behavior is presented in Figure 1–2. It shows how the many topics covered in this book can be combined into a meaningful study of organizational behavior. The model will appear again at the beginning of each major section of the book to highlight the upcoming section and to show how it relates to the remainder of the book.

The Organization's Environment

Organizations exist in societies and are created by societies. Figure 1–2 draws attention to the relationships between organizations and the society which creates and sustains them. Within a society, many factors impinge upon an organization, and management must be responsive to them. Every organization must respond to the needs of its customers or clients, to legal and political constraints, and to economic and technological changes and developments. The model reflects environmental forces interacting within the organization, and throughout our discussion of each aspect of the model, the relevant environmental factors will be identified and examined.

Behavior within Organizations: The Individual

Individual performance is the foundation of organizational performance. Understanding individual behavior is therefore critical for effective management, as illustrated in this account:

Ted Johnson has been a field representative for a major drug manufacturer since he graduated from college seven years ago. He makes daily
calls on physicians, hospitals, clinics, and pharmacies as a representative
of the many drugs his firm manufactures. During his time in the field,
prescription rates and sales for all of his firm's major drugs have increased and he has won three national sales awards given by the firm.
Yesterday, Ted was promoted to sales manager for a seven-state region.
He will no longer be selling but instead will be managing 15 other representatives. Ted accepted the promotion because he believes he knows
how to motivate and lead salespeople. He commented, "I know the personality of the salesperson. They are special people. I know what it
takes to get them to perform. Remember, I am one. I know their values

FIGURE 1–2

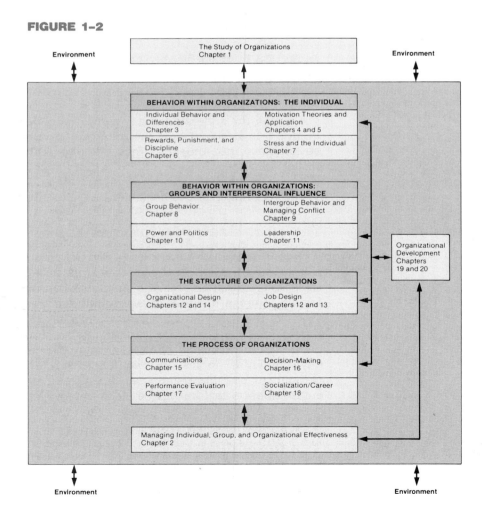

and attitudes and what it takes to motivate them. I know I can motivate a sales force."

In his new job, Ted Johnson will be trying to maximize the individual performances of 15 sales representatives. In doing so, he will be dealing with several facets of individual behavior. Our model includes four important influences on individual behavior and motivation in organizations: individual characteristics, individual motivation, rewards, and stress.

Individual Characteristics. Because organizational performance depends on individual performance, managers such as Ted Johnson must have more than a passing knowledge of the determinants of individual performance. Psychology and social psychology contribute a great deal of relevant knowledge about the relationships among attitudes, perceptions, personality, values, and individual performance. Individual capacity for learning and for coping with stress has become more and more important in recent years. Managers cannot ignore the necessity for acquiring and acting on knowledge of the individual characteristics of both their subordinates and themselves.

Individual Motivation. Motivation and ability to work interact to determine performance. Motivation theory attempts to explain and predict how the behavior of individuals is aroused, started, sustained, and stopped. Unlike Ted Johnson, not all managers and behavioral scientists agree on what is the "best" theory of motivation. In fact, motivation is so complex that it may be impossible to have an all-encompassing theory of how it occurs. However, managers must still try to understand it. They must be concerned with motivation because they must be concerned with performance.

Rewards. One of the most powerful influences on individual performance is an organization's reward system. Management can use rewards (or punishment) to increase performance by present employees. It can also use rewards to attract skilled employees to join the organization. Pay checks, raises, and bonuses are important aspects of the reward system, but they are not the only aspects. Ted Johnson makes this point very clear in the account when he states, "I know what it takes to get them to perform." Performance of the work itself can provide employees with rewards, particularly if job performance leads to a sense of personal responsibility, autonomy, and meaningfulness.

Stress. Stress is an important result of the interaction between the job and the individual. Stress in this context is a state of imbalance within an individual that often manifests itself in such symptoms as insomnia, excessive perspiration, nervousness, and irritability. Whether stress is positive or negative depends on the individual's tolerance level. People react differently to situations that outwardly seem to induce the same physical and psychological demands. Some individuals respond positively through increased motivation and commitment to finish the job. Other individuals respond less desirably by turning to such outlets as alcoholism and drug abuse. Hopefully, Ted Johnson will respond positively to the stresses of his new job.

Management's responsibility in managing stress has not been clearly defined, but there is growing evidence that organizations are devising programs to deal with work-induced stress.

Behavior within Organizations: Groups and Interpersonal Influence

Group behavior and interpersonal influence are also powerful forces affecting organizational performance. The effects of these forces are illustrated in the following account:

> Kelly McCaul spent 2½ years as a teller in the busiest branch of First National Bank. During that time she developed close personal friendships with her co-workers. These friendships extended off the job as well. Kelly and her friends formed a wine-and-cheese club as well as the top team in the bankwide bowling league. In addition, several of them took ski trips together each winter.
>
> Two months ago Kelly was promoted to branch manager. She was excited about the new challenge but was a little surprised that she got the promotion since some other likely candidates in the branch had been with the bank longer. She began the job with a great deal of optimism and believed her friends would be genuinely happy for her and supportive of her efforts. However, since she became branch manager, things haven't seemed quite the same. Kelly can't spend nearly as much time with her friends because she is often away from the branch attending management meetings at the main office. Because of a training course that she must attend two evenings a week, she has missed the last two wine-and-cheese club meetings. And she senses that some of her friends have been acting a little differently toward her lately.
>
> Recently, Kelly said, "I didn't know that being part of the management team could make that much difference. Frankly, I never really thought about it. I guess I was naive. I'm seeing a totally different perspective of the business and have to deal with problems I never knew about."

Kelly McCaul's promotion has made her a member of more than one group. In addition to being a member of her old group of friends at the branch, she is also a member of the management team. She is finding out that group behavior and expectations have a strong impact on individual behavior and interpersonal influence. Our model includes four important aspects of group and interpersonal influence on organizational behavior: group behavior, intergroup behavior and conflict, power and politics, and leadership.

Group Behavior. Groups form because of managerial action, but also because of individual efforts. Managers create work groups to carry out assigned jobs and tasks. Such groups, created by managerial decisions, are termed *formal groups*. The group that Kelly McCaul manages at her branch is a group of this kind.

Groups also form as a consequence of employees' actions. Such groups, termed *informal groups,* develop around common interests and friendships. The wine-and-cheese club at Kelly McCaul's branch is an informal group. Though not sanctioned by management, groups of this kind can affect organizational and individual performance. The effect can be positive or negative, depending on the intention of the group's members. If the group at Kelly's branch decided informally to slow the work pace, this norm would exert pressure on individuals who wanted to remain a part of the group. Effective managers recognize the consequences of individuals' need for affiliation.

Intergroup Behavior and Conflict. As groups function and interact with other groups, they develop their own unique set of characteristics, including structure, cohesiveness, roles, norms, and processes. As a result, groups may cooperate or compete with other groups, and intergroup competition can lead to conflict. If the management of Kelly's bank instituted an incentive program with cash bonuses to the branch bringing in the most new customers, this might lead to competition and conflict among the branches. While conflict among groups can have beneficial results for an organization, too much or the wrong kinds of intergroup conflict can have very negative results. Thus, managing intergroup conflict is an important aspect of managing organizational behavior.

Power and Politics. Power is the ability to get someone to do something you want done or to make things happen in the way you want them to happen. Many people in our society are very uncomfortable with the concept of power. Some are very offended by it. This is because the essence of power is control over others. To many Americans, this is an offensive thought. However, power is a reality in organizations. Managers derive power from both organizational and individual sources. Kelly McCaul has power by virtue of her position in the formal hierarchy of the bank. She controls performance evaluations and salary increases. However, she may also have power because her co-workers respect and admire the abilities and expertise she possesses. Managers must therefore become comfortable with the concept of power as a reality in organizations and managerial roles.

Leadership. Leaders exist within all organizations. Like the bank's Kelly McCaul, they may be found in formal groups, but they may also be found in informal groups. They may be managers or nonmanagers. The importance of effective leadership for obtaining individual, group, and organizational performance is so critical that it has stimulated a great deal of effort to determine the causes of such leadership. Some people believe that effective leadership depends on traits and certain behaviors—separately and in combination; other people believe that one leadership style is effective in all situations; still others believe that each situation requires a specific leadership style.

The Structure of Organizations

To work effectively in organizations, managers must have a clear understanding of the organizational structure. Viewing an organization chart on a piece of paper or framed on a wall, one sees only a configuration of positions, job duties, and lines of authority among the parts of an organization. However, organizational structures can be far more complex than that, as illustrated in the following account:

> Dr. John Rice was recently appointed dean of the business school at a major university. Prior to arriving on campus, Rice spent several weeks studying the funding, programs, faculty, students, and organizational structure of the business school. He was trying to develop a list of priorities for things that he believed would require immediate attention during his first year as dean. The president of the university had requested that he have such a list of priorities available when he arrived on campus.
>
> During his first official meeting with the president, Rice was asked the question he fully expected to be asked: "What will be your number one priority?" Rice replied: "Although money is always a problem, I believe the most urgent need is to reorganize the business school. At present, students can major in only one of two departments, accounting and business administration. The accounting department has 20 faculty members. The business administration department has 43 faculty members, including 15 in marketing, 16 in management, and 12 in finance. I foresee a college with four departments—accounting, management, marketing, and finance—each with its own chairperson. First, I believe such a structure will enable us to better meet the needs of our students. Specifically, it will facilitate the development of programs of majors in each of the four areas. Students must be able to major in one of the four functional areas if they are going to be prepared adequately for the job market. Finally, I believe such an organizational structure will enable us to more easily recruit faculty, since they will be joining a group with interests similar to their own."

As this account indicates, an organization's structure is the formal pattern of activities and interrelationships among the various subunits of the organization. Our model includes two important aspects of organizational structure: job design and organizational design.

Job Design. Job design refers to the process by which managers specify the contents, methods, and relationships of jobs to satisfy both organizational and individual requirements. Dr. Rice will have to define the content and duties of the newly created chairperson position and the relationship of that position to the dean's office and to the individual faculty members in each department.

Organizational Design.   Organizational design refers to the overall organization structure. Dr. Rice plans to alter the basic structure of the business school. The result of his efforts will be a new *structure* of tasks and authority relationships that he believes will channel the behavior of individuals and groups toward higher levels of performance in the business school.

The Processes of Organization

Certain behavioral processes give life to an organizational structure. When these processes do not function well, unfortunate problems can arise, as illustrated in this account:

> When she began to major in marketing as a junior in college, Connie Vick knew that someday she would work in that field. Once she completed her MBA, she was more positive than ever that marketing would be her life's work. Because of her excellent academic record, she received several outstanding job offers. She decided to accept the job offer that she received from one of the nation's largest consulting firms. She believed that this job would allow her to gain experience in several areas of marketing and to engage in a variety of exciting work. Her last day on campus, she told her favorite professor, "This has got to be one of the happiest days of my life, getting such a great career opportunity."
>
> Recently, while visiting the college placement office, the professor was surprised to hear that Connie had told the placement director that she was looking for another job. Since she had been with the consulting company less than a year, the professor was somewhat surprised. He decided to call Connie and find out why she wanted to change jobs. This is what she told him: "I guess you can say my first experience with the real world was a 'reality shock.' Since being with this company, I have done nothing but gather data on phone surveys. All day long, I sit and talk on the phone, asking questions and checking off the answers. In graduate school I was trained to be a manager, but here I am doing what any high school graduate can do. I talked to my boss, and he said that all employees have to pay their dues. Well, why didn't they tell me this while they were recruiting me? To say there was a conflict between the recruiting information and the real world would be a gross understatement. I'm an adult—why didn't they provide me with realistic job information and then let me decide if I wanted it? A little bit of accurate communication would have gone a long way."

Our model includes four behavioral processes that contribute to effective organizational performance: communication, decision making, performance evaluation, and socialization and career.

Communication Process.   Organizational survival is related to the ability of management to receive, transmit, and act on information. The communication process links the organization to its environment as well as to its parts. Information flows to and from the organization as well as within the organization. Information integrates the activities of the organization with the demands of the environment. But information also integrates the internal activities of the organization. Connie Vick's problem arose because the information that flowed *from* the organization was different from the information that flowed *within* the organization.

Decision-Making Process. The quality of decision making in an organization depends on selecting proper goals and identifying means for achieving them. With good integration of *behavioral* and *structural* factors, management can increase the probability that high-quality decisions will be made. Connie Vick's experience illustrates inconsistent decision making by different organizational units (personnel and marketing) in the hiring of new employees. Organizations rely on individual decisions as well as group decisions, and effective management requires knowledge about both types of decisions.

Performance Evaluation Process. Managers must evaluate the performance of individuals and groups within their organizations. Unfortunately for Connie Vick, her superior would be evaluating her using criteria different from the criteria that Connie had expected when she took the job. The model in Figure 1–2 indicates that individual, group, and organizational performance are the outcomes, or dependent variables, of organizational behavior, structure, and processes. The system that management installs to evaluate performance serves such purposes as deciding on rewards (pay, promotions, transfers), identifying training needs, and providing feed-back to employees. Many methods exist to evaluate performance, and the challenge to management is to select the appropriate one.

Socialization and Career Process. Individuals enter organizations to work and to pursue their personal career goals. Connie Vick joined the consulting firm because she believed that it was presenting her with a great career opportunity. Organizations employ individuals to perform certain tasks—the jobs of the organization structure. Thus, individual and organizational interests and goals must be brought into congruence if both are to be effective. Connie Vick's goals are, at this time, incongruent with those of her organization. Individuals move through time and jobs along career paths more or less prescribed by the organization. The extent to which an individual is successful in a career depends, in part at least, on the extent to which he or she adapts to the organization's demands.

The process by which the individual is made aware of the organization's expectations is termed *socialization.* Connie Vick's socialization consisted of an abrupt statement from her boss that all employees had to "pay their dues." Socialization may be formal, as when orientation programs are established for new employees, or informal, as when the manager and co-workers tell the new employee relevant details about the organization's expectations. Career development and socialization are interrelated activities that affect the performance of both the organization and the individual.

Performance Outcomes: Individual, Group, and Organizational

Individual performance contributes to group performance, which in turn contributes to organizational performance. In truly effective organizations, however, management helps create a positive synergy, that is, a whole that is greater than the sum of its parts.

No one measure, or criterion, adequately reflects performance at any level. The next chapter introduces the idea that organizational performance must be considered in terms of multiple measures within a time frame. But ineffective performance at any level is a signal to management to take corrective actions. All of management's corrective actions will focus on elements of organizational *behavior, structure,* or *processes.*

Organizational Development and Change

Managers must sometimes consider the possibility that proper performance can be achieved only by making significant changes in the total organization. Organizational change is the planned attempt by management to improve the overall performance of individuals, groups, and the organization by altering structure, behavior, and processes. If the change is correctly implemented, individuals and groups should move toward more effective performance. Concerted, planned, and evaluated efforts to improve performance have great potential for success.

SUMMARY AND INTRODUCTION TO THIS BOOK

The focus of this book is on the developing subdiscipline of the field of management known as organizational behavior. Organizational behavior studies the behavior of individuals and groups in organizational settings. The framework within which the contents of this book are presented is based on three characteristics common to *all* organizations: the *behavior* of individuals and groups, the *structure* of organizations (that is, the design of the fixed relationships that exist among the jobs in the organization), and the *processes* (for example, communication and decision making) that make the organization "tick" and give it life. Our model, presented in Figure 1–2, has evolved from our concept of what all organizations are.

Thus, our purpose in this book is to review theory and research on what we describe as the behavior, structure, and processes of organizations.[3] A major interest of this book will be the behavioral sciences that have produced theory and research concerning human behavior in organizations. However, no attempt will be made here to write a book that will teach the reader "behavioral science." The continuous theme throughout the book will be *the management of organizational behavior.* Given this theme, our task is to *interpret* behavioral science materials so that students of management can comprehend the behavior, structure, and process phenomena as these are affected by actions of managers.[4] It is our intention to provide the reader with a basis for applying the relevant contributions of behavioral science to the management of organizations.

Since our goal is to help you become a more effective manager, the next chapter deals with this topic: managing organizations effectively. It serves as the foundation for studying the remainder of the book.

---

[3] See Ronald G. Corwin and Karen Seashore Louis, "Organizational Barriers to the Use of Research," *Administrative Science Quarterly,* December 1982, pp. 623–40.

[4] Paul Shrivastava and Ian I. Mitroff, "Enhancing Organizational Research Utilization: The Role of Decision Maker's Assumptions," *Academy of Management Review,* January 1984, pp. 18–26.

DISCUSSION AND REVIEW QUESTIONS

1. Do you believe that organizations pervade your life? List each organization to which you belong. Do these organizations have any impact on your life? List and discuss each impact.

2. In dealing with many organizations today, we are often faced with red tape, inefficiency, and a generally unresponsive, inefficient, and ineffective organization. One of the goals of management is to achieve the opposite: an efficient and effective organization. What has happened?

3. What are your attitudes and feelings about organizations? What has influenced your attitudes?

4. Think of a particularly frustrating experience that you've had recently with an organi-

zation. It may have been an experience that occurred at school or at work, or it may have been experience that occurred when you were dealing with an organization as a customer, patient, or citizen. Describe the experience, and try to outline what may have been some of the causes.

5. "The kinds of problems that are faced by America today are such that they can only be solved by organizations." Comment.

6. Discuss the relationships among individual performance, group performance, and organizational performance.

7. Discuss, in your own words, our model for this book (Figure 1–2).

ADDITIONAL REFERENCES

Argyris, D. *The Applicability of Organizational Society.* New York: Cambridge University Press, 1972.

Bartunek, J. M.; J. R. Gordon; and R. P. Weathersby. "Developing Complicated Understanding in Administrators." *Academy of Management Review,* 1983, pp. 273–84.

Conner, P. E. "Research in the Behavioral Sciences: A Review Essay." *Academy of Management Journal,* 1972, pp. 219–28.

Cummings, L. L. "The Logics of Management." *Academy of Management Review,* 1983, pp. 532–38.

Downey, H. K., and R. D. Ireland. "Quantitative versus Qualitative: The Case of Environmental Assessment in Organizational Studies." *Administrative Science Quarterly,* 1979, pp. 630–37.

Dubin, R. "Management: Meanings, Methods, and More." *Academy of Management Review,* 1982, pp. 371–79.

Massarik, F., and B. E. Kreuger. "Through the Labyrinth: An Approach to Reading in Behavioral Science." *California Management Review,* 1970, pp. 70–75.

Meltzer, H., and W. Nord. "The Present Status of Industrial and Organizational Psychology." *Personnel Psychology,* 1973, pp. 11–29.

Mills, P. K. "Self-Management: Its Control and Relationship to Other Organizational Properties." *Academy of Management Review,* 1982, pp. 445–53.

Mitroff, I. I. "Archetypal Social Systems Analysis: On the Deeper Structure of Human Systems." *Academy of Management Review,* 1982, pp. 387–97.

————. "Reality as a Scientific Strategy: Revising Our Concepts of Science." *Academy of Management Review,* 1980, pp. 513–16.

Pettigrew, A. "On Studying Organizational Cultures." *Administrative Science Quarterly,* 1979, pp. 570–81.

Schein, E. H. "Behavioral Sciences for Management." In *Contemporary Management,* ed. J. W. McGuire. Englewood Cliffs, N.J.: Prentice-Hall, 1974.

Seashore, S. E. "Field Experiments within Formal Organizations." *Human Organization,* 1974, pp. 164–70.

Webber, R. A. "Behavioral Science and Management: Why the Troubled Marriage?" *Proceedings of the Academy of Management,* 1970, pp. 377–95.

Weiland, G. F. "The Contributions of Organizational Sociology to the Practice of Management." *Academy of Management Journal,* 1975, pp. 318–33.

Weiss, R. M. "Weber on Bureaucracy: Management Consultant or Political Theorist?" *Academy of Management Review,* 1983, pp. 242–48.

Chapter 2

After completing Chapter 2, you should be able to:

Define   individual, group, and organizational effectiveness.

Describe   the role of management in the attainment of effective performance.

Discuss   the importance of organizational culture.

Compare   the goal approach and the systems theory approach to organizational effectiveness.

Identify   the short-, intermediate-, and long-run criteria of effectiveness.

Managing Individual, Group, and Organizational Effectiveness

Management Makes a Difference

Argument For*

Thomas J. Peters and Robert H. Waterman, Jr., believe that management is the difference between successful and unsuccessful business organizations. Their book *In Search of Excellence* presents their evidence and conclusions. The book, which topped best-seller lists for most of 1983, must have struck a responsive chord in management as well as nonmanagement groups. Its optimistic theme has great appeal at a time when America suf-

---

* Based on Thomas J. Peters and Robert H. Waterman, Jr., *In Search of Excellence* (New York: Harper & Row, 1982).

fers economic instability and erosion of commercial dominance.

The appeal of the theme, "management makes a difference," is that business has the power to reverse the trend of economic decay. All that needs to be done is to adopt the managerial practices of firms that have achieved high levels of success. Peters and Waterman set out to demonstrate the differences in managerial practice that make a difference in organizational performance.

They first identified a group of firms that had achieved uncommon success as measured by six criteria. The six criteria were: (1) asset growth, (2) equity growth, (3) ratio of market price to book value, (4) return on total capital, (5) return on equity, and (6) return on sales. The firms that scored highest on these six criteria included IBM, Texas Instruments, Dana Corporation, and Procter & Gamble. The authors identify 36 firms that achieved the highest levels of performance on the six criteria during the period 1961–80.

What managerial practices were unique to these 36 firms? Peters and Waterman listed eight. Corporate excellence, they wrote, is achieved by managers who:

1. Emphasize the importance of fast action.
2. Stay in close contact with the needs and problems of their customers.
3. Encourage a spirit of autonomy and entrepreneurship among employees.
4. Believe in and act on the attitude that people are the keys to productivity.
5. Create simple organizations.
6. Develop a corporate culture that gives meaning to the work of each employee.
7. Encourage the existence of both loose and tight control.
8. Stick to the basic business of the organization.

The lesson is clear: Less successful organizations can be transformed into successful organizations by managers who can implement the eight practices.

On the question of whether management makes a difference, Peters and Waterman come down on the positive side. Managers do make a difference, they contend. Indeed, they are *the* difference.

Argument Against†

If management does make a difference, Peters and Waterman have not demonstrated it, their critics charge. Peters and Waterman fail to make the case for their position because of inadequacies in evidence and logic. The evidence that supports the case is narrow and anecdotal. The narrowness is due to their criteria of "success," which are six measures of financial success. Other measures of success, such as effectiveness, could yield a different sample of firms. Moreover, if a different time frame were used, for example, 1951–70, would the sample be different? If firms drop out of the list of "excellently managed," does this mean that they are no longer managed according to the eight practices?

Peters and Waterman's thesis that management makes the difference is the only logical explanation because they examined *only* management differences. They failed to include consideration of other causes of success, such as technology, market dominance, control of critical raw materials, national policy, and culture. Critics of Peters and Waterman point out that no firm will be able to achieve success against IBM, for example, without some protected technological edge, no matter how consistently its management applies the eight practices. But because such potential sources of corporate success are not analyzed, Peters and Waterman can only infer that management is the cause. It was the *only* cause they analyzed.

But what about the analysis itself? Is the evidence conclusive? According to one critic, Daniel T. Carroll, the analysis relies on secondary and anecdotal evidence. The secondary evidence includes articles appearing in the *New York Times, Fortune,* and the *Harvard Business Review.* While the ideas expressed in these articles may reflect truth or at least informed opinion, they cannot be accepted as preferable to evidence gathered from the firms themselves. Perhaps more damaging to Peters and Waterman's case is the fact that many points are supported with anecdotes. For example, Carroll has pointed out how Peters and Waterman support their conclusion about McDonald's concern for product quality. They rely on the recollections of a young business executive who worked for the fast-food chain as a 17-year-old high school student. The case for Hewlett-Packard's customer orientation is based on remarks overheard in a Palo Alto bar.

The point is not whether McDonald's is concerned for product quality or whether Hewlett-Packard is customer-oriented. The point is that the evidence *cited* does not make the case. Thus, even though managers may make a difference, the case is yet to be proved. But who is willing to say that managers make *no* difference?

† Based on Daniel T. Carroll, "A Disappointing Search for Excellence," *Harvard Business Review,* November–December 1983, pp. 78, 79, 83, 84, and 88.

effectiveness
Judgments we make regarding the performance of individuals, groups, and organizations. The closer their actual performance is to the desired performance, the more effective we judge them to be.

This chapter discusses how managers influence individual, group, and organizational effectiveness. Since a major purpose of this text is to contribute to the academic preparation of future managers, this issue must be introduced at this stage to lay the groundwork for the chapters to follow. As the Organizational Issue for Debate suggests, whether managers do (or can) influence **effectiveness** is difficult to determine, even though many instances of corporate excellence achieved through management excellence can be cited. We are reluctant to infer general principles from these instances. Although many writers on management and organizational behavior have attempted to develop a general theory of management, no such theory exists at present. But much is known about management and its role in organizations. This textbook is based on the belief that valuable insights about management can be found in the literature of organizational behavior.

As noted in the previous chapter, the field of organizational behavior identifies three *levels of analysis:* (1) individual, (2) group, and (3) organizational. Theorists and researchers in organizational behavior have accumulated a vast amount of information about each of these levels. These three levels of analysis also coincide with the three levels of managerial responsibility. That is, managers are responsible for the effectiveness of individuals, groups of individuals, and organizations themselves. For example, Lee Iacocca, the widely respected president of Chrysler Motors, took on the difficult task of improving the effectiveness of Chrysler Motors (the organizational level of responsibility). By all accounts, Iacocca met that responsibility. But how did he do it? And by what criteria do we assess the degree to which Chrysler became more effective? Iacocca might respond that Chrysler become more effective because individuals on the assembly lines produced a higher quality product (the individual level of responsibility) and because the engineering divisions designed more reliable automobiles (the group level of responsibility) and because the federal government guaranteed loans that forestalled bankruptcy (the organizational level of responsibility).

Each of these explanations for the improved effectiveness of Chrysler Motors involves different levels of analysis. Each of these levels involves a different perspective on effectiveness. The next section discusses these perspectives in greater detail.

PERSPECTIVES ON EFFECTIVENESS

Three perspectives on effectiveness can be identified. At the most basic level is *individual* effectiveness. The individual perspective emphasizes the task performance of specific employees or members of the organization. The tasks to be performed are parts of jobs or positions in the organization. Managers routinely assess individual effectiveness through performance evaluation processes. These are the bases for salary increases, promotions, and other rewards available in the organization.

Individuals seldom work in isolation from others in the organization. In fact, the usual situation is for individuals to work together in groups. Thus, you must consider yet another perspective on effectiveness: *group* effectiveness. In some instances, the effectiveness of a group is simply the sum of the contributions of all its members. For example, a group of scientists working on unrelated projects would be effective to the extent that each individual scientist is effective. In other instances, group effectiveness is more than the sum of the individual contributions. An example is an assembly line, which produces a finished product as a result of the contributions of each individual.

The third perspective is that of *organizational* effectiveness. Since organizations consist of individuals and groups, organizational effectiveness is a function of individual and group effectiveness. However, organizational effectiveness is more than the sum of individual and group effectiveness. Organizations are able to obtain higher levels of performance than the sum of the performance of their parts. In fact, the rationale for using organizations as means for doing the work of society is that they can accomplish more than is possible through individual efforts.

From the standpoint of society, the effectiveness of business organizations is critical. Publications that report business and economic events occasionally survey opinions about business performance. One such survey is reported in the following Close-Up.

ORGANIZATIONS: CLOSE-UP

Fortune's Survey of the Most Admired Corporations

In 1983, *Fortune* magazine polled 7,000 corporate executives, directors, and financial analysts to determine which corporations they held in highest esteem. Half of these officials responded to *Fortune's* request to rate 10 corporations in their respective industries on eight "attributes of reputation." These eight attributes were: (1) quality of management; (2) quality of products or services; (3) innovativeness; (4) long-term investment value; (5) financial soundness; (6) ability to attract, develop, and keep talented people; (7) community and environmental responsibility; and (8) use of corporate assets. The respondents to the survey rated each company from 0 (poor) to 10 (excellent) on each of the eight attributes.

According to *Fortune*, International Business Machines (IBM) was the most admired company. The respondents, all of whom were officials in other companies in the electronics industry, gave IBM an average of 8.53 on the eight attributes. Other corporations rated very high were Dow-Jones (8.35), Hewlett-Packard (8.24), Merck (8.17), Johnson & Johnson (8.15), Time, Inc. (7.99), General Electric (7.96), Anheuser-Busch (7.91), Coca-Cola (7.87), and Boeing (7.79).

Although IBM had the highest average rating, it did not rate highest on all eight attributes. The respondents rated IBM either first, second, or third on all attributes except quality of products or services and innovativeness.

Source: Nancy J. Perry, "America's Most Admired Corporations," *Fortune,* January 9, 1984, pp. 50–62.

The relationship among the three perspectives on effectiveness is shown in Figure 2–1.[1] The connecting arrows imply that group effectiveness depends on individual effectiveness and that organizational effectiveness depends on group effectiveness. The exact relationships among the three perspectives vary depending on such factors as the type of organization, the work it does, and the technology used in doing that work. The figure reflects the cumulative effects of the three perspectives. Thus, group effectiveness is larger than the sum of individual effectiveness because of the gains realized through the combined efforts of individuals and groups.

The job of management is to identify the *causes* of organizational, group, and individual effectiveness. As noted in Figure 2–2, each level

FIGURE 2–1

Three Perspectives on Effectiveness

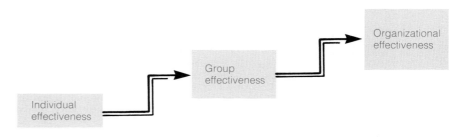

---

[1] The following discussion is based on David J. Lawless, *Effective Management: A Social Psychological Approach* (Englewood Cliffs, N.J.: Prentice-Hall, 1972), pp. 391–99.

FIGURE 2-2

Causes of Effectiveness

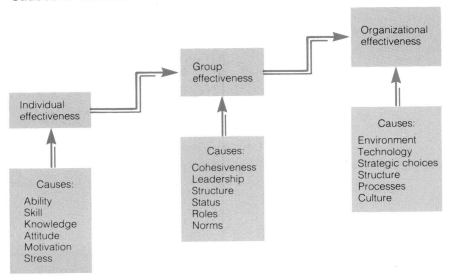

of effectiveness can be considered a variable that is caused by other variables, namely, the causes of effectiveness. Sources of individual effectiveness include ability, skill, knowledge, attitude, motivation, and stress. Individual differences in these areas account for most of the differences in individual effectiveness. Some of the most common causes of the differences in group and organizational effectiveness are also noted in Figure 2–2.[2] Potential sources of effectiveness are discussed at length in subsequent chapters. However, the reality of organizational life is that there are few unambiguous cause-effect relationships. In most instances, to make evaluation judgments, you must take into account multiple causes and circumstances.[3]

There is no universal agreement as to what the term *effectiveness* means, in either a theoretical sense or a practical sense. How you define effectiveness, however, can reflect adherence to one of two gen-

---

[2] One of the more ambitious attempts to determine the causes of organizational effectiveness is reported in John Child, "Managerial and Organizational Factors Associated with Company Performance—Part I," *Journal of Management Studies*, October 1974, pp. 175–89; and John Child, "Managerial and Organizational Factors Associated with Company Performance—Part II: A Contingency Analysis," *Journal of Management Studies*, February 1975, pp. 12–27. This study did not reach definitive conclusions, due no doubt to the inherent complexity of the concept organizational effectiveness.

[3] Jeffrey D. Ford and Deborah A. Schnellenberg, "Conceptual Issues of Linkage in Assessment of Organizational Performance," *Academy of Management Review*, January 1982, pp. 49–58.

eral approaches: the goal approach and the systems theory approach. These two approaches to defining effectiveness are most often contrasted in both the literature and the practice of organizational behavior.[4]

THE GOAL APPROACH

goal approach
This approach emphasizes the importance of goal achievement as the criterion for judging effectiveness.

The **goal approach** to defining and measuring effectiveness is the oldest and most widely used evaluation technique.[5] In the view of this approach, an organization exists to accomplish goals. An early and influential practitioner and writer on management and organizational behavior stated: "What we mean by effectiveness . . . is the accomplishment of recognized objectives of cooperative effort. The degree of accomplishment indicates the degree of effectiveness."[6] The idea that organizations, as well as individuals and groups, should be evaluated in terms of goal accomplishment has widespread appeal. The goal approach reflects purposefulness, rationality, and achievement—the fundamental tenets of contemporary Western societies.

Many management practices are based on the goal approach. One widely used practice is management by objectives. Using this practice, managers specify in advance the goals that they expect their subordinates to accomplish and periodically evaluate the degree to which the subordinates have accomplished these goals. The actual specifics of management by objectives vary from case to case. In some instances, the manager and subordinate discuss the objectives and attempt to reach mutual agreement. In other instances, the manager simply assigns the goals. The idea of management by objectives is to specify in advance the goals that are to be sought.

Yet the goal approach, for all of its appeal and apparent simplicity, has problems.[7] These are some of its more widely recognized difficulties:

1. Goal achievement is not readily measurable for organizations that do not produce tangible outputs. For example, the goal of a college may be "to provide a liberal education at a fair price." The question

---

[4] Kim Cameron, "Critical Questions in Assessing Organizational Effectiveness," *Organizational Dynamics*, Autumn 1980, pp. 66–80, identifies two other approaches: the internal process approach and the strategic constituencies approach. The former can be subsumed under the systems theory approach, and the latter is a special case of the multiple-goal approach.

[5] Stephen Strasser, J. D. Eveland, Gaylord Cummins, O. Lynn Deniston, and John H. Romani, "Conceptualizing the Goal and System Models of Organizational Effectiveness," *Journal of Management Studies*, July 1981, p. 323.

[6] Chester I. Barnard, *The Functions of the Executive* (Cambridge, Mass.: Harvard University Press, 1938), p. 55.

[7] E. Frank Harrison, *Management and Organization* (Boston: Houghton Mifflin, 1978), pp. 404–14, is an excellent survey of limitations of the goal approach.

is, How would one know whether the college achieves that goal? What is a liberal education? What is a fair price? For that matter, what is education?

2. Organizations attempt to achieve more than one goal, and achievement of one goal often precludes or diminishes their ability to achieve other goals. A business firm may state that its goal is to attain a maximum profit and to provide absolutely safe working conditions. These two goals are in conflict, because each of these goals is achieved at the expense of the other.

3. The very existence of a common set of "official" goals to which all members are committed is questionable. Various researchers have noted the difficulty of obtaining consensus among managers as to the specific goals of their organization.[8]

Despite the problems of the goal approach, it continues to exert a powerful influence on the development of management and organizational behavior theory and practice. Saying that managers should achieve the goals of the organization is easy. Knowing *how* to do this is more difficult. The alternative to the goal approach is the systems theory approach. Through systems theory, the concept of effectiveness can be defined in terms that enable managers to take a broader view of the organization and to understand the causes of individual, group, and organizational effectiveness.

THE SYSTEMS THEORY APPROACH

systems theory
This approach emphasizes the importance of adaptation to external demands as the criterion for judging effectiveness.

Systems theory enables you to describe the behavior of organizations both internally and externally. Internally, you can see how and why people within organizations perform their individual and group tasks. Externally, you can relate the transactions of organizations with other organizations and institutions. All organizations acquire resources from the outside environment of which they are a part and, in turn, provide goods and services demanded by the larger environment. *Managers must deal simultaneously with the internal and external aspects of organizational behavior.* This essentially complex process can be simplified, for analytical purposes, by employing the basic concepts of systems theory.

In systems theory, the organization is seen as one element of a number of elements that act interdependently. The flow of inputs and outputs is the basic starting point in describing the organization. In the simplest terms, the organization takes resources (inputs) from the larger system (environment), processes these resources, and returns

---

[8] Terry Connolly, Edward J. Conlon, and Stuart Jay Deutsch, "Organizational Effectiveness: A Multiple-Constituency Approach," *Academy of Management Review,* April 1980, p. 212.

FIGURE 2–3

The Basic Elements of a System

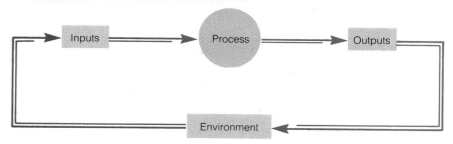

them in changed form (output). Figure 2–3 displays the fundamental elements of the organization as a system.

Systems theory can also describe the behavior of individuals and groups. The "inputs" of individual behavior are "causes" that arise from the workplace. For example, the cause could be the directives of a manager to perform a certain task. The input (cause) is then acted on by the individual's mental and psychological processes to produce a particular outcome. The outcome that the manager prefers is, of course, compliance with the directive, but depending on the states of the individual's processes, the outcome could be noncompliance. Similarly, you can describe the behavior of a group in systems theory terms. For example, the behavior of a group of employees to unionize (outcome) could be explained in terms of perceived managerial unfairness in the assignment of work (input) and the state of the group's cohesiveness (process). We use the terms of systems theory throughout this text to describe and explain the behavior of individuals and groups in organizations.

Systems Theory and Feedback

The concept of the organization as a system that is related to a larger system introduces the importance of feedback. As mentioned, the organization is dependent on the environment not only for its inputs, but also for the acceptance of its outputs. It is critical, therefore, that the organization develop means for adjusting to environmental demands. The means for adjustment are information channels that enable the organization to recognize these demands. In business organizations, for example, market research is an important *feedback* mechanism. Other forms of feedback are customer complaints, employee comments, and financial reports.

In simplest terms, feedback refers to information that reflects the outcomes of an act or a series of acts by an individual, a group, or an organization. Throughout this text, you will see the importance of feedback. Systems theory emphasizes the importance of responding to the content of the feedback information.

Examples of the Input-Output Cycle

The business firm has two major categories of inputs: *human* and *natural resources.* Human inputs consist of the people who work in the firm. They contribute their time and energy to the organization in exchange for wages and other rewards, tangible and intangible. Natural resources consist of the nonhuman inputs processed or used in combination with the human element to provide other resources. A steel mill must have people and blast furnaces (along with other tools and machinery) to process iron ore into steel and steel products. An auto manufacturer takes steel, rubber, plastics, and fabrics and—in combination with people, tools, and equipment—uses them to make automobiles. A business firm survives as long as its output is purchased in the market in sufficient quantities and at prices that enable it to replenish its depleted stock of inputs.

Similarly, a university uses resources to teach students, to do research, and to provide technical information to society. The survival of a university depends on its ability to attract students' tuitions and taxpayers' dollars in sufficient amounts to pay the salaries of its faculty and staff as well as the costs of other resources. If a university's output is rejected by the larger environment, so that students enroll elsewhere and taxpayers support other public endeavors, or if a university is guilty of expending too great an amount of resources in relation to its output, it will cease to exist. Like a business firm, a university must provide the right output at the right price if it is to survive.[9]

Systems theory emphasizes two important considerations: (1) the ultimate survival of the organization depends on its ability to *adapt to the demands of its environment,* and (2) in meeting these demands, the *total cycle of input-process-output must be the focus of managerial attention.* Therefore, the criteria of effectiveness must reflect each of these two considerations, and you must define effectiveness accordingly. The systems approach accounts for the fact that resources have to be devoted to activities that have little to do with achieving the organization's primary goal.[10] In other words, *adapting to the environ-*

---

[9] Kim Cameron, "Measuring Organizational Effectiveness in Institutions of Higher Education," *Administrative Science Quarterly,* December 1978, pp. 604–29.

[10] Amitai Etzioni, "Two Approaches to Organizational Analysis: A Critique and a Suggestion," in *Assessment of Organizational Effectiveness,* ed. Jaisingh Ghorpade (Santa Monica, Calif.: Goodyear Publishing, 1971), p. 36.

ment and maintaining the input-process-output flow require that resources be allocated to activities that are only indirectly related to that goal.

THE TIME DIMENSION MODEL OF ORGANIZATIONAL EFFECTIVENESS

The concept of organizational effectiveness presented in this book relies on the previous discussion of systems theory, but we must develop one additional point: the dimension of time. Recall that two main conclusions of systems theory are (1) that effectiveness criteria must reflect the entire input-process-output cycle, not simply output, and (2) that effectiveness criteria must reflect the interrelationships between the organization and its outside environment. Thus:

1. Organizational effectiveness is an all-encompassing concept that includes a number of component concepts.
2. The managerial task is to maintain the optimal balance among these components.

Much additional research is needed to develop knowledge about the components of effectiveness. There is little consensus not only about these relevant components but about the interrelationships *among them* and about the effects of managerial action on them.[11] In this textbook, we attempt to provide the basis for asking the right questions about what constitutes effectiveness and how those qualities that characterize it interact.

According to systems theory, an organization is an element of a larger system, the environment. With the passage of time, every organization takes, processes, and returns resources to the environment. The ultimate criterion of organizational effectiveness is whether the organization survives in the environment. Survival requires adaptation, and adaptation often involves predictable sequences. As the organization ages, it will probably pass through different phases. Some writers suggest that an organization passes through a life cycle. It forms, develops, matures, and declines in relation to environmental circumstances. Organizations and entire industries do rise and fall. Today, the personal computer industry is on the rise and the steel industry is declining. Marketing experts acknowledge the existence of product-market life cycles. Organizations also seem to have life

---

[11] J. Barton Cunningham, "Approaches to the Evaluation of Organizational Effectiveness," *Academy of Management Review,* July 1977, pp. 463–74; and Richard M. Steers, "Problems in Measurement of Organizational Effectiveness," *Administrative Science Quarterly,* December 1975, pp. 546–58.

FIGURE 2-4

Time Dimension Model of Effectiveness

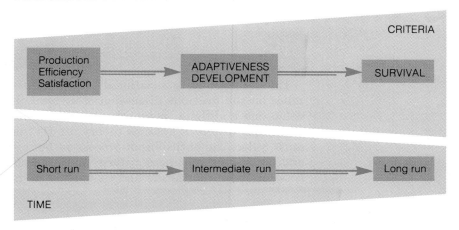

cycles. Consequently, the appropriate criteria of effectiveness must reflect the stage of the organization's life cycle.[12]

Managers and others with interests in the organization must have indicators that assess the probability of the organization's survival. In actual practice, managers use a number of short-run indicators of long-run survival. Among these indicators are measurements of productivity, efficiency, accidents, turnover, absenteeism, quality, rate of return, morale, and employee satisfaction.[13] Any of these criteria can be relevant for particular purposes. For simplicity, we will use three criteria of short-run effectiveness as representative of all such criteria. They are *production, efficiency,* and *satisfaction.*

Two other criteria complete the time dimension model: *adaptiveness* and *development.* These criteria reflect effectiveness in the intermediate time period. The relationships between these criteria and the time dimension are shown in Figure 2–4.

CRITERIA OF EFFECTIVENESS

In the time dimension model, criteria of effectiveness are typically stated in terms of the short run, the intermediate run, and the long

[12] Kim S. Cameron and David A. Whetten, "Perceptions of Organizational Effectiveness over Organizational Life Cycles," *Administrative Science Quarterly,* December 1981, pp. 525–44; and R. E. Quinn and Kim Cameron, "Organizational Life Cycles and Shifting Criteria of Effectiveness: Some Preliminary Evidence," *Management Science,* January 1983, pp. 33–51.

[13] John P. Campbell, "On the Nature of Organizational Effectiveness," in *New Perspectives on Organizational Effectiveness,* ed. Paul S. Goodman and Johannes M. Pennings (San Francisco: Jossey-Bass, 1979), pp. 36–39.

run. Short-run criteria are those referring to the results of actions that conclude in a year or less. Intermediate-run criteria are applicable when you judge the effectiveness of an individual, group, or organization for a longer time period, perhaps five years. Long-run criteria are those for which the indefinite future is applicable. We will discuss five general categories of effectiveness criteria, beginning with those of a short-run nature.

Production

production
As an effectiveness criterion, production refers to measures of the organization's primary output.

As used here, **production** reflects the ability of the organization to produce the quantity and quality of output that the environment demands. The concept excludes any consideration of efficiency, which is defined below. The measures of production include profit, sales, market share, students graduated, patients released, documents processed, clients served, and the like. These measures relate directly to the output that is consumed by the organization's customers and clients.

Efficiency

efficiency
As an effectiveness criterion, efficiency refers to measures of the organization's use of scarce resources.

Efficiency is defined as the ratio of outputs to inputs. This short-run criterion focuses attention on the entire input-process-output cycle, yet it emphasizes the input and process elements. Among the measures of efficiency are rate of return on capital or assets, unit cost, scrappage and waste, downtime, occupancy rates, and cost per patient, per student, or per client. Measures of efficiency must inevitably be in ratio terms; the ratios of benefit to cost or to time are the general forms of these measures.

Satisfaction

satisfaction
As an effectiveness criterion, satisfaction gauges the success of the organization in meeting the needs of employees and members.

The idea of the organization as a social system requires that some consideration be given to the benefits received by its participants as well as its customers and clients. **Satisfaction** and morale are similar terms referring to the extent to which the organization meets the needs of employees. We use the term *satisfaction* to refer to this criterion. Measures of satisfaction include employee attitudes, turnover, absenteeism, tardiness, and grievances.

Adaptiveness

adaptiveness
As an effectiveness criterion,

Adaptiveness is the extent to which the organization *can and does* respond to internal and external changes. Adaptiveness in this context refers to management's ability to sense changes in the environment

adaptiveness is a
measure of the
organization's
responsiveness to
required change.

as well as changes within the organization itself. Ineffectiveness in achieving production, efficiency, and satisfaction can signal the need to adapt managerial practices and policies. Or the environment may demand different outputs or provide different inputs, thus necessitating change. To the extent that the organization cannot or does not adapt, its survival is jeopardized.

How can one really know whether the organization is effectively adaptive? There are short-run measures of effectiveness, but there are no specific and concrete measures of adaptiveness. Management can implement policies that encourage a sense of readiness for change, and there are certain managerial practices that, if implemented, facilitate adaptiveness. For example, managers can invest in employee training programs and career counseling. They can encourage and reward innovativeness and risk-taking behavior. Yet, when the time comes for an adaptive response, the organization either adapts or it does not adapt—and that is the ultimate measure.

Development

development
As an effectiveness
criterion,
development
measures the
organization's
commitment to
enlarging its capacity
and potential for
growth.

This criterion measures the ability of the organization to increase its capacity to deal with environmental demands. An organization must invest in itself to increase its chances of survival in the long run. The usual **development** efforts are training programs for managerial and nonmanagerial personnel, but more recently the range of organizational development has expanded to include a number of psychological and sociological approaches.[14]

Time considerations enable you to evaluate effectiveness in the short, intermediate, and long run. For example, you could evaluate a particular organization as effective in terms of production, satisfaction, and efficiency criteria but as ineffective in terms of adaptiveness and development. A manufacturer of buggy whips may be optimally effective because it can produce buggy whips better and faster than any other producer in the short run, but with little chance of survival because no one wants to buy them. *Thus, maintaining optimal balance means, in part, balancing the organization's performance over time.*

The time dimension model of effectiveness enables us to understand the work of managers in organizations. The basic job of managers is to identify and influence the causes of individual, group, and organizational effectiveness in the short, intermediate, and long run. Let us examine the nature of managerial work in that light.

---

[14] Raymond A. Katzell and Richard A. Guzzo, "Psychological Approaches to Productivity Improvement," *American Psychologist,* April 1983, pp. 468–72.

THE NATURE OF MANAGERIAL WORK

Theories describing managerial work are many and varied.[15] The first attempts to describe managerial work were undertaken in the early 1900s by writers of the Classical School of Management.[16] The writers of the Classical School proposed that managerial work consists of distinct, yet interrelated, *functions* that taken together constitute the *managerial process.* The view has prevailed that management should be defined, described, and analyzed in terms of what managers do.

management
Management is the process of getting work done through people.

Management can be defined as a *process,* a series of actions, activities, or operations that lead to some end. The definition of management should also recognize that the process is undertaken by more than one person in most organizations. The definition should be broad enough to describe management wherever it is practiced, yet specific enough to identify differences in the relative importance of the functions associated with a particular manager's job.

The concept of management developed here is based on the assumption that the necessity for managing arises whenever work is specialized and is undertaken by two or more persons. Under such circumstances, the specialized work must be *coordinated,* and this creates the necessity for performing managerial work. The nature of managerial work, then, is to coordinate the work of others by performing four management functions: *planning, organizing, leading,* and *controlling.*

Planning Effective Performance

The planning function includes defining the ends to be achieved and determining *appropriate means to achieve the defined ends.* Planning activities can be complex or simple, implicit or explicit, impersonal or personal. For example, the sales manager who is forecasting the demand for the firm's major product may rely on complex econometric models or on casual conversations with salespersons in the field. The intended outcomes of planning activities are mutual under-

---

[15] Discussions of the history of management thought can be found in Daniel A. Wren, *The Evolution of Management Thought* (New York: Ronald Press, 1972); and Claude S. George, Jr., *The History of Management Thought* (Englewood Cliffs, N.J.: Prentice-Hall, 1968).

[16] The term *Classical School of Management* refers to the ideas developed by a group of practitioners who wrote of their experiences in management. Notable contributors to these ideas include Frederick W. Taylor, *Principles of Management* (New York: Harper & Row, 1911); Henri Fayol, *General and Industrial Management,* trans. J. A. Conbrough (Geneva: International Management Institute, 1929); James D. Mooney, *The Principles of Organization* (New York: Harper & Row, 1947); and James D. Mooney, *The Elements of Administration* (New York: Harper & Row, 1944).

standings about what the members of the organization should be attempting to achieve. These understandings may be reflected in the form of complicated plans that specify the intended results, or they may be reflected in a general agreement among the members.

Discussions of planning are often hampered by the absence of definitions of such terms as mission, goal, and objective. In some instances, the terms are used interchangeably, particularly *goal* and *objective*. In other instances, the terms are defined specifically, but there is no general agreement over the definitions. Depending on their backgrounds and purposes, managers and authors will use the terms differently. However, the pivotal position of planning as a management function requires us to make very explicit the meanings of these key concepts.

missions
The ultimate purposes of an organization.

Mission. Society expects organizations to serve specific purposes. These purposes are the missions of organizations. **Missions** are criteria for assessing the long-run effectiveness of an organization. Effective managers will state the mission of their organization in terms of those conditions that, if realized, will assure the organization's survival. Statements of mission are to be found in laws, articles of incorporation, and other extraorganizational sources. Mission statements are broad, abstract, and value-laden, and as such they are subject to various interpretations. For example, the mission of a state public health department as expressed in the law that created it mandates the agency to "protect and promote the health and welfare of the citizens of the Commonwealth." It is from this source that the organization will create its specific programs.

goals
A relatively long-run state or condition that, if achieved, contributes to the organization's mission.

Goals. **Goals** are future states or conditions that contribute to the fulfillment of the organization's mission. A goal is somewhat more concrete and specific than a mission. Goals can be stated in terms of production, efficiency, and satisfaction. For example, one goal of a public health agency could be stated as "the eradication of tuberculosis as a health hazard by the end of 1990." In a business setting, a goal might be "to have viable sales outlets established in every major population center of the country by the end of 1988." It is entirely possible for an organization to have multiple goals that contribute to its mission. For example, a hospital may pursue patient care, research, and training. Universities typically state three significant goals: teaching, research, and community service. The existence of multiple goals places great pressure on managers not only to coordinate the routine operations of the units that strive for these goals but also to plan and allocate scarce resources to the goals.

objectives
Enable managers to gauge the short-run progress of the

Objectives. **Objectives** refer to statements of accomplishment that are to be achieved in the short run, usually one year. The public health agency's objective can be stated as "to reduce the incidence of tuberculosis from 6 per 10,000 to 4 per 10,000 by the end of the

organization toward its goals. Objectives, are more specific and concrete than goals.

current year." The firm seeking to have sales outlets in all major population centers could state its current year's objective as "to have opened and begun operations in Chicago, Los Angeles, Louisville, and New York." Thus, goals are derived from the organization's mission, and objectives are derived from the goals.

A coherent set of missions, goals, and objectives defines the scope and direction of the organization's activities. Planning involves specifying not only where the organization is going, but also how it is to get there. Alternatives must be analyzed and evaluated in terms of criteria that follow from the mission, goals, and objectives. Thus, managers by their own decisions can affect how they and their organizations will be evaluated. They determine what ends are legitimate and therefore what criteria are relevant. And once the determination of appropriate means has been completed, the next managerial function—organizing—must be undertaken.

Organizing Effective Performance

The organizing function incudes *all managerial activities that are taken to translate the required planned activities into a structure of tasks and authority*. In a practical sense, the organizing function involves specific activities.

Defining the Nature and Content of Each Job in the Organization. The tangible results of this activity are job specifications, position descriptions, or task definitions. These indicate what is expected of jobholders in terms of responsibilities, outcomes, and objectives. In turn, the skills, abilities, and training required to meet the defined expectations are also specified.

Determining the Bases for Grouping Jobs Together. The essence of defining jobs is specialization, that is, dividing the work. But once the overall task has been subdivided into jobs, the jobs must be put into groups, or departments. The managerial decision involves selecting the appropriate bases. For example, all of the jobs that require similar machinery may be grouped together, or the manager may decide to group all of the jobs according to the product or service they produce.

Deciding the Size of the Group. The purpose of grouping jobs is to enable a person to supervise the group's activities. Obviously, there is a limit on the number of jobs that one person can supervise, but the precise number will vary depending on the situation. For example, it is possible to supervise a greater number of similar, simple jobs than of dissimilar, complex jobs. The supervisor of hourly workers can manage up to 25–30 employees, but the director of research scientists can manage far fewer, perhaps only 8 to 10.

authority
The legitimate right
to make decisions
without higher
approval.

Delegating Authority to the Assigned Manager. The preceding activities create groups of jobs with defined tasks. It then becomes necessary to determine the extent to which managers of the groups should be able to make decisions and use the resources of the group without higher approval. This is **authority.**

Once the structure of task and authority is in place, it must be given life. People perform jobs, and management must recruit and select the appropriate individuals who will perform the jobs. The process of finding and placing people in jobs is termed staffing. In some large organizations, specialized units such as personnel perform staffing activities. An important cause of individual effectiveness is a good fit between job requirements and individual abilities. Thus, even when staffing is done in a specialized unit, the activity remains an important management responsibility.

The interrelationships between planning and organizing are apparent. The planning function results in the determination of organizational ends and means; that is, it defines the "whats" and "hows." The organizing function results in the determination of the "whos," that is, *who will do what with whom to achieve the desired end results.* The structure of tasks and authority should facilitate the fulfillment of planned results if the next management function, leading, is performed properly.

Leading Effective Performance

Leading *involves the manager in close day-to-day contact with individuals and groups.* Thus, leading is uniquely personal and interpersonal. Even though planning and organizing provide guidelines and directives in the form of plans, job descriptions, organization charts, and policies, it is people who do the work. And people are frequently unpredictable. They have unique needs, aspirations, personalities, and attitudes. Thus, they each perceive the workplace and their jobs differently. Managers must take into account these unique perceptions and behaviors and somehow direct them toward common purposes.

Leading places the manager squarely in the arena of individual and group behavior. To function in this arena, you must have knowledge of individual differences and motivation, group behavior, power, and politics. In short, being a leader requires knowledge of ways to influence individuals and groups to accept and pursue organizational objectives, often at the expense of personal objectives.

Leading involves the day-to-day interactions between managers and their subordinates. In these interactions, the full panorama of human behavior is evident: individuals work, play, communicate, compete, accept and reject others, join groups, leave groups, receive rewards, and cope with stress. Of all the management functions, leading is the most humanly oriented.

Controlling Effective Performance

The controlling function includes *activities that managers undertake to assure that actual outcomes are consistent with planned outcomes.* Three basic conditions must exist to undertake control.

Standards. Norms of acceptable outcomes, *standards,* must be spelled out. These standards reflect goals and objectives and are usually found in accounting, production, marketing, financial, and budgeting documents. In more specific ways, standards are reflected in procedures, performance criteria, rules of conduct, professional ethics, and work rules. Standards therefore reflect desirable levels of achievement.

Information. Actual and planned outcomes must be compared using appropriate and reliable information. Many organizations have developed sophisticated information systems that provide managers with control data. Prime examples are standard cost accounting and quality control systems used extensively by modern manufacturing firms. In other instances, the sources of information consist of nothing more than managers' observations of the behavior of people assigned to their department.

Corrective Action. If actual outcomes are ineffective, managers must take corrective action. Without the ability to take corrective action, the controlling function has no point or purpose. It becomes an exercise without substance. Corrective action is made possible through the organizing function if managers have been assigned the authority to take action.

Simply stated, managers undertake control to determine *whether* intended results are achieved and if not, *why* not. The conclusions managers reach because of their controlling activities are that the planning function is faulty or that the organizing function is faulty, or both. Controlling is, then, the completion of a logical sequence. The activities that controlling comprises include employee selection and placement, materials inspection, performance evaluation, financial statement analysis, and other well-recognized managerial techniques.

Describing management in terms of the four functions of planning, organizing, leading, and controlling is certainly not complete. There is nothing in this description that indicates the specific behaviors or activities associated with each function. Nor is there any recognition of the relative importance of these functions for overall organizational effectiveness. However, these four functions conveniently and adequately define management.

The functions of management require the application of technical and administrative skills. They also require the application of human relations skills, the ability to deal with and relate to *people*. The literature of organizational behavior stresses the importance of people. Many observers and practioners of management believe that managing people effectively is the key to improving the performance of contemporary corporations. The following Close-Up lends some support to that idea.

ORGANIZATIONS: CLOSE-UP

The Importance of Good Human Resource Management

A number of major U.S. corporations recently have made major changes that take into account the importance of people—human resources. For example:

1. In the mid-1970s Citicorp planned to change from a banking institution to a financial services business, but it faced some major problems. One problem was the result of a survey of customer service satisfaction that showed Citibank to be last among the 30 banks surveyed. Management immediately analyzed the causes of this low ranking. The important causes were people-oriented—jobs, working conditions, and salaries. Jobs were redesigned so that employees could provide complete services for a smaller number of clients. Work stations were redesigned to accommodate the latest microcomputer technology. And employee status was upgraded from clerical to professional. The results were positive changes in efficiency and customer satisfaction.

2. General Electric provides employee counseling and support throughout an employee's career. The company recruits highly trained, technically oriented people and makes major investments in their career development. Because the company has fostered its reputation for effective and sincere human resource management, it is able to attract and keep scientific and engineering personnel.

Source: Charles Gitzendanner, Kenneth F. Misa, and R. Timothy Stein, "Management's Involvement in the Strategic Utilization of the Human Resource," *Management Review,* October 1983, pp. 13–17.

Managerial Work and the Behavior, Structure, and Processes of Organizations

The concept of managerial work developed in the preceding pages can now be brought into perspective. This textbook focuses on the *behavior of individuals and groups in organizations.* The purpose of managers in organizations is to achieve coordinated behavior so that an organization is judged effective by those who evaluate its record. Those who evaluate organizations can be concerned with any number of specific or general criteria and with output, process, or input measures.[17] To achieve coordinated behavior and to satisfy evaluators, managers engage in activities intended to *plan, organize, lead,* and *control* behavior. Major factors in determining individual and group behavior are task and authority relationships.[18] Therefore, managers must design organizational *structures* and *processes* to facilitate communication among employees.

The relationships among management, organizations, and effectiveness seem to be straightforward. Effective individual, group, and organizational performance should result from good planning, organizing, leading, and controlling. But organizations are not that simple. Such management writers as Peters and Waterman (whose ideas are the subject of the Organizational Issue for Debate) have brought to our attention the importance of organizational *culture*.[19]

ORGANIZATIONAL CULTURE

culture
The unique system of values, beliefs, and norms that members of an organization share. Cultures can be an important cause of effectiveness.

According to Peters and Waterman, effective organizations have internal cultures that reinforce the importance of excellence. **Culture** has various meanings. For our purpose, it means a system of shared *values* and *beliefs* that produce *norms* of behavior.[20] Values (what is important) and beliefs (how things work) interact to cause norms (how we *should* do things). Every organization has a culture, and, according to Peters and Waterman, that culture can be either a positive or a negative force in achieving effective performance.

Here are two examples of organizational culture:[21]

1. IBM's dominant value is customer service, and it keeps everyone from the CEO to the factory worker pulling in the same direction. An IBM field engineer will not hesitate to spend his or her own money for traveling to service a customer complaint. The engineer knows that IBM will reimburse such outlays without hesitation.
2. Entrepreneurship is Hewlett-Packard's dominant value and belief. Consequently, every H-P employee acts as an entrepreneur—ex-

---

[17] Frank Hoy and Don Hellriegel, "The Kilmann and Herden Model of Organizational Effectiveness for Small Business Managers," *Academy of Management Journal,* June 1982, pp. 308–22.

[18] Gregory H. Gaertner and S. Ramnarayan, "Organizational Effectiveness: An Alternate Perspective," *Academy of Management Review,* January 1983, pp. 97–107.

[19] Thomas J. Peters and Robert H. Waterman, Jr., *In Search of Excellence* (New York: Harper & Row, 1982).

[20] Linda Smircich, "Concepts of Culture and Organizational Analysis," *Administrative Science Quarterly,* September 1983, p. 342.

[21] Bro Uttal, "The Corporate Culture Vultures," *Fortune,* October 17, 1983, p. 66.

perimenting with new ideas, taking risks, courting failure. The employees do these things because they know that H-P stands for and supports entrepreneurial behavior. H-P ranks right behind IBM as one of America's most admired business organizations.

Negative cultures are counterproductive to management efforts to bring about performance improvements. Consider what can happen in the banking industry. Although there are exceptions, on the whole the cultures of contemporary banks emphasize values and beliefs that discourage the behavior required to compete in the recently deregulated banking industry. Bank cultures that value conservative, status quo behavior are incompatible with the need to be aggressive and competitive in the marketplace. Some banks have attempted major overhauls in their corporate cultures to make them more dynamic. First Chicago and Bank of America are among the major banks that have gone through extensive efforts to redirect their cultures.[22]

The realization that organizational culture is an important cause of organizational effectiveness is widespread in management practice.[23] Not so widespread, however, is understanding of how management can change organizational culture when it inhibits organizational effectiveness. Many management practitioners and consultants in the field are experimenting with alternative change approaches.[24] And much more will be known as managers move through the 1980s. At this point, however, some tentative guidelines for changing culture can be suggested.[25]

First, you must understand that organizational culture—the system of shared values, beliefs, and norms—is the product of the interaction among the managerial functions; the organization's behavior, structure, and process; and the larger environment in which the organization exists. As shown in Figure 2–5, organizational culture encompasses both the managerial functions and organizational characteristics. Management is both a cause of and a part of organizational culture. The existing culture of any organization reflects past and present managerial planning, organizing, leading, and controlling activities. For example, contemporary bank cultures that value operations efficiency (keeping track of the customers' deposits and checking activity) do so because bank managers have stated missions, goals, and objectives in those terms. These managers evaluate employees in terms of accuracy—for example, "minimum teller errors"—and they

---

[22] Ibid., p. 71.

[23] See "Corporate Culture: The Hard-to-Change Values That Spell Success or Failure," *Business Week*, October 27, 1980, pp. 148–60.

[24] Uttal, "Corporate Culture Vultures."

[25] Vijay Sathe, "Some Action Implications of Corporate Culture: A Manager's Guide to Action," *Organizational Dynamics*, August 1983, pp. 4–23.

FIGURE 2–5

Organizational Culture and Effectiveness

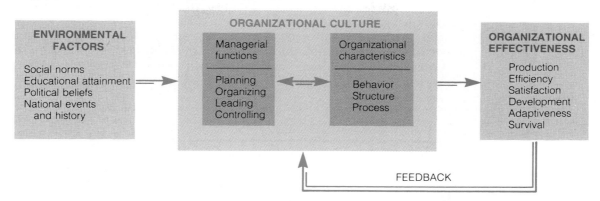

publicly proclaim the importance of doing things right. Banking executives have created the culture by virtue of their own managerial actions, and they hire and socialize employees to adopt and accept the important beliefs and values of that culture.

If management can create organizational culture, management should be able to change it by the same means. Or so it would seem. But it is not that simple or easy. Cultures are self-reinforcing. Once in place, cultures provide stability and certainty for their members. Individuals know what is expected, what is important, and what to do. They quite naturally resist any threatened disruption of the existing culture.

Managers must practice planning, organizing, leading, and controlling that are consistent with the beliefs and values of the desired culture. All four functions can contribute to changing the culture, but it is generally agreed that *leading* is the most important. By personal example and behavior, managers can demonstrate how things should be done. But they must be *capable* managers and *respected* leaders.

Thus, the issue raised in the opening debate, whether management makes a difference, would seem to be moot. Managers can influence effectiveness. Whether they do so in a positive manner seems to depend upon their own effectiveness as managers. How skillful and able they are as planners, organizers, leaders, and controllers would certainly affect individual, group, and organizational effectiveness. However, the *relative* contribution of managers can probably never be fully known.

The intended effect of organizational structure and processes is to predetermine what people will do, with whom they will do it, what decisions they will make, what information they will receive, and when, how, and how often they will perform certain actions and make certain decisions. Managers interact with other managers and with nonmanagers in individual and group settings to establish plans, policies, procedures, rules, job descriptions, reporting channels, and lines of authority and communication. All of these actions and interactions create an organizational culture that will have a significant impact, both positive and negative, on individual, group, and organizational effectiveness.

SUMMARY OF KEY POINTS

A. Concepts of effectiveness, managerial process, and organizational culture have been developed in this chapter. These three concepts are key ideas underlying the practice of management based on organizational behavior theory and research.

B. An overriding consideration documented in many studies of managerial work is that the managerial process is inherently a human process—people relating to people. The recognition of this fact establishes the importance of understanding human behavior in the workplace. The behavior of individuals and groups is important principally for achieving effective organizational performance, but the behavior of managers themselves must also be understood.

C. Managerial techniques are directed toward improving effectiveness. But to understand the impact of these techniques, you must develop an understanding of the concept of effectiveness. Although the term *effectiveness* is widely used, its meaning is not widely understood.

D. Two competing concepts of effectiveness derive from two competing theories of organizations. The goal theory is based on the idea that organizations are rational, purposive entities that pursue specific missions, goals, and objectives. Accordingly, how well organizations function, that is, how effective they are, is reckoned in terms of how successful they are in achieving their purposes. The systems theory assumes that organizations are social entities that exist as parts of a larger environment and that in order to survive they must function to satisfy the demands of that environment.

E. The time dimension model of effectiveness is based on systems theory and adds to it the effects that occur as the organization moves through time. As the organization does so, there must be short- and intermediate-run indicators of its progress toward long-run survival. These indicators are the criteria of effectiveness, and they apply in the evaluation of individual, group, and organizational effectiveness.

F.   Managerial work evolves from the need to coordinate work in organizations. By their nature, organizations exploit the benefits of specialization, but specialization requires coordination. Managers coordinate specialized work through the application of planning, organizing, leading, and controlling functions. These functions require that managers determine and influence the causes of individual, group, and organizational effectiveness.

G.   Management work focuses on the behavior of individuals and groups and on the process and structure of organizations. The considerable interdependence of behavior, process, and structure complicates the efforts of management.

H.   The interaction of managerial functions and organizational behavior, structure, and processes creates an organizational culture. This culture embodies the values, beliefs, and norms that influence the behavior of individuals and groups. The managerial challenge is to create and maintain organizational cultures that contribute to organizational effectiveness.

DISCUSSION AND REVIEW QUESTIONS

1. Can the evaluation of the effectiveness of an organization ever be made in absolute terms or is it always necessary to state effectiveness criteria in relative terms? Explain, and give examples to support your argument.

2. Is the distinction between short-run, intermediate-run, and long-run criteria meaningful for evaluating the effectiveness of a college course? Explain.

3. "An organization is effective if its employees believe that it is." Discuss.

4. If you were a training director responsible for instructing first-line supervisors in the techniques of supervision, how would you evaluate the effectiveness of your training program?

5. "Effectiveness criteria are relevant only in terms of the evaluator. For example, the state legislators look for some things, the federal people look for other things. I give each group whatever it wants." Comment on this statement, which was made by the administrator of a state governmental agency.

6. Explain why the effectiveness criteria of departments such as production, sales, and engineering tend to emphasize short run rather than long run measures of performance.

7. How would you evaluate the effectiveness of contemporary American society in terms of production, efficiency, satisfaction, adaptiveness, and development? Rate each crite-

rion on a five-point scale, and compare your evaluation with those of classmates.

8. Describe the process by which society makes known its expectations for the missions of universities. Based on your knowledge of the university or college you attend, how satisfactorily is it achieving its mission?

9. A public official with a talent for simplifying matters stated: "Planning is concerned with doing the right things. Organizing is concerned with doing things right." Comment.

10. Describe the culture of an organization that you belong to or relate to in some capacity. What are the shared values, beliefs, and norms? Are they consistent with, and do they contribute to, the organization's criteria of effectiveness? Explain your answers.

ADDITIONAL REFERENCES

Angle, H. L., and J. L. Perry. "An Empirical Assessment of Organizational Commitment and Organizational Effectiveness." *Administrative Science Quarterly,* 1981, pp. 1–14.

Bluedorn, A. C. "Cutting the Gordian Knot: A Critique of the Effectiveness Tradition in Organizational Research." *Sociology and Social Research,* 1980, pp. 477–96.

Coulter, P. B. "Organizational Effectiveness in the Public Sector: The Example of Municipal Fire Protection." *Administrative Science Quarterly,* 1979, pp. 65–81.

Deal, T. E., and A. A. Kennedy. *Corporate Cultures.* Reading, Mass.: Addison-Wesley Publishing, 1982.

Gregory, K. L. "Native-View Paradigms: Multiple Cultures and Culture Conflicts in Organizations." *Administrative Science Quarterly,* 1983, pp. 359–76.

Katz, D., and R. L. Kahn. *The Social Psychology of Organizations.* New York: John Wiley & Sons, 1966.

McGuire, J. W., ed. *Contemporary Management: Issues and Viewpoints.* Englewood Cliffs, N.J.: Prentice-Hall, 1974.

Mahoney, T. A. "Managerial Perceptions of Organizational Effectiveness." *Management Science,* 1967, pp. 76–91.

Markus, M. L. *Systems in Organizations.* Marshfield, Mass.: Pitman Publishing, 1984.

Mendelow, A. L. "Setting Corporate Goals and Measuring Organizational Effectiveness: A Practical Approach." *Long-Range Planning,* 1983, pp. 70–76.

Nash, M. *Managing Organizational Performance.* San Francisco: Jossey-Bass, 1983.

Neuhauser, D. "Hospital Effectiveness." *Health Services Research,* 1983, pp. 13–15.

Pondy, L. R.; P. Frost; G. Morgan; and T. Dandridge, eds. *Organizational Symbolism.* Greenwich, Conn.: JAI Press, 1983.

Price, J. L. "The Study of Organizational Effectiveness." *Sociological Quarterly,* 1972, pp. 3–15.

Quinn, R. E., and J. Rohrbaugh. "A Spatial Model of Effectiveness Criteria." *Management Science,* 1983, pp. 363–77.

Rice, A. K. *The Enterprise and Its Environment: A System Theory of Management Organization.* London: Tavistock Publications, 1963.

Robinson, R. B., Jr. "Measures of Small Firm Effectiveness for Strategic Planning Research." *Journal of Small Business Management,* 1983, pp. 22–29.

Shipper, F., and C. S. White. "Linking Organizational Effectiveness and Environmental Change." *Long-Range Planning,* 1983, pp. 99–106.

Snow, C. C., and L. G. Hrebiniak. "Strategy, Distinctive Competence, and Organizational

Performance." *Administrative Science Quarterly,* 1980, pp. 317–36.

Staw, B. M.; P. I. McKechnie; and S. M. Puffer. "The Justification of Organizational Performance." *Administrative Science Quarterly,* 1983, pp. 582–600.

Urwick, L. F. *The Pattern of Management.* Minneapolis: University of Minnesota Press, 1956.

Webb, R. J. "Organizational Effectiveness and the Voluntary Organization." *Academy of Management Journal,* 1974, pp. 663–77.

Wilkins, A. "The Culture Audit: A Tool for Understanding Organizations." *Organizational Dynamics,* 1983, pp. 24–38.

Yuchtman, E., and S. E. Seashore. "A Systems Resource Approach to Organizational Effectiveness." *American Sociological Review,* 1967, pp. 891–903.

Zander, A. *Making Groups Effective.* San Francisco: Jossey-Bass, 1983.

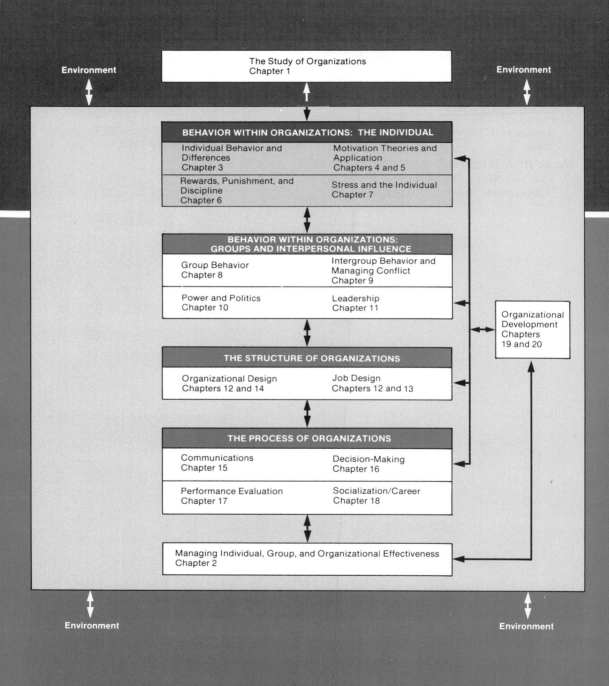

Environment

Environment

The Study of Organizations
Chapter 1

BEHAVIOR WITHIN ORGANIZATIONS: THE INDIVIDUAL

Individual Behavior and
Differences
Chapter 3

Motivation Theories and
Application
Chapters 4 and 5

Rewards, Punishment, and
Discipline
Chapter 6

Stress and the Individual
Chapter 7

**BEHAVIOR WITHIN ORGANIZATIONS:
GROUPS AND INTERPERSONAL INFLUENCE**

Group Behavior
Chapter 8

Intergroup Behavior and
Managing Conflict
Chapter 9

Power and Politics
Chapter 10

Leadership
Chapter 11

THE STRUCTURE OF ORGANIZATIONS

Organizational Design
Chapters 12 and 14

Job Design
Chapters 12 and 13

THE PROCESS OF ORGANIZATIONS

Communications
Chapter 15

Decision-Making
Chapter 16

Performance Evaluation
Chapter 17

Socialization/Career
Chapter 18

Managing Individual, Group, and Organizational Effectiveness
Chapter 2

Organizational
Development
Chapters
19 and 20

Environment

Environment

BEHAVIOR WITHIN ORGANIZATIONS: THE INDIVIDUAL

Chapter 3

After completing Chapter 3, you should be able to:

Define perception and explain the role it plays in understanding and coping with organizational life.

Describe how personality influences an individual's organizational behavior.

Discuss what research findings indicate about the relationship between job satisfaction and performance.

Compare the meanings of ability and skill.

Identify why it is very difficult to change a person's attitude.

Individual Behavior and Differences

Individual Personality Theories

Argument For

The individual personality theorists propose that there are individual differences in personalities that are not just transient but enduring. These differences are believed to be consistent over time and across situations. Thus, a person who respected and obeyed his or her father would probably continue to do so in any situation and would probably display the same attitude toward other father-like figures. That is, the person would submit to the wishes or orders of authority figures.

For example, the individual personality theorists would explain the behavior of employees named Jim, Mary, and Paul in terms of early childhood development, or by reference to general patterns of thinking and behaving, or by the development of self-actualization. Jim's needs, patterns of behavior, and self-development made him a unique individual. Jim's uniqueness, like Mary's uniqueness, or Paul's uniqueness, are important for a manager to recognize. By understanding the role of individual differences in shaping behavior, a manager would be able to explain an employee's behavior as well as help the individual match his or her unique strengths to a work situation.

Individual differences is the term used by theorists and researchers to refer to three related assumptions about people like Jim, Mary, and Paul: (1) individuals differ from one another in significant ways; (2) any particular individual's difference from others will hold true in many situations; and (3) individuals will maintain their characteristic differences over a considerable period of time.

53

Although a manager is unable to administer and interpret a personality test to measure individual differences, he or she needs to look closely at behavior patterns, similarities and differences, and consistency of behavior over time. The manager's observation and understanding of individual differences will permit him or her to work effectively with employees. Ignoring the fact that individual differences exist tends to encourage the practice of "robot management"—that is, managing every subordinate in the same manner. Since everyone is the same—"like a robot"—the manager treats everyone in the same way.

Argument Against

The individual personality theories are assumed to be too narrow by such people as the world-famous behaviorist B. F. Skinner. Skinner's approach and other social psychology approaches differ significantly, but they share a common set of assumptions that are contrary to the individual difference assumptions. The more recently developed social personality theories assume (1) that the major influences on human behavior come from the environment and therefore (2) that situational rather than individual differences should be the primary focus of attention.

Skinner and others believe that the individual is open to his or her environment and significantly influenced by it. The major vocabulary used in these theories include such terms as stimulus, interaction, reinforcement, and imitation. Terms that describe the individual as having drives, cognitions, and needs are used by only some of the environmental or social personality theorists. The theories of Skinner and others are often referred to as "social theories of personality" because of the importance that these theories attach to social interactions in an individual's environment.

According to Skinner's view, it makes no sense to talk about the needs, drives, and attitudes of Jim, Mary, and Paul. The causes of their behavior lie outside them, in the environment. Thus, individual differences are a moot point or issue. External rewards and punishments shape the way Jim, Mary, and Paul behave on the job.

Some claim that with an emphasis on the environment and situational differences instead of on individual differences, reinforcement theory and social learning theory can answer the question of why people behave as they do. The person is interacting with the "real world" and not operating in isolation in some kind of "vacuum tube" insulated from events, other people, and situations.

Any attempt to learn why people behave as they do in organizations requires some understanding about individual differences. Managers spend considerable time making judgments about the fit between individuals, job tasks, and effectiveness. Such judgments are typically influenced by both the manager's and the subordinate's characteristics. Making decisions about who will perform what tasks in a particular manner—without some understanding of behavior—can lead to irreversible long-run problems.

Each employee is different in many respects. A manager needs to ask how such differences influence the behavior and performance of subordinates. This chapter highlights some of the individual differences that can explain why one person is a significantly better performer than another person. The chapter also pays close attention to several of the more crucial individual differences that managers should consider.

Despite the contention of the opening Organizational Issue for Debate that on the one hand individual differences need to be studied and understood and that on the other hand the environment is the key to understanding behavior, we feel that both viewpoints have merit. In this chapter, we will help answer the question "Why do individual differences exist?" We will also talk about how the environment affects individual differences. Individual differences and the environment are inextricably intertwined. It is incorrect to assume that individual differences have no connection at all with the environment—work, family, community, and society.

THE BASIS FOR UNDERSTANDING BEHAVIOR

A manager's observation and analysis of individual behavior and performance require the consideration of three sets of variables that directly influence individual behavior or what an employee does (e.g., produces output, sells automobiles, services machines). The three sets of variables are classified as being individual, psychological, and organizational. Within each set are a number of subsets. For example, the individual variables include abilities and skills, background, and demographic variables. Figure 3–1 illustrates that an employee's behavior is complex because it is affected by such diverse variables, experiences, and events. Figure 3–1 presents such factors as the abilities and skills of employees, the psychological makeup of employees, and the response of employees to organizational variables such as the rewards being distributed and the design of the job itself.

Whether any manager can modify, mold, or reconstruct behaviors is a much-debated issue among behavioral scientists and managerial

FIGURE 3–1

**Variables That Influence Behavior
and Performance**

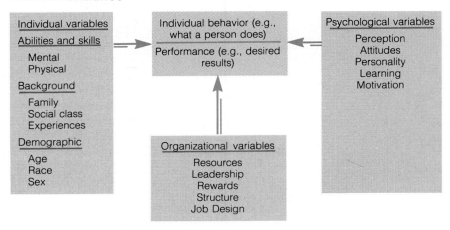

practitioners. For example, it is usually agreed that changing any of the psychological variables requires thorough diagnosis, skill, patience, and understanding on the part of a manager. There is no universally agreed-upon method that managers can use to change personalities, attitudes, perceptions, or learning patterns. The behavior patterns of people are always changing, although slightly. And any manager would certainly like to bring about behavior changes that result in improved performance.

Human behavior is too complex to be explained by a generalization that applies to all people. Therefore, only a sampling of some of the relevant variables that influence human behavior is presented in Figure 3–1. Even so, coverage of each of the variables presented in this figure is beyond the scope of this book. Most of our attention will be given to three major psychological variables—perception, attitudes, and personality. These variables form the foundation for our discussion of motivation, group behavior, and leadership. The learning and motivation variables will be discussed in Chapters 4 and 5. A presentation of the organizational variables will be found in other chapters of the book.

Figure 3–1 suggests that effective managerial practice requires that individual behavior differences be recognized and, when feasible, taken into consideration while carrying out the job of managing organizational behavior. To understand **individual differences,** a manager must (1) observe and recognize the differences, (2) study relationships between variables that influence individual behavior, and (3) discover

**individual
differences**
Individuals are

similar, but they are also unique. The study of individual differences such as attitudes, perceptions, and abilities helps a manager explain differences in performance levels.

relationships. For example, a manager would be in a better position to make optimal decisions if he or she knew what the attitudes, perceptions, and mental abilities of employees were, as well as how these and other variables were related. It would also be important to know how each variable influenced performance. Being able to observe differences, understand relationships, and predict linkages would facilitate managerial attempts to improve performance.

Behavior as outlined in Figure 3–1 is anything that a person does. *Talking* to a manager, *listening* to a co-worker, *filing* a report, *typing* a memo, and *placing* a completed unit in inventory are "behaviors." So are *daydreaming, reading* this book, and *learning* how to use a firm's accounting system. The general framework indicates that behavior depends on the types of variables shown in Figure 3–1. Thus, it can be stated that $B = f(I, O, P)$. Figure 3–1 suggests that an employee's behavior (B) is a function of individual (I), organizational (O), and psychological (P) variables. The behavior that results on the job is unique to each individual, but the underlying process is basic to all people.

After years of theory building and research, it is generally agreed that:

1. Behavior is caused.
2. Behavior is goal-directed.
3. Behavior that can be observed is measurable.
4. Behavior that is not directly observable (for example, thinking, perceiving) is also important in accomplishing goals.
5. Behavior is motivated.

To emphasize these points of agreement, consider the case of Jim (mentioned in the Organizational Issue for Debate), who is usually an average performer but who has recently become a high performer. A manager's analysis of this behavior change might be the following. Jim recently increased his efforts to perform. He has expressed more interest in his work, and he has expressed interest in a new vacancy in another department. This suggests that the improved performance occurred because Jim wanted and became motivated to work harder to gain a possible promotion.

The desired result of any employee's behavior is performance. An important part of a manager's job is to define performance in advance—that is, to state what results are desired. In organizations, individual, organizational, and psychological variables affect not only behavior but also performance. Performance-related behaviors are those that are directly associated with job tasks and that need to be accomplished to achieve a job's objectives. For a manager, performance-related behavior would include such actions as identifying performance problems; planning, organizing, and controlling the work of employees; and creating a motivational climate for subordinates.[1]

Since the manager's attention is focused on performance-related behaviors, he or she searches for ways to achieve optimal performance. If employees are not performing well or consistently, the manager must investigate the problem. There are six questions that will help the manager focus on performance problems. They are:

1. Does the employee have the skills and abilities to perform the job?
2. Does the employee have the necessary resources to perform the job?
3. Is the employee aware of the performance problem?
4. When did the performance problem surface?
5. What is the reaction of the employee's co-workers to the performance problem?
6. What can I (the manager) do to help alleviate the performance problem?

These questions and their answers again call attention to the complexity of individual behavior and performance differences. They also indicate that when performance problems are identified, some form of managerial action is required.

INDIVIDUAL VARIABLES

The individual variables presented in Figure 3–1 are classified as abilities and skills, background, and demographic. Each of these classes of variables helps explain individual differences in behavior and performance. However, only abilities and skills will be discussed in this chapter. Background and demographic variables will be discussed throughout the book.

Abilities and Skills

Some employees, even though highly motivated, simply do not have the abilities or skills to perform well. Abilities and skills play a major role in individual behavior and performance. An **ability** is a trait (inate or learned) that permits a person to do something mental or physical. **Skills** are task-related competences, such as the skill to operate a lathe or a computer. In most cases, the terms *abilities* and *skills* are used interchangeably in this book. Remember that B = f (I, O, P). Table 3–1 identifies a set of 10 mental abilities that make up what

ability
An ability is an innate or learned trait that allows an individual to complete a job.

---

[1] Robert Albanese and David D. Van Fleet, *Organizational Behavior: A Managerial Viewpoint* (Hinsdale, Ill.: Dryden Press, 1983), p. 52.

TABLE 3–1

Mental Abilities = Intelligence

Mental Ability	Description
1. Flexibility and speed of closure	The ability to "hold in mind" a particular visual configuration
2. Fluency	The ability to produce words, ideas, and verbal expressions
3. Inductive reasoning	The ability to form and test hypotheses directed at finding relationships
4. Associative memory	The ability to remember bits of unrelated material and to recall
5. Span memory	The ability to recall perfectly for immediate reproduction a series of items after only one presentation of the series
6. Number facility	The ability to manipulate numbers in arithmetic operations rapidly
7. Perceptual speed	Speed in finding figures, making comparisons, and carrying out simple tasks involving visual perceptions
8. Deductive reasoning	The ability to reason from stated premises to their necessary conclusion
9. Spatial orientation and visualization	The ability to perceive spatial patterns and to manipulate or transform the image of spatial patterns
10. Verbal comprehension	Knowledge of words and their meaning as well as the application of this knowledge

Source: Adapted from M. D. Dunnette, "Aptitudes, Abilities, and Skills," in *Handbook of Industrial and Organizational Psychology,* ed. M. D. Dunnette (Skokie, Ill.: Rand McNally, 1976), pp. 481–83.

skill
A job-related competence that a person possesses and uses when appropriate.

job analysis
A formal process used in organizations to define, study, and learn all of the specifics of a job.

is commonly referred to as intelligence.[2] An issue that a manager faces is whether these mental abilities are needed to be successful on the job and what types of mental abilities are required.

Table 3–2 presents a number of physical skills . The job of a secretary may require many of the mental abilities presented in Table 3–1, as well as various physical skills that are needed in order to handle word processing equipment.

Managers must attempt to match a person with abilities and skills with the job requirements. The matching process is important since no amount of leadership, motivation, or organizational resources can make up for deficiencies in abilities or skills. **Job analysis** is a widely used technique that takes some of the guesswork out of matching. Job analysis is the process of defining and studying a job in terms

[2] M. D. Dunnette, "Aptitudes, Abilities, and Skills," in *Handbook of Industrial and Organizational Psychology,* ed. M. D. Dunnette (Skokie, Ill.: Rand McNally, 1976), pp. 481–82.

TABLE 3–2

Sample of Physical Skills

Physical Skill	Description
1. Dynamic strength	Muscular endurance in exerting force continuously or repeatedly
2. Extent flexibility	The ability to flex or stretch trunk and back muscles
3. Gross body coordination	The ability to coordinate the action of several parts of the body while the body is in motion
4. Gross body equilibrium	The ability to maintain balance with nonvisual cues
5. Stamina	The capacity to sustain maximum effort requiring cardiovascular exertion

Source: Adapted from Edwin A. Fleishman "On the Relation between Abilities, Learning, and Human Performance," *American Psychologist*, November 1972, pp. 1017–32.

of tasks or behaviors and specifying the responsibilities, education, and training needed to perform the job successfully.[3]

PSYCHOLOGICAL VARIABLES

Unraveling the complexity of psychological variables such as perception, attitudes, and personality is an immense task. Thus, the purpose here is to present basic knowledge about each of these psychological variables. Even psychologists have a difficult time agreeing on the meaning and importance of these variables, so our goal is to provide meaningful information about them that managers can use in solving on-the-job behavior and performance problems.

Perception

perception
The cognitive process that individuals use to interpret and understand the world around them.

Perception, as depicted in Figure 3–2, is the cognitive process by which an individual gives meaning to the environment. Because each person gives his or her own meaning to stimuli, different individuals will "see" the same thing in different ways.[4] The way an employee sees the situation often has much greater meaning for understanding behavior than does the situation itself. Stated more thoroughly:

---

[3] For a complete discussion of job analysis, see John M. Ivancevich and William F. Glueck, *Foundations of Personnel/Human Resource Management* (Plano, Tex.: Business Publications, 1983), chap. 4, pp. 96–129.

[4] W. R. Nord, ed., *Concepts and Controversy in Organizational Behavior* (Santa Monica, Calif.: Goodyear Publishing, 1976), p. 22.

The cognitive map of the individual is not, then, a photographic representation of the physical world; it is, rather, a partial, personal construction in which certain objects, selected out by the individual for a major role, are perceived in an individual manner. Every perceiver is, as it were, to some degree a nonrepresentational artist, painting a picture of the world that expresses his individual view of reality.[5]

FIGURE 3-2

The Perceptual Process

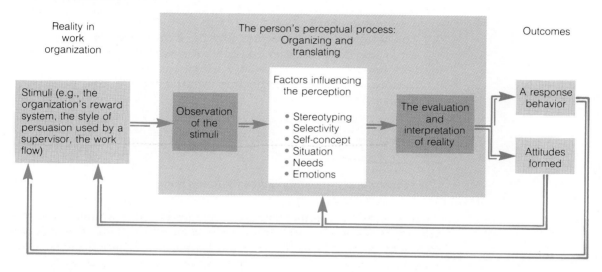

Since perception refers to the acquisition of specific knowledge about objects or events at any particular moment, it occurs whenever stimuli activate the senses. Perception involves cognition (knowledge). Thus, perception includes the interpretation of objects, symbols, and people in the light of pertinent experiences. In other words, perception involves receiving stimuli, organizing the stimuli, and translating or interpreting the organized stimuli so as to influence behavior and form attitudes.

Each person selects various cues that influence his or her perceptions of people, objects, and symbols. Because of these factors and their potential imbalance, people often misperceive another person, group, or object. To a considerable extent, people interpret the behavior of others in the context of the setting in which they find themselves.

The following are some organizational examples that point out how perception influences behavior:

[5] David Krech, Richard S. Crutchfield, and Egerton L. Ballachey, *Individual Society* (New York: McGraw-Hill, 1962), p. 20.

1. A manager believes that an employee is given opportunities to use his judgment about how to do the job, while the employee feels that he has absolutely no freedom to make judgments.
2. A subordinate's response to a supervisor's request is based on what she thought she heard the supervisor say, not on what was actually requested.
3. The manager considers the product sold to be of high quality, but the customer making a complaint feels that it is poorly made.
4. An employee is viewed by one colleague as a hard worker who gives good effort and by another colleague as a poor worker who expends no effort.
5. The salesperson regards her pay increase as totally inequitable, while the sales manager considers it a very fair raise.
6. One line operator views the working conditions as miserable; a co-worker right across the line regards the working conditions as pleasant.

These are a few of the numerous daily examples of how perception can differ. The fact that perceptual differences exist should be recognized by managers. Figure 3–3 on page 63 illustrates an example of how perception works.

A study clearly showing that managers and subordinates often have different perceptions was reported by Likert. He examined the perceptions of superiors and subordinates to determine the amounts and types of recognition that subordinates received for good performance. Both supervisors and subordinates were asked how often superiors provided rewards for good work. The results are presented in Table 3–3.

TABLE 3–3

The Perceptual Gap between Supervisors and Subordinates

Types of Recognition	Frequency with which supervisors say they give various types of recognition for good performance	Frequency with which subordinates say supervisors give various types of recognition for good performance
Gives privileges	52%	14%
Gives more responsibility	48	10
Gives a pat on the back	82	13
Gives sincere and thorough praise	80	14
Trains for better jobs	64	9
Gives more interesting work	51	5

Source: Adapted from Rensis Likert, *New Patterns in Management* (New York: McGraw-Hill, 1961), p. 91.

FIGURE 3–3

Perceptual Differences and Behavior

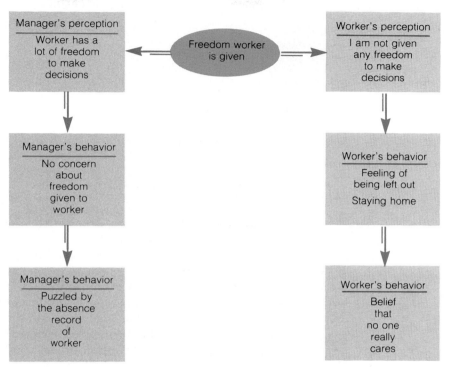

There were significant differences in what the two groups perceived. Each group viewed the type of recognition being given at a different level. The subordinates in most cases reported that very little recognition was being provided by their supervisors and that rewards were provided infrequently. The superiors saw themselves as giving a wide variety of rewards for good performance. The study points out that marked differences existed between the superiors' and the subordinates' perceptions of the superiors' behavior.

Perceptual Organization. An important aspect of what is perceived involves organization.[6] One of the most elemental organizing principles of perception is the tendency to pattern stimuli in terms of *figure-ground* relationships. Not all stimuli reach one's awareness with equal clarity. The factor focused on is called the *figure*. That which is experienced and is out of focus is called the *ground*. Figure 3–4 shows how in certain situations the figure-ground relationship is ambiguous. Do

---

[6] M. W. Levine and J. M. Shefner, *Fundamentals of Sensation and Perception* (Reading, Mass.: Addison-Wesley Publishing, 1981), p. 17.

FIGURE 3–4

Perceptual Differences and Behavior

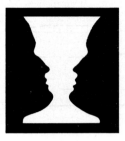

you see faces or a wineglass? As you read this text, your perceptions are organized in terms of figure and ground. In every perceptual act, the figure-ground principle is operating.[7] A figure-ground workplace example would be a union organizer who stands out more than other workers. As the union pushes to organize the work force, the organizer stands out more and more to management. In most cases, a union organizer would stand out and be considered a troublemaker by management.

The organizing nature of perception is also apparent when similar stimuli are grouped together and when stimuli in close proximity are grouped. Another grouping principle that shapes perceptual organization is called *closure*. This refers to the tendency to want to close something with missing parts. There is a strong need in some individuals to complete a configuration, a job, or a project. For example, if a person with a high need for closure is prevented from finishing a job or task, this could lead to frustration or a more drastic behavior such as quitting. Figure 3–5 is an example of closure. Do you feel the need to complete the drawing of the tiger?

Stereotyping. The manner in which managers categorize others is often a reflection of a perceptual bias. The term **stereotype** has been used to describe judgments made about people on the basis of their ethnic group membership. Other stereotypes also need to be guarded against.

For example, men stereotype women executives, managers stereotype union stewards, and women stereotype men. Most people engage in stereotyping. Age has been the basis for stereotyping employees. Researchers have found that managerial actions against older workers are influenced by stereotyping.[8] This type of action could proceed as

stereotype
A set of beliefs about the characteristics of people in a particular group that is generalized to all members of the group.

[7] B. V. H. Gilmer, *Applied Psychology* (New York: McGraw-Hill, 1975), p. 229.

[8] Benson Rosen and Thomas H. Jerdee, "The Influence of Age Stereotypes on Managerial Decisions," *Journal of Applied Psychology*, August 1976, pp. 428–32.

FIGURE 3–5

Perceptual Closure

follows: Suppose that a new job opening involves travel, long hours, and attending a lot of meetings. A manager with a negative bias against older candidates might decide that what is needed to accomplish the job is someone with a lot of energy and good health. Since the manager assumes that older workers lack energy and are usually not in good health, he or she will not even consider them. Thus, a perceptual bias excludes from consideration any worker past whatever age the manager considers as being old. Such stereotyping can result in implementing improper programs for promotion, motivation, job design, or performance evaluation.

The following Close-Up presents a classroom example and a job example that show the power of stereotyping. Each of us engages in stereotyping. Unfortunately, there are flaws in stereotyping that we fail to recognize or accept.

ORGANIZATIONS: CLOSE-UP

Stereotyping Is Deeply Rooted

Gordon Allport, the noted Harvard psychologist, told a story about a child who had come to believe that people who lived in Minneapolis were called monopolists. From his father, he had learned that monopolists were evil folk. It wasn't until years later, when he discovered his confusion, that his dislike of Minneapolis residents vanished.

Allport knew, of course, that it was not so easy to wipe out erroneous stereotypes. Because stereotyping is buried deep in human character, only a restructuring of education can begin to correct its influence. It is hard to deny that stereotyping is very common. When people first meet others, they typically notice highly visible and distinct characteristics: sex, race, physical appearance, and the like. Despite people's best intentions, their initial impressions of others are shaped by their assumptions about such characteristics. What is critical is that these assumptions are not merely beliefs or attitudes that exist in a vacuum; they are reinforced by the behavior of both prejudiced people and the targets of their prejudice.

The power of one person's beliefs to make other people conform to them has been demonstrated in real life. In the 1960s, researchers Robert Rosenthal and Lenore Jacobson entered elementary school classrooms and identified one out of every five pupils in each room as a child who would be expected to show significant intellectual improvement during the school year. What the teachers did not know was that the "gifted pupils" had been chosen on a random basis. Nevertheless, something happened in the relationships between the designated gifted pupils and their teachers that led to dramatic gains in test performance.

The same type of dramatic gain has occurred on the job. Albert King, a professor of management, informed a welding instructor in a vocational training center that five men in the program had unusually high aptitude. These five had been chosen at random and knew nothing of their being designated as high-aptitude trainees. They were absent less often than were colleagues, learned the basics of the welder's trade in about half the usual time, and scored a full 10 points higher than other trainees on a welding test. Also, other trainees singled out the five as their preferred co-workers.

These studies suggest that expectations can influence relationships between managers and workers. For example, managers who believe that men are better suited to some jobs and women to others may treat their workers (wittingly or unwittingly) in ways that encourage them to perform their jobs in accordance with stereotypes about differences between men and women. In fact, these stereotypes may determine who gets which job in the first place.

Source: Adapted from Mark Snyder, "Self-Fulfilling Stereotypes," *Psychology Today,* July 1982, pp. 60–68.

Selective Perception.   The concept of selective perception is important to managers since they often receive large amounts of information and data. Consequently, they may tend to select information that supports their viewpoints. People tend to ignore information or cues that might make them feel discomfort. For example, a skilled manager may be concerned primarily with an employee's final results or output. Since the employee is often cynical and negative when interacting with the manager, other managers may conclude that the employee will probably receive a poor performance rating. However, this manager selects out the negative features or cues and rates the subordinate on the basis of results. This is a form of selective perception.

The Manager's Characteristics.   People frequently use themselves as benchmarks in perceiving others. Research suggests that (1) knowing oneself makes it easier to see others accurately,[9] (2) one's own characteristics affect the characteristics identified in others,[10] and (3) persons who accept themselves are more likely to see favorable aspects of other people.[11]

Basically, these conclusions suggest that managers perceiving the behavior and individual differences of employees are influenced by their own traits. If they understand that their own traits and values influence perception, they can probably perform a more accurate evaluation of their subordinates. A manager who is a perfectionist tends to look for perfection in subordinates, while a manager who is quick in responding to technical requirements looks for this ability in his subordinates.

Situational Factors. The press of time, the attitudes of the people a manager is working with, and other situational factors will all influence perceptual accuracy. If a manager is pressed for time and has to immediately fill an order, then her perceptions will be influenced by the time constraints. The press of time will literally force the manager to overlook some details, to rush certain activities, and to ignore certain stimuli such as requests from other managers or from superiors.

Needs and Perceptions. Perceptions are significantly influenced by needs and desires. In other words, the employee, the manager, the vice president, and the director see what they want to see. Like the mirrors in the fun house at the amusement park, the world can be distorted; the distortion is related to needs and desires.

The influence of needs in shaping perceptions has been studied in laboratory settings. Subjects at various stages of hunger were asked to report what they saw in ambiguous drawings flashed before them. It was found that as hunger increased up to a certain point, the subjects saw more and more of the ambiguous drawings as articles of food. The hungry subjects saw steaks, salads, and sandwiches, while the subjects who had recently eaten saw nonfood images in the same drawings.[12]

Emotions and Perceptions. A person's emotional state has a lot to do with perceptions. A strong emotion, such as total distaste for

---

[9] R. D. Norman, "The Interrelationships among Acceptance-Rejection, Self-Other Identity, Insight into Self, and Realistic Perception of Others," *Journal of Social Psychology,* May 1953, pp. 205–35.

[10] J. Bossom and A. H. Maslow, "Security of Judges as a Factor in Impressions of Warmth in Others," *Journal of Abnormal and Social Psychology,* July 1957, pp. 147–48.

[11] K. T. Omivake, "The Relation between Acceptance of Self and Acceptance of Others Shown by Three Personality Inventories," *Journal of Consulting Psychology,* 1954, pp. 443–46.

[12] J. A. Deutsch, W. G. Young, and T. J. Kalogeris, "The Stomach Signals Satiety," *Science,* April 1978, pp. 23–33.

an organizational policy, can make a person perceive negative characteristics in most company policies and rules. Determining a person's emotional state is difficult. Yet managers need to be concerned about what issues or practices trigger strong emotions within subordinates. Strong emotions often distort perceptions.

Attitudes

attitude
An attitude is learned over a period of time. It is organized around experience and exerts a specific influence on a person's behavior.

Attitudes are determinants of behavior, because they are linked with perception, personality, and motivation. An **attitude** is a mental state of readiness, learned and organized through experience, exerting a specific influence on a person's response to people, objects, and situations with which it is related. Each of us has attitudes on numerous topics—unions, jogging, restaurants, friends, jobs, religion, the government, income taxes.

This definition of attitude has certain implications for the manager. First, attitudes are learned. Second, attitudes define one's predispositions toward given aspects of the world. Third, attitudes provide the emotional basis of one's interpersonal relations and identification with others. And fourth, attitudes are organized and are close to the core of personality. Some attitudes are persistent and enduring. Yet, like each of the psychological variables, attitudes are subject to change.[13]

Attitudes are intrinsic parts of a person's personality. However, a number of theories attempt to account for the formation and change of attitudes. One such theory proposes that people "seek a congruence between their beliefs and feelings toward objects," and suggests that the modification of attitudes depends on changing either the feelings or the beliefs.[14] The theory further assumes that people have structured attitudes that are composed of various affective and cognitive components. The interrelatedness of these components means that a change in one will set in motion a change in the others. When these components are inconsistent or exceed the person's "tolerance level," instability results. Instability can be corrected by (1) disavowal of a message designed to influence attitudes, (2) "fragmentation" of the attitudes, or (3) acceptance of the inconsistency so that a new attitude is formed.

The theory proposes that affect, cognition, and behavior determine attitudes and that attitudes, in turn, determine affect, cognition, and behavior. *Affect,* the emotional, or "feeling," component of an attitude, is learned from parents, teachers, and peer group members. One study

---

[13] M. Fishbein and I. Ajzen, *Belief, Attitude, Intention, and Behavior: An Introduction to Theory and Research* (Reading, Mass.: Addison-Wesley Publishing, 1975).

[14] M. J. Rosenberg, "A Structural Theory of Attitudes," *Publishing Opinion Quarterly,* Summer 1960, pp. 319–40.

FIGURE 3–6

The Three Components of Attitudes

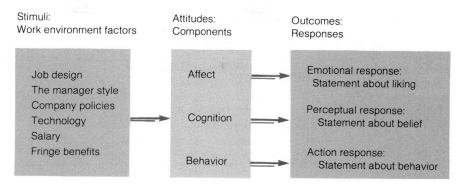

displays how the affective component can be measured. A question-naire was used to survey the attitudes of a group of students toward the church. The students then listened to tape recordings that either praised or disparaged the church. At the time of the tape recordings, the emotional responses of the students were measured with a galvanic skin response (GSR) device. Both prochurch and antichurch students responded with greater emotion (displayed by GSR changes) to state-ments that contradicted their attitudes than to those that reflected their attitudes.[15]

The *cognitive* component of an attitude consists of the person's per-ceptions, opinions, and beliefs. It refers to the thought processes with special emphasis on rationality and logic. An important element of cognition is the evaluative beliefs held by a person. Evaluative beliefs are manifested in the form of favorable or unfavorable impressions that a person holds toward an object or person.

The *behavioral* component of an attitude refers to the tendency of a person to act toward someone or something in a certain way. A person can act toward someone or something in a friendly, warm, aggressive, hostile, or apathetic way or in any of a number of other ways. Such actions could be measured or assessed to examine the behavioral component of attitudes.

Figure 3–6 presents the three components of attitudes in terms of work environment factors such as job design, company policies, and fringe benefits. These stimuli trigger an affect (emotional), cognitive (thought), and behavioral response. In essence, the stimuli result in

[15] H. W. Dickson and E. McGinnies, "Affectivity and Arousal of Attitudes as Measured by Galvanic Skin Responses," *American Journal of Psychology,* October 1966, pp. 584–89.

the formation of attitudes, which then lead to one or more responses—affect, cognitive, or behavioral.

The theory of affective, cognitive, and behavioral components as determinants of attitudes and attitude change has a significant implication for managers, namely, that the manager must be able to demonstrate that the positive aspects of contributing to the organization outweigh the negative aspects. It is through attempts to develop generally favorable attitudes toward the organization and the job that many managers achieve effectiveness.

There are many sources of attitudes. Attitudes are formed from family, peer groups, society, and previous job experiences. Early *family* experiences help shape the attitudes of individuals. The attitudes of young children usually correspond to those of their parents. As children reach their teen years, they begin to be more strongly influenced by *peers*. Peer groups are able to influence attitudes because individuals want to be accepted by others. Teenagers seek approval by sharing similar attitudes or by modifying attitudes to comply with those of a group.

Culture, mores, and language influence attitudes. The attitudes of French Canadians toward France, of Americans toward Iranians, and of Russians toward capitalism are learned in society. Within the United States, there are subcultures of ethnic communities, ghetto communities, and religious groups that help shape the attitudes of people.

Individuals learn attitudes through job experiences. They develop attitudes about such factors as pay equity, performance review, managerial capabilities, job design, and work group affiliation. Previous experiences can account for some of the individual differences in attitudes toward performance, loyalty, and commitment.

Individuals strive to maintain consistency among the components of attitudes. However, contradictions and inconsistency often occur. When this happens, a state of disequilibrium results. The tension resulting from such a state is reduced only when some form of consistency is achieved.

The term **cognitive dissonance** describes a situation where there is a discrepancy between the cognitive and behavioral components of an attitude.[16] Any form of inconsistency is uncomfortable; therefore, individuals will attempt to reduce dissonance. *Dissonance,* then, is viewed as a state within a person that, when aroused, elicits actions designed to return the person to a state of equilibrium. As an example, take the case of the chief executive officer (CEO) of a cigarette company. He may experience cognitive dissonance if he believes that he is honest and hardworking but that cigarettes contribute to lung cancer. He

cognitive dissonance
Being in a state of cognitive dissonance means that the person is experiencing a discrepancy between the components of a particular attitude. The person will be aroused to correct the cognitive dissonance.

Attitudes "hereidity"

---

[16] Leon Festinger, *A Theory of Cognitive Dissonance* (Evanston, Ill.: Row Peterson, 1957).

may think, "I am a good human being, but I am in charge of a firm producing a cancer-contributing product." These thoughts create inconsistency. Instead of quitting and giving up his successful career, he is more likely to modify his thoughts or cognitions. He could state, "Our firm has manufactured a cigarette that is now very safe and free of cancer-producing products." Or he may think that cigarette smoking actually improves the mental well-being of smokers, that it helps them reduce or cope with stress. What this example shows is that when there is inconsistency in a person's attitudes, he or she can attempt to work the problem out cognitively or behaviorally. The CEO used a cognitive process to reduce his dissonance.

Cognitive dissonance has important organizational implications. First, it helps explain choices made by individuals when attitude inconsistency is present. For example, if the elements underlying the dissonance are of little importance, the person will not be under pressure to reduce the dissonance.

Second, cognitive dissonance theory can help predict a person's propensity to change attitudes. If individuals are required, for example, by the design of their jobs or occupations to say or do things that contradict their personal attitudes, they will tend to change those attitudes to make them more compatible with what they have said or done.

Changing Attitudes. Managers are often faced with the task of changing attitudes because previously structured attitudes hinder job performance. Although many variables affect attitude change, they can all be described in terms of three general factors—trust in the sender, the message itself, and the situation.[17] If employees do not trust the manager, they will not accept the manager's message or change an attitude. Similarly, if the message is not convincing, there will be no pressure to change.

The greater the prestige of the communicator, the greater the attitude change that is produced.[18] A manager who has little prestige and is not shown respect by peers and superiors will be in a difficult position if the job requires changing the attitudes of subordinates so that they will work more effectively.

Liking the communicator produces attitude change because people try to identify with a liked communicator and tend to adopt attitudes and behaviors of the liked person.[19] Not all managers, however, are fortunate enough to be liked by each of their subordinates. Therefore,

---

[17] Jonathan L. Freedman, J. Merrill Carlsmith, and David O. Sears, *Social Psychology* (Englewood Cliffs, N.J.: Prentice-Hall, 1974), p. 271. Also see D. Coon, *Introduction to Psychology* (St. Paul, Minn.: West Publishing, 1977), pp. 626–29.

[18] Ibid., p. 272.

[19] H. C. Kelman, "Process of Opinion Change," *Public Opinion Quarterly*, Spring 1961, pp. 57–78.

it is important to recognize the importance of trust in the manager as a condition for liking the manager.

Even if a manager is trusted, presents a convincing message, and is liked, the problems of changing people's attitudes are not solved. An important factor is the strength of the employee's commitment to an attitude. A worker who has decided not to accept a promotion is committed to the belief that it is better to remain in his or her present position than to accept the promotion. Attitudes that have been expressed publicly are more difficult to change because the person has shown commitment, and to change would be to admit a mistake.

How much you are affected by attempts to change your attitude depends in part on the situation. When people are listening to or reading a persuasive message, they are sometimes distracted by other thoughts, sounds, or activities. Studies indicate that if people are distracted while they are listening to a message, they will show more attitude change because the distraction interferes with silent counterarguing.[20]

Distraction is just one of many situational factors that can increase persuasion. Another factor that makes people more susceptible to attempts to change attitudes is pleasant surroundings. The pleasant surroundings may be associated with the attempt to change the attitude.

Attitudes and Values. Values are linked to attitudes in the sense that a value serves as a way of organizing a number of attitudes. *Values* are defined "as the constellation of likes, dislikes, viewpoints, shoulds, inner inclinations, rational and irrational judgments, prejudices, and association patterns that determine a person's view of the world."[21] Certainly, the work that a person does is an important aspect of his or her world. Moreover, the importance of a value constellation is that, once internalized, it becomes, consciously or subconsciously, a standard or criterion for guiding one's actions. The study of values, therefore, is fundamental to the study of managing. Some evidence exists that values are also extremely important for understanding effective managerial behavior.[22]

Values will affect not only the perceptions of appropriate ends but

---

[20] R. A. Osterhouse and T. C. Brock, "Distraction Increases Yielding to Propaganda by Inhibiting Counterarguing," *Journal of Personality and Social Psychology*, March 1977, pp. 344–58.

[21] Edward Spranger, *Types of Men* (Halle, Germany: Max Niemeyer Verlag, 1928), as quoted in Vincent S. Flowers et al., *Managerial Values for Working* (New York: American Management Association, 1975), p. 11.

[22] Flowers et al. undertook a questionnaire study of members of the American Management Association. Questionnaires were mailed to 4,998 members, and the researchers were able to use 1,707 replies. Based on these results and other studies, Flowers et al. state that the impact of values on managerial and nonmanagerial behavior is sufficiently important to account for some variation in the relative effectiveness of managers.

also the perceptions of appropriate means to those ends. From the design and development of organizational structures and processes to the utilization of particular leadership styles and the evaluation of the performance of subordinates, value systems will be pervasive. An influential theory of leadership is based on the argument that managers cannot be expected to adopt a particular leadership style if it is contrary to their "need-structures," or value orientations.[23] Moreover, when managers evaluate the performance of subordinates, the effects of the managers' values will be noticeable. For example, one researcher reports that managers can be expected to evaluate subordinates with values similar to their own as more effective than subordinates with values dissimilar from their own.[24] The impact of values will be more pronounced in decisions involving little objective information and, consequently, a greater degree of subjectivity.

Another aspect of the importance of values occurs when the interpersonal activities of managers bring them into a confrontation with different, and potentially contradictory, values. Studies have shown that assembly-line workers, scientists, and persons in various professional occupations are characterized by particular, if not unique, value orientations.[25] Day-to-day activities will create numerous situations in which managers must relate to others having different views of what is right and wrong. Conflicts between managers and workers, administrators and teachers, and line and staff personnel have been documented and discussed in the literature of management. The manner in which these conflicts are resolved is particularly crucial to the effectiveness of the organization.[26]

Attitudes and Job Satisfaction. Job satisfaction is an attitude that individuals have about their jobs. It results from their perception of their jobs. Thus, job satisfaction stems from various aspects of the job, such as pay, promotion opportunities, supervisor, and co-workers. Job satisfaction also stems from factors of the work environment, such as the supervisor's style, policies and procedures, work group affilia-

job satisfaction
An attitude that employees develop over time about various facets of their jobs, such as pay, supervisory style, and co-workers.

---

[23] Fred E. Fiedler, *A Theory of Leadership Effectiveness* (New York: McGraw-Hill, 1967).

[24] John Senger, "Managers' Perceptions of Subordinates' Competence as a Function of Personal Value Orientations," *Academy of Management Journal,* December 1971, pp. 415–24.

[25] For example, see Flowers et al., *Managerial Values,* and Renato Tagiuri, "Value Orientations and Relationships of Managers and Scientists," *Administrative Science Quarterly,* June 1965, pp. 39–51.

[26] There has been an increasing tendency of American firms to use foreign nationals to manage overseas offices. This has created a concern for understanding the impact of culture on managers' values. See William T. Whitely and George W. England, "A Comparison of Value Systems of Managers in the U.S.A., Japan, Korea, India, and Australia," in *Proceedings of the Thirty-Fourth Annual Meeting of the Academy of Management,* 1974, p. 11; and Richard B. Peterson, "A Cross-Cultural Perspective of Supervisory Values," *Academy of Management Journal,* March 1972, pp. 105–17.

tion, working conditions, and fringe benefits. While numerous dimensions have been associated with job satisfaction, five in particular have crucial characteristics.[27] These five dimensions are:

Pay—the amount of pay received and the perceived equity of pay.

Job—the extent to which job tasks are considered interesting and provide opportunities for learning and for accepting responsibility.

Promotion opportunities—the availability of opportunities for advancement.

Supervisor—the abilities of the supervisor to demonstrate interest in and concern about employees.

Co-workers—the extent to which co-workers are friendly, competent, and supportive.

These five job satisfaction dimensions have been measured in some studies by using the Job Descriptive Index (JDI). Employees are asked to respond "yes," "no," or "?" (can't decide) in describing whether or not a word or phrase describes their attitudes about their jobs. Of the 72 items on the JDI, 20 are presented in Figure 3–7. A scoring procedure is used to arrive at a score for each of the five dimensions. These five scores are then totaled to provide a measure of overall satisfaction.

A major reason for studying job satisfaction is to provide managers with ideas about how to improve employee attitudes. Many organizations use attitude surveys to determine the levels of employee job satisfaction. National surveys indicate that, in general, workers are satisfied with their jobs.[28] In one report, no substantial change in job satisfaction was found between 1972 and 1978. Respondents answered this question: "On the whole, how satisfied are you with the work you do? Would you say that you are very satisfied, moderately satisfied, a little dissatisfied, or very dissatisfied?" In no year did less than 85 percent of the respondents indicate that they were satisfied or did less than 48 percent state that they were "very satisfied."[29]

Of course, national surveys, though interesting, may not reflect the degree of job satisfaction in a specific department or organization. There is also the problem that arises from simply asking people how satisfied they are. There is a bias toward giving a positive answer, since anything less indicates that the person is electing to stay in a dissatisfying job.

---

[27] P. C. Smith, L. M. Kendall, and C. L. Hulin, *The Measurement of Satisfaction in Work and Retirement* (Skokie, Ill.: Rand McNally, 1969).

[28] Karen E. DeBats, "The Continuing Personnel Challenge," *Personnel Journal,* May 1982, pp. 332–44.

[29] Charles N. Weaver, "Job Satisfaction in the United States in the 1970's," *Journal of Applied Psychology,* June 1980, pp. 364–67.

FIGURE 3–7

Sample Items from the 72-Item Job Descriptive Index with "Satisfied" Responses Indicated

Work		Supervision	
N	Routine	Y	Asks my advice
Y	Creative	Y	Praises good work
N	Tiresome	N	Doesn't supervise enough
Y	Gives sense of accomplishment	Y	Tells me where I stand

People		Pay	
Y	Stimulating	Y	Income adequate for normal
Y	Ambitious		expenses
N	Talk too much	N	Bad
N	Hard to meet	N	Less than I deserve
		N	Highly paid

Promotions	
Y	Good opportunity for advancement
Y	Promotion on ability
N	Dead-end job
N	Unfair promotion policy

Source: The Job Descriptive Index is copyrighted by Bowling Green State University. The complete forms, scoring key, instructions, and norms can be obtained from Dr. Patricia C. Smith, Department of Psychology, Bowling Green State University, Bowling Green, Ohio 43404. Reprinted with permission.

Satisfaction and Job Performance. One of the most debated and controversial issues in the study of job satisfaction is its relationship to job performance. Three views have been advanced: (1) satisfaction causes performance; (2) performance causes satisfaction; and (3) rewards intervene, and there is no inherent relationship.[30] Figure 3–8 shows these three viewpoints.

The first two views are supported weakly by research. A review of 20 studies dealing with the performance-satisfaction relationship found a low association between performance and satisfaction.[31] This evidence is rather convincing that a satisfied worker is not necessarily a high performer. Managerial attempts to make everyone satisfied will not yield high levels of production. Likewise, the assumption that a high-performing employee is likely to be satisfied is not supported. The third view, that factors such as rewards mediate the performance-satisfaction relationship, *is* supported by research findings.

[30] Charles N. Greene, "The Satisfaction-Performance Controversy," *Business Horizons,* October 1972, pp. 31–41.

[31] Victor H. Vroom, *Work and Motivation* (New York: John Wiley & Sons, 1964).

FIGURE 3-8

Satisfaction-Performance Relationships: Three Views

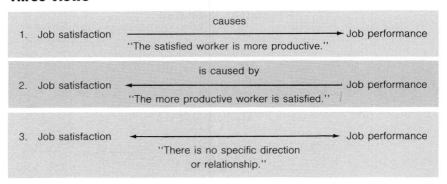

This means that performance is not a consequence of satisfaction, or vice versa. From a practical standpoint, however, most managers would like to have satisfied and productive workers. Accomplishing this, however, requires a lot of effort and sound decision making on the manager's part.

Personality

The relationship between behavior and personality is perhaps one of the most complex matters that managers have to understand. **Personality is significantly influenced by cultural and social factors.** Regardless of how personality is defined, however, certain principles are generally accepted among psychologists. These are:

personality
A unique patterning of behavioral and mental processes that characterize the individual.

1. Personality is an organized whole; otherwise, the individual would have no meaning.
2. Personality appears to be organized into patterns which are to some degree observable and measurable.
3. Although personality has a biological basis, its specific development is a product of social and cultural environments.
4. Personality has superficial aspects, such as attitudes toward being a team leader, and a deeper core, such as sentiments about authority or the Protestant work ethic.
5. Personality involves both common and unique characteristics. Every person is different from every other person in some respects, while being similar to other persons in other respects.

These five ideas are included in the following definition of personality:

An individual's personality is a relatively stable set of characteristics, tendencies, and temperaments that have been significantly formed by inheritance and by social, cultural, and environmental factors. This set of variables determines the commonalities and differences in the behavior of the individual.[32]

A review of each of the determinants that shapes personality (Figure 3–9) will indicate that managers have little control over these determi-

FIGURE 3–9

Some Major Forces Influencing Personality

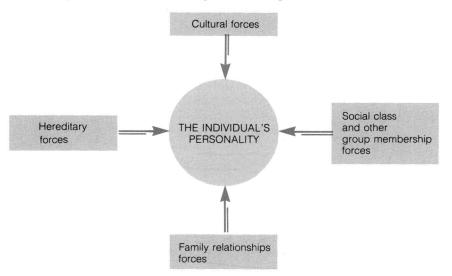

nants. However, no manager should conclude that personality is an unimportant factor in workplace behavior simply because it is formed outside the organization. The behavior of an employee cannot be understood without considering the concept of personality. In fact, personality is so interrelated with perception, attitudes, learning, and motivation that any analysis of behavior or any attempt to understand behavior is grossly incomplete unless personality is considered.

Theories of Personality.   Three theoretical approaches to understanding personality are: the trait approach, the psychodynamic approach, and the humanistic approach.

Trait Theories.   Just as the young child always seems to be searching for labels by which to classify the world, adults also label and classify

[32] This definition is based on Salvatore R. Maddi, *Personality Theories: A Comparative Analysis* (Homewood, Ill.: Dorsey Press, 1980), p. 41.

people by their psychological or physical characteristics. Classification helps to organize diversity and reduce the many to a few.

Allport was the most influential of the trait theorists. In his view, traits are the building blocks of personality, the guideposts for action, the source of the individual's uniqueness. *Traits* are defined as inferred predispositions that direct the behavior of an individual in consistent and characteristic ways. Furthermore, traits produce consistencies in behavior because they are enduring attributes, and they are general or broad in scope.[33]

The psychologist Cattell has for decades studied personality traits. He has gathered many measures of traits through behavioral observation, records of people's life histories, questionnaires, and objective tests.[34] On the basis of his research, Cattell has concluded that 16 basic traits underlie individual differences in behavior. The research resulted in the development of Cattell's 16PF (Sixteen Personality Factor) questionnaire, which is used to measure the degree to which people have these traits. Among the traits that Cattell identified are reserved-outgoing, practical-imaginative, relaxed-tense, and humble-assertive. All 16 of Cattell's traits are bipolar; that is, each trait has two extremes (e.g., relaxed-tense).

Trait theories have been criticized as not being real theories in that they do not explain how behavior is caused. The mere identification of such traits as tough-minded, conservative, expedient, reserved, or outgoing does not offer insight into the development and dynamics of personality. Furthermore, trait approaches have not been successful in predicting behavior across a spectrum of situations. This is due to the fact that situations (the job, the work activities) are largely ignored in trait theories.

Psychodynamic Theories. The dynamic nature of personality was not addressed seriously until Sigmund Freud's work was published. Freud accounted for individual differences in personality by suggesting that people deal with their fundamental drives differently. To highlight these differences, he pictured a continuing battle between two parts of personality, the id and the superego, moderated by the ego.[35]

The *id* is the primitive, unconscious part of the personality, the storehouse of fundamental drives. It operates irrationally and impulsively without considering whether what is desired is possible or morally acceptable.

---

[33] R. B. Cattell, *Personality and Mood by Questionnaire* (San Francisco: Jossey-Bass, 1973); and R. B. Cattell, *The Scientific Analysis of Personality* (Chicago: Aldine Publishing, 1966).

[34] Ibid.

[35] Sigmund Freud, "Psychopathology of Everyday Life," in *The Standard Edition of the Complete Psychological Works of Sigmund Freud*, ed. J. Strachey (London: Hogarth Press, 1960).

TABLE 3–4

Some Ego Defense Mechanisms

Mechanism	How It Is Applied in an Organization
Rationalization	Attempting to justify one's behavior as being rational and justifiable. (I had to violate company policies to get the job finished.)
Identification	Increasing feelings of worth by identifying self with person or institution of illustrious standing. (I am working for Jim, who is really the best manager in the country.)
Compensation	Covering up weakness by emphasizing desirable traits or making up for frustration in one area by overgratification in another. (I may be a harsh manager, but I play no favorites.)
Denial of reality	Protecting self from unpleasant reality by refusing to perceive it. (There is no chance that because of the economy this company will have to let people go.)

The *superego* is the storehouse of an individual's values, including moral attitudes shaped by society. The superego corresponds roughly to conscience. The superego is often in conflict with the id. The id wants to do what feels good, while the superego insists on doing what is "right."

The *ego* acts as the arbitrator of the conflict. It represents the person's picture of physical and social reality, of what will lead to what and of which things are possible in the perceived world. Part of the ego's job is to choose actions that will gratify id impulses without having undesirable consequences.

Often, the ego has to compromise and try to satisfy the id and the superego. Sometimes, this involves using ego defense mechanisms. These are mental processes that attempt to resolve conflict among psychological states and external realities. Table 3–4 presents some of the ego defense mechanisms that are used by individuals.

Even Freud's critics admit that he made contributions to the modern understanding of behavior. His emphasis on unconscious determinants of behavior is important. The significance he attributed to early-life origins of adult behavior gave impetus to the study of child development. In addition, his method of treating neurosis through psychoanalysis has added to our understanding of how to get people back on the right track toward effective functioning.[36]

Humanistic Theories. Humanistic approaches to understanding personality are characterized by an emphasis on the growth and self-

---

[36] Philip G. Zimbardo, *Psychology and Life* (Glenview, Ill.: Scott, Foresman, 1979), p. 484.

actualization of the individual. These theories emphasize the importance of how people perceive their world and all of the forces influencing them.

Carl Rogers' approach to understanding personality is humanistic or people-centered.[37] His advice is to listen to what people say about themselves and to attend to these views and their significance in the person's experiences. Rogers believes that the most basic drive of the human organism is toward *self-actualization*—the constant striving to realize one's inherent potential.

It is difficult to criticize theories that are so people-centered. However, some critics complain that the humanists never explain clearly the origin of the mechanism for attaining self-actualization. Other critics point out that people must operate in an environment that is largely ignored by the humanists. An overemphasis on self neglects the reality that an individual must function in a complex environment.

It might help to consider how each of the major theoretical approaches improves our understanding of personality. Trait theories provide a catalog that *describes* the individual. Psychodynamic theories integrate the characteristics of people and *explain* the dynamic nature of personality development. Humanist theories emphasize the *person* and the importance of self-actualization to personality. Each theoretical approach attempts to highlight the unique qualities of an individual that influence his or her behavior patterns.

Personality tests measure emotional, motivational, interpersonal, and attitudinal characteristics. Hundreds of such tests are available to organizations. One of the most widely used tests is the Minnesota Multiphasic Personality Inventory (MMPI). It consists of statements, to which a person responds: "true," "false," or "cannot say." The MMPI items cover such areas as health, psychosomatic symptoms, neurological disorders, and social attitudes, as well as many well-known neurotic or psychotic manifestations, such as phobias, delusions, and sadistic trends.[38]

Projective tests are also used to assess personality. These tests have a person respond to a picture, an inkblot, or a story. In order to encourage the person to respond freely, only brief, general instructions are given. For the same reason, the test pictures or stories are vague. The underlying reason for this is that the individual perceives and interprets the test material in a manner that will display his or her personality. That is, the individual will project his or her attitudes, needs, anxieties, and conflicts.

---

[37] Carl Rogers, *On Personal Power: Inner Strength and Its Revolutionary Impact* (New York: Delacorte, 1977).

[38] A. Anastasi, *Psychological Testing* (New York: Macmillan, 1976), chaps. 17, 18, and 19.

TABLE 3-5

**Sample Items from an Early Version
of Rotter's Test of Internal-
External Locus of Control**

1a Promotions are earned through hard work and persistence.
1b Making a lot of money is largely a matter of getting the right breaks.

2a When I am right, I can convince others.
2b It is silly to think that one can really change another person's basic attitudes.

3a In my case, the grades I make are the results of my own efforts; luck
    has little or nothing to do with it.
3b Sometimes I feel that I have little to do with the grades I get.

4a Getting along with people is a skill that must be practiced.
4b It is almost impossible to figure out how to please some people.

Personality and Behavior.   An issue of interest to behavioral scientists and researchers is whether the personality factors measured by such inventories as the MMPI or the 16PF questionnaire or by projective tests can predict behavior or performance in organizations. Using a total inventory to examine whether personality is a factor in explaining behavior is rarely done in organizational behavior research. Typically, a few select personality factors such as locus of control, creativity, Machiavellianism, or androgyny are used to examine behavior and performance.

locus of control
Describes the degree to which individuals believe that what happens to them is or is not within their personal control.

Locus of Control.   The **locus of control** of individuals determines the degree to which they believe that their behaviors influence what happens to them. Some people believe that they are autonomous— that they are masters of their own fate and bear personal responsibility for what happens to them. They see the control of their lives as coming from inside themselves. Rotter calls these people *internalizers*.[39]

Rotter also holds that many people view themselves as helpless pawns of fate, controlled by outside forces over which they have little, if any, influence. Such people believe that the locus of control is external rather than internal. Rotter calls them *externalizers*.

Rotter devised a scale containing 29 items to identify whether people are internalizers or externalizers.[40] The statements are concerned with success, failure, misfortune, and political events. One statement reflects a belief in internal control, and the other reflects a belief in external control. Four pairs of statements on the Rotter scale are shown in Table 3–5.

A study of 900 employees in a public utility found that internally

---

[39] J. R. Rotter, "Generalized Expectancies for Internal versus External Control of Reinforcement," *Psychological Monographs* 1, no. 609 (1966), p. 80.

[40] J. B. Rotter, "External Control and Internal Control," *Psychology Today,* June 1971, p. 37.

controlled employees were more satisfied with their jobs, more likely to be in managerial positions, and more satisfied with a participative management style than were employees who perceived themselves to be externally controlled.[41]

In an interesting study of 90 entrepreneurs, locus of control, perceived stress, coping behaviors, and performance were examined.[42] The study was done in a business district over a 3½-year period following flooding by Hurricane Agnes. Internalizers were found to perceive less stress than did externalizers and to employ more task-centered coping behaviors and fewer emotion-centered coping behaviors. In addition, the task-oriented coping behaviors of internalizers were associated with better performance.

Creativity.   There are a number of ways to view creativity. First, you can consider the creative person as mad. The madness of such creative artists as Van Gogh or Nijinsky is often cited as proof of this view. Research evidence, however, offers no support for it. Instead, it has been found that creative people have superior ego strength and handle problems constructively. Second, you can see the creative person as being disconnected from the art of creativity. Creativity, in this view, is a mystical act. Third, you can conclude that to be creative, a person must be intelligent. However, research shows that some intelligent people are creative and that others are not.[43] Or, finally, you can view creativity as a possibility open to every person, as an expression of personality that can be developed.[44]

Many studies have examined creativity. Life histories, personality characteristics, and tests are often scrutinized to determine a person's degree of creativity. In a typical test, subjects might be asked to examine a group of drawings and then answer what the drawings represent. Figure 3–10 presents a sample of a line drawing test that is used to determine the creativity of young children.[45] Novel and unusual answers are rated as being creative.

If management adopts the first two views of creativity, it might attempt to keep creative people out of the organization. Adoption of

[41] T. R. Mitchell, C. M. Smyser, and S. E. Weed, "Locus of Control: Supervision and Work Satisfaction," *Academy of Management Journal,* September 1975, pp. 623–31.

[42] C. R. Anderson, "Locus of Control, Coping Behaviors, and Performance in a Stress Setting: A Longitudinal Study," *Journal of Applied Psychology,* August 1977, pp. 446–51.

[43] L. M. Terman and M. Oden, *The Gifted Child at Midlife* (Stanford, Calif.: Stanford University Press, 1959).

[44] S. S. Gryskiewicz, "Restructuring for Innovation," *Issues and Observations,* November 1981, p. 1; and Isaac Asimov, "Creativity Will Dominate Our Time after the Concepts of Work and Fun Have Been Blurred by Technology," *Personnel Administrator,* December 1983, p. 42.

[45] M. A. Wallace and N. Kogan, *Modes of Thinking in Young Children* (New York: Holt, Rinehart & Winston, 1965).

FIGURE 3–10

Testing Creativity

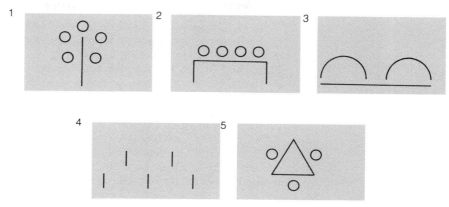

For item 1, "lollipop bursting into pieces" is a unique response, while "flower" is not. For item 2, "foot and toes" is a unique suggestion, while "table with things on top" is not. In response to item 3, "two haystacks on a flying carpet" is a unique suggestion, while "two igloos" is not. For item 4, "five worms hanging" is a unique response, while "raindrops" is not. For item 5, "three mice eating a piece of cheese" is a unique response, while "three people sitting around a table" is not.

the third view, which is not fully supported, might result in the hiring of only highly intelligent people. However, if management views creativity as a personality factor that can be developed, then it would move ahead to initiate development procedures.

The following Close-Up illustrates Roger von Oech's belief that creativity can be taught. von Oech has convinced a number of clients that each person has some creativity. In most cases, unfortunately, this creativity is not encouraged in organizations.

ORGANIZATIONS: CLOSE-UP

Creativity Can Be Taught: A New Training Concept

Many people feel that creativity can no more be taught or instilled by training than can ambidexterity, perfect pitch, or a taste for cod liver oil. They believe that creativity is a kind of neurochemical quality that you either have at birth or never. Roger von Oech (rhymes with *heck*) disagrees with the "you are born with it" theory. His position is: (1) we are all born with a creativity quality, but society and its institutions regulate and socialize us into noncreative thought patterns; and (2) these patterns can be broken by the use of certain techniques, exercises, and training.

von Oech is known in the business world as a creative-thinking consultant. His corporate clients, which appear to agree with his methods, include Apple, Atari, Du Pont, IBM, ITT, Kaiser, NASA, Sears, Wells Fargo, and Xerox. His creative training seminars run about two days, involve about 15 people each, and address high-tech engineering and marketing problems. The usual seminar begins with a film, which is followed by a lecture and creativity exercises. Von Oech believes that people learn creative thinking, not by being talked to, but by doing.

The von Oech method of training attempts to unlock a number of attitudes that stifle creativity in organizations. The "mental locks" discussed in the seminar were first treated in his now best-selling book entitled *A Whack on the Side of the Head*. Some of these locks are:

The right answer. This is a fallacy. Thinking that there is only one correct answer halts the search for other ideas.

Be practical. In other words, stifle your imagination. This is another idea killer.

To err is wrong. Not to err is not to experiment.

Play is frivolous. This is nonsense. People with playful attitudes come up with many good ideas.

Don't be foolish. This is bad advice. If we never tried anything that might make us look ridiculous, we would still be in caves.

I'm not creative. This is the worst mental lock. Self-condemnation stifles everything.

Just as Steven Jobs (founder of Apple) and Nolan Bushnell (founder of Atari) are originators of new industries, von Oech is the founder of the idea industry. He is convinced, as are a number of his clients, that creativity can be taught and should be encouraged. In a short time, he has become known as Silicon Valley's guru of creative-thought training and development.

Source: Adapted from Robert S. Wieder, "How to Get Great Ideas," *Success,* November 1983, pp. 29–31, 59–60.

Organizations can do a number of things to help develop creativity.[46] They are:

1. *Buffering.* Managers can look for ways to absorb the risks of creative decisions.
2. *Organizational time-outs.* Give people time off to work on a problem, and allow them to think things through.
3. *Intuition.* Give half-baked ideas a chance.

[46] Gryskiewicz, "Restructuring for Innovation," p. 3.

4. *Innovative attitudes.* Encourage everyone to think of ways to solve problems.
5. *Innovative organizational structures.* Let employees see and interact with many managers and mentors.

Managerial interest in developing creativity seems worthwhile. A review of research findings indicates that creative individuals share a number of important characteristics. Creative individuals are self-confident and motivated to succeed; they approach life enthusiastically; and they push on even when they must overcome obstacles.[47] These characteristics are important and valuable in any organization.

Machiavellianism. Imagine yourself in the following situation with two other people. Thirty new $1 bills are on the table to be distributed in any way the group decides. The game is over as soon as two of you agree to how it will be divided. Obviously, the fairest distribution would be $10 each. However, a selfish party could cut out the third person, and the other two would each end up with $15. Suppose that one person suggests this alternative to you and that before you can decide, the left-out person offers to give you $16, taking $14 as his or her share and cutting out the other person. What would you do?

Machiavellianism, a concept derived from the writings of Niccolò Machiavelli, helps answer the question.[48] Machiavelli was concerned with the manipulation of people and with the orientations and tactics used by manipulators versus nonmanipulators.[49]

From anecdotal descriptions of power tactics and the nature of influential people, various scales have been constructed to measure **Machiavellianism.** In one scale, the questions are organized around a cluster of beliefs about tactics, people, and morality. The following Close-Up presents the short form of the MACH scale. Remember, this is only a brief scale, so interpretation of your score should be done with caution.

Machiavellianism
A manipulative and cynical style of behavior toward others.

ORGANIZATIONS: CLOSE-UP

Measuring Your Machiavellian Tendencies

Organizations are interested in the Machiavellian tendencies of their managers. A number of scales can provide a general idea of these tenden-

---

[47] F. H. Barron, *Creativity and Personal Freedom* (New York: Van Nostrand Reinhold, 1968); and D. W. MacKinnon, "Personality and the Realization of Creative Potential," *American Psychologist,* March 1963, pp. 273–81.

[48] R. Christie and F. L. Geis, eds., *Studies in Machiavellianism* (New York: Academic Press, 1970).

[49] Ibid.

cies. The 10-item scale listed below will provide you with your own score for Machiavellianism. Take a few minutes, and complete the 10 items. Indicate your reactions to each of the statements shown below by circling one number for each statement. The key to answering is as follows:

1 = Disagree a lot.
2 = Disagree a little.
3 = Neutral.
4 = Agree a little.
5 = Agree a lot.

1. The best way to handle people is to tell them what they want to hear.   1   2   3   (4)   5

2. When you ask someone to do something for you, it is best to give the real reasons for wanting it rather than giving reasons that might carry more weight.   1   2   (3)   4   5

3. Anyone who completely trusts anyone else is asking for trouble.   1   (2)   3   4   5

4. It is hard to get ahead without cutting corners here and there.   (1)   2   3   4   5

5. It is safest to assume that all people have a vicious streak and it will come out when given a chance.   1   2   3   4   (5)

6. One should take action only when sure it is morally right.   1   2   3   4   (5)

7. Most people are basically good and kind.   1   (2)   3   4   5

8. There is no excuse for lying to someone else.   (1)   2   3   4   5

9. Most people forget more easily the death of a parent than the loss of their property.   (1)   2   3   4   5

10. Generally speaking, individuals will not work hard unless they're forced to do so.   1   2   3   (4)   5

Now that you have completed the scale, you can score it. First, add the numbers you circled for items 1, 3, 4, 5, 9, and 10. For your responses to items 2, 6, 7, and 8, reverse the score so that 5 becomes 1, 4 becomes 2, and so on. Second, add up your scores on the 10 items. This is your total MACH score. An average score on this form is about 25. If you scored much higher than this, say 38, you would be classified as a HIGH MACH. If you scored much lower than a 25, you would be classified as a LOW MACH.

Remember, this is not a test that can provide the final answer about your Machiavellian tendencies. Accurately assessing personality is much more difficult.

Source: Richard Christie and Florence L. Geis, *Studies in Machiavellianism* (New York: Academic Press, 1970). Reprinted by permission.

This particular MACH scale differentiates between high and low Machiavellians on the basis of the extent to which people endorse Machiavelli's rules of conduct.[50] In the money allocation game, the individuals who get the lion's share are those who score high on this scale. The low-MACH scorers get only slightly less than would be expected by a fair, one-third split.

Androgyny.   In our society, males are supposed to be masculine or macho, while females are supposed to be feminine. We are born with a sexual gender, but we are trained to develop a sexual identity that fits the inherited gender. This training begins before birth with the selection of clothes, furniture, and room colors for the newborn: blue for a boy and pink for a girl. When our behavior is not in step with the traditional sex role, our very self-concept is questioned.

androgyny
The blending of masculine and feminine traits and characteristics.

The concept of **androgyny** refers to the blending of the behaviors and personality traits traditionally associated with one or the other sexual identity. The androgynous person is both masculine and feminine, and is able to respond to situational demands with the most effective behavior for the particular situation. The androgynous person can be tender and gentle in one situation and hard-nosed and aggressive in another. That is, androgyny implies an adaptable personality.

Bem has pioneered and influenced the thinking on the androgynous personality. She developed the Bem Sex Role Inventory (BSRI), a series of 60 adjectives to measure androgyny patterns.[51] The BSRI includes 20 masculine adjectives (e.g., ambitious, self-reliant), 20 feminine adjectives (e.g., affectionate, gentle), and 20 neutral adjectives (e.g., truthful, happy). The average number of points assigned by the person to the feminine items is the femininity score, and the average number of points assigned to the masculine items is the masculinity score. Androgyny is defined as having high scores on both the masculine and feminine dimensions.

Studies using the BSRI have shown that androgynous individuals are more independent, nurturant, and supportive than those who score high on either the femininity or masculinity scales.[52] It has also been found that the self-esteem, social competence, and achievement orientations of androgynous men and women are higher than those of non-androgynous men and women.

The Organizational Issue for Debate that opened this chapter represented two views about personality. The content of the chapter indicates that both views make reasonable points. First, you must understand individual differences before you worry about how the person

---

[50] F. L. Geis and T. H. Moon, "Machiavellianism and Deception," *Journal of Personality and Social Psychology,* October 1981, pp. 766–75.

[51] S. L. Bem, "The Measurement of Psychological Androgyny," *Journal of Consulting and Clinical Psychology,* April 1974, pp. 155–62.

[52] J. R. Spence and R. L. Helmreich, *Masculinity and Femininity: Their Psychological Dimensions, Correlates, and Antecedents* (Austin: University of Texas Press, 1978).

interacts with the work environment. This was a point made by advocates of the individual difference approach. Second, as shown by the framework used to review influences on behavior (Figure 3–1), environmental (organizational) variables directly influence behavior. No individual operates in a vacuum. The "real world" consists of people, environmental forces, and situational events. Thus, instead of choosing sides in the debate, it is more reasonable to consider the merits of both sides.

Now that we have explored the notion of individual differences, it is time that we addressed a specific behavioral concern—motivation (Chapters 4 and 5). In order to understand such topics as motivation, rewards, and stress, the psychological and other variables discussed in this chapter must be a part of the manager's knowledge base. Attempting to motivate employees, or to distribute meaningful rewards, or to help subordinates cope with the stresses of work life without a sound, fundamental grasp of and insight into abilities, skills, perception, attitudes, and personality is like groping in the dark. The uninformed manager is likely to eventually find his way, but there will be a lot of bumps, bruises, and wrong turns. The knowledgeable manager, on the other hand, possesses the insight and wisdom needed to move efficiently, to make better decisions, and to be on the lookout for inevitable individual differences among his or her subordinates. As we proceed through the next four individual level chapters, think about how abilities, skills, perception, attitudes, and personality help shape the behavior and performance of employees.

SUMMARY OF KEY POINTS

A. Employees joining an organization must adjust to a new environment, new people, and new tasks. The manner in which people adjust to situations and other people will depend largely on their psychological makeup and their personal backgrounds.

B. Individual perceptual processes help the person face the realities of the world. People are influenced by other people and by situations, needs, and past experiences. While a manager is perceiving employees, they are also perceiving the manager.

C. Attitudes are linked with behavioral patterns in a complex manner. They are organized, and they provide the emotional basis for most of a person's interpersonal relations. Changing attitudes is extemely difficult and requires, at the very least, trust in the communicator and strength of message.

D. Job satisfaction is the attitude workers have about their jobs. Managers should be aware of research findings that a satisfied worker is not necessarily a higher performer.

E. Personality is developed long before a person joins an organization. It is influenced by hereditary, cultural, and social determinants. To assume that personality can be modified easily can result in managerial frustration and ethical problems. The manager should try to cope with personality differences among people and not try to change personalities to fit his or her model of the ideal person.

F. A number of personality variables, such as locus of control, creativity, androgyny, and Machiavellianism have been found to be associated with behavior and performance. Although difficult to measure, these variables appear to be important in explaining and predicting individual behavior.

DISCUSSION AND REVIEW QUESTIONS

1. Some people believe that perception is a more important explanation of behavior than is "reality." Why would this assumption about perception be made?

2. Explain why managers who are not treated favorably by their superiors would have problems in changing their subordinates' negative attitudes toward the organization.

3. Would abilities and skills be considered important in analyzing differences in high-technology jobs (e.g., computer specialist, robotics engineer)? In skilled work (e.g., machine lathe operator)?

4. Provide some examples of selective perception that would be used in purchasing a new automobile and in accepting a new position with an organization.

5. Some people state that being too concerned with individual differences can cause chaos in an organization. Do you agree? Why?

6. Why is it difficult to measure differences in personality and other individual differences?

7. Is a happy worker necessarily the most productive worker? Why?

8. Why would a manager act differently in leading a subordinate who is an internalizer than in leading another subordinate who is an externalizer?

9. Are the value systems of an employee largely developed before he or she begins to work for an organization? What are the managerial implications of your answer?

10. How could a manager encourage individual creativity among subordinates? Outline a reasonable plan of action.

ADDITIONAL REFERENCES

Bateman, T. S., and D. W. Organ. "Job Satisfaction and the Good Soldier: The Relationship between Affect and Employee 'Citizenship.' " *Academy of Management Journal,* 1983, pp. 487–95.

Block, J., "Some Enduring and Consequential Structures of Personality. In *Further Explorations in Personality,* ed. A. I. Rabin et al. New York: John Wiley & Sons, 1981.

Brewer, J., and C. Dubnicki. Relighting the Fires with an Employee Revitalization Program." *Personnel Journal,* 1983, pp. 812–18.

Cooper, W. H. "Ubiquitous Halo." *Psychological Bulletin,* 1981, pp. 218–44.

Eagly, A. H., and W. Wood. "Inferred Sex Differences in States as a Determinant of Gender Stereotypes about Social Influence." *Journal of Personality and Social Psychology,* 1982, pp. 915–28.

Fisher, K. W. "A Theory of Cognitive Development: The Control and Construction of Hierarchies of Skills." *Psychological Review,* 1980, pp. 477–531.

Jones, R. A. "Perceiving Other People: Stereotyping as a Process of Social Cognition." In *In the Eye of the Beholder: Contemporary Issues in Stereotyping* ed. A. G. Miller. New York: Praeger Publishers, 1982.

Major, B., and K. Deaux. "Individual Differences in Justice Behavior." In *Equity and Justice in Social Behavior,* ed. J. Greenberg and R. Cohen. New York: Academic Press, 1982.

Rubin, Z. "Does Personality Really Change after 20?" *Psychology Today,* 1981, pp. 18–27.

CASE FOR ANALYSIS

Affirmative Action: Inaccurate Perceptions or a Real Problem?

Nick Troc is the accounting department manager of Mid-States Telephone Corporation, a large telephone utility. Nick is 36 years old and a college graduate. He joined Mid-States one year ago, after working for Southern Lines Telephone Company for eight years. The accounting department employs about 230 female and 125 male clerks, 8 female and 15 male first-line supervisors, 6 female and 14 male second-line supervisors, and 1 female and 6 male third-line supervisors. Recently, Nick sensed some problems in working with and understanding the third-level supervisors, and he believed that the problems might have been caused by the firm's attempts to implement an affirmative action promotion policy. Each of these supervisors had been in his or her present position for less than 15 months. The third supervisory level was created by the executive committee to improve efficiency and provide managers at Mid-States with additional opportunities for promotion. Prior to this change, only two levels of supervision existed. Many of the promotable employees were leaving Mid-States because of the lack of advancement opportunities.

Discussions with various employees had not revealed why the third-level supervisor group did not seem to be working effectively as a team. After searching for answers to this problem, Nick decided to ask the personnel department for some information about each of the third-level supervisors. Below is a listing taken from the labor force inventory data bank. The data bank is used to acquire a background summary on present employees who are candidates for promotion and to examine the records of employees who have retired in the past five years.

Labor Force Inventory Summary: Third-Level Supervisors

Dennis Balinger: Age 46; time in present position, 12 months; graduate of Myers High School and Lee Junior College. Has worked at Mid-States for 21 years; rated in top 80 percentile for last 6 years of performance appraisal; present salary, $27,000.

Sam Turkla: Age 51; time in present position, 6 months; graduate of Wilcox High School. Has worked at Mid-States for 8 years; rated in top 65 percentile for last 3 years of performance appraisal; present salary, $28,400.

Mark Hardesty: Age 40; time in present position, 15 months; graduate of Midwest University. Has worked at Mid-States for 14 years; rated in top 84 percentile for last 6 years of performance appraisal; present salary, $28,250; CPA.

John Jackson: Age 50; time in present position, 8 months; graduate of the University of the South. Has worked at Mid-States for 8 months; present salary, $30,500; CPA.

Doris Riska: Age 44; time in present position, 9 months; graduate of Tuley High School. Has worked at Mid-States for 22 years; rated in top 75 percentile for last 5 years in performance appraisal; present salary, $28,400.

Willis Rogers: Age 42; time in present position, 14 months; graduate of Walker High School and Darby Junior College. Has worked at Mid-States for 12 years; rated in top 78 percentile for last 4 years in performance appraisal; present salary, $27,600.

Rudy Ramirez: Age 44; time in present position, 12 months; graduate of Northeast University. Has worked at Mid-States for 16 years; rated in top 75 percentile for last 3 years in performance appraisal; present salary, $28,200; CPA.

Nick's Analysis

Nick, in carefully reviewing the labor force inventory information, noted that three of the supervisors were CPAs, that Doris was a female, that Willis was a black, that Rudy was a Chicano, and that Sam was the oldest at 51. Whether these obvious individual differences had resulted in the lack of coordination among the supervisors was puzzling Nick. He did not accept the premise that such differences could influence behavior and performance on the job. This assumption caused him to discuss some of the problems with a few of the third-line supervisors. A summary of three of these discussions is presented. The discussion with Willis was as follows:

Nick: Willis, I'm trying to "dig out" what I believe is a problem among the third-level supervisors in accounting.

Willis: Nick, what problem are you talking about?

Nick: Well, you and the others just do not seem to be working well with each other.

Willis: I don't know what you mean by "working well with each other." I thought that we each worked on our assigned jobs and were performing quite well.

Nick: Well, I don't know. Perhaps your background is getting in the way of working together.

Willis: Background! I don't know what you mean. I'm from Chicago, and I like soul food. Is that what you mean?

Nick: No, Willis. I mean that each of you is so different in age, education, and overall qualifications. Let me think this out a little more, and I will get back to you.

Willis: OK, Nick, but I think you're making something out of nothing. Give us a chance to "click," and we will.

The conversation with Doris proceeded in this manner:

Nick: Doris, I need your help with a problem.

Doris: What kind of problem?

Nick: Well, I've been thinking that the third-level supervisors group is too diverse to work well together.

Doris: Nick, I'm female and the others are male, and this is the only difference that I can see.

Nick: Some of you are CPAs and college graduates.

Doris: So what? I do my job and perform any accounting task that has to be done. Are you telling me to get a CPA and a degree? This was not the way this job was presented to me nine months ago.

Nick: Doris, you're jumping to conclusions.

Doris: Nick, you're the one who called me in. Of course, I am jumping to conclusions. You call me in, and in one swoop you starting talking about certificates, degrees, and problems. I think that you are making a problem because you think one is present.

At this time, Doris was called out of the session with Nick because of some problems in her unit. The discussion between John and Nick proceeded as follows:

Nick: John, I wanted to discuss some problems that exist with the third-level supervisors.

John: You're right on target, Nick. These guys and Doris are a pain. They just are not top-quality people. They lack the abilities and the skills to do the job. There are also other problems.

Nick: What problems do you perceive?

John: They want to run their own small world. They are not cooperative, and they hold back relevant information from me. If I were you, I'd bust them up good and not let these practices go too far. They can become such a problem that accounting services can become a tangled mess.

Nick: John, how long have you been faced with these difficulties?

John: Since the day I set foot in the door. The reception I received was miserable. These people all come on as aristocracy.

Nick: Thanks for your ideas. I'll get back to you later.

Nick sat and thought about his discussions with the supervisors. He just didn't want to accept the idea that Mid-State's affirmative action program, which included promoting minority employees, was the cause of the problem that he felt existed. Willis, Rudy, and Doris were all fine people, but they did not appear to be working as a team. In addition, the other four supervisors were not working as a team.

Questions for Consideration

1. What individual differences that are being overlooked appear to be important in this case?

2. Why do you believe that Nick is overlooking the individual differences identified in your answer to the first question?

3. Do you feel that Nick is communicating effectively the problems that he believes exist? Why?

EXPERIENTIAL EXERCISE

SELF-PERCEPTION: ARE YOU ON TARGET?

Objectives

1. To learn how you perceive yourself.
2. To determine the perceptions that others have of you.
3. To find areas in which your self-perception and the perceptions that others have of you do not match.

Related Topics

The perceptions we have of others, our jobs, and our families are all projected onto other people or things. We also have self-perceptions, our own internal picture of what we are. Sometimes, we are surprised that others do not perceive us as we think they do.

Starting the Exercise

Individually complete the list by writing on a separate sheet of paper the statements that best describe you. Some of the statements may not apply to you. If they do not, do not place them on your sheet.

Have a classmate do the same thing—write down the statements that describe you on a separate sheet of paper. Also have a close friend or a family member prepare a list of statements that describe you.

Collect the lists from the classmate and the friend or the family member. Analyze the results. What differences in your self-perception or others' perceptions of you did you find?

Exercise Procedures

1. Form into groups of three members each to discuss what you each found. Did the others find discrepancies in their perceptions versus what others perceived?
2. Discuss why these discrepancies were found. What common error do we make in perceiving ourselves and the way others perceive us? Are you someone who:
    a. Listens carefully to what others say?
    b. Tends to make snap judgments?
    c. Is rushed by time?
    d. Prefers to work alone?
    e. Daydreams a lot?
    f. Is competitive?
    g. Is argumentative?
    h. Has a good sense of humor?

    i. Is satisfied with life?
    j. Is defensive?
    k. Has trouble relaxing?
    l. Is emotional?
  m. Is warm and friendly?
    n. Wants to finish the job on time?
    o. Is independent?
    p. Becomes upset easily?
    q. Can't keep a secret?
    r. Always asks for help?
    s. Is friendly?
    t. Gets nervous under pressure?

Chapter 4

LEARNING OBJECTIVES

After completing Chapter 4, you should be able to:

Define the meaning of content theories of motivation.

Describe the difference between Maslow's need hierarchy and Alderfer's ERG theory of motivation.

Discuss why McClelland believes that his theory of learned needs is important.

Identify the principles of operant conditioning.

Compare four content theories and how they explain motivation.

Motivation: Content Theories and Applications

Can Self-Actualization Be Achieved?

Argument For

You will read in this chapter that Maslow proposed a five-level need hierarchy. He suggested that once the first four levels of needs have been satisfied, an individual's behavior would be motivated by the self-actualization need. This is the need to fulfill oneself by maximizing the full use of one's abilities, skills, and potential. The picture Maslow gives us of the self-actualized person is a very positive one. The self-actualized person is no longer motivated by deficiencies but is motivated to grow and become all that he or she is capable of becoming.

Maslow spent considerable effort in attempting to define and clarify the major characteristics of the self-actualized person. He based his conclusions on the informal study of personal acquaintances, friends, and public and historic figures such as Abraham Lincoln and Thomas Jefferson. Some of the individual characteristics he identified in self-actualized persons were:

1. The ability to perceive people and events accurately.
2. The ability to remove themselves from the normal turmoils of life.
3. A problem and task orientation. They seemed to have a mission in life to do something that was worthwhile.
4. The ability to derive personal satisfaction from their own personal development in doing something worthwhile.
5. The capacity to love and experience life in a very intense manner.
6. An interest in the goals toward which they

were working, but in many instances the way in which the goals were pursued was itself a goal.

7. Being highly creative in their work.

Maslow's self-actualized person had mastered the lower needs and was motivated by what Maslow and Alderfer (also discussed in this chapter) called growth motivation. It was Maslow's belief that many people do not reach the stage of self-actualization because of poor environmental conditions. There is also the need to take risks in order to grow, which Maslow believed was a difficult step to take. Maslow believed that self-actualization could be achieved with the proper environmental conditions and a willingness to take risk in order to grow personally.

Argument Against

Maslow's views about the attainability of self-actualization are a pipe dream, according to critics. In terms of scientifically studying self-actualization, Maslow's attempt is not even partially acceptable. Maslow was subjective and biased in every procedure that he used. In fact, many of the living individuals whom he studied preferred to remain anonymous, so that other researchers could not check the accuracy of his conclusions. The historic figures were dead, requiring reliance on written accounts that were often self-serving.

There is also a strong elitist orientation in Maslow's view of self-actualization. People confined by a meager education, blue-collar jobs, or societal expectations are very unlikely to approach a state of self-actualization. The millions of blue-collar workers and even many managers would never be able to self-actualize. Maslow's claim that everyone from Abraham Lincoln to the least skilled manufacturing line worker has the potential to self-actualize is really stretching our imagination.

Thus, critics believe that Maslow's claim that a motivation to self-actualize exists in the general population is overstated. Some individuals certainly have the drive to self-actualize, but many others possess no such drive. In fact, in the blue-collar world of the 1980s, self-actualization may not even be feasible. Workers are concerned about job security, self-esteem, and working conditions. There is also the issue of the perfect state of self-actualization. In reading Maslow's list of characteristics, one is impressed with the view that being self-actualized is a perfect state. There undoubtedly have been and are self-actualized individuals who are tyrannical, unethical, ruthless, boring, and irritating. For the most part, these self-actualized misfits are not even described or mentioned in Maslow's writings.

In summary, Maslow's view that most people have an intense drive and the potential to self-actualize (1) has not been supported by research, (2) is elitist in tone, and (3) is not of any value to managers attempting to create a positively charged atmosphere of motivation. Don't waste time on such an unsupported view of people.

An important determinant of individual performance is motivation. It is not the only determinant; other variables such as effort expended, ability, and previous experience also influence performance. This chapter, however, concentrates on the motivation process as it affects behavior and individual performance.

A continual and perplexing problem facing managers is why some employees perform better than others. A number of interesting and important variables have been used to explain performance differences among employees. For example, variables such as ability, instinct, aspiration levels, and personal factors such as age, education, and family background explain why some employees perform well and others are poor performers.

Despite the obvious importance of motivation, it is difficult to define and to analyze. One definition proposes that motivation has to do with (1) the direction of behavior; (2) the strength of the response (i.e., effort), once an employee chooses to follow a course of action; and (3) the persistence of the behavior, or how long the person continues to behave in a particular manner.[1]

Another view suggests that the analysis of motivation should concentrate on the factors that incite and direct a person's activities.[2] One theorist emphasizes the goal-directedness aspect of motivation.[3] Another states that motivation is "concerned with how behavior gets started, is energized, is sustained, is directed, is stopped, and what kind of subjective reaction is present in the organism while all this is going on."[4]

A careful examination of each of these views leads to a number of conclusions about motivation:

1. Theorists present slightly different interpretations and place emphasis on different factors.
2. It is related to behavior and performance.
3. It involves goal directedness.
4. Physiological, psychological, and environmental differences are important factors to consider.

[1] John P. Campbell, Marvin D. Dunnette, Edward E. Lawler III, and Karl E. Weick, *Managerial Behavior, Performance, and Effectiveness* (New York: McGraw-Hill, 1970), p. 340.

[2] J. W. Atkinson, *An Introduction to Motivation* (Princeton, N.J.: D. Van Nostrand, 1964).

[3] D. Bindra, *Motivation: A Systematic Reinterpretation* (New York: Ronald Press, 1959).

[4] M. R. Jones, ed., *Nebraska Symposium on Motivation* (Lincoln: University of Nebraska Press, 1955), p. 14.

WHAT IS MOTIVATION?

Imagine that you are driving past a favorite fast-food restaurant. You notice your best friend's car parked outside, and glancing at your watch, you see that it is 12:45 P.M. You assume that your friend is "hungry" and is eating lunch. The assumption about hunger concerns your friend's motivation. You stop, enter the restaurant to visit your friend, and find him talking to the store manager. Based on this observation, you are not sure that your assumption about your friend's motivation is correct.

motivation
A concept that describes the forces acting on an employee that initiate and direct behavior.

First of all, when you saw your friend's car parked outside the restaurant, you assumed that it was there for a purpose. **Motivation** is the concept we use when we describe the forces acting on or within an individual to initiate and direct behavior. We use the concept to explain differences in the intensity of behavior, regarding more intense behaviors as the result of more intense levels of motivation. In addition, we often use the concept of motivation to indicate the *direction* of behavior. When you are tired or sleepy, you direct your behavior to get some sleep.

Motivation is an explanatory concept that we use to make sense out of the behaviors we observe. It is important to note that motivation is inferred. Instead of measuring it directly, we manipulate certain conditions and observe how behavior changes.[5] From the changes we observe, we improve our understanding of the underlying motivation. You assumed that your best friend had made a quick stop to eat lunch when you saw the car parked outside the fast-food restaurant. But your inference was not correct, because your friend was actually talking to the manager about a job on weekends. The lesson is clear: we must always be cautious in making motivational inferences. As more and more information is accumulated, however, our inferences become more accurate because we can eliminate alternative explanations.

THE STARTING POINT: THE INDIVIDUAL

Most managers must consider motivating a diverse, and in many respects unpredictable, group of people. The diversity results in different behavioral patterns that are in some manner related to needs and goals.

needs
Needs are deficiencies that an individual is aware of at a particular moment in time.

Needs refer to deficiencies that an individual experiences at a particular point in time. The deficiencies may be physiological (e.g., a need

---

[5] Herbert Petri, *Motivation: Theory and Research* (Belmont, Calif.: Wadsworth, 1979), p. 4.

for food), psychological (e.g., a need for self-esteem), or sociological (e.g., a need for social interaction). Needs are viewed as energizers or triggers of behavioral responses. The implication is that when need deficiencies are present, the individual is more susceptible to managers' motivational efforts.

The importance of *goals* in any discussion of motivation is apparent. The motivational process, as interpreted by most theorists, is goal directed. The goals, or outcomes, that an employee seeks are viewed as forces that attract the person. The accomplishment of desirable goals can result in a significant reduction in need deficiencies.

As illustrated in Figure 4–1, people seek to reduce various need deficiencies. Need deficiencies trigger a search process for ways to reduce the tension caused by the deficiencies. A course of action is selected, and goal (outcome)-directed behavior occurs. After a period of time, managers assess that behavior. The performance evaluation results in some type of reward or punishment. Such outcomes are weighed by the person, and the need deficiencies are reassessed. This, in turn, triggers the process, and the circular pattern is started again.

FIGURE 4–1

The Motivational Process: An Initial Model

MOTIVATION THEORIES: A CLASSIFICATION SYSTEM

content theories
Attempt to determine what factors within the individual energize, direct, sustain, and stop behavior.

process theories
Attempt to describe how behavior is energized, directed, sustained, and stopped.

Each person is attracted to some set of goals. If a manager is to predict behavior with any accuracy, it is necessary to know something about an employee's goals and about the actions that the employee will take to achieve them. There is no shortage of motivation theories and research findings that attempt to provide explanations of the behavior-outcome relationship. Two categories can be used to classify theories of motivation.[6] The **content theories** focus on the factors *within* the person that energize, direct, sustain, and stop behavior. They attempt to determine the specific needs that motivate people. The second category includes what are called the **process theories.** These theories provide a description and analysis of *how* behavior is energized, directed, sustained, and stopped. Both categories have important implications for managers, who are by the nature of their jobs involved with the motivational process. This chapter will cover some of the most publicized content theories, while the next chapter will discuss some process theories of motivation. Table 4–1 concisely summarizes the basic characteristics of content and process theories of motivation from a managerial perspective.

Four important content theories of motivation are Maslow's need hierarchy, Alderfer's ERG theory, Herzberg's two-factor theory, and McClelland's learned needs theory. Each of these four theories has an impact on managerial practices.

MASLOW'S NEED HIERARCHY

The crux of Maslow's theory is that needs are arranged in a hierarchy.[7] The lowest level needs are the physiological needs, and the highest level needs are the self-actualization needs. These needs are defined to mean the following:

1. *Physiological:* The need for food, drink, shelter, and relief from pain.
2. *Safety and security:* The need for freedom from threat, that is, the security from threatening events or surroundings.
3. *Belongingness, social, and love:* The need for friendship, affiliation, interaction, and love.
4. *Esteem:* The need for self-esteem and for esteem from others.
5. *Self-actualization:* The need to fulfill oneself by maximizing the use of abilities, skills, and potential.

---

[6] Campbell et al., *Managerial Behavior,* pp. 340–56.

[7] A. H. Maslow, "A Theory of Human Motivation," *Psychological Review,* July 1943, pp. 370–96; and A. H. Maslow, *Motivation and Personality* (New York: Harper & Row, 1954).

TABLE 4–1

**Managerial Perspective of Content and
Process Theories of Motivation**

Theoretical Base	Theoretical Explanation	Founders of the Theories	Managerial Application
Content	Factors within the person that energize, direct, sustain, and stop behavior. These factors can only be inferred	Maslow–five-level need hierarchy Alderfer–three-level hierarchy (ERG) Herzberg—two major factors called hygiene-motivators McClelland—three learned needs acquired from the culture: achievement, affiliation, and power	Managers need to be aware of differences in needs, desires, and goals because there is uniqueness among individuals
Process	Describes, explains, and analyzes how behavior is energized, directed, sustained, and stopped	Vroom—an expectancy theory of choices Skinner—reinforcement theory concerned with the learning that occurs as a consequence of behavior Adams—equity theory based on comparisons that individuals make Locke—goal-setting theory that conscious goals and intentions are the determinants of behavior	Managers need to understand the *process* of motivation and how individuals make choices based on preferences, rewards, and accomplishments

Maslow's theory assumes that a person attempts to satisfy the more basic needs (physiological) before directing behavior toward satisfying upper level needs (self-actualization). The importance of the self-actualization need in motivation was highlighted in the opening Organizational Issue for Debate. Are you satisfying or can you satisfy the self-actualization need on the job, at school, or at home? The lower order needs must be satisfied before a higher order need such as self-actualization begins to control the behavior of a person. A crucial point in

Maslow's thinking is that a satisfied need ceases to motivate. When a person decides that he or she is earning enough pay for contributing to the organization, money loses its power to motivate.

The Maslow theory is built on the premise that people have a need to grow and develop. This assumption may be true for some employees, but not for others. An inherent problem with the theory is that it was not scientifically tested by its founder. This point was made in the Organizational Issue for Debate at the beginning of this chapter. In a declarative manner, Maslow proposed that the typical adult had satisfied 85 percent of the physiological need; 70 percent of the safety and security need; 50 percent of the belongingness, social, and love need; 40 percent of the esteem need; and 10 percent of the self-actualization need. As presented in the Organizational Issue for Debate, critics believe that thinking in terms of satisfying even 10 percent of the self-actualization need is absurd when discussing the need satisfaction of blue-collar workers. These workers are simply trying to survive. Maslow's assertion is highlighted in Figure 4–2.

An implication of the high degree of need deficiency in the self-actualization and esteem categories (Figure 4–2) is that managers should focus attention on strategies to correct that deficiency. This logic assumes that attempts to rectify deficiencies in these categories have a higher probability of succeeding than does directing attention to the already satisfactorily fulfilled lower order needs.

Furthermore, needs whose satisfaction is highly deficient are a potential danger for managers. An unsatisfied need can cause frustration,

FIGURE 4–2

**The Typical Person's Need Deficiency
and Satisfaction**

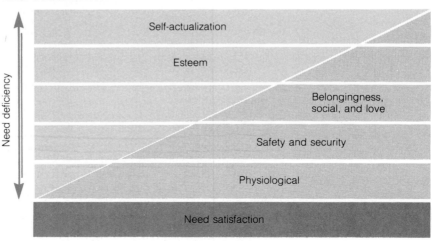

conflict, and stress. The skilled technician in a research laboratory who is given paperwork assignments instead of more challenging project assignments is being blocked from satisfying self-actualization needs. This type of blockage in the fulfillment of needs can lead to frustration and stress that may eventually result in undesirable performance. Individuals often cope with blockages of goal attainment by using ego defense mechanisms.

Selected Need Hierarchy Research

A number of research studies have attempted to test the need hierarchy theory. The first reported field research that tested a modified version of Maslow's need hierarchy was performed by Porter.[8] At the time of the initial studies, he assumed that physiological needs were being adequately satisfied for managers, so he substituted a higher order need called autonomy, defined as the person's satisfaction with opportunities to make independent decisions, set goals, and work without close supervision. The following Close-Up provides a portion of the needs assessment scale that Porter developed.

ORGANIZATIONS: CLOSE-UP

Assessing the Importance of Needs

Questionnaires have been developed for use in research studies, training programs, and discussion groups to provide insight into needs and motivation based on Maslow's need hierarchy. One of the most widely used of these questionnaires was prepared by Lyman W. Porter. Although you may not be working in an organization at present, it might be interesting to see how important various need characteristics are to you. If you are not currently working, use the most recent job you had in answering the following questions.

You are to indicate how important each characteristic is to you. Answer according to your feelings about the most recent job you had or about the job you currently hold. Circle the number on the scale that represents your feeling—1 (very unimportant) to 7 (very important).

1. The feeling of self-esteem a person gets from being in that job   1 2 3 4 5 6 7
2. The opportunity for personal growth and development in that job   1 2 3 4 5 6 7

[8] Lyman W. Porter, "A Study of Perceived Need Satisfaction in Bottom and Middle Management Jobs," *Journal of Applied Psychology,* February 1961, pp. 1–10.

3. The prestige of the job inside the company (that is, regard received from others in the company)   1 2 3 4 5 6 7

4. The opportunity for independent thought and action in that job   1 2 3 4 5 6 7

5. The feeling of security in that job   1 2 3 4 5 6 7

6. The feeling of self-fulfillment a person gets from being in that position (that is, the feeling of being able to use one's own unique capabilities, realizing one's potential)   1 2 3 4 5 6 7

7. The prestige of the job outside the company (that is, the regard received from others not in the company)   1 2 3 4 5 6 7

8. The feeling of worthwhile accomplishment in that job   1 2 3 4 5 6 7

9. The opportunity in that job to give help to other people   1 2 3 4 5 6 7

10. The opportunity in that job for participation in the setting of goals   1 2 3 4 5 6 7

11. The opportunity in that job for participation in the determination of methods and procedures   1 2 3 4 5 6 7

12. The authority connected with the job   1 2 3 4 5 6 7

13. The opportunity to develop close friendships in the job   1 2 3 4 5 6 7

Now that you have completed the questionnaire, score it as follows:

Rating for question 5 = ____ . Divide by 1 = ____ security.

Rating for questions 9 and 13 = ____ . Divide by 2 = ____ social.

Rating for questions 1, 3, and 7 = ____ . Divide by 3 = ____ esteem.

Rating for questions 4, 10, 11, and 12 = ____ . Divide by 4 = ____ autonomy.

Rating for questions 2, 6, and 8 = ____ . Divide by 3 = ____ self-actualization.

The instructor has national norm scores for presidents, vice presidents, and upper middle-level, lower middle-level, and lower level managers with which you can compare your *mean* importance scores. How do your scores compare with the scores of managers working in organizations?

Source: Adapted from Lyman W. Porter, *Organizational Patterns of Managerial Job Attitudes* (New York: American Foundation for Management Research, 1964), pp. 17, 19.

Since the early Porter studies, other studies have reported:

1. Managers higher in the organization chain of command place greater emphasis on self-actualization and autonomy.[9]
2. Managers at lower organizational levels in small firms (less than 500 employees) are more satisfied than their counterpart managers in large firms (more than 5,000 employees); however, managers at upper levels in large companies are more satisfied than their counterparts in small companies.[10]
3. American managers overseas are more satisfied with autonomy opportunities than are their counterparts working in the United States.[11]

Despite these findings, a number of issues remain regarding the need hierarchy theory. First, data from managers in two different companies provided little support that a hierarchy of needs exists.[12] The data suggested that only two levels of needs exist: one is the physiological level and the other a level which includes all other needs. Further evidence also disputes the hierarchy notions.[13] Researchers found that as managers advance in an organization, their needs for security decrease, with a corresponding increase in their needs for social interaction, achievement, and self-actualization.

ALDERFER'S ERG THEORY

Alderfer agrees with Maslow that individuals have needs that are arranged in a hierarchy.[14] However, his need hierarchy involves only three sets of needs:

1. *Existence:* These are needs that are satisfied by such factors as food, air, water, pay, and working conditions.

[9] Lyman W. Porter, *Organizational Patterns of Managerial Job Attitudes* (New York: American Foundation for Management Research, 1964).

[10] Lyman W. Porter, "Job Attitudes in Management: Perceived Deficiencies in Need Fulfillment as a Function of Size of the Company," *Journal of Applied Psychology,* December 1963, pp. 386–97.

[11] John M. Ivancevich, "Perceived Need Satisfactions of Domestic versus Overseas Managers," *Journal of Applied Psychology,* August 1969, pp. 274–78.

[12] Edward L. Lawler III and J. L. Suttle, "A Causal Correlation Test of the Need Hierarchy Concept," *Organizational Behavior and Human Performance,* April 1972, pp. 265–87.

[13] Douglas T. Hall and K. E. Nougaim, "An Examination of Maslow's Need Hierarchy in an Organizational Setting," *Organizational Behavior and Human Performance,* February 1968, pp. 12–35.

[14] Clayton P. Alderfer, "An Empirical Test of a Need Theory of Human Needs," *Organizational Behavior and Human Performance,* April 1969, pp. 142–75; and Clayton P. Alderfer, *Existence, Relatedness, and Growth: Human Needs in Organizational Settings* (New York: Free Press, 1972).

2. _Relatedness:_ These are needs that are satisfied by meaningful social and interpersonal relationships.
3. _Growth:_ These are needs that an individual satisfies by making creative or productive contributions.

ERG theory
A content motivation theory that proposes that individuals have Existence (E), Relatedness (R), and Growth (G) needs.

Alderfer's explanation differs from Maslow's in a number of ways. First, instead of a five-need hierarchy, Alderfer proposes a three-need hierarchy—Existence (E), Relatedness (R), and Growth (G), or **ERG.** The existence needs are similar to Maslow's physiological and safety categories; the relatedness needs are similar to the belongingness, social, and love category; and the growth needs are similar to the esteem and self-actualization categories. The growth category is what is being discussed in the following Close-Up.

ORGANIZATIONS: CLOSE-UP

Blue-Collar Growth Need Satisfaction

On the wall of Hangar No. 10 at John F. Kennedy International Airport is an anonymous poem that reads:

> We all know the name of Lindbergh
> And we've read of his flight to fame
> But think if you can of his maintenance man
> Can you remember his name?

The repair work of maintenance personnel for airlines is vital. Two mechanics were blamed for engine failures during an Eastern Airlines flight from Miami to Nassau in April 1983. A preliminary investigation found that the mechanics apparently failed to detect and replace missing seals on oil plugs in the plane's engines. Before the crew managed to restart one engine and land in Miami, the L–1011 with 172 people aboard rapidly lost altitude and nearly "ditched" into the Atlantic Ocean.

Despite their importance, the men and women who have helped keep the U.S. airline industry's record among the best in the world consider themselves unappreciated and unrecognized. They feel a low amount of satisfaction for their significant contributions to safe air travel.

Nick is a 20-year veteran maintenance man for Trans World Airlines (he is one of 44,000 airline mechanics). He feels that his job requires precision, since any given plane is subject to hundreds of potential defects, all of which must be checked out and repaired before takeoff. His work is boring, odious, dangerous—or immensely challenging, depending on the day's duty roster. Much of it is done against punishing time pressures and deadlines. Even a minor error in judgment or a sloppy bit of work could lead to a fatal crash.

Nick earns about $35,000 a year for a 40-hour week. Though much of the diagnostic work on TWA's planes is now completed with automated cockpit gauges and computerized inspection gear, Nick still plays a role as a troubleshooter. In 1981, Nick found a crack in the inlet case of a jet engine. The engine had to be replaced immediately. In 1982, he found a crack in a brake part that, undetected, could have caused a tire blowout. Perhaps these two finds saved many lives, and this is the sense of contribution that Nick derives from his job.

The poem on the wall in Hangar 10 suggests that although Nick and thousands like him are anonymous, they derive self-actualization from their work. Perhaps more recognition should be given to workers like Nick who contribute so much to the safety and well-being of millions of air travelers annually.

Source: Adapted from John D. Williams, "Airline Mechanics' Job Is Put in the Spotlight by Episode off Miami," *The Wall Street Journal*, May 10, 1983, pp. 1, 20.

Second, ERG theory and Maslow's need hierarchy differ on how people move through the different sets of needs. Maslow proposed that unfulfilled needs are predominant and that the next higher level of needs is not activated or triggered until the predominant need is adequately satisfied. Thus, a person progresses up the need hierarchy once satisfaction of the lower level need is adequate for that particular person. In contrast, Alderfer's ERG theory suggests that in addition to the *satisfaction-progression* process that Maslow proposed a *frustration-regression* process is also at work. That is, if a person is continually frustrated in attempts to satisfy growth needs, relatedness needs will

FIGURE 4–3

ERG Theory Relationships among Frustration, Importance, and Satisfaction of Needs

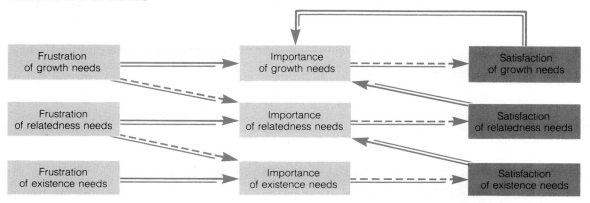

Source: Adapted from F. J. Landy and D. A. Trumbo, *Psychology of Work Behavior,* rev. ed. (Homewood, Ill.: Dorsey Press, 1980).

reemerge as a major motivating force causing the individual to redirect his or her efforts toward satisfying a lower order need category. Thus, the *frustration* leads to a *regression* because it results in attempts to satisfy lower order needs. Figure 4–3 graphically presents the ERG type of relationships.

Alderfer's ERG explanation of motivation provides an important suggestion to managers about behavior. If it is observed that a subordinate's higher order needs (e.g., growth) are being blocked, perhaps because of a company policy or the lack of resources, then it is in the manager's best interest to attempt to redirect the subordinate's efforts toward relatedness or existence needs. The ERG theory implies that individuals will be motivated to engage in behavior to satisfy one of the three sets of needs.

ERG Research: Limited Research to Date

The ERG theory has not stimulated a large number of research studies. Thus, empirical verification has not reached the point where it can be claimed that the ERG explanation has validity. Salancik and Pfeffer propose that need models such as Maslow's and Alderfer's have become popular because they are consistent with other theories of rational choice and because they attribute freedom to individuals.[15] The idea that individuals shape their actions to satisfy unfulfilled needs gives individual activity purpose and direction. Furthermore, Salancik and Pfeffer claim that need explanations are also popular, despite little research verification, because they are simple, easily expressed views of human behavior. This implies that managers or practitioners are less impressed by research-verified explanations than by simple, commonsense explanations.

Alderfer certainly doesn't accept the Salancik and Pfeffer critique of need explanations of motivation.[16] He proposes that available research evidence supports at least the conceptualization of the ERG theory. Other evidence to support portions of the ERG theory has been added to the literature since Alderfer's debate with Salancik and Pfeffer.

One study examined ERG theory with regard to the human life cycle.[17] Using Levinson's theory of life-cycle development, which in-

---

[15] Gerald R. Salancik and Jeffrey Pfeffer, "An Examination of Need-Satisfaction Models of Job Attitudes," *Administrative Science Quarterly,* September 1977, pp. 427–56.

[16] Clayton P. Alderfer, "A Critique of Salancik and Pfeffer's Examination of Need-Satisfaction Theories," *Administrative Science Quarterly,* December 1977, pp. 658–69.

[17] Clayton P. Alderfer and Richard A. Guzzo, "Life Expectancies and Adults' Enduring Strength of Desires in Organizations," *Administrative Science Quarterly,* September 1979, pp. 347–61.

cludes seven stages (e.g., early adult transition, 18–22 years old, midlife transition, 40–45 years old), the ERG theory of motivation was examined. The results indicated that (1) individuals with parents of higher educational levels had significantly higher scores for strength of desire for growth, (2) men had higher scores for strength of existence needs and lower scores for strength of relatedness than did women, and (3) black participants showed significantly higher existence needs than did whites.

In another study of ERG theory, researchers collected data from 208 employees working in 13 different jobs in a telephone company.[18] In general, the ERG categories were supported. However, the researchers found that there was a more rigid need hierarchy than that proposed by Alderfer. For example, relatively few individuals (17 out of 208) reported high growth need satisfaction when relatedness and existence needs were either "moderate" or "low." Alderfer placed much less emphasis on the hierarchy notion than had Maslow.

APPLICATION OF NEED THEORIES

The Maslow need hierarchy and Alderfer's ERG theory suggest that managers should be sensitive to the differences and desires among subordinates since every individual has his or her unique pattern of needs, values, and goals. As a result, what motivates one person may have absolutely no effect or even a negative effect on another person. Thus, managers must recognize and take into account individual differences in needs when designing and implementing programs. One example of a program that has been designed to take into consideration the various needs of subordinates is the modified or compressed workweek.

The Modified or Compressed Workweek

In recent years, three related innovations in work scheduling have been applied in organizations. First, there has been a move to shorten the workweek (i.e., fewer days per week and/or fewer hours per day). This is called the modified or compressed workweek. The most common modified schedule is a 10-hour day, often designed as the 4/40.

flexitime
Flexitime permits variations in starting

The second is discretionary working time or staggered or flexible working hours. **Flexitime,** also known as gliding time, is extremely popular. It allows employees to choose when they come to work and

[18] John P. Wanous and Abram Zwany, "A Cross-Sectional Test of Need Hierarchy Theory," *Organizational Behavior and Human Performance,* February 1977, pp. 78–97.

and quitting times but assumes that a constant number of hours will be worked. For a worker who starts at 10:00 A.M., quitting time will be 7:00 P.M., while a worker who starts at 7:00 A.M. will quit at 4:00 P.M.

leave work, within contraints set by management. Flexitime schedules attempt to shift some control over working time to the employee. These schedules give some autonomy, self-management, and decision making to employees. Thus, satisfying security, social, esteem, and self-actualization needs is one potential value of the flextime arrangement.

The third recent theme in work scheduling relates to part-time employment. The most rapid increase in part-time employment has been among women aged 18 to 44. Since 1965, about 34 million women in this age group have been added to the part-time work force.[19] For some employees, part-time employment is a solution to the problem of doing two things at once. For example, it permits homemakers to perform home and family roles while pursuing a career. It also lets students acquire new knowledge while they still earn some income. For some organizations, part-time employment lets managers tailor the size of the work force to the size of the workload.[20]

In this discussion of motivation programs designed to satisfy managerial and employee needs, each of these three themes could be developed. They each have powerful motivational potential. However, the modified workweek will be covered as simply one example of this potential motivational technique that has not been rigorously examined by researchers.[21]

Description of the Modified Workweek. The 4/40 (there are also the 3/36 and the 4/32) is a regular full-time workweek of 40 hours that are worked in four 10-hour days instead of five 8-hour days. Four-day and other compressed workweeks began to be used in the United States around 1970.

The 4/40 plan provides the employee with long weekends throughout the year. The incentive for the 4/40 is the belief that the system will lead to increased productivity. The employee will benefit from increased leisure time and from more freedom to pursue personal business, a family life, and educational objectives. Theoretically, the plan could satisfy the full range of the needs proposed by Maslow and Alderfer.

Modified workweeks are suitable for some situations. They can help businesses that have costly start-ups and shutdowns, unutilized capital equipment, and long travel time to job sites. For example, police departments could use three 10-hour shifts per day to get 6 hours of

---

[19] Nancy S. Barrett, "Part-Time Will Increase, Bring Change to Social Mores and Standards of Compensation," *Personnel Administrator,* December 1983, pp. 94–98, 104.

[20] Stanley D. Nollen, "What Is Happening to Flexitime, Flexihour, Gliding Time, the Variable Day? and Permanent Part-Time Employment? and the Four-Day Work Week?" *Across the Board,* April 1980, pp. 6–21.

[21] Randall B. Dunham and Jon L. Pierce, "The Design and Evaluation of Alternative Work Schedules," *Personnel Administrator,* April 1983, p. 67.

double staffing during high-crime night hours. Road construction crews could go out for four days for 10 hours at a time to cut down the number of trips made to work sites. Computer operators could use two 12-hour shifts, each working three consecutive days, to get round-the-clock utilization on Monday–Saturday.

Modified Workweek Research. A review of the research on the modified workweek indicates that 14 studies can be consulted to examine the impact of such a scheduling plan.[22] Nine studies investigated some aspect of job satisfaction. Five of these studies found that satisfaction with the job improved after the modified workweek was installed.

Of the nine studies measuring the effects of age, five reported that younger workers were more favorable than older workers; the remainder reported no differences. Eight studies investigated the role of sex. Two found that men were more favorable than women; the remainder indicated no difference. Of the six studies investigating the effect of the modified workweek on home and personal life, four reported a positive effect.

Six studies surveyed changes in leisure and recreational activities after installation of modified workweeks. All reported positive results. Of the five studies reporting the effects of the modified workweek on fatigue, all reported that fatigue had increased. This is consistent with expectations that working a longer day will be more tiring.

The research for the most part suggests that in some situations the modified workweek has a positive impact on job satisfaction, home/personal life satisfaction, and leisure/recreation satisfaction. However, it can also increase employee fatigue, which could be a problem in jobs where alertness is important (e.g., air traffic controller, police officer).

The Modified Workweek: An Application in a Manufacturing Company. An experimental-control group design and test of the 4/40 workweek was studied at a medium-sized manufacturing plant in the Midwest.[23] The company executive committee decided to establish two divisions as 4/40 units and two divisions as 5/40 units. It was expected that the 4/40 units would show increased satisfaction, lower job anxiety-stress, decreased absenteeism, and increased job performance.

To follow the impact of the application of the 4/40 versus the 5/40 units, data were collected and analyzed before the change to the

---

[22] Simcha Ronen and Sophia B. Primps, "The Compressed Work Week as Organizational Change: Behavioral and Attitudinal Outcomes," *Academy of Management Review,* January 1981, pp. 61–74.

[23] John M. Ivancevich, "Effects of the Shorter Work Week on Selected Satisfaction and Performance Measures," *Journal of Applied Psychology,* December 1974, pp. 717–21; and John M. Ivancevich and Herbert L. Lyon, "The Shortened Work Week: A Field Experiment," *Journal of Applied Psychology,* February 1977, pp. 34–37.

modified workweek, 3 months after the change, 12 months after the change, and 24 months after the change. Approximately 12 months after the 4/40 changes occurred, there was improvement in autonomy, personal worth, security, and pay satisfaction in the modified workweek units. There was also a reduction in the anxiety-stress in these units. However, these improvements were not sustained over time. Apparently, in this application of the modified workweek there was only a pronounced short-run satisfaction improvement. The long-run results, 24 months after the application of the 4/40, indicated very little differences between the units. This application suggests that the effects of the 4/40 can wear off. If satisfaction, anxiety-stress, and absenteeism improvements are to be sustained, more managerial work than simply applying a 4/40 schedule appears to be needed.

A Brief Critique of the Modified Workweek. For workers, the four-day workweek yields two clear advantages: a three-day weekend and one less commuting trip per week. There are problems in providing customer service and covering necessary duties on the fifth day that limit 4/40 applications to only some jobs. There are also problems associated with a longer day—fatigue, higher accident proneness, less time for evening meetings during the week.

The results of research on the modified workweek are mixed. There seem to be short-run improvements in need satisfaction and absenteeism. Even such short-run improvements, of course, are welcomed by any organization. However, are these enough to change a system from a 5/40 to a 4/40? Each organization must answer this question for itself.

Despite the mixed research results on the 4/40, a renewed energy crunch or a stronger move to energy conservation could make the modified workweek more popular during the remainder of the 1980s. In addition, if laws are eventually passed that do not force an employer to pay employees an overtime premium for all hours worked beyond eight in a day, the 4/40 may be used in more organizations.

HERZBERG'S TWO-FACTOR THEORY

Herzberg developed a content theory that is called the two-factor theory of motivation.[24] The two factors are called the dissatisfiers-satisfiers or the hygiene-motivators or the extrinsic-intrinsic factors, depending on the discussant of the theory. The original research testing this theory included a group of 200 accountants and engineers. Herzberg used interview responses to questions like "Can you describe, in detail, when you felt exceptionally good about your job?" and "Can you describe, in detail, when you felt exceptionally bad about your

---

[24] Frederick Herzberg, B. Mausner, and B. Synderman, *The Motivation to Work* (New York: John Wiley & Sons, 1959).

extrinsic
Extrinsic job
conditions, such as
pay or working
conditions, are
external to the job
itself.

job?" Rarely were the same kinds of experiences categorized as both good and bad. This systematic procedure resulted in the development of two distinct kinds of experiences—satisfiers and dissatisfiers.

The initial Herzberg study resulted in two specific conclusions about the theory. First, there is a set of **extrinsic** conditions, the job context, which result in *dissatisfaction* among employees when they are not present. If these conditions are present, this does not necessarily motivate employees. These conditions are the *dissatisfiers* or *hygiene* factors since they are needed to maintain at least a level of "no dissatisfaction." They include:

a. Salary.
b. Job security.
c. Working conditions.
d. Status.
e. Company procedures.
f. Quality of technical supervision.
g. Quality of interpersonal relations among peers, with superiors, and with subordinates.

intrinsic
Intrinsic job
conditions, such as
the challenge of the
work or the sense of
achievement from
doing a good job, are
built into the job
itself.

Second, a set of **intrinsic** conditions, the job content, when present in the job, builds strong levels of motivation that can result in good job performance. If these conditions are not present, they do not prove highly dissatisfying. The factors in this set are called the *satisfiers* or *motivators*. They include:

a. Achievement.   d. Advancement.
b. Recognition.   e. The work itself.
c. Responsibility. f. The possibility of growth.

Herzberg's model basically assumes that job satisfaction is not a unidimensional concept. His research leads to the conclusion that two continua are needed to correctly interpret job satisfaction. Figure

FIGURE 4–4

Traditional versus Herzberg View of Job Satisfaction

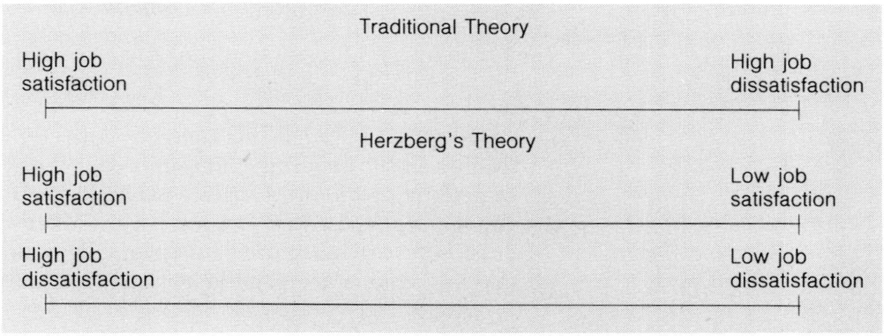

Traditional Theory	
High job satisfaction	High job dissatisfaction

Herzberg's Theory	
High job satisfaction	Low job satisfaction
High job dissatisfaction	Low job dissatisfaction

4–4 presents graphically two different views of job satisfaction. Prior to Herzberg's work those studying motivation viewed job satisfaction as a unidimensional concept; that is, they placed job satisfaction at one end of a continuum and job dissatisfaction at the other end of the same continuum. This meant that if a job condition caused job satisfaction, removing it would cause job dissatisfaction; similarly, if a job condition caused job dissatisfaction, removing it would cause job satisfaction.

The following Close-Up presents the recognition program of Tanner Company. Managers in this firm believe that recognition is a motivator, as suggested by Herzberg. This success of the Tanner program indicates that recognition awards for some individuals can influence behavior.

ORGANIZATIONS: CLOSE-UP

Recognition Awards at Tanner Company

Some managers have been successful in using recognition as a motivational tool. These managers have learned how to use recognition programs to praise and increase the performance accomplishments of subordinates, the philosophy being that "people work for money, but they live for recognition." In some organizations, recognition begins with a welcome award once a new hiree successfully completes a training and probationary period. Receiving an award early plants the seeds of future success.

O. C. Tanner Company of Salt Lake City, Utah, has been a pioneer in implementing a company-wide recognition program. The Tanner approach emphasizes motivation elements in that:

It applies the need for recognition.

It reinforces specific desired behaviors.

It focuses attention on expected results.

It concentrates on individual achievement.

Tanner managers have found that the success of their program is built on a number of key elements:

1. *A recognition symbol, the company logo.* By using the logo, Tanner focuses on the meaning of recognition. When the symbol is fashioned in gold, it provides a tangible example for the award program.
2. *Display options.* The Tanner program provides an attractive gift or accessory to recognized employees. Pens, jewelry, desk accessories, and key chains are popular options that employees can choose.

3. *Meaningful presentations.* A lasting influence results when a key corporate officer makes a recognition presentation. Working peers are present when the presentations are made.
4. *Program promotion.* Announcements, bulletin boards, house newspapers, and personal letters are used to promote the recognition program.
5. *Review and updating.* Periodic evaluation keeps the Tanner program fresh. New accessories and gifts, new promotional efforts, and new ways of presenting awards, all help build excitement.

The recognition program at Tanner has a "ripple" effect. As an employee sees others working in the same department receive recognition awards, that experience becomes a positive incentive. At Tanner the recognition program is believed to have instilled company pride and enhanced morale.

Source: Adapted from David J. Cherrington and B. Jackson Wixon, Jr., "Recognition Is Still a Top Motivator," *Personnel Administrator*, May 1983, pp. 87–91.

One appealing aspect of Herzberg's explanation of motivation is that the terminology is work-oriented. There is no need to translate psychological terminology into everyday language. Despite this important feature, Herzberg's work has been criticized for a number of reasons. First, the theory was originally based on a sample of accountants and engineers. Critics ask whether this limited sample can justify generalizing to other occupational groups. The technology, environment, and backgrounds of the two occupational groups are distinctly different from those of such groups as nurses, medical technologists, salespeople, computer programmers, clerks, and police officers.[25]

Second, some researchers believe that Herzberg's work oversimplifies the nature of job satisfaction. Dunnette et al. state:

Results show that the Herzberg two-factor theory is a grossly oversimplified portrayal of the mechanism by which job satisfaction or dissatisfaction comes about. Satisfaction or dissatisfaction can reside in the job context, the job content, or both jointly. Moreover, certain job dimensions—notably Achievement, Responsibility, and Recognition—are more important for both satisfaction and dissatisfaction than certain other

---

[25] For critiques of the Herzberg theory, see Robert J. House and L. Wigdor, "Herzberg's Dual-Factor Theory of Job Satisfaction and Motivation: A Review of the Empirical Evidence and a Criticism," *Personnel Psychology*, Winter 1967, pp. 369–80; and Joseph Schneider and Edwin Locke, "A Critique of Herzberg's Classification System and a Suggested Revision," *Organizational Behavior and Human Performance*, July 1971, pp. 441–58.

job dimensions—notably Working Conditions, Company Policies and Practices, and Security.[26]

Other critics focus on Herzberg's methodology, which requires people to look at themselves retrospectively. Can people be aware of all that motivated or dissatisfied them? These critics believe that subconscious factors are not identified in Herzberg's analysis. The "recency of events" bias of being able to recall the most recent job conditions and feelings is embedded in the methodology.[27]

Another criticism of Herzberg's work is that little attention has been directed toward testing the motivational and performance implications of the theory.[28] In the original study of engineers and accountants, only self-reports of performance were used and in most cases the respondents were reporting on job activities that had occurred over a long period of time. Herzberg has offered no explanation as to why various extrinsic and intrinsic job factors should affect performance. The two-factor theory also fails to explain why various job factors are important. In reality, the theory, because of its heavy emphasis on job factors, is basically a theory of determinants of job dissatisfaction and satisfaction.

McCLELLAND'S LEARNED NEEDS THEORY

McClelland has proposed a theory of motivation that is closely associated with learning concepts. He believes that many needs are acquired from the culture.[29] Three of these **learned needs** are the need for achievement (n Ach), the need for affiliation (n Aff), and the need for power (n Pow).

McClelland proposes that when a need is strong in a person, its effect is to motivate the person to use behavior that leads to its satisfaction. For example, having a high n Ach encourages an individual to set challenging goals, to work hard to achieve the goals, and to use the skills and abilities needed to achieve them.

How is what McClelland has labeled as the need for achievement (n Ach) measured? It is not enough to assume that those who work

learned needs
By living within a culture, a person acquires needs through learning. McClelland proposes three culturally learned needs—achievement, affiliation, and power.

---

[26] Marvin Dunnette, John Campbell, and M. Hakel, "Factors Contributing to Job Dissatisfaction in Six Occupational Groups," *Organizational Behavior and Human Performance,* May 1967, p. 147.

[27] Abraham K. Korman, *Industrial and Organizational Psychology* (Englewood Cliffs, N.J.: Prentice-Hall, 1971), pp. 148–50.

[28] Edward E. Lawler III, *Motivation in Work Organizations* (Monterey, Calif.: Brooks/Cole Publishing, 1973), p. 72.

[29] David C. McClelland, "Business Drive and National Achievement," *Harvard Business Review,* July–August 1962, pp. 99–112.

FIGURE 4–5

Adapted with permission of the Tests and Scoring Division, McBer and Company, 137 Newbury Street, Boston, Massachusetts 02116.

Thematic Apperception Test (TAT)
The TAT is a projective test that is used in McClelland's research to determine a person's achievement, affiliation, and power needs.

hard and long have it, while those who work slowly or in spurts do not. Interestingly, to assess individual differences in n Ach the **Thematic Apperception Test (TAT)** is used.[30] A person is shown pictures and asked to write a story about what is portrayed in them. The person's achievement, affiliation, or power needs are inferred from how he or she responds to the pictures. The person is asked to answer these questions about the pictures: What is happening? Who are the people? What has led to this situation? What has happened in the past? What are the people thinking? What is wanted?

The picture in Figure 4–5 is one that McClelland has used to elicit responses. McClelland states:

> If you want to understand motives behind . . . actions, find out what's on a person's mind. If you want to find out what's on a person's mind, don't ask him, because he can't always tell you accurately. Study his fantasies and dreams. If you do this over a period of time, you will

---

[30] R. Murray, *Thematic Apperception Test Pictures and Manual* (Cambridge, Mass.: Harvard University Press, 1943).

discover the themes to which his mind returns again and again. And these themes can be used to explain his actions.[31]

The story written by the individual is scored by trained evaluators. They develop objective measures of the strength of each of the needs, using a scoring technique developed by McClelland.[32] To be coded as a need achievement theme, a person's story about the picture has to reveal concern to do better, to improve performance. By contrast, social need affiliation themes reveal concern for establishing, maintaining, and repairing social relations. And power need themes are displayed by concern with reputation, influence, and impact.

An important feature of McClelland's n Ach is his contention that needs can be learned. McClelland cites instances in which individuals with a low initial n Ach were subjected to training or learning experiences that increased the n Ach. He proposes that entire economically backward cultures (nations) can be dramatically improved by stimulating the need for achievement in the populace. If McClelland is correct, and some research supports his theory, his approach could have a significant impact on motivation in general. Motivation could be taught in organizational and nonorganizational settings.

Research on n Ach

Most of the research evidence offered in support of McClelland's learned needs theory has been provided by McClelland or his associates. The research has provided a profile of the high achievers in society.[33] The descriptive profile suggests that:

- Those who are high n Ach prefer to set their own performance goals.
- High n Ach persons prefer to avoid easy and difficult performance goals. They actually prefer moderate goals that they think they can achieve.
- High n Ach persons prefer immediate and efficient feedback on how they are performing.
- The high n Ach persons like to be responsible for solving problems.

In a very ambitious project, researchers attempted to raise the achievement motivation of businessmen in an entire village in India. This program, called the Kakinada project, consisted of encouraging

---

[31] David C. McClelland, *Motivational Trends In Society* (Morristown, N.J.: General Learning Press, 1971).

[32] David C. McClelland, *The Achievement Motive* (New York: Appleton-Century-Crofts, 1953).

[33] David McClelland and D. Burnham, "Power Is the Great Motivator," *Harvard Business Review,* March–April 1976, pp. 100–11; and McClelland, *Achievement Motive.*

the businessmen to have high-achievement fantasies, to make plans that would help them realize the goals of a successful entrepreneur, and to communicate with one another about their goals and their methods of reaching them. The businessmen became more productive as entrepreneurs, starting several large industries, enlarging their businesses, and hiring more than 5,000 of their neighbors. In a 10-year reassessment of the program, achievement motivation levels and results were still exceptional.[34]

Research has not only provided the basis for developing a profile of those with high n Ach, but it has also pointed out the complexity of the achievement motive. Differences have been found between individuals with high n Ach who focus on attaining success and individuals who focus on avoiding failure.[35] Those who focus on attaining success tend to set more realistic goals and to choose tasks of moderate difficulty.

In most of the research on n Ach, the subjects have been men. In one study, however, the objective was to compare the achievement needs of college men and women.[36] It was determined in this study that women appeared to fear success more than men did. Students were asked to complete a story that began, "At the end of first-term finals, Anne finds herself at the top of her medical school class." For male subjects, John was the name used. When the male and female stories prepared by the students were analyzed, 62 percent of the women expressed conflict over Anne's success, while only 9 percent of the men expressed conflict over John's success. It was concluded that women had a greater negative imagery about success because their stories contained significantly more references to social rejection, anxiety, or a negative self-image.

The "fear of success hypothesis" was sensationalized by the popular press as an example of a personality type created by sexist ideology. Since this study was conducted, over 200 studies followed up on various aspects of women's fear of success.[37] The conclusion reached was that fear of success (achievement) is not a personality attribute of women. Rather, it is better conceived as a strong avoidance reaction in both women and men, triggered by certain social-economic-historic conditions.

---

[34] David C. McClelland, "Managing Motivation to Expand Human Freedom," *American Psychologist*, March 1978, pp. 201–10; and David C. McClelland and D. G. Winter, *Motivating Economic Achievement* (New York: Free Press, 1969).

[35] W. V. Meyer, "Achievement Motive Research," in *Nebraska Symposium on Motivation*, ed. W. J. Arnold (Lincoln: University of Nebraska Press, 1968).

[36] M. S. Horner, "Fail: Bright Women," *Psychology Today*, November 1969, pp. 36–38.

[37] D. Tresemer, ed., "Current Trends in Research on Fear of Success," *Sex Roles*, Spring 1976, entire issue.

Instead of measuring a fear of success, Horner may have actually been measuring a person's assessment of the negative consequences associated with deviation from traditional sex roles. A fear that the woman who deviates from sex-role standards will be rejected by men may be particularly strong among women. One study found that some men do indeed fear being "outdone" by women and so prefer to work alone on achievement tasks rather than with a woman.[38]

Based on theory and research, McClelland has made specific suggestions about developing a positive high need for achievement, that is, a high n Ach where there is no fear of success. He suggests that people do the following:

1. Arrange tasks so that they receive periodic feedback on performance. This will provide information that will enable them to make modifications or corrections.
2. Seek good models of achievement. They should search for achievement heroes, the successful people, the winners, and use them as models.
3. Modify their self-image. The high n Ach person likes himself or herself and seeks moderate challenges and responsibilities.
4. Control their imagination. They should think in realistic terms and think positively about how they will accomplish goals.

There are a number of criticisms of McClelland's work. First, the use of the projective TAT test to determine three needs has been questioned. While projective techniques have some advantages over self-report questionnaires, the interpretation and weighing of a story is at best an art. The validation of such analysis is extremely important and often neglected. Recently, a critical incident technique has been used to examine motivation in a developing country.[39] More research will be needed to determine whether critical incidents or other methods can be used as a measurement method for assessing the McClelland-type needs.

McClelland's claim that n Ach can be learned conflicts with a large body of literature that argues that the acquisition of motives normally occurs in childhood and is very difficult to alter in adulthood. McClelland acknowledges this problem, but points to evidence in politics and religion to indicate that adult behaviors can be changed.[40]

Third, McClelland's notion of learned needs is questioned on the ground of whether the needs are permanently acquired. Research is needed to determine whether acquired needs last over a period of

---

[38] J. Condry and S. Dyer, "Fear of Success: Attribution of Cause to the Victim," *Journal of Social Issues,* Summer 1976, pp. 63–83.

[39] Peter D. Machungiva and Neal Schmitt, "Work Motivation in a Developing Country," *Journal of Applied Psychology,* February 1983, pp. 31–42.

[40] McClelland, *Achievement Motive.*

time. Can something learned in a training and development program be sustained on the job?[41] This is the issue that McClelland and others have not been able to clarify.

A SYNOPSIS OF THE FOUR CONTENT THEORIES

Each of the four content theories attempts to explain behavior from a slightly different perspective. None of the theories has been accepted as the sole basis for explaining motivation. Although some critics are skeptical, it appears that people have innate and learned needs and that various job factors result in a degree of satisfaction. Thus, each

FIGURE 4–6

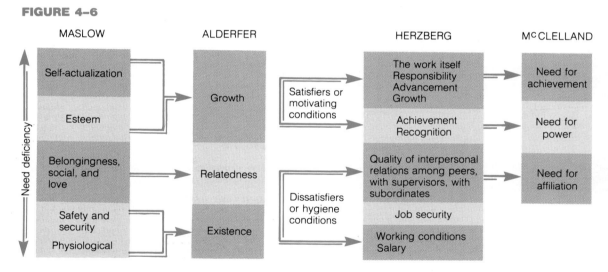

of the theories provides the manager with some understanding of behavior and performance.

The four theories are compared in Figure 4–6. McClelland proposed no lower order needs. However, his needs for achievement and power are not identical with Herzberg's motivators, or Maslow's higher order needs, or Alderfer's growth needs, but there are some similarities. A major difference between the four content theories is McClelland's

---

[41] Paul R. Lawrence and Jay W. Lorsh, *Developing Organizations: Diagnosis and Action* (Reading, Mass.: Addison-Wesley Publishing, 1969).

emphasis on socially acquired needs. The Maslow theory offers a static need hierarchy system; Alderfer presents a flexible three-need classification approach; and Herzberg discusses intrinsic and extrinsic job factors.

Now think back to the Organizational Issue for Debate about self-actualization. Clearly, each of the theories presented—Maslow's need hierarchy, Alderfer's ERG theory, Herzberg's two-factor theory, and McClelland's achievement, affiliation, and power needs—can be criticized because of the methods used and the conclusions reached. Whether we are discussing self-actualization, growth needs, recognition, or the need for achievement, there will be problems of empirical support, bias in interpretation, and creating workplace conditions that can aid in the satisfaction of the particular need. Despite these and other problems, it is still important for managers to understand what motivation involves. Each of the content theorists believes that he has presented the clearest, most meaningful, and most accurate explanation of motivation.

SUMMARY OF KEY POINTS

A. Any attempt to improve the job performance of individuals must invariably utilize motivation theories. This results from the fact that motivation is concerned with behavior or, more specifically, goal-directed behavior.

B. A major reason why behaviors of employees differ is that the needs and goals of people vary. Social, cultural, hereditary, and job factors influence behaviors. In order to understand the circular nature of motivation, the manager must learn about the needs of subordinates.

C. The theories of motivation can be classified as being either content theories or process theories. In this chapter, four of the more widely cited content theories are presented. These theories focus on factors within the person (e.g., needs, goals, motives) that energize, direct, sustain, and stop behavior.

D. The Maslow theory assumes that people have a need to grow and develop. The implication is that motivational programs will have a higher probability of success if the upper level need deficiencies are reduced. Although Maslow's need hierarchy has not met most of the standards of scientific testing, it appears that an adequately fulfilled need does not provide a good target for managers in building motivators that can influence performance.

E. Alderfer offers a three-level need hierarchy of existence, relatedness, and growth needs. In addition to the satisfaction-progression process proposed by Maslow, Alderfer states that there is also a frustration-regression process at work that plays a major role in motivating people.

F. Herzberg's two-factor theory of motivation identifies two types of factors in the workplace, satisfiers and dissatisfiers. One apparent weakness of the theory is that its findings have not been replicated by other researchers. Despite this and other shortcomings, it does focus on job-related factors in managerial terminology.

G. McClelland has proposed a theory of learned needs. The behavior associated with the needs for achievement, affiliation, and power is instrumental in the job performance of an individual. A manager should attempt to acquire an understanding of these needs.

DISCUSSION AND REVIEW QUESTIONS

1. Which content theory of motivation would have the most promise for explaining motivation and helping in the economic growth of developing Third World countries? Explain.

2. Could a modified workweek be helpful in satisfying the three levels of needs suggested by Alderfer? How?

3. Describe the major differences between Maslow's need hierarchy and Alderfer's ERG explanation of motivation.

4. The "fear of success' finding of Horner was reported and sensationalized in the popular press in the early 1970s. Do you feel that there is stronger, weaker, or absolutely no "fear of success" today among women and men? Explain.

5. Why would it be interesting to examine and compare the needs discussed by McClelland in young, middle-aged, and older people in the United States, Japan, China, Egypt, Argentina, and Sweden?

6. Is there any value to a manager in understanding the suggestions made by Herzberg's two-factor theory?

7. Why is it so difficult to accurately measure the needs of an employee?

8. In your opinion, how common is it for a manager to be faced with subordinates who have different predominant needs? If this is the situation facing a manager, what does he or she have to do?

9. Why is it important to understand that a manager must *infer* the motivation level of subordinates?

10. Why is Maslow's need hierarchy still the most publicized theory of motivation?

ADDITIONAL REFERENCES

Cosgrove, D. J., and R. L. Dinerman. "There Is No Motivational Magic." *Management Review,* 1982, pp. 58–61.

Dunham, R. B., and J. L. Pierce. "The Design and Evaluation of Alternative Work Schedules." *Personnel Administrator,* 1983, pp. 67–75.

Garlitz, G. F. "Temporary Workers: A Changing Industry." *Personnel Administrator,* 1983, pp. 47–48.

Hellriegel, D.; J. W. Slocum, Jr.; and R. W. Woodman. *Organizational Behavior.* St. Paul, Minn.: West Publishing, 1983.

Matsui, T.; A., Okada; and T. Kakuyama. "Influence of Achievement Need on Goal Setting, Performance, and Feedback Effectiveness." *Journal of Applied Psychology,* 1982, pp. 645–48.

Nelson, D. E. "Employee Control IS an Important Option in Variable Work Schedules." *Personnel Administrator,* 1983, pp. 118–23.

Smith, W. C. "Unifying Customer Needs with Worker Satisfaction." *Management Review,* 1983,. pp. 49–52.

Szilagyi, A. D., Jr., and M. J., Wallace, Jr. *Organizational Behavior and Performance.* Glenview, Ill.: Scott, Foresman, 1983.

CASE FOR ANALYSIS

A Motivator of People Must Be Replaced: The Aftermath

The McLaughlin Engineering Corporation employs approximately 1,200 operating employees. The plant is old, but is kept reasonably clean and is known as one of the better production facilities in the area. The plant has a research and development department, an industrial relations department, an accounting and financial control department, a distribution department, and four operating departments that produce valves, metal brackets, metal shelves, and pistons. Exhibit 1 is an organization chart of a typical operating department.

The plant manager, Joe Ruggio, was responsible for all production, maintenance, and engineering work performed in the departments. The department supervisor of the unit represented in Exhibit 1 was Clyde Campbell. He reported directly to Joe and had two support units—maintenance and engineering. Clyde also had three team supervisors reporting directly to him. These men were each responsible for one of the three shifts—days (8–4), afternoons (4–12), nights (12–8).

The maintenance team consisted of 8 mechanics and 10 apprentice mechanics who worked on maintaining the machinery. They worked closely with the engineering team, which worked primarily on experimenting with new equipment, new plant layouts, and other problems of technological change. Although the engineers were college graduates, they worked extremely well with the mechanics and respected their technical knowledge.

The mechanics and engineers also respected the team supervisors, who worked hard and were interested in task accomplishment and people problems. The smooth coordination and mutual respect among the managerial and operating employees were certainly trademarks of McLaughlin. At the annual

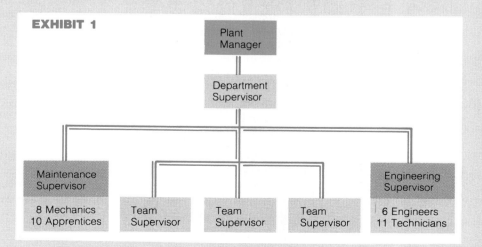

EXHIBIT 1

supervisory conference, the founder, Tommy McLaughlin, would mention the importance of respect, trust, and confidence. This message was continually presented in the company newspaper and at almost every annual award dinner.

Clyde had worked with McLaughlin for 18 years and had a reputation of being a technical expert in every phase of production. In fact, all of the four operating department supervisors were known throughout the organization for their technical and engineering skills.

The company has been one of the most popular within the community. In fact, the personnel department typically has an employment waiting list of at least 50 engineers, 100 mechanics, and 300 operating employees. Generally, about 80 percent of these people are qualified, but turnover is so low that there has been little hiring in the past three years.

The engineering group had no desire to unionize, and the mechanics, who were unionized, did not become involved in union politics. The plant has never had a strike, although other plants in the area are continually striking for better wages, fringe benefits, and related matters.

The performance of the plant had been improving in every area—in quality, quantity, and costs—for the past 10 years. The operating employees said that they respected the company and the management team because the managers knew what the employees' problems were all about. The managers were viewed as possessing technical knowledge and not just "paper shuffling" expertise.

Clyde became seriously ill around Christmas. He tried to come back to work in March, but was too weak physically and eventually had to take a disability leave in June. The three team supervisors were all considered for promotion to Clyde's position, but it was felt that they lacked experience to handle the job. The selection committee felt that promoting an engineer to the department supervisory position might be interpreted as favoritism by the mechanics. Thus, Nelson Morley, a 43-year-old engineer from Staley Engineering Corporation was hired to replace Clyde.

Nelson changed a few of Clyde's operating procedures concerning the reporting of productivity. The performance report procedure was one major change that many people disliked. Nelson would meet with the team supervisors once a month to go over reports on the performance of the three shifts. Clyde had met with the managers only as a team and did not meet separately with supervisors, engineers, and mechanics. There had been no regularity in Clyde's arrangement; the teams might meet once a week, twice a month, or once every six months.

Even before Nelson joined the company, a number of mechanics, engineers, and operating employees had said that they would leave if Clyde did not return. They believed that they performed well because of him. He was what they described as a "motivator of men."

Nelson was called an "outside renegade" behind his back. The quality of work and timeliness in filling orders suffered significantly after Nelson took over. The total team had been split because of his practice of only meeting with team supervisors. The engineers and mechanics began to quarrel with the supervisors about standards and procedures. These disagreements seemed to be most intense immediately after the monthly meetings between Nelson and the team supervisors.

One supervisor said, "Nelson is now the boss, and we must get into step and follow his procedures." This feeling was not shared by any of the mechanics or engineers. It appeared to them that the team supervisors were joining up with Nelson.

Joe was very concerned with the turn of events in the department and asked Nelson to visit with him. The objective of the meeting was to work out a plan so that performance and satisfaction would return to more acceptable levels.

Questions for Consideration

1. What type of plan could Joe and Nelson develop to correct the situation ?
2. Will Nelson be viewed as a "motivator of men" in this situation? Explain your answer in terms of a need satisfaction model.

EXPERIENTIAL EXERCISE
APPLYING MOTIVATION THEORY

Objectives

1. To evaluate the merits of different motivation theories.
2. To emphasize the decisions that must be made by managers in motivating people.
3. To apply motivation principles.

Related Topics

The manager must make decisions to succeed.
The difficulty of diagnosing situations.

Starting the Exercise

Set up groups of five to eight students to read the facts and the situation facing Margo Williams.

The Facts

In the chapter, a number of popular content theories were discussed. Some of the major points raised were the following:

Maslow: Motivation involves satisfying needs in a hierarchical order.
Herzberg: Some job factors are intrinsically satisfying and motivate individuals.

McClelland: Motives are acquired from a person's culture.

Alderfer: In addition to the satisfaction-progression process proposed by Maslow, there is a frustration-regression process at work.

With these four theories in mind, review the work situation that is currently facing Margo Williams.

Margo Williams is a project engineer director in a large construction company. She is responsible for scheduling projects, meeting customers, reporting progress on projects, controlling costs, and developing subordinates. A total of 20 men and 8 women report to Margo. All of them are college graduates and have had at least eight years of job experience. Margo is a Ph.D. engineer, but she has only had four years of project engineering experience.

The biggest problems facing Margo involve the lack of respect and response that she receives from her subordinates. Margo's supervisor has considered these problems and assumes that her moderate record of success could be improved if she could correct the situation. Margo is now considering a course of action that could motivate her subordinates to show more respect and respond more favorably to her requests.

Exercise Procedures

1. Set up small discussion groups of five to eight students to develop a motivation plan for Margo. The group should work on developing a plan that uses the motivation principles discussed in this chapter.
2. After the group has worked together for about 30 minutes, a group leader should present the plan to the class.
3. Discuss each group's plan for the remainder of the class period.

Chapter 5

After completing Chapter 5, you should be able to:

Define the meaning of learning.

Describe why goal setting has become a popular motivation application in organizations.

Discuss how comparisons are made in the equity explanation of motivation.

Compare expectancy and goal-setting explanations of motivation.

Identify operants that managers can work with in organizations.

Motivation: Process Theories and Applications

Skinner's Approach to Reinforcement

Argument For

Some researchers and managers believe that Skinner's work has been overlooked, misinterpreted, and misapplied. They point out that since the major concern of managers of human resources is to predict and control the behavior of organizational participants, it is curious to find that people with such a concern are extremely conversant with McGregor and Maslow and totally ignorant of Skinner.* The increasing attention that is be-

* Walter Nord, "Beyond the Teaching Machine: The Neglected Area of Operant Conditioning in the Theory and Practice of Management," *Organizational Behavior and Human Performance*, November 1969, p. 375.

ing given to Skinnerian behaviorism in the applied organizational behavior literature should reduce the misinterpretation of Skinner's work.

At the heart of Skinnerian behaviorism is a major contention: Behavior is a function of its consequences. Skinner's approach emphasizes the effect of environmental consequences on objective, observable behavior. Skinner believes that behavioral scientists should abandon their preoccupation with the inner thoughts of a person and concentrate more on the interactions between the person and the environment.

According to Skinner's approach, work behavior is shaped and maintained by its consequences; these consequences (reinforcers) can be either positive or negative, but positive reinforcers are more effective. Through the use of reinforcers, behavior can be learned. A learned behavior is called an *operant* because it operates on the environment to produce a consequence. Skinner called unlearned behavior *respondent behavior.*

The advocates of Skinner's principles have recommended that operant conditioning be applied to motivation attempts and programs, training and personal development, job design, compensation, organizational design, and performance appraisal. They believe that managers who take the time to study Skinner's principles of behavior control will see the potential managerial applications. They state that even Skinner's critics admit that his behavior principles work in organizations.†

Argument Against

The critics of Skinnerian behaviorism are numerous. One of the most respected and articulate critics is William F. Whyte. Whyte contends that Skinner's operant conditioning theory tells us little about the prediction and control of behavior and that it also fails to deal with four crucial elements of real-life behavior in organizations. These are:

1. *The cost-benefit ratio.* In using pigeons to develop his principles, Skinner would disregard the costs of the action to the actor. The costs were trifling compared to the benefits (food) that the experimental pigeons received as a consequence of action. However, people generally weigh what they receive for their efforts in terms of personal investments. Thus, providing positive reinforcers for production is much more complex than giving pigeons food.

2. *Conflicting stimuli.* Employees face conflicting stimuli from such organizational sources as the reward system, requests from subordinates, and schedules. They do indeed respond, as Skinner argues, in terms of the consequences of past behavior. But in many situations conflicting stimulus conditions exist, and managers cannot easily predict any response simply by analyzing the relationship between the individual and the anticipated reinforcement.

3. *Time lag and trust.* Few of a person's acts bring immediate rewards. The time span between behavior and reinforcement in organizations can be quite long. Given the time lag between behavior and rewards, the individual must have trust in the person applying reinforcers. Time lag and trust are not issues when experimental animals are used.

4. *One-body problem.* In the Skinner laboratory experiments, the researcher's attention is confined to the environmental conditions that induce the pigeon to behave in a certain way. When working with people, the contingencies to which an individual responds are provided by another person or persons. Thus, it is necessary to learn to deal with the contingencies that affect the behavior of the person initiating the reinforcers and the workers.

Whyte does not want to discard Skinner's theory, but he asks that it be treated cautiously. He would like Skinner and his supporters not to make grandiose claims, since the claims do not serve to develop what is an important set of ideas regarding motivation.‡

† For support for applying behavior modification to organizations, see Fred Luthans and Robert Kreitner, *Organizational Behavior Modification* (Glenview, Ill.: Scott, Foresman, 1975); and Everett E. Adam, Jr., "Behavior Modification in Quality Control," *Academy of Management Journal*, December 1975, pp. 662–79.

‡ Whyte's position appears in William F. Whyte, "Skinnerian Theory in Organizations," *Psychology Today*, April 1972, pp. 67–68, 96–100; and "An Interview with William F. Whyte," *Organizational Dynamics*, Spring 1975, pp. 51–66.

The previous chapter examined four content theories of motivation. These theories are concerned about what specific things motivate people. In this chapter, we will examine four process theories of motivation. These theories attempt to explain and describe how behavior is <u>energized</u>, how it is directed, how it is sustained, and how it is stopped. Currently, the four major process theories of motivation are ① reinforcement, ② expectancy, ③ equity, and ④ goal setting. Each of these theories will be presented in terms of how the motivation process works in organizational settings. However, before we address these theories, let us first examine *learning,* an important concept in explaining any process of motivation.

The Organizational Issue for Debate examines Skinner's ideas on learning. Skinner is not interested in whether Mike has a high esteem need or is comparing his work effort and salary with Mary's. Skinner is interested in answering the question "How can I get Mike to do *X?*" Getting Mike to change—moving him from where he is to where you want him—is how Skinner's behaviorism views learning and motivation.

LEARNING

Learning is one of the fundamental processes underlying behavior. Most of the behavior within organizations is learned behavior. Perceptions, attitudes, goals, and emotional reactions are learned. Skills— for example, programming a computer or counseling a troubled employee—can be learned. The meanings and uses of language are learned.

learning
The process of changing behavior through practice.

Learning can be defined as the process by which a relatively enduring change in behavior occurs as a result of practice. The words *relatively enduring* signify that the change in behavior is more or less permanent. The term *practice* is intended to cover both formal training and uncontrolled experiences. The changes in behavior that characterize learning may be <u>adaptive and promote effectiveness,</u> or they may be <u>nonadaptive and ineffective</u>. The definition also indicates that learning is a process in which certain changes in behavior occur. The process cannot be directly observed. It must be inferred from changes in behavior.

Types of Learning

Three types of learning are considered important in developing and altering behavior. These are classical conditioning, operant conditioning, and observational learning.

In understanding each of these types of learning, four basic concepts need to be clearly understood. First, the _drive_ of the person must be considered. A drive is an aroused condition within the person. It can result from deprivation or some specific stimulation. Primary drives, such as hunger, are unlearned. On the other hand, secondary drives, such as being anxious about attending a performance review feedback session, are learned. Once a drive has been learned, it serves to trigger behavior.

A second basic concept is stimulus. A _stimulus_ is a cue that is the occasion for a response. A supervisor's request is a stimulus to complete a job. The time on the clock is a stimulus to get up and go to a committee meeting. Stimuli, then, set the stage for a response or a series of responses. In some cases, the stimulus that calls forth a response is obvious. In other cases, the stimulus for a particular response is obscure.

Another basic concept is the response. A _response_ is the behavioral result of stimulation. It is any activity of the person, regardless of whether the stimulus is identifiable or the activity is observable. Responses become linked to stimuli, so that when stimulu occur, the responses are likely to follow. Responses in work organizations may be oral, written, manual, or attitudinal. The attitudinal response is often covert and difficult to detect. The cognitive and affective components of attitude cannot be seen.

reinforcer
Anything that a manager uses to increase or maintain a particular individual response.

The final basic concept is the reinforcer. A **reinforcer** is any object or event that serves to increase or sustain the strength of a response. Among the common reinforcers used in organizations are praise from a supervisor, a merit increase in pay, and transfer to a desirable job.

Classical Conditioning.   The study of classical conditioning began with the work of the Russian physiologist Pavlov around the turn of the 20th century. While studying the automatic reflexes associated with digestion, Pavlov noticed that his laboratory dog salivated not only in the presence of food but also at the presentation of other stimuli before food was placed in its mouth. He reasoned that food automatically produced salivation. This phenomenon was an unlearned association; Pavlov therefore labeled food an _unconditioned stimulus_ and salivation an _unconditioned response_. Since he believed that the response of salivating to other, seemingly unrelated stimuli had to be learned, he labeled it a _conditioned response_ initiated by a _conditioned stimulus_.

As part of his experiments, Pavlov rang a bell (conditioned stimulus) and then placed food in the dog's mouth (unconditioned stimulus). Soon the bell alone evoked salivation. Thus, salivation produced by food is an unconditioned response, whereas salivation produced by the bell alone is a conditioned (or learned) response. Figure 5–1 graphically presents Pavlov's work on classical conditioning.[1]

Operant Conditioning.   The name most closely associated with operant conditioning is that of B. F. Skinner, the world-famous behaviorist. This form of conditioning is concerned with learning that occurs as a *consequence of behavior*. In classical conditioning, the sequence of events is *independent of* the subject's behavior. Behaviors that can be controlled by altering the consequences (reinforcers and punishments) that follow them are referred to as *operants*. An operant is strengthened (increased) or weakened (decreased) as a function of the events that follow it. Most workplace behaviors are operants. Examples of operant behaviors are performing job-related tasks, reading a budget report, or coming to work on time. Operants are distinguished by virtue of being controlled by their consequences.

FIGURE 5–1

The Pavlov Procedure for Classical Conditioning

Before training
    Ringing a bell ⎯⎯⎯⎯⎯⎯⎯⎯⎯⎯⎯→ No salivation (no response)
Training
    Bell rings, and food (uncon-
    ditioned stimulus) is provided ⎯⎯⎯⎯→ Salivation (unconditioned response)
After training
    Bell rings (conditioned stimulus) ⎯⎯⎯→ Salivation (conditioned response)

In classical conditioning, the response to be learned (salivating) is already present in the animal and may be triggered by the presentation of the appropriate unconditioned stimulus (food). In operant conditioning, however, the desired response may not be present in the subject. Teaching a subordinate to prepare an accurate weekly budget report is an example of operant conditioning. There is no identifiable stimulus that will automatically evoke the response of preparing the budget. The manager works with the subordinate and reinforces him or her for preparing an accurate budget. Figure 5–2 illustrates the operant conditioning process.

The relationships of $S_1 \longrightarrow R_1 \longrightarrow S_2 \longrightarrow R_2$ are referred to as the

---

[1] An excellent presentation of the conditioning process is given in Bernard M. Bass and James A. Vaughn, *Training in Industry: The Management of Learning* (Monterey, Calif.: Brooks/Cole Publishing, 1966). Also see Alan E. Kazdin, *Behavior Modification in Applied Settings* (Homewood, Ill.: Richard D. Irwin, 1980).

FIGURE 5–2

An Example of Operant Conditioning

S_1 $\longrightarrow$	R_1 $\longrightarrow$	S_2 $\longrightarrow$	R_2
A memo that instructs subordinate to prepare budget	Preparing weekly budgets	Receiving valued praise from the superior	A sense of satisfaction
Conditioned stimulus	Conditioned operant response	Reinforcing stimulus	Unconditioned response
(Antecedent)	(Behavior)	(Consequence)	

contingencies of reinforcement.[2] This sequence is also described as the A----B----C operant mode. A designates the antecedent or stimulus that precedes the behavior, B. And C is the consequence, or what results from the behavior. Skinner believes that such consequences will be acted out in the future.[3] This notion lends itself particularly well to the study of various learning principles such as reinforcement and knowledge of results.

Observational Learning. Many professional golfers and baseball players improve their ability to hit the ball by taking a lot of practice swings. In fact, the best professional golfers and batters study and observe how others swing the club or the bat. Today, most major league baseball teams film the batting habits of players and then study the films to observe each part of the swing. These teams are using a form of observational learning. This type of learning occurs when an individual observes a model's behavior (it may be his own behavior on film) and attempts to duplicate that behavior.

Major corporations such as Exxon, Westinghouse, Union Carbide, and Federated Department Stores are teaching managers to apply motivation principles on the job through observational learning. Such attempts and empirical research on them are expected to increase in the 1980s. The "how-to" results orientation has impressed those organizations that are in the forefront of efforts to use observational learning.[4]

Observational learning has significant potential in organizational

[2] See W. Clay Hamner, "Reinforcement Theory and Contingency Management in Organizational Settings," in *Organizational Behavior and Management: A Contingency Approach,* ed. Henry L. Tosi and W. Clay Hamner (Chicago: St. Clair Press, 1974), pp. 86–112.

[3] B. F. Skinner, *Beyond Freedom and Dignity* (New York: Alfred A. Knopf, 1971); and B. F. Skinner, *Contingencies of Reinforcement: A Theoretical Analysis* (New York: Appleton-Century-Crofts, 1969).

[4] Bernard L. Rosenbaum, "Common Misconceptions about Behavior Modeling and Supervisory Skill Training (SST)," *Training and Development Journal,* August 1979, pp. 40–48.

settings, especially in training programs. It has already been used in training programs designed to improve interpersonal skills, supervisory practices, and managerial use of positive reinforcement.[5] Other uses that seem to be suited for modeling and observational learning are:

Training managers to conduct performance appraisal sessions.

Training individuals to engage in goal-setting processes.

Training individuals to interview properly.

Training sales personnel to practice sound selling procedures.

Learning, then, is strongly involved in the development and direction of the behaviors of individuals in organizational settings.[6] We have touched only briefly on three important types of learning that can influence workplace behavior and performance. Of the three, operant conditioning has stimulated the most interest and controversy.

REINFORCEMENT THEORY

The basic assumption of operant conditioning is that behavior is influenced by its consequences. B. F. Skinner's work with animals led to the use of the term *operant conditioning*. The term more often used to describe operant conditioning principles applied to individuals is *behavior modification* (also called B-mod and behavior mod). Thus, **behavior modification** is individual learning by reinforcement.

behavior modification
The application of operant conditioning principles.

Organizational behavior modification, or "OB Mod," is a more general term coined to designate "the systematic reinforcement of desirable organizational behavior and the nonreinforcement or punishment of unwanted organizational behavior."[7] Thus, OB Mod is an operant approach to organizational behavior. The term *organizational* has been added to the term *behavior modification* to indicate that the operant approach is being used in the work setting. We will use the terms *behavior modification* and *organizational behavior modification* interchangeably.

There are a number of important principles of operant conditioning that can aid the manager attempting to influence behavior. *Reinforcement* is an extremely important principle of learning. In a general sense, motivation is an internal cause of behavior, while

---

[5] For a review of behavior modeling uses in organizations, see six articles in *Personnel Psychology,* Autumn 1976, pp. 325–70.

[6] Patricia Sanders and John N. Yanouzas, "Socialization to Learning," *Training and Development Journal,* July 1983, pp. 14–21.

[7] Fred Luthans and Robert Kreitner, *Organizational Behavior Modification* (Glenview, Ill.: Scott, Foresman, 1975), p. 15; and Fred Luthans, *Organizational Behavior* (New York: McGraw-Hill, 1981), p. 268.

reinforcement is an external cause of behavior. Thus, reinforcement is anything that both increases the strength of response and tends to induce repetitions of the behavior that preceded the reinforcement.[8] It can be stated that without reinforcement no measurable modification of behavior takes place. Managers often use *positive reinforcers* to modify behavior. In some cases the reinforcers work as predicted, while in other cases they do not modify behavior in the desired direction because of competing reinforcement contingencies. When reinforcers are not made contingent on the behavior desired by the manager, desired behaviors do not occur. Also, giving reinforcers long after the occurrence of the desired behaviors decreases the probability of their recurrence.

Negative reinforcement refers to an increase in the frequency of a response following removal of a negative reinforcer immediately after the response. An event is a *negative reinforcer* only if its removal after a response increases the performance of that response. A familiar example of negative reinforcement in the summer months in Phoenix and Houston is turning on the automobile air conditioner on a stifling hot day. Turning on the air conditioner (the behavior) usually minimizes or terminates an aversive condition, namely being hot (negative reinforcer). This increases the probability of having an operating air conditioning system in the summer months. Similarly, exerting high degrees of effort to complete a job may be negatively reinforced by not having to listen to a nagging boss.

punishment
When a manager administers something unpleasant or withdraws something pleasant (subtracts pay for tardiness), he or she is engaged in applying punishment.

Punishment is an uncomfortable consequence of a particular behavioral response.[9] It is certainly a controversial method of behavior modification. Some people believe that punishment is the opposite of reward and is just as effective in changing behavior.

Punishment may be a poor approach to learning because:

1. The results of punishment are not as predictable as those of reward.
2. The effects of punishment are less permanent than those of reward.
3. Punishment is frequently accompanied by negative attitudes toward the administrator of the punishment, as well as toward the activity that led to the punishment.

Despite the costs of using punishment, it has been and will continue to be used as a method of altering behavior. In situations where the costs of not punishing outweigh the advantages, punishment may be an appropriate method. For example, punishing a worker who deliberately slows down the flow of work is a costly way of altering behavior.

---

[8] Luthans, *Organizational Behavior,* p. 250.

[9] W. E. Craighead, A. E. Kazdin, and M. J. Mahoney, *Behavior Modification* (Boston: Houghton Mifflin, 1976), pp. 112–20.

However, there might be ways of dealing with the problem other than punishment. The point is, however, that punishment and its use depend on the situation and on the manager's style of altering behavior. Punishment will be discussed in more detail in the next chapter.

extinction
Not reinforcing a behavior so that the behavior eventually stops.

Extinction reduces undesired behavior. When positive reinforcement for a learned response is withheld, individuals will continue to practice that behavior for some period of time. If not reinforcing the behavior continues, the behavior decreases and will eventually disappear. The decline in the response rate because of nonreinforcement is defined as extinction.

An important base for these four important principles is Thorndike's proposed *law of effect*. This law is stated as follows:

> Of several responses to the same situation, those that are accompanied or closely followed by satisfaction (reinforcement) . . . will be more likely to recur; those which are accompanied or closely followed by discomfort (punishment) . . . will be less likely to occur.[10]

The idea that the consequences of behavior, reward or punishment, are critical in determining future behavior remains an important foundation for the use of operant conditioning in organizational settings.

Reinforcement Schedules

It is extremely important to properly time the rewards or punishments used in an organization. The timing of these outcomes is called *reinforcement scheduling*. In the simplest schedule, the response is reinforced each time it occurs. This is called *continuous reinforcement*. If reinforcement occurs only after some instances of a response and not after each response, an *intermittent reinforcement* schedule is being used.

Continuous and intermittent reinforcement schedules produce important differences in performance. First, during the initial development of a response (e.g., learning and applying a new job skill), continuous reinforcement is preferred because it accelerates early performance. Second, when trying to sustain a response (e.g., good performance), intermittent schedules are more effective.

Examples of relatively continuous reinforcement might be receiving praise after every unit is produced or being greeted warmly every day by the supervisor. Examples of intermittent reinforcement occur in connection with preparing a report for the boss (only occasionally will he or she compliment you) or running for an elected union position (only occasionally do you win these elections).

---

[10] Edward L. Thorndike, *Animal Intelligence* (New York: Macmillan, 1911), p. 244.

Types of Intermittent Schedules

Intermittent reinforcement can be scheduled in a number of ways. Reinforcers can be delivered by a manager on the basis of a time interval. This is referred to as an *interval schedule*, meaning that

FIGURE 5–3

Intermittent Schedules of Reinforcement Used by Managers

1. Fixed interval schedule

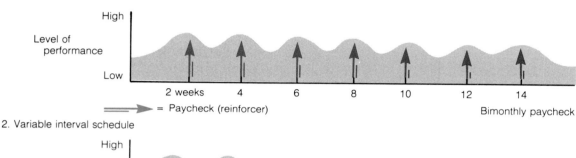

2. Variable interval schedule

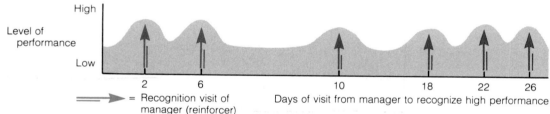

3. Fixed ratio schedule

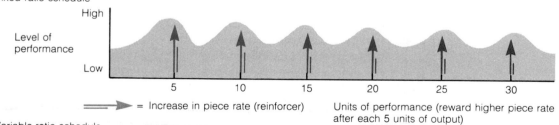

4. Variable ratio schedule

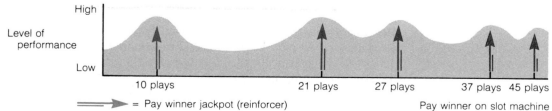

Source: Based on Dennis W. Organ and W. Clay Hamner, *Organizational Behavior* (Plano, Tex.: Business Publications, 1982), p. 76.

the response will be reinforced after a specified time interval. Reinforcers can also be delivered after a certain number of responses. This is referred to as as *ratio schedule* because the schedule specifies the number of responses required for each reinforcement.

Interval schedules can be either *fixed* or *variable*. A fixed interval schedule requires that an unvarying time interval must pass before the reinforcer is available. Figure 5–3 highlights the types of intermittent schedules that managers can use. The *fixed interval schedule* is illustrated by an employee receiving a bimonthly paycheck. Every two weeks the individual is paid (reinforced). A *variable interval schedule* uses an interval that varies around an average. For example, reinforcers become available after 2, 6, 10, 18, 22, and 26 days. This averages to a reinforcer every 14 days.

A *fixed ratio* reinforcement schedule involves issuing a reinforcer after a fixed number of responses have occurred. For example, every fifth response or unit of output is reinforced. A *variable ratio* schedule also requires that a certain number of responses occur before the manager delivers a reinforcer. However, the number varies around an average. The example in Figure 5–3 shows that over the 140 plays

TABLE 5–1

Reinforcement Schedules and Their Effects on Behavior

Schedule	Description	When Applied to Individual	When Removed by Manager	Organizational Example
Continuous	Reinforcer follows every response	Fastest method for establishing new behavior	Fastest method to cause extinction of new behavior	Praise after every response, immediate recognition of every response
Fixed interval	Response after specific time period is reinforced	Some inconsistency in response frequencies	Faster extinction of motivated behavior than variable schedules	Weekly, bimonthly, monthly paycheck
Variable interval	Response after varying period of time (an average) is reinforced	Produces high rate of steady responses	Slower extinction of motivated behavior than fixed schedules	Transfers, promotions, recognition
Fixed ratio	A fixed number of responses must occur before reinforcement	Some inconsistency in response frequencies	Faster extinction of motivated behavior than variable schedules	Piece rate, commission on units sold
Variable ratio	A varying number (average) of responses must occur before reinforcement	Can produce high rate of response that is steady and resists extinction	Slower extinction of motivated behavior than fixed schedules	Bonus, award, time off

Source: Adapted from O. Behling, C. Schriesheim, and J. Tolliver, "Present Theories and New Directions in Theories of Work Effort," *Journal of Supplement Abstract Service of the American Psychological Association,* 1974, p. 57.

the average reinforcement occurs every 28 plays: 10, 21, 27, 37, and 45, or 140, divided by five reinforcements.

Research has shown that higher rates of response are usually achieved with ratio rather than interval schedules. This finding is understandable since high response rates do not necessarily speed up the delivery of a reinforcer in an interval schedule, as they do with ratio schedules. A summary of the effects that the various reinforcement schedules have on behavior is presented in Table 5–1.

Description of Behavior Modification: A Managerial Perspective

Behavior modification assumes that behavior is more important than its "psychological causes," such as the needs, motives, and values held by individuals.[11] Thus, a behaviorist such as B. F. Skinner focuses on specific behaviors and not on such intangibles as esteem needs or personality structure. For example, if a behaviorist is told that an employee is not performing well, he or she would probably ask, "What specific behaviors led to this conclusion?" Discrete and distinguishable behaviors are the most important bases in developing any behavior modification plan to correct a performance problem.

In addition to the attention devoted to discrete and distinguishable behaviors, there is an emphasis on the consequences of behavior. For example, suppose that all new management trainees are given a two-day training program on preparing budget reports but that shortly after the training sessions have been completed, it is noticed that few reports are prepared correctly. One explanation may be that the training program was ineffective. This may be the problem.

However, the behaviorist might approach the problem from a different direction. First, he or she could determine whether the trainees understand the importance of correct reports. He or she might then find out which trainees are turning in correct reports and what consequences are being incurred by these trainees. It could be that turning in correct reports results in nothing, that there are no observable consequences. In the same manner, submitting an incorrect report may also result in no consequences, positive or negative. This finding might result in developing a program of positive and negative consequences (e.g., recognition, praise, a meeting with the boss to go over mistakes). The behaviorist believes that people tend to repeat behaviors that lead to positive consequences. This principle could serve as a cornerstone in improving the report accuracy of trainees.

The proposed application of behavior modification in organizations

---

[11] Ron Zemke, "So Long, Skinner . . . Hello Cog Sci?" *Training,* February 1983, pp. 40–42, 44–45.

FIGURE 5-4

**Applied Behavior Modification: A
Manager's Step-by-Step Procedure**

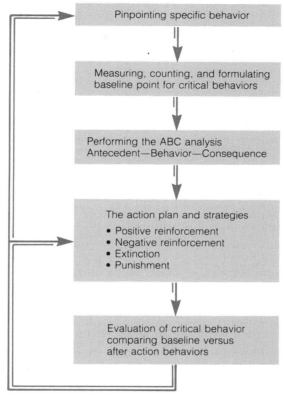

Feedback to make changes

follows a problem-solving process.[12] Figure 5–4 shows a problem-solving model that emphasizes five major points. First, the manager must identify and define the specific behavior. A behavior is pinpointed when it can be accurately and reliably observed and recorded. To be pinpointed as an important behavior, there must be positive answers to these questions: (1) <u>Can it be seen?</u> and (2) <u>Can it be measured?</u>[13]

Second, the manager must measure or count the occurrences of

---

[12] Two excellent and very similar behavior modification problem-solving processes are found in Lawrence M. Miller, *Behavior Management* (New York: John Wiley & Sons, 1978), pp. 64–66; and Luthans, pp. 270–89.

[13] Discussed in Luthans, *Organizational Behavior;* and Fred Luthans and Jason Schweizer, "How Behavior Modification Techniques Can Improve Total Organizational Performance," *Management Review,* September 1979, pp. 43–50.

TABLE 5–2
Performance Analysis Questions

Antecedent
Does the employee know what is expected?
Are the standards clear?
Have they been communicated?
Are they realistic?

Behavior
Can the behavior be performed?
Could the employee do it if his or her life depended upon it?
Does something prevent its occurrence?

Consequence
Are the consequences weighted in favor of performance?
Are improvements being reinforced?
Do we note improvement even though the improvement may still leave the employee below company standards?
Is reinforcement specific?

Source: Thomas K. Connellan, *How to Improve Human Performance: Behaviorism in Business* (New York: Harper & Row, 1978), p. 51.

the pinpointed behavior. This count provides the manager with a clear perspective of the strength of the behavior under the present or before-change situation. The count serves as the means of evaluating any changes in behavior that may occur later on. Managers can graph these data to determine whether the behavior is increasing, decreasing, or remaining the same.

Third, the manager conducts an analysis of the ABCs of the behavior.[14] This is also called functionally analyzing the behavior.[15] The A designates analyzing the antecedents of the actual behavior, B. The B designates the pinpointed critical behaviors. Finally, the C indicates the contingent consequence. Specific analyses of the ABCs attempt to determine where the problems lie. Connellan has developed a set of performance analysis questions to get at the problem source.[16] These are presented in Table 5–2.

The ABC analysis permits the manager to consider performance analysis questions that are important in formulating any specific program. In analyzing absenteeism, for example, the manager using a question format and the type of framework displayed in Table 5–3 is systematically viewing the problem of absenteeism in terms of antecedents, behaviors, and consequences.

---

[14] Thomas K. Connellan, *How to Improve Human Performance: Behaviorism in Business and Industry* (New York: Harper & Row, 1978), pp. 48–75.

[15] Luthans, *Organizational Behavior*, p. 276.

[16] Connellan, *How to Improve Human Performance*, p. 51.

TABLE 5–3

Using the ABCs Analysis: An Absenteeism Problem

A Antecedent(s)	B Behavior(s)	C Consequence(s)

Family problems: wife, children
Personal health
Illness
Jury duty
No transportation
Company policies
Group norm
Friends visiting
Injured on way to work
Hangover
No child care facilities
Do not have proper tools
  or clothing
	Staying home
	Shopping
	Overslept
	Getting up late
	Attending sporting
	  event
	Working at home
	Visiting
	Served on jury
	In emergency room
	  at hospital
	At doctor's office
		Public reprimand
		Private reprimand
		Written record
		  and reprimand
		Reduction in pay
		Suspension
		Firing
		Social isolation
		  from group

Source: Adapted from Fred Luthans and Mark Martinko, "An Organizational Behavior Modification Analysis of Absenteeism," *Human Resources Management*, Fall 1976.

FIGURE 5–5

Reinforcement Strategies Applying the ABCs

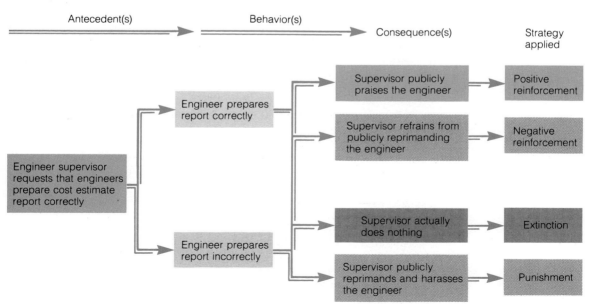

Fourth, the first three steps in an applied behavior modification program set the stage for the actual step. The goal of operant conditioning is to strengthen desirable and observable critical performance behaviors and to weaken undesirable behaviors. The strategies for accomplishing these goals were discussed under the heading of reinforcement theory. Included as strategies are positive reinforcers, negative reinforcers, punishment, and extinction. The application of these four strategies is presented in terms of the ABCs in Figure 5–5.

Positive reinforcement is the preferred strategy in most applied behavior modification programs. However, it is not always easy to identify positive reinforcers. The most obvious approach is to ask subordinates what is rewarding. Another identification method is to use attitude surveys asking about job reward preferences.

An example of the application of reinforcers is found in the gambling casinos of Atlantic City and Las Vegas. The owners may not be at all familiar with the details of reinforcement, but they sure can apply them in the casinos. The following Close-Up shows how reinforcers encourage gamblers to keep playing.

ORGANIZATIONS: CLOSE-UP

The Use of Behavior Modification in Atlantic City and Las Vegas

There seems to be some knowledge about how reinforcement works among casino owners in Atlantic City and Las Vegas. These owners seem to know how people (the visitors, compulsive gamblers, the amateurs) react to reinforcement (a jackpot).

Most players of slot machines assume that jackpots occur according to some random reinforcement schedule. If the casino owners set the machines to pay off on a fixed ratio schedule, then counting the number of pulls between each jackpot would be a successful technique. If the slot were on a fixed interval schedule, then the player would simply have to watch the clock and time the occurrence of jackpots. The casino owners know that staying with the machine and feeding in coins are more likely to occur if there is a random reinforcement schedule. Then the players have no idea when they will strike it rich. They must keep playing to win, even once or twice. Thus, what we find in Atlantic City and Las Vegas is a program of random reinforcement.

The casino owners also know the value of atmosphere in keeping players at the machine. An atmosphere of excitement is created because people all around seem to be winning. The owners have accomplished this excitement by connecting each slot machine to a central control. Why? So that when any single slot machine hits a jackpot, sirens wail, lights flash, bells sound off, and screams of joy are heard and seen by everyone. This display informs everyone that it pays to keep playing. Keep inserting those coins. The payoff is money. If you want to be a winner and there are winners all around, keep feeding those coins.

Does it work? The casino owners think so. Many of them may never have heard of B. F. Skinner, but he sure provided some reinforcement principles that work. The slot machines are so popular that many visitors to Atlantic City and Las Vegas spend all their time feeding those coins and waiting for the bells to go off.

The final applied behavior modification step involves evaluation. A major weakness in many applied motivational programs is that formal evaluations are not conducted. The evaluation of an applied program permits the manager to trace and review changes in behavior before and after the implementation of an action program. The use of evaluation permits managers to measure performance on an ongoing basis. Furthermore, evaluation can provide feedback to the manager on the behaviors being exhibited. This feedback can enable the manager to make necessary and timely corrections in the program.

Research on Reinforcement Theory

The application of operant conditioning in organizations (i.e., behavior modification or organizational behavior modification) has given rise to a limited number of field research studies. The available research on reinforcement theory applications is often limited to small samples, single organizations, and limited periods of time. Furthermore, it has on a number of occasions resulted in unexpected findings. For example, one study compared the effects of continuous and variable ratio piece rate bonus pay plans. Contrary to predictions, the continuous schedule yielded the highest level of performance. One reason cited for the less than expected effectiveness of the variable ratio schedules was that some employees working on these schedules were opposed to the pay plan. They perceived the plan as a form of gambling, and this was not acceptable to them.[17]

A characteristic of behavior modification research is its emphasis on the use of the scientific approach. Researchers take extreme care to clearly define concepts, carefully classify variables, and present results so that the data trends and changes can be easily distinguished.

---

[17] G. Yukl, K. N. Wexley, and J. E. Seymore, "Effectiveness of Pay Incentives under Variable Ratio and Continuous Reinforcement Schedules," *Journal of Applied Psychology*, February 1972, pp. 19–23.

FIGURE 5–6

Impact of Behavior Modification Training

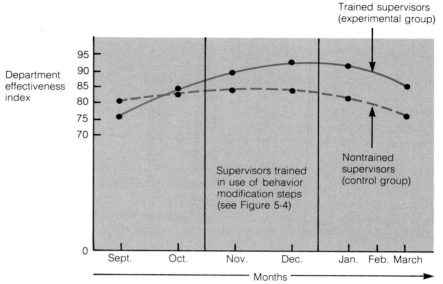

Source: Adapted from Robert Otteman and Fred Luthans, "An Experimental Analysis of the Effectiveness of an Organizational Behavior Modification Program in Industry." *Academy of Management Proceedings,* 1975, p. 141.

An example of these features is found in the reports of behavior modification research in a manufacturing plant.[18]

Two groups of production supervisors were used in the study (placed into either an experimental or a control group). The experimental group received training in how to conduct an applied behavior modification program with subordinates. The training emphasized the types of steps spelled out in Figure 5–4. The departments of the trained managers appeared to improve behaviors related to effectiveness. Their performance after the supervisors returned from training revealed fewer complaints, a lower scrap rate, and fewer rejects. Figure 5–6 shows these results.

Unfortunately, this study (1) was conducted in a single firm (can the results be replicated in other firms?), (2) used only two groups of nine production supervisors (is the procedure manageable with larger groups?), (3) covered only a seven-month period as presented (do the

---

[18] Robert Otteman and Fred Luthans, "An Experimental Analysis of the Effectiveness of an Organizational Behavior Modification Program in Industry," *Academy of Management, Proceedings,* 1975, pp. 140–42. For a more complete discussion, see Fred Luthans and Robert Kreitner, *Organizational Behavior Modification* (Glenview, Ill.: Scott, Foresman, 1975), pp. 150–59.

results hold or sustain themselves for longer periods of time?), and (4) failed to discuss the costs and benefits of the training (it is assumed that the improvement saved money, but what did the training and research cost?).[19]

Despite apparent problems associated with the application of behavior modification, the list of users includes Michigan Bell Telephone, Ford Motor Company, American Can, United Airlines, Warner-Lambert, Chase Manhattan Bank, Procter & Gamble, and Standard Oil of Ohio. The results of some of these applications of behavior modification principles are summarized in Table 5–4.

A review of the results summarized in Table 5–4 discloses some noticeable features of most applied behavior modification programs. First, for the most part the programs are applied at the operating employee level (e.g., mechanics, maintenance employees, clerks). The tasks of operating employees are compatible with the features of behavior modification—identifying critical behaviors, performing the ABC analysis, and evaluating changes in behavior. Second, each of the programs has specified goals. Goal setting is extremely important in behavior modification. Third, most of the programs focus on absenteeism and performance. Fourth, the feedback cycle is usually short—daily or weekly—again indicating that behavior modification may be more suitable at operating levels, where short-run criteria are typically used to evaluate performance, than at middle and upper managerial levels, where feedback is not on such a short cycle.

Fifth, the popular set of positive reinforcers used in applied programs centers on praise, recognition, and self-feedback. Money is less widely used in applied behavior modification programs. Finally, most reports of applied behavior modification (especially when a company is identified) present successful results. It is interesting and rare to find a reported result such as that of the Connecticut General Life Insurance Company, where some divisions stopped using positive reinforcement (see Table 5–4).

Of the many reported applications of behavior modification principles, the most publicized has been the program implemented at Emery Air Freight Company under the direction of Edward Feeney, a company executive.[20] The approach he used was (1) to regularly inform employees how well they were meeting specific goals and then (2) to reward improvement with praise and recognition.

Feeney closely examined the processing of parcels at Emery and

---

[19] These comments do not apply only to behavior modification research. A significant amount of organizational behavior research could be reviewed in this same manner. However, since the vast majority of the research in this applied area has these characteristics, they are mentioned at this point.

[20] "At Emery Air Freight: Positive Reinforcement Boosts," *Organizational Dynamics*, Winter 1973, p. 43.

TABLE 5-4

Results of Applying Behavior Modification Programs in Organizations: A Summary

The Organization	Types of Employees	Goals of Program	Frequency of Feedback	Positive Reinforcers Applied	Results
Michigan Bell	Operating level (e.g., mechanics, maintenance workers)	a. Decrease turnover and absenteeism b. Increase productivity c. Improve union-management relations	a. Lower level—daily and weekly b. Higher level—monthly and quarterly	a. Praise and recognition b. Opportunity to see oneself improve	a. Attendance performance has improved by 50 percent b. Productivity and efficiency have continued to be above standard where positive reinforcement is being used
Connecticut General Life Insurance Company	Clerical and first-line supervisors	a. Decrease absenteeism b. Decrease lateness	Immediate	a. Self-feedback b. System feedback c. Earned time off	a. Chronic absenteeism and lateness have been drastically reduced b. Some divisions refused to use positive reinforcement because it was "outdated"
General Electric	Employees at all levels	a. Meet EEO objectives b. Decrease absenteeism and turnover c. Improve training d. Increase productivity	Immediate—uses modeling and role play as training tools to teach users	a. Praise b. Rewards c. Constructive feedback	a. Cost savings b. Increased productivity c. Increased self-esteem in minority groups d. Decreased direct labor cost
B. F. Goodrich Chemical Company	Manufacturing employees at all levels	a. Better meeting of schedules b. Increase productivity	Weekly	a. Praise b. Recognition c. Freedom to choose one's own activity	Production increases of over 300 percent

Source: Adapted from W. Clay Hamner and Ellen P. Hamner, "Behavior Modification on the Bottom Line," *Organizational Dynamics*, Spring 1976, pp. 12–14.

found discrepancies between what should have been done and what was being done. For example, in the airfreight business small shipments intended for the same destination fly at lower shipping rates when they are shipped together in containers (rather than as a single parcel). Thus, by encouraging employees to accumulate their shipments and use containers, the firm could ship at lower rates.

A "performance audit" showed that workers used containers (with a lower cost of shipping) only about 45 percent of the time, although they thought they were using them about 90 percent of the time. Overall, half of the containers were being shipped significantly below capacity. Management's program was established complete with a workbook for managers that specified how to provide praise, rewards, and feedback to their subordinates.

The results of the program were impressive. In 80 percent of the situations where it was applied, container usage increased from 45 percent to 95 percent. Savings from container usage alone amounted to over $500,000 a year and increased to $2 million during the first three years. As a result of these findings, Emery began using a similar system for handling customer problems on the telephone and for estimating the container sizes needed for shipment of lightweight packages.

While the use of praise, recognition, and feedback was initially successful at Emery, their effects diminished over time. Their use became too routine. As a result, Emery had to introduce other reinforcers. These included invitations to business luncheons, public recognition for good performance such as a letter sent home or placed on the bulletin board, assignment to a more desirable job after completing a less desirable one, and special time off from the job. Again, as with other applied motivation programs, managers had to be creative enough to introduce new reinforcers or techniques to keep the program fresh and meaningful.

Criticisms of Behavior Modification

Critics of behavior modification have attacked it on a number of grounds. A frequent concern with the use of reinforcers is that there is no "real" change in behavior. The person is just being "bribed" to perform. Bribery refers to the illicit use of rewards to corrupt someone's conduct. This is not really what is meant by reinforcement. In reinforcement, outcomes are delivered for behaviors that it is generally agreed will benefit the person and the organization. Thus, this criticism is logical, but it really does not apply to the types of reinforcers usually used in organizations.

One critic believes that to view reinforcements as modifying responses automatically, independent of a person's beliefs, values, or mental processes, is simply a wrong way to view human behavior. Locke claims that this theory is simple and appealing but that the facts do not support it. He claims that people can learn by seeing others get reinforcement. People can also learn by imitating others who are not reinforced. There is also self-reinforcement, which operant conditioning theorists ignore.[21]

Another criticism focuses on the point that individuals can become too dependent on extrinsic reinforcers (e.g., pay). Thus, behavior may become dependent on the reinforcer and never performed without the promise of the reinforcer. The point is also made that when reinforcement is no longer provided, the behavior will eventually become extinct. However, there are some studies available that show that when reinforcers are terminated, extinction does not always occur.[22] Unfortunately, these studies for the most part involve children and mental patients. Whether the same results can be expected of normal adults has not been adequately tested.

EXPECTANCY THEORY

One of the more popular expectancy explanations of motivation was developed by Victor Vroom.[23] Over 50 studies have been done to test the accuracy of expectancy theory in predicting employee behavior.[24]

Vroom defines *motivation* as a process governing choices among alternative forms of voluntary activity. In his view, most behaviors are considered to be under the voluntary control of the person and are consequently motivated.

---

[21] Edwin A. Locke, "The Myths of Behavior Mod in Organizations," *Academy of Management Review,* October 1977, pp. 543–53. In addition to Locke's critique of operant conditioning, also see Jerry L. Gray, "The Myths of the Myths about Behavior Mod in Organizations: A Reply to Locke's Criticisms of Behavior Modification," *Academy of Management Review,* January 1979, pp. 121–29; and Marcia Parmerlee and Charles Schwenk, "Radical Behaviorism: Misconceptions in the Locke-Gray Debate," *Academy of Management Review,* October 1979, pp. 601–7.

[22] See G. L. Paul and R. J. Lentz, *Psychosocial Treatment of Chronic Mental Patients: Milieu versus Social Learning Programs* (Cambridge, Mass.: Harvard University Press, 1977); and D. C. Russo and R. L. Koegel, "A Method for Integrating an Autistic Child into a Normal Public School Classroom," *Journal of Applied Behavior Analysis,* October 1977, pp. 579–90.

[23] Victor H. Vroom, *Work and Motivation* (New York: John Wiley & Sons, 1964). For earlier work, see Kurt Lewin, *The Conceptual Representation and the Measurement of Psychological Forces* (Durham, N.C.: Duke University Press, 1938); and E. C. Tolman, *Purposive Behavior in Animals and Men* (New York: Appleton-Century-Crofts, 1932).

[24] David A. Nadler and Edward E. Lawler III, "Motivation: A Diagnostic Approach," in *Perspectives on Behavior in Organizations,* ed. J. R. Hackman, E. E. Lawler III, and L. W. Porter (New York: McGraw-Hill, 1977), pp. 26–38. Also see Edwin A. Locke, "Personnel Attitudes and Motivation," *Annual Review of Psychology* (1973), pp. 457–80; and Abraham K. Korman, Jeffrey H. Greenhaus, and Irwin J. Badin, "Personnel Attitudes and Motivation," *Annual Review of Psychology* (1977), pp. 175–96.

In order to understand expectancy theory, it is necessary to define the important terms in the theory and explain how they operate. The most important terms are the following:

First- and Second-Level Outcomes

The first-level outcomes resulting from behavior are those associated with doing the job itself. These outcomes include productivity, absenteeism, turnover, and quality of productivity. The second-level outcomes are those events (rewards or punishments) that the first-level outcomes are likely to produce, such as merit pay increase, group acceptance or rejection, and promotion.

Instrumentality

instrumentality
The strength of a person's belief that one action leads to a second outcome.

This is the perception by an individual that first-level outcomes will be associated with second-level outcomes. Vroom suggests that **instrumentality** can take values ranging from -1, indicating a perception that attainment of the second level is certain without the first outcome and impossible with it, to $+1$, indicating that the first outcome is necessary and sufficient for the second outcome to occur. Since this reflects an association, it can be thought of in terms of correlation.

Valence

valence
The strength of an individual's desire for a particular outcome.

This term refers to the preferences for outcomes as seen by the individual. For example, a person may prefer a 9 percent merit increase over a transfer to a new department, or the transfer over a relocation to a new facility. An outcome is *positively* valent when it is preferred and *negatively* valent when it is not preferred or is avoided. An outcome has a **valence** of zero when the individual is indifferent to attaining or not attaining it. The valence concept applies to first- and second-level outcomes. For example, a person may prefer to be a high-performing (first-level outcome) employee because he or she believes that this will lead to a merit increase in pay (second-level outcome).

Expectancy

expectancy
A person has an expectancy or a *belief* that a chance exists that a certain effort will lead to a

Expectancy refers to the individual's belief concerning the likelihood or subjective probability that a particular behavior will be followed by a particular outcome. That is, it refers to the assigned chance of something occurring because of the behavior. Expectancy has a value ranging from 0, indicating no chance that an outcome will occur after the behavior or act, to $+1$, indicating certainty that a particular

particular level of
performance. This
is the effort-
performance
expectancy. He or
she also has the
expectancy (belief)
that performance will
lead to certain
outcomes. This is the
performance-
outcome expectancy.

outcome will follow an act or a behavior. Expectancy is considered
in terms of probability.

In the work setting, an effort-performance expectancy is held by
individuals. This expectancy represents the individual's perception
of how hard it will be to achieve a particular behavior (say, completing
the budget on time) and the probability of achieving that behavior.
For example, the person may have a high expectancy that if she works
around the clock, she could complete the budget on time. On the other
hand, she may perceive that her chances of finishing on time are
about 40 percent if she works only during the day.

Given a number of alternative levels of behavior to finish the budget
(working 8 hours, 10 hours, or around the clock) she will choose the
level of performance that has the greatest motivational force associated with it. In other words, when faced with *choices* about behavior,
the person preparing the budget goes through a process of questioning:
Can I perform at that level if I give it a try? If I perform at that
level, what will happen? Do I prefer the things that will happen?

There is also a performance-outcome expectancy. In the individual's
mind, every behavior is associated with outcomes (rewards or punishments). For example, an individual may have an expectancy that if
the budget is completed on time, she will receive a day off next week.

The term *force* is equated with motivation. The intent of expectancy
theory is to assess the magnitude and direction of all the forces acting
on the individual. The act with the greatest force is the one that is
most likely to occur.

The term *ability* designates a person's potential for doing the job
or work. That potential may or may not be utilized. It refers to the
person's physical and mental abilities to do the job and not to what
the person will do.

Principles of Expectancy Theory

When the important expectancy theory concepts are integrated,
three major principles are generated.[25] They are:

1. $P = f (M \times A)$. Performance is considered to be a multiplicative
    function of motivation (the force) and ability.
2. $M = f (V_1 \times E)$. Motivation is a multiplicative function of the
    valence for each first-level outcome (V_1) and the perceived expec-
    tancy that a given behavior will be followed by a particular first-
    level outcome. If expectancy is low, there will be little motivation.

[25] W. Clay Hamner and Dennis W. Organ, *Organizational Behavior: An Applied Psychological Approach* (Plano, Tex.: Business Publications, 1978), p. 144.

Similarly, if the valence of an outcome is zero, neither the absolute value nor variations in the strength of the expectancies of accomplishing it will have any effect.

3. $V_1 = (V_2 \times I)$. The valence associated with various first-level outcomes is a multiplicative function of the sum of the valences attached to all second-level outcomes and the instrumentalities that attainment of the first-level outcome has for achieving each second-level outcome.

Figure 5–7 presents the general expectancy model and includes the two expectancy points (E——→P and P——→0). However, instead of developing this complex model, we prefer, for illustrative purposes, to use the simpler expectancy-performance (E——→P) version. Thus, Figure 5–8 uses numerical values to illustrate how expectancy theory works conceptually. The situation portrayed involves an employee faced with various first- and second-level outcomes. Starting at the second-level outcome point (the right side), the valence associated with finishing the budget on time is calculated by $V_1 + V_2 \times I$, or $V_1 = (6 \times 0.6) + (3 \times 1.0) + (1 \times 0.3)$, or 6.9. All of these values were assigned by the

FIGURE 5–7

Expectancy Theory

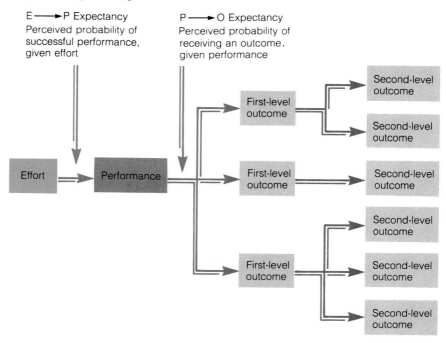

FIGURE 5–8

Expectancy Theory Applied

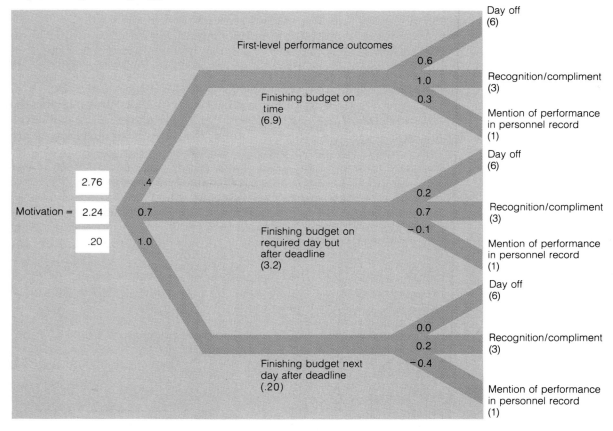

Key: Motivation = Force to performance.
  E = Expectancy of success if this choice is made (only E→P expectancy is used in this problem).
  V_1 = Valence of first-level outcomes.
  I = Instrumentality (relationships between V_1 and V_2).
  V_2 = Valence of second-level outcomes.

Work problem from right to left to reach motivation values of 2.76, 2.24, and 0.20.

authors to show how the theory works. The motivational force is calculated by $M = f(V_1 \times E)$, or $M = 6.9 \times 0.4$, or 2.76. The motivation force for finishing the budget on the required day but after the deadline is 2.24, while finishing the budget the day after the deadline has a force of 0.20. Thus, the strongest force or motivation would be directed toward finishing the budget on time.

Research on Expectancy

The empirical research to test expectancy theory continues each year. A few studies have used students in laboratory experiments. However, most of the research has been conducted in field settings. For example, one interesting study examined performance-outcome instrumentality in a temporary organization.[26] The experiment used either an hourly rate of pay (low instrumentality) or a piece rate (high instrumentality). After individuals had worked for three four-hour days under one pay system, they were shifted to the other system and worked three more days. Immediately following the shift in pay systems, and for all three subsequent days, the performance of the subjects who were shifted to the high-instrumentality system was higher than their own performance under the low-instrumentality system and higher than the performance of the subjects who were shifted to the low-instrumentality system.

Another area that has been researched focuses on the valence and behavior portion of the model. The results have been mixed. However, it appears that three conditions must hold for the valence of outcomes to be related to effort. Performance-outcome instrumentalities must be greater than zero; effort-performance expectancies must be greater than zero; and there must be some variability in the valence of outcomes.[27]

Criticisms of Expectancy theory

Theorists, researchers, and practitioners (to a lesser extent) continue to work on defining, measuring, and applying expectancy concepts. Many difficulties are encountered when testing the model. One problem involves the issue of effort or motivation itself. The theory attempts to predict choice or effort. However, there is no clear specification of the meaning of effort, and consequently there is no adequate measurement of the variable. Typically, self, peer, or supervisor ratings of effort are used. Unfortunately, each study seems to have its own definition, measurement, and research design.

Another difficulty concerns the issue of first-level outcomes. Expectancy theory is a process theory and does not specify which outcomes are relevant to a particular individual in a situation. Each researcher

---

[26] R. D. Pritchard and P. J. DeLeo, "Experimental Test of the Valence-Instrumentality Relationships in Job Performance," *Journal of Applied Psychology,* April 1973, pp. 264–79.

[27] J. P. Campbell and R. D. Pritchard, "Motivation Theory in Industrial and Organizational Psychology," in *Handbook of Industrial and Organizational Psychology,* ed. M. D. Dunnette (Skokie, Ill.: Rand McNally, 1976), pp. 84–95.

is expected to address this issue and does so in a unique way. Consequently, no systematic approach is being used or refined.

Furthermore, there is an implicit assumption in the expectancy approach that all motivation is conscious. The individual is assumed to consciously calculate the pleasure or pain that he or she expects to attain or avoid. Then a choice is made. Certainly, it is generally accepted that individuals are not always conscious of their motives, expectancies, and perceptual processes. Expectancy theory says nothing about subconscious motivation, and this is a point that has been for the most part neglected in the theory.

Most of the available field studies testing the model have relied on employees from a single organization who were doing the same or similar jobs. It seems that these types of studies would seriously limit and restrict the range of expectancies and instrumentalities. This type of research also raises the issue of whether results from these studies can be generalized to other samples. Is it valid to make generalizations?

Thus, although the research results have been promising, there are some major problems with the theory, research, and application of expectancy motivation. Over the years, the additions to the original model have made the expectancy theory a complex model to understand and apply.

EQUITY THEORY

equity
A state of equity exists in the mind of an individual when he or she feels that the ratio of efforts to rewards is equivalent to the ratio of comparison individuals.

The essence of **equity** theory is that employees compare their efforts and rewards with those of others in similar work situations. This theory of motivation is based on the assumption that individuals are motivated by a desire to be equitably treated at work. The individual works in exchange for rewards from the organization.

Four important terms in this theory are:

1. *Person:* The individual for whom equity or inequity is perceived.
2. *Comparison other:* Any group or persons used by Person as a referent regarding the ratio of inputs and outcomes.
3. *Inputs:* The individual characteristics brought by Person to the job. These may be achieved (e.g., skills, experience, learning) or ascribed (e.g., age, sex, race).
4. *Outcomes:* What Person received from the job (e.g., recognition, fringe benefits, pay).

Equity exists when employees perceive that the ratios of their inputs (efforts) to their outcomes (rewards) are equivalent to the ratios of other employees. Inequity exists when these ratios are not equivalent; an individual's own ratio of inputs to outcomes could be greater than

FIGURE 5–9

The Equity Theory of Motivation

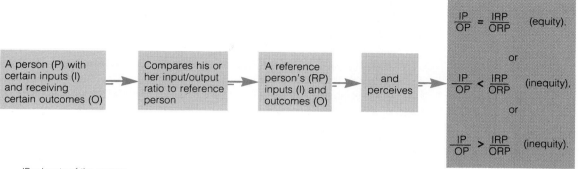

IP = Inputs of the person.
OP = Outputs of the person.
IRP = Inputs of reference person.
ORP = Outputs of reference person.

or less than that of others.[28] Figure 5–9 illustrates the equity theory of motivation.

Change Procedures to Restore Equity

Equity theory suggests a number of alternative ways that can be used to restore a feeling or sense of equity. Some examples of restoring equity would be:

1. *Changing inputs.* The employee may decide that he or she will put less time or effort into the job.
2. *Changing outputs.* The employee may decide to produce more units since a piece rate pay plan is being used.
3. *Changing attitudes.* Instead of changing inputs or outputs, the employee may simply change the attitude that he or she has. Instead of actually putting in more time at work, the employee may decide that "I put in enough time" to make a good contribution.
4. *Changing the reference person.* The reference person can be changed by making comparisons with the input/output ratios of some other person. This change can restore equity.
5. *Changing the inputs or outputs of the reference person.* If the reference person is a co-worker, it might be possible to attempt to

---

[28] J. Stacy Adams, "Toward an Understanding of Equity," *Journal of Abnormal and Social Psychology,* November 1963, pp. 422–36.

change his or her inputs or outputs. Asking the reference person to slow down or not be a rate-buster would be an example of such an attempt.

6. *Changing the situation.* Quitting the job can alter feelings of inequity. There is also the possibility of transferring to get away from an inequitable situation.

Each of these methods is designed to reduce or change the feelings of discomfort and tension created by inequity. Equity theory proposes that when inequity exists, a person will be motivated to take one or more of these six steps.

Research on Equity

Most of the research on equity theory has focused on pay as the basic outcome.[29] The failure to incorporate other relevant outcomes limits the impact of the theory in work situations. A review of the studies also reveals that the comparison person is not always clarified. A typical research procedure is to ask a person to compare his or her inputs and outcomes with those of a specific person. In most work situations, an employee selects the comparison person after working for some time in the organization. Two issues to consider are whether comparison persons are within the organization and whether comparison persons change during a person's work career.

Several individuals have questioned the extent to which inequity that results from overpayment (rewards) leads to perceived inequity . Locke argues that employees are seldom told they are overpaid. He believes that individuals are likely to adjust their idea of what constitutes an equitable payment to justify their pay.[30] Campbell and Pritchard point out that employer-employee exchange relationships are highly impersonal when compared to exchanges between friends. Perceived overpayment inequity may be more likely when friends are involved. Thus, individuals will probably react to overpayment inequity only when they believe that their actions have led to a friend's being treated unfairly. The individual receives few signals from the organization that it is being treated unfairly.[31]

---

[29] Paul S. Goodman and Abraham Friedman, "An Examination of Adam's Theory of Inequity," *Administrative Science Quarterly,* December 1971, pp. 271–88.

[30] Edwin A. Locke, "The Nature and Causes of Job Satisfaction," in *Handbook of Industrial and Organizational Psychology,* ed. M. Dunnette (Skokie, Ill.: Rand McNally, 1976), pp. 1297–1349.

[31] Campbell and Pritchard, "Motivation Theory," pp. 63–130.

Most equity research focuses on short-term comparisons.[32] What is needed is longitudinal research that examines inequity over a period of time. What happens over time as the inequity remains, or is increased, or is decreased? These types of questions and research to answer them could provide insight into the dynamic character of equity theory and individual responses.[33]

Despite limitations, equity theory provides a relatively insightful model to help explain and predict employee attitudes about pay. The theory has also emphasized the importance of comparisons in the work situation. The identification of comparison persons seems to have some potential value when attempting to restructure a reward program. Equity theory also raises the issue of methods for resolving inequity. An inequitable situation can cause morale, turnover, and absenteeism problems.

GOAL SETTING

goal setting
As individuals, we set goals and then work to accomplish them. This goal orientation determines our behavior.

There has been considerable and growing interest in applying goal setting to organizational problems and issues since Locke presented what is now considered a classic paper in 1968.[34] Locke proposed that **goal setting** was a cognitive process of some practical utility. Locke's view is that an individual's conscious goals and intentions are the primary determinants of behavior. It has been noted that "one of the commonly observed characteristics of intentional behavior is that it tends to keep going until it reaches completion."[35] That is, once a person starts something (e.g., a job, a new project), he or she pushes on until a goal is achieved. Intention plays a prominent role in goal-setting theory. Also, goal-setting theory places specific emphasis on the importance of conscious goals in explaining motivated behavior. Locke has used the notion of intentions and conscious goals to propose and provide research support for the thesis that harder conscious goals will result in higher levels of performance if these goals are accepted by the individual.

Descriptions of Goal Setting

A goal is the object of an action. For example, the attempt to produce four units on a production line, or to cut direct costs by $3,000, or

[32] Robert Vecchio, "Predicting Worker Performance in Inequitable Settings," *Academy of Management Review*, January 1982, pp. 103–10.

[33] Richard A. Cosier and Dan R. Dalton, "Equity Theory and Time: A Reformulation," *Academy of Management Review*, April 1983, pp. 311–19.

[34] Edwin A. Locke, "Toward a Theory of Task Motivation and Incentives," *Organizational Behavior and Performance*, May 1968, pp. 157–89.

[35] Thomas A. Ryan, *Intentional Behavior* (New York: Ronald Press, 1970), p. 95.

to decrease absenteeism in a department by 12 percent, is a goal. Frederick W. Taylor has had a direct influence on the current thinking about goals and goal-setting practices.

Locke states that Taylor used assigned goals as one of his key techniques of scientific management. Each employee was assigned a challenging but attainable goal based on the results of time and motion study. The methods by which the individual achieved the assigned goal (e.g., the tools used, the work procedures, followed the pacing needed to do the job) were spelled out in detail.[36]

Thus, Locke points out the significant influence of Taylor in his formulation of goal setting. Locke also carefully describes the attributes of the mental (cognitive) processes of goal setting. The attributes he highlights are goal specificity, goal difficulty, and goal intensity. *Goal specificity* is the degree of quantitative precision (clarity) of the goal. *Goal difficulty* is the degree of proficiency or the level of performance that is sought. *Goal intensity* pertains to the process of setting the goal or of determining how to reach it.[37] To date, goal intensity has not been widely studied, although a related concept, *goal commitment,* has been considered in a number of studies. *Goal commitment* is the amount of effort used to achieve a goal.

Figure 5–10 portrays applied goal setting from a managerial perspective and the sequence of events for such a goal-setting program. The key steps in applying goal setting are (1) *diagnosis* for readiness (determining whether the people, the organization, and the technology are suited for goal setting; (2) *preparing* employees via increased interpersonal interaction, communication, training, and action plans for goal setting; (3) *emphasizing* the attributes of goals that should be understood by a manager and subordinates; (4) *conducting* intermediate reviews to make necessary adjustments in established goals; and (5) performing a final review to check the goals set, modified, and accomplished. Each of these steps needs to be carefully planned and implemented if goal setting is to be an effective motivational technique. In too many applications of goal setting, steps outlined in or issues suggested by Figure 5–10 are ignored.

Goal-Setting Research

Between 1968 and 1984, the amount of research on goal setting increased considerably. Locke's 1968 paper on goal setting certainly contributed to the increase in laboratory and field research on goal

---

[36] Frederick W. Taylor, *The Principles of Scientific Management* (New York: W. W. Norton, 1947).

[37] Edwin A. Locke, Karyll N. Shaw, Lise M. Saari, and Gary P. Latham, "Goal Setting and Task Performance: 1969–1980," *Psychological Bulletin,* July 1981, p. 129.

FIGURE 5-10

Goal Setting as Applied in Organizations

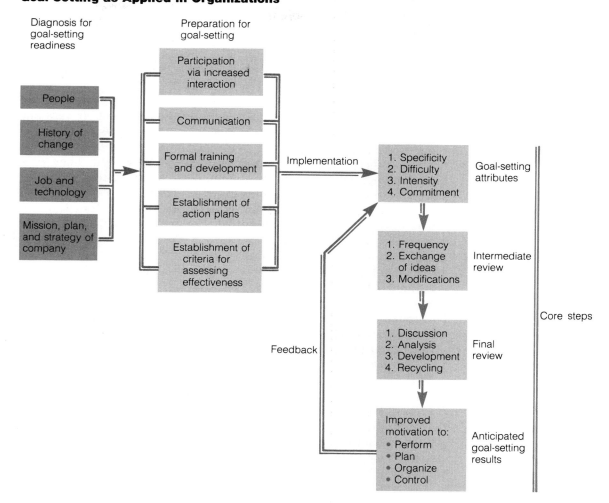

setting. Another force behind the increase in interest and research was the demand of managers for practical and specific techniques that they could apply in their organizations. Goal setting offered such a technique for some managers.[38]

Research has found that specific goals lead to higher output than

---

[38] Edwin A. Locke, "The Ubiquity of the Technique of Goal Setting in Theories of and Approaches to Employee Motivation," *Academy of Management Review,* July 1978, p. 600.

do vague goals such as "Do your best."[39] Field experiments using clerical workers, maintenance technicians, marketing personnel, truckers,
engineering personnel, typists, and manufacturing employees have
compared specific versus do-your-best goal-setting conditions.[40] The
vast majority of these studies support partly or in total the hypothesis
that specific goals lead to better performance than do vague goals.
In fact, in 99 out of 110 studies reviewed by Locke and his associates,
specific goals produced better results.[41]

One study in particular highlights the practical significance of setting specific goals.[42] As part of a logging operation, truck drivers had
to load logs and drive them to a mill for processing. An analysis of
the performance of each trucker showed that the truckers were often
not filling their trucks to the maximum allowable weight. They were
underloading. For the three months in which underloading was being
studied, the trucks were seldom loaded in excess of 58 to 63 percent
of capacity.

The researchers believed that underloading resulted from management's practice of simply instructing the truckers to do their best in
loading the trucks. The researchers concluded that simply setting a
specific goal could be the operational impetus needed to improve the
situation. They decided that a specific goal of 94 percent of capacity
would be assigned to the drivers. it was agreed that no driver would
be disciplined for failing to reach the assigned goal. No monetary
rewards or fringe benefits other than praise from the supervisor were
given for improvements in performance. No specific training or instruction was given to the managers or the drivers.

Within the first month after the goal was assigned, performance
increased to 80 percent of the truck's limit. After the second month,
however, performance decreased to 70 percent. Interviews with the
drivers indicated that they were testing management's promise not
to take disciplinary action if goals were not met. After the third month,
performance exceeded 90 percent of the truck's limit. This performance was being maintained seven years after the original research.

The results of this field experiment are impressive. They suggest
that setting specific goals can be a powerful force. The value of goal
setting is reflected in a statement of the researchers:

> The setting of a goal that is both specific and challenging leads to an
> increase in performance because it makes it clearer to the individual
> what he is supposed to do. This in turn may provide the worker with

---

[39] Locke, "Task Motivation and Incentives."

[40] For a complete analysis, see Locke et al., "Goal Setting."

[41] Ibid.

[42] Gary Latham and J. James Baldes, "The Practical Significance of Locke's Theory
of Goal Setting," *Journal of Applied Psychology*, February 1975, pp. 122–24.

a sense of achievement, recognition, and commitment, in that he can compare how well he is doing now versus how well he has done in the past and in some instances, how well he is doing in comparison to others.[43]

Goal Difficulty. It is generally agreed that the more difficult the goal, the higher the level of performance. The important point, however, is that this holds true only if the goals are accepted. A point of diminishing returns appears to be a real issue in goal difficulty. Although laboratory and field studies find that people with high (difficult) goals consistently perform better, there is a critical point.[44] If and when a goal is perceived as so difficult that it is virtually impossible to attain, the result is often frustration rather than achievement.

The difficulty of the fund raising goals of the United Fund points up the issue of frustration.[45] The more difficult the goal, the more money was raised. This was true only when the goals were seen as attainable. When they were viewed as unattainable, the morale of fund raisers suffered.

Locke has contrasted goal setting with the expectancy and need for achievement explanations of motivation.[46] Figure 5–11 highlights the differences in the explanations of the goal difficulty–performance relationship proposed by these three theories. Expectancy theory predicts that increased performance will be the result of easier goals, since the probability of success (and also the probability of being rewarded) increases. The need for achievement prediction is that difficult goals will improve performance up to a point but that when goals are too difficult, performance will suffer.

Locke's most recent explanation of the goal difficulty–performance relationship is presented as III in Figure 5–11. Locke predicts that performance will increase as goal difficulty increases, assuming that the person is committed and has the ability to perform. A ceiling of performance (B) is reached. Individuals who lack commitment to difficult goals will have decreasing or poor performance (C).

Individual Differences. Scattered throughout the goal-setting literature are studies that examine the effects of individual differences on goal setting. Most of these studies have dealt with the effects of education, race, and job tenure on the goal-setting process. In one study involving electronics technicians, it was found that goal difficulty (challenge) was significantly related to performance only for those

---

[43] Ibid. p. 124.

[44] Locke et al., "Goal Setting."

[45] A. Zander and T. T. Newcomb, Jr., "Goal Levels of Aspirations in United Fund Campaigns," *Journal of Personality and Social Psychology,* June 1967, pp. 157–62.

[46] Edwin A. Locke and Gary P. Latham, *Goal Setting: A Motivational Technique That Works* (Englewood Cliffs, N.J.: Prentice-Hall, 1984), p. 22.

FIGURE 5–11

**The Goal Difficulty–Performance
Relationship: Three Motivation Views**

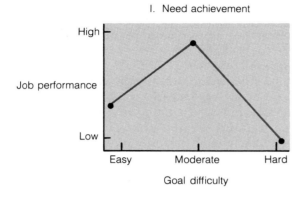

I. Need achievement

II. Expectancy theory

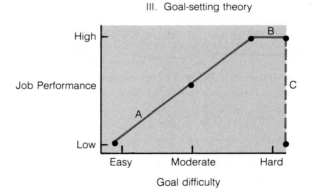

III. Goal-setting theory

technicians with 12 or more years of education. The technicians with
less education reported that goal clarity (e.g., having a clear understanding of the goal) and goal feedback (e.g., receiving feedback on
how results matched the goal) were significantly related to
performance.[47]

In a field experiment, loggers working under assigned, participative,
and do-your-best conditions were compared. It was found that participative goal setting affected the performance of the less educated loggers but did not affect the performance of the more educated loggers.[48]

---

[47] John M. Ivancevich and J. Timothy McMahon, "Education as a Moderator of Goal-
Setting Effectiveness," *Journal of Vocational Behavior,* August 1977, pp. 83–94.

[48] Gary P. Latham and Gary A. Yukl, "Assigned versus Participative Goal Setting
with Educated and Uneducated Wood Workers," *Journal of Applied Psychology,* June
1975, pp. 299–302.

One study examined race as a goal-setting variable. Goal clarity and goal feedback were found to be related to performance for blacks only.[49] On the other hand, goal difficulty (challenge) was found to be related to performance for whites only. It was proposed by the researchers that clarity and feedback may have affected the black goal setters because they had a higher need for security. Goal clarity and accurate feedback are ways of increasing security.

Thus far, individual difference studies on goal setting have been inconclusive. There is no clear-cut evidence that education, race, tenure, sex, age, need for achievement, self-esteem, or any of the other variables studied are significant.

Goal Setting: An Application at Tenneco

Tenneco is a large, diversified, multiindustry company operating in eight major industries.[50] The Tenneco companies include J. I. Case, manufacturer and marketer of farm and construction equipment, and Packaging Corporation of America, a vertically integrated supplier of paperboard, folding cartons, and corrugated containers. Unlike most users of goal setting, Tenneco decided to emphasize not only performance goals but also personal development goals in its program.

The chairman of the board at Tenneco issued statements, memos, and guidelines on the goal-setting effort. The emphasis on personal development was to be accomplished through a program whose goals focused on performance and development criteria of success for managers. The program was designed by a task force representing each of Tenneco's companies.

One phase that was especially stressed at Tenneco was formally training the goal-setting participants (managers) in "how to do it." A corporate-level training package was prepared. However, each company altered, added to, or subtracted from the corporate training package. The training package presented what goal setting was, how it was to be used, and the skills that were needed to be effective in goal setting.

Reexamine Figure 5–10, since this is basically the sequence of events and the framework of Tenneco's goal-setting program. Management systematically diagnosed, prepared for goal setting, and implemented each of the core steps—goal setting, intermediate reviews, and a final review. The evaluations of the Tenneco goal-setting program found:

---

[49] John M. Ivancevich and J. Timothy McMahon, "Black-White Differences in a Goal Setting Program," *Organizational Behavior and Human Performance*, December 1977, pp. 287–300.

[50] Based on the detailed study as presented in unpublished reports and executive summaries and in John M. Ivancevich, J. Timothy McMahon, J. William Streidl, and Andrew D. Szilagyi, Jr., "Goal Setting: The Tenneco Approach to Personnel Development and Management Effectiveness," *Organizational Dynamics*, Winter 1978, pp. 58–80.

1. Improved morale after the program was implemented.
2. A more relaxed work environment (less job tension) for users of the goal-setting program.
3. More success in those Tenneco units in which management (supervisors) actively participated in and supported goal setting.
4. A necessity to spend time in diagnosis, training, and evaluation so that proper alterations in procedures and types of goals set could be made.
5. That many individuals had difficulty in establishing personal development goals. This difficulty may have been caused by a climate that for years overemphasized performance. Many individuals had not had to think in terms of their own personal development. Thus, there was some initial difficulty in setting personal development goals.
6. That patience was needed before declaring an applied goal-setting program such as Tenneco's a success or a failure. Those using goal setting should use time periods of longer than six months or even a year before reaching any conclusions. At Tenneco, numerous improvements and some negative results (irritation with paperwork, feelings of not being trained properly or long enough to do the goal setting) did not show up until one to two years after the program had been initiated.

Tenneco is not presented as either a success or a failure of applied goal setting. Instead, it provides a view of the complexities, details, and hard work associated with goal setting. There is no easy or ideal way to apply goal setting. Advance preparation for successes, failures, and changes along the way seems to be the best way to approach goal setting in work organizations.

Criticisms of Goal Setting

Unfortunately, there are some arguments against using goal setting or becoming too enthusiastic about it. Some managers and researchers have found that:

Goal setting is rather *complex* and *difficult to sustain.* The Tenneco case displayed how difficulties across divisions became somewhat disruptive when use of a corporate set of guidelines for action was implemented.

Goal setting works well for simple jobs—clerks, typists, loggers, and technicians—but not for complex jobs. Goal setting with jobs in which goals are not easily measured (e.g., teaching, nursing, engineering, accounting) has posed some problems.

Goal setting encourages game playing. Setting low goals so as to look good later is one game played by subordinates who do not want to be caught short. Managers play the game of setting an initial goal that is generally not achievable and then finding out how subordinates react.

Goal accomplishment can become an obsession. In some situations, goal setters have become so obsessed with achieving their goals that they neglect other important areas of their jobs.

Goal setting is used as another check on employees. It is a control device to monitor performance.

Goal setting can be a very powerful technique for motivating employees. When used correctly, carefully monitored, and actively supported by managers, goal setting can improve performance. However, neither goal setting nor any other technique can be used to correct every problem. No applied motivational approach can be *the* technique to solve all performance problems. This, unfortunately, is what some enthusiastic advocates have turned goal setting into—a panacea for everything.

REVIEWING MOTIVATION

In Chapters 4 and 5, eight popular theories of motivation were portrayed. The theories are typically pitted against one another in the literature. This is unfortunate since each theory can help managers better understand workplace motivation. Each theory attempts to organize in a meaningful manner major variables associated with explaining motivation in work settings.

The *content* theories are individual-oriented in that they place primary emphasis on the characteristics of people. Each of the *process* theories has a specific orientation. Reinforcement theory focuses on the work environment. The notion of individual needs and attitudes is virtually ignored by this theory. Expectancy theory places emphasis on individual, job, and environmental variables. It recognizes differences in needs, perceptions, and beliefs. Equity theory primarily addresses the relationship between attitudes toward inputs and outputs and reward practices. Goal-setting theory emphasizes the cognitive processes and the role of intentional behavior in motivation.

Each of the eight theories that we have presented has something to offer managers. It is also important to notice that various parts of the theories are, in many respects, complementary. Despite the abundance of theories, research, and complementarity, there are still many managers who continue to ignore the topic of motivation.

The following Close-Up points out that each of the motivation theories discussed to this point has value if it is used correctly. The psychologists and social psychologists who formulated these theories were

ORGANIZATIONS: CLOSE-UP

Should Managers Be Psychologists? NO!

Do you have to be a psychologist to understand and use the motivation theories presented in this chapter? We hope not. The theories point out that managers are not able to know with certainty what goes on inside the person's head. Motivation is merely an abstract concept invented from evidence taken from observed behavior, which supposedly explains that behavior. Yes, motivation is something that comes from within, but managers still do not know exactly what goes on inside.

Some believe that it's up to the manager and the company to set the stage, to create the atmosphere that allows the employee's internal motivation to appear. To do so, managers need to tailor rewards to individual motivation. The manager has to search and find out what makes an individual tick, what triggers the internal state that is eventually observed by managers as higher performance or less absenteeism.

The details, complexities, and problems associated with needs, motives, values, and physical responses to work are not really in the domain of managers. The manager is an amateur in this arena. This arena is really better suited for the professional psychologist. Likewise, the psychologist is an amateur when it comes to the day-to-day operations of managing people and creating stimulating work environments.

Thus, the psychologist is the expert who is best prepared to discuss, analyze, and interpret needs, drives, and values. On the other hand, the manager is the expert when it comes to creating the atmosphere in which an employee's internal motivation can grow and be sustained. Experts in one area can look rather foolish and even be dangerous in another area. Managers need to beware and use their expertise where they are experts.

experts in explaining needs, motives, and values but were really not so astute at explaining what managers could do to motivate employees.

If anything, Chapters 4 and 5 indicate that instead of ignoring motivation, managers must take an active role in motivating their employees. Four specific conclusions are offered here:

1. Managers can influence the motivation state of employees. If performance needs to be improved, then managers need to intervene and help create an atmosphere that encourages, supports, and sustains improvement.

2. Managers need to be sensitive to variations in employees' needs, abilities, and goals. They must also consider differences in preferences (valences) for rewards.

3. Continual monitoring of needs, abilities, goals, and preferences of employees is each individual manager's responsibility and is not the domain of personnel/human resources managers only.

4. Managers need to work on providing employees jobs that offer task challenge, diversity, and a variety of opportunities for need satisfaction.

In simple terms, the theme of our discussion of motivation is that the *manager needs to be actively involved.* If motivation is to be energized, sustained, and directed, managers will have to know about needs, intentions, preferences, goals, reinforcement, and comparison. Failure to learn and understand these types of concepts will result in many missed opportunities to help motivate employees in a positive manner.

We have concluded that it is important to understand the cognitive view of motivation. At the outset, in the Organizational Issue for Debate, cognitive and noncognitive approaches were introduced. Certainly, Skinner's noncognitive approach provides some valuable insights about motivating employees. He has definitely displayed to managers that differentiating levels of needs, expectancies, or goals is not enough to motivate subordinates. Calling attention to reinforcement and its impact on behavior and performance is in itself a valuable contribution in the study of motivation in organizational settings. However, ignoring the cognitively based needs, goals, and preferences of individuals is unrealistic in this era of greater manager-employee communication, openness, and sharing.

SUMMARY OF KEY POINTS

A. Reinforcement theory relies on applying the principles of operant conditioning to motivate people. A major assumption of operant conditioning is that behavior is influenced by its consequences.

B. The nature of rewards or punishments and how they are employed influences behavior. Thus, reinforcement scheduling or the timing of consequences is an important feature of motivation.

C. The expectancy theory of motivation is concerned with the expectations of a person and how they influence behavior. One value of this theory is that it can provide the manager with a means for pinpointing desirable and undesirable outcomes associated with task performance.

D. Equity theory focuses on comparisons, tension, and tension reduction. To date, most of the research work on equity theory has involved pay. Equity theory is a more straightforward and understandable explanation of employee attitudes about pay than expectancy theory. The manager should be aware of the fact that people compare their rewards, punishments, job tasks, and other job-related dimensions to those of others.

E. Locke's goal-setting theory proposes that an individual's goals and intentions are the primary determinants of behavior.

F. Despite an impressive number of supportive studies, goal setting has been criticized as working primarily for easy jobs, encouraging game playing, and operating as another control check on employees.

DISCUSSION AND REVIEW QUESTIONS

1. Vroom's expectancy model includes the concepts of valence, expectancy, and instrumentality. What are the meanings of these concepts, and how could a manager apply these concepts to motivate his or her subordinates?

2. Could a manager who understands equity theory utilize this knowledge in developing pay programs? How?

3. What stigma is associated with behavior modification? What do you think is necessary to reduce some of the managerial resistance to this approach?

4. For what types of jobs would it be difficult to establish goals? Why?

5. What ethical considerations should be considered before using a behavior modification program in a work setting?

6. What types of reinforcement schedules can be used by managers? Explain.

7. Why would it be difficult to use a "change the situation" approach to restore equity during hard economic times?

8. Compare the research results on behavior modification and goal setting. Are there differences in the kinds of research that are being conducted on these two approaches?

9. Why is it important to pinpoint critical behaviors in any behavior modification application?

10. Why would one conclude that the motivation theories presented in Chapters 4 and 5 are to some extent complementary?

ADDITIONAL REFERENCES

Duchon, D., and A. Jago. "Equity and Performance of Major League Baseball Players: An Extension of Lord & Horkenfeld." *Journal of Applied Psychology,* 1981, pp. 728–32.

Erez, M., and F. H. Kanfer. "The Role of Goal Acceptance in Goal Setting and Task Performance. *Academy of Management Review,* 1983, pp. 454–63.

Freedman, S. R., and J. R. Montanari. "An Integrative Model of Managerial Reward Allocation." *Academy of Management Review,* 1980, pp. 381–90.

Garland, H. "Goal Levels and Task Performance: A Compelling Replication of Some Compelling Results." *Journal of Applied Psychology,* 1982, pp. 245–58.

Greenberg, J., and S. Ornstein. "High Status Job Title as Compensation for Underpayment: A Test of Equity Theory." *Journal of Applied Psychology,* 1983, pp. 285–97.

Lawler, E. E. *Pay and Organization Development.* Reading, Mass.: Addison-Wesley Publishing, 1981.

Mento, A. J.; N. D. Cartledge; and E. A. Locke. "Maryland vs. Michigan vs. Minnesota: Another Look at the Relationship of Expectancy and Goal Difficulty to Task Performance." *Organizational Behavior and Human Performance,* 1980, pp. 419–40.

Mitchell, T. R. "New Directions for Theory, Research, and Practice." *Academy of Management Review,* 1982, pp. 80–88.

Vecchio, R. P. "An Individual-Difference Interpretation of the Conflicting Predictions Generated by Equity Theory and Expectancy Theory." *Journal of Applied Psychology,* 1981, pp. 470–81.

Walker, L. R., and K. W. Thomas. "Beyond Expectancy Theory: An Integrative Motivational Model from Health Care." *Academy of Management Review,* 1982, pp. 187–94.

CASE FOR ANALYSIS

A Lottery for Clerical Employees: Does It Work?

Brown and Ferris Insurance Company was faced with a pressing absentee-ism problem among clerical workers. On Mondays and Fridays, approximately 26 percent of the clerical personnel were absent from their jobs. Through discussions with clerical supervisors, management determined that absentee-ism was now a part of the accepted norm. The employees simply wanted some time off, regardless of losing a day's pay. They liked to be able to choose for themselves when they would be absent.

The three-day weekend gave the employees some time to attend to personal business. Tom Amoss, the director of human resources at Brown and Ferris, had just attended an executive development program at the local university. One idea that really caught his attention was applied behavior modification. Brown and Ferris's estimated costs of absenteeism were running about $8,000 per week. Tom felt that maybe behavior modification could reduce some of this expense.

Tom presented his plan to combat absenteeism to Randy Pandlers, the vice president of administrative services. Randy thought that Tom had really gone off the deep end. Tom's plan went like this. Each Friday at 3:00 P.M., a weekly lottery drawing would be held. The time cards of all clerical employees who had worked every day that week would be placed in a drum and five winners drawn at random. The five winners would receive prizes such as certificates for $150 of groceries, cameras, and a television set. At the end of a month, a monthly lottery would be held. To be eligible, employees had to have one month of perfect attendance. There would be one card drawn, and the winner would receive a prize of $1,000 cash. A six-month lottery (an all-expense-paid, one-week vacation for two at a famous resort hotel) and an annual lottery (a $4,000 prize) were also included in the plan.

After listening to Tom and doing some fast calculations, Randy agreed to go ahead with the plan. He felt that it just might work. The plan has been in effect for four months, and absenteeism on Monday and Friday is now averaging about 6 percent on each day. However, one problem has emerged. Some employees are coming to work when they are really sick. Some actually drag themselves out of sickbeds to get to work and remain eligible for the lottery. They are just not able to do the work, and they are actually presenting a health hazard to other employees.

Questions for Consideration

1. Why do you think this behavior modification plan has had some success?

2. Do you believe that the success can be continued over a long period of time—a year? Why?

3. What about the issue of ill employees coming to work? What would you do to correct this problem?

4. Is this lottery plan a form of bribery? Explain.

EXPERIENTIAL EXERCISE

GOAL SETTING: HOW TO DO IT AND A CRITIQUE

Objectives

1. To present what is meant by the term *goal*.
2. To illustrate guidelines for preparing goals.
3. To involve the reader with some hints for evaluating the quality of a goal.

Related Topics

Goals are statements of measurable results that a person is attempting to accomplish. They help a person develop a plan to turn expectations and wishes into reality. Goals are found in most motivation applications in organizations. In behavior modification programs, for example, goals are the targets of behavior changes.

Starting the Exercise

Each person is to work alone for at least 30 minutes with this exercise. After sufficient time has elapsed for each person to work through the exercise, the instructor will go over each goal and ask for comments from the class or group. The discussion should display the understanding of goals that each participant has and what will be needed to improve his or her goal-writing skills.

The facts

Writing and evaluating goals seem simple, but they are often not done well in organizations. The press of time, previous habits, and little concern about the attributes of a goal statement are reasons why goals are often poorly constructed.* Actually, a number of guidelines should be followed in preparing goals. Remember these points:

---

* For a discussion of how to set goals, see George Morrisey, *Getting Your Act Together* (New York: John Wiley & Sons, 1980); especially see chap. 7.

1. A well-presented goal statement contains four elements:
   - a. An action or accomplishment verb.
   - b. A single and measurable result.
   - c. A date of completion.
   - d. A cost in terms of effort, resources, or money or some combination of these factors.
2. A well-presented goal statement is short; it is not a paragraph. It should be presented in a sentence.
3. A well-presented goal statement specifies only what and when and doesn't get into how or why.
4. A well-presented goal statement is challenging and attainable. It should cause the person to stretch his or her skills, abilities, and efforts.
5. A well-presented goal statement is meaningful and important. It should be a priority item.
6. A well-presented goal statement must be acceptable to you so that you will try hard to accomplish the goal.

The goal statement model should be:

To (action or accomplishment verb) (single result) by (a date—keep it realistic) at (effort, use of what resource, cost).

An example for a production operation:

To reduce the production cost per unit of Mint toothpaste by at least 3 percent by March 1, at a changeover of equipment expense not to exceed $45,000.

Examine the next four statements that are presented as goal statements. Below each goal write a critique of the statement. Is it a good goal statement? Why? Discuss your viewpoints in the class group discussion.

To reduce my blood pressure to an acceptable level.

_____
_____
_____

To make financial investments with a guaranteed minimum return of at least 16 percent.

_____
_____
_____

To spend a minimum of 45 minutes a day on a doctor-approved exercise plan, starting Monday, lasting for six months, at no expense.

_____
_____
_____

To spend more time reading non-work-related novels and books during the next year.

_____
_____
_____
_____

Chapter 6

After completing Chapter 6, you should be able to:

Define What is meant by the term *discipline.*

Describe the main objectives of organizational reward programs.

Discuss the association between satisfaction and rewards.

Compare the effectiveness of salary and bonus pay plans.

Identify the major strengths and weaknesses of cafeteria-style fringe benefits, banking time-off, and all-salaried reward plans.

Rewards, Punishment, and Discipline

The Pay for Performance Controversy*

Argument For

Merit pay or "pay for job performance" as a basis for rewarding employees is a widely accepted management practice. Merit pay is defined as any compensation system that bases an individual's wage or salary on the measured performance of that individual. Although some argue about the relative impor-

tance of pay compared with other extrinsic and intrinsic rewards, there is general agreement in management circles that pay is an important reward for most employees. If two employees are hired to perform the same job and one is a better performer, surely the high performer should be paid more for his or her superior performance.

Almost all managerial employees and many nonmanagers are paid using a merit pay system. One approach is to set a minimum level of pay for each job and then provide incremental increases until an upper level of compensation is reached. This approach is criticized because it has little motivational power. Under such a plan, an employee is rewarded with pay increases simply for attending and staying on the job. Under a pay for performance plan, the highest performers receive the largest increases and the poorest performers receive the smallest increases or no increases at all. Thus, management has available a "carrot" or a "stick" to motivate better performance. The carrot is used for high performers, and the stick is applied to low performers.

---

* For more on this debate, see Richard E. Kopelman, "The Case for Merit Rewards" and William L. Mihal, "Merit Pay: A Good Idea but Does It Work?" both in *Personnel Administrator,* October 1983, pp. 60–68 and 61–67.

Argument Against

Despite the logical attractiveness of the pay for performance plan, experience shows clearly that it is a pipe dream. Typically, managers give small rewards to individuals in the same job, regardless of performance differences.

A major problem with merit pay plans is the fact that an employee's increases are based primarily on supervisory judgments. It is assumed that a supervisor can make reliable and valid distinctions between the job performances of individuals. Who actually accepts the judgments of others about personal matters such as job performance? Are the judgments really reliable and valid? Critics of merit pay do not believe that performance appraisals are good enough to clearly show a relationship between pay and performance.

Another problem with the pay for performance approach is that it forces employees to compete for rewards. Since pay dollars are limited, a system of paying for performance forces employees to think in win-lose terms: "If I win a raise, someone else loses a raise." Unfortunately, this mentality is usually detrimental to organizational effectiveness.

Thus, although the evidence suggests that pay for performance makes good sense, there are too many factors that make it impossible to practice. If pay for performance is to be a successful motivational practice, organizations must have accurate performance appraisal systems, agreed-upon criteria (for both managers and subordinates), trust and openness, and evaluative follow-up research. At present, these requirements are rarely met by organizations.

Organizations use a variety of rewards to attract and retain people and to motivate them to achieve their personal and organizational goals.[1] The manner and timing of distributing rewards are important issues that managers must address almost daily. Managers distribute such rewards as pay, transfers, promotions, praise, and recognition. They can also help create the climate that results in more challenging and satisfying jobs. Because these rewards are considered important by employees, they have significant effects on behavior and performance. In this chapter, we are concerned with how rewards are distributed by managers. The reactions of people to rewards are also discussed, and the response of employees to rewards received in organizational settings is examined. Administering rewards is another topic that we review. The role of rewards in organizational membership, absenteeism, turnover, and commitment is presented.

Remarkably little has been written about punishment and discipline in organizations. Unfortunately, managers are frequently faced with the task of eliminating undesirable behavior and performance. Although punishment and discipline are controversial topics, they will be discussed in this chapter. Failure to include such a discussion would deny the reality of what occurs in organizational settings.

To attract people to join the organization, to keep coming to work, and to motivate them to perform at high levels, managers reward employees. Employees exchange their time, ability, skills, and effort for valued rewards. This relationship between the organization and its employees has been called the psychological contract. Schein states the psychological contract as follows:

> The individual has a variety of expectations of the organization and the organization a variety of expectations of him or her. These expectations not only cover how much work is to be performed for how much pay, but also involve the whole pattern of rights, privileges, and obligations between the worker and the organization.[2]

A MODEL OF INDIVIDUAL REWARDS

A model that illustrates how rewards fit into the overall policies and programs of an organization can prove useful to managers. The main objectives of reward programs are (1) to attract qualified people to *join* the organization, (2) to *keep* employees coming to work, and (3) *to motivate* employees to achieve high levels of performance. Figure

---

[1] Kae H. Chung and Leon G. Megginson, *Organizational Behavior* (New York: Harper & Row, 1981), p. 363.

[2] Edgar H. Schein, *Organizational Psychology* (Englewood Cliffs, N.J.: Prentice-Hall, 1970), p. 12.

6–1 presents a model that attempts to integrate satisfaction, motivation, performance, and rewards. Reading Figure 6–1 from left to right suggests that the motivation to exert effort is not enough to cause acceptable performance. Performance results from a combination of the effort of an individual and the individual's level of ability, skill, and experience. The performance results of the individual are evaluated either formally or informally by management. As a result of the evaluation, two types of rewards can be distributed, intrinsic or extrinsic. The rewards are evaluated by the individual. To the extent that the rewards are satisfactory and equitable, the individual achieves a level of satisfaction.

A significant amount of research has been done on what determines whether individuals will be satisfied with rewards. Lawler has summarized five conclusions based on the behavioral science research literature. They are:

1. *Satisfaction with a reward is a function both of how much is received and of how much the individual feels should be received.* This conclusion has as its basis the comparisons that people make. When individuals receive less than they feel they should, there is some dissatisfaction.

2. *An individual's feelings of satisfaction are influenced by comparisons with what happens to others.* People tend to compare their efforts, skills, seniority, and job performance with those of others. They then attempt to compare rewards. That is, they compare their own inputs with the inputs of others relative to the rewards received. This type of input-outcome comparison was discussed

FIGURE 6–1

The Reward Process

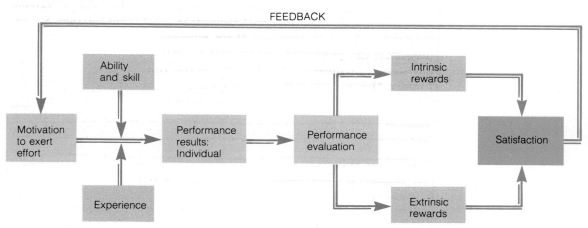

when the equity theory of motivation was introduced in Chapter 5.

3. *Satisfaction is influenced by how satisfied employees are with both intrinsic and extrinsic rewards. Intrinsic rewards* are rewards that are valued in and of themselves and are related to performing the job. Examples would be feelings of accomplishment and achievement. *Extrinsic rewards* are external to the work itself. They are administered externally. Examples would be salary and wages, fringe benefits, and promotions. There is some debate among researchers as to whether intrinsic or extrinsic rewards are more important in determining job satisfaction. The debate has not been settled, because most studies suggest that both types of rewards are important.[3] One clear message from the research is that extrinsic and intrinsic rewards satisfy different needs.

4. *People differ in the rewards they desire and in how important different rewards are to them.* Individuals differ on what rewards they prefer. In fact, preferred rewards vary at different points in a person's career, at different ages, and in various situations.

5. *Some extrinsic rewards are satisfying because they lead to other rewards.* There are some extrinsic rewards that lead to other, more preferred rewards. For example, a large office or an office that has carpeting or drapes is often considered a reward because it indicates the individual's status and power. Money is a reward that leads to such other things as prestige, autonomy and independence, security, and shelter.[4]

The relationship between rewards and satisfaction is not perfectly understood, nor is it static in nature. It changes because people and the environment change. There are, however, some important considerations that managers could use to develop and distribute rewards. First, the rewards available must be sufficient to satisfy basic human needs. Federal legislation, union contracts, and managerial fairness have provided at least minimal rewards in most work settings. Second, individuals tend to compare their rewards with those of others. If inequities are perceived, dissatisfaction will occur. People make comparisons regardless of the quantity of the rewards that they receive. Finally, the managers distributing rewards must recognize individual differences. Unless individual differences are considered, it is likely that the reward process will invariably be less effective than desired. Any reward package should (1) be sufficient to satisfy basic needs

add when typing ① ② ③ to 1), 2), 3) →

[3] Terence R. Mitchell, "Motivation: New Directions for Theory, Research, and Practice," *Academy of Management Review,* January 1982, pp. 80–88.

[4] Edward E. Lawler III, "Reward Systems," in *Improving Life at Work,* ed. J. Richard Hackman and J. Lloyd Suttle (Santa Monica, Calif.: Goodyear Publishing, 1977), pp. 163–226.

(e.g., food, shelter, clothing), (2) be considered equitable, and (3) be individually oriented.[5] An interesting approach to rewarding employees is presented in the following: Close-Up, which presents Sheraton's Superstar program.

ORGANIZATIONS: CLOSE-UP

Sheraton's Superstar Program

The Sheraton Corporation is in the hotel business. The firm's management knows that when employees do not perform, guests do not receive necessary services. Thus, management wanted to identify and reward the employees who were superperformers. It wanted these employees to know that management cared about them and recognized when they did a good job.

The result of management's concern was the Superstar program. Hotel guests are given a "star card" when they check in, at the food and beverage outlets, and in their rooms so that they can vote for the most efficient and pleasant employees. The votes are totaled monthly, and a total of 20 superstars are chosen. The winners are announced at a monthly meeting and awarded a certificate and $100.

A super superstar employee of the month is chosen from the 20 finalists and is awarded a $100 check and a trophy. At the end of the year, 1 of the 12 monthly winners is selected as the employee of the year and receives a $1,000 check and a trophy.

In addition to being announced at the monthly employee meetings, superstar winners are announced in the superstar newsletter. This again calls specific attention to the best performers at Sheraton. The superstar performance and special reward program is going strong. Management is satisfied with the results, and most employees are satisfied that the program is fair and meaningful.

Source: "Superstars at Sheraton," *Personnel Journal,* February 1981, p. 104.

INTRINSIC AND EXTRINSIC REWARDS

The rewards shown in Figure 6–1 are classified into two broad categories, *extrinsic* and *intrinsic.* Whether we are discussing extrinsic rewards or intrinsic rewards, it is important to first consider the rewards *valued* by the person. An individual will put forth little effort unless

---

[5] Ibid., p. 168.

the reward has *value*. Both extrinsic and intrinsic rewards can have value.[6]

Extrinsic Rewards

extrinsic rewards
Rewards that come from the job but are not part of the job are extrinsic. They include money, status, promotion, and respect.

Financial Rewards: Salary and Wages. Money is a major extrinsic reward. It has been said that "although it is generally agreed that money is the major mechanism for rewarding and modifying behavior in industry . . . very little is known about how it works."[7] To really understand how money modifies behavior, the perceptions and preferences of the person being rewarded must be understood. Of course, this is a challenging task for a manager to complete successfully. It requires careful attention and observation of the person. In addition, the manager must be trusted, so that the person will communicate his or her feelings about financial rewards.

Unless employees can see a connection between performance and merit increases, money will not be a powerful motivator. The point made in the Organizational Issue for Debate on the need for a sound performance appraisal system shouldn't be underestimated. A well-designed appraisal system can make the pay-performance connection clear in the minds of employees.

Many organizations utilize some type of incentive pay plan to motivate employees. Lawler presents the most comprehensive summary of the various pay plans and their effectiveness as motivators.[8] Each plan is evaluated on the basis of the following questions:

1. How effective is it in creating the perception that pay is related to performance?
2. How well does it minimize the perceived negative consequences of good performance?
3. How well does it contribute to the perception that important rewards other than pay (e.g., praise and interest shown in the employee by a respected superior) result in good performance? A summary of Lawler's ideas is presented in Table 6–1.

When each criterion is looked at separately, some interesting patterns evolve. The individual salary and bonus plans seem to be best if management is attempting to link pay and performance. The least effective way of accomplishing this is to implement a total organizational salary

---

[6] Richard A. Guzzo, "Types of Rewards, Cognitions, and Work Motivation," *Academy of Management Review,* January 1979, pp. 75–86.

[7] R. L. Opsahl and M. D. Dunnette, "The Role of Financial Compensation in Industrial Motivation," *Psychological Bulletin,* August 1966, p. 114.

[8] Edward L. Lawler III, *Pay and Organizational Effectiveness* (New York: McGraw-Hill, 1971), pp. 164–70.

TABLE 6–1

Evaluation of Pay-Incentive Plans in Organizations

Type of Pay Plan	Performance Criteria	Perceived Pay-Performance Linkage	Minimization of Negative Consequences	Perceived Relationship between Other Rewards and Performance
Salary plan				
For individuals	Productivity	Good	Neutral	Neutral
	Cost effectiveness	Fair	Neutral	Neutral
	Superiors' rating	Fair	Neutral	Fair
For group	Productivity	Fair	Neutral	Fair
	Cost effectiveness	Fair	Neutral	Fair
	Superiors' rating	Fair	Neutral	Fair
For total organization	Productivity	Fair	Neutral	Fair
	Cost effectiveness	Fair	Neutral	Fair
	Profits	Neutral	Neutral	Fair
Bonus plan				
For individuals	Productivity	Excellent	Poor	Neutral
	Cost effectiveness	Good	Poor	Neutral
	Superiors' rating	Good	Poor	Fair
For group	Productivity	Good	Neutral	Fair
	Cost effectiveness	Good	Neutral	Fair
	Superiors' rating	Good	Neutral	Fair
For total organization	Productivity	Good	Neutral	Fair
	Cost effectiveness	Good	Neutral	Fair
	Profits	Fair	Neutral	Fair

Source: Adapted from Edward E. Lawler III, *Pay and Organizational Effectiveness* (New York: McGraw-Hill, 1971), table 9–3, p. 165.

plan. This makes sense because the individual may not perceive his or her impact on organizational outcomes such as productivity, cost effectiveness, and profits.

The bonus plans are generally more effective than the salary plans. This is especially noticeable for the first objective of linking pay and performance. Bonus plans are typically related to the current performance of employees. Salary plans, on the other hand, are often related to past performance. Neither bonus plans nor salary plans minimize the potential negative consequences of linking pay and performance. Perhaps it is futile to think about developing a perfect pay plan.

If management is attempting to relate nonpay rewards to performance, the group and total organization plans seem more suitable than the individual plans. In essence, if people believe that other rewards stem from performance, they would tend to encourage improved performance among peers throughout the organization.

This discussion should clearly illustrate that no one plan can accomplish every desirable objective. The evidence indicates that bonus plans, where they can be used, are generally the best type of salary or wage plan. Also, individually based plans, seem to be superior to group and organizational plans.

A widely publicized incentive plan has existed at Lincoln Electric Company since 1907. Some of the background on the plan is presented in the following Close-Up.

ORGANIZATIONS: CLOSE-UP

Lincoln Electric Company's Pay Incentive System

In 1907, Lincoln Electric initiated a motivation plan that it still uses. The company relies on incentives. It pays most of its 2,500 employees on a piecework basis. Based on performance, bonuses may exceed regular pay, and Lincoln applies bonuses far more extensively than do most firms. A secretary's mistakes, for example, can reduce her bonus.

Some employees complain of pressure because of the pay plan. However, turnover is only 0.3 percent per month. The Cleveland company has no unions and no strikes. In 1981, employees earned an average of about $45,000 including the bonus.

Employees can buy stock at book value, but if they leave, they must sell it at the book value. About 70 percent of the employees own stock, and together they hold about 50 percent of all outstanding shares.

John C. Lincoln founded the company in 1895 to make an electric motor he had developed. His brother, James, joined the firm in 1907 and began emphasizing employee motivation and commitment.

The company produces electric motors, which means that it is in a weak industrial market. Therefore, employees average only 30 hours of work per week. At the average manufacturing wage of $8.69 an hour in 1982, an employee working full time every week would earn just over $18,000. However, the bonus based on performance adds many more dollars to the pay package.

Each employee is responsible for the quality of his or her work. Parts are inspected and defects corrected by the responsible employee. The company keeps detailed records on who worked on each piece of equipment. Defects that slip by the worker and are discovered by customers or by Lincoln's quality control people lower the worker's merit rating, bonus, and pay.

There is a price to pay for Lincoln's motivation system. Some employees complain that it is physically and mentally tough. There are also complaints that the pay-bonus system generates unfriendly employee competition. A number of merit points are allotted to each department. An unusually high rating for one person usually means a lower rating for another.

Despite these complaints, the company plans to continue use of the system. Turnover is low, sales keep increasing, and customers praise Lincoln's products, which are good reasons to continue the system. Other firms would like their own motivation systems to have the success that Lincoln has had since 1907.

Source: Adapted from Maryann Mrowca, "Ohio Firm Relies on Incentive-Pay System To Motivate Workers and Maintain Profits," *The Wall Street Journal*, August 12, 1983, p. 17.

Financial Rewards: Fringe Benefits.   In most cases, fringe benefits are primarily financial. There are some fringe benefits, however, such as IBM's recreation program for employees and General Mills' picnic grounds, that are not entirely financial. The major financial fringe benefit in most organizations is the pension plan. For most employees, the opportunity to participate in the pension plan is a valued reward. Fringe benefits such as pension plans, hospitalization, and vacations are not usually contingent on the performance of employees. In most cases, fringe benefit plans are based on seniority or attendance.

Interpersonal Rewards.   The manager has some power to distribute such interpersonal rewards as status and recognition. By assigning individuals to prestigious jobs, the manager can attempt to improve or remove the status a person possesses. However, if co-workers do not believe that a person merits a particular job, it is likely that status will not be enhanced. By reviewing performance, managers can in some situations grant what they consider to be job changes that improve status. The manager and co-workers both play a role in granting job status.

Much of what was just stated about status also applies to recognition. In a reward context, **recognition** refers to managerial acknowledgment of employee achievement that could result in improved status. Recognition from a manager could include public praise, expressions of a job well done, or special attention.[9] The extent to which recognition is motivating depends, as do most rewards, on its perceived value and on the connection that the individual sees between it and behavior.

Promotions.   For many employees, promotion does not happen often; some employees never experience it in their careers. The manager making a promotion reward decision attempts to match the right person with the job. Criteria that are often used to reach promotion decisions are performance and seniority. Performance, if it can be accu-

recognition
Managerial use of recognition involves a manager's acknowledgment of a job well done.

---

[9] Philip M. Podsakoff, William D. Tudor, and Richard Skov, "Effects of Leader Contingent and Noncontingent Reward and Punishment Behaviors on Subordinate Performance and Satisfaction," *Academy of Management Journal*, December 1982, pp. 810–21.

rately assessed, is often given significant weight in promotion reward allocations.

Intrinsic Rewards

intrinsic rewards
Rewards that are part of the job itself are intrinsic. They include a sense of completion, achievement, autonomy, and growth.

Completion.   The ability to start and finish a project or job is important to some individuals. These people value what is called *task completion*. The effect that completing a task has on a person is a form of self-reward. Some people have a need to complete tasks. Opportunities that allow such people to complete tasks can have a powerful motivating effect.

Achievement.   Achievement is a self-administered reward that is derived when a person reaches a challenging goal. McClelland has found that there are individual differences in striving for achievement.[10] Some individuals seek challenging goals, while others

TABLE 6–2

Types and Sources of Selected Extrinsic and Intrinsic Rewards

Type	Source of Reward		
	Manager	Group	Individual
I. Extrinsic			
A. Financial			
1. Salary and wages	D		
2. Fringe benefits	D		
B. Interpersonal	D	D	
C. Promotion	D		
II. Intrinsic			
A. Completion	I		D
B. Achievement	I		D
C. Autonomy	I		D
D. Personal growth	I		D

D = The direct source of the reward.
I = The indirect source of the reward.

tend to seek moderate or low goals. In goal-setting programs, it has been proposed that difficult goals result in a higher level of individual performance than do moderate goals. However, even in such programs individual differences must be considered before reaching conclusions about the importance of achievement rewards.

Autonomy.   There are some people who want jobs that provide them with the right and privilege to make decisions and operate without

---

[10] David C. McClelland, *The Achieving Society* (New York: D. Van Nostrand, 1961).

being closely supervised. A feeling of autonomy could result from the freedom to do what the employee considers best in a particular situation. In jobs that are highly structured and controlled by management, it is difficult to create tasks that lead to a feeling of autonomy.

Personal Growth.   The personal growth of any individual is a unique experience. An individual who is experiencing such growth senses his or her development and can see how his or her capabilities are being expanded. By expanding capabilities, a person is able to maximize or at least satisfy skill potential. Some people often become dissatisfied with their jobs and organizations if they are not allowed or encouraged to develop their skills.

The rewards included in this section are distributed or created by managers, work groups, or the individual. Table 6–2 summarizes the rewards we have discussed. As the table indicates, the manager can play either a direct or an indirect role in developing and administering the rewards.

THE INTERACTION OF INTRINSIC AND EXTRINSIC REWARDS

The general assumption has been that intrinsic and extrinsic rewards have an independent and additive influence on the motivation of individuals. That is, motivation is determined by the sum of the person's intrinsic and extrinsic sources of motivation.[11] This straightforward assumption has been questioned by several researchers. Some researchers have suggested that in situations in which individuals are experiencing a high level of intrinsic rewards, the addition of extrinsic rewards for good performance may cause a decrease in motivation.[12] Basically, the person who is receiving self-administered feelings of satisfaction is performing because of intrinsic rewards. Once extrinsic rewards are added, the feelings of satisfaction change because performance is now thought to be occurring because of the extrinsic rewards. The addition of the extrinsic rewards tends to reduce the extent to which the individual will experience self-administered intrinsic rewards.

The argument concerning the potential negative effects of extrinsic rewards has stimulated a number of research studies. Unfortunately, these studies report contradictory results. Some researchers report

[11] Daniel C. Feldman and Hugh J. Arnold, *Managing Individual and Group Behavior in Organizations* (New York: McGraw-Hill, 1983), p. 164.

[12] E. L. Deci, "The Effects of Externally Mediated Rewards on Intrinsic Motivation," *Journal of Personality and Social Psychology,* April 1971, pp. 105–15; E. L. Deci, *Intrinsic Motivation* (New York: Plenum, 1975); and B. M. Staw, *Intrinsic and Extrinsic Motivation* (Morristown, N.J.: General Learning Press, 1975).

That there is a reduction in intrinsic rewards following the addition of extrinsic rewards for an activity.[13] Other researchers have failed to observe such an effect.[14] A review of the literature found that 14 of 24 studies supported the theory that extrinsic rewards reduced intrinsic motivation.[15] However, 10 of the 24 studies found no support for the reducing effect theory. It should be noted that of the 24 studies reviewed, only two used actual employees as subjects. All of the other studies used college students or grade school students. In studies of telephone operators and clerical employees, the reducing effect theory was not supported.[16] In fact, managers need to be aware of the point that there is not yet a scientifically based and reported study showing that the introduction of extrinsic rewards has a negative effect on intrinsic motivation.

ADMINISTERING REWARDS

Managers are faced with the decision of how to administer rewards. Three major theoretical approaches to reward administration are: (1) positive reinforcement, (2) modeling and social imitation, and (3) expectancy.[17]

Positive Reinforcement

As discussed in Chapter 5, in administering a positive reinforcement program, the emphasis is on the desired behavior that leads to job performance, rather than performance alone. The basic foundation of administering rewards through positive reinforcement is the rela-

---

[13] Deci, "Effects of Externally Mediated Rewards"; and B. M. Staw, "The Attitudinal and Behavior Consequences of Changing a Major Organizational Reward," *Journal of Personality and Social Psychology,* June 1974, pp. 742–51.

[14] Cynthia D. Fisher, "The Effects of Personal Control, Competence, and Extrinsic Reward Systems on Intrinsic Motivation," *Organizational Behavior and Human Performance,* June 1978, pp. 273–87; and James S. Phillips and Robert G. Lord, "Determinants of Intrinsic Motivation: Locus of Control and Competence Information as Component's of Deci's Cognitive Evaluation Theory," *Journal of Applied Psychology,* April 1980, pp. 211–18.

[15] Kimberly B. Boone and Larry L. Cummings, "Cognitive Evaluation Theory: An Experimental Test of Processes and Outcomes," *Organizational Behavior and Human Performance,* December 1981, pp. 289–310.

[16] E. M. Lopez, "A Test of Deci's Cognitive Evaluation Theory in an Organizational Setting," paper presented at the 39th Annual Convention of the Academy of Management, Atlanta, August 1979; and Fisher, "Effects of Personal Control, Competence, and Extensive Reward Systems."

[17] Lyman W. Porter, "Turning Work into Nonwork: The Rewarding Environment," in *Work and Nonwork in the year 2001,* ed. M. D. Dunnette (Belmont, Calif.: Wadsworth, 1973) p. 122, suggests three approaches. Porter introduces operant conditioning. We believe that when rewards are being discussed, positive reinforcement should be used.

tionship between behavior and its consequences. Consequences are viewed as outcomes in an employee's environment that are related to the demonstration of certain behaviors. If a consequence increases the occurrence of a behavior, it is called a reinforcer. If a manager can identify behavior that leads to high levels of performance, select the most effective positive reinforcers that shape the behavior, and distribute the reinforcers on some form of effective schedule, job performance can be improved.

While positive reinforcement can be a useful method of shaping desired behavior, other considerations concerning the type of reward schedule to use are also important. We have already discussed schedules of positive reinforcement in Chapter 5. Suffice it to say that managers should explore the possible consequences of different types of reward schedules for individuals. It is important to know how employees respond to continuous, fixed interval, and fixed ratio schedules. In addition, managers could benefit from understanding how individuals respond to different forms of monetary and nonmonetary positive reinforcers.

Modeling and Social Imitation[18]

There is little doubt that many human skills and behaviors are acquired by observational learning or, simply, imitation. This form of learning was presented in Chapter 5.[19] Observational learning equips a person to duplicate a response, but whether the response is actually imitated depends on whether the model person was rewarded or punished for particular behaviors. If a person is to be motivated, he or she must observe models receiving reinforcements that are valued.

In order to use modeling to administer rewards, managers would need to determine who responds to this approach. In addition, selecting appropriate models would be a necessary step. Finally, the context in which modeling occurs needs to be considered. That is, if high performance is the goal and it is almost impossible to achieve that goal because of limited resources, the manager should conclude that modeling is not appropriate. Some managers using modeling have attempted to force it on employees when the situation did not warrant such an approach. Managers must judge the appropriateness of using modeling to administer rewards.

---

[18] The discussion of Porter, "Turning Work Into Nonwork," was used in the development of this section.

[19] A. Bandura and R. H. Walters, *Social Learning and Personality Development* (New York: Holt, Rinehart & Winston, 1963).

Expectancy Theory

Expectancy theory is incorporated in Figure 6–1. It states that the effort expended by an employee to perform a job is a joint function of both the value that the employee attaches to obtaining rewards (extrinsic and intrinsic) and the expectation (perceived chance or probability) that a specific level of energy will be enough to receive the rewards.

The expectancy approach, like the other two methods of administering rewards, requires managerial action. Managers must determine the kinds of rewards employees desire and do whatever is possible to distribute those rewards or create conditions so that what is available in the form of rewards can be applied. In some situations, it is just not possible to provide the rewards that are valued and preferred. Therefore, managers often have to increase the desirability of other rewards.

A manager can and often will use principles from each of the three methods of administering rewards—positive reinforcement, modeling, and expectancy. Each of these methods indicates that the job performance of employees is a result of the application of effort. To generate the effort to perform, managers can use positive reinforcers, modeling, and expectations. It should be remembered that performance may never be satisfactorily accomplished if employees are deficient in problem-solving skills, specific abilities, and experience. To get the most from administering rewards, a manager needs to have employees who have the ability, skill, and experience to perform.

REWARDS AND ORGANIZATIONAL MEMBERSHIP

As stated earlier, a major objective of a reward system is to attract people to join or become members of an organization. This involves people making organizational and job choices. The notion of how an individual moves from outside to inside an organization is called **organizational entry**.[20] There are a number of research studies that examine the organizational entry decisions of employees. Most of these studies indicate that people are attracted to an organization that is rated highest on their goals and values and on their expectations about what the organization will be like. It appears that people will choose the organization that they believe will result in the best set

organizational entry
Researchers have provided managers with useful information to explain why people become members of organizations.

---

[20] John P. Wanous, "Organizational Entry: The Individual's Viewpoint," in *Perspectives on Behavior in Organizations*, ed. J. Richard Hackman, Edward E. Lawler III, and Lyman W. Porter (New York: McGraw-Hill, 1977), pp. 126–35; and John P. Wanous, *Organizational Entry* (Reading, Mass.: Addison-Wesley Publishing, 1979).

of outcomes or rewards. This behavior seems reasonable because being able to obtain valued rewards leads to high levels of satisfaction.

In an interesting study of job choice, individuals were asked to rate the jobs they were considering in terms of their chances of achieving a number of goals. These individuals were also asked to rank the goals in order of importance. The data showed that these individuals were attracted to organizations that were seen as being instrumental in the attainment of their preferred goals.[21]

The attraction of members to an organization depends to some extent on how people in the external market view the possible rewards offered by the organization. If the reward image of the company is clear and people value the potential rewards, there will be attraction. Just as rewards can be used to attract people to join an organization, they can and are used to motivate individuals to remain with the organization.

REWARDS AND TURNOVER AND ABSENTEEISM

Some managers assume that low turnover is a mark of an effective organization. This view is somewhat controversial because a high quit rate means more expense for an organization. However, some organizations would benefit if disruptive and low performers quit.[22] Thus, the issue of turnover needs to focus on the *frequency* and on *who* is leaving.

Ideally, if managers could develop reward systems that retained the best performers and caused poor performers to leave, the overall effectiveness of an organization would improve.[23] To approach this ideal state, an equitable and favorably compared reward system must exist. The feeling of *equity* and *favorable comparison* has an external orientation. That is, the equity of rewards and favorableness involves comparisons with external parties. This orientation is used because quitting most often means that a person leaves one organization for an alternative elsewhere. Of course, if an organization had an endless stream of extrinsic and intrinsic rewards and could increase the level of rewards distributed, high performers could usually be retained. This is a very costly reward strategy that most organizations are not able to afford.

---

[21] Victor H. Vroom, "Organizational Choice: A Study of Pre- and Post-Decision Processes," *Organizational Behavior and Human Performance,* December 1966, pp. 212–25.

[22] Dan R. Dalton, David M. Krackhardt, and Lyman W. Porter, "Functional Turnover: An Empirical Assessment," *Journal of Applied Psychology,* December 1981, pp. 716–21.

[23] Dan R. Dalton and William D. Tudor, "Turnover: A Lucrative Hard Dollar Phenomenon," *Academy of Management Review,* April 1982, p. 212.

merit
Paying someone on
the basis of merit
means that good
performance is being
recognized and
rewarded.

There is no perfect means for retaining high performers. It appears that a reward system based on **merit** should encourage most of the better performers to remain with the organization. There also has to be some differential in the reward system that discriminates between high and low performers, the point being that the high performers must receive significantly more extrinsic and intrinsic rewards than the low performers.

Absenteeism, no matter for what reason, is a costly and disruptive problem facing managers.[24] It is costly because it reduces output and disruptive because it requires that schedules and programs be modified. It is estimated that absenteeism in the United States results in the loss of over 400 million workdays per year, or about 5.1 days per employee.[25] Employees go to work because they are motivated to do so. The level of motivation will remain high if an individual feels that attendance will lead to more valued rewards and fewer negative consequences than alternative behaviors.

There has been some research on reward systems and attendance. In an interesting study, researchers used a poker incentive plan to improve attendance. Each day as an employee came to work and was on time, he was allowed to select one card from a regular playing deck. At the end of a five-day week, the employees who attended every day on time would have a regular five-card hand. The highest hand won $20.[26] There were eight winners, one for each department. This plan seemed to result in a decrease of absenteeism of 18.7 percent. The study did not compare the poker incentive plan with any other system, so whether it would be better than some other reward system is not known. However, it was better than when no bonus or prize was distributed for attendance.

Another study reported the effects of an employee-developed bonus plan on attendance. Three work groups developed a plan that offered a cash bonus to workers who attended work regularly.[27] The results indicated that job attendance improved significantly. Further data from the study showed what happened when a plan developed by some individuals was imposed on other people. The plan developed by the three groups was applied to two other groups in the organiza-

---

[24] Gary Johns and Nigel Nicholson, "The Meanings of Absence: New Strategies for Theory and Research," in *Research In Organizational Behavior,* ed. B. M. Staw and L. L. Cummings (Greenwich, Conn.: JAI Press, 1982), pp. 127–72.

[25] Richard M. Steers and Susan R. Rhodes, "A New Look at Absenteeism," *Personnel,* November–December 1980, pp. 60–65.

[26] E. Pedalino and V. Gamboa, "Behavior Modification and Absenteeism: Intervention in One Industrial Setting," *Journal of Applied Psychology,* December 1974, pp. 694–98.

[27] Edward E. Lawler III and J. Richard Hackman, "The Impact of Employee Participation in the Development of Pay Incentive Plans: A Field Experiment," *Journal of Applied Psychology,* December 1969, pp. 467–71.

tion. The findings indicated that it was not effective in reducing absenteeism. The success of a reward plan involving employee participation was linked to where the plan was developed.

In one company, employees are paid a bonus if they have no absences for four weeks. The firm also doesn't pay for absences for the first eight hours of absence due to illness. This plan has resulted in over 3,000 hours of reduced absenteeism.[28]

Managers appear to have some influence over attendance behavior. They have the ability to punish, establish bonus systems, and allow employee participation in developing plans. Whether these or other approaches will reduce absenteeism is determined by the value of the rewards perceived by employees, the amount of the rewards, and whether employees perceive a relationship between attendance and rewards. These same characteristics appear every time we analyze the effects of rewards on organizational behavior.

REWARDS AND JOB PERFORMANCE

There is agreement among behaviorists and managers that extrinsic and intrinsic rewards can be used to motivate job performance. It is also clear that certain conditions must exist if rewards are to motivate good job performance: the rewards must be *valued* by the person, and they must be related to the level of job performance that is to be motivated.[29]

In Chapter 5, expectancy motivation theory was presented. It was stated that according to the theory, every behavior has associated with it (in a person's mind) certain outcomes or rewards or punishments. In other words, an assembly-line worker may believe that by behaving in a certain way, he or she will get certain things. This is a description of the *performance-outcome expectancy.* The worker may expect that a steady performance of 10 units a day will eventually result in a transfer to a more challenging job. On the other hand, the worker may expect that a steady performance of 10 units a day will result in being considered a rate-buster by co-workers.

Each outcome has a *valence* or value to the person. Outcomes such as pay, promotion, a reprimand, or a better job have different values for different people. This occurs because each person has different needs and perceptions. Thus, in considering which rewards to use, a manager has to be astute at considering individual differences. If valued rewards are used to motivate, they can result in the exertion of effort to achieve high levels of performance.

---

[28] Darron H. Harvey, Judy A. Schultze, and Jerome F. Rogers, "Rewarding Employees for Not Using Sick Leave," *Personnel Administrator,* May 1983, pp. 55–59.

[29] Lyman W. Porter, Edward E. Lawler III and J. Richard Hackman, *Behavior in Organizations* (New York: McGraw-Hill, 1975), p. 352.

REWARDS AND ORGANIZATIONAL COMMITMENT

commitment
An employee's commitment indicates identification with the organization's goals, feelings about being involved in the firm, and a sense of loyalty.

There is little research on the relationship between rewards and organizational commitment. **Commitment** to an organization involves three attitudes: (1) a sense of identification with the organization's goals, (2) a feeling of involvement in organizational duties, and (3) a feeling of loyalty for the organization.[30] There is research evidence that the absence of commitment can reduce organizational effectiveness.[31] People who are committed are less likely to quit and accept other jobs. Thus, the costs of high turnover are not incurred. In addition, committed and highly skilled employees require less supervision. Close supervision and a rigid monitoring control process are time-consuming and costly. Furthermore, a committed employee perceives the value and importance of integrating individual and organizational goals. The employee thinks of his or her goals and the organization's goals in personal terms.

A study of upper middle managers in large organizations reported some of the organizational rewards that significantly influenced commitment.[32] Some of these rewards were:

Personal importance. The experience of being considered a valuable member of an organization increased commitment.

Realization of expectations. Those managers who were able to fulfill expectations because the organization fulfilled its promises reported more commitment.

Job challenge. Challenging, interesting, and self-rewarding job assignments appeared to strengthen commitment. The study also found that the job experience in the first year continued to shape the attitudes of managers into the future.

Intrinsic rewards are important for the development of organizational commitment. Organizations able to meet employee needs by providing achievement opportunities and by recognizing achievement when it occurs have a significant impact on commitment. Thus, managers need to develop intrinsic reward systems that focus on personal importance or self-esteem, to integrate individual and organizational goals, and to design challenging jobs.

---

[30] Bruce Buchanan, "To Walk an Extra Mile: The Whats, Whens, and Whys of Organizational Commitment," *Organizational Dynamics,* Spring 1975, pp. 67–80.

[31] R. T. Mowday, L. W. Porter, and R. M. Steers, *Employee-Organization Linkages* (New York: Academic Press, 1982).

[32] Buchanan, "To Walk an Extra Mile."

INNOVATIVE REWARD SYSTEMS

The typical list of rewards that managers can and do distribute in organizations has been discussed above. We all know that pay, fringe benefits, and opportunities to achieve challenging goals are considered rewards by most people. It is also generally accepted that rewards are administered by managers through such processes as reinforcement, modeling, and expectancies. What are some of the newer and innovative, yet largely untested, reward programs that some managers are experimenting with? Three different approaches to rewards are providing cafeteria fringe benefits, banking time-off, and paying all employees a salary. The strengths and weaknesses of these three approaches are summarized in Table 6–3.

Cafeteria-Style Fringe Benefits

In a cafeteria-style plan, management places an upper limit on how much the organization is willing to spend on fringe benefits. The em-

TABLE 6–3

Three Innovative Reward Approaches: A Summary and Comparison

Reward Approach	Major Strengths	Major Weaknesses	Research Support
Cafeteria-style fringe benefits	Since employees have different desires and needs, a program can be tailored that fits the individual.	The administration can become complex and costly. The more employees involved, the more difficult it is to efficiently operate the approach	Limited since only a few programs have been scientifically examined
Banking time-off	Can be integrated with performance in that time-off credits can be made contingent on performance achievements	Requires that an organization have a valid, reliable, and equitable performance appraisal program.	Extremely limited
All-salaried team	Eliminates treating some employees as insiders and some as outsiders. Everyone is paid a salary and is a member of the team.	Assumes that everyone wants to be a team member and paid a salary. Some individuals value being nonmanagers and nonsalaried.	None available

ployee is then asked to decide how he or she would like to receive the total fringe benefit amount. The employee is able to develop a personally attractive fringe benefit package. Some employees take all of the fringes in cash or purchase special medical protection plans. The cafeteria plan provides individuals with the benefits they prefer rather than the benefits that someone else establishes for them. A cafeteria-style program is discussed in the following Close-Up.

ORGANIZATIONS: CLOSE-UP

American Can's Benefits Program

American Can Company now has nearly 9,000 salaried employees who design their own personal benefits packages. The company provides a core of nonoptional benefits, and then employees can select from a group of options on the basis of flexible "credits" that are allocated to each participant in the plan. Employees enrolled in the program are also able to buy additional benefits through payroll deductions.

American Can keeps a close watch on how employees spend their money. Management at first feared that employees would make foolish choices. However, the profile of how the benefits are selected is really fairly predictable. Young single employees take more time off. So do married women, who usually want the same number of vacation days as their husbands have. Those with young families tend to choose more medical and life insurance coverage. Older employees are more concerned with savings, first for their children's education and later, as their children leave home, for their retirement.

Benefit options can be changed once a year. In September, every employee receives a form stating his or her existing program and the credits earned. Employees may then choose to remain with the same options or elect completely different options. Changes go into effect January 1.

Since the program has been in effect, employees seem to understand their benefits much more than they used to. A survey conducted before the flexible benefits program was introduced showed little understanding among the employees about benefits. Many employees believed that the benefits had little value. However, since the plan was implemented, employees have come to recognize the significant value of their benefits. They also discuss the fringe benefits thoroughly with spouses. The American Can program has certainly made employees aware of and interested in fringe benefits.

Source: Gerard Tavernier, "How American Can Manages Its Flexible Benefits Program," *Management Review*, August 1980, pp. 9–13.

There are some administrative problems associated with cafeteria plans.[33] Because of the different preferences of employees, records become more complicated. For a large organization with a cafeteria plan, a computer system is almost essential to do the record keeping. Another problem involves group insurance premium rates. Most life and medical insurance premiums are based on the number of employees participating. It is difficult to determine what the participation level will be under a cafeteria plan.

TRW Corporation has placed approximately 12,000 employees on a cafeteria plan. It allows employees to rearrange and redistribute their fringe benefit packages every year. Over 80 percent of the TRW participants have changed their benefit packages since the plan was initiated.[34]

Banking Time-Off

A time-off feature is attractive to most people. In essence, most companies have a time-off system built into their vacation programs. Employees receive different amounts of time off based on the number of years they have worked for the organization. An extension of such a time-off reward could be granted for certain levels of performance. That is, a bank of time-off credits could be built up contingent on performance achievements.

Today, some organizations are selecting their best performers to attend educational and training programs. One company in Houston selects the best performers and provides them with an opportunity to attend an executive educational program. Being eligible is largely contingent on the performance record of the individual. Those finally selected are given two Fridays off a month to attend classes.

The All-Salaried Team

In most organizations, managers are paid salaries and nonmanagers receive hourly wages. The practice of paying all employees a salary is supposed to improve loyalty, commitment, and self-esteem. The notion of being a part of a team is projected by the salary-for-everyone practice. One benefit of the all-salary practice considered important by nonmanagers is that it eliminates punching a time clock. To date, rigorous investigations of the influence, if any, of the all-salary practice are not available. It does seem to have promise when applied to some employees.

---

[33] James H. Shea, "Cautions about Cafeteria-Style Benefit Plans," *Personnel Journal*, January 1981, p. 37.

[34] Lawler, "Reward Systems," p. 182.

The link between the performance evaluation system and reward distribution was shown in Figure 6–1. The discussion of this and other linkages in the reward process suggests the complexity of using rewards to motivate better performance. Managers need to use judgment, diagnosis, and the resources available to reward their subordinates. As shown, administering rewards is perhaps one of the most challenging and frustrating tasks that managers must perform.

PUNISHMENT AND DISCIPLINE

The analysis and discussion of job motivation in organizational behavior and management focus primarily on eliciting desired behavior and performance. However, managers are occasionally faced with eliminating undesired behavior and inadequate performance. Despite their unpleasant connotations, punishment and disciplinary measures are used in organizations to eliminate undesired behavior and poor performance.[35] Some managers and researchers argue that there is no justification for the use of punishment in organizational settings. Other individuals believe that there are times when punishment is

TABLE 6–4

Punishable Behaviors

Absenteeism	Insubordination
Tardiness	Abusing customers
Leaving work station	Work slowdown
Theft	Refusing to work with co-workers
Sleeping on the job	Refusing to work overtime
Fighting	Possession and use of drugs on
Threatening management	the job
Repeated poor performance	Damaging equipment
Violating safety rules and	Profane language
policies	Illegal strike

the most efficient and effective way to change behavior. Table 6–4 presents a partial list of behaviors that have been punished in organizations.

Punishment is the presentation of an aversive event or the removal of a positive event following a response that decreases the frequency of the response.[36] A relationship or contingency exists between some

[35] Richard D. Arvey and John M. Ivancevich, "Punishment in Organizations: A Review, Propositions, and Research Suggestions," *Academy of Management Journal,* January 1980, pp. 123–32.

[36] A. E. Kazdin, *Behavior Modification in Applied Settings* (Homewood, Ill.: Dorsey Press, 1975), pp. 33–34.

defined response and some aversive consequence or stimulus (e.g., a pay reduction for being absent, a publicized memo informing you of poor performance). The resistance of some to the use of punishment is based on moral grounds, the moral position being that pain is bad and should always be avoided. **Discipline** is the use of some form of punishment or sanction when employees deviate from the rules. Not all disciplinary measures are a form of punishment.[37] For example, suppose that frequent absence results in a three day suspension from work. If the person suspended doesn't like his job and prefers to stay home, he will not regard the suspension as aversive. In such a situation, the disciplined person has not been punished.

discipline
Discipline is a form of punishment. It differs from punishment, however, in that the recipient does not always view discipline as aversive, whereas punishment is always considered aversive.

Instead of discussing discipline programs, we prefer to discuss punishment. The theoretical framework and basis for organizational progressive discipline programs (whereby a sequence of penalties for violations is administered, each one slightly more severe than the previous one) are found in the punishment literature. It should be noted that managers prefer to acknowledge that their firms have discipline programs as opposed to admitting that punishment is used.

Punishment and Behavior

The earliest theoretical explanation of punishment was advanced by Thorndike.[38] Thorndike proposed that punishment exerted its effect on behavior by weakening the connection between a stimulus and a response. According to this theory, the proverbial child caught with a hand in the cookie jar and immediately punished would on subsequent occasions no longer be under the influence of the cookie jar or the cookies in it. The jar and the cookies would have lost their power to control the behavior of reaching into the jar. Later, Thorndike reexamined this commonsense view that punishment would reduce the tendency to repeat the behavior that it immediately followed.[39] He decided that punishment really had no weakening effect on behavior.

Thorndike's reevaluation of punishment was arrived at by his questioning of his original position. He argued that wherever punishment appears to weaken a response, it is an indirect effect. Punishment may or may not weaken a response, but it clearly cannot be the mirror

[37] Ira G. Asherman, "The Corrective Discipline Process," *Personnel Journal,* July 1982, p. 528.

[38] E. L. Thorndike, *Educational Psychology,* vol. 2 H: *The Psychology of Learning* (New York: Columbia University Teachers College Bureau of Publications, 1913).

[39] E. L. Thorndike, *Reward and Punishment in Animal Learning,* Contemporary Psychological Monograph, 1983, *8,* no. 39.

image of the action of reward. For example, if an employee's response is rewarded, it is apparent that repetition of this response may also be rewarding; but if an employees' response is punished, it is not clear to the person which of the other available responses will be rewarded. In effect, Thorndike suggested that punishment does an exemplary job of telling a person what not to do but by itself carries no information that tells an individual which particular alternative course of behavior should be followed.

What happens, however, when the only response that is appropriate for a particular motivational state of affairs is punished? The youngster who is punished for taking the cookies may not know any other way to satisfy a craving for sweets. No matter how many raps on the knuckles (or elsewhere) the youngster may receive, the cookies lose none of their attraction, and the child is probably not likely to find another way of getting cookies.

Arguments against Using Punishment

Besides the moral reasons cited against the use of punishment, other reasons for using it have been advanced. First, the purpose of punishment is presumably to reduce the occurrence of the specific behavior being punished. However, if the punishment is severe enough and is applied over sufficient time, it may also suppress the occurrence of socially desirable behaviors.

Suppression effects can be important from an organizational perspective. Assume that a new employee has limited technical ability and that, in fact, it is desirable for him to work as much and as closely with others as possible. To engage in these behaviors, the employee must be away from the work station. Punishment for not being at the work station might lead to generalized inhibition of observing, talking, and working with persons who have technical skills. To forestall potentially damaging effects on technical skill development, it would be important to teach the new employee to discriminate between the times when being away from his work station is inappropriate and the times when it is appropriate.

Second, it is assumed by some that the use of punishment will result in undesirable side effects (e.g., anxiety, aggressiveness). In addition, those being punished may attempt to escape or avoid (e.g., absenteeism, turnover) or show hostility toward (e.g., sabotage) management.

Research support concerning the undesirable emotional side effects of punishment is not particularly strong. A review of the literature of numerous studies indicates that only one study supported this assumption.[40] The review indicated that improvement in subject be-

[40] J. M. Johnson, "Punishment of Human Behavior," *American Psychologist*, November 1972, pp. 1033–54.

havior rather than undesirable emotional side effects occurred as a result of punishment. Perhaps undesirable emotional side effects are more likely to occur if managers are indiscriminately and unfairly punitive.[41]

Third, punishment effects are only temporary, and once the threat of punishment is removed, the undesirable response will return full force. Thus, the threat of punishment must always be there or be used. The fact is that punishment does work, and this may produce positive reinforcement for the managers to continue its use.

Fourth, through observational learning, punishment may result in negative responses from peers of the punished person. For example, individuals observing a manager punishing a colleague may imitate this behavior among themselves or toward management. In effect, the manager would be teaching employees aggressive, impersonal behavior, which is exactly what punishment is designed to eliminate.

Conditions of Punishment

Although there are logical arguments against the use of punishment in organizations, there are conditions that can make its use feasible and more effective.

Timing. The time at which punishment is administered is important.[42] Punishment can be introduced during the punished response, immediately after the punished response or some time after the response. Research suggests that the effectiveness of punishment is enhanced when the aversive event is delivered close in time to the punished response.

Intensity. Punishment achieves greater effectiveness when the aversive stimulus is relatively intense. The implication of this condition is that in order to be effective, punishment should get the immediate attention of the person being punished.[43] High-intensity punishment may, however, create a level of anxiety and fear in the workplace that stifles taking nonroutine actions in completing a job. That is, it may inhibit generally preferred behaviors because it is so severe.

Scheduling. The effects of punishment depend on the schedule. Punishment can occur after every response (continuous schedule), a variable or fixed period of time after the undesired behavior occurred (variable or fixed interval schedules), or after a variable or fixed number of responses have occurred (variable or fixed ratio schedules). Some

---

[41] Philip M. Podsakoff, "Determinants of a Supervisor's Use of Rewards and Punishments: A Literature Review and Suggestions for Further Research," *Organizational Behavior and Human Performance,* February 1982, pp. 58–83.

[42] A. Trenholme and A. Baron, "Immediate and Delayed Punishment of Human Behavior by Loss of Reinforcement," *Learning and Motivation,* February 1975, pp. 62–79.

[43] Johnson, "Punishment of Human Behavior."

research indicates that punishment is most effective if administered on a continuous schedule. In one study, employees who were disciplined consistently for absenteeism demonstrated less absenteeism than did employees who received discipline haphazardly or not at all.[44]

The notion of consistency in using any type of punishment schedule is important. Are managers consistent in punishing the same undesired behavior over time? Are managers consistent in applying punishment across employees? It is important for managers to punish fairly and equitably. A manager who punishes inequitably is more likely to set off undesirable emotional side effects than is one who punishes fairly.

Clarifying the Reasons. Cognition plays an important role in punishment.[45] Providing clear, unambiguous reasons why the punishment occurred and notice of future consequences if the response recurs has been shown to be particularly effective. Providing reasons emphasizes to the person which specific response is responsible for the manager's action. It essentially informs the person exactly what not to do.

Impersonal. Punishment should focus on a specific response, not on the person or general patterns of behavior.[46] The more impersonal the punishment, the less likely is the person punished to experience undesirable emotional side effects and permanent strains in the relationship with the manager. It takes extreme self-control and patience for any person administering punishment to do so in an impersonal manner. However, the consequences of applying punishment in an impersonal manner are likely to be much more positive than those of applying punishment in an emotional manner.

What we have attempted to do in this section is to clarify the issue of punishment in organizations. Certainly, we prefer the predominant use of positive reinforcement. However, when a manager is faced with stopping a persistently undesirable response, positive reinforcement, negative reinforcement, or extinction alone may not be enough. These and other suggested alternatives may all be ineffective or costly. In such cases, punishment is used and will undoubtedly continue to be used. Although punishment is a complex and controversial process, continuing to ignore its use is not likely to enhance management's understanding of its application.

The opening Organizational Issue for Debate focused on the pay for performance controversy. This chapter illustrated that the practice of paying for performance is appealing but is not as simple as it ap-

---

[44] A. L. Gray, "Industrial Absenteeism: An Evaluation of Three Methods of Treatment," *Personnel Journal*, March 1971, pp. 252–53.

[45] Dennis W. Organ and W. Clay Hamner, *Organizational Behavior* (Plano, Tex.: Business Publications, 1982), pp. 97–98.

[46] Michael Domjan and Barbara Burkhard, *The Principles of Learning and Behavior* (Monterey, Calif.: Brooks/Cole Publishing, 1982), p. 264.

pears. Individual employee attitudes toward merit pay, other rewards, and punishment differ. These differences make management's job much more challenging and complex than it would be if employee attitudes on these matters were identical.

SUMMARY OF KEY POINTS

A. The major objectives of the reward processes are to attract people to join the organization, to keep them coming to work, and to motivate them to perform at high levels.

B. It is general knowledge that certain reward process issues should be addressed if any objectives are to be accomplished. Namely, there must be enough rewards to satisfy basic needs, people make comparisons between what rewards they receive and what others receive, and individual differences in reward preferences are important issues for consideration.

C. Management can and must distribute both extrinsic and intrinsic rewards. *Extrinsic* rewards are those that are external to the job, such as promotions, fringe benefits, and pay. *Intrinsic* rewards are associated with doing the job. They include responsibility, challenge, and meaningful work.

D. If extrinsic o   631048   e to motivate good job performance, th   ie employee and linked to the
level of p   ted.

E. Manager   dministering extrinsic and intrinsic re   popular methods are positive
reinforcem   application of expectancy theory princip

F. Rewards, i   fect such organizational behaviors as me   nteeism, and commitment. The
research   vards influence these behaviors
is still ra

G. Some inn   used by managers include cafe-
teria-styl   g time-off, and an all-salaried
work forc   not been thoroughly examined
by resear

H. Punishmen   ganizations, but its use is not
widely publicized because of the negative connotation of the word itself.

I. Punishment is the presentation of an aversive event or the removal of a positive event following a response that decreases the frequency of the response.

J. Arguments against the use of punishment under any circumstance include suppression effects, undesirable emotional side effects, its temporary influence, and its influence on peers of the punished individual.

K. The use of punishment in an organization requires the consideration of timing, intensity, scheduling, clarification of reasons, and impersonality.

DISCUSSION AND REVIEW QUESTIONS

1. Most managers use an array of rewards and punishment to accomplish desired outcomes. However, most systems are designed around a number of features such as merit, seniority, or attendance. Why is it almost impossible to distribute rewards on the basis of merit?

2. Develop a list of extrinsic and intrinsic rewards that are important to you. What kind of organization and job would be able to provide you with these rewards?

3. Have you ever been rewarded by modeling? Present a personal experience that shows how modeling influenced you.

4. The timing of a reward is especially important when implementing positive reinforcement. Why?

5. Is punishment justified as a managerial strategy for correcting behaviors? Why?

6. What managerial skills and abilities are needed to derive the most benefit from administering rewards?

7. It has been said that distributing rewards carefully and equitably is an investment in the most important organizational resource, people. Do you agree?

8. Some of the newer reward plans such as cafeteria-style fringe benefits and banking time-off have not really met the test of science. What type of research is needed to determine whether these kinds of plans are organizationally successful?

9. Can rewards and punishment be integrated into a unified program to motivate employees? Explain.

10. If equity and favorable comparisons are so important in reward systems, how can an organization develop a program that is generally viewed as equitable and favorable?

ADDITIONAL REFERENCES

Belohav, J. "Realities of Successful Employee Discipline." *Personnel Administrator*, 1983, pp. 74–77, 92.

Clegg, C. W. "Psychology of Employee Lateness, Absence, and Turnover: A Methodological

Critique and an Empirical Study." *Journal of Applied Psychology,* 1983, pp. 88–101.

Crystal, G. S. "Pay for Performance—Even If It's Just Luck." *The Wall Street Journal,* March 2, 1981, p. 16.

Ellig, B. R. "Perquisites: The Intrinsic Form of Pay." *Personnel,* 1981, pp. 23–31.

Kerr, S. "On the Folly of Rewarding A, While Hopping for B." *Academy of Management Journal,* 1975, pp. 769–83.

Kopelman, R. E. "Linking Pay to Performance Is a Proven Management Tool." *Personnel Administrator,* 1983, pp. 60–68.

Latham, G. P.; L. L. Cummings; and T. R. Mitchell. "Behavioral Strategies to Improve Productivity." *Organizational Dynamics,* 1981, pp. 4–23.

Mihal, W. L. "More Research Is Needed: Goals May Motivate Better." *Personnel Administrator,* 1983, pp. 61–67.

Mirvis, P. H., and E. E. Lawler III. "Measuring the Financial Impact of Employee Attitudes." *Journal of Applied Psychology,* 1977, pp. 1–8.

Mobley, W. H.; R. W. Griffeth; H. H. Hand; and B. H. Meglino. "Review and Conceptual Analysis of the Turnover Process." *Psychological Bulletin,* 1979, pp. 493–522.

Mowday, R. T.; R. M. Steers; and L. W. Porter. "The Measurement of Organizational Commitment." *Journal of Vocational Behavior,* 1979, pp. 224–47.

Pulich, M. A. "Train First-Line Supervisors to Handle Discipline." *Personnel Journal,* 1983, pp. 980–86.

Rusbult, C. E., and D. Farrell. "A Longitudinal Test of the Investment Model: The Impact of Job Satisfaction, Job Commitment, and Turnover of Variations in Rewards, Costs, Alternatives, and Investments." *Journal of Applied Psychology,* 1983, pp. 429–38.

CASE FOR ANALYSIS

The Effort-Performance-Pay Dilemma at Justis Corporation

John Hankla is a generator assembler working for the Justis Manufacturing Corporation. The company employs approximately 4,200 nonunionized workers and 495 managerial personnel. Justice manufactures repair parts and generators that are used for construction equipment.

The assemblers in what has become known as the Arco unit work the day shift and have worked for the company an average of 15 years. Each of the assemblers has worked for the company for at least eight years and is paid an hourly wage. The wage program for assemblers is related primarily to seniority and performance. The new plant manager, Paul Slanker, wants to continue integrating the performance of assemblers with the wage increases that are granted every 12 to 15 months.

The performance of assemblers in the Arco unit is evaluated by the shift supervisor, Randy Jones, and Paul. They use an evaluation form that focuses on quantity of output, quality control, promptness of completing task assignments, and intragroup aid provided by idle assemblers. The intragroup factor is concerned with the steps taken by assemblers who have completed their work on the generator to help others on the line who have fallen behind for some reason.

The line is a straight flow processing arrangement with six work stations. These stations are arranged as shown in Exhibit 1.

The wages of the 12 assemblers range from $3.98 to $6.25 an hour. Each assembler is trained and able to work at any of the six work stations. The assemblers typically work at one station for periods of up to four months and then rotate to another station on the line. Randy and Paul believe that John is without doubt the best performer. He has continually helped others on conveyor 1 and 2 to reduce the backlogs that often occur.

Paul and Randy believe that with current inflationary conditions an increase in pay would be a desirable reward for any of the assemblers. They further believe that competition is a force that needs to be examined carefully, especially with regard to productivity per person. Although Justis has much the same equipment as its two competitors, it is top management's opinion that the performance and the effort expended by Justis's employees are not up to the level of the competition. Top management wants supervisors to improve the effort and performance of their subordinates.

The plan for improving performance focuses on wages. Paul and Randy have decided to raise John's merit increase by 10 percent above that of any other assembler. They believe that Joyce, Marko, and Tom have the same ability and skill as John but do not exert the effort needed to perform as well. Pete, Alice, Al, and Mick are just slightly less skilled than the high-skill group but do not seem to be motivated to improve their skill levels. Tony, Mike, Dot, and Will just do not have the same level of skills as the others.

The assemblers, because of their close proximity to one another, often ex-

EXHIBIT 1

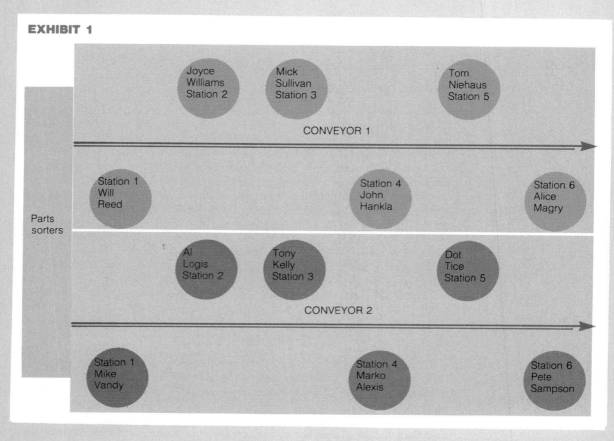

change thoughts about the job, the company, the management, and the pay-performance-ability linkage in the organization. This has led to comparisons and in some instances arguments about who is the best worker, the best company person, and the person most likely to be promoted to the supervisory level of management. In the past eight years, four people have been promoted to management positions from the Arco unit.

The first person to be notified about this year's merit increase was Joyce Wiliams. She received a raise of 4.8 percent. Next was Tom Niehaus, who received a raise of 5.0 percent. The third person was Al Logis, who received a raise of 4.4 percent. John, the fourth person, was notified of his merit increase plus his supplemental increase for superior performance, which resulted in a total merit increase of 16.4 percent. The other raises ranged from 4.0 to 6.4 percent.

The notification of merit increases took five weeks to complete. The assembly-line gossip immediately identified a difference between most of the increases and John's. Almost immediately, the Arco unit's productivity decreased and its backlogs increased. Its monthly production over the past two years is shown in Exhibit 2. Current production is shown by the darker line; last year's production is shown by the lighter line.

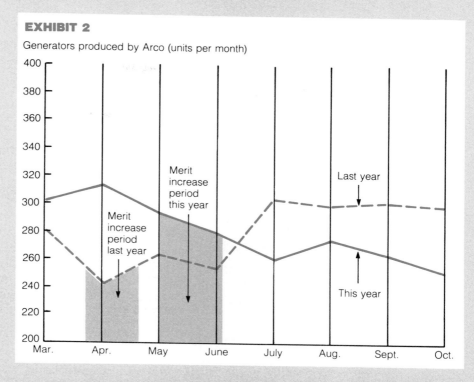

EXHIBIT 2

Generators produced by Arco (units per month)

Merit increase period this year

Merit increase period last year

Last year

This year

Although Paul knew he was no statistician, the decrease in productivity and the sustained lower level of output between June and October worried him. He called Randy in to discuss the problems in the Arco unit. Paul wanted to work out a motivation plan that would get the unit "pointed in the right direction" again.

Questions for Consideration

1. Do you believe that it is possible to think about the problems identified in this situation in terms of a need satisfaction model? Explain.

2. Should the decrease in productivity have been expected by Paul and Randy? Why?

3. Is the type of work performed by the Arco unit suited for the type of performance evaluation and pay plan used by management? Explain.

EXPERIENTIAL EXERCISE

MAKING CHOICES ABOUT REWARDS

Objectives

1. To illustrate individual differences in reward preferences.
2. To emphasize how both extrinsic and intrinsic rewards are considered important.
3. To enable people to explore the reasons for the reward preferences of others.

Related Topics

Since rewards are so pervasive in organizational settings, they tend to be linked to merit, seniority, and attendance. In fact, they are so related to organizational behavior that few issues of work life can be discussed without mentioning rewards.

Starting the Exercise

Initially individuals will work alone establishing their own list of reward preferences after reviewing Exhibit A. Then the instructor will set up groups of four to six students to examine individual preferences and complete the exercise.

The Facts

It is possible to develop an endless list of on-the-job rewards. Presented in a random fashion in Exhibit A are some of the rewards that could be available to employees.

EXHIBIT A

Some Possible Rewards for Employees

Company picnics	Recognition	Participation in decisions
Watches	Smile from manager	Stock options
Trophies	Feedback on performance	Vacation trips for
Piped-in music	Feedback on career progress	performance
Job challenge	Larger office	Manager asking for advice
Achievement opportunity	Club privileges	Informal leader asking for
Time-off for performance	More prestigious job	advice
Vacation	More job involvement	Office with a window
Autonomy	Use of company recreation	The privilege of completing a
Pay increase	facilities	job from start to finish

Exercise Procedures

Phase I: 25 minutes

1. Each individual should set up from Exhibit A a list of extrinsic and intrinsic rewards.
2. Each person should then rank-order from most important to least important the two lists.
3. From the two lists, rank the *eight* most important rewards. How many are extrinsic, and how many are intrinsic?

Phase II: 30 minutes

1. The instructor will set up groups of four to six individuals.
2. The two lists in which the extrinsic and intrinsic categories were developed should be discussed.
3. The final rank orders of the eight most important rewards should be placed on a board or chart at the front of the room.
4. The rankings should be discussed within the groups. What major differences are displayed?

Chapter 7

After completing Chapter 7, you should be able to:

Define in the form of a working definition the meaning of the term *stress*.

Describe in terms of the general adaptation syndrome a person's responses to stress.

Discuss some of the organizational effects of stress.

Compare the characteristics of quantitative and qualitative overload.

Identify the characteristics of the Type A Behavior Pattern.

Stress and the Individual

Avoiding Stress and Remaining Healthy

Argument For

It has long been a common opinion that prolonged strain resulting from job stress can make a person sick. Medical researchers have collected some evidence that job-related stress can be and is a contributor to chronic illnesses such as heart disease and peptic ulcers. Managers being bombarded by stress-producing job demands, and nonmanagers being prodded by demanding managers, may eventually become statistics in reports on coronary heart disease or other illnesses. Thus, advice is being offered that stressful jobs or hard-charging lifestyles should be avoided.

The hard-driving, competitive perfectionist who is valued by organizations is considered a prime candidate for an early coronary. If not a coronary, it may be migraines, ulcers, asthma, ulcerative colitis, or even adult acne. The hard-charger has been called a Type A Behavior Pattern (TABP). He (a male in most cases, but women in growing numbers are beginning to fit the TABP classification) marches to a "drummer" who requires winning at all costs. The Type A style is to wade in, do the job, enjoy the taste of success, and move on to the next challenge. This "race-horse" style means that the TABP person has a 1 in 5 chance of having a heart attack before reaching his 60th birthday. The message here is that avoiding excessive amounts of stress can prolong life.

Argument Against

Unfortunately, there is a great deal of confusion about what stress is and how individuals

217

deal with it. We hear a great deal about the dangers of TABP. However, others claim that the "racehorse" can't be a "turtle" without suffering anxiety and stress. Individual differences must be considered when discussing stress and how people react to it. It would be far more stressful for many Type As to change their style than to continue being hard-chargers.

There is also some concern over the practice of classifying individuals. Can we be sure that the measurements being used are accurate? Dr. Hans Selye, a leading medical authority on stress, believes that all of the stress inventories used to classify respondents are flawed because they fail to give enough weight to individual differences. He states that each individual is really the best judge of his or her stress threshold. Instead of using an inventory to detect stress tolerance or stress conditions, each person should be the

judge. Self-awareness is the best way to deal with stress conditions. The Type A may know without a doubt that he or she is a hard-charger, competitive, and a perfectionist. This person may also know how healthy he or she feels physically and psychologically. There are some individuals who just need stress, long hours, and a lot of work pressure. Instead of stating that TABP is bad, it is more accurate to state that some people are not suited to be Type As.

Unless a TABP person voluntarily wants to change, no organization, physician, or other individual has the right or the authority to intervene. TABP is a personal matter unless it affects others in an organization. If it does, then the organization has not only the right, but also the responsibility, to intervene. The problem, however, is that few intervention programs have proved successful in altering TABP.

nterest in occupational stress has become widespread in recent years. However, the experience of stress is not new; our cave-dwelling ancestors experienced it every time they left their caves and encountered their enemy, the saber-toothed tigers. The tigers of yesteryear are gone, but they have been replaced by other predators—work overload, a nagging boss, time deadlines, excessive inflation, poorly designed jobs, marital disharmony, the drive to keep up with the Joneses. These work and nonwork predators interact and create stress for individuals on and off the job. This chapter will focus primarily on the individual at work in organizations and on the stress created in this setting. Much of the stress experienced by people in our industrialized society originates in organizations; much of the stress that originates elsewhere affects our behavior and performance in these same organizations.

WHAT IS STRESS?

Stress means an incredibly different array of things to different people. The businessperson thinks of stress as frustration or emotional tension; the air traffic controller thinks of it as a problem of alertness and concentration; the biochemist thinks of it as a purely chemical event. In an uncomplicated way, it is best to consider stress as something that involves the interaction of the individual with the environment.[1] Most definitions of stress recognize the individual and the environment in terms of a stimulus interaction, a response interaction, or a stimulus-response interaction.

Stimulus Definition

A stimulus definition of stress would be the following: *Stress* is the force or stimulus acting on the individual that results in a response of strain, where strain is pressure or, in a physical sense, deformation. One problem with this definition is that it fails to recognize that two people subjected to the same level of stress may show far different levels of strain.

Response Definition

A response definition of stress would be the following: *Stress* is the physiological or psychological response of an individual to an environmental stressor, where a *stressor* is an external event or situation

---

[1] John M. Ivancevich and Michael T. Matteson, *Stress at Work: A Managerial Perspective* (Glenview, Ill.: Scott, Foresman, 1980), p. 6.

that is potentially harmful. In the stimulus definition, stress is an external event; here it is an internal response. This definition fails to enable anyone to predict the nature of the stress response or even whether there will be a stress response.

Stimulus-Response Definition

An example of a stimulus-response definition would be that *stress* is the consequence of the *interaction* between an environmental stimulus and the response of the individual. Stress is viewed as more than either a stimulus or a response; it is the result of a unique interaction between stimulus conditions in the environment and the individual's predisposition to respond in a certain way.

A Working Definition

Each of the three definitions offers important insights into what constitutes stress. Therefore, each is used to develop a working definition for this chapter. We define stress as:

> an adaptive response, mediated by individual differences and/or psychological processes, that is, a consequence of any external (environmental) action, situation, or event that places excessive psychological and/or physical demands on a person.

This working definition portrays stress in a more negative light than do most definitions. That is, stress is a neutral word in most discussions. We have, however, included the term *excessive* in our definition. Certainly, not all stress is negative. The positive stress that Dr. Hans Selye refers to as **eustress** (from the Greek *eu*, meaning good, as in *euphoria*) is stimulating in a positive sense. Eustress is necessary in our lives. However, because of space constraints we are not able to develop our discussion of eustress in this chapter.

eustress
In most discussions, positive stress is overlooked. Stress that has a positive impact on a person is called eustress.

The above working definition allows us to focus attention on specific environmental conditions that are potential sources of stress. Such conditions are called *stressors*. Whether stress is felt or experienced by a particular individual will depend on that individual's unique characteristics. Furthermore, the definition emphasizes an *adaptive response*. The vast majority of our responses to stimuli in the work environment do not require adaptation and thus are not really potential sources of stress.

An important point to keep in mind is that a variety of dissimilar situations—work effort, fatigue, uncertainty, fear, emotional arousal—are capable of producing stress. Therefore, it is extremely difficult to isolate a single factor as the sole cause.[2]

---

[2] Rita E. Numerof, *Managing Stress* (Rockville, Md.: Aspen Publications, 1983), p. 7.

THE PSYCHOPHYSIOLOGY OF STRESS

If for some reason you happened to place your hand on a hot stove, a number of predictable events would occur. There would be pain. There would also be tissue damage as successive layers of skin were exposed to the stove. Depending on your reaction time, the hand would be pulled away from the stove. You might even give off a few choice words.

This event displays an interaction between you and the environment. It is an event that results in physical and psychological consequences. It is also an event that magnifies what stress is and how we respond to it—physically and psychologically.

The General Adaptation Syndrome

Dr. Hans Selye, the pioneer of stress research, conceptualized the psychophysiological responses to stress.[3] Selye considered stress a non-specific response to any demand made upon an organism. He labeled the three phases of the defense reaction that a person establishes when stressed as the **General Adaptation Syndrome (GAS).** Selye called the defense reaction *general* because stressors had effects on several areas of the body; *adaptation* refers to a stimulation of defenses designed to help the body adjust to or deal with the stressors; and *syndrome* indicates that individual pieces of the reaction occur more or less together. The three distinct phases are called *alarm, resistance,* and *exhaustion.*

The *alarm stage* is the initial mobilization by which the body meets the challenge posed by the stressor. When a stressor is recognized, the brain sends forth a biochemical message to all of the body's systems. Respiration increases, blood pressure rises, pupils dilate, muscles tense up, and so forth.

If the stressor continues, the GAS proceeds to the *resistance stage.* Signs of being in the resistance stage include fatigue, anxiety, and tension. The person is now fighting the stressor. While resistance to a particular stressor may be high during this stage, resistance to other stressors may be low. A person has only finite sources of energy, concentration, and ability to resist stressors. Individuals are often more ill-ness-prone during periods of stress than at other times.[4]

The final GAS stage is *exhaustion.* Prolonged and continual exposure to the same stressor may eventually use up the adaptive energy available, and the system fighting the stressor becomes exhausted. The three stages of the GAS are presented in Figure 7–1.

General Adaptation Syndrome The father of stress research, Hans Selye, introduced a three-phase defense mechanism that a person uses to combat stress. The three phases—alarm, resistance, and exhaustion—make up the General Adaptation Syndrome (GAS).

[3] Hans Selye, *The Stress of Life* (New York: McGraw-Hill, 1976); and Hans Selye, *Stress without Distress* (Philadelphia: J. B. Lippincott, 1974).

[4] Selye, *Stress without Distress,* p. 5.

FIGURE 7–1

Selye's General Adaptation Syndrome (GAS)

Krau

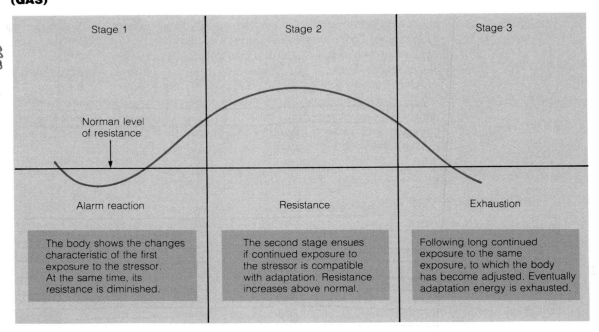

Stage 1	Stage 2	Stage 3
Norman level of resistance		
Alarm reaction	Resistance	Exhaustion
The body shows the changes characteristic of the first exposure to the stressor. At the same time, its resistance is diminished.	The second stage ensues if continued exposure to the stressor is compatible with adaptation. Resistance increases above normal.	Following long continued exposure to the same exposure, to which the body has become adjusted. Eventually adaptation energy is exhausted.

It is important to keep in mind that the activation of the GAS places extraordinary demands on the body. Clearly, the more frequently the GAS is activated and the longer it remains in operation, the more wear and tear there is on the psychophysiological mechanisms. The body and mind have limits. The more frequently a person is alarmed, resists, and becomes exhausted by work, nonwork, or the interaction of these activities, the more susceptible the person becomes to fatigue, disease, aging and other negative consequences.

STRESS AND WORK: A MODEL

For most employed individuals, work is more than a 40-hour-a-week commitment. Even if the actual work time is 40 hours, when work-related activities such as travel time, preparation for work, and lunch time are added in, most individuals spend 10 or more hours a day on work-related activities.

Not only is a lot of time spent on work-related activities, but many individuals find a substantial portion of their satisfaction and identity in their work. Consequently, work and nonwork activities are interdependent. The distinction between stress at work and stress at home is an artificial one at best. Sources of stress at work spill over into a person's nonwork activities. As a consequence of stressors experienced at work, the individual may come home irritable, short-tempered, and fatigued. This may result in arguments with the spouse. Marital conflict may be a source of subsequent stress that in turn negatively affects job performance. Thus, stress at work and stress away from work are often interrelated. However, our main concern here is with stressors at work.

In order to better understand the link between stressors, stress, and consequences, we have developed an integrative model of stress and work. A managerial perspective is used to develop the parts of the model shown in Figure 7–2. The model divides stressors at work

FIGURE 7-2

Stress and Work: A Working Model

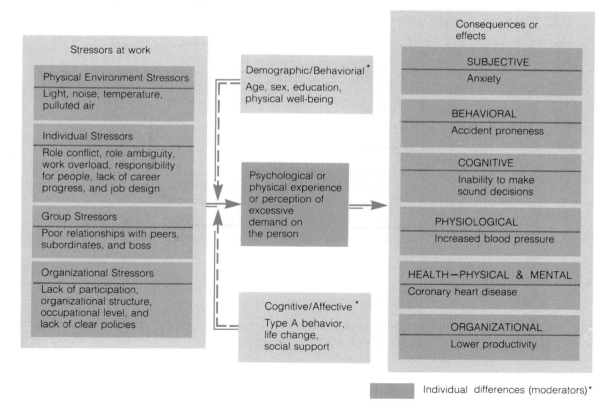

* Only some of these variables will be discussed in the chapter. For a more complete discussion of these stressors and moderators, see John M. Ivancevich and Michael T. Matteson, *Stress and Work: A Managerial Perspective* (Glenview, Ill.: Scott, Foresman, 1980).

into four categories: physical, individual, group, and organizational. The model also presents five potential categories of the effects of stress. In this book, we are concerned primarily with the effects that influence job performance.

The model introduces **moderators**.[5] The moderator variables that have been investigated by occupational stress researchers include age, sex, work addiction, self-esteem, and community involvement. We have elected to discuss the three moderators that have received the most research attention—Type A, life change events, and social support.

moderators
Variables that influence the relationship between two other variables.

Consequences of Stress

The mobilization of the body's defense mechanisms are not the only potential consequences of contact with stressors. The effects of stress are many and varied. Some, of course, are positive, such as self-motivation, stimulation to work harder, and increased inspiration to live a better life. However, many are disruptive and potentially dangerous. Cox has identified five types of potential consequences of effects of stress.[6] His categories include:

Subjective Effects. Anxiety, aggression, apathy, boredom, depression, fatigue, frustration, loss of temper, low self-esteem, nervousness, feeling alone.

Behavioral effects. Accident proneness, alcoholism, drug abuse, emotional outbursts, excessive eating, excessive smoking, impulsive behavior, nervous laughter.

Cognitive effects. Inability to make sound decisions, poor concentration, short attention span, hypersensitivity to criticism, mental blocks.

Physiological effects. Increased blood glucose levels, increased heart rate and blood pressure, dryness of the mouth, sweating, dilation of pupils, hot and cold flashes.

Organizational effects. Absenteeism, turnover, low productivity, alienation from co-workers, job dissatisfaction, reduced organizational commitment and loyalty.

These five types are not all-inclusive; nor are they limited to those effects on which there is universal agreement and for which there is clear scientific evidence. They merely represent some of the potential effects that are frequently associated with stress. It should not be

---

[5] Robert R. Holt, "Occupational Stress," in *Handbook of Stress,* ed. L. Goldberger and S. Breznitz (New York: Free Press, 1982), pp. 419–44.

[6] T. Cox, *Stress* (Baltimore: University Park Press, 1978), p. 92.

inferred, however, that stress always causes the effects listed above.

From a managerial perspective, each of the five categories of stress effects shown in Figure 7–2 is important. However, withdrawal and nonproductive behaviors such as absenteeism, turnover, alcoholism, and drug abuse are specially troublesome in terms of lost productivity and costs.

Withdrawal.   Being absent and quitting are two forms of withdrawal behavior that can temporarily reduce job stress in some cases. Some research indicates a relationship between job stress and absenteeism and turnover. For example, one study indicated that over a 15-year period there was a 22 percent increase in absenteeism attributed to physical health problems, while absenteeism associated with psychological health problems increased 152 percent for men and 302 percent for women.[7]

A study of 175 hospital employees examined stress as a predictor of turnover. Organizational commitment, job satisfaction, and working conditions were unable to predict turnover. However, high levels of stress were a significant predictor of intentions to leave the hospital. The researchers concluded that employees with low stress levels had expectations of longer tenure at the hospital.[8]

Alcoholism.   Alcoholism is a disease characterized by repeated excessive drinking that interferes with an individual's health and work behavior.[9] Probably no one factor can cause alcoholism, which is a complex entity. In terms of costs to society and lost productivity, alcoholism is an expensive disease. The suicide rate among alcoholics is 58 times that of the general public. The cost in terms of workdays lost and talent wasted is estimated at over $10 billion annually.[10] North American Rockwell Corporation, with 100,000 employees, placed the cost of alcoholism to its operations at $250 million. The Illinois Bell Telephone Company sets wage replacements due to alcoholism at $418,500.[11] To curb this type of cost, an increasing number of employers have been establishing alcohol control programs. Over 12,000 occupational helping programs are now being operated in organizations. One successful program is presented in the following Close-up.

---

[7] J. D. Kearns, *Stress in Industry* (London: Priory Press, 1973).

[8] Jack F. McKenna, Paul L. Oritt, and Howard K. Wolff, "Occupational Stress as a Predictor in the Turnover Decision," *Journal of Human Stress*, December 1981, pp. 12–17.

[9] Joseph Follman, *Alcoholics and Business* (New York: American Management Association, 1976).

[10] J. R. Milam and K. Ketcham, *Under the Influence: A Guide to the Myths and Realities of Alcoholism* (Seattle: Madrove Publishers, 1981).

[11] Steven H. Applebaum, "A Human Resources Counseling Model: The Alcoholic Employee," *Personnel Administrator*, August 1982, p. 35.

ORGANIZATIONS: CLOSE-UP

Digital Equipment Corporation's One-Man Gang

Digital Equipment Corporation (DEC) is a $4 billion computer giant with 70,000 employees that has attacked alcoholism and drug abuse problems. Jim Kelly, an employee with an interesting background, is largely responsible for DEC's active participation in helping troubled employees. Kelly is a former drug user, a reformed alcoholic, and an individual who had undergone 10 major abdominal surgeries by the time he was 40 years old. He persuaded DEC management to let him help co-workers who were afflicted with alcohol and drug problems.

Kelly's efforts were highly informal at first. The word was passed around that he was available during lunch and coffee breaks to anyone with an alcohol or drug problem. His informed "counseling center" consisted of a workbench and a few stools set in an inconspicuous corner of the plant. Workers began to visit Kelly once they realized that what they told him would be kept in confidence and that Kelly and the company (which is nonunion) were there to help them. With DEC paying the bills, Kelly earned state certification as an alcoholism counselor.

Kelly now devotes full time to counseling and referring employees who need help. He sees an average of 10 employees a day. His concern and attitude have spread throughout DEC. The organization now has employee assistance programs in 24 other locations, most of which are run by outside professionals.

DEC will not say what the programs cost, and the corporate manager of the programs says that the firm doesn't even bother to guess how much it gains because of them. DEC is one company that has recognized that alcohol and drug problems exist in the workplace. If the problems exist in society, they also exist at DEC and in most organizations across the nation. Recognizing the problems and taking action are the steps that DEC has willingly initiated.

Adapted from "Taking Drugs on the Job," *Newsweek*, August 22, 1983, p. 58.

There are no established correlations of specific types of work stress with the use of alcohol as a response to stress. However, researchers have found that alcoholics have a high need for emotional support, make aggressive demands, show impulsivity with easy decision making, and engage in efforts at control by repression and suppression.[12] Surprisingly, alcoholism is not always accompanied by deteriorating

---

[12] J. C. Finney, D. F. Smith, D. E. Skeeters, and C. Auvenshine, "MMPI and Alcoholic Scales," *Quarterly Journal of Studies on Alcohol*, November 1971, pp. 1055–60.

job performance in the early stages of the disease. As the disease progresses, the quantity and quality of job performance eventually suffer.[13]

Early identification of alcoholism is important because the prognosis for successful treatment is more favorable if treatment is initiated at the early stages of the disease. Managers can look for various signs of alcoholism, which include:

1. Excessive absenteeism patterns: Mondays, Fridays, and days before and after holidays.
2. Unexcused and frequent absences.
3. Tardiness and early departures.
4. Poor judgment and bad decisions.
5. Sloppy personal appearance.
6. Marked increase in nervousness and occasional hand tremors.
7. Marked increase in hospital-medical-surgical claims.

These signs can signal a problem to alert managers. It is important for managers to understand that job stress can contribute to a person's need for and use of alcohol. It is also important for managers to know that professional help needs to be applied early if the individual is to be successfully treated. Furthermore, although the use of alcohol develops in response to stress and serves to alleviate it, as the pattern of use progresses into alcoholism, drinking can become a source of stress.

Drug Abuse. Organizations appear to be finally waking up to the drug abuse problem.[14] Some firms have admitted that drug abuse occurs at work and have been using a variety of means to combat the problem. Drug-sniffing dogs to search work areas are used by Mobay Chemical Corporation in Baytown, Texas. Humphrey & Associates, an electrical firm in Dallas, gives blood tests to anyone who has an accident on the job, and Sunkist Products Group of Ontario, California, requires employees who behave strangely on the job to take urine tests.[15] These types of drug detection programs have their critics and raise some serious legal questions. However, more and more organizations have been getting on the antidrug bandwagon for humanitarian reasons and because of the enormous estimated loss of $16.6 billion annually due to drug abuse.[16]

One of the causes of drug abuse is stress stemming from the job.

---

[13] Mark B. Sobell and Linda C. Sobell, "Functional Analysis of Alcohol Problems," in *Medical Psychology: Contributions to Behavioral Medicine,* ed. C. K. Prokop and L. A. Bradley (New York: Academic Press, 1981), pp. 81–90.

[14] James W. Schreier, "A Survey of Drug Abuse in Organizations," *Personnel Journal,* June 1983, pp. 478–84.

[15] "Taking Drugs on the Job," *Newsweek,* August 22, 1983, p. 53.

[16] Ibid., p. 55.

Stimulants and hallucinogens (e.g., marijuana and cocaine), narcotics (e.g., heroin and Demerol), and sedative-hypnotics (e.g., barbiturates and Valium) are taken by employees across all job categories to relieve job boredom, excessive stress, and related work problems. In order to combat drug abuse, management has to first recognize that work-related stress can lead or contribute to drug abuse. Next, it is in management's interest to combat drug abuse with a humane and effective program. Unfortunately, drug abuse exists not only in the workplace but across society. Combating drugs will require managers to focus primarily on the effects of drug use on job performance. Other suggestions based on the experiences of companies that are fighting the drug abuse problem are:

1. *Establish and communicate a clear policy on drug use.* Management must inform employees about the health and safety risks caused by drugs and the danger posed in the workplace by drug abuse. Management must also communicate that it is determined to obey the law.
2. *Reinforce the drug abuse policy.* Higher level management must back supervisors who enforce the firm's drug policy.
3. *Anticipate the problem, and do not be surprised by it.* A company needs to be aware of the magnitude of the drug abuse problem in society, articulate its drug policy, and enforce that policy consistently.
4. *Maintain good relationships with law enforcement agencies.* The police are needed to take action in cases and should be viewed as a part of the team that is fighting drug abuse in the workplace.
5. *Don't attempt to deal with the problem on your own; seek professional advice.*[17] Most organizations lack the investigative capability and skill needed to investigate and assemble evidence on drug abuse.

Organizations that have developed and implemented antidrug programs have accepted the role of helping employees with drug problems who are willing to seek assistance. This is not only good employee relations; it is also good from an economic standpoint. Retraining, hiring, and arbitration costs are avoided, and a favorable public image results from a well-run antidrug program.[18]

Physical and Mental Health

Of the potential consequences of stress, those classified as physiological are perhaps the most controversial and organizationally dysfunc-

---

[17] Peter B. Bensinger, "Drugs in the Workplace," *Harvard Business Review,* November–December 1982, pp. 48–60.

[18] Research Triangle Institute, *The Study of the Economic Costs to Society of Alcohol, Drugs, and Mental Disorders* (Research Triangle Park, N.C., 1981).

tional. Those who hypothesize a link between stress and physical health problems are, in effect, suggesting that an emotional response is responsible for producing a physical change in an individual.[19] In fact, most medical textbooks attribute between 50 and 75 percent of illness to stress-related origins.[20]

Perhaps the most significant of the potential stress–physical illness relationships is that of coronary heart disease (CHD). Although virtually unknown in the industrialized world 60 years ago, CHD now accounts for half of all deaths in the United States. The disease is so pervasive that American males who are now between the ages of 45 and 55 have one chance in four of dying from a heart attack in the next 10 years.

Traditional risk factors such as obesity, smoking, heredity, high cholesterol, and high blood pressure can account for no more than about 25 percent of the incidence of coronary heart disease. There is growing medical opinion that job and life stress may be a major contributor in the remaining 75 percent.[21]

Even this brief overview of the health consequences of stress would be incomplete without some mention of mental health effects. Kornhauser studied extensively the mental health of industrial workers.[22] He did not find a relationship between mental health and such factors as salary, job security, and working conditions. Instead, clear associations between mental health and job satisfaction emerged. Poor mental health was associated with frustration growing out of not having a satisfying job.

In addition to frustration, the anxiety and depression that may be experienced by individuals under a great deal of stress may manifest itself in the form of alcoholism (about 5 percent of the adult population are problem drinkers), drug dependency (over 150 million tranquilizer prescriptions are written in the United States annually), hospitalization (over 25 percent of occupied hospital beds have people with psychological problems), and, in extreme cases, suicide.[23] Even the relatively minor mental disruptions produced by stress, such as the inability to concentrate or reduced problem-solving capabilities, may prove very costly to an organization.

Before we examine parts of the stress and work model in more

[19] P. Astrand and K. Rodahl, *Textbook of Work Physiology* (New York: McGraw-Hill, 1970).

[20] M. H. Brenner, "The Stressful Price of Prosperity," *Science News,* March 18, 1978, p. 166.

[21] David C. Glass, *Behavior Patterns, Stress, and Coronary Disease* (Hillsdale, N.J.: Erlbaum Associates, 1977), pp. 5–6.

[22] A. Kornhauser, *Mental Health of the Industrialized Worker* (New York: John Wiley & Sons, 1965).

[23] Herbert Peyser, "Stress and Alcohol," in *Handbook of Stress,* ed L. Goldberger and S. Breznitz (New York: Free Press, 1982), p. 586.

detail, several caveats are in order. This model, or any model attempting to integrate stress and work phenomena, is not totally complete. There are so many important variables that a complete treatment would require much more space. Furthermore, the variables that will be discussed are offered only as ones that provide managerial perspectives on stress. They are certainly not the only appropriate variables to consider. Finally, accurate and reliable measurement is extremely important because management-initiated programs to manage stress at optimal levels will depend on how well these and other variables are measured.[24]

Physical Environmental Stressors

Physical environment stressors are often termed *blue-collar stressors* because they are more a problem in blue-collar occupations.[25] Over 14,000 workers die annually in industrial accidents (nearly 55 a day, or 7 people every working hour); over 100,000 workers are permanently disabled every year; and employees report more than 5 million occupational injuries annually.[26] New estimates of the toll of workplace chemicals, radiation, heat stress, pesticides, and other toxic materials lead the National Institute of Occupational Safety and Health (NIOSH) to estimate that about 100,000 workers may die annually from industrial diseases that could have been prevented.

Many blue-collar workers are nervous and stressed by the alleged health consequences of working in their present jobs. Since the passage in 1970 of the Occupational Safety and Health Act (OSHA), some of the stress experienced by individuals has been reduced. Gains can be traced to employers' increased acceptance of OSHA regulations. In addition, many unions enthusiastically support the act. Problems still exist, and management is now being held responsible by the courts for stress that is related to the physical and general work environment. Jury compensation awards to workers have become more widespread. The following Close-Up illustrates the increasing role of the courts in job stress cases. We expect the courts' role to become even more significant in the future.[27]

---

[24] Roy Payne, Todd D. Jick, and Ronald J. Burke, "Whiter Stress Research? An Agenda for the 1980s," *Journal of Occupational Behavior,* January 1982, pp. 131–45.

[25] E. C. Poulton, "Blue-Collar Stressors," in *Stress at Work,* ed. C. L. Cooper and R. Payne (New York: John Wiley & Sons, 1978), pp. 51–80.

[26] Arthur B. Shostak, *Blue-Collar Stressors* (Reading, Mass.: Addison-Wesley Publishing, 1980), p. 19.

[27] John M. Ivancevich and Michael T. Matteson, "Employee Claims for Damages Add to the High Cost of Job Stress," *Management Review,* November 1982, pp. 9–13.

ORGANIZATIONS: CLOSE-UP

Job Stress Is Now a Legal Issue

Feeling stress on the job? File a claim!

Many workers are, and they're winning workers' compensation payments for emotional illness traced to the pressures of their jobs.

"It's a major concern for employers and insurance companies," says Andre Maisonpierre, vice president of the Alliance of American Insurers, a trade group. He warns that psychiatric injury awards "could have some major cost implications."

Following court decisions, about 15 states now make disability payments in cases where severe anxiety, depression, or other mental problems have been caused by work stress. The most common, clear-cut case is compensation for the shock suffered when a worker sees a co-worker fall to his or her death.

In one significant case, the Michigan Supreme Court recently granted lifetime workers' compensation to a General Motors Corporation parts inspector who was considered to be a "compulsive perfectionist." He suffered mental strain when assembly-line workers insisted on installing parts that he had labeled defective.

Are stress claims valid? Answers vary. Consider some cases in which workers won compensation.

A Burroughs Corporation secretary became hysterical when her boss constantly criticized her for going to the bathroom too often. She said he also asked prying questions about her new husband's family. The state workers' disability compensation bureau awarded her $7,000. Her attorney hopes to get a larger settlement from an appeal board.

After working with radioactive materials for 30 years and developing cancer in one eye, a Los Alamos Scientific Laboratory technician feared that he would die from the exposure. The New Mexico Supreme Court decided that his anxiety neurosis had totally disabled him; he received $75,000.

A Maine state trooper's duties involved cruising around a quiet, rural area. But he became severely depressed because he was on call 24 hours a day. He claimed that his home life deteriorated because he never knew when the phone would ring. The state supreme court approved the officer's claim for total, permanent disability, but the attorney general asked the court to reconsider—and then settled out of court for $5,000.

Source: Joann S. Lublin, "On-the-Job Stress Leads Many Workers to File—and Win—Compensation Awards," *The Wall Street Journal*, September 17, 1980.

Individual Stressors

individual stressors
Stressors that have a direct and indirect impact on the individual are classified as individual-level stressors.

Stressors at the individual level have been studied more than any other category presented in Figure 7–2. Role conflict is perhaps the most widely studied **individual stressor.**[28] **Role conflict** is present whenever compliance by an individual to one set of expectations about the job is in conflict with compliance to another set of expectations. Facets of role conflict include being torn by conflicting demands from a supervisor about the job, and being pressured to get along well with people with whom you are not compatible. Regardless of whether role conflict results from organizational policies or from other persons, it can be a significant stressor for some individuals.

role conflict
An employee is faced with role conflict when two or more sets of expectations are in conflict with one another.

Kahn et al. report on an interview survey of a national sample of male wage and salary employees that revealed that 48 percent of the participants experienced role conflict.[29] In a study at Goddard Space Flight Center, it was determined that about 67 percent of the employees reported some role conflict. The study also found that workers who suffered more role conflict had lower job satisfaction and higher job-related tension.[30] It is interesting to note that the researchers also found that the greater the power or authority of the people sending the conflicting role messages, the greater was the job dissatisfaction produced by role conflict. A larger and more medically oriented study found that for white-collar workers role conflict was related to abnormal electrocardiographic readings.[31] In Chapter 8, "Group Behavior," we shall see that role conflict is also important in the conflict that occurs within groups.

role ambiguity
Not knowing what to do, being confused, and being unsure is called role ambiguity.

In order to perform their jobs well, employees need certain information regarding what they are expected to do and not to do. Employees need to know their rights, privileges, and obligations. **Role ambiguity** is a lack of understanding about the rights, privileges, and obligations that a person has for doing the job. Studies have addressed the question of role ambiguity. In the study at Goddard Space Flight Center, administrators, engineers, and scientists completed a role ambiguity stress scale. Blood samples, blood pressure, and pulse rate readings were obtained.[32] It was found that role ambiguity was significantly related to low job satisfaction and to feelings of job-related threat to one's

---

[28] John R. P. French and Robert D. Caplan, "Organizational Stress and Individual Strain," in *The Failure of Success*, ed. J. Marrow (New York: AMACOM, 1973), pp. 30–66.

[29] R. L. Kahn, D. M. Wolfe, R. P. Quinn, J. D. Snoek, and R. A. Rosenthal, *Organizational Stress: Studies in Role Conflict and Ambiguity* (New York: John Wiley & Sons, 1964), p. 94.

[30] Ibid.

[31] John R. P. French and Robert D. Caplan, "Psychosocial Factors in Coronary Heart Disease," *Industrial Medicine*, September 1970, pp. 383–97.

[32] Kahn et al., *Organizational Stress*.

mental and physical well-being. Furthermore, the more ambiguity a person reported, the lower was the person's utilization of intellectual skills, knowledge, and leadership skills.

Everyone has experienced *work overload* at one time or another. Overload may be of two different types: quantitative or qualitative. Having too many things to do or insufficient time to complete a job is *quantitative* overload. *Qualitative* overload, on the other hand, occurs when individuals feel that they lack the ability needed to complete their jobs or that performance standards are too high.

From a health standpoint, studies as far back as 1958 established that quantitative overload might cause biochemical changes, specifically, elevations in blood cholesterol levels.[33] It has also been suggested that overload is most harmful to those who experience the lowest job satisfaction.[34] Still another study found overload to be associated with lowered confidence, decreased work motivation, and increased absenteeism. Overload may also be indirectly responsible for decreases in decision-making quality, deteriorating interpersonal relations, and increases in accidents.[35]

One study examined the relationship of overload, underload, and stress among 1,540 executives of a major corporation. Those executives in the low and high ends of the stress ranges reported and had more significant medical problems. This study suggests that the relationship between stressors, stress, and disease may be curvilinear. That is, those who are underloaded and those who are overloaded represent two ends of a continuum, each with a significantly elevated number of medical problems.[36] The underload/overload continuum is presented in Figure 7–3. The optimal stress level provides the best balance of challenge, responsibility, and reward.

Any type of *responsibility* can be a burden for some people. Different types of responsibility apparently function differently as stressors. One way of categorizing this variable is in terms of responsibility for people versus responsibility for things. The intensive care unit nurse, the neurosurgeon, and the air traffic controller each have a high responsibility for people. One study found support for the hypothesis that responsibility for people contributes to job-related stress.[37] The more responsibility for people reported, the more likely the person was to

---

[33] B. L. Margolis, W. M. Kroes, and R. P. Quinn, "Job Stress: An Untested Occupational Hazard," *Journal of Occupational Medicine,* October 1974, pp. 659–61.

[34] Stephen M. Sales, "Organizational Role as a Risk Factor in Coronary Disease," *Administration Science Quarterly,* September 1969, pp. 325–36.

[35] S. Kasl, "Work and the Mental Health," in *Work and Quality of Life,* ed. James O'Toole (Cambridge, Mass.: MIT Press, 1974), pp. 171–96.

[36] Clinton Weiman, "A Study of Occupational Stressors and the Incidence of Disease/Risk," *Journal of Occupational Medicine,* February 1977, pp. 119–22.

[37] French and Caplan, "Psychosocial Factors," p. 387.

FIGURE 7–3

The Underload/Overload Continuum

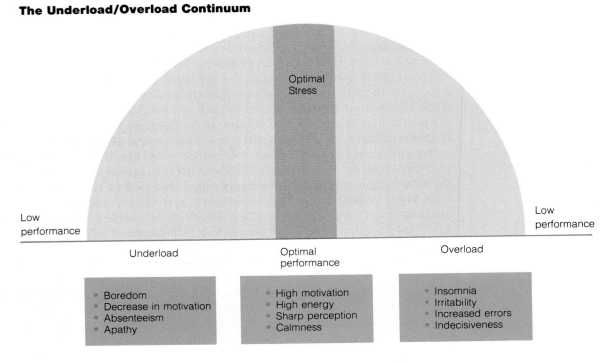

smoke heavily, have high blood pressure, and show elevated cholesterol levels. Conversely, the more responsibility for things the employee reported, the lower were these indicators.

Group Stressors

The effectiveness of any organization is influenced by the nature of the relations among groups. There are many group characteristics that can be powerful stressors for some individuals. A number of behavioral scientists have suggested that good relationships among the members of a work group are a central factor in individual well-being.[38] Poor relations include low trust, low supportiveness, and low interest in listening to and trying to deal with the problems that confront an employee.[39] Studies in this area have reached the same conclusion: mistrust of the persons one works with is positively related to high

[38] Chris Argyris, *Integrating the Individual and the Organization* (New York: John Wiley & Sons, 1964); and Cary L. Cooper, *Group Training and Organizational Development* (Basel, Switzerland: Karger, 1973).

[39] French and Caplan, "Psychosocial Factors."

role ambiguity, which leads to inadequate communications among people and low job satisfaction.

Organizational Stressors

A problem in the study of organizational stressors is identifying which are the most important ones. Participation in decision making is considered to be an important part of working within organizations for some individuals. *Participation* refers to the extent that a person's knowledge, opinions, and ideas are included in the decision process. Participation can contribute to stress. Some people may be frustrated by the delays often associated with participative decision making. Others may view shared decision making as a threat to the traditional right of a supervisor or manager to have the final say.

Organizational structure is another stressor that has rarely been studied. One available study of trade salespersons examined the effects of tall (bureaucratically structured), medium, and flat (less rigidly structured) arrangements on job satisfaction, stress, and performance. It was determined that salespersons in the least bureaucratically structured arrangement experienced less stress and more job satisfaction and performed more effectively than did salespersons in the medium and tall structures.[40]

A number of studies have examined the relationship of organizational level to health effects. The majority of these studies suggest the notion that the risk of contracting such health problems as coronary heart disease increases with organizational level.[41] Not all researchers, however, support the notion that the higher one is in an organization hierarchy, the greater is the health risk. A study of Du Pont employees found that the incidence of heart disease was inversely related to salary level.[42]

The nature of the classifications used in these studies has contributed to the confusion of the results.[43] The trend now is to look in more detail at significant job components, as a way of explaining the effects of stress. Several studies, for example, have tried to assess whether inactivity or increased intellectual and emotional job demands contribute most to the increased risk of coronary heart disease. One early

---

[40] John M. Ivancevich and James H. Donnelly, "Relation of Organizational Structure to Job Satisfaction, Anxiety-Stress, and Performance," *Administrative Science Quarterly,* June 1975, pp. 272–80.

[41] R. V. Marks, "Social Stress and Cardiovascular Disease," *Milbank Memorial Fund Quarterly,* April 1976, pp. 51–107.

[42] S. Pell and C. A. D'Alonzo, "Myocardial Infarction in a One-Year Industrial Study," *Journal of the American Medical Association,* June 1958, pp. 332–37.

[43] Cary L. Cooper and Judi Marshall, "Occupational Sources of Stress: A Review of the Literature Relating to Coronary Heart Disease and Mental Ill Health," *Journal of Occupational Psychology,* March 1976, pp. 11–28.

study contributed to this form of analysis in that it found that downtown bus drivers (sedentary jobs) and conductors (active jobs) had higher coronary heart disease than did their suburban counterparts.[44] More research is needed to determine whether emotional job demands are more powerful than inactivity in explaining the incidence of health problems.

We have considered only a very small sample of the tremendous amount of behavioral and medical research that is available on stressor, stress, and effects linkages. The information available, like other organizational research, is contradictory in some cases. However, what is available implies a number of important points. These points are:

1. There is a relationship between stressors at work and physical, psychological, and emotional changes in individuals.
2. The adaptive responses to stressors at work have been measured by self-rating, performance appraisals, and biochemical tests. Much more work must be done in properly measuring stress at work.
3. There is no universally acceptable list of stressors. Each organization has its own unique set that should be examined.
4. Individual differences explain why the same stressor that is disruptive and unsettling to one person is challenging to another person.

MODERATORS

Stressors evoke different responses from different people. Some individuals are better able to cope with a stressor than others; they can adapt their behavior in such a way as to meet the stressor head-on. On the other hand, some individuals are predisposed to stress; that is, they are not able to adapt to the stressor.

The model presented in Figure 7–2 suggests that various factors moderate the relationship between stressors and stress. A moderator is a condition, behavior, or characteristic that qualifies the relationship between two variables. The effect may be to intensify or weaken the relationship. The relationship between the number of gallons of gasoline used and total miles driven, for example, is affected by the variable speed (a moderator). Likewise, an individual's personality may moderate or affect the extent to which that individual experiences stress as a consequence of being in contact with a particular stressor.

Type A Behavior Pattern (TABP)

Cardiovascular disease is the leading cause of death in the United States. Nearly 1 million Americans die of cardiovascular disease each

[44] J. N. Morris et al., "Coronary Heart Disease and Physical Activity at Work: Coronary Heart Disease in Different Occupations," *Lancet*, October 1953, pp. 1053–57.

year, and more than 40 million Americans are afflicted with some form of the disease.[45]

In the 1950s, two medical cardiologists and researchers, Meyer Friedman and Ray Rosenman, discovered what they called the **Type A Behavior Pattern** (TABP).[46] They searched the medical literature and found that traditional coronary risk factors such as dietary cholesterol, blood pressure, and heredity could not totally explain or predict coronary heart disease (CHD). Coronary heart disease is the term given to cardiovascular diseases that are characterized by an inadequate supply of oxygen to the heart. Other factors seemed to them to be playing a major role in CHD. Through interviews with, and observation of, patients, they began to uncover a pattern of behavior or traits. They eventually called this the Type A Behavior Pattern (TABP).

The person with TABP has these characteristics:

Chronically struggles to get as many things done as possible in the shortest time period.

Is aggressive, ambitious, competitive, and forceful.

Speaks explosively, rushes others to finish what they are saying.

Is impatient, hates to wait, considers waiting a waste of precious time.

Is preoccupied with deadlines and is work-oriented.

Is always in a struggle, with people, things, events.

The converse Type B individual is mainly free of the TABP characteristics and generally feels no pressing conflict with either time or persons. The Type B may have considerable drive, wants to accomplish things, and works hard. The Type B has a confident style that allows him or her to work at a steady pace and not to race against the clock. The Type A has been likened to a racehorse, the Type B to a turtle.

As cardiologists, Friedman and Rosenman observed numerous coronary patients, most of whom were Type As. One incident highlighted to them what individuals with TABP were like. They called an upholsterer to fix the seats and chairs in their reception room. After inspecting the chairs, the man asked what sort of physicians they were. They informed him that they were cardiologists. He then told them that he noticed a peculiar thing about the wear and tear on the office furniture. Only the front edge of each seat was worn out. Friedman and Rosenman interpreted this to indicate the impatience of their patients sitting on the edge of their seats to see the doctor. Type As would tend to do such things while waiting impatiently in an office. Since the early work of Friedman and Rosenman on TABP, a number

Type A Behavior Pattern Individual characteristics such as aggressiveness, impatience, competitiveness, and explosive speech indicate what is called the Type A Behavior Pattern.

---

[45] Virginia A. Price, *Type A Behavior Pattern* (New York: Academic Press, 1982), p. 3.

[46] Meyer Friedman and Ray H. Rosenman, *Type A Behavior and Your Heart* (New York; Alfred A. Knopf, 1974).

of studies have found it to be a significant predictor of premature CHD.[47] In fact, recent literature reviews and studies strongly suggest that Type A individuals have approximately twice the risk of developing CHD as Type B individuals.[48] Furthermore, this doubled CHD risk factor for Type A persons is independent of the influence of the traditional coronary risk factors.

Western Collaborative Group Study. A longitudinal study called the Western Collaborative Study was initiated in the early 1960s. This study used over 3,000 employees from 11 corporations. It is an excellent example of some of the research that has been done to study TABP. The subjects (all male, ages 39 to 59) were free of coronary disease at the start of the study. Each year they underwent a physical exam and their behavior patterns were assessed.

The first follow-up data were reported after 2½ years.[49] Of the original sample, 70 participants had heart disease and 77 percent of these were Type As (compared with 50 percent for the entire sample). The TABP was particularly predictive for the younger subjects. In the 39- to 49-year-old group, Type A men experienced 6½ times the incidence of heart disease that Type Bs did.

The data after 4½ years of follow-up included 133 participants with heart disease.[50] The predictive link between coronary problems and Type A behavior was still present. It was also found that at the eight-year data point Type A men had more than twice the rate of coronary disease that Type B men did.

Type A Measurement. Several methods have been developed for assessing TABP. Self-report scales and structured interview procedures are the most popular.[51] Friedman and Rosenman strongly urge the use of their structured interview. For example, individuals are asked about their reactions to working with a slow partner and to waiting in long lines. The interviewer also asks challenging questions, and assesses voice stylistics, nonverbal mannerisms, and verbal con-

---

[47] For a thorough review and appraisal, see Karen A. Matthews, "Psychological Perspectives on the Type A Behavior Pattern," *Psychological Bulletin,* March 1982, pp. 293–323; and Michael T. Matteson and John M. Ivancevich, "The Coronary-Prone Behavior Pattern: A Review and Appraisal," *Social Science and Medicine,* July 1980, pp. 337–51.

[48] Ibid., p. 343.

[49] R. H. Rosenman, M. Friedman, W. Straus, M. Wurm, R. Kositchek, W. Hahn, and N. T. Werthessen, "A Predictive Study of Coronary Heart Disease," *Journal of the American Medical Association,* February 1964, pp. 15–22.

[50] R. Rosenman et al., "Coronary Heart Disease in the Western Collaborative Group Study: A Follow-Up Experience of 4½ Years," *Journal of Chronic Diseases,* April 1970, pp. 173–d90.

[51] James M. MacDougall, Theodore M. Dembroski, and Linda Musante, "The Structured Interview and Questionnaire Methods of Assessing Coronary-Prone Behavior in Male and Female College Students," *Journal of Behavioral Medicine,* March 1979, pp. 71–84.

tent. Two widely used self-report scales are the 10-item Framingham Type A scale and the 50-item Jenkins Activity Survey. The structured interview, Framingham, and Jenkins measures all appear to be reliable. On the other hand, the association among the three measures, which supposedly measure the same construct, is less than impressive. Thus, it is incorrect to assume that the three most popular Type A measures assess the same aspect of the behavior pattern.[52]

Susceptible Type A Individuals. Research is being conducted to determine which individual differences are associated with Type A tendencies. There are some indications that TABP is associated with age. In one study of males and females, it was found that the older half of the sample had lower mean Type A scores.[53] In a similar study, the 36- to 55-year-old group had the strongest Type A tendencies.[54]

Some research has found that TABP is more prevalent in males than in females.[55] However, as more women enter the work force and move into nontraditional roles for females (e.g., top-level management, project directors, research engineers, legal counsel), it is expected that TABP will become increasingly common among women. Even today, studies show that there is a strong association between TABP in women and the onset of coronary heart disease.[56] Interestingly, one study revealed that, unlike men, working women showed maximum Type A scores between the ages of 30 and 35 years.[57] The researchers suggested that this "age peak" was due to the fact that more Type B females tended to leave their jobs when having children before the age of 30. Therefore, it was the Type A women who tended to continue with their careers.

For the most part, the research to date on TABP has shown association of TABP with CHD, but not a cause and effect relationship between them. Thus, specific predictions are not advised at this time. Furthermore, few studies have thus far focused on women, and virtually none have examined the extent to which Type A behavior constitutes a risk factor among blacks, Mexican-Americans, and other minority populations. There are also critics of the methods used to classify

---

[52] Matthews, "Psychological Perspectives," p. 296.

[53] M. A. Chesney and R. H. Rosenman, "Type A Behavior in the Work Setting," in *Current Concerns in Occupational Stress,* ed. C. Cooper and R. Payne (New York: John Wiley & Sons, 1980), pp. 187–212.

[54] J. H. Howard, D. A. Cunningham, and P. A. Rechnitzer, "Work Patterns Associated with Type A Behavior: A Managerial Population," *Human Relations,* September 1977, pp. 825–36.

[55] I. Waldron, "The Coronary-Prone Behavior Pattern, Blood Pressure, and Socio-Economic Studies in Women," *Journal of Psychosomatic Research,* March 1978, pp. 79–87.

[56] Chesney and Rosenman, "Type A Behavior."

[57] I. Waldron, S. Zyzanski, R. B. Shekelle, et al., "The Coronary Prone Behavior Pattern in Employed Men and Women," *Journal of Human Stress,* January 1977, pp. 2–18.

people as Type A or Type B. These critics claim that the classification system is based on faulty measurement and subjective conclusions.[58]

The accumulated evidence at this point strongly suggests that managers attempting to manage stress should include TABP in their assessments. Failure to include TABP would ignore some of the better interdisciplinary research (behavioral and medical) that has been conducted over the past 25 years. Of all the moderators that could or should be included in a stress model, TABP seems to be one of the most promising for additional consideration.

Life Change Events

There is a commonsense proposition that when individuals undergo extremely stressful changes in their lives, their personal health is likely eventually to suffer. Research work on this intriguing proposition was initiated by Holmes and Rahe.[59] Their work led to the development of the Schedule of Recent Life Events, of which a later version was titled the Social Readjustment Rating Scale (SRRS). Through research and analysis, Holmes and Rahe weighted the SRRS. An individual is asked to indicate which of the listed events has happened to him or her in the past 12 months. The SRRS is presented in Table 7–1.

life change units
Each of us undergoes changes. Adding up the changes in the form of life change units (LCUs) and weighting the LCUs can predict future health, according to two researchers, Holmes and Rahe.

Holmes and Rahe found that individuals reporting **life change units** totaling 150 points or less generally had good health the following year. However, those reporting life change units totaling between 150 and 300 points had about a 50 percent chance of developing a serious illness the following year. And among individuals scoring 300 or more points, there was at least a 70 percent chance of contracting a major illness the following year.

The relationships found between life change event scores and personal health problems have not been overwhelming.[60] The correlations in most studies between the total score and major health problems the following year have been relatively low.[61] Of course, many individuals who are exposed to many life changes show absolutely no subsequent health problems. That is, they are hardy enough to withstand the consequences of life changes.

---

[58] J. J. Ray and R. Bozek, "Dissecting the A–B Personality Type," *British Journal of Medical Psychology*, June 1980, pp. 181–86.

[59] T. H. Holmes and R. H. Rahe, "Social Readjustment Rating Scale," *Journal of Psychosomatic Research*, 1967, pp. 213–18.

[60] Scott M. Monroe, "Major and Minor Life Events as Predictors of Psychological Distress: Further Issues and Findings," *Journal of Behavioral Medicine*, June 1983, pp. 189–205.

[61] David V. Perkins, "The Assessment of Stress Using Life Events Scales," in *Handbook of Stress*, ed. L. Goldberger and S. Breznitz (New York: Free Press, 1982), pp. 320–31.

TABLE 7–1

Social Readjustment Rating Scale

Rank	Life Event	Mean Value
1	Death of spouse	100
2	Divorce	73
3	Marital separation	65
4	Jail term	63
5	Death of close family member	63
6	Personal injury or illness	53
7	Marriage	50
8	Fired at work	47
9	Marital reconciliation	45
10	Retirement	45
11	Change in health of family member	44
12	Pregnancy	40
13	Sex difficulties	39
14	Gain of new family member	39
15	Business readjustment	39
16	Change in financial state	38
17	Death of close friend	37
18	Change to different line of work	36
19	Change in number of arguments with spouse	35
20	Mortgage over $10,000	31
21	Foreclosure of mortgage or loan	30
22	Change in responsibilities at work	29
23	Son or daughter leaving home	29
24	Trouble with in-laws	29
25	Outstanding personal achievement	28
26	Wife beginning or stopping work	26
27	Beginning or ending school	26
28	Change in living conditions	25
29	Revision of personal habits	24
30	Trouble with boss	23
31	Change in work hours or conditions	20
32	Change in residence	20
33	Change in schools	20
34	Change in recreation	19
35	Change in church activities	19
36	Change in social activities	18
37	Mortgage or loan less than $10,000	17
38	Change in sleeping habits	16
39	Change in number of family get-togethers	15
40	Change in eating habits	15
41	Vacation	13
42	Christmas	12
43	Minor violations of the law	11

The amount of life stress that a person has experienced in a given period of time, say one year, is measured by the total number of life change units (LCUs). These units result from the addition of the values (shown in the right-hand column) associated with events that the person has experienced during the target time period.

Source: Thomas H. Holmes and Richard H. Rahe, "The Social Readjustment Rating Scale," *Journal of Psychosomatic Research,* 1967, pp. 213–18.

Kobasa proposed that individuals who experienced high life change unit scores without becoming ill might differ, in terms of personality, from individuals who had subsequent health problems.[62] She refers to the personality characteristic as "hardiness." The individuals with the hardiness personality seem to possess three important characteristics. First, they believe that they can control the events they encounter. Second, they are extremely committed to the activities in their lives. Third, they treat change in their lives as a challenge.

In a longitudinal study to test the three-characteristic theory of hardiness, managers were studied over a two-year period. It was determined that the more managers possessed hardiness characteristics, the smaller was the negative impact of life change units on their personal health.[63] Hardiness appeared to buffer the negative impact of life changes.

Social Support

social support
Supportive co-workers enable us to cope with job-related stress.

Numerous literature reviews link social support with many aspects of health, illness, and quality of life.[64] The literature offers a number of definitions of social support. Some of these definitions focus on the exchange of information or material, the availability of a confidant, and gratification of basic social needs. **Social support** is defined as the comfort, assistance, or information that one receives through formal or informal contacts with individuals or groups.[65] This definition would apply to a co-worker listening to a friend who failed to receive a desired promotion, a group of recently laid-off workers helping each other find new employment, or an experienced employee helping a new hiree learn a job.

Social support has been operationalized as the number of people one interacts with, the frequency of contact with other individuals, or the individual's perceptions about the adequacy of interpersonal contact. The limited amount of research using these operationalizations suggests that social support protects or buffers individuals from the negative consequences of stressors. One study showed significant interactions of social support and work stress for factory workers.

[62] S. C. Kobasa, "Stressful Life Events, Personality, and Health: An Inquiry Into Hardiness," *Journal of Personality and Social Psychology,* January 1979, pp. 1–11.

[63] S. C. Kobasa, S. R. Maddi, and S. Kahn, "Hardiness and Health: A Prospective Study," *Journal of Personality and Social Psychology,* January 1982, pp. 168–77.

[64] R. D. Caplan, "Patient, Provider, and Organization: Hypothesized Determinants of Adherence," *New Directions in Patient Compliance,* ed. S. J. Cohen (Lexington, Mass.: D. C. Heath, 1979); and W. B. Carveth and B. H. Gottlieb, "The Measurement of Social Support and Its Relation to Stress," *Canadian Journal of Behavioral Science,* July 1979, pp. 179–88.

[65] Barbara S. Wallston, Sheryle W. Alagna, Brenda M. DeVellis, and Robert F. DeVellis, "Social Support and Physical Health," *Health Psychology,* Fall 1983, pp. 367–91.

The support of co-workers moderated the relationship between role conflict and health complaints.[66] The higher the level of social support reported, the fewer were the health complaints reported.

The best evidence to date on the importance of social support derives from the literature on rehabilitation, recovery, and adaptation to illness.[67] For example, better outcomes have been found in alcohol treatment programs when the alcoholic's family was supportive and cohesive.[68] Managerial use of social support research in reducing stress will be expanded as more organizationally based research is conducted.[69]

ORGANIZATIONAL PROGRAMS TO MANAGE STRESS

An astute manager never ignores a turnover or absenteeism problem, workplace drug abuse, a decline in performance, reduced quality in production, or any other sign that the organization's performance goals are not being met. The effective manager, in fact, views these occurrences as symptoms and looks beyond them to identify and correct the underlying causes. Yet most managers today are likely to search for traditional causes such as poor training, defective equipment, or inadequate instructions on what needs to be done. In all likelihood, stress is not on the list of possible problems. Thus, the very first step in any program to manage stress so that it remains within tolerable limits is recognition that it exists. Any intervention program to manage stress must first determine whether stress exists and what is contributing to its existence. A few examples of organizational programs will be presented in this section.

Role Analysis and Clarification

In the model presented in Figure 7–2, the importance of how the employee sees the job is highlighted. Is it clear? What is expected of me? Can I do a good job with these expectations? These and similar questions emphasize the role that a person is expected to perform.

[66] J. M. La Rocco, J. S. House, and J. R. P. French, "Social Support, Occupational Stress, and Health." *Journal of Health and Social Behavior,* June 1980, pp. 202–18.

[67] R. E. Mitchell, A. G. Billings, and R. H. Moos, "Social Support and Well Being: Implications for Prevention Programs," *Journal of Primary Prevention,* February 1982, pp. 77–98; and E. L. Cowen, "Help Is Where You Find It: Four Informal Helping Groups," *American Psychologist,* April 1982, pp. 385–95.

[68] Benjamin H. Gottlieb, *Social Support Strategies* (Beverly Hills, Calif.: Sage Publications, 1983).

[69] James J. House, Work Stress and Social Support (Reading, Mass.: Addison-Wesley Publishing, 1981).

It has been suggested that when excessive stress exists in a role, adaptive responses can be initiated by management. Three such responses are: to redefine the person's role, to reduce role overload by redistributing the work, and to implement procedures for reducing stress when it occurs (e.g., allow the employee to have a meeting with those who are causing problems so that a solution can be worked out).[70]

Each of these methods attempts to improve the fit between the person in a particular role and the job or organizational environment. This same logic is used in job enrichment programs. Job enrichment involves redefining and restructuring a job so as to make it more meaningful, challenging, and intrinsically rewarding (see Chapter 13). In the context of job stress, the objective of job enrichment is to make the job more stimulating and challenging. The jobholder would be assigned tasks that are intrinsically rewarding, and a fit between the person and the job would result.

Company-Wide Programs

Stress-management programs can be offered on a company-wide basis. Some programs indicate the specific problem on which they are focused: alcohol or drug abuse program, job relocation program, career counseling program, and so forth. Others are more general: the Emotional Health Program of Equitable Life, the Employee Assistance Center at B. F. Goodrich, the Illinois Bell Health Evaluation Program, and the Caterpillar Tractor Special Health Services.[71]

Originally, labels such as mental health were used. However, to get away from the connotation of serious psychiatric disease, companies have changed the names of their programs. Today a popular name is stress-management. Two prototypes of stress-management programs appear to be in use: clinical and organizational. The former is initiated by the firm and focuses on individual problems. The latter deals with units or groups in the work force and focuses on problems of the group or the total organization.

Clinical Programs. These programs are based on the traditional medical approach to treatment. Some of the elements in the programs include:

Diagnosis. Person with problem asks for help. Person or people in employee health unit attempt to diagnose problem.

Treatment. Counseling or supportive therapy is provided. If staff within company can't help, employee is referred to professionals in community.

---

[70] French and Caplan, "Organizational Stress."

[71] Andrew J. J. Brenna, "Worksite Health Promotion Can Be Cost Effective," *Personnel Administrator,* April 1983, pp. 39–42.

Screening. Periodic examination of individuals in highly stressful jobs is provided to detect early indications of problems.

Prevention. Education and persuasion is used to convince employees at high risk that something must be done to help them cope with stress.

Clincial programs must be staffed by competent personnel if they are to provide benefits. The trust and respect of users must be earned. This is possible if a qualified staff exists to provide diagnosis, treatment, screening, and prevention. An example of one organization's stress-management program is outlined in the following Close-Up.

ORGANIZATIONS: CLOSE-UP

Kaiser-Permanente's Management of Stress Program

Kaiser-Permanente, a health maintenance organization (HMO), is using a clinical/organizational hybrid type of stress preventive program for staff personnel at its Los Angeles Medical Center. The original program was developed by a physician, a private therapist, a nurse, and psychiatric personnel. So far it has been available to nursing directors and supervisors, middle-level managers, and a group of physicians and nurses.

The program takes place over four consecutive days (eight hours twice and four hours twice) and combines educational and experiential components. Two principal sources of stress are emphasized—intrapersonal (from within individual employees) and interpersonal.

In lectures and seminars, the participants are given a basic understanding of the mechanics of stress, its sources, and its consequences. Principles of illness prevention are discussed, and the group is taught relaxation and breathing techniques to lower the "stress response threshold." In addition, the participants engage in role playing, psychodrama, and assertiveness training.

Each participant is given cassette tapes with relaxation instructions, a Stress Symptom Checklist, and materials for constructing his or her own stress profile. The participants are instructed to keep daily stress journals, recording situations (stressors) that arouse stress, the symptoms evoked, and other factors.

These diaries are kept for four weeks following the workshops; then the participants meet in a follow-up session to review what was learned, how they coped, and what they will do next.

Source: Philip Goldberg, *Executive Health* (New York: McGraw-Hill, 1978), p. 240.

Organizational Programs. Organizational programs are aimed more broadly at an entire employee population. They are sometimes extensions of the clinical program. Often they are stimulated by problems identified in a group or a unit or by some impending change such as the relocation of a plant, the closing of a plant, or the installation of new equipment. Such programs are found in IBM, Dow Chemical, Control Data, and Equitable Life.

A variety of programs can be used to manage work stress. Included in a list of such organizational programs would be management by objectives, organizational development programs, job enrichment, redesigning the structure of the organization, establishing autonomous work groups, establishing variable work schedules, and providing employee health facilities. For example, such companies as Xerox, Rockwell International, Weyerhaeuser, and Pepsi-Cola are spending thousands of dollars for gyms equipped with treadmills, exercise bicycles, jogging tracks, and full-time physical educational and health care staffs. One of the more impressive programs is found at Kimberly-Clark, where $2.5 million has been invested in a 7,000-square-foot health testing facility and a 32,000-square-foot physical fitness facility staffed by 15 full-time health care personnel.[72]

INDIVIDUAL APPROACHES TO STRESS

There are also a vast variety of individual approaches to managing stress. To see this, all one has to do is visit any bookstore and look at the self-improvement section. It will be stocked with numerous "how to do it" books for reducing stress. We have selected only a few of the more popularly cited methods for individually managing stress. They have been selected because (1) some research is available on their impact, (2) they are widely cited in both the scientific and the popular press, and (3) scientifically sound evaluations of their effectiveness are under way.

Relaxation

Just as stress is an adaptive response of the body, there is also an adaptive antistress response, "a relaxation response."[73] Benson reports that in this response muscle tension decreases, heart rate and blood pressure decrease, and breathing slows.[74] The stimuli necessary to

---

[72] Ivancevich and Matteson, *Stress at Work*, p. 215.

[73] Herbert Benson, *The Relaxation Response* (New York: William Morrow, 1975).

[74] Herbert Benson and Robert L. Allen, "How Much Stress Is Too Much?" *Harvard Business Review*, September–October 1980, p. 88.

produce relaxation include *(a)* a quiet environment, *(b)* closed eyes, *(c)* a comfortable position, and *(d)* a repetitive mental device.

Meditation

A form of meditation that has attracted many individuals is called transcendental meditation, or TM. Its originator, Maharishi Mahesh Yogi, defines it as turning the attention toward the subtler levels of thought until the mind transcends the experience of the subtlest state of thought and arrives at the source of thought.[75]

The basic procedure used by TM is simple, but the effects claimed for it are extensive. One simply sits comfortably with closed eyes and engages in the repetition of a special sound (a mantra) for about 20 minutes twice a day. Studies are available that indicate that TM practices are associated with reduced heart rate, lowered oxygen consumption, and decreased blood pressure.[76]

Biofeedback

Individuals can be taught to control a variety of internal body processes by a technique called biofeedback. In biofeedback, small changes occurring in the body or brain are detected, amplified, and displayed to the person. Sophisticated recording and computer technology makes it possible for a person to attend to subtle changes in heart rate, blood pressure, temperature, and brain-wave patterns that would normally be unobservable.[77] Most of these processes are affected by stress.

The ongoing biological processes are made available to the individual by the feedback that he or she receives. The person is able to monitor what is biologically occurring. The ability to gain insight and eventual control over one's bodily processes can lead to significant changes.

Despite the results of some generally well-designed research studies, individuals using biofeedback devices must remain cautious. It is unlikely that the average employee could alter any biological process without proper training.

Individual and organizational approaches have been used in attempts to modify the Type A Behavior Pattern. Recall from the opening Organizational Issue for Debate that the argument against position was that some individuals were suited to be Type As. The approaches

---

[75] P. Carrington, *Freedom in Meditation* (New York: Anchor Press, 1978).

[76] D. Kuna, "Meditation and Work," *Vocational Guidance Quarterly,* June 1975, pp. 342–46.

[77] Philip G. Zimbardo, *Psychology and Life* (Glenview, Ill.: Scott, Foresman, 1979), p. 551.

used to change a person from a Type A to more of a Type B have to date not been successful.[78]

SUMMARY OF KEY POINTS

A. As individuals, we establish a defense reaction to stress. It has been called the General Adaptation Syndrome (GAS). The three phases of the GAS are called alarm, resistance, and exhaustion.

B. The consequences of stress are numerous and can be classified as subjective, behavioral, cognitive, physiological, health, and organizational.

C. Stress at work influences a person's nonwork activities. The interrelatedness of work and nonwork stress must be considered when attempting to explain and understand employee behavior and performance.

D. Three especially counterproductive effects of stress are withdrawal behaviors (absenteeism and turnover), alcoholism, and drug abuse.

E. Alcoholism has been estimated to cost about $50 billion annually in terms of economic waste, while drug abuse has been estimated to cost over $16 billion annually.

F. Stressors are external events that are potentially, but not necessarily, harmful to individuals. One way to classify stressors at work is on the basis of physical environment, individual level, group level, and organizational level.

G. Stressors at work evoke different responses from different people. Figure 7–2 shows a number of moderators of the stressor-stress and stress-effects relationships.

H. Three publicized and scientifically studied moderators are the Type A Behavior Pattern (TABP), life change events, and social support.

I. Some research based on medical and behavioral science suggests that TABP is associated with coronary heart disease.

J. Numerous programs sponsored and initiated by organizations are available for managing work stress. The most popular include role analysis and clarification practices, company-wide clinical programs, and the provision of physical health facilities for employees.

---

[78] Price, *Type A Behavior Pattern.*

K. Individual intervention programs for managing stress are numerous. The more promising programs of this kind include relaxation, meditation, and biofeedback.

DISCUSSION AND REVIEW QUESTIONS

1. Why should a manager consider moderator variables when investigating what are assumed to be consequences of job stress?

2. Would it be difficult to change or modify an individual's style from a Type A Behavior Pattern to a Type B Behavior Pattern? Why?

3. What role would self-motivation play in any individually based program to manage stress?

4. Why would the goal of eliminating *all* stress in the workplace be contrary to organizational effectiveness?

5. Should managers be concerned about the potential health effects of job stress? Why?

6. In what occupations, other than those discussed in this chapter, would responsibility for people be stressful for many job occupants?

7. Should management be concerned about and involved in drug detection of the workplace? Why?

8. What principles of operant conditioning are used in the biofeedback approach to managing individual stress?

9. Could an individual's work unit be an important social support system for buffering stress? Explain.

10. Why is the measurement of stress difficult?

ADDITIONAL REFERENCES

Barnes, V.; E. H. Potter; and F. E. Fiedler. "Effect of Interpersonal Stress on Prediction of Academic Performance." *Journal of Applied Psychology,* 1983, pp. 686–97.

Boyd, D. P., and D. E. Gumpert. "Coping with Entrepreneurial Stress." *Harvard Business Review,* 1983, pp. 44–46, 52, 56, 58, 62, 64.

Friedman, M., and D. Ulmer. *Treating Type A Behavior and Your Heart.* New York: Knopf, 1984.

Gaines, J., and J. M. Jermeir. "Emotional Exhaustion in a High Stress Organization." *Academy of Management Journal,* 1983, pp. 567–86.

Ganster, D. C.; B. T. Mayes; W. E. Sime; and G. D. Tharp. "Managing Organizational Stress: A Field Experiment." *Journal of Applied Psychology,* 1982, pp. 533–42.

Jackson, S. E., and C. Maslach. "After-Effects of Job Related Stress: Families as Victims." *Journal of Occupational Behavior,* 1982, pp. 63–77.

Kafry, D., and A. Pines. "The Experience of Tedium in Life and Work." *Human Relations,* 1980, pp. 477–503.

Kahn, R. L. *Work and Health.* New York: John Wiley & Sons, 1981.

Kimball, C. P. "Stress and Psychosomatic Illness." *Journal of Psychosomatic Research,* 1982, pp. 63–67.

Maslach, C. "Understanding Burnout: Definitional Issues in Analyzing a Complex Phenomenon." In *Job Stress and Burnout: Research, Theory, and Intervention Perspectives,* ed. W. S. Paine. Beverly Hills, Calif.: Sage Focus Editions, 1982.

Parker, D. F., and T. DeCotiis. "Organizational Determinants of Job Stress." *Organizational Behavior and Human Performance,* 1983, pp. 160–77.

Seers, A.; G. W. McGee; T. T. Serey; and G. B. Graen. "The Interaction of Job Stress and Social Support: A Strong Inference Investigation." *Academy of Management Journal,* 1983, pp. 273–84.

Shaw, J. B., and J. H. Riskind. "Predicting Job Stress Using Data from the Position Analysis Questionnaires." *Journal of Applied Psychology,* 1983, pp. 253–61.

Wrich, J. T. *Guidelines for Developing an Employee Assistance Program.* New York: American Management Association, 1982.

CASE FOR ANALYSIS

Am I a Success or a Failure?

At age 46, Jim Roswell is a self-made man. Although he never graduated from college, Jim was recently promoted to vice president of operations of a manufacturing firm with annual sales of $80 million. He is known around the firm as a take-charge, no-nonsense man who likes both adults and children. Jim is very active in the Boy Scouts, Little League baseball, and local business groups. He is married and has a son who is in college and a daughter who is a senior in high school.

Recently, Jim has been experiencing what he calls a midlife breakdown in health. He has complained about breathing difficulties, lower back pain, insomnia, and recurring and intense headaches. His physician has found no physiological basis for the problems and is considering asking Jim to see a psychiatrist.

Jim worked his way up through the ranks. He started with the company 23 years ago as an assembler. Through hard work, his ability to work with people, and his thorough way of doing things, he received one promotion after another. His last two promotions required him to move first from Miami to Atlanta and then to Colorado Springs. His wife, who was very active in the Miami community, became very upset with the move to Atlanta.

As Jim's responsibilities grew, he found that he had to delegate more and more authority. Since some of his subordinates were not well trained, he worked hard helping them do their jobs. This extra work took him away from his family. His wife began to experience frequent bouts of depression. Finally, under a physician's care, she began to take antidepressant medication. One of the side effects of the medication was that she was always fatigued.

Jim feels that his world is caving in around him. His son recently informed him that he was getting married and thinking about dropping out of school for a few years. His daughter has become very antagonistic about life in general, and her grades have slipped badly this year.

The situation facing Jim seems very bleak to him. He is having difficulty in justifying all the hard work he put in trying to be successful. He thinks he has been successful in the organizational world, but he is at a loss to explain what went wrong at home. He is really fighting against becoming a regular visitor to a psychiatrist. He feels that all his life he made adjustments, and he is puzzled about his current inability to cope with his problems.

Questions for Consideration

1. What stressors in Jim's life are having an effect on his thinking, behavior, and performance?

2. Explain how work and nonwork stressors are influencing Jim's view of the world?

3. Is Jim going to be able to solve his problems on hiw own? Why?

EXPERIENTIAL EXERCISE

ANALYSIS OF YOUR TYPE A TENDENCIES

Objectives

1. To provide each student with a view of his or her Type A Behavior Pattern.
2. To enable students to compare their TABP scores with those of others in the class.

Related Topics

TABP has been associated with various behavioral characteristics, such as impatience, time urgency, competitiveness, and hard driving. It has also been associated with coronary heart disease. Those with more pronounced TABP appear to have a greater chance of contracting coronary heart disease.

Starting the Exercise

Each student should complete the behavior activity profile. The instructor has the scoring Key and some norms for the student to use.

Exercise Procedures

Phase I: 15 minutes
Individually complete and score the behavior activity profile.

Phase II: 20 or more minutes
Meet in small groups (four to six people), and discuss the behavior activity profile—yours and those of other members of the group.

Behavior Activity Profile

Because we are all unique individuals, we have different ways of behaving and acting, as well as different values, thought patterns, approaches to relationships, even ways of moving. The behavior activity profile is designed to access the characteristic style or approach that you exhibit in a number of situations. There are no "right" or "wrong" answers. The best answer to each item is the response that most nearly describes the way you really feel, behave, or think.

Instructions.   For each item in the profile, you will be presented with two alternatives. You are asked to indicte which of the two alternatives is more descriptive of you. For some items, you may feel that

Behavior Activity Profile *(continued)*

the two alternatives are equally descriptive; for other items, you may feel that neither alternative is descriptive. Nonetheless, try to determine which alternative is relatively more descriptive. For each item, you have five points, which you may distribute between the two alternatives in any of the following ways:

If X is totally descriptive of you and Y is not at all descriptive, place a 5 in the X box and a 0 in the Y box.

X	Y
5	0

If X is mostly descriptive of you and Y is somewhat or reasonably descriptive, place a 4 in the X box and a 1 in the Y box.

X	Y
4	1

If X is slightly more descriptive of you than Y is, place a 3 in the X box and a 2 in the Y box.

X	Y
3	2

Each of the above three combinations can be reversed. Thus, if Y is slightly more descriptive of you than X, place a 2 under X and a 3 under Y, and so on for X = 1, Y = 4, and X = 0, Y = 5.

Thus, there are six possible combinations for responding to each pair of alternatives. Whatever combination you use, be sure that the total points you allocate sum to 5. Remember, answer on the basis of what you honestly feel is descriptive—not how you feel you should be or how you would like to be.

X Y

1. ☐☐

    X. I guess I'm just interested in what other people have to say—I seldom find my attention wandering when someone is talking to me.

                    or

    Y. Many times when someone is talking to me, I find myself thinking about other things.

X Y

2. ☐☐

    X. When I talk, I tend to accent words with increased volume and my delivery is staccato, but rapid.

                    or

    Y. My speech usually flows slowly in a smooth amplitude, without changes in speed.

Behavior Activity Profile *(continued)*

X Y

3. ☐☐

    X. I like to enjoy whatever it is I'm doing; the more relaxed and noncompetitive I can be, the more I enjoy the activity.

        or

    Y. In just about everything I do, I tend to be hard driving and competitive.

X Y

4. ☐☐

    X. I prefer being respected for the things that I accomplish.

        or

    Y. I prefer being liked for whom I am.

X Y

5. ☐☐

    X. I let people finish what they are doing or saying before I respond in any way—no use in jumping the gun and making a mistake.

        or

    Y. I usually anticipate what a person will do or say next; for example, I'll start answering a question before it has been completely asked.

X Y

6. ☐☐

    X. Probably my behavior is seldom or never governed by a desire for recognition and influence.

        or

    Y. If I were really honest about it, I'd have to admit that a great deal of what I do is designed to bring me recognition and influence.

X Y

7. ☐☐

    X. Frankly, I frequently get upset or angry with people even though I may not show it.

        or

    Y. I rarely get upset with people; most things simply aren't worth getting angry about.

Behavior Activity Profile *(continued)*

8. X Y ☐☐

    X. Quite candidly, I frequently feel impatient toward others either for their slowness or for the poor quality of their work.

              or

    Y. While I may be disappointed in the work of others, I just don't let it frustrate me.

9. X Y ☐☐

    X. My job provides me with my primary source of satisfaction; I don't find other activities nearly as gratifying.

              or

    Y. While I like my job, I regularly find satisfaction in numerous pursuits such as spectator sports, hobbies, friends, and family.

10. X Y ☐☐

    X. If I had to identify one thing that really frustrates me, it would be having to stand in line.

              or

    Y. Quite honestly, I find it kind of amusing the way some people get upset about waiting in line.

11. X Y ☐☐

    X. I don't have to control my temper; it's just not a problem for me.

              or

    Y. Quite frankly, I frequently find it hard to control my temper, although I usually manage to do so.

12. X Y ☐☐

    X. I work hard at my job because I have a very strong desire to get ahead.

              or

Behavior Activity Profile *(concluded)*

Y. I work hard at my job because I owe it to my employer, who pays my salary.

X Y
13. ▢▢

X. It's very unusual for me to have difficulty getting to sleep because I'm excited, keyed up, or worried about something.

or

Y. Many times I'm so keyed up that I have difficulty getting to sleep.

X Y
14. ▢▢

X. I may not be setting the world on fire, but I don't really want to either.

or

Y. I often feel uncomfortable or dissatisfied with how well I am doing in my job or career.

X Y
15. ▢▢

X. It really bothers me when for some reason plans I've made can't be executed.

or

Y. Few plans I make are so important that I get upset if something happens and I can't carry them out.

X Y
16. ▢▢

X. Such things as achieving peace of mind or enjoyment of life are as worthy ambitions as a desire to get ahead.

or

Y. People who do not want to get ahead professionally or careerwise simply don't have any ambition.

Source: This survey was developed by Michael T. Matteson and John M. Ivancevich, and it is copyrighted by STress RESearch Systems, P.O. Box 883, Spring, Texas 77373.

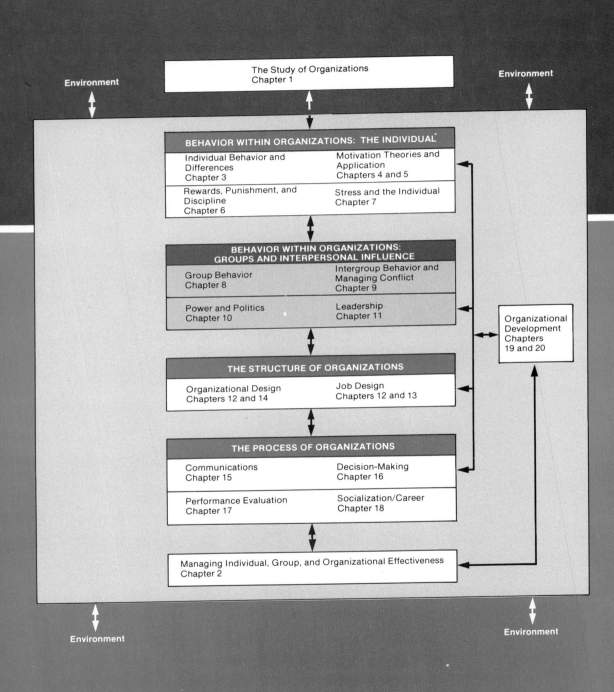

BEHAVIOR WITHIN ORGANIZATIONS: GROUPS AND INTERPERSONAL INFLUENCE

PART THREE

Chapter 8

After completing Chapter 8, you should be able to:

Define what is meant by the term group.

Describe various types of groups that exist in organizations.

Discuss why people form groups.

Compare the various stages of group development

Identify the major characteristics of groups in organizations.

Group Behavior

Does Allowing Work Groups More Freedom Improve Group Performance?

Argument for

The management of a paper mill believed that autonomous work groups were a better way to utilize human resources and increase member satisfaction. The idea was to break away from the one-person, one-machine organization and have a small group monitor several machines. The experiment began in the chemical pulp department, with the division of 35 workers into four continuous shift groups of 8 to 9 workers. Supervisors were eliminated, and the number of managers was cut in half. Workers were trained in quality control and information handling.

The experiment worked. In six years, it spread virtually throughout the plant and reduced turnover from 25 to 6 percent a year, while doubling productivity. It gave management much more flexibility in scheduling work and enabled the plant to stay open through holiday periods.

Argument Against

The management of a steel fabricating plant believed that autonomous work groups would improve performance. Attempts were made to break away from the one-person, one-machine organization. Workers were allowed to move among the various machines and to be responsible for some equipment maintenance.

This experiment did not work. Both workers and middle managers were hostile to the idea. In one instance, one of five workers was ill for two weeks. The remaining workers handled the five machines and in addition produced more than all five workers had done previously. Unfortunately, the experiment was halted because both workers and middle managers were unwilling to alter the basic work patterns or wage structure.*

* *Behavioral Sciences Newsletter*, August 8, 1977, p. 1. For recent research and discussion on this and related issues, see G. P. Latham and T. P. Steele, "The Motivational Effects of Participation versus Goal Setting on Performance," *Academy of Management Journal*, September 1983, pp. 406–17; J. M. Ivancevich and J. T. McMahon, "The Effects of Goal Setting, External Feedback, and Self-Generated Feedback on Outcome Variables: A Field Experiment," *Academy of Management Journal*, June 1982, pp. 354–72; and W. F. Muhs, "Worker Participation in the Progressive Era: An Assessment by Harrington Emerson," *Academy of Management Review*, January 1982, pp. 99–102.

This chapter examines groups in organizations. While the existence of groups in organizations probably does not alter the individual's motivations or needs, the group does influence the behavior of individuals in an organizational setting. As the chapter-opening Organizational Issue for Debate indicates, organizational behavior is more than the logical composite of the behavior of individuals. It is not their sum or product but rather a much more complex phenomenon, a very important part of which is the group. This chapter will provide you with a model for understanding the nature of groups in organizations. The chapter explores the various types of groups, the reasons for their formation, the characteristics of groups, and some end results of group membership.

THE NATURE OF GROUPS

No generally accepted definition of a group exists. Instead, a range of available views can be presented, and from these a comprehensive definition of a group can be developed.

A Group in Terms of Perception

Many behavioral scientists believe that to be considered a group, the members of a group must perceive their relationships to others. For example:

> A small group is defined as any number of persons engaged in interaction with one another in a single face-to-face meeting or series of such meetings, in which each member receives some impression or perception of each other member distinct enough so that he can, either at the time or in later questioning, give some reaction to each of the others as an individual person, even though it may be only to recall that the other was present.[1]

This view points out that the members of a group must perceive the existence of each member as well as the existence of the group.

A Group in Terms of Organization

Sociologists view the group primarily in terms of organizational characteristics. For example, according to a sociological definition, a group is

---

[1] R. F. Bales, *Interaction Process Analysis: A Method for the Study of Small Groups* (Reading, Mass.: Addison-Wesley Publishing, 1950), p. 33.

an organized system of two or more individuals who are interrelated so that the system performs some function, has a standard set of role relationships among its members, and has a set of norms that regulate the function of the group and each of its members.[2]

This view emphasizes some of the important characteristics of groups, such as roles and norms, which will be discussed later in this chapter.

A Group in Terms of Motivation

A group that fails to aid its members in satisfying their needs will have difficulty in remaining viable. Employees who are not satisfying their needs in a particular group will search for other groups to aid in important need satisfactions. This view defines a group as

a collection of individuals whose existence as a collection is rewarding to the individuals.[3]

As pointed out in an earlier chapter, it is difficult to ascertain clearly what facets of the work organization are rewarding to individuals. The problem of identifying individual needs is a shortcoming of defining a group solely in terms of motivation.

A Group in Terms of Interaction

Some theorists assume that interaction in the form of interdependence is the core of "groupness." A view that stresses interpersonal interactions is the following:

We mean by a group a number of persons who communicate with one another often over a span of time, and who are few enough so that each person is able to communicate with all the others, not at second-hand, through other people, but face-to-face.[4]

All of these four views are important, since they all point to key features of groups. Furthermore, it can be stated that if a group exists in an organization, its members:

1. Are motivated to join.
2. Perceive the group as a unified unit of interacting people.

---

[2] J. W. McDavid and M. Harari, *Social Psychology: Individuals, Groups, Societies* (New York: Harper & Row, 1968), p. 237.

[3] Bernard M. Bass, *Leadership, Psychology, and Organizational Behavior* (New York: Harper & Row, 1960), p. 39.

[4] G. C. Homans, *The Human Group* (New York: Harcourt Brace Jovanovich, 1950, p. 1.

group
A collection of individuals is a group if the behavior and/or performance of one member is influenced by the behavior and/or performance of other members.

3. Contribute in various amounts to the group processes (i.e., some people contribute more time or energy to the group).

4. Reach agreements and have disagreements through various forms of interaction.

In this textbook, a **group** is defined as

> two or more employees who interact with each other in such a manner that the behavior and/or performance of a member is influenced by the behavior and/or performance of other members.[5]

TYPES OF GROUPS

formal groups
Formal groups are created by managerial decision to accomplish the stated goals of the organization.

An organization has technical requirements that arise from its stated goals. The accomplishment of these goals requires that certain tasks be performed and that employees be assigned to perform these tasks. As a result, most employees will be members of a group based on their position in the organization. These are **formal groups.** On the other hand, whenever individuals associate on a fairly continuous basis, there is a tendency for groups to form whose activities may be different from those required by the organization. These are **informal groups.** Both formal groups and informal groups, it will be shown, exhibit the same general characteristics.

informal groups
Informal groups arise from individual efforts and develop around common interests and friendships rather than deliberate design.

Formal Groups

The demands and processes of the organization lead to the formation of different types of groups. Specifically, two types of formal groups exist: command and task.

Command Group.   The command group is specified by the organization chart. The group comprises the subordinates who report directly to a given supervisor. The authority relationship between a department manager and the supervisors, or between a senior nurse and her subordinates, is an example of a command group.

Task Group.   A task group comprises the employees who work together to complete a particular task or project. For example, the activities of clerks in an insurance company when an accident claim is filed are required tasks. These activities create a situation in which several clerks must communicate and coordinate with one another if the claim is to be handled properly. These required tasks and interactions facilitate the formation of a task group. The nurses assigned to duty in the emergency room of a hospital usually constitute a task group, since certain activities are required when a patient is treated.

---

[5] See M. E. Shaw, *Group Dynamics: The Psychology of Small Group Behavior,* 2d ed. (New York: McGraw-Hill, 1976).

Informal Groups

Informal groups are natural groupings of people in the work situation in response to social needs. In other words, informal groups do not arise as a result of deliberate design but rather evolve naturally. Two specific types of informal groups exist: interest and friendship.

Interest Groups. Individuals who may not be members of the same command or task group may affiliate to achieve some mutual objective. Employees grouping together to present a unified front to management for more benefits and waitresses "pooling" their tips are examples of interest groups. Also, note that the objectives of such groups are not related to those of the organization but are specific to each group.

Friendship Groups. Many groups form because the members have something in common, such as age, political beliefs, or ethnic background. These friendship groups often extend their interaction and communication to off-the-job activities.

If employees' affiliation patterns were documented, it would become readily apparent that they belong to numerous and often overlapping groups. A distinction has been made between two broad classifications of groups: formal and informal. The major difference between them is that formal groups (command and task) are designated by the formal organization and are a means to an end, while informal groups (interest and friendship) are important for their own sake. They satisfy a basic human need for association.

WHY PEOPLE FORM GROUPS

Formal and informal groups form for various reasons. Some of the reasons involve needs, proximity, attraction, goals, and economics.

The Satisfaction of Needs

The desire for need satisfaction can be a strong motivating force leading to group formation.[6] Specifically, the security, social, esteem, and self-actualization needs of some employees can be satisfied to a degree by their affiliation with groups.

Security. Without the group to lean on when various management demands are made, certain employees may assume that they are standing alone, facing management and the entire organization system. This "aloneness" leads to a degree of insecurity. By being a member

---

[6] For a discussion of the group as an instrument for satisfaction of individual needs, see C. Gratton Kemp, *Perspectives on Group Processes* (Boaston: Houghton Mifflin, 1970), pp. 26–29. Also see Linda N. Jewell and H. Joseph Reitz, *Group Effectiveness in Organizations* (Glenview, Ill.: Scott, Foresman, 1981). This is an excellent comprehensive work devoted entirely to the subject of groups in organizational settings.

of a group, the employee can become involved in group activities and discuss management demands with other members who hold supportive views. The interactions and communications existing among the members of the group serve as a buffer to management demands. The need for a buffer may be especially strong in the case of a new employee. He or she may depend heavily on the group for aid in correctly performing the job.

Social.   The gregariousness of people stimulates the need for affiliation. The desire to be a part of a group points up the intensity of social needs. The need to socialize exists not only on the job but away from the workplace, as evidenced by the vast array of social, political, civic, and fraternal organizations that one can join.

Esteem.   In a particular work environment, a certain group may be viewed by employees as having a high level of prestige for a variety of reasons (technical competence, outside activities, and so on). Consequently, membership in this group carries with it a certain status not enjoyed by nonmembers. For employees with high esteem needs, membership in such a group can provide much-needed satisfaction.[7]

Proximity and Attraction

Interpersonal interaction can result in group formation. Two important facets of interpersonal interaction are proximity and attraction. *Proximity* involves the physical distance between employees performing a job. *Attraction* designates the attraction of people to each other because of perceptual, attitudinal, performance, or motivational similarity.

Individuals who work in close proximity have numerous opportunities to exchange ideas, thoughts, and attitudes about various on- and off-the-job activities. These exchanges often result in some type of group formation. This proximity also makes it possible for individuals to learn about the characteristics of other people. To sustain the interaction and interest, a group is often formed.

Group Goals

A group's goals, if clearly understood, can be reasons why an individual is attracted to it. For example, an individual may join a group that meets after work to become familiar a new personal computer system. Assume that this system is to be implemented in the work organization over the next two years. The person who voluntarily

---

[7] See K. W. Mossholder, A. G. Bedian, and A. A. Armenakis, "Group Process—Work Outcome Relationships: A Note on the Moderating Effects of Self-Esteem," *Academy of Management Journal,* September 1982, pp. 575–85.

joins the after-hours group believes that learning the new system is a necessary and important goal for employees.

It is not always possible to identify group goals. The assumption that formal organizational groups have clear goals must be tempered by the understanding that perception, attitudes, personality, and learning can distort goals. For example, a new employee may never be formally told the goals of the unit that he or she has joined. By observing the behavior and attitudes of others, individuals may conclude what they believe the goals to be. These perceptions may or may not be accurate. The same can be said about the goals of informal groups.

Economic Reasons

In many cases, groups form because individuals believe that they can derive greater economic benefits from their jobs if they organize. For example, individuals working at different points on an assembly line may be paid on a group-incentive basis where the production of the group determines the wages of each member. By working and cooperating as a group, the individuals may obtain higher economic benefits.

In numerous other instances, economic motives lead to group formation: workers in nonunion organizations form a group to exert pressure on top management for more benefits; top executives in a corporation form a group to review executive compensation. Whatever the circumstances, the group members have a common interest—increased economic benefits—that leads to group affiliation.

STAGES OF GROUP DEVELOPMENT

Groups learn, just as individuals do. The performance of a group depends both on individual learning and on how well the members learn to work with one another. For example, a new product committee formed for the purpose of developing a response to a competitor may evolve into a very effective team, with the interests of the company being most important. However, it may also be very ineffective if its members are more concerned about their individual departmental goals than about developing a response to a competitor. This section describes some general stages through which groups develop and points out that some kind of sequential developmental process is involved.

One model of group development assumes that groups proceed through four stages of development: (1) mutual acceptance, (2) communication and decision making, (3) motivation and productivity, and

(4) control and organization.[8] Although competing models of group development exist, we believe that the model presented here is the most useful for students of organizational behavior.

Mutual Acceptance

In the early stages of group formation, members are generally reluctant to communicate with one another. Typically, they are not willing to express opinions, attitudes, and beliefs. This is similar to the situation facing a faculty member at the start of a new semester. Until the class members accept and trust one another, very little interaction and class discussion are likely to occur.

Communication and Decision Making

After a group reaches the point of mutual acceptance, its members begin to communicate openly with one another. This communication results in increased confidence and even more interaction within the group. The discussions begin to focus more specifically on problem-solving tasks and on the development of alternative strategies to accomplish the tasks.[9]

Motivation and Productivity

This is the stage of development in which effort is expended to accomplish the group's goals. The group is working as a cooperative unit and not as a competitive unit.

Control and Organization

At this point, group affiliation is valued and members are regulated by group norms. The group goals take precedence over individual goals, and the norms are compiled with, or sanctions are exercised. The ultimate sanction is ostracism for not complying with the group goals or norms. Other forms of control include temporary isolation from the group or harassment by the other members.

---

[8] Bernard M. Bass, *Organizational Psychology* (Boston: Allyn & Bacon, 1965), pp. 197–98; and J. M. Ivancevich and J. T. McMahon, "Group Development, Trainer Style, and Carry-Over Job Satisfaction and Performance," *Academy of Management Journal,* September 1976, pp. 395–412. For an opposing viewpoint, see J. A. Seeger, "No Innate Phases in Group Problem Solving," *Academy of Management Review,* October 1983, pp. 683–89.

[9] See Ralph Katz, "The Effects of Group Longevity on Project Communication and Performance," *Administrative Science Quarterly,* March 1982, pp. 81–104.

CHARACTERISTICS OF GROUPS

As groups evolve through their various stages of development, they begin to exhibit certain characteristics. To understand group behavior, you must be aware of these general characteristics. They are: structure, status hierarchy, roles, norms, leadership, cohesiveness, and conflict.

Structure

Within any group, some type of structure evolves over a period of time. The group members are differentiated on the basis of such factors as expertise, aggressiveness, power, and status. Each member occupies a *position* in the group. The pattern of relationships among the positions constitutes a *group structure*. Members of the group evaluate each position in terms of its prestige, status, and importance to the group. In most cases, there is some type of status difference among positions such that the group structure is hierarchical. Status in formal groups is usually based on the position in the formal organization, while in informal groups status can be based on anything relevant to the group (e.g., golf scores, ability to communicate with management). The occupant of each position is expected by the members to enact certain behaviors. The set of expected behaviors associated with a position in the structure constitutes the role of that position's occupant.

Status Hierarchy

Status and position are so similar that the terms are often used interchangeably. The status *assigned* to a particular position is typically a consequence of certain characteristics that differentiate one position from other positions. In some cases, a person is assigned status because of such factors as job seniority, age, or assignment. For example, the oldest worker may be perceived as being more technically proficient and is attributed status by a group of technicians. Thus, assigned status may have nothing to do with the formal status hierarchy.[10]

Roles

Each position in the group structure has an associated role that consists of the expected behaviors of the occupant of that position.

---

[10] For a recent relevant study, see L. A. Nikolai and J. D. Bazley, "An Analysis of the Organizational Interaction of Accounting Departments," *Academy of Management Journal*, December 1977, pp. 608–21.

The director of nursing services in a hospital is expected to organize and control the department of nursing. The director is also expected to assist in preparing and administering the budget for the department. A nursing supervisor, on the other hand, is expected to supervise the activities of nursing personnel engaged in specific nursing services, such as obstetrics, pediatrics, and surgery. These expected behaviors generally are agreed on not only by the occupants, the director of nursing and the nursing supervisor, but by other members of the nursing group and other hospital personnel.[11]

An *expected role* is only one type of role. There are also a "perceived role" and an "enacted role." The *perceived role* is the set of behaviors that a person in a position believes he or she should enact. In some cases, the perceived role may correspond to the expected role. As discussed in Chapter 3, perception can, in some instances, be distorted or inaccurate. The *enacted role,* on the other hand, is the behavior that a person actually carries out. Thus, three possible role behaviors can result. Conflict and frustration may result from differences in these three role types. In fairly stable or permanent groups, there is typically good agreement between expected and perceived roles. When the enacted role deviates too much from the expected role, the person can either become more like the expected role or leave the group.

Because of membership in different groups, individuals perform multiple roles. First-line supervisors are members of the management team but are also members of the group of workers they supervise. These multiple roles result in a number of expected role behaviors. In many instances, the behaviors specified by the different roles are compatible. When they are not, however, the individual experiences role conflict. There are several types of role conflict and some important consequences. Role conflict will be discussed later in the chapter.

Norms

norms
Group norms are generally agreed-upon standards of individual and group behavior that have developed as a result of member interaction over time.

Norms are the standards that are shared by the members of a group. Norms have certain characteristics that are important to group members. First, norms are formed only with respect to things that have significance for the group. They may be written, but very often they can be verbally communicated to members. In many cases, they may never be formally stated but somehow are known by group members. If production is important, then a norm will evolve. If helping other group members complete a task is important, then a norm will develop.[12] Second, norms are accepted in various degrees by group

---

[11] For example, see C. E. Schneier and P. W. Beatty, "The Influence of Role Prescriptions on the Performance Appraisal Process," *Academy of Management Journal,* March 1978, pp. 129–34.

[12] For examples, see R. J. Burke, T. Weir, and G. Duncan, "Informal Helping Relationships in Work Organizations," *Academy of Management Journal,* September 1976, pp. 370–77.

members. Some norms are completely accepted by all members, while other norms are only partially accepted. And third, norms may apply to every group member, or they may apply to only some group members. For example, every member may be expected to comply with the production norm, while only group leaders may be permitted to disagree verbally with a management directive.

Norm Conformity.   An issue of concern to managers is why employees conform to group norms.[13] This is especially important when a person with skill and capability is performing significantly below his or her capacity so that group norms are not violated. Four general classes of variables influence conformity to group norms:

1. The personality of group members.
2. The stimuli that evoke the response.
3. Situational factors.
4. Intragroup relationships.

Personality can influence whether an individual conforms to group norms. For example, research indicates that persons of high intelligence are less likely to conform than the less intelligent and that authoritarian individuals (those favoring obedience to authority) conform more than do nonauthoritarians.[14]

Stimulus factors includes all of the organizational factors that are related to the norm to which the group member is conforming. The more ambiguous the stimulus, the greater will be the conformity to group norms. For example, suppose that top management adopts a new type of performance appraisal interview. The group of managers who are to conduct the interviews may initially be unsure of the process because of its newness and complexity. This lack of clarity of the stimulus may result in the group utilizing the old group performance appraisal procedures rather than the new ones as outlined by top management. The managers conform to the old group norm until the new process is clarified and key group members begin to utilize the new procedure.

Situational factors pertain to such variables as the size and structure of the group. Conformity to group norms may be more difficult in larger groups or in groups whose members are separated geographically.

Intragroup relationships include such factors as the kind of group pressure exerted, how successful the group has been in achieving desired goals, and the degree to which a member identifies with the group.

---

[13] Daniel C. Feldman, "The Development and Enforcement of Group Norms," *Academy of Management Review,* January 1984, pp. 47–53.

[14] Salvatore R. Maddi, *Personality Theories: A Comparative Analysis* (Homewood, Ill.: Dorsey Press, 1980), chap. 7.

Potential Consequences of Conforming to Group Norms. The research on conformity distinctly implies that conformity is a requirement of sustained group membership. The member who does not conform to important norms is often punished by a group. One form of punishment is to isolate or ignore the presence of the nonconformist. There are some potential negative and positive consequences of conformity. Conformity can result in a loss of individuality and the establishment of only moderate levels of performance. This type of behavior can be costly to an organization that needs above-average levels of performance to remain competitive.

There are, of course, potential positive consequences of conformity to group norms. If no conformity existed, a manager would have a difficult, if not impossible, time in predicting a group's behavior patterns. This inability to estimate behavior could result in unsuccessful managerial attempts to channel the group's efforts toward the accomplishment of organizational goals. This, of course, is a problem facing managers of formal groups. They have no systematic way to predict such behavior as a group's response to a new computer system or a new performance appraisal system if there is a lack of conformity to group norms.

Leadership

The leadership role in groups is an extremely crucial group characteristic. The leader of a group exerts some influence over the members of the group. In the formal group, the leader can exercise legitimately sanctioned power. That is, the leader can reward or punish members who do not comply with the directives, orders, or rules.

The leadership role is also a significant factor in an informal group. The person who becomes an informal group leader is generally viewed as a respected and high-status member who:

1. Aids the group in accomplishing its goals.
2. Enables members to satisfy needs.
3. Embodies the values of the group. In essence, the leader is a personification of the values, motives, and aspirations of the members.
4. Is the choice of the group members to represent their viewpoint when interacting with other group leaders.
5. Is a facilitator of group conflict and an initiator of group actions and is concerned with maintaining the group as a functioning unit.

Cohesiveness

Formal and informal groups seem to possess a closeness or commonness of attitude, behavior, and performance. This closeness has been

cohesiveness
The strength of the members' desires to remain in the group and their commitment to the group determine the cohesiveness of the group.

referred to as **cohesiveness.** It is generally regarded as a force acting on the members to remain in a group that is greater than the forces pulling the member away from the group. A cohesive group, then, involves individuals who are attracted to one another. A group that is low in cohesiveness does not possess interpersonal attractiveness for the members.

There are, of course, numerous sources of attraction to a group. A group may be attractive to an individual because:

1. The goals of the group and the members are compatible and clearly specified.
2. The group has a charismatic leader.
3. The reputation of the group indicates that the group successfully accomplishes its tasks.
4. The group is small enough to permit members to have their opinions heard and evaluated by others.
5. The members are attractive in that they support one another and help one another overcome obstacles and barriers to personal growth and development.[15]

These five factors are related to need satisfaction. As discussed earlier, one of the reasons for group formation is to satisfy needs. If an individual is able to join a cohesive group, then there should be an increase in the satisfaction of needs through this group affiliation.

Since highly cohesive groups are composed of individuals who are motivated to be together, there is a tendency to expect effective group performance. This logic is not supported conclusively by research evidence. In general, as the cohesiveness of a work group increases, the level of conformity to group norms also increases. But these norms may be inconsistent with those of the organization. The group pressures to conform are more intense in the cohesive group. The question of whether managers should encourage or discourage group cohesiveness will be examined later in the chapter.

The importance of group cohesiveness was indicated in an early study conducted by the Tavistock Institute in Great Britain.[16] The

---

[15] D. Cartwright and A. Zander, *Group Dynamics: Research and Theory* (New York: Harper & Row, 1968).

[16] E. L. Trist and K. W. Bamforth, "Some Social and Psychological Consequences of the Longwall Method of Coal Getting," *Human Relations*, February 1951, pp. 3–38. For other important research on group cohesiveness, see S. E. Seashore, *Group Cohesiveness in the Industrial Work Group* (Ann Arbor: Institute for Social Research, University of Michigan, 1954); A. J. Lott and B. E. Lott, "Group Cohesiveness as Interpersonal Attraction: A Review of Relationships with Antecedent and Consequent Variables," *Psychological Bulletin*, October 1965, pp. 259–309; and S. M. Klein, *Workers under Stress: The Impact of Work Pressure on Group Cohesion* (Lexington: University of Kentucky Press, 1971).

coal mining industry in England introduced a number of changes in mining equipment and procedures after World War II. Prior to the arrival of this new technology, miners had worked together as teams. Each group of miners dug out the coal, loaded it into cars, and moved it to a station where it was taken from the mine. The tasks, physical proximity, and dangers of mining were forces that resulted in the development of cohesive teams. The teams provided the members with opportunities to interact. Thus, highly cohesive groups had developed prior to the introduction of the new equipment.

The new technology disrupted the groups. The machinery did some of the tasks previously accomplished by the miners. It also destroyed many of the opportunities for miners to socialize. Without the support of the highly cohesive groups, and with an increase in physical distance between workers, the coal miners began to slow down their production. Other groups or teams formed, but they were less attractive to the miners than the traditional teams that worked close to each other. This research clearly indicated the impact of group cohesiveness on group performance.

The recognition of the impact of groups on performance is a vital one for managers.[17] The following Close-Up outlines the productive utilization of work groups in the banking industry.

ORGANIZATIONS: CLOSE-UP

Using Groups to Solve Problems in the Banking Industry

One hour each week, several teams meet at Society National Bank of Cleveland. The teams consist of 4 to 12 members each, plus a group leader. The bank's top management decided to create these "quality circles," as the teams are called, to help solve problems. Management believes that the program has improved communications throughout the bank, increased the total awareness of all employees, decreased turnover and absenteeism, and generally aided the development of human resources and customer relations.

The concept of quality circles is based on the premise that it is not *what* people can do that is important; rather, it is what they *want* to do. By developing the participative management program, the bank has seen improvement in the attitudes and behavior of people at all levels of the organization.

---

[17] Karen A. Brown, "Explaining Group Poor Performance: An Attributional Analysis," *Academy of Management Review,* January 1984, pp. 54–63.

More than 130 officers and employees are currently involved in the bank's quality circle program. Each team receives 14 weeks' training in group decision making, communications skills, and human relations skills. The team members then put their skills to use to solve work problems and improve bank performance. Some recent accomplishments are:

Branch Team—reduced balancing time from 45 minutes to 20 minutes at the end of each business day.

Domestic Collection Team—developed new ways of processing redemption coupons in-house for a savings of $45,000.

Customer Service Team—reduced customer calls from 3 percent to 1 percent; and reduced the percentage of calls answered by recorded messages from 5 percent to 2 percent.

The executive vice president and chief financial officer of the bank concluded: "We are convinced that employees and managers who are involved in shaping how they do their work achieve a superior work output. Today's world requires people who will acknowledge that they are responsible for their efforts and respond accordingly."

Source: "Quality Circles Solve Problems at Society National Bank," *American Banker*, May 6, 1983, pp. 5, 10.

Cohesiveness and Performance. The concept of cohesiveness is important for understanding groups in organizations. The degree of cohesiveness in a group can have positive or negative effects, depending on how group goals match up with those of the formal organization. In fact, four distinct possibilities exist, as illustrated in Figure 8–1.

Figure 8–1 indicates that if cohesiveness is high and the group ac-

FIGURE 8–1

The Relationship between Group Cohesiveness and Agreement with Organizational Goals

		Agreement with Organizational Goals	
		Low	High
Degree of Group Cohesiveness	Low	Performance oriented away from organizational goals.	Performance probably oriented toward achievement of organizational goals.
	High	Performance probably oriented away from organizational goals.	Performance oriented toward achievement of organizational goals.

cepts and agrees with formal organization goals, then group behavior will probably be positive from the formal organization standpoint. Such a situation appears to exist at Society National Bank in the Organizations: Close-Up. However, if the group is highly cohesive but with goals that are not congruent with those of the formal organization, then group behavior will probably be negative from the formal organization's standpoint.

Figure 8–1 also indicates that if a group is low in cohesiveness and the members have goals that are not in agreement with those of management, then the results will probably be negative from the standpoint of the organization. Behavior will be more on an individual basis than on a group basis because of the low cohesiveness. On the other hand, it is possible to have a group low in cohesiveness where the members' goals agree with those of the formal organization. Here the results will probably be positive, although again more on an individual basis than on a group basis.

When the goals of a cohesive group conflict with those of management, some form of intervention by management is usually necessary. Intervention techniques will be discussed in detail in the next chapter.

groupthink
Groupthink occurs when a cohesive group's desire for agreement interferes with the group's consideration of alternative solutions.

outside experts excluded

Groupthink.　Highly cohesive groups are very important forces in organizational behavior. In other words, it is a good idea to place people with many similarities in an isolated setting, give them a common goal, and reward them for performance. On the surface, this may look like a good idea. One author has provided a very provocative account about highly cohesive groups.[18] In his book, Irving Janis has analyzed foreign policy decisions made by a number of presidential administrations and concluded that these groups were highly cohesive and close-knit. He has labeled their decision-making process **"groupthink."** Janis defines groupthink as the "deterioration of mental efficiency, reality testing, and moral judgement" in the interest of group solidarity.[19] He described the following characteristics.

Illusion of Invulnerability.　Members of one group believed that they were invincible. For example, on the eve of the disastrous attempt to invade Cuba in April 1961 (the Bay of Pigs invasion), Robert Kennedy stated that with the talent in the group, they could overcome whatever challenged them with "common sense and hard work" and "bold new ideas."

Tendency to Moralize.　The group studied had a general tendency to view the United States as the leader of the free world. Any opposition to this view was characterized by the group's members as weak, evil, or unintelligent.

---

[18] Irving Janis, *Victims of Groupthink: A Psychological Study of Foreign Policy Decisions and Fiascos* (Boston: Houghton Mifflin, 1973).

[19] Ibid., p. 9.

Feeling of Unanimity. The group reported that each member of the Executive Committee supported the president's decisions. Later on, however, members indicated that they had had serious doubts at the time the decisions were being made. For example, Arthur Schlesinger and Theodore Sorensen both reported that they had had reservations about the decisions being made with respect to Southeast Asia during the Kennedy years. Both men admitted regretting their hesitancy to let their views be known at the time. However, at the time they believed that everyone else was in total agreement and that they had the only differing view. Rather than appear weak or soft, each kept his view to himself. This indicates how the pressure toward group solidarity can distort the judgment of individual members.

Pressure to Conform. Occasionally, President Kennedy would bring in an expert to respond to questions that members of the group might have. The purpose was to have the expert in effect silence the critic instead of actively encouraging discussion of divergent views. Other forms of informal pressures to conform were also used on cabinet and staff members. In one instance, Arthur Schlesinger reported that Robert Kennedy had mentioned informally to him that while he could see some problems associated with a particular decision, the president needed unanimous support on the issue. There was a strong perceived need for group solidarity. Thus, groups can exert great pressure to conform on individual members.

Opposing Ideas Dismissed. Any individual or outside group that criticized or opposed a decision or policy received little or no attention from the group. Even valid ideas and relevant arguments were often dismissed prematurely. Janis notes that much evidence indicated strongly that the invasion of Cuba would fail but it was given little consideration. Thus, conflicting information with group goals can be distorted or ignored as individual members strive for agreement and solidarity.

Certainly, some level of group cohesiveness is necessary for a group to tackle a problem. If seven individuals from seven different organizational units are assigned a task, the task may never be completed effectively. The point, however, is that more cohesiveness may not necessarily be better. While members of task groups may redefine solving a problem to mean reaching agreement rather than making the best decision, members of cohesive groups may redefine it to mean preserving relations among group members and preserving the image of the group. The decision to invade Cuba as described by Janis is an example of the negative impact of group pressures on the quality of the decisions made by the group.

Groupthink illustrates the impact of group dynamics and cohesiveness on group performance. As a summary, the sometimes negative effects of these phenomena can be observed in another setting, in the following Close-Up.

ORGANIZATIONS: CLOSE-UP

How Group Pressure Can Have Negative Effects

Research has indicated that through a process similar to that described as groupthink, corporations may eventually be led to criminal activities such as price fixing and bribery. The first step toward such behavior appears to come amid an atmosphere of intense competition of trying financial times. At this point, when the chief executive officer should be exhibiting high ethical standards, a lowered moral tone may appear and begin to permeate the entire organization. Performance pressures on managers are intense, and this combination of factors may lead to an atmosphere that rewards improper means of attaining corporate goals.

Finally, a member of top management begins engaging in specific illegal activities. Other key people become involved, and most others tend to go along with the situation and do what is asked of them. Anyone in management who objects is merely excluded. As in the process of groupthink, in situations such as these we see a deterioration of mental efficiency and moral judgment as the pressure to conform increases. The impact of group pressures on the individual should never be underestimated.

Source: Summarized from M. David Ermann and Richard J. Lundman, *Corporate and Governmental Deviance* (New York: Oxford University Press, 1982), pp. 3–18.

Intergroup Conflict

An important characteristic of groups is that they frequently conflict with other groups in an organization. There are many reasons why groups conflict with one another, and the consequences of this conflict can be good for the organization, or it can be extremely negative.

This chapter is concerned mainly with what happens *within* groups: the types and characteristics of groups as they develop. What happens *between* groups (intergroup behavior) is the subject of the next chapter.

THE CONCEPT OF ROLE

role
An individual's role is an organized set of behaviors.

The concept of **role** is very important to the understanding of organizational behavior. Role refers to the expected behavior patterns attributed to a particular position in an organization.

The roles of wife and husband are familiar to everyone. Those roles are culturally defined expectations associated with particular positions. A role may include attitudes and values as well as specific kinds of behavior. It is what an individual must do in order to validate his or her occupancy of a particular position. In other words, what kind of a husband or wife an individual is depends a great deal on how he or she performs the culturally defined role associated with the position. For example, consider your own perceptions of the roles associated with physicians, law enforcement officers, military officers, politicians, college professors, and business executives.

Certain activities are expected of every position in the formal organization. These activities constitute the role for that position from the standpoint of the organization. The organization develops job descriptions that define the activities of a particular position and how it relates to other positions in the organization. However, roles may not be set forth explicitly and yet be clearly understood by group members. For example, members of the marketing department in a bank may know that only the director of marketing represents the bank at national conventions and that they have no chance of attending even though this has never been explicitly stated. This is true both for formal (task and command) groups and for informal (interest and friendship) groups. Thus, whether they are formally or informally established, status hierarchies and accompanying roles are integral parts of every organization.

Multiple Roles and Role Sets

multiple roles
Because most people hold many positions in a variety of organizations, they perform multiple roles. One person may play the role of manager, parent, church leader, and subordinate.

Most of us play many roles simultaneously. This is because we occupy many different positions in a variety of organizations—home, work, church, civic, and so forth. Within each of these organizations, we occupy and perform certain roles. Most individuals perform **multiple roles.** We may simultaneously be playing the role of parent, mate, supervisor, and subordinate. For each position, there may be different role relationships. For example, the position of college professor involves not only the role of teacher in relation to students but also numerous other roles relating the position to administrators, peers, the community, and alumni. Each group may expect different things. For example, students may expect good classroom performance; administrators may expect classroom performance, research, and publication; the college community may expect community service; and alumni may expect help in recruiting students and athletes. This we term the **role set.** A role set refers to those individuals who have expectations for the behavior of the individual in the particular role. The more expectations, the more complex is the role set. For example, a college professor probably has a more complex role set than that of a forest ranger but one less complicated than that of a politician.

role set
Because most groups have their own role expectations, most individuals have a

role set that consists of those individuals who have expectations for the behavior of the individual in a role.

Multiple roles refer to different roles, while role set refers to the different expectations associated with one role. Therefore, an individual involved in many different roles, each with a complex role set, faces the ultimate in complexity of individual behavior. The concepts of multiple roles and role sets are important because there may be complications that make it extremely difficult to define specific roles, especially in organizational settings.[20] This can often result in *role conflict* for the individual. As we saw in Chapter 6, role conflict is a major cause of individual stress in organizations.

Role Perception

You can understand how different individuals have different perceptions of the behavior associated with a given role. In an organizational setting, accuracy in role perception can have a definite impact on performance.[21] This matter is further complicated in an organization because there may be three different perceptions of the same role: that of the formal organization, that of the group, and that of the individual. For example, a college dean has perceptions of the role of professors, as do students and the professors themselves. As we saw in our discussion of role sets above, student perceptions of the role of a professor may be very different from those of the college administrators. This increases even further the possibility of role conflict.

The Organization.   The positions that individuals occupy in an organization are the sum total of their organizationally defined roles. This includes the position in the chain of command, the amount of authority associated with the position, and the functions and duties of the position. These roles are defined by the organization and relate to the position and not to a particular individual.

The Group.   Role relationships develop that relate individuals to the various groups to which they belong. These may be formal and informal groups, and the expectations evolve over time and may or may not match up with the organization's perception of the role. In a group of salespeople, for example, the individual with the longest time in the field may be expected to represent the group to the district manager, although this person may not be the most successful salesperson in the company. In this respect, the role relationships are similar to group norms.

---

[20] An important work in this field is R. L. Kahn, D. M. Wolfe, R. P. Quinn, and J. D. Snoek, *Organizational Stress: Studies in Role Conflict and Ambiguity* (New York: John Wiley & Sons, 1964), pp. 12–26.

[21] For a relevant study, see A. D. Szilagyi, "An Empirical Test of Causal Inference between Role Perceptions, Satisfaction with Work, and Organizational Level," *Personnel Psychology,* Autumn 1977, pp. 375–88.

The Individual.   Every individual who occupies a position in an organization or group has a clearly defined perception of his or her role. This perception will be influenced greatly by background and social class, since they affect the individual's basic values and attitudes. These are brought to the organization and will affect the individuals' perception of their roles. For example, because of social class background and values, a newly promoted first-line supervisor may perceive his or her role as being that of a representative of the group "to" management rather than that of a representative "of" management to the group.

Role Conflict

role conflict
Role conflicts arise when a person in an organization receives incompatible messages regarding appropriate role behavior.

Because of the multiplicity of roles and role sets, it is possible for an individual to face a situation of the simultaneous occurrence of two or more role requirements for which the performance of one precludes the performance of the others. When this occurs, the individual faces a situation known as **role conflict.** Several forms of role conflict can occur in organizations.

Person-Role Conflict.   Person-role conflict occurs when role requirements violate the basic values, attitudes, and needs of the individual occupying the position. A supervisor who finds it difficult to dismiss a subordinate with a family and an executive who resigns rather than engage in some unethical activity are examples of individuals experiencing this type of role conflict.[22]

Intrarole Conflict.   Intrarole conflict occurs when different individuals define a role according to different sets of expectations, making it impossible for the person occupying the role to satisfy all of them. This is more likely to occur when a given role has a complex role set (many different role relationships). The supervisor in an industrial situation has a rather complex role set and thus may face intrarole conflict. On one hand, top management has a set of expectations that stresses the supervisor's role in the management hierarchy. However, the supervisor may have close friendship ties with members of the command group who may be former working peers. This is why supervisors are often described as being "in the middle."[23]

---

[22] For example, see N. Keeley, "Subjective Performance Evaluation and Person-Role Conflict under Conditions of Uncertainty," *Academy of Management Journal,* June 1977, pp. 301–14. For an analysis of some of the organizational implications of this type of conflict, see L. Roos and F. Starke, "Roles in Organizations," in *Handbook of Organizational Design,* ed. W. Starbuck and P. Nystrom (Oxford, England: Oxford University Press, 1980).

[23] For classic discussions of the conflict-laden position of foremen, see F. J. Roethlisberger, "The Foreman: Master and Victim of Double Talk," *Harvard Business Review,* September–October 1965, pp. 23 ff.; and F. C. Mann and J. K. Dent, "The Supervisor: Member of Two Organizational Families," *Harvard Business Review,* November–December 1954, pp. 103–12.

Interrole Conflict. Interrole conflict can result from facing multiple roles. It occurs because individuals simultaneously perform many roles, some of which have conflicting expectations. A scientist in a chemical plant who is also a member of a management group might experience role conflict of this kind. In such a situation, the scientist may be expected to behave in accordance with the expectations of management as well as the expectations of professional chemists. A physician placed in the role of hospital administrator may also experience this type of role conflict. In the next chapter, you will see that this type of role conflict is also often the cause of conflict between groups in many organizations.

The Results of Role Conflict

Behavioral scientists agree that an individual confronted with role conflict will experience psychological stress that may result in emotional problems and indecision. These problems were outlined in detail in Chapter 7. While there are certain kinds of role conflict that managers can do little to avoid, many role conflicts can be minimized. For example, some types of role conflict (especially intrarole conflict) can be the result of violations in the classical principles of chain of command and unity of command. The rationale of the early management writers for these two principles was that violation would probably cause conflicting pressures on the individual. In other words, when individuals are faced with conflicting expectations or demands from two or more sources, the likely result will be a decline in performance.

In addition, interrole conflict can be generated by conflicting expectations of formal or informal groups, with results similar to those of intrarole conflict. Thus, a highly cohesive group with goals not consistent with those of the formal organization can cause a great deal of interrole conflict for its members.

One final point must be made concerning role conflict. Research has shown that role conflict does occur frequently and with negative effects on performance over a wide spectrum of occupations.[24]

---

[24] R. G. Corwin, "The Professional Employee: A Study of Conflict in Nuursing Roles," *American Journal of Sociology,* May 1961, pp. 604–15; J. M. Ivancevich and J. H. Donnelly, Jr., "A Study of Role Clarity and Need for Clarity for Three Occupational Groups," *Academy of Management Journal,* March 1974, pp. 28–36; R. H. Miles, "A Comparison of the Relative Impacts of Role Perceptions of Ambiguity and Conflict by Role," *Academy of Management Journal,* March 1976, pp. 25–34; L. Chonko, "The Relationship of Span of Control to Sales Representatives' Experienced Role Conflict and Role Ambiguity," *Academy of Management Journal,* June 1982, pp. 452–56; and P. J. Nicholson, Jr., and S. C. Goh, "The Relationship of Organization Structure and Interpersonal Attitudes to Role Conflict and Ambiguity in Different Work Environments," *Academy of Management Journal,* March 1983, pp. 148–56.

AN INTEGRATED MODEL OF GROUP FORMATION AND DEVELOPMENT

Figure 8–2 summarizes what has been discussed to this point. In effect, it supports both sides of the chapter-opening Organizational Issue for Debate by indicating that performance (positive or negative) is an important impact of group behavior. Figure 8–2 indicates all of the potential end results of group behavior: individual performances, group performances, and overall organizational effectiveness and performance. The model also includes feedback from the potential behavioral consequences and each of the other elements in the model. Note that each segment can influence each of the other segments.

FIGURE 8–2

A Model of Group Formation and Development

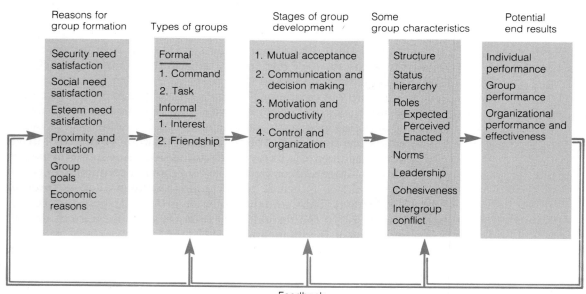

SUMMARY OF KEY POINTS

A. A group can be viewed in terms of perception, organization, motivation, or interaction. You should consider a group as employees who interact in such a manner that the behavior or performance of one group member is influenced by the behavior or performance of other group members.

B. By being aware of group characteristics and behaviors, managers can be prepared for the potential positive and negative results of group activities. In a proactive sense, a manager can intervene to modify the perceptions, attitudes, and motivations that precede the results.

C. People are attracted to groups because of their potential for satisfying needs, their physical proximity and attraction, and the appeal of group goals and activities. In essence, people are attracted to one another; this is a natural process.

D. Groups develop at different rates and with unique patterns that depend on the task, the setting, the members' individual characteristics and behavioral patterns, and the manager's style of managing.

E. Some characteristics of groups are:

1. Structure.
2. Status hierarchy.
3. Roles.
4. Norms.
5. Leadership.
6. Cohesiveness.
7. Intergroup conflict.

These characteristics pervade all groups. In an informal group these characteristics emerge from within the unit, while in a formal group they are established by the managerial process. The characteristics provide a degree of predictability for the members that is important to the group and to outsiders (e.g., management, other groups). A group that is unstable or unpredictable is a problem for its members and for others who interact with it.

F. Each group possesses some degree of cohesiveness. This attractiveness of the group can be a powerful force in influencing individual behavior and performance.

G. Research studies indicate that cohesive groups can formulate goals and norms that may or may not agree with those of management. When these goals and norms are incongruent, some form of managerial intervention is necessary.

H. The concept of role is vital to an understanding of group behavior. A role is the expected behavior patterns that are attributed to a particular position. Most individuals perform multiple roles, each with its own role set (expectations of others for the role). An individual involved in many different roles, each having a complex role set, faces the ultimate in complexity of individual behavior.

I. In organizations, there may be as many as three perceptions of the same role: the organization's, the group's, and the individual's. When an individual faces the simultaneous occurrence of two or more role requirements for which the performance of one precludes the performance of the others, he or she experiences role conflict. Three different types of role conflict—person-role conflict, intrarole conflict, and interrole conflict—can occur in organizational settings. Research has shown that the consequences of role conflict to the individual include increased psychological stress and other emotional reactions. Management can minimize certain types of role conflicts and should be continually aware that the consequences to the organization can include ineffective performance by individuals and groups.

DISCUSSION AND REVIEW QUESTIONS

1. Think of an informal group to which you belong. Does a status hierarchy exist in the group? What is it based on?

2. For the group you have selected above, can you describe any evolution or developmental process such as was described in the chapter? Discuss.

3. What are some of the attitudes, beliefs, and so forth, that you held when you first joined the class in which you are using this book? Describe them, and then indicate whether you believe that they have had any impact on your behavior and performance in the class.

4. Are there any cohesive subgroups in your class? How do you know? Do you think that this has influenced the behavior or performance of their members in the class?

5. Describe some sources of person-role conflict, intrarole conflict, and interrole conflict that you have either experienced personally or watched others experience.

6. Why is it important for a manger to be familiar with concepts of group behavior?

7. Why is cohesiveness an important concept in managing group behavior?

ADDITIONAL REFERENCES

Cobb, A. T. "Informal Influence in the Formal Organization: Perceived Sources of Power among Work Unit Peers." *Academy of Management Journal*, 1980, pp. 155–60.

Cohen, A. R.; S. L. Fink; H. Gadon; and R. D. Willits. *Effective Behavior in Organizations.* Homewood, Ill.: Richard D. Irwin, 1980.

Delbecq, A. L., and A. VandeVen. "A Group Process Model for Problem Identification and Program Planning." *Journal of Applied Behavioral Science,* 1971, pp. 466–92.

Fairhurst, G. T., and B. K. Snavely. "Majority and Token Minority Group Relationship: Power Acquisition and Communication." *Academy of Management Review,* 1983, pp. 292–300.

Gandy, J., and V. V. Murry. "The Experience of Workplace Politics." *Academy of Management Journal,* 1980, pp. 237–51.

Graham, G. H. "Interpersonal Attraction as a Basis of Informal Organization." *Academy of Management Journal,* 1971, pp. 483–95.

Hackman, J. R. "Group Influences on Individuals." In *Handbook of Industrial and Organizational Psychology,* ed. M. D. Dunnette. Skokie, Ill.: Rand McNally, 1976.

Lewis, G. H. "Role Differentiation." *American Sociological Review,* 1972, p. 424–34.

Liddell, W. W., and J. W. Slocum, Jr. "The Effects of Individual-Role Compatibility upon Group Performance: An Extension of Schutz's FIRO Theory." *Academy of Management Journal,* 1976, pp. 413–26.

Malcolm, A. *The Tyranny of the Group.* Totowa, N.J.: Littlefield, Adams, 1975.

Munchus, G., III. "Employer-Employee Based Quality Circles in Japan: Human Resource Policy Implications for American Firms." *Academy of Management Review,* 1983, pp. 255–61.

Rahim, M. A. "A Measure of Styles of Handling Interpersonal Conflict." *Academy of Management Journal,* 1983, pp. 368–76.

Smith, P. B. *Groups within Organizations.* New York: Harper & Row, 1973.

Steiner, I. D. *Group Processes and Productivity.* New York: Academic Press, 1972.

Turner, A. N. "A Conceptual Scheme for Describing Work Group Behavior." In *Organizational Behavior and Administration,* ed. P. R. Lawrence et al. Homewood, Ill.: Richard D. Irwin, 1961.

CASE FOR ANALYSIS

The "No Martini" Lunch

Jim Lyons had just completed his second month as manager of an important office of a nationwide sales organization. He believed that he had made the right choice in leaving his old company. This new position offered a great challenge, excellent pay and benefits, and tremendous opportunity for advancement. In addition, his family seemed to be adjusting well to the new community. However, in Jim's mind there was one very serious problem that he believed must be confronted immediately, or it could threaten his satisfaction in the long run.

Since taking the job, Jim had found out that the man he replaced had made an institution of the hard-drinking business lunch. He and a group of other key executives had virtually a standing appointment at various local restaurants. Even when clients were not present, they would have several drinks before ordering their lunches. When they returned, it was usually well into the afternoon, and they were in no condition to make the decisions or take the actions that were often the pretext of the lunch in the first place. This practice had also spread to the subordinates of the various executives, and it was not uncommon to see various groups of salespersons doing the same thing a few days each week. Jim decided that he wanted to end the practice, at least for himself and the members of his group.

Jim knew that this was not going to be an easy problem to solve. The drinking had become institutionalized with a great deal of psychological pressure from a central figure—in this case, the man he replaced. He decided to plan the approach that he would take and then discuss the problem and his approach for solving it with his superior, Norm Landy.

The following week, Jim made an appointment with Norm to discuss the situation. Norm listened intently as Jim explained the drinking problem but did not show any surprise at learning about it. Jim then explained what he planned to do.

"Norm, I'm making two assumptions on the front end. First, I don't believe it would do any good to state strong new policies about drinking at lunch or to lecture my people about the evils of the liquid lunch. About all I'd accomplish there would be to raise a lot of latent guilt that would only result in resentment and resistance. Second, I am assuming that the boss is often a role model for his subordinates. Unfortunately, the man I replaced made a practice of the drinking lunch. The subordinates close to him then conform to his drinking habits and exert pressure on other members of the group. Before you know it, everyone is a drinking buddy and the practice becomes institutionalized even when one member is no longer there.

"Here is what I intend to do about it. First, when I go to lunch with the other managers, I will do no drinking. More importantly, however, for the members of my group, I am going to establish a new role model. For example, at least once a week we have a legitimate reason to work through lunch. In the past, everyone has gone out anyway. I intend to hold a business lunch and have sandwiches and soft drinks sent in. In addition, I intend to make it a regular practice to take different groups of my people to lunch at a no-alcohol coffee shop.

"My goal, Norm, is simply to let my subordinates know that alcohol is not a necessary part of the workday and that drinking will not win my approval. By not drinking with the other managers, I figure that sooner or later they too will get the point. As you can see, I intend to get the message across by my behavior. There will be no words of censure. What do you think, Norm?"

Norm Landy pushed himself away from his desk and came around and seated himself beside Jim. He then looked at Jim and whispered, "Are you crazy? I guarantee you, Jim, that you are going to accomplish nothing but cause a lot of trouble. Trouble between your group and other groups if you succeed, trouble between you and your group, and trouble between you and the other managers. Believe me, Jim, I see the problem, and I agree with you that it is a problem. But the cure might kill the patient. Will all that conflict and trouble be worth it?"

Jim thought for a moment and said, "I think it will be good for the organization in the long run."

Questions for Consideration

1. Do you agree with Norm Landy or with Jim Lyons? Why?

2. Do you think that anything can be done about this situation? Why? What is your opinion of Jim's plan?

3. What would you do in Jim's situation? Be specific.

Chapter 9

After completing Chapter 9, you should be able to:

Define functional conflict and dysfunctional conflict.

Describe the impact of intergroup conflict on organizational performance.

Discuss why intergroup conflict occurs.

Compare the consequences of intergroup conflict *within* groups and *between* groups.

Identify various techniques that can be used to manage intergroup conflict.

Intergroup Behavior and Managing Conflict

Should Management Seek to Eliminate Conflict?*

Argument For

Many practicing managers view group conflict negatively and thus seek to resolve or eliminate all types of disputes. These managers contend that conflict disrupts the organization and prevents optimal performance. As such, conflict is a clear indication that something is wrong with the organization and that sound principles are not being applied in managing the activities of the organization.

Since their desire was to eliminate conflict, early organizational writers based their approaches on the principles of authority and unity of command. They believed that conflict could be eliminated or avoided by recruiting the right people, carefully specifying job descriptions, structuring the organization in such a way as to establish a clear chain of command, and establishing clear rules and procedures to meet various contingencies.

Many writers believe that this view is held today by the majority of practicing managers. These managers view all conflict as disruptive, and they think that their task is to eliminate it.

---

* The first view is discussed in detail in C. B. Derr, *A Historical Review of Management Organization Conflict* (Boston: Graduate School of Education, Harvard University, 1972), pp. 1–22. The opposing view is discussed in detail in M. Olson, *The Logic of Collective Action* (Cambridge, Mass.: Harvard University Press, 1965). Also see M. Deutsch, "Conflicts: Productive and Destructive," in *Conflict Resolution through Communication*, ed. F. Jandt (New York: Harper & Row, 1973), pp. 155–97.

Argument Against

Many managers believe that a more realistic view of conflict is that it cannot be avoided. They believe that conflict is inevitable and that it can result from numerous factors, including the structure of the organization itself, the performance evaluation system, and even something as seemingly unimportant as the physical design of an office and its furnishings.

In fact, these individuals believe that a certain amount of conflict is not only useful but that optimal organizational performance *requires* a moderate level of conflict. Without conflict, there would be no sensing of a need to change and attention would not be called to problem areas.

Obviously, these individuals realize that too much conflict is undesirable. Thus, they believe that conflict can either "add to" or "detract from" organizational performance in varying degrees. In other words, conflict can be positive or negative for the organization, depending on the amount and kind. Under this viewpoint, management's task becomes one of managing the level of conflict in order to achieve optimal performance.

For any organization to perform effectively, interdependent individuals and groups must establish working relationships across organizational boundaries, between individuals, and among groups. Individuals or groups may depend on one another for information, assistance, or coordinated action. But the fact is that they are interdependent. Such interdependence may foster cooperation or conflict.

For example, the production and marketing executives of a firm may meet to discuss ways to deal with foreign competition. Such a meeting may be reasonably free of conflict. Decisions get made, strategies are developed, and the executives return to work. Thus, there is intergroup cooperation to achieve a goal. However, this may not be the case if sales decline because the firm is not offering enough variety in its product line. The marketing department desires broad product lines to offer more variety to customers, while the production department desires narrow product lines to keep production costs at a manageable level and to increase productivity. Conflict is likely to occur at this point because each function has its own goals which, in this case, conflict. Thus, groups may cooperate on one point and conflict on another.

The focus of this chapter is on conflict that occurs between groups in organizations.[1] Intergroup problems are not the only type of conflict that can exist in organizations. Conflict between individuals, however, can usually be more easily resolved through existing mechanisms. Troublesome employees can be fired, transferred, or given new work schedules.

This chapter begins with an examination of attitudes toward conflict. Reasons for the existence of intergroup conflict and its consequences are also presented. Finally, we shall outline various techniques that have been used to successfully manage intergroup conflict.

A REALISTIC VIEW OF INTERGROUP CONFLICT

Conflict is inevitable in organizations. Intergroup conflict, however, can be both a positive and a negative force, so management should *not* strive to eliminate all conflict, only conflict that will have disruptive effects on the organization's efforts to achieve goals. Some type or degree of conflict may prove beneficial if it is used as an instrument for change or innovation. In Chapter 7, you saw that individuals have differing abilities to withstand stress. Thus, it appears that the critical

---

[1] See Clayton Alderfer and Ken K. Smith, "Studying Intergroup Relations Embedded in Organizations," *Administrative Science Quarterly,* March 1982, pp. 35–64.

issue is not conflict itself but rather how it is managed. Using this approach, we can define conflict in terms of the *effect it has on the organization.* In this respect, we shall discuss both *functional* and *dysfunctional* conflict.[2]

Functional Conflict

functional conflict
When the results of a conflict or confrontation between groups proves beneficial to the organization, it is functional conflict from the organization's standpoint.

A **functional conflict** is a confrontation between groups that enhances and benefits the organization's performance. For example, two departments in a hospital may be in conflict over the most efficient and adaptive method of delivering health care to low-income rural families. The two departments agree on the goal but not on the *means* to achieve it. Whatever the outcome, low-income rural families will probably end up with better medical care once the conflict is settled. Without this type of conflict in organizations, there would be little commitment to change and most groups would probably become stagnant. Thus, functional conflict can be thought of as a type of "creative tension."

Dysfunctional Conflict

dysfunctional conflict
When the results of a conflict or confrontation between groups hinder organizational performance, it is dysfunctional conflict from the organization's standpoint.

A **dysfunctional conflict** is any confrontation or interaction between groups that harms the organization or hinders the achievement of organizational goals. Management *must* seek to eliminate dysfunctional conflicts. Beneficial conflicts can often turn into bad conflicts. In most cases, the point at which functional conflict becomes dysfunctional is impossible to identify precisely. Levels of stress and that conflict that may help create a healthy and positive movement toward goals in one group may prove extremely disruptive and dysfunctional in another group (or a different time for the same group). A group's tolerance for stress and conflict can also depend on the *type* of organization it serves. Automobile manufacturers, professional sports teams, and crisis organizations such as police and fire departments would have different points where functional conflict becomes dysfunctional than would organizations such as universities, research and development firms, and motion picture production firms.

Dysfunctional conflict can have a negative impact on the performance of individuals, groups, and organizations. Such a situation is illustrated vividly in the following Close-Up.

---

[2] This view reflects current thinking among management theorists and a growing number of practitioners. It has been labeled the *interactionist* view. For a major work devoted entirely to the subject of organizational conflict that discusses this and other views, see Stephen P. Robbins, *Managing Organizational Conflict* (Englewood Cliffs, N.J.: Prentice-Hall, 1974). Also see K. W. Thomas, "Organizational Conflict," in *Organizational Behavior,* ed. S. Kerr (Columbus, Ohio: Grid, 1979), pp. 151–81.

ORGANIZATIONS: CLOSE-UP

Dysfunctional Conflict: PATCO versus the Government

In what was one of the most shocking labor conflicts in recent years, 11,500 air traffic controllers walked off their jobs on August 3, 1981. The Reagan administration, pointing to a law that forbade strikes by federal employees, insisted on no negotiations. Conflict between the Professional Air Traffic Controllers Organization (PATCO) and the Federal Aviation Administration (FAA) reached its peak in the summer of 1981. Instead of open and constructive bargaining, there were threats, hostility, and disruptive actions. Despite a 48-hour "window" in which the controllers could return to their jobs, only a handful did return. The conflict ended with the 11,500 air traffic controllers quitting their jobs and then being fired by the president.

There were apparently no winners as a result of the conflict. Air travelers were stranded for days; airline schedules were in chaos for months; the air traffic controllers lost their jobs; and government had to hire and train new air traffic controllers.

Source: David G. Bowers, "What Would Make 11,500 People Quit Their Jobs," *Organizational Dynamics*, Winter 1983, pp. 5–19.

Dysfunctional conflict also can occur in situations much less visible than the PATCO/government conflict. One such source of disruption is described in the following Close-Up.

ORGANIZATIONS: CLOSE-UP

Office Romances Result in Dysfunctional Conflict

Recent research has found that love affairs between managers can ruin careers, disrupt the organization's chain of command, and cause conflict between individuals and groups as group members choose sides. As a result, communication between the affected groups can break down.

In four specific case studies, the women eventually left the organization following long, bitter periods of intergroup conflict, gossip, and backbiting. According to the researcher, the incidence of such problems is growing as more and more women join executive ranks. With better education and social standing, the women executives in the study were equal partners in the relationship and not the object of a sexual fling.

Conflict and Organizational Performance

Conflict may have either a positive or negative impact on organizational performance, depending on the nature of the conflict and how it is managed. For every organization, there is an optimal level of conflict that can be considered highly functional: it helps generate positive performance. When the conflict level is *too low,* performance can suffer. Innovation and change are difficult, and the organization may have difficulty in adapting to change in its environment. If this low conflict level continues, the very survival of the organization can be threatened. On the other hand, if the conflict level becomes *too high,* the resulting chaos can also threaten the organization's survival. An example is the popular press coverage of the results of "dissension" in labor unions and its impact on performance. If fighting between rival factions in the union becomes too great, it can render the union less effective in pursuing its mission of furthering its members' interests. The proposed relationship between level of intergroup conflict and organizational performance is presented in Figure 9–1 and explained for three hypothetical situations.

Views toward Intergroup Conflict in Practice

Some organizational researchers contend that dysfunctional conflict should be eliminated and functional conflict encouraged. However, this is not what actually happens in most organizations.[3] In practice, most managers attempt to eliminate all types of conflict, whether dysfunctional or functional. Why is this the case? Some reasons are:

1. Anticonflict values have historically been reinforced in the home, school, and church. Traditionally, conflict between children or between children and parents has, for the most part, been discouraged. In school systems, conflict has been discouraged. Teachers had all the answers, and both teachers and children were rewarded for orderly

[3] K. W. Thomas and W. H. Schmidt, "A Survey of Managerial Interests with Respect to Conflict," *Academy of Management Journal*, June 1976, pp. 315–18.

FIGURE 9–1

FIGURE 9–1

Proposed Relationship between Intergroup Conflict and Organizational Performance

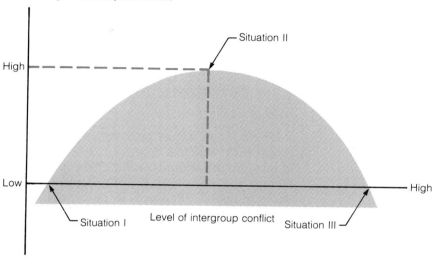

	Level of Intergroup Conflict	Probable Impact on Organization	Organization Characterized by	Level of Organizational Performance
Situation I	Low or none	Dysfunctional	Slow adaptation to environmental changes Few changes Little stimulation of ideas Apathy Stagnation	Low
Situation II	Optimal	Functional	Positive movement toward goals Innovation and change Search for problem solutions Creativity and quick adaptation to environmental changes	High
Situation III	High	Dysfunctional	Disruption Interference with activities Coordination difficult Chaos	Low

classrooms. Finally, most religious doctrines stress peace, tranquillity, and acceptance without questioning.

2. Managers are often evaluated and rewarded for the lack of conflict in their areas of responsibility. Anticonflict values, in fact, become part of the "culture" of the organization. Harmony and satisfaction are viewed positively, while conflicts and dissatisfaction are viewed negatively. Under such conditions, managers seek to avoid conflicts—functional or dysfunctional—that could disturb the status quo.[4]

WHY INTERGROUP CONFLICT OCCURS

Every group comes into at least partial conflict with every other group with which it interacts. This tendency is known as "the law of interorganizational conflict."[5] In this section, we shall examine four factors that contribute to group conflict: work interdependence, differences in goals, differences in perceptions, and the increased demand for specialists.

Interdependence

pooled interdependence Pooled interdependence requires no interaction among groups except through the total organization.

Work interdependence occurs when two or more organizational groups must depend on one another to complete their tasks. The conflict potential in such situations is high. Three distinct types of interdependence among groups have been identified.[6]

Pooled Interdependence. **Pooled interdependence** requires no interaction among groups because each group, in effect, performs separately. However, the pooled performances of all the groups determine how successful the organization is. For example, the staff of an IBM sales office in one region may have no interaction with their peers in another region. Similarly, two bank branches will have little or no interaction. In both cases, however, the groups are interdependent because the performance of each must be adequate if the total organization is to thrive. The conflict potential in pooled interdependence is relatively low, and management can rely on standard rules and procedures developed at the main office for coordination.

sequential interdependence Sequential interdependence requires one group to complete its task before another can complete its task, thereby increasing the likelihood of conflict.

Sequential Interdependence. **Sequential interdependence** requires one group to complete its task before another group can complete its task. Tasks are performed in a sequential fashion. In a manufacturing plant, for example, the product must be assembled before

---

[4] This section is based on Robbins, *Managing Organizational Conflict.*

[5] See Anthony Downs, *Inside Bureaucracy* (Boston: Little, Brown, 1968).

[6] J. Thompson, *Organizations in Action* (New York: McGraw-Hill, 1967).

it can be painted. Thus, the assembling department must complete its task before the painting department can begin painting.

Under these circumstances, since the output of one group serves as the input for another, conflict between the groups is more likely to occur. Coordinating this type of interdependence involves effective use of the management function of planning.

reciprocal interdependence Reciprocal interdependence requires one group's output to serve as another group's input, thereby providing a basis for great potential conflict.

Reciprocal Interdependence. Reciprocal interdependence requires the output of each group to serve as input to other groups in the organization. Consider the relationships that exist between the anesthesiology staff, nursing staff, technician staff, and surgeons in a hospital operating room. This relationship creates a high degree of reciprocal interdependence. The same interdependence exists among groups involved in space launchings. Another example is the interdependence between airport control towers, flight crews, ground operations, and maintenance crews. Clearly, the potential for conflict is great in any of these situations. Effective coordination involves management's skillful use of the organizational processes of communication and decision making.[7]

All organizations have pooled interdependence among groups. Complex organizations also have sequential interdependence. The most complicated organizations experience pooled, sequential, and reciprocal interdependence among groups. The more complex the organization, the greater are the potentials for conflict and the more difficult is the task facing management.

Differences in Goals

As the subunits of an organization become specialized, they often develop dissimilar goals. A goal of a production unit may include low production costs and few defective products. A goal of the research and development unit may be innovative ideas that can be converted into commercially successful new products. These different goals can lead to different expectations among the members of each unit. Because of their goal, production engineers may expect close supervision, while research scientists may expect a great deal of participation in decision making. Because of the different goals of these two groups, conflict can result when they interact. Finally, marketing departments usually have a goal of maximum gross income. On the other hand, credit departments seek to minimize credit losses. Depending on which department prevails, different customers might be selected. Here again, conflict can occur because each department has a different goal.

---

[7] For some recent research, see D. S. Cochran and D. D. White, "Intraorganizational Conflict in the Hospital Purchasing Decision," *Academy of Management Journal,* June 1981, pp. 324–32.

There are certain conditions that foster intergroup conflict because of differences in goals.

Limited Resources.   When resources are limited and must be allocated, mutual dependences increase and any differences in group goals become more apparent. If money, space, the labor force, and materials were unlimited, each group could pursue, at least to a relative degree, its own goals. But in virtually all cases, resources must be allocated or shared. What often occurs in limited resource situations is a win-lose competition that can easily result in dysfunctional conflict.

Reward Structures.   Intergroup conflict is more likely to occur when the reward system is related to individual group performance rather than to overall organizational performance. When rewards are related to individual group performance, performance is, in fact, viewed as an independent variable, although the performance of the group is in reality very interdependent. For example, in the situation described above, suppose that the marketing group is rewarded for sales produced and that the credit group is rewarded for minimizing credit losses. In such a situation, competition will be directly reinforced and dysfunctional conflict will inadvertently be rewarded.

Intergroup conflict arising from differences in goals can be dysfunctional to the organization as a whole. Depending on the type of organization, intergroup conflicts can also be dysfunctional to third-party groups—usually the clients the organization serves. An example of this is controversy in many teaching hospitals over the conflict between meeting the goals of quality health care for patients and meeting the teaching needs of future physicians.

Differences in Perceptions

The differences in goals can be accompanied by differing perceptions of reality, and disagreements over what constitutes reality can lead to conflict. For instance, a problem in a hospital may be viewed in one way by the administrative staff and in another way by the medical staff. Alumni and faculty may have different perceptions concerning the importance of a winning football program. Many factors cause groups in organizations to form differing perceptions of reality. The major factors include different goals, different time horizons, status incongruency, and inaccurate perceptions.

Different Goals.   Differences in group goals are an obvious contributor to differing perceptions. For instance, if the goal of marketing is to maximize sales, that department's personnel will certainly view a major breakdown in production differently than will the staff of the production department, whose goal is to minimize costs.

Different Time Horizons.   Time perspectives influence how a group perceives reality. Deadlines influence the priorities and importance that groups assign to their various activities. Research scientists working for a chemical manufacturer may have a time perspective of several years, while the same firm's manufacturing engineers may work within time frames of less than a year. A bank president might focus on 5- and 10-year time spans, while middle managers might concentrate on much shorter spans. With such differences in time horizons, problems and issues deemed critical by one group may be dismissed as not important by another, and conflicts may erupt.

Status Incongruency.   Conflicts concerning the relative status of different groups are common and influence perceptions. Usually, many different status standards are found in an organization, rather than an absolute one. The result is many status hierarchies. For example, status conflicts are often created by work patterns—which group initiates the work and which group responds. A production department, for instance, may perceive a change as an affront to its status because it must accept a salesperson's initiation of work. This status conflict may be aggravated deliberately by the salesperson. Academic snobbery is certainly a fact of campus life at many colleges and universities. Members of a particular academic discipline perceive themselves, for one reason or another, as having a higher status than others.

Inaccurate Perceptions.   Inaccurate perceptions often cause one group to develop stereotypes about other groups. While the differences between groups may actually be small, each group will tend to exaggerate them. Thus, you will hear that "all women executives are aggressive" or "all bank trust officers behave alike." When the differences between the groups are emphasized, the stereotypes are reinforced, relations deteriorate, and conflict develops.

The Increased Demand for Specialists

Conflicts between staff specialists and line generalists are probably the most common type of intergroup conflict. With the growing necessity for technical expertise in all areas of organizations, staff roles can be expected to expand and line and staff conflicts can be expected to increase. Line and staff persons simply view one another and their roles in the organization from different perspectives.[8] Table 9–1 summarizes some additional causes of conflict between staff specialists

---

[8] For a classic discussion, see L. A. Allen, "The Line-Staff Relationship," *Management Record,* September 1955, pp. 346–49.

TABLE 9-1

Common Causes of Line/Staff Conflict

Perceived Diminution of Line Authority. Line managers fear that specialists will encroach on their jobs and thereby diminish their authority and power. As a result, specialists often complain that line executives do not make proper use of staff specialists and do not give staff members sufficient authority.

Social and Physical Differences. Often, major differences exist between line managers and staff specialists with respect to age, education, dress, and attitudes. In many cases, staff specialists are younger than line managers and have higher educational levels or training in a specialized field.

Line Dependence on Staff Knowledge. Since line generalists often do not have the technical knowledge necessary to manage their departments, they are dependent on the specialist. The resulting gap between knowledge and authority may be even greater when the staff specialist is lower in the organizational hierarchy than the manager, which is often the case. As a result, staff members often complain that line managers resist new ideas.

Different Loyalties. Divided loyalties frequently exist between line managers and staff specialists. The staff specialist may be loyal to a discipline, while the line manager may be loyal to the organization. The member of the product development group may be a chemist first and a member of the organization second. The production manager's first loyalty, however, may be to the organization. When loyalties to a particular function or discipline are greater than loyalties to the overall organization, conflict is likely to occur.

and line generalists.[9] With the growth of sophistication, specialization, and complexity in most organizations, line/staff conflicts will continue to be a major concern in the management of organizational behavior.

---

[9] See M. Dalton, "Conflicts between Staff and Line Managerial Officers," *American Sociological Review,* June 1950, pp. 342–51; A. W. Gouldner, "Cosmopolitans and Locals: Toward an Analysis of Latent Social Roles," *Administrative Science Quarterly,* December 1957, pp. 281–306; A. Etzioni, ed., *Complex Organizations* (New York: Holt, Rinehard & Winston, 1961); A. Etzioni, *Modern Organization* (Englewood Cliffs, N.J.: Prentice-Hall, 1964); R. W. Scott, "Professionals in Bureaucracies: Areas of Conflict," in *Professionals,* ed. H. M. Vollmer and D. L. Mills (Englewood Cliffs, N.J.: Prentice-Hall, 1966); P. R. Lawrence and J. W. Lorsch, *Organization and Environment: Managing Differentiation and Intergration* (Boston: Graduate School of Business Administration, Harvard University, 1967); J. A. Balasco and J. A. Alutto, "Line and Staff Conflicts: Some Empirical Insights," *Academy of Management Journal,* March 1969, pp. 469–77: E. Rhenman, *Conflict and Cooperation in Business* (New York: John Wiley & Sons, 1970); P. K. Berger and A. J. Grimes, "Cosmopolitan-Local: A Factor Analysis of the Construct," *Administrative Science Quarterly,* June 1973, pp. 223–35; and J. E. Sorensen and T. L. Sorensen, "The Conflict of Professionals in Bureaucratic Organizations," *Administrative Science Quarterly,* March 1974, pp. 98–106.

THE CONSEQUENCES OF DYSFUNCTIONAL INTERGROUP CONFLICT

Behavioral scientists have spent more than three decades researching and analyzing how dysfunctional intergroup conflict affects those who experience it.[10] They have found that groups placed in a conflict situation tend to react in fairly predictable ways. We shall now examine a number of the changes that occur *within groups* and *between groups* as a result of dysfunctional intergroup conflict.

Changes within Groups

Many changes are likely to occur within groups involved in intergroup conflict. Unfortunately, these changes generally result in either a continuance or an escalation of the conflict.

Increased Group Cohesiveness. Competition, conflict, or external threat usually result in group members putting aside individual differences and closing ranks. Members become more loyal to the group, and group membership becomes more attractive.

Rise in Autocratic Leadership. In extreme conflict situations where threats are perceived, democratic methods of leadership are likely to become less popular. The members want strong leadership. Thus, the leaders are likely to become more autocratic. In the National Football League players strike in 1982 and the PATCO strike discussed earlier, the heads of each union had tremendous authority.

Focus on Activity. When a group is in conflict, its members usually emphasize doing what the group does and doing it very well. The group becomes more task-oriented. Tolerance for members who "goof off" is low and there is less concern for individual member satisfaction. The emphasis is on accomplishing the group's task and defeating the "enemy" (the other group in the conflict).

Emphasis on Loyalty. Conformity to group norms tends to become more important in conflict situations. Group goals take precedence over individual satisfaction as members are expected to demonstrate their loyalty. In major conflict situations, interaction with members of "the other group" may be outlawed.

---

[10] The classic work is M. Sherif and C. Sherif, *Groups in Harmony and Tension* (New York: Harper & Row, 1953). Their study was conducted among groups in a boys' camp. They stimulated conflict between the groups and observed the changes that occurred in group behavior. Also see their "Experiments in Group Conflict," *Scientific American,* March 1956, pp. 54–58.

Changes between Groups

During conflicts, certain changes will probably occur *between* the groups involved.

Distorted Perceptions. During conflicts, the perceptions of each group's members become distorted. Group members develop stronger opinions of the importance of their units. Each group sees itself as superior in performance to the other and as more important to the survival of the organization than other groups. In a conflict situation, nurses may conclude that they are more important to a patient than physicians, while physicians may consider themselves more important than hospital administrators. The marketing group in a business organization may think, "Without us selling the product, there would be no money to pay anyone else's salary." The production group meanwhile will say, "If we don't make the product, there is nothing to sell." Ultimately, none of these groups is more important, but conflict can cause their members to develop gross misperceptions of reality.

Negative Stereotyping. As conflict increases and perceptions become more distorted, all of the negative stereotypes that may have ever existed are reinforced. A management representative may say, "I've always said these union guys are just plain greedy. Now they've proved it." The head of a local teacher's union may say, "Now we know that what all politicians are interested in is getting reelected, not the quality of education." When negative stereotyping is a factor in a conflict, the members of each group see less differences *within* their unit than actually exist and greater differences *between* the groups than actually exist.

Decreased Communication. Communications between the groups in conflict usually break down. This can be extremely dysfunctional, especially where sequential interdependence or reciprocal interdependence relationships exist between groups. The decision-making process can be disrupted, and the customers or others whom the organization serves can be affected. Consider the possible consequences to patients, for instance, if a conflict between hospital technicians and nurses continues until it lowers the quality of health care.

While these are not the only dysfunctional consequences of intergroup conflict, they are the most common and they have been well documented in the research literature.[11] Other consequences, such as violence and aggression, are less common but also occur. When

---

[11] For additional discussion, see J. Litterer, "Conflict in Organizations: A Re-Examination," *Academy of Management Journal,* September 1966, pp. 178–86; J. W. Lorsch and J. J. Morse, *Organizations and Their Members: A Contingency Approach* (New York: Harper & Row, 1974); and E. Schein, "Intergroup Problems in Organizations," in *Organization Development: Theory, Practice, and Research,* 2d. ed. W. French, C. Bell, and R. Zawacki (Plano, Tex.: Business Publications, 1983), pp. 106–10.

intergroup conflicts take place, some form of managerial intervention is usually necessary. How managers can deal with these situations is the subject of the next section.

MANAGING INTERGROUP CONFLICT THROUGH RESOLUTION

Since managers must live with intergroup conflict, they must confront the problem of managing it.[12] In this section, you will examine techniques that have been used successfully in resolving intergroup conflicts that have reached levels dysfunctional to the organization.[13]

Problem Solving

The confrontation method of problem solving seeks to reduce tensions through face-to-face meetings of the conflicting groups. The purpose of the meetings is to identify conflicts and resolve them. The conflicting groups openly debate various issues and bring together all relevant information until a decision has been reached. For conflicts resulting from misunderstandings or language barriers, the confrontation method has proved effective. For solving more complex problems, (e.g., conflicts where groups have different value systems), the method has been less successful.

Superordinate Goals

superordinate goals
Superordinate goals cannot be achieved without the cooperation of the conflicting groups.

In the resolution of conflicts between groups, the **superordinate goals** technique involves developing a common set of goals and objectives. These goals and objectives cannot be attained without the cooperation of the groups involved. In fact, they are unattainable by one group singly and supersede all other goals of any of the individual groups involved in the conflict.[14] For example, several unions in the automobile and airline industries have, in recent years, agreed to forgo

---

[12] See David M. Herold, "Improving the Performance Effectiveness of Groups through a Task-Contingent Selection of Intervention Strategies," *Academy of Management Review,* April 1978, pp. 315–51; and R. A. Cosier and T. L. Ruble, "Research on Conflict-Handling Behavior: An Experimental Approach," *Academy of Management Journal,* December 1981, pp. 816–31.

[13] Based on Robbins, *Managing Organizational Conflict,* pp. 67–77.

[14] See M. Sherif and C. Sherif, *Social Psychology* (New York: Harper & Row, 1969), pp. 228–62, for a detailed discussion of this method. Sherif and Sherif conducted a number of sociopsychological experiments designed to determine effective ways of resolving conflict. Based on this research, they developed the concept of superordinate goals. Also see J. D. Hunger and L. W. Stern, "An Assessment of the Functionality of the Superordinate Goal in Reducing Conflict," *Academy of Management Journal,* December 1976, pp. 591–605.

increases and in some cases to accept pay reductions because the survival of their firm or industry was threatened. When the crisis is over, demands for higher wages will undoubtedly return, as they have at once-struggling Chrysler Corporation.

Expansion of Resources

As noted earlier, a major cause of intergroup conflict is limited resources. Whatever one group succeeds in obtaining is gained at the expense of another group. The scarce resource may be a particular position (e.g., the presidency of the firm), money, space, and so forth. For example, one major publishing firm decided to expand by establishing a subsidiary firm. Most observers believed that the major reason for the expansion was to allow the firm to become involved in other segments of the market. While this was partially correct, a stronger reason was to enable the firm to stem the exit of valued personnel. By establishing the subsidiary, the firm was able to double its executive positions, since the subsidiary needed a president, various vice presidents, and other executives. Expanding resources is a very successful technique for solving conflicts in many cases, since this technique may enable almost everyone to be satisfied. In reality, however, resources are usually not easily expanded.

Avoidance

Frequently, some way can be found to avoid conflict. While avoidance may not bring any long-run benefits, it certainly can work as a short-run solution. Avoiding a conflict neither effectively resolves it nor eliminates it. Eventually, the conflict will have to be faced. But in some circumstances avoidance may be the best temporary alternative.

Smoothing

The technique known as smoothing emphasizes the common interests of the conflicting groups and de-emphasizes their differences. The basic belief behind smoothing is that stressing shared viewpoints on certain issues facilitates movement toward a common goal. If the differences between the groups are serious, smoothing—like avoidance—is, at best, a short-run solution.

Compromise

Compromise is a traditional method for resolving intergroup conflicts.[15] With compromise, there is no distinct winner or loser and

---

[15] For a discussion of the problems associated with compromise, see W. Notz and F. Starke, "Final Offer vs. Conventional Arbitration as Means of Conflict Management," *Administrative Science Quarterly,* June 1978, pp. 189–203.

the decision reached is probably not ideal for either group. Compromise can be used very effectively when the goal sought (e.g., money) can be divided equitably. If this is not possible, one group must give up something of value as a concession. Compromise may also involve third-party interventions, as well as total group or representative negotiating and voting.[16] An example of resolving conflict through compromise is provided in the following Close-Up:

ORGANIZATIONS: CLOSE-UP

Resolving Conflict through Compromise at International Paper

To reduce the possibility of major conflicts between the two groups, the United Paper Workers Union and International Paper Company agreed on the need for "a system of cooperation that avoids confrontation." Leaders of both groups agreed to meet formally at least twice a year to discuss mutual problems. Each group must appoint three members to solve problems. The company agreed to steer clear of attempts to eliminate the union from certain plants and to rebuild existing unionized mills rather than build new ones when it expands. In return, the union was willing to grant the company a cheaper pension formula in contract talks at International Paper's southern mills and in future talks at its other operations.

Source: "Paper Avoids a Replay of J. P. Stevens," *Business Week*, June 1983, pp. 33–34.

Authoritative Command

The use of authority may be the oldest and most frequently used method for resolving intergroup conflict. Using this method, management simply resolves the conflict as it sees fit and communicates its desires to the groups involved. Subordinates will usually abide by a superior's decision, whether or not they agree with it. Thus, authoritative command usually works in the short run. As with avoidance, smoothing, and compromise, however, it does not focus on the cause of the conflict but rather on the results of it. If the causes of the conflict are still present, it will probably recur.

---

[16] For research on a different but related problem, see J. Sullivan, R. Peterson, N. Kameda, and J. Shimada, "The Relationship between Conflict Resolution Approaches and Trust—A Cross Cultural Study," *Academy of Management Journal*, December 1981, pp. 803–15.

Altering the Human Variable

Altering the human variable involves trying to change the behavior of the members of the groups involved. This method focuses on the cause or causes of the conflict and on the attitudes of the people involved. While the method is certainly difficult, it does center on the cause of the conflict. Part Six of this book focuses specifically on changing behavior. In it, we shall see that while altering the human variable is slower than other methods and often costly, the results can be significant in the long run.

Altering the Structural Variables

Another way to resolve intergroup disputes is to alter the structural variables. This involves changing the formal structure of the organization. Structure refers to the fixed relationships among the jobs of the organization and includes the design of jobs and departments. Altering the structure of the organization to resolve intergroup conflict involves such things as transferring, exchanging, or rotating members of the groups or having someone serve as a coordinator, liaison, or go-between who keeps groups communicating with one another.

Identifying a Common Enemy

In some respects, identifying a common enemy is the negative side of superordinate goals. Groups in conflict may temporarily resolve their differences and unite to combat a common enemy. The common enemy may be a competitor that has just introduced a clearly superior product. Conflicting groups in a bank may suddenly work in close harmony when government bank examiners make a visit. The common-enemy phenomenon is very evident in domestic conflicts. Most police officers prefer not to become involved in heated domestic conflicts because, in far too many cases, the combatants close ranks and turn on the police officer.

Whatever the techniques utilized to deal with intergroup conflict (and there are undoubtedly others), the important point is that you must learn how to recognize both the existence and the causes of intergroup conflict. You must also develop skills to deal with it. A program for training managers is discussed in the following Close-Up.

ORGANIZATIONS: CLOSE-UP

Conflict Management at Union Carbide

Union Carbide is concerned with how its managers manage conflict. Recently, it sent 200 managers to a three-day workshop to help them develop skills in conflict management. One technique used at the workshop for teaching managers how to deal with conflict in organizational settings is known as the egg drop exercise.

In this exercise, managers are divided into teams. Each team races against the clock as well as against other teams. The teams are instructed to build a device that will catch dropped eggs gently enough to keep them from breaking. The managers acquire the needed building materials from an auctioneer who "sells" such items as metal strips and pieces of string. Each team bids for the items with allocated funds. A videotape machine records the bidding, the discussion, and the construction of the egg-catching devices.

At the completion of the exercise, the managers view a replay. What they often see is bickering, arguing, mocking one another, hostility, impatience, and relying on authoritarian orders. While the objective of the exercise is to beat the other teams, the managers often discover that most of their conflicts were with persons on their own team.

Source: "Teaching How to Cope with Workplace Conflicts," *Business Week*, February 18, 1980, pp. 136, 139.

The most commonly used methods for managing intergroup conflict each have strengths and weaknesses and are effective or ineffective under different conditions and situations. What this chapter has said thus far about intergroup conflict is summarized in Figure 9–2. The figure illustrates the relationship between causes and types of intergroup conflict, the consequences of intergroup conflict, and techniques for resolution.

MANAGING INTERGROUP CONFLICT THROUGH STIMULATION

Throughout this chapter, we have stressed that some conflict is beneficial. This point is noted again in Figure 9–2, which focuses on some of the functional consequences of intergroup conflict. The figure indicates that change can develop out of conflict, from an awareness of problems and from creative search for alternative solutions. We have already examined a situation where conflict is dysfunctional because it is too high and requires resolution. It is also possible, however,

FIGURE 9–2

An Overview of Intergroup Conflict

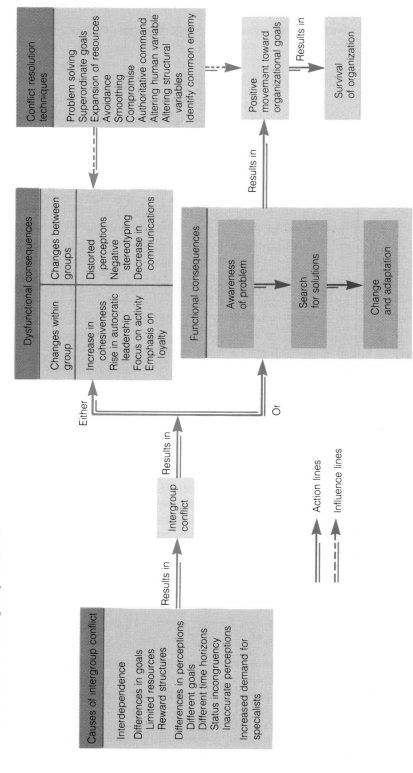

that intergroup conflict may be too low and require stimulation to generate action. The next section examines techniques that have been used successfully to stimulate conflict to a functional level, where it is contributing positively to organizational performance.[17]

Communication

By intelligent use of the organization's communication channels, a manager can stimulate beneficial conflict. Information can be placed carefully into formal channels to create ambiguity, reevaluation, or confrontation. Information that is threatening (e.g., a proposed budget cut) can stimulate functional conflict in a department and improved performance. Carefully planted rumors can also serve a useful purpose. For example, a hospital administrator may start a rumor about a proposed reorganization of the hospital. His purpose is twofold: (1) to stimulate new ideas on how to more effectively carry out the mission of the hospital and (2) to reduce apathy among the staff.

Bringing Outside Individuals into the Group

A technique widely used to "bring back to life" a stagnant organization or subunit of an organization is to hire or transfer in individuals whose attitudes, values, and backgrounds differ from those of the group's present members. Many college faculties consciously seek new members with different backgrounds and often discourage the hiring of graduates of their own programs. This is to ensure a diversity of viewpoints on the faculty. The technique of bringing in outsiders is also used widely in government and business. Recently, a bank president decided not to promote from within for a newly created position of marketing vice president. Instead, he hired a highly successful executive from the very competitive consumer products field. The bank president felt that while the outsider knew little about marketing financial services, her approach to, and knowledge of, marketing was what the bank needed to become a strong competitor.

Altering the Organization's Structure

Changing the structure of the organization can not only help resolve intergroup conflict; it is also excellent for *creating* conflict. For example, a school of business typically has several departments. One, named the Department of Business Administration, includes all of the faculty

---

[17] See Robbins, *Managing Organizational Conflict*, chap. 9.

members who teach courses in management, marketing, finance, production management, and so forth. Accordingly, the department is rather large, with 32 members under one department chairman, who reports to the dean. A new dean has recently been hired, and he is considering dividing the business administration unit into several separate departments (e.g., departments of marketing, finance, management), each with five or six members and a chairperson. The reasoning is that reorganizing in this manner will create competition among the groups for resources, students, faculty, and so forth, where none existed before because there was only one group. Whether this change will improve performance remains to be seen.

Stimulating Competition

Many managers utilize various techniques to stimulate competition among groups. The use of various incentives, such as awards and bonuses for outstanding performance, often stimulates competition. If properly utilized, such incentives may help maintain a healthy atmosphere of competition that may result in a functional level of conflict. Incentives can be given for least defective parts, highest sales, best teacher, greatest number of new customers, or in any area where increased conflict is likely to lead to more effective performance.

SUMMARY OF KEY POINTS

A. Conflict between groups is inevitable in organizations. This conflict may be positive or negative, depending on its impact on the organization's goal achievement.

B. Functional conflict represents a confrontation between groups that enhances and benefits the organization's performance.

D. Dysfunctional conflict results from a confrontation or interaction between groups that hinders the achievement of organizational goals.

D. While most managers try to eliminate conflict, evidence indicates that for most organizations an optimal level of conflict can positively influence organizational performance.

E. Intergroup conflict results from such factors as work interdependence, differences in goals, differences in perceptions, and the increasing demand for specialists.

F. Dysfunctional conflict causes changes to take place within and between the groups involved. Within the group, there may be an increase in group cohesiveness, a rise in autocratic leadership, a focus on the task, and an emphasis on loyalty. Changes occurring between the groups include distorted perceptions, negative stereotyping, and a decrease in communication.

G. One of the difficult tasks that a manager must confront is diagnosing and managing intergroup conflict. Some useful techniques for resolving intergroup conflict include problem solving, superordinate goals, expansion of resources, avoidance, smoothing, compromise, authority, and changing either the people or the organization's structure. Each of these techniques is useful in specific situations and circumstances.

H. Conflict management techniques also exist for situations where the manager diagnoses a level of conflict that is dysfunctional because it is too low. Conflict stimulation techniques include using the communication channels, hiring or transferring in outside individuals, and changing the organization's structure. The important point is that effective conflict management involves both resolution and stimulation.

DISCUSSION AND REVIEW QUESTIONS

1. From your personal experiences, describe situations where conflict was functional and situations where it was dysfunctional.

2. Is the competition for grades among students functional or dysfunctional? Why?

3. Some individuals believe that conflict is necessary for change to take place. Comment.

4. Why is union-management conflict often so dysfunctional?

5. Identify an intergroup conflict situation at your school. Is the conflict functional or dysfunctional? Why? If dysfunctional, what conflict management technique would you recommend to either resolve it or stimulate it?

6. Assume that you were chosen by the president of your school to recommend strategies for eliminating student apathy. What would your recommendation be?

7. What is meant when it is said that a manager must be able to diagnose intergroup conflict situations? How can a manager obtain these diagnostic skills?

8. Discuss your personal view of intergroup conflict in organizations.

ADDITIONAL REFERENCES

Aram, J. D., and P. J. Jalispante, Jr. "An Evaluation of Organizational Due Process in the Resolution of Employee/Employer Conflict." *Academy of Management Journal,* 1981, pp. 197–204.

Bacharach, S. B., and E. J. Lawler. *Bargaining: Power, Tactics, and Outcomes.* San Francisco: Jossey-Bass, 1981.

Boulding, E. "Further Reflections on Conflict Management." In *Power and Conflict in Organizations,* ed. R. Kahn and E. Boulding. New York: Basic Books, 1964.

Campbell, D. R. "Stereotypes and the Perception of Group Differences." *American Psychologist,* 1967, pp. 817–29.

Cherington, D. J. "Satisfaction in Competitive Behavior." *Organizational Behavior and Human Performance,* 1973, pp. 47–71.

Cosier, R. A., and G. L. Rose. "Cognitive Conflict and Goal Conflict Effects on Task Performance. *Organizational Behavior and Human Performance,* 1977, pp. 378–91.

Deutsch, M. "Conflicts: Productive and Destructive." In *Conflict Resolution through Communication,* ed. F. Jandt. New York: Harper & Row, 1973.

Doob, L. W., and W. J. Foltz. "The Belfast Workshop: An Application of Group Techniques to a Destructive Conflict." *Journal of Conflict Resolution,* 1973, pp. 489–512.

Dutton, J. M., and R. E. Walton. "Interdepartmental Conflict and Cooperation: Two Contrasting Studies." *Human Organization,* 1966, pp. 297–20.

French, W. L.; C. H. Bell; and R. A. Zawacki. *Organizational Development: Theory, Practice, Research.* Plano, Tex.: Business Publications, 1982.

Kelly, J. "Make Conflict Work for You." *Harvard Business Review,* 1970, pp. 103–13.

Kilmann, R. H., and K. W. Thomas. "Four Perspectives on Conflict Management: An Attributional Framework for Organizing Descriptive and Normative Theory." *Academy of Management Journal,* 1978, pp. 59–68.

Likert, R., and J. G. Likert. *New Ways of Managing Conflict.* New York: McGraw-Hill, 1976.

Mead, M. *Cooperation and Competition among Primitive Peoples.* New York: McGraw-Hill, 1961.

Pondy, L. "Organizational Conflict: Concepts and Models." *Administrative Science Quarterly,* 1967, pp. 296–320.

Robbins, S. P. "Conflict Management and Conflict Resolution Are Not Synonymous Terms." In *The Dynamics of Organizational Theory: Gaining a Macro Perspective,* ed. J. F. Veiga and J. N. Yanouzas. St. Paul, Minn.: West Publishing, 1979.

Schmidt, S. M., and T. A. Kochan. "Conflict: Toward Conceptual Understanding." *Administrative Science Quarterly,* 1972, pp. 359–70.

Thomas, K. W. "Conflict and Conflict Management." In *Handbook of Industrial and Organizational Psychology,* ed. M. Dunnette. Skokie, Ill.: Rand McNally, 1976.

————. "Toward Multi-Dimensional Values in Teaching: The Example of Conflict Behavior." *Academy of Management Review,* 1977, pp. 484–90.

————. "Introduction to Series on Conflict." *California Management Review,* 1978, pp. 488–90.

Twomey, D. F. "The Effects of Power Properties on Conflict Resolution." *Academy of Management Review,* 1978, pp. 144–50.

Zechmeister, K., and D. Druckman. "Determinants of Resolving a Conflict of Interest." *Journal of Conflict Resolution,* 1973, pp. 63–68.

CASE FOR ANALYSIS

We'll Just Let Them Show Their Stuff

Seven months ago, Captain Jon Shea announced that he would retire as police chief of Bay Ridge in one year. This advanced notice was to allow Mayor Foster Taff and the city commissioners time to initiate the search and selection process for his replacement. Captain Shea had come to Bay Ridge from a much larger city in Florida six years earlier. He had served as assistant police chief in that city for five years.

During his term as chief, Shea had initiated many changes in the department. For the most part, the changes had been accepted, and nearly everyone agreed that Shea had done a fine job. The crime rate was below the national average; citizen/police relations appeared good; and the morale of the police officers seemed high. The Bay Ridge Police Association (BRPA), the organization that represented the police officers, occasionally had minor disagreements with the chief and the city administration. However, these conflicts were small compared to the conflicts taking place in other cities. During the last five years, salaries for foot patrol officers had surpassed the national average for cities the size of Bay Ridge.

Many individuals were quite surprised at Shea's relative success. He had been the "outside candidate" for the job, and he had been selected over two veteran members of the force. The two inside candidates had engaged in bitter infighting that had divided the department at that time. One of them subsequently took a chief's position elsewhere. One city commissioner recently stated off the record, "I don't know how Shea did it. I didn't give him a snow-ball's chance six years ago. I thought he was crazy for taking the job and jumping in that hornet's nest. I guess being 1,000 miles away, he may not have known what he was getting into. But he sure has done one helluva job."

During the last seven months, an intensive search has been conducted. Applications have been received from all over the country. The search committee is made up of city officials. In addition, three professors from the management department of a local university have been hired as consultants to serve as an advisory committee to the search committee.

A total of 12 candidates were invited to interview personally for the job. Each candidate has been interviewed intensively by both committees. Surprisingly, both committees agree on the top three choices, although not in the same order. They are:

Phillip Kinney: 23 years on the Bay Ridge Police Force. Holds the rank of captain and has been the head of the Robbery Division for three years. Excellent record in the Robbery Division. Holds every departmental commendation. He is 51 years old, married, with three grown children. He is a graduate of Bay Ridge High School and was one of the final two inside candidates in the search seven years ago. According to inside sources, he barely missed getting appointed.

Anthony Jackson: holds the rank of lieutenant in the Narcotics Division. He has had an outstanding record of accomplishment since becoming the first black person on the police force 15 years ago. He is extremely popular in the black community and has been credited by the press with being instrumental in improving relations between the department and the black community. In fact, many black civic leaders have encouraged him to take a leave of absence to run for political office. He is 39 years old, married, with two young children. He holds a B.S. degree in law enforcement. He ran unsuccessfully for president of the BRPA in the last election.

Paul Stephens: 20 years in the department. Holds the rank of captain in the Homicide Division. He is considered to be one of the top homicide detectives in this region of the country, often serving as a consultant to police departments in other cities on difficult cases. Holds every departmental commendation. He is single at present and has one child by an earlier marriage. He holds a B.S. degree in law enforcement and is president of the BRPA.

The candidates have been presented to Mayor Taff by City Manager Bill Joslin, with the recommendation that he select one of the three to replace Shea. Joslin's first comment to Taff is, "Shea must have also developed some good people while he was here. None of the outside candidates made the cut."

"Who does Shea like?" the mayor asks. "He's not saying," Joslin replies. "He says that since he won't have to work for the guy, he shouldn't influence the selection. That's also why he declined to serve on the search committee. He also told that to the press this morning. Apparently, someone leaked the names of the three finalists to a TV station. Reporters cornered Shea on the way out of his house this morning."

"Which one do you like?" asks Joslin, adding, "I think you should announce your choice as soon as you've made it."

"No," says the mayor. "I think I'll wait. We've got about five months."

"Why wait?" asks Joslin. There is a short silence, and then the mayor replies, "We'll just let them show their stuff."

Questions for Consideration

1. What do you think of the mayor's decision to wait? Why?
2. What are the advantages of waiting? The disadvantages?
3. Could the mayor's decision have any positive or negative impact outside the department? Discuss.

Chapter 10

After completing Chapter 10, you should be able to:

Define the five interpersonal power bases.

Describe what is meant by the expression "two faces of power."

Discuss how subunits within an organization acquire and use power.

Compare the tactics used in the insurgency and counterinsurgency political games.

Identify the reasons why an illusion of power can influence a person's behavior.

Power and Politics

Sharing of Power: Possible or Impossible?*

Argument For

In this chapter, we will discuss the sharing of power, i.e., involving others in decision making. Power in the United States has traditionally resided with the ownership of property, so theoretically the owner is the one who has to share power. Realistically, however, most power in American organizations is in the hands of professional managers. It

---

* Adapted from Kenneth O. Alexander, "Democracy in the Workplace: An Elusive Goal," *Technology Review*, November–December 1983, pp. 12–15.

is these managers who must initiate the steps needed to share power with subordinates.

Managers today realize that the sharing of power is important to many workers. An example of a novel power-sharing idea took place in 1982, when General Motors and the United Auto Workers union agreed to encourage labor-management cooperation. The chairman of General Motors declared, "It moves us in a new direction—away from confrontation and toward cooperation. . . . It seeks to directly involve the union and its members in the effort to make GM more competitive." The contract was a step by the General Motors management to share power with the union.

Contracts like that of General Motors and a new wave of management enthusiasm about power sharing are assumed to be good for business. In order to compete and to remain productive, management must share more of its decision-making power with subordinates. An adversarial relationship between management and nonmanagement employees is costly, disruptive, and not at all conducive to long-term success.

It has taken management decades to realize that the sharing of power is a necessity. Today managers who refuse to share power will be faced with an alienated work force, employees who are likely to withhold productivity, and even employees who will turn to unionization as an answer to powerlessness.

Arguments for the sharing of power are so convincing with regard to productivity and satisfaction that it is not a matter of sharing power, but of when and how much power will be shared.

Argument Against

Top management sharing power with others (involving others in decision making) is a dream, a myth. There must be a power center of focal point in any organization. Sharing power creates confusion and a vacuum in an organization. Managers should control power so that order and efficiency are built into the organization. Some individuals cite the 1982 General Motors contract with the UAW as an example of power sharing. This is a totally inaccurate viewpoint. In fact, on the day the contract granting union concessions was announced, GM also announced an enhanced executive bonus plan. Management was considered by some, not to be sharing, but to be lining its own pockets with union concessions.

Management is not able to share power be-

cause it must make rapid and tough decisions. People have to be transferred, fired, passed over for promotion, and so on. You can't keep passing the buck on these kinds of tough business decisions. Democracy, participation, and power sharing are worthy goals when everything is operating smoothly and according to forecasts. However, this kind of "dream world" doesn't exist at U.S. Steel, Texas Instruments, General Motors, or any other firm.

There are some who claim that increased foreign competition encourages power sharing. Again, this seems to be a misguided claim. What is needed to combat foreign competition is strong management decision makers who take decisive action and who can make decisions without always attempting to reach a consensus. You just can't respond to any kind of competition if your hands are tied by worrying about sharing power with others.

Power sharing is like other theories; it raises some interesting points, but it is not very practical. Proponents of power sharing are just not able to support their assumptions and wishes with factual information. In the real organizational world, power sharing costs more than the benefits it generates. It costs in terms of slow decision making, clumsy decision making, and a management by consensus orientation. These costs are too much for any organization in a competitive, quick-moving environment to bear.

Power is a pervasive part of the fabric of organizational life. Managers and nonmanagers use it. They manipulate power to accomplish goals and, in many cases, to strengthen their own positions. A person's success or failure in using or reacting to power is largely determined by understanding power, knowing how and when to use it, and being able to anticipate its probable effects.

The purpose of this chapter is to learn about power and its uses in organizational settings. We will examine the bases of power, how power is used, the need for power, and the relationship between power and organizational politics. Warren Bennis, a behavioral scientist, has said this about power: "It is the organization's last dirty secret." This chapter will indicate that power is not a dirty secret but is actually a mechanism that is continually used to achieve organizational, group, and individual goals. Power is considered dirty because some use it to hurt other people or to achieve self-serving purposes. When power is used in an ethical and fair way, there is nothing dirty about it.

POWER AND AUTHORITY

The study of power and its effects is important to understanding how organizations operate. It is possible to interpret every interaction and every social relationship in an organization as involving an exercise of power.[1] How organizational subunits and individuals are controlled is related to the issue of power. **Power** is simply defined as the ability to get things done the way one wants them to be done. The power of a manager who wants an increased amount of financial resources is ability to get the desired resources. The power of a salesperson who wants his sales territory expanded is his ability to get the larger territory.

power
A person who can get someone to do something as he or she wants it done has power.

Power involves a relationship between two or more people. Robert Dahl, a political scientist, captures this important relational focus when he defines power as "A has power over B to the extent that he can get B to do something B would not otherwise do."[2] A person or group cannot have power in isolation; power has to be exercised or have the potential for being exercised in relation to some other person or group.

The opening Organizational Issue for Debate points out that some people feel that power can be used in isolation or by one person over other people. We agree with the power-sharing argument that unless

---

[1] W. Graham Astley and Paramjit S. Sachdeva, "Structural Sources of Intraorganizational Power: A Theoretical Synthesis," *Academy of Management Review,* January 1984, p. 104.

[2] Robert Dahl, "The Concept of Power," *Behavioral Science,* July 1957, pp. 202–3.

some amount of power is shared, there will be an increase in adversarial attitudes and relationships. However, this raises the problem of determining how power sharing can be implemented. It can't be forced on people. Power sharing is a process that will require some time to develop within an organization's culture. Time will be needed to develop (1) better lines of communication, (2) more trust, and (3) openness between the power sharers—managers and subordinates or subunits. Since organizations have for many years relied on authority hierarchies to accomplish goals, it is unreasonable to expect that managers will overnight and without some resistance simply begin sharing their power with others.

authority
A person in a position in the organizational hierarchy has formal authority because of the position.

In the literature, a distinction is made between power and authority. Weber called attention to differences between these two concepts.[3] He believed that power involved force and coercion. Authority, on the other hand, is a subset of power that is much narrower in scope. It does not carry the implication of force. Rather, it involves a "suspension of judgment" on the part of its recipients. **Authority** is the formal power that a person has because of the position that he or she holds in the organization. Directives or orders from a manager in an authority position are followed because they must be followed. That is, persons in higher positions have legal authority over subordinates in lower positions. In the authority hierarchy, the CEO is above the district manager, who is above the salesperson. Today authority is considered to have the following properties:

1. It is invested in a *person's position.* An individual has authority because of the position that he or she holds, not because of any specific personal characteristics.
2. *It is accepted by subordinates.* The individual in a legal authority position exercises authority and can gain compliance because he or she has a legitimate right.[4]
3. *Authority is used vertically.* Authority flows from the top down in the hierarchy of an organization.

Influence is a word that one often comes across when studying power. We agree with Mintzberg and others that making a distinction between influence and power adds little to understanding.[5] Therefore, we will use the terms *influence* and *power* interchangeably throughout this chapter.

---

[3] Max Weber, *Theory of Social and Economic Organization* (New York: Free Press, 1947), pp. 324–28.

[4] Andrew J. Grimes, "Authority, Power, Influence, and Social Control: A Theoretical Synthesis," *Academy of Management Review,* October 1978, pp. 724–35.

[5] Henry Mintzberg, *Power in and around Organizations* (Englewood Cliffs, N.J.: Prentice-Hall, 1983), p. 5.

POWER BASES

Power can be derived from many sources. How power is obtained in an organization depends to a large extent on the type of power being sought. Power can be derived from interpersonal, structural, and situational bases.

Interpersonal Power

French and Raven suggested five interpersonal bases of power: legitimate, reward, coercive, expert, and referent.[6]

Legitimate Power. Legitimate power is a person's ability to influence because of position. A person at a higher level has power over people below. In theory, organizational equals (e.g., all first-line supervisors) have equal legitimate power. However, each person with legitimate power uses it with a personal flair. Legitimate power is similar to Weber's concept of authority.

Subordinates play a major role in the exercise of legitimate power. If subordinates view the use of power as legitimate, they will comply. However, the culture, customs, and value systems of an organization determine the limits of legitimate power. A company president who suggests that all employees should vote for a particular political candidate may find that only some people comply with his suggestion.

Reward Power. This type of power is based on a person's ability to reward a follower for compliance. Reward power is used to back up the use of legitimate power. If followers value the rewards or potential rewards that the person can provide (recognition, a good job assignment, a pay raise, additional resources to complete a job), they may respond to orders, requests, and directions. For example, a sales manager who can reward salespeople with cash bonuses, expanded client lists, or additional entertainment funds can exert reward power.

coercive power
An individual who complies with someone's request because of fear is responding to coercive power.

Coercive Power. The opposite of reward power is **coercive power,** the power to punish. Followers may comply because of fear. A manager may block a promotion or harass a subordinate for poor performance. These practices and the fear that they will be used are coercive power. Although punishment may result in some unexpected side effects (discussed in Chapter 6), it is a form of coercive power that is still being used to bring about compliance or to correct nonproductive behavior in organizations.

Expert Power. A person has expert power when he or she possesses special expertise that is highly valued. Experts have power even when

---

[6] John R. P. French and Bertram Raven, "The Basis of Social Power," in *Studies in Social Power,* ed. D. Cartwright (Ann Arbor: Institute for Social Research, University of Michigan, 1959), pp. 150–67.

their rank is low. An individual may possess expertise on technical, administrative, or personal matters. The more difficult it is to replace the expert, the greater is the degree of expert power that he or she possesses.

Expert power is a personal characteristic, while legitimate, reward, and coercive power are largely prescribed by the organization. A secretary who has a relatively low-level organizational position may have high expert power because he or she knows the details of operating the business—knows where everything is or knows how to handle difficult situations.

referent power
A person with charisma, or a strong personality attraction, can exercise referent power.

Referent Power. Many individuals identify with and are influenced by a person because of the latter's personality or behavioral style. The charisma of the person is the basis of **referent power.** A person with charisma is admired because of his or her characteristics. The strength of a person's charisma is an indication of his or her referent power. Charisma is a term that is often used to describe politicians, entertainers, or sports figures. However, some managers are regarded as extremely charismatic by their subordinates.

The five bases of interpersonal power can be divided into two major categories: organizational and personal. Legitimate, reward, and coercive power are primarily prescribed by the organization, the position, formal groups, or specific interaction patterns. A person's legitimate power can be changed by transferring the person, rewriting the job description, or reducing the person's power by restructuring the organization. On the other hand, expert and referent power are very personal. A person has expertise, or he or she develops a set of credentials or image characteristic of an expert. Being admired because of the strength of your personality is difficult to tamper with or to modify or develop through training programs. A person has or does not have charisma. It is a *personal style* that is quite individualized.

The five types of interpersonal power are not independent. On the contrary, a person can use these power bases effectively in various combinations. Also, the use of a particular power base can affect the others. For example, a manager who uses coercive power to punish a subordinate may lose his referent power influence. Most individuals dislike and do not admire a manager who punishes them.

A field experiment involving 37 first-line managers and 392 subordinates in two plants was conducted to examine power.[7] The employees in one plant were asked to rate the reward, punishment, expert, referent, and legitimate power of their managers at two points in time. At the first point in time, an incentive pay plan was in effect. The

---

[7] Charles N. Greene and Philip M. Podsakoff, "Effects of Withdrawal of a Performance-Contingent Reward on Supervisory Influence and Power," *Academy of Management Journal,* September 1981, pp. 527–42.

plan was based on managerial evaluations, and through it employees could obtain a bonus of as much as 20 percent of their pay each month. At the second point in time, the company had abandoned the incentive pay plan. The researchers predicted that the abandonment of the plan would reduce the managers' reward power and that this would strongly affect subordinate ratings of managerial punishment, referent, and legitimate power.

The results of the study are presented in Figure 10–1, and it can be seen that they support the researchers' predictions. After the incentive pay plan was dropped (t_2), the subordinates felt that the managers' punishment power had increased. On the other hand, once the incentive pay plan was no longer available (t_2), the managers were considered to have less reward, referent, and legitimate power. No differences were found with regard to the t_1 and t_2 expert power comparisons.

FIGURE 10–1

The Relationship of Power Bases as Viewed by Managers' Subordinates

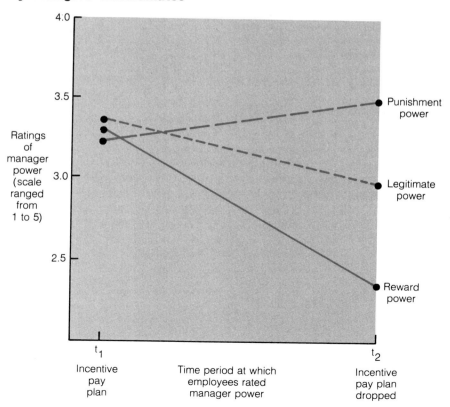

Similar results were not observed in a second comparison plant where the pay plan was retained. This study and other research shows that although interpersonal power stems from different sources and characteristics (reward, legitimate, punishment, or coercive), there is some interrelatedness. The field experiment suggests that legitimate and reward power are positively related, while punishment power is inversely related to legitimate and reward power.[8]

NEED FOR POWER

Throughout history, human beings have always been fascinated by power. In ancient Chinese writings, concern about power is clearly expressed—the taming power of the great, the power of light, the power of the dark. Early religious writings also contain numerous references to the person who possesses or acquires power. Historical records show that there have been differences in the extent to which individuals have pursued, feared, enjoyed, and misused power. Currently, the image of those who seek power is for the most part quite negative. For example, power seekers have been portrayed as:

Neurotics who are covering up feelings of inferiority, anxiety, hatred.

Substituting power for lack of affection, being alone, being deprived of friendship.

Attempting to compensate for some childhood deprivation.[9]

The power seeker has been labeled as being weak, neurotic, and troubled. This, of course, may be true for some power seekers (e.g., Adolf Hitler), but to place every power seeker in this category seems too broad sweeping and general.

McClelland proposes that power can be responsibly sought and used.[10] In addition to examining the need for achievement (discussed in Chapter 4), McClelland examined the **need for power,** or as he refers to it, n Pow. McClelland defines *n Pow* as the desire to have an impact on others. This type of impact may be shown basically in three ways: (1) by strong action, by giving help or advice, by controlling someone; (2) by action that produces emotion in others; and (3) by a concern for reputation.

need for power
Some individuals have a desire to influence others.

---

[8] Kurt Student, "Supervisory Influence and Work Group Performance," *Journal of Applied Psychology,* June 1968, pp. 188–94.

[9] David Kipnis, *The Powerholders* (Chicago: University of Chicago Press, 1976), pp. 149–56. Kipnis doesn't present these characteristics as fitting all power seekers but only as a summarization of the ugly and bland face of power seekers.

[10] David C. McClelland, *Power: The Inner Experience* (New York: Irvington Publishers, 1975), p. 7.

Research has been devoted to attempts at determining how people high in n Pow behave as contrasted with people low in n Pow. In general, individuals high in n Pow (1) are competitive and aggressive, (2) are interested in prestige possessions (e.g., a car), (3) prefer action situations, and (4) join a number of groups. Research on n Pow conducted by McClelland and his associates has revealed that the most effective organizational managers share these characteristics:

They have a high n Pow.

They use their power to achieve organizational goals.

They practice a participative or "coaching" style when interacting with followers.

They do not concentrate on developing close relations with others.[11]

The effective managers in McClelland's research were designated as *institutional managers* because they used their power to achieve organizational (institutional) goals. The institutional managers were more effective than the *personal power managers,* who used their power for personal gain, and the *affiliative managers,* who were more concerned with being liked than with using their power. Figure 10–2 summarizes the responses of subordinates of managers who were perceived to be using the three different power styles.

McClelland has also found that men who score high in n Pow, low in need for affiliation, and high in self-control are very effective. Young managers who displayed these characteristics when they entered AT&T were more likely to have been promoted to higher levels of management in the company after 16 years than were young managers who did not display these characteristics.[12]

The research work stimulated and conducted by McClelland presents evidence that is contrary to the negative image that has historically been attached to all power seekers. Stating that all power seekers are weak, neurotic, and troubled is as ridiculous as stating that all power seekers are effective, well adjusted, and highly motivated. There are what McClelland refers to as the "two faces of power." One face depicts power seekers in negative terms. The other face suggests that power can be used to accomplish goals, use resources efficiently, and help followers feel more powerful themselves. McClelland's view seems to be more realistic and correct than the view that all power seekers are weak and neurotic.

---

[11] David C. McClelland and David H. Burnham, "Power Is the Great Motivator," *Harvard Business Review,* March–April 1976, pp. 100–110.

[12] David C. McClelland, "Understanding Psychological Man," *Psychology Today,* May 1982, pp. 55–56.

FIGURE 10–2

Responses of Subordinates of Managers with Different Motive Profiles

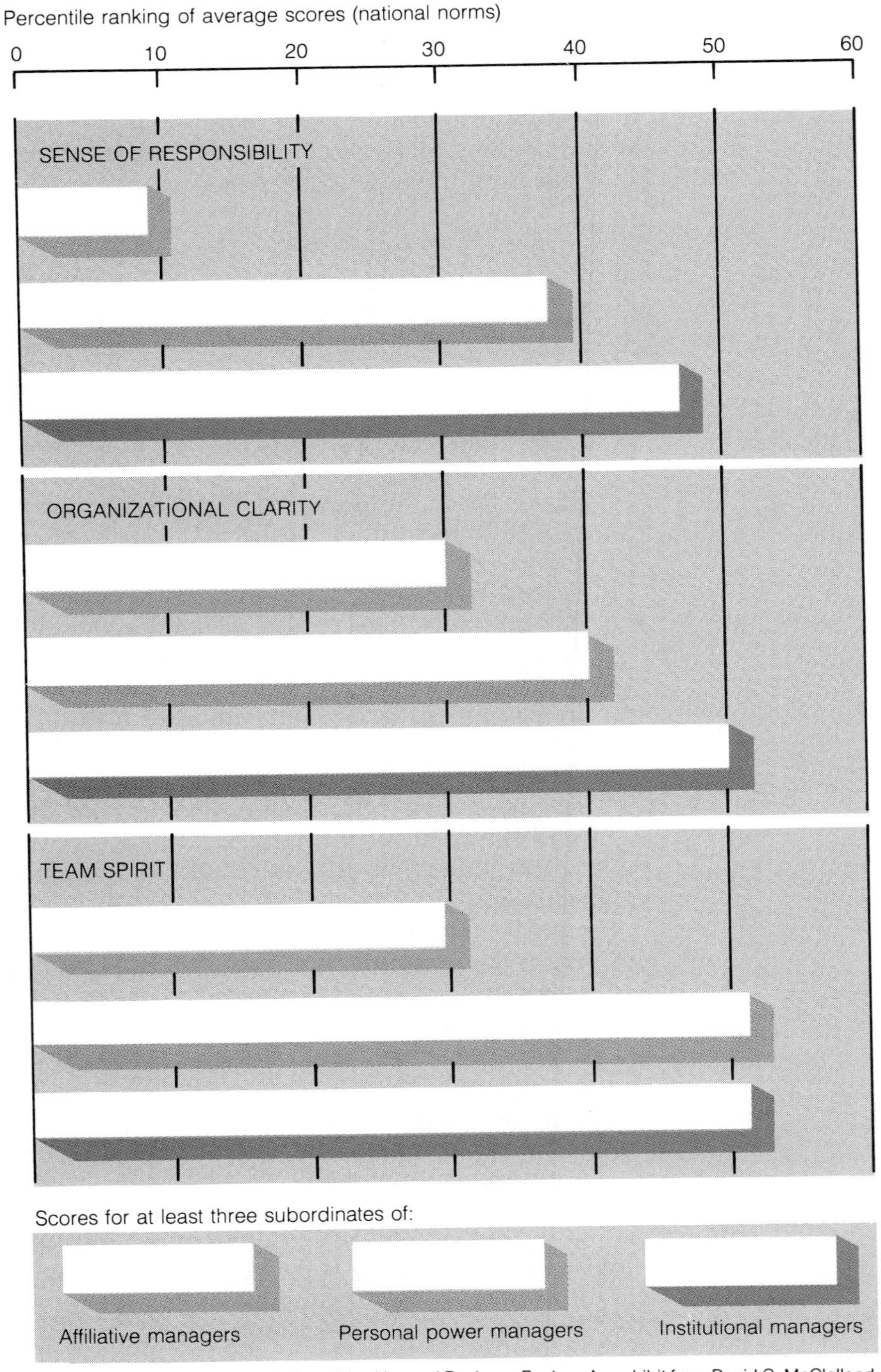

Percentile ranking of average scores (national norms)

Scores for at least three subordinates of:

Affiliative managers   Personal power managers   Institutional managers

STRUCTURAL AND SITUATIONAL POWER

Pfeffer has proposed that power is primarily prescribed by structure within the organization.[13] He regards the structure of an organization as the control mechanism by which the organization is governed. In the organization's structural arrangements, decision-making discretion is allocated to various positions. Also, the structure establishes the patterns of communication and the flow of information. Thus, organizational structure creates formal power and authority by specifying certain individuals to perform specific job tasks and make certain decisions and by encouraging informal power through its effect on information and communication structures within the system.[14]

We have already discussed how formal position is associated with power and authority. Certain rights, responsibilities, and privileges accrue from a person's position. Other forms of structural power exist because of resources, decision making, and information.[15]

Resources

Kanter argues quite convincingly that power stems from (1) access to resources, information, and support; and (2) the ability to get cooperation in doing necessary work.[16] Power occurs when a person has open channels to resources—money, human resources, technology, materials, customers, and so on. In organizations, vital resources are allocated downward along the lines of the hierarchy. The top-level manager has more power to allocate resources than do other managers further down in the managerial hierarchy. The lower level manager receives resources that are granted by top-level managers. In order to assure compliance with goals, top-level managers (e.g., presidents, vice presidents, directors) allocate resources on the basis of performance and compliance. Thus, a top-level manager usually has power over a lower level manager because the lower level manager must receive resources from above to accomplish goals.

The *dependency* relationship exists because of limited resources and

---

[13] Jeffrey Pfeffer, *Power in Organizations* (Marshfield, Mass.: Pitman Publishing, 1981), p. 117. See Pfeffer's excellent discussion in chap. 4 (pp. 99–135), on where power originates in organizational settings.

[14] Jeffrey Pfeffer, "The Micropolitics of Organizations," in *Environments and Organizations,* ed. M. W. Meyer et al. (San Francisco: Jossey-Bass, 1978), pp. 29–50.

[15] The discussion of these forms of structural power is based on Pfeffer, *Power in Organizations,* pp. 104–22; and Rosabeth M. Kanter, "Power Failures in Management Circuits," *Harvard Business Review,* July–August 1979, pp. 65–75.

[16] Kanter, "Power Failures."

division of labor.[17] Without adequate compliance with top-management goals and requests, a lower level manager is unable to receive the necessary resources to do the job. The division of labor (e.g., positions in the hierarchy) grants upper management, by position, the privilege of allocating limited resources.

Even a chief executive officer (CEO) is dependent in an organization. The following Close-Up discusses this dependency.

ORGANIZATIONS: CLOSE-UP

Even the Chief Executive Officer Has Limited Power

Chief executive officers (CEOs) have significant power and authority to do what they want. Well, we're not so sure. Although CEOs possess legal authority, they are not so sure of their power. A survey of nearly 400 CEOs showed that one in three worried about being removed from office. There is a high turnover rate among CEOs.

The uncertainty among CEOs about their power stems from dependence. Organizations were created to eliminate the arbitrary and unpredictable whim of rulers, but other forms of dependence were created. In a bureaucracy, the division of labor precludes any individuals from having everything (people, resources, skills) needed to complete the job. The scarcity of resources means that even CEOs must rely on other people who control needed resources. A president of a major bank commented, "Everyone has power until they try to use it. Then you see how real the power is. I appear to have it, but it is impossible to act unilaterally."

Vulnerability results from dependence. Like everyone else, CEOs are controlled by the power relationship. They must give orders that will be obeyed, justify personal whims to impersonal and collective groups, and act on their promises to reward or punish. Subordinates can withhold compliance from CEOs, thereby threatening and controlling their careers and influence.

On the other hand, dependence encourages CEOs to acquire power. CEOs are more vulnerable because all of the people below them are competing hard to be in their slots. So CEOs have to devote a lot of time and energy to power consolidation.

Becoming powerful and staying that way is not an easy task for CEOs. There are a number of traps that can make even CEOs powerless:

Planning for the future is an uncertain business. When CEOs pursue long-range goals with innovative ideas, they can gain respect. How-

[17] John P. Kotter, "Power, Dependence, and Effective Management," *Harvard Business Review,* July–August 1977, pp. 125–36.

ever, when such goals are abandoned, they lose credibility and consequently power.

The loss of contact with information invites isolation, dependence, and powerlessness.

The CEO comes under attack from pressure groups, called stakeholders. The CEO must clearly show these groups that he or she deserves to maintain the position of power. Thus, the CEO must learn as much as possible about each of these groups.

Although CEOs are powerful people, their hold on power is fragile. They can become powerless by falling into traps that must be avoided.

Adapted from David C. Calabra, "CEOs and the Paradox of Power," *Business Horizons*, January–February 1982, pp. 29–31.

Decision-Making Power

The degree to which individuals or subunits (e.g., a department or a special project group) can affect decision making determines the amount of power acquired. A person or subunit with power can influence how the decision-making process occurs, what alternatives are considered, and when a decision is made.[18] For example, when Richard Daley was mayor of Chicago, he was recognized as a power broker. He not only influenced the decision-making process, but he also had the power to decide which decision would be given priority in the city council and when decisions would be made.[19] He was a powerful politician because he was considered to be an expert at controlling each step in important decisions.

Information Power

Having access to relevant and important information is power. Accountants do not generally have a particularly strong or apparent interpersonal power base in an organization. Rather, accountants have power because they control important information. Information is the basis for making effective decisions. Thus, those who possess information needed to make optimal decisions have power. The accountant's position in the organization structure may not accurately portray the amount of power that he or she wields. A true picture of a person's

---

[18] For an organizationally oriented, concise, and excellent discussion of structural and situationally oriented sources of power, see Don Hellriegel, John W. Slocum, Jr., and Richard W. Woodman, *Organizational Behavior* (St. Paul, Minn.: West Publishing, 1983), pp. 433–37.

[19] Mike Royko, *Boss: Richard J. Daley of Chicago* (New York: E. P. Dutton, 1971).

power is provided not only by the person's position, but also by the person's access to relevant information.

A number of organizational situations can serve as the source of either power or powerlessness (not acquiring power). The powerful manager exists because he or she allocates required resources, makes crucial decisions, and has access to important information. He or she is likely to make things happen. The powerless manager, however, lacks the resources, information, and decision-making prerogatives needed to be productive. Table 10–1 presents some of the common symptoms and sources of powerlessness of first-line supervisors, staff professionals, and top-level managers.

TABLE 10–1

Symptoms and Sources of Powerlessness

Position	Symptoms	Sources
First-line supervisors (e.g., foreman, line supervisor)	Supervise too closely Fail to train subordinates Not sufficiently oriented to the management team Inclined to do the job themselves	Routine, rule-minded jobs Limited lines of communication Limited advancement opportunities for themselves and their subordinates
Staff professionals (e.g., corporate lawyer, personnel/human resources specialist)	Create islands and set themselves up as experts Use professional standards as basis for judging work that distinguishes them from others Resist change and become conservative risk-takers	Their routine tasks are only adjuncts to real line job Blocked career advancement Replaced by outside consultants for nonroutine work
Top-level managers (e.g., chief executive officer, vice president)	Short-term time horizon Top-down communication systems emphasized Reward followers to think like the manager, do not welcome bearers of bad news	Uncontrollable lines of supply Limited or blocked lines of information about lower managerial levels Diminished lines of support because of challenges to legitimacy

Source: Reprinted by permission of the Harvard Business Review. Adapted from "Power Failures in Management Circuits," by Rosabeth Moss Kanter (July–August 1979), p. 73. Copyright © 1979 by the President and Fellows of Harvard College; all rights reserved.

Table 10–1 indicates that a first-line manager will display a number of symptoms of powerlessness such as supervising very closely and not showing much concern about training or developing subordinates. If symptoms such as these persist, it is likely that the individual is powerless. For years, women as a group have not typically possessed significant organization power. In many situations, they have been powerless. The following Close-Up shows that this is changing. In fact, the Close-Up indicates that women can use power as effectively as men and consequently that there is no reason for powerlessness to be a common condition of women in organizational settings.

ORGANIZATIONS: CLOSE-UP

Women Managers and the Power Factor

Today a disproportionate number of women managers are found among first-line supervisors or staff professionals. Like men in these positions, they are likely to possess very little power. There are a number of ways in which women are kept relatively powerless in their managerial jobs. First, there is a tendency for other managers to patronizingly overprotect women by placing them in "safe jobs" out of harm's way, the view being that "it's really a jungle, and a woman shouldn't have to fight through the mess."

Second, women are easily bypassed because it is assumed that they "don't know the ropes." Women are often seen as being informed about the technical requirements of a job but as not being skilled in other areas. Third, until recently men have not felt comfortable about seeing women as businesspeople. They did not get the impression of women having the competence to handle power.

Finally, even when women are able to achieve some power on their own, they have not necessarily been able to build an organizational power base. Traditionally, neither men nor women have seen women as capable of sponsoring others. Women have been viewed as the recipients of sponsorship rather than as sponsors. This limits the ability of women to build up a power base of individuals whom they have sponsored.

How long it will take before myths and stereotypes about women are put to rest is not known. A growing number of women have exercised power very effectively. These women have shown that women are like men when it comes to power. Some use it effectively, while others abuse it. A sample of effective and powerful women includes:

Hanna Gray, the president of the University of Chicago.

Jeanne Kirkpatrick, U.S. ambassador to the United Nations.

Paige Rense, chief executive of a small publishing magazine empire. Mary Dolan, editor of the *Los Angeles Herald Examiner*.

Interviews with these four powerful women indicate some important attributes. All have possessed since childhood a strong sense of autonomy and independence. They point to some role model, male or female, who gave them early encouragement to actually believe that they could take on the world in any way they chose.

The women differ on the aspects of their high-powered jobs that they find hardest to handle. "The most difficult thing in the world is firing people," said Gray. Kirkpatrick must work hard to project a strong image. Rense finds that being diplomatic is difficult. Dolan works hard not to come across as a blunt, pushy person.

These four women and a growing number of other women show that the use and misuse of power are possibilities attached to organizational life. Women can use power as effectively as men, and they can misuse power as miserably as men.

Based on Patricia O'Brien, "Women and Power," *Collegiate Career Woman,* Winter 1982–83, pp. 17–20; and Rosabeth Moss Kanter, "Power Failures in Management Circuits," *Harvard Business Review,* July–August 1979, p. 60.

UPWARD FLOW OF POWER

Most people think of power as being exerted in a downward direction. It is true that individuals in positions at the lower end of the power hierarchy generally have less power than do individuals in higher level positions. However, power can also be exercised up the organization.[20] In sociological terms, a person exerting power upward has personal power but no authority. The power-sharing argument of the Organizational Issue for Debate suggests that power should flow not only downward but also upward if optimal performance is to be accomplished.[21]

The discussion of legitimate authority suggests that individuals in higher level positions (supervisors) can exert only as much power as individuals in lower level positions (subordinates) accept. The concept of subordinate power can be linked to expertise, location, and information. Significant upward power or influence can sometimes be exerted by a relatively low-ranking secretary, computer programmer, or clerk who possesses expertise, is in a position to interact with important

[20] Gary Yukl and Tom Taber, "The Effective Use of Managerial Power," *Personnel.* March–April 1983, pp. 37–44.

[21] Keith G. Provan, "Recognizing, Measuring, and Interpreting the Potential/Enacted Power Distinction in Organizational Research," *Academy of Management Review,* October 1980, pp. 549–59.

individuals, or has access to and control of important information.[22] Studies have shown that expertise, location, and information control are important determinants of the power potential of employees at lower levels of the hierarchy.[23]

An example of expertise power would be that of a research technician with rare talents and knowledge who becomes indispensable to a manager. The technician could demand certain privileges, working conditions, or considerations and would probably receive them because of his expertise. Power accumulation can also be linked to the physical location of an individual. An individual who is visible to and in contact with powerful individuals may be viewed by others as having power by association. Likewise, a person who has control of or access to the flow of important information may have power, no matter what his or her position in the hierarchy may be. For example, a clerk who has access to important and private files can in some situations acquire power and influence other employees.

Two important sources of upward influence have been referred to as manipulative persuasion and manipulation.[24] *Manipulative persuasion* is a person's direct attempt to disguise the true persuasion objective. This is the hidden agenda ploy. Through persuasion skills, the individual is able to accumulate power. For example, a manager who is trying to have a poor worker transferred may present only the strengths of the worker to a project manager who is looking for people for a new assignment. Although the manager's true objective is to unload the worker on someone else, that objective is hidden within the manager's presentation of the employee's strengths.

Manipulation refers to the form of influence in which both the objective and the attempt are concealed. For example, instead of providing customer complaints to a manager as they are received, the clerk receiving the complaints may arrange them as he or she desires. This can be done in such a way as to place other employees or a department in a more or less favorable light. If in this situation the clerk has arranged the incoming complaints so that the manager in charge would reprimand a departmental supervisor whom the clerk doesn't

---

[22] L. W. Porter, R. W. Allen and H. L. Angee, "The Politics of Upward Influence in Organizations," in *Research in Organizational Behavior*, ed. L. L. Cummings and B. M. Staw (Greenwich, Conn.: JAI Press, 1981), pp. 181–216.

[23] David Mechanic, "Sources of Power in Lower Participants in Organizations," *Administrative Science Quarterly*, September 1962, pp. 349–64; and Donald C. Pelz, "Influence: A Key to Effective Leadership in the First-Line Supervisor," *Personnel*, November 1952, pp. 209–17.

[24] For an excellent discussion of upward influence, see Richard S. Blackburn, "Lower Participant Power: Toward a Conceptual Integration," *Academy of Management Review*, January 1981, pp. 127–31; and Richard T. Mowday, "The Exercise of Upward Influence in Organizations," *Administrative Science Quarterly*, March 1978, pp. 137–56.

like, the clerk's action would be considered manipulation in the upward direction.

INTERORGANIZATIONAL POWER

The primary focus to this point has been on individual power and how it is obtained. However, it is also important to consider subunit or interdepartmental power. Even though all vice presidents of departments at the same level in the managerial hierarchy are supposed to have the same amount of power, this is not usually the case. Some vice presidents have more power because they are in a particular unit or department. Perrow surveyed managers in 12 industrial firms to study subunit power.[25] He was concerned about subunit power differences in production, sales and marketing, research and development, and finance and accounting departments. Perrow's survey results indicated that sales and marketing units had the most power. The subunit power rank ordering from most powerful to least powerful was (1) sales and marketing, (2) production, (3) finance and accounting, and (4) research and development.

strategic contingency
An event or activity that is of crucial importance to complete a project or accomplish a goal.

The strategic contingency theory developed by Hickson focused on subunit power. A **strategic contingency** is an event or activity that is extremely important for accomplishing organizational goals.[26] Crozier, a French sociologist, provided insight into the idea of strategic contingencies. He studied the relationships between workers in the production and maintenance departments of French tobacco processing plants. Crozier found that the production workers enjoyed job security because of tenure, were protected against unfair disciplinary action, and were not replaced or transferred arbitrarily. The production workers were less skilled than the maintenance workers. The maintenance workers were highly skilled and were recruited and selected only after going through a rigorous screening process.

The production workers were dependent on the maintenance workers. This power differential was explained in terms of the control exercised by the maintenance workers over an important contingency. If machines were shut down, the entire plant came to a halt. Efficiently functioning machines were needed to accomplish output goals. Since the maintenance workers, who at the request of the production workers, repaired machines that were down, they possessed significant power.

---

[25] Charles Perrow, "Departmental Power and Perspective in Industrial Firms," in *Power in Organizations,* ed. M. N. Zald (Nashville, Tenn.: Vanderbilt University Press, 1970), pp. 59–89.

[26] Michel Crozier, *The Bureaucratic Phenomenon* (Chicago: University of Chicago Press, 1964).

When machines were down, the job performance of the production workers suffered. Stoppages totally disrupted the workflow and the output of the production workers. Crozier proposed that the maintenance workers controlled a strategically contingent factor in the production process. Crozier's study provided clear evidence of subunit power differences. The study also stimulated other studies that eventually resulted in a strategic contingencies explanation of power differences.[27]

Hinnings et al. studied the strategic contingency explanation of power in 28 subunits of seven manufacturing organizations in Canada and the United States.[28] Engineering, marketing, production, and accounting departments were studied. Each of the subunits interacted with the three others. The researchers examined various indicators of power such as substitutability (ability of the subunit to obtain alternative performance for its activities), workflow pervasiveness (the degree to which the workflows of a subunit were linked to the workflows of other subunits), uncertainty (the lack of information about future events), and workflow immediacy (the speed and severity with which the workflow of a subunit affected the final outputs of the organization). The results indicated that only a combination of high values on all the power indicators gave a subunit dominant first-rank power. Thus, being able to deal with uncertainty alone or possessing substitutability power alone does not provide a subunit with dominant power over other subunits.

Using the work of Crozier and of Hickson and his associates, it is possible to develop a concise explanation of strategic contingencies. The model presented in Figure 10–3 suggests that subunit power, the power differential between subunits, is influenced by (1) the degree of ability to cope with uncertainty, (2) the centrality of the subunit, and (3) the substitutability of the subunit.

Coping with Uncertainty

Unanticipated events can create problems for any organization or subunit. It is, therefore, the subunits most capable of coping with uncertainty that typically acquire power. It has been stated that

---

[27] It should be noted that the strategic contingency theory was developed by D. J. Hickson and his colleagues. Other theorists and researchers have modified and discussed this approach. However, the reader is urged to use the original sources for a discussion of the complete and unmodified theory. See D. J. Hickson, C. R. Hinnings, C. A. Lee, R. E. Schneck, and J. M. Pennings, "A Strategic Contingency Theory of Intraorganizational Power," *Administrative Science Quarterly,* June 1971, pp. 216–29; and C. R. Hinnings, D. J. Hickson, J. M. Pennings, and R. E. Schneck, "Structural Conditions of Intraorganizational Power," *Administrative Science Quarterly,* March 1974, pp. 22–44.

[28] Hinnings et al., "Structural Conditions," p. 41.

FIGURE 10–3

A Strategic Contingency Model of Subunit Power

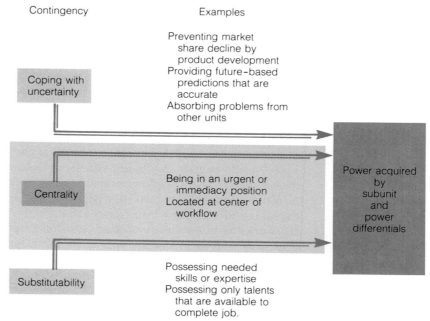

Contingency   Examples

Coping with uncertainty

Preventing market
share decline by
product development
Providing future-based
predictions that are
accurate
Absorbing problems from
other units

Centrality

Being in an urgent or
immediacy position
Located at center of
workflow

Substitutability

Possessing needed
skills or expertise
Possessing only talents
that are available to
complete job.

Power acquired
by
subunit
and
power
differentials

This figure is based on the detailed research work conducted by D. J. Hickson, C. R. Hinnings, C. A. Lee, R. E. Schneck, and J. M. Pennings, "A Strategic Contingency Theory of Intraorganizational Power," *Administrative Science Quarterly,* June 1971, pp. 216–29; and C. R. Hinnings, D. J. Hickson, J. M. Pennings, and R. E. Schneck, "Structural Conditions of Intraorganizational Power," *Administrative Science Quarterly,* March 1974, pp. 22–44.

uncertainty itself does not give power; coping gives power. If organizations allocate to their various subunits task areas that vary in uncertainty, then those subunits that cope most effectively with the most uncertainty should have the most power within the organization.[29]

There are three types of coping activities. First, there is *coping by prevention.* Here a subunit works at reducing the probability that some difficulty will arise. For example, designing a new product to prevent lost sales because of new competition in the marketplace is a coping technique. Another would be to hire two individuals when only one is actually needed. The overhiring is done because of expected turnover.

Second, there is *coping by information.* The use of forecasting is an example. Possessing timely forecasting information enables a sub-

---

[29] Hickson et al., "Strategic Contingency Theory," pp. 219–20.

unit to deal with such events as competition, strikes, shortages of materials, and consumer demand shifts. Planning departments conducting forecasting studies acquire power when their predictions prove accurate.

Third, there is coping by absorption. This coping approach involves dealing with uncertainty as it impacts the subunit. For example, one subunit might take a problem employee from another subunit and then attempt to retrain and redirect that employee. This is done as a favor, so that the other subunit will not have to go through the pain of terminating or continuing to put up with the employee. The subunit that takes in the problem employee gains the respect of other subunits, which results in an increase in power.

The relation of coping with uncertainty to power was expressed by Hickson as follows: "The more a subunit copes with uncertainty, the greater its power within the organization."[30]

Centrality

The subunits that are most central to the flow of work in an organization typically acquire power.[31] There is no subunit that has zero centrality since all subunits are somehow interlinked with other subunits. A measure of centrality is the degree to which the work of the subunit contributes to the final output of the organization.[32] Since a subunit is in a position to affect other subunits, it has some degree of centrality and therefore power.

Also, a subunit possesses power if its activities have a more immediate or urgent impact than that of other subunits. For example, Ben Taub is a major public hospital in Houston. The emergency and trauma treatment subunit is extremely important and crucial. It contains significant power within the hospital. Failures in this subunit could result in the death of emergency victims. On the other hand, the psychiatric subunit does important work, but not of the crucial and immediate type. Therefore, it has significantly less subunit power than the emergency and trauma treatment subunit.

The two main centrality propositions offered by Hickson et al. are as follows:

---

[30] Ibid., p. 39.

[31] L. C. Freeman, D. Roeder, and R. R. Mulholland, "Centrality in Social Networks: II. Experimental Results," *Social Networks*, June 1980, pp. 119–42.

[32] Richard L. Daft, *Organization Theory and Design* (St. Paul, Minn.: West Publishing, 1983), pp. 392–98. This source contains an excellent discussion of the strategic contingency perspective in terms of managerial and organizational theory. Daft's discussion is a concise and informative presentation of the original Hickson et al. theory and research.

The higher the pervasiveness of the workflows of a subunit the greater is its power within the organization.

The higher the immediacy of the workflows of a subunit, the greater is its power within the organization.[33]

Substitutability

substitutability
The degree of
substitution that is
available to perform
the job or task.

Substitutability refers to the ability of other subunits to perform the activities of a particular subunit. If an organization has or can obtain alternative sources of skill, information, and resources to perform the job done by a subunit, the subunit's power will be diminished. Training subunits lose power if training work can be done by line managers or outside consultants. On the other hand, if a subunit has unique skills and competencies (e.g., the maintenance workers in Crozier's study discussed above) that would be hard to duplicate or replace, this would tend to increase the subunit's power over other subunits.

Changes in the labor market may result in changes in a subunit's power. Today there is a shortage of robotic technical specialists. Since robotic technicians are difficult to replace, train, and substitute for, the robotic subunit of an organization possesses inordinate power. Of course, there are also other reasons for the emergence of powerful robotic subunits, such as their access to technical information, their centrality, and the improvements in productivity that they bring about.

Hickson et al. capture the importance of substitutability power when they propose that the lower the substitutability of the activities of a subunit, the greater is its power within the organization.[34]

THE ILLUSION OF POWER

Admittedly, some individuals and subunits have vast amounts of power to get others to do things the way they want them done. However, there are also illusions of power. Imagine that one afternoon your supervisor asks you to step into his office. He starts the meeting: "You know we're really losing money using that Beal stamping machine. I'd like you to do a job for the company. I want you to destroy the machine and make it look like an accident." Would you comply with this request? After all, this is your supervisor, and he is in charge of everything—your pay, you promotion opportunities, your job assignments. You might ask, Does my supervisor have this much power over me?

---

[33] Ibid., p. 41.
[34] Ibid., p. 40.

Where a person or subunit's power starts and stops is difficult to pinpoint. One might assume that the supervisor in the hypothetical example has the specific power to get someone to do this unethical and illegal "dirty work." However, even individuals who seemingly possess only a little power can influence others. A series of studies conducted by Milgram focused on the illusion of power.

Milgram conducted a number of highly controversial experiments on "obedience to authority."[35] The subjects in the experiments were adult men drawn from a variety of occupations and social positions in the New Haven, Connecticut, area. Upon arriving at the laboratory, each subject was introduced to his supposed cosubject, a man of about 50 who was actually a confederate working with Milgram. The two were asked to draw lots to determine who would be the "teacher" and who the "learner." The drawing was rigged. The real subject always became the teacher.

The experiment was ostensibly designed to find out about the effects of punishment on learning. Whenever the learner made a mistake, he was to be punished with an electric shock. A shock-generating machine was used. It had 30 switches on it, the first delivering 15 volts, the second 30, and so on up to 450 volts, where the switch was labeled, "Danger—Severe Shock—XXX."

The teacher (the real subject) then took his place at the shock-generating machine, where he could not see the learner (the confederate). The plan was for the learner to make many mistakes in repeating words given to him by the teacher. With each mistake, the teacher was told to increase the shocks. At 75 volts, the teacher could hear grunts coming from the learner, who was actually faking as instructed by Milgram. At 150 volts, the learner shouted, "Let me out," and said his heart couldn't stand the pain. He began to yell. He let out an agonizing scream at 285 volts and refused to go on, but seemingly kept trying and made even more mistakes.

Most of the teachers became very upset. Some asked the experimenter whether it was proper to continue. No matter what the teacher asked or how he protested, the experimenter only said, "The experiment requires that we go on." The subjects were also told, "You have no other choice; you must go on." Milgram wanted to know how many subjects would defy the orders to go on and how many would continue. Before these experiments were conducted, 40 psychiatrists were asked their opinions about whether the subjects would quit. Only 4 percent of the subjects, the psychiatrists predicted, would continue to shock

---

[35] S. Milgram, "Behavioral Study of Obedience," *Journal of Abnormal and Social Psychology,* October 1963, pp. 371–78; and S. Milgram, *Obedience to Authority* (New York: Harper & Row, 1974).

FIGURE 10–4

Results of Milgram's Classic Experiment on Obedience

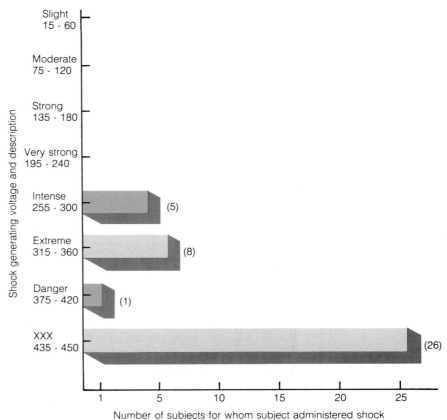

Source: Based on descriptions and data presented in S. Milgram, "Behavioral Study of Obedience," *Journal of Abnormal and Social Psychology,* October 1963, pp. 371–78.

the learner when he failed to respond. But look at Figure 10–4 to see what actually happened.

Out of a total of 40 subjects, 26, or 65 percent, obeyed the experimenter all the way to XXX, the very highest voltage level on the shock generator. These men were not abnormal. In fact, most showed extreme signs of emotional strain and psychological conflict during the experiment. They trembled, bit their lips, and dug their fingernails into the palms of their hands. They repeatedly asked for permission from the experimenter to stop. Yet they continued increasing the voltage. Milgram stated:

> I observed a mature and initially poised businessman enter the laboratory, smiling and confident; within 20 minutes he was reduced to a

twitching, stuttering wreck, who was rapidly approaching a point of nervous collapse . . yet he continued to respond to every word of the experimenter and obeyed to the end.[36]

After the experiment, the subjects were all told the truth. The shock-generating machine delivered "nothing at all"; it was a sham. During the experiment, however, every subject was convinced that the learner was another subject just like himself. Milgram's experiments have produced much controversy over the ethics of the procedure. Some opponents of this type of research maintain that many of the subjects suffered long-term psychological harm. Milgram flatly rejects this idea and points out that his sessions all ended with a complete briefing.

Why did the subjects obey the experimenter? Although the experimenter possessed no specific power over the subjects, he appeared to be a powerful person. He created an illusion of power. The experimenter dressed in a white lab coat, was addressed by others as "doctor," and was very stern. The subjects perceived the experimenter as possessing legitimacy to conduct the study. The experimenter apparently did an excellent job of projecting the illusion of having power.

The Milgram experiments indicate that possessing power in a legitimate way is not the only way that power can be exerted. Individuals who are perceived to have power may also be able to significantly influence others. Power is often exerted by individuals who have only minimum or no actual power. The "eye of the beholder" plays an important role in the exercise of power.[37]

POLITICAL STRATEGIES AND TACTICS

politically oriented behavior
When a person behaves outside the normal power system to benefit himself or herself or a subunit, that person is engaging in political behavior.

Individuals and subunits continually engage in **politically oriented behavior.**[38] What do we mean by politically oriented behavior? We mean a number of things:

1. *Behavior* that is usually outside the legitimate, recognized power system.
2. Behavior that is designed to benefit an individual or subunit, *often* at the expense of the organization in general.[39]
3. Behavior that is intentional and is designed to acquire and maintain power.

---

[36] Milgram, "Behavioral Study of Obedience," p. 377.

[37] S. H. Ng, *The Social Psychology of Power* (New York: Academic Press, 1980), p. 119.

[38] Manual Velasquez, Dennis J. Moberg, and Gerald F. Cavanagh, "Organizational Statesmanship and Dirty Politics: Ethical Guidelines for the Organizational Politician," *Organizational Dynamics*, Autumn 1983, p. 5.

[39] Mintzberg, *Power in and around Organizations*, p. 172.

As a result of politically oriented behaviors, the formal power that exists in an organization is often sidetracked or blocked. In the language of organizational theory, political behavior results in the displacement of power.[40]

Research on Politics

A number of studies have been conducted to explore political behavior and perceptions in organizations.[41] A study of 142 purchasing agents examined their political behavior. The job objective of the purchasing agents was to negotiate and fill orders in a timely manner. However, the purchasing agents also viewed their jobs as being a crucial link with the environment—competition, price changes, market shifts.[42] Thus, the purchasing agents considered themselves information processors. This vital link of the purchasing agents with the external environment placed them in conflict with the engineering department. As a result of the conflict, attempts to influence the engineering subunit were a regular occurrence.

A variety of political tactics used by the purchasing agents were discovered in this study. They included:

1. *Rule evasion.* Evading the formal purchase procedures in the organization.
2. *Personal-political.* Using friendships to facilitate or inhibit the processing of an order.
3. *Educational.* Attempting to persuade engineering to think in purchasing terms.
4. *Organizational.* Attempting to change the formal or informal interaction patterns between engineering and purchasing.

These political tactics were used by the purchasing agents to accomplish their goals. The tactics (1) were outside the legitimate power system (2) occasionally benefited the purchasing agent at the expense of the rest of the organization, and (3) were intentionally developed so that more power was acquired by the purchasing agent.

Another study of political behavior was conducted in the electronics industry in southern California. A total of 87 managers (30 chief execu-

[40] Ibid.

[41] Dan L. Madison, Robert W. Allen, Lyman W. Porter, Patricia A. Renwick, and Bronston T. Mayes, "Organizational Politics: An Exploration of Managers' Perceptions," *Human Relations,* February 1980, pp. 79–100; Jeffrey Gantz and Victor V. Murray, "The Experience of Workplace Politics," *Academy of Management Journal,* June 1980, pp. 237–51; and Robert W. Allen, Dan L. Madison, Lyman W. Porter, Patricia A. Renwick, and Bronston T. Mayes, "Organizational Politics: Tactics and Characteristics of Its Actors, *California Management Review,* 1979, pp. 77–83.

[42] George Strauss, "Tactics of the Lateral Relationship: The Purchasing Agent," *Administrative Science Quarterly,* 1962, pp. 161–86.

TABLE 10–2

Managerial Perceptions of Organizational Political Behavior

Tactic	Combined Groups	Chief Executive Officers	Staff Managers	Supervisors
Attacking or blaming others	54.0%	60.0%	50.0%	51.7%
Use of information	54.0	56.7	57.1	48.3
Image building/impression management	52.9	43.3	46.4	69.0
Developing base of support	36.8	46.7	39,3	24.1
Praising others, ingratiation	25.3	16.7	25.0	34.5
Power coalitions, strong allies	25.3	26.7	17.9	31.0
Associating with the influential	24.1	16.7	35.7	20.7
Creating obligations/reciprocity	12.6	3.3	14.3	30.7

Source: R. W. Allen, D. L. Madison, L. W. Porter, P. A. Renwick, and B. T. Mayes, "Organizational Politics: Tactics and Characteristics of Its Actors." Copyright 1979 by the Regents of the University of California. Reprinted from *California Management Review*, December 1979, p. 79 by permission of the Regents.

tive officers, 28 higher level staff managers, 29 supervisors) were interviewed and asked about political behavior.[43] Table 10–2 presents a summary of the eight categories of political tactics (behavior) that were mentioned most frequently by each of the three managerial groups.

The managers were also asked to describe the personal characteristics of the individuals who used political behavior effectively. Thirteen personal characteristics were identified as important. These characteristics are presented in Table 10–3.

The managers in this study were aware of political behavior because it was a part of their organizational experiences. As the researchers noted, the research was not designed to praise or disparage political behavior.[44] Instead, it was intended to show that politics is a fact of organizational existence.

Playing Politics

If anything, the available (yet scanty) research indicates that politics exists in organizations and that some individuals are very adept at political behavior. Mintzberg and others describe these adept politicians as playing games.[45] The games that managers and nonmanagers

---

[43] Allen et al., "Organizational Politics."

[44] Ibid.

[45] This discussion of games relies on the presentation in Mintzberg, *Power in and around Organizations*, chap. 13, pp. 171–271. Please refer to the source for a complete and interesting discussion of political games.

TABLE 10–3

Personal Characteristics of Effective Politicians

Personal Characteristics	Combined Groups	Chief Executive Officers	Staff Managers	Supervisors
Articulate	29.9%	36.7%	39.3%	12.8%
Sensitive	29.9	50.0	21.4	17.2
Socially adept	19.5	10.0	32.1	17.2
Competent	17.2	10.0	21.4	20.7
Popular	17.2	16.7	10.7	24.1
Extroverted	16.1	16.7	14.3	17.2
Self-confident	16.1	10.0	21.4	17.2
Aggressive	16.1	10.0	14.3	24.1
Ambitious	16.1	20.0	25.0	3.4
Devious	16.1	13.3	14.3	20.7
"Organization person"	12.6	20.0	3.6	13.8
Highly intelligent	11.5	20.0	10.7	3.4
Logical	10.3	3.3	21.4	6.9

Source: R. W. Allen, D. L. Madison, L. W. Porter, P. A. Renwick, and B. T. Mayes, "Organizational Politics: Tactics and Characteristics of Its Actors," Copyright 1979 by the Regents of the University of California. Reprinted from *California Management Review*, December 1979, p. 78, by permission of the Regents.

engage in are intended to (1) resist authority (e.g., the insurgency game), (2) counter the resistance to authority (e.g., the counterinsurgency game), (3) build power bases (e.g., the sponsorship game and the coalition-building game), (4) defeat rivals (e.g., the line versus staff game), and (5) effect organizational change (e.g., the whistle-blowing game). In all, Mintzberg describes and discusses 13 types of political games. Six of these will be briefly presented.

The Insurgency Game. This game is played to resist authority. For example, suppose that a plant foreman is instructed to reprimand a particular worker for violating company policies. The reprimand can be delivered according to the foreman's feelings and opinions about its worth and legitimacy. If the reprimand is delivered in a halfhearted manner, it will probably have no noticeable effect. On the other hand if it is delivered aggressively, it may be effective. Insurgency in the form of not delivering the reprimand as expected by a higher level authority would be difficult to detect and correct. Insurgency as a game to resist authority is practiced in organizations at all levels.

The Counterinsurgency Game. Often, a person in an authority position will fight back when faced with insurgency. The foreman's superior may have to carefully monitor whether policies concerning the reprimand are being followed. One tactic is to occasionally (not always) follow up requests given to subordinates with a detailed checking system. For example, the person with ultimate authority could ask the foreman on occasion whether the reprimand had been given, when it was given, what the person's reaction was, and how the foreman would make presentation improvements in the future. The foreman's superior could then also check with the person who was reprimanded to determine when and how the reprimand was given. The purpose of periodic monitoring is to encourage the foreman to deliver the reprimand according to company procedures.

The Sponsorship Game. This is a rather straightforward game in that a person attaches himself or herself to someone with power. The sponsor is typically the person's boss or someone else with higher power and status than those of the person. Typically, individuals attach themselves to someone who is on the move. There are a few rules involved in playing this game. First, the person must be able to show commitment and loyalty to the sponsor. Second, the person must follow each sponsor-initiated request or order. Third, the person must stay in the background and give the sponsor credit for everything. Finally, the person must be thankful and display gratitude to the sponsor. The sponsor is not only a teacher and trainer for the person, but also a power base. Some of the sponsor's power tends to rub off on the person because of his or her association with the sponsor.

The following Close-Up highlights the sponsorship game that was played at Bendix Corporation. This Close-Up shows that sponsorship can result in dirty politics, gossip, and suspicion.

ORGANIZATIONS: CLOSE-UP

Romance, Rumors, or Dirty Politics at Bendix Corporation

In June 1979, William Agee, chairman of Bendix Corporation, hired Mary Cunningham, a recent Harvard Business School graduate, to be his executive assistant. Only 28, she was described as unusually intelligent, ambitious, and politically savvy. Agee immediately assigned her to analyze some major Bendix acquisition leads. Within a year, Agee promoted Cunningham to vice president for corporate and public affairs. Her new position gave her unlimited access to Agee.

Although Cunningham's first year at Bendix was quite successful, other executives got nervous. Conflicts between Agee and William Panny, the president of Bendix, became frequent occurrences. Rumors were also circulated that Agee intended to implement a significant reorganization at Bendix. There was also office gossip about the relationship between Agee and Cunningham. Both had separated from their spouses.

The gossip suggested a more than professional relationship between the two. The fact that Cunningham was given the assignment of evaluating the strategic issue that had caused a rift between Agee and Panny fanned the rumor mill. Her seven-person task force was known around Bendix as "Snow White and the Seven Dwarfs."

In early September 1980, Agee fired Panny over a policy disagreement, and the vice president for strategic planning resigned within hours of Panny's firing. Agee announced that Cunningham was to be the new vice president for strategic planning. About the same time, Agee learned that someone had been sending anonymous letters to the Bendix board of directors about his relationship with Cunningham. Agee reacted quickly and arranged meetings with Bendix's top managers and with the board's executive committee. He claimed that the reference to his romantic involvement with Cunningham was false. In one meeting with Bendix employees, Agee stated: "I know it has been buzzing around that Mary Cunningham's rise in this company is very unusual and that it has something to do with a personal relationship we have. Sure it's unusual. Her rise in this company is unusual because she's a very unusual and very talented individual."

Eventually, the pressure, gossip, rumors, and insinuations became too much for Mary Cunningham. On October 9, 1980, she resigned from Bendix.

Adapted from Manuel Velasquez, Dennis J. Moberg, and Gerald F. Cavanagh, "Organizational Statesmanship and Dirty Politics: Ethical Guidelines for the Organizational Politician," *Organizational Dynamics*, Autumn 1983, pp. 65–80.

The Coalition-Building Game. A subunit such as a personnel/human resources management department or a research and development department may be able to increase its power by forming an alliance (a coalition) with other subunits. The strength in numbers idea is encouraged by coalition building. When such alliances are formed within the organization, there is an emphasis on common goals and common interests. However, forming coalitions with groups outside the organization can also enhance the power of a subunit.

An example of the building of an internal coalition can illustrate how power can be acquired. The personnel/human resources department in most organizations typically has limited power. However, current litigation involving employee relations and employee health problems associated with disability triggered by job stress is becoming a costly expense. Consequently, legal staffs in organizations have acquired power. These legal staffs do not have the information, daily contact with employees, and records needed to legally serve the firm. That is, they are not able to completely deal with needs of employees and with their inclination to file legal suits. Skills, abilities, and information to cope with employee-based uncertainties are more in the domain of the personnel/human resources department. Therefore, an alliance between the legal staff and the personnel/human resources department would enhance both their power bases. The coalition would enable the organization to effectively address legal issues.

Building a coalition with an external group can also enhance the power of various groups. The alumni office of most state universities interacts with alumni in fund raising, projecting a positive image, and providing service on community projects. The donations of alumni are extremely important for funding and supporting research programs conducted within a university. The alumni office would acquire more power by forming an alliance with major donors who actively support it. The university would be hard pressed to ignore requests that major donors made to the administration to support the alumni office, the implication being that failing to support the alumni office and its personnel would cause these donors to withhold donations.

The Line versus Staff Game. The line manager versus the staff adviser game has existed for years in organizations. In essence, it is a game that pits line authority to make operating decisions against the expertise possessed by staff advisers. There are also value differences and a clash of personality. Line managers are typically more experienced, more oriented to the bottom line and more intuitive in reaching decisions. On the other hand, staff advisers tend to be younger, better educated, and more analytical decision makers.[46] These differences result in viewing the organizational world from slightly different perspectives.

Withholding information, having access to powerful authority figures, creating favorable impressions, and identifying with organizational goals are tactics used by line and staff personnel. The line versus staff clash must be controlled in organizations before it reaches the point at which organizational goals are not being achieved because of the disruption.

The Whistle-Blowing Game. This game is played to bring about organizational change. If a person in an organization identifies a behavior that violates his or her sense of fairness, morals, ethics, or law, then he or she may blow the whistle. **Whistle-blowing** means that the person informs someone—a newspaper reporter, a government representative, a competitor—about an assumed injustice, irresponsible action, or violation of the law. The whistle-blower is attempting to correct the behavior or practice. By whistle-blowing, the person is bypassing the authority system within the organization. This is viewed in a negative light by managers who possess position power. Often,

whistle-blowing
Informing someone about an organizational practice or behavior if it conflicts with a personal opinion, value, or belief is called whistle-blowing.

---

[46] S. S. Hammond III, "The Roles of the Manager and Management Scientist in Successful Implementation," *Sloan Management Review,* Winter 1974, pp. 1–24.

whistle-blowing is done secretly so that retribution by the authority system is avoided.

Whistle-blowers come from all levels in the organization. For example, an Eastern Airlines pilot complained to management first and then to the public about defects in his plane's automatic pilot mechanisms. His complaints were attacked by management as being groundless. In another example, a biologist reported to the Environmental Protection Agency that his consulting firm had submitted false data to the agency on behalf of an electric utility company; he was fired. In still another publicized case, an engineer at Ford complained about the faulty design of the Pinto. Unfortunately, this whistle-blower was demoted. Many of the legal costs and settlements from Pinto crash victims might have been avoided if the whistle-blower's message had been taken more seriously.[47]

These six examples of political game playing are not offered as always being good or bad for the organization. They are games that occur with various degrees of frequency in organizations. They occur within and between subunits, and they are played by individuals representing themselves or a subunit. Certainly, political behaviors carried to an extreme can hurt individuals and subunits. However, it is unrealistic to assume that all political behavior can or should be eliminated through management intervention. Even in the most efficient, profitable, and socially responsible organizations and subunits, political behaviors and games are being acted out. Top-management encouragement of power sharing as presented in the opening Organizational Issue for Debate would seem to be a vehicle for minimizing the use of negative political gamesmanship in organizations.

SUMMARY OF KEY POINTS

A. Power is defined as the ability to get things done in the way that one wants them to be done.

B. Authority is a much narrower concept than power. Authority is a form of power that is made legitimate because it is accepted by subordinates or followers.

C. French and Raven introduced the notion of five interpersonal power bases—legitimate (position based), reward, coercive (pun-

---

[47] Alice L. Priest, "When Employees Think Their Company Is Wrong," *Business Week*, November 24, 1980, p. 2; and Andy Pasztor, "Speaking Up Gets Biologist into Big Fight," *The Wall Street Journal*, November 26, 1980, p. 29.

ishment based), expert, and referent (charismatic). These five bases can be divided into two major categories: organizational and personal. Legitimate, reward, and coercive power are primarily prescribed by an organization, while expert and coercive power are based on personal qualities.

D. Structural and situational power bases also exist. An organization's structural arrangement establishes patterns of communication and information flow that play an important role in power formation and use.

E. Historically, power seekers have been presented in negative terms. They have been portrayed as weak, neurotic, and troubled. However, research by McClelland on the need for power paints a different picture. McClelland has found that some managers with a high need for power are effective, use their power to accomplish organizational goals, and are involved heavily in coaching subordinates.

F. Power and influence can flow upward, from the bottom to the top, in an organization. Lower level employees can have significant power because of expertise, location, and access and control of information. Some lower level employees acquire power through persuasion and manipulation skills.

G. Subunits within organizations acquire and use power. The strategic contingency approach addresses subunit power. A strategic contingency is an event or activity that is extremely important for accomplishing organizational goals. The strategic contingency factors that have been disclosed by research include coping with uncertainty, centrality, and substitutability.

H. Coping with uncertainty is extremely important for acquiring, retaining, and using power.

I. Individuals can sometimes exercise power because of illusion. The Milgram "obedience to authority" experiments involving faked electric shocks illustrated how the illusion of power can bring about compliance.

J. Politics is present in all organizations. Politics comprises those activities that are used to acquire, develop, and use power and other resources to obtain one's preferred outcome when there is uncertainty or disagreement about choices.

K. Mintzberg introduced the notion of political game playing. Examples of political games are the insurgency game, the sponsorship game, and the coalition-building game.

DISCUSSION AND REVIEW QUESTIONS

1. Suppose that someone comments, "Power flows from the top to the bottom. The top levels have it; the lower levels would like to have it, but do not." Is this an accurate view of power in organizations?

2. Why would it be important to share power with others?

3. What changes in an organization's or subunit's environment would bring about changes in strategic contingencies?

4. Why would a manager have to engage in political behaviors to accomplish goals?

5. Why is it unrealistic to assume that little or no political game playing exists in an organization such as McDonald's or Chrysler?

6. Power and politics are two terms that elicit negative reactions. However, we believe that it is more accurate to regard power and politics as neutral terms. Why?

7. Charisma is a term that is used to explain the referent power base. Do you feel that it is possible to increase or improve a person's charisma? How?

8. Who in an organization has legal authority and therefore power according to Weber?

9. What power and political tactics are used to give an illusion of power? Is it ethical to create an illusion of power?

10. It has been claimed that when managers are faced with uncertainties in making decisions, there tends to be more political maneuvering and jockeying. Do you agree? Why?

ADDITIONAL REFERENCES

Allen, R. W., and L. W. Porter. *Organizational Influence Processes.* Glenview, Ill.: Scott, Foresman, 1983.

Blackburn, R. S. "Lower Participant Power: Toward a Conceptual Integration." *Academy of Management Review,* 1981, pp. 127–31.

Boyle, R. J. "Wrestling with Jellyfish." *Harvard Business Review,* 1984, pp. 74–83.

Ewing, D. L. *Do It My Way or You're Fired.* New York: John Wiley & Sons, 1983.

Jackson, C. N., and D. C. King. "The Effects of Representatives' Power within Their Own Organizations on the Outcome of a Negotiation." *Academy of Management Journal,* 1983, pp. 178–85.

Kanter, R. M. "The Middle Manager as Innovator." *Harvard Business Review,* 1982, pp. 95–105.

————. *The Changemasters: Innovation for Productivity in the American Mode.* New York: Simon & Schuster, 1983.

Main, J. "How to Be a Better Negotiator." *Fortune,* 1983, pp. 141–46.

Mitroff, I. *Stakeholders of the Organizational Mind.* San Francisco: Jossey-Bass, 1983.

Mizruchi, M. S. "Who Controls Whom? An Examination of the Relation between Management and Boards of Directors in Large American Corporations." *Academy of Management Review,* 1983, pp. 426–35.

Sanders, C. S., and R. Scamell. "Intraorganizational Distributions of Power: Replication Research." *Academy of Management Journal,* 1982, pp. 192–200.

Steiner, G. *The New CEO.* New York: Macmillan, 1983.

Vancil, R. F., and C. H. Green. "How CEOs Use Top Management Committees." *Harvard Business Review,* 1984, pp. 65–73.

Zand, D. E. *Information, Organization, and Power: Effective Management in the Knowledge Society.* New York: McGraw-Hill, 1981.

CASE FOR ANALYSIS

The Power Center at
Geico Corporation

John J. Byrne is chairperson of Geico Corporation, the Washington, D. C.,
auto insurer. He took over in 1976, when the firm was on the verge of bankruptcy. Within a few years, he succeeded in building a culture at Geico that
was based on consensus management and inflexible operator rules. He found,
however, that one of his inflexible rules stood in the way of Geico's sales
growth. Byrne could have used his authority as chief executive to change
the rule, but instead he chose to muddle. That way it took four years to
bring about a change that he could have commanded from his position of
power with a one-page memo.

Byrnes' career began at Lincoln National Life as a roving reinsurance actu-
ary. In 1967, he moved to the Traveler's Insurance. In six years, he was promoted to executive vice president. He describes himself as a pusher, a driver
who sometimes pushes his ideas too hard.

During his first few months at Geico, Byrne was putting out fires and not
really concerned about building a productive work culture. He was going
strictly by the books and relying on his position power to do the job. That
is, he was influencing others by the use of legitimate, reward, and coercive
power bases, the position power that is prescribed by the organization. He
hired and fired and put together his own Geico management team.

Byrne describes his muddling style as a blend of management by objectives
and consensus management. He believes that top management should not
make policy decisions by itself. Instead, it should create a company culture
and style in which power is shared and subordinates are trusted to perform
well.

Byrne is considered a politician by some managers. He has tailored Geico's
culture to fit his personality. He will yield and bend to group decisions, but
he stays in control of the decision-making process. Long before any major
issue is put to the group, Byrne will be moving from office to office, gently
nudging group members, listening, and getting to know what group members
are thinking and feeling. He is jockeying for advice, coaxing, and letting others
know what he thinks.

Byrne uses "challenge sessions" as a tool to stimulate and prod other managers. This is how they work. Each manager circulates copies of his or her
proposed budget and goals for the year to a group of other managers. Each
manager must sit alone at the front of the room presenting his or her proposals.
The other managers then attack the proposals from every direction. It is
not acceptable to simply "rubber-stamp" another manager's proposals. Managers are expected to sell their proposals to others. The challenge sessions last
12 to 16 hours a day, five days a week, for three weeks.

Based on Stratford P. Sherman, "Muddling to Victory at Geico," *Fortune*, September
5, 1983, pp. 66–80.

At the end of the challenge sessions, each manager has accepted responsibility for a one-year corporate operating plan. Byrne is firm about not rewarding with a bonus any manager who fails to meet his or her goals. If managers hold back and try to set lower goals at the challenge sessions, Byrne has a knack for spotting this and letting the manager know it. He wants his managers to perform and pushes them to set realistic, challenging objectives. His philosophy is that results are the key to success at Geico. He states that as long as the employee gets results, "I don't care if he shines his shoes with a brick."

Indoctrinated in Byrne's style of managing, Geico managers are cost cutters and realistic goal setters, and they perform their jobs with zeal. Byrne has pushed, led by example, subtly coerced, and motivated the Geico management team. In addition, he listens and shares power through the muddling process. Byrne is patient, and he will wait for managers to finally see the light.

Byrne prides himself on creating a corporate culture that permits power to be shared. The sharing has facilitated trust, internal communication, and realistic targets. Instead of relying on power, fear, and coercion, Byrne has taken another route. When he perceives a need for major changes, he waits for the lieutenants to see the need before issuing orders.

Questions for Consideration

1. Some critics of Byrne's muddling style claim that it can work in insurance but that if you tried it in a more volatile and unpredictable industry such as computers, automobiles, or clothing, competition would simply pass you by? What do you think?

2. What types of power bases does Byrne actually rely on to perform his job as chairperson at Geico?

3. Why would a manager making a formal presentation at a "challenge session" tend to feel powerless?

4. How does Byrne combine power and politics to perform his job?

EXPERIENTIAL EXERCISE
OCCUPATIONAL POWER DIFFERENCES AND TACTICS

Objectives

1. To examine the power bases of various occupations.
2. To illustrate the difference in opinion about power bases.

Starting the Exercise

Phase I: 5 minutes

Individually rank the following occupations according to the overall power that they would generally possess in their organizations. Place a 1 in front of the occupation that you feel to be the most powerful in its particular organization, a 15 in front of the occupation that you feel to be the least powerful in its particular organization, and numbers 2 through 14 in front of the remaining occupations.

_____ Nurse in a hospital
_____ President of major university
_____ Chief executive officer of major firm
_____ Medical technologist in hospital
_____ Counselor in personnel unit of major firm
_____ College professor in major university
_____ Machinist in major firm
_____ Accountant in hospital
_____ District sales manager in major firm
_____ Research and Development Scientist in High-Technology Firm
_____ Police officer
_____ Navy ensign
_____ Homemaker (full time)
_____ Secretary (president's) in major firm
_____ U.S. senator

Phase II: 15 minutes

Decide which of the occupations listed would have the strongest legitimate, reward, and coercive power bases. Write a 50-word report describing why you selected each of the occupations as the most powerful in each of the three categories of interpersonal power.

Phase III: 10 minutes

Select the least powerful occupation from your ranking, and develop a brief list of power and political tactics that could be used to enhance the power of this occupation.

Phase IV: 15 minutes

The instructor will form small groups of four, six, or eight students to discuss the rankings, the brief reports on power bases, and the lists of power and political tactics.

Phase V: 5–10 minutes

The instructor will wrap up the session by discussing briefly the findings of the small groups.

Chapter 11

After completing Chapter 11, you should be able to:

Define the term *leadership*.

Describe the difference in the trait versus the personal-behavioral approaches in explaining leadership effectiveness.

Discuss what is meant by substitutes for leader behavior.

Compare the situational factors used in discussions of the contingency, path-goal, and Vroom-Yetton approaches to leadership.

Identify the internal and external causes used in the attribution explanation of leadership.

Leadership: Theories, Models, and Applications

A General Description of Leadership

Argument For

There are writers who believe that a new type of person is taking over the leadership of the most technically advanced companies in the United States. In contrast to the "jungle fighter" industrialist of the past, the new leader is driven, not to build or preside over a large empire, but to plan, organize, and control winning teams. Unlike the security-seeking organization man of William H. Whyte, the new leader is excited by the chance to cut deals and to gamble. The new leader is called a *gamesman.*

The most dynamic companies with these innovative leaders are able to create their own markets. Organizations that can attract or develop the gamesman-type leader will be successful. They will be able to face tough competition and develop new products and technology.

By studying the different types of leaders who manage in organizations, students will be able to understand why the gamesman usually comes out on top. The predominant type of leaders found in organizations are:

1. *The craftsman.* This type of leader is production-oriented, concerned with quality, and interested in building a sound record.
2. *The jungle fighter.* This type of leader is interested in gaining power. Life and work are viewed as a jungle. Peers are viewed as accomplices or enemies. Two types of jungle fighters are the *lions,* who conquer and build, and the *foxes,* who move ahead by politicking.
3. *The company man.* This type of leader is interested in cooperation, commitment, and security.
4. *The gamesman.* This is the new type of leader who thrives on challenge, competitive activity, and new and fresh approaches and whose main goal is to be a winner. This type of leader is interested in developing the tactics and strategies needed to be a winner.

The suggestion offered here is that you should explore the virtues and value of being a gamesman. Experiment with the style, and attempt to improve your gamesman tactics.

Argument Against

Although books like *The Gamesman* become best-sellers, they do not improve our understanding of what effective leadership is in organizations around the world. Such books are imaginative but not very explanatory, scientifically based, or accurate. In fact, it is even dangerous to reach any conclusions on the basis of interviews conducted with only 250 managers. This is what Michael Maccoby, the author of *The Gamesman* (New York: Simon & Schuster, 1976), did to develop his conclusions about the craftsman, the jungle fighter, the company man, and the gamesman.

It may be true that some effective executives in organizations are gamesmen, but to suggest that this or any similarly developed framework adds to our knowledge is disappointing because the study of organizational leadership has advanced past the practice of listing descriptions of types of individuals. It has become rather clear that effective leadership is contingent on having the right person for the situation at hand and a particular group of subordinates. Leader behavior characteristics, subordinate characteristics, organizational climate, and goals must be considered. These situational variables are not investigated scientifically by Maccoby.

The failure to scientifically study situational variables results in just another list of descriptions of types of leaders. What is needed and more appropriate is a careful analysis of what leaders do and what the results of this behavior are in terms of performance.

Exploring the virtues or values of the gamesman approach is worthless. In fact, the concept is nothing more than an anecdote-based description. You would be better off by determining what your strengths and weaknesses are, how others respond to your influence, and how you can improve your leadership characteristics. Don't get involved in catchy terms. Invest your time in scientifically and thoroughly studying leadership.

In all of the groups to which you have belonged—family, sports team, social club, study group, work unit—there was typically a person who was more influential than the others. The most influential person in these groups was probably called a leader. Leaders are extremely important in a variety of organizational settings. Indeed, organizations would undoubtedly be less efficient without leaders, and in extreme cases they would be unable to accomplish purposeful goals. For these and similar reasons, leadership has been the center of attention of theorists, researchers, and practitioners.

Although leadership is important and has been studied by behavioral scientists for decades, it is still somewhat of a mystery.[1] Even after thousands of studies, there is still a lack of consensus among the experts on exactly what leadership is and how it should be analyzed. This chapter will examine leadership in organizational settings. A number of somewhat distinct perspectives of leadership will be presented. Each perspective will be explored theoretically, empirically, and from the standpoint of its application value. This type of exploration will suggest that (1) leadership is not the same as management; (2) leadership is a complex concept; (3) leadership attributes can be developed through experience, training, and analysis; (4) leadership effectiveness depends primarily on the fit between the leader, followers, and situations; and (5) leadership is substituted for in various settings and situations—that is, in some situations leadership isn't important or a significant influence.

The idea that leadership is a synonym for management is not completely valid. Leadership is a narrower concept than management. A manager in a formal organization is responsible and entrusted to perform such functions as planning, organizing, and controlling. However, leaders also exist in informal groups. Informal leaders are not always formal managers performing managerial functions that are required by the organization. Consequently, leaders are only in some instances actually managers.

The concept of role was clarified in Chapter 8 dealing with group behavior. In the formal organization, roles often have specific responsibilities associated with them. For example, the first-line supervisory role may be one in which the role occupant is responsible for the level and quality of production generated by a particular group of employees. Exactly how the supervisor fulfills the responsibility involves the occupant's style. Some first-line supervisors rely on the *authority* of the position to secure compliance with performance standards, while others use a more *participative* approach that involves

---

[1] Bernard M. Bass, *Stogdill's Handbook of Leadership* (New York: Free Press, 1982).

joint decision making on the part of the leader (manager) and followers (subordinates).

A hierarchy of roles also exists in informal groups. The informal leader is accepted as the person to carry out the duties of the position. Once again, how the leader brings about compliance from followers will depend largely on the leadership style used. What is effective for one leader may not be for another. This, in essence, is the crux of the leadership issue: What makes for effective leadership? As indicated earlier, there is no simple or single answer to this important question.

LEADERSHIP DEFINED

leadership
An attempt to use noncoercive types of influence to motivate individuals to accomplish some goal.

The five bases of interpersonal power discussed in Chapter 10 suggest that power can be defined as the ability to influence another person's behavior. Where one individual attempts to affect the behavior of a group without using the coercive form of power, we describe the effort as leadership. More specifically, **"Leadership** is an attempt at influencing the activities of followers through the communication process and toward the attainment of some goal or goals."[2] This definition implies that leadership involves the use of influence and that all relationships can involve leadership. A second element in the definition involves the importance of the communication process. The clarity and accuracy of communication affect the behavior and performance of followers.

Another element of the definition focuses on the accomplishment of goals. The effective leader may have to deal with individual, group, and organizational goals. Leader effectiveness is typically considered in terms of the degree of accomplishment of one or a combination of these goals. Individuals may view the leader as effective or ineffective in terms of the satisfactions they derive from the total work experience. In fact, acceptance of a leader's directives or requests rests largely on the followers' expectations that a favorable response will lead to an attractive outcome.

Reward and legitimate power are primarily specified by an individual's role in a hierarchy. This role can, of course, be in a formal or an informal group. The degree and scope of a leader's expert and referent power are dictated primarily by personal attributes. Some leaders, because of personality or communication difficulties, cannot influence others through expert or referent power.

Figure 11–1 summarizes the key sources and perceived bases of

---

[2] Edwin A. Fleishman, "Twenty Years of Consideration and Structure," in *Current Developments in the Study of Leadership,* ed. Edwin A. Fleishman and James G. Hunt (Carbondale: Southern Illinois University Press, 1973), p. 3.

FIGURE 11–1

A Leadership Model: Sources, Moderators, Outcomes

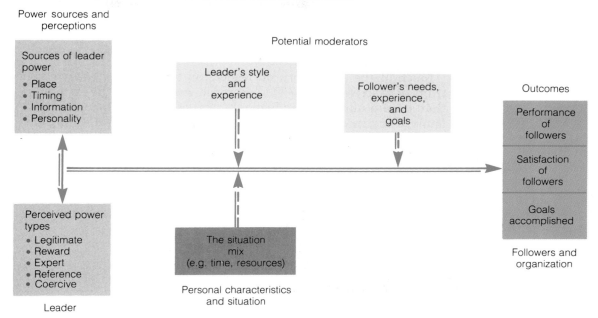

interpersonal power. It also presents some of the possible moderating factors between the sources and perceived bases of power and outcomes (goals). The model suggests that (1) a successful leader is one who is aware of sources of power and the importance of perceived power; (2) the leader doesn't rely on coercive power; (3) the sources of a leader's power include place, time, and information and personality characteristics; and (4) the accomplishment of goals will depend not only on power sources and perceptions but also on follower needs, the situation, and the experience of the leader.[3]

We agree with the "argument against" position in the Organizational Issue for Debate. To make broad, generalized statements about leadership after studying only 250 managers does not result in an improved understanding of leadership. Descriptions and listings are not very helpful in working toward a clear picture of leadership as practiced in organizations. Figure 11–1 is more meaningful than using a description of leadership. It calls attention to the sources of power used by leaders, factors that moderate the leader's effectiveness, and

---

[3] See Arthur G. Jago, "Leadership: Perspectives in Theory and Research," *Management Science,* March 1982, pp. 315–36.

the goals of leadership behavior. This type of perspective is more meaningful than simply classifying individuals as gamesmen or jungle fighters. We need to explain, understand, and trace gamesman behaviors and performance.

TRAIT THEORIES

Much of the early work on leadership focused on identifying the traits of effective leaders. This approach was based on the assumption that a finite number of individual traits of effective leaders could be found. Thus, most research was designed to identify intellectual, emotional, physical, and other personal traits of successful leaders. The personnel testing component of scientific management supported to a significant extent the trait theory of leadership.[4] In addition to being studied by personnel testing, the traits of leaders have been studied by observation of behavior in group situations, by choice of associates (voting), by nomination of rating by observers, and by analysis of biographical data.

Intelligence

In a review of 33 studies, Stogdill found a general trend that indicated that leaders were more intelligent than followers.[5] One of the most significant findings was that extreme intelligence differences between leaders and followers might be dysfunctional. For example, a leader with a relatively high IQ who is attempting to influence a group with members with average IQs may be unable to understand why the members do not comprehend the problem. In addition, such a leader may have difficulty in communicating ideas and policies. Being too intelligent would be a problem in some situations.

Personality

Some research results suggest that such personality traits as alertness, originality, personal integrity, and self-confidence are associated with effective leadership.[6] Ghiselli reported several personality traits that tend to be associated with leader effectiveness.[7] For example,

---

[4] Ralph M. Stogdill, "Historical Trends in Leadership Theory and Research," *Journal of Contemporary Business,* Autumn 1974, p. 4.

[5] Ralph M. Stogdill, *Handbook of Leadership* (New York: Free Press, 1974), pp. 43–44.

[6] For example, see Chris Argyris, "Some Characteristics of Successful Executives," *Personnel Journal,* June 1955, pp. 50–63; and J. A. Hornaday and C. J. Bunker, "The Nature of the Entrepreneur," *Personnel Psychology,* Spring 1970, pp. 47–54.

[7] Edwin E. Ghiselli, "The Validity of Management Traits in Relation to Occupational Level," *Personnel Psychology,* Summer 1963, pp. 109–13.

he found that initiative and the ability to act and initiate action independently were related to the level in the organization of the respondent. The higher the person went in the organization, the more important this trait became. Ghiselli also found that self-assurance was related to hierarchical position in the organization. Finally, he found that individuals who exhibited individuality were the most effective leaders. Some writers argue that personality is unrelated to leadership. This view is too harsh if we consider how personality has been found to be related to perception, attitudes, learning, and motivation. The problem is finding valid ways to measure personality traits. This goal has been difficult to achieve, but progress, although slow, is being made.[8]

Physical Characteristics

Studies of the relationship between effective leadership and physical characteristics such as age, height, weight, and appearance provide contradictory results. Being taller and heavier than the average of a group is certainly not advantageous for achieving a leader position.[9] However, many organizations believe that it requires a physically large person to secure compliance from followers. This notion relies heavily on the coercive or fear basis of power. On the other hand, Truman, Gandhi, Napoleon, and Stalin are examples of individuals of small stature who rose to positions of leadership.

Supervisory Ability

Using the leaders' performance ratings, Ghiselli found a positive relationship between a person's supervisory ability and level in the organizational hierarchy. The supervisor's ability is defined as the "effective utilization of whatever supervisory practices are indicated by the particular requirements of the situation."[10] Once again, a measurement of the concept is needed, and this is a difficult problem to resolve.

A summary of some of the most researched traits of leaders is presented in Table 11–1. These are some of the traits that have been found most likely to be characteristic of successful leaders. Some studies have reported that these traits contribute to leadership success.

---

[8] For example, see Robert W. Lundin, *Personality* (New York: Macmillan, 1974); and Leonard Krasner and Leonard P. Ullman, *Behavior Influence and Personality* (New York: Holt, Rinehart & Winston, 1973).

[9] Ralph M. Stogdill, "Personal Factors Associated with Leadership," *Journal of Applied Psychology*, January 1948, pp. 35–71.

[10] Edwin E. Ghiselli, *Exploration in Managerial Talent* (Santa Monica, Calif.: Goodyear Publishing, 1971).

TABLE 11-1

Traits Associated With Leadership Effectiveness

Intelligence	Personality	Abilities
Judgment	Adaptability	Ability to enlist cooperation
Decisiveness	Alertness	Cooperativeness
Knowledge	Creativity	Popularity and prestige
Fluency of speech	Personal integrity	Sociability (interpersonal skills)
	Self-confidence	Social participation
	Emotional balance and control	Tact, diplomacy
	Independence (nonconformity)	

Adapted from Bernard M. Bass, *Stogdill's Handbook of Leadership* (New York: Free Press, 1982), pp. 75–76.

However, to claim that leadership success is primarily or completely a function of these traits is oversimplified and too broad.[11]

Although traits such as those in Table 11–1 have in some studies differentiated effective from ineffective leaders, there still exist many contradictory research findings. There are a number of possible reasons for the contradictory results. First, the list of potentially important traits is endless. Every year new traits, such as the sign under which a person is born, handwriting style, and order of birth, are added to personality, physical characteristics, and intelligence. This continual "adding on" results in more confusion among those interested in identifying leadership traits. Second, trait test scores are not consistently predictive of leader effectiveness. Leadership traits do not operate singly, but in combination, to influence followers. This interaction influences the leader-follower relationship. Third, the patterns of effective behavior depend largely on the situation. The leadership behavior that is effective in a bank may be ineffective in a laboratory. Finally, the trait approach does not provide insight into what the effective leader does on the job. Observations are needed that describe the behavior of effective and ineffective leaders.

Despite these shortcomings, the trait approach is not completely invalid. Stogdill concisely captures the value of the trait approach in the following statement:

The view that leadership is entirely situational in origin and that no personal characteristics are predictive of leadership . . . seems to over-

---

[11] David A. Kenny and Stephen J. Zaccaro, "An Estimate of Variance due to Traits in Leadership," *Journal of Applied Psychology*, November 1983, pp. 678–85.

emphasize the situational and underemphasize the personal nature of leadership.[12]

However, after years of speculation and research on leadership traits, we are not even close to identifying a specific set of such traits. Thus, the trait approach appears to be interesting, but not very efficient for identifying and predicting leadership potential.

PERSONAL-BEHAVIORAL THEORIES

In the late 1940s, researchers began to explore the notion that how a person acts determines that person's leadership effectiveness. Instead of searching for traits, these researchers examined behaviors and their impact on the performance and satisfaction of followers. Today there are a number of well-known personal-behavioral theories of leadership. For each theory, we will outline how leadership behaviors were classified and studied.

The University of Michigan Studies: Job-Centered and Employee-Centered

In 1947, Likert began studying how best to manage the efforts of individuals to achieve desired performance and satisfaction objectives.[13] The purpose of most of the leadership research of the Likert-inspired team at the University of Michigan has been to discover the principles and methods of effective leadership. The effectiveness criteria used in many of the studies included:

Productivity per work hour or other similar measures of the organization's success in achieving its production goals.

Job satisfaction of members of the organization.

Turnover, absenteeism, and grievance rates.

Costs.

Scrap loss.

Employee and managerial motivation.

Studies have been conducted in a wide variety of organizations: chemical, electronics, food, heavy machinery, insurance, petroleum, public utilities, hospitals, banks, and government agencies. Data have been

---

[12] Stogdill, "Personal Factors," p. 72.

[13] For a review of this work, see Rensis Likert, *New Patterns of Management* (New York: McGraw-Hill, 1961); and Rensis Likert, *The Human Organization* (New York: McGraw-Hill, 1967).

obtained from thousands of employees doing different job tasks, ranging from unskilled work to highly skilled research and development work.

Through interviewing leaders and followers, the researchers identified two distinct styles of leadership, referred to as *job-centered* and *employee-centered.* The job-centered leader practices close supervision so that subordinates perform their tasks using specified procedures. This type of leader relies on coercion, reward, and legitimate power to influence the behavior and performance of followers. The concern for people is viewed as important but as a luxury that a leader cannot always afford.

The *employee-centered* leader believes in delegating decision making and aiding followers in satisfying their needs by creating a supportive work environment. The employee-centered leader is concerned with followers' personal advancement, growth, and achievement. These actions are assumed to be conducive to the support of group formation and development.

The Michigan series of studies does not clearly show that one particular style of leadership is always the most effective. Moreover, it only examines two aspects of leadership—task and people behavior.

The Ohio State Studies: Initiating Structure and Consideration

initiating structure
Leaders who initiate structure tend to establish exactly what they want their subordinates to do while performing the job.

consideration
A leader who scores high in consideration works hard at developing a close, personal relationship with followers.

Among the several large research programs on leadership that developed after World War II, one of the most significant was headed by Fleishman and his associates at Ohio State University. This program resulted in a two-factor theory of leadership.[14] The studies isolated two leadership factors, referred to as *initiating structure* and *consideration.* The definitions of these factors are as follows: **initiating structure** involves behavior in which the leader organizes and defines the relationships in the group, tends to establish well-defined patterns and channels of communication, and spells out ways of getting the job done. **Consideration** involves behavior indicating friendship, mutual trust, respect, warmth, and rapport between the leader and the followers.

These dimensions are measured by two separate questionnaires. The Leadership Opinion Questionnaire (LOQ) attempts to assess how lead-

[14] For a review of the studies, see Stogdill, *Handbook of Leadership,* chap. 11. Also see Edwin A. Fleishman, "The Measurement of Leadership Attitudes in Industry," *Journal of Applied Psychology,* June 1953, pp. 153–58; C. L. Shartle, *Executive Performance and Leadership* (Englewood Cliffs, N.J.: Prentice-Hall, 1956); Edwin A. Fleishman, E. F. Harris, and H. E. Burtt, *Leadership and Supervision in Industry* (Columbus: Bureau of Educational Research, Ohio State University, 1955); and Fleishman, "Twenty Years of Consideration and Structure."

FIGURE 11-2

The Scores of Five Leaders: Initiating Structure and Consideration

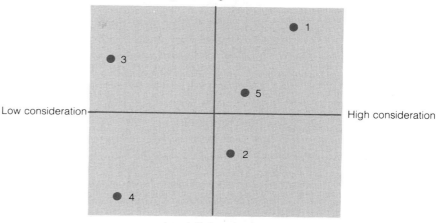

ers think they behave in leadership roles. The Leader Behavior Description Questionnaire (LBDQ) measures the perceptions of subordinates, peers, or superiors.

The initiating structure and consideration scores derived from the responses to the questionnaires provide a way to measure leadership style. Figure 11–2 provides a view of the behaviors of five different leaders. These points indicate that leaders have scores on both dimensions. Individual 1 is high on both initiating structure and consideration; individual 4 is low on both dimensions.

Since the original research undertaken to develop the questionnaire, there have been numerous studies of the relationship between these two leadership dimensions and various effectiveness criteria. Many of the early results stimulated the generalization that leaders above average in both consideration and initiating structure were more effective. In a study at International Harvester, however, the researchers began to find some more complicated interpretations of the two dimensions. In a study of supervisors, it was found that those scoring higher on initiating structure had higher proficiency ratings (ratings received from superiors) but also had more employee grievances. The higher consideration score was related to lower proficiency ratings and lower absences.[15]

The Ohio State personal-behavioral theory has been criticized be-

---

[15] Fleishman, Harris, and Burtt, *Leadership and Supervision.*

cause of simplicity (e.g., only two dimensions of leadership), lack of generalizability, and reliance on questionnaire responses to measure leadership effectiveness. The critique of Korman has been perhaps the most publicized.[16] Korman has criticized the Ohio State research on leadership in the following manner:

1. The researchers have made little attempt to conceptualize situational variables and their influence on leadership behavior.
2. Most of the research studies yield generally insignificant correlations between leader behavior measures and effectiveness criteria.
3. The theory has not provided any answer to the question of causality.

Some of the problems have been partially corrected.[17] For example, it has been pointed out in more recent research that many variables affect the relationship between leadership behavior and organizational effectiveness. These variables include employee experience, competence, job knowledge, expectations for leader behavior, the upward influence of leaders, the degree of autonomy, role clarity, and the urgency of time.[18]

A Synopsis of the Personal-Behavioral Theories

A review of the two prominent personal-behavioral theories and research indicates a number of common themes. The two theories each attempt to isolate broad dimensions of leadership behavior. The logic of this appears to be that multidimensions confound the interpretation of leadership behavior and complicate the research designs developed to test the particular theory.

The measurement of leadership style for the two theories is accomplished typically through paper-and-pencil questionnaire responses. This method of measurement is, of course, limited and controversial. The common bases of these theories are presented in Table 11–2.

The personal-behavioral approaches have provided practitioners

[16] Abraham K. Korman, "Consideration, Initiating Structure, and Organizational Criteria—A Review," *Personnel Psychology,* Winter 1966, pp. 349–61.

[17] Steven Kerr and Chester Schriescheim, "Consideration, Initiating Structure, and Organizational Criteria—An Update of Korman's 1966 Review," *Personnel Psychology,* Winter 1974, pp. 555–68.

[18] R. C. Cummins, "Leader-Member Relations as a Moderator of the Effects of Leader Behavior and Attitude," *Personnel Psychology,* Winter 1972, pp. 655–60; and James G. Hunt and V. K. C. Liebscher, "Leadership Preference, Leadership Behavior, and Employee Satisfaction," *Organizational Behavior and Human Performance,* February 1973, pp. 59–77.

TABLE 11-2

A Review of Two Personal-Behavioral Leadership Approaches

Leadership Factors	Prime Initiator(s) of the Theory	How Behavior Is Measured	Subjects Researched	Principal Conclusions
Employee-centered and job-centered	Likert	Through interview and questionnaire responses of groups of followers	Formal leaders and followers in public utilities, banks, hospitals, manufacturing, food, government agencies	Employee-centered and job-centered styles result in production improvements. However, after a brief period of time the job-centered style creates pressure that is resisted through absenteeism, turnover, grievance, and poor attitudes. The best style is *employee-centered.*
Initiating structure and consideration	Fleishman, Stogdill, and Shartle	Through questionnaire responses of groups of followers, peers, the immediate superior, and the leader	Formal leaders and followers in military, education, public utilities, manufacturing, and government agencies	The combination of initiating structure and consideration behavior which achieves individual, group, and organizational effectiveness depends largely on the situation.

with information on what behaviors leaders should possess. This knowledge has resulted in the establishment of training programs for individuals who perform leadership tasks. Each of the approaches is also associated with highly respected theorists, researchers, or consultants, and each has been studied in different organizational settings. Yet the linkage between leadership and such important performance indicators as production, efficiency, and satisfaction has not been conclusively resolved by either of the two personal-behavioral theories.

SITUATIONAL THEORIES

The search for the "best" set of traits or behavior has failed to discover an effective leadership mix and style for all situations. What has evolved are situation-leadership theories that suggest that leadership effectiveness depends on the fit between personality, task, power, attitudes, and perceptions.[19] There are three publicized and researched situation-oriented leadership approaches: the Fiedler contingency model, the Vroom-Yetton normative model, and the path-goal theory.

---

[19] Fleishman, "Twenty Years of Consideration and Structure."

The Situational Variable

The importance of the situation was studied more closely by those interested in leadership only when inconclusive and contradictory results evolved from much of the early trait and personal-behavioral research. Eventually, it became known that the type of leadership behavior needed to enhance performance depends largely on the situation. What is effective leadership in one situation may be disorganized incompetence in another situation. The situational theme of leadership is appealing, but it is certainly a challenging orientation to implement. Its basic foundation suggests that an effective leader must be flexible enough to adapt to the differences among subordinates and situations.

Deciding how to lead other individuals is difficult and requires an analysis of the leader, the group, and the situation. Managers aware of the forces they face are able to more readily modify their styles to cope with changes in the work environment. Three factors of particular importance are the forces on the managers, the forces in the subordinates, and the forces in the situation.[20] Tannenbaum and Schmidt state the situational theme in this way:

> Thus, the successful manager of men can be primarily characterized neither as a strong leader nor as a permissive one. Rather, he is one who maintains a high batting average in accurately assessing the forces that determine what his most appropriate behavior at any given time should be and in actually being able to behave accordingly.[21]

As the importance of situational factors and leader assessment of forces became more recognized, leadership research became more systematic and contingency models of leadership began to appear in the organizational behavior and management literature. Each model has its advocates, and each attempts to identify the leader behaviors most appropriate for a series of leadership situations. Also, each model attempts to identify the leader-situation patterns that are important for effective leadership.

THE CONTINGENCY LEADERSHIP MODEL

The contingency model of leadership effectiveness was developed by Fiedler.[22] The model postulates that the performance of groups is

---

[20] The following discussion is based on Robert Tannenbaum and Warren H. Schmidt, "How to Choose a Leadership Pattern," *Harvard Business Review*, May–June 1973, pp. 162–80.

[21] Ibid., p. 180.

[22] Fred E. Fiedler, *A Theory of Leadership Effectiveness* (New York: McGraw-Hill, 1967).

dependent on the interaction between leadership style and situational favorableness. Leadership is viewed as a relationship based on power and influence. Two important questions are considered: (1) To what degree does the situation provide the leader with the power and influence needed to be effective, or how favorable are the situational factors? and (2) To what extent can the leader predict the effects of his or her style on the behavior and performance of followers?

Some of Fiedler's views are captured in the following Close-Up. Do you agree with what Fiedler has to say?

ORGANIZATIONS: CLOSE-UP

Some Thoughts of Fiedler on Leadership

Fred Fiedler is recognized by managers as an expert on leadership. He has published more than 150 articles and papers and five books on the topic of leadership and organizational behavior. Listed below are a few of Fiedler's own thoughts.

What makes an effective leader? You really can't talk about leadership like that. Leadership isn't something that you have inside you like a gall bladder or a liver. It is a relationship between a person and other individuals. General George Patton was a very effective combat tank commander, but I doubt he'd be as good as a chairman of the PTA.

So a committee chairman may not make an effective chief elected officer of an association? You really can't generalize like that. Leadership is a very complicated issue that people have been thinking about ever since the time of Plato. In any leadership relationship, what we are concerned with is how much control and influence the leader has in a group or an organization. Some people do well with control, and others don't.

Can you give us an example of job engineering? Actually, people do this all the time. If you volunteer for things you like, you prevent other people from volunteering you for jobs you don't like. And if you like the job, chances are you are successful at it. You have engineered your job situation. Our motto for job engineering is: If you learn to avoid situations in which you are likely to fail, you will be a success.

Source: "How to Be a Successful Leader," *Toastmaster,* October 1980, pp. 11–14.

The Leader's Style

**Least-Preferred
Co-Worker Scale**
This is a
measurement
attempt by Fiedler to
determine how
positive or negative a
person is toward the
least-preferred co-
worker.

Fiedler was concerned about measuring the leadership orientation of an individual. He developed the **Least-Preferred Co-Worker Scale** (LPC) to measure two leadership styles: (1) task-oriented, or controlling, structuring leadership; and (2) relationship-oriented, or passive, considerate leadership. Take a few minutes before going on, and complete the LPC scale that appears in Figure 11–3.

FIGURE 11–3

Least-Preferred Co-Worker (LPC) Scale

Throughout your life, you will have worked in many groups with a wide variety of different people—on your job, in social groups, in church organizations, in volunteer groups, on athletic teams, and in many other situations. Some of your co-workers may have been very easy to work with in attaining the group's goals, while others were less so.

Think of all the people with whom you have ever worked, and then think of the person with whom you could work *least well.* He or she may be someone with whom you work now or with whom you have worked in the past. This does not have to be the person you liked least well, but should be the person with whom you had the most difficulty getting a job done, the *one* individual with whom you could work *least well.*

Describe this person on the scale that follows by placing an *X* in the appropriate space.

Look at the words at both ends of the line before you mark your *X. There are no right or wrong answers.* Work rapidly; your first answer is likely to be the best. Do not omit any items, and mark each item only once.

Now describe the person with whom you can work least well.

											Scoring
Pleasant	__	__	__	__	__	__	__	__	Unpleasant		___
	8	7	6	5	4	3	2	1			
Friendly	__	__	__	__	__	__	__	__	Unfriendly		___
	8	7	6	5	4	3	2	1			
Rejecting	__	__	__	__	__	__	__	__	Accepting		___
	1	2	3	4	5	6	7	8			
Tense	__	__	__	__	__	__	__	__	Relaxed		___
	1	2	3	4	5	6	7	8			
Distant	__	__	__	__	__	__	__	__	Close		___
	1	2	3	4	5	6	7	8			
Cold	__	__	__	__	__	__	__	__	Warm		___
	1	2	3	4	5	6	7	8			
Supportive	__	__	__	__	__	__	__	__	Hostile		___
	8	7	6	5	4	3	2	1			
Boring	__	__	__	__	__	__	__	__	Interesting		

FIGURE 11-3 *(concluded)*

	1	2	3	4	5	6	7	8		
Quarrelsome									Harmonious	___
	1	2	3	4	5	6	7	8		
Gloomy									Cheerful	___
	1	2	3	4	5	6	7	8		
Open									Guarded	___
	8	7	6	5	4	3	2	1		
Backbiting									Loyal	___
	1	2	3	4	5	6	7	8		
Untrustworthy									Trustworthy	___
	1	2	3	4	5	6	7	8		
Considerate									Inconsiderate	___
	8	7	6	5	4	3	2	1		
Nasty									Nice	___
	1	2	3	4	5	6	7	8		
Agreeable									Disagreeable	___
	8	7	6	5	4	3	2	1		
Insincere									Sincere	___
	1	2	3	4	5	6	7	8		
Kind									Unkind	___
	8	7	6	5	4	3	2	1		
									Total	___

Source: Adapted from Fred. E. Fiedler, Martin M. Chemers, and Linda Mahar, *Improving Leadership Effectiveness* (New York: John Wiley & Sons, 1976), p. 7.

To determine your score, sum the ratings you checked to obtain a score between 18 and 144. Fiedler states that someone with a score of 64 or higher is a high-LPC person. The high-LPC person is the type who can work with difficult people. The high-LPC person has a sensitivity toward others and is classified as a "relationship-motivated" leader.

If your score is 57 or lower, you are considered a low-LPC leader. You tend to classify the least-preferred co-worker in negative terms. The low-LPC person is a task-motivated leader. A score of 58 to 63 indicates a mix of motivations in your leadership style.

Fiedler proposes three situational factors that determine whether a high-LPC or low-LPC leader is more likely to be effective: leader-member relations, task structure, and position power. From a theoretical as well as an intuitive point of view, interpersonal relationships between leader and followers are likely to be the most important variable that determines power and influence. The leader's influence depends in part on acceptance by the followers. If others are willing to follow because of charisma, expertise, or mutual respect, the leader has little need to rely on task structure or position power. If, however, the leader is not trusted and is viewed negatively by the followers, the situation is considered less favorable in Fiedler's theory.

The **leader-member relations** factor refers to the degree of confidence, trust, and respect that the followers have in the leader. This situational variable reflects the acceptance of the leader.

The second most important measure of situational favorableness is referred to as **task structure.** This dimension includes the following components:

Goal clarity—the degree to which the tasks and duties of the job are clearly stated and known to the people performing the job.

Goal-path multiplicity—the degree to which the problems encountered in the job can be solved by a variety of procedures. An assembly-line worker solves problems within a systematic framework, while a scientist has a number of different ways to solve a problem.

Decision verifiability—the degree to which the "correctness" of the solutions or decisions typically encountered in a job can be demonstrated by appeal to authority, by logical procedures, or by feedback. A quality control inspector can show defective parts and clearly indicate why a part is sent back for reworking.

Decision-specificity—the degree to which there is generally more than one correct solution. An accountant preparing a balance sheet has few choices, while a research scientist may have numerous potentially correct alternatives to choose from.

The most obvious way in which the leader secures power is by accepting and performing the leadership role. The leader is recognized as having the right to direct, evaluate, reward, and punish followers, though this right must be exercised within defined boundaries. **Position power** in the contingency model refers to the power inherent in the leadership position. To determine leader position power, questions such as the following are asked:

Can the supervisor recommend subordinate rewards and punishments to his boss?

Can the supervisor punish or reward subordinates on his or her own?

Can the supervisor recommend promotion or demotion of subordinates?[23]

Fiedler contends that such questions provide a profile of high or low position power.

---

[23] Fred E. Fiedler and Martin M. Chemers, *Leadership and Effective Management* (Glenview, Ill.: Scott, Foresman, 1974).

Favorableness of the Situation

The three situational factors that seem to be the most important in determining the leader's power and influence are: (1) whether leader-member relations are good or poor, (2) whether the task is relatively structured or unstructured, and (3) whether the position power is relatively strong or weak. A few examples will show how Fiedler would determine the *favorableness* of the situation for a particular leader.

> *An office manager.* This individual has eight subordinates who like her. She structures the job by making work assignments and by setting goals for required outputs. She is also responsible for reviewing the work of subordinates and is the main spokesperson for and evaluator of the employees at merit review time.
>
> *A project engineer.* This individual was appointed as the leader of a five-person project study group. Each of the assigned members really does not want to serve in the group. The assigned members have other, more pressing jobs. As the appointed leader, the project engineer was actually given no power. His calls for meetings are generally unanswered, and when he gets the assigned members together, they are rather hostile, negative, and discourteous.
>
> *A registered nurse (supervisory).* This individual is well liked by her subordinates, but the physicians have taken almost total control of the work. They will not give permission to perform what the registered nurse feels are nursing activities. This nurse is in a constant battle with the physicians to let her do the job and stop interfering.

The classification of these three individuals according to Fiedler would be as shown in Figure 11–4. The office manager is in situation I, in which she is liked, has a structured task, and position power. The project engineer is in situation VIII, with poor leader-member relations, low task structure, and weak position power. The registered nurse is in situation IV. She is well liked, but she has no task-structure opportunities and no position power because of the physicians. The situation is more favorable for the situation I leader than for the situation VIII leader.

Fiedler contends that a permissive, more lenient (relationship-oriented) style is best when the situation is moderately favorable or moderately unfavorable. Thus, if a leader were moderately liked and possessed some power, and the job tasks for subordinates were somewhat vague, the leadership style needed to achieve the best results would be relationship-oriented.

In contrast, when the situation is highly favorable or highly unfavora-

FIGURE 11–4

Summary of Fiedler's Situational Variables and Their Preferred Leadership Styles

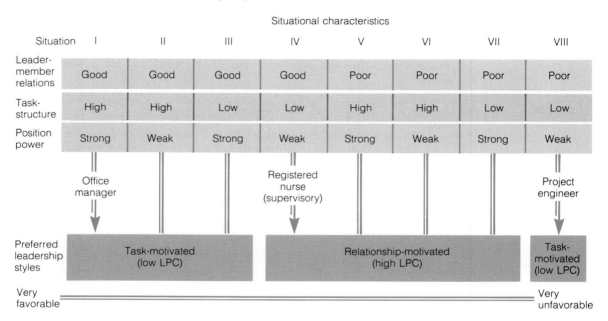

ble, a task-oriented approach generally produces the desired performance. The well-liked office manager, who has power and has clearly identified the performance goals, is operating in a highly favorable situation. The project engineer, who is faced with a group of suspicious and hostile subordinates and has little power and vague task responsibilities, needs to be task-oriented in this highly unfavorable situation.

Fiedler recommends that leaders do something about their situations. Table 11–3 presents some of Fiedler's suggestions for changing particular situational factors. What he is suggesting is that the leader can make changes that result in a more favorable situation.

RESEARCH ON FIEDLER'S MODEL

Over the past two decades, Fiedler and advocates of the contingency model have studied military, educational, and industrial leaders. In a summary of 63 studies based on 454 separate groups, Fiedler suggests

TABLE 11–3

Leadership Actions to Change Situations

Modifying Leader-Member Relations

1. Spend more—or less—informal time with your subordinates (lunch, leisure activities, etc.).
2. Request particular people for work in your group.
3. Volunteer to direct difficult or troublesome subordinates.
4. Suggest or effect transfers of particular subordinates into or out of your unit.
5. Raise morale by obtaining positive outcomes for subordinates (e.g., special bonuses, time-off, attractive jobs).

Modifying Task Structure

If you wish to work with less structured tasks, you can:

1. Ask your boss, whenever possible, to give you the new or unusual problems and let you figure out how to get them done.
2. Bring the problems and tasks to your group members, and invite them to work with you on the planning and decision-making phases of the tasks.

If you wish to work with more highly structured tasks, you can:

1. Ask your superior to give you, whenever possible, the tasks that are more structured or to give you more detailed instructions.
2. Break the job down into smaller subtasks that can be more highly structured.

Modifying Position Power

To raise your position power, you can:

1. Show your subordinates "who's boss" by exercising fully the powers that the organization provides.
2. Make sure that information to your group gets channeled through you.

To lower your position power, you can:

1. Call on members of your group to participate in planning and decision-making functions.
2. Let your assistants exercise relatively more power.

the kind of leadership that is the most appropriate for the situational conditions.[24] Figure 11–5 summarizes his analysis.

The situational characteristics are shown at the bottom of Figure 11–5. The vertical axis indicates the correlation between a leader's LPC score and the group's performance. A median correlation above the midline shows that the relationship-oriented leaders tend to per-

---

[24] Fred E. Fiedler, "How Do You Make Leaders More Effective? New Answers to an Old Puzzle," *Organizational Dynamics*, Autumn 1972, pp. 3–8.

FIGURE 11-5

A Summary of Contingency Model Research

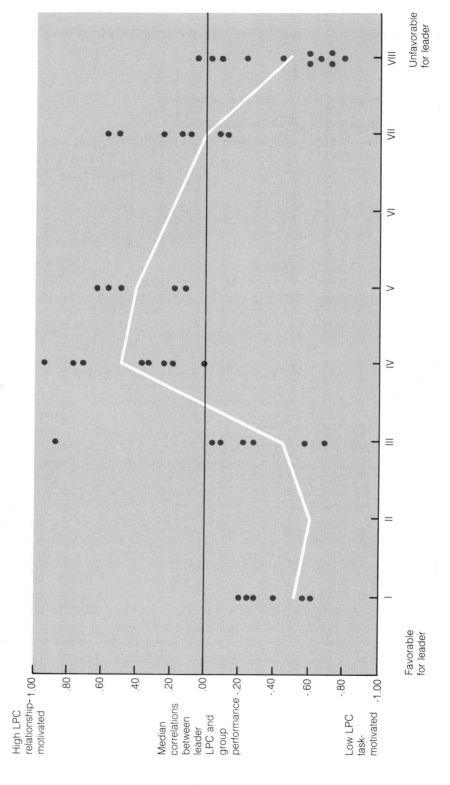

Source: Fred E. Fiedler, *A Theory of Leadership Effectiveness* (New York: McGraw-Hill, 1967), p. 146.

form better than the task-oriented leaders. A median correlation below the midline indicates that the task-oriented leaders perform better than the relationship-oriented leaders.

The data presented in Figure 11–5 imply a number of things about effective leaders. First, task-oriented leaders tend to perform better than relationship-oriented leaders in situations that are very favorable (I, II, III) and in situations that are unfavorable (VIII). Relationship-oriented leaders tend to perform better than task-oriented leaders in situations that are intermediate in favorableness (IV, V, and VII).[25] These findings support the notion that both types of leaders are effective in certain situations.

Can Leaders Be Trained?

Fiedler states:

> Fitting the man to the leadership job by selection and training has not been spectacularly successful. It is surely easier to change almost anything in the job situation than [to change] a man's personality and his leadership style.[26]

It is assumed that changing a leader's style through training is an extremely difficult task.

Fiedler contends that training programs and experience can improve a leader's power and influence if the situational favorableness is high. This means that a training program that improves a leader's power and influence may benefit the relationship-oriented person but could be detrimental to the task-oriented person.

Since training program–stimulated changes are so elusive, the better alternative is to change the favorableness of the situation. A first step recommended by Fiedler is to determine whether leaders are task- or relationship-oriented. Next, the organization needs to diagnose and classify the situational favorableness of its leadership positions. Finally, the organization must select the best strategy to bring about improved effectiveness. If leadership training is selected as an option, then it should devote special attention to teaching participants how to modify their environments and their jobs to fit their styles of leader-

---

[25] John K. Kennedy, Jr., "Middle LPC Leaders and the Contingency Model of Leadership Effectiveness," *Organizational Behavior and Human Performance,* August 1982, pp. 1–14.

[26] Fred E. Fiedler, "Engineering the Job to Fit the Manager," *Harvard Business Review,* September–October 1965, p. 115. Also see Fred E. Fiedler, "The Effects of Leadership Training and Experience: A Contingency Model Interpretation," *Administrative Science Quarterly,* December 1972, pp. 453–70; and Walter Hill, "Leadership Style: Rigid or Flexible?" *Organizational Behavior and Human Performance,* February 1973, pp. 35–47.

ship. That is, leaders should be trained to change their leadership situations. Fiedler's recent work indicates that when leaders can recognize the situations in which they are most successful, they can then begin to modify their own situations.[27]

A Critique of the Contingency Model

Fiedler's model and research have elicited a number of pointed criticisms and concerns. First, Graen and others present evidence that research support for the model is not strong, especially if studies conducted by researchers not associated with Fiedler are examined.[28] The earlier support and enthusiasm for the model came from Fiedler and his students, who conducted numerous studies of leaders. Second, a number of researchers have called attention to the questionable measurement of the LPC. These researchers claim that the reliability and validity of the LPC questionnaire measure are low.[29] Third, the meaning of the variables presented by Fiedler is not clear. For example, what is the point at which a "structured" task becomes an "unstructured" task? Who can define or display this point? Finally, critics claim that Fiedler's theory can accommodate nonsupportive results. This point is specifically made by one critic who states:

> Fiedler has revealed his genius twice; first, in devising the model, which stands like calculus to arithmetic compared with previous leadership models, and second, in his ability to integrate new findings into his models.[30]

Despite these incisive criticisms, Fiedler's contingency model has made significant contributions to the study and application of leadership principles. Fiedler called direct attention to the situational nature of leadership. His view of leadership stimulated numerous research studies and much-needed debate about the dynamics of leader behavior. Certainly, Fiedler has played one of the most prominent roles in encouraging the scientific study of leadership in work settings. He pointed the way and made others uncomfortably aware of the complexities of the leadership process.

---

[27] Fred E. Fiedler, "The Leadership Game: Matching the Man to the Situation," *Organizational Dynamics*, Winter 1976, pp. 6–16.

[28] G. Graen, J. B. Orris, and K. M. Alvares, "Contingency Model of Leadership Effectiveness: Some Experimental Results," *Journal of Applied Psychology*, June 1971, pp. 196–201.

[29] C. A. Schriesheim, B. D. Bannister, and W. H. Money, "Psychometric Properties of the LPC Scale: An Extension of Rice's Review," *Academy of Management Review*, April 1979, pp. 287–90.

[30] Joe Kelly, *Organizational Behavior: Its Data, First Principles, and Applications* (Homewood, Ill.: Richard D. Irwin, 1980), p. 367.

THE VROOM-YETTON MODEL OF LEADERSHIP

normative model
Vroom-Yetton
present a model that
describes how a
leader should lead in
various situations.
This model shows
that no single
leadership style is
applicable to all
situations.

Vroom and Yetton have developed a leadership decision-making model that indicates the kinds of situations in which various degrees of participative decision making would be appropriate.[31] In contrast to Fiedler, Vroom and Yetton attempt to provide a **normative model** that a leader can use in making decisions. Their approach assumes that single leadership style is appropriate for every situation. Unlike Fiedler, Vroom and Yetton assume that leaders must be flexible enough to change their leadership styles to fit situations. It was Fiedler's contention that the situation must be altered to fit the fairly rigid leadership style.

In developing their model, Vroom and Yetton made a number of assumptions. These were:

a. The model should be of value to leaders or managers in determining which leadership styles they should use in various situations.
b. No single leadership style is applicable to all situations.
c. The main focus should be the problem to be solved and the situation in which the problem occurs.
d. The leadership style used in one situation should not constrain the styles used in other situations.
e. There are a number of social processes that will influence the amount of participation by subordinates in problem solving.

Applying these assumptions resulted in a model that was concerned with leadership decision making.

Decision Effectiveness: Quality and Acceptance

The Vroom-Yetton model emphasizes two criteria of decision effectiveness: quality and acceptance. *Decision quality* refers to the objective aspects of a decision that influence subordinates' performance aside from any direct impact on motivation. Some kinds of job-related decisions are linked to performance, while other kinds of job-related decisions have relatively little effect on performance. For example, determining workflow patterns and layout, performance goals and deadlines, or work assignments usually has an important influence on group performance. On the other hand, selecting work area locations for water coolers or deciding what type of cafeteria furniture to buy has no effect on group performance. When decision quality is

---

[31] Victor H. Vroom and Philip Yetton, *Leadership and Decision Making* (Pittsburgh: University of Pittsburgh Press, 1973), © 1973 by the University of Pittsburgh Press.

important for performance and subordinates possess ability and information that the leader does not possess, the Vroom-Yetton model would indicate that the leader use a decision procedure that allows subordinate participation.

Decision acceptance is the degree of subordinate commitment to the decision. There are many situations in which a course of action, even if technically correct, can fail because it is resisted by those who have to execute it. In judging whether a problem requires subordinate commitment, the leader needs to look for two things: (1) Are subordinates going to have to execute the decision under conditions in which initiative and judgment will be required? and (2) Are subordinates likely to "feel strongly" about the decision? If the answer to either or both of these questions is yes, then the problem possesses an acceptance requirement. When subordinates can accept a decision as theirs, they will be more inclined to implement it effectively.

Five Decision-Making Styles of Leaders

The Vroom-Yetton model makes a distinction between two types of decision problem situations facing leaders: individual and group. Individual problem situations are those whose solutions affect only one of the leader's followers. Problem situations that affect several followers are classified as group problems. The five leadership decision styles that fit the individual and group situations are defined in Table 11–4.

A, designates autocratic decision systems; C, consultative decision systems; G, group decision systems; and D, delegative decision systems. The Roman numerals indicate variants of the same process. We will focus on group problem situations in presenting the Vroom-Yetton approach. This is done only because of space limitations.

The Diagnostic Procedure for Leaders

Vroom and Yetton suggest that leaders perform a diagnosis of the situation and problem by applying a number of decision rules. These rules will help determine which decision-making style of leadership is appropriate for the particular situation. By using a careful diagnosis, the leader would minimize the chances of reducing decision quality and acceptance. The diagnosis decision rules are presented in Table 11–5.

The seven decision rules in Table 11–5 are used in determining what procedures should not be used by a leader in a given situation. The first three rules are designed to protect decision quality. The re-

TABLE 11-4

Decision Styles for Leadership: Individuals and Groups

Individual Level	Group Level
AI. You solve the problem or make the decision yourself, using information available to you at that time.	**AI.** You solve the problem or make the decision yourself, using information available to you at that time.
AII. You obtain any necessary information from the subordinate, then decide on the solution to the problem yourself. You may or may not tell the subordinate what the problem is in getting the information from him. The role played by your subordinate in making the decision is clearly one of providing specific information that you request, rather than generating or evaluating alternative solutions.	**AII.** You obtain any necessary information from subordinates, then decide on the solution to the problem yourself. You may or may not tell the subordinates what the problem is in getting the information from them. The role played by your subordinates in making the decision is clearly one of providing specific information that you request, rather than generating or evaluating solutions.
CI. You share the problem with the relevant subordinate, getting ideas and suggestions. Then *you* make the decision. This decision may or may not reflect your subordinate's influence.	**CI.** You share the problem with the relevant subordinates individually, getting their ideas and suggestions without bringing them together as a group. Then *you* make the decision. This decision may or may not reflect your subordinates' influence.
GI. You share the problem with one of your subordinates, and together you analyze the problem and arrive at a mutually satisfactory solution in an atmosphere of free and open exchange of information and ideas. You both contribute to the resolution of the problem, with the relative contribution of each being dependent on knowledge rather than formal authority.	**CII.** You share the problem with your subordinates in a group meeting. In this meeting, you obtain their ideas and suggestions. Then *you* make the decision, which may or may not reflect your subordinates' influence.
DI. You delegate the problem to one of your subordinates, providing him or her with any relevant information that you possess, but giving him or her responsibility for solving the problem alone. Any solution that the person reaches will receive your support.	**GII.** You share the problem with your subordinates as a group. Together, you generate and evaluate alternatives and attempt to reach agreement (consensus) on a solution. Your role is much like that of chairman, coordinating the discussion, keeping it focused on the problem, and making sure that the critical issues are discussed. You do not try to influence the group to adopt "your" solution, and you are willing to accept and implement any solution that has the support of the entire group.

maining four rules are designed to protect decision acceptance. The application of the seven decision rules is illustrated by use of a decision-tree chart. One such chart is shown in Figure 11–6. The chart is read from left to right. Begin by considering the situation and asking question A. If the answer to A is no, question D is then asked, but if the

TABLE 11–5

Rules Underlying the Vroom-Yetton Model

RULES TO PROTECT THE QUALITY OF THE DECISION

1. **The leader information rule.** If the quality of the decision is important and the leader does not possess enough information or expertise to solve the problem by himself, then AI is eliminated from the feasible set.

2. **The goal congruence rule.** If the quality of the decision is important and subordinates are not likely to pursue the organization goals in their efforts to solve the problem, then GII is eliminated from the feasible set.

3. **The unstructured problem rule.** In decisions in which the quality of the decision is important, if the leader lacks the necessary information or expertise to solve the problem by himself and if the problem is unstructured, the method of solving the problem should provide for interaction among subordinates likely to possess relevant information. Accordingly, AI, AII, and CI are eliminated from the feasible set.

RULES TO PROTECT THE ACCEPTANCE OF THE DECISION

4. **The acceptance rule.** If the acceptance of the decision by subordinates is critical to effective implementation and if it is not certain that an autocratic decision will be accepted, AI and AII are eliminated from the feasible set.

5. **The conflict rule.** If the acceptance of the decision is critical, an autocratic decision is not certain to be accepted, and disagreement among subordinates in methods of attaining the organizational goal is likely, the methods used in solving the problem should enable those in disagreement to resolve their differences with full knowledge of the problem. Accordingly, under these conditions, AI, AII, and CI, which permit no interaction among subordinates and therefore provide no opportunity for those in conflict to resolve their differences, are eliminated from the feasible set. Their use runs the risk of leaving some of the subordinates with less than the needed commitment to the final decision.

6. **The fairness rule.** If the quality of the decision is unimportant but acceptance of the decision is critical and not certain to result from an autocratic decision, it is important that the decision process used generate the needed acceptance. The decision process used should permit the subordinates to interact with one another and negotiate over the fair method of resolving any differences, with full responsibility on them for determining what is fair and equitable. Accordingly, under these circumstances, AI, AII, CI, and CII are eliminated from the feasible set.

7. **The acceptance priority rule.** If acceptance is critical and not certain to result from an autocratic decision, and if subordinates are motivated to pursue the organizational goals represented in the problem, then methods that provide equal partnership in the decision-making process can provide greater acceptance without risking decision quality. Accordingly, AI, AII, CI, and CII are eliminated from the feasible set.

Source: "On the Validity of the Vroom-Yetton Model" by V. H. Vroom and A. G. Jago, *Journal of Applied Psychology,* April 1978, 151–62. Copyright © 1978 by the American Psychological Association. Reprinted by permission of the publisher and authors.

FIGURE 11-6

Decision Process Flowchart (Feasible Set)

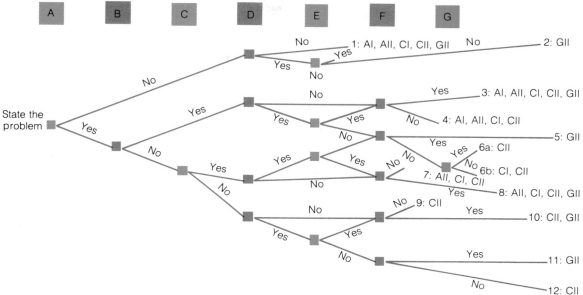

A. Does the problem possess a quality requirement?
B. Do I have sufficient information to make a high-quality decision?
C. Is the problem structured?
D. Is acceptance of the decision by subordinates important for effective implementation?
E. If I were to make the decision by myself, am I reasonably certain that it would be accepted by my subordinates?
F. Do subordinates share the organizational goals to be attained in solving the problem?
G. Is conflict among subordinates likely in preferred solutions?

answer to A is yes, ask question B. The leader would proceed from left to right until a terminal or end point is reached. For example, the feasible solutions at point 1 are AI, AII, CI, CII, and GII. On the other hand, the feasible solution suggested at point 11 is GII. Each of the styles suggested is likely to lead to a high-quality decision acceptable to subordinates. Since this is the case, most leaders and managers believe that it is wisest to choose the most autocratic of the styles. The leader can save time by doing so without risking decision quality or acceptance. The specific style of leadership attempted would be based on the time needed to make a decision, the leader's preference, and the ability, knowledge, and experience of subordinates. Vroom and Yetton have developed a time-efficient Model A version of the decision tree,[32] which would lead to the selection of the least time-

[32] Victor H. Vroom, "Can Leaders Learn to Lead?" *Organizational Dynamics,* Winter 1976, pp. 17–28.

consuming leadership style. The decision tree used in Figure 11–6 is the Model B or group development version. It maximizes the development of subordinates through increased participation in decision making when possible.

Application of the Vroom-Yetton Model

Vroom and Yetton have developed actual decision-making scenarios that portray how the model shown in Figure 11–6 can be applied. A person reading the scenarios is asked to assume the role of a leader or manager and to describe the behavior or style (e.g., AI, AII, CI, CII, or GII) that he or she would apply to the situation described. An example of a scenario is presented in the following Close-Up. Working through the flowchart shown in Figure 11–6 would result in a suggested leadership decision style of GII, a group participative process.

ORGANIZATIONS: CLOSE-UP

A Decision Scenario

You are supervising the work of 12 engineers. Their formal training and work experience are very similar, permitting you to use them interchangeably on projects. Yesterday, your manager informed you that a request had been received from an overseas affiliate for four engineers to go abroad on extended loan for a period of six to eight months. For a number of reasons, he argued, and you agreed, that this request should be met from your group. All of your engineers are capable of handling this assignment, and from the standpoint of present and future projects, there is no particular reason why any one should be retained over any other. The problem is somewhat complicated by the fact that the overseas assignment is in what is generally regarded in the company as an undesirable location.

Analysis (based on Figure 11–6)

Question A (Quality requirement?): NO
Question D (Subordinate acceptance critical?): YES
Question E (Is acceptance likely without participation?): NO
Feasible set of decision procedures: GII
Minimum time solution: GII

Source: Adapted from *Leadership and Decision-Making*, pp. 41–42, by Victor H. Vroom and Philip W. Yetton, by permission of the University of Pittsburgh Press. © 1973 by the University of Pittsburgh Press.

Research on the Vroom-Yetton Model

The Vroom-Yetton model is still relatively new, and many research questions raised by it need to be tested. However, the research to date can be divided into two types: (1) *verification*—which is aimed at verifying the model's prescriptions; and (2) *descriptive*—which attempts to identify the determinants of actual leader or managerial behavior and the degree to which such behavior conforms to the model's prescriptions.

Verification Research. One study examined 181 actual decision-making situations and behavior in these situations.[33] The model was then used to predict what decisions would be effective (i.e., those in which the manager's behavior was one of the acceptable styles) and which decisions would be ineffective (i.e., those in which the manager's behavior violated one of the seven decision rules pertaining to quality and acceptance). These predictions were then compared with the actual ratings of decision effectiveness. The results showed substantial support for the model. Of the decisions where the manager's behavior agreed with the feasible style of leadership, 68 percent were judged to have successful results. Of the decisions where the manager's behavior disagreed with the feasible style of leadership, only 22 percent had successful results.

A study involving 226 university business students tested the model without relying on self-report data collected from participants. In general, evidence was found that showed that decisions made with processes in the feasible set were significantly more effective than decisions made with processes outside the feasible set. Of the 105 decisions in which the leader's behavior agreed with the feasible set, 49 percent were effective, while only 36 percent of the decisions in which the leader's behavior disagreed with the feasible set were effective. A limitation of this study, however, is its nongeneralizability to managerial samples.[34]

Another test of the model was conducted in 45 retail franchises in the cleaning industry.[35] Store managers who exhibited conformity to the Vroom-Yetton leadership style prescriptions had more productive operations and more satisfied subordinates than did store managers exhibiting less conformity to the model.

Descriptive Research. Descriptive research has attempted to better understand how leaders or managers *do* behave rather than how managers *should* behave. The research suggests that most managers per-

[33] Victor H. Vroom and Arthur G. Jago, "On the Validity of the Vroom-Yetton Model," *Journal of Applied Psychology*, April 1978, pp. 151–62.

[34] R. H. George Field, "A Test of the Vroom-Yetton Normative Model of Leadership," *Journal of Applied Psychology*, October 1982, pp. 523–32.

[35] C. Margerison and R. Glube, "Leadership Decision Making: An Empirical Test of the Vroom and Yetton Model," manuscript, 1978.

mit a greater overall level of participative decision making than seems to be required.[36] Although the model suggests that the AI (autocratic) leadership style is appropriate for various situations, managers tend to avoid its use. On the other hand, managers seem to overuse the CI and CII styles.

Other research using the decision situation scenarios reveals that female managers are more participative than male managers[37] and that business school students are more participative than actual managers.[38] In addition, it has been found that managers higher in the managerial hierarchy are more participative than managers lower in the same hierarchy.[39]

A Critique of the Vroom-Yetton Model

The Vroom-Yetton model has been specifically criticized on a number of issues.[40] First, the reliance on self-report data is considered a major threat to the validity of the model. Leaders (managers) are asked to list the details of one successful and one unsuccessful decision-making situation that they personally faced. The experience reporting occurs after the manager has studied the five decision styles and rational problem solving and practiced choosing a decision process for each of 30 decision scenarios.

It has been proposed by one critic that managers report successful decisions as using a rational decision process that was appropriate to the situation, regardless of their actual behavior.[41] The self-reported behavior would tend to match the rational model, and the Vroom-Yetton model would thus be validated. Jago and Vroom report that subordinates' perceptions of managerial behavior do not correlate significantly with the superior's own descriptions of the same behavior.[42]

---

[36] Victor H. Vroom and Arthur G. Jago, "Decision Making as a Social Process: Normative and Descriptive Models of Leader Behavior," *Decision Sciences,* October 1974, pp. 743–69.

[37] Rick Steers, "Individual Differences in Participative Decision Making," *Human Relations,* September 1977, pp. 837–47.

[38] Arthur G. Jago and Victor H. Vroom, "Predicting Leader Behavior from a Measure of Behavioral Intent," *Academy of Management Journal,* December 1978, pp. 715–21.

[39] Arthur G. Jago, "Hierarchical Level Determinants of Participative Leader Behavior," Ph.D. dissertation, Yale University, 1977.

[40] R. H. George Field, "A Critique of the Vroom-Yetton Contingency Model of Leadership Behavior," *Academy of Management Review,* April 1979, pp. 249–57.

[41] Ibid.

[42] Arthur G. Jago and Victor H. Vroom. "Perceptions of Leadership Style: Superior and Subordinate Descriptions of Decision-Making Behavior," in *Leadership Frontiers,* ed. J. G. Hunt and L. L. Larson (Carbondale: Southern Illinois University Press, 1975), pp. 103–20.

This raises another question about the validity of manager (leader) behavior self-reports.

Second, the methods just described to determine a leader's view of successful and unsuccessful behavior are also subject to experimenter and social desirability effects. Since managers have previously studied rational problem solving, there may be an experimenter influence on the results. Furthermore, there may be a tendency to want to appear more participative than one actually is in decision-making situations. It is socially desirable to permit followers or subordinates to participate.

Despite the criticisms, the Vroom-Yetton approach to leadership is an important contribution. The model was developed after thorough experimentation with similar models. In addition, tests of the model are at least as rigorous and in most cases seem more carefully planned and executed than tests of other leadership approaches. Also, one important organizational implication of the model involves training. If current and future research support the validity of the model, more effective leadership will result if leaders are trained or instructed to use the model.[43] Training would enable leaders to choose the appropriate level of follower/subordinate participation.

PATH-GOAL MODEL

path-goal model
A leadership explanation that indicates that a leader's effectiveness depends on how well the leader can provide guidance, motivation, and support for accomplishing the goals of followers.

Like the other situational or contingency leadership approaches, the **path-goal model** attempts to predict leadership effectiveness in different situations. According to this model, leaders are effective because of their positive impact on followers' motivation, ability to perform, and satisfaction. The theory is designated path-goal because it focuses on how the leader influences the followers' perceptions of work goals, self-development goals, and paths to goal attainment.[44]

The foundation of path-goal theory is the expectancy motivation theory, discussed in Chapter 5. Some early work on the path-goal theory asserts that leaders will be effective by making rewards available to subordinates and by making those rewards contingent on the subordinates' accomplishment of specific goals.[45] It is argued that an

---

[43] Arthur G. Jago, "Leadership Perspectives in Theory and Research," draft paper in College of Business Working Paper Series, University of Houston, 1979, p. 31.

[44] Robert J. House, "A Path-Goal Theory of Leadership Effectiveness," *Administrative Science Quarterly,* September 1971, pp. 321–39. Also see Robert J. House and Terence R. Mitchell, "Path-Goal Theory of Leadership," *Journal of Contemporary Business,* Autumn 1974, pp. 81–98, which is the basis for the following discussion.

[45] Martin G. Evans, "The Effects of Supervisory Behavior on the Path-Goal Relationship," *Organizational Behavior and Human Performance,* May 1970, pp. 277–98. Also see Martin G. Evans. "Effects of Supervisory Behavior: Extensions of Path-Goal Theory of Motivation," *Journal of Applied Psychology,* April 1974, pp. 172–78.

important part of the leader's job is to clarify for subordinates the kind of behavior that is most likely to result in goal accomplishment. This activity is referred to as *path clarification*.

This early path-goal work led to the development of a complex theory involving four specific styles of leader behavior (directive, supportive, participative, and achievement) and three types of subordinate attitudes (job satisfaction, acceptance of the leader, and expectations about effort-performance-reward relationships.)[46] The *directive leader* tends to let subordinates know what is expected of them. The *supportive leader* treats subordinates as equals. The *participative leader* consults with subordinates and uses their suggestions and ideas before reaching a decision. The *achievement-oriented* leader sets challenging goals, expects subordinates to perform at the highest level, and continually seeks improvement in performance.

Research studies suggest that these four styles can be practiced by the same leader in various situations.[47] These findings are contrary to the Fiedler notion concerning the difficulty of altering style. The path-goal approach suggests more flexibility than the Fiedler contingency model. On the other hand, the path-goal approach is similar to that of Vroom and Yetton in that it also argues for flexibility in leader behavior.

The Main Path-Goal Propositions

The path-goal theory has led to the development of two important propositions:

1. Leader behavior is effective to the extent that the subordinates perceive such behavior as a source of immediate satisfaction or as instrumental to future satisfaction.
2. Leader behavior will be motivational to the extent that it makes satisfaction of subordinates' needs contingent on effective performance and it complements the environment of subordinates by providing the guidance, clarity of direction, and rewards necessary for effective performance.[48]

According to the path-goal theory, leaders should increase the number and kinds of rewards available to subordinates. In addition, the leader should provide guidance and counsel to clarify the manner in which these rewards can be obtained. This means that the leader

---

[46] Robert J. House and Gary Dessler, "The Path-Goal Theory of Leadership: Some Post Hoc and A Priori Tests," in *Contingency Approaches to Leadership*, ed. James G. Hunt (Carbondale: Southern Illinois University Press, 1974).

[47] House, "A Path-Goal Theory"; and House and Dessler, "Path-Goal Theory."

[48] These propositions are presented by House and Mitchell, "Path-Goal Theory of Leadership," p. 84.

should help subordinates clarify realistic expectancies and reduce the barriers to the accomplishment of valued goals. For example, counseling employees on their chances of receiving a promotion and helping them eliminate skill deficiencies so that a promotion becomes a more realistic possibility are appropriate leadership behaviors. The leader works at making the path to goals for subordinates as clear as possible. The style that is best suited to accomplish this is selected and applied. Thus, the path-goal approach requires flexibility from the leader to use whatever style is appropriate in a particular situation.

The Situational Factors

Two types of situational or contingency variables are considered in the path-goal theory. These variables are the *personal characteristics of subordinates* and the *environmental pressures and demands* with which subordinates must cope in order to accomplish work goals and derive satisfaction.

An important personal characteristic is subordinates' perception of their own ability. The higher the degree of perceived ability relative to the task demands, the less likely the subordinate is to accept a directive leader style. This directive style of leadership would be viewed as unnecessarily close. In addition, it has been discovered that a person's *locus of control* also affects responses. Individuals who have an internal locus of control (they believe that rewards are contingent upon their efforts) are generally more satisfied with a participative style, while individuals who have an external locus of control (they believe that rewards are beyond their personal control) are generally more satisfied with a directive style.[49]

The environmental variables include factors that are not within the control of the subordinate but are important to satisfaction or to the ability to perform effectively.[50] These include the tasks, the formal authority system of the organization, and the work group. Any of these environmental factors can motivate or constrain the subordinate. The environmental forces may also serve as a reward for acceptable levels of performance. For example, the subordinate could be motivated by the work group and receive satisfaction from co-workers' acceptance for doing a job according to group norms.

The path-goal theory proposes that leader behavior will be motivational to the extent that it helps subordinates cope with environmental uncertainties. A leader who is able to reduce the uncertainties of the job is considered to be a motivator because he or she increases the

---

[49] Ibid.

[50] Ibid., p. 87.

FIGURE 11-7

The Path-Goal Model

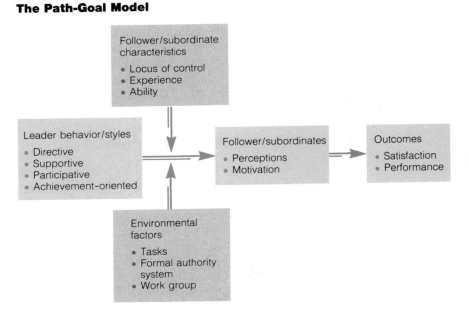

subordinates' expectations that their efforts will lead to desirable rewards.

Figure 11–7 presents the features of the path-goal approach. The path-goal approach has not been subjected to a complete test. Parts of the model, however, have been examined in field settings. One study found that when task structure (the repetitiveness or routineness of the job) was high, directive leader behavior was negatively related to satisfaction, whereas directive leader behavior was positively related to satisfaction when task structure was low. Also, when task structure was high, supportive leadership was positively related to satisfaction, whereas under low task structure there was no relationship between supportive leader behavior and satisfaction.[51]

A Critique of the Path-Goal Model

The path-goal model, like the Vroom-Yetton model, warrants further study. There is still some question about the predictive power of the path-goal model. One researcher suggested that subordinate performance might be the cause of changes in leader behavior instead of,

---

[51] House and Dessler, "Path-Goal Theory."

as predicted by the model, the other way around.[52] A review of the path-goal approach suggested that the model had resulted in the development of only a few hypotheses. These reviewers also point to the record of inconsistent research results associated with the model. They note that research has consistently shown that the higher the task structure of subordinate jobs, the higher will be the relationship between supportive leader behavior and subordinate satisfaction. However, the second main hypothesis of the path-goal model has not received consistent support. This hypothesis—the higher the task structure, the lower the relationship between directive leader behavior and subordinate satisfaction—has received only some support.[53]

On the positive side, one must admit that the path-goal model is an improvement over the trait and personal-behavioral theories. It attempts to indicate which factors affect the motivation to perform. In addition, the path-goal approach introduces both situational factors and individual differences when examining leader behavior and outcomes such as satisfaction and performance. The path-goal approach makes an effort to explain why a particular style of leadership works best in a given situation. As more research accumulates, this type of explanation will have practical utility for those interested in the leadership process in work settings.

COMPARISON OF THE SITUATIONAL APPROACHES

Three current models for examining leadership have been presented. These models have similarities and differences. they are similar in that they (1) focus on the dynamics of leadership, (2) have stimulated research on leadership, and (3) remain controversial because of measurement problems, limited research testing, or contradictory research results.

The themes of each model are summarized in Table 11–6. Fiedler's model has been the most tested and perhaps the most controversial. His view of leader behavior centers on task- and relationship-oriented tendencies and how these tendencies interact with task and position power. Vroom and Yetton view leader behavior in terms of autocratic, consultative, or group styles. Finally, the path-goal approach emphasizes the instrumental actions of leaders and four styles for conducting

---

[52] C. Greene, "Questions of Causation in the Path-Goal Theory of Leadership," *Academy of Management Journal,* March 1979, pp. 22–41.

[53] Chester A. Schriecheim and Angelo DeNisi, "Task Dimensions as Moderators of the Effects of Instrumental Leadership: A Two-Sample Replicated Test of Path-Goal Leadership Theory," *Journal of Applied Psychology,* October 1981, pp. 589–97.

TABLE 11-6

**A Comparison of Three Situational Approaches
to Leadership**

Approach	Leader Behavior/Style	Situational Factors	Outcome Criteria
Fiedler's contingency model	Task-oriented (low LPC) Relationship-oriented (high LPC)	Task-structure Leader-member relations Position power	Group's effectiveness
Vroom-Yetton	Autocratic Consultative Group	Quality of decision Information requirement Problem structure Followers' acceptance of decision Mutuality of follower and organizational goals Level of follower conflict	Quality of decision Acceptance of decision by followers Time to make decisions
Path-goal	Directive Supportive Participative Achievement-oriented	Follower characteristics Environmental factors	Satisfaction Performance

Source: Adapted from Edwin P. Hollander, *Leadership Dynamics* (New York: Free Press, 1978).

these actions—directive, supportive, participative, and achievement-oriented.

The situational variables discussed in each approach differ somewhat. There is also a different view of outcome criteria for assessing how successful the leader behavior has been. Fiedler discusses leader effectiveness; Vroom and Yetton discuss the quality of a decision, follower acceptance, and the timeliness of the decision; the path-goal approach focuses on satisfaction and performance.

SOME REMAINING ISSUES REGARDING LEADERSHIP

The trait, personal-behavioral, and situational theories have advanced the understanding of leadership and have stimulated important research studies. However, a number of gaps still remain in the current understanding of the process and outcomes of leadership in work organizations. Three particularly interesting leadership issues are: (1) What role does a leader's perception play in leadership effectiveness? (2) Does leadership cause or is it more significantly affected by follower satisfaction and performance? and (3) Are there substitutes for leadership that affect satisfaction and performance?

THE ATTRIBUTION THEORY OF LEADERSHIP

Attribution theory suggests that understanding and predicting how people will react to events around them are enhanced by knowing what their causal explanations for those events are. Kelley stresses that attribution theory is mainly concerned with the cognitive processes by which a person interprets behavior as being caused by (or attributed to) certain cues in the relevant environment.[54] The emphasis of attribution leadership theory is on "why" some behavior has occurred. Most causes of subordinate or follower behaviors are not directly observable; therefore, to determine causes requires reliance on perception. In attribution theory, individuals are assumed to be rational and to be concerned about the causal linkages in their environments.

The attributional approach starts with the position that the leader is essentially an *information processor*.[55] In other words, the leader is searching for informational cues that explain "why" something is happening. From these cues, the leader attempts to construct causal explanations that guide his or her leadership behavior. The process in simple terms appears to be follower behavior ⟶ leader attributions ⟶ leader behavior.

The Leader's Attributions

Kelley suggests that the primary attributional task of the leader is to categorize the causes of follower or subordinate behavior into three source dimensions: person, entity, or context. That is, for any given behavior, such as poor quality of output, the leader's job is to determine whether the poor quality was caused by the person (e.g., inadequate ability), the task (entity), or some unique set of circumstances surrounding the event (context).

The leader seeks three types of information when forming attributions about a follower's behavior-distinctiveness, consistency, and consensus. For any behavior, the leader first attempts to determine whether the behavior is *distinctive* to a task, that is, whether the behavior occurs on this task but not on other tasks. Next, the leader is concerned about *consistency,* that is how frequently the behavior

---

[54] H. H. Kelley, "Attribution Theory in Social Psychology," in *Nebraska Symposium on Motivation,* ed. D. Levine (Lincoln: University of Nebraska Press, 1967), p. 193.

[55] Stephen G. Green and Terence R. Mitchell, "Attributional processes of Leaders in Leader-Member Interactions," *Organizational Behavior and Human Performance,* June 1979, pp. 429–58.

occurs. Finally, the leader estimates the extent to which others behave in the same way; if the behavior is unique to one follower, it is said to have *low consensus;* if it is common to other followers, this reflects *high concensus.*

The Leader's Perception of Responsibility

The judgment of responsibility is considered to moderate the leader's response to an attribution. Clearly, the more a behavior is seen as caused by some characteristic of the follower (i.e., an internal cause) and the more the follower is judged to be responsible for the behavior, the more likely the leader is to take some action toward the follower. For example, it is possible to attribute an outcome (e.g., poor performance) to factors outside the control of a person, such as not having the tools to do the job well, or to internal causes, such as lack of effort.

An Attributional Leadership Model

Attribution theory appears to offer a framework for explaining leader behavior more insightfully than either the trait or personal-behavioral theories. Attribution theory attempts to explain *why* behaviors are happening.[56] The trait and personal-behavioral theories are more descriptive and do not focus on the why issue. Furthermore, attribution theory can offer some predictions about a leader's response to a follower's behavior. In Figure 11–8, an attributional leadership model is presented.

Two important linkages are emphasized in Figure 11–8. At the first linkage point, the leader attempts to make attributions about poor performance. These attributions are moderated by the three information sources—distinctiveness, consistency, and consensus. The second linkage point suggests that the leader's behavior or response is determined by the types of attributions that he or she makes. This relationship between attribution and leader behavior is moderated by the leader's perception of responsibility. Is the responsibility internal or external?

One empirical test of attribution leadership theory examined nursing supervisors who were also considered leaders. Distinctiveness, consistency, and consensus did influence the leader's attributions: leaders

---

[56] Terence R. Mitchell, Stephen C. Green, and Robert E. Wood, "An Attributional Model of Leadership and the Poor Performing Subordinate: Development and Validation," in *Research in Organizational Behavior,* ed. B. M. Staw and L. L. Cummings (Greenwich, Conn.: JAI Press, 1981).

FIGURE 11–8

An Attributional Leadership Model

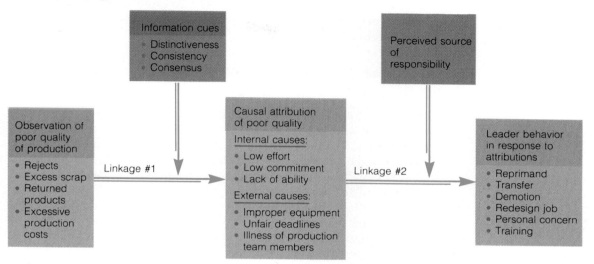

Source: Adapted from Terence R. Mitchell and Robert E. Wood, "An Empirical Test of an Attributional Model of Leader's Responses to Poor Performance," in *Academy of Management Proceedings*, 1979, ed. Richard C. Huseman, p. 94.

who made attributions of internal causes (e.g., lack of effort) tended to use more punitive behaviors, and leaders tended to make more internal attributions and to respond more harshly when the problems were serious.[57]

An interesting approach of researchers has been to include sex effects in the attributional model of leadership. It is emphasized that the sex of the leader and the sex of the subordinate have been largely neglected. A study of college students was conducted to examine whether the sex of the leader, the sex of the subordinate, and the interaction between these two factors would affect both the attributions made for employees' poor performance and the corrective action taken by leaders.[58] The researchers concluded that the sex composition of the leader-subordinate dyad was a critical and neglected variable in attributional research.

Currently, the research support for the attributional theory of lead-

[57] Terence R. Mitchell and Robert E. Wood, "An Empirical Test of an Attributional Model of Leader's Responses to Poor Performance," in *Academy of Management Proceedings*, 1979, ed. Richard C. Huseman pp. 94–98.

[58] Gregory H. Dobbins, Earl C. Pence, Joseph A. Orban, and Joseph A. Sgro, "The Effects of Sex of the Leader and Sex of the Subordinate on the Use of Organizational Control Policy," *Organizational Behavior and Human Performance*, December 1983, pp. 325–43.

ership is limited. There is a need to test the theory in more organizational settings.[59] Understanding the causes of leader behavior or at least searching for these causes seems more promising for managerial use than does simply adding another trait or descriptive theory to the leadership literature.

Is Leader Behavior a Cause or an Effect?

We have implied that leader behavior has an effect on the follower's performance and job satisfaction. There is, however, a sound basis from which one can argue that follower performance and satisfaction cause the leader to vary his or her leadership style. It has been argued that a person will develop positive attitudes toward objects that are instrumental to the satisfaction of his or her needs.[60] This argument can be extended to leader-follower relationships. For example, organizations reward leaders (managers) based on the performance of followers (subordinates). If this is the case, leaders might be expected to develop positive attitudes toward high-performing followers. Let us say that an employee, Joe, because of outstanding performance, enables his boss, Mary, to receive the supervisory excellence award, a bonus of $1,000. The expectation then is that Mary would think highly of Joe and reward him with a better work schedule or job assignment. In this case, Joe's behavior leads to Mary's being rewarded, and she in turn rewards Joe.

In a field study, data were collected from first-line managers and from two of each manager's first-line supervisors. The purpose of this research was to assess the direction of causal influence in relationships between leader and follower variables. The results strongly suggested that (1) leader consideration behavior caused subordinate satisfaction and (2) follower performance caused changes in the leader's emphasis on both consideration and the structuring of behavior-performance relationships.[61]

The research available on the cause-effect issue is still quite limited. It is premature to conclude that all leader behavior or even a significant portion of such behavior is a response to follower behavior. However, there is a need to examine the leader-follower relationship in

[59] John A. Pearce II and Angelo S. DeNisi, "Attribution Theory and Strategic Decision Making: An Application to Coalition Formation," *Academy of Management Journal*, March 1983, pp. 119–28.

[60] D. Katz and E. Stotland, "A Preliminary Statement to a Theory of Attitude Structure and Change," in *Psychology: A Study of Science*, ed. S. Koch (New York: McGraw-Hill, 1959).

[61] Charles N. Greene, "The Reciprocal nature of Influence between Leader and Subordinate," *Journal of Applied Psychology*, April 1975, pp. 187–93.

reciprocal causation

Do leaders cause or respond to behavior? The reciprocal causation position is that both views are correct.

substitutes for leadership

The position that there are substitutes for leader behaviors. That is, a leader will have little or no effect if certain situations, skills, or tasks exist.

terms of **reciprocal causation.** That is, leader behavior causes follower behavior and follower behavior causes leader behavior.

Substitutes for Leadership

A wide variety of individual, task, environmental, and organizational characteristics have been identified as factors that influence relationships between leader behavior and follower satisfaction and performance. Some of these variables (e.g., follower expectations of leader behavior) appear to influence which leadership style will enable the leader to motivate and direct followers. Others function, however, as **substitutes for leadership.** Substitute variables tend to negate the leader's ability to either increase or decrease follower satisfaction or performance.[62]

It is claimed that substitutes for leadership are prominent in many organizational settings. However, the dominant leadership approaches fail to include substitutes for leadership in discussing the leader behavior–follower satisfaction and performance relationship.

Table 11–7, based on previously conducted research, provides substitutes for only two of the more popular leader behavior styles—relationship-oriented and task-oriented. For each of these leader behavior styles, Kerr and Jermier present which substitutes (characteristics of the subordinate, the task, or the organization) will serve to neutralize the style.[63] For example, an experienced, well-trained and knowledgeable employee does not need a leader to structure the task (e.g., a task-oriented leader). Likewise, a job (task) that provides its own feedback doesn't need a task-oriented leader to inform the employee how he or she is doing. Also, an employee in a close-knit, cohesive group doesn't need a supportive, relationship-oriented leader. The group is a substitute for this type of leader.

Admittedly, we do not fully understand the leader-follower relationship in organizational settings. The need to continue searching for guidelines and principles is apparent. Such searching now seems to be centered on more careful analysis of a situational perspective of leadership and on issues such as the cause-effect question, the constraints on leader behavior, and substitutes for leadership. The descriptions offered by popular press anecdotes such as those found in *The Gamesman* (see the opening Organizational Issue for Debate) are interesting but not based on scientific findings. We feel that it is better to study leaders and substitutes for leaders than to use catchy descrip-

---

[62] Steven Kerr and John M. Jermier, "Substitutes for Leadership: Their Meaning and Measurement," *Organizational Behavior and Human Performance,* December 1978, pp. 376–403.

[63] Ibid.

TABLE 11-7

Substitutes for Leadership

Characteristic	Will Tend to Neutralize	
	Relationship-Oriented	Task-Oriented
Of the subordinate:		
1. Ability, experience, training, knowledge		X
2. Need for independence	X	X
3. "Professional" orientation	X	X
4. Indifference toward organizational rewards	X	X
Of the task:		
5. Unambiguous and routine		X
6. Methodologically invariant		X
7. Provides its own feedback concerning accomplishment		X
8. Intrinsically satisfying	X	
Of the organization:		
9. Formalization (explicit plans, goals, and areas of responsibility)		X
10. Inflexibility (rigid, unbending rules and procedures)		X
11. Highly specified and active advisory and staff functions		X
12. Close-knit, cohesive work groups	X	X
13. Organizational rewards not within the leader's control	X	X
14. Spatial distance between superior and subordinates	X	X

Source: Adapted from Steven Kerr and John M. Jermier, "Substitutes for Leadership: Their Meaning and Measurement," *Organizational Behavior and Human Performance,* December 1978, p. 378.

tions to identify leaders. This type of study and analysis can result in the development of programs to train, prepare, and develop employees for leadership roles.

This chapter should have clearly presented the idea that a single, universally accepted theory of leadership is not available. Each of the perspectives covered in the chapter provides insight into leadership. The fact is that various traits of leaders (e.g., intelligence, personality) influence how they behave with followers. Also situational variables and follower characteristics (e.g., needs, abilities, experience) affect a leader's behavior. Therefore, traits, personal-behavioral, and situational characteristics must be considered when attempting to understand leadership in organizational settings.

SUMMARY OF KEY POINTS

A. Leadership is an ability to influence followers that involves the use of power and the acceptance of the leader by the followers. This ability to influence followers is related to the followers' need satisfaction.

B. The trait approach has resulted in attempts to predict leadership effectiveness from physical, sociological, and psychological traits. The search for traits has led to studies involving effectiveness and such factors as height, weight, intelligence, and personality.

C. There continues to be a great deal of semantic confusion and overlap regarding the definition of leadership behavior. Such terms as *employee-centered, job-centered, initiating structure,* and *consideration* are classified as personal-behavioral descriptions of what the leader does.

D. Research studies have resulted in generally inconclusive findings about the relation of leader behavior to follower effectiveness. The evidence to date is in some cases suggestive. For example, most studies indicate that leaders who are considerate (employee-centered, concerned about people, supportive) will generally have more satisfied followers.

E. The personal-behavioral approaches suggest that situational variables such as the follower's expectations, skills, role clarity, and previous experiences should be seriously considered by leaders. Leaders can do little to improve effectiveness unless they can properly modify these variables or change their style of leadership.

F. The *situational approach* emphasizes the importance of forces within the leader, the subordinates, and the organization. These forces interact and must be properly diagnosed if effectiveness is to be achieved.

G. The *contingency model* proposes that the performance of groups is dependent on the interaction of leadership style and situational favorableness. The three crucial situational factors are leader-member relations, task structure, and position power.

H. Vroom and Yetton have developed a leadership model that can be used to select the amount of group decision-making participation needed in a variety of problem situations. The model suggests that the amount of subordinate participation depends on the leader's skill and knowledge, whether a quality decision is needed, the extent to which the problem is structured, and whether acceptance by subordinates is needed to implement the decision.

I. Research gathered to date on the Vroom-Yetton model has been supportive of the prescriptions offered by applying the various decision rules. In general, it appears that leaders permit a greater level of subordinate participation than seems to be required. The research also points out the need for leaders to be flexible so that high-quality decisions that are accepted by subordinates can be made in a reasonable amount of time.

J. The leader's role in the *path-goal theory* is (1) to increase the number and kinds of personal payoffs to subordinates and (2) to provide guidance and counsel for clarifying paths and reducing problems when seeking various outcomes.

K. The attribution theory of leadership is concerned with why a particular behavior has occurred. In this approach, the leader is considered to be an information processor.

L. There is some evidence that raises the question of whether leader behavior causes follower satisfaction or performance, or vice versa. Followers may have a significant impact on leader behavior or style.

M. Subordinates can be influenced by substitutes for leader behavior. Task, subordinate, and organizational substitutes exist. These substitutes include ability, experience, the routineness of the task, and group cohesiveness.

DISCUSSION AND REVIEW QUESTIONS

1. What is the major difference between attributional and personal-behavioral explanations of leader behavior?

2. Is it possible to train, in management or organizational behavior courses, leaders in the way to lead followers? Explain.

3. A number of the models presented in the chapter emphasize the need for leaders to be flexible. Are any potential problems associated with what would be classified as flexible leaders?

4. What type of research is needed to further develop and modify the Vroom-Yetton model?

5. According to the contingency theory, an alternative to modifying the style of leadership through training is changing the favorableness of the situation. What is meant by changing the favorableness of the situation?

6. Why are leadership theories becoming more complex?

7. Why should a leader examine the substitutes for leadership?

8. Why would a leader be replaced in a formal organizational group and in an informal group?

9. What are the similarities between the contingency model and the path-goal leadership approach?

10. Is personality an important factor in the contingency and path-goal theories of leadership? Explain.

ADDITIONAL REFERENCES

Ashour, A. S. "A Framework of a Cognitive-Behavioral Theory of Leader Influence and Effectiveness." *Organizational Behavior and Human Performance*, 1982, pp. 407–30.

Frost, D. E. "Role Perceptions and Behavior of the Immediate Superior: Moderating Effects on the Prediction of Leadership Effectiveness." *Organizational Behavior and Human Performance*, 1983, pp. 123–42.

Graeff, C. L. "The Situational Leadership Theory: A Critical Review." *Academy of Management Review*, 1983, pp. 285–91.

Hayes, J. L. *Memos for Management: Leadership.* New York: AMACOM, 1983.

Ilgen, D. R.; T. R. Mitchell; and J. W. Fredrickson. "Poor Performers: Supervisors' and Subordinates' Responses." *Organizational Behavior and Performance*, 1981, pp. 386–410.

Lombardo, M. M., and M. W. McCall, Jr. "The Intolerable Boss." *Psychology Today*, 1984, pp. 44–48.

Lord, R. G.; R. J. Foti; and J. S. Phillips. "A Theory of Leadership Categorization." In *Leadership: Beyond Establishment Views*, ed. J. G. Hunt, V. Sekaran, and C. Schriescheim. Carbondale: Southern Illinois University Press, 1982.

Phillips, J. S. "The Accuracy of Leadership Ratings: A Cognitive Categorization Perspective." *Organizational Behavior and Human Performance*, 1984, pp. 125–38.

Phillips, J. S., and R. G. Lord. "Causal Attributions and Perceptions of Leadership." *Organizational Behavior and Human Performance*, 1981, pp. 143–63.

Strube, M. J., and J. E. Garcia. "A Meta-Analytic Investigation of Fiedler's Contingency Model of Leader Effectiveness." *Psychological Bulletin*, 1981, pp. 307–21.

Weiss, H. M., and S. Allen. "Cognitive Complexity and the Structure of Implicit Leadership Theories. *Journal of Applied Psychology*, 1981, pp. 69–78.

Wood, R. E., and T. R. Mitchell. "Manager Behavior in a Social Context: The Impact of Impression Management on Attributions and Disciplinary Actions." *Organizational Behavior and Human Performance*, 1981, pp. 356–78.

Wooford, J. C., and T. N. Srinivasan. "Experimental Tests of the Leader-Environment-Follower Interaction Theory of Leadership." *Organizational Behavior and Human Performance*, 1983, pp. 35–54.

Yukl, G. A. *Leadership in Organizations.* Englewood Cliffs, N.J.: Prentice-Hall, 1981.

Zahn, G. L., and G. Wolf. "Leadership and the Art of Cycle Maintenance: A Simulation Model of Superior-Subordinate Interaction." *Organizational Behavior and Human Performance*, 1981, pp. 26–49.

CASE FOR ANALYSIS

A New Leadership Position

The Dancey Electronics Company is located in a suburb of Dallas. Management forecasts indicated that the company would enjoy moderate growth during the next 10 years. This growth rate would require the promotion of a number of individuals to newly created positions of general manager, which would, in turn, require them to spend most of their time working with departmental managers and less time on production, output, and cost issues.

A majority of the candidates for the three new general manager positions had been with the company for at least 15 years. They were all skilled in the production aspects of operations. Don Kelly, the vice president, felt, however, that none of the candidates had the training or overall insight into company problems to move smoothly into the general manager positions. The board of directors had decided that the three new general managers would be recruited from within Dancey despite these anticipated problems.

Dancey, in attempting to find the best candidates for the new position, hired a consulting firm, Management Analysis Corporation (MAC), to perform an internal search for qualified individuals. Through interviews, testing, and a review of company records, the consulting firm generated a list of six candidates.

One of the candidates found by MAC was Joe Morris. The analysis used to assess Joe involved the study of environmental variables and his current style of leadership. Exhibit 1 presents a profile of Joe's leadership style and various environmental factors that have some impact on this style.

Joe's present leadership style, which is high in task orientation and low in relationship orientation, is similar to the leadership styles of the other five general manager candidates. The expectations of the company, the potential subordinates of the general manager, and the new position of general manager are not consistent with Joe's or any of the other candidates' present leadership styles. The shaded, intersecting area indicates where the expectations of the company, the new position, and the subordinates would be consistent. This is assumed by MAC to be the ideal leadership style for candidates to use once they have been promoted to the general manager position.

If Joe or any of the other candidates accepted the general manager jobs, they would have to significantly increase their relationships orientation. If they did not change their orientation, there would be, according to the consulting firm, a high probability of failure.

Don Kelly was adamant about not going outside Dancey to find three potentially successful new general managers. He and the entire board of directors wanted to utilize a recruitment-from-within policy to secure the three best general managers. It was Don's belief that a leader could modify the style of leadership that he or she had used to meet new situational demands. This belief, and the internal recruitment plan, led Don to call a meeting to discuss a program to improve the compatibility between the three general managers finally selected—Joe Morris, Randy Cooper, and Gregg Shumate—and the environmental factors: the company, the subordinates, and the requirements of the new position.

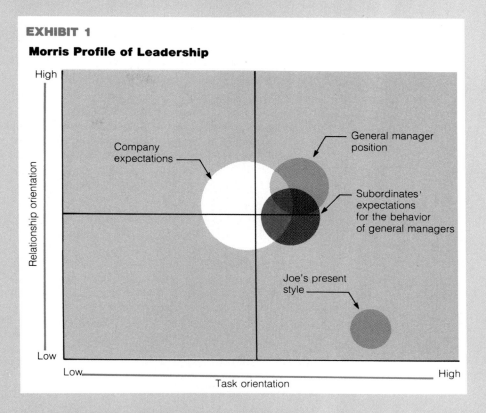

EXHIBIT 1

Morris Profile of Leadership

Questions for Consideration

1. Do you believe that the diagnosis and resulting profile prepared by the Management Analysis Corporation was a necessary step in the process of finding a potentially successful group of general managers? Explain.

2. What alternatives are available to modify the potential effectiveness of Joe Morris in the new general manager position?

3. Why will it be difficult for Joe Morris to modify his style of leadership?

EXPERIENTIAL EXERCISE

LEADERSHIP STYLE ANALYSIS

Objectives

1. To learn how to diagnose different leadership situations.
2. To learn how to apply a systematic procedure for analyzing situations.
3. To improve understanding of how to reach a decision.

Related Topics

Decision making and problem solving when given a number of facts about a situation.

Starting the Exercise

Review the "Decision Process Flowchart" in Figure 11–6. Also examine the "Decision Scenario," presented in the Organizations: Close-Up on page 388. The instructor will then form groups of four to five people to analyze each of the following three cases. Try to reach a group consensus on which decision style is best for the particular case. You are to select the best style based on use of the Vroom-Yetton model, available decision styles, and decision rules. Each case should take a group between 30 and 45 minutes to analyze.

Case I

Setting: Corporate Headquarters
Your Position: Vice President

As marketing vice president, you frequently receive nonroutine requests from customers. One such request, from a relatively new customer, is for extended terms on a large purchase ($2.5 million) involving several of your product lines. The request is for extremely favorable terms that you would not consider except for the high inventory level of most product lines at the present time due to the unanticipated slack period that the company has experienced over the last six months.

You realize that the request is probably a starting point for negotiations, and you have proved your abilities to negotiate the most favorable arrangements in the past. As preparation for these negotiations, you have familiarized yourself with the financial situation of the customer, using various investment reports that you receive regularly.

Reporting to you are four sales managers, each of whom has responsibility for a single product line. They know of the order, and like you, they believe that it is important to negotiate terms with minimum risk and maximum returns to the company. They are likely to differ on what constitutes an acceptable level of risk. The two younger managers have developed a reputation of being "risk takers," whereas the two more senior managers are substantially more conservative.

Case II

Setting: Toy Manufacturer
Your Position: Vice President, Engineering and Design

You are a vice president in a large toy manufacturing company, and your responsibilities include the design of new products that will meet the changing demand in this uncertain and very competitive industry. Your design teams, each under the supervision of a department head, are therefore under constant pressure to produce novel, marketable ideas.

At the opposite end of the manufacturing process is the quality control department, which is under the authority of the vice president, production. When quality control has encountered a serious problem that may be due to design features, its staff has consulted with one or more of your department heads to obtain their recommendations for any changes in the production process. In the wake of consumer concern over the safety of children's toys, however, the responsibilities of quality control have recently been expanded to ensure not only the quality but also the safety of your products. The first major problem in this area has arisen. A preliminary consumer report has "blacklisted" one of your new products without giving any specific reason or justification. This has upset you and others in the organization since it was believed that this product would be one of the most profitable items in the coming Christmas season.

The consumer group has provided your company with an opportunity to respond to the report before it is made public. The head of quality control has therefore consulted with your design people, but you have been told that they became somewhat defensive and dismissed the report as "overreactive fanatic nonsense." Your people told quality control that, while freak accidents were always possible, the product was certainly safe as designed. They argued that the report should simply be ignored.

Since the issue is far from routine, you have decided to give it your personal attention. Because your design teams have been intimately involved in all aspects of the development of the item, you suspect that their response was extreme and was perhaps governed more by their emotional reaction to the report than by the facts. You are not convinced that the consumer group is totally irresponsible, and you are anxious to explore the problem in detail and to recommend to quality control any changes that may be required from a design standpoint. The firm's image as a producer of high-quality toys could suffer a serious blow if the report were made public and public confidence were lost as a result.

You will have to depend heavily on the background and experience of your design teams to help you in analyzing the problem. Even though quality control will be responsible for the decision to implement any changes that you may ultimately recommend, your own subordinates have the background of design experience that could enable you to set standards for what is "safe" and to suggest any design modifications that would meet these standards.

Case III

Setting: Corporate Headquarters
Your Position: Vice President

The sales executives in your home office spent a great deal of time visiting regional sales offices. As marketing vice president, you are concerned that the expenses incurred on these trips are excessive—especially now, when the economic outlook seems bleak and general belt-tightening measures are being carried out in every department.

Having recently been promoted from the ranks of your subordinates, you are keenly aware of some cost-saving measures that could be introduced. You have, in fact, asked the accounting department to review a sample of past expense reports, and it has agreed with your conclusion that several highly favored travel "luxuries" could be curtailed. For example, your sales executives, could restrict first-class air travel to only those occasions when economy class is unavailable, and airport limousine service to hotels could be used instead of taxis where possible. Even more savings could be made if your personnel carefully planned trips such that multiple purposes could be achieved where possible.

The success of any cost-saving measures, however, depends on the commitment of your subordinates. You do not have the time (or the desire) to closely review the expense reports of these sales executives. You suspect, though, that they do not share your concerns over the matter. Having once been in their position, you know that they feel themselves to be deserving of travel amenities.

The problem is to determine which changes, if any, are to be made in current travel and expense account practices in light of the new economic conditions.

Exercise Procedures

Phase I: 10–15 minutes
Individually read case and select proper decision style, using Vroom-Yetton model.

Phase II: 30–45 minutes
Join group appointed by instructor, and reach group consensus.

Phase III: 20 minutes
Each group spokesperson presents group's response and rationale to other groups.

These phases should be used for each of the cases.

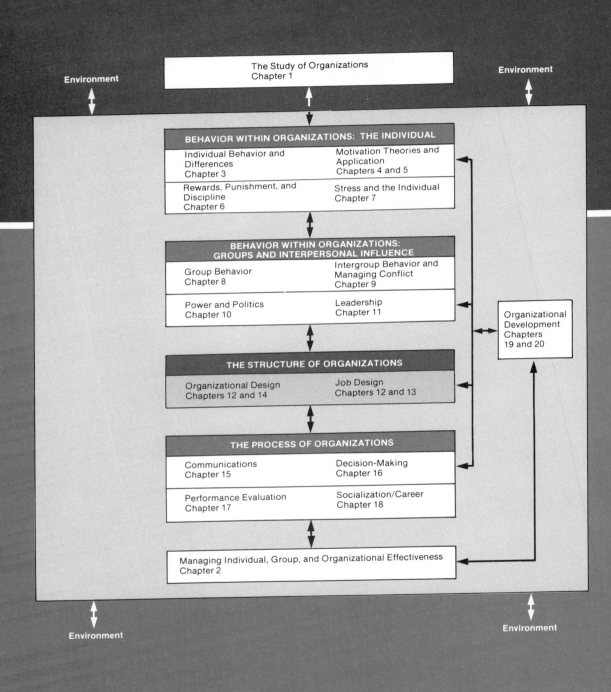

Environment

The Study of Organizations
Chapter 1

Environment

BEHAVIOR WITHIN ORGANIZATIONS: THE INDIVIDUAL

Individual Behavior and
Differences
Chapter 3

Motivation Theories and
Application
Chapters 4 and 5

Rewards, Punishment, and
Discipline
Chapter 6

Stress and the Individual
Chapter 7

**BEHAVIOR WITHIN ORGANIZATIONS:
GROUPS AND INTERPERSONAL INFLUENCE**

Group Behavior
Chapter 8

Intergroup Behavior and
Managing Conflict
Chapter 9

Power and Politics
Chapter 10

Leadership
Chapter 11

THE STRUCTURE OF ORGANIZATIONS

Organizational Design
Chapters 12 and 14

Job Design
Chapters 12 and 13

THE PROCESS OF ORGANIZATIONS

Communications
Chapter 15

Decision-Making
Chapter 16

Performance Evaluation
Chapter 17

Socialization/Career
Chapter 18

Managing Individual, Group, and Organizational Effectiveness
Chapter 2

Organizational
Development
Chapters
19 and 20

Environment

Environment

THE STRUCTURE OF ORGANIZATIONS

Chapter 12

After completing Chapter 12, you should be able to:

Define organizational structure.

Describe the relationship between a manager's span of control and potential interpersonal contacts.

Discuss the advantages and disadvantages of decentralization.

Compare alternative bases for departmentalization.

Identify the three dimensions of organizational structure.

Organizational Structure

The Fixed Optimal Span of Control*

Argument For

The argument regarding the optimal span of control has gone on for many years. The importance of the issue warrants the attention given it. The determination of how many people report to managers has implications for the behavior of the managers, the people reporting to them, and the organization itself. Some of the most influential writers on management and organizational behavior have argued that the optimal span of control is a

*Based on David D. Van Fleet, "Span of Management Research and Issues," *Academy of Management Journal,* September 1983, pp. 546–52.

fixed number—5, 6, or 10, depending on the writer.

The basis for these writers' views is that the ability of managers to supervise is limited. As more and more people are added to the units of managers, the proportionate amount of time that managers can spend on each individual decreases. Moreover, the number of possible interpersonal relationships is 50 times greater for a span of 10 than for a span of 5. Thus, it was apparent to some writers that no superior could supervise directly the work of more than 5 or, at the most, 10 subordinates.

The idea that the optimal span of control is a fixed, small number has several organizational implications. The most important of these is that the organization would tend to have many layers of management through which information and directives would pass. Consequently, the organization would be unable to respond to environmental changes as quickly as might be appropriate. Nevertheless, the disadvantages of tall, layered organizations are outweighed, accord-

415

ing to proponents of narrow spans, by the advantages of greater supervisory control.

Argument Against

Those writers and practitioners who argue against the fixed optimal span of control take exception to two points. First, they argue that wide spans of control and the resultant flat organizations foster greater employee participation and self-control. Since managers having relatively wide spans of control are unable to direct closely the work of their subordinates, the subordinates will therefore develop greater independence and learn to direct themselves. Moreover, the flatter organization structure enables managers to respond more quickly to environmental changes because information and directives will pass through fewer levels. These outcomes—greater employee initiatives and more responsive organizations—are advantages in their own right.

A second point of debate has to do with the view of contingency theories of organizational behavior. According to this view, the optimal span of control varies depending on numerous other variables (contingencies). Managerial ability is one such contingency, but there are others. For example, wider spans of control are possible if subordinates' jobs are highly routine, similar, formalized, and performed in one location. In such instances, the amount of supervision required tends to decline because the work, in effect, supervises itself. Thus, an optimal span of control may exist for any given situation, but it cannot be represented by a specific number without examining the state of the variables that determine it.

The subject of this section of the book is organizational *structure*. It is one of the three major subjects of the entire book (the other two are organizational *behavior* and organizational *processes*. In Chapter 1, we noted the importance of organizational **structure** as an influence on the behavior of the individuals and groups that the organization comprises. The importance of structure as a source of influence is so widely accepted that some experts define the concept in these terms: "Organizational structure for our purposes will be defined broadly as those features of the organization that serve to *control* or distinguish its parts."[1] Our common experience enables us to recognize some of the ways that structure controls the behavior of employees. Most of us have worked in organizational settings, and we know that in those settings our behavior was "controlled" in the sense that we were unable to make absolutely free choices in what we did and how we did it. We gave up free choice when we undertook the work necessitated by the *jobs* we held. Jobs are important features of any organization.

But jobs are not the only features of organizations. Again, our common experience informs us that organizations consist of departments, divisions, units, or any of a number of other terms that denote *groups* of jobs. No doubt the college or university you attend is made up of a number of academic departments—management, accounting, economics if you are in a business school. Each of these departments contains individuals who perform different jobs that combine to produce a larger outcome than is possible from the efforts of any single job or department. When you graduate, your education will have been made possible by the combined efforts of individual departments. But the point is not that these departments combine the effects of many different jobs; rather, what we are noting here is the effect of the departments on the behavior of the individuals in them. As members of departments, individuals must necessarily abide by commonly held agreements, policies, and rules and thereby give up the freedom to act with complete freedom.

The Organizational Issue for Debate that opened this chapter concerns how best to control the behavior of individuals through one seemingly innocent characteristic of groups—the number of individuals comprised by the groups. The number of individuals in a group is the number of individuals who must be managed, referred to as the span of control. The debatable issue is how many people a manager can effectively control. As the span of control decreases, the manager can exert greater supervision and consequently greater control over

structure
The pattern of jobs and groups of jobs. Structure is an important cause of individual and group behavior.

---

[1] Robert H. Miles, *Macro Organizational Behavior* (Santa Monica, Calif.: Goodyear Publishing, 1980), p. 18.

the individuals who report to him or her. But the cost of the additional control is to increase the number of managers (and managers' salaries). So we see that the issue of achieving control through manipulating the size of a department involves balancing the relative benefits and disbenefits of at least two desirable outcomes: control and efficiency. Controlling the behavior of employees is but one of those outcomes.

A second perspective on organizational structure must be introduced to provide a complete understanding of the concept. This perspective focuses on the *activities performed as consequences of the structure.* Defined from this perspective, "the concept of structure is usually understood to imply a configuration of activities that is characteristically enduring and persistent; the dominant feature of organizational structure is its patterned regularity."[2] Note that this definition states nothing about the reason for the "patterned regularity," only that it exists. The definition points out that within organizations certain activities can be counted on to occur routinely. For example, people come to work each morning at eight o'clock, clock in, go to their work stations, and begin doing the same work that they did the day before. They talk to the same people; they receive information from the same people; they are periodically, but predictably, evaluated for promotion and raises. Without these predictable activities, the work of the organization could not be achieved.

Definitions that focus on regularly occurring organizational activities emphasize the importance of what we term *organizational processes.* In the next section of the book, we will discuss the processes of communication, decision making, performance evaluation, socialization, and career. These processes occur with considerable regularity, and it is certainly possible and even useful to analyze the patterns of communication, decision making, and other processes. But it is also useful to distinguish between activity (or processes) and the causes of that activity. Thus, when we discuss structure in the following pages, we refer to a *relatively stable framework of jobs and departments that influences the behavior of individuals and groups toward organizational goals.*

Organizations are purposive and goal-oriented. It follows that the structure of organizations is likewise purposive and goal-directed. Our concept of organizational structure will take into account the existence of purposes and goals, and our attitude will be that management should think of structure in terms of its contribution to organizational effectiveness.

The statement that organizational structures facilitate the achieve-

[2] Stewart Ranson, Bob Hinings, and Royston Greenwood, "The Structuring of Organizational Structures," *Administrative Science Quarterly,* March 1980, p. 1.

ment of organizational goals assumes that managers know how to match organizational structures and goals and that they desire to do so. It is entirely reasonable to acknowledge that in many instances organizational structures do not contribute positively to organizational performance because managers are unable by training or intellect to design a structure that guides the behavior of individuals and groups to achieve high levels of production, efficiency, satisfaction, adaptiveness, and development. It is also reasonable to acknowledge that in some instances organizational structures reflect and contribute to the personal goals of managers at the expense of the goals of the organization. Thus, to say that organizational structures contribute positively to organizational effectiveness requires assumptions about the abilities and motivations of those who have power to design them. The structure of an organization is without doubt related to the achievement of organizational effectiveness, even though the exact nature of the relationship is inherently difficult to know.[3]

THE EFFECTS OF STRUCTURE ON INDIVIDUAL AND GROUP BEHAVIOR

The behavior of individuals and groups in organizations is affected in significant ways by the *jobs* they perform. The job itself provides powerful stimuli for individual behavior. The demands on, and expectations of, individuals can result in high levels of personal satisfaction or stress, anxiety, and physiological dysfunctions.[4] The jobs that people hold require them to perform activities in combination with other people in the organization. The activities can be routine or nonroutine; they can require high or low levels of skill; they can be perceived as challenging or as trivial. The required relationships can be with co-workers, managers, clients, suppliers, or buyers. The relationships can result in feelings of friendship, competition, cooperativeness, and satisfaction, or they can be causes of stress and anxiety. The determination of required job activities and relationships, a key managerial function, is covered in Chapter 13.

Structure also affects the behavior and functioning of groups in

---

[3] Dan R. Dalton, William D. Todor, Michael J. Spendolini, Gordon J. Fielding, and Lyman W. Porter, "Organization Structure and Performance: A Critical Review," *Academy of Management Review,* January 1980, pp. 49–64.

[4] Greg R. Oldham and J. Richard Hackman, "Relationships between Organizational Structure and Employee Reactions: Comparing Alternative Frameworks," *Administrative Science Quarterly,* March 1981, pp. 66–83; John M. Ivancevich and James H. Donnelly, Jr., "Relation of Organizational Structure to Job Satisfaction, Anxiety-Stress, and Performance," *Administrative Science Quarterly,* June 1975, pp. 272–80; and Larry L. Cummings and Chris J. Berger, "Organization Structure: How Does It Influence Attitudes and Performance?" *Organizational Dynamics,* Autumn 1976, pp. 34–49.

organizations.[5] Depending on the specific configuration of jobs and departments, groups can be either more or less cohesive, more or less communicative. For example, a department that contains 10 individuals performing the same job will act quite differently from one that contains 10 individuals, each performing a different job. Studies of organizational structure indicate that the group of people doing the same job will be less cohesive, less open to new ideas, and less communicative than the group of people doing different jobs. Thus, structure makes a difference in the ways groups act in organizations, and we cover that topic in Chapter 14.

DESIGNING AN ORGANIZATIONAL STRUCTURE

Managers who set out to design an organizational structure face difficult decisions. They must choose among a myriad of alternative frameworks of jobs and departments. *The process by which they make these choices is termed* **organizational design,** *which means quite simply the decisions and actions that result in an organizational structure.*[6] This process may be explicit or implicit; it may be "one-shot" or developmental; it may be done by a single manager or by a team of managers.

organizational design
Consists of managers' decisions and actions that result in a specific organizational structure.

However the actual decisions come about, the content of the decisions is always the same. The first two decisions focus on individual jobs; the next two decisions focus on departments, or groups of jobs.

1. Managers decide how to divide the overall task into successively smaller jobs. They divide the total activities of the task into smaller sets of related activities. The effect of this decision is to define jobs in terms of specialized activities and responsibilities. Although jobs have many characteristics, their most important characteristic is their degree of *specialization.*
2. Managers distribute authority among jobs. Authority is the right to make decisions without approval by a higher manager and to exact obedience from designated other people. All jobs contain the right to make decisions within prescribed limits. But not all jobs contain the right to exact obedience from others. The latter aspect of authority distinguishes managerial from nonmanagerial jobs. Managers can exact obedience; nonmanagers cannot.

The outcomes of these two decisions are jobs that management assigns to individuals. The jobs will have two distinct attributes: *activities*

---

[5] John A. Pearce II and Fred R. David, "A Social Network Approach to Organizational Design and Performance," *Academy of Management Review,* July 1983, pp. 436–44.

[6] Hugh C. Willmott, "The Structuring of Organizational Structures: A Note," *Administrative Science Quarterly,* September 1981, pp. 470–74.

and *authority*. The third and fourth decisions affect the manner in which the jobs are grouped into departments.

3. Managers decide the bases on which individual jobs are to be grouped together. This decision is much like any other classification decision, and it can result in groups containing jobs that are relatively homogeneous or heterogeneous.
4. Finally, managers decide the appropriate size of the group reporting to each superior. As we have already noted, this decision involves determining whether there are relatively few or many spans of control.

Thus, organizational structures vary depending on the choices that managers make. If we consider each of the four design decisions to be a continuum of possible choices, the alternative structures can be depicted as follows:

Division of Labor:	Specialization	
	High	Low
Authority	Delegation	
	High	Low
Departmentalization:	Basis	
	Homogeneous	Heterogeneous
Span of control:	Number	
	Few	Many

Generally speaking, organizational structures will tend toward one extreme or the other along each continuum. Structures tending to the left are characterized by a number of terms, including classical, formalistic, structured, bureaucratic, System 1, and mechanistic. Structures tending to the right are termed neoclassical, informalistic, unstructured, nonbureaucratic, System 4, and organic. These terms are in no way precise or universally understood; this imprecision provides evidence of the relative immaturity of the state of knowledge about organizational design.

DIVISION OF LABOR

Division of labor concerns the extent to which jobs are specialized. Managers divide the total task of the organization into specific jobs having specified *activities*. The activities define what the person performing a particular job is to do and to get done. For example the activities of the job "accounting clerk" can be defined in terms of the *methods* and *procedures* required to process a certain quantity of transactions during a specified period of time. Various accounting clerks could use the same methods and procedures to process *different types* of transactions. One accounting clerk could be processing accounts receivable; the others could be processing accounts payable. *Thus, jobs can be specialized both by method and by application of the method.*

A major decision in developing an organizational structure is determining how much division of labor should exist. Advocates of dividing work into a small number of tasks often cite the advantages of specialization. Two of the major advantages are:

1. If a job contains few tasks, it is easy to train replacements for terminated, transferred, or absent personnel. The minimum training effort results in a lower training cost.
2. When a job entails only a limited number of tasks, the employee can become proficient in performing these tasks. The employee's high level of proficiency is reflected in a better quality of output.

These two benefits are largely economic and technical, and they are usually applied to nonmanagerial jobs. However, similar benefits are applicable to specialized managerial positions.[7] For example, the jobs of marketing manager and production manager are different because of the advantages of specialization. The marketing manager specializes in the problems of promoting and selling a product; the production manager specializes in manufacturing it.

The economic advantages of dividing work into specialized jobs are the principal historical reasons for the creation of organizations. As societies became more and more industrialized and urbanized, craft production gave away to mass production. Mass production depends on the ability to obtain the economic benefits of specialized labor, and organizations are the most effective means for obtaining specialized labor. Although managers are concerned with more than the economic implications of jobs, they seldom lose sight of specialization as the rationale for dividing work among jobs.

DELEGATION OF AUTHORITY

Managers decide how much authority is to be delegated to each job and each jobholder. As we have noted, authority refers to the

---

[7] Michael Aiken, Samuel B. Bacharach, and J. Lawrence French, "Organization Structure, Work Process, and Proposal Making in Administrative Bureaucracies," *Academy of Management Journal*, December 1980, pp. 631–52.

right of individuals to make decisions without approval by higher management and to exact obedience from others. A sales manager can be delegated the right to hire salespersons (a decision) and the right to assign them to specific territories (obedience). Another sales manager may not have the right to hire but may have the right to assign territories. Thus, the degree of delegated authority can be relatively high or relatively low with respect to both aspects of authority. And for any particular job, there is a range of alternative configurations of authority delegation. Managers must balance the relative gains and losses of alternatives. Let us evaluate some of these.

First, relatively high delegation of authority encourages the development of professional managers. As decision-making authority is pushed down (delegated) in the organization, managers have opportunities to make significant decisions and to gain skills that enable them to advance in the company. By virtue of their right to make decisions on a broad range of issues, managers develop expertise that enables them to cope with problems of higher management. Managers with broad decision-making power often make difficult decisions. Consequently, they are trained for promotion into positions of even greater authority and responsibility. Upper management can readily compare managers on the basis of actual decision-making performance. The advancement of managers on the basis of demonstrated performance can eliminate favoritism and personality conflicts in the promotion process.

Second, high delegation of authority can lead to a competitive climate within the organization. Managers are motivated to contribute in this competitive atmosphere since they are compared with their peers on various performance measures. A competitive environment in which managers compete on how well they achieve sales, cost reduction, and employee development targets can be a positive factor in overall organizational performance. Competitive environments can also produce destructive behavior if the success of one manager occurs at the expense of another. But regardless of whether it is positive or destructive, significant competition exists only when individuals have authority to do those things that enable them to win.

Finally, high delegation of authority enables managers to exercise more autonomy, and thus satisfy their desires to participate in problem solving. This autonomy can lead to managerial creativity and ingenuity that contribute to the adaptiveness and development of the organization and managers. As we have seen in earlier chapters, opportunities to participate in setting goals can be positive motivators. But a necessary condition for goal setting is the authority to make decisions.

These are only three of the benefits associated with delegated authority. These benefits are not free of costs. Among the costs are the following:

First, managers must be trained to make the decisions that go with delegated authority. Formal training programs can be quite expensive, and that can more than offset the benefits.

Second, many managers are accustomed to making decisions and they resist delegating authority to their subordinates. Consequently, they may perform at lower levels of effectiveness because they believe that delegation of authority involves losing control.

Third, administrative costs are incurred because new or altered accounting and performance systems must be developed to provide top management with information about the effects of their subordinates' decisions. When authority is delegated to lower levels of management, top management must have some means of reviewing the use of that authority. Consequently, top management typically creates reporting systems that inform it.

These are, of course, only some of the costs. Like most managerial issues, whether authority should be delegated in high or low degrees cannot be resolved simply. As we see it, the issue has implications not only for individual jobs but also for the organization's information and decision-making process.

The following Close-Up illustrates one firm's experience with delegated authority.

ORGANIZATIONS: CLOSE-UP

Decentralization at Curtice-Burns, Inc.

Curtice-Burns, Inc., manages seven food manufacturing divisions with a headquarters staff of only 12 people. The headquarters staff, located in Rochester, New York, oversees the seven divisions through a decentralized organizational structure. Each division is considered a profit center, and each division's chief executive is completely responsible for the division. Completely delegated authority is the rule except in the area of major capital investments. Each division chief must request funds for capital improvements from the company's board of directors. Apart from this one constraint, each division is an autonomous unit with the authority to make all of the decisions necessary to run an independent business.

According to Hugh Cumming, president and CEO, "We manage by exception rather than by control. If there is a problem and the division CEO is a good manager, he's already briefed corporate management that he is taking a risk and may fail. We as managers have to have failures to learn. If every time you have a failure, corporate headquarters gets into the act, nobody is going to take any chances."

Since its inception, the company has grown to sales of over $300 million, primarily through acquisitions of other companies that subsequently became the company's divisions. Earnings per share have increased by over 700 percent. Although these impressive gains cannot be attributed solely to the organizational structure that Curtice-Burns has adopted, Cumming believes that it has been a major contributing factor.

Source: *Management Review*, November 1979, pp. 32–33.

Once management has defined a job in terms of its *activities* and its *authority,* the two principal components of the job will have been determined. These two components define not only the expectations of the job itself but also the *relationships* of the job to other jobs. For example, the job of the manager of a branch bank will be defined in terms of (1) what the manager must do and get done (activities), (2) what decisions and directives the manager can issue without seeking approval (authority), and (3) what individuals report to the manager as well as who the manager reports to (relationships). In organizational settings, managers must define jobs in these terms.

DEPARTMENTALIZATION

The process of defining the activities and authority of jobs is analytical; that is, the total task of the organization is broken down into successively smaller ones. But then management must combine the divided tasks into groups or departments.

The rationale for grouping jobs rests on the necessity for coordinating them. The specialized jobs are separate, interrelated parts of the total task, whose accomplishment requires the completion of each of the jobs. But the jobs must be performed in the specific manner and sequence intended by management when they were defined. As the number of specialized jobs in an organization increases, there comes a point when they can no longer be effectively coordinated by a single manager. Thus, to create manageable numbers of jobs, they are combined into smaller groups and a new job is defined, that of manager of the group. The crucial managerial consideration when creating departments is determining the *bases* for grouping jobs. These bases are termed departmentalization bases, and some of the more widely used ones are described in the following sections.

Functional Departmentalization

Managers can combine jobs according to the **functions** of the organization. Every organization must undertake certain activities in order

functions
The inherent tasks of specific organization types. The functions of a business organization include production, marketing, and finance.

to do its work. These necessary activities are the organization's functions. The necessary functions of a manufacturing firm include production, marketing, finance, accounting, and personnel. These functions are necessary to create, produce, and sell a product. The necessary functions of a commercial bank include taking deposits, making loans, and investing the bank's funds. The functions of a hospital include surgery, psychiatry, housekeeping, pharmacy, and personnel. Each of these functions can be a specific department, and jobs can be combined according to them. The functional basis of departmentalization is often found in relatively small organizations providing a narrow range of products and services. It is also widely used as the basis in divisions of large multiproduct organizations.

The Oldsmobile Division of General Motors is structured on a functional basis, as depicted in Figure 12–1. The functions are engineering, manufacturing, reliability, distribution, finance, personnel, public relations, and purchasing. The management of General Motors decided that these eight functions should be the bases for combining the jobs of the Oldsmobile Division. Other divisions of General Motors use different functional bases, depending on the decisions of management. The specific configuration of functions that appear as separate departments varies from organization to organization.

For comparative purposes, the organizational structure of U.S. Ireland Army Hospital is depicted in Figure 12–2. The departments of the hospital are divided into two broad categories: professional services and administrative services. The several departments comprised by each of these two main functions reflect the jobs that are necessary to provide patient care and to run a hospital. As is the case with business firms, the number and kinds of departments that hospital managers consider necessary reflect the size and scope of the hospital's activity. For example, a university teaching and research hospital and medical center will have more separate departments than a community hospital.

The principal advantage of functional departmentalization is its efficiency. That is, it seems logical to have a department that consists of experts in a particular field such as production or accounting. By having departments of specialists, management creates highly efficient units. An accountant is generally more efficient when working with accountants and other individuals who have similar backgrounds and interests. They can share expertise to get the work done.

A major disadvantage of this departmental basis is that because specialists are working with and encouraging one another in their area of expertise and interest, the organizational goals may be sacrificed in favor of departmental goals. Accountants may see only their problems and not those of production or marketing or the total organization. In other words, identification with the department and its cul-

FIGURE 12–1

Organizational Structure of Oldsmobile Division

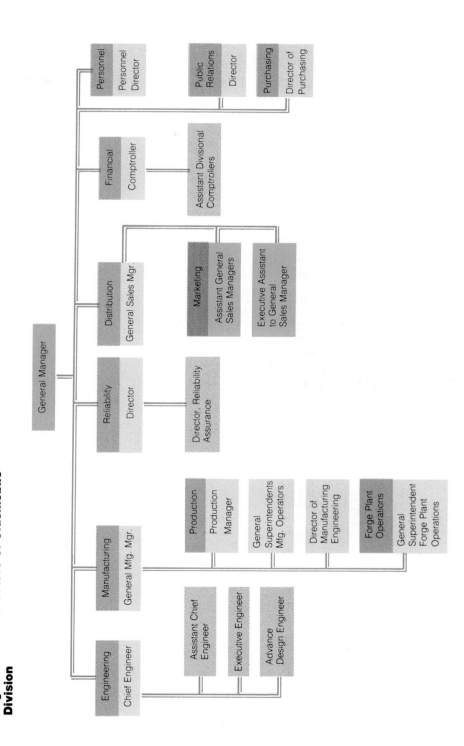

FIGURE 12–2

**Organizational Structure of U.S. Ireland
Army Hospital**

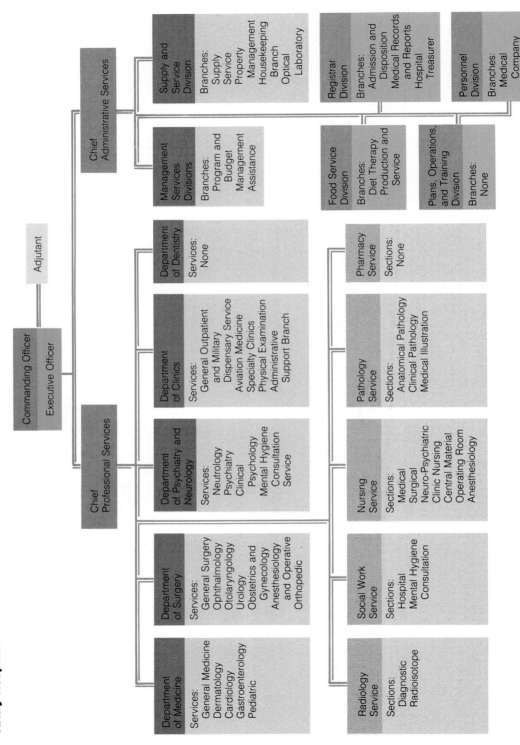

ture is often stronger than identification with the organization and its culture.

Territorial Departmentalization

Another commonly adopted method for departmentalizing is to establish groups on the basis of geographic area. The rationale for this method is that all activities in a given region should be assigned to a manager. This individual would be in charge of all operations in that geographic area.

In large organizations, territorial arrangements are advantageous because the physical dispersion of activities makes centralized coordination difficult. For example, it is extremely difficult for someone in New York to manage salespersons in Kansas City. It makes sense to assign the managerial job to someone in Kansas City. An example of a territorial structure is presented in Figure 12–3, which illustrates the organization chart of R. H. Macy & Co., Inc.

The divisions of the department store reflect the locations of Macy stores in eight states. The managers of individual stores in a specific city report to a regional president. The manager of Macy's in Sacramento reports to the president of Macy's California, whose offices are in San Francisco.

Territorial departmentalization provides a training ground for managerial personnel. The company is able to place managers in territories and then assess their progress in that geographic region. The experience that managers acquire in a territory away from headquarters provides valuable insights about how products and services are accepted in the field.

Product Departmentalization

Managers of many large diversified companies group jobs on the basis of product. All of the jobs associated with producing and selling a product or product line are placed under the direction of one manager. Product becomes the preferred basis as a firm grows by increasing the number of products it markets. As a firm grows, it becomes difficult to coordinate the various functional departments and it becomes advantageous to establish product units. This form of organization allows personnel to develop total expertise in researching, manufacturing, and distributing a product line. Concentration of the authority, responsibility, and accountability in a specific product department allows top management to coordinate actions.

The Consumer Products Division of Kimberly-Clark reflects product departmentalization. The specific product groups shown in Figure 12–4 include feminine hygiene, household, and commercial products.

FIGURE 12-3

Organizational Structure of R. H. Macy & Co., Inc.

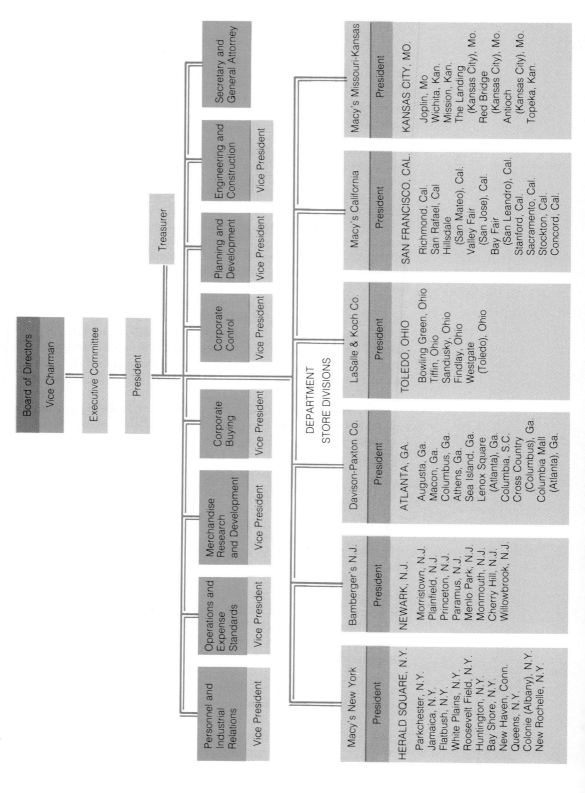

FIGURE 12-4

Organizational Structure of Consumer Products Division, Kimberly-Clark Corporation

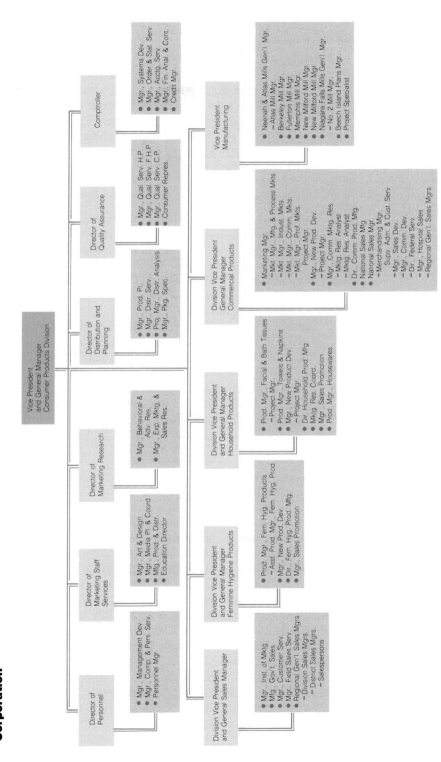

Within each of these units, we find production and marketing personnel. Since the managers of product divisions coordinate the sales, manufacturing, and distribution of a product, they become the overseers of a profit center. In this manner, profit responsibility is implemented in product-based organizations. Managers are often asked to establish profit goals at the beginning of a time period and then to compare actual profit with planned profit.

Customer Departmentalization

Customers and clients can be a basis for grouping jobs. Examples of customer-oriented departments are the organizational structures of educational institutions. Some institutions have regular (day and night) courses and extension divisions. In some instances, a professor will be affiliated solely with the regular division or the extension division. In fact, the title of some faculty positions often specifically mentions the extension division.

Another form of customer departmentalization is the loan department in a commercial bank. Loan officers are often associated with industrial, commercial, or agricultural loans. The customer will be served by one of these three loan officers.

Some department stores are departmentalized to some degree on a customer basis. They have such groupings as university shops, men's clothing, and boys' clothing. They have bargain floors that carry a lower quality of university, men's, and boys' clothing.

Mixed and Changing Departmentalization

The bases for departments do not remain unchanged in organizations. Because of the importance of departments, managers change the bases as conditions warrant. An organization chart should be viewed as much like a snapshot of a moving object: The action is "frozen" for a moment, but the viewer understands that the object continued in motion. Over time, organizations will use a mix of bases, at some time using function, at other times using product, territory, and customer. Moreover, within the same organization there will be different bases at different levels of management. For example, the departmental basis at the corporate level of General Motors is product type—compact and full-size cars, with an executive vice president heading up each division, The general managers of the Chevrolet and Pontiac divisions report to the compact car vice president; the general managers of the Buick, Oldsmobile, and Cadillac divisions report to the full-size car vice president. But below the general managers, function is the departmental basis, as we noted in Figure 12–1. The following Close-Up describes how the Textile Fibers Department of Du Pont changed departmental bases over time.

ORGANIZATIONS: CLOSE-UP

Changing Departmental Bases at Du Pont

At one time, the Textile Fibers Department was made up of five divisions, one for each of the five fibers that the department made and sold. Each division, under a division manager, had a sales division and a manufacturing division. The organizational structure at this point in time reflected product departmentalization. Each of the five divisions acted as a separate business, producing and selling a particular fiber.

Later, management combined the five divisions into six functional divisions: manufacturing, control, personnel and industrial relations, sales, planning, and research. The directors and managers of each of these divisions had authority over their counterparts in the fiber product groups. This functional organization is shown in Figure 12–5.

Eventually, management changed the sales division and added a merchandising unit. The merchandising unit consisted of six groups: men's wear, women's wear, home furnishings, industrial merchandising, advertising and promotion, and marketing research. As shown in Figure 12–6, the merchandising unit is but one of five divisions reporting to the general director. These five divisions contain all four departmentalization bases:

The Research Division has functional departments.

The Sales Programs Division has product departments.

The Merchandising Division has customer departments.

The Sales Division has territorial departments.

And the Technical Service Section has a mixture of product and functional departments.

The degree of coordination that management achieves depends greatly on having appropriate department bases at each level in the organization. As illustrated in the Close-Up on the experience of the Textile Fibers Department, the appropriate bases change with time and circumstances. The changes in the Textile Fibers Department reflect the relative importance of making and selling fibers (product departments), obtaining efficiency and greater control (functional departments), and meeting the special needs of different segments of

FIGURE 12–5

**Organizational Structure of Textile Fibers
Department, Du Pont**

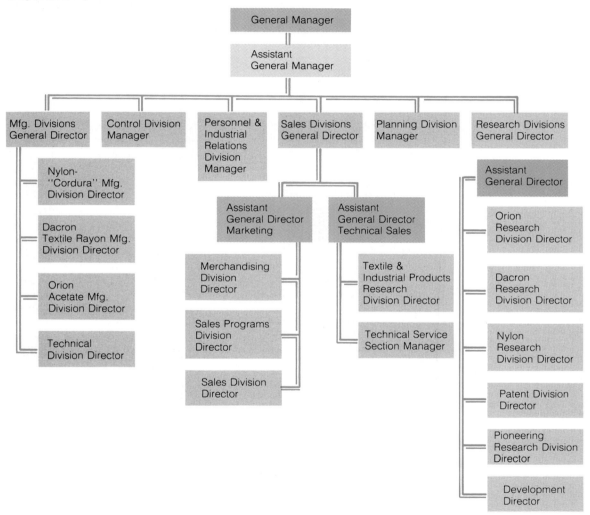

the market (the merchandising unit's customer departments). Departmentmentalization is a key decision in organizational design. An equally
important decision is the determination of each manager's span of
control.

SPAN OF CONTROL

The determination of appropriate bases for departmentalization establishes the *kinds* of jobs that will be grouped together. But it does

FIGURE 12–6

**Organizational Structure of Sales Divisions
of Textile Fibers Department, Du Pont**

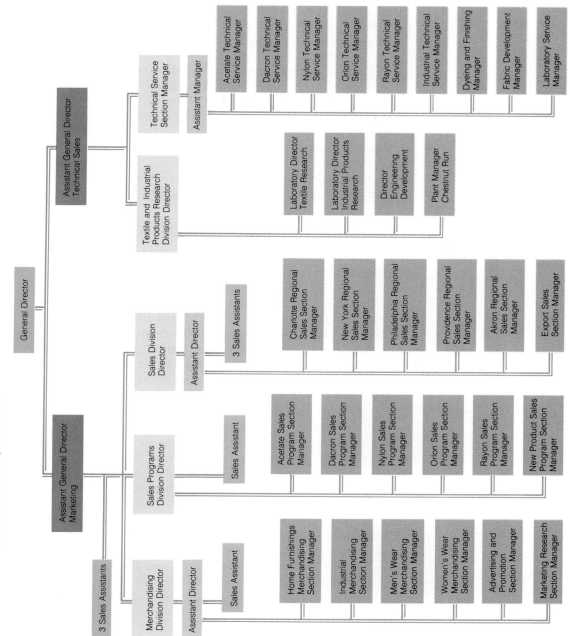

not establish the *number* of jobs to be included in a specific group. That determination is the issue of span of control. Generally, the issue comes down to the decision of how many people a manager can oversee; that is, will the organization be more effective if the span of control is relatively wide or narrow? This question is basically concerned with determining the volume of interpersonal relationships that the department's manager is able to handle. Moreover, the span of control must be defined to include not only formally assigned subordinates but also those who have access to the manager. A manager may not only be responsible for immediate subordinates but may also be the chairperson of several committees and task groups that take time.[8]

The number of *potential* interpersonal relationships between a manager and subordinates can be calculated as follows:

$$R = N\left(\frac{2^N}{2} + N - 1\right)$$

where R designates the number of relationships and N is the number of subordinates assigned to the manager's command group.[9] This formula is simply a method for counting the number of potential relationships that can exist. Table 12–1 shows the results of using the formula to calculate the potential relationships between 1 manager and 1 through 9 and 18 subordinates. The relationship is not arithmetic or proportional. Note that as the number of subordinates increases from 2 to 3, the number of relationships increases from 6 to 18. More dramatic is the increase in relationships associated with doubling the number of subordinates from 9 to 18. Clearly, the rate of change in potential relationships increases *geometrically* as the number of subordinates increases *arithmetically*.

The calculation assumes that managers potentially contend with three types of interpersonal relationships: (1) direct single, (2) direct group, and (3) cross. Direct single relationships occur between the manager and each subordinate individually, that is in a "one-on-one" setting. Direct group relations occur between the manager and each possible permutation of subordinates. Finally, cross relationships occur when subordinates interact with one another. These potential relationships are illustrated in Figure 12–7 for a manager (M) and two subordinates (A and B) and for a manager and three subordinates (A, B, and C). Direct group relationships differ depending on which subordinate (A, B, or C) assumes the leadership role in interaction with the

---

[8] William G. Ouchi and John B. Dowling, "Defining the Span of Control," *Administrative Science Quarterly,* September 1974, pp. 357–65.

[9] A. V. Graicunas, "Relationships in Organization," in *Papers on the Science of Administration,* ed. Luther Gulick and Lyndall F. Urwick (New York: Columbia University Press, 1947), pp. 183–87.

TABLE 12-1

Potential Relationships

Number of Subordinates	Number of Relationships
1	1
2	6
3	18
4	44
5	100
6	222
7	490
8	1,080
9	2,376
18	2,359,602

manager. And depending on the issue to be discussed or the problem to be solved, we would expect different group members to emerge as leader.

The critical consideration in determining the manager's span of control is not the number of *potential* relationships. Rather, it is the frequency and intensity of the *actual* relationships that are important. Not all relationships will occur, and those that do will vary in importance. If we shift our attention from potential to actual relationships

FIGURE 12-7

Potential Relationships among a Manager and Two/Three Subordinates

Direct single	1. M → A	Direct single	1. M → A
	2. M → B		2. M → B
			3. M → C
Direct group	3. M → A with B	Direct group	4. M → A with B
	4. M → B with A		5. M → A with C
			6. M → B with A
			7. M → B with C
			8. M → C with A
			9. M → C with B
			10. M → A with B and C
			11. M → B with A and C
			12. M → C with A and B
Cross	5. A → B	Cross	13. A → B
	6. B → A		14. A → C
			15. B → A
			16. B → C
			17. C → A
			18. C → B

as the bases for determining optimum span of control, at least three factors appear to be important.

1. Required Contact. In research and development, medical, and production work, there is a need for frequent contact and a high degree of coordination between a superior and subordinates. The use of conferences and other forms of consultation often aid in the attainment of goals within a constrained time period. For example, the research and development team leader may have to consult frequently with team members so that a project is completed within a time period that will allow the organization to place a product on the market by a certain date. Thus, instead of relying on memos and reports, it is in the best interest of the organization to have as many in-depth contacts with the team as possible. A large span of control would preclude contacting subordinates so frequently, and this could delay the completion of the project. In general, the greater the inherent ambiguity that exists in an individual's job, the greater is the need for supervision to avoid conflict and stress.[10]

2. Degree of Specialization. The degree of specialization among employees is a critical consideration in establishing the span of control at all levels of management. It is generally accepted that a manager at a lower organizational level can oversee more subordinates because work at the lower level is more specialized and less complicated than work at higher levels of management. Management can combine highly specialized and similar jobs into relatively large departments because the employees who do those jobs may not need close supervision.

3. Ability to Communicate. Instructions, guidelines, and policies must be communicated verbally to subordinates in most work situations. The need to discuss job-related factors influences the span of control. An individual who can clearly and concisely communicate with subordinates is able to manage more people than one who cannot do so.

The following Close-up describes the importance of span of control in Dana Corporation's organization structure.

ORGANIZATIONS: CLOSE-UP

Spans of Control at Dana Corporation

Dana Corporation of Toledo, Ohio, has in recent years undergone some changes in its organizational structure. One of the objectives of Dana's

---

[10] Lawrence B. Chonko, "The Relationship of Span of Control to Sales Representatives' Experienced Role Conflict and Role Ambiguity," *Academy of Management Journal,* June 1982, pp. 452–56.

top management is to reduce the total number of managerial jobs. A promising approach to achieve that goal is to increase spans of control. According to John M. Toth, communications manager, top management is encouraging plant managers to organize according to how many people a manager can supervise, rather than by what functions coincide with a manager's title. Plant managers evaluate the supervisory skills of each manager and assign him or her a correspondingly appropriate number of individuals. Thus, a quality control manager may supervise people involved in maintenance and shipping, for example, instead of only six or so quality control inspectors. The people who perform work other than quality control can be assigned to the manager because of his or her supervisory skill. The concept that underlies Dana Corporation's approach is that management should be defined in terms of control, rather than as boxes on an organization chart.

Source: John M. Toth, "How Dana Is Reducing Number of Managers Despite Its Growth," *Management Review*, November–December 1982, pp. 29, 36.

Even though it is possible to identify some of the specific factors that relate to optimal spans of control, the search for the full answer continues.[11] In Chapter 14, "Organizational Design," we will see that span of control *and* departmentalization bases are different both among and within organizations.

DIMENSIONS OF STRUCTURE

The four design decisions (division of labor, delegation of authority, departmentalization, and span of control) result in a structure of organizations. Researchers and practitioners of management have attempted to develop their understanding of relationships between structures and performance, attitudes, satisfaction, and other variables thought to be important. The development of understanding has been hampered not only by the complexity of the relationships themselves, but also by the difficulty of defining and measuring the concept of organizational structure.

Although universal agreement on a common set of dimensions that measure differences in structure is neither possible nor desirable, some suggestions can be made. At present, three dimensions are often used in research and practice to describe structure. They are *formalization, centralization,* and *complexity.*[12]

---

[11] Robert D. Dewar and Donald P. Simet, "A Level-Specific Prediction of Spans of Control Examining the Effects of Size, Technology, and Specialization," *Academy of Management Journal,* March 1981, pp. 5–24.

[12] Richard S. Blackburn, "Dimensions of Structure: A Review and Reappraisal," *Academy of Management Review,* January 1982, pp. 59–66.

Formalization

formalization
The extent to which an organization relies on written rules and procedures to predetermine the actions of employees.

The dimension of **formalization** refers to the extent to which expectations regarding the means and ends of work are specified and written. An organizational structure that is described as highly formalized would be one in which rules and procedures are available to prescribe what each individual should be doing. Organizations with such structures would have written standard operating procedures, specified directives, and explicit policies. In terms of the four design decisions, formalization is the result of high specialization of labor, high delegation of authority, the use of functional departments, and wide spans of control.[13]

1.   High specialization of labor such as exists in the auto industry is amenable to the development of written work rules and procedures. The jobs are so specialized as to leave little to the discretion of the jobholder.

2.   High delegation of authority creates the need to have checks on its use. Consequently, the organization will write guidelines for decision making and will insist upon reports that describe the use of authority.

3.   Functional departments are made up of jobs that have great similarities. Such departments bring together members of the same occupation—accountants, engineers, machinists, and the like. Because of the similarity of the jobs and the rather straightforward nature of the functional department's activities, management can develop written documents to govern those activities.

4.   Wide spans of control discourage one-on-one supervision. There are simply too many subordinates for managers to keep up with on a one-to-one basis. Consequently, managers will require written reports to inform them.

Although formalization is defined in terms of the existence of written rules and procedures, it is important to understand how these are viewed by the employees. In organizations with all the appearances of formalization, complete with thick manuals of rules, procedures, and policies, employees may not perceive the manuals as affecting their behavior. Thus, even though rules and procedures exist, they must be enforced if they are to affect behavior.[14]

centralization
A dimension of structure that describes whether top management delegates authority to make decisions.

Centralization

Centralization refers to the location of decision-making authority in the hierarchy of the organization. More specifically, the concept

---

[13] See Peter H. Grinyear and Masoud Yasai-Ardekani, "Dimensions of Organizational Structure: A Critical Replication," *Academy of Management Journal*, September 1980, pp. 405–21, for discussion of formalization in relation to centralization.

[14] Eric J. Walton, "The Comparison of Measures of Organization Structure," *Academy of Management Review*, January 1981, pp. 155–60.

refers to the delegation of authority among the jobs in the organization. Typically, researchers and practitioners think of centralization in terms of (1) decision making and (2) control. Despite the apparent simplicity of the concept, it can be complex.

The complexity of the concept derives from three sources. First, people at the same level can have different decision-making authority. Second, not all decisions are of equal importance in organizations. For example, a typical management practice is to delegate authority to make routine operating decisions (i.e., decentralization) but to retain authority to make strategic decisions (i.e. centralization). Third, individuals may not perceive that they really have authority even though their job descriptions include it. Thus, objectively they have authority, but subjectively they do not.[15]

The relationships between centralization and the four design decisions are generally as follows:

1. The higher the specialization of labor, the greater the centralization. This relationship holds because highly specialized jobs do not require the discretion that authority provides.

2. The less the delegation of authority, the greater the centralization. By definition, centralization involves retaining authority in the top-management jobs rather than delegating it to lower levels in the organization.

3. The greater the use of functional departments, the greater the centralization. The use of functional departments requires that the activities of the interrelated departments be coordinated. Consequently, authority to coordinate them will be retained in top management.

4. The wider the spans of control, the greater the centralization. Wide spans of control are associated with relatively specialized jobs, which, as we have seen, have little need for authority.

Complexity

complexity
Describes how many different job titles and authority levels exist in an organization.

Complexity is the direct outgrowth of dividing work and creating departments. Specifically, the concept refers to the number of distinctly different job titles, or occupational groupings, and the number of distinctly different units, or departments. The fundamental idea is that organizations with a great many different kinds and types of jobs and units create more complicated managerial and organizational problems than do those with fewer jobs and departments.

Complexity, then, relates to *differences* among jobs and units. It is not surprising, therefore, that *differentiation* is often used synony-

---

[15] Jeffrey D. Ford, "Institutional versus Questionnaire Measures of Organizational Structure," *Academy of Management Journal,* September 1979, pp. 601–10.

FIGURE 12-8

**Organizational Dimensions and
Organizational Decisions**

High formalization:	Results from:	1.	High specialization
		2.	Delegated authority
		3.	Functional departments
		4.	Wide spans of control
High centralization:	Results from:	1.	High specialization
		2.	Centralized authority
		3.	Functional departments
		4.	Wide spans of control
High complexity:	Results from:	1.	High specialization
		2.	Delegated authority
		3.	Territorial, customer, and product departments
		4.	Narrow spans of control

mously with complexity. Moreover, it has become standard practice to use the term *horizontal differentiation* to refer to the number of different units at the same level;[16] *vertical differentiation* refers to the number of levels in the organization. The relationships between complexity (horizontal and vertical differentiation) and the four design decisions are generally as follows:

1. The greater the specialization of labor, the greater the complexity of the organization. Specialization is the process of creating different jobs, and thus more complexity. Specialization of labor contributes primarily to horizontal differentiation.

2. The greater the delegation of authority, the greater the complexity. Delegation of authority is typically associated with a lengthy chain of command, that is, with a relatively large number of managerial levels. Thus, delegation of authority contributes to vertical differentiation.

3. The greater the use of territorial, customer, and product bases, the greater the complexity. These bases involve the creation of self-sustaining units that operate much like freestanding organizations. Consequently, there must be considerable delegation of authority, and thus considerable complexity.[17]

4. Narrow spans of control are associated with high complexity. This relationship holds because narrow spans are necessary when the

---

[16] Richard L. Daft and Patricia J. Bradshaw, "The Process of Horizontal Differentiation: Two Models," *Administrative Science Quarterly*, September 1980, pp. 441–56.

[17] Dennis S. Mileti, Doug A. Timmer, and David F. Gillespie, "Intra- and Interorganizational Determinants of Decentralization," *Pacific Sociological Review*, April 1982, pp. 163–83, provides evidence to suggest the importance of territorial departmentalization in decentralized organizations.

jobs to be supervised are quite different from one another. A supervisor can manage more people in a simple organization than in a complex organization. Thus, as suggested by the opening Organizational Issue for Debate, the apparently simple matter of span of control can have profound effects on organizational and individual behavior. Hence, we should expect the controversy that surrounds it.

The discussion of the relationships between dimensions of organizational structure and the four design decisions is summarized in Figure 12–8. The figure notes only the causes of *high* formalization, centralization, and complexity. However, the relationships are symmetrical: the causes of *low* formalization, centralization, and complexity are the opposite of those shown in Figure 12–8.

As we will see in the next two chapters, organizations differ in their degree of formalization, centralization, and complexity. The important managerial issue is the relationship between these dimensions and individual, group, and organizational effectiveness.

SUMMARY OF KEY POINTS

A. The structure of an organization consists of relatively fixed and stable relationships among jobs and groups of jobs. The primary purpose of organizational structure is to influence the *behavior* of individuals and groups so as to achieve effective performance.

B. Four key managerial decisions determine organization structures. These decisions are dividing work, delegating authority, departmentalizing jobs into groups, and determining spans of control.

C. The four key decisions are interrelated and interdependent, although each has certain specific problems that can be considered apart from the others.

D. Dividing the overall task into smaller related tasks, jobs, depends initially on the technical and economic advantages of specialization of labor.

E. Delegating authority enables an individual to make decisions and exact obedience without approval by higher management. Like other organizing issues, delegated authority is a relative, not absolute, concept. All individuals in an organization, whether managers or nonmanagers, have some authority. The question is whether they have enough to do their jobs.

E. The grouping of jobs into departments requires the selection of common bases such as function, territory, product, or customer.

Each basis has advantages and disadvantages that must be evaluated in terms of overall effectiveness.

F. The optimal span of control is no one specific number of subordinates. Although the number of *potential* relationships increases geometrically as the number of subordinates increases arithmetically, the important considerations are the frequency and intensity of the actual relationships.

G. Organizational structures differ as a consequence of the four management decisions. In order to measure these differences, it is necessary to identify measurable attributes, or dimensions, of structure. Three often used dimensions are complexity, centralization, and formalization.

H. Complexity refers to the extent to which the jobs in the organization are relatively specialized; centralization refers to the extent to which authority is retained in the jobs of top management; and formalization refers to the extent to which policies, rules, and procedures exist in written form.

DISCUSSION AND REVIEW QUESTIONS

1. Describe the process of designing an organization by discussing how the manager of a retail store would analyze the four subproblems of the design decision.

2. Compare functional and product departmentalization in terms of relative efficiency, production, satisfaction, adaptiveness, and development. Consider particularly the possibility that one basis may be superior in achieving one aspect of effectiveness, yet inferior in achieving another.

3. Describe the process by which a business firm changes its departmental bases as it grows in size.

4. Discuss the statement that in order to manage effectively a person must have the authority to hire subordinates, assign them to specific jobs, and reward them on the basis of performance. Interview any chairperson of an academic department, and determine whether he or she has this authority.

5. The terms *responsibility, authority,* and *ac-* *countability* appear in the management and organization literature. What is your understanding of these terms? Are they different? Do they refer to fundamental questions of organizational design.

6. How can a manager know that the organizational design is ineffective? Is there any difference between *designing* and *changing* organizational structure? Explain.

7. Explain the relationships between decentralization and divisional organizational structures. Is it possible to create divisional organizations without delegating considerable authority to divisional managers? Explain.

8. Explain how you could use the three dimensions of structure to compare two organizations.

9. Describe the managerial skills and behaviors that would be required to manage effectively in a functional department. Are these skills and behaviors different from those required in a product department? Explain.

ADDITIONAL REFERENCES

Allen, R. W., and L. W. Porter. *Organizational Influence Processes.* Glenview, Ill.: Scott, Foresman, 1983.

Argyris, C. *Integrating the Individual and the Organization.* New York: John Wiley & Sons, 1964.

Blau, P. M. *On the Nature of Organizations.* New York: John Wiley & Sons, 1974.

Chandler, A. D., Jr. *Strategy and Structure.* Cambridge, Mass.: MIT Press, 1962.

Daft, R. L. *Organization Theory.* St. Paul, Minn.: West Publishing, 1983.

Galbraith, J. *Organization Design.* Reading, Mass.: Addison-Wesley Publishing, 1977.

Hall, R. H. *Organizations: Structure and Process.* Englewood Cliffs, N.J.: Prentice-Hall, 1977.

Hrebiniak, L. G. *Complex Organizations.* St. Paul, Minn.: West Publishing, 1978.

Jackson, J. H., and C. Morgan. *Organization Theory.* Englewood Cliffs, N.J.: Prentice-Hall, 1978.

Kilmann, R. H.; L. R. Pondy; and D. P. Slevin, eds. *The Management of Organization Design: Strategies and Implementation,* vol. 1. New York: Elsevier-North Holland Publishing, 1976.

Krupp, S. *Pattern in Organization Analysis: A Critical Examination.* New York: Holt, Rinehart, & Winston, 1961.

Kuhn, A., and R. D. Beam. *The Logic of Organization.* San Francisco: Jossey-Bass, 1982.

Meyer, M. W. *Theory of Organization Structure.* Indianapolis, Ind.: Bobbs-Merrill, 1977.

Miner, J. B. *Theories of Organizational Structure and Processes.* New York: CBS Educational and Professional Publishing, 1982.

Mintzberg, H. *Structure in Fives: Designing Effective Organizations.* Englewood Cliffs, N.J.: Prentice-Hall, 1983.

Morris, J. H.; R. M. Steers; and J. L. Koch. "Influence of Organizational Structure on Role Conflict and Ambiguity for Three Occupational Groupings." *Academy of Management Journal,* 1979, pp. 58–71.

Nystrom, P. C., and W. H. Starbuck. *Handbook of Organizational Design,* vols. 1 and 2. New York: Oxford University Press, 1983.

Perkins, D. N. T.; V. F. Nieva; and E. E. Lawler III. *Managing Creation: The Challenge of Building a New Organization.* New York: John Wiley and Sons, 1983.

Pfeffer, J. *Organizations and Organization Theory.* Marshfield, Mass.: Pitman Publishing, 1982.

Sathe, V. "Institutional versus Questionnaire Measures of Organizational Structure." *Academy of Management Journal,* 1978, pp. 227–38.

Scott, W. R. *Organizations: Rational, Natural, and Open Systems.* Englewood Cliffs, N.J.: Prentice-Hall, 1981.

Tosi, H. *Theories of Organization.* New York: John Wiley & Sons, 1984.

Urwick, L. F. "V. A. Graicunas and the Span of Control." *Academy of Management Journal,* 1974, pp. 349–54.

Zey-Ferrell, M. *Dimensions of Organizations: Environment, Context, Structure, Process, and Performance.* Santa Monica, Calif.: Goodyear Publishing, 1979.

CASE FOR ANALYSIS

Selecting between Function and Product as Basis for Departmentalization

Recently, the top management of a rapidly expanding consumer products company met to consider organizational issues. The present organization structure was departmentalized according to functions as shown in Exhibit 1.

The company's product line had expanded some 10 times during the previous 16 years, and although the current economic conditions caused some concern, management believed that the company's products were well established. Moreover, it anticipated even greater expansion during the next 20 years.

The present organization structure was the topic of discussion, because despite the growth and success of prior years management believed that in many instances the company had not been as responsive to opportunities as it might have been. Changes in consumer tastes, new manufacturing techniques, and engineering breakthroughs had not been exploited because of apparent isolation of the functional departments from the rest of the company. Each of the functional departments tended to emphasize its own goals and objectives; if new developments had not been included in the annually prepared operating plan, they could not be acted upon. Top management believed that it should attempt to restructure the organization to emphasize the importance of its products.

The organizational planning staff, a part of the personnel function, was instructed to prepare an analysis of alternative structures. It returned six months later with the recommendation that the company adopt a product-based structure. The structure, often termed a *divisional organization structure,* would place under the authority of a single manager all of the functions necessary to produce and sell a product or a line of products. The recommended structure is shown in Exhibit 2.

Reporting to each vice president would be the heads of the marketing, production, finance, engineering, and personnel departments. These function heads would carry out the work necessary to produce and sell one or more

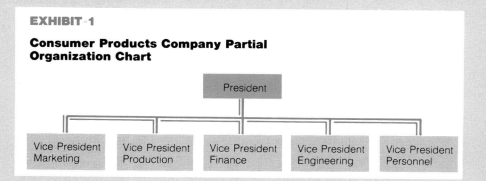

EXHIBIT·1

Consumer Products Company Partial Organization Chart

President

| Vice President Marketing | Vice President Production | Vice President Finance | Vice President Engineering | Vice President Personnel |

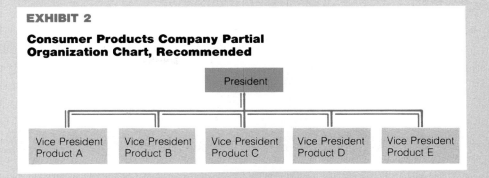

EXHIBIT 2

Consumer Products Company Partial Organization Chart, Recommended

complementary products. The organizational planning staff stated that its review of the literature on organizational structure indicated that product-based organizations were superior to function-based organizations in their ability to respond to external changes, but that they were somewhat less efficient. The impact of the recommended structure on the profit and loss statement would be slightly higher unit costs because the size of the individual units would not be sufficient to take advantage of the economies of scale. It would also mean that the functional experts would have to be less specialized. For example, the marketing personnel would have to become involved in product development as well as selling. But the advantages of increased adaptability should offset the disadvantages of reduced efficiency.

The potential impact of the product-based organization on the satisfaction of employees was noted. According to the staff, the employees would suffer some decrease in satisfaction and some increase in feelings of stress because they would have to orient their thinking toward the products and away from their specialties. The specialists would have to interact more often with other specialists in the integration of their functions. Consequently, some of the bases for positive job satisfaction would be undermined. The staff could not predict how the reduction in satisfaction would affect turnover, absenteeism, or tardiness. It did state that employees should experience a greater sense of involvement in the total operations of the product departments.

Questions for Consideration

1. Has the organizational planning staff moved in the right direction in its analysis? Is its recommended structure appropriate, given the nature of the company's environment?

2. How can management determine the relative advantages of the proposed organization if it cannot determine the relationships among the measures of effectiveness?

3. What differences in the two structures other than those identified by the staff would you expect?

Chapter 13

After completing Chapter 13, you should be able to:

Define job design.

Describe alternative job redesign approaches that organizations use to improve job performance.

Discuss the various factors and relationships that link job design and job performance.

Compare job enrichment, job enlargement, and job redesign strategies.

Identify specific individual differences that account for different perceptions of job content.

Job Design

Job Redesign: Was It Successful?*

Argument For

General Foods Corporation's new pet-food plant in Topeka, Kansas, was designed to minimize supervision by delegating authority to workers to make job assignments,

* Based on Richard E. Walton, "The Topeka Work System: Optimistic Visions, Pessimistic Hypotheses, and Reality," in *The Innovative Organization*, ed. Robert Zager and Michael P. Rosow (Elmsford, N.Y.: Pergamon Press, 1982), pp. 260–87.

schedule coffee breaks, interview prospective employees, and decide pay raises. The system, installed in the plant by a company task force with the assistance of Richard E. Walton, Harvard University, assigns three areas of responsibility—processing, packaging and shipping, and office duties—to self-managing teams of 7 to 14 workers.

The teams, directed by a "team leader," share responsibility for a variety of tasks, including tasks typically performed by staff personnel, for example, equipment maintenance and quality control. The team members rotate between dreary and meaningful jobs. Pay is related to the number of tasks that each individual masters. The teams performed much of the work assigned to managerial and staff personnel. As stated by J. W. Bevans, Jr., manager of organizational development, the system attempted "to balance the needs of the people with the needs of the business."

449

The success of the program is unquestionable according to the former manager of pet-food operations, Layman D. Ketchum: "From the standpoint of humanistic working life and economic results, you can consider it a success." As evidence of the claim, the plant's unit costs are 5 percent less than those of comparable sites, amounting to an annual saving of $1 million. Employee turnover is only 8 percent, and the plant went for almost four years before experiencing a lost-time accident.

Argument Against

Whether General Foods' experience with job redesign was successful depends on whom you talk to. One employee states emphatically, "The system went to hell. It didn't work." According to the critics, problems arose because the system came up against the company's bureaucracy. Lawyers, fearing reactions from the National Labor Relations Board, opposed allowing workers to vote on pay raises. Personnel managers resented having workers make hiring decisions; engineers resented having workers do engineering work. These resentments resulted in power struggles among and between corporate-level staff, plant managers, and workers. Several managers, including three from the pet-food plant itself, quit General Foods.

As a consequence of the pressures, the Topeka system began to change—workers participated less, job classifications were added, and supervisors supervised. These changes were perceived as a weakening of management's commitment to the philosophy underlying the system. Quality has dipped; teams have fewer team meetings; and competition among shifts has increased. A major contribution to competition has been jealousy, particularly as reflected in pay decisions. Workers have found it particularly difficult to discard their subjective judgments of friends when considering their work performance. Workers at Topeka have also argued that they should share in the financial success of Topeka through the provision of bonuses tied to cost savings.

The critics observe that their negative evaluations of the Topeka system must have merit. They note as evidence that General Foods no longer permits reporters inside the Topeka plant despite the fact that management once encouraged publicity. The critics also point out that the Topeka system has not been implemented in any other General Foods plant. One manager has predicted that "the future of that plant [Topeka] is to conform to the company norm."

The building blocks of organizational structures are the jobs that people perform. There are many causes of individual, group, and organizational effectiveness. A major cause is the job performance of employees. Job design refers to the process by which managers decide individual job tasks and authority. Apart from the very practical issues associated with job design, that is, issues that relate to effectiveness in economic, political, and monetary terms, we can appreciate its importance in social and psychological terms. As noted in earlier chapters, jobs can be sources of psychological stress and even mental and physical impairment. On a more positive note, jobs can provide income, meaningful life experiences, self-esteem, esteem from others, regulation of our lives, and association with others.[1] Thus, the well-being of organizations and people depends on how well management is able to design jobs.

JOB DESIGN AND QUALITY OF WORK-LIFE

In recent years, the issue of designing jobs has gone beyond the determination of the most efficient way to perform tasks. The concept of quality of work-life is now widely used to refer to "the degree to which members of work organizations are able to satisfy important personal needs through their experiences in organizations."[2] The emphasis on satisfaction of personal needs does not imply de-emphasis of organizational needs. Instead, contemporary managers are finding that when the personal needs of employees are satisfied, the performance of the organization itself is enhanced.

As America moves into the mid-1980s, the challenge to managers is to provide for both quality of work-life and improved production and efficiency through reindustrialization. At present, the trade-offs between the gains in human terms from improved quality of work-life and the gains in economic terms from reindustrialization are not fully known. There are those who believe that it will be necessary to defer quality of work-life efforts so as to make the American economy more productive and efficient.[3] Others observe that reindustrialization can present opportunities to combine quality of work-life with reindustrialization efforts.[4]

---

[1] David F. Smith, "The Functions of Work," *Omega*, 1975, pp. 383–93.

[2] J. Richard Hackman and J. Lloyd Suttle, eds., *Improving Life at Work* (Santa Monica, Calif.: Goodyear Publishing, 1977), p. 4.

[3] Amitai Etzioni, "Choose America Must—Between 'Reindustrialization and Quality of Life,'" *Across the Board*, October 1980, pp. 43–49.

[4] D. J. Skrovan, ed., *Quality of Work Life* (Reading, Mass.: Addison-Wesley Publishing, 1983).

Job design and redesign techniques attempt (1) to identify the most important needs of employees and the organization and (2) to remove obstacles in the workplace that frustrate those needs. Managers hope that the results are jobs that (1) fulfill important individual needs and (2) contribute to individual, group, and organizational effectiveness. The Organizational Issue for Debate that opens this chapter notes that managers are, in fact, redesigning jobs and job settings. But whether the outcomes of those managerial actions are positive is debatable. Obviously, designing and redesigning jobs is complex. The remainder of this chapter reviews the important theories, research, and practices of job design. As will be seen, contemporary management has at its disposal a wide range of techniques that facilitate the achievement of personal and organizational performance.

A CONCEPTUAL MODEL OF JOB DESIGN

The conceptual model depicted in Figure 13–1 is based on the extensive research literature that has appeared in the last 20 years. The model includes the various terms and concepts that appear in the current literature. When linked together, these concepts describe the important determinants of job performance and organizational effectiveness. The model takes into account a number of sources of complexity. It recognizes that individuals react differently to jobs. While one person may derive positive satisfaction from a job, another may not. It also recognizes the difficult trade-offs between organizational and individual needs. For example, the technology of manufacturing (an

FIGURE 13–1

Job Design and Job Performance

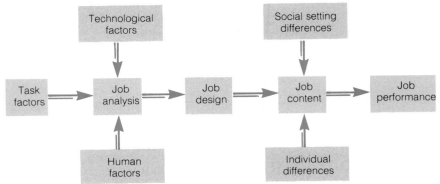

environmental difference) may dictate that management adopt assembly-line mass-production methods and low-skilled jobs to achieve optimal efficiency. Such jobs, however, may result in great unrest and worker discontent. Perhaps these costs could be avoided by a more careful balancing of organizational and individual needs.

The ideas reflected in Figure 13–1 are the bases for this chapter. We will present each important factor that is the cause or the effect of job design, beginning with job analysis.

JOB ANALYSIS

Job analysis is the process of decision making that translates task, human, and technological factors into job designs. Either managers or personnel specialists undertake the process, and a number of approaches exist to assist them. Two of the more widely used approaches are functional job analysis (FJA) and the position analysis questionnaire (PAQ).

Functional Job Analysis

functional job analysis
The classification of jobs according to task and technology factors. It focuses on what the worker does, what methods and medium the worker uses, and what the worker produces.

Functional job analysis focuses attention on task and technological factors. FJA directs attention to the following four aspects of each job or class of jobs:

1. What the worker *does* in relation to data, people, and jobs.
2. What *methods* and *techniques* the worker uses.
3. What *machines, tools,* and *equipment* the worker uses.
4. What *materials, products, subject matter,* or *services* the worker produces.

The first three aspects relate to job *activities.* The fourth aspect relates to job *performance.* FJA provides descriptions of jobs that can be the bases for classifying jobs according to any one of the four dimensions. In addition to defining what activities, methods, and machines make up the job, FJA also defines what the individual doing the job should produce. FJA can, therefore, be the basis for defining standards of performance.

FJA is the most popular and widely used of the job analysis methods.[5] In addition, it is the basis for the most extensive available list of occupational titles.[6]

---

[5] Marc J. Wallace, Jr., N. Fredric Crandall, and Charles H. Fay, *Administering Human Resources* (New York: Random House, 1982), p. 196.

[6] U.S. Department of Labor, *Dictionary of Occupational Titles,* 4th ed. (Washington, D.C.: U.S. Government Printing Office, 1977).

Position Analysis Questionnaire

position analysis questionnaire
The classification of jobs according to human *and* task and technology factors. It focuses on informational and interpersonal requirements as well as physical requirements and working conditions.

The **position analysis questionnaire** takes into account human as well as task and technological factors. PAQ has been the object of considerable attention by researchers and practitioners who believe that accurate job analysis must take human factors into account.[7] PAQ analysis attempts to identify the following six job aspects:

1. Information sources critical to job performance.
2. Information processing and decision making critical to job performance.
3. Physical activity and dexterity required of the job.
4. Interpersonal relationships required of the job.
5. Physical working conditions and the reactions of individuals to those conditions.
6. Other job characteristics such as work schedule and work responsibilities.

It is important to note that FJA and PAQ overlap considerably. Each attempts to identify job activities that are necessary, given the task to be done and the technology to do it with. But PAQ also considers the individual's psychological responses to the job and its environment. Thus, PAQ acknowledges that job designs should combine the effects of all three factors.

Numerous methods exist to perform job analysis. PAQ and FJA appear to be two of the most popular ones. A recent survey of the opinions of expert job analysts bear out the popularity of PAQ and FJA. But the survey also suggests that different methods make different contributions to organizational purposes.[8]

Job Analysis in Different Settings

People perform their jobs in a variety of settings. It is not possible to discuss all of the settings. We will, instead, discuss two significant job settings—the factory and the office. One has historical significance; the other has future significance.

Jobs in the Factory. Job analysis began in the factory. Industrialization created the setting in which individuals performed many hundreds of specialized jobs. The earliest attempts to do job analysis followed the ideas advanced by the proponents of scientific management.

---

[7] E. J. McCormick, P. R. Jeanneret, and R. C. Mecham, "A Study of Job Characteristics and Job Dimensions as Based on the Position Analysis Questionnaire (PAQ)," *Journal of Applied Psychology*, August 1972, pp. 347–68.

[8] Edward L. Levine, Ronald A. Ash, Hardy Hall, and Frank Sistrunk, "Evaluation of Job Analysis Methods by Experienced Job Analysts," *Academy of Management Journal*, June 1983, pp. 339–48.

They were industrial engineers who, at the turn of the 20th century, began to devise ways to analyze industrial jobs.

The major theme of scientific management was that objective analyses of facts and data collected in the workplace could provide the bases for determining the *one best way* to design work.[9] F. W. Taylor stated the essence of scientific management as follows:

> First: Develop a science for each element of a man's work which replaces the old rule-of-thumb method.
>
> Second: Scientifically select and then train, teach, and develop the workman, whereas in the past he chose his own work and trained himself as best he could.
>
> Third: Heartily cooperate with the men so as to insure all of the work being done in accordance with the principles of the science which has been developed.
>
> Fourth: There is almost an equal division of the work and the responsibility between the management and the workmen. The management takes over all work for which they are better fitted than the workmen, while in the past, almost all of the work and the greater part of the responsibility were thrown upon the men.[10]

These four principles express the theme of scientific management methods. Management should take into account task and technology to determine the best way to do each job and then train people to do the job that way.

Scientific management produced many techniques that are in current use. Motion and time study, work simplification, and standard methods are at the core of job analysis in factory settings. Functional job analysis reflects the scientific management philosophy in that it excludes consideration of the human factor.

Jobs in the Office. In the short space of time since the advent of scientific management, the American economy has shifted from factory-oriented to office-oriented work. The fastest growing segment of jobs is secretarial, clerical, and information work. The growth of these jobs is due to technological breakthroughs in both factory and office settings.

Technological breakthroughs in automation, robotics, and computer-assisted manufacturing have reduced the need for industrial jobs. But

---

[9] The literature of scientific management is voluminous. The original works and the subsequent criticisms and interpretations would make a large volume. Of special significance are the works of the principal authors, including Frederick W. Taylor, *Principles of Scientific Management* (New York: Harper & Row, 1911); Harrington Emerson, *The Twelve Principles of Efficiency* (New York: Engineering Magazine, 1913); Henry L. Gantt, *Industrial Leadership* (New Haven, Conn.: Yale University Press, 1916); Frank B. Gilbreth, *Motion Study* (New York: D. Van Nostrand, 1911); and Lillian M. Gilbreth, *The Psychology of Management* (New York: Sturgis & Walton, 1914).

[10] Taylor, *Principles*, pp. 36–37.

those same breakthroughs have increased the need for office jobs. However, the modern office is not a mere extension of the traditional factory.

The modern office reflects the new computer technology. Its most striking feature is the replacement of paper with some electronic medium, usually a visual display terminal (VDT). One individual interacts with the VDT to do a variety and quantity of tasks that in earlier times would have required many individuals. A significant aspect of job analysis in modern offices is the creation of *work modules*, interrelated tasks that can be assigned to a single individual. The following Close-Up describes the work module approach in the "back office" of a large bank.

ORGANIZATIONS: CLOSE-UP

Work Modules at Continental Illinois National Bank & Trust Company

Christine Szczesniak, a Continental Illinois National Bank and Trust employee, worked for 17 years doing one task over and over. She and her co-employees sat at one position on a check-processing line. Day in and day out, she processed hundreds of checks. She was a highly competent and productive employee, but now she is even more productive. As a consequence of changes in job designs at the bank, Christine works at a computer terminal and performs a complete work module. She completes all of the tasks necessary to handle checks sent in by companies that do business with Continental's corporate clients. She now processes checks that arrive in the mail, deposits them in customers' accounts, and informs clients of the current status of their accounts. Her expanded job was made possible not only by computer technology, but also by management's willingness to redefine her job. Christine remarks that she is more satisfied with her new job because she sees the work from beginning to end. Not only is the work more satisfying, but her error ratio has also been reduced. Thus, the work module has not only provided a more satisfying job; it has also provided a more efficient one.

Source: "A Work Revolution in U.S. Industry," *Business Week*, May 16, 1983, p. 103.

Not all experiences with VDT have been positive. In recent times, managers and researchers have found that human factors must be given special attention when analyzing jobs in the electronic office. VDT operators report that they suffer problems such as headaches, "burning" eyes, and shoulder and backaches.[11] The sources of these problems seem to be in the design of the workplace, particularly the interaction between the individual and the VDT.

Job analysis in the office must pay particular attention to human factors. The tendency is to overemphasize the technological factor—in this case, the computer—and to analyze jobs only as extensions of the technology. As was true of job analysis in factories, it is simply easier to deal with the relatively fixed nature of tasks and technology than to deal with the variable human nature.[12]

JOB DESIGNS

Job designs are the results of job analysis. They specify three characteristics of jobs: range, depth, and relationships.

Range and Depth

range
Job range varies from few to many different tasks. Jobs with relatively few tasks are more specialized than those with many tasks.

depth
Job depth varies from little to considerable discretion in the choice of activities and outcomes. Relatively little depth is a characteristic of relatively specialized jobs.

The **range** of a job refers to the number of tasks that a jobholder performs. The person who performs eight tasks to complete a job has a wider job range than does the person who performs four tasks. In most instances, the greater the number of tasks performed, the longer it takes to complete the job.

A second job characteristic is **depth,** the amount of discretion that an individual has to decide job activities and job outcomes. In many instances, job range relates to personal influence as well as delegated authority. Thus, an employee with the same job title and at the same organizational level as another employee may possess more, less, or the same amount of job depth because of personal influence.

Job range and depth distinguish one job from another not only within the same organization but also among different organizations. To illustrate how jobs differ in range and depth, Figure 13–2 depicts the differences for selected jobs of business firms, hospitals, and universities. For example, business research scientists, hospital chiefs of surgery, and university presidents generally have high job range and significant job depth. Research scientists perform a large number of tasks and are usually not closely supervised. Chiefs of surgery have significant job range in that they oversee and counsel on many diverse surgical matters. In addition, they are not supervised closely and they

---

[11] Barbara S. Brown, Key Dismukes, and Edward J. Rinalducci, "Video Display Terminals and Vision of Workers: Summary and Review of a Symposium," *Behavior and Information Technology,* April–June 1982, pp. 121–40.

[12] David A. Buchanon and David Boddy, "Advanced Technology and the Quality of Working Life: The Effects of Word Processing on Video Typists," *Journal of Occupational Psychology,* March 1982, pp. 1–11; and Walter B. Kleeman, "The Future of the Office," *Environment and Behavior,* September 1982, pp. 593–610.

FIGURE 13-2

Job Depth and Range

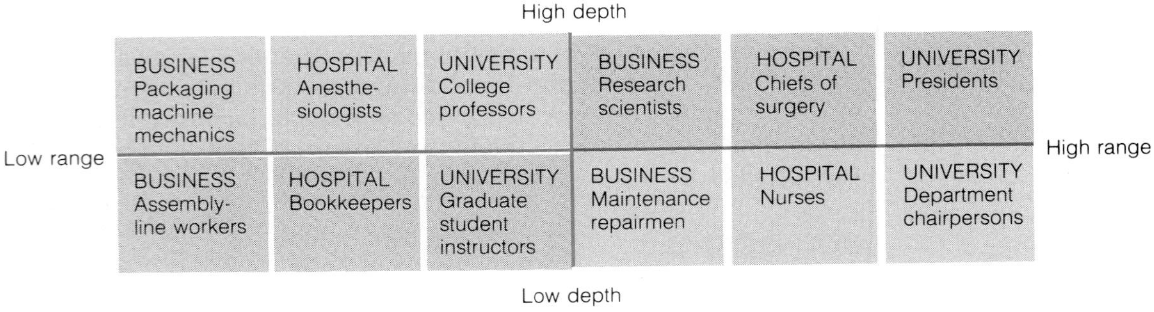

have the authority to influence hospital surgery policies and procedures.

University presidents have a large number of tasks to perform. They speak to alumni groups, politicians, community representatives, and students. They develop, in consultation with others, policies on admissions, fund raising, and adult education. They can alter the faculty recruitment philosophy and thus alter the course of the entire institution. For example, a university president may want to build an institution that is noted for high-quality classroom instruction and for the excellent services that it provides to the community. This thrust may lead to recruiting and selecting professors who want to concentrate on these two specific goals. In contrast, another president may want to foster outstanding research and high-quality classroom instruction. Of course, still another president may attempt to develop an institution that is noted for instruction, research, and service. The critical point is that university presidents have sufficient job depth to alter the course of a university's direction.

Examples of jobs that have high depth and low range are those of packaging machine mechanics, anesthesiologists, and faculty members. Mechanics perform the limited tasks that pertain to repairing and maintaining packaging machines. But they can decide how breakdowns on the packaging machines are to be repaired. This discretion means that the mechanics have relatively high job depth.

Anesthesiologists also perform a limited number of tasks. They are concerned with the rather restricted task of administering anesthetics to patients. However, they can decide what type of anesthetic will be administered in a particular situation, a decision indicative of high job depth.

University professors specifically engaged in classroom instruction have relatively low job range. Teaching involves comparatively more tasks than the work of the anesthesiologist, but fewer tasks than the work of the business research scientist. However, the job depth of professors is greater than that of graduate student instructors. This follows from the fact that they determine how they will conduct the class, what materials will be presented, and what standards will be used in evaluating students. Graduate students typically do not have complete freedom in the choice of class materials and procedures. Professors decide these matters for them.

Highly specialized jobs are those that have few tasks to accomplish and use prescribed means to accomplish them. Such jobs are quite routine; they also tend to be controlled by specified rules and procedures (low depth). A highly despecialized job (high range) has many tasks to accomplish and discretion regarding means and ends (high depth). Within an organization, there are typically great differences among jobs in both range and depth. Although there are no precise equations that managers can use to decide job range and depth, they can follow this guideline: Given the economic and technical requirements of the organization's mission, goals, and objectives, what is the optimal point along the continuum of range and depth for each job?

Job Relationships

Job relationships are determined by managers' decisions regarding departmentalization bases and spans of control. It becomes the manager's responsibility to coordinate the resulting groups toward organizational purposes. The decisions regarding departmentalization bases and spans of control determine the nature and extent of jobholders' interpersonal relationships, individually and within groups. As we have already seen in the discussion of groups in organizations, group performance is effected in part by group cohesiveness. And the degree of group cohesiveness depends on the quality and kinds of interpersonal relationships established by jobholders assigned to a task or command group.

The wider the span of control, the larger is the group and consequently the more difficult it is to establish friendship and interest relationships. People in larger groups are less likely to communicate (and interact sufficiently to form interpersonal ties) than people in smaller groups. Without the opportunity to communicate, people will be unable to establish cohesive work groups. Thus, an important source of satisfaction may be lost for individuals who seek to fulfill social and esteem needs through relationships with co-workers.

The basis for departmentalization that management selects also has important implications for job relationships. The functional basis places jobs with similar depth and range in the same groups, while the product, territory, and customer bases place jobs with dissimilar depth and range in the same groups. Thus, people in functional departments will have much the same specialty. Product, territory, and customer departments, however, comprise heterogeneous jobs. Individuals who work in heterogeneous departments experience feelings of dissatisfaction, stress, and involvement more intensely than do individuals who work in homogeneous, functional departments. People with homogeneous backgrounds, skills, and training have more common interests than do people whose backgrounds, skills, and training are heterogeneous. Thus, it is easier for them to establish satisfying social relationships with less stress, but also with less involvement in the department's activities.

Job designs describe the *objective* characteristics of jobs. That is, through job analysis techniques such as FJA and PAQ, managers can describe jobs in terms of the activities required to produce a specified outcome. But before we can understand the relationship between jobs and performance, we must consider yet another factor—job content.

JOB CONTENT

Taylor proposed that the way to improve work, that is, to make it more efficient, is to determine (1) the "best way" to do a task (motion study) and (2) the standard time for completion of the task (time study). Motion study determines preferred work activities in relation to raw materials, product design, order of work, tools, equipment, and workplace layout. Time study determines the preferred time for performing each job activity. Through motion and time study, practitioners of scientific management design jobs solely in terms of technical data.

The belief that the design of a job can be based solely on technical data ignores the very large role played by the individual who performs the job. In this section, the issue of **job content** is examined. As we will see, the manner in which individuals react to their jobs depends on their unique characteristics.

job content
The characteristics of a job as perceived by the individuals who perform them. Job characteristics can have both objective and subjective properties.

Job content refers to the aspects of a job that define its general nature as *perceived by the jobholder as influenced by the social setting.* It is important to distinguish between the *objective* properties of jobs and the *subjective* properties of jobs as reflected in the perceptions of the people who perform them.[13] Managers cannot understand the causes of job performance without considering such individual differences as personality, needs, and span of attention.[14] According to Fig-

---

[13] Kenneth R. Brousseau, "Toward a Dynamic Model of Job-Person Relationships: Findings, Research Questions, and Implications for Work System Design," *Academy of Management Review,* January 1983, pp. 33–45.

[14] Donald P. Schwab and L. L. Cummings, "A Theoretical Analysis of the Impact of Task Scope on Employee Performance," *Academy of Management Review,* April 1976, pp. 31–32.

ure 13–1, job content precedes job performance. Thus, if managers desire to increase job performance by changing job content, they can change job design, individual perceptions, or social settings—all of which are causes of job content.

If management is to understand perceived job content, some method for measuring it must exist.[15] In response to this need, organizational behavior researchers have attempted to measure job content in a variety of work settings. The methods that researchers use rely on questionnaires, completed by jobholders, that measure the jobholders' perceptions of certain job *characteristics*.

Job Characteristics

The pioneering effort to measure job content through employee responses to a questionnaire resulted in the identification of six characteristics: variety, autonomy, required interaction, optional interaction, knowledge and skill required, and responsibility.[16] The index of these six characteristics is termed the Requisite Task Attribute Index (RTAI). The original RTAI has been extensively reviewed and analyzed. One important development was the review by Hackman and Lawler, who revised the index to include the six characteristics shown in Table 13–1.[17]

Variety, task identity, and *feedback* are perceptions of job range; *autonomy* is the perception of job depth; and *dealing with others* and *friendship opportunities* reflect perceptions of job relationships. Employees sharing similar perceptions, job designs, and social settings should report similar job characteristics. Employees whose perceptions are different, however, report different job characteristics of the *same* job. For example, an individual with a high need for social belonging would perceive "friendship opportunities" differently than would another individual with a low need for social belonging.

Measuring Job Content

Two approaches currently exist to measure perceived job content. The Job Characteristics Index (JCI) attempts to measure jobholders'

---

[15] Thomas W. Ferratt, Randall B. Dunham, and Jon L. Pierce, "Self-Report Measures of Job Characteristics and Affective Responses: An Examination of Discriminant Validity," *Academy of Management Journal,* December 1981, pp. 780–94.

[16] Arthur N. Turner and Paul R. Lawrence, *Industrial Jobs and the Worker: An Investigation of Response to Task Attributes* (Cambridge, Mass.: Harvard University Press, 1965).

[17] J. Richard Hackman and Edward W. Lawler III, "Employee Reactions to Job Characteristics," *Journal of Applied Psychology,* June 1971, pp. 259–86; and J. Richard Hackman and Greg R. Oldham, "Development of the Job Diagnostic Survey," *Journal of Applied Psychology,* April 1975, pp. 159–70.

TABLE 13-1

Selected Job Characteristics

Variety. The degree to which a job requires employees to perform a wide range of operations in their work and/or the degree to which employees must use a variety of equipment and procedures in their work.

Autonomy. The extent to which employees have a major say in scheduling their work, selecting the equipment they will use, and deciding on procedures to be followed.

Task identity. The extent to which employees do an entire or whole piece of work and can clearly identify with the results of their efforts.

Feedback. The degree to which employees, as they are working, receive information that reveals how well they are performing on the job.

Dealing with others. The degree to which a job requires employees to deal with other people to complete their work.

Friendship opportunities. The degree to which a job allows employees to talk with one another on the job and to establish informal relationships with other employees at work.

Source: Henry P. Sims, Jr., Andrew D. Szilagyi, and Robert T. Keller, "The Measurement of Job Characteristics," *Academy of Management Journal*, June 1976, p. 197.

perceptions of the six characteristics shown in Table 13–1.[18] A more widely used approach is the Job Diagnostic Survey (JDS).[19] The JDS measures variety, autonomy, task identity, feedback, and significance. Unlike the JCI, which includes job relationship dimensions, the JDS attempts to measure only the "core" dimensions of job content. In doing so, it includes an additional dimension, significance, which reflects the perceived importance of the work to the organization or to others. The JDS has been widely used by researchers,[20] although some evidence exists that the JCI is an alternative measure.[21] Subsequent studies will no doubt improve the measurement of job content, but it is doubtful that any perceptual measurement will ever eliminate the effects of individual differences. The effect of individual differences is to "provide filters such that different persons perceive the same objective stimuli in different manners."[22]

[18] Henry P. Sims, Jr., Andrew Szilagyi, and Robert T. Keller, "The Measurement of Job Characteristics," *Academy of Management Journal*, June 1976, pp. 195–212.

[19] Hackman and Oldham, "Development of the Job Diagnostic Survey."

[20] K. H. Roberts and W. Glick, "The Job Characteristics Approach to Task Design: A Critical Review," *Journal of Applied Psychology*, April 1981, pp. 193–217; and Ramon J. Aldag, Steve H. Barr, and Arthur P. Brief, "Measurement of Perceived Task Characteristics," *Psychological Bulletin*, November 1981, pp. 415–31.

[21] Jon L. Pierce and Randall B. Dunham, "The Measurement of Perceived Job Characteristics: The Job Diagnostic Survey versus the Job Characteristics Inventory," *Academy of Management Journal*, March 1978, pp. 123–28.

[22] Randall B. Dunham, Ramon J. Aldag, and Arthur P. Brief, "Dimensionality of Task Design as Measured by the Job Diagnostic Survey," *Academy of Management Journal*, June 1977, p. 222.

Individual differences in need strength, particularly the strength of growth needs, have been shown to influence the perception of task variety. Employees with relatively weak higher order needs are less concerned with performing a variety of tasks than are employees with relatively strong growth needs. Thus, managers expecting higher performance to result from increased task variety would be disappointed if the jobholders did not have strong growth needs. Even individuals with strong growth needs cannot respond continuously to the opportunity to perform more and more tasks. At some point, performance turns down as these individuals reach the limits imposed by their abilities and time. For such individuals, the relationship between performance and task variety is likely to be curvilinear.[23]

Differences in the social settings of work also affect perceptions of job content. Examples of such differences include leadership style[24] and what other people say about the job.[25] More than one research study has pointed out that how one perceives a job is greatly affected by what other people say about it. Thus, if one's friends state that their jobs are boring, one is likely to state that his or her job is also boring. If the individual perceives the job as boring, job performance would no doubt suffer. Job content, then, results from the interaction of many factors in the work situation.

JOB PERFORMANCE

Job performance includes a number of outcomes. In this section, we will discuss performance outcomes that have value to the organization and to the individual.

Objective Outcomes

Quantity and quality of output, absenteeism, tardiness, and turnover are objective outcomes that can be measured in quantitative terms. For each job, implicit or explicit standards exist for each of these objective outcomes. Industrial engineering studies establish standards for daily quantity, and quality control specialists establish tolerance limits for acceptable quality. These aspects of job performance account

---

[23] Joseph E. Champoux, "A Three Sample Test of Some Extensions to the Job Characteristics Model of Work Motivation," *Academy of Management Journal*, September 1980, pp. 466–78.

[24] Ricky W. Griffin, "Supervisory Behavior as a Source of Perceived Task Scope," *Journal of Occupational Psychology*, September 1981, pp. 175–82.

[25] Joe Thomas and Ricky W. Griffin, "The Social Information Processing Model of Task Design: A Review of the Literature," *Academy of Management Review*, October 1983, pp. 672–82; Ricky W. Griffin, "Objective and Subjective Sources of Information in Task Redesign: A Field Experiment," *Administrative Science Quarterly*, June 1983, pp. 184–200; and Jeffrey Pfeffer, "A Partial Test of the Social Information-Processing Model of Job Attitudes," *Human Relations*, July 1980, pp. 457–76.

for characteristics of the product, client, or service for which the job-holder is responsible. But job performance includes other outcomes.

Personal Behavior Outcomes

The jobholder reacts to the work itself by either attending regularly or being absent, by staying with the job, or by quitting. Moreover, physiological and health-related problems can be consequences of job performance. Stress related to job performance can contribute to physical and mental impairment. Accidents and occupationally related disease can also result from job performance.

Intrinsic and Extrinsic Outcomes

Job outcomes may be intrinsic or extrinsic. The distinction between intrinsic and extrinsic outcomes is important for understanding the reactions of people to their jobs.[26] In a general sense, intrinsic outcomes are objects or events that follow from the worker's own efforts and do not require the involvement of any other person. More simply, they are outcomes that are clearly related to action on the worker's part. Such outcomes are typically thought to be solely in the province of professional and technical jobs; yet all jobs potentially have opportunities for intrinsic outcomes. Intrinsic outcomes involve feelings of responsibility, challenge, and recognition and result from such job characteristics as variety, autonomy, identity, and significance.

Extrinsic outcomes, however, are objects or events that follow from the worker's own efforts in conjunction with other factors that are not directly involved in the job itself. Pay, working conditions, co-workers, and even supervision are characteristics of the workplace that are potentially job outcomes but are not a fundamental part of the work itself. Dealing with others and friendship interactions are sources of extrinsic outcomes.

Job Satisfaction Outcome

Job satisfaction depends on the levels of intrinsic and extrinsic outcomes and on how the jobholder views them. These outcomes have different values for different people. For some people, responsible and challenging work may have neutral or even negative value. For other people, such work outcomes may have high positive value. People differ in the importance that they attach to job outcomes. That differ-

[26] Arthur P. Brief and Ramon J. Aldag, "The Intrinsic-Extrinsic Dichotomy: Toward Conceptual Clarity," *Academy of Management Review,* July 1977, pp. 496–500.

ence alone would account for different levels of job satisfaction for essentially the same job tasks.

Another important individual difference is job involvement.[27] People differ in the extent to which (1) work is a central life interest, (2) they actively participate in work, (3) they perceive work as central to self-esteem, and (4) they perceive work as consistent with their self-concept. Persons who are not involved in their work cannot be expected to realize the same satisfaction as those who are. This variable accounts for the fact that two workers could report different levels of satisfaction for the same performance levels.

A final individual difference is the perceived equity of the outcome in terms of what the jobholder considers a fair reward. If the rewards are perceived to be unfair in relation to those of others in similar jobs requiring similar effort, the jobholder will experience dissatisfaction and will seek means to restore the equity, either by seeking greater rewards (primarily extrinsic) or by reducing effort.

Thus, we see that job performance includes many potential outcomes. Some are of primary value to the organization—the objective outcomes, for example. Others are of primary importance to the individual—for example, job satisfaction. Job performance is without doubt a complex variable that depends on the interplay of numerous factors. Managers can make some sense of the issue by understanding the motivational implications of jobs.

MOTIVATIONAL PROPERTIES OF JOBS AND JOB PERFORMANCE

The interest of organizational behavior researchers and managers in the motivational properties of jobs is based on the understanding that job performance depends on more than the ability of the jobholder. Specifically, job performance is determined by the interaction of ability and motivation as expressed by the equation:

$$\text{Job performance} = \text{Ability} \times \text{Motivation}$$

The equation reflects the fact that one person's job performance can be greater than that of another person because of greater ability, greater motivation, or both. It also reflects the possibility that job performance could be zero even if the jobholder has ability; in such instances, motivation would have to be zero. Thus, it is imperative that management consider the potential impact of the motivational properties of jobs. The following Close-Up illustrates one company's efforts to include motivational properties in employees' first jobs.

[27] S. D. Saleh and James Hosek, "Job Involvement: Concepts and Measurements," *Academy of Management Journal,* June 1976, pp. 213–24.

ORGANIZATIONS: CLOSE-UP

Job Design Research at General Electric

The research carried on at General Electric under the direction of Dr. Thomas D. Hollmann, manager of personnel research, has confirmed the importance of an individual's first job. According to Hollmann, people who experienced challenging work on their first jobs and received good counseling tended to be productive and to stay with the company. To determine what constitutes challenging work, Hollmann and his colleagues interviewed employees with two to four years' experience with GE. These employees came from such diverse functions as engineering, manufacturing, and marketing. They were asked to describe their most and least challenging work experiences and to specify what their managers had done to encourage their career development.

The concept of challenging work that emerged from these interviews stressed the importance of skill utilization, personal involvement, opportunities to interact with others, and a sense of accomplishment. With this idea of what is meant by challenging work, Hollmann was able to go to GE managers and ask them to verify the concept and then to identify the problems associated with providing such work experiences in their units. Since the purpose of the entire effort was to *provide* challenging work to new employees rather than to *define* it, the managers were encouraged to propose solutions for the removal of barriers to such work.

Source: *Management Review,* June 1980, p. 30.

The field of organizational behavior has advanced a number of suggestions for improving the motivational properties of jobs. Invariably, the suggestions, termed *job redesign strategies,* attempt to improve job performance through changes in job range and depth. In the next section, the more significant job redesign strategies are reviewed.

REDESIGNING JOB RANGE: JOB ROTATION AND JOB ENLARGEMENT

The earliest attempts to redesign jobs date to the scientific management era. The efforts at that time emphasized efficiency criteria. As a result, the individual tasks that a job comprised were made limited, uniform, and repetitive. This practice led to narrow job range and, consequently, to reported high levels of job discontent, turnover, absenteeism, and dissatisfaction. Accordingly, strategies were devised that widened job range by increasing the requisite activities of jobs. Two of these strategies were *job rotation* and *job enlargement*.

Job Rotation

job rotation
The practice of moving individuals from job to job to reduce their potential boredom and to increase their potential motivation.

The managers of such organizations as Western Electric, Ford, Bethelehem Steel, and TRW Systems have utilized different forms of the **job rotation** strategy. This strategy involves rotating an individual from one job to another. Thus, the individual is expected to complete more job activities since each job includes different tasks. Job rotation involves increasing the range of jobs and the perception of variety in the job content. Increasing task variety should, according to expectancy theory, increase the valence associated with job satisfaction. However, the practice of job rotation does not change the basic characteristics of the assigned jobs. Critics state that this approach involves nothing more than having people perform several boring and monotonous jobs rather than one. An alternative strategy is job enlargement.

Job Enlargement

The pioneering Walker and Guest study was concerned with the social and psychological problems associated with mass-production jobs in automobile assembly plants.[28] Walker and Guest found that many workers were dissatisfied with their highly specialized jobs. In particular, they disliked mechanical pacing, the repetitiveness of operations, and the lack of a sense of accomplishment.

job enlargement
The practice of increasing the number of tasks for which an individual is responsible. Job enlargement increases job range to reduce monotony and increase motivation.

Walker and Guest also found a positive relationship between job range and job satisfaction. The findings of their study gave early support for those motivation theories that predicted that increases in job range would increase job satisfaction and other objective job outcomes. **Job enlargement** strategies focus on the opposite of dividing work—they are a form of despecialization, or increasing the number of tasks that an employee performs. For example, a job is designed so that the individual performs six tasks instead of three.

Although, in many instances, an enlarged job requires a longer training period, it usually increases job satisfaction because boredom is reduced. The implication, of course, is that this will lead to improvement in other performance outcomes.

The concept and practice of job enlargement have become considerably more sophisticated. In recent years, effective job enlargement has involved more than simply increasing task variety. In addition,

---

[28] Charles R. Walker and Robert H. Guest, *The Man on the Assembly Line* (Cambridge, Mass.: Harvard University Press, 1952).

it has been necessary to redesign certain other aspects of job range. For example, machine-paced control has been replaced by worker-paced control.[29] Each of the changes that have been made has involved balancing the gains and losses of varying degrees of division of labor.

Some employees cannot cope with enlarged jobs because they cannot comprehend complexity; moreover, their attention span may be so short that they cannot stay with and complete an enlarged set of tasks. However, if employees are known to be amenable to job enlargement and if they have the requisite ability, then job enlargement should increase satisfaction and product quality and decrease absenteeism and turnover. These gains are not without costs, including the likelihood that employees will demand larger salaries in exchange for their performance of enlarged jobs. Yet these costs must be borne if management desires to implement *job enrichment,* the redesign strategy that enlarges job depth. Job enlargement is a necessary precondition for job enrichment.

REDESIGNING JOB DEPTH: JOB ENRICHMENT

job enrichment
The practice of increasing the discretion of an individual to select job activities and outcomes. Job enrichment increases job depth to increase the fulfillment of growth and autonomy needs.

The impetus for redesigning job depth was provided by Herzberg's two-factor theory of motivation.[30] The basis of this theory is that the factors that meet individuals' need for psychological growth, especially responsibility, job challenge, and achievement, must be characteristic of their jobs. The application of Herzberg's theory is termed **job enrichment.**

The implementation of job enrichment is realized through direct changes in job depth. Managers can provide employees with greater opportunities to exercise discretion by making the following changes:

1. *Direct feedback.* The evaluation of performance should be timely and direct.
2. *New learning.* A good job enables people to feel that they are growing. All jobs should provide opportunities to learn.
3. *Scheduling.* People should be able to schedule some part of their own work.
4. *Uniqueness.* Each job should have some unique qualities or features.
5. *Control over resources.* Individuals should have some control over their job tasks.

---

[29] Kae H. Chung and Monica F. Ross, "Differences in Motivational Properties between Job Enlargement and Job Enrichment," *Academy of Management Review,* January 1977, pp. 114–15.

[30] Frederick Herzberg, "The Wise Old Turk," *Harvard Business Review,* September–October 1974, pp. 70–80.

6. *Personal accountability.* People should be provided with an opportunity to be accountable for the job.

As defined by the executive in charge of a pioneering job enrichment program at Texas Instruments, job enrichment is a process that (1) encourages employees to behave like managers in managing their jobs and (2) redesigns the job to make such behavior feasible.[31] The job enrichment process as implemented in TI is continuous and pervades the entire organization. Every one of the jobs in TI is viewed as subject to analysis to determine whether it can be enriched to include managerial activities and thereby made more meaningful. Moreover, as the jobs of nonmanagerial personnel are redesigned to include greater depth, the jobs of managers must be redesigned. The redesigned managerial jobs emphasize the training and counseling of subordinates and de-emphasize control and direction.

An application of job enrichment in a nonmanufacturing setting is illustrated in the following Close-Up.

ORGANIZATIONS: CLOSE-UP

Job Enrichment at Citibank

Citibank recently undertook an extensive change in the ways its employees did their work. According to George E. Seegers, a bank vice president, a customer survey indicated that the bank scored very low on "customer service." Upon examining the causes of the problem, the bank management concluded that the reason was that its employees didn't "feel like somebody." They were dissatisfied with their rather mundane jobs, created in part by the decision of the bank some time ago to introduce automatic teller machines. Building on the idea that everybody wants to feel like somebody, the bank undertook extensive changes designed to recognize the individuality of employees as well as customers.

Among the many changes implemented were the following:

Encouraging communications between the functional departments: operations, marketing, and servicing.

Decentralizing operations so that one person could handle an entire transaction from the time it came into the bank until the time it left.

Putting the employees who did the job in direct contact with the customers and the computers.

Asking the people who did the job what was boring or troublesome *before* the bank automated.

---

[31] M. Scott Myers, *Every Employee a Manager* (New York: McGraw-Hill, 1970), p. xii.

Undertaking considerable training and education for the entire work force.

These changes in job design were made over a two-year period. The changes were accompanied by training sessions that taught the new skills. It was also necessary to develop new attitudes among the management personnel, including the attitude that employee opinions were valuable and desirable inputs into decisions.

Source: Roy W. Walters, "The Citibank Project: Improving Productivity through Work Design," in *The Innovative Organization,* ed. Robert Zager and Michael P. Rosow (Elmsford, N.Y.: Pergamon Press, 1982).

As the theory and practice of job enrichment have evolved, managers have become aware that successful applications require numerous changes in the way work is done. Some of the more important changes include delegating greater authority to workers to participate in decisions, to set their own goals, and to evaluate their (and their work groups') performance. Job enrichment also involves changing the nature and style of managers' behavior. Managers must be willing and able to delegate authority. Given the ability of employees to carry out enriched jobs and the willingness of managers to delegate authority, gains in performance can be expected. These positive outcomes are the result of increasing employees' expectancies that efforts will lead to performance, that performance will lead to intrinsic and extrinsic rewards, and that these rewards will have the power to satisfy needs.[32]

REDESIGNING JOB RANGE AND DEPTH: COMBINED APPROACH

Job enrichment and job enlargement are not competing strategies. Job enlargement, but not job enrichment, may be compatible with the needs, values, and abilities of some individuals. Yet job enrichment, when appropriate, necessarily involves job enlargement. A promising new approach to job redesign that attempts to integrate the two approaches is the job characteristic model. Hackman, Oldham, Janson, and Purdy devised the approach and based it on the Job Diagnostic Survey, cited in an earlier section.[33]

The model attempts to account for the interrelationships among

---

[32] Kae H. Chung, *Motivational Theories and Practices* (Columbus, Ohio: Grid, 1977), p. 204.

[33] J. Richard Hackman, Greg Oldham, Robert Janson, and Kenneth Purdy, "New Strategy for Job Enrichment," *California Management Review,* Summer 1975, pp. 57–71; and Hackman and Oldham, "Development of the Job Diagnostic Survey."

FIGURE 13-3

The Job Characteristics Model

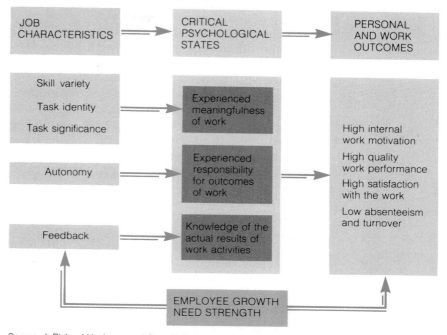

Source: J. Richard Hackman and Greg R. Oldham, "Development of the Job Diagnostic Survey," *Journal of Applied Psychology* 60(1975): 159–170.

(1) certain job characteristics; (2) psychological states associated with motivation, satisfaction, and performance; (3) job outcomes; and (4) growth need strength. Figure 13–3 describes the relationships among these variables. The core dimensions of the job consist of characteristics first described by Turner and Lawrence.[34] According to this model, although variety, identity, significance, autonomy, and feedback do not completely describe job content, they sufficiently describe those aspects of job content that management can manipulate to bring about gains in productivity.

work modules
Enable individuals to complete a whole piece of work so as to increase the sense of accomplishment.

The steps that management can take to increase the core dimensions of the job include combining task elements, assigning whole pieces of work (i.e., **work modules**), allowing discretion in the selection of work methods, and permitting self-paced control. These actions increase task variety, identity, and significance; consequently, they increase the "experienced meaningfulness of work." Permitting em-

---

[34] Turner and Lawrence, *Industrial Jobs.*

ployee participation and self-evaluation and creating autonomous work groups increases the feedback and autonomy dimensions along with the psychological states "experienced responsibility" and "knowledge of actual results."

The positive benefits of these redesign efforts are moderated by individual differences in the strength of employees' growth needs. That is, employees with strong need for accomplishment, learning, and challenge will respond more positively than employees with relatively weak growth needs. In other, more familiar, terms, employees who have high need for self-esteem and self-actualization are the more likely candidates for job redesign. If employees who lack either the need strength or the ability to perform redesigned jobs are forced to participate in job redesign programs, they may experience stress, anxiety, adjustment problems, erratic performance, turnover, and absenteeism.

The available research on the interrelationships among individual differences, job content, and performance is meager. It is apparent, however, that managers must cope with significant problems in matching employee needs and differences with organizational needs.[35] The difficulty of doing this is indicated by the finding of one study that of the 125 firms surveyed, only 5 had made any efforts to redesign jobs.[36] Among the problems associated with job redesign are the following:[37]

1. The program is time-consuming and costly.
2. Unless lower level needs are satisfied, people will not respond to opportunities to satisfy higher level needs. And even though our society has been rather successful in providing food and shelter, these lower level needs regain importance when the economy moves through periods of recession and inflation.
3. Job redesign programs are intended to satisfy needs that are typically not satisfied in the workplace. As workers are told to expect higher order need satisfaction, they may raise their expectations beyond what is possible. As a result, dissatisfaction with the failure of job redesign programs to meet these expectations may displace dissatisfaction with their jobs.
4. Finally, job redesign may be resisted by labor unions that see the effort as an attempt to get more work for the same pay.

---

[35] William E. Zierden, "Congruence in the Work Situation: Effects of Growth Needs, Management Style, and Job Structure on Job-Related Satisfactions," *Journal of Occupational Behavior,* October 1980, pp. 297–310.

[36] Fred Luthans and W. E. Reif, "Job Enrichment: Long on Theory, Short on Practice," *Organizational Dynamics,* Fall 1974, pp. 30–43.

[37] Chung, *Motivational Theories and Practices,* pp. 211–12.

Despite these problems, some companies have turned to job redesign as a way to improve productivity and satisfaction.

APPLICATIONS OF JOB REDESIGN

In this section, we will review actual attempts to implement job redesign. The most publicized efforts have occurred in the Volvo and General Motors automobile manufacturing plants.

The Volvo Experience: Work Modules

When Pehr Gyllenhammar joined Volvo in 1971 as its managing director, performance indicators such as productivity, absenteeism, and turnover were unsatisfactory.[38] The company was the largest employer in Sweden, with some 65,000 employees, and in 1976 it ranked 61st on *Fortune*'s international 500 list. Gyllenhammar took a keen interest in the experiments in job rotation (termed job alternation in Volvo) that were being conducted by Ingvar Barrby, head of the upholstery department. The reduction in turnover from 35 percent to 15 percent encouraged the new managing director to adopt other aspects of job redesign.[39] For example, group management and work modules were used at the Torslanda car assembly plant. Employees, in groups, followed the same auto body for either seven or eight work stations along the line for a total period of 20 minutes.

The concepts of group management and natural work modules were more highly developed at a truck assembly plant. Here groups of 5 to 12 people with common work assignments elected their own supervisors, scheduled their output, distributed work to their own members, and were responsible for their own quality control. Group piece rates, rather than individual piece rates, were the bases for wages, and everyone except the elected supervisor earned the same amount. Subsequently, absenteeism and turnover decreased and quality improved—due, in Gyllenhammar's opinion, to the effects of the job redesign program.

Job redesign at Volvo reached a major milestone when the Kalmar assembly plant opened. Gyllenhammar had been personally and visibly behind the design and construction phases of the new plant to assure that opportunities to provide job enrichment were parts of the physical and technological layout. The plant incorporated a technology

---

[38] John M. Roach, "Why Volvo Abolished the Assembly Line," *Management Review*, September 1977, p. 50.

[39] William F. Dowling, "Job Redesign on the Assembly Line: Farewell to Blue-Collar Blues?" *Organizational Dynamics*, Autumn 1973, pp. 51–67.

of assembly in which overhead carriers moved the auto body, chassis, and subassemblies to assembly team areas. There, work teams of 20 to 25 employees completed major segments of auto assembly—electrical systems, instrumentation, finishing, and so on. Each group was responsible for a whole piece of work. The groups functioned as autonomous units, in much the same way as those at the truck assembly plant.[40]

The General Motors Experience: Work Teams

General Motors became involved with job redesign in 1971.[41] The company was formulating plans for building the GM mobile home, a new product in a rapidly growing market. GM management believed that the new product was amenable to new design concepts as well as innovative approaches to work organization. After analyzing several factors, including the expected production rate, technological complexity, and size of the new operation, management determined that the work teams concept would be applicable.

The plan called for the creation of 8 six-person teams to produce 32 vehicles per shift in the body-upfit area; 14 three-person teams would complete the same number of chassis; and 4 four-person teams would install air conditioning. Implementation of the plan began with the selection of a nucleus of 30 hourly employees who would build the pilot vehicles and later be the team leaders and trainers of the expanded work force. The pilot phase ended in December 1972, and additional employees were recruited to fill out the work teams.

Problems arose shortly thereafter. Efficiency and quality never reached acceptable levels. The teams were unable to maintain discipline, and some team members did not carry their fair share of the load. Absenteeism, turnover, and job dissatisfaction increased. Some team members were unable to keep pace, due in large part to inadequate training and poor work layout. Management had underestimated the complexity of the assembly process and the training required to complete work cycles of up to 18 half-hour sequences.

The discouraging outcomes resulted in the phasing out of the team concept, beginning in 1973. Three years later, only a few people continued to work in teams. In this instance, the failure of job design was the consequence of flaws in implementing the concept rather than

---

[40] See Pehr Gyllenhammar, *People at Work* (Reading, Mass.: Addison-Wesley Publishing, 1977), for a full account of the Volvo experience.

[41] Noel M. Tichy and Jay N. Nisberg, "When Does Job Restructuring Work?" *Organizational Dynamics*, Summer 1976, pp. 63–80; and Richard L. Cherry, "The Development of General Motors' Team-Based Plants," in *The Innovative Organization*, ed. Robert Zager and Michael P. Rosow (Elmsford, N.Y.: Pergamon Press, 1982), pp. 125–48.

the concept itself. Here we see the importance of *management skill at coordinating work* to be a crucial moderator of the effects of job redesign on organizational effectiveness and job satisfaction.

When considering the experience of job redesign approaches, one reaches the conclusion that, in general, they are relatively successful in increasing quality of output, but not quantity. This conclusion is valid, however, only if the reward system already satisfies lower level needs. Otherwise, employees cannot be expected to experience upper level need satisfaction (intrinsic rewards) through enriched job content.

Since a primary source of organizational effectiveness is job performance, managers should design jobs according to the best available knowledge. At present, the strategies for designing and redesigning jobs have evolved from scientific management approaches to work design that emphasize quality of work-life issues. Job enlargement and job enrichment are important, but often incomplete, strategies. Strategies that take into account individual differences probably have the greatest probability of success, assuming compatible environmental, situational, and management conditions. As suggested in the Organizational Issue for Debate, the outcomes of work redesign efforts are often controversial. Minimizing these side effects requires managers who can diagnose their own people and organizations to determine the applicability of specific job design approaches.

SUMMARY OF KEY POINTS

A. Job design involves managerial decisions and actions that specify objective job depth, range, and relationships to satisfy organizational requirements as well as the social and personal requirements of jobholders.

B. Contemporary managers must consider the issue of quality of work-life when designing jobs. This issue reflects society's concern for work experiences that contribute to the personal growth and development of employees.

C. Strategies for increasing the potential of jobs to satisfy the social and personal requirements of jobholders have gone through an evolutionary process. The initial efforts were directed toward job rotation and job enlargement. These strategies produced some gains in job satisfaction but did not change primary motivators such as responsibility, achievement, and autonomy.

D. During the 1960s, job enrichment became a widely recognized strategy for improving quality of work-life factors. This strategy, based on Herzberg's motivation theory, involves increasing the *depth* of jobs through greater delegation of authority to jobholders. Despite some major successes, job enrichment is not universally applicable because it does not consider individual differences.

E. Individual differences are now recognized as crucial variables to consider when designing jobs. Experience, cognitive complexity, needs, values, and perceptions of equity are some of the individual differences that influence the reactions of jobholders to the scope and relationships of their jobs. When individual differences are combined with environmental, situational, and managerial differences, job design decisions become increasingly complex.

F. The most recently developed strategy of job design emphasizes the importance of core job characteristics as perceived by jobholders. Although measurements of individual differences remain a problem, managers should be encouraged to examine ways to increase positive perceptions of variety, identity, significance, autonomy, and feedback. Doing so increases the potential for high-quality work performance and high job satisfaction, given that jobholders possess relatively high growth need strength.

G. Many organizations, including Volvo, Saab, General Motors, and General Foods, have attempted job redesign with varying degrees of success. The current state of research knowledge is inadequate for making broad generalizations regarding the exact causes of success and failure in applications of job redesign. Managers must diagnose their own situations to determine the applicability of job redesign in their organizations.

DISCUSSION AND REVIEW QUESTIONS

1. Explain the difficulties that management would encounter in attempting to redesign existing jobs as compared to designing new jobs.

2. Explain the relationships between job depth and perceived autonomy and significance.

3. Is it possible to increase job depth without decreasing managers' authority? Explain.

4. What are the characteristics of individuals who would respond favorably to job enlargement but not to job enrichment?

5. Explain why it is necessary to enlarge a job before it can be enriched.

6. Explain the relationships between feedback and personal goal setting. Is personal goal setting possible without feedback? Explain.

7. What specific core dimensions of jobs could be changed to increase employees' perceptions of instrumentalities and expectancies?

8. Which of the core dimensions do you now value most highly? Explain, and list them in the rank order of their importance to you.

9. Compare the Volvo and General Motors experiences with job redesign, and explain why Volvo's experience has been relatively more successful.

10. In your opinion, was the General Foods experience with job redesign a success or a failure? Explain.

ADDITIONAL REFERENCES

Abdel-Halin, A. A. "Effects of Role Stress–Job Design–Technology Interaction on Employee Work Satisfaction." *Academy of Management Journal,* 1981, pp. 260–73.

Aldag, R. J., and A. P. Brief. *Task Design and Employee Motivation.* Glenview, Ill.: Scott, Foresman, 1979.

Becherer, R. C. "The Job Characteristics of Industrial Salespersons: Relationship to Motivation and Satisfaction." *Journal of Marketing,* 1982, pp. 125–35.

Blau, G. J., and R. Katerberg. "Toward Enhancing Research with the Social Information Processing Approach to Task Design." *Academy of Management Review,* 1982, pp. 543–50.

Brief, A. P., and R. J. Aldag. "Employee Reactions to Job Characteristics: A Constructive Replication." *Journal of Applied Psychology,* 1975, pp. 182–86.

Buchanan, D. A. *The Development of Job Design Theories.* Farnborough: Saxon House, 1979.

Crystal, J. C., and Deems, R. S. "Redesigning Jobs." *Training and Development Journal,* 1983, pp. 44–46.

Dainoff, M. J. "Occupational Stress Factors in Visual Display Terminal (VDT) Operations: A Review of Empirical Research." *Behavior and Information Technology,* 1982, pp. 141–76.

Davis, L. E. "Optimizing Organizational Plant Design: A Complementary Structure for Technical and Social Systems." *Organizational Dynamics,* 1979, pp. 3–15.

Griffin, R. W. "A Longitudinal Investigation of Task Characteristics Relationships." *Academy of Management Journal,* 1981, pp. 99–113.

———. *Task Design.* Glenview, Ill.: Scott, Foresman, 1982.

Hackman, J. R., and G. R. Oldham. "Motivation through the Design of Work: Test of a Theory." *Organizational Behavior and Human Performance,* 1976, pp. 250–79.

Hedge, A. "The Open-Plan Office: A Systematic Investigation of Employee Reactions to Their Work Environment." *Environment and Behavior,* 1982, pp. 519–42.

Hutton, M., and R. Collins. "Job Design: Australian Practice and Prospects." *Practising Manager,* 1983, pp. 11–15.

Konz, S. *Work Design.* Santa Monica, Calif.: Goodyear Publishing, 1979.

Lawler, E. E. "Job Design and Employee Motivation." *Personnel Psychology,* 1969, pp. 415–44.

———; **J. R. Hackman; and S. Kaufman.** "Effects of Job Design: A Field Experiment." *Journal of Applied Social Psychology,* 1973, pp. 46–62.

O'Connor, E. J.; C. J. Rudolph; and L. H. Peters. "Individual Differences and Job Design Reconsidered: Where Do We Go from Here?"

Academy of Management Review, 1980, pp. 249–54.

Poza, Ernesto J., and M. Lynne Markus. "Success Story: The Team Approach to Work Restructuring." *Organizational Dynamics,* 1980, pp. 2–25.

Shaw, J. B. "An Information-Processing Approach to the Study of Job Design." *Academy of Management Review,* 1980, pp. 41–48.

Staw, B. M. *Intrinsic and Extrinsic Motivation.* Morristown, N.J.: General Learning Press, 1976.

Steers, R. M. "Effects of Need for Achievement on the Job Performance–Job Attitude Relationship." *Journal of Applied Psychology,* 1975, pp. 678–82.

———. "Factors Affecting Job Attitudes in a Goal-Setting Environment." *Academy of Management Journal,* 1976, pp. 6–16.

Umstot, D. D.; C. H. Bell; and T. R. Mitchell. "Effects of Job Enrichment and Task Goals on Satisfaction and Productivity: Implications for Job Design." *Journal of Applied Psychology,* 1976, pp. 379–94.

CASE FOR ANALYSIS

Work Redesign in an Insurance Company

The executive staff of a relatively small life insurance company was considering a proposal to install an electronic data processing system. The proposal to install the equipment was presented by the assistant to the president, John Skully. He had been charged with studying the feasibility of the equipment after a management consultant had recommended a complete overhaul of the jobs within the company.

The management consultant had been engaged by the company to diagnose the causes of high turnover and absenteeism. After reviewing the situation and speaking with groups of employees, the management consultant had recommended that the organization structure be changed from a functional to a client basis. The change in departmental basis would enable management to redesign jobs to reduce the human costs associated with highly specialized tasks.

The present organization included separate departments to issue policies, collect premiums, change beneficiaries, and process loan applications. Employees in these departments had complained that their jobs were boring, insignificant, and monotonous. They had stated that the only reason they stayed with the company was because they liked the small company atmosphere. They felt that the management had a genuine interest in their welfare but that the trivial nature of their jobs contradicted that feeling. As one employee said, "This company is small enough to know almost everybody. But the job I do is so boring that I wonder why they even need me to do it." This and similar comments had led the consultant to believe that the jobs must be altered to provide greater motivation. But he also recognized that work redesign opportunities were limited by the organization structure. He had therefore recommended that the company change to a client basis. In such a structure, each employee would handle every transaction related to a particular policyholder.

When the consultant had presented his views to the members of the executive staff, they had been very much interested in his recommendation. And, in fact, they had agreed that his recommendation was well founded. They had noted, however, that a small company must pay particular attention to efficiency in handling transactions. The functional basis enabled the organization to achieve the degree of specialization necessary for efficient operations. The manager of internal operations stated: "If we move away from specialization, the rate of efficiency must go down because we will lose the benefit of specialized effort. The only way we can justify redesigning the jobs as suggested by the consultant is to maintain our efficiency; otherwise, there won't be any jobs to redesign because we will be out of business."

The internal operations manager had explained to the executive staff that despite excessive absenteeism and turnover, he was able to maintain acceptable productivity. The narrow range and depth of the jobs reduced training time to a minimum. It was also possible to hire temporary help to meet peak loads and to fill in for absent employees. "Moreover," he said, "changing the jobs our people do means that we must change the jobs our managers do. They are experts in their own functional areas, but we have never attempted to train them to oversee more than two operations."

A majority of the executive staff had believed that the consultant's recommendations should be seriously considered. At that point, the group had directed John Skully to evaluate the potential of electronic data processing (EDP) as a means of obtaining efficient operations in combination with the redesigned jobs. He had completed the study and presented his report to the executive staff.

"The bottom line," Skully said, "is that EDP will enable us to maintain our present efficiency, but with the redesigned jobs we will not obtain any greater gains. If my analysis is correct, we will have to absorb the cost of the equipment out of earnings because there will be no cost savings. So it comes down to what price we are willing and able to pay for improving the satisfaction of our employees."

Questions for Consideration

1. What core characteristics of the employees' jobs will be changed if the consultant's recommendations are accepted? Explain.

2. What alternative redesign strategies should be considered? For example, job rotation and job enlargement are possible alternatives; what are the relevant considerations for these and other designs in the context of this company?

3. What would be your decision in this case? What should the management be willing to pay for employee satisfaction? Defend your answer.

EXPERIENTIAL EXERCISE
PERSONAL PREFERENCES

Objectives

1. To illustrate individual differences in preferences about various job design characteristics.
2. To illustrate how your preferences may differ from those of others.
3. To examine the most important and least important job design characteristics and how managers would cope with them.

Related Topics

This exercise will be related to intrinsic and extrinsic reward topics. The job design characteristics considered could be viewed as either intrinsic or extrinsic job issues.

Starting the Exercise

First, you will respond to a questionnaire asking about your job design preferences and how you view the preferences of others. After you have worked through the questionnaire *individually*, small groups will be formed. In the groups, discussion will focus on the individual differences in preferences expressed by group members.

The Facts

Job design is concerned with a number of attributes of a job. Among these attributes are the job itself, the requirements of the job, the interpersonal interaction opportunities on the job, and performance outcomes. There are certain attributes that are preferred by individuals. Some prefer job autonomy, while others prefer to be challenged by different tasks. It is obvious that individual differences in preferences would be an important consideration for managers. An exciting job for one person may be a demeaning and boring job for another person. Managers could use this type of information in attempting to create job design conditions that allow organizational goals and individual goals and preferences to be matched.

The Job Design Preferences form is presented below. Please read it carefully, and complete it after considering each of the characteristics listed. Due to space limitations, not all job design characteristics are included for your consideration. Use only those that are included on the form.

Job Design Preferences

A. Your Job Design Preferences

Decide which of the following characteristics is most important to you. Place a *1* in front of the most important characteristic. Then decide which characteristic is the second most important to you and place a *2* in front of it. Continue numbering the items in order of importance until the least important is ranked *10*. There are no right answers since individuals differ in their job design preferences. Do not discuss your individual rankings until the instructor forms groups.

_____ Variety in tasks

_____ Feedback on performance from doing the job

_____ Autonomy

_____ Working as a team

_____ Responsibility

_____ Developing friendships on the job

_____ Task identity

(continued)

_____ Task significance

_____ Having the resources to perform well

_____ Feedback on performance from others (e.g., the manager, co-workers)

B. Others' Job Design Preferences

In the A section, you have provided your job design preferences. Now number the items as you think others would rank them. Consider others who are in your course, class, or program, that is, who are also completing this exercise. Rank the factors from 1 (most important) to 10 (least important).

_____ Variety in tasks

_____ Feedback on performance from doing the job

_____ Autonomy

_____ Working as a team

_____ Responsibility

_____ Developing friendships on the job

_____ Task identity

_____ Task significance

_____ Having the resources to perform well

_____ Feedback on performance from others (e.g., the manager, co-workers)

Exercise Procedure

Phase I: 15 minutes

1. Individually complete the A and B portions of the Job Design Preferences form.

Phase II: 45 minutes

1. The instructor will form groups of four to six students.
2. Discuss the differences in the rankings individuals made on the A and B parts of the form.
3. Present each of the A rank orders of group members on a flip chart or the blackboard. Analyze the areas of agreement and disagreement.
4. Discuss what implications the A and B rankings would have to a *manager* who would have to supervise a group such as the one you are in. That is, what could a manager do to cope with the individual differences displayed in the above steps?

Chapter 14

After completing Chapter 14, you should be able to:

Define organizational design.

Describe the important conclusions from studies of the relationship between structure and technology and environmental uncertainty.

Discuss the way organizations respond to the need to process information about their environments.

Compare the mechanistic and organic models of organizational design.

Identify the circumstances that would cause an organization to evolve into a matrix design.

Organizational Design

The Technological Imperative

Argument For

Since the pathbreaking studies of Joan Woodward, the view that technology *determines* structure has been debated. According to this view, an optimal organizational design exists for each technological type; managers, therefore, should match the design with the technology. Woodward's studies indicated that the mechanistic design proposed by classical theorists is optimal only for mass-production-type technology; the organic design strategy is appropriate for job order and process technologies. These studies cast consid-

erable doubt on the view that there is a one universally best way to organize.

The evidence that technology is the compelling force behind design decisions accumulated as other researchers tested Woodward's findings in other settings. Although subsequent research studies differed in some respects, the conclusions were consistent. Studies of industrial organizations in the Minneapolis–St. Paul area, for example, confirmed that when management failed to match structure with technology, additional costs were incurred that resulted in lower organizational performance.

The finding that technology determines structure prompted theorists to devise explanations for the relationship. Their theories attempt to provide general frameworks for thinking about the relationships between structure and technology. Thus, it is possible to argue that in nonmanufacturing as well as manufacturing business firms technology is the most important determinant of optimal organizational structure.

Argument Against

The argument against the technological imperative is based on research that indicates that although technology is important, other considerations must be taken into account. The most compelling counterargument is that technology is the important variable for designing organizational units that directly produce the product or service. Thus, the production department or division should be designed to meet technological demands, but other units in the organization face different, nontechnological demands. This view is based on the theory that organizations must deal with various subenvironments, each posing different constraints.

The view that technology is the primary influence on structure is not borne out by studies of very large organizations. Woodward's studies, and those of supportive researchers, included firms of relatively small size. The impact of technology is more noticeable in smaller firms than in larger ones since larger firms create staff units—research, marketing, and information, for example—to deal with nonproduction environments. The larger the organization, the less influential technology becomes. Thus, according to one counterargument, size, not technology, is the principal determinant of structure.

Organizational design refers to managerial decision making to determine the structure and processes that coordinate and control the jobs of the organization. The outcome of organizational design decisions is a system of jobs and work groups, including the processes that link them. Among these linking processes are authority relationships, communication networks, and specific planning and controlling techniques. In effect, organizational design implies the creation of a superstructure within which the work of the organization takes place.

Organizational design has been at the core of managerial work since the earliest efforts to develop management theory. The importance of design decisions has stimulated a great deal of interest in the issue. Managers and organizational behavior theorists and researchers have contributed to what is now a considerable body of literature. The manager who faces the necessity of designing an organizational structure is at no loss for ideas. Quite the contrary. The literature of organizational design contains numerous and conflicting ideas as to how an organization should be designed to achieve optimal effectiveness.

The Organizational Issue for Debate that opens this chapter summarizes some of the arguments for and against the importance of technology as a factor to be taken into account in design decisions. But technology is, as we will see, only one of numerous design factors. Other design factors include the nature of the work itself, the characteristics of the people who will do the work, the demands of the environment in which the organization exists, the need to receive and process information from that environment, and the overall strategy that the organization chooses in order to relate to its environment.

To make some sense of this apparent complexity, the flow of the discussion will be as follows. We will first describe two general models of organizational design: the mechanistic and the organic models. Next, we will examine three important factors that managers must take into account when designing the organizational structure: technology, environmental uncertainty, and information processing requirements. Finally, we will discuss an emerging form of organization, the matrix organization.

MECHANISTIC AND ORGANIC MODELS OF ORGANIZATIONAL DESIGN

The two models of organizational design that will be described in this section are important ideas in management theory and practice. Because of their importance, they receive considerable theoretical and practical attention. Nevertheless, there is little uniformity in the terms that are used to designate the two models. The two terms that we use here, mechanistic and organic, are relatively descriptive of the important features of the models.[1]

The Mechanistic Model

During the early part of the 20th century, a body of literature emerged that considered the problem of designing the structure of an organization as but one of a number of managerial tasks, including planning and controlling. The objective of the contributors to that body of literature was to define *principles* that could guide managers in the performance of their tasks. One of these early writers, Henri Fayol, proposed a number of principles that he had found useful in the management of a large coal mining company in France.[2] Some of Fayol's principles dealt with the management function of organizing, and four of them are relevant for understanding the **mechanistic model**.

mechanistic model
Emphasizes the importance of achieving high levels of production and efficiency. This organizational design makes use of extensive rules and procedures, centralized authority, and high specialization.

The Principle of Specialization.   Fayol stated that specialization was the best means for making use of individuals and groups of individuals. At the time of Fayol's writings, the limit of specialization, that is, the optimal point, had not been definitively determined. As we say in the preceding chapter, scientific management popularized a number of methods for implementing the specialization of labor. These methods, such as work standards and motion and time study, emphasized technical (not behavioral) dimensions of work.

The Principle of Unity of Direction.   According to this principle, jobs should be grouped according to specialty. Engineers should be grouped with engineers, salespersons with salespersons, accountants with accountants. The departmentalization basis that most nearly implements this principle is the functional basis.

The Principle of Authority and Responsibility.   Fayol believed that a manager should be delegated sufficient authority to carry out his or her assigned responsibilities. Because the assigned responsibilities of top managers are considerably more important to the future of the organization than those of lower management, the application of the principle inevitably leads to centralized authority. Centralized authority is a logical outcome not only because of top management's larger responsibilities but also because the work at this level is more

[1] Tom Burns and G. M. Stalker, *The Management of Innovation* (London: Tavistock Publications, 1961). Burns and Stalker are largely responsible for the terms *mechanistic* and *organic.*

[2] Henri Fayol, *General and Industrial Management,* trans. J. A. Conbrough (Geneva: International Management Institute, 1929). The more widely circulated translation is that of Constance Storrs (London: Pitman Publishing, 1949).

complex, the number of workers involved is greater, and the relationship between actions and results is remote.

The Scalar Chain Principle.   The natural result of the implementation of the three preceding principles is a graded chain of managers from the ultimate authority to the lowest ranks. The scalar chain is the route for all vertical communications in an organization. Accordingly, all communications from the lowest level must pass through each superior in the chain of command. Correspondingly, communications from the top must pass through each subordinate until they reach the appropriate level.

Fayol's writings became part of a literature that, although each contributor made unique contributions, had a common thrust. Writers such as Mooney and Reiley,[3] Follett,[4] and Urwick[5] all shared the common objective of defining the principles that should guide the design and management of organizations. A complete review of their individual contributions will not be attempted here. However, we will review the ideas of one individual who made important contributions to the mechanistic model: Max Weber. Weber described applications of the mechanistic model and coined the term *bureaucracy.*

Bureaucracy has various meanings. The traditional usage is the political science concept of government by bureaus but without participation by the governed. In the layperson's terms, bureaucracy refers to the negative consequences of large organizations, such as excessive "red tape," procedural delays, and general frustration.[6] But in Max Weber's writings, bureaucracy refers to a particular way of organizing collective activities.[7] Weber's interest in bureaucracy reflected his concern for the ways in which society developed hierarchies of control so that one group could, in effect, dominate other groups.[8] Organizational design involves domination in the sense that authority involves the legitimate right to exact obedience from others. Weber's search for the forms of domination that evolve in society led him to the study of bureaucratic structure.

According to Weber, the bureaucratic structure is "superior to any other form in precision, in stability, in the stringency of its discipline

[3] James D. Mooney and Allan C. Reiley, *Onward Industry* (New York: Harper & Row, 1939). Subsequently revised as James D. Mooney, *The Principles of Organization* (New York: Harper & Row, 1947).

[4] Henry C. Metcalf and Lyndall Urwick, eds., *Dynamic Administration: The Collected Papers of Mary Parker Follett* (New York: Harper & Row, 1940).

[5] Lyndall Urwick, *The Elements of Administration* (New York: Harper & Row, 1944).

[6] Michael Crozier, *The Bureaucratic Phenomenon* (Chicago: University of Chicago Press, 1964), p. 3.

[7] Max Weber, *The Theory of Social and Economic Organization*, trans. A. M. Henderson and Talcott Parsons (New York: Oxford University Press, 1947).

[8] Richard M. Weiss, "Weber on Bureaucracy: Management Consultant or Political Theorist?" *Academy of Management Review*, April 1983, pp. 242–48.

and its reliability. It thus makes possible a high degree of calculability of results for the heads of the organization and for those acting in relation to it."[9] The bureaucracy compares to other organizations "as does the machine with nonmechanical modes of production."[10] In these words are captured the essence of the mechanistic model of organizational design.

Weber believed that in order to achieve the maximum benefits of the bureaucratic design an organization must have the following characteristics.

1. All tasks are divided into highly specialized jobs. Through specialization, jobholders become expert in their jobs and management can hold them responsible for the effective performance of their duties.

2. Each task is performed according to a system of abstract rules to assure uniformity and the coordination of different tasks. The rationale for this practice is that it enables the manager to eliminate uncertainty in task performance due to individual differences.

3. Each member or office of the organization is accountable for job performance to one, and only one, manager. Managers hold their authority because of their expert knowledge and because it is delegated from the top of the hierarchy. An unbroken chain of command exists.

4. Each employee of the organization relates to other employees and clients in an impersonal, formalistic manner, maintaining a social distance with subordinates and clients. This assures that personalities and favoritism will not interfere with the efficient accomplishment of the organization's objectives.

5. Employment in the bureaucratic organization is based on technical qualifications and is protected against arbitrary dismissal. Similarly, promotions are based on seniority and achievement. Employment in the organization is viewed as a lifelong career, and a high degree of loyalty is engendered.

These five characteristics of bureaucracy describe organizations of the kind that Fayol believed to be most effective. Both Fayol and Weber described the same type of organization, one that functioned in a machinelike manner to accomplish the organization's goals in a highly efficient manner. Thus, the term *mechanistic* aptly describes such organizations.

The following Close-Up describes United Parcel Service's use of the mechanistic model.

---

[9] Weber, *Theory of Social and Economic Organization*, p. 334.

[10] H. H. Gerth and C. W. Mills, eds. and trans., *From Max Weber: Essays in Sociology* (New York: Oxford University Press, 1946), p. 214.

ORGANIZATIONS: CLOSE-UP

United Parcel's Mechanistic Design

United Parcel Service (UPS) is in direct competition with the U.S. Postal Service in the delivery of small packages. Even though the Postal Service is subsidized and pays no taxes, UPS has been able to compete successfully by stressing efficiency of operations. It apparently achieves great efficiencies through a combination of automation and organizational design. Specialization and formalization are highly visible characteristics of the UPS structure. UPS makes use of clearly defined jobs and an explicit chain of command. The jobs are arranged in a hierarchy of authority consisting of eight managerial levels. The high degree of specialization enables management to use many forms of written reports such as daily work sheets that record each employee's work quotas and performance. Company policies and practices are in written form and are routinely consulted in hiring and promotion decisions. Apparently, UPS has found the mechanistic form of organization to be well suited to its purposes.

Source: Richard L. Daft, *Organization Theory and Design* (St. Paul, Minn.: West Publishing, 1983), pp. 126–27.

The mechanistic model achieves high levels of efficiency due to its structural characteristics. It is highly complex because of its emphasis on specialization of labor; it it highly centralized because of its emphasis on authority and accountability; and it is highly formalized because of its emphasis on function as the primary basis of departmentalization. These organizational characteristics and practices underlie a widely used organizational model. But the mechanistic model is not the only one that is used.

The Organic Model

organic model
Emphasizes the importance of achieving high levels of adaptiveness and development. This organizational design makes little use of rules and procedures, centralized authority, or high specialization.

The **organic model** of organizational design stands in sharp contrast to the mechanistic model. The organizational characteristics and practices that underlie the organic model are distinctly different from those that underlie the mechanistic model. The most distinct differences between the two models result from the different effectiveness criteria that each seeks to maximize. While the mechanistic model seeks to maximize efficiency and production, the organic model seeks to maximize flexibility and adaptability.

The organic organization is flexible and adaptable to changing environmental demands because its design encourages greater utilization of the human potential. Managers are encouraged to adopt practices that tap the full range of human motivations through job design that stresses personal growth and responsibility. Decision making, control, and goal-setting processes are decentralized and are shared at all levels of the organization. Communications flow throughout the organization, not simply down the chain of command. These practices are intended to implement a basic assumption of the organic model, which states that an organization will be effective to the extent that its structure is "such as to ensure a maximum probability that in all interactions and in all relationships with the organization, each member, in the light of his background, values, desires, and expectations, will view the experience as supportive and one which builds and maintains a sense of personal worth and importance."[11]

An organizational design that provides individuals with this sense of personal worth and motivation and that facilitates flexibility and adaptability would have the following characteristics:

1. It would be relatively simple because of its deemphasis on specialization and its emphasis on increasing job range.
2. It would be relatively decentralized because of its emphasis on delegation of authority and increasing job depth.
3. And it would be relatively informalized because of its emphasis on product and customer as bases for departmentation.

Honeywell, Inc., has used the organic design with considerable success, as noted in the following Close-Up.

ORGANIZATIONS: CLOSE-UP

Honeywell's Organic Structure

Honeywell, Inc.'s Defense and Marine Systems Group (DMSG) is opening a new plant in Joliet, Illinois. The organizational design of the new plant will have many of the features of an organic structure. A major characteristic of the plant will be jobs that have relatively wide range and depth. All employees will participate in policy formulation and goal setting. There will be no time clocks and no status hierarchy. Jobs will be loosely defined, and employees will be encouraged to take on any task that they are competent to complete. Information and communications will flow throughout the organization to assure that individuals are involved fully in the plant's activities and decisions. Many task groups will exist to involve individuals across specialties. In some instances, quality circles will be used; in other instances, task forces and

---

[11] Rensis Likert, *New Patterns of Management* (New York: McGraw-Hill, 1961); and Rensis Likert, *The Human Organization* (New York: McGraw-Hill, 1967).

committees will be used. The exact form of Honeywell's interpretation of the organic design varies from plant to plant, but the Joliet plant is a milestone in the company's experience with it.

Source: Richard J. Boyle, "Designing the Energetic Organization: How a Honeywell Unit Stimulated Change and Innovation," *Management Review*, August 1983, pp. 20–25.

One of the leading spokespersons and developers of ideas supporting applications of the organic model is Rensis Likert. The studies that Likert carried out at the University of Michigan led him to argue that organic organizations (Likert uses the term *System 4*) differed markedly from mechanistic organizations (Likert uses the term *System 1*) along a number of structural dimensions.[12] The important differences are shown in Table 14–1.

There is no question that Likert's views are widely shared by researchers and practitioners. The literature has been filled with reports of efforts to implement organic designs in actual organizations.[13] Likert himself has reported many of these studies.[14] Likewise, there is no question that the proponents of the organic organization believe that it is universally applicable; that is, they regard the organic model as the "one best way" to design an organization. In this regard, the proponents of both the mechanistic and organic models are equally zealous in their advocacy.

CONTINGENCY DESIGN THEORIES

A current trend in management research and practice is to design organizations to be congruent with the demands of the situation.[15] The demands of a situation are termed "contingencies." Accordingly, neither the mechanistic nor the organic model is necessarily the more effective organizational design; either can be the better approach, depending on the situation. The contingency point of view provides an opportunity to get away from the dilemma of choosing between the

---

[12] Likert, *New Patterns of Management,* p. 103.

[13] See in particular A. J. Marrow, D. G. Bowers, and S. E. Seashore, eds., *Strategies of Organization Change* (New York: Harper & Row, 1967); and William F. Dowling, "At General Motors: System 4 Builds Performance and Profits," *Organizational Dynamics,* Winter 1975, pp. 23–28.

[14] Likert, *New Patterns of Management;* and Likert, *Human Organization.*

[15] W. Alan Randolph and Gregory G. Dess, "The Congruence Perspective of Organization Design: A Conceptual Model and Multivariate Research Approach," *Academy of Management Review,* January 1984, pp. 114–27.

TABLE 14–1

Mechanistic and Organic Structure

Mechanistic Structure	Organic Structure
1. *Leadership process* includes no perceived confidence and trust. Subordinates do not feel free to discuss job problems with their superiors, who in turn do not solicit their ideas and opinions.	1. *Leadership process* includes perceived confidence and trust between superiors and subordinates in all matters. Subordinates feel free to discuss job problems with their superiors, who in turn solicit their ideas and opinions.
2. *Motivational process* taps only physical, security, and economic motives through the use of fear and sanctions. Unfavorable attitudes toward the organization prevail among employees.	2. *Motivational process* taps a full range of motives through participatory methods. Attitudes are favorable toward the organization and its goals.
3. *Communication process* is such that information flows downward and tends to be distorted, inaccurate, and viewed with suspicion by subordinates.	3. *Communication process* is such that information flows freely throughout the organization—upward, downward, and laterally. The information is accurate and undistorted.
4. *Interaction process* is closed and restricted; subordinates have little effect on departmental goals, methods, and activities.	4. *Interaction process* is open and extensive; both superiors and subordinates are able to affect departmental goals, methods, and activities.
5. *Decision process* occurs only at the top of the organization; it is relatively centralized.	5. *Decision process* occurs at all levels through group process; it is relatively decentralized.
6. *Goal-setting process* is located at the top of the organization, discouraging group participation.	6. *Goal-setting process* encourages group participation in setting high, realistic objectives.
7. *Control process* is centralized and emphasizes fixing of blame for mistakes.	7. *Control process* is dispersed throughout the organization and emphasizes self-control and problem solving.
8. *Performance goals* are low and are passively sought by managers who make no commitment to developing the human resources of the organization.	8. *Performance goals* are high and are actively sought by superiors, who recognize the necessity for making a full commitment to developing, through training, the human resources of the organization.

Source: Adapted from Rensis Likert, *The Human Organization* (New York: McGraw-Hill, 1967), pp. 197–211.

contingency design approach
Emphasizes the importance of designing an organization to fit the demands of the environment.

mechanistic model and the organic model. As such, it represents an evolution of ideas whose bases can be found in the work of earlier writers.

The essence of the **contingency design approach** is expressed by this question: Under what circumstances and in what situations is either the mechanistic or the organic model more effective? The answer to this question requires the manager to specify the factors in a situation that influence the relative effectiveness of a particular design.

Obviously, the contingency approach is quite complicated because of the many factors that must be considered.[16] Technology is one of the more important of these factors.

TECHNOLOGY AND ORGANIZATIONAL DESIGN

technology
The actions taken by an individual to change the form or content of an object.

The effects of **technology** on organizational structure can be readily understood at an abstract level of analysis. Although various definitions of technology exist, it is generally understood to be "the *actions that an individual performs upon an object with or without the aid of tools or mechanical devices, in order to make some change* in that object."[17] A compatible, yet even broader, definition is that "technology is the application of knowledge to perform work."[18] Thus, organizational structures reflect technology in the ways that jobs are designed (the division of labor) and grouped (departmentalization). In this sense, the current state of knowledge regarding the appropriate actions to change an object acts as a constraint on management.

The literature of organizational theory includes a number of studies that examine the relationship between technology and organizational structure. We cannot possibly survey all of these studies in this section; to do so would take considerable space and would go beyond the intent of our discussion. Rather, we will briefly review one study that stimulated a number of follow-up studies and has become quite important in the literature of organizational design.

The Woodward Research Findings

Joan Woodward gained considerable attention when she released the findings of analyses of the organizational structures of 100 manufacturing firms in southern England.[19] While she and her colleagues had sought to answer a number of questions regarding the contributions of organizational structure to organizational effectiveness, it was their conclusions regarding technology and structure that were widely acclaimed.

---

[16] Sang M. Lee, Fred Luthans, and David L. Olson, "A Management Science Approach to Contingency Models of Organizational Structure," *Academy of Management Journal,* September 1982, pp. 553–66.

[17] Charles Perrow, "A Framework for the Comparative Analysis of Organizations," *American Sociological Review,* April 1967, p. 195. See Michael Withey, Richard L. Daft, and William H. Cooper, "Measures of Perrow's Work-Unit Technology: An Empirical Assessment and A New Scale," *Academy of Management Journal,* March 1983, pp. 45–63.

[18] Denise M. Rousseau, "Assessment of Technology in Organizations: Closed versus Open Systems Approaches," *Academy of Management Review,* October 1979, p. 531.

[19] Joan Woodward, *Industrial Organization: Theory and Practice* (London: Oxford University Press, 1965).

Woodward and her team of researchers had set out to determine whether there were structural differences between the more and less effective firms. They used a number of measures of effectiveness to classify the firms they studied into three categories: above average, average, and below average. But when they compared the organizational structures within each category, no consistent pattern emerged.

It was then that the team began analyzing the information relating to technology—"the methods and processes of manufacture."[20] The team measured technology in terms of three related variables: "(1) stages in the historical development of production processes, (2) the interrelationship between the items of equipment used for these processes, and (3) the extent to which the operations performed in the processes were repetitive or comparable from one production cycle or sequence to the next."[21] The application of these measures to the information about the firm's manufacturing methods resulted in a continuum, with job-order manufacturing and process manufacturing at the extremes and mass-production manufacturing in the middle.

The research team classified the firms according to the three categories of technology. It then discovered that the three categories were characterized by differences in organizational structures. The important differences were:[22]

1. The organizations at each end of the continuum were more flexible; that is, they resembled the organic model, with job duties and responsibilities being less clearly defined. The organizations in the middle of the continuum were more specialized and formalized; that is, they resembled the mechanistic model.

2. The organizations at each end of the continuum made greater use of verbal communications than of written communications; the organizations in the middle made greater use of written communications and were more formalized. This pattern was also consistent with the distinctions between organic and mechanistic models.

3. The managerial positions were more highly specialized in mass-production manufacturing than in either job-order or process manufacturing. First-level supervisors engaged primarily in direct supervision, leaving the technical decisions to staff personnel. In contrast, the managers in job-order firms were expected to have greater technical exper-

---

[20] Ibid., p. 35.

[21] J. J. Rackham, "Automation and Technical Change—The Implications for the Management Process," in *Organizational Structure and Design*, ed. Gene W. Dalton, Paul R. Lawrence, and Jay W. Lorsch (Homewood, Ill.: Richard D. Irwin and Dorsey Press, 1970), p. 299.

[22] Joan Woodward, *Management and Technology, Problems of Progress in Industry, no. 3* (London: Her Majesty's Stationery Office, 1958), pp. 4–30; and in Gary A. Yukl and Kenneth N. Wexley, eds., *Readings in Organizational and Industrial Psychology* (New York: Oxford University Press, 1971), p. 19.

tise and the managers in process manufacturing were expected to have greater scientific expertise.

4. Consistent with the preceding point, the actual *control of production* in the form of schedule making and routing was separated from the *supervision of production* in mass-production firms. The two managerial functions were more highly integrated in the role of the first-level supervisor in organizations at the extremes of the continuum.

Thus, the data indicated sharp organizational differences due to technological differences. But how is it that technology affects organization? We offer our interpretation in the next section.

An Interpretation of Woodward's Findings

The relationship between technology and organizations can be understood with reference to the natural business functions—product development, production, and marketing. The job-order firm produces according to customer specifications; the firm must secure the order, develop the product, and manufacture it. The cycle begins with marketing and ends with production.

This sequence requires the firm to be especially adept at sensing market changes and at adjusting to those changes. But more important, the product development function holds the key to the firm's success. This function must convert customer specifications into products that are acceptable to both the customer and the production personnel. The organic design is more effective than the mechanistic design in promoting the kinds of interactions and communication patterns required to meet the market and product development problems associated with job-order or unit production.

At the other extreme of the technological continuum are the process manufacturing firms. In these firms, the cycle begins with product development. The key to success is the ability to discover through scientific research a new product—a new chemical, gasoline additive, or fabric—that can be produced by already existing facilities or by new facilities once a market has been established. The development, marketing, and production functions in process manufacturing all tend to demand scientific personnel and specialized competence at the highest levels in the organization. Since the success of process manufacturing firms depends on adjustment to new scientific knowledge, the organic design is more effective than the mechanistic design.

The mechanistic design is effective for firms that use mass-production technology. The market exists for more or less standardized products—autos, foods, clothing—and the task is to manufacture the products through fairly routine means, efficiently and economically. The workers tend machines that are designed and paced by engineering standards. The actual control of the workflow is separated from the supervision of the work force. In mass-production firms, the ideas of scientific management and mechanistic design are most applicable.

Subsequent research to test the effect of technology on structure has produced mixed results. The most complete replication was undertaken by Zwerman.[23] His findings lend support to Woodward's. Another supportive study, completed by Harvey, found that as technological diffuseness decreased, that is, as fewer product changes occurred over time, there was an *increase* in the number of specialized subunits, the number of managerial levels, the ratio of managerial to nonmanagerial personnel, and the extent of formalized rules and communication channels.[24] But other studies have produced inconsistent relationships between technology and structure.

The fact that the studies attempting to discern the effects of technology have produced mixed results can be explained, at least partially. Recent critical reviews of the literature on technology and structure have noted a number of explanations.[25] One explanation is the confusion over level of analysis. Some studies have focused on the effects of technology on the individual task, while other studies have focused on the effects of technology on groups and organizations.[26] Another explanation is the tendency of researchers to define technology only in terms of the conversion phases of a technical system, with little regard to either the input or output phases.[27] Finally, there is the inherent difficulty of distinguishing between technology as a *cause* of structural differences rather than as the *effect* of such differences. For example, by increasing the degree of participation in decision making (decentralization of authority), a human service organization changed the manner in which clients were treated (technology).[28] These research and theoretical issues must be taken into account when attempting to reconcile studies of technology and structure.

Recent studies have indicated that the relationship between technology and structure is moderated by at least two factors, *size* and *mana-*

[23] William L. Zwerman, *New Perspectives in Organization Theory* (Westport, Conn.: Greenwood Publishing, 1970).

[24] Edward Harvey, "Technology and the Structure of Organizations," *American Sociological Review*, April 1968, pp. 247–59.

[25] Donald Gerwin, "The Comparative Analysis of Structure and Technology: A Critical Appraisal," *Academy of Management Review*, January 1979, pp. 41–51; and Louis W. Fry, "Technology-Structure Research: Three Critical Issues," *Academy of Management Journal*, September 1982, pp. 532–52.

[26] Peggy Leatt and Rodney Schneck, "Nursing Subunit Technology: A Replication," *Administrative Science Quarterly*, June 1981, pp. 225–36.

[27] Rousseau, "Assessment of Technology," pp. 531–42; and Peter K. Mills and Dennis J. Moberg, "Perspectives on the Technology of Service Organizations," *Academy of Management Review*, July 1982, pp. 467–78.

[28] Charles A. Glisson, "Dependence of Technological Routinization on Structural Variables in Human Service Organizations," *Administrative Science Quarterly*, September 1978, pp. 383–95.

gerial choice. The effect of size is to reduce the impact of technology on the total organization structure. This relationship was noted in the Aston studies[29] and subsequently in the studies by Blau and his associates.[30] The structures of small organizations have not reached the stage of growth that permits the creation of support units such as engineering, research and development, product development, and public relations. Consequently, the effect of technology on structure is more apparent in firms whose goals and functions are related to the production process.[31]

The effect of managerial choice takes into account the range of choices that managers have in designing an organization.[32] The choices are constrained by such factors as technology and economies of scale, but managers have considerable discretion within those constraints.[33] This point of view reconfirms the importance of management decision making for organizational performance. More important, it identifies technology as only one, albeit significant, factor in the organization's environment.

ENVIRONMENT AND ORGANIZATIONAL DESIGN

The relationship between technology and effective organizational design was firmly established in the Woodward study. Yet, as we saw,

---

[29] The original Aston studies were carried out from 1961 to 1973 by the Industrial Administration Unit of the University of Aston in Birmingham. The significant papers of this research are presented in Derek S. Pugh and David J. Hickson, *Organizational Structure in Its Context* (Westmead, England: Saxon House, D. C. Heath, 1976); and Derek S. Pugh and Charles R. Hinings, *Organizational Structure: Extensions and Replications* (Westmead, England: Saxon House, D. C. Heath, 1976). A recent review of the Aston Group's measure of structure is Peter H. Grinyer and Masoud Yasai-Ardekani, "Some Problems with the Measurement of Macro-Organizational Structure," *Organization Studies,* vol. 2, no. 3, 1981, pp. 287–96.

[30] Peter M. Blau, Cecilia M. Falbe, William McKinley, and K. Tracy Phelps, "Technology and Organization in Manufacturing," *Administrative Science Quarterly,* March 1976, pp. 20–30.

[31] Bernard C. Reimann, "Organizational Structure and Technology in Manufacturing: System versus Work Flow Level Perspectives," *Academy of Management Journal,* March 1980, pp. 61–77; Steven K. Paulson, "Organization Size, Technology, and Structure: Replication of a Study of Social Service Agencies among Small Retail Firms," *Academy of Management Journal,* June 1980, pp. 341–47; and Robert M. Marsh and Hiroshi Mannari, "Technology and Size as Determinants of the Organization Structures of Japanese Firms," *Administrative Science Quarterly,* March 1981, pp. 33–57.

[32] John R. Montanari, "An Expanded Theory of Structural Determination: An Empirical Investigation of the Impact of Managerial Discretion on Organization Structure," (DBA dissertation, University of Colorado, 1976); and Donald C. Hambrick, "Environment, Strategy, and Power within Top Management Teams," *Administrative Science Quarterly,* June 1981, pp. 253–76.

[33] H. Randolph Bobbitt and Jeffrey D. Ford, "Decision-Maker Choice as a Determinant of Organizational Structure," *Academy of Management Review,* January 1980, pp. 13–23.

the interpretation of that relationship required that the *environment* of organizations be taken into account. Thus, the more basic explanation for differences in organization is differences in the environment. This line of reasoning has been pursued by a number of researchers, notably Lawrence and Lorsch. We shall review their theory and some of their research findings in this section.

The Lawrence and Lorsch Findings

Lawrence and Lorsch based their findings on detailed case studies of firms in the plastics, food, and container industries.[34] An initial exploratory study consisted of case studies of six firms operating in the plastics industry. Lawrence and Lorsch analyzed these studies to answer the following questions.[35]

1. How are the environmental demands facing various organizations different, and how do environmental demands relate to the design of effective organizations?
2. Is it true that organizations in certain or stable environments make more exclusive use of centralized authority to make key decisions, and, if so, why? Is it because fewer key decisions are required, or is it because in certain or stable environments key decisions can be made more effectively at higher organizational levels or by fewer people?
3. Is the same degree of specialization and differences in orientation among individuals and groups found in organizations in different industrial environments?
4. If greater specialization and differences among individuals and groups are found in different industries, does this influence the problems of coordinating the organizations' parts? Does it influence the organizations' means of achieving integrations?

To arrive at answers to these questions, Lawrence and Lorsch undertook their research of structure in the plastics, food, and container industries. In the course of their investigation, they coined three terms that have since become widely used in the theory and practice of organizational design. These terms are: *differentiation, integration,* and *environment.*

---

[34] Paul R. Lawrence and Jay W. Lorsch, "Differentiation and Integration in Complex Organizations," *Administrative Science Quarterly,* June 1967, pp. 1–47; Jay W. Lorsch, *Product Innovation and Organization* (New York: Macmillan, 1965); Paul R. Lawrence and Jay W. Lorsch, *Organization and Environment* (Homewood, Ill.: Richard D. Irwin, 1969); and Paul R. Lawrence, "The Harvard Organization and Environment Research Program," in *Perspectives on Organization Design and Behavior,* ed. Andrew H. Van de Ven and William Joyce (New York: Wiley Interscience, 1981), pp. 311–37.

[35] Lawrence and Lorsch, *Organization and Environment,* p. 16.

differentiation
The degree of the differences among the units of an organization. The differences are due to different structural and behavioral characteristics.

Differentiation. The "state of segmentation of the organizational system into subsystems, each of which tends to develop particular attributes in relation to the requirements posed by its relevant external environment," is termed **differentiation.**[36] This concept refers in part to the idea of specialization of labor, specifically to the degree of departmentalization. But it is broader, and it also includes the behavioral attributes of the employees of subsystems, or departments. Lawrence and Lorsch were interested in three behavioral attributes:

1. They believed that the employees in some departments would be more or less task- or person-oriented than the employees in other departments. This belief reflects the ideas found in Fiedler's situational theory of leadership.
2. They proposed that the employees in some departments would have longer or shorter time horizons than the employees in other departments. They believed that these differences could be explained by different environmental attributes, specifically to differences in the length of time between action and the feedback of results.
3. They expected to find some employees more concerned with the goals of their department than with the goals of the total organization.

The organization of each department in six firms was classified along a continuum from mechanistic to organic. The employees in the mechanistically organized departments were expected to be more oriented toward tasks and to have shorter time horizons than the employees in the organic departments.

integration
The integration of differentiated units is achieved through rules, procedures, planning, and leadership.

Integration. The "process of achieving unity of effort among the various subsystems in the accomplishment of the organization's task" is defined as **integration,** and it can be achieved in a variety of ways.[37] The proponents of the mechanistic model argue for integration through the creation of rules and procedures to govern the behavior of the subsystem members. But this method of integration can be effective only in relatively stable and predictable situations.[38] Rules and procedures lose their effectiveness as the environment becomes more unstable; thus, integration by *plans* takes on greater significance. But as we approach the highly unstable environment, integration is achieved by mutual adjustment. Mutual adjustment requires a great deal of communication through open channels throughout the organi-

---

[36] Lawrence and Lorsch, "Differentiation and Integration in Complex Organizations," pp. 3–4.

[37] Ibid., p. 4.

[38] James D. Thompson, *Organizations in Action* (New York: McGraw-Hill, 1967), p. 56.

zation, a characteristic of organically designed organizations. In terms of the Lawrence and Lorsch research, the type of integrative devices that managers use should be related to the degree of differentiation. Highly differentiated organizations would tend to use mutual adjustment as a means of achieving integration.

Environment. Lawrence and Lorsch conceptualized the independent variable, environment, from the perspective of the organization's members as they looked outward. Consequently, they assumed that a basic reason for differentiating an organization into subsystems was to deal more effectively with subenvironments. They identified three main subenvironments: the *market* subenvironment, the *technical-economic* subenvironment, and the *scientific* subenvironment. These three subenvironments correspond to the sales, production, and research and development functions within organizations. Most organizations create separate departments for sales, production, and research and development. These departments represent parts of the total organization, or in the researchers' terms, "subsystems of the total system."

The researchers believed that the degree of differentiation within each subsystem would vary depending on specific attributes of the relevant subenvironment. Specifically, the subenvironment could vary along three dimensions: (1) the rate of change of conditions over time, (2) the certainty of information about conditions at any particular time, and (3) the time span of feedback on the results of employee decisions.[39]

Figure 14–1 depicts the idea that an organization consists of separate parts, usually departments, that must deal with different aspects of the total environment. Lawrence and Lorsch identify the organizational parts, or subsystems, as marketing, production, and research. They identify the environmental parts, or subenvironments as market, technical-economic, and science. The subsystems must be organized in such a way as to deal effectively with their relevant subenvironments. The greater the differences among the three subenvironments in terms of rate of change, certainty of information, and time span of feedback, the greater will be the differences among the three subsystems in terms of organizational structure and behavioral attributes. That is, the greater these differences, the more differentiated are the three subsystems and the more important is the task of integrating these subsystems.

An Interpretation of Lawrence and Lorsch's Findings

The differentiation-integration approach is based on the fundamental viewpoint that organizations must be designed to cope with environ-

---

[39] Lawrence and Lorsch, "Differentiation and Integration in Complex Organizations," pp. 7–8.

FIGURE 14-1

A Conceptualization of the Lawrence and Lorsch Model

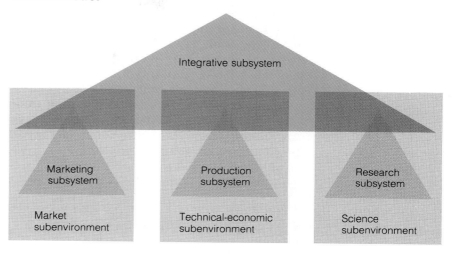

mental demands. But this approach goes further to show that different organizational designs can and often do exist within a single large organization. A manufacturing firm may find it necessary to design its production department quite differently from its research and development department. In some instances, for example in mass production, the production department must be designed according to the mechanistic model, but the research and development department may be designed according to the organic model. The differences in the designs are due to the differences in the environmental uncertainty that each department confronts. Because the production environment is relatively certain, there is no need to stress adaptability and the department can be designed to achieve high levels of efficiency. But the research and development environment is likely to be highly uncertain, with considerable need to cope flexibly with unforeseen changes.

The process of departmentalizing creates the necessity for integrating the activities of the departments. The integration of separate, yet interdependent, activities is a familiar problem in the management of organizations. Mechanistic design proponents believe that integration can be achieved through the creation of rules, procedures, plans, and a hierarchical chain of command that places managers in the position of integrators. The solutions of organic design proponents, differ, however. They believe that committees, task groups, cross-functional teams, integrators, and group-centered decision making are better approaches. According to Lawrence and Lorsch, either approach is appropriate depending on the situation.

Other studies have established the relationship of environmental factors to organizational structure.[40] But there are inconsistencies and contradictions in these studies. The causes of these inconsistencies are much like the causes of the inconsistencies associated with studies of technology. For example, some studies have used qualitative measures of environmental uncertainty, and others have used quantitative measures; some studies have used questionnaire responses as completed by participants in the organization, and others have used objective indexes of uncertainty.[41] It is necessary to evaluate critically the studies reporting environmental effects before drawing any final conclusions. It is also necessary to consider in detail the precise effects of environmental uncertainty on the organization. One approach is to evaluate the effects of uncertainty on the organization's information processing requirements.

ENVIRONMENTAL UNCERTAINTY, INFORMATION PROCESSING, AND ADAPTIVE DESIGN STRATEGIES

The relationships among environment, technology, and organizational structure can be synthesized. The key concept is *information*, and the key idea is that organizations must effectively receive, process, and act on information to achieve performance. Information flows into the organization from its environments. That information enables the organization to respond to market, technological, and resource changes.[42] The more rapid the changes, the greater is the necessity for information and the greater is the need for flexible and innovative organizational design.[43]

As we noted above, organizations existing in relatively certain and

---

[40] Lawrence G. Hrebiniak and Charles C. Snow, "Industry Differences in Environmental Uncertainty and Organizational Characteristics Related to Uncertainty," *Academy of Management Journal*, December 1980, pp. 750–59; and Howard L. Smith, Stephen M. Shortell, and Borje O. Saxberg, "An Empirical Test of the Configurational Theory of Organization," *Human Relations*, August 1979, pp. 667–88.

[41] H. Kirk Downey and R. Duane Ireland, "Quantitative versus Qualitative Environmental Assessment in Organizational Studies," *Administrative Science Quarterly*, December 1979, pp. 630–37; and Richard Blackburn and Larry L. Cummings, "Cognitions of Work-Unit Structure," *Academy of Management Journal*, December 1982, pp. 836–54.

[42] The development of theory relating information processing and organizational structure has been discussed in various sources. The more recent and most publicized sources are Jay Galbraith, *Designing Complex Organizations* (Reading, Mass.: Addison-Wesley Publishing, 1973); and Jay Galbraith, *Organization Design* (Reading, Mass.: Addison-Wesley Publishing, 1977).

[43] Jay R. Galbraith, "Designing the Innovative Organization," *Organizational Dynamics*, Winter 1982, pp. 5–25; Richard L. Daft, "Bureaucratic versus Nonbureaucratic Structure and the Process of Innovation and Change," *Research in the Sociology of Organizations*, vol. 1, no. 1, 1982, pp. 129–66; and William G. Egelhoff, "Strategy and Structure in Multinational Corporations: An Information Processing Approach," *Administrative Science Quarterly*, September 1982, pp. 453–58.

unchanging environments rely on centralized authority, rules and procedures, and planning to coordinate departments. These coordinative methods are effective as long as the environment remains stable and predictable. The information-processing requirements are relatively modest in such environments. For example, firms manufacturing and selling paper containers can plan production schedules with relative assurance that sudden shifts in demand, resource supply, or technology will not disrupt the schedules. The information requirements of such firms consist almost solely of projections from historical sales, cost, and engineering data.

Organizations existing in dynamic and complex environments, however, are unable to rely on traditional information-processing and control techniques. Changes in market demand, resource supplies, and technology disrupt plans and require adjustments *during* task performance. On-the-spot adjustments to production schedules and task performance disrupt such organizations. Coordination is made more difficult because it is impossible to preplan operations and to devise rules and procedures. It is imperative to acquire information that reflects environmental changes; "the greater the uncertainty, the greater the amount of information that must be processed among decision makers during task completion in order to achieve a given level of performance."[44]

From a managerial perspective, one effect of environmental uncertainty and increased flow of information is to overload the organization with problems requiring top management's attention. As a greater number of consequential nonroutine problems occur in the organization's environment, managers are more and more drawn into day-to-day operating matters. But neither the managers nor the organization can cope with the overload.

Some organizations are designed from their inception to deal with information-processing demands; most, however, must confront the problem at a point in time subsequent to their creation. For organizations that discover that their present design is incapable of dealing with the demands of changing environments, the problem becomes one of selecting an appropriate adaptive strategy. The two general approaches are (1) to reduce the need for information and (2) to increase the capacity to process information.

Strategies to Reduce the Need for Information

Managers can reduce the need for information by reducing (1) the number of exceptions that occur and (2) the number of factors to be

---

[44] Jay Galbraith, "Organization Design: An Information Processing View," *Interfaces,* May 1974, p. 28.

considered when the exceptions do occur. These two ends can be achieved by creating slack resources or by creating self-contained units.[45]

Creating Slack Resources.   Slack resources can be created by stockpiling materials, personnel, and other capabilities that enable the organization to respond to uncertainty. Slack resources can also be created by lengthening planning periods, production schedules, and lead times. These practices limit the number of exceptional cases by increasing the time span within which a response is necessary. For example, job-order manufacturers can intentionally overestimate the time required to complete a customized product, thus allowing time to deal with any difficulties that arise.

From the standpoint of organizational design, the effect of slack resources is to reduce the interdependence between units within the organization. If inventory is available to meet unexpected sales, no interaction is required between production and sales units. If inventory is not available, production and sales units must necessarily interact and coordinate their activities. Thus, through the creation of slack resources, management changes the nature of two of its subenvironments from uncertain to certain. As a consequence, the two departments can be integrated by mechanistic methods such as planning.

Creating Self-Contained Units.   Creating self-contained units involves a complete reorganization away from functional bases and toward product, customer, or territorial bases. Each unit is provided with its own resources—manufacturing, personnel, marketing, and engineering. Ordinarily, accounting, finance, and legal functions would remain centralized and made available to the new units on an "as needed" basis. Reorganization around products, customers, or territories enables the organization to achieve desired flexibility and adaptability; as you now know, these departmental bases are typically found in organic organizational design.

Strategies to Increase Capacity to Process Information

Instead of reducing the amount of information needed, managers may choose to increase the organization's capacity to process it. Two strategies accomplish this objective: (1) invest in information systems, or (2) create boundary-spanning roles.

Investing in Information Systems.   One result of increased environmental uncertainty is information overload. Managers are simply inundated with information that requires action of some kind. A strate-

---

[45] Based on Galbraith, "Organization Design."

gic response to the problem is to invest in information-processing systems, such as computers, clerks, and executive assistants. These resources process information more quickly and format the data in more efficient language. But the organizational design implications of this strategy are increased complexity (as more specialized jobs are designed) and increased formalization (processing information involves forms as well as formats!).

Creating Boundary-Spanning Roles. As the necessity for increased coordination among functional units intensifies, decisions must be made that cross departmental boundaries. The primary purpose of **boundary-spanning roles** is to facilitate joint decision making among the functional units, but without the loss of efficiency due to specialization. Individuals in boundary-spanning roles perform two functions: (1) they gather information; and (2) they represent the organization.[46]

boundary-spanning roles

Jobs that require the employee to relate to people in different units, both inside and outside the organization.

Internal boundary roles exist within the organization at the interface between such subunits as functional and product departments. Product managers, expediters, integrators, and liaison personnel are examples of roles that exist between subunits. Organizations cope with environmental uncertainty and increased information by establishing these types of roles.

External boundary roles exist at the interface of the organization and its external environments. Sales personnel, purchasing agents, lobbyists, public relations personnel, marketing researchers, and personnel recruiters are a few of the job titles that gather information and represent the organization.

The demands on those in boundary-spanning positions are qualitatively different from the demands on others in the organization. These unique demands result from the fact that boundary spanners must deal with conflicting expectations but lack the authority to settle the disagreements that arise.[47]

Role Conflict. Boundary spanners are often caught between people who expect different, and often incompatible, behaviors. Product managers, for example, must balance the interests of marketing personnel who want high-quality products against the interest of production personnel who desire manufacturing efficiency. Since the product manager has authority over neither group, he or she must balance these

---

[46] Howard Aldrich and Diane Herker, "Boundary Spanning Roles and Organization Structure," *Academy of Management Review,* April 1977, p. 218; and Michael L. Tushman and Thomas J. Scanlan, "Boundary Spanning Individuals: Their Role in Information Transfer and Antecedents," *Academy of Management Journal,* June 1981, pp. 289–305.

[47] The following discussion is based on Dennis W. Organ, "Linking Pins between Organizations and Environment," in *The Applied Psychology of Work Behavior,* ed. Dennis W. Organ (Plano, Tex.: Business Publications, 1978), 509–19.

interests and reach effective decisions through informal influence based on expertise. The company negotiator must deal simultaneously with the demands of both fellow managers and union spokespersons. Each segment of the environment or the organization has its own set of goals, beliefs, and values. To the extent that there are great differences among these sets, the boundary-spanning role is made more difficult. People having a high tolerance for ambiguity and a desire for relative freedom from close supervision, that is, autonomy, would have the greatest chance of performing the boundary-spanning role effectively because they would be able to cope with the conflict.

Lack of Authority.   Boundary spanners do not have position power; that is, authority is not delegated to them. They must achieve their performance levels through other means. An industrial salesperson, for example, can attempt to influence customer demand by becoming extremely knowledgeable about the customers' technical and production methods. By doing so, he or she is able to influence the customers' decisions with respect to purchasing the organization's products.

Agents of Change.   Some boundary-spanning positions are created to facilitate change and innovation. For example, key roles in research and development labs are those that link the labs to the various informational sources in the environment.[48] We have already noted the manner in which organizations respond to the necessity for product innovation by creating product task forces, teams, and managers. Indeed, the need to innovate arises coincidentally with environmental and technological pressures and demands. Yet the fact that boundary spanners are advocates for change places them in conflict with organizational subunits that desire stable operations, such as manufacturing, data processing, and personnel departments. An example of internal boundary-spanning roles is provided in the following Close-Up.

ORGANIZATIONS: CLOSE-UP

Product Managers at General Mills

The concept of product (or brand) managers was first introduced in 1927, when Procter & Gamble assigned a man to oversee Camay soap. Today product managers exist in a variety of multiproduct firms. Although the product manager's role differs from company to company, at General Mills he or she acts as a business manager, collecting all the necessary information that might affect the product and setting

---

[48] Michael L. Tushman, "Special Boundary Roles in the Innovation Process," *Administrative Science Quarterly,* December 1977, pp. 587–605.

goals and establishing strategies for achieving those goals. Seemingly, a product manager at General Mills is a full-fledged manager. Such, however, is not the case. A product manager *represents* the product in the organization and must obtain internal resources by means other than formal authority. In a real sense, the product manager has considerable responsibility but no authority over the production and marketing functions necessary to carry out that responsibility.

Product managers compete with one another for financial and staff support for their products. They also compete for promotions to the next tier of management—marketing director. At present, there are 33 product managers at General Mills; only 8 or 9 of them will be promoted to the next level. About half of those not promoted will go to another company; the other half will move to other positions in General Mills. The system at General Mills does a good job of preparing future general managers in the marketing aspects of the business, but it is less successful in providing training and experience in the production and finance areas.

Basically, product management is management by persuasion. For example, if a product manager needs special support from the sales force and additional output from manufacturing to implement an aggressive advertising campaign, he or she must sell the idea to people who report to the managers of marketing and manufacturing. If the product manager believes that the product needs different packaging, new recipe testing, or a reformulation of basic ingredients, he or she must persuade the appropriate support personnel to take action on the product. To be effective in the role of product manager, the individual must be effective in dealing with people up and down the line. The individual must be able to cross the boundaries of the various functional areas and obtain the support needed to carry out the plans for the product.

Source: Ann M. Morrison, "The General Mills Brand of Managers," *Fortune*, January 12, 1981 pp. 99–107.

Thus, we see that the adaptation of organizations to increasing uncertainty and the need for information requires some changes in the organizational design. Reducing the need for information and increasing the capacity to process information are, however, partial strategies. They are effective only when the environmental pressures are episodic or temporary. If the environmental pressures are persistent and permanent, more complete solutions are called for. In particular, management will begin to develop a matrix organization. Figure 14–2 summarizes the discussion to this point.

matrix organization
An organizational design that overlays product or project departments on existing functional departments.

MATRIX ORGANIZATIONAL DESIGN

An emerging organizational design, termed **matrix organization,** attempts to maximize the strengths and minimize the weaknesses of

FIGURE 14–2

Management's Responses to Environmental Demands for Increased Information Processing

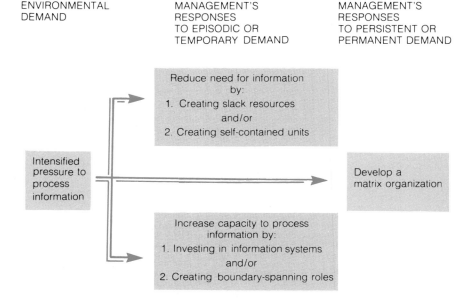

ENVIRONMENTAL
DEMAND

MANAGEMENT'S
RESPONSES
TO EPISODIC OR
TEMPORARY DEMAND

MANAGEMENT'S
RESPONSES
TO PERSISTENT OR
PERMANENT DEMAND

Intensified pressure to process information

Reduce need for information by:
1. Creating slack resources and/or
2. Creating self-contained units

Increase capacity to process information by:
1. Investing in information systems and/or
2. Creating boundary-spanning roles

Develop a matrix organization

both the mechanistic and organic designs. In practical terms, the matrix design combines functional and product departmental bases.[49] Among the many companies that use matrix organization are American Cyanamid, Avco, Carborundum, Caterpillar Tractor, Hughes Aircraft, ITT, Monsanto Chemical, National Cash Register, Prudential Insurance, TRW, and Texas Instruments. Public sector users include public health and social service agencies.[50] Although the exact meaning of matrix organization is not well established, the most typical meaning sees it as a balanced compromise between functional and product organization, between departmentalization by process and by purpose.[51]

The matrix organizational design achieves the desired balance by superimposing, or overlaying, a horizontal structure of authority, influence, and communication on the vertical structure. The arrange-

[49] Richard L. Daft, *Organization Theory and Design* (St. Paul: West Publishing, 1983), p. 237.

[50] Kenneth Knight, "Matrix Organization: A Review," *Journal of Management Studies,* May 1976, p. 111.

[51] Ibid., p. 114.

FIGURE 14–3

Matrix Organizations

Projects, Products	Functions			
	Manufacturing	Marketing	Engineering	Finance
Project or product A				
Project or product B				
Project or product C				
Project or product D				
Project or product E				

ment can be described as in Figure 14–3; personnel assigned in each cell belong not only to the functional department but also to a particular product or project. For example, manufacturing, marketing, engineering, and finance specialists will be assigned to work on one or more projects or products A, B, C, D, and E. As a consequence, personnel will report to two managers, one in their functional department and one in the project or product unit. The existence of a *dual authority* system is a distinguishing characteristic of matrix organization.

Matrix structures are found in organizations that require responses to rapid change in two or more environments, such as technology and markets; that face uncertainties generating high information-processing requirements; and that must deal with financial and human resources constraints.[52] Managers confronting these circumstances must obtain certain advantages that are most likely to be realized with matrix organizations.[53]

Advantages of Matrix Organization

A number of advantages can be associated with the matrix design. Some of the more important ones are as follows.

Efficient Use of Resources. Matrix organization facilitates the utilization of highly specialized staff and equipment. Each project or product unit can share the specialized resource with other units, rather than duplicating it to provide independent coverage for each. This

---

[52] Paul R. Lawrence, Harvey F. Kolodny, and Stanley M. Davis, "The Human Side of the Matrix," *Organizational Dynamics*, September 1977, p. 47.

[53] The following discussion is based on Knight, "Matrix Organization."

is particularly advantageous when projects require less than the full-time efforts of the specialist. For example, a project may require only half of a computer scientist's time. Rather than having underutilized computer scientists assigned to each of several projects, the organization can keep fewer computer scientists fully utilized by shifting them from project to project.

Flexibility in Conditions of Change and Uncertainty. Timely response to change requires information and communication channels that efficiently get the necessary information to the right people at the right time. Matrix structures encourage constant interaction among project unit and functional department members. Information is channeled vertically and horizontally as people exchange technical knowledge. The result is quicker response to competitive conditions, technological breakthroughs, and other environmental conditions.

Technical Excellence. Technical specialists interact with other specialists while assigned to a project. Such interaction encourages cross-fertilization of ideas, as when a computer scientist must discuss the pros and cons of electronic data processing with a financial accounting expert. Each specialist must be able to listen to, understand, and respond to the views of the other. At the same time, specialists maintain ongoing contact with members of their own discipline because they are also members of a functional department.

Freeing Top Management for Long-Range Planning. An initial stimulus for the development of matrix organizations is that top management becomes increasingly involved with day-to-day operations. Environmental changes tend to create problems that cross functional and product departments and that cannot be resolved by the lower level managers. For example, when competitive conditions create the need to develop new products at faster rates, the existing procedures become bogged down. Top management is then called on to settle conflicts among the functional managers. Matrix organization makes it possible for top management to delegate ongoing decision making, thus providing more time for long-range planning.

Improving Motivation and Commitment. Project and product groups comprise individuals with specialized knowledge. On the basis of their expertise, management assigns these individuals responsibility for specific aspects of the work. Consequently, decision making within project and product groups tends to be more participative and democratic than in hierarchical settings. The opportunity to participate in key decisions fosters high levels of motivation and commitment, particularly for individuals with acknowledged professional orientations.

Providing Opportunities for Personal Development. Members of matrix organizations are given considerable opportunity to develop their skills and knowledge. They are placed in groups consisting of individuals representing diverse parts of the organization. They must, therefore, come to appreciate the different points of view expressed by these individuals; each group member becomes more aware of the total organization. Moreover, members of matrix organizations have opportunities to learn something of other specialties. Engineers develop knowledge of financial issues; accountants learn about marketing. The experience broadens each specialist's knowledge, not only of the organization, but of other scientific and technical disciplines.

Different Forms of Matrix Organization

Matrix organization forms can be depicted as existing in the middle of a continuum that has mechanistic organizations at one extreme and organic organizations at the other. Organizations can move from mechanistic to matrix forms or from organic to matrix forms. Ordinarily, the process of moving to matrix organization is evolutionary. That is, as the present structure proves incapable of dealing with rapid technological and market changes, management attempts to cope by establishing procedures and positions that are outside the normal routine.

Galbraith describes this evolutionary process as follows:

Task Force. When a competitor develops a new product that quickly captures the market, a rapid response is necessary. In a mechanistic organization, however, new product development is often too time-consuming because of the need to coordinate the various units that must be involved. A convenient approach is to create a task force of individuals from each functional department and to charge it with the responsibility for expediting the process. The task force achieves its objective and dissolves, as members return to their primary assignment.

Teams: If product or technological breakthrough generates a family of products that move through successive stages of new and improved products, the temporary task force concept is ineffective. A typical next step is to create permanent teams that consist of representatives from each functional department. The teams meet regularly to resolve interdepartmental issues and to achieve coordination. When not involved with issues associated with new product development, the team members work on their regular assignments.

Product Managers. If the persistence of the technological breakthrough makes new product development a way of life, top management will create the roles of product managers. In a sense, product managers chair the teams, but they are not permanent positions. Ordinarily, they report to top management, but they have no formal authority over the team members. They must rely on their expertise and interpersonal skill to influence the team members. Companies such as General Foods, Du Pont, and IBM make considerable use of the product management concept.

Product Management Departments. The final step in the evolution to matrix organization is the creation of product management departments. Figure 14–4 depicts the organization that has a product manager reporting to top management and subproduct managers for each product line. In some instances, the subproduct managers are selected from specific functional departments and continue to report directly to their functional managers. There is considerable diversity in the application of matrix organization, yet the essential feature is the creation of overlapping authority and the existence of dual authority.

Exactly where along the continuum an organization stops in the evolution depends on factors in the situation. Specifically and primarily important are the rates of change in technological and product developments. The resultant uncertainty and the information required to deal with the uncertainty vary. The following Close-Up illustrates how one firm used a form of matrix organization.

ORGANIZATIONS: CLOSE-UP

Matrix Organization at IM&CC, Inc.

Anthony E. Cascino, vice chairman of International Minerals & Chemical Corporation, recounts how a crisis that threatened to break down the company's decision-making processes led him to adapt matrix organization to meet the crisis. At the time of the crisis, Cascino was an executive vice president who relied on two key managers: the vice president of marketing and the vice president of operations. Within a two-week period of time, both vice presidents left the company, and no qualified successors were available. Cascino had been removed from day-to-day operations for several years and was quite reluctant to try to do the work of the vice presidents who were no longer with the company.

The task of personally overseeing the activities of five operating divisions and five marketing divisions was impossible without some form of coordination. Since most of the causes for adjustment were generated from within the marketing divisions, Cascino brought together the heads of the five marketing divisions and asked them to collectively assume the responsibility for coordination of their divisions. He asked them to select their own chairperson, to meet as often as necessary, and to seek his intervention only when they were unable to find solutions to their problems. The informal arrangement soon became a permanent part of the organizational structure as the benefits of horizontal collaboration were recognized. The "Coordinating Committee" came to include representatives from the production divisions, and several improvements in performance criteria were traceable, according to Cascino, to this form of matrix organization as it evolved in IM&CC.

Source: Anthony E. Cascino, "How One Company 'Adapted' Matrix Management in a Crisis," *Management Review*, November 1979, pp. 57–61.

FIGURE 14–4

Fully Evolved Matrix Organization

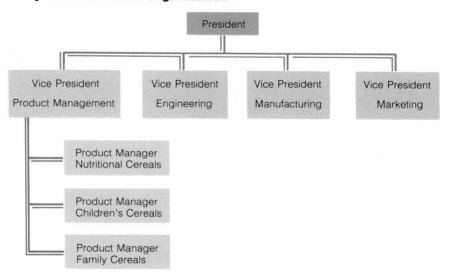

AN INTEGRATIVE FRAMEWORK

Managers must consider many complex factors and variables to design an optimal organization structure. The most important of these factors and variables are shown in Figure 14–5. The material presented in Chapters 12, 13, and 14 reflects the current state of knowledge regarding the issues of organizational design. As we have seen, the *key design decisions* are division of labor, departmentalization, spans of control, and delegation of authority. These decisions, which reflect *environmental* and *managerial* interactions, are complex; managers do not have the luxury of designing a one best way structure. Instead, the optimal design depends on the situation as determined by the interaction of size, environmental, and managerial factors. Matching

FIGURE 14-5

**An Integrative Framework for Organizational
Design**

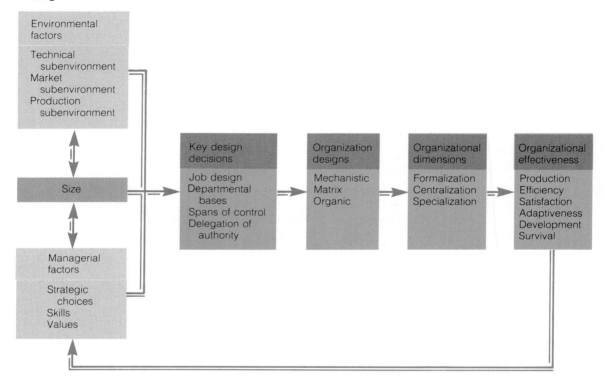

the appropriate structure to these factors is the essence of *contingency
design* theory and practice.

The overall structure of tasks and authority that results from the
key decisions is a specific *organization design*. The alternative designs
range along a continuum, with mechanistic design at one extreme
and organic design at the other. The matrix design, at the midpoint,
represents a balance between the two extremes.

Organizational structures differ on many dimensions, the more important being shown in Figure 14–5. In general, mechanistic organizations are more formalized, centralized, and specialized than organic
organizations. They are also less differentiated, and they achieve integration through hierarchy, rules and procedures, and planning. Organic organizations, however, must achieve integration through more
complex methods, including boundary-spanning roles, task groups,
committees, and other forms of mutual adjustment. Regardless of the
specific configuration of organizational dimensions and integration
strategies, the overriding purpose of organizational design is to chan-

nel the behavior of individuals and groups into patterns which contribute to effective organizational performance.

Thus, managerial decision making plays a key role in organizational design.[54] In fact, much of what has been stated in this section can be summarized in the idea that structure follows strategy[55] and that maximum performance is achieved when there is congruence between strategy and structure.[56] Managerial strategy involves the choice of what products and services the organization will supply to specific customers and markets. Thus, managers who decide to supply a single product to a specific set of customers can be expected to design a far simpler organizational structure than will be designed by managers of a highly diversified company serving multiple markets with multiple products and services.[57] Moreover, the strategic choice affects not only organizational design but also job design[58] and, apparently, leadership behavior[59] as well. Organizational design is the consequence of many variables, but despite that complexity some general conclusions apply, as noted in this chapter.

SUMMARY OF KEY POINTS

A. The task and authority relationships among jobs and groups of jobs must be defined and structured according to rational bases. Practitioners and theorists have recommended two specific, yet contradictory, theories for designing organizational structures.

B. One theory, termed *mechanistic design,* is based on the assumption that the more effective organizational structure is characterized by highly specialized jobs, homogeneous departments, narrow spans of control, and relatively centralized authority. The bases

---

[54] L. J. Bourgeois, "Strategy and Environment: A Conceptual Integration," *Academy of Management Review,* January 1980, pp. 25–39.

[55] Alfred Chandler, *Strategy and Structure* (Cambridge, Mass.: MIT Press, 1962).

[56] This relationship has been analyzed in a series of studies, including Richard Rumelt, *Strategy, Structure, and Economic Performance* (Boston, Mass.: Division of Research, Harvard Business School, 1974); and, more recently, Peter Grinyer, Shawki Al-Bazzaz, and Masoud Yasai-Ardekani, "Strategy, Structure, the Environment, and Financial Performance in 48 United Kingdom Companies," *Academy of Management Journal,* June 1980, pp. 193–220.

[57] Jay R. Galbraith and Daniel A. Nathanson, *Strategy Implementation: The Role of Structure and Process* (St Paul, Minn.: West Publishing, 1978).

[58] Jon L. Pierce, Randall B. Dunham, and Richard S. Blackburn, "Social System Structure, Job Design, and Growth Need Strength: A Test of the Congruence Model," *Academy of Management Journal,* June 1979, pp. 223–40.

[59] Ricky W. Griffin, "Relationships among Individual, Task Design, and Leader Behavior Variables," *Academy of Management Journal,* December 1980, pp. 665–83.

for these assumptions are to be found in the historical circumstances within which this theory developed. It was a time of fairly rapid industrialization that encouraged public and private organizations to emphasize the production and efficiency criteria of effectiveness. To achieve these ends, classical design theory proposes a single best way to structure an organization.

C. In recent years, beginning with the human relations era of the 1930s and sustained by the growing interest of behavioral scientists in the study of management and organization, an alternative to mechanistic design theory has been developed. This alternative theory, termed *organic design*, proposes that the more effective organization has relatively despecialized jobs, heterogeneous departments, wide spans of control, and decentralized authority. Such organizational structures, it is argued, achieve not only high levels of production and efficiency but also satisfaction, adaptiveness, and development.

D. The design of an effective organizational structure cannot be guided by a "one best way" theory. Rather, the manager must adopt the point of view that either the mechanistic or organic design is more effective for the total organization or for subunits within its organization.

E. The manager must identify and describe the relevant subenvironments of the organization. These subenvironments determine the relationships within units, among units, and between units and their subenvironments.

F. The manager must evaluate each subenvironment in terms of its rate of change, relative certainty, and time span of feedback. These conditions are the key variables for determining the formal structure of tasks and authority.

G. Each subunit structure is designed along the mechanistic-organic continuum in a manner consistent with the state of environmental conditions. Specifically, slower rates of change, greater certainty, and shorter time spans of feedback are compatible with the mechanistic design; the converse is true for the organic design.

H. Concurrent with the design of subunit structures is the design of integrative techniques. The appropriate techniques, whether rules, plans, or mutual adjustment, depend on the degree of subunit differentiation. The greater the differentiation, the greater is the need for mutual adjustment techniques. The smaller the differentiation, the greater is the need for rules and plans.

I. Information processing is required of all organizations, given their size, technology, and environments. Thus, information processing, as a concept, summarizes the contingency theory of organizational design.

DISCUSSION AND REVIEW QUESTIONS

1. Explain the rationale for the argument that there is "one best way" to design an organization.

2. "Anytime a group forms to accomplish a task, a hierarchy of authority *must* be created." Comment.

3. All organizations have elements of bureaucracy. Can you think of any instance for which this statement is not true?

4. What is the basis of the argument that bureaucracies tend to become conservative in their actions?

5. What is the basis of the argument that organic organization is the one best way to organize? Do you agree?

6. Do you believe that it would be easier to change an organization from mechanistic to organic, or from organic to mechanistic? Explain.

7. Do you believe that any real-world organizations can be termed organic? Do you believe that there are any "ideal type" bureaucracies? If not, of what use are these concepts?

8. Use the characteristics of mechanistic and organic organization to describe two different organizations that you know about. After you have determined the organizational differences, see whether you can relate the differences to technological and environmental differences.

9. What are the counterparts to the market, technical-economic, and scientific subenvironments of a university? A hospital? A professional football team?

10. What criteria of effectiveness were used in the Woodward research? Compare these with the criteria used in the Lawrence and Lorsch research.

11. Discuss the manner in which technology and environmental certainty interact to determine the most effective organization.

12. Although this has not been the main focus of the chapter, we have suggested ways in which the structure of an organization is related to such processes as communications, interactions, and time orientations. As a general rule, are you prepared to accept the argument that the structure does, in fact, determine important aspects of these processes? Discuss your reasoning.

13. Based on whatever information is at your disposal, rank from high to low the environmental uncertainty of a college of arts and sciences, a college of engineering, a college of business, and a college of education. What does your ranking suggest about the integration techniques that would be appropriate in each college?

ADDITIONAL REFERENCES

Blau, P. M. "A Formal Theory of Differentiation in Organizations." *American Sociological Review*, 1970, pp. 201–18.

Burns, T., and G. W. Stalker. *The Management of Innovation.* London: Tavistock Publications, 1961.

Chase, R. B., and D. A. Tansik. "The Customer Contact Model for Organization Design." *Management Science,* 1983, pp. 1037–50.

Corey, E. R., and S. H. Star. *Organization Strategy: A Marketing Approach.* Boston: Division of Research, Harvard Business School, 1971.

Cremer, A. J. "A Partial Theory of the Optimal Organization of a Bureaucracy." *Bell Journal of Economics,* 1980, pp. 683–93.

Driver, M. J. "A Human Resource Data-Based Approach to Organizational Design." *Human Resource Planning,* 1983, pp. 169–82.

Gordon, L. V. "Correlates of Bureaucratic Orientation." *Manpower and Applied Psychology,* 1969, pp. 54–59.

Harvey, E. "Technology and Structure in Organizations." *American Sociological Review,* 1968, pp. 247–49.

Jelinek, M., and M. Burstein. "The Production Administrative Structure." *Academy of Management Review,* 1982, pp. 242–51.

Jurkovich, R. "A Core Typology of Organization Environments." *Administrative Science Quarterly,* 1974, pp. 380–94.

Lynch, B. P. "An Empirical Assessment of Perrow's Technology Construct." *Administrative Science Quarterly,* 1974, pp. 338–56.

Mills, P. K., and D. J. Moberg. "Perspectives on the Technology of Service Organizations." *Academy of Management Review,* 1982, pp. 467–78.

Mintzberg, H. "Organization Design: Fashion or Fit?" *Harvard Business Review,* 1981, pp. 103–16.

Mohr, L. B. "Organizational Technology and Organizational Structure." *Administrative Science Quarterly,* 1970, pp. 444–59.

Osborn, R. N., and J. G. Hunt. "Environment and Organizational Effectiveness." *Administrative Science Quarterly,* 1974, pp. 231–46.

Pearce, J. A., II, and F. R. David. "A Social Network Approach to Organization Design —Performance." *Academy of Management Review,* 1983, pp. 436–44.

Pennings, J. M. "The Relevance of the Structural-Contingency Model for Organizational Effectiveness." *Administrative Science Quarterly,* 1975, pp. 393–410.

Pheysey, D. C.; R. L. Payne; and D. S. Pugh. "Influence of Structure on Organizational and Group Levels." *Administrative Science Quarterly,* 1971, pp. 61–73.

Reimann, B. D. "Dimensions of Structure in Effective Organizations." *Academy of Management Journal,* 1974, pp. 693–708.

Segal, M. "Organization and Environment: A Typology of Adaptability and Structure." *Public Administration Review,* 1974, pp. 212–20.

Simon, M. E. "Matrix Management in the U.S. Consumer Products Safety Commission." *Public Administration Review,* 1983, pp. 357–61.

Thompson, J. D., ed. *Approaches to Organizational Design.* Pittsburgh: University of Pittsburgh Press, 1966.

Urwick, L. *Notes on the Theory of Organization.* New York: American Management Association, 1952.

CASE FOR ANALYSIS

Defining the Role of a Liaison Officer

Recently, the governor of a southeastern state created the Department for Human Resources. It was in fact a combination of many formerly distinct state agencies that carried out health and welfare programs. The organization chart of the department is shown in Exhibit 1. The functions of each of the bureaus as noted in the governor's press release are as follows:

The Bureau for Social Insurance will operate all income maintenance and all income supplementation programs of the Department for Human Resources. That is, it will issue financial support to the poor, unemployed, and needy, and it will issue food stamps and pay for medical assistance.

The Bureau for Social Services will provide child welfare services, foster care, adoptions, family services, and all other general counseling in support of families and individuals who require assistance for successful and adequate human development.

The Bureau for Health Services will operate all programs of the Department that provide health service, including all physical and mental health programs. This bureau will take over the functions of the Department of Health, the Department of Mental Health, and the Commission for Handicapped Children.

The Bureau for Manpower Services will operate all manpower development and job placement programs of the Department, including all job recruitment and business liaison functions, job training, and worker readiness functions and job counseling and placement.

EXHIBIT 1

Department for Human Resources

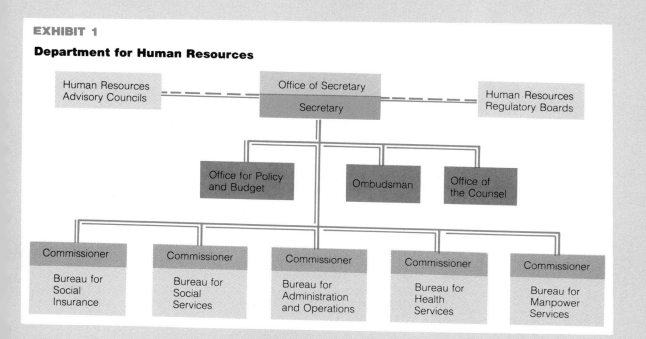

The Bureau for Administration and Operations will consolidate numerous support services now furnished by 19 separate units such as preaudits, accounting, data processing, purchasing, and duplicating, for all the Departments.

Very soon after the department began to operate in its reorganized form, it became apparent that major problems were traceable to the Bureau for Administration and Operations (BAO). Prior to reorganization, each department had had its own support staffs—data processing, accounting, personnel, and budgeting. Those staffs and equipment had all been relocated and brought under the direction of the BAO commissioner. Employees who had once specialized in the work of one area, such as mental health, were now expected to perform work for all the bureaus. In addition, it was necessary to revise forms, procedures, computer programs, accounts, and records to conform to the new department's policies.

Consequently, the department began to experience administrative problems. Payrolls were late and inaccurate; payments to vendors and clients were delayed; and personnel actions got lost in the paperwork. Eventually, the integrity of the department service programs was in jeopardy.

The executive staff of the department, consisting of the secretary, commissioner, and administrator of the Office for Policy and Budget, soon found itself spending more time dealing with these administrative problems than with policy formulation. It was apparent that the department's effectiveness would depend on its ability to integrate the functions of BAO with the needs of the program bureaus. It was also apparent that the executive staff was not the appropriate body to deal with these issues. Aside from the inordinate amount of time that was being spent on the administrative problems, a great deal of interpersonal conflict was being generated among the commissioners.

The BAO commissioner was instructed by the secretary to give his full-time attention to devising a means for integrating the administrative functions. After consultation with his staff, the idea of an administrative liaison officer was formulated. The staff paper that described this new job is shown in Exhibit 2. The BAO commissioner presented the paper to the executive

EXHIBIT 2

Description of Responsibilities, Administrative Liaison Officer

Introduction

Executive Order 78–777 abolished the former human resources agencies and merged their functions into a new single department. A prime element in the organizational concept of the new department is the centralization of administrative and support activities into a Bureau for Administration and Operations which supports the four program bureaus of the Department. While the centralization of these administrative and support activities only included those functions that were located in centralized administrative units in the former human resources agencies, the size of the Department for Human Resources dictates that extra levels of effort be applied to ensure close coordination and cooperation between the four program bureaus and the Bureau for Administration and Operations.

EXHIBIT 2 (*continued*)

As one element in the comprehensive range of efforts now being applied to ensure a high level of responsiveness and cooperation between the Bureau for Administration and Operations and each program bureau, there will be created within the Office of the Commissioner for Administration and Operations four positions for administrative liaison officers, one of which will be assigned responsibility for liaison with each program bureau.

Responsibilities

1. Each administrative liaison officer will provide assistance to the program bureau commissioner and other officials of the program bureau to which assigned in the:

    a. Identification and definition of the administrative and operational support needs of that program bureau.
    b. Determination of the relative priorities of those needs for services.
    c. Identification of programmatic and operational requirements of the program bureau that may be assisted by the enforcement of administrative regulations by the Bureau for Administration and Operations.
    d. Identification of resources available within the Bureau for Administration and Operations that may be of value to the program bureau.
    e. Coordination of the delivery of services by the various divisions of the Bureau for Administration and Operations to the program bureau.
    f. Interpretation of data and information provided by the Bureau for Administration and Operations.
    g. Interpretation and distribution of administrative regulations and procedures issued by the Bureau for Administration and Operations with respect to its responsibilities under policies delineated by the secretary and the commissioners of the Department for Human Resources.

2. Each administrative liaison officer will provide assistance to the Commissioner for Administration and Operations and other officials of the Bureau for Administration and Operations in the:

    a. Development of strategies for providing the maximum possible quality and quantity of support services that can be made available to the officer's particular program bureau within budgetary and policy constraints.
    b. Understanding of special needs and problems of respective program bureaus.
    c. Identification of new procedures and systems whereby services rendered to the program bureau can result in improved coordination between all organizational units of the Department for Human Resources.
    d. Identification of inadequacies or gaps in presently available services provided by the Bureau for Administration and Operations.
    e. Direction and/or coordination of task forces and other temporary organizational units created within the Bureau for Administration and Operations assigned to provide resources specific to the program bureau.
    f. Supervision of all personnel of the Bureau for Administration and Operations that may be on a temporary duty assignment to the program bureau to which the officer is assigned.

Operational Arrangement

1. The administrative liaison officer will be appointed to a position within the Office of the Commissioner for Administration and Operations.
2. The assignment of an administrative liaison officer to a program bureau will require the concurrence of the commissioner of that program bureau.

EXHIBIT 2 (*concluded*)

3.   The Office of the Administrative Liaison Officer will be physically located within the suite of offices of the program bureau commissioner to whom the officer is assigned.
4.   The administrative liaison officer will attend all staff meetings of the commissioner of the program bureau to which assigned and all staff meetings of the Commissioner for Administration and Operations.

staff for discussion and adoption. According to the BAO commissioner, there was simply no procedural or planning means for integrating the administrative functions. Rather, it would continue to be a conflict-laden process that would require the undivided attention of an individual assigned to each of the four bureaus.

Questions for Consideration

1.   Evaluate the concept of "administrative liaison officer" as a strategy for achieving integration. Is this an example of the mutual adjustment strategy?
2.   How will the officers achieve integration when they will have no authority over either the administrative functions or the programs that are to be integrated?
3.   What would be the most important personal characteristics to look for in an applicant for these positions?

EXPERIENTIAL EXERCISE

ORGANIZING A NEW BUSINESS

Objectives

To increase the readers' understanding of the organizational design problem in the context of a new business.

Related Topics

Chapters 12, 13, and 14 provide the reader with sufficient information.

Starting the Exercise

Form groups of five to eight individuals toward the end of a class meeting. Each group will meet for 5–10 minutes and identify a specific type of business that will be the focus of its exercise. For convenience, the groups can be encouraged to select one of the fast-food franchise restaurants. Most readers are familiar with these businesses and have sufficient knowledge of their operations to complete the exercise.

In the interim, before the next meeting, each group member will complete the six steps of the exercise. The groups will meet during class time to share answers and to prepare a group report. The reports will be presented at the second class meeting.

Instructions for the Exercise

1. State the primary mission of your business. What functions must be performed to accomplish the mission?

2. Describe the environment in which your business must operate in terms of the relevant subenvironments. Identify the relative certainty with which information about these subenvironments will be received.

3. Write job descriptions for each class of jobs for each function, including managerial and nonmanagerial jobs.

4. Draw an organization chart, and describe how the roles and functions will be integrated.

5. What important knowledge and skills will be required for each of the key roles in the organization?

6. What crucial decisions are to be made that will determine the success of the business?

7. Meet in assigned groups, and share your work. Prepare a group plan that embodies the best ideas generated by the group members. Compare your plan with those of other groups, and modify it if you think this is necessary.

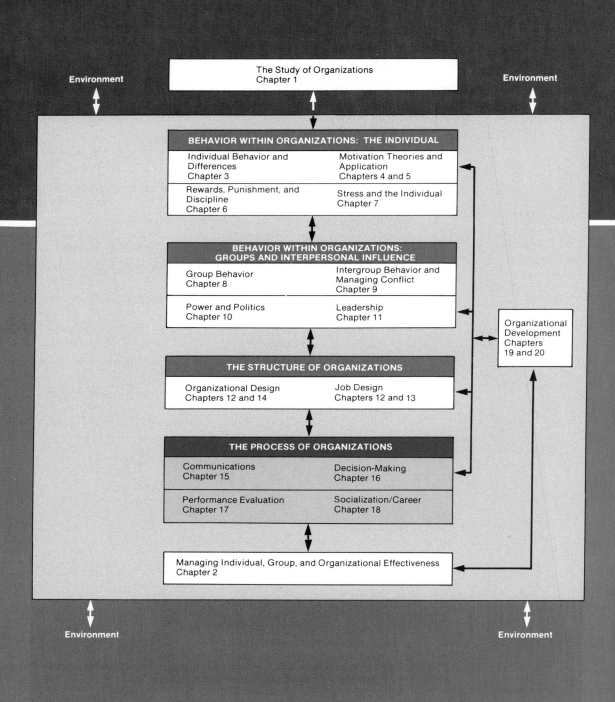

THE PROCESSES OF ORGANIZATIONS

Chapter 15

After completing Chapter 15, you should be able to:

Define the term *communication.*

Describe how the process of communication works.

Discuss the major elements in the process of communication.

Compare the various forms that communication takes within organizations.

Identify the major barriers to effective communication and means to overcome these barriers.

Communication Processes

An Organizational Issue for Debate

The Value of Upward Communication*

Argument For

While the classical organizational structure formally provides for downward and upward communication, the downward system seems

* For research and discussion on this issue, see H. J. Leavitt and R. A. H. Mueller, "Some Effects of Feedback on Communications," *Human Relations*, November 1951, pp. 401–10; W. V. Haney, "A Comparative Study of Unilateral and Bilateral Communication," *Academy of Management Journal*, June 1964, pp. 128–36; W. V. Haney, *Communication in Organizational Behavior* (Homewood, Ill.: Richard D. Irwin, 1973); and K. H. Roberts and C. A. O'Reilly III, "Failures in Upward Communication in Organizations: Three Possible Culprits," *Academy of Management Journal*, June 1974, pp. 205–15.

to dominate in most organizations. As a result, most organizational communication is one-way, from higher to lower levels without obtaining any reactions or questions from subordinates. In addition, traditional systems—grievance procedures, suggestion systems, employee publications, and "open-door" policies—instituted in many organizations have not worked.

As a result, managers must encourage the free flow of upward communication and encourage subordinates to express their opinions and offer suggestions for improvement. They must seek to develop an atmosphere of trust between themselves and their subordinates. Research has indicated that two-way communication is more accurate than one-way communication. However, how accurate it is depends a great deal on the amount of trust that the subordinate has in the superior. Under the right conditions, communication could take the form of summaries, proposals, and recommendations from subordinates. This will improve not only decision making and organizational performance but also the attitudes and satisfaction of subordinates.

529

Argument Against

The studies indicating that two-way communication is more effective have always involved complex problems requiring two-way communication for solution. They have also been conducted mostly in laboratory situations, and they have involved problems that have nothing to do with those faced by individuals in most organizations.

In the majority of situations, understanding is easy to achieve and two-way communication is not critical. Besides, two-way communication takes time, and that is a cost most organizations cannot afford. Time is a valuable resource in most organizations. In highly structured organizations, where the problems are routine, one-way communication is more than adequate if care is taken. This is not to say that the situation might not be different in a scientific laboratory than in a police or fire department.

We must also remember the realities of organizational life. Subordinates often purposely withhold information that they think is unpleasant or would displease their superior. Also, distortions and cover-ups occur because subordinates want to avoid looking incompetent to superiors.

One of the important purposes of an organizational *structure* is to facilitate the *process* of communication. The opening Organizational Issue for Debate stresses the necessity of both downward and upward communication. This chapter will focus on the process of organizational communication, while the process of decision making will be the subject of the next chapter. However, both processes are similar in that they pervade everything managers do. The managerial functions of planning, organizing, leading, and controlling all involve managers in specific decisions and communication. In fact, the management functions of planning, organizing, leading, and controlling become operationalized only through communicative activity. When making decisions, managers must both acquire and disseminate information. Thus, communication is critical since managers rarely work with "things" but rather with "information about things."

THE IMPORTANCE OF COMMUNICATION

"You said to get to it as soon as I could—how did I know you meant now!" "How did I know she was really serious about resigning!" In these and similar situations, someone usually ends up saying, "What we have here is a failure to communicate." This statement has meaning to everyone because each of us has faced situations in which the basic problem was communication. Whether on a person-to-person basis, nation-to-nation, in organizations, or in small groups, breakdowns in communication are pervasive.

It would be extremely difficult to find an aspect of a manager's job that does not involve communication. Serious problems arise when directives are misunderstood, when casual kidding in a work group leads to anger, or when informal remarks by a top-level manager are distorted. Each of these situations is a result of a breakdown somewhere in the process of communication.

Accordingly, the pertinent question is not whether managers engage in communication or not, because communication is inherent to the functioning of an organization. Rather, the pertinent question is whether managers will communicate well or poorly. In other words, communication itself is unavoidable in an organization's functioning; only *effective* communication is avoidable. *Every manager must be a communicator.* In fact, everything that a manager does communicates something in some way to somebody or some group. The only question is, "With what effect?" While this may appear an overstatement at this point, it will become apparent as you proceed through the chapter. Despite the tremendous advances in communication and information technology, communication among people in organizations leaves much to be desired. Communication among people does not depend on technology, but rather on forces in people and their surroundings. It is a "process" that occurs "within" people.

THE COMMUNICATION PROCESS

The general process of communication is presented in Figure 15–1. The process contains five elements—the communicator, the message, the medium, the receiver, and feedback. It can be simply summarized as: Who . . . says what . . . in what way . . . to whom . . . with what effect?[1] To appreciate each element in the process, we must examine how communication works.

FIGURE 15–1

The Communication Process

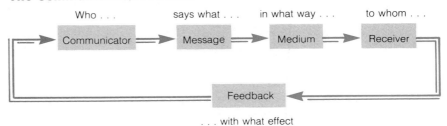

. . . with what effect

How Communication Works

Communication experts tell us that effective communication is the result of a common understanding between the communicator and the receiver. In fact, the word **communication** is derived from the Latin *(communis),* meaning "common." The communicator seeks to establish a "commonness" with a receiver. Hence we can define communication as the *transmission of information and understanding through the use of common symbols.* The common symbols may be verbal or nonverbal. We shall see later that in the context of an organizational structure information can flow up and down (vertical), across (horizontal), and down and across (diagonal).

The most widely used contemporary model of the process of communication has evolved mainly from the work of Shannon and Weaver,

communication
Communication is successful only if the communicator transmits understanding to the receiver.

---

[1] These five questions were first suggested in H. D. Lasswell, *Power and Personality* (New York: W. W. Norton, 1948), pp. 37–51.

FIGURE 15–2

A Communication Model

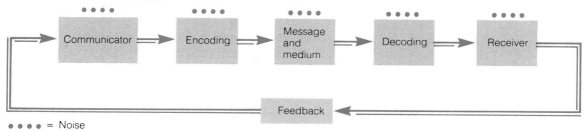

●●●● = Noise

and Schramm.[2] These researchers were concerned with describing the general process of communication that could be useful in all situations. The model that evolved from their work is useful for understanding communication. The basic elements include a communicator, an encoder, a message, a medium, a decoder, a receiver, feedback, and noise. The model is presented in Figure 15–2. Each element in the model can be examined in the context of an organization.

The Elements of Communication

Communicator.   In an organizational framework, the communicator is an employee with ideas, intentions, information, and a purpose for communicating.

Encoding.   Given the communicator, an encoding process must take place that translates the communicator's ideas into a systematic set of symbols—into a language expressing the communicator's purpose. The major form of encoding is language. For example, a manager often takes accounting information, sales reports, and computer data and translates them into one message. The function of encoding, then, is to provide a form in which ideas and purposes can be expressed as a message.

Message.   The result of the encoding process is the message. The purpose of the communicator is expressed in the form of the message—either *verbal* or *nonverbal*. Managers have numerous purposes for communicating, such as to have others understand their ideas, to understand the ideas of others, to gain acceptance of themselves or their

---

[2] Claude Shannon and Warren Weaver, *The Mathematical Theory of Communication* (Urbana: University of Illinois Press, 1948); and Wilbur Schramm, "How Communication Works," in *The Process and Effects of Mass Communication,* ed. Wilbur Schramm (Urbana: University of Illinois Press, 1953), pp. 3–26.

ideas, or to produce action. The message, then, is what the individual hopes to communicate to the intended receiver, and the exact form it takes depends to a great extent on the medium used to carry the message. Decisions relating to the two are inseparable.

Not as obvious, however, are *unintended messages* that can be sent by silence or inaction on a particular issue as well as decisions of which goals and objectives not to pursue and which methods not to utilize. For example, a decision to utilize one type of performance evaluation method rather than another may send a "message" to certain people. An instructor's decision not to give a final examination may send an unintended "message" to certain students that the course is too easy. This is what we meant earlier when we said that everything a manager does communicates.

Medium.   The medium is the carrier of the message. Organizations provide information to members in a variety of ways, including face-to-face communication, telephone, group meetings, computers, memos, policy statements, reward systems, production schedules, and sales forecasts.

Decoding-Receiver.   For the process of communication to be completed, the message must be decoded in terms of relevance to the receiver. *Decoding* is a technical term for the receiver's thought processes. Decoding, then, involves interpretation. Receivers interpret (decode) the message in light of their own previous experiences and frames of reference. Thus, a salesperson is likely to decode a memo from the company president differently than a production manager. A nursing supervisor is likely to decode a memo from the hospital administrator differently than the chief of surgery. The closer the decoded message is to the intent desired by the communicator, the more effective is the communication. This underscores the importance of the communicator being "receiver-oriented."

Feedback.   Provision for feedback in the communication process is desirable.[3] *One-way* communication processes are those that do not allow receiver-to-communicator feedback. This may increase the potential for distortion between the intended message and the received message.[4] A feedback loop provides a channel for receiver response that enables the communicator to determine whether the message has been received and has produced the intended response. *Two-way* communication processes provide for this important receiver-to-com-

---

[3] For a theoretical discussion of feedback, see D. M. Herold and M. M. Greller, "Feedback: The Definition of a Construct," *Academy of Management Journal,* March 1977, pp. 142–47.

[4] For the classic experimental study comparing one-way and two-way communications, see Harold J. Leavitt and R. A. H. Mueller, "Some Effects of Feedback on Communications," *Human Relations,* November 1951, pp. 401–10. Also see H. J. Leavitt, *Managerial Psychology* (Chicago: University of Chicago Press, 1978).

municator feedback. This is an important part of the argument for upward communication in our opening Organizational Issue for Debate. For the manager, communication feedback may come in many ways. In face-to-face situations, *direct* feedback through verbal exchanges is possible, as are such subtle means of communication as facial expressions of discontent or misunderstanding. In addition, *indirect* means of feedback (such as declines in productivity, the poor quality of production, increased absenteeism or turnover, and a lack of coordination and/or conflict between units) may indicate communication breakdowns.

Noise. In the framework of human communication, noise can be thought of as those factors that distort the intended message. Noise may occur in each of the elements of communication. For example, a manager who is under a severe time constraint may be forced to act without communicating or may communicate hastily with incomplete information. Or a subordinate may attach a different meaning to a word or phrase than was intended by the manager. These are examples of noise in the communication process.

The elements discussed in this section are essential for communication to occur. They should not, however, be viewed as separate. They are, rather descriptive of the acts that have to be performed for any type of communication to occur. The communication may be vertical (superior-subordinate, subordinate-superior) or horizontal (peer-peer), or it may involve one individual and a group, but the elements discussed here must be present.

Nonverbal Messages

nonverbal communication
Nonverbal communication can be as important as verbal communication. Nonverbal messages can be sent with body posture, facial expressions, and hand and eye movements.

The information sent by a communicator that is unrelated to the verbal information—that is, *nonverbal messages* or **nonverbal communication**—is a relatively recent area of research among behavioral scientists. The major interest has been in the *physical cues* that characterize the communicator's physical presentation, such as hand movements, facial expressions, and eye movements. These cues are viewed as important influences on the receiver's interpretations of the message. Figure 15–3 presents the factors that research has shown to provide nonverbal information.

Research indicates that facial expressions and eye contact and movements generally provide information about the *type* of emotion, while such physical cues as distance, posture, and gestures indicate the *intensity* of the emotion. These conclusions are important to managers. They indicate that communicators often send a great deal more information than is obtained in these verbal messages. To increase the effectiveness of our communication, we must be aware of the nonverbal as well as the verbal content of our messages.

FIGURE 15-3

Modes of Transmitting Nonverbal Messages

1. *Head, face, and eye behavior.* When used in combination, the head, face, and eyes provide the clearest indications of attitudes toward other people. Maintaining eye contact with another person improves communication with that person. In order to maintain eye contact, it is usually necessary to move your head and face. Moving your head, face, and eyes away from another person is often interpreted as defensiveness or lack of self-confidence.

2. *Posture.* Leaning toward another individual suggests that you are favorably disposed toward his or her messages; leaning backward suggests the opposite. Opening the arms or legs is an indicator of liking or caring. In general, people establish close postures (arms folded and legs crossed) when speaking to people they dislike. Standing up straight generally reflects high self-confidence. Stooping or slouching could mean a poor self-image.

3. *Distance.* If you want to convey positive attitudes to another person, get physically close to that person. People located in relatively close proximity are seen as warmer, friendlier, and more understanding than people located farther away.

4. *Gestures.* Positive attitudes are shown by frequent hand movements. At the other extreme, dislike or lack of interest usually produces few gestures.

5. *Tone of voice.* Anger is often perceived when the source speaks loudly, quickly, and with irregular inflection and clipped enunciation. Boredom is often indicated by moderate volume, pitch, and rate. Joy is often indicated by loud volume, high pitch, fast rate, and upward inflection.

6. *Environmental cues.* Location (for example, office or hallway), room color, temperature, lighting, and furniture arrangement can influence the receiving of a message. For example, a person sitting behind a large, uncluttered desk appears more powerful than a person sitting behind a small, cluttered desk.

7. *Clothing, dress, and appearance.* Dress is often said to influence the appearance of power to others. For example, a woman wearing a tailored suit with blazer jacket appears more powerful than one wearing a dress with frills. A man in a three-piece gray pin-striped suit sends out more power signals than does a man in a loud plaid sport jacket and slacks.

8. *Use of time.* A subtle mode of nonverbal communication in organizations is the use of time. If we are late for a meeting, we might be regarded as careless, uninvolved, or unambitious. However, the lateness of a high-ranking official might be perceived as evidence of his or her importance. Looking at your watch is usually interpreted as a sign of boredom or restlessness.

Source: Summarized from Andrew J. DuBrin, *Contemporary Applied Management* (Plano, Tex.: Business Publications, 1982), pp. 127–34.

COMMUNICATING WITHIN ORGANIZATIONS

The design of an organization should provide for communication in four distinct directions: downward, upward, horizontal, and diagonal. Since these directions of communication establish the framework within which communication in an organization takes place, let us briefly examine each one. This will enable us to better appreciate the barriers to effective organizational communication and means to overcome these barriers.[5]

downward communication
Downward communication flows from higher to lower levels in an organization and includes management policies, instructions, and official memos.

Downward Communication. **Downward communication** flows from individuals in higher levels of the hierarchy to those in lower levels. The most common forms of downward communication are job instructions, official memos, policy statements, procedures, manuals, and company publications. In many organizations, downward communication is often both inadequate and inaccurate. This is evidenced in the often-heard statement among organization members that "we have absolutely no idea what's happening." Such complaints indicate inadequate downward communication and the need of individuals for information relevant to their jobs. The absence of job-related information can create unnecessary stress among organization members.[6] A similar situation is faced by a student who has not been told the requirements and expectations of an instructor.

upward communication
Upward communication flows from lower to higher levels in an organization and includes suggestion boxes, group meetings, and grievance procedures.

Upward Communication. An effective organization needs **upward communication** as much as it needs downward communication.[7] In such situations, the communicator is at a lower level in the organization than the receiver. We shall see later that effective upward communication is difficult to achieve, especially in larger organizations. However, as was indicated in the opening Organizational Issue for Debate, successful upward communication is often necessary for sound decision making. Some of the most common upward communication flows are suggestion boxes, group meetings, and appeal or grievance procedures. In their absence, people somehow find ways to adapt to nonexistent or inadequate upward communication channels. This has been evidenced by the emergence of "underground" employee publications in many large organizations.

---

[5] For a recent general discussion, see S. B. Bacharach and M. Aiken, "Communication in Administrative Bureaucracies," *Academy of Management Journal*, September 1977, pp. 365–77.

[6] J. M. Ivancevich and J. H. Donnelly, Jr., "A Study of Role Clarity and Need for Clarity in Three Occupational Groups," *Academy of Management Journal*, March 1974, pp. 28–36.

[7] For an example, see Warren K. Schilit and Edwin Locke, "A Study of Upward Influence in Organizations," *Administrative Science Quarterly*, January 1982, pp. 304–16.

horizontal communication
Horizontal communication flows across functions in an organization. It is necessary for coordinating and integrating diverse organizational functions.

Horizontal Communication. Often overlooked in the design of most organizations is provision for **horizontal communication.** When the chairperson of the accounting department communicates with the chairperson of the marketing department concerning the course offerings in a college of business administration, the flow of communication is horizontal. Although vertical (upward and downward) communication flows are the primary considerations in organizational design, effective organizations also need horizontal communication. Horizontal communication—for example, communication between production and sales in a business organization and among the different departments or colleges within a university—is necessary for the coordination and integration of diverse organizational functions.

Since mechanisms for assuring horizontal communication ordinarily do not exist in an organization's design, its facilitation is left to individual managers. Peer-to-peer communication is often necessary for coordination and can also provide social need satisfaction.

diagonal communication
Diagonal communication cuts across functions and levels in an organization and is important in situations where members cannot communicate through upward, downward, or horizontal channels.

Diagonal Communication. While probably the least used channel of communication in organizations, **diagonal communication** is important in situations where members cannot communicate effectively through other channels. For example, the comptroller of a large organization may wish to conduct a distribution cost analysis. One part of that task may involve having the sales force send a special report directly to the comptroller rather than going through the traditional channels in the marketing department. Thus, the flow of communication would be diagonal as opposed to vertical (upward) and horizontal. In this case, a diagonal channel would be the most efficient in terms of time and effort for the organization.

INTERPERSONAL COMMUNICATIONS

interpersonal communications
Interpersonal communications flows between individuals in face-to-face and group situations and are an important influence on interpersonal behavior.

Within an organization, communication flows from individual to individual in face-to-face and group settings. Such flows are termed **interpersonal communications** and can vary from direct orders to casual expressions. Interpersonal behavior could not exist without interpersonal communication. Interpersonal communication connects individuals.

The problems that arise when managers attempt to communicate with other people can be traced to *perceptual differences* and *interpersonal style differences*. We know from Chapter 3 that each manager perceives the world in terms of his or her background, experiences, personality, frame of reference, and attitude. The primary way in which managers relate to and learn from the environment (including the people in that environment) is through information received and transmitted. And the way in which managers receive and transmit information depends, in part, on how they relate to two very important *senders* of information, *themselves* and *others*.

Interpersonal Styles

interpersonal style
The manner in which we relate to other persons is known as our interpersonal style.

Interpersonal style refers to *the way in which an individual prefers to relate to others.* The fact that much of the relationship among people involves communication indicates the importance of interpersonal style.

Let us begin by recognizing that information is held by oneself and by others but that each of us does not fully have or know that information. The different combinations of knowing and not knowing relevant information are shown in Figure 15–4. The figure identifies four combinations, or regions, of information known and unknown by the self and others and is popularly known as the Johari Window.[8]

FIGURE 15–4

The Johari Window: Interpersonal Styles and Communications

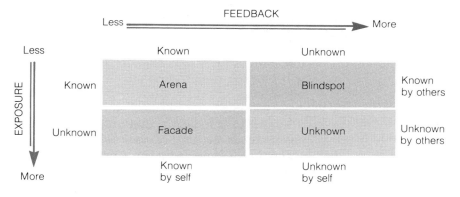

The Arena. The region most conducive to effective interpersonal relationships and communication is termed the *Arena*. In this setting, all of the information necessary to carry on effective communication is known to both the communicator (self) and the receivers (others). For a communication attempt to be in the Arena region, the parties involved must share identical feelings, data, assumptions, and skills.

---

[8] Joseph Luft, "The Johari Window," *Human Relations and Training News,* January 1961, pp. 6–7. The discussion here is based on a later adaptation. See J. Hall, "Communication Revisited," *California Management Review,* Fall 1973, pp. 56–67.

Since the Arena is the area of common understanding, the larger it becomes, the more effective communication will be.

The Blindspot. When relevant information is known to others but not to the self, a *Blindspot* area results. This constitutes a handicap for the self, since one can hardly understand the behaviors, decisions, and potentials of others if he or she doesn't have the information on which these are based. Others have the advantage of knowing their own reactions, feelings, perceptions, and so forth, while the self is unaware of these. Consequently, interpersonal relationships and communications suffer.

The Facade. When information is known to the self but unknown to others, a person (self) may react to superficial communications, that is, present a "false front" or facade. Information that we perceive as potentially prejudicial to a relationship or that we keep to ourselves out of fear, desire for power, or whatever, makes up the *Facade*. This protective front, in turn, serves a defensive function for the self. Such a situation is particularly damaging when a subordinate "knows" and an immediate supervisor "does not know." The Facade, like the Blindspot, diminishes the Arena and reduces the possibility of effective communication.

The Unknown. This region constitutes that portion of the relationship where relevant information is not known by the self or by other parties. As is often stated, "I don't understand them, and they don't understand me." It is easy to see that interpersonal communication will be poor under such circumstances. Circumstances of this kind often occur in organizations when individuals in different specialties must communicate to coordinate what they do.

Figure 15–4 indicates that an individual can improve interpersonal communications by utilizing two strategies, exposure and feedback.

Exposure. Increasing the Arena area by reducing the Facade area requires that the individual be open and honest in sharing information with others. The process that the self uses to increase the information known to others is termed exposure because it sometimes leaves the self in a vulnerable position. Exposing one's true feelings by "telling it like it is" will often involve risks.

Feedback. When the self does not know or understand, more effective communications can be developed through feedback from those who do know. Thus, the Blindspot can be reduced, with a corresponding increase in the Arena. Of course, whether the use of feedback is possible depends on the individual's willingness to "hear" it and on the willingness of others to give it. Thus, the individual is less able to control the provision of feedback than the provision of exposure. Obtaining feedback is dependent on the active cooperation of others, while exposure requires the active behavior of the communicator and the passive listening of others.

Managerial Styles and
Interpersonal Styles

Type A
Type A managers are often poor interpersonal communicators. Often, they are autocratic leaders who are aloof and cold toward others.

The day-to-day activities of managers place a high value on effective interpersonal communications. Managers provide *information* (which must be *understood*); they give *commands* and *instructions* (which must be *obeyed* and *learned*); and they make *efforts to influence* and *persuade* (which must be *accepted* and *acted on*). Thus, the way in which managers communicate, both as senders and receivers, is crucial for obtaining effective performance.

Theoretically, managers who desire to communicate effectively can use both exposure and feedback to enlarge the area of common understanding, the Arena. As a practical matter, such is not the case. Managers differ in their ability and willingness to use exposure and feedback. At least four different managerial styles can be identified.

Type A. Managers who use neither exposure nor feedback are said to have a **Type A** style. The Unknown region predominates in this style because such managers are unwilling to enlarge the area of their own knowledge or the knowledge of others. Type A managers exhibit anxiety and hostility and give the appearance of aloofness and coldness toward others. If an organization has a large number of such managers in key positions, then we would expect to find poor and ineffective interpersonal communications and a loss of individual creativity. Type A managers often display the characteristics of autocratic leaders.

Type B
Type B managers seek good relationships with subordinates but are unable to openly express their feelings. The interpersonal communication of Type B managers is often ineffective because subordinates realize that these managers are not expressing their feelings.

Type B. Some managers desire some degree of satisfying relationships with their subordinates, but because of their personalities and attitudes these managers are unable to open up and express their feelings and sentiments. Consequently, they cannot use exposure and they must rely on feedback. The Facade is the predominant feature of interpersonal relationships when managers overuse feedback to the exclusion of exposure. The subordinates will probably distrust such managers because they realize that these managers are holding back their own ideas and opinions. **Type B** behavior is often displayed by managers who desire to practice some form of permissive leadership.

Type C. Managers who value their own ideas and opinions, but not the ideas and opinions of others, will use exposure at the expense of feedback. The consequence of this style is the perpetuation and enlargement of the Blindspot. Subordinates will soon realize that such managers are not particularly interested in communicating, only in telling. Consequently, **Type C** managers usually have subordinates who are hostile, insecure, and resentful. Subordinates soon learn that such managers are mainly interested in maintaining their own sense of importance and prestige.

Type C
Type C managers are interested only in their own ideas and not in the ideas and opinions of others. They are usually not effective communicators because subordinates soon realize that these managers are interested only in telling, not communicating.

Type D. The most effective interpersonal communication style is one that uses a balance of exposure and feedback. Managers who are

Type D
Type D managers feel free to express their feelings to others and to have others express their feelings. They are the most effective at interpersonal communication.

secure in their positions will feel free to expose their own feelings and to obtain feedback from others. To the extent that a manager practices **Type D** behavior successfully, the Arena region becomes larger and communication becomes more effective.

To summarize our discussion, we should emphasize the importance of interpersonal styles in determining the effectiveness of interpersonal communication. The primary force in determining the effectiveness of interpersonal communication is the attitude of managers toward exposure and feedback. The most effective approach is that of the Type D manager. Types A, B, and C managers resort to behaviors that are detrimental to the effectiveness of communication and to organizational performance.

BARRIERS TO EFFECTIVE COMMUNICATION

A good question at this point is, "Why does communication break down?" On the surface, the answer is relatively easy. We have identified the elements of communication as the communicator, encoding, the message, the medium, decoding, the receiver, and feedback. If noise exists in these elements *in any way,* complete clarity of meaning and understanding will not occur. A manager has no greater responsibility than to develop effective communications. In this section, we shall discuss the following barriers to effective communications: frame of reference, selective listening, value judgments, source credibility, semantic problems, filtering, in-group language, status differences, time pressures, and overload. These sources of noise can exist in both organizational and interpersonal communications.

Frame of Reference

Different individuals can interpret the same communication differently, depending on their previous experiences. This results in variations in the encoding and decoding processes. Communication specialists agree that this is the most important factor that breaks down the "commonness" in communications. When the encoding and decoding processes are not alike, communication tends to break down. Thus, while the communicator is actually speaking the "same language" as the receiver, the message conflicts with the way the receiver "catalogs" the world. This problem is depicted in Figure 15–5. The interior areas in this diagram represent the accumulated experiences of the participants in the communication process. If a large area is shared in common, effective communication is facilitated. If a large area is

FIGURE 15-5

Overlapping Fields of Experience

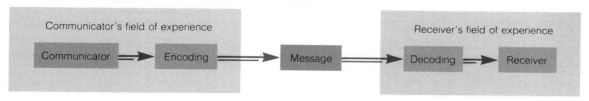

not shared in common—if there has been no common experience—then communication becomes impossible, or at best highly distorted. The important point is that communicators can encode and receivers can decode only in terms of their experiences.[9]

As a result, distortion often occurs because of differing frames of reference. Teenagers perceive things differently than do their parents, and college deans perceive problems differently than do faculty members. People in various organizational *functions* interpret the same situation differently. A business problem will be viewed differently by the marketing manager than by the production manager. An efficiency problem in a hospital will be viewed by the nursing staff from their frame of reference and experiences, which may result in interpretations different from those of the physician staff. Different *levels* in the organization will also have different frames of reference. First-line supervisors have frames of reference that differ in many respects from those of vice presidents. They are in different positions in the organization structure, and this influences their frames of reference.[10] As a result, their needs, values, attitudes, and expectations will differ, and this will often result in unintentional distortion of communication. This is not to say that either group is wrong or right. All it means is that in any situation individuals will choose the part of their own past experiences that relates to the current experience and that is helpful in forming conclusions and judgments. Unfortunately, incongruencies in encoding and decoding result in barriers to effective communication. We shall see that many of the other barriers examined in this section are also the result of variations in encoding and decoding.

---

[9] For a recent related study, see J. D. Hatfield and R. C. Huseman, "Perceptual Congruence about Communication as Related to Satisfaction: Moderating Effects of Individual Characteristics," *Academy of Management Journal,* June 1982, pp. 349–58.

[10] See K. M. Watson, "An Analysis of Communication Patterns: A Method for Discriminating Leader and Subordinate Roles," *Academy of Management Journal,* March 1982, pp. 107–20.

Selective Listening

This is a form of selective perception in which we tend to block out new information, especially if it conflicts with what we believe. Thus, when we receive a directive from management, we notice only those things that reaffirm our beliefs. Those things that conflict with our preconceived notions we either do not note at all or we distort to confirm our preconceptions.

For example, a notice may be sent to all operating departments that costs must be reduced if the organization is to earn a profit. The communication may not achieve its desired effect because it conflicts with the "reality" of the receivers. Thus, operating employees may ignore or be amused by such information in light of the large salaries, travel allowances, and expense accounts of some executives. Whether or not they are justified is irrelevant; what is important is that such preconceptions result in breakdowns in communication. In other words, if we only hear what we want to hear, we cannot be disappointed.

Value Judgments

In every communication situation, value judgments are made by the receiver. This basically involves assigning an overall worth to a message prior to receiving the entire communication. Value judgments may be based on the receiver's evaluation of the communicator or previous experiences with the communicator or on the message's anticipated meaning. For example, a hospital administrator may pay little attention to a memorandum from a nursing supervisor because "she's always complaining about something." A college professor may consider a merit evaluation meeting with the department chairperson as "going through the motions" because the faculty member perceives the chairperson as having little or no power in the administration of the college. A cohesive work group may form negative value judgments concerning all actions by management.

Source Credibility

Source credibility is the trust, confidence, and faith that the receiver has in the words and actions of the communicator. The level of credibility that the receiver assigns to the communicator in turn directly affects how the receiver views and reacts to words, ideas, and actions of the communicator.

Thus, how subordinates view a communication from their manager is affected by their evaluation of the manager. This, of course, is heavily influenced by previous experiences with the manager. Again, we see that everything done by a manager communicates. A group of hospital medical staff who view the hospital administrator as less than honest, manipulative, and not to be trusted are apt to assign nonexistent motives to any communication from the administrator. Union leaders who view management as exploiters and managers who view union leaders as political animals are likely to engage in little real communication.

Semantic Problems

Communication has been defined as the transmission of *information* and *understanding* through the use of *common symbols*. Actually, we cannot transmit understanding. We can only transmit information in the form of words, which are the common symbols. Unfortunately, the same words may mean entirely different things to different people. The understanding is in the receiver, not in the words.

Because different groups use words differently, communication can often be impeded. This is especially true with abstract or technical terms or phrases. A "cost-benefit study" would have meaning to those involved in the administration of the hospital but would probably mean very little to the staff physicians. In fact, it might even carry a negative meaning. Such concepts as "trusts," "profits," and "Treasury bills" may have concrete meaning to bank executives but little or no meaning to bank tellers. Thus, because words mean different things to different people, it is possible for a communicator to speak the same language as a receiver but still not transmit understanding.

Filtering

Filtering is a common occurrence in upward communication in organizations. It refers to the "manipulation" of information so that the receiver perceives it as positive. Subordinates "cover up" unfavorable information in messages to their superiors. The reason for such filtering should be clear; this is the direction (upward) that carries control information to management. Management makes merit evaluations, grants salary increases, and promotes individuals based on what it receives by way of the upward channel. The temptation to filter is likely to be strong at every level in the organization.

In-Group Language

Each of us has undoubtedly had associations with experts and been subjected to highly technical jargon, only to learn that the unfamiliar words or phrases described very simple procedures or very familiar objects. Many students are asked by researchers to "complete an instrument as part of an experimental treatment." The student soon learns that this involves nothing more than filling out a paper-and-pencil questionnaire.

Often, occupational, professional, and social groups develop words or phrases that have meaning only to members. Such special language can serve many useful purposes. It can provide members with feelings of belongingness, cohesiveness, and, in many cases, self-esteem. It can also facilitate effective communication *within* the group. The use of in-group language can, however, result in severe communication breakdowns when outsiders or other groups are involved. This is especially the case when groups use such language in an organization, not for the purpose of transmitting information and understanding, but rather to communicate a mystique about the group or its function.

Status Differences

Organizations often express hierarchical rank through a variety of symbols—titles, offices, carpets, and so on. Such status differences can be perceived as threats by persons lower in the hierarchy, and this can prevent or distort communication. Rather than look incompetent, a nurse may prefer to remain quiet instead of expressing an opinion or asking a question of the nursing supervisor.

Many times, superiors, in an effort to utilize their time efficiently, make this barrier more difficult to surmount. The governmental administrator or bank vice president may be accessible only by making an advance appointment or by passing the careful quizzing of a secretary. This widens the communication gap between superiors and subordinates.

Time Pressures

The pressure of time is an important barrier to communication. An obvious problem is that managers do not have the time to communicate frequently with every subordinate. However, time pressures can often lead to far more serious problems than this. *Short-circuiting* is a failure of the formally prescribed communication system that often results from time pressures. What it means is simply that someone has been left out of the formal channel of communication who would normally be included.

For example, suppose a salesperson needs a rush order for a very important customer and goes directly to the production manager with the request, since the production manager owes the salesperson a favor. Other members of the sales force get word of this and become upset over this preferential treatment and report it to the sales manager. Obviously, the sales manager would know nothing of the "deal" since the sales manager has been short-circuited. In some cases, however, going through formal channels is extremely costly or is impossible from a practical standpoint. Consider the impact on a hospital patient if a nurse had to report a critical malfunction in life support equipment to the nursing team leader, who in turn had to report it to the hospital engineer, who would instruct a staff engineer to make the repair.

Communication Overload

One of the vital tasks performed by a manager is decision making. One of the necessary conditions for effective decisions is *information*. Because of the advances in communication technology, the difficulty is not in generating information. In fact, the last decade has often been described as the "Information Era" or the "Age of Information." Managers often feel "buried" by the deluge of information and data that they are exposed to. As a result, people cannot absorb or adequately respond to all of the messages that are directed to them. They "screen out" the majority of messages, which in effect means that these messages are never decoded. Thus, the area of organizational communication is one in which "more" is not always "better."[11]

The barriers to communication that have been discussed here, while common, are by no means the only ones. Figure 15–6 illustrates the

FIGURE 15–6

Barriers to Effective Communication

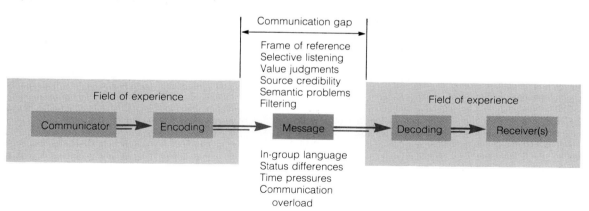

---

[11] See Charles A. O'Reilly III, "Individuals and Information Overload in Organizations: Is More Necessarily Better?" *Academy of Management Journal*, December 1980, pp. 684–96.

[12] For a recent study on the importance of communication, see P. M. Muchinsky, "Organizational Communication: Relationships to Organizational Climate and Job Satisfaction," *Academy of Management Journal*, December 1977, pp. 592–607.

impact of these barriers on the process of communication. Examining each barrier indicates that they are either *within individuals* (e.g., frame of reference, value judgments) or *within organizations* (e.g., in-group language, filtering). This point is important because attempts to improve communication must of necessity focus on changing people and/or changing the organization structure.[12] This is clearly illustrated in the following Close-Up.

ORGANIZATIONS: CLOSE-UP

Improving Communication at International Paper Company

Recently, International Paper Company successfully negotiated several labor agreements that included numerous critical changes in the operations of its pulp and paper mills. The firm credits much of the success in reaching the agreements to its revamped approach to employee communication.

One reason for the breakthrough is that both employees and union officials now receive realistic information about the company long before they enter into negotiations. A company executive stated that "objectives can only be met with the constructive and active support of employees. Management's chief means for getting that support is effective communication."

International Paper has made employee communication a top priority for line managers. Managers must hold regular meetings with subordinates to inform them of new developments, their decisions and the reasons for them, or any changes in objectives, and to answer all questions.

To support the line managers, the company has strengthened its employee communication department. It has also developed tighter controls over communications flow within the organization, so that it is better coordinated, more consistent, and produced more efficiently. The result, according to the company, has been relevant, timely, and honest information.

Source: Gerard Tavernier, "Using Employee Communications to Support Corporate Objectives," *Management Review,* November 1980, pp. 8–13.

IMPROVING COMMUNICATION IN ORGANIZATIONS

Managers striving to become better communicators have two separate tasks that they must accomplish. First, they must improve their *messages*—the information they wish to transmit. Second, they must seek to improve their own *understanding* of what other people are trying to communicate to them. What this means is that they must become better encoders and decoders. *They must strive not only to be understood but also to understand.* The techniques discussed here will contribute to accomplishing these two important tasks.

Following Up

This involves assuming that you are misunderstood and, whenever possible, attempting to determine whether your intended meaning was actually received. As we have seen, meaning is often in the mind of the receiver. An accounting unit leader in a government office passes on to accounting staff members notices of openings in other agencies. While longtime employees may understand this as a friendly gesture, a new employee might interpret it as an evaluation of poor performance and a suggestion to leave.

Regulating Information Flow

This involves the regulation of communication to ensure an optimum flow of information to managers, thereby eliminating the barrier of "communication overload."[13] Communication is regulated in terms of both quality and quantity. The idea is based on the *exception principle* of management, which states that only significant deviations from policies and procedures should be brought to the attention of superiors. In terms of formal communication, then, superiors should be communicated with only on matters of exception and not for the sake of communication. An example of regulating information flow is presented in the following Close-Up.

ORGANIZATIONS: CLOSE-UP

Regulating Information Flow at Old South Bank

Most managers realize that no matter how extensive their computer systems are, the secret of increasing human productivity lies within the flow and *use* of information. However, the pressure to install systems and produce information often causes managers to ignore how their systems are being received and whether or not they are being used.

---

[13] This is described as the principle of "sufficiency" by William G. Scott and Terence R. Mitchell, *Organizational Theory: A Structural and Behavioral Analysis* (Homewood, Ill.: Richard D. Irwin, 1972), p. 161.

Data processing users pay a high price for information, but often what they get is not what they need—at least not in the way they want it.

The Bank of the South in Atlanta decided to do something about it and hired a consultant to help minimize "information overload" and regulate the flow of communication. The result was three simple, one-page reports for each bank manager.

1. The Performance Feedback Report (PFR) consolidates all of the manual or computer-generated reports relevant to each manager. Every key factor that he or she ought to review is in it. The performance indexes describe about 80 percent of the manager's important duties.

2. The Performance Exception Report (PER) highlights the positive and negative exceptions of the Performance Feedback Report. This report tells the manager how he or she is doing, pointing out strengths and weaknesses. It also indicates how far up the organization the exceptional performance has been reported.

3. The Performance Management Report (PMR) is intended to help senior managers manage subordinates. Every supervisor, manager, and vice president receives it. One part tells managers how their immediate subordinates are doing, with strengths, weaknesses, and trends specified. The other part indicates how subordinates at lower levels are doing.

Source: R. Khadem and J. Dewberry, "Have Your Reports and Use Them, Too," *ABA Banking Journal,* August 1983, pp. 35–43.

As we saw in the section on the structure of organizations, certain types of organizational structures would be more amenable to this principle than would other types. Certainly, in an organic organization with its emphasis on free-flowing communication, this principle would not apply. However, mechanistic organizations would find the principle useful.

Utilizing Feedback

Earlier in the chapter, feedback was identified as an important element in effective two-way communication. It provides a channel for receiver response that enables the communicator to determine whether the message has been received and has produced the intended response.

In face-to-face communication, direct feedback is possible. In downward communication, however, inaccuracies often occur because of insufficient opportunity for feedback from receivers. Thus, a memorandum addressing an important policy statement may be distributed to all employees, but this does not guarantee that communication has occurred. One might expect that feedback in the form of upward communication would be encouraged more in organic organizations, but the mechanisms discussed earlier that can be utilized to encourage upward communication are found in many different organizational designs. A healthy organization needs effective upward communication if its downward communication is to have any chance of being effective. The point is that developing and supporting mechanisms for feedback involves far more than following up on communications.

Empathy

This involves being receiver-oriented rather than communicator-oriented. The form of the communication should depend largely on what is known about the receiver. Empathy requires communicators to place themselves in the shoes of the receiver in order to anticipate how the message is likely to be decoded.

It is vital that a manager understand and appreciate the process of decoding. Decoding involves perceptions, and the message will be "filtered" through the person. Empathy is the ability to put oneself in the other person's role and to assume that individual's viewpoints and emotions. For vice presidents to communicate effectively with supervisors, for faculty to communicate effectively with students, and for government administrators to communicate effectively with minority groups, empathy is often an important ingredient. Empathy can reduce many of the barriers to effective communication that have been discussed. Remember that the greater the gap between the experiences and background of the communicator and the receiver, the greater is the effort that must be made to find a common ground of understanding—where there are overlapping fields of experience.[14]

Repetition

Repetition is an accepted principle of learning. Introducing repetition or redundancy into communication (especially that of a technical nature) ensures that if one part of the message is not understood, other parts will carry the same message. New employees are often provided with the same basic information in several different forms when first joining an organization. Likewise, students receive much redundant information when first entering a university. This is to ensure that registration procedures, course requirements, and new terms such as matriculation and quality points are communicated.

---

[14] A technique known as *sensitivity training* has been utilized for many purposes in organizations, one of which is to improve the ability of managers to empathize. The technique will be discussed in Chapter 20.

Encouraging Mutual Trust

We know that time pressures often negate the possibility that managers will be able to follow up communication and encourage feedback or upward communication every time they communicate. Under such circumstances, an atmosphere of mutual confidence and trust between managers and their subordinates can facilitate communication.[15] Subordinates judge for themselves the quality of the relationship with their superior that they perceive. Managers who develop a climate of trust will find that following up on each communication is less critical and that no loss in understanding will result among subordinates from a failure to follow up on each communication. This is because they have fostered high "source credibility" among subordinates. Some organizations initiate formal programs designed to encourage mutual trust. One example is provided in the following Close-Up.

ORGANIZATIONS: CLOSE-UP

Encouraging Mutual Trust at Manufacturers Hanover Bank

At Manufacturers Hanover Trust Company in New York City, small groups of volunteers from the funds transfer department meet once a week on bank time to discuss departmental problems and their solutions. According to a bank vice president, "The benefits are numerous. About 97 percent of them involve improved staff communications."

Such meetings—known popularly as quality circles—have produced some encouraging results at many banks. At Manufacturers Hanover, "Anything goes except discussion of personalities and items related to compensation and benefits." Each group has a "facilitator" whose job is to pull all parts of the discussion together and guarantee communication with all levels of management. Over one half of this person's time is spent in communicating with management. The role of the facilitator is to promote the exchange of the proposal between the group and the management level empowered to act on it.

At Manufacturers Hanover, the groups are instructed to make their presentations to management as thorough as possible, backed up with data to substantiate their recommendations. Management always has the option of saying no to any recommendation, but it must cite reasons

---

[15] See Karlene H. Roberts and Charles A. O'Reilly III, "Failures in Upward Communication in Organizations: Three Possible Culprits," *Academy of Management Journal*, June 1974, pp. 205–15; and Leland P. Bradford, Jack R. Gibb, and Kenneth D. Benne, eds., *T-Group Theory and Laboratory Method: Innovation in Re-Education* (New York: John Wiley & Sons, 1965), pp. 285–86.

for its actions and it must also respond rapidly to recommendations. This is believed to be an important incentive in encouraging trust in sharing ideas with management.

Source: "At MHT Quality Circles Improves Staff Communications," *American Banker,* December 16, 1981, p. 32.

Effective Timing

Individuals are exposed to thousands of messages daily. Many of these messages are never decoded and received because of the impossibility of taking in all the messages. It is important for managers to note that while they are attempting to communicate with a receiver, other messages are being received simultaneously. Thus, the message that managers send may not be "heard." Messages are more likely to be understood when they are not competing with other messages.

Many organizations use "retreats" when important policies are being made or important changes are taking place. A group of executives may be sent to a resort to resolve an important corporate policy issue, or a group of college faculty may "retreat" to an off-campus site to design a new curriculum. On an everyday basis, effective communication can be facilitated by properly timing major announcements. The barriers discussed earlier are often the result of poor timing that results in distortions and value judgments.

Simplifying Language

Complex language has been identified as a major barrier to effective communication. Students often suffer when their teachers use technical jargon that transforms simple concepts into complex puzzles.

Universities are not the only place, however, where this occurs. Government agencies are also known for their often incomprehensible communications. We have already noted instances where professional people use in-group language in attempting to communicate with individuals outside their group. Managers must remember that effective communication involves transmitting *understanding* as well as information. If the receiver does not understand, then there has been no communication. In fact, many of the techniques discussed in this section have as their sole purpose the promotion of understanding. Managers must encode messages in words, appeals, and symbols that are meaningful to the receiver.

Effective Listening

It has been said that to improve communication, managers must seek to be understood but also to *understand*. This involves listening.

One method of encouraging someone to express true feelings, desires, and emotions is to listen. Just listening is not enough; one must listen with understanding. Can managers develop listening skills? There are numerous pointers for effective listening that have been found to be effective in organizational settings. For example, one writer cites "Ten Commandments for Good Listening": stop talking; put the speaker at ease; show the speaker you want to listen; remove distractions; empathize with the speaker; be patient; hold your temper; go easy on argument and criticism; ask questions; and stop talking.[16] Note that to stop talking is both the first and the last commandment.

Such guidelines can be useful to managers. More important, however, is the *decision to listen*. The above guidelines are useless unless the manager makes the conscious decision to listen. The realization that effective communication involves being understood as well as understanding is probably far more important than guidelines. Then and only then can guidelines become useful. The importance of listening skills is illustrated in the following Close-Up.

ORGANIZATIONS: CLOSE-UP

Developing Listening Skills at Sperry Corporation

The Sperry Corporation has initiated an ongoing series of programs designed to heighten the listening skills of its managers. They deal with both responding to internal corporate situations and responding effectively to outsiders.

The training concentrates on specific on-the-job applications showing how Sperry employees in various real-life situations can do a better job of responding—the end product of the listening process. R. L. Robertson, staff vice president—public affairs, states that "listening occurs in four stages—sensing (hearing the message), understanding (interpreting it), evaluating (appraising it), and responding (doing something with it). The ultimate point of the training is that the fourth of these stages—the intelligent, sincere response—is the basic commitment we are making and provides a valuable payoff to both the sender and the receiver."

Source: *Management Review*, April 1980, p. 40.

---

[16] Keith Davis, *Human Behavior at Work* (New York: McGraw-Hill, 1980), p. 394.

Using the Grapevine

The grapevine is an important informal communication channel that exists in all organizations. It basically serves as a bypassing mechanism, and in many cases it is faster than the formal system it bypasses. It has been aptly described in the following manner: "With the rapidity of a burning train, it filters out of the woodwork, past the manager's office, through the locker room, and along the corridors."[17] Because it is flexible and usually involves face-to-face communication, the grapevine transmits information rapidly. The resignation of an executive may be common knowledge long before it is officially announced.

For management, the grapevine may frequently be an effective means of communication. It is likely to have a stronger impact on receivers because it is face-to-face and allows for feedback. Because it satisfies many psychological needs, the grapevine will always exist. No manager can do away with it. Over 75 percent of the information in the grapevine is accurate. Of course, the 25 percent that is distorted can be devastating. The point, however, is that if the grapevine is inevitable, managers should seek to utilize it or at least attempt to increase its accuracy. One way to minimize the undesirable aspects of the grapevine is to improve other forms of communication. If information exists on issues relevant to subordinates, then damaging rumors are less likely to develop.

In conclusion, it would be hard to find an aspect of a manager's job that does not involve communication. If everyone in the organization had common points of view, communicating would be easy. Unfortunately, this is not the case. Each member comes to the organization with a distinct personality, background, experience, and frame of reference. The structure of the organization itself influences status relationships and the distance (levels) between individuals, which in turn influence the ability of individuals to communicate.

In this chapter, we have tried to convey the basic elements in the process of communication and what it takes to communicate effectively. These elements are necessary whether the communication is face-to-face or written and communicated vertically, horizontally, or diagonally within an organizational structure. Thus, we support the argument for upward communication in the chapter-opening Organizational Issue for Debate. Several common communication barriers and several means to improve communication were discussed. Figure 15–7 illustrates the means that can be used to facilitate more effective communication. We realize that often there is not enough time to utilize many of the techniques for improving communication and that

---

[17] Ibid., p. 267.

FIGURE 15-7

**Improving Communication in Organizations
(Narrowing the Communication Gap)**

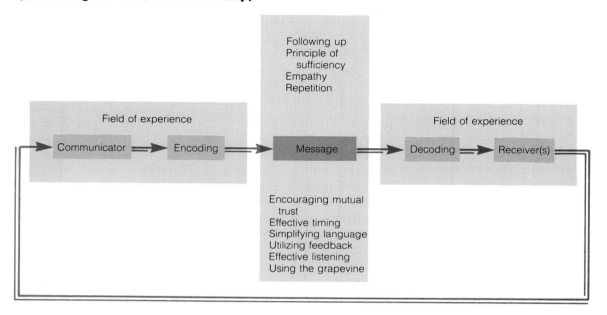

skills such as empathy and effective listening are not easy to develop. The figure does, however, illustrate the challenge of communicating effectively and suggest what is required. It shows that communicating is a matter of transmitting and receiving. Managers must be effective at both. They must understand as well as be understood.

SUMMARY OF KEY POINTS

A. Communication is one of the vital processes that breathe life into an organizational structure. Communication is unavoidable in an organization's work; only *effective* communication is avoidable.

B. The quality of managerial decisions depends in large part on the quality of information available. Communication is the transmission of information and understanding through the use of common symbols.

C. Everything that a manager does communicates. The only question is, "With what effect?" Every manager is a communicator.

D. The process of communication consists of several basic elements that must always be present if effective communication is to result. These elements are the communicator, the message, the medium, the receiver, and feedback.

E. Organizational design and the communication process are inseparable. The design of an organization must provide for communication in three distinct directions: vertical, horizontal, and diagonal.

F. When the encoding and decoding processes are homogeneous, communication is most effective. When they become heterogeneous, communication tends to break down. Numerous barriers exist that contribute to communication breakdowns. Managers must be aware of the barriers that are relevant to their situations.

G. Numerous techniques exist that aid in improving communication and can be utilized by managers. However, a prerequisite to their use is the conscious realization by the individual manager that communication involves understanding as well as being understood. An effective communicator must also be an effective receiver.

DISCUSSION AND REVIEW QUESTIONS

1. What do we mean when we say that everything a manager does communicates?

2. Discuss why organizational design and communication flow are so closely related.

3. Discuss how communication flow and the contingency view of organizational design are related.

4. Think of a classroom situation in terms of the basic elements of communication: communicator, encoding, message, medium, decoding, receiver, and feedback. Identify each element, and discuss the activities involved. For example, who the communicator is, what the message is, and who the receiver is. Is

effective communication occurring? Why? Identify where, if at all, breakdowns are occurring and why.

5. Think of a situation from your own life in which communication between yourself and another individual or group was not possible. Identify the barriers. What might you have done to overcome these barriers?

6. Discuss what the following statement means to you. "To communicate effectively, one must be understood but must also understand."

7. Think of a situation in which you have been the receiver in a one-way communication pro-

cess. Describe the situation. Can you think of some reasons why certain individuals might not like it? Why might some people prefer it?

8. Choose a technique discussed in the chapter that you believe can help you become a more effective communicator. Why have you chosen it? How do you plan to implement it?

ADDITIONAL REFERENCES

Carlson, R. O. "Is Business Really Facing a Communication Problem?" *Organizational Dynamics,* 1973, pp. 35–52.

Ellis, D. S. *Management and Administrative Communication.* New York: Macmillan, 1978.

Ericson, R. F. "Organizational Cybernetics and Human Values." *Academy of Management Journal,* 1970, pp. 49–66.

Goldhaber, G. M. *Organizational Communications.* Dubuque, Iowa: Wm. C. Brown, 1974.

Greenbaum, H. H. "The Audit of Organizational Communication." *Academy of Management Journal,* 1974, pp. 737–54.

———. "Management's Role in Organizational Communication Analysis." *Journal of Business Communication,* 1972, pp. 39–52.

Guetzkow, H. "Communication in Organizations." In *Handbook of Organizations,* ed. J. G. March. Skokie, Ill.: Rand McNally, 1965.

Mears, P. "Structuring Communication in a Working Group." *Journal of Communication,* 1974, pp. 71–79.

Poole, M. S. "An Information-Task Approach to Organizational Communication." *Academy of Management Review,* 1978, pp. 493–504.

Roberts, K. H., and C. A. O'Reilly III. "Some Correlates of Communication Roles in Organizations." *Academy of Management Journal,* 1979, pp. 42–57.

Rockey, E. H. *Communicating in Organizations.* Cambridge, Mass.: Winthrop Publishers, 1977.

Rogers, C. *On Becoming a Person.* Boston: Houghton Mifflin, 1961.

Saunders, C. S. "Management Information Systems, Communications, and Departmental Power: An Integrative Model." *Academy of Management Journal,* 1981, pp. 431–42.

Schemerhorn, J. R. "Information Sharing as an Interorganizational Activity." *Academy of Management Journal,* 1977, pp. 148–53.

Schneider, A. E.; W. C. Donaghy; and P. J. Newman. *Organizational Communication.* New York: McGraw-Hill, 1975.

Tubbs, S. L., and S. Moss. *Human Communication.* New York: Random House, 1977.

Tushman, M. L. "Impacts of Perceived Environmental Variability on Patterns of Work Related Communication." *Academy of Management Journal,* 1979, pp. 482–500.

Watson, K. "An Analysis of Communication Patterns: A Method for Discriminating Leader and Subordinate Roles," *Academy of Management Journal,* 1982, pp. 107–20.

Wiener, N. *Cybernetics: or, Control and Communication in the Animal and the Machine.* New York: John Wiley & Sons, 1948.

———. *The Human Use of Human Beings.* New York: Anchor Books, 1954.

Wofford, J. C.; E. A. Gerloff; and R. C. Cummins. *Organizational Communication: The Keystone to Managerial Effectiveness.* New York: McGraw-Hill, 1977.

Wolf, M. P.; D. F. Keyser; and R. R. Aurner. *Effective Communication in Business.* Cincinnati: South-Western Publishing, 1979.

CASE FOR ANALYSIS

Leigh Randell

Leigh Randell is supervisor of in-flight services at the Atlanta base of Omega Airlines. Omega Airlines is a very successful regional air carrier with routes throughout the South and Southwest. In addition to its base in Atlanta, it has bases in six other major cities.

Ms. Randell's job involves supervision of all in-flight services and personnel at the Atlanta base. She has been with the airline for seven years and in her present job for two years. After having served as a flight attendant for five years, she was asked by management to assume her present management position. While preferring flying to a permanent ground position, she decided to try the management position. In her job, she reports directly to Kent Davis, vice president of in-flight services.

During the last year, Leigh has observed what she believes is a great deal of duplication of effort betwen flight attendants and passenger-service personnel (in-terminal personnel) with respect to the paperwork procedures for boarding passengers. This, she believes, has resulted in unnecessary delays in the departures of many flights. This has especially appeared to be the case with through flights, those that do not originate or terminate in Atlanta. Since most of Omega's flights of this type are in Atlanta, she believes that such delayed departures are probably not a major problem at Omega's other bases or at smaller airports. Thus, she has decided to try to develop a more efficient procedure for coordinating the efforts of flight attendants and passenger-service personnel that would simplify the boarding procedures, thereby reducing ground time and increasing passenger satisfaction through closer adherence to departure times.

In this respect, she has, on three occasions during the last two months, written memos to Tom Ballard, passenger services representative for Omega at the Atlanta base. Tom's job involves supervision of all passenger-service personnel. He has been with Omega for five years, having joined its management training program immediately after graduating from college. He reports directly to Alan Brock, vice president of passenger services at the Atlanta base. Exhibit 1 presents the organizational structure for the Atlanta base. Each time, Leigh has requested information regarding specific procedures, time, and costs for the boarding of passengers on through flights. She has received no reply from Tom Ballard.

Last week, Leigh wrote a memo to Kent Davis in which she stated:

> For several months, I have been trying to develop a new method for facilitating the boarding of passengers on through flights by more closely coordinating the efforts of In-Flight Services and Passenger Services. The results would be a reduction in clerical work, costs, and ground time and closer adherence to departure times for through flights. Unfortunately, I have received no cooperation at all in my efforts from the passenger services representative. I have made three written requests for information, each of which has been ignored. Needless to say, this has been very frustrating to me. While I realize that my beliefs may

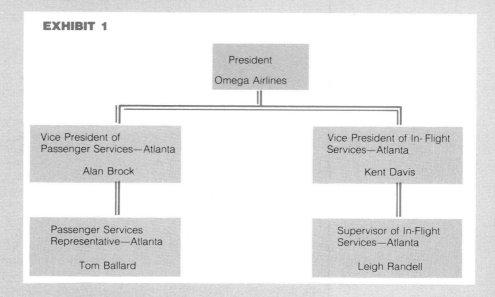

EXHIBIT 1

President
Omega Airlines

Vice President of
Passenger Services—Atlanta

Alan Brock

Vice President of In- Flight
Services—Atlanta

Kent Davis

Passenger Services
Representative—Atlanta

Tom Ballard

Supervisor of In-Flight
Services—Atlanta

Leigh Randell

not always be correct, in this instance I am only trying to initiate something that will be beneficial to everyone involved: Passenger Services, In-Flight Services, and most important, Omega Airlines. I would like to meet with you to discuss this matter and the possibility of my transferring back to flight duty.

Kent Davis summoned Alan Brock and Tom Ballard to a hastily called conference. Tom Ballard was mildly asked why he had not furnished the information that Leigh had requested.

"Too busy," he said. "Her questions were out of sight. There was no time for me to answer this sort of request. I've got a job to do. Besides, I don't report to her."

"But Tom, you don't understand," Kent Davis said. "All Ms. Randell is trying to do is improve the present system of boarding passengers on through flights. She has taken the initiative to work on something that might benefit everyone."

Tom Ballard thought for a moment. "No," he replied, "it didn't look like that to me. You know I've also had ideas on how to improve the system for quite some time. Anyway, she's going about it all wrong."

Questions for Consideration

1. What barriers to effective communication do you detect in this case?

2. Is anyone "wrong" in this situation? By what other means could Leigh have requested the information from Tom Ballard? What do you think of Tom Ballard's reaction? Why?

3. While communicating information vertically up or down the organization does not present a major problem, why is it that horizontal and diagonal

communication are more difficult to attain? What would you recommend that the management of Omega Airlines do to remedy this situation? Why do you believe that your recommendations would improve communication in the organization?

EXPERIENTIAL EXERCISE
FRUSTRATION, CLARITY, ACCURACY

Objectives

1. To display the features of the communication process.
2. To identify the differences between one-way and two-way communications.
3. To examine the reactions of individuals to one- and two-way communications.

Related Topics

The communication process is pervasive in any organization. Therefore, communication is related to any topic discussed in organizational behavior, organizational theory, or management.

Starting the Exercise

The instructor will give the same message to two separate groups. These groups will receive the private message only one time. They are not permitted to ask the instructor any questions about the message.

The Facts

The instructor will serve as the initiator of a message to two separate groups of three or four students. The groups will attempt to develop a clear understanding of what the instructor said. They will then return to the main classroom, where other students will serve as communication chains for the message. Both a one-way chain and a two-way chain will be used. To complete both the one- and two-way communication versions of this exercise, a minimum of 22 students will be needed. If a class does not have 22 students, the instructor will need to make some modifications.

Exercise Procedures

Phase I: Group Communication: 10 minutes

Group 1 and Group 2, consisting of three or four students, will be selected. The groups should be isolated from each other to receive the message. The instructor will read *one time* the same message to the two groups in their separate rooms or isolated areas. Each group will discuss the message for no more than five minutes.

Phase II: One-Way Communication: 10 minutes

Four students who are not in Groups 1 or 2 will serve as the *chain* for one of the groups, and four other students will serve as the chain for the other group. A representative of Group 1 will whisper the message to the first person in the four-person chain, who, in turn, will pass on the private message to the second member, and so on. Talking between members in the chain is not permitted. Only one person, the transmitter, is permitted to speak. The last person in the chain will write the message down and hand it to the instructor. The same one-way communication process will be followed in Group 2.

Phase III: Two-Way Communication: 20 minutes

Four new students who have not participated in either Phases 1 or 2 will serve as the Group 1 chain. A representative of Group 1 will discuss the message with the first person in the chain. The representative and the first person can discuss the message privately from other members in the chain. When the discussants are ready and within the allocated time limit, the first person in the chain will then discuss the message privately with the second person in the chain. These private two-way discussions will continue until the time allotted has expired or until the last person in the chain hears the message and writes it for the instructor. The same two-way communication process will be followed in Group 2.

Phase IV: Analysis of the Exercise: 20 minutes

Each participant should evaluate the exercise. Some of the issues to consider are:

a. One-way versus two-way communication accuracy.
b. Attitudes of the different participants. Were any participants frustrated? About what?
c. What were some of the barriers to effective communication?

Chapter 16

After completing Chapter 16, you should be able to:

Define the terms *programmed decision* and *nonprogrammed decision*.

Describe the process of decision making.

Discuss the major behavioral influences on the process of decision making.

Compare group decision making and individual decision making.

Identify the various methods that managers can use to stimulate creativity in group decision making.

Decision-Making Processes

The Decision Participation Controversy*

Argument For

Many researchers and managers believe that most organization members desire opportu-

---

* Much research and opinion exists on this issue. For comprehensive reviews, see V. H. Vroom and P. W. Yetton, *Leadership and Decision-Making* (Pittsburgh: University of Pittsburgh Press, 1973); and P. Blumberg, *Industrial Democracy: The Sociology of Participation* (New York: Schocken Books, 1974). Also see J. W. Driscoll, "Trust and Participation in Organizational Decision Making as Predictors of Satisfaction," *Academy of Management Journal*, March 1978, pp. 44–56; and R. S. Schuler, "A Role and Expectancy Perception Model of Participation in Decision Making," *Academy of Management Journal*, June 1980, pp. 331–40.

nities to participate in the process of decision making. They believe that increased decision participation increases commitment to the organization, job satisfaction, personal growth and development, and acceptance of change. Thus, the manager's mode of influence is based more on reciprocity and collaboration than on authority.

Besides leading to greater satisfaction, and as a result, greater effort, performance, and effectiveness, decision participation has an additional rationale according to the supporters of this viewpoint. They point out that many of the problems faced by organizations are becoming increasingly complex, requiring knowledge in sophisticated areas, and are of types that the organization has not faced in the past. These problems may be technological, human, or societal. As a result, knowledge and expertise in many different areas are needed to solve these problems. Since knowledge and expertise are widely distributed throughout the organization, wider participation would probably increase the quality of managerial decisions.

Argument Against

Many practicing managers and researchers believe that in organizational settings people prefer a great amount of clarity in what is expected of them. This need for security in knowing what behavior is expected results in a great deal more respect for the manager who acts decisively. These managers and researchers believe that trying to achieve consensus in a group is upsetting to the group and a waste of organizational resources and time. Since managers are a dominant mode of influence in the organization, they must recognize this and act on it. The world of a decision maker may be a lonely one, but managers must accept the responsibility that the "buck stops" with them. Nothing is more dysfunctional than the "participation ritual" that many managers engage in. Here managers go through the process of participation for the purpose of selling decisions that have already been made, by making them look like group decisions. If managers fail to take charge of group activities, they abdicate their role as manager and performance will be negatively affected.

The focus of this chapter is on decision making. The quality of the decisions that managers reach is the yardstick of their effectiveness. Thus, the flow of the preceding material leads logically to a discussion of decision making: that is, people behave as *individuals* and as members *of groups, within* an *organizational structure,* and they *communicate* for many reasons, an important one of which is to *make decisions.* This chapter, therefore, will describe and analyze decision making in terms that reflect the ways in which people decide as a consequence of the information they receive both through the organizational *structure* and through the *behavior* of important other persons and groups.

TYPES OF DECISIONS

While managers in various kinds of organizations may be separated by background, lifestyle, and distance, sooner or later they must all make decisions. The opening Organizational Issue for Debate focuses on whether managers should encourage subordinates to participate in the process of decision making. However, regardless of the stand you may take on this debate, it is managers who are ultimately responsible for the outcomes of a decision. That is, they face a situation involving several alternatives and their decision involves a comparison between the alternatives and an evaluation of the outcome. In this section, our purpose is to move away from a general definition of a decision and to present a classification system into which various kinds of decisions can be placed.

programmed decisions
Programmed decisions are specific procedures that have been developed for repetitive and routine problems.

nonprogrammed decisions
Many management problems are unique and complex. Such problems require nonprogrammed decisions.

Specialists in the field of decision making have developed several ways of classifying different types of decisions. For the most part, these classification systems are similar, differing mainly in terminology. We shall use the widely adopted distinction suggested by Herbert Simon.[1] Simon distinguishes between two types of decisions:

1. *Programmed decisions.* If a particular situation occurs often, a routine procedure will usually be worked out for solving it. Thus, decisions are **programmed** to the extent that they are repetitive and routine and a definite procedure has been developed for handling them.

2. *Nonprogrammed decisions.* Decisions are **nonprogrammed** when they are novel and unstructured. Thus, there is no established procedure for handling the problem, either because it has not arisen in exactly the same manner before or because it is complex or extremely important. Such decisions deserve special treatment.

While the two classifications are broad, they point out the importance of differentiating between programmed and nonprogrammed

---

[1] Herbert A. Simon, *The New Science of Management Decision* (New York: Harper & Row, 1960), pp. 5–6.

TABLE 16-1

Types of Decisions

	Programmed Decisions	Nonprogrammed Decisions
Type of problem	Frequent, repetitive, routine, much certainty regarding cause and effect relationships	Novel, unstructured, much uncertainty regarding cause and effect relationships
Procedure	Dependence on policies, rules, and definite procedures	Necessity for creativity, intuition, tolerance for ambiguity, creative problem solving
Examples	*Business firm:* Periodic reorders of inventory	*Business firm:* Diversification into new products and markets
	University: Necessary grade-point average for good academic standing	*University:* Construction of new classroom facilities
	Health care: Procedure for admitting patients	*Health care:* Purchase of experimental equipment
	Government: Merit system for promotion of state employees	*Government:* Reorganization of state government agencies

decisions. The managements of most organizations face great numbers of programmed decisions in their daily operations. Such decisions should be treated without expending unnecessary organizational resources on them. On the other hand, the nonprogrammed decision must be properly identified as such since it is this type of decision that forms the basis for allocating billions of dollars worth of resources in our economy every year. Unfortunately, it is the human process involving this type of decision that we know the least about.[2] Table 16-1 presents a breakdown of the different types of decisions, with examples of each type in different kinds of organizations. It indicates that programmed and nonprogrammed decisions require different kinds of procedures and apply to distinctly different types of problems.

Traditionally, programmed decisions have been handled through rules, standard operating procedures, and the structure of the organization that develops specific procedures for handling them. More recently, operations researchers through the development of mathematical models have facilitated the handling of these types of decisions.

On the other hand, nonprogrammed decisions have traditionally been handled by general problem-solving processes, judgment, intuition, and creativity. Unfortunately, the advances that modern management techniques have made in improving nonprogrammed decision

---

[2] Stephen A. Stumpf, Dale E. Zand, and Richard D. Freedman, "Designing Groups for Judgmental Decisions," *Academy of Management Review,* October 1979, pp. 589–600.

making have not been nearly as great as the advances that they have made in improving programmed decision making.[3]

Ideally, the main concern of top management should be nonprogrammed decisions, while first-level management should be concerned with programmed decisions. Middle managers in most organizations concentrate mostly on programmed decisions, although in some cases they will participate in nonprogrammed decisions. In other words, the nature, frequency, and degree of certainty surrounding a problem should dictate at what level of management the decision should be made.

Obviously, problems arise in those organizations where top management expends much time and effort on programmed decisions. One unfortunate result of this practice is a neglect of long-range planning. In such cases, long-range planning is subordinated to other activities whether the organization is successful or is having problems. If the organization is successful, this justifies continuing the policies and practices that achieved success. If the organization experiences difficulty, its current problems have first priority and occupy the time of top management. In either case, long-range planning ends up being neglected.

Finally, the neglect of long-range planning usually results in an overemphasis on short-run control. This results in a lack of delegation of authority to lower levels of management, which often has adverse effects on motivation and satisfaction.

THE DECISION-MAKING PROCESS

decision
A decision is a means to achieve some result or to solve some problem. It is the outcome of a process that is influenced by many forces.

Decisions should be thought of as *means* rather than ends. They are the *organizational mechanisms* through which an attempt is made to achieve a desired state. They are, in effect, an *organizational response* to a problem. Every decision is the outcome of a dynamic process that is influenced by a multitude of forces. This process is presented diagrammatically in Figure 16–1. The reader should not, however, interpret this to mean that decision making is a fixed procedure. It is a sequential process rather than a series of steps. This enables us to examine each element in the normal progression that leads to a decision.

Examination of Figure 16–1 reveals that it is more applicable to nonprogrammed decisions than to programmed decisions. Problems that occur infrequently, with a great deal of uncertainty surrounding the outcome, require that the manager utilize the entire process. For problems that occur frequently it is not necessary to consider the

---

[3] See Herbert A. Simon, *The Shape of Automation* (New York: Harper & Row, 1965); and I. L. Janis and L. Mann, *Decision Making: A Psychological Analysis of Conflict, Choice, and Commitment* (New York: Free Press, 1977).

FIGURE 16–1

The Decision-Making Process

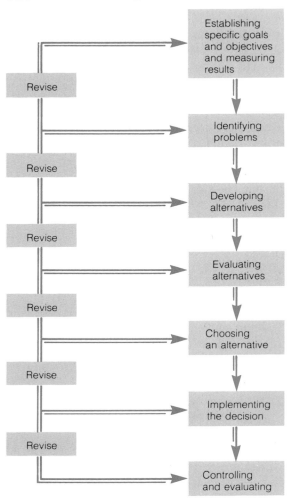

entire process. If a policy is established to handle such problems, it will not be necessary to develop and evaluate alternatives each time a problem of this kind arises.

Establishing Specific Goals and Objectives and Measuring Results

Organizations need goals and objectives in each area where performance influences the effectiveness of the organization. If goals and objectives are adequately established, they will dictate what results must be achieved and what measures will indicate whether or not they have been achieved.

Identifying Problems

A necessary condition for a decision is a problem. That is, if problems did not exist, then there would be no need for decisions.[4] This underscores the importance of establishing goals and objectives. How critical a problem is for the organization is measured by the gap between the levels of performance specified in the organization's goals and objectives and the levels of performance attained. Thus, a gap of 20 percent between a sales volume objective and the volume of sales actually achieved signifies that some problem exists.

It is easy to understand that some problem exists when a gap occurs between desired results and actual results. However, certain factors often lead to difficulties in identifying exactly what the problem is.[5] These factors are:

1. Perceptual Problems. As noted in Chapter 3, individual perceptions may act in such a way as to protect or defend us from unpleasant perceptions. Thus, negative information may be selectively perceived in such a way as to distort its true meaning. It may also be totally ignored. For example, a college dean may fail to identify increasing class sizes as a problem while at the same time being sensitive to problems faced by the president of the university in raising funds for the school.

2. Defining Problems in Terms of Solutions. This is really a form of jumping to conclusions. For example, a sales manager may say, "The decrease in profits is due to our poor product quality." The sales manager's definition of the problem suggests a particular solution: the improvement of product quality in the production department. Certainly, other solutions may be possible. Perhaps the sales force has been inadequately selected or trained. Perhaps competitors have a superior product.

3. Identifying Symptoms as Problems. "Our problem is a 32 percent decline in orders." While it is certainly true that orders have declined, the decline in orders is really a symptom of the real problem. When the manager identifies the real problem, the cause of the decline in orders will be found.

---

[4] Two excellent references on this and related problems are W. E. Pounds, "The Process of Problem Finding," *Industrial Management Review,* Fall 1969, pp. 1–19; and C. E. Watson, "The Problems of Problem Solving," *Business Horizons,* August 1976, pp. 88–94.

[5] See G. P. Huber, *Managerial Decision Making* (Glenview, Ill.: Scott, Foresman, 1980).

Problems are usually of three types: opportunity, crisis, or routine.[6] *Crisis* and *routine* problems present themselves and must be attended to by the managers. *Opportunities,* on the other hand, must usually be found. They await discovery, and they often go unnoticed and are eventually lost by an inattentive manager. This is because, by their very nature, most crises and routine problems demand immediate attention. Thus, a manager may spend a great deal of time in handling minor crises and solving routine problems and not have time to pursue important new opportunities. Many well-managed organizations try to draw attention away from crises and routine problems and toward longer range issues through planning activities and goal-setting programs. The following Close-Up illustrates one organization's approach.

ORGANIZATIONS: CLOSE-UP

Threat Analysis at IBM

IBM is one organization that formally trains managers to anticipate what the future may hold in the relevant environments that influence the manager's area of performance. This "threat analysis" or "what if?" type of thinking, it is believed, fosters a future orientation whereby various possible situations or states of nature are identified, analyzed, and incorporated into the decision-making process.

It is true that many of the problems faced by managers may be the result of external forces beyond their control. However, like IBM, many organizations train managers to make decisions and solve problems in the present but also train them to anticipate future problems.

Developing Alternatives

Before a decision is made, feasible alternatives should be developed (actually these are potential solutions to the problem) and the potential consequences of each alternative should be considered. This is really a search process in which the relevant internal and external environments of the organization are investigated to provide information that can be developed into possible alternatives. Obviously, this search is conducted within certain time and cost constraints since only so much effort can be devoted to developing alternatives.[7]

---

[6] H. Mintzberg, D. Raisinghavi, and A. Theoret, "The Structure of 'Unstructured' Decision Processes," *Administrative Science Quarterly,* Spring 1976, pp. 246–75.

[7] For a recent example, see Howard M. Weiss, Daniel R. Ilgen, and Michael E. Sharbaugh, "Effects of Life and Job Stress on Information Search Behavior of Organizational Members," *Journal of Applied Psychology,* February 1982, pp. 60–66.

For example, a sales manager may identify an inadequately trained sales force as the cause of declining sales. The sales manager would then identify possible alternatives for solving the problem, such as (1) a sales training program conducted at the home office by management, (2) a sales training program conducted by a professional training organization at a site away from the home office, and (3) more intense on-the-job training.

Evaluating Alternatives

Once alternatives have been developed, they must be evaluated and compared. In every decision situation, the objective in making a decision is to select the alternative that will produce the most favorable outcomes and the least unfavorable outcomes. This again points up the necessity of objectives and goals, since in selecting from among alternatives, the decision maker should be guided by the previously established goals and objectives. The alternative-outcome relationship is based on three possible conditions:

1. *Certainty.* The decision maker has complete knowledge of the probability of the outcome of each alternative.
2. *Uncertainty.* The decision maker has absolutely no knowledge of the probability of the outcome of each alternative.
3. *Risk.* The decision maker has some probabilistic estimate of the outcomes of each alternative.

Decision making under conditions of risk is probably the most common situation. It is in evaluating alternatives under these conditions that statisticians and operations researchers have made important contributions to decision making. Their methods have proved especially useful in the analysis and ranking of alternatives. The following Close-Up describes an actual high-risk decision.

ORGANIZATIONS: CLOSE-UP

Napco's Risky Decision

Very few companies would risk what Napco Industries did when it completely rebuilt its corporate strategy five years ago. In a group decision five years ago, management decided to sell the business that produced two thirds of sales—axles and electronic products—and to enter a new service business—distributing nonfood products as well as pricing and keeping inventory tabs on them for supermarkets. It established a successful network in the South and the Central Plains. Napco has been so successful that it has begun to expand westward, aiming to become the first national service merchandiser. Napco's risky decision paid off.

Source: "Napco: Seeking a National Network as a Nonfood Supermarket Supplier," *Business Week*, November 8, 1982, pp. 70, 74.

Choosing an Alternative

The purpose in selecting an alternative is to solve a problem in order to achieve a predetermined objective. This point is an important one. It means that a decision is not an end in itself but only a means to an end. While the decision maker chooses the alternative that is expected to result in the achievement of the objective, the selection of that alternative should not be as an isolated act. If it is, the factors that led to and lead from the decision are likely to be excluded. Specifically, the steps following the decision should include implementation, control, and evaluation. The critical point is that decision making is *more* than an act of choosing; it is a dynamic process.[8]

Unfortunately for most managers, situations rarely exist in which one alternative achieves the desired objective without having some positive or negative impact on another objective.[9] Situations often exist where two objectives cannot be optimized simultaneously. If one objective is *optimized,* the other is *suboptimized.* In a business organization, for example, if production is optimized, employee morale may be suboptimized, or vice versa. Or a hospital superintendent optimizes a short-run objective such as maintenance costs at the expense of a long-run objective such as high-quality patient care. Thus, the multiplicity of organizational objectives complicates the real world of the decision maker.[10]

A situation could also exist where attainment of an organizational objective would be at the expense of a societal objective. The reality of such situations is clearly seen in the rise of ecology groups, environmentalists, and the consumerist movement. Apparently, these groups question the priorities (organizational as against societal) of certain organizational decision makers. In any case, whether an organizational

---

[8] This important point is discussed in detail in E. F. Harrison, *The Managerial Decision-Making Process* (Boston: Houghton Mifflin, 1975); and Huber, *Managerial Decision Making.* These are excellent comprehensive works on the subject of managerial decision making.

[9] For a study, see F. Luthans and R. Koester, "The Impact of Computer-Generated Information on the Choice Activity of Decision Makers," *Academy of Management Journal,* June 1976, pp. 328–32.

[10] See R. L. Daft, "System Influence on Organizational Decision Making: The Case of Resource Allocation," *Academy of Management Journal,* March 1978, pp. 6–22.

objective conflicts with another organizational objective or with a societal objective, the values of the decision maker will strongly influence the alternative chosen. Individual values were discussed earlier, and their influence on the decision-making process should be clear.

Thus, in managerial decision making, *optimal* solutions are often impossible. This is because the decision maker cannot possibly know all of the available alternatives, the consequences of each alternative, and the probability of occurrence of these consequences. Thus, rather than being an *optimizer*, the decision maker is a *satisficer*, selecting the alternative that meets an acceptable (satisfactory) standard.[11]

Implementing the Decision

Any decision is little more than an abstraction if it is not implemented. In other words, a decision must be effectively implemented in order to achieve the objective for which it was made. It is entirely possible for a "good" decision to be hurt by poor implementation. In this sense, implementation may be more important than the actual choice of the alternative.

Since in most situations implementing decisions involves people, the test of the soundness of a decision is the behavior of the people involved relative to the decision. While a decision may be technically sound, it can easily be undermined by dissatisfied subordinates. Subordinates cannot be manipulated in the same manner as other resources. Thus, a manager's job is not only to choose good solutions but also to transform such solutions into behavior in the organization. This is done by effectively communicating with the appropriate individuals and groups.[12]

Control and Evaluation

Effective management involves periodic measurements of results. Actual results are compared with planned results (the objective), and if deviations exist, changes must be made. Here again, we see the importance of measurable objectives. If such objectives do not exist, then there is no way to judge performance. If actual results do not match planned results then changes must be made in the solution chosen, in its implementation, or in the original objective if it is deemed unattainable. If the original objective must be revised, then the entire decision-making process will be reactivated. The important point is

---

[11] For a comprehensive discussion devoted solely to this problem, see Janis and Mann, *Decision Making,* chap. 2.

[12] P. L. Hunsaker and J. S. Hunsaker, "Decision Styles—in Theory, in Practice," *Organizational Dynamics,* Autumn 1981, pp. 23–26.

that once a decision is implemented, a manager cannot assume that the outcome will meet the original objective. Some system of control and evaluation is necessary to make sure the *actual results* are consistent with the *results planned for* when the decision was made.

BEHAVIORAL INFLUENCES ON INDIVIDUAL DECISION MAKING

Several behavioral factors influence the decision-making process. Some of these factors influence only certain aspects of the process, while others influence the entire process. However, each may have an impact and, therefore, must be understood in order to fully appreciate decision making as a process in organizations. Four individual behavioral factors—values, personality, propensity for risk, and potential for dissonance—will be discussed in this section. Each of these factors has been shown to have a significant impact on the decision-making process.

Values

values
A decision maker's values are the basic guidelines and beliefs that he or she uses when confronted with a situation in which a choice must be made.

In the context of decision making, **values** can be thought of as the guidelines that a person uses when confronted with a situation in which a choice must be made. Values are acquired early in life and are a basic (often taken for granted) part of an individual's thoughts. The influence of values on the decision-making process is profound:

In *establishing objectives*, it is necessary to make value judgments regarding the selection of opportunities and the assignment of priorities.

In *developing alternatives*, it is necessary to make value judgments about the various possibilities.

In *choosing an alternative*, the values of the decision maker influence which alternative is chosen.

In *implementing* a decision, value judgments are necessary in choosing the means for implementation.

In the *evaluation and control* phase, value judgments cannot be avoided when corrective action is taken.[13]

It is clear that values pervade the decision-making process. They are reflected in the decision maker's behavior before making the decision, in making the decision, and in putting the decision into effect.

---

[13] Harrison, *Managerial Decision-Making Process*, p. 42.

Personality

Decision makers are influenced by many psychological forces, both conscious and subconscious. One of the most important of these forces is their personality, which is strongly reflected in the choices they make. Some studies have examined the effect of selected personality variables on the process of decision making.[14] These studies have generally focused on the following sets of variables:

1. *Personality variables.* These include the attitudes, beliefs, and needs of the individual.
2. *Situational variables.* These pertain to the external, observable situations in which individuals find themselves.
3. *Interactional variables.* These pertain to the momentary state of the individual as a result of the interaction of a specific situation with characteristics of the individual's personality.

The most important conclusions concerning the influence of personality on the decision-making process are as follows:

It is unlikely that one person can be equally proficient in all aspects of the decision-making process. The results suggest that some people will do better in one part of the process, while others will do better in another part.

Such characteristics as intelligence are associated with different phases of the decision-making process.

The relation of personality to the decision-making process may vary for different groups on the basis of such factors as sex and social status.

An important contribution of this research is that it determined that the personality traits of the decision maker combine with certain situational and interactional variables to influence the decision-making process.

Propensity for Risk

From personal experience, the reader is undoubtedly aware that decision makers vary greatly in their propensity for taking risks. This one specific aspect of personality strongly influences the decision-making process. A decision maker who has a low aversion to risk will

---

[14] Orville C. Brun, Jr., et al., *Personality and Decision Processes* (Stanford, Calif.: Stanford University Press, 1962). Also see P. A. Renwick and H. Tose, "The Effects of Sex, Marital Status, and Educational Background on Selected Decisions," *Academy of Management Journal,* March 1978, pp. 93–103; and A. A. Abdel-Halim, "Effects of Task and Personality Characteristics on Subordinate Responses to Participative Decision Making," *Academy of Management Journal,* September 1983, pp. 477–84.

establish different objectives, evaluate alternatives differently, and select different alternatives than will another decision maker in the same situation who has a high aversion to risk. The latter will attempt to make choices where the risk or uncertainty is low or where the certainty of the outcome is high. We shall see later in the chapter that many people are bolder and more innovative and advocate greater risk-taking in groups than as individuals. Apparently, such people are more willing to accept risk as members of a group.

Potential for Dissonance

While much attention has been focused on the forces and influences on the decision maker before a decision is made, and on the decision itself, only recently has attention been given to what happens after a decision has been made. Specifically, behavioral scientists have focused attention on the occurrence of postdecision anxiety.

cognitive dissonance
Cognitive dissonance often occurs when there is a conflict between what we believe and reality. Most individuals are motivated to reduce dissonance and achieve consonance.

Such anxiety is related to what Festinger calls **"cognitive dissonance."**[15] Festinger's theory states that there is often a lack of consistency or harmony among an individual's various cognitions (attitudes, beliefs, and so on) after a decision has been made. That is, there will be a conflict between what the decision maker knows and believes and what was done, and as a result the decision maker will have doubts and second thoughts about the choice that was made. In addition, there is a likelihood that the intensity of the anxiety will be greater when any of the following conditions exist:

1. The decision is an important one psychologically or financially.
2. There are a number of foregone alternatives.
3. The foregone alternatives have many favorable features.

Each of these conditions is present in many decisions in all types of organizations. We can expect, therefore, that post-decision dissonance will be present among many decision makers, especially those at higher levels in the organization.

When dissonance occurs, it can, of course, be reduced by admitting that a mistake has been made. Unfortunately, many individuals are reluctant to admit that they have made a wrong decision. These individuals will be more likely to use one or more of the following methods to reduce their dissonance:

1. Seek information that supports the wisdom of their decision.
2. Selectively perceive (distort) information in a way that supports their decision.

---

[15] Leon Festinger, *A Theory of Cognitive Dissonance* (New York: Harper & Row, 1957), chap. 1.

3. Adopt a less favorable view of the foregone alternatives.
4. Minimize the importance of the negative aspects of the decision and exaggerate the importance of the positive aspects.[16]

While each of us may resort to some of this behavior in our personal decision making, it is easy to see how a great deal of it could be extremely harmful in terms of organizational effectiveness. The potential for dissonance is influenced heavily by one's personality, specifically one's self-confidence and persuasibility. In fact, all of the behavioral influences are closely interrelated and are only isolated here for purposes of discussion. For example, what kind of a risk-taker you are and your potential for anxiety following a decision are very closely related, and both are strongly influenced by your personality, your perceptions, and your value system. Before managers can fully understand the dynamics of the decision-making process, they must appreciate the behavioral influences on themselves and other decision makers in the organization when they make decisions.

GROUP DECISION MAKING

The first parts of this chapter focused on individuals making decisions. In most organizations, however, a great deal of decision making is achieved through committees, teams, task forces, and other kinds of groups. This is because managers frequently face situations in which they must seek and combine judgments in group meetings. This is especially true for nonprogrammed problems, which are novel, with much uncertainty regarding the outcome. In most organizations, it is unusual to find decisions on such problems being made by one individual on a regular basis. The increased complexity of many of these problems requires specialized knowledge in numerous fields, usually not possessed by one person. This requirement, coupled with the reality that the decisions made must eventually be accepted and implemented by many units throughout the organization, has increased the use of the collective approach to the decision-making process. The result for many managers has been an endless amount of time spent in meetings of committees and other groups. It has been found that many

---

[16] W. J. McGuire, "Cognitive Consistency and Attitude Change," *Journal of Abnormal and Social Psychology,* May 1960, pp. 345–53. Also see J. S. Adams, "Reduction of Cognitive Dissonance by Seeking Consonant Information," *Journal of Abnormal and Social Psychology,* January 1961, pp. 74–78; D. S. Holmes and B. K. Houston, "Effectiveness of Situation Redefinition and Affective Isolation in Coping with Stress," *Journal of Personality and Social Psychology,* August 1974, pp. 212–18; and C. A. O'Reilly III, "Variations in Decision Makers' Use of Information Sources: The Impact of Quality and Accessibility of Information," *Academy of Management Journal,* December 1982, pp. 756–71.

managers spend as much as 80 percent of their working time in committee meetings.[17]

Individual versus Group Decision Making

There has been considerable debate over the relative effectiveness of individual versus group decision making. Groups usually take more time to reach a decision than individuals do, but bringing together individual specialists and experts has its benefits since the mutually reinforcing impact of their interaction results in better decisions. In fact, a great deal of research has shown that consensus decisions with five or more participants are superior to individual decision making, majority vote, and leader decisions.[18] Unfortunately, open discussion has been found to be negatively influenced by such behavioral factors as the pressure to conform: the influence of a dominant personality type in the group; "status incongruity," as a result of which, lower status participants are inhibited by higher status participants and "go along" even though they believe that their own ideas are superior; and the attempt of certain participants to influence others because these participants are perceived to be expert in the problem area.[19]

Certain decisions appear to be better made by groups, while others appear better suited to individual decision making. Nonprogrammed decisions appear to be better suited to group decision making. Such decisions usually call for pooled talent in arriving at a solution; the

---

[17] A. H. Van de Ven, *An Applied Experimental Test of Alternative Decision-Making Processes* (Kent, Ohio: Center for Business and Economic Research Press, Kent State University, 1973).

[18] For examples, see Charles Holloman and Harold Henrick, "Adequacy of Group Decisions as a Function of The Decision-Making Process," *Academy of Management Journal*, June 1972, pp. 175–84; Andrew H. Van de Ven and André Delbecq, "Nominal versus Interacting Group Processes for Committee Decision-Making Effectiveness," *Academy of Management Journal*, June 1972, pp. 203–12; and B. M. Staw, "The Escalation of Commitment to a Course of Action," *Academy of Management Review*, October 1981, pp. 577–88.

[19] For examples, see Soloman Asch, "Studies of Independence and Conformity," *Psychological Monographs*, 1956, pp. 68–70; Normal Dalkey and Olaf Helmer, "An Experimental Application of Delphi Method to Use of Experts," *Management Science*, April 1963, pp. 458–67; E. M. Bridges, W. J. Doyle, and D. J. Mahan, "Effects of Hierarchical Differentiation on Group Productivity, Efficiency, and Risk-Taking," *Administrative Science Quarterly*, Fall 1968, pp. 305–39; Victor Vroom, Lester Grant, and Timothy Cotten, "The Consequences of Social Interaction in Group Problem-Solving," *Organizational Behavior and Human Performance*, February 1969, pp. 77–95; P. A. Collaras and L. R. Anderson, "Effect of Perceived Expertise upon Creativity of Members of Brainstorming Groups," *Journal of Applied Psychology*, April 1969, pp. 159–63; Richard A. Guzzo and James A. Waters, "The Expression of Affect and the Performance of Decision Making Groups," *Journal of Applied Psychology*, February 1982, pp. 67–74; and D. Tjosvold and R. H. G. Field, "Effects of Social Context on Consensus and Majority Vote Decision Making," *Academy of Management Journal*, September 1983, pp. 500–506.

decisions are so important that they are usually made by top managers and to a somewhat lesser extent by middle managers. An example of this type of decision making is provided in the following Close-Up.

ORGANIZATIONS: CLOSE-UP

Group Decision Making in a Large Retail Organization

The leading retailer J. C. Penney Company utilizes group decision making at the top levels of the organization. A committee consisting of 14 top managers debates and reaches decisions on such important issues as planning, managerial selection, merchandise selection, and public relations.

The executives at Penney believe that there are some risks in having a group make key decisions. The group decision-making process takes longer, costs more in executive time, and often results in compromises that are less than perfect. The executives also believe that the process has solved some very difficult problems such as how to allocate costs among divisions, which merchandise mix alternatives to pursue, and how to compensate headquarters management.

Group decision making is also credited with improving the firm's profit picture, implementing the use of computers at a faster rate, and reducing an excessive number of staff positions. Finally, inventories, profit margins, and enthusiasm have all improved because of the group decision-making approach, according to Penney's board of directors.

Management expects to continue utilizing group decision making. All key decisions are now reached by the management committee. At J. C. Penney, apparently, "14 heads are better than 1."

Source: "Teamwork Pays Off at Penneys," *Business Week*, April 12, 1982, pp. 107–8.

In terms of the decision-making process itself, the following points concerning group processes for nonprogrammed decisions can be made:

1. In *establishing objectives,* groups are probably superior to individuals because of the greater amount of knowledge available to groups.
2. In *identifying alternatives,* the individual efforts of group members are necessary to ensure a broad search in the various functional areas of the organization.
3. In *evaluating alternatives,* the collective judgment of the group, with its wider range of viewpoints, seems superior to that of the individual decision maker.

4. In *choosing an alternative,* it has been shown that group interaction and the achievement of consensus usually result in the acceptance of more risk than would be accepted by an individual decision maker. In any event, the group decision is more likely to be accepted as a result of the participation of those affected by its consequences.

5. *Implementation* of a decision, whether or not it is made by a group, is usually accomplished by individual managers. Thus, since a group cannot be held responsible, the responsibility for implementation necessarily rests with the individual manager.

Figure 16–2 summarizes the research on group decision making. It presents the relationship between the probable quality of a decision and the method utilized to reach the decision. It indicates that as we move from "individual" to "consensus," the quality of the decision improves. Note also that each successive method involves a higher level of mutual influence by group members. Thus, for a complex problem requiring pooled knowledge, the quality of the decision is likely to be higher as the group moves toward achieving consensus.

FIGURE 16–2

Probable Relationship between Quality of Group Decision and Method Utilized

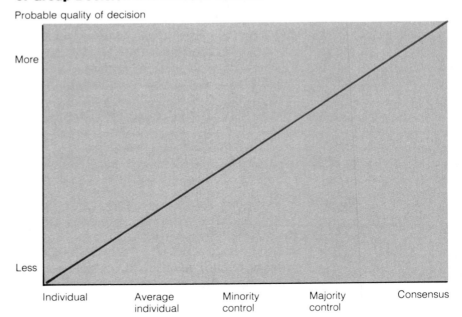

Probable quality of decision

Creativity in Group Decision Making

If groups are better suited to nonprogrammed decisions than individuals, then it is important that an atmosphere fostering group creativity be created. In this respect, group decision making may be similar to brainstorming in that discussion must be free flowing and spontaneous. All group members must participate, and the evaluation of individual ideas must be suspended in the beginning to encourage participation. However, a decision must be reached, and this is where group decision making differs from brainstorming. Figure 16–3 presents guidelines for developing the permissive atmosphere that is important for creative decision making.

Techniques for Stimulating Creativity

It seems safe to say that in many instances group decision making is preferable to individual decision making. But we have all heard the statement "A camel is a racehorse designed by a committee." Thus while the necessity and the benefits of group decision making are recognized, numerous problems are also associated with it, some of which have already been noted. Practicing managers are in need of specific techniques that will enable them to increase the benefits from group decision making while reducing the problems associated with it.

We shall examine three techniques that, when properly utilized, have been found to be extremely useful in increasing the creative capability of a group in generating ideas, understanding problems, and reaching better decisions. Increasing the creative capability of a group is especially necessary when individuals from diverse sectors of the organization must pool their judgments in order to create a satisfactory course of action for the organization. The three techniques are known as brainstorming, the Delphi technique, and the nominal group technique.

brainstorming
Brainstorming promotes creativity by encouraging idea generation through noncritical discussion.

Brainstorming. In many situations, groups are expected to produce creative or imaginative solutions to organizational problems. In such instances, **brainstorming** has often been found to enhance the creative output of the group. The technique of brainstorming includes a strict series of rules. The purpose of the rules is to promote the generation of ideas while at the same time avoiding the inhibitions of members that are usually caused by face-to-face groups. The basic rules are:

No idea is too ridiculous. Group members are encouraged to state any extreme or outlandish idea.

Each idea presented belongs to the group, not to the person stating it. In this way, it is hoped that group members will utilize and build on the ideas of others.

FIGURE 16-3

Creative Group Decision Making

Group Structure

The group is composed of heterogeneous, generally competent personnel who bring to bear on the problem diverse frames of reference, representing channels to each relevant body of knowledge (including contact with outside resource personnel who offer expertise not encompassed by the organization), with a leader who facilitates the creative process.

Group Roles

Each individual explores with the entire group all ideas (no matter how intuitively and roughly formed) that bear on the problem.

Group Processes

The problem-solving process is characterized by:

1. Spontaneous communication between members (not focused on the leader).
2. Full participation from each member.
3. Separation of idea generation from idea evaluation.
4. Separation of problem definition from generation of solution strategies.
5. Shifting of roles, so that interaction that mediates problem solving (particularly search activities and clarification by means of constant questioning directed both to individual members and to the whole group) is not the sole responsibility of the leader.
6. Suspension of judgment and avoidance of early concern with solutions, so that the emphasis is on analysis and exploration, rather than on early commitment to solutions.

Group Style

The social-emotional tone of the group is characterized by:

1. A relaxed, nonstressful environment.
2. Ego-supportive interaction, where open give-and-take between members is at the same time courteous.
3. Behavior that is motivated by interest in the problem, rather than concern with short-run payoff.
4. Absence of penalties attached to any espoused idea or position.

Group Norms

1. Are supportive of originality and unusual ideas and allow for eccentricity.
2. Seek behavior that separates source from content in evaluating information and ideas.
3. Stress a nonauthoritarian view, with a realistic view of life and independence of judgment.
4. Support humor and undisciplined exploration of viewpoints.
5. Seek openness in communication, where mature, self-confident individuals offer "crude" ideas to the group for mutual exploration without threat to the individuals for "exposing" themselves.
6. Deliberately avoid giving credence to short-run results or short-run decisiveness.
7. Seek consensus but accept majority rule when consensus is unobtainable.

Source: Andre L. Delbecq, "The Management of Decision Making within the Firm: Three Strategies for Three Types of Decision Making," *Academy of Management Journal*, December 1967, pp. 334–35.

No idea can be criticized. The purpose of the session is to generate, not evaluate, ideas.

Brainstorming is widely used in advertising and some other fields, where it is apparently effective. In other situations, it has been less successful because there is no evaluation or ranking of the ideas generated. Thus, the group never really concludes the problem-solving process.[20]

The Delphi Technique. This technique involves the solicitation and comparison of anonymous judgments on the topic of interest through a set of sequential questionnaires that are interspersed with summarized information and feedback of opinions from earlier responses.[21]

Delphi process
The Delphi process promotes creativity by using anonymous judgment of ideas to reach a consensus decision.

The **Delphi process** retains the advantage of having several judges while removing the biasing effects that might occur during face-to-face interaction. The basic approach has been to collect anonymous judgments by mail questionnaire. For example, the members independently generate their ideas to answer the first questionnaire and return it. The staff members summarize the responses as the group consensus, and feed this summary back along with a second questionnaire for reassessment. Based on this feedback, the respondents independently evaluate their earlier responses. The underlying belief is that the consensus estimate will result in a better decision after several rounds of anonymous group judgment. While it is possible to continue the procedure for several rounds, studies have shown essentially no significant change after the second round of estimation.[22]

The Nominal Group Technique (NGT). NGT has gained increasing recognition in health, social service, education, industry, and government organizations.[23] The term **Nominal Group Technique** was adopted by earlier researchers to refer to processes that bring people together but do not allow them to communicate verbally. Thus, the collection of people is a group "nominally," or "in name only." We shall see, however, that NGT in its present form combines both verbal and nonverbal stages.

Nominal Group Technique
The Nominal Group Technique promotes creativity by bringing people together in a very structured meeting that does not allow for much verbal communication. The group decision is the mathematically pooled outcome of individual votes.

Basically, NGT is a structured group meeting that proceeds as follows: A group of individuals (7 to 10) sit around a table but do not speak to one another. Rather, each person writes ideas on a pad of paper. After five minutes, a structured sharing of ideas takes place.

---

[20] For a review of research on brainstorming, see T. J. Bouchard, "Whatever Happened to Brainstorming?" *Journal of Creative Behavior*, Fall 1971, pp. 182–89.

[21] Norman Dalkey, *The Delphi Method: An Experimental Study of Group Opinion* (Santa Monica, Calif.: Rand Corporation, 1969). This is a classic work on the Delphi method.

[22] Norman Dalkey, *Experiments in Group Prediction* (Santa Monica, Calif.: Rand Corporation, 1968).

[23] See André L. Delbecq, Andrew H. Van de Ven, and David H. Gustafson, *Group Techniques for Program Planning* (Glenview, Ill.: Scott, Foresman, 1975). The discussion here is based on this work.

Each person around the table presents one idea. A person designated as recorder writes the ideas on a flip chart in full view of the entire group. This continues until all of the participants indicate that they have no further ideas to share. There is still no discussion.

The output of this phase is a list of ideas (usually between 18 and 25). The next phase involves structured discussion in which each idea receives attention before a vote is taken. This is achieved by asking for clarification or stating the degree of support for each idea listed on the flip chart. The next stage involves independent voting in which each participant, in private, selects priorities by ranking or voting. The group decision is the mathematically pooled outcome of the individual votes.

Both the Delphi technique and NGT are relatively new, but each has had an excellent record of successes. Basic differences between them are:

1. Delphi participants are typically anonymous to one another, while NGT participants become acquainted.
2. NGT participants meet face-to-face around a table, while Delphi participants are physically distant and never meet face-to-face.
3. In the Delphi process, all communication between participants is by way of written questionnaires and feedback from the monitoring staff. In NGT, communication is direct between participants.[24]

Practical considerations, of course, often influence which technique is used. For example, such factors as the number of working hours available, costs, and the physical proximity of participants will influence which technique is selected.

Our discussion here has not been designed to make the reader an expert in the Delphi process or NGT.[25] Our purpose throughout this section has been to indicate the frequency and importance of group decision making in every type of organization. The three techniques discussed are practical devices whose purpose is to improve the *effectiveness* of group decisions.

The use of creativity-generating techniques in organizations has been growing, and it is expected to continue to grow during the next decade. However, their use appears to be even greater among European organizations than among American organizations, as the following Close-Up suggests.

---

[24] *Ibid.*, p. 18.

[25] The reader desiring to learn more about each of these techniques is encouraged to consult Delbecq, Van de Ven, and Gustafson, *Group Techniques for Program Planning;* and Frederick C. Miner, Jr., "A Comparative Analysis of Three Diverse Groups' Decision-Making Approaches," *Academy of Management Journal*, March 1979, pp. 81–93.

ORGANIZATIONS: CLOSE-UP

Stimulating Creativity in European Firms

European companies—struggling with stagnant economies, stiff competition, and complex labor-management problems—have been using creativity-generating techniques to a far greater extent than many of their American counterparts. Battelle Institute in Frankfurt indicates that brainstorming—the freewheeling, anything goes technique—is still the most popular method for stimulating creativity and generating ideas among the managements of European companies.

Another method, often called Delphi, is based on the assumption that an honest consensus cannot be reached when people attempt to resolve a problem face-to-face. Using Delphi, individual members anonymously provide their suggestions, which are then compared. The process is repeated until a true consensus is reached.

Third is a method known as morphological analysis, which is the most popular method among the research and development organizations in Europe. A team using this approach begins by breaking a problem down into all of its independent variables. A solution derives from scrutinizing every possible question that any of the variables may raise.

Source: *Management Review,* January 1980, p. 4.

Decision making is a common responsibility shared by all executives, regardless of functional area or management level. Every day, managers are required to make decisions that shape the future of their organization as well as their own futures. The quality of these decisions is the yardstick of their managers' effectiveness. Some of these decisions may have a strong impact on the organization's success, while others will be important but less crucial. However, *all* of the decisions will have some effect (positive or negative, large or small) on the organization.

SUMMARY OF KEY POINTS

A. Decision making is a fundamental process in organizations. Managers make decisions on the basis of the information (communication) that they receive through the organizational structure and the behavior of individuals and groups within it.

B. Decision making distinguishes managers from nonmanagers. The quality of the decisions that managers make determines their effectiveness as managers.

C. Decisions may be classified as programmed or nonprogrammed depending on the type of problem. Most programmed decisions should be made at the first level in the organization while nonprogrammed decisions should be made mostly by top management.

D. Decision making should not be thought of as an end but as a *means* to achieve organizational goals and objectives. Decisions are organizational responses to problems.

E. Decision making should be viewed as a multiphased *process* of which the actual choice is only one phase.

F. The decision-making process is influenced by numerous environmental and behavioral factors. Different decision makers may select different alternatives in the same situation because of different values, perceptions, and personalities.

G. A great deal of nonprogrammed decision making is carried on in group situations. Much evidence exists to support the claim that in most instances group decisions are superior to individual decisions. Three relatively new techniques (brainstorming, the Delphi technique, and the Nominal Group Technique) have the purpose of improving the effectiveness of group decisions. The management of collective decision making must be a vital concern for future managers.

DISCUSSION AND REVIEW QUESTIONS

1. In terms that are satisfactory to you, define a decision.

2. Describe two situations that you have faced that called for programmed decisions on your part and two that called for nonprogrammed decisions. What were some of the differences between them? Did this influence your decision-making approach? How?

3. Think of a decision that you made recently in response to a problem you faced. Describe it in terms of the decision-making process presented in Figure 16–1.

4. For decision-making purposes, why are goals and objectives so important?

5. Think of a major decision that you made recently. It may have involved your personal life, a major purchase, and so on. Do you believe there were any behavioral influences on your decision? Discuss them.

6. What is your attitude toward risk? Has that attitude ever influenced a decision you made? What are the implications of your attitude toward risk?

7. Have you ever been a member of a committee or a task force that was charged with making some type of decision? Describe this experience in terms of your satisfactions, dissatisfactions, problems, and so forth.

ADDITIONAL REFERENCES

Alutto, J., and D. Vredenburgh. "Characteristics of Decisional Participation by Nurses." *Academy of Management Journal,* 1977, pp. 341–47.

Archer, E. R. "How to Make a Business Decision: An Analysis of Theory and Practice." *Management Review,* 1980, pp. 56–61.

Bouchard, R. J., and M. Hare. "Size, Performance, and Potential in Brainstorming Groups." *Journal of Applied Psychology,* 1970, pp. 51–55.

Collins, B. E., and H. Guetzkow. *A Social Psychology of Group Processes for Decision Making.* New York: John Wiley & Sons, 1964.

Delbecq, A. L. "The Management of Decision Making within the Firm: Three Strategies for Three Types of Decision Making." *Academy of Management Journal,* 1967, pp. 329–39.

Garnier, G. H. "Context and Decision Making Autonomy in the Foreign Affiliates of U.S. Multinational Corporations." *Academy of Management Journal,* 1982, pp. 893–908.

Gerwin, D., and F. D. Tuggle. "Modeling Organization Decisions Using the Human Problem-Solving Paradigm." *Academy of Management Journal,* 1978, pp. 762–73.

Gifford, W. E.; H. R. Bobbitt; and J. W. Slocum, Jr. "Message Characteristics and Perceptions of Uncertainty by Organizational Decision Makers." *Academy of Management Journal,* 1979, pp. 458–81.

Gustafson, D. H.; R. M. Shukla; A. L. Delbecq; and G. W. Walster. "A Comparative Study of Differences in Subjective Likelihood Estimates Made by Individuals, Interacting Groups, Delphi Groups, and Nominal Groups." *Organizational Behavior and Human Performance,* 1973, pp. 280–91.

Hall, E. J.; J. Mouton; and R. R. Blake. "Group Problem-Solving Effectiveness under Conditions of Pooling versus Interaction." *Journal of Social Psychology,* 1963, pp. 147–57.

Halter, A. N., and G. W Dean. *Decisions under Uncertainty with Research Applications.* Cincinnati: South-Western Publishing, 1971.

Harrison, F. L. "Decision Making in Conditions of Extreme Uncertainty." *Journal of Management Studies,* 1977, pp. 169–78.

Huber, G., and A. L. Delbecq. "Guidelines for Combining the Judgment of Individual Members in Decision Conferences." *Academy of Management Journal,* 1972, pp. 161–74.

King, J. L. "Cost-Benefit Analysis for Decision Making." *Journal of Systems Management,* 1980, pp. 12–14.

Kogan, N., and M. A. Wallach. *Risk-Taking: A Study in Cognition and Personality.* New York: Holt, Rinehart & Winston, 1964.

Lang, J. R.; J. E. Dittrich; and S. E. White. "Managerial Problem Solving Models: A Review and a Proposal." *Academy of Management Review,* 1978, pp. 854–66.

Lindley, D. V. *Making Decisions.* New York: John Wiley & Sons, 1971.

Miller, D. W., and M. K. Starr. *The Structure of Human Decisions.* Englewood Cliffs, N.J.: Prentice-Hall, 1967.

Provan, K. "Interorganizational Linkages and Influence over Decision Making." *Academy of Management Journal,* 1982, pp. 443–51.

Rosen, B., and T. H. Jerdee. "Effects of Decision Performance on Managerial Willingness to Use Participation." *Academy of Management Journal,* 1978, pp. 722–24.

Shull, F. A.; A. L. Delbecq; and L. L. Cummings. *Organizational Decision Making.* New York: McGraw-Hill, 1970.

Simon, H. A. *Models of Man.* New York: John Wiley & Sons, 1957.

———. *Sciences of the Artificial.* Cambridge, Mass.: MIT Press, 1969.

Tersine, R. J., and W. E. Riggs. "The Delphi Technique: A Long-Range Planning Tool." *Business Horizons,* 1976, pp. 51–56.

Van de Ven, A. H. *Group Decision Making and Effectiveness: An Experimental Study.* Kent, Ohio: Kent State University Press, 1974.

White, J. K. "Generalizability of Individual Difference Moderators of the Participation in Decision Making—Employee Response Relationship." *Academy of Management Journal,* 1978, pp. 36–43.

CASE FOR ANALYSIS

The Faculty Decision

Tom Madden slipped into his seat at the meeting of the faculty of the College of Business Administration of Longley University. He was 10 minutes late because he had come completely across campus from another meeting that had lasted 1¼ hours. "Boy!" he thought, "if all of these meetings and committee assignments keep up, I won't have time to do anything else."

"The next item of importance," said the dean, "is consideration of the feasibility report prepared by the assistant dean, Dr. Jackson, for the establishment of our Latin American MBA program."

"What's that?" Tom whispered to his friend Jim Lyon, who was sitting next to him.

"Ah, Professor Madden," winked Lyon as he passed the 86-page report to Tom, "evidently you've not bothered to read this impressive document. Otherwise, you'd know."

"Heck, Jim, I've been out of town for two weeks on a research project, and I've just come from another meeting."

"Well, Tom," chuckled Jim, "the report was circulated only three days ago to, as the dean put it, 'ensure that we have faculty input into where the college is going.' Actually, Tom, I was hoping you had read it because then you could have told me what was in it."

"Dr. Jackson," said the dean, "why don't you present a summary of your excellent report on what I believe is an outstanding opportunity for our college, the establishment of an MBA program in Latin America."

"Hey, Jim," said Tom, "they've got to be kidding. We're not doing what we should be doing with the MBA we've got here on campus. Why on earth are we thinking about starting another one 3,000 miles away?"

Jim shrugged. "Some friend of the dean's or Jackson's from down there must have asked them, I guess."

While the summary was being given, Tom thumbed through the report. He noted that the college was planning to offer the same program that it offered in the United States. "Certainly," he thought, "their students' needs are different from ours." He also noted that faculty were going to be sent from the United States on one- to three-year appointments. "You would think that whenever possible they would seek local instructors who were familiar with the needs of local industry," Tom thought. He concluded in his own mind, "Actually, why are we even getting involved in this thing in the first place? We don't have the resources."

When Jackson finished the summary, the dean asked, "Are there any questions?"

"I wonder how many people have had the time to read this report in three days and think about it," Tom thought to himself.

"Has anybody thought through this entire concept?" Tom spoke up. "I mean . . ."

"Absolutely, Professor Madden," the dean answered. "Dr. Jackson and I have spent a great deal of time on this project."

"Well, I was just thinking that . . ."

"Now, Professor Madden, surely you don't question the efforts of Dr. Jackson and myself. Had you been here when this meeting started, you would know all about our efforts. Besides, it's getting late and we've got another agenda item to consider today, the safety and security of final examinations prior to their being given."

"No further questions," Tom said.

"Wonderful," said the dean. "Then I will report to the president that the faculty of the College of Business Administration unanimously approves the Latin American MBA program. I might add, by the way, that the president is extremely pleased with our method of shared decision making. We have made it work in this college, while other colleges are having trouble arriving at mutually agreed-upon decisions.

"This is a great day for our college. Today we have become a multinational university. We can all be proud."

After the meeting, as Tom headed for the parking lot, he thought, "What a way to make an important decision. I guess I shouldn't complain though, I didn't even read the report. I'd better check my calendar to see what committee meetings I've got the rest of the week. If I've got any more, I'll . . ."

Questions for Consideration

1. Analyze this case, and outline the factors that influenced the faculty decision in this case—either positively or negatively.

2. Does this case indicate that shared decision making cannot be worthwhile and effective? How could it be made more effective in the College of Business Administration?

3. Do you believe that decision making of this type may be more worthwhile and effective in some types of organizations than in others? Discuss.

EXPERIENTIAL EXERCISE
LOST ON THE MOON: A GROUP DECISION EXERCISE

Objective

After reading the "Situation" below, you will first individually, and then as a member of a team, rank in importance a number of items available for carrying out your mission. Your objective is to come as close as possible to the "best solution" as determined by experts of the National Aeronautics and Space Administration.

Instructions

Phase I: 15 minutes

Read the "Situation" below and the directions that follow it. Then, in column 2 (Your Ranks) of the work sheet, assign priorities to the 15 items listed. Use a pencil since you may wish to change your rankings. Somewhere on the sheet it may be useful to note your logic for each ranking.

Phase II: 25 minutes

Your instructor will assign you to a team. The task of each team is to arrive at a consensus on the rankings. Share your individual solutions, and reach a consensus—one ranking for each of the 15 items that best satisfies all of the team members. Thus, by the end of Phase II, all members of the team should have the same set of rankings in column 4 (Group Ranks). Do *not* change your individual rankings in column 2.

Phase III

Your instructor will provide you with the "best solution" to the problem, that is, the set of rankings determined by the NASA experts, along with their reasoning. Each person should note this set of rankings in column 1 (NASA's Ranks). (Note: While it is fun to debate the experts' rankings and their reasoning, don't forget that the objective of the game is to learn more about decision making, not how to survive on the moon!)

Evaluation

It is time now to see how well you did, individually and as a team. First, find your individual score by taking the absolute difference between Your Ranks (column 2) and NASA's Ranks (column 1) and writing it in the first

---

Source: Special permission for reproduction of the above material is granted by the author, Jay Hall, Ph.D., and the publisher, Teleometrics, International. All rights reserved.

Error Points column (column 3). (Thus, if you ranked "Box of matches" 3 and NASA ranked it 8, you would put a 5 in column 3 next to "Box of matches." Then total the error points in column 3 and write the total in the space at the bottom of the column.

LOST ON THE MOON
The Situation

Your spaceship has just crash-landed on the moon. You were scheduled to rendezvous with a mother ship 200 miles away on the lighted surface of the moon, but the rough landing has ruined your ship and destroyed all of the equipment aboard, except for the 15 items listed below.

Your crew's survival depends on reaching the mother ship, so you must choose the most critical items available for the 200-mile trip. Your task is to rank the 15 items in terms of their importance for survival. Place number 1 by the most important item, number 2 by the second most important, and so on through number 15, the least important.

Work Sheet Items	1 NASA's Ranks	2 Your Ranks	3 Error Points	4 Group Ranks	5 Error Points
Box of matches	___	___	___	___	___
Food concentrate	___	___	___	___	___
Fifty feet of nylon rope	___	___	___	___	___
Parachute silk	___	___	___	___	___
Solar-powered portable heating unit	___	___	___	___	___
Two .45-caliber pistols	___	___	___	___	___
One case of dehydrated Pet milk	___	___	___	___	___
Two 100-pound tanks of oxygen	___	___	___	___	___
Stellar map (of the moon's constellation)	___	___	___	___	___
Self-inflating life raft	___	___	___	___	___
Magnetic compass	___	___	___	___	___
Five gallons of water	___	___	___	___	___
Signal flares	___	___	___	___	___
First-aid kit containing injection needles	___	___	___	___	___
Solar-powered FM receiver-transmitter	___	___	___	___	___

Total error points   Individual _____   Group _____

Next, score your group performance in the same way, this time taking the absolute differences between Group Ranks (column 4) and NASA's Ranks (column 1) and writing them in the second Error Points column (column 5). Total the group error points. (Note that all members of the team will have the same group error points.)

Finally, prepare three pieces of information to be submitted to your instructor when he calls on your team:

1. Average individual error points (the average of the points in the last space in column 3. One team member should add these figures and divide by the number of team members to get the average).
2. Group error points (the figure at the bottom of column 5).
3. Number of team members who had fewer individual error points than the group error points.

Using this information, your instructor will evaluate the results of the exercise and discuss your performance with you. Together, you will then explore the implications of this exercise for the group decision-making process.

Chapter 17

After completing Chapter 17, you should be able to:

Define   what is meant by the term *job analysis*.

Describe   how a behaviorally anchored rating scale is developed.

Discuss   the role that federal laws play in performance evaluation.

Compare   the features or points of interest of various performance evaluation methods (e.g., graphic rating scales, checklists, MBO, assessment centers).

Identify   the reasons why the performance evaluation feedback interview is important.

Performance Evaluation Processes

Using a Trait-Oriented Performance Evaluation

Argument For

An important decision that managers make is to determine how performance evaluations will be used. Performance evaluation programs have been used to assess employee traits, behavior, and output. Many organizations make decisions using systems that evaluate such traits as dependability, technical competence, commitment, and initiative.

The assumption made by some of the individuals who use traits for performance evaluation is that there is a relationship between the traits selected and individual job performance. The trait-oriented evaluation system is assumed by some users to be relatively inexpensive to implement, informative, and as accurate as behavior- or results-oriented programs. Since subjectivity cannot be completely eliminated from any performance evaluation system, there is sufficient reason to employ the least expensive program.

Another argument supporting a trait-oriented system focuses on the overemphasis on results. Overemphasizing bottom-line results has dysfunctional consequences and is not conducive to the actual development of employees. It can be reasoned that if quality of work-life improvements are to occur, there must be less emphasis on bottom-line results.

Argument Against

The opponents of trait-oriented performance evaluation programs believe that results-oriented evaluations are needed. They agree that certain traits are important in perform-

597

ing some jobs. However, they argue that traits are so ingrained and difficult to determine that few managers can successfully evaluate them or alter them significantly. Any rater who uses a trait evaluation must make many inferences. The rater must translate the trait into behaviors that are linked to performance. Critics believe this task is beyond the capabilities of most individuals. It would require a genius, with perfect insight and assessment skills, to be able to generate the trait-behavior-performance linkages. For example, what is the relationship between an attitude (a trait), working extra hours (a behavior), and the final number of units produced (a performance output). Can any person really measure attitudes? What is the connection between attitudes and behavior? These and similar questions are so complex that trait-based systems do nothing but confuse the issue. That is, by using a trait-based system, a manager is unable to answer any questions about why an employee is behaving or performing in a particular manner. Until traits are translated into behaviors and results, they should be left out of performance appraisal.

Traits are less helpful for use in coaching and feedback sessions involving a rater and ratee. The rater is not able to cite examples of specific job behaviors that can be corrected or modified to improve performance. Being unable to cite behavioral examples creates significant strain in the rater-ratee dialogue. A ratee wants to know why he or she received a particular evaluation. Answering that question requires being able to cite specific examples.

The Organizational Issue for Debate indicates that trait systems are still very popular and are widely used. Their simplicity accounts for some of this popularity. The courts, however, have raised serious questions about the validity, reliability, and relevance of trait-based evaluations. This chapter will show that trait systems have serious flaws and drawbacks. If such systems are used in combination with other programs, they may provide some subjective impressions that a rater could use. However, sole reliance on typically vague and subjective trait systems will not result in a sound performance evaluation program.

This chapter focuses on the uses, types, and applications of formal performance evaluation systems. The challenge facing managers involves finding an evaluation system that provides an equitable, legally correct, and informative basis for evaluating the performance of employees. This is not a small challenge, because every system has strengths, weaknesses, and costs that need to be evaluated carefully. In some organizations, there may be a need to use more than one evaluation system. The important theme of the chapter is not whether formal evaluation systems should be used but what ones should be used and how they should be used.

Since performance evaluation is inevitable and is to some degree subjective, managers need to gather information that is relevant, accurate, and sufficiently complete. Managers who gather such information will eventually have to address the following questions: (1) What is the purpose of the evaluation? (2) What criteria should be evaluated? (3) What pitfalls of evaluation should be avoided? (4) What methods of evaluation are best suited to accomplish the purpose? and (5) How can evaluation become a development experience for subordinates?

performance evaluation
The systematic, formal evaluation of an employee's job performance and potential for future development.

Many varieties of **performance evaluation** systems are now being used in organizations. In most organizations, the evaluation system is designed to provide both the ratee and the rater (manager) with information about job performance.[1] However, before any performance evaluation system is selected, there should be a clear understanding among raters and ratees about the objectives of the system. Two broadly stated purposes of performance evaluation are to reach an *evaluative* or *judgmental* conclusion about job performance and to *develop* employees through the system.[2] These two broadly stated purposes are compared in Table 17–1. Notice the differences in the time orientation, objectives, and roles of the ratee and rater.

---

[1] Gary P. Latham and Kenneth N. Wexley, *Increasing Productivity through Performance Appraisal* (Reading, Mass.: Addison-Wesley Publishing, 1981).

[2] L. L. Cummings and Donald P. Schwab, *Performance in Organizations* (Glenview, Ill.: Scott, Foresman, 1973), p. 5.

TABLE 17-1

Two Major Purposes of Performance Evaluation: A Comparison

Points of Comparison	Major Purposes	
	Judgmental	Developmental
Time orientation	Past performance	Preparation for future performance
Objective	Improving performance by changing behavior through reward system	Improving performance through self-learning and personal growth
Method	Use of rating scales, comparisons, and frequency distributions	Counseling, mutual trust, goal setting, and career planning
Supervisor's role (rater)	A judge who appraises	A supportive counseling and encouraging person who listens, helps, and guides
Subordinate's role (ratee)	Listener, reacts and attempts to defend past performance	Actively involved in charting future job performance plans

Source: Adapted from L. L. Cummings and Donald P. Schwab, *Performance In Organizations* (Glenview, Ill.: Scott, Foresman, 1973), p. 5.

Organizations are becoming increasingly aware that raters must clearly identify the purpose of the performance evaluation program.[3] The judgmental and developmental purposes are certainly not mutually exclusive. In fact, surveys of practices indicate that a growing number of organizations use performance evaluations for both judgmental and developmental purposes.[4]

Managers are continually faced with making judgments concerning the job performance of subordinates. For example, judgments are made about promotions and pay raises. Most experts recommend that evaluation sessions addressing salary or promotion should be kept separate from those dealing with personal and career development. The rationale for the separation is the differences in the judgmental and developmental purposes of performance evaluation illustrated in Table 17-1.

A well-designed and -implemented performance evaluation program can certainly have a motivational impact on ratees. It can encourage improvement, develop a sense of responsibility, and increase organizational commitment. Performance evaluation can also be motivational

[3] Angelo S. DeNisi and George E. Stevens, "Profiles of Performance, Performance Evaluations, and Personnel Decisions," *Academy of Management Journal*, September 1981, pp. 596–602.

[4] William Schiemann, *Managing Human Resources/1983 and Beyond* (Chestnut Hill, Mass.: Opinion Research Corporation, 1983).

TABLE 17–2

Specific Purposes of Performance Evaluation

Motivation	Identifying training and development needs
Promotion	
Termination	Evaluating effectiveness of selection and placement decisions
Salary increases	
Wage increases	Transfer
Improved managerial awareness of subordinate's job tasks and problems	Human resource planning
	Layoff
Improved understanding by subordinate of management's view of his or her performance	

if it provides ratees with some understanding of what is expected of them.

Another specific purpose of performance evaluation is the improvement of managerial understanding. A formal program encourages managers to observe the behavior of subordinates. Through increased and more thorough observations, improved mutual understanding between supervisors and subordinates can result.

Performance evaluation information also provides a basis for planning, training, and development. Weaknesses in such areas as technical competence, communication skills, and problem-solving techniques can be identified and analyzed.

A research purpose can also be accomplished through performance evaluation. The accuracy of selection decisions can be determined by comparing performance evaluations with such selection devices as test scores and interviewers' ratings.

Although the two broad purposes of performance evaluation are judgmental and developmental, the specific reasons for using it transcend the organization. Some of these more *specific* purposes are summarized in Table 17–2.

One other important purpose of performance evaluation is to reduce favoritism in making important decisions. This reason is not shown in Table 17–2, but it is extremely important to many employees. It is not shown in Table 17–2 because it is a subjective factor, while the other purposes cited are specific and related to the broad judgmental and developmental categories. The negative effects of perceived favoritism include strained supervisor-subordinate relationships, low morale, and dissatisfaction with company policies.[5]

---

[5] P. Pigors and C. A. Myers, *Personnel Administration* (New York: McGraw-Hill, 1977), p. 270.

THE PERFORMANCE CRITERION
ISSUE OF EVALUATION

criterion
A rule or standard
that is used to
determine how well
or poorly a person is
performing.

The performance evaluation program at any level within the organizational hierarchy must at some point focus on the criterion issue. A **criterion** is a standard or test by which something will be judged. For example, in golf a criterion of a golfer's competence is his score. The lower the score, the better the golfer's performance.[6] In organizations, the criterion should reflect the employee's contribution to the job. In performance evaluation, the criterion is the dependent or predicted measure (e.g., standard) for appraising the effectiveness of an individual employee.

Requirements of a
Performance Criterion

There are a number of requirements that should be met before a variable qualifies as a performance criterion. First, a criterion should be *relevant* to the individual and the organization. Determining what is relevant is itself controversial. Some person or group must make a judgment about what constitutes relevance. Once the relevant criterion has been selected, an effort must be made to develop a sound and valid measure of the variable.

Second, the criterion must be reliable. This involves agreement between evaluations made at different points in time. If the results from the two evaluations show little agreement, there would be some uncertainty about whether the criterion was stable.

Third, a performance criterion may be relevant and reliable and still be useless in evaluating employees. A criterion is useful only if it can *discriminate* between good performers and poor performers. If all employees are good performers, then there is no need to discriminate. If, however, there are good, average and poor performers, then the evaluation criterion must disciminate.

Finally, the criterion must be *practical*. The criterion must mean something to the rater and ratee. If the criterion serves no practical function, then it becomes something that is evaluated but offers no meaning.

Meeting these four requirements does not provide the answer to two questions: (1) Should one criterion be used to measure job performance? and (2) Should the criterion be an economic, physiological, or some other variable?

---

[6] Robert M. Guion, *Personnel Testing* (New York: McGraw-Hill, 1965), p. 90.

Criterion or Criteria?

The use of the term *criterion,* a single noun, has resulted from the search for years to find the "ultimate criterion." Thorndike stated:

> The ultimate criterion for a production line worker might be that he performs his task, maintaining the tempo of the line, with the minimum of defective products requiring rejection upon inspection, that he be personally satisfied with the task.[7]

This statement adequately represents the view of those who believe that a single criterion exists for every job.

In general, there is ample evidence to support either the single criterion or multiple criteria arguments. In some situations, especially at the policymaking level, a single criterion is needed to reach a managerial decision. In other situations, involving promotion, salary and wage decisions, transfer, and counseling, multiple criteria can be useful in illustrating why a particular decision is made or a specific development program recommended. It would be extremely difficult to explain a promotion decision on the basis of a single criterion. Of course, if the employee receives the promotion, he or she may not mind the use of an ultimate criterion for reaching the decision.

Some Other Issues Involving Criteria

Selecting appropriate criteria to use in performance evaluation is further complicated by the fact that criteria are often dynamic. That is, criteria that are valid, reliable, and practical at one point in an employee's career may become inappropriate over a period of time. For example, during the first year or so on the job producing 15 units a week may be acceptable for an employee. However, as the employee acquires experience, confidence, and career goals, this level of production may become inappropriate. An experienced employee might be expected to average about 25 units a week.

Another controversial issue concerning criteria involves the activities versus results debate. A performance evaluation program that concentrates on either activities or results to the exclusion of the other often produces problems because employees learn what is important and work at that aspect of the job.[8] For example, if production output is a major criterion for assessing performance, assembly-line workers may produce as many units as possible so that they will receive

---

[7] R. L. Thorndike, *Personnel Selection* (New York: John Wiley & Sons, 1949), p. 11.

[8] Lyman W. Porter, Edward E. Lawler III, and J. Richard Hackman, *Behavior in Organizations* (New York: McGraw-Hill, 1975), pp. 324–25, has an excellent discussion of the activities versus results controversy.

a good evaluation. This production quantity orientation may cause poor quality products to be manufactured at high costs because of the excessive number of rejects.

On the other hand, a program of performance evaluation that appraises only activities also has limitations. First, if would encourage only activities and disregard accomplishments. For example, if our assembly-line worker is evaluated only on whether safety rules were followed and his or her work area was properly prepared for production, too few units may be made for eventual sale.

It seems appropriate to suggest that whenever possible, performance evaluation criteria should be established for both activities and results. If any performance evaluation program addresses either activities or results criteria at the exclusion of the other, little attention may be paid to organizational and personal goal accomplishment. Organizations often focus on results, while activities seem to be important to groups and individuals. Therefore, so that all parties can benefit as much as possible from the performance evaluation program, both results and activities criteria should be developed whenever possible.[9]

PERFORMANCE CRITERIA AND THE LAW

The Equal Employment Opportunity Commission (EEOC), the federal agency responsible for administering and enforcing the Civil Rights Act of 1964, issued the Uniform Guidelines on Employment Selection Procedures in 1978. These guidelines have an impact on performance evaluation because they view evaluations as a selection procedure.[10] The guidelines state that a procedure such as a performance evaluation must not have an adverse impact on any person or group protected by the Civil Rights Act.

Most performance evaluation procedures rely on paper-and-pencil methods to identify specific work behavior, although assessment centers are a procedure by which participants experience numerous simulations (i.e., exercises) reflecting the demands and skills of a given position. These simulations are evaluated by trained raters.[11] Management uses the outcomes of evaluations (e.g., paper and pencil, observation, or assessment centers) to make promotion, pay, transfer, and other human resource decisions (see Table 17–2). In making these decisions, there is the potential for bias and poor judgment in many

---

[9] Ibid., p. 326.

[10] Richard Henderson, *Performance Appraisal* (Reston, Va.: Reston Publishing, 1984), p. 337.

[11] Frederic D. Frank and James R. Preston, "The Validity of the Assessment Center Approach and Related Issues," *Personnel Administrator,* June 1982, p. 87.

parts of the evaluation process. For example, managers who are serving as raters could use criteria that are not important in performing a job or could place too little weight on significant job performance criteria.

Since employers have been losing many race, sex, and age discrimination cases, understanding the law seems to be a major concern. Court rulings provide managers with guidelines on the issues of criteria, validity, and reliability. These three concepts are extremely important if a case reaches the courts.

A number of cases involving performance evaluation have reached the courts. The U.S. circuit court in *Brito* v. *Zia Company* (1973) found that Zia Company was in violation of Title VII of the Civil Rights Act of 1964 when a disproportionate number of a protected group were laid off on the basis of low performance scores.[12] Zia also failed in accordance with the law to "introduce evidence of validity . . . consistency of empirical data. . . . The court found that the evaluations were based on best judgments and opinions . . . but not on any specific performance that were supported by some kind of record."[13]

In the *Jackson* v. *Kreps* (1979) case, performance evaluation was ruled to be discriminatory.[14] The court found that four white applicants for a promotion were classified "highly qualified," while no blacks received more than a "qualified" rating. The court awarded the employee (Jackson) back pay and promotion to the next vacancy that occurred.

These and other court cases and rulings emphasize the importance of validity in any performance evaluation system.[15] The principal kinds of validity that are relevant for making performance evaluations are briefly presented in Table 17–3. As shown, numerous types of validity exist.[16] The important point to note is that validity is inferred and not directly measured. The manager has to make a judgment about the validity of the criteria he or she is using. The federal courts are now insisting that proper consideration be given to the validity and reliability of performance evaluation instruments.

In order to comply with federal laws regarding performance evaluation, the criteria, validity, and reliability issues must be carefully considered. Managers also need to review previous court rulings. In addi-

---

[12] *Brito* v. *Zia Company,* 478 F. 2d 1200 (1973).

[13] Ibid.

[14] *Jackson* v. *Kreps,* 20 FEP 1532 (1979).

[15] L. S. Kleiman and R. L. Durham, "Performance Appraisal, Promotion, and the Courts: A Critical Review," *Personnel Psychology,* Spring 1981, pp. 103–21.

[16] For an excellent and brief discussion of the validity and reliability of performance criteria, see Henderson, *Performance Appraisal,* pp. 221–24; and Richard I. Henderson, *Compensation Management* (Reston, Va.: Reston Publishing, 1982), pp. 378–400.

TABLE 17–3

**Types of Validity Used in Determining
Acceptability of Performance Evaluation Criteria**

Type of Validity	Brief Description
Concurrent	Statistical correlation between a predictor (an item on the evaluation form) and actual job performance.
Content	The degree to which scores or ratings on the evaluation are a representative sample of all the job behaviors required to perform the job.
Criterion-related	Whenever individual difference measures are used, criterion-related validity should be examined. Scores or ratings on the evaluation are related to some criterion (e.g., expert judgment). If the criterion is available at the same time that the predictor is measured, concurrent validity is being assessed.
Predictive	In contrast to concurrent validity, if criterion data are not available until after predictor scores are obtained, then predictive validity is being measured. Thus, predictive validity is oriented toward the future, while concurrent validity is oriented toward the present.
Construct	The degree to which scores may be interpreted as measuring a property such as potential, motivation, or commitment. It is important to obtain a degree of objectivity in assessing construct validity.
Convergent	The correlation between the same properties or traits as rated by different raters is significantly different from zero.
Discriminant	The correlation between the same traits as rated by different raters should be higher than the correlation between different traits as rated by the same rater. Also, the correlation between the same traits as rated by different raters should be higher than the correlation between different traits as rated by different raters.

tion to addressing the validity and reliability issues, managers must make sure that:

The overall performance evaluation process is standardized and as objective as possible.

The performance evaluation is as job-related as possible.

A thorough, formal job analysis for all positions is carefully done.

Subjective ratings are considered as only one input in the evaluation decisions.

Raters are trained to use the performance evaluation forms and process.

Raters have daily contact with and are able to frequently observe ratees.

The evaluation is conducted independently by more than one rater for each ratee.[17]

The evaluation system is validated.

A mechanism for employee appeal is provided.[18]

The law and the need for a formal performance evaluation system have greatly affected what organizations are now using. In essence, no matter what process is used, managers or raters must make judgments about ratees. Furthermore, these judgments need to be based on scientifically derived criteria. Figure 17–1 displays the central im-

FIGURE 17–1

The Four Main Phases of Performance Evaluation

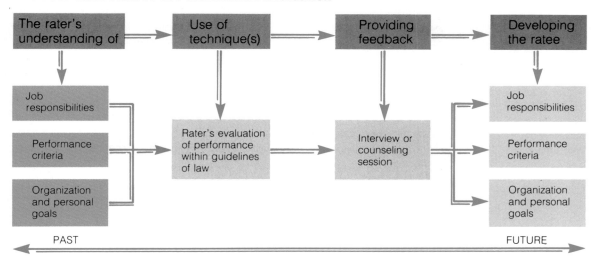

portance of criteria in the performance evaluation process. Furthermore, the importance of the law, the role of the rater in providing feedback to and developing ratees, and the part played by the ratee in understanding responsibilities, criteria, and goals are emphasized.

[17] Duane E. Thompson, Charles R. Klasson, and Gary L. Lubben, "Performance Appraisal and the Law: Policy and Research Implications of Court Cases," paper presented at Academy of Management Meetings, Atlanta, Georgia, August 9, 1979, pp. 5–6.

[18] Wayne F. Cascio and H. John Bernardin, "Implications of Performance Appraisal Litigation for Personnel Decisions," *Personnel Psychology*, Summer 1981, pp. 211–26.

JOB ANALYSIS AND PERFORMANCE EVALUATION

In Figure 17–1, the importance of criteria development in performance evaluation is identified. One needs to examine jobs and how the organization divides its tasks into individual jobs before reliable, valid, and practical criteria emerge. The description of how one job differs from another in terms of the demands, activities, and skills required is *job analysis.*

job analysis
The procedures used to examine the details and characteristics of a job. Job analysis offers a method for differentiating one job from another.

Broadly stated, **job analysis** is devoted to the gathering and analysis of job-specific information. The job analyst is interested in specifying the unique characteristics that differentiate one job from another. By careful analysis of the job's characteristics, a summary statement of what an employee on the job actually does is developed. This statement is called a *job description.* Furthermore, a dollar value is attached to the job, enabling the organization to relate the dollar value of the job to the dollar value of other jobs. The assignment of dollar values is called **job evaluation.** Performance evaluation distinguishes the performance and potential among employees on the basis of various criteria. Figure 17–2 presents the relationships between job analysis and performance evaluation.

job evaluation
Once jobs have been analyzed and classified, a dollar value is assigned to them. This assignment of dollar value is called job evaluation.

Through job analysis, a manager is provided with clues about which criteria can be used to evaluate job performance. Several kinds of criteria are commonly used in organizations. The type of criteria used depends on such factors as the type of job, the time period covered

FIGURE 17–2

**Job Analysis and Performance Evaluation:
A Relationship**

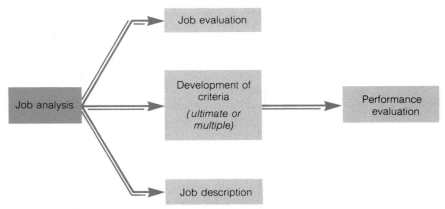

Source: Adapted from Frank J. Landy and Don A. Trumbo, *Psychology of Work Behavior* (Homewood, Ill.: Dorsey Press, 1980), p. 104.

by the evaluation, and the purposes to be served by the evaluation program. The criteria used to evaluate the research and development scientist (e.g., new discoveries, funds allocation) working in an organizational laboratory are different from the criteria used to evaluate the first-line supervisor (e.g., units output, cost of output) or the salesperson (e.g., sales revenue, customers called on).

PERFORMANCE EVALUATION METHODS: TRADITIONAL

If pressed for an answer, most managers could offer a general description of the job performance of subordinates. However, a more formal and systematic procedure than asking for the opinions of managers or supervisors is generally used.[19] Managers usually attempt to select a performance evaluation procedure that will minimize conflict with ratees, provide relevant feedback to ratees, and contribute to the achievement of organizational goals. Basically, the manager attempts to find, develop, and implement a performance evaluation program that can benefit the employee, other managers, the work group, and the organization.

There are no universally accepted methods of performance evaluation that fit every purpose, person, or organization. What is effective in IBM will not necessarily work in General Mills. In fact, what is effective within one department or for one group in a particular organization will not necessarily be effective for another unit or group in the same organization. The only important point is that some type of measuring device or procedure should be used to record data on a number of performance criteria so that subjectivity in reward, development, and other managerial decisions is minimized.

Graphic Rating Scales

The oldest and most widely used performance evaluation procedure, the scaling technique, appears in many forms. Generally, the rater is supplied with a printed form, one for each subordinate to be rated. The form contains a number of job performance qualities and characteristics that are to be rated. The rating scales are distinguished by (1) how exactly the categories are defined, (2) the degree to which the person interpreting the ratings can tell what response was intended by the rater, and (3) how carefully the performance dimension is defined for the rater.

---

[19] For an excellent discussion of performance evaluation methods, see Frank J. Landy and James L. Farr, "Performance Rating," *Psychological Bulletin,* February 1980, pp. 72–107.

Figure 17–3 presents samples of some of the common **graphic rating scales.** The first distinguishing feature among rating scales, the meaning of the possible response categories, is usually handled by the use of anchor statements or words placed at points along a scale. Rating scales (a), and (b), (c), (d), and (h) use anchors.

The second distinguishing feature among rating scales is the degree to which the person interpreting the ratings can tell what response was intended. The clarity of response intention is exemplified in scales (e), (f), and (g).

Quality of work can be interpreted differently by various raters. Therefore, a performance dimension needs to be defined for each rater. Scales (a), (b), (e), and (g) give the rater little performance dimension definition. Scales (c) and (h) provide the rater with a fairly good definition of the performance dimension.

Ranking Methods

Some managers use a rank order procedure to evaluate all subordinates. The subordinates are ranked according to their relative worth to the company or unit on one or more performance dimensions. The procedure followed usually involves identifying the best performer and the worst performer. They are ranked in the first and last positions on the ranking list. The next best and next poorest performers are then filled in on the list. This rank ordering continues until all subordinates are placed on the list. The rater is forced to discriminate by the rank ordering performance evaluation method.

There are some problems with the ranking method. It is likely that ratees in the central portion of the list will not be much different from each other on the performance rankings. Another problem involves the size of the group of subordinates being evaluated. It becomes more difficult to rank large groups of subordinates.

Other ranking methods are also used. For example, in the *paired comparison* method, every subordinate is compared with every other. The supervisor is asked to identify the best performer from each pair. If a supervisor had eight subordinates, he or she would have:

$$\text{Pairs} = \frac{N(N-1)}{2}$$

or

$$\frac{8(8-1)}{2} = 28$$

Weighted Checklists

The weighted-checklist rating consists of a number of statements that describe various types and levels of behavior for a particular

FIGURE 17-3

Some Samples of Rating Scale Formats

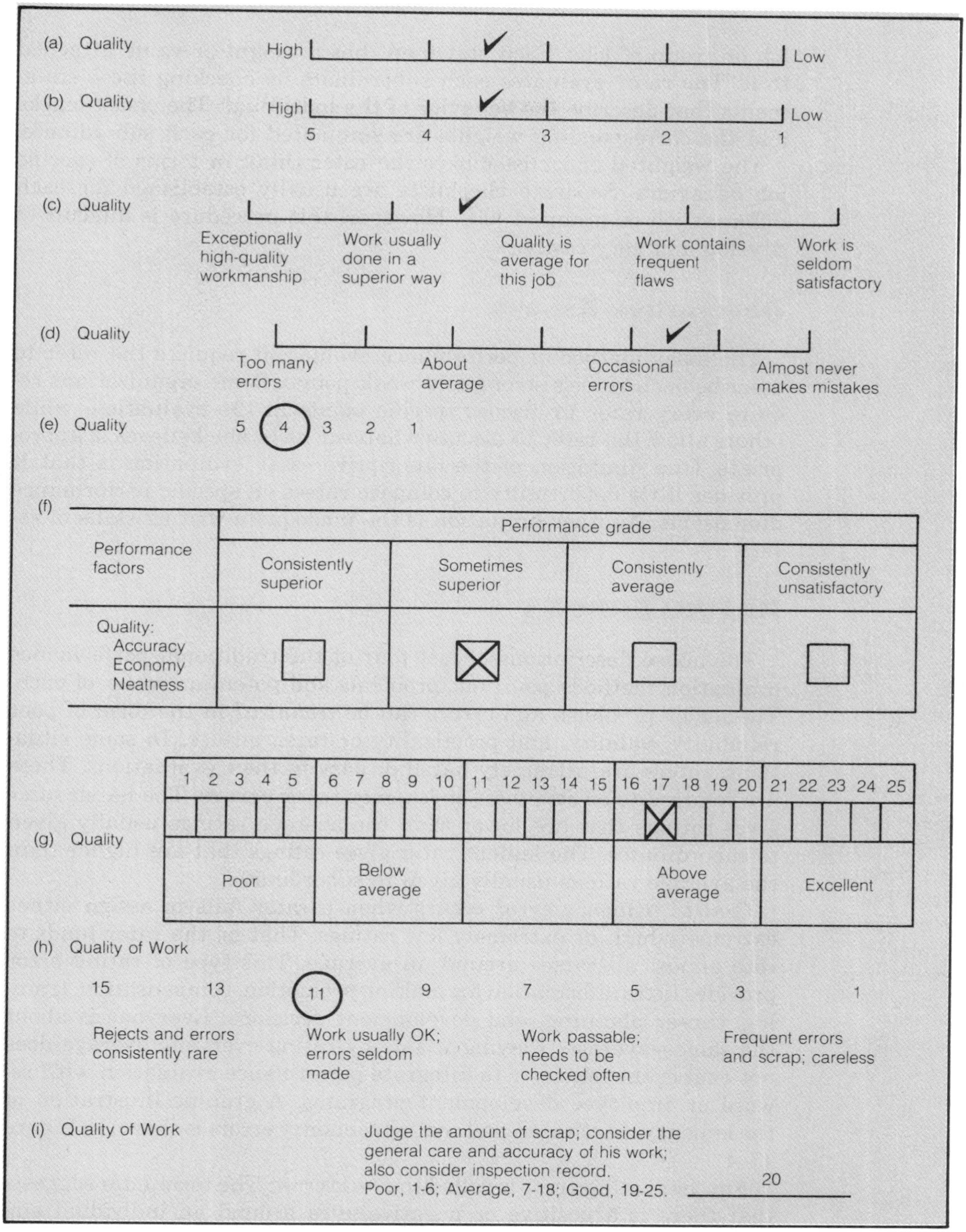

(a) Quality   High |_____|_____✔_____|_____|_____| Low

(b) Quality   High |_____|_____✔_____|_____|_____| Low
                    5   4   3   2   1

(c) Quality |_____|_____✔_____|_____|_____|

Exceptionally   Work usually   Quality is   Work contains   Work is
high-quality   done in a   average for   frequent   seldom
workmanship   superior way   this job   flaws   satisfactory

(d) Quality |____|____|____|____|____✔____|

Too many   About   Occasional   Almost never
errors   average   errors   makes mistakes

(e) Quality   5 ④ 3 2 1

(f)

Performance factors	Performance grade			
	Consistently superior	Sometimes superior	Consistently average	Consistently unsatisfactory
Quality: Accuracy Economy Neatness	☐	☒	☐	☐

1 2 3 4 5	6 7 8 9 10	11 12 13 14 15	16 17 18 19 20	21 22 23 24 25
☐☐☐☐☐	☐☐☐☐☐	☐☐☐☐☐	☒☐☐☐☐	☐☐☐☐☐

(g) Quality

Poor	Below average		Above average	Excellent

(h) Quality of Work

15   13   ⑪   9   7   5   3   1

Rejects and errors   Work usually OK;   Work passable;   Frequent errors
consistently rare   errors seldom   needs to be   and scrap; careless
                         made   checked often

(i) Quality of Work   Judge the amount of scrap; consider the
                          general care and accuracy of his work;
                          also consider inspection record.   20
                          Poor, 1-6; Average, 7-18; Good, 19-25. _____

Variations on a graphic rating scale; each line represents one way in which a judgment of the quality of a person's work may be given. From Robert M. Guion, *Personnel Testing* (New York: McGraw-Hill, 1965), p. 98, Copyright 1965, McGraw-Hill Book Company.

job or group of jobs. Each statement has a weight or value attached to it. The rater evaluates each subordinate by checking those statements that describe the behavior of the individual. The check marks and the corresponding weights are summated for each subordinate.

The weighted checklist makes the rater think in terms of specific job behaviors. Separate checklists are usually established for each different job or group of jobs. However, this procedure is difficult to develop and very costly.

Descriptive Essays

The essay method of performance evaluation requires the rater to describe each ratee's strong and weak points. Some organizations require every rater to discuss specific points in the evaluation, while others allow the rater to discuss whatever he or she believes is appropriate. One limitation of the descriptive essay evaluation is that it provides little opportunity to compare ratees on specific performance dimensions. Another limitation is the inadequate writing skills of raters.

RATING ERRORS

rater errors
The tendency to make errors in rating exists for any rater. Errors result from the use of poor scales, personal rater characteristics, and personal rater biases.

The above descriptions of just four of the traditional performance evaluation methods point out problems and potential errors of each. The major problems and errors can be *technical* in the form of poor reliability, validity, and practicality or rater misuse. In some situations, raters are extremely harsh or easy in their evaluations. These are referred to as *strictness or leniency* **rater errors.** The harsh rater gives ratings that are lower than the average ratings usually given to subordinates. The lenient rater gives ratings that are higher than the average ratings usually given to subordinates.

Central tendency error occurs when a rater fails to assign either extremely high or extremely low ratings. That is, the rater tends to rate almost all ratees around an average. This type of rating error provides little information for making promotion, compensation, training, career planning, and development decisions. Everyone is about the same—average. Playing it safe by rating everyone average does not enable the manager to integrate performance evaluation with reward or employee development programs. A graphic illustration of the leniency, harshness, and central tendency errors is shown in Figure 17–4.

Another rating error is called the *halo error*. The term *halo* suggests that there is a positive or negative aura around an individual employee. This aura influences the rater's evaluation in about the same way for all of the performance dimensions being considered. Halo

FIGURE 17-4

Examples of Leniency, Central Tendency, and Harshness Errors on Seven-Point Scale

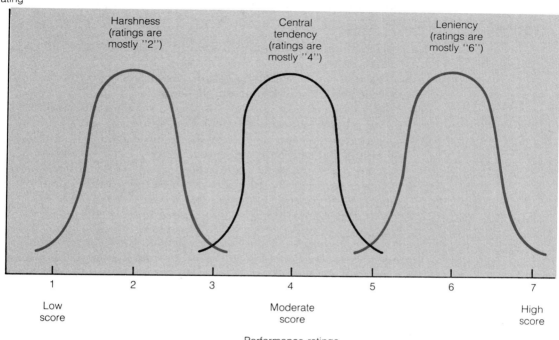

Performance ratings distributions by raters

error is caused by the rater's inability to discriminate between the different dimensions being rated. It is also caused by the rater assuming that a particular dimension is extremely important. The rating on this dimension influences the rater's evaluations of all the other dimensions.

In many performance evaluation programs, the most recent behaviors of ratees tend to color ratings. Using only the most recent behaviors to make evaluations can result in what is called the *recency of events* error. Forgetting to include important past behaviors can introduce a strong bias into the evaluation. Ratees are usually aware of this tendency and become visible, interested, productive, and cooperative just before the formal evaluation occurs.

A *time delay error* can influence ratings. In many situations, it is not uncommon for performance ratings to be obtained through limited observations but not to be recorded or documented immediately.

Rather, the rating documentation occurs a week, a month, or even longer after the observation. With the passage of time, observations are less accurately recalled.[20] Consequently, the longer the delay between observation, recall, and documentation, the greater the performance rating errors are likely to be.

According to research findings,[21] rating errors are likely to be minimized if

1. Each dimension addresses a single job activity rather than a group of activities.
2. The rater on a regular basis can observe the behavior of the ratee while the job is being accomplished.
3. Terms like *average* are not used on a rating scale, since different raters have different reactions to such terms.
4. The rater does not have to evaluate large groups of subordinates. Fatigue and difficulty in discriminating between ratees become major problems when large groups of subordinates are evaluated.
5. Raters are formally trained to avoid such errors as leniency, harshness, halo, central tendency, and recency of events.
6. The dimensions being evaluated are meaningful, clearly stated, and important.

Another interesting idea is to provide raters with feedback on their rating tendencies and patterns.[22] Feedback on how a rater's scores compare with those of other raters, how a rater's procedures compare with those of other raters, and what ratees feel about the equity, timeliness, and accuracy of the ratings could be informative. Auditing the ratings given by raters in order to identify trends or tendencies is one source of feedback. For example, if over a two-year period no women working for a manager (rater) received a high evaluation, this might signal a potential rating error. The problem could be that the rater is overly harsh with female subordinates or that the women need training to improve their performance. In any event, it appears that some benefits could result from providing feedback to raters about their rating tendencies and errors. The intent of providing such feed-

---

[20] Robert L. Heneman and Kenneth N. Wexley, "The Effects of Time Delay in Rating and Amount of Information Observed on Performance Rating Accuracy," *Academy of Management Journal*, December 1983, pp. 677–86.

[21] For discussions of minimizing rating errors, see H. J. Bernardin and C. S. Walter, "The Effects of Rater Training and Diary Keeping on Psychometric Error in Ratings," *Journal of Applied Psychology*, February 1977, pp. 64–69; and R. G. Burnaska and T. D. Hollman, "An Empirical Comparison of the Relative Effects of Rater Response Bias on Three Rating Scale Formats," *Journal of Applied Psychology*, June 1974, pp. 307–12.

[22] Mark R. Edwards and J. Ruth Sproull, "Rating the Raters Improves Performance Appraisals," *Personnel Administrator*, August 1983, pp. 77–82.

back would be to reduce errors and to make the evaluation experience more beneficial for both the rater and the ratee.

The following Close-Up portrays how Syborn Corporation has attempted to improve its performance evaluation system. This firm, like a growing number of other firms, has decided to use formal training to improve the accuracy of its raters.

ORGANIZATIONS: CLOSE-UP

Performance Evaluation at Syborn Corporation

Syborn Corporation was like most firms—not very satisfied with its performance evaluation program. It appeared that most raters did not know how to evaluate subordinates effectively and objectively. There seemed to be a preference for rushing through the evaluations in a matter of minutes. Rushing led to making more errors and more dissatisfaction with the program.

Syborn decided to provide the managers doing the rating with a training program designed to improve rating skills and the motivation to set objectives. The first part of the training involved managers in interpersonal skill exercises and in learning procedures for setting evaluation reviews and substantiating goals. The firm used lectures, discussions, and videotaping in this part of the program.

The second part of the training presented to the managers involved five general principles to improve their managerial performance. The five principles were presented, discussed, and critiqued. They were:

1. Maintain and enhance self-esteem.
2. Focus on behavior, not personality.
3. Use reinforcement techniques to shape behavior.
4. Listen actively.
5. Maintain communication, and set specific follow-up dates.

Since only 8 or 10 managers participate in each course, there is time for total involvement, thus reinforcing the goals of the program.

Source: "Syborn Trains Managers to Improve Performance Appraisals," *Management Review,* January 1981, pp. 32–33.

In addition to the guidelines presented above, attempts have been made to minimize rating errors by using other forms of performance evaluation. Two of the more publicized approaches are behaviorally anchored ratings scales (BARS) and management by objectives (MBO).

PERFORMANCE EVALUATION METHODS: BARS AND MBO

In an effort to improve the reliability, validity, and practicality of traditional performance evaluations, some organizations have used various behaviorally based and objective-setting programs.[23] The behaviorally based programs attempt to examine what the employee does in performing the job. The objective, or goal-oriented programs typically examine the results or accomplishments of the employee.

Behaviorally Anchored Rating Scales

critical incident
Any observed behavior that is important in performing a job.

Smith and Kendall developed a procedure that is referred to as behaviorally anchored rating scales (BARS) or behaviors expectation scales (BES).[24] The BARS approach relies on the use of **critical incidents** to construct the rating scale. A critical incident is "any observable human activity that is sufficiently complete in itself to permit inferences and predictions to be made about the person performing the work."[25] Once the important areas of performance have been identified and defined by employees who know the job, critical incident statements are used as anchors to discriminate between high, moderate, and low performance. The BARS rating form usually covers 6 to 10 specifically defined performance dimensions, each with various descriptive anchors. Each dimension is based on observable behaviors and is meaningful to the employees being evaluated.

An example of a BARS for engineering competence is presented in Figure 17–5. The dimension is defined for the rater; the anchors define the particular response categories for the rater; and the response made by the rater is specific and easy to interpret. If the ratee is given a 7 on this dimension, he or she is provided with the specific performance incident that the rater used to make such a rating.

Proposed Advantages of BARS

Some thorough reviews of the literature have concluded that BARS are (1) costly to construct, (2) require significant time to put into use, and (3) are not much better in improving rating errors than graphic-

---

[23] Stuart Murray, "A Comparison of Results-Oriented and Trait-Based Performance Appraisals," *Personnel Administrator*, June 1983, pp. 100–105.

[24] P. C. Smith and L. M. Kendall, "Retranslation of Expectations: An Approach to the Construction of Unambiguous Anchors for Ratings Scales," *Journal of Applied Psychology*, April 1963, pp, 149–55.

[25] John C. Flanagan, "The Critical Incident Technique," *Psychological Bulletin*, April 1954, p. 329.

FIGURE 17–5

A BARS Performance Dimension for an Engineer

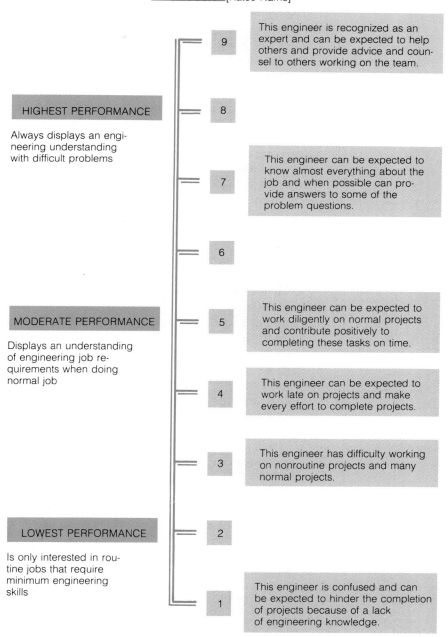

Engineering Competence
(the technical ability and skill
utilization as applied to any assigned job)
Place a single X on the appropriate
point on the vertical scale.
_____[Ratee Name]

9 — This engineer is recognized as an expert and can be expected to help others and provide advice and counsel to others working on the team.

8

HIGHEST PERFORMANCE

Always displays an engineering understanding with difficult problems

7 — This engineer can be expected to know almost everything about the job and when possible can provide answers to some of the problem questions.

6

MODERATE PERFORMANCE

Displays an understanding of engineering job requirements when doing normal job

5 — This engineer can be expected to work diligently on normal projects and contribute positively to completing these tasks on time.

4 — This engineer can be expected to work late on projects and make every effort to complete projects.

3 — This engineer has difficulty working on nonroutine projects and many normal projects.

LOWEST PERFORMANCE

Is only interested in routine jobs that require minimum engineering skills

2

1 — This engineer is confused and can be expected to hinder the completion of projects because of a lack of engineering knowledge.

rating scales or weighted checklists.[26] Despite some discouraging research findings and constructive criticisms, BARS are still being used by numerous organizations. The continued popularity of BARS is based on various proposed advantages. It is assumed that since job-knowledgeable employees participate in the actual development steps, the final form will be reliable, valid, and meaningful. It should also cover the full domain of the job. A common problem of traditional performance evaluation programs is that they do not tap the full domain of the job.[27]

The use of BARS is also valuable for providing insights when developing training programs. The skills to be developed are specified in terms of actual behavioral incidents rather than abstract or general skills. Trainees in a BARS-based program could learn what behaviors are expected and how job performance is evaluated.[28]

The literature also implies that leniency, halo, and central tendency errors will be reduced through the use of a behaviorally anchored system. These errors are assumed to be minimized because of the independence between the dimensions rated and the reliability of BARS.[29] However, some critics of BARS present results indicating that this approach is not always the most reliable, valid, and practical. They also suggest that more research is needed comparing BARS with other traditional evaluation methods.[30]

It is suggested that a BARS program can minimize subordinate or ratee defensiveness toward evaluation. By being involved in the development of a BARS, subordinates can make their inputs known. These inputs can be incorporated into the final BARS. As McGregor pointed out, many superiors are uncomfortable about judging someone and acting out the role of an evaluator.[31] The BARS development steps could include both superiors and subordinates. In a sense, then, all of the parties involved can contribute to the creation of the evaluation criteria and the behavioral incidents used as anchors.

[27] J. P. Campbell, M. D. Dunnette, R. D. Arvey, and L. W. Hellervik, "The Development and Evaluation of Behaviorally Based Rating Scales," *Journal of Applied Psychology,* February 1973, pp. 15–22.

[28] M. R. Blood, "Spin-Offs from Behavioral Expectation Scale Procedures," *Journal of Applied Psychology,* August 1974, pp. 513–15.

[29] S. Zedeck and H. T. Baker, "Nursing Performance as Measured by Behavioral Expectation Scales: A Multitrait-Multirater Analysis," *Organizational Behavior and Human Performance,* June 1972, pp. 457–66.

[30] Peter W. Hom, Angelo S. DeNisi, Angelo V. Kinicki, and Brendan D. Bannister, "Effectiveness of Performance Feedback from Behaviorally Anchored Rating Scales," *Journal of Applied Psychology,* October 1982, pp. 568–76; and D. P. Schwab, H. G. Heneman III, and T. A. DeCotiis, "Behaviorally Anchored Rating Scales: A Review of the Literature," *Personnel Psychology,* Winter 1975, pp. 549–62.

[31] D. McGregor, "An Uneasy Look at Performance Appraisal," *Harvard Business Review,* May–June 1957, pp. 89–94.

[26] R. Jacobs, D. Kafry, and S. Zedeck, "Expectations of Behaviorally Anchored Rating Scales," *Personnel Psychology,* Autumn 1980, pp. 595–640.

Management by Objectives

management by objectives
A performance evaluation system in which superiors and subordinates jointly set objectives (goals) for job performance and career (personal) development.

Some managers believe that a results-based system is more efficient and informative than other evaluation systems. One popular results-based program is called **management by objectives** (MBO). An MBO program typically involves the establishment of objectives (also referred to as goals) by the supervisor alone or jointly by the supervisor and the subordinate.

MBO is far more than just an evaluation approach. It is usually a part of an overall motivational program, planning technique, or organizational change and development program. More details on MBO will be presented in Chapter 20.

An MBO performance evaluation program focuses on what an employee achieves. The key features of a typical MBO program are as follows:

1. Superior and subordinate meet to discuss and jointly set goals for subordinate for a specified period of time (e.g., six months or one year).
2. Both the superior and the subordinate attempt to establish goals that are realistic, challenging, clear, and comprehensive. The goals should also be related to organizational and personal needs.
3. The criteria for measuring and evaluating the goals are agreed on.
4. The superior and subordinate establish some intermediate review dates when the goals will be reexamined.
5. The superior plays more of a coaching, counseling, and supportive role and less the role of a judge and jury.
6. The entire process focuses on results accomplished and on the counseling of subordinates and not on activities, mistakes, and organizational requirements.

MBO-type programs have been used in organizations throughout the world.[32] Approximately 40 percent of Fortune's 500 largest industrial firms reported using MBO-type programs.[33] As with each of the performance evaluation programs already discussed, both benefits and potential costs are associated with using MBO. The assumed benefits include better planning and improved motivation. Because of knowledge of results, evaluation decisions based on results instead of on traits, improves commitment through participation, and improves supervisory skills in such areas as listening, counseling, and evaluating. These are certainly significant benefits, but they are not always accomplished in MBO programs. Using MBO is no sure way to improve upon the problems associated with performance evaluation programs.

---

[32] Dale D. McConkey, *How to Manage by Results* (New York: AMACOM, 1983).
[33] J. Singular, "Has MBO Failed?" *MBA*, October 1975, pp. 47–50.

It too has some potential and real problems. The fact that MBO stresses results is a benefit that can also be a problem. Focusing only on results may take attention away from how to accomplish the goals. A subordinate receiving feedback about what has been achieved may still not be certain about how to make performance corrections.

Other problems that have been linked to MBO programs include: improper implementation, lack of top-management involvement, too much emphasis on paperwork, failure to use an MBO system that best fits the needs of the organization and the employees, and inadequate training preparation for employees who are asked to establish goals.[34]

A final limitation of MBO is that comparisons of subordinates are difficult. In traditional performance evaluation programs, all subordinates are rated on common dimensions. In MBO, each individual usually has a different set of objectives that is difficult to compare across a group of subordinates. The superior must make reward decisions not only on the basis of objectives achieved but also on his or her conception of the kinds of objectives that were accomplished. The feeling of achieving objectives will generally wear thin among subordinates if the accomplishment is not accompanied by meaningful rewards.

PERFORMANCE EVALUATION: THE ASSESSMENT CENTER

assessment center
A standardized evaluation of behavior that is based on multiple rater judgments is conducted in an assessment center.

The **assessment center** technique was pioneered by Douglas Bray and his associates at American Telephone and Telegraph Company in the mid-1950s. By the 1970s, it had become a popular evaluation technique used in organizations of all sizes. The foundation of this technique is a series of situational exercises in which candidates for promotion, training, or other managerial programs take part over a two- to three-day period while being observed and rated. The exercises are simulated management tasks and include such techniques as role playing and case analysis. In some assessment centers, personal interviews and psychological tests are also used to make evaluations.[35] The assessment center is unique as an evaluation technique in that it focuses on the future instead of on past performance. Thus, it is a technique that attempts to evaluate a ratee's potential.

[34] J. M. Ivancevich, "Different Goal Setting Treatments and Their Effects on Performance and Job Satisfaction, *Academy of Management Journal,* September 1977, pp. 406–19; and J. M. Ivancevich, J. H. Donnelly, Jr., and J. L. Gibson, "Evaluating MBO: The Challenges Ahead," *Management by Objectives,* Winter 1976, pp. 15–24.

[35] R. B. Finkle, "Managerial Assessment Centers," in *Handbook of Industrial and Organizational Psychology,* ed. M. D. Dunnette (Skokie, Ill.: Rand McNally, 1976), pp. 861–88.

Purposes of Assessment Centers

Since individual ratees are observed in a controlled setting (the center), raters can compare the performance of candidates. It is estimated that over 5,000 organizations now use assessment centers.[36] The centers are used:

1. To identify individuals who are suited for a particular type or level of management job.
2. To determine individual and group training and development needs.
3. To identify individuals for promotion to positions that are quite different from their current positions, for example, salespeople, technicians, or engineers being considered for managerial positions. Because the new managerial jobs would require such different skills and abilities than those required by the candidates' current jobs, it is difficult to determine the candidates' suitability for the new jobs before the promotion. The assessment center attempts to identify some indicators of managerial ability before the promotion decision is made.

Dimensions Measured by Assessment Centers

There are different dimensions measured in assessment centers depending on the purpose of the evaluation. Such dimensions as interpersonal skills, communication ability, creativity, problem-solving skills, tolerance for stress and ambiguity, and planning ability are among the commonly assessed dimensions.

A study in a large manufacturing plant was designed to evaluate supervisors in an assessment center. The assessment center was used to determine whether the supervisors possessed the skills and characteristics that years of performance evaluation had determined to be necessary for effective supervision.[37] The skills and characteristics assessed included decision making, communication, leadership, adaptability to the job, self-confidence, and assertiveness. Twelve individuals were in each assessment group. Each group was assessed by a four-person evaluation team. The results indicated that each of the supervisors was evaluated globally instead of by using a separate score for each trait/skill. Thus, instead of evaluating each supervisor's commu-

---

[36] George C. Thorton and W. C. Byham, *Assessment Centers and Managerial Performance* (New York: Academic Press, 1982).

[37] Janet J. Turnage and Paul M. Muchinsky, "Transsituational Variability in Human Performance within Assessment Centers," *Organizational Behavior and Human Performance,* October 1982, pp. 174–200.

nication, self-confidence, and assertiveness separately, the evaluators simply rated the overall assessment center performance of the supervisor.

IBM has conducted studies of its assessment center programs. In general, the results indicate a positive relationship between center ratings and various criteria of success.[38] Such variables as energy level, communication skills, aggressiveness, and self-confidence have been rated in the IBM program.

The Chevrolet sales divisions select candidates for assessment centers by using nine dimensions for measuring managerial potential. Among these dimensions are judgment, use of time, job knowledge, and interpersonal communications. The candidates that are rated the highest on the nine dimensions are selected for the assessment center evaluation. In the center, the candidates' potential for assuming a higher level position is rated.[39]

A Typical Program

No universally used set of exercises is applied in assessment centers. An example of an assessment center schedule is presented in Figure 17-6.

After the assessment program, the raters meet to discuss and evaluate all candidates. The assessment center raters are usually managers two or more levels above the ratees. They are used because they are familiar with the jobs for which the ratees are being considered and because they can improve their evaluation skills and techniques by participating.

Problems of Assessment Centers

Again, it must be stated that evaluating employee performance in any setting is extremely difficult. One of the potential problems of the assessment center evaluation procedure is that it is so pressure-packed. Outstanding employees who have contributed to the organization may simply not perform well in the center. Raters may be embarrassed because of their inability to justify ratings or because of their limited ability to identify key behaviors.

One evaluation of assessment center experiences showed that both high scorers and low scorers generally found benefits in the center experience. This study is presented in the following Close-Up.

---

[38] W. E. Dodd, "Summary of IBM Assessment Validations," paper presented as part of the symposium "Validity of Assessment Centers" at the 79th annual convention of the American Psychological Association, 1971.

[39] F. M. McIntyre, "Unique Program Developed by Chevrolet Sales," *Assessment and Development,* January 1975.

FIGURE 17-6

Format for a Typical 2½-Day Assessment Center

Day 1	Day 2	Day 3
A. Orientation of approximately 12 ratees. B. Breakup into groups of six or four to play management simulated game (*Raters* observe planning ability, problem-solving skill, interaction skills, and communication ability.) C. Psychological testing—measure verbal and numerical skills. D. Interview with raters. (*Raters* discuss goals, motivation, and career plans.) E. Small group discussion of case incidents. (*Raters* observe confidence, persuasiveness, and decision-making flexibility.)	A. Individual decision-making exercise—ratees are asked to make a decision about some problem that must be solved. (*Raters* observe fact-finding skill, understanding of problem-solving procedures, and risk-taking propensity.) B. In-basket exercise. (*Raters* observe decision making under stress, organizing ability, memory, and ability to delegate.) C. Role-play of performance evaluation interview. (*Raters* observe empathy, ability to react, counseling skills, and how information is used.) D. Group problem solving (*Raters* observe leadership ability and ability to work in a group.)	A. Individual case analysis and presentation. (*Raters* observe problem-solving ability, method of preparation, ability to handle questions, and communication skills.) B. Evaluation of other ratees. (Peer evaluations.)

ORGANIZATIONS: CLOSE-UP

Are Assessment Centers Pressure Cookers?

How do assessment center participants react to their experiences? Are assessment centers pressure-packed fishbowls in which individuals must perform or else? There is some opinion that they are. However, a study that used subjects from four organizations provides some interesting results. Thirty-seven people who had participated in an assessment center were studied—19 high scorers (they did well) and 18 poor scorers; moderate scorers were excluded. The subjects worked for the Orange County Human Services Agency, Western Airlines, the San Diego County Department of Public Welfare, and the San Francisco City and County Department of Social Services. Twenty-five of the subjects were female, and 12 were male.

All of the subjects were interviewed by the researcher. They were told that the purpose of the interview was simply to obtain their opinions about the quality and value of their assessment center experiences. The results indicated that both high and low scorers reacted positively to their assessment center experiences. The high scorers, however, were generally more favorable. The two groups did differ significantly in their responses to two questions. The high scorers felt that their performance in the center accurately reflected how they performed on the job, while the low scorers felt that their center performance was not an accurate reflection of their on-the-job performance. Also, the high scorers thought the assessors' evaluations were accurate, while only some of the low scorers thought that this was the case.

All of the participants in the center received feedback on their center performance in personal interviews. The interviews were held 6 to 12 weeks after the center, and they lasted from 30 minutes to two hours. Most of the participants felt that this feedback had been beneficial. There were complaints, however, that the feedback should have been provided more promptly. Also, the participants felt that to increase the objectivity of the ratings, only assessors who had had no prior contact with them should have been used.

This study indicated that the assessment center participants, regardless of scores, reacted favorably to their assessment experiences. As expected, the high scorers reacted more favorably, but a majority of the low scorers felt that their participation had been a positive and informative experience.

Adapted from Kenneth S. Teel and Henry DuBois, "Participants' Reactions to Assessment Centers," *Personnel Administrator*, March 1983, pp. 85–91.

Another problem involves the feelings of individuals who receive mediocre or poor evaluations. Employees who receive a poor evaluation may leave the organization or be demoralized for an extended period of time. It is natural for the highly rated participants in centers to be identified as "comers" or individuals to develop. The poorly rated participants may be viewed as "losers."

Basing promotion decisions or the identification of individuals with high potential on the results of a single assessment center experience is questionable. The research evidence on the reliability and validity of assessment centers is still somewhat mixed.[40] Until more evidence is available, the assessment center may be useful for only some situations and some evaluation decisions. It is another evaluation procedure that has both potential benefits and potential problems.[41]

---

[40] R. J. Klimoski and W. J. Strickland, "Assessment Centers—Valid or Merely Prescient?" *Personnel Psychology*, Autumn 1977, pp. 353–61.

[41] Joyce D. Ross, "A Current Review of Public Sector Assessment Centers: Cause for Concern," *Public Personnel Management*, January–February 1979, p. 41.

A REVIEW OF POTENTIAL PERFORMANCE EVALUATION PROGRAMS

Table 17–4 summarizes the main points of the various performance evaluation approaches that have been discussed. The usefulness of each method is debatable. In some organizations, one system is more useful because of the types of individuals doing the rating or because of the criteria being used. Every program discussed thus far has both costs and benefits. Since performance evaluation is such an integral part of managing within organizations, recognizing the strengths, weaknesses, and best uses for a particular program is an important job for managers.

TABLE 17–4

Managerial Points of Interest When Selecting a Performance Evaluation Program

Point of Interest	Programs						
	Graphic Rating Scales	Ranking	Checklists	Essay	BARS	MBO	Assessment Centers
Acceptability to subordinates	Fair	Fair/poor	Fair	Poor	Good	Generally good	Generally good
Acceptability to management	Fair	Fair/poor	Fair	Poor	Good	Generally good	Generally good
Useful in reward allocations	Poor	Poor	Fair	Fair	Good	Good	Fair/good
Useful in counseling and developing subordinates	Poor	Poor	Poor	Fair	Good	Good	Good
Meaningful dimensions	Rarely	Rarely	Sometimes	Rarely	Often	Often	Often
Ease of developing actual program	Yes	Yes	Yes	No	No	No	No
Development costs	Low	Low	Low	Moderately high	High	High	High

DEVELOPING EMPLOYEES THROUGH PERFORMANCE EVALUATION FEEDBACK

A performance evaluation program conducted solely for the sake of rating employees will soon lose any potential value or motivational impact unless it becomes integrated with the main emphasis of the organization. The judgment and development purposes will be achieved when both the ratees and the raters understand each other's roles in the process. The rater must clarify, coach, counsel, and provide feedback. The ratee must understand the rater's expectations, his or her own strengths and weaknesses, and the goals that need to be accomplished. These various roles can become clear if the performance evaluation program is considered a continual process that focuses both on task accomplishment and on personal development.

Regardless of how individual job performance information is collected—whether by a BARS, an assessment center, or a rating scale—the rater must provide formal feedback to the ratee. Managers provide informal feedback that can have an impact on performance and job attitudes. Instead of addressing both formal and informal feedback, we have elected to focus only on formal performance evaluation feedback because of space limitations.[42] An example of how formal performance feedback is used is presented in the following Close-Up.

ORGANIZATIONS: CLOSE-UP

Performance Evaluation in Greensboro, North Carolina, City Government

The city of Greensboro, North Carolina, implemented a performance planning and appraisal system (PPA) for managers and subordinates. A main feature of PPA was to acquire information about performance and to provide that information to subordinates. The first step in PPA was the establishment of a work plan for each subordinate. This plan identified the job responsibilities of each subordinate and then required the supervisor and subordinate mutually to set challenging goals.

Another part of PPA called for the supervisor to provide regular feedback to employees. There were quarterly and annually scheduled feedback sessions. The basis of these feedback sessions was the work plan objectives that were set at the beginning of the cycle and the actual accomplishments of the subordinates. The feedback sessions provided a forum to examine the progress of subordinates in three areas: new projects, routine tasks, and personal development. The supervisor and subordinate in the feedback sessions exchanged comments, expectations, and concerns about the progress being made and not being made in the three target areas.

The Greensboro PPA program is an example of a program that incorporated feedback sessions from the outset. Unfortunately, many perfor-

---

[42] An excellent and detailed model that addresses informal performance feedback is found in John R. Larson, Jr., "The Performance Feedback Process: A Preliminary Model," *Organizational Behavior and Human Performance*, February 1984, pp. 42–76.

mance evaluation programs fail to emphasize or even use formal feed-back sessions. Without formal feedback, it is difficult to imagine ratees making the necessary modifications in their activities and behaviors to improve performance accomplishments.

Source: Richard Henderson, *Performance Appraisal* (Reston, Va.: Reston Publishing, 1980), pp. 205–6.

The performance evaluation feedback interview should be part of any program from the beginning. It should focus on the job performance of the ratee. Generally, raters feel uncomfortable about discussing ratee weaknesses or problems. On the other hand, ratees often become defensive when personal weaknesses or failures are pointed out by a rater.[43] Kay, Meyer, and French reviewed the relationship between comments focusing on subordinate weaknesses in a feedback interview and defensive comments made by the ratees.[44] They found that as critical comments increased, subordinate defensiveness increased. Furthermore, they concluded that praise in the feedback sessions was ineffective. They assumed that since most raters first praise, then criticize, and finally praise to end the feedback session, ratees become conditioned to this sequence. In essence, praise becomes a conditioned stimulus preceding criticism.

If the performance evaluation program is acceptable to the rater and the ratee, there is a higher probability that the feedback interview can be more than a praise-criticism-praise sequence. The acceptability of any program depends on such factors as (1) how the evaluation will be used, (2) who developed the program, (3) whether the criteria are fair, (4) how good the rater is in evaluating performance, and (5) whether the rater has sufficient time to spend in planning for, implementing, and providing feedback in the program. It should be noted that providing effective performance feedback information requires skill, time, and patience.[45] Feedback has both positive and negative consequences. Poorly presented performance evaluation feedback can result in distrust, hostility, dissatisfaction, and turnover. Effective performance evaluation feedback can be motivational and can encourage the development of ratees as they pursue valued goals.[46]

---

[43] Stanley D. Truskie, "Get Better Results from Performance Reviews," *The Wall Street Journal,* October 4, 1982, p. 28.

[44] E. Kay, H. Meyer, and J. R. P. French, "Effects of Threat in a Performance Appraisal Interview," *Journal of Applied Psychology,* October 1965, pp. 311–17.

[45] Douglas Cederblom, "The Performance Appraisal Interview: A Review, Implications, and Suggestions," *Academy of Management Review,* April 1982, pp. 219–27.

[46] Susan J. Ashford and Larry L. Cummings, "Feedback as an Individual Resource: Personal Strategies of Creating Information," *Organizational Behavior and Human Performance,* December 1983, pp. 370–98.

Too often, performance evaluation interviews focus on the past year or on plans for the short run. Rarely do a manager and a subordinate discuss careers.[47] Recall that in our presentation of the performance evaluation process (Figure 17–1) the future development of the ratee is considered extremely important. It is important for managers to have knowledge about the various career tracks that are available within the organization and their requirements. The creation of challenging tasks will help prepare subordinates for future jobs that require the use of more skills and abilities. Basically, it seems worthwhile for managers to consider and be prepared to discuss the lifelong sequence of job experiences and jobs of subordinates, as part of the evaluation interview. Only through managerial consideration of career goals can the evaluation process become a development experience as well as a judgmental analysis of job performance.

SUMMARY OF KEY POINTS

A. Performance evaluation occurs in most organizations. It is a formal process that involves the systematic evaluation of subordinates' job performance and potential for future development.

B. Performance evaluation is used in a broad sense to make judgments and to develop subordinates. In a more specific sense, it has motivational, improved knowledge, research, promotion, and training and development purposes.

C. Federal laws play a major role in performance evaluation. Managers are advised to examine carefully the validity and reliability of the techniques and programs that they use to evaluate subordinate performance.

D. An important step in developing any performance evaluation program involves the establishment of criteria. A criterion is a dependent or predicted measure for appraising the effectivensss of employees. A good criterion must be relevant, stable, able to discriminate between ratees, and practical.

E. A few of the widely used performance evaluation programs are graphic rating scales, ranking procedures, weighted checklists, and descriptive essays. These procedures often result in rating errors. The most common errors are harshness and leniency, halo effect, central tendency, and recency of events. The available

---

[47] G. W. Dalton, P. H. Thompson, and R. L. Price, "A New Look at Performance by Professionals," *Organizational Dynamics*, Summer 1977, pp. 19–42.

methods for reducing these errors include eliminating terms such as *average* on the scales. having raters rate a small number of individuals instead of many people, and training raters to recognize the most common error tendencies.

F. The behaviorally anchored rating scale (BARS) is a form of evaluation that uses critical incidents or examples of specific job behaviors to determine various levels of performance. The development of BARS is time-consuming and costly, but it can involve the joint participation of raters and ratees. This joint effort can result in more acceptance of the evaluation program by ratees.

G. A results-based performance evaluation program is called management by objectives (MBO) or goal setting. The program typically involves a superior/subordinate meeting to discuss and jointly set goals for subordinates for a specified period of time. The superior plays more of a coaching and supportive role in this results-based program.

H. The assessment center technique has become a popular evaluation technique in the past two decades. The foundation of this program is a set of exercises in which candidates for promotion, training, or other managerial programs take part—over a two- to three-day period—while being observed and rated. One major problem with this program involves the participants who are rated low. They can become extremely demoralized about their future careers in the organization.

I. The performance evaluation feedback interview is an essential part of any program. Feedback provides information about how others view the ratee's job performance. Without feedback, knowledge about progress and development and clarity about expectations are difficult to attain. Another important part of feedback involves relating performance and progress to career development. Feedback of recent results and activities plus events for the near future should be combined with discussions about organizational career tracks and requirements for the long run.

DISCUSSION AND REVIEW QUESTIONS

1. Some courts have ruled that performance evaluation is a test. How could a court reach such a conclusion?

2. How can common rating errors result in problems in a performance evaluation program?

3. What are the main differences between a behaviorally anchored rating scale (BARS) and a graphic rating scale?

4. What role can subordinates play in developing the evaluation system that will be used by their superiors?

5. Why is it important for the rater to be able to observe behavior in most performance evaluation programs?

6. It is often stated that any performance evaluation program contains some degree of subjectivity. Do you agree?

7. Why is development considered an important purpose of performance evaluation?

8. Some claim that the assessment center is a pressure-packed experience or a fishbowl exercise. Why are these statements made?

9. Why is job analysis an important antecedent to the development of criteria and the actual performance evaluation program used?

10. Why is the performance evaluation feedback interview such an important part of the process of appraisal?

ADDITIONAL REFERENCES

Beatty, R. W., and Schneier, C. E. *Personnel Administration: An Experiential Skill-Building Approach.* Reading, Mass.: Addison-Wesley Publishing, 1981.

Beer, M. "Performance Appraisal: Dilemmas and Possibilities." *Organizational Dynamics,* 1981, pp. 24–36.

Bernardin, H. J.; R. L. Cardy; and J. J. Carlyle. "Cognitive Complexity and Appraisal Effectiveness: Back to the Drawing Board?" *Journal of Applied Psychology,* 1982, pp. 151–60.

Block, J. R. *Performance Appraisal on the Job.* Englewood Cliffs, N.J.: Prentice-Hall, 1982.

DeNisi, A. S., W. A. Randolph; and A. G. Blencoe. "Potential Problems with Peer Ratings." *Academy of Management Journal,* 1983, pp. 457–64.

Ivancevich, J. M. "Longitudinal Study of the Effects of Rater Training on Psychometric Error in Ratings." *Journal of Applied Psychology,* 1979, pp. 502–8.

———. "A Longitudinal Study of Behavioral Expectation Scales: Attitudes and Performance." *Journal of Applied Psychology,* 1980, pp. 139–46.

———. "Subordinates' Reactions to Performance Appraisal Interviews: A Test of Feedback and Goal-Setting Techniques." *Journal of Applied Psychology,* 1982, pp. 581–87.

———. "Contrast Effects in Performance Evaluation and Reward Practices." *Academy of Management Journal,* 1983, pp. 465–76.

Murphy, K. R.; M. Garcia; S. Kerkar; C. Martin; and W. K. Balzer. "Relationship between Observational Accuracy and Accuracy in Evaluating Performance." *Journal of Applied Psychology,* 1982, pp. 320–25.

Wells, R. G. "Guidelines for Effective and Defensible Performance Appraisal Systems." *Personnel Journal,* 1982, pp. 766–82.

Wexley, K. N., and R. Klimoski. "Performance Appraisal: An Update." In *Research in Personnel and Human Resources Management,* ed. K. M. Rowland and G. D. Ferris. Greenwich, Conn.: JAI Press, 1984.

CASE FOR ANALYSIS

The Evaluation of a Performance Evaluation Program

Mike Pecaro, the project manager for a new power plant being constructed for the Atlanta, Georgia, area, was called into the vice president's office to discuss some complaints about the company's performance evaluation program. In order to determine whether the complaints of engineers, technicians, and machinists were justified, Mike was asked to critique the present evaluation system. The system used eight dimensions that were assumed to be associated with good performance. The rating scale being used ranged from one to seven, with seven being the rating given for the highest level of performance. The three highest rated engineers in Mike's group were used as reference points for purposes of discussion. The ratings are presented in Exhibit 1.

EXHIBIT 1

Ratings for Three Best Performers in Mike Pecaro's Group

Performance Dimension	Bob Lowry	Tony Nelson	Randy Anderson
Quality of work	6	6	7
Dependability	6	7	7
Cooperation	7	6	7
Customer interaction	7	7	7
Meeting budget requirements	6	7	7
Development of subordinates	7	6	6
Problem-solving skill	6	7	6
Technical competence	7	7	7
Total score	52	53	54

Don Baker, the vice president, wanted Mike to critique the soundness of the overall performance evaluation program. He was interested in whether the performance dimensions were meaningful to the engineers, technicians, and machinists. The same dimensions were being used for each group. One of the major and loudest complaints had to do with the relevance of some of the dimensions. Listed below are some of the complaints received from employees:

Machinist: The evaluation dimensions mean nothing since I have no control over some of them. I never interact with customers. Why am I rated on this dimension?

Technician: Everyone is rated about average, so the rating system is really a failure.

Technician: The performance dimensions are a mystery to all of us. What does dependability mean? What is an example of problem-solving skill?

Engineer: My supervisor never provides me with any feedback on progress. I have to guess at how I am doing. I have no idea of where I am going in the company.

Engineer: The performance evaluation never covers the long run. It only focuses on the short run or yesterday's results. I do not like this emphasis.

Engineer: My supervisor really doesn't know how to use the evaluation program. He uses it just to exercise tighter control of my activities. Shouldn't it be used to help me make improvements?

Mike was not surprised to hear these kinds of complaints since he also felt uneasy about the performance evaluation program. He told Don that most of the comments were on target. He rated the present system unreliable, inaccurate, and uninformative. The present rating system had some flaws that could be eliminated. Based on the seemingly endless list of complaints, Mike recommended that the present system be reevaluated by a committee of supervisors and subordinates. Don wanted some time to think about the possible solutions to the growing negative reactions to the present system.

Questions for Consideration

1. What type of system is presently being used to evaluate performance?
2. What problems and errors with the present system of evaluation are displayed in the list of complaints?
3. What are some of the possible solutions available for correcting the shortcomings of the present program?

EXPERIENTIAL EXERCISE
THE FACTS OF ORGANIZATIONAL LIFE

Objectives

1. To illustrate how difficult it is to use performance evaluation when making promotion choices.
2. To emphasize the impact of outside forces on performance evaluation programs.
3. To consider how a performance evaluation decision may become complex.

Related Topics

The government's role in performance evaluation is illustrated in this exercise. The difficulty of informing individuals is they will not be promoted is considered.

Starting the Exercise

Set up groups of five to eight students for the 40- to 60-minute first phase of the exercise. If possible, include men and women in all groups. The groups should be separated from one another and asked to reach a decision within the group. Before the groups are established, each person should read the facts of the situation.

The Facts

The Sebring Electronics Corporation is located in Baton Rouge, Louisiana. Over the past five years, the company has incorporated a performance evaluation program for operating employees that is generally viewed as a fair system. The company has maintained a steady rate of growth and has reached a point where two new supervisors are needed. Since the company motto is to "hire, develop, promote, and reward from within," it is now the job of a management committee to locate the best two new supervisors.

The performance evaluation program was designed to provide needed information to make promotion, wage and salary, training and development, and career planning decisions. Recently, the federal government has applied pressure on Sebring to play down the role of performance evaluation in making various decisions. It wants Sebring to initiate affirmative action to promote more females, blacks, and Chicanos. At present, of the 96 managerial personnel in the Baton Rouge facility, six are females, three are blacks, and two are Chicanos.

The six employees being considered for the two supervisory vacancies are considered the best within the company for the promotions. They are:

Tony Santos: Chicano; age 37; married; 4 children; 2 years college; 9 years with Sebring.

EXHIBIT A

Two-Year Performance Evaluation of Six Top Candidates for Promotion

Candidate for Promotion	Objective Performance Dimensions*				Subjective Performance Dimensions			
	Quantity†	Quality (percent)‡	Cost§	Absences (unexcused percent)‖	Develops Assistants	Potential for Promotion	Cooperative Attitude	Communication Skills
Tony Santos	138.7	87.4	1.61	5.1	Good	Good	Fair	Good
Barbara Golding	106.4	85.8	1.74	8.1	Good	Good	Good	Fair
Mark Petro	110.8	89.6	1.39	6.2	Good	Good	Good	Excellent
Denny Slago	165.7	94.6	1.02	3.0	Excellent	Excellent	Good	Good
Bobby Green	120.8	86.8	1.41	5.9	Excellent	Good	Fair	Good
George Nelson	169.7	95.1	1.00	2.1	Good	Good	Excellent	Good

* The quantity, quality, and cost measures are weekly averages. The absence indicator is the average of four six-month periods of review.
† Higher mean score indicates more quantity.
‡ Higher mean score indicates better quality.
§ Lower mean score indicates better cost control.
‖ Lower mean score indicates better absence record.

Barbara Golding: White; age 32; married; 1 child; 3 years college; 6 years with Sebring.

Mark Petro: White; age 38; married; 2 children; 1 year college; 7 years with Sebring.

Denny Slago: White; age 39; single; high school graduate; 10 years with Sebring.

Bobby Green: Black; age 38; married; 2 years college; 8 years with Sebring.

George Nelson: White; age 40; single; 3 years college; 7 years with Sebring.

The performance records of these six individuals have been carefully scrutinized. Average performance over a two-year period is presented in Exhibit A. These data are being weighed heavily by the committee that is to make the final choices.

Exercise Procedures

Phase I: 40 to 60 minutes

1. Each group is to select two employees for promotions. A group consensus should be the final step in reaching agreement. The group should also develop a statement supporting its decision.
2. The group decisions should be placed on a board or chart in front of all class members and discussed.

Phase II: 40 minutes

1. Assume that Barbara Golding and Bobby Green were selected for the promotion.
2. Select two people from the class to role-play an interview between the chairperson of the promotion committee and Denny Slago.
3. Denny is concerned about the decision and is very upset about not being selected. The committee chairperson's role is to explain to Denny why he was not selected.
4. If possible, use two different role-play groups. Have one group wait outside the room during the first role play. In one role play have a woman play the role of the chairperson. In the second role play, have a woman act out the role of Denny.
5. As a class, consider the impact of any promotion decision at Sebring on the four employees who were not selected. Also consider whether any performance evaluation program would make the Sebring decision any easier.

Chapter 18

After completing Chapter 18, you should be able to:

Define organizational socialization and careers.

Describe the way in which socialization stages correspond with career stages.

Discuss the different experiences and activities that correspond to each career stage.

Compare alternative socialization practices for each socialization stage.

Identify the characteristics of effective socialization practice.

Socialization and Career Processes

Building Loyalty through Socialization*

Argument For

In recent years, organizations have found it more and more difficult to obtain loyalty and commitment from their managers. For obvious reasons, organizations value loyal and committed employees: such employees work harder and achieve greater success than do disloyal and uncommitted ones. But organizations cannot count on loyalty; they must *socialize* new employees so that they become loyal. Socialization processes that en-

course and reward loyalty take many forms and involve specific organizational practices.

One particularly effective form of socialization involves four key elements:

First, the organization induces employees to choose to be loyal by offering rewards.

Second, the organization influences employees to remain loyal by enticement, not force.

Third, the organization draws employees away from their own values and goals toward the organization's values and goals.

Fourth, the organization creates the appearance that the individual exercises free choice when hiring on and remaining in the job.

The organization implements this form of socialization by hiring only those individuals who have apparent inclinations to accept the organization's values and goals. Once such an individual has been hired, he or she is provided with opportunities to work in high-status, challenging, responsible, enriched jobs. If the individual performs satisfactorily,

* Based on Roy J. Lewicki, "Organizational Seduction: Building Commitment to Organizations," *Organizational Dynamics*, Autumn 1981, pp. 5–21.

637

he or she is highly rewarded through monetary compensation, plush working conditions, and job perks.

Through this process, the organization engenders a high level of loyalty. Individuals, in fact, feel obligated to be loyal to such benevolent organizations.

The purpose of the status system and the enriched jobs is to constantly reinforce the value of loyalty. People in lower levels of the status hierarchy must reaffirm their commitment as a condition for advancement. Enriched jobs with their associated responsibilities are so demanding and time-consuming that individuals can seldom see beyond them. The reward system is the payoff for their hard work. As a consequence of these practices, individuals become loyal employees. In return for all the benefits of employment, they are willing to suspend their judgments and accept those of the organization.

Argument Against

Critics of socialization that secures loyalty and commitment through inducement and enticement note aptly that it is a form of "organizational seduction." Practices that manipulate individuals to suspend their own values and goals involve not only organizational issues but ethical issues as well.

The ethical issues relate to whether individuals really exercise free will or whether the abundance of opportunities and rewards inexorably draws them into behaviors that they would otherwise not choose. Would individuals react favorably if the organization explained the purposes of its practices? The critics believe that they would feel manipulated if they were told that the price of status and rewards is their own seduction.

The organizational issues relate to long-range effects. One effect is to promote to top management those individuals who demonstrate the greatest loyalty and commitment. They may not, however, be the most creative, the best decision makers, the most effective problem solvers. Not only will such managers fail to perform at high levels, but they are likely to expect undue loyalty and commitment from their subordinates. Consequently, they impose a confining, if not closed, mentality on those below them. Those who do not make it up the ladder and who are insufficiently loyal either withdraw from or leave the organization. Anger and bitterness follow unfulfilled expectations, and there are bound to be unfulfilled expectations because there is less room at the top of the status hierarchy than there are candidates.

But perhaps the greatest cost of organizational seduction is the loss of dissent. Loyalty and dissenting opinion are uneasy companions. In fact, managers often view dissent as disloyalty and violation of the "team player" idea. Insistence on agreement fosters an ever-narrowing range of alternatives and perspectives to be considered. Under such circumstances, organizational effectiveness must decline.

Organizational socialization and individual career development are important processes. Through socialization, the organization attempts to achieve high levels of individual performance, although group and organizational performance are also enhanced by effective socialization efforts. Specifically, organizational socialization "is the process by which an individual comes to appreciate the values, abilities, expected behaviors, and social knowledge essential for assuming an organizational role and for participating as an organization member."[1] The specific activities of socialization vary among organizations, yet the purpose remains the same: to integrate individual and organizational interests.

The Organizational Issue for Debate that opens the chapter raises an interesting question regarding socialization: To what extent are socialization efforts intended to reshape the individual's values to coincide with organizational values? If organizations do indeed obtain employee loyalty through seductive practices, important ethical issues must be confronted.

From the perspective of the individual, the socialization process is related to career development. That is to say, the individual looks to the organization for opportunities to achieve satisfying work experiences that constitute a satisfying career. The socialization process attempts to focus an individual's perception of satisfying work activities on those that lead to effective group and organizational performance. Thus, individual career development and organizational socialization processes are interrelated.

Because the two processes are interrelated, we will discuss them together. We begin with the career process and discuss contemporary ideas regarding the concept of career, the meaning of career effectiveness, career stages, and career paths. Next, we take up organizational socialization and discuss socialization stages and criteria to evaluate the effectiveness of organizational socialization.

ORGANIZATIONAL CAREERS

The popular meaning of the term **career** is reflected in the idea of moving upward in one's chosen line of work. Moving upward implies commanding larger salaries, assuming more responsibility, and acquiring more status, prestige, and power. Although the career concept is

---

[1] Meryl R. Louis, "Surprise and Sense Making: What Newcomers Experience in Entering Unfamiliar Organizational Settings," *Administrative Science Quarterly*, June 1980, pp. 229–30. This definition of socialization in organizational settings is generally accepted and reflects the view of Edgar H. Schein, "Organizational Socialization and the Profession of Management," *Industrial Management Review*, January 1968, pp. 1–16.

career
The sequence of job-related experiences and activities that create certain attitudes and behaviors in the individual.

typically restricted to lines of work that involve gainful employment, we can certainly relate the concept to homemakers, mothers, fathers, volunteer workers, civic leaders, and the like. These people also advance in the sense that their knowledge and skills grow with time, experience, and training. Here we will restrict our attention to the careers of those in organizations; however, doing so does not deny the existence of careers in other contexts.

The definition of the term *career* as used in this discussion is as follows:

> The career is the individually perceived sequence of attitudes and behaviors associated with work-related experiences and activities over the span of the person's life.[2]

This definition emphasizes that a career consists of both attitudes and behaviors and that it is an ongoing sequence of work-related activities. Yet even though the career concept is clearly work-related, it must be understood that a person's nonwork life and roles play a significant part in it. For example, a mid-career manager 50 years old can have quite different attitudes about job advancement involving greater responsibilities than a manager nearing retirement. A bachelor's reaction to a promotion involving relocation is likely to be quite different from that of a father of school-age children.

Although careers have typically been thought of in terms of upward mobility, recent ideas have enlarged the career concept. For example, it is evident that an individual can remain in the same job, acquiring and developing skills, but without moving upward in an organizational or professional hierarchy. It is also possible for an individual to move among various jobs in different fields and organizations.[3] Thus, the concept of career must be broad enough to include not only traditional work experiences but also the emerging work styles and lifestyles. Contemporary career development practices recognize the diversity of individual choices and career alternatives.[4]

CAREER CHOICES

How do people get into particular occupations and professions? Is it by chance or by choice? Although the matter of matching individuals and careers is vitally important for individuals, organizations, and

---

[2] Douglas T. Hall, *Careers in Organizations* (Santa Monica, Calif.: Goodyear Publishing, 1976), p. 4.

[3] Meryl R. Louis, "Career Transitions: Varieties and Commonalities," *Academy of Management*, July 1980, p. 330.

[4] Kathryn M. Bartol, "Vocational Behavior and Career Development, 1980: A Review," *Journal of Vocational Behavior*, October 1981, pp. 123–62; and Edwin L. Herr, "Comprehensive Career Guidance: A Look to the Future," *Vocational Guidance Quarterly*, June 1982, pp. 371–76.

society, career guidance and counseling is far from a precise science. The most obvious complication is the inherent tendency of individuals to change their interests, motivations, and abilities. But equally obvious in this day and age is the fact of changing career demands. Technology has brought irrevocable change, for example, to the demands on those seeking careers in office work, factories, medicine, banking, and government service. Thus, an individual may prepare for a career, but subsequently discover that technology has made that preparation obsolete and irrelevant.

A reasonable way to understand career choice is that individuals tend toward careers that are consonant with their personal orientations. This line of thinking underlies an imporant theory of career choices that John Holland developed.[5]

According to Holland, individuals can be classified as having one of six personality types that coincides with one of six occupational types. If people do in fact tend to gravitate toward those occupational types that coincide with their personality types, and if Holland's personality and occupational types are valid, these individuals can make informed career choices. Holland's personality types and compatible occupations are shown in Figure 18–1.

Holland and others have devised paper-and-pencil tests that, when scored, identify an individual's primary orientation. Many counseling centers in high schools and universities use such a test as *one basis* for advising students as to educational and career tracks. The idea is rather straightforward: Individuals whose career choices match their personality types will probably persist in the required educational preparation and prosper in the subsequent career.

Holland's theory and the counseling practices based on it are not, in all instances, valid. But they are sufficiently widespread to command considerable attention. The theory and practices have been subjected to continued study to validate their applicability for both initial and subsequent career choices. The importance of career choice decisions as a factor in career effectiveness cannot be overvalued.[6]

CAREER EFFECTIVENESS

In organizational settings, career effectiveness is judged not only by the individual but also by the organization itself. But what is meant

---

[5] John L. Holland, *Making Vocational Choices: A Theory of Careers* (Englewood Cliffs, N.J.: Prentice-Hall 1973). The discussion of Holland's theory is based on Hall, *Careers in Organizations*, pp. 13–15. Manuel London, "Toward a Theory of Career Motivation," *Academy of Management Review*, October 1983, pp. 620–30, is an extensive review of the literature.

[6] William L. Mihal, Patricia A. Sorce, and Thomas E. Comte, "A Process Model of Individual Career Decision Making," *Academy of Management Review*, January 1984, pp. 95–103; and London, "Toward a Theory of Career Motivation."

FIGURE 18-1

Holland's Six Personality Types and Compatible Occupations

Type	Characteristics	Occupations
Realistic	Aggressive behavior; prefers activities requiring skill, strength, and coordination	Forestry, farming, architecture
Investigative	Cognitive behavior; prefers thinking, organizing, and understanding activities	Biology, mathematics, oceanography
Social	Interpersonal behavior; prefers feeling and emotional activities	Clinical psychology, foreign service, social work
Conventional	Structured behavior; prefers to subordinate personal needs to other's needs	Accounting, finance
Enterprising	Predictable behavior; prefers power and status acquisition activities	Management, law, public relations
Artistic	Self-expressive behavior; prefers artistic, self-expressive, and individualistic activities	Art, music, education

Source: Douglas T. Hall, *Careers in Organization* (Pacific Palisades, Calif.: Goodyear Publishing, 1976), p. 13.

career effectiveness Judgments by individuals regarding how closely their careers match their expectations.

by career effectiveness? Under what circumstances will individuals state that they have had "successful" or "satisfying" careers? And will the organization share the individuals' views about their careers? Although numerous characteristics of **career effectiveness** could be listed, four are often cited. They are performance, attitude, adaptability, and identity.

Career Performance

Salary and position are the more popular indicators of career performance. Specifically, the more rapidly one's salary increases and the more rapidly one advances up the hierarchy, the higher is the level of career performance. The higher one advances, the greater is the responsibility in terms of employees supervised, budget allocated, and revenue generated. The organization is, of course, vitally interested in career performance since it bears a direct relation to organizational effectiveness. That is, the rate of salary and position advancement reflects in most instances the extent to which the individual has contributed to the achievement of organizational performance.

Two points should be made. First, to the extent that the organization's performance evaluation and reward processes do not fully recognize performance, individuals may not realize this indicator of career effectiveness. Thus, individuals may not receive the rewards, salary, and promotion that are associated with career effectiveness because the organization either does not or cannot provide them. Many employees discover that organizations often state that they reward performance when, in fact, they reward other, nonperformance outcomes.[7] Second, the organization may have expectations for the individual's performance that the individual is unwilling or unable to meet. The organization may accurately assess the individual's potential as being greater than present performance, yet because the individual has other, nonjob interests (for example, family, community, religious), performance does not match potential. In such instances, the individual may be satisfied with career performance, yet the organization is disappointed. This mismatch occurs as a consequence of the individual's *attitudes* toward the career.

Career Attitudes

Career attitudes refers to the ways in which individuals perceive and evaluate their careers. Individuals who have positive career attitudes will also have positive perceptions and evaluations of their careers. Positive career attitudes have important implications for the organization because individuals with such attitudes are more likely to be committed to the organization and involved in their jobs. The manner in which individuals come to have positive career attitudes is a complex psychological and sociological process; a full development of that process is beyond the scope of this discussion. However, it is evident that positive career attitudes are likely to coincide with career demands and opportunities that are consistent with an individual's interests, values, needs, and abilities.

Career Adaptability

Few professions are stagnant and unchanging. On the contrary, the condition of change and development more accurately describes contemporary professions. Changes occur in the profession itself, requiring new knowledge and skills to practice it; for example, medicine and engineering have advanced and will continue to advance in the utilization of new information and technology. Other professions have likewise changed markedly. Individuals unable to *adapt* to such changes and to *adopt* them in the practice of their careers run the risk of early obsolescence. It goes without saying that organizations benefit through the *adaptiveness* of their employees. An expression

---

[7] Roy J. Lewicki, "Organizational Seduction: Building Commitment to Organizations," *Organizational Dynamics*, Autumn 1981, p. 9.

of the mutual benefits derived from career adaptability is the dollars expended by organizations for employee training and development. Thus, career adaptability implies the application of the latest knowledge, skills, and technology in the work of a career.

Career Identity

Career identity comprises two important components. The first is the extent to which individuals have clear and consistent awareness of their interests, their values, and their expectations for the future. The second is the extent to which individuals view their lives as consistent through time, the extent to which they see themselves as extensions of their pasts. The idea expressed in this concept is, "What do I want to be, and what do I have to do to become what I want to be?"[8] Individuals who have arrived at satisfactory resolutions of this question are likely to have effective careers and to make effective contributions to the organizations that employ them.

Effective careers in organizations, then, are likely to occur for individuals with high levels of performance, positive attitudes, adaptiveness, and identity resolution. Moreover, effective careers are without doubt linked to organizational performance.

Figure 18–2 suggests some possible relationships between the characteristics of career effectiveness and criteria of organizational effectiveness. The degree to which these relationships are generally valid cannot be stated with certainty, yet some suggestions are warranted.

Career performance would seem to be related to organizational production and efficiency. In most organizations, the performance evaluation process places primary emphasis on these two criteria, and career performance effectiveness is judged accordingly. Positive career attitudes would imply commitment to production and efficiency and, perhaps by definition, satisfaction. Individuals with positive career attitudes who work in organizations that place emphasis on employee growth and development would no doubt be effective; thus, connective arrows could also be drawn from attitudes to adaptiveness and development. Career adaptability is directly related to organizational adaptiveness and development, particularly for those occupations and organizations that are subject to rapid change. Finally, career identity is directly related to satisfaction; it may be related to other criteria, but one can reach a level of identity resolution that excludes production and efficiency activities. The importance of career effectiveness as a source of organizational effectiveness supports the allocation of resources to career programs.[9]

---

[8] Erik H. Erikson, "The Concept of Identity in Race Relations: Notes and Queries," *Daedalus 95* (1966), p. 148, as cited in Hall, *Careers in Organizations,* p. 95.

FIGURE 18–2

Suggested Relationships between Characteristics of Career Effectiveness and Criteria of Organizational Effectiveness

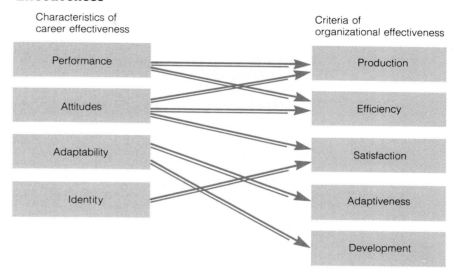

CAREER STAGES

career stages
The orderly sequence of distinctly different sets of experiences and activities that are associated with all careers.

Individuals typically move through four distinct **career stages:** *establishment, advancement, maintenance,* and *withdrawal.*[10] The establishment stage occurs at the onset of the career. The advancement stage is a period of moving from job to job, both inside and outside the organization. Maintenance occurs when the individual has reached the limits of advancement and concentrates on the job that he or she is doing. Finally, at some point prior to actual retirement, the individual goes through the withdrawal stage. The duration of these stages varies among individuals, but in general they each go through all of them.

Needs and expectations change as individuals move through each

---

[9] Mary Ann Von Glinow, Michael J. Driver, Kenneth Brousseau, and J. Bruce Pine, "The Design of a Career-Oriented Human Resource System," *Academy of Management Review,* January 1983, pp. 23–32; and Carol L. Parker, "Facilitating Career Development in Small Business," *Vocational Guidance Quarterly,* September 1982, pp. 86–89.

[10] Lloyd Baird and Kathy Kram, "Career Dynamics: Managing the Superior/Subordinate Relationship," *Organizational Dynamics,* Spring 1983, p. 47.

career stage. A study of managers in American Telephone and Telegraph (AT&T) found that they expressed considerable concern for security needs during the *establishment* stage.[11] During establishment, individuals require and seek support from others, particularly their managers. It is important for managers to recognize this need and to respond by assuming the role of mentor.[12] During the *advancement* stage, the AT&T managers expressed considerably less concern for security need satisfaction and more concern for achievement, esteem, and autonomy. Promotions and advancement to jobs with responsibility and opportunity to exercise independent judgment are characteristics of this stage. But the specific factors that explain why some individuals advance, while others do not, remain obscure.[13]

The *maintenance* stage is marked by efforts to stabilize the gains of the past. In some respects, this stage is analogous to a plateau—no new gains are made, yet it can be a period of creativity since the individual has satisfied many of the psychological and financial needs associated with the earlier stages. Although each individual and career will be different in actuality, it is reasonable to assume that esteem is the most important need in the maintenance stage. Many people experience what is termed the *mid-career crisis* during this stage. Such people are not successfully achieving satisfaction from their work and may, consequently, experience physiological and psychological discomfort. They may experience poor health and a heightened sense of anxiety. They no longer desire to advance, and consequently they underperform. They then lose the support of their managers, which further intensifies the health and job problems.[14]

The maintenance stage is followed by the *retirement stage*. The individual has, in effect, completed one career and may move on to another.[15] During this stage, the individual may have opportunities to experience self-actualization through activities that it was impossible to pursue while working. Painting, gardening, volunteer service, and quiet reflection are among the many positive avenues available to retirees.

Some of the important characteristics of career stages are summarized in Figure 18–3. This figure depicts careers in the context of orga-

---

[11] Douglas T. Hall and Khalil Nougaim, "An Examination of Maslow's Need Hierarchy in an Organizational Setting," *Organizational Behavior and Human Performance 3* 1968, pp. 12–35.

[12] David M. Hunt and Carol Michael, "Mentorship: A Career Training and Development Tool," *Academy of Management Review,* July 1983, pp. 475–85.

[13] John F. Veiga, "Mobility Influences during Managerial Career Stages," *Academy of Management Journal,* March 1983, pp. 64–85.

[14] Janet P. Near, "Work and Nonwork Correlates of the Career Plateau," *Academy of Management Proceedings,* 1983, pp. 380–84.

[15] James B. Shaw, "The Process of Retiring: Organizational Entry in Reverse," *Academy of Management Review,* January 1981, pp. 41–47.

FIGURE 18–3

Characteristics of General Career Stages

Stage	Establishment	Advancement	Maintenance	Withdrawal
Age	18 - 24	25 - 39	40 - 54	55 - 65
Primary work- related activities	Obtaining job- related skills and knowledge	Becoming an independent contributor	Developing the skills of others	Sharing work experiences with others
Primary psychlogical demands	Being dependent upon others for rewards	Being dependent upon self for rewards	Being dependent upon others for need satisfaction	Letting go of work identity
Primary need satisfaction	Security	Achievement autonomy	Esteem	Self-neutralization

nizations. It also reflects the passage of an individual along a traditional career path.

Career Paths

career paths
Jobs linked together along a continuum of increasing responsibility and authority.

Effective advancement through career stages involves moving along **career paths.** From the perspective of the organization, career paths are important inputs into human resource planning. An organization's future human resource needs depend on the projected passage of individuals through the ranks. From the perspective of the individual, a career path is the sequence of jobs that he or she desires to undertake to achieve personal and career goals. It is virtually impossible to integrate completely the needs of both the organization and the individual in the design of career paths, yet systematic career planning has the potential for closing the gap.

In the traditional sense, career paths emphasize upward mobility in a single occupation or functional area, as reflected in Figure 18–4. When recruiting personnel, the organization's representative will speak of engineers', accountants', or marketers' career paths. In these contexts, the recruiter will describe the different jobs that typical individuals will hold as they work their way progressively upward in an organization. Each job, or rung, is reached when the individual has accumulated the necessary experience and ability and has demon-

FIGURE 18–4

Career Path, General Management

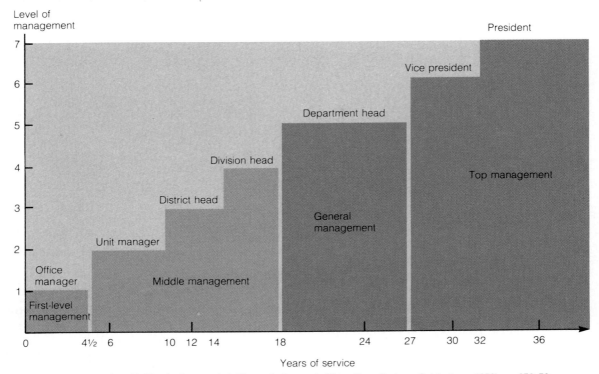

Source: Based on William F. Glueck, *Personnel: A Diagnostic Approach* (Plano, Tex.: Business Publications, 1978) pp. 272–73.

strated that he or she is ready for promotion. Implicit in such career paths are attitudes that failure results whenever an individual does not move on up after an elapsed time.

The idea of career path reflects the idea of moving upward in the organization along one "path." That path is usually the managerial, or line, path. Employees in staff position are often prevented from moving upward unless they give up their specialty and move into a line position. Some organizations are beginning to recognize the importance of multiple paths, as noted in the following organizational Close-Up.

ORGANIZATIONS: CLOSE-UP

Career Ladders at BDM Corporation

BDM Corporation provides more than one way to get to the top. The company has created three career ladders, each comprising successively higher level (and higher paying) positions. The three ladders enable employees to advance in their technical and administrative specialties. Typically, advancement upward to the executive suite requires technical and administrative personnel to relinquish their specialty and move into line management. They then move up the management hierarchy. But BDM views the typical practice as wasteful of specialized talent. As an alternative, the company provides comparable upward advancement for all three talents: technical, administrative, and management. The company's practice gives all employees opportunities for advancement without sacrificing expertise.

Source: John P. Riceman, "How to Operate a Successful Career Development Program," *Management Review*, May 1982, pp. 21–24.

Organizational Careers in Perspective

Upon reflection, the achievement of career effectiveness is a complex process. At a minimum, the following complexities can be noted:

1. Career effectiveness consists of four criteria (performance, attitudes, adaptability, and identity) that are interrelated in different ways for different individuals. It cannot be said with certainty that, for example, achieving high levels of performance will lead to or is the result of positive career attitudes. Individual differences in perception and personality account for differences in career effectiveness criteria.

2. The relative importance of career effectiveness criteria varies among individuals, but also among organizations. Some individuals (and organizations) may value performance at the expense of adaptability, while other individuals (and organizations) may value adaptability over performance. Thus, career effectiveness requires individual and organizational agreement as to the importance of criteria.

3. The organization provides opportunities in the form of career paths for the realization of career effectiveness. The passage of individuals along career paths coincides with the passage of career stages. Thus, the coincidence of career paths and career stages reinforces

the interrelationship and interdependence between the individual and the organization. An important linkage between the individual and the organization is the socialization process.

SOCIALIZATION: A LINKAGE BETWEEN CAREER EFFECTIVENESS AND ORGANIZATIONAL EFFECTIVENESS

socialization
Activities undertaken by the organization to integrate individual and organizational purposes.

The **socialization** process goes on throughout an individual's career. As the needs of the organization change, for example, its employees must adapt to those new needs; that is, they must be socialized. But even as we recognize that socialization is ever present, we must also recognize that it is more important at some times then at others. For example, socialization is most important when an individual first takes a job or first takes a different job in the same organization. The socialization process occurs throughout the career stages and at every step along career paths, but individuals are more aware of it when they change jobs or change organizations.[16] The parallelism between careers and socialization efforts implies the existence of socialization stages corresponding to career stages.

Socialization Stages

The stages of socialization coincide generally with the stages of a career. For convenience, three stages sufficiently describe the socialization process: (1) anticipatory socialization, (2) accommodation, and (3) role management.[17] Each stage involves specific activities that, if undertaken properly, increase the individual's chances of having an effective career. Moreover, these stages occur continuously and often simultaneously.

Anticipatory Socialization. The first stage involves all of the activities that the individual undertakes prior to entering the organization or prior to taking a different job in the same organization. The primary purpose of these activities is to acquire information about the new

---

[16] Daniel C. Feldman and Jeanne M. Brett, "Coping with New Jobs: A Comparative Study of New Hires and Job Changers," *Academy of Management Journal,* June 1983, pp. 258–72.

[17] These stages are identified by Daniel C. Feldman, "A Contingency Theory of Socialization," *Administrative Science Quarterly,* September 1976, pp. 434–35. The following discussion is based heavily on this work as well as on Daniel C. Feldman, "A Practical Program for Employee Socialization," *Organizational Dynamics,* Autumn 1976, pp. 64–80; and Daniel C. Feldman, "The Multiple Socialization of Organization Members," *Academy of Management Review,* June 1981, pp. 309–18.

organization and/or the new job. This stage of socialization corresponds to the prework career stage, and the information-gathering activities include formal schooling, actual work experience, and the recruiting efforts of organizations attempting to attract new employees.

People are vitally interested in two kinds of information prior to entering a new job or organization. First, they want to know as much as they can about what working for the organization is really like. Second, they want to know whether they are suited to the jobs available in the organization. Individuals seek out this information with considerable effort when they are faced with the decision to take a job, whether it be their first one or one that comes along in the way of transfer or promotion. At these times, the information is specific to the job or the organization. But we should understand that we also form impressions about jobs and organizations in less formal ways. For example, our friends and relatives talk of their experiences. Parents impart both positive and negative information to their offspring regarding the world of work. Thus, we continually receive information about this or that job or organization, but we are more receptive to such information when we are faced with the necessity of making a decision.

It is desirable, of course, that the information transmitted and received during the anticipatory stage be such that the organization and the job are accurately and clearly depicted. However, we know that individuals differ considerably in the way they decode and receive information. Yet if the fit between the individual and the organization is to be optimal, two conditions are necessary. The first condition is *realism*. That is to say, both the individual and the organization must portray themselves realistically. The second condition is *congruence*. This condition is present when the individual's skills, talents, and abilities are fully utilized by the job. Either their overutilization or their underutilization results in incongruence and, consequently, poor performance.[18]

The necessity of obtaining realism and congruence during the anticipatory socialization stage places special emphasis on the organization's recruitment efforts. It is through recruitment that the organization attracts the kinds and types of people on whom it depends for future performance. All too often, the recruitment process is undertaken from the perspective of "getting warm bodies" or "filling slots." The result is that the organization is portrayed unrealistically. The recruits are simply not told the whole story, only the good parts. The predictable outcome is the creation of unrealistic expectations. Individuals are led to believe that certain things will happen to them, and when

---

[18] Feldman, "A Practical Program," pp. 65–66.

they do not, the natural outcome is lowered satisfaction and production.

One way to counteract the unrealistic expectations of new recruits is to provide realistic information during their recruiting process. This practice is based on the idea that people should know both the bad and the good things to expect from their jobs and their organizations. Through **realistic job previews** (RJPs), recruits are given opportunities to learn not only the benefits that they may expect but also the nonbenefits. Studies have shown that the recruitment rate is the same for those who receive RJPs as for those who do not. More important, those who receive RJPs are more likely to remain on the job and to be satisfied with it than are those who have been selected in the usual manner.[19] The practice of "telling it like it is" is used by a number of organizations, including the Prudential Insurance Company, Texas Instruments, and the U.S. Military Academy.[20]

Accommodation. The second stage of socialization occurs after the individual becomes a member of the organization, after he or she takes the job. During this stage, the individual sees the organization and the job for what they actually are. Through a variety of activities, the individual attempts to become an active participant in the organization and a competent performer on the job. This breaking-in period is ordinarily stressful for the individual because of anxiety created by the uncertainties inherent in any new and different situation. Apparently, the closer the individual came to realism and congruence during the anticipatory stage, the greater is the likelihood that some of the stress will be lessened. Nevertheless, the demands on the individual do indeed create situations that induce stress.

The accommodation stage comprises four major activities. All individuals must, to a degree, engage in (1) establishing new interpersonal relationships with both co-workers and supervisors, (2) learning the tasks required to perform the job, (3) clarifying their role in the organization and in the formal and informal groups relevant to that role, and (4) evaluating the progress that they are making toward satisfying the demands of the job and the role. Readers who have been through the accommodation stage will recognize these four activities and will recall more or less favorable reactions to them.

If all goes well in this stage, the individual will feel a sense of acceptance by co-workers and supervisors and will experience competence in performing the tasks for the job. The breaking-in period will, if successful, also result in role definition and congruence of evaluation.

---

realistic job previews
The means for providing accurate, realistic, and pertinent information to prospective employees.

[19] John P. Wanous, *Organizational Entry* (Reading, Mass.: Addison-Wesley Publishing, 1980); and Paula Popovich and John P. Wanous, "The Realistic Job Preview as a Persuasive Communication," *Academy of Management Review,* October 1982, pp. 570–78.

[20] James A. Breaugh, "Realistic Job Previews: A Critical Appraisal and Future Research Directions," *Academy of Management Review,* October 1983, pp. 612–19.

These four outcomes of the accommodation stage (acceptance, competence, role definition, and congruence of evaluation) are experienced by all new employees to a greater or lesser extent. However, the relative "value" of each of these outcomes varies from person to person.[21] For example, acceptance by the group may be a less valued outcome for an individual whose social need is satisfied off the job. Regardless of these differences due to individual preferences, each of us will experience the accommodation stage of socialization and will ordinarily move on to the third stage.

Role Management.   The third stage of socialization, role management, coincides with the third stage of careers, stable work. In contrast to the accommodation stage, which requires the individual to adjust to the demands and expectations of the immediate work group, the role management stage takes on a broader set of issues and problems. Specifically, the third stage requires the individual to resolve two types of conflicts. First, there is the conflict that arises between the individual's work and home lives. For example, the individual must allocate time and energy between the job and his or her role in the family. Since the amount of time and energy are fixed and the demands of work and family seem insatiable, conflict is inevitable. Employees who are unable to resolve these conflicts are often forced to leave the organization or to perform at an ineffective level. In either case, the individual and the organization are not well served by unresolved conflict between work and family.

The second source of conflict that arises during the role management stage is between the individual's work group and other work groups in the organization. This source of conflict can be more apparent for some employees than for others. For example, as an individual moves up in the organization's hierarchy, he or she is required to interact with various types of groups both inside and outside the organization. Each group can and often does place different demands on the individual, and to the extent that these demands are beyond the individual's ability, stress will result. The tolerance for the level of stress induced by these conflicting and irreconcilable demands varies among individuals, but it can generally be assumed that the existence of unmanaged stress works to the disadvantage of the individual and the organization.

The Outcomes of Socialization

If an individual moves through each stage of the socialization process in a positive manner, then the groundwork is laid for an effective

---

[21] Gareth R. Jones, "Psychological Orientation and the Process of Organizational Socialization: An Interactionist Perspective," *Academy of Management Review,* July 1983, pp. 464–74.

career. Note that what results from socialization is the groundwork, or beginnings. Socialization processes contribute to some aspects of one's reaction to a job and an organization, but not to all reactions. For example, general satisfaction, the degree to which an individual is satisfied and happy in his or her work, is related to high congruence, role definition, resolution of conflicting demands of work groups, and resolution of work-family conflicts. Congruence is an activity of the anticipatory stage; role definition occurs during the accommodation stage; and the conflict resolution activities are the primary characteristics of the role management stage. Thus, each stage of the socialization process contributes to general satisfaction.

The same research that found the relationships noted above also found that socialization activities are unrelated to two very important variables: internal work motivation and job involvement. Thus, an individual may have positive or negative experiences with an organization's socialization processes and at the same time have positive or negative work motivation and job involvement. The most likely explanation for this finding is that motivation and involvement are the results of the nature of the work itself. Our discussion of job design in Chapter 13 noted the importance of job-related factors such as task identity, task significance, job freedom, and feedback to the sense of job satisfaction that employees experience. Thus, while organizational socialization processes can contribute to building a solid foundation for effective careers, they cannot guarantee such careers. It is possible to incorporate motivating factors into the socialization process, and organizations that are committed to providing maximum career opportunities will do so.

CHARACTERISTICS OF EFFECTIVE SOCIALIZATION AND CAREER PROCESSES

Organizational socialization processes vary in form and content from organization to organization. Even within the same organization, different individuals experience different socialization processes. For example, the accommodation stage for a college-trained management recruit is quite different from that of a member of the lowest-paid occupation in the organization. As Van Maanen has pointed out, socialization processes are not only extremely important in shaping the individuals who enter an organization; they are also remarkably different from situation to situation.[22] This variation reflects either the

---

[22] J. Van Maanen, "People Processing: Strategies for Organizational Socialization," *Organizational Dynamics,* Summer 1978, pp. 18–36.

lack of attention by management to the socialization process, or it reflects the uniqueness of the process as related to organizations and individuals. Either explanation permits the suggestion that while uniqueness is apparent, some general principles can be implemented in the socialization process.[23]

Effective Anticipatory Socialization

The organization's primary activities during the first stage of socialization are *recruitment* and *selection and placement* programs. If these programs are effective, then new recruits in an organization should experience the feeling of *realism* and *congruence*. In turn, accurate expectations about the job result from realism and congruence.

Recruitment programs are directed toward new employees, those not now in the organization. It is desirable to give these prospective employees not only information about the job but also information about those aspects of the organization that will affect them as individuals. It is nearly always easier for the recruiter to stress job-related information to the exclusion of organization-related information. Job-related information is usually specific and objective, whereas organization-related information is usually general and subjective. Nevertheless, the recruiter should, to the extent possible, convey factual information about such matters as pay and promotion policies and practices, objective characteristics of the group that the recruit is likely to work with, and other information that reflects the recruit's concerns.

Selection and placement practices, in the context of anticipatory socialization, are important conveyers of information to employees already in the organization. Of prime importance is the manner in which individuals view career paths in the organizations. As noted earlier, the stereotypical career path is one that involves advancement up the managerial hierarchy. However, this concept does not take into account the differences among individuals with regard to such moves. Greater flexibility in career paths would require the organization to consider the following alternatives.[24]

Lateral transfers involve moves at the same organizational level from one department to another. A manager who has plateaued in production could be transferred to a similar level in sales, engineering, or some other area. The move would require the manager to learn quickly the technical demands of the new position, and there would be a period of reduced performance as this learning occurred. But

---

[23] The following discussion reflects the research findings of Feldman, "A Practical Program."

[24] Douglas T. Hall and Francine S. Hall, "What's New in Career Management," *Organizational Dynamics,* Summer 1976, pp. 21–27.

once qualified, the manager would bring the perspectives of both areas to bear on decisions.

Downward transfers are associated in our society with failure; an effective manager simply does not consider a move downward to be a respectable alternative. Yet downward tranfers are in many instances not only respectable alternatives but entirely acceptable alternatives, particularly when one or more of the following conditions exist:

> The manager values the quality of life afforded by a specific geographic area and may desire a downward transfer if this is required in order to stay in or move to that area.
>
> The manager views the downward transfer as a way to establish a base for future promotions.
>
> The manager is faced with the alternatives of dismissal or a downward move.
>
> The manager desires to pursue autonomy and self-actualization in non-job-related activities—such as religious, civic, or political activities—and for that reason may welcome the reduced responsibility (and demands) of a lower level position.

The use of *fallback positions* is a relatively new way to reduce the risk of lateral and downward transfers. The practice involves identifying in advance a position to which the transferred manager can return if the new position does not work out. By identifying the fallback position in advance, the organization informs everyone who is affected that some risk is involved but that the organization is willing to accept some of the responsibility for it and that returning to the fallback job will not be viewed as failure. Such companies as Heublein, Procter & Gamble, Continental Can, and Lehman Brothers have used fallback positions to remove some of the risk of lateral and upward moves. The practice appears to have considerable promise for protecting the careers of highly specialized technicians and professionals who make their first move into general management positions.

An alternative to traditional career pathing is realistic career pathing. This practice bases career progression on real-world experiences and individualized preferences. Such career paths would have several characteristics:[25]

1. They would include lateral and downward possibilities not tied to "normal" rates of progress, as well as upward possibilities.
2. They would be tentative and responsive to changes in organizational needs.

---

[25] James W. Walker, "Let's Get Realistic about Career Paths," *Human Resource Management,* Fall 1976, pp. 2–7.

3. They would be flexible enough to take into account the qualities of individuals.
4. Each job along the path would be specified in terms of acquirable skills, knowledge, and other specific attributes—not merely educational credentials, age, or work experience.

Realistic career paths, rather than traditional ones, are necessary for effective anticipatory socialization. In the absence of career path information, the employee can only guess at what is available.

Effective Accommodation Socialization

Effective accommodation socialization comprises five activities. They are (1) designing orientation programs, (2) structuring training programs, (3) providing performance evaluation information, (4) assigning challenging work, and (5) assigning demanding bosses.

Orientation programs are seldom given the attention they deserve. The first few days on the new job can have very strong negative impacts or very strong positive impacts on the new employee. Taking a new job involves not only new job tasks but also new interpersonal relationships. The new employee comes into an ongoing social system that has evolved a unique set of values, ideals, frictions, conflicts, friendships, coalitions, and all the other characteristics of work groups. If left alone, the new employee must cope with the new environment in ignorance, but if given some help and guidance, he or she can cope more effectively.[26]

Thus, the organization should design orientation programs that enable the new employee to meet the rest of the employees as soon as possible. Moreover, specific individuals should be assigned the task of orientation. These individuals should be selected for their social skills and given time off from their own work to spend with the new people. The degree to which the orientation program is formalized will vary, but in any case the program should not be left to chance.

Training programs are invaluable in the breaking-in stage. There is no question that training programs are necessary to instruct new employees in proper techniques and to develop requisite skills. Moreover, effective training programs provide frequent feedback as to progress in acquiring the necessary skills. What is not so obvious is the necessity of integrating the formal training with the orientation program.

Most jobs involve not only the use of technical skills but also the

---

[26] Cynthia D. Fisher, "The Role of Social Support in Organizational Socialization," *Academy of Management Proceedings,* 1983.

use of social skills. Most of us must work with other people to get our work done. But the people whom we have to work with have unique personalities that must be understood. For example, nurses must learn about the personalities and preferences of the physicians with whom they work in order to perform their nursing duties effectively. Yet it takes nurses considerably longer to learn about physicians than it takes them to learn the technical skills of their jobs. Thus, to the extent possible, training programs should include both the technical and the social information required to perform specific jobs.[27] Career development training programs need not be elaborate, as the following organizational Close-Up illustrates.

ORGANIZATIONS: CLOSE-UP

Career Development at the University of Minnesota

William C. Thomas was assistant vice president for administration and personnel at the University of Minnesota. He implemented a career development program in the University of Minnesota personnel department whose primary purpose was to develop people in the jobs they now hold and whose secondary purpose was to prepare these people for advancement to other jobs. The program itself contained no particularly unusual features. Its basic characteristic was the annual discussion between supervisors and employees, at which time career development objectives were mutually agreed on.

However, it is the translation of these objectives into developmental activities that sets this effort apart from other career development programs. The budget of the University of Minnesota contained no provision for employee career development activities. Therefore, any unit wishing to undertake such efforts must come up with the money through cost cutting and increased efficiency. Thomas stressed low-cost techniques such as one-to-one supervisory coaching, internal small group workshops, individual self-help reading courses, training seminars taught by the unit's own employees, and job rotation. The strength of the program was its involvement of the employees in their own developmental activities and the discussion that was annually held between each employee and his or her supervisor. Perhaps as important was the fact that the program demonstrated that career development need not be an expensive fringe benefit, but rather can be undertaken through the combined efforts of both the employees and the organization. The University of Minnesota program therefore put into practice the idea that career devel-

---

[27] B. Kaye, "Career Development Puts Training in Its Place," *Personnel Journal,* February 1983, pp. 132–37.

opment involves benefits to both the individual and the organization and that both should be expected to share in the cost of the program.

Source: W. C. Thomas, "A Career Development Program that Works," *Management Review*, May 1980, pp. 38–40.

Performance evaluation, in the context of socialization, provides important feedback about how well the individual is getting along in the organization. Inaccurate or ambiguous information regarding this important circumstance can only lead to performance problems. To avoid these problems, it is imperative that performance evaluation sessions take place in face-to-face meetings between the individual and manager and that the performance criteria be as objective as possible in the context of the job. Management by objectives and behaviorally anchored rating scales are particularly applicable in these sessions.

Feedback on performance is an important managerial responsibility. Yet many managers are inadequately trained to meet this responsibility. They simply do not know how to evaluate the performance of their subordinates. This management deficiency is especially damaging to new managers. They have not been in the organization long enough to be socialized by their peers and other employees. They are not as yet sure of what they are expected to believe, what values to hold, or what behaviors are expected of them. They naturally look to their own managers to guide them through this early phase. But when their managers fail to evaluate their performance accurately, they remain ignorant and confused as to whether they are achieving what the organization expects of them. The following Close-Up depicts one approach to the integration of performance evaluation and career development.

ORGANIZATIONS: CLOSE-UP

Career Development at Exxon Corporation

The executive succession plan at Exxon Corporation has been developed over the past 30 years. It has produced nearly everyone now on the board of directors and the top 200 executives.

At least once a year, each of Exxon's 50,000 management and professional employees from 13 organizations in 100 countries is assessed by at least four different superiors. According to Frank Gaines, Jr., Exxon's executive development coordinator, the pooling of these judgments results in considerable consistency. Although executive potential is difficult to define, it is evidently easy to recognize.

The heart of the system is a process by which each individual is ranked in order of potential and performance at each managerial level. The rankings are filed on standardized forms that include suggested training, recommended additional experience, and ultimate potential. For example, a particular manager may, as a result of the review, be advised that he or she needs additional training in human relations and experience in an overseas branch and has the potential for reaching the level of director or higher. Also included on the form is the individual's projected career path over the next five years.

The system attempts to take into account the wishes and needs of the individuals themselves. For example, a manager with a child in school may not be amenable to a career move involving geographic relocation. However, it is possible that one with a child in difficulty in the present school system might view a relocation as a means to get the youngster into a new school situation. At present, Exxon has not experienced too many difficulties with the dual-career family. But Gaines expects that problems will arise in the next 10 to 15 years. He predicts that many people will opt to change companies rather than to relocate for career purposes, particularly when the move would create hardships for one of the dual careerists.

Source: *Career Development Bulletin,* Center for Research in Career Development, 2, no. 1 (1980).

Assigning challenging work to new employees is a principal feature of effective socialization programs. The first jobs of new employees often demand far less of them than they are able to deliver. Consequently, they are unable to demonstrate their full capabilities, and in a sense they are being stifled. This is especially damaging if the recruiter was overly enthusiastic in "selling" the organization when they were recruited.

Some individuals are able to *create* challenging jobs even when their assignments are fairly routine. They do this by thinking of ways to do their jobs differently and better. They may also be able to persuade their managers to give them more leeway and more to do. Unfortunately, many recent college graduates are unable to create challenge. Their previous experiences in school were typically experiences in which challenge had been given to them by their teachers. The challenge had been created for them, not *by* them.

Job enrichment is an established practice for motivating employees with strong growth and achievement needs. If the nature of the job to be assigned is not intrinsically challenging, the manager of the newly hired individual can enrich the assignment. The usual ways to enrich a job include giving the new employee more authority and responsibility, permitting the new employee to interact directly with customers and clients, and enabling the new employee to implement his or her own ideas (rather than merely recommending them to the boss).

Assigning demanding bosses is a practice that seems to have considerable promise for increasing the retention rate of new employees. In this context, "demanding" should not be interpreted as "autocratic." Rather, the type of boss most likely to get new hirees off in the right direction is one who has high but achievable expectations for their performance. Such a boss instills the understanding that high performance is expected and rewarded and, equally important, that the boss is always ready to assist through coaching and counselling.

The socialization programs and practices that are intended to retain and develop new employees can be used separately or in combination. A manager would be well advised to establish the policies that would be most likely to retain those recent hirees who have the highest potential to perform effectively. The likelihood of that result is improved if those policies include realistic orientation and training programs, accurate performance evaluation feedback, and challenging initial assignments supervised by supportive, performance-oriented managers. Although such practices are not perfect, they are helpful not only in retaining employees but also in avoiding the problems that may arise during the role management stage of socialization.

Effective Role Management Socialization

Organizations that effectively deal with the conflicts associated with the role management stage recognize the impact of these conflicts on job satisfaction and turnover. Even though motivation and high performance may not be associated with socialization activities, satisfaction and turnover are, and organizations can ill afford to lose capable employees.

The retention of employees beset by off-job conflicts is enhanced in organizations that provide professional counseling services and that schedule and adjust work assignments for those with particularly difficult conflicts at work and home. Of course, these practices do not guarantee that the employees will be able to resolve or even cope with the conflicts. The important point, however, is for the organization to show good faith and to make a sincere effort to adapt to the problems of its employees. Table 18–1 summarizes what managers can do to encourage effective socialization.

TABLE 18–1

A Checklist of Effective Socialization Practices

Socialization Stage	Practices
Anticipatory socialization	1. Recruitment using realistic job previews 2. Selection and placement using realistic career paths
Accommodation socialization	1. Tailor-made and individualized orientation programs 2. Social as well as technical skill training 3. Supportive and accurate feedback 4. Challenging work assignments 5. Demanding, but fair supervisors
Role management socialization	1. Provision of professional counseling 2. Adaptive and flexible work assignments 3. Sincere person-oriented managers

SUMMARY OF KEY POINTS

A. Socialization and career development processes occur in all organizations, and through them the interests of individuals and organizations are identified and confronted. Socialization emphasizes the interests of the organization, while career development emphasizes the interests of the individual. The preferred outcome is integration of organizational and individual interests.

B. Although the popular meaning of career development can include any occupation, vocation, or lifework, in the context of the present discussion career development is restricted to organizational careers. Here we are interested in the careers of individuals who choose to spend their working lives in organizations. A career in this context refers to a sequence of individually perceived attitudes and behaviors associated with organizationally relevant work-related experiences.

C. The dynamics of career choices are but vaguely understood. One of the more influential theories of career choice is that which Holland advances. According to his theory, individuals choose careers that are compatible with their personality types. Moreover, according to the theory, there are definite relationships between certain personality types and occupational characteristics.

D. The concept of career in organizations must be broad enough to include emerging patterns of work and nonwork life. Some of these patterns include the willingness of individuals to trade career experiences for family and personal experiences, a concern for the quality of life in all its facets, and the existence of multiple careers in the same household.

E. Effective careers include the characteristics of performance, attitudes, adaptability, and identity. These characteristics of individual career effectiveness can be related to criteria of organizational effectiveness to the extent that individual and organizational effectiveness criteria are congruent.

F. Most individuals move through their careers in generally predictable patterns. Each career stage involves specific activity, psychological, and behavioral demands. Moreover, the relative importance of specific needs changes as the individual progresses through each stage. For example, the needs of the initial hire are much different from those of the veteran employee. Organizational career development practices must take these differences into account.

G. Organizational socialization processes coincide with the stages of careers. Anticipatory socialization occurs with the prework career stage. Accommodation occurs with the establishment and advancement career stages, and role management occurs with the maintenance stage. The coincidence of socialization and career development stages enables management to implement practices that maximize the chances for achieving the mutual needs of the individual and the organization.

H. The success of organizational socialization depends on how well the socialization activities meet the needs of the individual and the organization at each career stage. Usual organizational practices such as recruitment, selection, placement, promotion, and transfer can be important parts of an effective socialization process if management thinks of them in terms of meeting individual as well as organizational needs.

DISCUSSION AND REVIEW QUESTIONS

1. "Socialization in organizations will occur regardless of what managers do, one way or the other." Comment on this statement.

2. Describe the ways in which socialization and career processes are interrelated.

3. What factors in contemporary society do you think have contributed to the increasing interest in nontraditional career paths?

4. Rank the relative importance of the four characteristics of effective careers from the perspective of the individual and from the perspective of the organization. Explain your rankings.

5. What, in your opinion, is the ethical responsibility of organizations in the area of providing career counseling to employees?

6. Which of the three socialization stages is most important for developing high-performing employees? Explain your answer.

7. What characteristics of the role management stage create difficulties for an organization that desires to help its employees through the stage?

8. Why are leaders and peers considered the most important actors in socialization processes?

9. Based on your own work experience, have managers or peers been more important in socializing you into an organization?

10. If there is validity to the finding that socialization contributes to satisfaction but not to production or efficiency, how can an organization justify expending resources for formal socialization programs?

ADDITIONAL REFERENCES

Badawy, M. K. "Managing Career Transition." *Research Management,* 1983, pp. 28–31.

Bolles, R. *What Color Is Your Parachute? A Practical Manual for Job Hunters and Career Changers.* Rev. ed. Berkeley, Calif: Ten Speed Press, 1977.

Bradford, L. P. "Emotional Problems in Retirement and What Can Be Done." *Group and Organizational Studies,* 1979, pp. 429–39.

Driver, M. "Career Concepts and Career Management in Organizations." In *Behavioral Problems in Organizations,* ed. C. L. Cooper. Englewood Cliffs, N.J.: Prentice-Hall, 1979.

Dugoni, B. L., and D. R. Ilgen. "Realistic Job Previews and the Adjustment of New Employees." *Academy of Management Journal,* 1981, pp. 579–91.

Feldman, D. C. "A Socialization Process That Helps Recruits Succeed." *Personnel,* 1980, pp. 11–23.

Hamner, W. C. *Organizational Shock.* New York: John Wiley & Sons, 1980.

Hunt, J. W. "The Costs of Corporate Dependence: Managers Caught in the Middle." *Managerial Psychology,* 1981, pp. 13–22.

Jelinek, M. "Career Management and Women." *Communication Research and Broadcasting,* 1980, pp. 114–25.

Korman, A. K.; U. Wittig-Berman; and D. Lang. "Career Success and Personal Failure: Alienation in Professionals and Managers." *Academy of Management Journal,* 1981, pp. 342–60.

Kotter, J.; V. Faux; and C. McArthur. *Self-Assessment and Career Development.* Englewood Cliffs, N.J.: Prentice-Hall, 1978.

Lee, Y., and L. Larwood. "The Socialization of Expatriate Managers in Multinational Firms." *Academy of Management Journal,* 1983, pp. 657–65.

Pulakos, E. D., and N. Schmitt. "A Longitudinal Study of a Valence Model Approach for the Prediction of Job Satisfaction of New Employees." *Journal of Applied Psychology,* 1983, pp. 307–12.

Reilly, R. R.; B. Brown; M. Blood; and C. Maletesta. "The Effects of Realistic Job Previews: A Study and Discussion of the Literature." *Personnel Psychology,* 1981, pp. 823–34.

Rhodes, S. R., and M. Doering. "An Integrated Model of Career Motivation." *Academy of Management Review,* 1983, pp. 631–39.

Schein, E. *Career Dynamics: Matching Individual and Organizational Needs.* Reading, Mass.: Addison-Wesley Publishing, 1978.

Sheehy, G. *Passages: Predictable Crises of Adult Life.* New York: E. P. Dutton, 1976.

Sholl, R. W. "Career Lines and Employment Stability." *Academy of Management Journal,* 1983, pp. 86–103.

Skorholt, T. M., and J. I. Morgan. "Career Development: An Outline of Issues for Men." *Personnel and Guidance Journal,* 1981, pp. 231–37.

Sonnenfeld, J., and J. P. Kotter. "The Maturation of Career Theory." *Human Relations,* 1982, pp. 19–46.

Souerwine, A. H. *Career Strategies: Planning for Personal Achievement.* New York: AMACOM, 1978.

Super, D. E., and D. T. Hall. "Career Development: Exploration and Planning." *Annual Review of Psychology,* 1978, pp. 333–72.

Wanous, J. P. *Organizational Entry: Recruitment, Selection and Socialization of Newcomers.* Reading, Mass.: Addison-Wesley Publishing, 1980.

CASE FOR ANALYSIS

Refusing a Promotion

Ron Riddell, 36 years old, is a project manager for the Dowling Products Corporation and has established a reputation as a conscientious, prompt, and creative manager. At present, he is working on a new cleansing product that can be used to clean sink tops. The cleanser is expected to generate gross sales of $3 million the first year it is on the market.

Ron has a permanent team of eight men and three women and a temporary team of two women and two men assigned to him only for the important cleansing product. The team plans, organizes, and controls the various project phases from development to pilot market testing. The team must work closely with engineers, chemists, production managers, sales directors, and marketing research specialists before a quality product can be finally marketed.

In the past eight years, Ron has directed four projects that have been considered outstanding market successes and one that has been considered a "super-loser" financially. His supervisor is Norma Collins, Ph.D., a chemical engineer. Norma has direct responsibility for seven projects, three of which are considerably smaller than Ron's and three of which have about the same potential and size as Ron's.

Norma has recently been selected to be the overseas divisional coordinator of research and development. She and three top executives have met for the past two weeks and have decided to offer Norma's present position to Ron. They believe that the new job for Ron will mean more prestige and authority, and certainly an increase in salary.

Norma has been given the task of offering the position to Ron. This is the discussion that occurs in Norma's office:

Norma: Ron, how is the cleansing project going?

Ron: As good as could be expected. I sometimes think that Joe Rambo is trying to slow down our progress. He is just a "bear" to get along with.

Norma: Well, everyone has been a little concerned because of the main competitor's progress on their cleansing product. I'm sure we can put everything together and effectively compete in the market.

Ron: I know we can.

Norma: I wanted to talk to you about a new job that is becoming vacant in 30 days. The executive selection committee unanimously believes that Ron Riddell is the right person for the job.

Ron: What new job are you talking about?

Norma: My job, Ron. I have been promoted to overseas divisional coordinator of research and development. We want to begin turning over my job to you as soon as possible. If we drag our feet, the cleansing project may not be the success that we need to bolster our financial picture.

Ron: I am flattered by this opportunity and really believe that professionally I can handle the challenge. My real concern is the personal problems I'm having.

Norma: Do you mean personal problems here at Dowling?

Ron: No, I mean problems in my family that have led to sleepless nights, arguments with my wife, and hostility between myself and my best neighbor. My brother Mark has been arrested two times recently, once for vagrancy and once for possession of narcotics. As you know, my dad died four years ago and my mother just can't handle the kid. So I have pitched in and am trying to straighten the kid out. Connie, my wife, is fed up with the time I spend here at work and my meddling into my brother's problems. She has even threatened to leave me and take the kids with her to Denver. The new job is really interesting, but I'm afraid it would be the "straw that breaks the camel's back."

Norma: I'm sorry to hear about these problems, Ron. I know that it is hard to separate outside problems and pressures from Dowling problems and pressures. If you are going to become a more important part of the management team, that separation will be mandatory. The new job is the challenge that we have trained you for and is a reward for your outstanding past performance. Please think over the job offer and let me know in three days. We need your talents, experience, and leadership.

Ron left Norma's office with a sick feeling in his stomach. He had worked hard for years, and the goal he was striving for was within his reach. All he had to do was to say yes to Norma. He thought about the additional money, status, and authority attached to the new job. Then he thought about his wife, who had become more depressed about his working on Saturdays and Sundays; his daughter, whom he really had not talked to for six months; his mother, who had helped pay for his college education; and his brother, who always called and asked him to play golf or shoot pool only to be told, "I have to work, Steve. Sorry."

After thinking over the offer for three days, Ron walks into Norma's office.

Norma: Come on in, Ron, and relax.

Ron: I can't relax, because I am extremely nervous. I really want the job, but my family must come first. My daughter, wife, and mother have helped me get to my present position. I just feel that taking on this new job will lead to so many problems that I must turn it down.

Norma: I sympathize with your dilemma and wish you the best of luck. I want you to understand, however, that this type of opportunity may never happen again. The company needs your talents now. Can't you get your wife and mother to understand the importance of this job in your career? I just can't believe that they would not understand.

Ron: Norma, we all have priorities and personal backgrounds that just can't be ignored.

Norma: Ron, you are sounding like a behavioral scientist. I know that just as well as you. What I'm saying is that you have worked this long and hard and now decide not to accept the challenge. That is what puzzles me.

Questions for Consideration

1. What organizational responsibilities does Norma believe that Ron is shirking by turning down the new job offer?

2. Why would the behavioral orientations of Ron and Norma differ?

3. Do you consider personal needs and problems as more important than organizational needs and problems? Why?

4. Should organizations force an employee like Ron to fit their plans for him? Why?

EXPERIENTIAL EXERCISE

REORIENTING AN EXCELLENT PERFORMER

Objectives

1. To examine the process of reviewing career planning decisions.
2. To illustrate some of the major problems facing individuals involved in the career planning process.

Related Topics

Career planning is related to such organizational behavior topics as goal setting, individual growth, and group development.

Starting the Exercise

Each student should first consider his or her own career and plans for the future. This will set the theme for participating in the exercise.

The Facts

Roger Belhurst is a 50-year-old district sales manager for Rockhurst Corporation. He has been in his present position for 10 years. His superior rates Roger as outstanding in every area in the performance evaluation program. Unfortunately, order cutbacks and the lack of promotion opportunities have kept Roger in his current position. In addition, Roger's superior has stated that "Roger is in a position that uses his skills and abilities optimally." Roger disagrees and believes that he is being put on the shelf and will not be promoted. His present attitudes about the company, his job, and the future are poor.

Exercise Procedures

Phase I: Group analysis: 15 minutes

The instructor will select two groups of five to seven people. Each group will analyze the Roger Belhurst case. The groups should develop a career plan that would result in an improvement in Roger's overall attitudes. Each group will make a five-minute presentation to the class.

Phase II: Evaluation: 15 minutes

A third group of three to five people will serve as evaluators of the analysis presented by the two groups. The evaluators should develop a set of criteria and apply these to the two five-minute presentations. They should then decide which presentation is better. When one group is presenting the solution to Roger's career plan, the second group should not be present in the room.

Phase III: Critique: 20–30 minutes

The entire class should reflect and critique the presentations and the evaluations. During the critique, the following questions should be answered:

a. Why was one group's analysis and career plan better than the other group's?
b. What criteria were used by the evaluators to rate the two group presentations?
c. What would be Roger's reaction to the career plan?

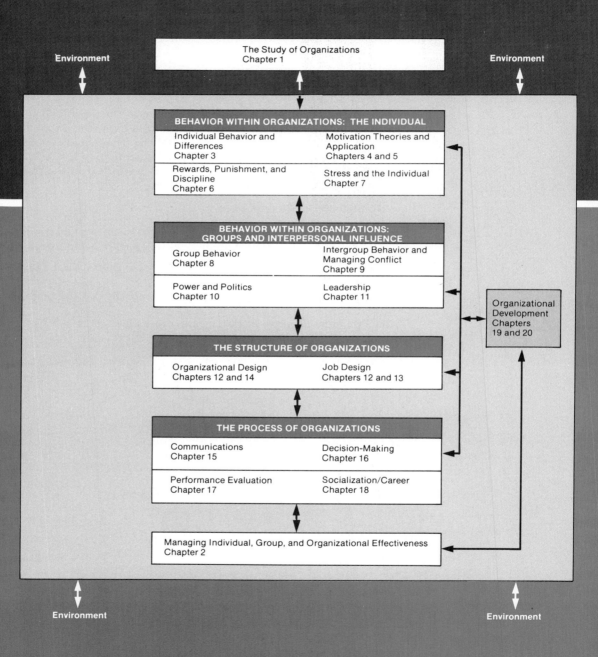

DEVELOPING ORGANIZATIONAL EFFECTIVENESS

PART SIX

Chapter 19

LEARNING OBJECTIVES

After completing Chapter 19, you should be able to:

Define the concept of organizational development.

Describe the distinguishing characteristics of organizational development presented in Figure 19–1.

Discuss alternative strategies for managing organizational development.

Compare the alternative organizational development techniques.

Identify the role of the change agent in organizational development.

Organizational Development: Improving Performance

External Change Agents Are Necessary for Successful OD

Argument For

Successful instances of organizational development (OD) are always (or at least usually) the result of intervention by a person or group external to the organization itself. The rationale for this position is that external persons are not caught up in the day-to-day operations of the organization and are able to see problems and causes of problems more clearly than those who must work within it. The change agent is able to see the problems because he or she is neutral and impartial, having no vested interest or personal stake in the organization. Managers and staff personnel already in the organization are unable to see the problems clearly, and indeed may be part of them.

Moreover, so the argument goes, only external change agents are able to undertake the necessary steps that bring about development. They alone are able to present unbiased information that indicates the necessity of changing attitudes and behaviors. Through attitude defreezing and refreezing, successful organizational development occurs. But managers whose attitudes require change cannot themselves be the catalyst for changing the attitudes of others.

Support for this position is to be found in research studies and case histories. One researcher documented the differences to be found in the strategies associated with successful versus unsuccessful OD efforts. He concluded that successful OD strategy was invariably associated with the use of an external change agent.

Argument Against

The "argument against" is based on the idea that organizational development efforts vary from company to company. In some instances, the developmental effort may involve nothing more than changes in job descriptions and departmental bases. In other instances, that effort may involve fundamental changes in personal and interpersonal variables. Thus, the necessity for an external change agent depends upon the magnitude of the intended change.

Alternatives to the exclusive use of external change agents include establishing a corporate-level organization-development department, hiring an OD specialist, training a member of the personnel department, and assigning OD responsibility to the management-development department. Each of these alternatives has advantages and disadvantages. Although the existence of internal change agents does not preclude the use of external change agents, it provides reasonable alternatives to the exclusive use of external parties.

The process by which managers sense and respond to the necessity for change has been the focus of much research and practical attention in recent years. If managers were able to design perfect sociotechnical organizations and if the scientific, market, and technical environments were stable and predictable, there would be no pressure for change. But such is not the case. The statement that "we live in the midst of constant change" has become a well-worn but relevant cliché. Of course, the need for change affects organizations differently; those that operate in relatively certain environments need to be less concerned with change than those that operate in less certain environments. But even managers in certain environments must continually combat the problems of complacency. Apparently, complacency is such a problem in some organizatio s that external "change agents" are often brought in from outside the organization to initiate change efforts. This point of view is expressed in the opening Organizational Issue for Debate.

The literature and practice that deal with the process of organizational change cannot be conveniently classified because of the yet unsettled nature of this aspect of organizational behavior. Various conceptualizations and theories and their meanings and interpretations are subject to considerable disagreement.[1] The current trend is to use the term **organizational development** (OD) to refer to the process of preparing for and managing change. Since we will use the term in this and the next chapter, it is important that we clarify our meaning and interpretation.

In its most restrictive usage, OD refers to *sensitivity* training.[2] In this context, OD stresses the process by which people in organizations become more aware of themselves and others. The emphasis is on the psychological states of employees that inhibit their ability to communicate and interact with other members of the organization. The assumption is that organizational effectiveness can be increased if people can engage in honest and open discussion of issues. We will have more to say about sensitivity training in the following chapter.

A slightly more encompassing definition of OD states:

> Using knowledge and techniques from the behavioral sciences, organizational development is a process which attempts to increase organizational effectiveness by integrating individual desires for growth and de-

organizational development
Most managers must live in a world of change. Organizational development helps managers prepare for and manage change.

---

[1] For an insightful recent discussion, see James G. March, "Footnotes to Organizational Change," *Administrative Science Quarterly,* December 1981, pp. 563–77.

[2] For a discussion of the history of organizational development, see Wendell L. French, "The Emergence and Early History of Organization Development: With Reference to Influences on and Interaction among Some of the Key Actors," *Group and Organizational Studies,* September, 1982, pp. 261–78.

velopment with organizational goals. Typically, this process is a planned change effort which involves a total system over a period of time, and these change efforts are related to the organization's mission.[3]

This definition acknowledges the existence of methods other than sensitivity training. For example, participative management, job enrichment, management by objectives, and the managerial grid are some alternative methods for integrating individual and organizational objectives. The definition also acknowledges the fact that OD is a planned process over time that must be justified in terms of organizational effectiveness. The definition, however, is still incomplete for our purposes.

The concept of OD must be broad enough to include not only the behavioral approach but others as well. The following definition identifies all the significant aspects of OD:

> The term "Organizational development" . . . implies a normative, reeducation strategy intended to affect systems of beliefs, values, and attitudes within the organization so that it can adapt better to the accelerated rate of change in technology, in our industrial environment and society in general. It also includes formal organizational restructuring which is frequently initiated, facilitated and reinforced by the normative and behavioral changes.[4]

The three subobjectives of OD are "changing attitudes or values, modifying behavior, and inducing change in structure and policy."[5] However, it is conceivable that the OD strategy might well emphasize one or another of these subobjectives. For example, if the structure of an organization is optimal in management's view, the OD process might attempt to educate personnel to adopt behaviors consistent with that structure. Such would be the case for leadership training in participative management in an organization that already has an organic structure.

Moreover, the concept of OD must include the possibility of programs aimed at providing personnel with technical skills. It is entirely possible that effective change is not forthcoming simply because people in the organization do not have the technical skills needed to cope

---

[3] W. Warren Burke and Warren H. Schmidt, "Management and Organizational Development," *Personnel Administration,* March 1971, p. 45. Also see Alan Sheldon, "Organizational Paradigms: A Theory of Organizational Change," *Organizational Dynamics,* Winter 1980, pp. 61–80.

[4] Alexander Winn, "The Laboratory Approach to Organizational Development: A Tentative Model of Planned Change," paper read at the annual conference, British Psychological Society, Oxford, September 1968, and cited in Robert T. Golembiewski, "Organizational Development in Public Agencies: Perspectives on Theory and Practice," *Public Administration Review,* July–August 1969, p. 367.

[5] Ibid., p. 367.

with it. Management may determine that attitudes, behavior, and structure are appropriate, yet the organization cannot respond to change because key personnel simply do not have the skills needed to respond. The skill training programs of industry and government are important application of OD.

Organizational development, as the term is used in contemporary management practice, has certain distinguishing characteristics:

1. *It is planned.* OD is a data-based approach to change that involves all of the ingredients that go into managerial planning. It involves goal setting, action planning, implementation, monitoring, and taking corrective action when necessary.
2. *It is problem-oriented.* OD attempts to apply theory and research from a number of disciplines, including behavioral science, to the solution of organizational problems.
3. *It reflects a systems approach.* OD is both systemic and systematic. It is a way of more closely linking the human resources and potential of an organization to its technology, structure, and management processes.
4. *It is an integral part of the management process.* OD is not something that is done to the organization by outsiders. It becomes a way of managing organizational change processes.
5. *It is not a "fix-it" strategy.* OD is a continuous and ongoing process. It is not a series of ad hoc activities designed to implement a specific change. It takes time for OD to become a way of life in the organization.
6. *It focuses on improvement.* The emphasis of OD is on improvement. It is not just for "sick" organizations or for "healthy" ones. It is something that can benefit almost any organization.
7. *It is action-oriented.* The focus of OD is on accomplishments and results. Unlike approaches to change that tend to describe how organizational change takes place, the emphasis of OD is on getting things done.
8. *It is based on sound theory and practice.* OD is not a gimmick or a fad. It is solidly based on the theory and research of a number of disciplines.[6]

These characteristics of contemporary organizational development indicate that managers who implement OD programs are committed to making fundamental changes in organizational behavior. The following Close-Up illustrates one company's commitment to organizational development.

---

[6] Newton Margulies and Anthony P. Raia, *Conceptual Foundations of Organizational Development* (New York: McGraw-Hill, 1978), p. 25.

ORGANIZATIONS: CLOSE-UP

Organizational Development at B. F. Goodrich

Roger J. Howe, Mark G. Mindell, and Donna L. Simmons were members of the organizational development staff of the B. F. Goodrich Tire and Rubber Company, a major multinational corporation. They represent B. F. Goodrich's commitment to implement permanent and ongoing organizational development efforts in the corporation. That commitment to ongoing organizational development is reflected in its statement of operating principles, a public statement that directs management in the development of strategic plans. The statement includes the following: "The company will stress the technology of management and organization development, with specific focus on interpersonal relationships among individuals and business groups."

The program at B. F. Goodrich involved training some 60 individuals in the process and methods of organizational development. These individuals are then located throughout the organization, in both line and staff departments. Their primary function is to assist the managers of the departments in the diagnosis and identification of organizational development needs. The basic idea is that internal people will have a better chance of gaining acceptance for OD efforts and will also be able to diagnose problems in terms that are consistent with the problems of the specific manager and the department. At B. F. Goodrich, organizational development is an integral part of the company's practices and policies. It represents not only a commitment to the development of individuals and groups but also the recognition that a major internal innovation requires much the same commitment as a new product innovation. The OD program at B. F. Goodrich enables the line manager to call on the OD personnel whenever a new process or policy is to be introduced that will affect the way in which individuals or groups perform their assigned tasks.

Source: Roger J. Howe, Mark G. Mindell, and Donna L. Simmons, "Introducing Innovation through OD," *Management Review* February 1978, pp. 52–56.

LEARNING PRINCIPLES IN THE CONTEXT OF OD PROGRAMS

To better understand how changes are brought about in individuals, it is essential to comprehend the various principles of learning discussed in Chapter 5. Managers can design a theoretically sound OD program and not achieve any of the anticipated results because they overlooked the importance of providing reinforcement or continuous feedback to employees. These are principles of learning, and they should be tailored to the needs of the group that is affected by the OD program.

Expectations and Motivations

People must want to learn. They may need more skill in a particular job or more understanding of the problems of other units of the firm. Some people recognize this need and are receptive to experiences that will aid them in developing new skills or new empathies. Others reject the need or play it down, because learning is to them an admission that they are not completely competent in their jobs. These kinds of people face the prospect of change with different expectations and motivations. Determining the expectations and motivations of people is not an easy task. It is, however, a task that must be undertaken. The point to remember is that not everyone wants to participate in a change program and that it is management's responsibility to show employees why they should want to change.

Reinforcement and Feedback

An important principle of learning is that of reinforcement. This principle suggests that when people receive positive rewards, information, or feelings for doing something, it becomes more likely that they will do the same thing in the same or a similar situation.[7] The other side of the coin involves the impact of punishment for a particular response. It is assumed that punishment will decrease the probability of doing the same thing at another time. The principle, then, implies that it would be easier to achieve successful change through the use of positive rewards. Reinforcement can also occur when the knowledge or skill acquired in a training program is reimparted through a refresher course.

A major problem associated with reinforcement is the determination of reinforcers. That is, what will serve as the appropriate reinforcer of desired behavior? Money or praise is an effective reinforcer for some people, while others are more responsive to a refresher type of training experience. Once again, situations and individuals determine what means of reinforcement will prove effective. Employees generally desire knowledge on how they are doing. This is especially true after a change program has been implemented. Providing information about

---

[7] See B. F. Skinner, *About Behaviorism* (New York: Alfred A. Knopf, 1974).

the progress of a unit or a group of employees lets the employees take corrective action. A number of studies indicate that employees perform more effectively on a variety of tasks when they have feedback than when it is absent.[8] The timing of feedback is a factor that should be considered. Most college students want to know their course grade as soon as possible after the final examination. The same need to know exists for managers who have set their objectives for the next year. They want to know immediately whether their objectives are acceptable. Thus, the immediacy of feedback is an issue to consider. Providing feedback a long time after an action has occurred will probably not be as effective as providing feedback immediately after the action. As one might anticipate, individuals differ in their receptivity to feedback concerning their actions. In general, it is more favorably received by employees who are motivated to improve themselves or their unit.

Management must guard against the possibility that what a person has learned at a training site is lost when that person is transferred to the actual work site. If things have gone well, only a minimum amount will be lost in this necessary transfer. A possible strategy for keeping the loss to a minimum is to make the training situation similar to the actual workplace environment. Another strategy is to reward the newly learned behavior. If the colleagues and superiors of newly trained people approve new ideas or new skills, these people will be encouraged to continue to behave in the new way. If colleagues and superiors behave negatively, the newly trained people will be discouraged from persisting with attempts to use what they have learned. This is one of the reasons why it has been suggested that superiors be trained before subordinates. The superior, if trained and motivated, can serve as a reinforcer and feedback source for the subordinate who has left the training confines and is now back on the job.

There are numerous other principles of learning that will prove invaluable when attempting to manage OD programs. Those noted above, however, are principles that are currently being discussed in the OD literature. The manager who fails to consider them when introducing an OD program will have a difficult time in improving organizational effectiveness.

An OD program must be designed systematically. This argues for an analytical approach that breaks down the OD process into constituent steps, logically sequenced. For this purpose, a model is proposed that identifies the key elements and decision points that managers can follow. This model is described in the next section, and the remainder of this chapter elaborates on each of the steps in the model.

---

[8] Victor H. Vroom and Philip Yelton, *Leadership and Decision Making* (Pittsburgh: University of Pittsburgh Press, 1973).

FIGURE 19–1

A Model for the Management of Organizational Development

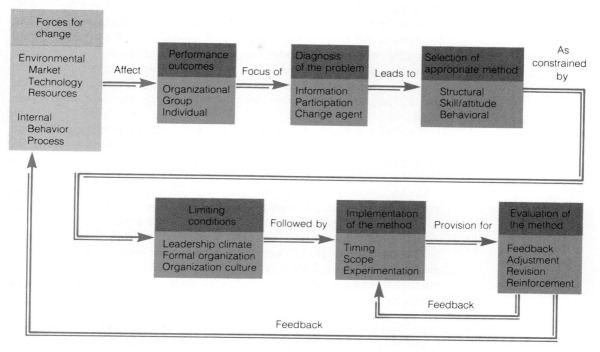

A MODEL FOR MANAGING ORGANIZATIONAL DEVELOPMENT

The model that we propose is described in Figure 19–1 and consists of eight steps that are linked in a logical sequence. A manager considers each of them, either explicitly or implicitly, to undertake an OD program. The prospects of initiating successful change can be enhanced when the manager explicitly and formally goes through each successive step.[9]

The model presumes that forces for change continually act on the organization; this assumption reflects the dynamic character of the modern world. At the same time, it is the manager's responsibility to sort out the information that reflects the magnitude of change

---

[9] Equivalent models for managing organizational development are discussed in Eric L. Herzog, "Improving Productivity via Organizational Development," *Training and Development Journal*, April 1980, pp. 36–39; and Roland L. Warren, *Social Change and Human Purpose: Toward Understanding and Action* (Skoku, Ill.: Rand McNally, 1977).

forces.[10] The information is the basis for recognizing when change is needed; it is equally desirable to recognize when change is not needed. But once managers recognize that something is malfunctioning, they must diagnose the problem and identify relevant alternative techniques. The selected technique must be appropriate to the problem, as constrained by limiting conditions. One example of a limiting condition that we have discussed in an earlier chapter is the prevailing character of group norms. The informal groups may support some change techniques but may sabotage others. Other limiting conditions include leadership behavior, legal requirements, and economic conditions.

Finally, the manager must implement the change and monitor the change process and change results. The model includes feedback to the implementation step and to the forces for change step. These feedback loops suggest that the change process itself must be monitored and evaluated. The mode of implementation may be faulty and may lead to poor results, but responsive action could correct the situation. Moreover, the feedback loop to the initial step recognizes that no change is final. A new situation is created within which problems and issues will emerge; a new setting is created that will itself become subject to change. The model suggests no "final solution"; rather, it emphasizes that the modern manager operates in a dynamic setting wherein the only certainty is change itself.

FORCES FOR CHANGE

The forces for change can be classified conveniently into two groups. They are: (1) environmental forces and (2) internal forces. **Environmental forces** are beyond the control of management. Internal forces operate inside the firm and are generally within the control of management.

environmental forces
Environmental forces for change include marketplace actions, technological changes, and social and political changes.

Environmental Forces

The manager of a business firm has historically been concerned with reacting to changes in the *marketplace*. Competitors introduce new products, increase their advertising, reduce their prices, or increase their customer service. In each case, a response is required unless the manager is content to permit the erosion of profit and market share. At the same time, changes occur in customer tastes and incomes. The firm's products may no longer have customer appeal;

---

[10] Sara Kiesler and Lee Sproull, "Managerial Response to Changing Environments: Perspectives on Problem Solving from Social Cognition," *Administrative Science Quarterly*, December 1982, pp. 548–70.

customers may be able to purchase less expensive, higher quality forms of the same products.

The enterprise system generally eliminates from the economic scene those firms that do not adjust to market conditions. The isolated-from-reality manager who ignores the signals from the market will soon confront the more vocal (and louder) signals of discontented stockholders. By that time, however, the appropriate change may well be dissolution of the firm—the final solution.

Suppliers of the organization's resources are another market force to be dealt with. A change in the quality and quantity of human resources can dictate changes in the firm. For example, the adoption of automated processes can be stimulated by a decline in the supply of labor. The techniques of coal mining and tobacco farming have greatly changed during recent years due to labor shortages. Changes in the supply of materials can cause the firm to substitute one material for another. Rayon stockings and synthetic rubber tires were direct outgrowths of war-induced shortages in raw materials. We need not catalog the whole range of possible changes in the resource markets that stimulate organizational change. The potential is great, however, and it must be recognized.

The second source of environmental change forces is *technology*. The knowledge explosion has introduced new technology for nearly every business function. Computers have made possible high-speed data processing and the solution to complex production problems. New machines and new processes have revolutionized the way in which many products are manufactured and distributed. Computer technology and automation have affected not only the technical conditions of work, but the social conditions as well. New occupations have been created, and others have been eliminated. Slowness to adopt new technology that reduces costs and improves quality will show up in the financial statements sooner or later. Technological advance is a permanent fixture in the business world, and as a force for change it will continue to demand attention.

The third source of environmental change forces is *social* and *political* change. Business managers must be "tuned in" to the great movements over which they have no control but which, in time, influence their firm's fate. Sophisticated mass communications and international markets create great potential for business, but they also pose great threats to those managers who are unable to understand what is going on. Finally, the relationship between government and business becomes much closer as new regulations are imposed. These pressures for change reflect the increasing complexity and interdependence of modern living. The traditional functions of organizations are being questioned, and new objectives are being advanced. No doubt, the events of the future will intensify external environmental forces for change. The following Close-Up illustrates some impacts of external environmental forces on the rapidly changing banking industry.

ORGANIZATIONS: CLOSE-UP

The Impact of Environmental Forces on the Banking Industry

As the banking industry enters an age of rapid changes, banks must help employees deal with their opportunities and plans, according to Diane H. Frank, senior vice president for human resources at the First Interstate Bank of California, Los Angeles. Frank believes that deregulation, new services, bank acquisitions, and new competition will contribute to change and feelings of uncertainty for many employees.

"We have employees hired 25 years ago who will be facing forced retraining," Frank said. These employees as well as their managers and their banks will be facing some very dramatic changes. "For example, my own bank recently acquired a small bank in a very small town in Texas," Frank said. "Those people probably never thought they'd be affected by all this, but here they are, owned by a big bank in California."

Source: "Personnel Divisions and Coming of Age," *American Banker*, September 16, 1983, p. 3.

internal forces
Internal forces for change can usually be traced to behavioral problems, such as absenteeism, and to turnover or process problems, such as breakdowns in communication and decision making and interpersonal and interdepartmental conflicts.

To cope effectively with external changes, an organization's boundary functions must be sensitive to these changes. These boundary functions must bridge the external environment with units of the organization.[11] *Boundary roles* such as marketing research, labor relations, personnel recruiting, purchasing, and some areas of finance must sense changes in the external environment and convey information on these changes to managers.

Internal Forces

Internal forces for change, which occur within the organization, can usually be traced to *process* and *behavioral* problems. The process problems include breakdowns in decision making and communications. Decisions are not being made, are made too late, or are of poor quality.

---

[11] For a recent related study, see David F. Caldwell and Charles A. O'Reilly III, "Boundary Spanning and Individual Performance: The Impact of Self-Monitoring," *Journal of Applied Psychology*, February 1982, pp. 124–27.

Communications are short-circuited, redundant, or simply inadequate. Tasks are not undertaken or not completed because the person responsible did not "get the word." Because of inadequate or nonexistent communications, a customer order is not filled, a grievance is not processed, or an invoice is not filed and the supplier is not paid. Interpersonal and interdepartmental conflicts reflect breakdowns in organizational processes.

Low levels of morale and high levels of absenteeism and turnover are symptoms of behavioral problems that must be diagnosed. A wildcat strike or a walkout may be the most tangible sign of a problem, yet such tactics are usually employed because they arouse management to action. A certain level of employee discontent exists in most organizations, and a great danger is to ignore employee complaints and suggestions. But the process of change includes the *recognition* phase, and it is at this point that management must decide to act or not to act.

In many organizations, the need for change goes unrecognized until some major catastrophe occurs. The employees strike or seek the recognition of a union before the management finally recognizes the need for action. Whether it takes a whisper or a shout, the need for change must be recognized by some means; and once that need has been recognized, the exact nature of the problem must be diagnosed. If the problem is not properly understood, the impact of change on people can be extremely negative, as illustrated in the following Close-Up.

ORGANIZATIONS: CLOSE-UP

Organizational Change and Its Human Impact in the Banking Industry

By 1990, 5,400 banks and 2,500 savings and loan associations are expected to be involved in mergers. As a result, the lives of nearly 822,000 people will change. Many people believe that bankers have built up their financial, strategic, and legal planning to deal effectively with the coming wave of merger activity but that the human side of change has been ignored.

Betty Wishard, a former banker who is now a consultant to banks on organizational development, believes that to understand the dynamics of a merger, it is essential to view how this change affects people—individually and organizationally. Wishard believes that change in any form represents a loss. A merger is a major life change in which the loss is multiplied—personally, socially, and professionally. Overnight, employees lose self-worth and intangible values that come from identity with a company.

According to Wishard, takeover shock turns into a bitter struggle for survival. People on both sides of a takeover try to define what is going to happen and where they fit in as key executives leave and power bases are realigned. Teamwork breaks down.

What was once a collaborative effort now becomes a question of "sides." This is complicated by the fact that often mergers are not a clean absorption of one organization into another but a "trade-off" of strengths, structures, systems, people, resources, and culture.

Uncertainty spawns a "who will go next" attitude. Friendships with people laid off or displaced become the reason for indulging in pettiness and interdepartmental conflict. Morale declines. Performance plummets as sickness, tardiness, and absenteeism rise. Productivity declines as employees lose interest and involvement and avoid risks. Wishard believes that management sensitivity to these "people" aspects of organizational change is crucial if mergers are to be effected smoothly and without an exodus of key employees.

Source: Betty Wishard, "In Mergers, Remember that the Human Element Is Vital," *American Banker,* September 16, 1983, pp. 4, 15, 16.

DIAGNOSIS OF A PROBLEM

Appropriate action is necessarily preceded by diagnosis of the symptoms of the problem. Experience and judgment are critical to this phase unless the problem is readily apparent to all observers. Ordinarily, however, managers can disagree on the nature of the problem. There is no formula for accurate diagnosis, but the following questions point the manager in the right direction:

1. What is the problem as distinct from the symptoms of the problem?
2. What must be changed to resolve the problem?
3. What outcomes (objectives) are expected from the change, and how will those outcomes be measured?

The answers to these questions can come from information ordinarily found in the organization's information system. Or it may be necessary to generate ad hoc information through the creation of committees or task forces. Meetings between managers and employees provide a variety of viewpoints that can be sifted through by a smaller group. Technical operational problems may be easily diagnosed, but more subtle behavioral problems usually entail extensive analysis. One approach for diagnosing such problems is the attitude survey.

Attitude surveys can be administered to the entire work force or to a representative sample. The attitude survey permits the respondents to evaluate and rate management, pay and pay-related items, working conditions, equipment, and other job-related factors. The appropriate use of such a survey requires that the questionnaire be completed anonymously so that employees can express their views freely and without threat, whether real or imagined. The objective of the survey is to pinpoint the problem or problems as perceived by the members of the organization. Subsequent discussions of the survey results, at all levels of the organization, can add further insights into the nature of the problem.[12]

The survey is a useful diagnostic approach if the potential focus of change is the total organization. If smaller units or entities are the focus of change, the survey technique may not be a reliable source of information. For example, if the focus of change is a relatively small work group, diagnosis of the problem is better accomplished through individual interviews followed by group discussion of the interview data. In this approach, the group becomes actively involved in sharing and interpreting perception of problems.

Identification of the problems of individual employees comes about through interviews and personnel department information. Consistently low performance evaluations are indicators that such problems exist, but it is often necessary to go into greater detail. Identification of individuals' problems is far more difficult than identification of organizational problems. Thus, the diagnostic process must stress the use of precise and reliable information.

Managers must make two key decisions prior to undertaking the diagnostic phase. They must determine the degree to which subordinates will participate in the process, and they must decide whether a change agent will be used. These two decisions have implications not only for the diagnosed process but also for the eventual success of the entire program.

The Degree of Subordinate Participation

The degree to which subordinates participate in decisions that affect their activities has been the subject of much practical and theoretical discussion. Fayol, for example, spoke of the principle of centralization in terms of the extent to which subordinates contribute to decision making. The researchers at the Hawthorne plant discovered the positive impact of supervisory styles that permit employees some say in the way they do their work. In fact, the Hawthorne studies produced

---

[12] Ernest C. Miller, "Attitude Surveys: A Diagnostic Tool," *Personnel*, May–June 1978, pp. 4–10.

the first scientific evidence of the relationship between employee participation and production. Other studies followed, including the classic Coch and French[13] and Lewin[14] research, which provided evidence that participation by subordinates could lead to higher levels of production, satisfaction, and efficiency.

Despite the considerable research, many unanswered questions remain regarding the relationships between subordinate participation, production, and acceptance of change. Moreover, whether actual participation or perceived participation is the more important factor bearing on organizational effectiveness has not yet been completely settled. It may be that not all subordinates aspire to participate but that all subordinates do desire the *opportunity* to do so when the occasion arises.[15] Nevertheless, the tendency in much of the current literature on development methods and strategies is to take the position that active participation is a requirement for successful OD programs. This position is much more a matter of espousing a set of values than a matter of scientific evidence.

Changing Values. The values held by those who espouse participative management are reflected in Table 19–1. These values are in transition and though not completely accepted in managerial practice, they are being adopted by ever-increasing numbers of managers. These values reflect the growing importance of the humanistic point of view. One can see that important implications follow if the new set of values is adopted, that is, if one accepts the idea that subordinates are basically good, with untapped abilities that can be used in active problem solving for the organization's benefit, subordinates will be actively involved in the development program from its very inception.

The *degree* to which subordinates are actively involved in the development program can be constrained by situational factors. But the strategic decision regarding subordinate participation is not simply an either-or decision. A continuum more aptly describes the decision, as shown in Figure 19–2. The figure identifies two extreme positions (unilateral and delegated) and a middle-of-the-road approach (shared) to change.[16]

---

[13] Lester Coch and John R. P. French, Jr., "Overcoming Resistance to Change," *Human Relations,* August 1948, pp. 512–32.

[14] Kurt Lewin, "Frontiers in Group Dynamics," *Human Relations,* June 1947, pp. 5–41.

[15] See T. O. Jacobs, *Leadership and Exchange in Formal Organizations* (Alexandria, Va.: Human Resources Research Organization, 1971), pp. 204–9, for a review of research bearing on this issue. For a recent study, see Aaron J. Nurick, "Participation in Organizational Change: A Longitudinal Field Study," *Human Relations,* May 1982, pp. 413–29.

[16] Larry E. Greiner, "Patterns of Organization Change," *Harvard Business Review,* May–June 1967, pp. 119–30.

TABLE 19–1

The Transition of Values Underlying OD Strategy

Away from:	*Toward:*
1. A view of man as essentially bad.	1. A view of man as basically good.
2. Avoidance or negative evaluation of individuals.	2. Confirming them as human beings.
3. A view of individuals as fixed.	3. Seeing them as being in process.
4. Resisting and fearing individual differences.	4. Accepting and utilizing them.
5. Utilizing an individual primarily with reference to his or her job description.	5. Viewing him or her as a whole person.
6. Walling off the expression of feelings.	6. Making possible both appropriate expression and its effective use.
7. Maskmanship and game-playing.	7. Authentic behavior.
8. Use of status for maintaining power and personal prestige.	8. Use of status for organizationally relevant purposes.
9. Distrusting people.	9. Trusting them.
10. Avoidance of facing others with relevant data.	10. Making appropriate confrontation.
11. Avoidance of risk taking.	11. Willingness to risk.
12. A view of process work as being unproductive effort.	12. Seeing it as essential to effective task accomplishment.
13. A primary emphasis on competition.	13. Much greater emphasis on collaboration.

unilateral
The unilateral approach for introducing change does not allow for participation by subordinates. Management identifies the problem and proposes the solution.

Unilateral Approach.   At one extreme, subordinates make no contribution to the development, or change, program. The definition and solution to the problem are proposed by management. The use of **unilateral** authority can appear in three forms:

1. *By decree.* This a simply a situation in which the superior dictates a program. There is little upward communication, and subordinates are expected to accept the program without asking questions. This form assumes that subordinates will accept the program be-

FIGURE 19–2

Strategies for Introducing Major and/or Minor Changes

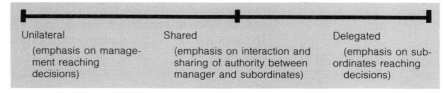

Unilateral	Shared	Delegated
(emphasis on management reaching decisions)	(emphasis on interaction and sharing of authority between manager and subordinates)	(emphasis on subordinates reaching decisions)

cause it is being stated by authority figure that they deal with—
the "boss."

2. *By replacement.* This form involves the replacement of personnel
and is based on the premise that key personnel are the crucial
factors in developing the organization. The replacement decision
is a top-down decision since top-level executives develop the plan
for replacing personnel.

3. *By structure.* This form attempts to alter the organizational structure by administrative fiat. An example is when a manager's span
of control is increased or decreased.

Delegated Approach.   At the other extreme from the unilateral approach is the **delegated** approach. In this approach, the subordinates
actively participate in the development program, in one of two forms:[17]

delegated
The delegated
approach for
introducing change
allows subordinates
to actively
participate in the
change effort.

1. *The discussion group.* Managers and their subordinates meet, discuss the problem, and identify the appropriate development
method. The managers refrain from imposing their own solution
upon the group. The assumption of this approach is that two-way
discussion and problem solving among subordinates and managers
result in more motivated groups.

2. *The T-group.* The emphasis of the T-group is on increasing the
individual's self-awareness. The T-group is less structured than
the discussion group, but in this context the T-group is designed
to initiate the development program and it is not the central focus.
For example, the T-group could identify MBO as the development
method to be implemented.

The delegated approach focuses on having the subordinates interact
with the superior and eventually work out a development approach.
If used correctly, it is a major step in creating a climate of full subordinate participation.

shared
The shared approach
for introducing
change focuses on the
sharing of decision-
making authority
between managers
and subordinates.

Shared Approach.   The **shared** approach is built on the assumption
that authority is present in the organization and must be exercised
after, and only after, giving careful consideration to such matters as
the magnitude of the development effort, the people involved, and
the time available for introducing the method. This approach also
focuses on the sharing of authority to make decisions. It is employed
in two slightly different formats:

1. *Group decision making.* The problem is defined by management
and communicated to the subordinates. The subordinates are then
free to develop alternative solutions and to select what they believe
is the best method to be implemented. It is assumed that the subor-

---

[17] Ibid., pp. 121–22.

dinates will feel a greater commitment to the solution selected because they participated in its selection.

2. *Group problem solving.* This form stresses both the definition of the problem and the selection of a possible solution. Here authority is shared throughout the process, from problem identification to problem solution. It is assumed that because the group is involved in the entire decision process, it will have increased insight into the development program that is finally implemented.

A survey of published cases of organizational change notes that the shared approach was relatively more successful than the unilateral or delegated approaches.[18]

The Shared Approach: Some Preconditions. Before the shared strategy can be successful, certain preconditions with respect to the employees must exist. They are:

1. An intuitively obvious factor is that the employees must want to become involved. They may, for any number of reasons, reject the invitation to participate. For example, they may have other needs, such as getting on with their own work. Or they may view the invitation as a subtle (but not too subtle) attempt by managers to manipulate them toward a predetermined solution. If the organizational culture encourages perceptions of mistrust and insincerity, any attempt to involve the employees will be viewed by them in cynical terms.

2. The employees must be willing and able to voice their ideas. In addition, they must have some expertise in some aspect of the analysis. Certainly, the technical problems associated with a computer installation or automated manufacturing processes are beyond the training of typical employees, yet they may have valuable insights into the impact of such equipment on their jobs.

3. The managers must feel secure in their positions. If they feel insecure, then they will perceive any participation by employees as a threat to their authority. They may view employee participation as indicating weakness or as undermining their status. They must be able to give credit for good ideas and to explain why other ideas are of questionable merit. As is evident, the managers' personalities and leadership styles must be compatible with the shared authority approach if it is to be a successful strategy.

4. Finally, the managers must be open-minded to employees' suggestions. If the managers have predetermined the solution, the participation by employees will soon be recognized for what it is. Certainly, the managers have the final responsibility for the outcome, but they can control the situation by specifying beforehand the latitude of the

---

[18] Ibid., pp. 119–30.

employees. They may define objectives, establish constraints, or whatever, so long as the participants know what is expected of them.

Successful organizational development strategies emphasize sharing authority among managers and employees. The shared approach involves the personnel in a process that not only minimizes resistance to change but also maximizes acceptance through the application of basic learning principles.

The Role of Change Agents

change agent
A change agent brings an outsider's perspective to the organization's change situation. The change agent may be from outside the organization (external change agent) or may be employed in some other part of the organization (internal change agent). Combination teams of external and internal change agents are also used.

Because there is a tendency to seek answers in traditional solutions, the intervention of an outsider is usually necessary. The intervener, or **change agent,** brings a different perspective to the situation and serves as a challenge to the status quo.

The success of any change program rests heavily on the quality and workability of the relationship between the change agent and the key decision makers within the organization. Thus, the form of intervention is a crucial phase.

To intervene is to enter into an ongoing organization, or among persons, or between departments, for the purpose of helping them improve their effectiveness.[19] A number of forms of intervention are used in organizations. First, there is the *external* change agent who is asked to intervene and provide recommendations for bringing about change. As we saw in the chapter-opening Organizational Issue for Debate, there is considerable disagreement over both the necessity and the effectiveness of external change agents. Second, there is the *internal* change agent. This is an individual who is working for the organization and knows something about its problems. Finally, a number of organizations have used a combination *external-internal* change team to intervene and develop programs. This approach attempts to use the resources and knowledge base of both external and internal change agents.

Each of the three forms of intervention has advantages and disadvantages. The external change agent is often viewed as an outsider. When this belief is held by employees inside the company, there is a need to establish rapport between the change agent and decision makers. The change agent's views on the problems faced by the organization are often different from the decision maker's views, and this leads to problems in establishing rapport. The differences in viewpoints often result in a mistrust of the external change agent by the policymakers or a segment of the policymakers.

---

[19] See Chris Argyris, *Intervention Theory and Method* (Reading, Mass.: Addison-Wesley Publishing, 1970); and Fritz Steele, *Consulting for Organizational Change* (Amherst: University of Massachusetts Press, 1975).

The internal change agent is often viewed as being more closely associated with one unit or group of individuals than with any other. This perceived favoritism leads to resistance to change by those who are not included in the internal change agent's circle of close friends. The internal change agent, however, is familiar with the organization and its personnel, and this knowledge can be valuable in preparing for and implementing change.[20]

The third type of intervention, the combination external-internal team, is the rarest, but it seems to have an excellent chance for success. In this type of intervention, the outsider's objectivity and professional knowledge are blended with the insider's knowledge of the organization and its human resources. This blending of knowledge often results in increased trust and confidence among the parties involved. The ability of the combination external-internal team to communicate and develop a more positive rapport can reduce the resistance to any change that is forthcoming.

The change agent, whether internal or external to the organization, can relate to the organization according to one or more models.[21]

The Medical Model. Perhaps the most basic of all models, the medical model places the change agent in the role of adviser. The organization asks the change agent to assist in clarifying the problems, diagnosing the causes, and recommending courses of action, but retains the responsibility for accepting or rejecting the change agent's recommendations. The relationship is analogous to the physician-consultant arrangement; that is, the physician may seek opinions from other experts, but the choice of therapy remains with the physician.

The Doctor-Patient Model. The application of this model places the organization in the position of a "patient" who suspects that something is wrong. The change agent—the "doctor"—diagnoses and prescribes a solution that, of course, can be rejected by the patient. Yet by virtue of the relationship, the organization will usually adopt the change agent's recommendations. The change agent engages in diagnostic and problem-identification activities jointly with the organization. The more involved the organization is in the process, the more likely management will be to accept the recommended solution.

The Engineering Model. This model is used when the organization has performed the diagnostic work and has decided on a specific solution. For example, management desires to implement a MBO or job enrichment program and it seeks the services of experts to aid in the implementation. An alternative form of the model exists when

---

[20] Jerome Adams and John J. Sherwood, "An Evaluation of Organizational Effectiveness: An Appraisal of How Army Internal Consultants Use Survey Feedback in a Military Setting," *Group and Organization Studies*, June 1979, pp. 170–82.

[21] Based on Margulies and Raia, *Conceptual Foundations*, pp. 108–14.

the organization has defined the problem—excessive turnover, inter-group competition, or ineffective leadership behavior, for example—and requests the change agent to specify a solution. The general characteristic of the model, however, is that the diagnostic phase is undertaken by management.

The Process Model. This model is widely used by OD consultants. It involves the actual *collaboration* of the change agent and the organization through which management is encouraged to see and understand organizational problems. Through joint efforts, managers and change agents try to comprehend the factors in the situation that must be changed to improve performance. The change agent avoids taking sole responsibility for either diagnosis or prescription; rather, the emphasis is placed on enabling management to comprehend the problems. The change agents' emphasis is on teaching management *how* to diagnose rather than on doing the diagnosing for management.

The choice of an appropriate model depends on characteristics of the change agent, the organization, and the situation. It is not a matter of one model being superior in all instances; for any given circumstance, a particular model is appropriate.

Change agents facilitate the diagnostic phase by gathering, interpreting, and presenting data. Although the accuracy of data is extremely important, of equal importance is the way in which the data are interpreted and presented. This is generally accomplished in one of two ways. First, the data are discussed with a group of top managers, who are asked to make their own diagnosis of the information; or, second, the change agents may present their own diagnoses without making explicit their frameworks for analyzing the data. A difficulty with the first approach is that top management tends to see each problem separately. Each manager views his or her problem as being the most important and fails to recognize other problem areas. The second approach has inherent problems of communication. External change agents often have difficulty with the second approach because they become immersed in theory and various conceptual frameworks that are less realistic than the managers would like.[22]

A more general difficulty with either of these approaches derives from the close relationship between diagnosis and action.[23] One important guideline for managers of OD programs is that the method should not be separated from the diagnosis. In many OD programs, the empha-

---

[22] See Danny Miller and Peter H. Friesen, "Structural Change and Performance: Quantum versus Piecemeal Incremental Approaches," *Academy of Management Journal,* December 1982, pp. 867–92.

[23] Jay W. Lorsch and Paul Lawrence, "The Diagnosis of Organizational Problems," in *Organizational Development,* ed. Margulies and Raia, p. 219.

sis appears to be on the implementation of a particular method, with little concern for whether it is appropriate. For example, Blake and Mouton concentrate on implementing the managerial grid across different companies,[24] and Seashore and Bowers designed an action program based on participative management for the Banner organization prior to diagnosing specific problem areas.[25] Instead of a "canned" approach in which the diagnosis and method are the same for different companies, a more "tailored" approach to change is needed. That is, interventions should fit the particular problems of an organization.

ALTERNATIVE DEVELOPMENT TECHNIQUES

The choice of a particular development technique depends on the nature of the problem that management has diagnosed. Management must determine which alternative is most likely to produce the desired outcome, whether it be improvement in skills, attitudes, behavior, or structure. As we have noted, diagnosis of the problem includes specification of the outcome that management desires from the change. In the following chapter, we will describe a number of change techniques, some of which have been discussed in previous chapters. These techniques will be classified according to whether their major focus is to change skills, attitudes, behavior, or structure. This classification of techniques for organizational change in no way implies a distinct division among the areas of change. On the contrary, the interrelationships among skills, attitudes, behavior, and structure must be acknowledged and anticipated.

An important contribution of behavioral research has been the documentation of the impact of structure on attitudes and behavior. Overspecialization and narrow spans of control can lead to low levels of morale and low production. At the same time, the technology of production, distribution, and information processing can affect the structural characteristics of the firm as well as attitudes and behaviors. These interrelationships might suggest a weakness in our classification scheme; in defense of that scheme, however, we would note that the various development techniques can be distinguished on the basis of their major thrust or focus—whether skills, attitudes, behavior, or structure.

---

[24] Robert R. Blake and Jane S. Mouton, *The Managerial Grid* (Houston: Gulf Publishing, 1964).

[25] Stanley Seashore and David Bowers, *Changing the Structure and Functioning of an Organization: Report of a Field Experiment* (Ann Arbor: Survey Research Center, University of Michigan, 1963).

RECOGNITION OF LIMITING CONDITIONS

The selection of any developmental technique should be based on diagnosis of the problem, but the choice is tempered by certain conditions that exist at the time. Scholars identify three sources of influence on the outcome of management development programs that can be generalized to cover the entire range of organizational development efforts, whether attitudinal, behavioral, or structural. The three sources are leadership climate, formal organization, and organizational culture.

Leadership climate refers to the nature of the work environment that results from "the leadership style and administrative practices" of superiors. Any OD program that does not have the support and commitment of management has only a slim chance of success.[26] We can also understand that the style of leadership may itself be the subject of change; for example, the managerial grid and System 4 are direct attempts to move managers toward a certain style—open, supportive, and group-centered. But it must be recognized that the participants may be unable to adopt such styles if the styles are not compatible with their own superior's style.

The *formal organization* must also be compatible with the proposed change. The formal organization includes the philosophy and policies of top management, as well as legal precedent, organizational structure, and the systems of control. Of course, each of these sources of impact may itself be the focus of a change effort; the important point is that a change in one must be compatible with all of the others. For example, a change in structure that will eliminate employees contradicts a policy of guaranteed employment.

The *organizational culture* refers to the impact on the environment resulting from group norms, values, and informal activities. The impact of traditional behavior that is sanctioned by groups norms, but not formally acknowledged, was first documented in the Hawthorne studies. A proposed change in work methods or the installation of an automated device can run counter to the expectations and attitudes of the work group, and if such is the case, the OD strategy must anticipate the resulting resistance.

Implementation of OD that does not consider the contraints imposed by prevailing conditions within the present organization may, of

---

[26] Bernard J. White and V. Jean Ramsey, "Some Unintended Consequences of 'Top Down' Organizational Development," *Human Resources Management*, Summer 1978, pp. 7–14, note potential problems associated with extensive involvement of top management in the diagnostic phase of organizational development. Also see Robert T. Golembiewski, Carl W. Proehl and David Sink, "Estimating the Success of OD Applications," *Training and Development Journal*, April 1982, pp. 86–95.

course, amplify the problem that triggered the developmental process. If OD is implemented in this way, the potential for subsequent problems is greater than would ordinarily be expected. Taken together, the prevailing conditions constitute the climate for change, and they can be positive or negative.

IMPLEMENTING THE METHOD

timing
Timing is critical in implementing organizational development methods. Timing refers to the point in time that has been selected to initiate the change method.

scope
Scope is critical in implementing organizational development methods. Scope refers to the scale on which the change is implemented (e.g., throughout the entire organization, level by level, department by department).

The implementation of the OD method has two dimensions—**timing** and **scope.** Timing refers to the selection of the appropriate time at which to initiate the method, and scope refers to the selection of the appropriate scale. The matter of timing depends on a number of factors, particularly the organization's operating cycle and the groundwork that has preceded the OD program. Certainly, if a program is of considerable magnitude, it is desirable that it not compete with day-to-day operations; thus, the change might well be implemented during a slack period. On the other hand, if the program is critical to the survival of the organization, then immediate implementation is in order. The scope of the program depends on the strategy. The program may be implemented throughout the organization. Or it may be phased into the organization level by level or department by department. The shared strategy makes use of a phased approach, which limits the scope but provides feedback for each subsequent implementation.

The method that is finally selected is usually not implemented on a grand scale; rather, it is implemented on a small scale in various units throughout the organization. For example, an MBO program can be implemented in one unit or at one level at a time. The objective is to experiment with the method, that is, to test the validity of the diagnosed solution. As management learns from each successive implementation, the total program is strengthened. Not even the most detailed planning can anticipate all the consequences of implementing a particular method. Thus, it is necessary to experiment and to search for new information that can bear on the program.

As the experimental attempts provide positive signals that the program is proceeding as planned, there is a reinforcement effect. The personnel will be encouraged to accept the change required of them and to enlarge the scope of their own efforts. Acceptance of the change is facilitated by its positive results.

EVALUATING THE PROGRAM

An OD program represents an expenditure of organizational resources in exchange for some desired result. The resources take the form of money and time that have alternative uses. The result is in the form of increased organizational effectiveness—production, efficiency, and satisfaction in the short run; adaptiveness and development in the intermediate run; survival in the long run. Accordingly, some provision must be made to evaluate the program in terms of expenditures and results. The evaluation phase has two problems to overcome: the acquisition of data that measure the desired results[27] and the determination of the expected trend of improvement over time.

The acquisition of information that measures the sought-after result is the easier problem to solve, although it certainly does not lend itself to naive solutions. As we have come to understand, the stimulus for change is the deterioration of performance criteria that management has traced to structural and behavioral causes. The criteria may be any number of effectiveness indicators, including profit, sales volume, absenteeism, turnover, scrappage, or costs. The major source of feedback for those variables is the organization's information system. But if the change includes the expectation that employee satisfaction must be improved, the usual sources of information are limited, if not invalid. It is quite possible for a change to induce increased production at the expense of declining employee satisfaction. Thus, if the manager relies on the naive assumption that production and satisfaction are directly related, the change may be incorrectly judged successful when cost and profit improve.

To avoid the danger of overreliance on production data, the manager can generate ad hoc information that measures employee satisfaction. The benchmark for evaluation would be available if an attitude survey was used in the diagnosis phase. The definition of acceptable improvement is difficult when evaluating attitudinal data, since the matter of "how much more" positive the attitude of employees should be is quite different from the matter of "how much more" productive should they be. Nevertheless, if a complete analysis of results is to be undertaken, attitudinal measurements must be combined with production and other effectiveness measurements.

The second evaluation problem is the determination of the trend of improvement over time. The trend itself has three dimensions: (1) the first indication of improvement, (2) the magnitude of improvement, and (3) the duration of improvement. In Figure 19–3, three different patterns of change for a particular effectiveness criterion are illustrated.

In the change illustrated by the lighter solid line, improvement is slight during the early periods of time, but rises and maintains itself

---

[27] Arthur G. Bedeian, Achilles A. Armenakis, and Robert W. Gibson, "The Measurement and Control of Beta Change," *Academy of Management Review,* October 1980, pp. 561–66.

FIGURE 19–3

Three Patterns of Change in Results through Time

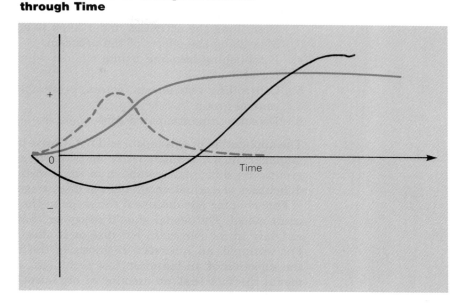

at a positive level. The dashed line illustrates a marked increase but followed by deterioration and a return to the original position. The darker solid line describes a situation in which the early signs indicate a decrease, but followed by a sharp rise toward substantial improvement. The patterns demonstrate only three of a number of possible relationships. A well-devised OD program would include an analysis of what change pattern can be expected. The actual pattern can then be compared with the expected pattern.

In a practical sense, the effectiveness of an OD program cannot be evaluated if objectives have not been established before it is implemented. A program that is undertaken to make the organization "a better place to work" or to develop the "full potential of the employees" cannot be evaluated. If, on the other hand, measurable criteria that are valid indicators of "better places to work" and "full employee potential" are collected during the diagnostic phase and subsequently tracked as the program is undertaken, bases for evaluation exist. A considerable body of literature exists that describes methods of evaluation, and managers of OD programs should consult it for guidance in program evaluation.[28]

---

[28] Achilles A. Armenakis, Hubert S. Feild, and Don C. Mosely, "Evaluation Guidelines for the OD Practitioner," *Personnel Journal*, Spring 1975, pp. 39–44; and William M. Evan, ed., *Organizational Experiments* (New York: Harper & Row, 1971).

Generally, an evaluation model would follow the steps of evaluative research. The steps include:

1. Determining the objectives of the program.
2. Describing the activities undertaken to achieve the objectives.
3. Measuring the effects of the program.
4. Establishing baseline points against which changes can be compared.
5. Controlling extraneous factors, preferably through the use of a control group.
6. Detecting unanticipated consequences.

The application of this model will not always be possible. For example, managers do not always specify objectives in precise terms and control groups are difficult to establish in some instances. Nevertheless, the difficulties of evaluation should not discourage attempts to evaluate.[29]

This chapter has discussed the steps in the organizational development model. The reader should recognize that each step is important not only in its own right but also as it affects each subsequent step. For example, an incorrect diagnosis of the problem could result in the selection of an inappropriate technique. Actual experience documents the fact that no amount of organizational restructuring will resolve problems that are rooted in attitude and skill deficiencies. Similarly, the development of attitudes and behaviors cannot have long-lasting effects if the task structure and the authority relationships are hostile to the newly learned attitudes and behaviors.

There are no guarantees that correct managerial decisions will be forthcoming from the use of any model. Much is left to managerial judgment. Nevertheless, the model presented in this chapter does introduce the appropriate questions and issues.

SUMMARY OF KEY POINTS

A. The need to consider organizational development arises from changes in the inter- and extraorganizational environment. Changes in input, output, technological, and scientific subenvironments may indicate the need to consider the feasibility of a long-

---

[29] James A Terborg, George S. Howard, Scott E. Maxwell, "Evaluating Planned Organizational Change: A Method for Assessing Alpha, Beta, and Gamma Changes," *Academy of Management Review*, January 1980, pp. 109–22; and Wendell L. French, "A Checklist for Organizing and Implementing an OD Effort," in *Organization Development: Theory, Practice, Research,* ed. W. L. French, C. H. Bell, Jr., and R. A. Zawacki (Plano, Tex.: Business Publications, 1983), pp. 451–59.

term, systematically managed program for changing the structure, process, and behavior of the organization. Even in the absence of environmental changes, organizational processes and behavior may become dysfunctional for achieving organizational effectiveness.

B. The diagnosis of present and potential problems involves the collection of information that reflects the level of organizational effectiveness. Data that measure the current state of production, efficiency, satisfaction, adaptiveness, and development must be gathered and analyzed. The purpose of diagnosis is to trace the causes of the problem.

C. In addition to serving as the bases for problem identification, the diagnostic data also establish the basis for subsequent evaluation of the organizational development effort.

D. The problem must be diagnosed, and managers can undertake the analysis by considering these questions:

1. What is the problem as distinct from its symptoms?
2. What must be changed to resolve the problem?
3. What outcomes are expected, and how will these outcomes be measured?

The managerial response to these questions should be stated in terms of criteria that reflect organizational effectiveness. Measurable outcomes such as production, efficiency, satisfaction, adaptiveness, and development must be linked to skill, attitudinal, behavioral, and structural changes that are necessitated by the problem identification.

E. Managers must evaluate the impact of limiting conditions. For example, if the organizational climate is conducive to the shared strategy, the employees would be brought into the diagnostic process and would participate with management from that point on. Through shared authority, the problem would be associated with skill, attitude, behavioral, and structural causes and the appropriate method selected. If employee participation is inappropriate because the necessary preconditions do not exist, management must unilaterally define the problem and select the appropriate method. Whether the problem is related to skill, attitude, behavioral, or structural causes, the strategy must include provision for the learning principles of feedback, reinforcement, and transfer.

F. The last step of the OD process is the decision to provide for an evaluation procedure. The ideal situation would be to structure the procedure in the manner of an experimental design. That is, the end results should be operationally defined and measurements should be taken, before and after, in both the organization undergoing development and in a second organization (the "control group"). Or, if the scope of the program is limited to a subunit, a second subunit could serve as a control group. The purpose of an evaluation is not only to enable management to account for its use of resources but also to provide feedback. Corrections can be taken in the implementation phase based on this feedback.

DISCUSSION AND REVIEW QUESTIONS

1. It is correct to argue that if either Maslow's or Herzberg's theory of motivation is valid, then management should expect employees to have a need to participate in decision making? Explain your answer.

2. Is it correct to argue that if employees desire to participate, they should be permitted to do so? Explain your answer.

3. Critique your instructor's teaching approach in terms of his or her utilization of learning principles.

4. Under what circumstances would the unilateral strategy be appropriate for implementing an OD method? Use the concept of leadership climate in your answer.

5. Assume that you are responsible for implementing an MBO system in an organization and that a unilateral strategy has been used. What problems of employee commitment can you anticipate, and how would you overcome these problems?

6. "The benefits derived from traditional training programs are so intangible that it makes little sense to measure them." Comment on this statement made by the training officer of a large corporation.

7. Identify the learning principles that are implemented in the shared strategy.

8. What OD strategy would probably be used in an organization that tends toward bureacracy? Explain your answer in terms of the alternative strategies that are available.

9. Explain the difficulties that you would encounter in attempting to obtain diagnostic information from the members of two groups who believe that they are competing for scarce resources.

10. Describe the factors that would sustain the process model of change agent behavior.

ADDITIONAL REFERENCES

Armenakis, A. A.; A. O. Bedian; and S. P. Pond. "Research Issues in OD Evaluation: Past, Present, and Future." *Academy of Management Review*, 1983, pp. 320–28.

Bennis, W. G. *Changing Organizations.* New York: McGraw-Hill, 1966.

Burke, W., ed. *Contemporary Organizational Development.* Washington, D.C.: NTL Institute for Applied Behavioral Science, 1972.

French, W. L.; C. H. Bell, Jr.; and R. A. Zawacki. *Organization Development: The-*

ory, Practice, Research. Plano, Tex.: Business Publications, 1983.

Friedlander, F., and L. Brown. "Organizational Development." *Annual Review of Psychology,* 1974, pp. 219–341.

Glassman, A. M., and S. McCoy. "Organizational Development in a Social Service Agency: Preparing for the Future." *Public Personnel Management,* 1981, pp. 324–32.

Halal, W. "Organizational Development in the Future." *California Management Review,* 1974, pp. 35–41.

Havelock, R. G., and M. G. Havelock. *Training for Change Agents.* Ann Arbor, Mich.: Center for Research on Utilization of Scientific Knowledge, 1973.

Herman, S. M., and M. Korenich. *Authentic Management: A Gestalt Orientation to Organizations and Their Management.* Reading, Mass.: Addison-Wesley Publishing, 1977.

Kilmann, R. H., and R. P. Herden. "Toward a Systemic Methodology for Evaluating the Impact of OD Interventions on Organization Effectiveness." *Academy of Management Review,* 1976 pp. 87–98.

King, A. S. "Expectation Effects in Organizational Change." *Administrative Science Quarterly,* 1974, pp. 221–30.

Lippitt, G. L. *Organization Renewal.* New York: Appleton-Century-Crofts, 1969.

Lippitt, R.; J. Waton; and B. Westly. *The Dynamics of Planned Change.* New York: Harcourt Brace Jovanovich, 1958.

Martinko, M. J., and P. D. Tolchinsky. "Critical Issues for Planned Change in Human Service Organizations: A Case Study and Analysis." *Group and Organizational Studies,* 1982, pp. 179–82.

Nicholas, J. M. "The Comparative Impact of Organization Development Interventions on Hard Criteria Measures." *Academy of Management Review,* 1982, pp. 531–42.

Patten, T. H., and L. E. Dorey. "Long-Range Results of a Team Building OD Effort." *Public Personnel Journal,* 1977, pp. 31–50.

Roberts, N. C., and J. I. Porras. "Progress in Organization Development Research." *Group and Organizational Studies,* 1982, pp. 91–116.

Schein, V. E. "Political Strategies for Implementing Change." *Group and Organizational Studies,* 1977, pp. 42–48.

Sirota, D., and A. D. Wolfson. Pragmatic Approach to People Problems." *Harvard Business Review,* 1973, pp. 120–28.

Sofer, C. *The Organization from Within.* London: Quandrangle Books, 1962.

Tichy, N. M. "How Different Types of Change Agents Diagnose Organizations." *Human Relations,* 1975, pp. 771–79.

Varney, G. *An Organization Development Approach to Management Development.* Reading, Mass.: Addison-Wesley Publishing, 1976.

White, L. P., and K. C. Wooten. "Ethical Dilemmas in Various Stages of Organizational Development." *Academy of Management Review,* 1983, pp. 690–97.

CASE FOR ANALYSIS

Evaluation of an MBO Program

Attitude survey data that a state health department collected as a part of its OD program served as a basis for evaluating the program. The program was based on the MBO method, and it was designed to develop the managerial capabilities of program directors, among other objectives. The initial diagnosis had indicated that the program directors were, by and large, not involved in decision making because the division directors, their immediate supervisors, preferred the directive style of management. One of the consequences of this style was the relatively short supply of program directors who were promotable to more responsible positions.

The OD program was designed to develop, through training and experience, the division directors' ability to work with their program directors in less directive, more participative ways. It was also anticipated that the program directors would need training in how to accept and implement their increased authority. The external change agent also believed, and the top management agreed with him, that the program must build in the opportunities for division and program directors to meet and make decisions.

Accordingly, the program provided for meetings of the division directors and the commissioner on a regular basis. During these meetings, they studied the literature on participative management and MBO. Equally important, they also learned the commissioner's philosophy and attitudes toward management. Training materials containing journal articles and case studies were provided and discussed during the sessions. And to focus the discussion of the group on real rather than hypothetical problems, the attitude survey data were analyzed and evaluated by the division directors.

During this period, the division directors were expected to train the program directors of their respective divisions. They were to meet the first or second day after each of their sessions with their program directors and to discuss, interpret, and elaborate the materials that they themselves had been studying. In this manner, the division directors not only assumed the roles of coaches, but the program directors were also made aware of the commissioner's intent to develop a climate that encouraged and supported participative management and increased delegation of authority.

The training period preceded by six months the development of goal statements for each division. These statements were to serve as the bases for allocating the department's budget among the divisions. It was expected that the division directors would develop these statements jointly with the program directors and that this experience would reinforce the learning presumed to have occurred during the training sessions.

Two months after the completion of the training sessions and the funding decisions, a second attitude survey was undertaken. The questionnaire was completed by all employees. The respondents remained anonymous except for the designation of certain demographic and job information, including level in the managerial hierarchy. Thus, it was possible to combine the responses of program and division directors to obtain group means. The change agent presented the data from the second attitude survey to the division directors. He noted one result that he believed they should discuss and analyze. That result seemed to indicate that one of the objectives of the program had not been attained, namely, the intended downward delegation of authority to program directors.

A number of questions on the questionnaire measured the perceived amount of authority. Generally, the program directors indicated that their authority had declined since the first attitude survey. One particularly interesting question, to which all of the directors responded on both occasions, was stated as follows:

> How much "say" do you think each of the following people usually has in deciding the work objectives of the departmental program? *Circle one in each line across.*

	Usually Has a Great Deal of Say	Quite a Bit of Say	Some Say	Just a Little Say	Usually Has No Say at All
Program directors	1	2	3	4	5
Division heads	1	2	3	4	5
The commissioner's office	1	2	3	4	5

Exhibits 1 and 2 present the group means to this question for the division directors (solid line) and the program directors (dashed line). Plainly, the

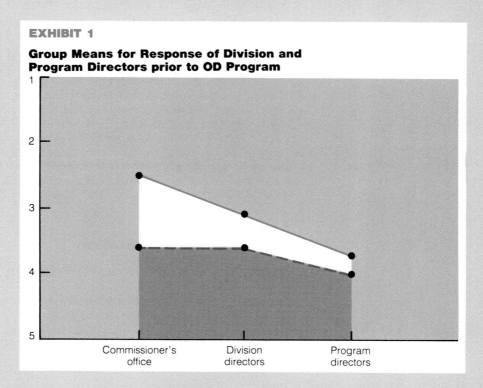

EXHIBIT 1

Group Means for Response of Division and Program Directors prior to OD Program

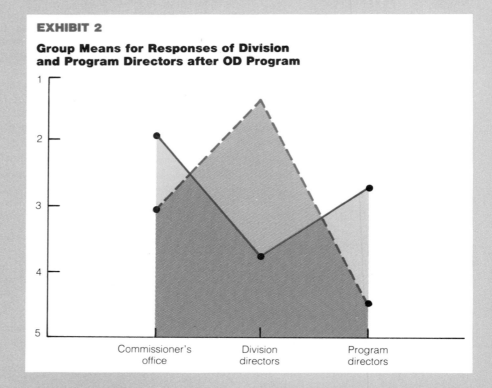

EXHIBIT 2

Group Means for Responses of Division and Program Directors after OD Program

program directors' perceptions of what had happened during the previous year were contrary to what was supposed to happen. They believed, as indicated by their responses, that not only did they have less say in their programs but that the division directors had considerably more say than before. And the division directors reported that they had considerably less say and that the program directors had more say in deciding work objectives.

The division directors were confused by the questionnaire results. How could it be, they asked the change agent, that despite our efforts they believe that we have more say and they have less authority? Are the data reliable? Is there any other evidence to indicate that the program has backfired, at least as it was to affect the program directors? What do we do now? Scrap it and start all over?

Questions for Consideration

1. What would be your answers to the division directors if you were the change agent?

2. What other kinds and sources of information would be useful in determining the validity of the attitude survey data?

3. How likely is it that efforts that managers undertake to delegate authority will be perceived by subordinates as efforts to centralize authority?

Chapter 20

After completing Chapter 20, you should be able to:

Define the "depth of intended change."

Describe the actual process that some organizations use to implement the System 4 structural change method.

Discuss the differences between the managerial grid and team-building methods for developing effective group performance.

Compare alternative skill and attitude development training approaches.

Identify the circumstances that underlie the choice of sensitivity training as a method for improving interpersonal skills.

Methods and Applications of Organizational Development

Sensitivity Training Is an Effective OD Technique

Argument For*

Sensitivity training is a learning experience that emphasizes human relations skills. The training is designed to help good managers become better managers. The proponents of sensitivity training believe that the inability to deal with others—subordinates, superiors, peers, and clients—is a major cause of organizational problems. The learning that

---

* Based on Leslie This and Gordon L. Lippitt, "Managerial Guidelines to Sensitivity Training, *Training and Development Journal*, June 1981, pp. 144–50.

occurs in sensitivity training sessions provides managers with greater awareness of their own values, motives, and assumptions.

The evidence for the effectiveness of sensitivity training is testimonial in nature. That is, participants state that they have learned to cope with frustrations, anxieties, and stress in their jobs as a consequence of their sensitivity training. As one participant stated, "Through becoming more aware of others' problems, I found that my problems were not unique. As a result, I achieved more inner peace and ability to face some of the problems of our team."

Wives of executives often participate with their husbands. As one executive's wife stated, "I gained a deeper understanding of the tremendous stress and strain my husband is constantly under. I had not understood his problems before and tended to blame him for poor communication. Now we both realize our joint responsibility for communication and, more importantly, how we can go about it." This wife's reaction to the training is shared by many others who have gone through it.

Argument Against†

Critics of sensitivity training believe that testimonials are inadequate evidence. They state that these claims must be validated by rigorous research. Specifically, they believe that research should evaluate the impact of sensitivity training on participants, and they have carried out research to do so. The conclusion of the research is that there is little evidence to indicate changes in participants'

attitudes, values, outlooks, and interpersonal sensitivity. Thus, even though participants often report that they believe that these changes have occurred as a consequence of sensitivity training, there are no objective facts to support that belief.

Another claim of sensitivity training is that participants are better able to analyze problems, synthesize information, face and resolve interpersonal conflict, and implement solutions. At present, no research evidence exists to support these claims, largely because researchers have evaluated only the human relations effects of sensitivity training. Thus, even though much personal testimonial evidence supports sensitivity training, empirical research data tend to support the counterargument.

† Based on Peter B. Smith, "Controlled Studies in the Outcomes of Sensitivity Training," *Psychological Bulletin*, July 1975, pp. 597–622.

As we noted in the previous chapter, effective organizational development requires the active involvement of managers. They must designate objectives, select methods to achieve those objectives, and implement the methods. Managers can state objectives in terms of improved production, efficiency, satisfaction, adaptiveness, and development, separately or in some combination. Managers can implement one or more organizational development methods depending on the objectives. This chapter focuses on the issues and problems associated *with alternative development methods.*

Each of these methods has strengths and weaknesses, advantages and disadvantages, advocates and detractors. The Organizational Issue for Debate describes the controversy surrounding one method—sensitivity training. We cover this method more completely later in the chapter. The point to be made here is that any of the methods we discuss could be the subject of an Organizational Issue for Debate. Organizational development is a complex and people-oriented process. Consequently, controversy is bound to pervade its practice.

DEPTH OF INTENDED CHANGE

Depth of intended change refers to the scope and intensity of the organizational development efforts. The idea is depicted in Figure 20–1, which likens the organization to an iceberg. This analogy draws attention to two important components: the *formal* and *informal* aspects of organizations. The formal components of an organization are analogous to the part of an iceberg that is "above water"; the informal components lie "below water," unseen, but there nevertheless. As indicated in Figure 20–1, the formal components are observable, rational, and oriented to structural factors. The informal components are, on the other hand, not observable to all people, affective, and oriented to process and behavioral factors.

Generally speaking, the greater the scope and intensity of a problem, the more likely it is that the problem will be found in the informal components. Thus, depth of intended change refers to how far management must go into the organizational iceberg to solve the problem. At one extreme are problems that lie with the structure of the organization. Managers can solve such problems by changing job definitions, departmentalization bases, spans of control, and delegated authority. At the other extreme are problems that lie with the *behavior* of groups and individuals. These problems are related to personal views, value orientations, feelings, and sentiments as well as activities, sentiments, and roles within and among groups. And while these behaviors can certainly be affected by changes in structure, they are ordinarily deep-seated and management must confront them more directly.

FIGURE 20–1

The Organizational Iceberg

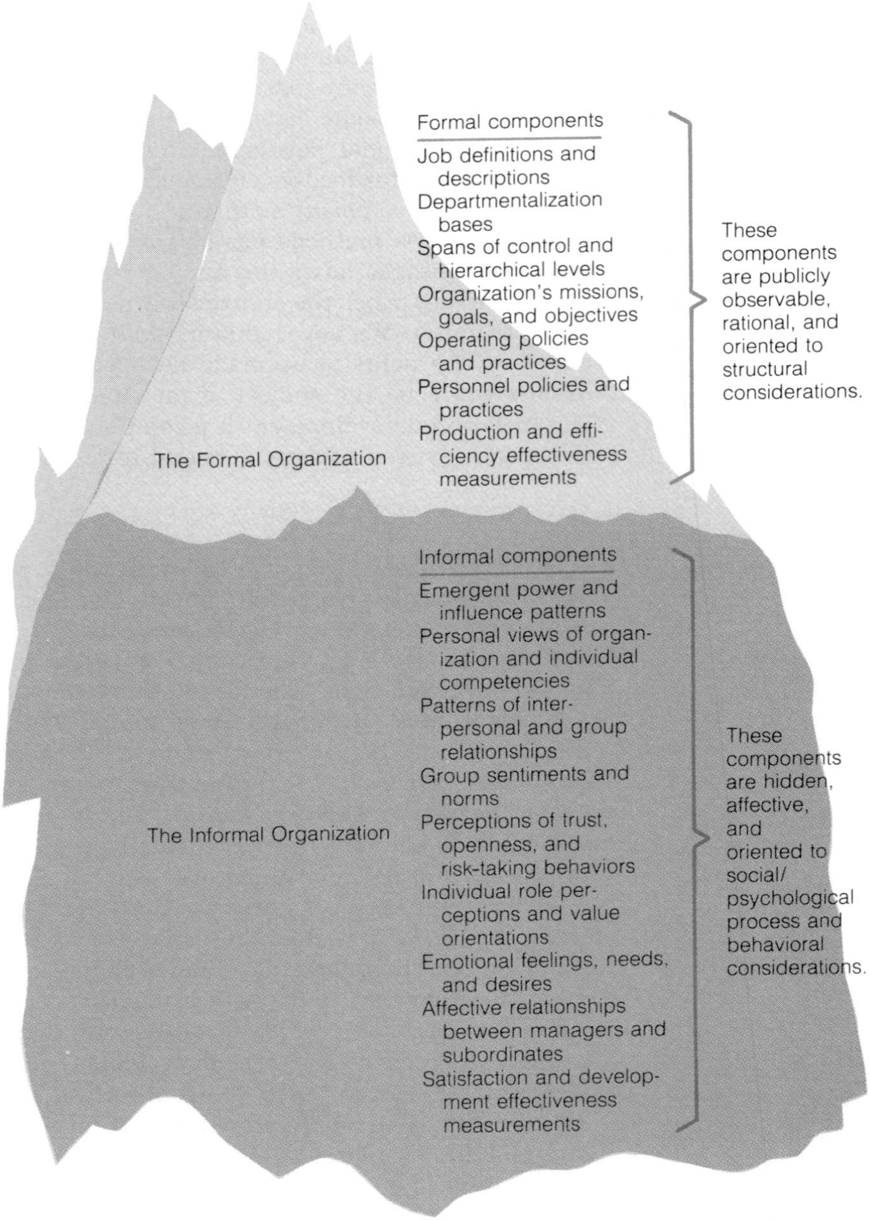

The Formal Organization

Formal components

Job definitions and
   descriptions
Departmentalization
   bases
Spans of control and
   hierarchical levels
Organization's missions,
   goals, and objectives
Operating policies
   and practices
Personnel policies and
   practices
Production and effi-
   ciency effectiveness
   measurements

These
components
are publicly
observable,
rational, and
oriented to
structural
considerations.

The Informal Organization

Informal components

Emergent power and
   influence patterns
Personal views of organ-
   ization and individual
   competencies
Patterns of inter-
   personal and group
   relationships
Group sentiments and
   norms
Perceptions of trust,
   openness, and
   risk-taking behaviors
Individual role per-
   ceptions and value
   orientations
Emotional feelings, needs,
   and desires
Affective relationships
   between managers and
   subordinates
Satisfaction and develop-
   ment effectiveness
   measurements

These
components
are hidden,
affective,
and
oriented to
social/
psychological
process and
behavioral
considerations.

Source: Adapted from Richard J. Selfridge and Stanley L. Sokolik, "A Comprehensive View of Organizational Development," *MSU Business Topics,* Winter 1975, p. 47.

FIGURE 20–2

Model of Organizational Development Targets

STRUCTURAL TARGETS						→ BEHAVIORAL TARGETS			
Level I	*Level II*	*Level III*	*Level IV*	*Level V*	*Level VI*	*Level VII*	*Level VIII*	*Level IX*	*Level X*
Organizational structure	Operating policies and practices	Personnel policies and practices	Job performance appraisal and improvement	Management attitudes and skills	Non-management attitudes and skills	Intergroup behavior	Intragroup behavior	Individual behavior	Individual-group behavior

LOW ← Depth of intended change → HIGH

Adapted from Richard J. Selfridge and Stanley L. Sokolik, "A Comprehensive View of Organizational Development," *MSU Business Topics*, Winter 1975. p. 49.

The relationship between source of problem and degree of intended change is illustrated in Figure 20–2; it suggests that there are 10 levels, or targets, of an OD program. As the target moves from left to right and, consequently, deeper into the organization, the OD program becomes more person- and group-centered. It will rely more on sociopsychological and less on technical-economic knowledge. Levels I through IV involve formal components, including structure, policies, and practices of the organization. Levels V and VI involve both formal and informal components, including skills and attitudes of managerial and nonmanagerial personnel. Levels VII through X involve informal components, including the behavior of groups and individuals. For each of these levels, one or more OD *methods* can be possible solutions. These methods are based on current behavioral science theory and practice. Only after the problem and its level have been diagnosed should the method be selected. Figure 20–2 relates the target levels and the more popular methods. These methods are the focus of the remaining discussion.

Despite an ever-increasing knowledge base, organizational development practitioners are not absolutely certain that a specific method will have its intended effects. In fact, there are many instances of failure, and some of these instances will be discussed in the sections to follow. Recently, a number of reviews have been undertaken to discern the relative success of OD methods, particularly in terms of whether they have affected the intended target in the intended manner. These reviews suggest that OD methods do not always obtain the desired changes in the targets of intervention.[1] Thus, even though there is growing sophistication in the OD theory and practice, there is yet room for caution,[2] as suggested by the following Close-Up.

ORGANIZATIONS: CLOSE-UP

Failure at Rushton

Paul S. Goodman, in his book *Addressing Organizational Change: The Rushton Quality of Work Experiment*, traces the history of a quality

---

[1] William A. Pasmore and Donald C. King, "Understanding Organizational Change: A Comparative Study of Multifaceted Interventions," *Journal of Applied Behavioral Sciences,* October–December 1978, pp. 455–68; and Jerry I. Porras, "The Comparative Impact of Different OD Techniques and Intervention Intensities," *Journal of Applied Behavioral Science,* April–June 1979, pp. 156–78.

[2] Mark L. McConkle, "Classifying and Reviewing the Empirical Work on MBO: Some Implications," *Group and Organization Studies,* December 1979, pp. 461–75.

of work-life experiment that allowed three eight-member crews in one section of a coal mine to direct their own work, subject only to safety regulations. The experiment was an attempt to enrich the work of coal miners by providing increased autonomy, self-direction, and team problem solving. The experiment was concerned not only with improving the quality of work-life but also with improving productivity. For a period of about three years, the experiment was deemed successful: indicators of morale, safety, and productivity all improved. Then the experiment began to fail, and new it has been virtually disbanded. The causes for the failure have little to do with the experiment itself, according to Goodman.

The failure was due to a series of union walkouts over issues that were unrelated to the experiment but nevertheless produced tensions between management and labor. However, there were also difficulties that could be traced to the experiment. For example, the external consulting team failed to train adequately the miners so that they could continue the program after the consultants left; a program that would share the gains from the program with the miners was promised but never implemented; and basic antagonisms developed between members of the experimental and control work teams. Nevertheless, and despite the failure of the Rushton experiment, Goodman believes that management should not hesitate to attempt quality of work-life improvement programs. If managed properly, the results can be positive for both management and labor.

STRUCTURAL DEVELOPMENT METHODS

Structural development in the context of organizational change refers to managerial action that attempts to improve effectiveness through a change in the formal structure of task and authority relationships. The organizational structure creates the bases for relatively stable human and social relationships. These relationships can in time become irrelevant for organizational effectiveness. For example, the jobs that people do may become obsolete, and thus irrelevant. But to change the jobs also changes the relationships among the employees. Members of the organization may resist efforts to disrupt these relationships.

Structural changes affect some aspects of the formal task and authority definitions. As we have seen, the design of an organization involves the definition and specification of job range and depth, the grouping of jobs in departments, the determination of the size of the groups reporting to a single manager, and the delegation of authority. Three methods designed to change all or some aspect of the organizational structure are discussed in this section. They are management by objectives (MBO), System 4, and MAPS. These methods are appropriate for consideration when the problem is diagnosed as being in Levels I through IV.

Management by Objectives

Management by objectives encourages managers to participate in the establishment of objectives for themselves and their units.[3] The process can also include the participation of nonmanagers in the determination of their specific objectives. Successful use of MBO depends on the ability of participants to define their objectives in terms of their contribution to the total organization and to be able to accomplish them.

The original work of Drucker[4] and subsequent writings by others[5] provide the basis for three guidelines for implementing MBO:

1. Superiors and subordinates meet and discuss objectives that contribute to overall goals.
2. Superiors and subordinates jointly establish attainable objectives for the subordinates.
3. Superior and subordinates meet at a predetermined later date to evaluate the subordinates' progress toward the objectives.

The exact procedures employed in implementing MBO vary from organization to organization and from unit to unit. However, the basic elements of objective setting, participation of subordinates in objective setting, and feedback and evaluation are usually parts of any MBO program. The intended consequences of MBO include improved contribution to the organization, improved attitudes and satisfaction of participants, and greater role clarity. MBO is highly developed and widely used in business, health care, and governmental organizations. In this section, we will describe an OD project that was undertaken in a

---

[3] Original statements of MBO may be found in Peter Drucker, *The Practice of Management* (New York: Harper & Row, 1954); George Odiorne, *Management by Objectives* (New York: Pitman Publishing, 1965); and W. J. Reddin, *Effective Management by Objectives* (New York: McGraw-Hill, 1970).

[4] See Ronald G. Greenwood, "Management by Objectives: As Developed by Peter Drucker, Assisted by Harold Smiddy," *Academy of Management Review,* April 1981, pp. 225–30.

[5] For discussions of applications of MBO in a variety of settings, see *First Tango in Boston: A Seminar on Organizational Change and Development* (Washington, D.C.: National Training and Development Services, 1973); "Management by Objectives in the Federal Government," *Bureaucrat,* Winter 1974; Kevin W. Mossholder and H. Dudley Dewhirst, "The Appropriateness of Management-by-Objectives for Development and Research Personnel," *Journal of Management,* Fall 1980, pp. 145–56; and David E. Terpstra, Philip D. Olson, and Brad Lockeman, "The Effects of MBO on Levels of Performance and Satisfaction among University Faculty," *Group and Organizational Studies,* September 1982, pp. 353–66.

state department of health and resulted in the implementation of an MBO system.

The project began with the administration of an attitude questionnaire to all employees in the state department of health. The purpose of the attitude survey was twofold: to provide information for pinpointing problems and to provide baseline measurements for follow-up studies. The same attitude questionnaire was administered to all employees in the state department of mental health. The two departments were quite similar in mission and in employee characteristics such as age, educational level, and length of service. The mental health department was the comparison group for purposes of gauging the effects of the health department's OD program.

The attitude data became the focus of discussion in training sessions attended by the division directors and the commissioner of health. In effect, the commissioner and the division directors made up the management team that implemented the program. Management teams are often the implementers of MBO.[6] The results of the survey were made known to the division directors in keeping with the generally accepted practice in the use of attitude surveys.[7]

The division directors focused their discussion on the problems identified in the attitude survey. It was found, for example, that there was considerable ambiguity in the minds of employees about their job expectations and objectives. This finding suggested to the division directors that MBO should be implemented in the health department. They then undertook an intensive training program to learn the basics of MBO.

Subsequent to the training sessions, the division directors, in consultation with their program directors, prepared goal statements that listed in order of priority the major objectives of each division. The number of objectives depended on the scope of each division's activities and ranged from 5 to 15. In addition, the division directors estimated the resource requirement for each objective. Each division director met with the commissioner to discuss the goal statements. The outcome of the discussions was mutually agreed-upon objectives and resource allocations.

At the six-month review, discussions between the commissioner and each of the division directors indicated the necessity for revisions in light of revised priorities and planning premises. The revised objectives prevailed during the next six months, and the cycle began anew.

---

[6] Will Ellis, "Use of a Management Team System to Implement MBO in an Airline," *Journal of Organizational Behavior Management,* Fall–Winter 1982, pp. 65–80.

[7] James F. Gavin and Paul A. Krois, "Content and Process of Survey Feedback Sessions and Their Relation to Survey Responses: An Initial Study," *Group and Organizational Studies,* June 1983, pp. 221–47.

The program undertaken in the health department reflected the main features of OD as we have defined it here:

1. The program was long-term and systematically planned.
2. The managerial personnel at all levels confronted organizational problems as revealed by diagnostic data (the attitude survey).
3. The training sessions were designed to facilitate the discussion of mutual problems, with technical literature serving as a source of help in the resolution of these problems.
4. The MBO method was integrated into the organization only after careful consideration.

System 4 Organization

System 4 organization
A widely used approach to develop organic design characteristics in an ongoing organization.

System 4 organization is an important application of the organic organizational design. Moreover, according to Likert, System 4 is an "ideal type" of organization for achieving high levels of performance and any deviation from the ideal, System 4, represents reduced levels of performance. Thus, managers should develop their organizations toward System 4 characteristics. According to Likert, an organization can be described in terms of eight characteristics.[8] They are:

1. Leadership.
2. Motivation.
3. Communication.
4. Interaction.
5. Decision making.
6. Goal setting.
7. Control.
8. Performance.

Furthermore, each of these characteristics can be measured through the use of a questionnaire, which members of the organization (usually managers) complete. The averages of each response category are calculated and plotted to produce an organizational profile, as shown in Figure 20–3.

To diagnose the extent to which a particular organization approximates the System 4 structure, Likert has devised a 51-item questionnaire, which is completed by the employees of an organization. The employees indicate their perceptions of the extent to which the characteristics that define the System 4 organization are present in their own organization. The means of the responses are calculated and plotted along the continua that describe the eight characteristics. Figure 20–3 illustrates the profiles of two manufacturing firms.

The profiles illustrate the differences that can occur in organizational characteristics. In Likert's terms, the organization described by the lighter line clearly tends toward a mechanistic design (a System 1), whereas the organization defined by the darker line tends toward

---

[8] Rensis Likert, *The Human Organization* (New York: McGraw-Hill, 1967).

FIGURE 20-3

Organizational Profiles for Two Manufacturing Firms

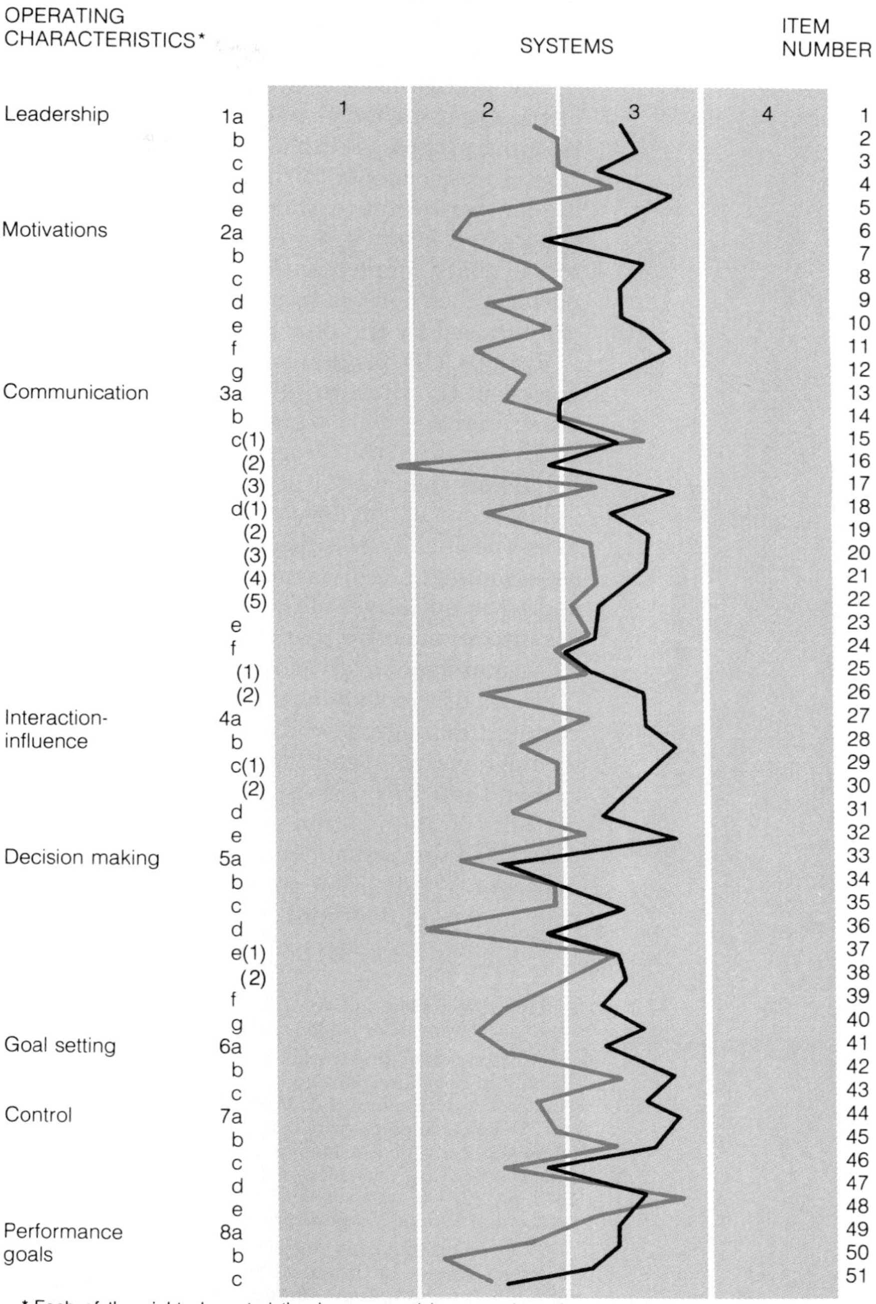

OPERATING CHARACTERISTICS*

SYSTEMS

ITEM NUMBER

Operating Characteristics		Item Number
Leadership	1a	1
	b	2
	c	3
	d	4
	e	5
Motivations	2a	6
	b	7
	c	8
	d	9
	e	10
	f	11
	g	12
Communication	3a	13
	b	14
	c(1)	15
	(2)	16
	(3)	17
	d(1)	18
	(2)	19
	(3)	20
	(4)	21
	(5)	22
	e	23
	f	24
	(1)	25
	(2)	26
Interaction-influence	4a	27
	b	28
	c(1)	29
	(2)	30
	d	31
	e	32
Decision making	5a	33
	b	34
	c	35
	d	36
	e(1)	37
	(2)	38
	f	39
	g	40
Goal setting	6a	41
	b	42
	c	43
Control	7a	44
	b	45
	c	46
	d	47
	e	48
Performance goals	8a	49
	b	50
	c	51

* Each of the eight characteristics is measured by a number of items. Leadership, for example, is measured by five questionnaire items (1a–1e).

an organic design (System 4). If the System 4 theory is valid, the organization on the right will be more effective than the one on the left. Furthermore, both organizations could be improved by a developmental plan that would move them closer to the right, or closer to System 4.

The change toward System 4 involves measuring the present state of the organization through the use of the questionnaire. Subsequent training programs emphasize the concepts of System 4 and the application of the concepts to the present organization. According to Likert, higher performance should ordinarily result through the use of (1) supportive, group-oriented leadership; and (2) equalization of authority to set goals, implement control, and make decisions. The improved performance derives from positive changes in employee attitudes that are induced by the changes in organizational structure.[9]

Various OD programs utilizing System 4 concepts have been reported in the literature.[10] Here we will describe a program that combined management training (Level V) and structural change (Level I). Essentially, the program was designed to develop attitudes and behaviors that would be compatible with a System 4 organization.[11]

The focus of the development effort was the sales unit of a business firm, specifically 16 sales managers. The group consisted of a national sales manager, 2 divisional managers, and 13 regional managers. The short-run objectives of the program were (1) to integrate the 16 managers into an effective team following the appointment of a new national sales manager, a divisional manager, and three regional managers; (2) to facilitate the development and acceptance of new roles for the regional managers, who, with the introduction of a new product line, would have to spend 90 percent of their time in managerial work, rather than the present 40 percent; and (3) to confront and resolve certain communication and interpersonal problems that remained as a result of the personnel changes. The main difficulty was the regional managers' perception that the new national head was so aggressive that he would dominate the divisional managers.

The long-run goals of the program were:

---

[9] Heinz Weihrich and André-Sean Rigny, "Toward System-4 through Transactional Analysis," *Journal of Systems Management,* July 1980, pp. 30–36.

[10] An important illustration is reported in Alfred J. Marrow, David G. Bowers, and Stanley E. Seashore, *Management by Participation* (New York: Harper & Row, 1967). This report documents the effort of the Harwood company management to transform the Weldon company, which it purchased in 1961, into a System 4 organization. A follow-up study of the Harwood experience is reported in Stanley E. Seashore and David G. Bowers, "Durability of Organizational Change," *American Psychologist,* March 1970, pp. 227–33. Also see W. F. Dowling, "At General Motors: System 4 Builds Performance and Profits," *Organizational Dynamics,* Winter 1975, pp. 23–28.

[11] This OD program is reported in Robert T. Golembiewski and Stokes B. Carrigan, "Planned Change in Organization Style Based on the Laboratory Approach," *Administrative Science Quarterly,* March 1970, pp. 79–93.

1. To make actual and preferred behaviors more congruent (the managers feared that mistrust and secrecy would be required in order to succeed in the organization, but they preferred trusting and open relationships).
2. To move the organization toward the System 4 end of the continuum.
3. To experiment with a "bottom-up" approach to OD (the usual approach is "top-down," as in the case of the health department OD program).

To get at these objectives, the sales managers engaged in training during which they experimented with the kinds of behaviors appropriate to a System 4 organization. Learning exercises that emphasized interpersonal and intergroup relations were an important part of the training since these were the key relationships involved in building integrated work groups. The training sessions culminated in a confrontation between the regional and divisional managers and between the divisional managers and the national sales manager. These confrontations encouraged the managers to share and to test the value of openness and problem solving in the organization. However, the real test of openness and problem solving would come in the context of the everyday work of the organization; that is, the real test would be whether the behavior learned in the training sessions could be transferred back to the workplace.

To obtain some indication of the lasting effects of the training session and to gauge progress toward the development of a System 4 organization, the managers completed the organizational profile questionnaire prior to the training session and again four months later. There was no control group available. Obviously, the absence of a control group limited the analysis and the results had to be validated by other means, such as observation of actual workplace behavior. The differences between the before and after measures indicated that movement had been made toward the System 4 organization and that this movement had been facilitated by the training methodology. Thus, the behavior learned in the training sessions appears to have been made a part of the organization structure.

MAPS Design Technology

MAPS
A method for designing an organization based on relationships that individuals state as necessary to perform their tasks.

Organizational development, as we have noted, involves management in a long-term, collaborative process to improve the performance of organizations, groups, and individuals. Moreover, typical OD methods are based on specific humanistic values and assumptions. **MAPS** is a relatively recent development that embodies the ideas of organizational development in the design of organizational structure. MAPS—

an acronym for multivariate analysis, participation, and structure—
attempts to apply humanistic theories of motivation to create organizational structures.[12]

Although the method has not fully evolved, at present its proponents
suggest that an organizational structure can be designed (or redesigned) by going through the following steps. These steps should be
undertaken by members of the organization with the aid of an external
consultant familiar with the MAPS approach.[13]

1. Diagnosing the organization to determine whether organizational
   structure is a cause of performance problems.
2. Determining whether the total organizational structure or selected work-group structures should be changed and developed.
3. Specifying the objectives to be accomplished by the effort; these
   objectives would be related to performance criteria and to the
   diagnosed problems.
4. Matching the specific MAPS approach to the diagnosed problems
   and objectives. The approach varies depending on the change
   target, the problem diagnosis, and the stated objectives.[14]
5. Developing a questionnaire that lists the various specific tasks
   that the organization or group must accomplish. The list of tasks
   is produced in a *participative* collaborative effort by all the members of the organization *and,* in some instances, by customers
   and/or clients. The purpose of this step is to account fully for
   the total range of tasks necessary to achieve effective organizational or group performance.
6. Administering the questionnaire to all members of the organization or group. Each member indicates his or her strength of preference for working on specific tasks as well as preference of other
   individuals with whom to work on these preferred tasks.
7. Analyzing the questionnaire data through *multivariate statistics*
   (and a computer) to identify "clusters" of tasks and people. The
   clusters reflect the preferences of individuals for working on specific tasks with specific other people. The idea is to permit people
   to choose their tasks and co-workers. These individual choices
   are the bases for work clusters.
8. Selecting a specific set of clusters of tasks and people. It is inevitable that different combinations of tasks and people clusters will

---

[12] Ralph H. Kilmann, *Social System Design: Normative Theory and the MAPS Design
Technology* (New York: North-Holland Publishing, 1977), p. 23.

[13] Ralph H. Kilmann, "On Integrating Knowledge Utilization with Knowledge Development: The Philosophy behind the MAPS Design Technology," *Academy of Management Review,* July 1979, pp. 420–21.

[14] See Kilmann, *Social System Design,* for a complete discussion of this quite technical
aspect of MAPS.

result from the application of different rules for combining them. The ultimate decision is based on discussion among all of the individuals who are vitally affected by the outcome, thus providing additional opportunity for *participation.*

9. Implementing the selected set of clusters—the organizational design—by providing resources and support that enable the members of the newly formed groups to learn to work together.

10. Monitoring the entire implementation process to detect problems that can be resolved at early stages.

11. Evaluating the realized results of the change in terms of the objectives originally set forth during the diagnostic stage.

12. Rediagnosing the new structure in recognition of the fact that solutions to old problems become sources of new problems.

A careful reading of the 12 steps of the MAPS method indicates the manner in which the method implements effective OD strategy. Steps 1–4 and 8–12 apply the change strategy, discussed in Chapter 19, that has been associated with instances of successful change efforts. *Thus, MAPS represents an integration of a specific method with a more general OD strategy.*

The MAPS design technology is a relatively new development in organizational development. The first reported application was in the redesign of a university departmental structure.[15] Since that first application, several other attempts have been reported.[16] Although it is too early to establish the potential significance of MAPS, its initial effects have been promising.

SKILL AND ATTITUDE DEVELOPMENT METHODS

The most widely used methods for developing employee productivity are training programs.[17] These programs are designed to improve participants' knowledge, skills, and attitudes toward their jobs and the organization. The training may be part of a larger effort such as MBO, MAPS, or System 4 programs, or it may be directed toward specific objectives. In the usual case, managerial training is directed toward the development of communication and decision-making skills, thus improving the organization's fundamental processes.

---

[15] Bill McKelvey and Ralph H. Kilmann, "Organization Design: A Participative Multivariate Approach," *Administrative Science Quarterly,* March 1975, pp. 24–36.

[16] See Kilmann, "On Integrating Knowledge Utilization"; and Ralph H. Kilmann, "The Costs of Organization Structure: Dispelling the Myths of Independent Divisions and Organization-Wide Decision-Making," *Accounting, Organization, and Society,* 1983, pp. 341–60, for a review of these and other studies.

[17] Stephen R. Michael, "Organizational Change Techniques: Their Present, Their Future," *Organizational Dynamics,* Summer 1982, pp. 67–80.

Because of the multiplicity of training programs, we will describe only some of the more representative and widely publicized types in this section. Some of the advantages and disadvantages associated with each type will be described. The attainment of desired objectives such as knowledge acquisition or improvement in job performance will also be examined.

On-the-Job Training

A popular philosophy over the years has been to train employees on the job. It is assumed that if training occurs off the job, there will be a loss in performance when the trainees are transferred back to the job. It is also proposed that on-the-job training is best from an economic standpoint, since employees are producing while they undergo training.

Corning Glass Works has an extensive on-the-job training program. It begins with an assessment of the needs for training as identified by department heads. The training unit then matches the identified training needs with classroom instruction. The classroom instructor then moves to the workplace, where the classroom instruction is reinforced by actual on-the-job application. As employees master each job requirement, they receive credits that become part of their performance evaluation.[18]

On-the-job training has a number of shortcomings. First, employees may be placed in a stress-laden situation even before learning the job. This may result in accidents or poor initial attitudes about the job. Second, the areas in which employees are being trained are often congested. Finally, if a number of trainees are learning in various job locations, the trainer must move around constantly to monitor their performance.

Job-Instruction Training.   Formulated during World War II by the War Manpower Board, this program provides a set of guidelines for undertaking on-the-job training for white- and blue-collar employees. After trainees are introduced to the job, they receive a step-by-step review and demonstration of the job functions. When trainees are sufficiently confident that they understand the job, they demonstrate their ability to perform the job. This demonstration continues until the trainees reach a satisfactory level of performance.

The objective of this approach is to bring about a positive change in performance that is reflected in higher production, lower scrap costs, and so on. This type of training is best suited for jobs that have specific content. Variations of this program are used in universities

---

[18] John G. Dickey, "Training with a Focus on the Individual," *Personnel Administration,* June 1982, pp. 37–38.

in preparing doctoral candidates for teaching and research careers and in hospitals in preparing nurses for new job duties. A crucial point to recognize is that the trainer must have the technical skill to perform the job that the trainee is performing. Note also that the trainer must understand the importance of repetition, active participation, and immediate constructive feedback.

Junior Executive Boards. This technique, popularized by the McCormick Company, concentrates on providing junior-level (middle- and lower-level managers) with top-level management problem-solving experience. The junior executive may serve on a committee or junior board that is considering some major decision concerning investments or personnel planning. The assumption in this type of training is that the trainee will acquire an appreciation for the decisions being made "upstairs" and that this can be translated into a better overall view of the organization's direction and difficulties. In addition, the ability of the junior executive to contribute to problem solving can be assessed. In effect, management is teaching the trainee and determining the trainee's ability to cope with major problems. The value of such a program depends on the trainee's readiness to cope with such problems and on the feedback received about performance.

Off-the-Job Training

Traditionally, organizations have found that it is necessary to provide training that supplements on-the-job efforts. Some of the advantages of off-the-job training are:

1. It lets executives get away from the pressures of the job and work in a climate in which "party line" thinking is discouraged and self-analysis is stimulated.
2. It presents a challenge to executives that, in general, enhances their motivation to develop themselves.
3. It provides resource people and resource material—faculty members, fellow executives, and literature—that contribute suggestions and ideas for the executives to "try on for size" as they attempt to change, develop, and grow.

The theme of the advantages cited above is that trainees are more stimulated to learn by being away from job pressures. This is certainly debatable since it is questionable whether much of what is learned can be transferred back to the job. Attending a case problem-solving program in San Diego is quite different from facing irate customers in Detroit.

However, despite the difficulty of transferring knowledge from the classroom-type environment to the office, plant, or hospital, off-the-job training programs are still very popular and widely utilized.

The Lecture Method. This is probably the most widely used method of training because it is a relatively inexpensive way to distribute information in programs in which knowledge acquisition by participants is the objective. However, if changing attitudes is the primary objective of a training program, it would seem that the lecture method could not accomplish this objective by itself.

A main attraction of the lecture method is its simplicity and the control it is supposed to give to the trainer. The lecture can be prepared weeks or months ahead of time, and the material can be used again and again. Despite the advantage of preparing the lecture before presentation, the procedure doesn't ensure that learning will occur. A critical point often forgotten is that the audience must be motivated to learn. In training programs that participants are required to attend, their presence doesn't ensure motivation. The best-developed and planned lecture may not achieve any impact if the participants are not ready to learn.

The Discussion or Conference Approach. This method provides the participants with opportunities to exchange ideas and recollections of experiences. Through the interaction in the sessions, the participants stimulate one another's thinking, broaden their outlook, and improve their communicative abilities.

The role of participants is relatively passive in the lecture method, while in the discussion group trainees have many opportunities to participate. The trainer serves as a resource person and provides immediate feedback. Because of the interaction between trainer and participants, the trainer must be highly skilled. If interpersonal skills are to be improved and knowledge acquired, the trainer must understand the importance of reinforcing positive behavior and feeding back clearly the contribution of each participant to the group discussion.

The Case Study and Role-Playing Method. This method provides trainees with a description of some events that actually occurred in an organization. The case may describe the manner in which a nursing supervisor tried to motivate subordinates or the type of wage and salary program that was implemented in a retail store. Trainees read the case, identify the problems, and reach solutions.

In role playing, trainees are asked to participate actively in the case study. That is, they act out a case as if it were a play. This form of learning is an application of experiential learning that is based on the concept of learning by doing.[19] One participant may be the nurse supervisor, and three other participants may play the roles of subordinates. The rationale is that role playing enables the participants to actually "feel" what the cases are all about.

---

[19] P. Jervis, "Analysing Decision Behavior: Learning Models and Learning Styles as Diagnostic Aids," *Personnel Review*, 1983, pp. 26–38.

The process of organizational change and development inevitably includes some form of training. Organizational development requires *learning* new skills and attitudes. Thus, whether formal or informal, training and learning precede change. In some instances, the training is the central focus in the transition to a new, preferred state. The following Close-Up illustrates the importance of training in organizational development efforts at Aluminum Company of America.

ORGANIZATIONS: CLOSE-UP

Change-Oriented Training at Alcoa

Aluminum Company of America (Alcoa) relies on training to bring about changes in the way it manages. Alcoa's human resources department designed training programs that encourage managers to accept women and minorities as peers and comanagers. These "consciousness-raising" programs are part of a larger effort to develop skills in problem solving and teamwork. The training of all managers emphasizes the improvement of productivity through the development of a corporate-wide philosophy of participative management. The training includes the usual lecture, discussion and role-playing methods, but it also includes computer simulations and videotapes of role-playing exercises. Alcoa is striving to make a significant change in managerial skills and attitudes through training.

Source: Carol Hymowitz, "Tradition-Bound Alcoa Develops Training to Challenge Concern's Old-Boy Network," *The Wall Street Journal,* November 15, 1980, p. 35.

BEHAVIORAL DEVELOPMENT METHODS

Levels VII through X require methods that delve deeply into group and individual behavior processes. Intergroup, intragroup, individual-group, and individual behavior often involve emotional and perceptual processes that interfere with effective organizational functioning. These development targets have received the greatest amount of attention from OD experts, and a considerable number of methods have therefore been devised for attacking them. Instead of cataloging all these methods, we will discuss only four of them in detail—the managerial grid, sensitivity training, team building, and life planning. These are the more widely used methods since they tend to span at least two and potentially three levels or targets.

The Managerial Grid

managerial grid program
A program that combines leadership training and group development exercises.

The **managerial grid program** is based on a theory of leadership behavior.[20] The two dimensions of leadership that the developers of the program, Blake and Mouton, identify are concern for production and concern for people. A balanced concern for production and people, is the most effective leadership style according to Blake and Mouton. The managerial grid program requires not only the development of this style *but also the development of group behavior that supports and sustains it.* The entire program consists of six sequential phases that are undertaken over a three- to five-year period.

The six phases can be separated into two major segments. The first two phases provide the foundation for the four later phases.

1.   Laboratory-Seminar Training.   This is typically a one-week conference designed to introduce the manager to the grid philosophy and objectives. From 12 to 48 managers are assigned as members of problem-solving seminars. These seminars are conducted by line managers of the company who have already been through this initial grid training phase.

The seminar begins by determining and reviewing each participant's style of leadership behavior concerning production and people. It continues with 50 hours of problem solving, focusing on situations involving interpersonal behavior and its influences on task performance. Each group regularly assesses its problem-solving performance. This immediate face-to-face feedback sets the stage for phase 2.

2.   Intragroup Development.   In this phase, superiors and their immediate subordinates explore their managerial styles and operating practices as a group. It is anticipated that the climate of openness and candor that was established in phase 1 will carry over into phase 2. Taken together, the first two phases provide conditions that are designed to:

Enable managers to learn managerial grid concepts as an organizing framework for thinking about management practices.

Build improved relationships between groups, among colleagues at the same level, and between superiors and subordinates.

Make managers more critical of outworn practices and precedents while extending their problem-solving capacities in interdependent situations.

Such words as *involvement* and *commitment* become real in terms of day-to-day tasks.

---

[20] Robert R. Blake and Jane S. Mouton, *The Versatile Manager* (Homewood, Ill.: Richard D. Irwin, 1982).

3. *Intergroup Development.* This phase involves group-to-group working relationships and focuses on building effective group roles and norms that improve relationships among groups within the organization. Situations are established whereby tensions that typically exist between groups are identified and discussed by group members.

The objective of this phase is to move the groups from the usual "we win–you lose" patterns to a joint problem-solving activity. This procedure also helps link managers who are at the same management level but belong to different work units.

4. *Organizational Goal Setting.* The immediate objective of the fourth phase is to set up a model of an effective organization for the future. The development of an organizational blueprint involves developing convictions about ideal management practices by testing existing practices and setting attainable objectives. Through the focus on the total organization, it is hoped that planned goals at each level will be linked.

5. *Goal Attainment.* This phase uses some of the group and educational procedures that were used in phase 1, but the major concern is the total organization. Once the special task groups define the problem areas, other groups are set up throughout the organization. These groups are given a written "task paragraph" that describes the problem and the goal. The group members are given packets of information on the issue under discussion. They study the packets and then are given a test on the contents. Once the information is understood and agreement has been reached within the group, the group begins to work on corrective steps.

6. *Stabilization.* The final phase is a period of stabilizing the changes brought about in prior phases. A period of time, perhaps as long as a year, is necessary after the first five phases to identify weaknesses and take corrective actions on the goals set and the plans implemented. This phase also enables management to evaluate the total program.

The longevity of the managerial grid method suggests that it is more than a fad to practicing managers. Thus, it would appear that more rigorous studies of what it can and cannot accomplish are required. Only by properly studying this approach can those interested in implementing it as a developmental method generally understand how it can change employee behavior.

team building
A management technique that includes a number of specific methods for developing effective teamwork both within and among work groups.

Team Building

The managerial grid approach develops a group process to support and sustain a particular leadership style. It is not necessary, however, to develop group behavior around any one leadership style. Rather, group processes can develop to perform more effectively through **team**

building.[21] Whereas the managerial grid is a comprehensive technique, the focus of team building is the work group, as illustrated by the following Close-Up.

ORGANIZATIONS: CLOSE-UP

Quality of Work-Life at Tarrytown

To keep unionized organizations effective, organizational efforts must involve the union as well as management. In 1973, General Motors and the United Auto Workers established the National Committee to Improve the Quality of Work Life. The committee consists of two high-placed union officials and two top-management people. The purpose of the committee is to encourage and sponsor efforts at the local plant level that are designed to improve and develop the quality of work-life.

An example of the results produced by the joint committee is the improvement in performance at the Tarrytown, New York, plant, where the company assembles the front-wheel-drive Chevrolet Citation. The plant had a history of union-management adversity, excessive costs, and poor overall performance. Gus Beirne, former superintendent of the plant, recalls: "Workers and bosses were constantly at each others' throats." Something had to be done. With the support and encouragement of the national committee, the Tarrytown plant established its own joint committee and began discussions regarding ways to overcome the difficulties that beset the plant.

A significant outcome of the local committee's deliberations was the initiation of a three-day training program for all of the employees at Tarrytown. The primary focus of the training program was the development of skills in team problem solving. But the training sessions also enabled management and union officials to talk to the participants about the plant and about how their jobs were related to other jobs in the plant. Attendance at the program was voluntary, but nearly all of the 3,800 employees attended during 1½-year duration.

The effort is credited with much of the improvement in the Tarrytown plant's performance indicators. Satisfaction has improved; absenteeism has dropped; and grievances are only a fraction of what they were before the training sessions. Top management now considers Tarrytown to be one of the best-performing assembly plants in General Motors. The clear lesson of the Tarrytown experience is that management and labor can cooperate to their mutual advantage to increase both job satisfaction and productivity.

Source: "Stunning Turnaround at Tarrytown," *Time*, May 5, 1980, p. 87.

---

[21] S. Jay Liebowitz and Kenneth P. de Meuse, "The Application of Team Building," *Human Relations*, January 1982, pp. 1–18.

The purpose of team building is to enable work groups to get their work done more effectively, to improve their performance.[22] The work groups may be existing, or relatively new, command and task groups. The specific aims of the intervention include setting goals and priorities, analyzing the ways the group does its work, examining the group's norms and processes for communicating and decision making, and examining the interpersonal relationships within the group. As each of these aims is undertaken, the group is placed in the position of having to recognize explicitly the contributions, positive and negative, of each group member.[23]

The process by which these aims is achieved begins with *diagnostic* meetings. Often lasting an entire day, the meetings enable each group member to share with other members his or her perceptions of problems. If the group is large enough, subgroups engage in discussion and report their ideas to the total group. The purpose of these sessions is to obtain the views of all members and to make these views public. That is, diagnosis, in this context, implies the value of "open confrontation" of issues and problems that were previously talked about in relative secrecy.

Problem identification, and consensus as to their priority, is an initial and important step. However, a *plan of action* must be agreed on. The action plan should call on each of the group members, individually or as part of a subgroup, to undertake a specific action to alleviate one or more of the problems. If, for example, an executive committee agrees that one of the problems is lack of understanding of and commitment to a set of goals, a subgroup can be appointed to recommend goals to the total group at a subsequent meeting. Other group members can work on other problems. For example, if problems are identified in the relationships among the members, a subgroup initiates a process for examining the roles of each member.[24]

Team-building interventions do not always require a complex process of diagnostic and action meetings. For example, the chief executive of a large manufacturing firm recognized that conflict within his executive group was creating defensiveness among the functional departments. He also recognized that his practice of dealing on a one-to-one basis with each of the executive group members, each of whom

---

[22] Richard W. Woodman and John J. Sherwood, "Effects of Team Development Intervention: A Field Experiment," *Journal of Applied Behavioral Science,* April–June 1980, pp. 211–17; and R. Wayne Boss, "Organizational Development in the Health-Care Field: A Confrontational Team-Building Design," *Journal of Health and Human Resources Administration,* Summer 1983, pp. 72–91.

[23] Richard L. Hughes, William E. Rosenbach, and William H. Clover, "Team Development in an Intact, Ongoing Work Group," *Group and Organizational Studies,* June 1983, pp. 161–81.

[24] Virginia E. Schein and Larry E. Greiner, "Can Organization Development Be Fine-Tuned to Bureaucracies?" *Organizational Dynamics,* Winter, 1977, p. 54.

headed a functional department, contributed to the defensiveness and conflict. Rather than viewing themselves as team members having a stake in the organization, the department heads viewed one another as competitors. The chief excutive's practice of dealing with them individually confirmed their belief that they managed relatively independent units.

To counteract the situation, the chief executive adopted the simple expedient of requiring the top group to meet twice weekly. One meeting focused on operating problems, the other on personnel problems. The ground rule for these meetings was that the group must reach consensus on decisions. After one year of such meetings, company-oriented decisions were being made and the climate of interunit competition had been replaced by cooperation.

Team building is also effective when new groups are being formed. Problems often exist when new organizational units, project teams, or task forces are created. Typically, such groups have certain characteristics that must be overcome if the groups are to perform effectively. For example:

1. Confusion exists as to roles and relationships.
2. Members have a fairly clear understanding of short-term goals.
3. Group members have technical competence that puts them on the team.
4. Members often pay more attention to the tasks of the team than to the relationships among the team members.

The result of these characteristics is that the new group will focus initially on task problems but ignore the relationship issues. By the time the relationship problems begin to surface, the group is unable to deal with them and performance begins to deteriorate.

To combat these tendencies, the new group should schedule team-building meetings during the first weeks of its life. The meetings should take place away from the work site; one- or two-day meetings are often sufficient. The format of such meetings varies, but essentially their purpose is to provide time for the group to work through its timetable and the roles of members in reaching the group's objectives. An important outcome of such meetings is to establish understanding about each member's contribution to the team and about the reward for that contribution. Although the reports of team building indicate mixed results, the evidence suggests that group processes improve through team-building efforts.[25] This record of success accounts for the increasing use of team building as an OD method.[26]

---

[25] Kenneth P. de Meuse and S. Jay Liebowitz, "An Empirical Analysis of Team-Building Research," *Group and Organizational Studies*, September 1981, pp. 357–78.

[26] W. J. Heisler, "Patterns of OD in Practice," in *Organization Development*, ed. Daniel Robey and Steven Altman (New York: Macmillan, 1982), pp. 23–29.

Life Planning

Problems at the individual level are often diagnosed as the result of mismatches between what people want out of life and what they get. People grow and change; throughout their lives, they develop skills, attitudes, and beliefs that may be incompatible with their lifestyles, including the style of their work lives. Life situations change away from the workplace as children come and go, as marriages strengthen or decay. The intertwining of work and living creates dynamic forces that affect job performance.

life planning
A development method that encourages and enables individuals to take an active role in integrating their career and life activities toward satisfying outcomes.

Initial career choices reflect a person's interests, personality, self-identify, and social background at the time such choices are made. But these factors change. **Life planning** techniques are not only a reflection of an organization's commitment to the aspirations of its employees but are also valid responses to ineffective individual performance.[27]

Life planning and development involve an intervention process that encourages individuals to focus on their past, present, and future states. Specifically, the process enables individuals to consider the following points:

1. An assessment of one's life at the present time, including important events and choices as well as personal strengths and weaknesses.
2. A formulation of future goals as related to the desired lifestyle and career path.
3. The establishment of a plan that specifies goals, action steps, and target dates.

Each individual considers these points after engaging in exercises that require explicit analyses. Although the specific format of the exercise may vary, the following is representative.

First Phase

1. Draw a straight line from left to right to represent your life span. The length represents your total life experience and your future expectations.
2. Indicate on the line where you are now.
3. Prepare an inventory of important happenings, including:
   a. Peak experiences you have had.
   b. Things you do well.
   c. Things you do poorly.
   d. Things you would like to stop doing.
   e. Things you would like to learn to do well.

---

[27] Douglas T. Hall, *Careers in Organizations* (Santa Monica, Calif.: Goodyear Publishing 1976), pp. 11–22.

   f. Peak experiences you would like to have.
   g. Values you want to achieve.
   h. Things you would like to start doing now.
4. Discussion of each person's statements in subgroups.

Second Phase

1. Write your own obituary.
2. Form pairs, and write an eulogy for your partner.
3. Discussion in subgroups.

The value of providing opportunities for employees to assess their lives depends largely on the commitment of organizations. The forms of that commitment are money and time—money to sponsor the training and time of employees to participate. But if life planning is done properly, benefits can accrue to individuals and organizations. For example, life planning:

Demonstrates the large social responsibility of a mature organization.

Indicates to employees that the organization cares about them.

Prepares individuals for change in society, organizations, and themselves.

Releases the potential of the individual on behalf of the organization.[28]

Life planning is closely related to management by objectives, but it focuses on life accomplishments rather than job accomplishments. This technique commits the organization to a process that recognizes the value of each individual and to an effort to integrate individual and organizational aspirations.

Sensitivity Training

sensitivity training
A widely used method for assisting people to learn how they can improve their interpersonal skills.

This highly publicized and widely used development method focuses on individual and individual-group problems.[29] "Sensitivity" in this context means sensitivity to self and to self-other relationships. An assumption of **sensitivity training** is that the causes of poor task performance are the emotional problems of the people who must collectively achieve the goal. Consequently, eliminating these problems removes a major impediment to task performance. Sensitivity training stresses the *process* rather than the *content* of training and focuses

---

[28] Gordon L. Lippitt, "Developing Life Plans: A New Concept and Design for Training and Development," *Training and Development Journal,* May 1970, p. 3.

[29] Kenneth N. Wexley and Gary P. Latham, *Developing and Training Human Resources in Organizations,* (Glenview, Ill.: Scott, Foresman, 1981), p. 184.

on *emotional* rather than *conceptual* training. Thus, this form of training is quite different from traditional forms of training that emphasize the acquisition of a predetermined set of concepts with immediate application to the workplace.

The process of sensitivity training includes a group (a T-group) that in most cases meets at some place away from the job. The group, under the direction of a trainer, can engage in a group dialogue that has no agenda and no focus. The objective is to provide an environment that produces its own learning experiences.[30] As group members engage in the dialogue, they are encouraged to learn about themselves as they deal with others. They explore their needs and their attitudes as revealed through their behavior toward others in the group and through the behavior of others in the group toward them. The T-group may be highly unstructured. As one who participated in sensitivity training points out, "It [sensitivity training] says, 'Open your eyes. Look at yourself. See how you look to others. Then decide what changes, if any, you want to make and in which direction you want to go.'"

A critical test of sensitivity training is whether the experience itself is a factor leading to improvement in task performance. Although studies confirm that such training induces positive changes in the participant's sensitivity to self and others,[31] nevertheless such behavior may be either impossible or impermissible back in the workplace. The participant must deal with the same environment and the same people as before the training. The open, supportive, and permissive environment of the training sessions may not be found on the job or even back in one's home.[32] Even so, the proponent of sensitivity training would reply that the participants are better able to deal with the environment and to understand their own relationship to it. We would also recognize that sensitivity training may well induce negative changes in some participants' ability to perform their organizational task; the training sessions can be occasions of extreme stress and anxiety. The capacity to deal effectively with stress varies among individuals, and the outcome may be dysfunctional for these participants.[33]

The scientific evidence to date suggests mixed results for the effec-

---

[30] Elliot Aronson, "Communication in Sensitivity Training Groups," in *Organization Development,* ed. Wendell L. French, Cecil H. Bell, Jr., and Robert A. Zawacki, (Plano, Tex. Business Publications, 1983), pp. 249–53.

[31] Peter B. Smith, "Controlled Studies in the Outcomes of Sensitivity Training," *Psychological Bulletin,* July 1975, pp. 597–622.

[32] Peter B. Smith, "Back-Home Environment and With-Group Relationships as Determinants of Personal Change," *Human Relations,* January 1983, pp. 53–67.

[33] Gary L. Cooper, "How Psychologically Dangerous Are T-Groups and Encounter Groups?" *Human Relations,* April 1975, pp 249–60; and Carl A. Bramlette and Jeffrey H. Tucker, "Encounter Groups: Positive Change or Deterioration? More Data and a Partial Replication," *Human Relations,* April 1981, pp. 303–14.

tiveness of sensitivity training as a change method.[34] Managers must critically examine this technique in terms of the kinds of changes that they desire and in terms of the changes that are possible given the existence of conditions that limit the range of possible changes. In this light, managers must determine whether the changes induced by sensitivity training are instrumental for organizational purposes and whether prospective participants are able to tolerate the potential anxiety of the training.

The inconclusive results regarding the relationships between sensitivity training and organizational effectiveness have caused managers to become skeptical about its use.[35] That skepticism and the concern of OD experts to improve their methods have led to a number of variations on the basic sensitivity approach. These variations tend to delve less deeply into the non-work-related feelings and sentiments of the participants and instead focus only on task-relevant behavior. These variants have not been fully evaluated in terms of organizational effectiveness, nor is there widespread understanding of *how* sensitivity training brings about the changes. Nevertheless, the use of sensitivity training–type approaches in organizational development is firmly established.

MULTIMETHOD OD PROGRAMS

In the previous sections, we have reviewed the characteristics of a number of organizational development methods. The success of OD efforts depends in part on matching the method and the depth of intervention. Thus, a manager should be wary of the claims of proponents for all-purpose methods. Each method, whether System 4, MBO, or sensitivity training, has a primary focus, or target, of change. Managers will be disappointed if they expect changes in targets that are not affected by the method. If the change required is broad-based, involving several targets, or depths of intervention, then the OD program must incorporate more than one method.

A recent review of the record of OD interventions in bringing about change concluded that multimethod approaches had had better success than single-method ones.[36] Nichols compared the effects of sensitivity training, team building, job enrichment, and job redesign and concluded that no one method was successful in all instances (an expected

---

[34] Smith, "Controlled Studies in the Outcomes of Sensitivity Training."

[35] William J. Kearney and Desmond D. Martin, "Sensitivity Training: An Established Management Development Tool?" *Academy of Management Journal,* December 1974, pp. 755–60.

[36] John M. Nicholas, "The Comparative Impact of Organization Development Interventions on Hard Criteria Measures," *Academy of Management Review,* October 1982, pp. 531–42.

conclusion, given what we have said above). But he also found that significant changes occurred when several methods were combined. One such combination includes three discrete steps that involve all levels of the organization. The three steps are: (1) all employees participate in goal-setting, decision-making, and job redesign; (2) employee collaboration is developed through team building; and (3) the organizational structure is reorganized to accommodate the new levels of participation and collaboration. The application of these three steps can go a long way toward meeting some of the arguments against specific OD methods (e.g., the arguments in the opening Organizational Issue for Debate, which highlighted sensitivity training). The overriding managerial concern is transfer of learning to the work environment. Only under these circumstances can OD methods be considered effective.

The idea that organizational development involves multilevels and multifunctions coincides with the conclusions of systems theory. All parts of an organization *are* connected to all other parts, and change in one part involves change in all parts. The following Close-Up describes a multimethod OD program at American Telephone and Telegraph (AT&T).

ORGANIZATIONS: CLOSE-UP

Multimethod OD at AT&T

Since 1981, a work unit of AT&T has been involved in organizational development. The unit consists of 16 employees who set prices for AT&T's Private Line Interstate Digital Service. The unit's job requires considerable teamwork under stressful circumstances. The OD program aims at the improvement of teamwork through improvement of communications, individual growth, and job involvement. To achieve these purposes, the unit's manager implemented several different OD methods, including (1) routinely scheduled staff meetings that encourage participation, (2) clarification of job responsibilities, (3) individually tailored career plans, (4) increased delegation of authority, (5) increased emphasis on in-service training, (6) management literature review sessions that require participants to read and report articles pertaining to management theory and practice, (7) development of multidirectional communications channels, (8) stress reduction programs such as meditation and relaxation, (9) management by objectives, and (10) after-work functions such as softball and football games. The unit's manager believes that a broad-gauged approach is necessary to achieve fully the expected outcomes.

Source: Robert R. Craver, "AT&T's QWL Experiment: A Practical Case Study," *Management Review,* June 1983, pp. 12–16.

Effective organizational development requires accurate diagnosis of problems, the selection of appropriate targets for change, and the application of appropriate, usually multiple, OD methods. The valued outcome of OD is an organization whose separate parts are directed toward common purposes. Integrated, multimethod OD programs are promising means for achieving that outcome.[37]

SUMMARY OF KEY POINTS

A. After diagnosing the problem and identifying the targets for change, management must select the most promising development method. The philosophy of OD emphasizes that the correct order of analysis is problem to method, not method to problem.

B. Management must tailor the OD program to the problems and personnel of the organization. Throughout our discussions of organizational design, motivation, and leadership, we have stressed the contingency approach. This point of view is fundamental to the process of organizational development and change.

C. Inherent in the contingency approach is the understanding that each organization must adapt in unique ways to its environment. Accordingly, conditions exist that limit the range of the development methods and strategies available to management. A development method such as sensitivity training or System 4 will fail if management does not support the behavioral changes induced by the OD program.

D. Analysis of the problem, identification of alternatives, and recognition of constraints lead to the selection of the most promising method and strategy. The selection is based on the principle of maximizing expected returns to the organization.

E. Although there is by nature considerable overlap among the levels for which a particular method is appropriate, each has a primary focus. One would not expect, for example, that MBO will be effective in changing behaviors at level X, although it may have some effect on behaviors at levels VII and VIII.

F. The number of OD methods is considerable and is constantly increasing. Only a few of the more widely used ones have been

---

[37] Mark Mendenhall and Gary Oddou, "The Integrative Approach to OD: McGregor Revisited," *Group and Organizational Studies,* September 1983, pp. 291–302.

discussed. Managers considering the possibility of OD should consult a more detailed description of them. Several such descriptions appear in the citations and additional references of this chapter.

DISCUSSION AND REVIEW QUESTIONS

1. Do you believe that changes are required in processes, behaviors, or structure in the college you attend?

2. Which organizational development method described in the chapter would you recommend to your university's president for implementation? Why?

3. What are the implicit value judgments of the organizational development techniques described in this chapter? Do you agree with them?

4. Could professors use MBO in the management of their classrooms? Could they negotiate different course objectives for each student. What difficulties might they encounter?

5. Describe how you would go about designing a managerial grid training program for a group of campus student leaders.

6. What are the differences between MAPS and System 4 organization? Are the differences simply matters of emphasis, or are there fundamental differences?

7. What would be the most serious limiting condition for each of the development methods discussed in this chapter?

8. What specific motivation theories explain the apparent success of MBO? Develop your answer fully.

9. Explain how team-building exercises apply group-development theory as explained in Chapter 8.

ADDITIONAL REFERENCES

Armenakis, A. A., A. G. Bedeian, and S. B. Pond III. "Research Issues in OD Evaluation: Past, Present and Future." *Academy of Management Review,* 1983, pp. 320–28.

Brush, D. H., and B. J. Licata. "The Impact of Skill Learnability on the Effectiveness of Managerial Training and Development." *Journal of Management,* 1983, pp. 27–39.

Connor, P. E. "A Critical Inquiry into Some Assumptions and Values Characterizing OD." *Academy of Management Review,* 1977, pp. 635–44.

Covaleski, M. A., and M. W. Dirsmith. "MBO and Goal-Directedness in a Hospital Context." *Academy of Management Review,* 1981, pp. 409–18.

Cummings, G., E. S. Molloy, and R. H. Glen. "Intervention Strategies for Improving Productivity and the Quality of Work Life." *Organizational Dynamics,* 1975, pp. 52–68.

Davis, H. J., and K. M. Weaver. *Alternate Workweek Patterns: An Annotated Bibliography of Selected Literature.* Washington, D.C.: National Council for Alternative Work Patterns, 1978.

Fordyce, J. D., and R. Weil. *Managing with People: A Manager's Handbook of Organizational Development Methods.* Reading, Mass.: Addison-Wesley Publishing, 1979.

French, W. L., C. H. Bell, Jr., and Robert A. Zawacki, eds. *Organization Development.* Rev. ed. Plano, Tex.: Business Publications, 1983.

Galbraith, J. R. "Designing the Innovating Organization." *Organizational Dynamics.* 1982, pp. 5–25.

Glassman, A. M., and S. McCoy. "Organizational Development in a Social Service Agency: Preparing for the Future." *Public Personnel Management,* 1981, pp. 324–32.

Greenbaum, H. H. "Organizational Structure and Communication Processes: A Study of Change." *Group and Organizational Studies,* 1983, pp. 61–82.

Hornstein, H. A., and N. M. Tichy. "Developing Organization Development for Multinational Organizations." *Columbia Journal of World Business,* 1976, pp. 474–95.

Hughes, R. L.; W. E. Rosenbach; and W. H. Clover. "Team Building in an Intact, Ongoing Work Group." *Group and Organizational Studies,* 1983, pp. 161–86.

Jackson, J. H. "Using Management by Objectives: Case Studies of Four Attempts." *Personnel Administrator,* 1981, pp. 78–81.

Kaufman, R. "Organizational Improvement: A Review of Models and an Attempted Synthesis." *Group and Organizational Studies,* 1976, pp. 474–95.

Kondrasuk, J. N. "Studies in MBO Effectiveness." *Academy of Management Review,* 1981, pp. 419–30.

Lindell, M. K., and J. A. Drexler. "Equivocality of Factor Incongruence as an Indicator of Type of Change in OD Interventions." *Academy of Management Review,* 1980, pp. 105–8.

Moore, P. D., and T. Staton. "Management by Objectives in American Cities." *Public Personnel Management,* 1981, pp. 223–32.

Nadler, D. A. "The Use of Feedback for Organizational Change." *Group and Organizational Studies,* 1976, pp. 177–86.

Plovnick, M. S.; R. S. Fry; and W. W. Burke. *Organization Development.* Boston: Little, Brown, 1982.

Pringle, C. D., and J. G. Longenecker. "Ethics in MBO." *Academy of Management Review,* 1982, pp. 305–12.

Robey, D., and S. Altman. *Organization Development.* New York: Macmillan, 1982.

Ruth, S. R., and W. W. Brooks. "Who's Using MBO in Management?" *Journal of Systems Management,* 1980, pp. 30–36.

Schein, V. E.; E. H. Maurer; and J. F. Novak. "Impact of Flexible Working Hours on Productivity." *Journal of Applied Psychology,* 1977, pp. 463–65.

Schneier, C. E. "Behavior Modification in Management: A Review and Critique." *Academy of Management Journal,* 1974, pp. 528–48.

Scott, D. "Productive Partnership: Coupling MBO and TA." *Management Review,* 1976, pp. 12–19.

Seashore, S. E.; E. E. Lawler III; P. H. Mirvis, and C. Cammann. *Assessing Organizational Change: A Guide to Methods, Measures, and Practices.* New York: John Wiley & Sons, 1983.

Stephenson, T. E. "Organization Development— A Critique." *Journal of Management Studies,* 1975, pp. 249–65.

Tichy, N. M. *Managing Strategic Change: Technical, Political, and Cultural Dynamics.* New York: John Wiley and Sons, 1983.

Umstot, D. D. "Organization Development Technology and the Military: A Surprising Merger?" *Academy of Management Review,* 1980, pp. 189–201.

Warrick, D. D. "Applying OD to the Public Sector." *Public Personnel Management,* 1976, pp. 186–90.

White, L. P., and K. C. Wooten. "Ethical Dilemmas in Various Stages of Organizational Development." *Academy of Management Review,* 1983, pp. 690–97.

White, S. E., and T. R. Mitchell. "Organization: A Review of Research Content and Design." *Academy of Management Review,* 1976, pp. 57–73.

Zager, R., and M. P. Rosow. *The Innovative Organization.* New York: Pergamon Press, 1982.

CASE FOR ANALYSIS

Developing Effective Work Teams

The Saga Administrative Corporation was created in the 1940s to provide food service to universities and other institutions. The organization of the company was along territorial lines; the food service managers at institutions reported to district managers, who in turn report to regional managers. The vice president for food service, located in Menlo Park, California, had responsibility for food service operations and was the ultimate source of authority for all decisions regarding food service.

The rapid expansion of the company had caused considerable upheaval in the way Saga typically functioned. The philosophy of the chairman of the board reflected that of the company's founders; it stated, essentially, that the "Saga way" was to prosper by promoting within the company a sense of respect for the dignity of each individual employee and by encouraging a spirit of entrepreneurism. Employees throughout the organization should be made to feel that they had contributions to make and that they should exercise initiative and independent action. The company's top management knew from experience that the food service manager at a particular institution faced unique problems and must be willing and able to make decisions. But apparently this philosophy had been lost during the expansion period. More and more, it seemed to top management, managers all down the line looked to headquarters for decisions. Attitude surveys were undertaken, and they indicated that managers viewed headquarters as a "Big Daddy" that always knew best.

In response to their own views of the situation and the results of the attitude surveys, Saga's executives met with two OD experts from the UCLA faculty. That meeting was the initial step in the development of an OD program in Saga. But at that time there was no commonly held view as to exactly what was wrong or what was required to correct it. The executives simply felt that a more effective organization was needed and that they wanted to do whatever was required to develop it.

As a first step, the executive group appointed one of their own members to direct the program. His first task was to diagnose the problems and then select a method or set of methods that would be appropriate for Saga. He held meetings throughout the country with managers from all levels of the hierarchy. The focus of the meetings was the data from the attitude surveys. The managers were encouraged to express their interpretations of the meanings of the attitudes reflected in the data. The issues that continually emerged from these meetings centered on feelings of isolation and aloneness. The food service managers at institutions simply felt that they no longer were parts of the organization. Resentment and frustration were prevalent emotions. The institutional food service managers were particularly vocal and stated that if they bucked decisions up the line, it was because headquarters wanted it that way.

The director of the OD effort listened carefully to the discussions at these meetings. It was apparent that the OD method must focus on the philosophy of Saga and make it real in the company's operations. A concept was needed, and it seemed that Likert's idea of interlocking work teams would fit Saga's situation. The geographic dispersion of the company made it possible to think of teams of food service managers and their district managers that would function as decision-making groups. But to build these teams required more than simply stating that they existed and defining their authority. It was necessary to restore the confidence of managers in the good intentions of top management.

The team-building program was thus defined as a method for developing individual, group, and individual-group behavior. The mechanics of the program were as follows:

1. The vice president for food services and his four area managers met first and confronted the issues and problems that kept them from functioning effectively.
2. The area managers met with their district managers. Like the initial meetings held with the vice presidents, these meetings created a renewed sense of trust and confidence. The groups confronted their problems, and communication was more frank and open than in previous meetings.
3. Finally, the district managers and institutional food service managers met. The meetings were based on materials and experience obtained from earlier sessions between upper level management.

The process of team building began at the top and moved successively down into the organization. Information was shared at every level; expectations, attitudes, and feelings were confronted and discussed. The underlying assumption was that the teams could function effectively only if they were able to communicate openly. As one manager observed: "What's changed is not that problems go away but that we can now find out about them for ourselves, we can discuss them openly, and we don't have to conduct an attitude survey to know how we feel."

Questions for Consideration

1. What were the fundamental problems that the Saga OD program sought to resolve?
2. Must any rapidly expanding company experience problems similar to those of Saga?
3. What value orientation underlies the "Saga way" philosophy?

EPILOGUE

Chapter 21

Epilogue:
Organizations:
Behavior,
Structure,
Processes

We have now completed our presentation of *Organizations: Behavior, Structure, Processses*. As mentioned at the outset, we live in an organized society. It is now virtually impossible to escape organizations. Most of us work in organizations and will spend the remainder of our working years in them. Therefore, the intent of this book was to study, examine, and review organizations and what takes place within them. The theme of the book centers on three characteristics of organizations—behavior, structure, and processes.

The main actors throughout our presentation have been people—specifically, the employees of organizations, the managers and nonmanagers. It is *people* who conduct the affairs, transactions, and productive work in organizations. It is *people* who perform well or slow down production or quit to join other organizations. It is *people* who make decisions. It is *people* who lead others, engage in political behavior, distribute rewards, and grow and develop. Thus, this book purposefully focused on the behavior of people in organizations.

As you know by now, theories of human behavior are numerous, sometimes confusing, and often contradictory. Nevertheless, theorists, researchers, and managers continue the search to become more knowledgeable about people. In fact, the field of study now called organizational behavior has evolved because managers and society want to know more about people within organizations.

PEOPLE IN ORGANIZATIONS

The concern for people performing jobs in organizations is not new. What is relatively new, however, is that we are finally becoming more scientific in our study of people within organizations. The importance and use of the scientific approach have been emphasized throughout this book.

The scientific approach to the study of people in organizations is the result of such factors as (1) the managers' need for more than simple, intuitive opinions to make decisions and solve problems, (2) the contributions of a number of behavioral disciplines, (3) a trend away from a "one best way" philosophy and description of people toward a more contingency-based approach, and (4) shifts in the political, economic, international, and competitive environments in which organizations are attempting to survive. Although the scientific approach will not always provide the perfect answer, it does provide a useful framework for the study and analysis of people in organizations.

THE MANAGER: THEORIST, RESEARCHER, AND PRACTITIONER

As indicated throughout this book, more and more managers need to know and use theories, review relevant research findings, and apply techniques that work. Furthermore, to be successful, managers need to acquire and develop diagnostic skills. Managers in organizational settings diagnose perceptions, attitudes, group norms, intergroup conflict, power relationships, political tactics, noncompliance, creativity, low morale, exceptional performance, rating errors, and other topics covered throughout the book. As suggested, these are difficult factors to diagnose.

Managers usually perform their diagnostic tasks in settings that are occasionally turbulent, ambiguous, and unreceptive. This suggests that managers' lives are challenging but also potentially troublesome. For example, research findings indicate that managers:

Work long hours.

Are extremely busy.

Perform work that is fragmented.

Have numerous tasks to perform.

Are primarily involved with oral communication.

Use a lot of interpersonal contact.

Are not the best reflective planners.

Are not generally aware of how they use their time.

The manager's job is exciting. It is dynamic, filled with challenges and uncertainty, and involves people. This excitement is what we hope was portrayed in the book. We admit that managing organizational behavior is difficult, but we also know that managers are extremely important in our society.

ORGANIZATIONAL BEHAVIOR: REVISITED

We pointed out early that many of the theories, research findings, and practical applications that managers review, use, and modify have evolved from the behavioral disciplines. As a result of this evolution, we have now reached a point where the field of organizational behavior is recognized as an integrative attempt to apply the behavioral sciences.

In Chapter 1, we defined organizational behavior (OB) as:

The study of human behavior, attitudes, and performance within an organizational setting; drawing on theory, methods, and principles from such disciplines as psychology, sociology, and cultural anthropology to learn about *individual* perceptions, values, learning capacities, and actions while working in *groups* and within the total *organization;* analyzing the external environment's effect on the organization and its human resources, missions, objectives, and strategies.

Each part of this definition was covered in the book. However, as we noted in Chapter 1, it is valuable to consider OB as: (1) a way of thinking, (2) an eclectic field of study, (3) humanistic, (4) performance-oriented, (5) concerned about how the environment affects people, and (6) scientifically based. These features spell out why OB is now considered an applied field of study.

The integration of the behavioral sciences into OB has significant value to practicing managers. It provides them with theories, research, and techniques that they can use and modify in their unique organizational context. Figure 21–1 presents many of the topics discussed in the chapters in the context of OB.

The Trend Away from Simple Answers

The prominence of the contingency theme indicates that simple, universally accepted answers do not exist. There are simple explanations that can provide insight about people in organizations, but they are often incomplete, misleading, and unrealistic. For example, the trait theories of leadership are concise but are considered unrealistic and nonpredictive. In their place have emerged more complex, yet unproved theories of leadership such as the path-goal and Vroom-Yetton models.

The trend away from the simple toward the more complex is found at every level of analysis—individual, group, and organizational—and for most organizational behavior topics from individual perception to goal setting to team building to career planning. Unfortunately, many theorists and researchers have failed to explain their more complex theories and models to managers. In many cases, they have instead added jargon and complexity at the expense of clarity, practical utility, and meaningfulness. This is unfortunately a verdict reached by too many managers. Consequently, managers in many cases have refused to permit the testing of these theories and models in their organizations. If additional knowledge is to be gained from scientifically testing more complex theories and models, there will be a need to improve the clarity of these approaches.

Certainly, simple answers are not sufficient for most organizational problem areas. However, there is nothing sacred about a more complex approach. Each approach will have to meet three tests: (1) Is it understandable? (2) Is it better than the simpler approaches? and (3) Can

FIGURE 21-1

The Manager's Guide to Applied Organizational Behavior

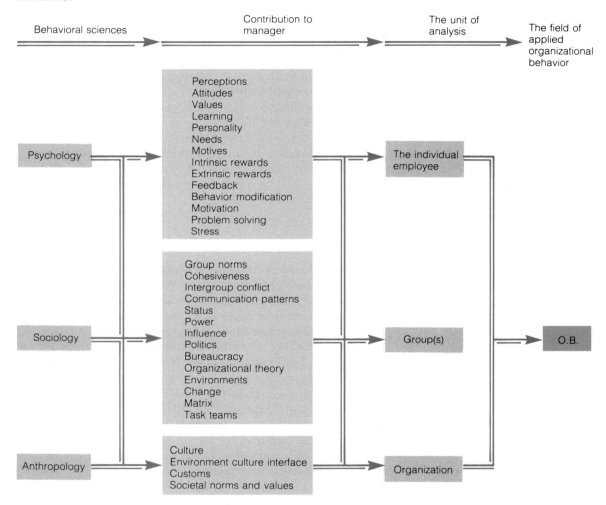

it be applied by managers? Conduct your own evaluation of some of the more complex theories and models that we presented—behavior modification, matrix design, strategic power contingencies, BARS, career planning, superordinate goals, the attribution theory of leadership. Being understandable means that the approach can be explained.

THE ENVIRONMENT

In an era of inflation, international conflict, increasing foreign competition, and growing concern about the quality of life, managers are searching for better insight into and answers to problems. These shifting environmental forces have led to the growth of interest in the kind of environmental topics covered in *Organizations: Behavior, Structure, Processes*. In addition, more and more organizations are scientifically monitoring environmental forces. This monitoring provides a source of information that is vitally needed to make changes within organizations.

Managers now realize that environmental forces operate on the internal functioning of an organization—the individuals, groups, and total system. There is acceptance of the thesis that the interaction of multiple forces causes people, groups, and the organization to behave. The exact nature of this causality is not yet clear. However, managers now accept the premise that environmental forces must be considered when examining the behaviors occurring within organizations. Studying how people behave within organizations without considering the environment results in unrealistic, incomplete, and misleading conclusions.

ADDITIONAL WORK TO BE DONE

Instead of offering just another set of predictions about what the future holds for managers, organizations, and society, we prefer to spell out some areas for additional theorizing, research, and application. We have tried to provide an analysis of people working in organizations. Hopefully, you can distill from the chapters, cases, exercises, and actual organizational situations a sense of (1) what organizations are, (2) what organizations have (i.e., behavior, structure, processes), and (3) what organizations do. Furthermore, the book should have pointed out many areas that need to be developed further. There are many questions that need to be asked and studied in each of these areas.[1] Some of the areas in need of additional work will be briefly identified.

Theories

Well-articulated theories that are relevant to managerial practice need to be developed more completely for understanding individual, group, and organizational characteristics. These theories must be coherent, use managerial language, be testable, and possess reasonable generalizability from one setting to the next. The theories will have to incorporate the changing nature of society, the labor force, and economic conditions.

For example, Maslow's need hierarchy has a commonsense appeal,

---

[1] John P. Campbell, Richard L. Daft, and Charles L. Hulin, *What to Study: Generating and Developing Research Questions* (Beverly Hills, Calif.: Sage Publications, 1982).

but does it apply to women, blacks, handicapped employees, over-worked managers, and employees in dangerous occupations? The questionable validity of the theory should cause serious doubts. Is it possible to develop or use a more complex explanation of motivation? We believe that it is possible if more effort is made to expand the domain of a theory without increasing its jargon. Clarity of presentation should be a major criterion in the development of theories in the field of organizational behavior.

History

We propose that more attention be paid to the history of organizations. The way in which organizations operate today and will operate tomorrow is significantly influenced by past events. We need to take a closer look at the actions of key managers and leaders—at how strategic policy decisions were reached, how managers responded to various crises, and what skills seemed valuable in solving problems. There seems to be a reluctance to even consult history, and what is lost is some of the explanation of how an organization became what it is today. We need a historical branch in the field of organizational behavior as much as we need a theoretical, research, and application orientation.

Measurement

The measurement techniques for studying behavior and testing theories need to be improved. Sole reliance on self-report surveys is questionable and not highly recommended. We now have the theoretical, psychometrical, and statistical capabilities to develop more valid, reliable, and practical techniques than the self-report survey. We need to work on measurement in conjunction with managers so that measuring procedures are developed that not only have psychometric power but also appeal to managers. We are not suggesting the elimination of self-report surveys, only the redirection of effort toward other techniques such as observation, interviewing, and the use of documents and records. The use of qualitative research methods is discussed in Appendix A.

Costs versus Benefits

The economic and psychological costs versus benefits of such techniques as goal setting, leadership training, rater training, career pathing, job enrichment, and matrix organizational structures need to be seriously evaluated. Few studies even estimate the costs of such techniques. We need to begin evaluating techniques in terms of costs (economic and noneconomic) and benefits (economic and noneconomic). Accountants and economists have much to offer the field of organizational behavior in terms of methods for analyzing costs and benefits. Since managers are held accountable for their actions, it seems important to work more systematically on the issue of costs versus benefits.

Applied organizational behavior programs need to be carefully scrutinized so that their short- and long-term contributions can be pinpointed. It is to the manager's benefit to take advantage of available methods for demonstrating costs versus benefits. Top management is likely to increase requests for data and analyses on the costs versus benefits of applied organizational behavior practices.

Technological

Managing people in organizations in the 1980s, as in the past, is not easy. At the same time that so many businesses have been failing or teetering, new industries have been born: biotechnology, fiber optics, electronics, satellite teleconferencing, and many more. What's fueling these new industries? People—people with imagination, the need to excel, and a willingness to work hard and put in long hours.

Just as crop rotation brought a revolution to the farm, as machines and engines ushered in the industrial revolution, we are in the middle of a new revolution. The center of that revolution is people. The present technological revolution is not based on acts of physical labor but on the art of thinking. The major resource is the mind. Evidence of the revolution is everywhere—in robotics, in computers, in laser technology. What will be needed are strategies, programs, and procedures to harness, control, and monitor technological wizardry and power. The management of that wizardry and power so that the human condition will improve will require the use of theories, research, and applications offered by organizational behavioralists.

Managers will need to be prepared for the utilization of the new technologies. New theories of motivation, leadership, and organizational change will be needed to take optimum advantage of the new technologies. An experimental, scientific method-oriented mind-set will be needed to properly assess, modify, and put into practice the new technologies. What is the best organizational arrangement? What kinds of people are productive in that arrangement? How should people be rewarded in such an arrangement? Who will be displaced by new organizational arrangements? What will be the social and work impact of technological and structural changes? These and similar questions will have to be explored if the full benefits of technological growth and change are to be realized. The quantitative and qualitative tools, techniques, and methods for such exploration are what organizational behavioralists can provide.

Training and Development

The training of managers to recognize important contingencies and appropriate responses needs to be undertaken. Managers need to be trained in problem-solving and decision-making skills to make the most efficient use of organizational resources. Unless managers are properly trained, goal attainment will be placed in serious jeopardy, productivity will suffer, and the quality of work-life will decline. Not only must formal training occur, but there must also be scientific evaluation of its effectiveness. Are managers more successful, more responsive to contingency factors, more aware of the environment, and more thorough problem solvers after training? These questions can only be answered if the training is evaluated with valid and reliable measures.

Foreign Management Practices

The economic development and growth of such nations as Japan, Canada, West Germany, and Australia are the result of many factors including government policies, favorable trade pacts with other nations, sound planning and forecasting, and effective managerial practices. The classic view of an economic miracle is the story of Japan. "Made in Japan" was once the mark of shoddy merchandise. However, it is now a badge of quality for everything from compact automobiles to videotape recorders. Are there any lessons for those interested in people working in organizations? We believe so.

There is a need in the field of OB to learn from the experience of foreign organizations as well as domestic organizations. Study and analysis of the relationship between workers and their companies in Japan and elsewhere can provide insight into the managerial techniques being used. Why do Japanese workers have a sense that the company is the base of their lives? Can this feeling be generated for the U.S. worker? Should this feeling be generated? These and similar questions need to be studied at the individual, group, and organizational levels. We are suggesting that the application of OB can be improved by examining what has been successfully used and how it was used in other organizations around the world.

Some American companies have begun experimenting with Japanese-style management techniques. What is now needed are careful and long-term analyses of these experiments. We need to scientifically study foreign management practices so that we can separate fact from fiction. We believe that the wonders of foreign management practices have been exaggerated to the point of fantasy and fable in some cases. We must examine these practices to learn and to analyze how and why a management practice operates as it does.

There are major differences in the economic and political systems and cultures of such nations as Japan, Canada, West Germany, and the United States. Some of the managerial techniques that are successful in one nation may not be successful in other nations. We need to find out why some things work and others fail. Studies on these matters should be conducted by using the scientific approach encouraged in this book. Furthermore, inquiring into what works and what doesn't should proceed at three levels of analysis—the individual, the group, and the organization.

Women and Minorities

Since the early 70s, more and more women and minorities have moved into organizational careers. As a result of this development, the following kinds of questions are being asked: Do women fear success? Can blacks effectively manage white subordinates? How do Mexican-Americans feel about working for women managers? Do men and women differ in aggressiveness, risk-taking propensity, commitment, and the work ethic?

It would be foolish to deny that at present women and minorities working in organizations are relatively misunderstood. What is needed are sound, scientific investigations of men, women, blacks, Mexican-Americans, and others performing managerial and nonmanagerial jobs in organizational settings. We need data to examine and locate differences in style and characteristics if they do exist. Preconceptions, tacit assumptions, and personal opinions should be replaced with comparative research that is based on sound quantitative and qualitative procedures.

These are only a few of the areas that need more dialogue, debate, theory building, research, and experimentation. Instead of suggesting an ideal model of organizational behavior as the foremost need, we have elected to call attention to a few specific areas of interest and concern. Of course, work must proceed in integrating concepts, variables, and causal linkages in the field of organizational behavior. However, just as important is the need to study and analyze more thoroughly people working within organizations. We need theories, frameworks, and techniques to manage more effectively, but we should never lose sight of people as individuals, working in groups, and as part of the total organization.

> "Only the supremely wise and the abysmally ignorant do not change."
>
> Confucius

APPENDIX A Procedures and Techniques for Studying Organizations:

Behavior, Structure, Processes

SOURCES OF KNOWLEDGE
ABOUT ORGANIZATIONS

The vast majority of the research reports and writing on organizations are contained in technical papers known as journals. Some of these journals, such as the *Academy of Management Review,* are devoted entirely to topics of management and organization, while such journals as *Organizational Behavior and Human Performance* are devoted largely to the results of laboratory studies. Such journals as the *Harvard Business Review,* are general business journals, while the *American Sociological Review* and the *Journal of Applied Psychology* are general behavioral science journals. These general business and behavioral science journals often contain articles of interest to students of management. Table A–1 presents a selective list of journals.

The sources in Table A–1 provide information, data, and discussion about what is occurring within and among organizations. This knowledge base provides managers with available research information that could prove useful in their own organizations or situations.

HISTORY AS A WAY OF KNOWING
ABOUT ORGANIZATIONS

The oldest approach to the study of organizations is through the history of organizations, societies, and institutions. Organizations are as old as human history. Throughout time, people have joined with others to accomplish their goals, first in families, later in tribes and other more sophisticated political units. Ancient peoples constructed pyramids, temples, and ships; they created systems of government, farming, commerce, and warfare. For example, Greek historians tell us that it took 100,000 men to build the great pyramid of Khufu in Egypt. The project took over 20 years to complete. It was almost as high as the Washington Monument and had a base that would cover eight football fields. Remember, these people had no construction equipment or computers. One thing they did have, though, was *organization.* While these "joint efforts" did not have formal names such as "XYZ Corporation," the idea of "getting organized" was quite widespread throughout early civilizations. The literature of the times refers to such managerial concepts as planning, staff assistance, division of labor, control, and leadership.[1]

The administration of the vast Roman Empire required the application of organization and management concepts. In fact, it has been

---

[1] For an excellent discussion of organizations in ancient societies, see Claude S. George., Jr., *The History of Management Thought* (Englewood Cliffs, N.J.: Prentice-Hall, 1968), pp. 3–26.

TABLE A-1

Selected Sources of Writing and Research on Organizations

1.	Academy of Management Journal	17.	Journal of Applied Behavioral Science
2.	Academy of Management Review		
3.	Administrative Management	18.	Journal of Applied Psychology
4.	Administrative Science Quarterly	19.	Journal of Business
5.	Advanced Management Journal	20.	Journal of Human Resources
6.	American Sociological Review	21.	Journal of Management Studies
7.	Business Horizons	22.	Management International Review
8.	Business Management	23.	Management Review
9.	California Management Review	24.	Management Science
10.	Fortune	25.	Organizational Behavior and Human Performance
11.	Harvard Business Review		
12.	Hospital and Health Services Administration	26.	Organizational Dynamics
		27.	Personnel
13.	Human Organization	28.	Personnel Journal
14.	Industrial and Labor Relations Review	29.	Personnel Psychology
		30.	Public Administration Review
15.	Industrial Engineering	31.	Public Personnel Review
16.	Industrial Management Review	32.	Training and Development Journal

said that "the real secret of the greatness of the Romans was their genius for organization."[2] This is because the Romans used certain principles of organization to coordinate the diverse activities of the empire.

If judged by age alone, the Roman Catholic Church would have to be considered the most effective organization of all time. While its success is the result of many factors, one of these factors is certainly the effectiveness of its organization and management. For example, a hierarchy of authority, a territorial organization, specialization of activities by function, and use of the staff principle were integral parts of early church organization.

Finally, it is not surprising that some important concepts and practices in modern organizations can be traced to military organizations. This is because, like the church, military organizations were faced with problems of managing large, geographically dispersed groups. As did the church, military organizations early adopted the concept of staff as an advisory function for line personnel.

Knowledge of the history of organizations in earlier societies can be useful for the future manager. In fact, many of the early concepts and practices are being utilized successfully today. However, one may ask whether heavy reliance on the past is a good guide to the present

[2] James D. Mooney, *The Principles of Organization* (New York: Harper & Row, 1939), p. 63.

and future. We shall see that time and organizational setting have much to do with what works in management.

Experience as a Way of Knowing About Organizations

Some of the earliest books on management and organizations were written by successful practitioners. Most of these individuals were business executives, and their writings focused on how it was for them during their time with one or more companies. They usually put forward certain general principles or practices that had worked well for them. Although using the writings and experiences of practitioners sounds "practical," it has its drawbacks. Successful managers are susceptible to the same perceptual phenomena as each of us. Their accounts are therefore based on their own preconceptions and biases. No matter how objective their approaches, the accounts may not be entirely complete or accurate. In addition, the accounts may also be superficial since they are often after-the-fact reflections of situations in which, when the situations were occurring, the managers had little time to think about how or why they were doing something. As a result, the suggestions in such accounts are often oversimplified. Finally, as with history, what worked yesterday may not work today or tomorrow.[3]

Science as a Way of Knowing About Organizations

We have noted that a major interest in this book was the behavioral sciences which have produced theory, research, and generalizations concerning the behavior, structure, and processes of organizations. The interest of behavioral scientists in the problems of organizations is relatively new, becoming popular in the early 1950s. It was at that time that an organization known as the Foundation for Research on Human Behavior was established. The objectives of this organization were to promote and support behavioral science research in business, government, and other types of organizations.

Many advocates of the scientific approach believe that practicing managers and teachers have accepted prevalent practices and principles without the benefit of scientific validation. They believe that scientific procedures should be used whenever possible to validate practice. Because of their work, many of the earlier practices and principles have been discounted or modified and others have been validated.

---

[3] An excellent article on this subject is W. H. Gruber and J. S. Niles, "Research and Experience in Management," *Business Horizons*, Fall 1973, pp. 15–24.

Research in the Behavioral Sciences

Present research in the behavioral sciences is extremely varied with respect to the scope and methods used. One common thread among the various disciplines is the study of human behavior through the use of scientific procedures. Thus, it is necessary to examine the nature of science as it is applied to human behavior. There are those who believe that a science of human behavior is unattainable and that the scientific procedures used to gain knowledge in the physical sciences cannot be adapted to the study of humans, especially humans in organizations.

The authors do not intend to become involved in these arguments. However, we believe that the scientific approach is applicable to management and organizational studies.[4] Furthermore, as we have already pointed out, there are means other than scientific procedures that have provided important knowledge concerning people in organizations.

The manager of the future will draw from the behavioral sciences just as the physician draws from the biological sciences. The manager must know what to expect from the behavioral sciences, their strengths and weaknesses, just as the physician must know what to expect from bacteriology and how it can serve as a diagnostic tool. However, the manager, like the physician, is a practitioner who must make decisions in the present, whether or not science has all the answers, and certainly cannot wait until it finds them before acting.

The Scientific Approach

Most current philosophers of science define "science" in terms of what they consider to be its one universal and unique feature: *method*. The greatest advantage of the scientific approach is that it has one characteristic that no other method of attaining knowledge has: *self-correction*.[5] It is an objective, systematic, and controlled process with built-in checks all along the way to knowledge. These checks control and verify the scientist's activities and conclusions to enable the attainment of knowledge independent of the scientist's own biases and preconceptions.

---

[4] A similar debate has taken place for years over the issue of whether management is a science. For relevant discussions, the interested reader should consult R. E. Gribbons and S. D. Hunt, "Is Management a Science?" *Academy of Management Review,* January 1978, pp. 139–43; O. Behling, "Some Problems in the Philosophy of Science of Organizations," *Academy of Management Review,* April 1978, pp. 193–201; and O. Behling, "The Case for the Natural Science Model for Research in Organizational Behavior and Organization Theory," *Academy of Management Review,* October 1980, pp. 483–90.

[5] See Fred N. Kerlinger, *Foundations of Behavioral Research* (New York: Holt, Rinehart & Winston, 1973), p. 6.

TABLE A–2

Characteristics of the Scientific Approach

1. *The procedures are public.* A scientific report contains a complete description of what was done, to enable other researchers in the field to follow each step of the investigation as if they were actually present.

2. *The definitions are precise.* The procedures used, the variables measured, and how they were measured must be clearly stated. For example, if examining motivation among employees in a given plant, it would be necessary to define what is meant by motivation and how it was measured (for example, number of units produced, number of absences).

3. *The data collecting is objective.* Objectivity is a key feature of the scientific approach. Bias in collecting and interpreting data has no place in science.

4. *The findings must be replicable.* This enables another interested researcher to test the results of a study by attempting to reproduce them.

5. *The approach is systematic and cumulative.* This relates to one of the underlying purposes of science, to develop a unified body of knowledge.

6. *The purposes are explanation, understanding, and prediction.* All scientists want to know "why" and "how." If they determine "why" and "how" and are able to provide proof, they can then predict the particular conditions under which specific events (human behavior in the case of behavioral sciences) will occur. Prediction is the ultimate objective of behavioral science, as it is of all science.

Source: Bernard Berelson and Gary A. Steiner, *Human Behavior: An Inventory of Scientific Findings* (New York: Harcourt Brace Jovanovich, 1964), pp. 16–18.

Most scientists agree that there is no single scientific method but rather several methods that scientists can and do use. Thus, it probably makes more sense to say that there is a scientific approach. Table A–2 summarizes the major characteristic of this approach. While only an "ideal" science would exhibit all of them, they are nevertheless the hallmarks of the scientific approach. They exhibit the basic nature—objective, systematic, controlled—of the scientific approach, which enables others to have confidence in research results. What is important is the overall fundamental idea that the scientific approach is a controlled rational process.

Methods of Inquiry Used by Behavioral Scientists

How do behavioral scientists gain knowledge about the functioning of organizations? Just as physical scientists have certain tools and methods for obtaining information, so too do behavioral scientists. These are usually referred to as *research designs.* In broad terms, there are three basic designs used by behavioral scientists: the case study, the field study, and the experiment.

Case Study. A case study attempts to examine numerous characteristics of one or more people, usually over an extended time period. For years, anthropologists have studied the customs and behavior of various groups by actually living among them. Some organizational researchers have done the same thing. They have actually worked and socialized with the groups of employees that they were studying.[6] The reports on such investigations are usually in the form of a case study. For example, a sociologist might report the key factors and incidents that led to a strike by a group of blue-collar workers.

The chief limitations of the case study approach for gaining knowledge about the functioning of organizations are:

1. Rarely can you find two cases that can be meaningfully compared in terms of essential characteristics. In other words, in another firm of another size the same factors might not have resulted in a strike.

2. Rarely can case studies be repeated or their findings verified.

3. The significance of the findings is left to the subjective interpretation of the researcher. Like the practitioner, the researcher attempts to describe reality, but it is reality as perceived by one person (or a very small group). The researcher has training, biases, and preconceptions that can inadvertently distort the report. A psychologist may give an entirely different view of a group of blue-collar workers than would be given by a sociologist.

4. Since the results of a case study are based on a sample of one, the ability to generalize from them may be limited.[7]

Despite these limitations, the case study is widely used as a method of studying organizations. It is extremely valuable in answering exploratory questions.

Field Study. In attempts to add more reality and rigor to the study of organizations, behavioral scientists have developed several systematic field research techniques such as personal interviews, observation, archival data, and questionnaire surveys. These methods are used individually or in combination. They are used to investigate current practices or events, and with these methods, unlike some other methods, the researcher does not rely entirely on what the subjects say. The researcher may personally interview other people in the organization—fellow workers, subordinates, and superiors—to gain a more balanced view before drawing conclusions.[8] In addition, archival data, rec-

---

[6] See E. Chinoy, *The Automobile Worker and the American Dream* (Garden City, N.Y.: Doubleday Publishing, 1955); and D. Roy, "Banana Time—Job Satisfaction and Informal Interaction," *Human Organization,* 1960, pp. 158–69.

[7] Based in part on Robert J. House, "Scientific Investigation in Management," *Management International Review,* 1970, pp. 141–42. The interested reader should see G. Morgan and L. Smircich, "The Case for Qualitative Research," *Academy of Management Review,* October 1980, pp. 491–500; and L. R. Jauch, R. N. Osborn, and T. N. Martin, "Structured Content Analysis of Cases: A Complementary Method for Organizational Research," *Academy of Management Review,* October 1980, pp. 517–26.

[8] See G. R. Salancik, "Field Stimulations for Organizational Behavior Research," *Administrative Science Quarterly,* December 1979, pp. 638–49, for an interesting approach to field studies.

ords, charts, and statistics on file may be used to analyze a problem or hypothesis.

A very popular field study technique involves the use of expertly prepared questionnaires. Not only are such questionnaires less subject to unintentional distortion than personal interviews, but they also enable the researcher to greatly increase the number of individuals participating. Figure A–1 presents part of a questionnaire that is used in organizations to evaluate ratee perceptions of a performance appraisal interview program. The questionnaire enables the collection of data on particular characteristics that are of interest (for example, equity, accuracy, and clarity). The seven-point scales measure ratee perceptions of the degree to which the performance appraisal interviews possess a given characteristic.

In most cases, surveys are limited to a description of the current state of the situation. However, if researchers are aware of factors that may account for survey findings, they can make conjectural statements (known as hypotheses) about the relationship between two or more factors and relate the survey data to those factors. Thus, instead of just describing ratee perceptions of performance evaluation, the researchers could make finer distinctions (for example, distinctions regarding job tenure, salary level, or education) among groups of ratees. Comparisons and statistical tests could then be applied to determine differences, similarities, or relationships. Finally, *longitudinal* studies involving observations made over time are used to describe changes that have taken place. Thus, in the situation described here, we can become aware of changes in overall ratee perceptions of appraisal interviews over time as well as ratee perceptions relating to individual managers.[9]

Despite their advantages over many of the other methods of gaining knowledge about organizations, field studies are not without problems. Here again, researchers have training, interests, and expectations that they bring with them.[10] Thus, a researcher may inadvertently ignore a vital technological factor when conducting a study of employee morale while concentrating on only behavioral factors. Also, the fact that a researcher is present may influence how the individual responds. This weakness of field studies has long been recognized and is noted in some of the earliest field research in organizations.

Experiment.   The experiment is potentially the most rigorous of scientific techniques. For an investigation to be considered an experiment,

---

[9] The design of surveys and the development and administration of questionnaires are better left to trained individuals if valid results are to be obtained. The interested reader might consult Seymour Sudman and Norman M. Bradburn, *Asking Questions: A Practical Guide to Questionnaire Design* (San Francisco: Jossey-Bass, 1982).

[10] For an excellent article on the relationship between what researchers want to see and what they do see, consult G. Nettler, "Wanting and Knowing," *American Behavioral Scientist,* July 1973, pp. 5–26.

FIGURE A–1

Scale for Assessing GANAT Appraisal Interviews

Part A: Appraisal Interview

The following items deal with the formal appraisal interview used in conjunction with the GANAT project program. Please circle the number that best describes your opinion of the most recent interview session.

	Very False						Very True
1. The appraisal interview covered my entire job.	1	2	3	4	5	6	7
2. The discussion of my performance during the appraisal interview was covered equitably.	1	2	3	4	5	6	7
3. The appraisal interview was accurately conducted.	1	2	3	4	5	6	7
4. I didn't have to ask for any clarification.	1	2	3	4	5	6	7
5. The interview was fair in every respect.	1	2	3	4	5	6	7
6. The interview really raised my anxiety level.	1	2	3	4	5	6	7
7. The interview's purpose was simply not clear to me.	1	2	3	4	5	6	7
8. The appraisal interview really made me think about working smarter on the job.	1	2	3	4	5	6	7
9. The appraisal interview was encouraging to me personally.	1	2	3	4	5	6	7
10. I dreaded the actual interview itself.	1	2	3	4	5	6	7
11. The boss was totally aboveboard in all phases of the interview.	1	2	3	4	5	6	7
12. The interview gave me some direction and purpose.	1	2	3	4	5	6	7
13. The interview really pinpointed areas for improvement.	1	2	3	4	5	6	7
14. The interview was disorganized and frustrating.	1	2	3	4	5	6	7
15. I disliked the interview because the intent was not clear.	1	2	3	4	5	6	7
16. The appraisal interviewer (boss) was not well trained.	1	2	3	4	5	6	7
17. The interview has been my guide for correcting weaknesses.	1	2	3	4	5	6	7
18. I understood the meaning of each performance area better after the interview.	1	2	3	4	5	6	7
19. The interview time was too rushed.	1	2	3	4	5	6	7
20. I received no advanced notice about the interview.	1	2	3	4	5	6	7
21. During the interview, my performance was fairly analyzed.	1	2	3	4	5	6	7
22. I was often upset because the interview data were not accurate.	1	2	3	4	5	6	7
23. My record as it was introduced in the interview contained no errors.	1	2	3	4	5	6	7

Source: This interview appraisal form was developed by John M. Ivancevich and sponsored by research funds provided by the GANAT Company.

it must contain two elements—manipulation of some variable (independent variable) and observation or measurement of the results (dependent variable) while maintaining all other factors unchanged. Thus, in an organization a behavioral scientist could change one organizational factor and observe the results while attempting to keep everything else unchanged.[11] There are two general types of experiments.

In a *laboratory experiment,* the environment is created by the researcher. For example, a management researcher may work with a small voluntary group in a classroom. The group may be students or managers. They may be asked to communicate, perform tasks, or make decisions under different sets of conditions designated by the researcher. The laboratory setting permits the researcher to control closely the conditions under which observations are made. The intention is to isolate the relevant variables and to measure the response of dependent variables when the independent variable is manipulated. Laboratory experiments are useful when the conditions required to test a hypothesis are not practically or readily obtainable in natural situations and when the situation to be studied can be replicated under laboratory conditions. For such situations, many schools of business have behavioral science laboratories where such experimentation is done.

In a *field experiment,* the investigator attempts to manipulate and control variables in the natural setting rather than in a laboratory. Early experiments in organizations included manipulating physical working conditions such as rest periods, refreshments, and lighting, while today behavioral scientists attempt to manipulate a host of additional factors.[12] For example, a training program might be introduced for one group of managers but not for another. Comparisons of performance, attitudes, and so on could be obtained later at one point or at several different points (a longitudinal study) to determine what effect, if any, the training program had on the managers' performances and attitudes.

The experiment is especially appealing to many researchers because it is the prototype of the scientific approach. It is the ideal toward which every science strives. However, while its potential is still great,

---

[11] For a volume devoted entirely to experiments in organizations, see W. M. Evan, ed., *Organizational Experiments: Laboratory and Field Research* (New York: Harper & Row, 1971). Also see J. A. Waters, P. F. Salipante, Jr., and W. W. Notz, "The Experimenting Organization: Using the Results of Behavioral Science Research," *Academy of Management Review,* July 1978, pp. 483–92.

[12] See an account of the classic Hawthorne studies in Fritz J. Roethlisberger and W. J. Dickson, *Management and the Worker* (Boston: Division of Research, Harvard Business School, 1939). The original purpose of the studies, which were conducted at the Chicago Hawthorne Plant of Western Electric, was to investigate the relationship between productivity and physical working conditions.

it has not produced a great breadth of knowledge about the functioning of organizations. Laboratory experiments suffer the risk of "artificiality." The results of such experiments often do not extend to real organizations. Teams of business administration or psychology students working on decision problems may provide a great deal of information for researchers. Unfortunately, it is questionable whether this knowledge can be extended to a group of managers or nonmanagers making decisions under severe time constraints.[13]

Field experiments also have drawbacks. First, researchers cannot "control" every possible influencing factor (even if they knew them all) as they can in a laboratory. Also, here again the fact that a researcher is present may make people behave differently, especially if they are aware that they are participating in an experiment. Experimentation in the behavioral sciences, and more specifically, experimentation in organizations, is a complex matter.

In a *true experiment*, the researcher has complete control over the experiment: the who, what, when, where, and how. A *quasi-experiment*, on the other hand, is an experiment in which the researcher lacks the degree of control over conditions that is possible in a true experiment. In the vast majority of organizational studies, it is impossible to completely control everything. Thus, quasi-experiments are typically the rule when organizational behavior is studied via an experiment.

Finally, with each of the methods of inquiry utilized by behavioral scientists, some type of *measurement* is usually necessary. For knowledge to be meaningful, it must often be compared with or related to something else. As a result, research questions (hypotheses) are usually stated in terms of how differences in the magnitude of some variable are related to differences in the magnitude of some other variable.

The variables studied are measured by research instruments. Those instruments may be psychological tests, such as personality or intelligence tests; questionnaires designed to obtain attitudes or other information, such as the questionnaire shown in Figure A–1; or in some cases electronic devices to measure eye movement or blood pressure.

It is very important that a research instrument be both *reliable* and *valid*. Reliability is the consistency of the measure. In other words, repeated measures with the same instrument should produce the same results or scores. Validity is concerned with whether the research instrument actually measures what it is supposed to be measuring. Thus, it is possible for a research instrument to be reliable but not valid. For example, a test designed to measure intelligence could yield

---

[13] See K. E. Weick, "Laboratory Experimentation with Organizations: A Reappraisal," *Academy of Management Review*, January 1977, pp. 123–27, for a discussion of this problem.

consistent scores over a large number of people but not be measuring intelligence.

RESEARCH DESIGNS

A number of designs are used in experiments to study organizational behavior. To illustrate some of the available designs, we shall use the example of a training program being offered to a group of first-line supervisors. Suppose that the task of the researcher is to design an experiment that will permit the assessment of the degree to which the program influenced the performance of the supervisors. We will use the following symbols in our discussion:

S = The subjects, the supervisors participating in the experiment
O = The observation and measurement devices used by the researcher (that is, ratings of supervisors' performance by superiors)
X = The experimental treatment, the manipulated variable (that is, the training program)
R = The randomization process.[14]

One-Shot Design

If we assume that all supervisors go through the training program, it will be difficult for the researchers to evaluate it. This is because the researchers cannot compare the group with another group that did not undergo the training program. This design is called a *one-shot* design and is diagrammed as follows:

X   O

The letter *X* stands for the experimental treatment (that is, the training program) and the letter *O* for the observation of performance on the job. The measure of performance could be in the form of an average score based on ratings of superiors. However, the researchers can in no way determine whether performance was influenced at all by the training program. This experimental design is rarely used because of its weaknesses.

One-Group Pretest-Posttest Design

The previous design can be improved upon by first gathering performance data on the supervisors, instituting the training program, and

[14] R. H. Helmstader, *Research Concepts in Human Behavior* (New York: Appleton-Century-Crofts, 1970); William C. Scott and Terence R. Mitchell, *Organization Theory: A Structural and Behavioral Analysis* (Homewood, Ill.: Richard D. Irwin, 1976); and D. W. Emory, *Business Research Methods* (Homewood, Ill.: Richard D. Irwin, 1980).

TABLE A–3

Some Sources of Error in Experimental Studies

Factor	Definition
1. History	Events other than the experimental treatment (X) that occurred between pretest and posttest.
2. Maturation	Changes in the subject group with the passage of time that are not associated with the experimental treatment (X).
3. Testing	Changes in the performance of the subjects because measurement of their performance makes them aware that they are part of an experiment (that is, measures often alter what is being measured).
4. Instrumentation	Changes in the measures of participants' performance that are the result of changes in the measurement instruments or the conditions under which the measuring is done (for example, wear on machinery, boredom, fatigue on the part of observers).
5. Selection	When participants are assigned to experimental and control groups on any basis other than random assignment. Any selection method other than random assignment will result in systematic biases that will result in differences between groups that are unrelated to the effects of the experimental treatment (X).
6. Mortality	If some participants drop out of the experiment before it is completed, the experimental and control groups may not be comparable.
7. Interaction effects	Any of the above factors may interact with the experimental treatment, resulting in confounding effects on the results. For example, the types of individuals withdrawing from a study (mortality) may differ for the experimental group and the control group.

then remeasuring their performance. This is diagramed as follows:

$$O_1 \quad X \quad O_2$$

Thus, a pretest is given in time period 1, the program is administered, and a posttest is administered in time period 2. If $O_2 > O_1$, the differences can be attributed to the training program.

There are numerous factors that can confound the results obtained with this design. For example, suppose new equipment has been installed between O_1 and O_2. This could explain the differences in the performance scores. Thus, a *history* factor may have influenced our results. There are numerous other factors that could also influence our results. The most recurrent factors are listed along with their definitions in Table A–3.[15] Examination of Table A–3 indicates that results achieved in this design may also be confounded by *maturation* (the supervisors may learn to do a better job between O_1 and O_2, which would increase their performance regardless of training), *testing* (the

---

[15] Ibid.

measure of performance in O_1 may make the supervisors aware that they are being evaluated, which may make them work harder and increase their performance), and *instrumentation* (if the performance observations are made at different times of the day, the results could be influenced by fatigue). Each of these factors offers explanations for changes in performance other than the training program. Obviously, this design can be improved upon.

Static-Group Comparison Design

In this design, half of the supervisors would be allowed to enroll for the training. Once the enrollment reached 50 percent of the supervisors, the training program would begin. After some period of time, the group of supervisors who enrolled in the program would be compared with those who did not enroll. This design is diagramed as follows:

$$X \quad O$$
$$O$$

Since the supervisors were not randomly assigned to each group, it is highly possible that the group that enrolled consisted of the more highly motivated or more intelligent supervisors. Thus, *selection* is a major problem with this design. However, note that the addition of a *control group* (comparison group) has eliminated many of the error factors associated with the first two designs. The problem here is that the subjects were not randomly assigned to the experimental group (undergoing training) and the control group (no training). Therefore, it is possible that differences may exist between the two groups that are not related to the training.

The three designs discussed thus far (one-shot, one-group pretest-posttest, static-group comparisons) have been described as "pseudo-experimental" or "quasi-experimental" designs. When true experimentation cannot be achieved, these designs (especially the last two) are preferred over no research at all or over relying on personal opinion. The following three designs can be considered "true" experimental designs because the researcher has complete control over the situation in the sense of determining precisely who will participate in the experiment and which subjects will or will not receive the experimental treatment.

Pretest-Posttest Control Group Design

This design is one of the simplest forms of true experimentation used in the study of human behavior. It is diagramed as follows:

$$R \quad O_1 \quad X \quad O_2$$
$$R \quad O_1 \qquad \;\; O_2$$

Note that this design is similar to the one-group pretest-posttest design except that a control group has been added and the participants have been randomly assigned to both groups. Which group is to receive the training (experimental group) and which will not (control group) is also randomly determined. The two groups may be said to be equivalent at the time of the initial observations, and at the time the final observations are made, and different only in that one group has received training, while the other has not. In other words, if the change from O_1 to O_2 is greater in the experimental group than in the control group, we can attribute the difference to the training program rather than selection, testing, maturation, and so forth.

The major weakness of the pretest-posttest control group design is one of *interaction* (selection and treatment), where individuals are aware that they are participating in an experiment. In other words, being observed the first time makes all of the participants work more diligently, both those who are in the training group and those who are in the control group. Here the participants in the training program will be more receptive to training because of the pretest. This problem of interaction can be overcome by using a posttest-only control group design.

Posttest-Only Control Group Design

In this design, the participants are randomly assigned to two groups, the training is administered to one group, and the scores on the posttests are compared (performance envaluated). It is diagramed as follows:

$$R \quad X \quad O$$
$$R \qquad \;\; O$$

This eliminates the problem of the previous design by not administering a pretest. However, the dependent variable (performance) is an ultimate rather than a relative measure of achievement. Also, the researcher does not have a group that was pretested and posttested without receiving the experimental treatment (training program). Such a group can provide valuable information on the effects of history, maturation, instrumentation, and so on. However, where a pretest is difficult to obtain or where its use is likely to make the participants aware that an experiment is being carried on, this approach may be much preferred to the pretest-posttest control group design.

Solomon Four-Group Design

This design is a combination of the previous two designs and is diagramed as follows:

Group 1	R	O_1	X	O_2
Group 2	R	O_1		O_2
Group 3	R		X	O_2
Group 4	R			O_2

Where gain or change in behavior is the desired dependent variable, this design should be used. This design is the most desirable of all the designs examined here. While it does not control any more sources of invalid results, it does permit the estimation of the extent of the effects of some of the sources of error. In our example here, the supervisors are randomly assigned to four groups, two of which will receive the training, one with a pretest and one without. Therefore, the researcher can examine, among other things, the effects of history (Group 1 to Group 2), testing (Group 2 to Group 4), and testing-treatment interaction (Group 2 to Group 3). Clearly, this design is the most complex, utilizing more participants, and it will be more costly. The added value of the additional information will have to be compared to the additional costs.[16]

QUALITATIVE RESEARCH

Instead of using experimental designs and concentrating on measurement issues, some researchers also use qualitative research procedures. The notion of applying qualitative research methods to studying behavior within organizations has recently been addressed in leading research outlets.[17] The term *qualitative methods* is used to describe an array of interpretative techniques that attempt to describe and clarify the meaning of naturally occurring phenomena. It is by design rather open-ended and interpretative. The researcher's interpretation and description are the significant data collection acts in a qualitative study. In essence, qualitative data are defined as those (1) whose meanings are subjective, (2) that are rarely quantifiable, and (3) that are difficult to use in making quantitative comparisons.

The quantitative approach to organizational behavior research is

---

[16] For a complete coverage of this area, see Kerlinger, *Foundations of Behavioral Research,* pp. 300–76; Helmstader, *Research Concepts in Human Behavior,* pp. 91–121; and Emory, *Business Research Methods,* pp. 330–65.

[17] John Van Maanen, ed., *Qualitative Methodology* (Beverly Hills, Calif.: Sage Publications, 1983).

exemplified by precise definitions, control groups, objective data collection, use of the scientific method, and replicable findings. These characteristics are presented in Table A-2. The importance of reliability, validity, and accurate measurement is always stressed. On the other hand, qualitative research is more concerned with the meaning of what is observed. Since organizations are so complex, a range of quantitative and qualitative techniques can be used side by side to learn about individual, group, and organizational behavior.[18]

Qualitative methodology uses the experience and intuition of the researcher to describe the organizational processes and structures that are being studied. The data collected by a qualitative researcher requires him or her to become very close to the situation or problem being studied. For example, a qualitative method that is used is called by anthropologists the *ethnographic method*.[19] When this method is used, the researcher typically studies a phenomenon for long periods of time as a *participant-observer*. The researcher becomes part of the situation being studied in order to feel what it is like for the people in that situation. The researcher becomes totally immersed in other people's realities.

Participant observation is usually supplemented by a variety of quantitative data collection tools such as structured interviews and self-report questionnaires. A variety of techniques are used so that the researcher can cross-check the results obtained from observation and recorded in field notes.

In training researchers in the ethnographic method, it is a common practice to place them in unfamiliar settings. A researcher may sit with and listen to workers on a production line, drive around in a police car to observe police officers, or do cleanup work in a surgical operating room. The training is designed to improve the researcher's ability to record, categorize, and code what is being observed.

An example of qualitative research involvement is presented in Van Maanen's participant-observer study of a big city police department. He went through police academy training and then accompanied police officers on their daily rounds. He functioned with police officers in daily encounters. Thus, he was able to provide vivid descriptions of what police work was like.[20]

Other qualitative techniques include content analysis (e.g., the researcher's interpretation of field notes), informal interviewing, archi-

---

[18] Richard L. Daft, "Learning the Craft of Organizational Research," *Academy of Management Review*, October 1983, pp. 539–46.

[19] Anthony F. C. Wallace, "Paradigmatic Processes in Cultual Change," *American Anthropologist*, 1972, pp. 467–78.

[20] John Van Maanen, J. M. Dobbs, Jr., and R. R. Faulkner, *Varieties of Qualitative Research* (Beverly Hills, Calif.: Sage Publications, 1982).

val data surveys and historical analysis, and the use of unobtrusive measures (e.g., data whose collection is not influenced by a researcher's presence). An example of the last would be the wear and tear on a couch in a cardiologist's office. As reported in the discussion of the Type A Behavior Pattern in Chapter 7, the wear and tear was on the edges of the couch, which suggested anxiety and hyperactive behavior. Qualitative research appears to rely more on multiple sources of data than on any one source. The current research literature suggests a number of characteristics associated with qualitative research.[21]

1. *Analytical induction.* Qualitative research begins with the close-up, firsthand inspection of organizational life.
2. *Proximity.* Researchers desire to witness firsthand what is being studied. If the application of rewards is what is being studied, the researcher would want to observe episodes of reward distribution.
3. *Ordinary behavior.* The topics of research interest should be ordinary, normal, routine behaviors.
4. *Descriptive emphasis.* Qualitative research seeks descriptions for what is occurring in any given place and time. The aim is to disclose and reveal, not merely to order data and to predict.
5. *Shrinking variance.* Qualitative research is geared toward the explanation of similarity and coherence. There is a greater emphasis on commonality and on things shared in organizational settings than on things not shared.
6. *Enlighten the consumer.* The consumer of qualitative research could be a manager. A major objective is to enlighten without confusing him or her. This is accomplished by providing commentary that is coherent and logically persuasive.

Researchers and managers do not have to choose either quantitative or qualitative research data and interpretation. There are convincing and relevant arguments that more than one method of research should be used when studying organizational behavior. Quantitative and qualitative research methods and procedures have much to offer practicing managers. Blending and integrating quantitative and qualitative research are what researchers and managers must do in the years ahead to better understand, cope with, and modify organizational behavior.

---

[21] Van Maanen, *Qualitative Methodology*, pp. 255–56.

APPENDIX B Selected Comprehensive Cases

CASE METHOD: HOW TO ADDRESS
THE CASES

The "real world" cases in the book place the student in an organization as a manager, leader, or nonmanager who must make decisions. A *case* is "a story of organizational issues which actually have been faced by people, together with facts, opinions, and prejudices upon which decisions must be made. A key feature of a case is that decisions that require action must be made."[1]

With the case method, the process of arriving at an answer is more important than the answer itself. It is anticipated that by working through cases, the student will develop an understanding of the process of reaching decisions and be able to support and communicate these decisions to others. Instead of sitting back and reacting to the comments made by an instructor, the student is asked to make decisions, typically with incomplete information and in a limited time period, which is usually the situation faced by most managers.

There are no ideal solutions to any of the cases used in this book. Searching for the perfect answer will be futile. Instead, the student should learn to think through the issues, problems, facts, and other information presented in the cases. *Critical* thinking is required to make better decisions. *Thorough* thinking is needed so that the decisions reached can be communicated and intelligently discussed in classroom discussions. Classroom discussions about the cases should clearly illustrate the thinking processes used by the student.

The preparation for classroom discussion of the cases in this book could follow a set pattern. One suggested pattern would be to:

1. *Read* the case rather quickly to get a feel for what is involved.
2. *Reread* the case and sort out the assumptions, hunches, and facts. Since all of the cases are incomplete, the student will need to make plausible assumptions about the situation. List those assumptions, and be able to support their plausibility. The assumptions will enable you to "fill in the blanks" that exist in the case. Remember that in organizations decisions are generally made with incomplete information and some uncertainty.
3. *Identify* the major *problems* and subproblems that must be considered in the case.
4. *List* the problems in the order of their importance or priority. That is, show what problems have to be solved first.
5. *Develop* a list of alternative courses of action that would minimize or eliminate the problems. If possible, have at least two fully developed alternatives that are feasible solutions.

---

[1] Kenneth L. Bernhardt and Thomas C. Kinnear, *Cases in Marketing Management* (Plano, Tex. Business Publications, 1978), p. 3.

6. In developing the alternative courses of action, *outline* the constraints (e.g., resources, historical precedent, competition, skill limitations, attitudes) that will limit success.
7. *Select* the course of action that is best for the problems identified in step 3. Show how the course of action would work, and be able to discuss why it would be the most successful alternative to solve the problems.

DICK SPENCER*

After the usual banter when old friends meet for cocktails, the conversation between a couple of university professors and Dick Spencer, a former student who was now a successful businessman, turned to Dick's life as a vice president of a large manufacturing firm.

"I've made a lot of mistakes, most of which I could live with, but this one series of incidents was so frustrating that I could have cried at the time," Dick said in response to a question. "I really have to laugh at how ridiculous it is now, but at the time I blew my cork."

Spencer was plant manager of Modrow Company, a Canadian branch of the Tri-American Corporation. Tri-American was a major producer of primary aluminum, with integrated operations ranging from the mining of bauxite through the processing to fabrication of aluminum into a variety of products. The company also made and sold refractories and industrial chemicals. The parent company had wholly owned subsidiaries in five separate U.S. locations and had foreign affiliates in 15 different countries.

Tri-American mined bauxite in Jamaica and shipped the raw material by commercial vessels to two plants in Louisiana, where it was processed into alumina. The alumina was then shipped to reduction plants in one of three locations for conversion into primary aluminum. Most of the primary aluminum was then moved to the company's fabricating plants for further processing. Fabricated aluminum items included sheet, flat, coil, and corrugated products; siding; and roofing.

Tri-American employed approximately 22,000 employees in the total organization. The company was governed by a board of directors, which included the chairman, the vice chairman, the president, and 12 vice presidents. However, each of the subsidiaries and branches functioned as an independent unit. The board set general policy, which was then interpreted and applied by the various plant managers. In a sense,

* This case was developed and prepared by Dr. Margaret Fenn, Graduate School of Business Administration, University of Washington. Reprinted by permission.

the various plants competed with one another as though they were independent companies. This decentralization in organizational structure increased the freedom and authority of the plant managers, but increased the pressure for profitability.

The Modrow branch was located in a border town in Canada. The total work force in Modrow was 1,000. This Canadian subsidiary was primarily a fabricating unit. Its main products were foil and building products such as roofing and siding. Aluminum products were gaining in importance in architectural plans, and increased sales were predicted for this branch. Its location and its stable work force were the most important advantages it possessed.

In anticipation of estimated increases in sales, Modrow had recently completed a modernization and expansion project. At the same time, its research and art departments combined talents in developing a series of 12 new patterns of siding that were being introduced to the market. Modernization and pattern development had been costly undertakings, but the expected return on investment made the project feasible. However, the plant manager, who was a Tri-American vice president, had instituted a campaign to cut expenses wherever possible. In his introductory notice of the campaign, he emphasized that cost reduction would be the personal aim of every employee at Modrow.

Salesman.   The plant manager of Modrow, Dick Spencer, was an American who had been transferred to this Canadian branch two years previously, after the start of the modernization plan. Dick has been with the Tri-American Company for 14 years, and his progress within the organization was considered spectacular by those who knew him well. Dick had received a master's degree in business administration from a well-known university at the age of 22. Upon graduation, he had accepted a job as a salesman for Tri-American. During his first year as a salesman, he succeeded in landing a single, large contract that put him near the top of the sales volume leaders. In discussing his phenomenal increase in sales volume, several of his fellow salesmen concluded that his looks, charm, and ability on the golf course had contributed as much to his success as his knowledge of the business or his ability to sell the products.

During the second year of his sales career, Dick continued to set a fast pace. Although his record set difficult goals for the other salesmen, he was considered a "regular guy" by them and both he and they seemed to enjoy the few occasions when they socialized. However, by the end of the second year of constant traveling and selling, Dick began to experience some doubt about his future.

His constant involvement in business matters disrupted his marital life, and his wife divorced him during his second year with Tri-American. Dick resented her action at first, but he gradually seemed to recognize that his career at present depended on his freedom to travel unencumbered. During that second year, he ranged far and wide in his sales territory and successfully closed several large contracts. None of them was as large as his first year's major sale, but in total volume he was again well up near the top of salesmen for the year. Dick's name became well known in the corporate headquarters, and he was spoken of a "the boy to watch."

Dick had met the president of Tri-American at a company conference during his first year as a salesman. After three days of golfing and socializing, they developed a relaxed camaraderie that was considered unusual by those who observed the developing friendship. Although their contacts were infrequent after the conference, their easy relationship seemed to blossom the few times that they did meet. Dick's friends kidded him about his ability to make use of his new friendship to promote himself in the company, but Dick brushed aside their gibes and insisted that he'd make it on his own abilities, not on someone's coattail.

By the time he was 25, Dick began to suspect that he did not look forward to a life as a salesman for the rest of his career. He talked about his unrest with his friends, and they suggested that he groom himself for sales manager. "You won't make the kind of money you're making from commissions," he was told, "but you will have a foot in the door from an administrative standpoint, and you won't have to travel quite as much as you do now." Dick took their suggestions lightly and continued to sell the product, but he was aware that he felt dissatisfied and he did not seem to get the satisfaction out of his job that he had once enjoyed.

By the end of his third year with the company, Dick was convinced that he wanted a change in direction. As usual, he and the president spent quite a bit of time on the golf course during the annual company sales conference. After their match one day, the president kidded Dick about his game. The conversation drifted back to business, and the president, who seemed to be in a jovial mood, started to kid Dick about his sales ability. In a joking way, he implied that anyone could sell products as good as Tri-American's, but that it took real "guts and know-how" to make the products. The conversation drifted to other things, but this remark stuck with Dick.

Sometime later, Dick approached the president formally with a request for a transfer out of the sales division. The president was surprised and hesitant about this change in career direction for Dick. He recognized Dick's superior sales ability, but he was unsure that Dick was willing or able to assume responsibilities in any other division of the organization. Dick sensed the hesitancy but continued to push his request. He later remarked that the initial hesitancy of the president seemed to have convinced him that he needed an opportunity to prove himself in a field other than sales.

Troubleshooter.   Dick was finally transferred back to the home office of the organization and indoctrinated into productive and administrative roles in the company as a special assistant to the senior vice president of production. As a special assistant, Dick was assigned several troubleshooting jobs. He acquitted himself well in this role, but in the process he succeeded in gaining a reputation as a ruthless headhunter among the branches where he had performed a series of amputations. His reputation as an amiable, genial, easygoing guy from the sales department was the antithesis of the reputation of a cold, calculating headhunter that he earned in his troubleshooting role. The vice president, who was Dick's boss, was aware of the reputation that Dick had earned but was pleased with the results that were obtained. The faltering departments that Dick had worked in seemed to bloom with new life and energy after Dick's recommended amputations. As a result, the vice president began to sing Dick's praises and the president began to accept Dick in his new role in the company.

Management Responsibility.   About three years after Dick's switch from sales, he was given an assignment as assistant plant manager of an English branch of the company. Dick, who had remarried, moved his wife and family to London, and they attempted to adapt to their new routine. The plant manager was English, as were most of the other employees. Dick and his family were accepted with reservations into the community life as well as into the plant life. The difference between British and American philosophy and performance within the plant was marked for Dick, who was imbued with modern managerial concepts and methods. Dick's directives from headquarters were to update and upgrade performance in this branch. However, his power and authority were less than those of his superior, so he constantly found himself in the position of having to soft-pedal or withhold suggestions that he would have liked to make or innovations that he would have liked to introduce. After a frustrating year and a half, Dick was suddenly made plant manager of an old British company that had just been purchased by Tri-American. He left his first English assignment with mixed feelings and moved from London to Birmingham.

As the new plant manager, Dick operated much as he had in his troubleshooting job for the first couple of years of his change from sales to administration. Training and reeducation programs were instituted for all of the supervisors and managers who survived the initial purge. Methods were studied and simplified or redesigned whenever possible, and new attention was directed toward production that better met the needs of the sales organization. A strong controller helped to straighten out the profit picture through stringent cost control; and, by the end of the third year, the company showed a small profit for the first time in many years. Because he felt that this battle was won, Dick requested transfer back to the United States. This request was partially granted when nine months later he was awarded a junior vice president title and was made manager of a subsidiary Canadian plant, Modrow.

Modrow Manager. Prior to Dick's appointment as plant manager at Modrow, extensive plans for plant expansion and improvement had been approved and started. Although Dick had not been in on the original discussions and plans, he inherited all of the problems that accompany large-scale changes in any organization. Construction was slower than had been planned originally; equipment arrived before the building was finished; employees were upset about the extent of the change expected in their work routines with the installation of additional machinery; and in general, morale was at a low ebb.

Various versions of Dick's former activities had preceded him, and on his arrival he was viewed with dubious eyes. The first few months after his arrival were spent in a frenzy of catching up. This entailed attending constant conferences and meetings, reading volumes of past reports, becoming acquainted with the civic leaders of the area, and handling a plethora of dispatches to and from the home office. Costs continued to climb unabated.

By the end of Dick's first year at Modrow, the building program had been completed, although behind schedule, the new equipment had been installed, and some revamping of cost procedures had been incorporated. The financial picture at this time showed a substantial loss, but since it had been budgeted as a loss, this was not surprising. The managers of the various divisions had worked closely with their supervisors and accountants in planning the budget for the following year, and Dick began to emphasize his personal interest in cost reduction.

As he worked through his first year as plant manager, Dick developed the habit of strolling around the organization. He was apt to leave his office and appear wherever there was activity concerned with Modrow—on the plant floor, in the design offices, at the desk of a purchasing agent or accountant, or in the plant cafeteria rather than the executive dining room. During his strolls, he looked, listened, and became acquainted. If he observed activities that he wanted to talk about or heard remarks that gave him clues to future action, he did not reveal this at the time. Rather, he had a nod, a wave, or a smile for the people near him but a mental note to talk to his supervisors, managers, and foremen in the future. At first, his presence disturbed those who noted him coming and going, but after several exposures to him without any noticeable effect, the workers came to accept his presence and continue their usual activities. The supervisors, managers, and foremen, however, felt less comfortable when they saw him in the area.

Their feelings were aptly expressed by the manager of the siding department one day when he was talking to one of his foremen: "I wish to hell he'd stay up in the front office where he belongs. Whoever heard of a plant manager who had time to wander around the plant all the time? Why doesn't he tend to his paperwork and let us tend to our business?"

"Don't let him get you down," joked the foreman. "Nothing ever comes of his visits. Maybe he's just lonesome and looking for a friend. You know how these Americans are."

"Well, you may feel that nothing ever comes of his visits, but I don't. I've been called into his office three separate times within the last two months. The heat must really be on from the head office. You know these conferences we have every month where he reviews our financial progress, our building progress, our design progress, and so forth? Well, we're not really progressing as fast as we should be. If you ask me, we're in for continuing trouble."

In recalling his first year at Modrow, Dick said that he had constantly felt pressured and badgered. He had always sensed that the Canadians he worked with resented his presence since he was brought in over the heads of the operating staff. At the same time that he had felt this subtle resistance from his Canadian work force, he had believed that the president and his friends in the home office were constantly on the alert, waiting for him to prove himself or fall flat on his face. Because of the constant pressures and demands of the work, he had literally dumped his family into a new community and had withdrawn into the plant. In the process, he had built up a wall of resistance toward the demands of his wife and children, who, in turn, had felt that he was abandoning them.

During the course of the conversation with his university friends, Dick began to recall a series of incidents that had probably resulted from the conflicting pressures. When describing some of these incidents, he continued to emphasize the fact that his attempt to be relaxed and casual had backfired. Laughingly, Dick said, "As you know, both human relations and accounting were my weakest subjects during the master's program, and yet they are the two fields I felt I needed most at Modrow at this time." He described some of the cost procedures that he would have liked to incorporate. However, without the support and knowledge furnished by his former controller, he had busied himself with details that were unnecessary. One day, as he described it, he had overheard a conversation between two of the accounting staff members with whom he had been working very closely. One of them commented to the other, "For a guy who's a vice president, he sure spends a lot of time breathing down our necks. Why doesn't he simply tell us the kind of systems he would like to try, and let us do the experimenting and work out the budget?" Without commenting on the conversation he had overheard, Dick then described himself as attempting to spend less time and be less directive in the accounting department.

Another incident he described that apparently had had real meaning for him was one in which he had called a staff conference with his top-level managers. They had been going "hammer and tongs" for better than an hour in his private office and in the process of the heated conversation had loosened ties, taken off coats, and really rolled up their sleeves. Dick himself had slipped out of his shoes. In the midst of this, his secretary had reminded him of an appointment with public officials. Dick had rapidly finished up his conference with his managers, straightened his tie, donned his coat, and wandered out into the main office in his stocking feet.

Dick fully described several occasions when he had disappointed, frustrated, or confused his wife and family by forgetting birthdays, appointments, dinner engagements, and so on. He seemed to be describing a pattern of behavior that had resulted from continuing pressure and frustration. He was setting the scene to describe his baffling and humiliating position in the siding department. In looking back and recalling his activities during this first year, Dick commented on the fact that his frequent wanderings throughout the plant had resulted in a nodding acquaintance with the workers but had probably also resulted in foremen and supervisors spending more time in getting ready for his visits and in reading meaning into them afterward than in attending to their specific duties. His attempts to know in detail the accounting procedures being used had required long hours of concentration and detailed conversations with the accounting staff that had been time-consuming and very frustrating for him, as well as for them. His lack of attention to his family life had resulted in continued pressure from both wife and family.

The Siding Department Incident. Siding was the product that had been budgeted as a large profit item of Modrow. Aluminum siding was gaining in popularity among both architects and builders, because of its possibilities in both decorative and practical uses. Panel sheets of siding were shipped in standard sizes on order; large sheets of the coated siding were cut to specifications in the trim department, packed, and shipped. The trim shop was located near the loading platforms, and Dick often cut through the trim shop on his wanderings through the plant. On one of his frequent trips through the area, he suddenly became aware of the fact that several workers responsible for the disposal function were spending countless hours at high-speed saws cutting scraps into specified lengths to fit into scrap barrels. The narrow bands of scrap that resulted from the trim process varied in length from 7 to 27 feet and had to be reduced in size to fit into the disposal barrels. Dick, in his concentration on cost reduction, picked up one of the thin strips, bent it several times, and fittied it into the barrel. He tried this with another piece, and it bent very easily. After assuring himself that bending was possible, he walked over to a worker at the saw and asked why he was using the saw when material could easily be bent and fitted into the barrels, resulting in a saving of time and equipment. The workers response was, "We've never done it that way, sir. We've always cut it."

Following his plan of not commenting or discussing matters on the floor, but distressed by the reply, Dick returned to his office and asked the manager of the siding department if he could speak to the foreman of the scrap division. The manager said, "Of course. I'll send him up to you in just a minute."

After a short time, the foreman, very agitated at being called to the plant manager's office, appeared. Dick began questioning him about the scrap disposal process and received the standard answer: "We've always done it that way." Dick then proceeded to review cost-cutting objectives. He talked about the pliability of the strips of scrap. He called for a few pieces of scrap to demonstrate the ease with which it could be bent and ended what he thought was a satisfactory conversation by requesting the foreman to order heavy-duty gloves for his workers and use the bending process for a trial period of two weeks to check the cost saving possible.

The foreman listened throughout most of this hour's conference, offered several reasons why it wouldn't work, raised some questions about the record-keeping process for cost purposes, and finally left the office with the forced agreement to try the suggested new method of bending, rather than cutting, for disposal. Although Dick was immersed in many other problems, his request was forcibly brought home to him one day as he cut through the scrap area. The workers were using power saws to cut scraps. He called the manager of the siding department and questioned him about the process. The manager explained that each foreman was responsible for his own processes, and since Dick had already talked to the foreman, perhaps he had better talk to him again. When the foreman arrived, Dick began to question him. He received a series of excuses and some explanations of the kinds of problems that they were meeting by attempting to bend the scrap material. "I don't care what the problems are," Dick nearly shouted. "When I request a cost-reduction program instituted, I want to see it carried through."

Dick was furious. When the foreman left, he phoned the maintenance department and ordered the removal of the power saws from the scrap area immediately. A short time later, the foreman of the scrap department knocked on Dick's door to report his astonishment at having maintenance men step into his area and physically remove the saws. Dick reminded the foreman of his unavailing request for a trial at cost reduction and ended the conversation by saying that the power saws were gone and would not be returned and that the foreman had damned well better learn to get along without them. After a stormy exit by the foreman, Dick congratulated himself on having solved a problem and turned his attention to other matters.

A few days later, Dick had cut through the trim department and literally stopped to stare. As he described it, he had been completely nonplussed to discover gloved workmen using hand shears to cut each piece of scrap.

HOVEY AND BEARD COMPANY*

Part 1

The Hovey and Beard Company manufactured wooden toys of various kinds: wooden animals, pull toys, and the like. One part of the manufacturing process involved spraying paint on the partially assembled toys.

The toys were cut, sanded, and partially assembled in the wood room. Then they were dipped into shellac, following which they were painted. The toys were predominantly two-colored; a few were made in more than two colors. Each color required an additional trip through the paint room.

For a number of years, production of these toys had been entirely handwork. However, to meet tremendously increased demand, the painting operation had recently been reengineered so that the eight workers who did the painting sat in a line by an endless chain of hooks. These hooks were in continuous motion, past the line of workers and into a long horizontal oven. Each worker sat at a separate painting booth so designed as to carry away fumes and to backstop excess paint. Workers would take a toy from the tray beside them, position it in a jig inside the painting cubicle, spray on the color according to a pattern, then release the toy and hang it on the hook passing by. The rate at which the hooks moved had been calculated by the engineers so that each worker, when fully trained, would be able to hang a painted toy on each hook before it passed beyond her reach. (All of the workers were women.)

The employees working in the paint room were on a group bonus plan. Since the operation was new to them, they were receiving a learning bonus that decreased by regular amounts each month. The

* From W. F. Whyte, *Money and Motivation* (New York: Harper & Row, 1955), pp. 90–94. Used by permission.

learning bonus was scheduled to vanish in six months, by which time it was expected that they would be on their own—that is, able to meet the standard and to earn a group bonus when they exceeded it.

Part 2

By the second month of the training period, trouble had developed. The employee's learned more slowly than had been anticipated, and it began to look as though their production would stabilize far below what was planned for. Many of the hooks were going by empty. The workers complained that they were going by too fast and that the time study man had set the rates too high. A few people quit and had to be replaced with new workers, which further aggravated the learning problem. The team spirit that the management had expected to develop automatically through the group bonus was not in evidence except as an expression of what the engineers called "resistance." One worker, whom the group regarded as its leader (and the management regarded as the ringleader), was outspoken in making the various complaints of the group to the supervisor: the job was a messy one, the hooks moved too fast, the incentive pay was not being correctly calculated, and it was too hot working so close to the drying oven.

Part 3

A consultant who was brought into this picture worked entirely with and through the supervisor. After many conversations with the consultant, the supervisor felt that the first step should be to get the workers together for a general discussion of the working conditions. He took this step with some hesitation, but he took it on his own volition.

The first meeting, held immediately after the shift was over at four o'clock in the afternoon, was attended by all eight workers. They voiced the same complaints again: the hooks went by too fast; the job was too dirty; the room was hot and poorly ventilated. For some reason, it was this last item that they complained of most. The supervisor promised to discuss the problem of ventilation and temperature with the engineers, and he scheduled a second meeting to report back to the employees. In the next few days, the supervisor had several talks with the engineers. They and the superintendent felt that this was really a trumped-up complaint and that the expense of any effective corrective measure would be prohibitively high.

The supervisor came to the second meeting with some apprehensions. The workers, however, did not seem to be much put out, perhaps because they had a proposal of their own to make. They felt that if several large fans were set up so as to circulate the air around their feet, they would be much more comfortable. After some discussion, the supervisor agreed that the idea might be tried out. The supervisor and the consultant discussed the question of the fans with the superintendent, and three large propeller-type fans were purchased.

Part 4

The fans were brought in. The workers were jubilant. For several days, the fans were moved about in various positions until they were placed to the satisfaction of the group. The employees seemed completely satisfied with the results, and relations between them and the supervisor improved visibly.

The supervisor, after this encouraging episode, decided that further meetings might also be profitable. He asked the workers whether they would like to meet and discuss other aspects of the work situation. They were eager to do this. The meeting was held, and the discussion quickly centered on the speed of the hooks. The employees maintained that the time study man had set them at an unreasonably fast speed and that they would never be able to reach the goal of filling enough of them to make a bonus.

The turning point of the discussion came when the group's leader frankly explained that the point wasn't that they couldn't work fast enough to keep up with the hooks but that they couldn't work at that pace all day long. The supervisor explored the point. The workers were unanimous in their opinion that they could keep up with the belt for short periods if they wanted to. But they didn't want to because if they showed they could do this for short periods, they would be expected to do it all day long. The meeting ended with an unprecedented request: "Let us adjust the speed of the belt faster or slower depending on how we feel." The supervisor agreed to discuss this with the superintendent and the engineers.

The reaction of the engineers to the suggestion was negative. However, after several meetings it was granted that there was some latitude within which variations in the speed of the hooks would not affect the finished product. After considerable argument with the engineers, it was agreed to try out the workers' ideas.

With misgivings, the supervisor had a control with a dial marked "low, medium, fast" installed at the booth of the group leader; she could now adjust the speed of the belt anywhere between the lower and upper limits that the engineers had set.

Part 5

The workers were delighted, and they spent many lunch hours deciding how the speed of the belt should be varied from hour to hour throughout the day. Within a week, the pattern had settled down to one in which the first half hour of the shift was run on what the employees called a medium speed (a dial setting slightly above the point marked "medium"). The next 2½ hours were run at high speed; the half hour before lunch and the half hour after lunch were run at low speed. The rest of the afternoon was run at high speed with the exception of the last 45 minutes of the shift, which was run at medium.

In view of the workers' reports of satisfaction and ease in their work, it is interesting to note that the constant speed at which the engineers had originally set the belt was slightly below medium on the dial of the control that had been given the employees. The average speed at which they were running the belt was on the high side of the dial. Few, if any, empty hooks entered the oven, and inspection showed no increase of rejects from the paint room.

Production increased, and within three weeks (some two months before the scheduled ending of the learning bonus) the workers were operating at 30 to 50 percent above the level that had been expected under the original arrangement. Naturally, their earnings were correspondingly higher than anticipated. They were collecting their base pay, a considerable piece rate bonus, and the learning bonus, which, it will be remembered, had been set to decrease with time and not as a function of current productivity. They were earning more now than many skilled workers in other parts of the plant.

Part 6

Management was besieged by demands that this inequity be taken care of. With growing irritation between superintendent and supervisor, engineers and supervisor, superintendent and engineers, the situation came to a head when the superintendent revoked the learning bonus and returned the painting operation to its original status: the hooks moved again at their constant, time-studied designated speed; production dropped again; and within a month all but two of the eight original workers had quit. The supervisor himself stayed on for several months but, feeling aggrieved, then left for another job.

A CASE OF MISUNDERSTANDING:
MR. HART AND MR. BING*

In a department of a large industrial organization, there were seven workers (four men and three women) engaged in testing and inspecting

* Reproduced by permission of the President and Fellows of Harvard College.

panels of electronic equipment. In this department, one of the workers, Bing, was having trouble with his immediate supervisor, Hart, who had formerly been a worker in the department. Had we been observers in this department, we would have seen Bing carrying two or three panels at a time from the racks where they were stored to the bench where he inspected them together. For this activity, we would have seen him charging double or triple setup time. We would have heard him occasionally singing at work. Also, we would have seen him usually leaving his work position a few minutes early to go to lunch, and noticed that other employees sometimes accompanied him. And had we been present on one specific occasion, we would have heard Hart telling Bing that he disapproved of these activities and that he wanted Bing to stop engaging in them. However, not being present to hear the actual verbal exchange that took place in this interaction, let us note what Bing and Hart each said to a personnel representative.

What Bing Said

In talking about his practice of charging double or triple setup time for panels that he inspected all at one time, Bing said:

> This is a perfectly legal thing to do. We've always been doing it. Mr. Hart, the supervisor, has other ideas about it, though; he claims it's cheating the company. He came over to the bench a day or two ago and let me know just how he felt about the matter. Boy, did we go at it! It wasn't so much the fact that he called me down on it, but more the way in which he did it. He's a sarcastic bastard. I've never seen anyone like him. He's not content just to say in a manlike way what's on his mind, but he prefers to do it in a way that makes you want to crawl inside a crack in the floor. What a guy! I don't mind being called down by a supervisor, but I like to be treated like a man, and not humiliated like a schoolteacher does a naughty kid. He's been pulling this stuff ever since he's been promoted. He's lost his friendly way and seems to be having some difficulty in knowing how to manage us employees. He's a changed man over what he used to be like when he was a worker on the bench with us several years ago.
>
> When he pulled this kind of stuff on me the other day, I got so damn mad I called in the union representative. I knew that the thing I was doing was permitted by the contract, but I was intent on making some trouble for Mr. Hart, just because he persists in this sarcastic way of handling me. I am about fed up with the whole damn situation. I'm trying every means I can to get myself transferred out of this group. If I don't succeed and I'm forced to stay on here, I'm going to screw him in every way I can. He's not going to pull this kind of kid stuff any longer on me. When the union representative questioned him on the case, he finally had to back down, because according to the contract an employee can use any timesaving method or device in order to speed up the process as long as the quality standards of the job are met.

You see, he knows that I do professional singing on the outside. He hears the people talking about my career in music. I guess he figures I can be so cocky because I have another means of earning some money. Actually, the employees here enjoy having me sing while we work, but he thinks I'm disturbing them and causing them to "goof off" from their work. Occasionally, I leave the job a few minutes early and go down to the washroom to wash up before lunch. Sometimes, several others in the group will accompany me, and so Mr. Hart automatically thinks I'm the leader and usually bawls me out for the whole thing.

So, you can see, I'm a marked man around here: He keeps watching me like a hawk. Naturally, this makes me very uncomfortable. That's why I'm sure a transfer would be the best thing. I've asked him for it, but he didn't give me any satisfaction at the time. While I remain here, I'm going to keep my nose clean, but whenever I get the chance, I'm going to slip it to him, but good.

What Hart Said

Here, on the other hand, is what Hart told the personnel representative:

Say, I think you should be in on this. My dear little friend Bing is heading himself into a showdown with me. Recently, it was brought to my attention that Bing has been taking double and triple setup time for panels that he is actually inspecting at one time. In effect, that's cheating, and I've called him down on it several times before. A few days ago it was brought to my attention again, and so this time I really let him have it in no uncertain terms. He's been getting away with this for too long, and I'm going to put an end to it once and for all. I know he didn't like me calling him on it because a few hours later he had the union representative breathing down my back. Well, anyway, I let them both know I'll not tolerate the practice any longer. I'm inclined to think the guy's mentally deficient, because talking to him has actually no meaning to him whatsoever. I've tried just about every approach to jar some sense into that guy's head, and I've just about given it up as a bad deal.

I don't know what it is about the guy, but I think he's harboring some deep feelings against me. For what, I don't know, because I've tried to handle that bird with kid gloves. But his whole attitude around here on the job is one of indifference, and he certainly isn't a good influence on the rest of my group. Frankly, I think he purposely tries to agitate them against me at times, too. It seems to me he may be suffering from delusions of grandeur, because all he does all day long is sit over there and croon his fool head off. Thinks he's a Frank Sinatra! No kidding! I understand he takes singing lessons and he's working with some of the local bands in the city. All of which is OK by me; but when his outside interests start interfering with his efficiency on the job, then I've got to start paying closer attention to the situation.

For this reason, I've been keeping my eye on that bird, and if he steps out of line any more, he and I are going to part ways.

You know there's an old saying, "You can't make a silk purse out of a sow's ear." The guy is simply unscrupulous. He feels no obligation to do a real day's work. Yet I know the guy can do a good job, because for a long time he did. But in recent months he's slipped, for some reason, and his whole attitude on the job has changed. Why, it's even getting to the point now where I think he's inducing other employees to "goof off" a few minutes before the lunch whistle and go down to the washroom and clean up on company time. I've called him on it several times, but words just don't seem to make any lasting impression on him. Well, if he keeps it up much longer, he's going to find himself on the way out. He's asked me for a transfer, so I know he wants to go. But I didn't given him an answer when he asked me, because I was storming mad at the time, and I may have told him to go somewhere else.

A COLLAPSE OF SHELVING AND ITS UNUSUAL AFTERMATH*

Crawford's has 39 stores (catalog showrooms) in Alabama, Florida, Georgia, Louisiana, Mississippi, and Texas. Since its Georgia incorporation in October 1962, the Atlanta firm had experienced steady annual growth until its sales and profits were $260 million and $5.6 million, respectively. Crawford's success paralleled that of other discount merchandisers operating on a high-volume, low-margin principle. Net sales by product categories showed the following percentage composition: jewelry, 30.9; house and gifts, 33.4; cameras and electronics, 15.6; toys, 11.4; and sporting goods, 8.7. Diamonds and jewelry produced the firm's largest profits.

Crawford's is organized on a geographic basis, with each store being in a local district, while districts are grouped into regions. Part of the Atlanta regional office is the four-store Birmingham district, with stores in Bessemer, Hoover, Mountain Brook, and Roebuck Shopping Center. (Exhibit 1 depicts the Birmingham organizational arrangement of Crawford's.)

In February 1976, John G. Rutledge, the Bessemer store manager, was promoted to district manager, in addition to being named manager of the Roebuck catalog showroom. Rutledge was touted for big things in the organization if the rumors preceding him were accurate.

---

* This case was prepared by Associate Professor Charles W. Langdon and Chris Lind, a student of the University of New Orleans, as a basis for discussion rather than to illustrate either effective or ineffective handling of an administrative situation. Copyright © by the University of New Orleans.

EXHIBIT 1

Crawford Company Organization Chart—Birmingham District

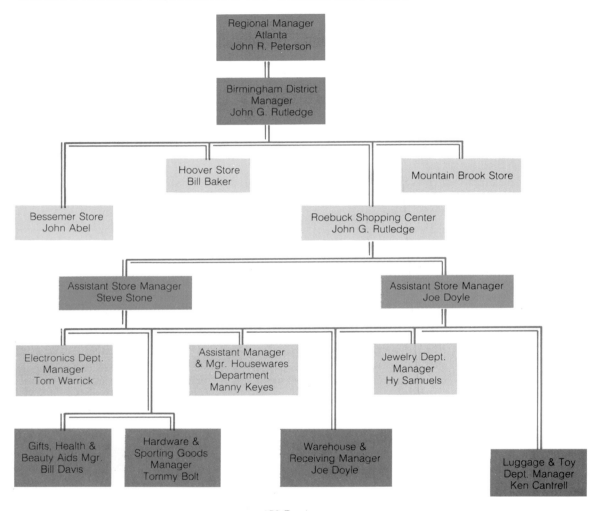

150 Employees

After the new district manager adjusted to his new position, he was seldom seen by the showroom employees unless they went to his office, and this was not likely because he kept the door closed most of the day. His communication was primarily by telephone to his own regional supervisor and his store managers. "Notice how red Rutledge's ear is?" declared Jeff Larson, toy department assistant manager to Steve Stone, assistant store manager.

"He spends 75 to 80 percent of his time every day on the phone," replied Stone.

"He's always bragging about how much clout he has with Atlanta, but he never gives us any information from the home office. Do you think that's where all those calls are going to?" queried Larson.

"Look, I'm not even sure they're all business calls, but what *really* bothers me is that his office door is always closed when he's on the phone, so I'm, forced to wait for long periods to get his approval, even for minor matters. Jeff, you know how reluctant Rutledge is to relinquish authority," continued Stone.

Stone Notes Turnover Problems

A 38-year old native of Michigan, Stone had arrived in Birmingham three years earlier and shortly afterward had obtained employment at Robert Hall (a unit of a national retail chain). He was a seasoned merchandising manager when he left in October 1976 to assume his present position at Crawford's Roebuck catalog showroom. "This system was simple to understand because of my training and previous experience, and I felt quite confident in it after 30 days," he related.

The Roebuck catalog showroom had a normal personnel complement of 150, which was about equally balanced between full- and part-time employees. The latter were mostly high school and college students, but while most employees were young adults, there was a significant percentage of older employees as well. From the beginning of his service, Stone had noted that like other retail outlets in the region the Roebuck store encountered a high rate of turnover. As a result, it was nearly always understaffed, thereby creating problems, primarily customer-related ones. "One day you'd open the store and be short a cashier," declared Joe Doyle, assistant store manager. "Then you'd have to start swapping around," One consequence of such shifting was that many employees worked overtime, which normally shouldn't have been necessary. In the final analysis, this reduced sales for the Roebuck store and caused expenses to exceed the budgeted figures.

During his first Christmas season under Rutledge, Larson was budgeted for 1,300 employee-hours in the toy department, but he ended up receiving only about half that number. Though turnover was high, a big stack of applications for work in the Roebuck store was always awaiting processing. Though Crawford's use of the polygraph test (closely supervised by Rutledge) was one of the steps that lengthened the screening process, the real bottleneck resulted from Rutledge's practice of making the ultimate decision on hiring. "I could have interviewed 30 to 60 applicants in the time it takes him to talk to one," said Stone, who added that it was common for Rutledge to spend two hours interviewing one applicant. Applicants were asked mostly personal questions, with job description information seldom entering the conversation.

Rutledge at 35 was short, heavyset, and balding—which he attempted to conceal by combing his hair in an upswept manner. Married and the father of three, Rutledge was a graduate of Florida State University. He had been employed by J. C. Penney Company before joining Crawford's. As manager of the Bessemer store, he had impressed his superiors enough to be promoted to the position of Birmingham district manager. At the Roebuck store, he was often heard to exclaim, "All I have to do is call Atlanta, and they'll give me what I want."

Crawford's Centralization and Problems at Individual Stores

In following Crawford's purchasing policies, its buyers at the Atlanta headquarters contract for large quantities of stock items from manufacturers or suppliers of those goods. The headquarters staff unilaterally determines the allocations to the catalog showrooms of all stock items, be they attaché cases, cameras, or fishing rods. A 400-page mail-order catalog showing these items is made available to Crawford's customers.

Stock supply and replenishment are an inherent problem for mass-marketing chains, and Crawford is no exception. After the initial shipment of an item becomes exhausted, the procedure for replenishment seldom operates satisfactorily. (To make matters worse, department managers have no authority to deal with local wholesalers to buy "fill-in" merchandise.) Customers seeking an out-of-stock item are given a "rain check" that can be used after a store receives its replenishment order. Even though buyers are given timely notice of out-of-stock items, months may go by before the replacement stock comes in. "I've had as many as 300 rain checks on some items," remarked Larson.

The purchase of store supplies is also highly centralized. Though many supplies could be purchased locally in Birmingham, all but the smallest orders have to be routed to Atlanta on purchase requisition.

Rutledge and Detailed Decision Making

It can only be conjectured whether the company's inclination for close control influenced Rutledge to adopt the same stance or merely reinforced an inbred characteristic. In any case, regardless of the level of operation, he wanted to be in complete charge. Thus, for example, he kept control of petty cash disbursements.

One Christmas season, the toy department was inundated with orders for gym sets. A very bulky item, the gym set was too large to fit *in* a customer's car, so it was determined that it would have to be *tied* on the roof of the automobile. Larson decided that he had to make an outside purchase of twine from a nearby variety store (a five-minute trip away) at a cost of about $8. Since all purchases through petty cash required the approval of the store manager, Larson set out to get such authorization. Rutledge balked at buying twine from the nearby store because he knew it could be purchased much more cheaply at another outlet, the name of which, unfortunately, he could not remember. The only way to find the name, Rutledge decided, was to flip through several years of vendor sales slips and petty cash vouchers. After four hours of patient search, the voucher was uncovered and the company name was ascertained. It was located in Bessemer, approximately a 45-minute drive from the Roebuck Shopping Center. Since it took another two hours to determine how the petty cash vouchering would be handled, the whole transaction absorbed nearly all of Larson's day.

The problem of a breakdown of the store's computer was exaggerated by Rutledge's refusal to delegate. Normal procedure for such an event was to phone the computer maintenance firm. The authorization for such a call could have been given to several personnel, especially the two assistant store managers. But since Rutledge felt obliged to monitor this vital functions, his standing instructions were that he was to be the only person qualified to call the computer servicemen. Since these breakdowns occurred two or three times a week, valuable time was often lost in this manner.

How to Straighten Out Ken?

Only a short time after he assumed his position at Crawford's, Stone realized that two of his six department heads needed to be replaced. One of these was Ken Cantrell, manager of the toy department. In addition to this department's declining sales, Stone noticed Ken was frequently away from the department. Most of this time was spent in conversation with Rutledge in the latter's office (with the door closed) or in the employees' lounge gossiping with other employees. Ostensibly, however, Ken went to the lounge to check the time cards of his 25–30 subordinates or to prepare their work schedules for the coming week.

Frequently, Ken would fail to show up for work on Saturday, blaming illness. His friends said he played the piano late at night and envisioned himself as a coming Elvis Presley, even combing his hair in the "duckbill" style of his rock'n'roll idol.

"I'll bet Ken's on another drunk. Do you think Rutledge knows?"

said Joe Doyle on a Saturday morning that Ken failed to arrive for work. Even though Rutledge's popularity with most of his subordinates had declined considerably, Doyle's loyalty to his boss remained unaltered. Nevertheless, he was strongly opposed to what he considered Rutledge's "pampering" of Ken over the past year, and both Stone and Doyle had expressed the belief that Ken ought to be discharged. Of course, Rutledge had always vetoed the suggestion.

Weeks later, when Ken had failed to report one Saturday, Stone and Doyle informed Rutledge and wrung from the latter the promise that he himself "would try to straighten Ken out." A few days later, the two assistant managers learned that Ken had been given a raise to become the highest-paid department manager in the store. Doyle and Stone were dumbfounded.

Collapse of the Shelving and Its Impact

In December 1977, Crawford's was readying a new store (in Mountain Brook) for opening in early 1978. Rutledge became involved in decision making at the very lowest level. He had decided that money could be saved on shelving for merchandise by collecting excess bins and racks from other stores, rather than buying new, custom-made shelving. Unfortunately, the surplus shelving did not match either in size or color, and one evening collapsing shelves caused a serious accident with extensive damage and nearly injured one employee as well. When word of this got back to Atlanta, Rutledge was told to stay away from the outfitting of the Mountain Brook store.

A month later, as the furnishing of the new store was proceeding and tensions had abated, Stone began thinking about applying for the position of manager of the Mountain Brook showroom. When Stone asked Larson for his opinion, Larson replied skeptically, "Steve, you'd still be under Rutledge, and he'd want you to clear everything with him."

"I'm inclined to disagree, Jeff, for two reasons," replied Stone. "First, Rutledge is much more subdued now. He was really burned on that shelving deal, and his boss Peterson in Atlanta will have him under much closer scrutiny now. Second, I believe he's decided he must delegate a bit more in the future. For the last six months, he's let me do the hiring, thank goodness! He's stopped having those ridiculous two-hour interviews. Jeff, I'm kind of optimistic about a changing climate around here." As they parted, Larson remarked, "You know, Steve, the change may be more apparent than real. It may be just temporary. He may snap back like an elastic to his original disposition."

Glossary of Terms

ABC Analysis. The analysis of antecedents, behavior, and consequences when investigating work- or job-related issues.

Ability. A trait, biological or learned, that permits a person to do something mental or physical.

Accommodation Stage Socialization. Socialization activities undertaken or experienced after an individual takes a job or enters an organization.

Adaptiveness. A criterion of effectiveness that refers to the ability of the organization to respond to change that is induced by either internal or external stimuli. An equivalent term is *flexibility*, although adaptiveness connotes an intermediate time frame, whereas flexibility is ordinarily used in a short-run sense.

Alcoholism. A disease characterized by repeated excessive drinking that interferes with an individual's health and work behavior.

Anticipatory Stage Socialization. Socialization activities undertaken or experienced prior to taking a job or entering an organization.

Assembly-Line Technology. A form of manufacturing in which component parts are brought together and combined into a single unit of output. It is used to produce relatively standard products that have a mass market.

Assessment Centers. An evaluation technique that uses situational exercises to identify promotable, trainable, and high-potential employees.

Attitudes. Mental states of readiness for need arousal

Attribution Leadership Theory. A theory of the relationship between individual perception and interpersonal behavior. The theory suggests that understanding and predicting how people will react to events around them are enhanced by knowing what their causal explanation for those events is.

Authority. Authority resides in the relationship between positions and in the role expectations of the position occupants. Thus, an influence attempt based on authority is generally not resisted because when joining an organization, individuals become aware that the exercise of authority is required of supervisors and that compliance is required of subordinates. The recognition of authority is necessary for organizational effectiveness and is a cost of organizational membership.

Banking Time-Off. A reward practice of allowing employees to build up time-off credits for such things as good performance or attendance. The employees would then receive the time-off in addition to the regular vacation time granted by the organization because of seniority.

Baseline. The period of time before a change is introduced.

Behavior. Anything that a person does, such as talking, walking, thinking, or daydreaming.

Behavior Modification. An approach to motivation that uses the principles of operant conditioning.

Behaviorally Anchored Rating Scales (BARS). Rating scales developed by raters and/or ratees that use critical behavioral incidents as interval anchors on each scale. Approximately 6 to 10 scales with behavioral incidents are used to derive the evaluation.

Boundary-Spanning Role. The role of an individual who must relate to two different systems, usually an organization and some part of its environment.

Brainstorming. The generation of ideas in a group through noncritical discussion.

Bureaucratic Theory. The theory developed by Max Weber that defines the characteristics of an organization that maximize a the stability and controllability of its members. The ideal-type bureaucracy is an organization that contains all of these characteristics to a high degree.

Cafeteria Fringe Benefits. The employee is allowed to develop and allocate a personally attractive fringe benefit package. The employee is informed of what the total fringe benefits allowed will be and then distributes the benefits according to his or her preferences.

Career. The individually perceived sequence of attitudes and behaviors associated with work-related experiences and activities over the span of a person's life.

Career Effectiveness. The extent to which the sequence of career attitudes and behaviors is satisfying to the individual.

Career Paths. Different jobs and/or positions associated with a specific career.

Career Stages. Distinctly different, yet related, stages in the progression of a career.

Case Study. An examination of numerous characteristics of a person, group, or organization usually over an extended time period.

Central Tendency Error. The tendency to rate all ratees around an average score.

Centralization. A dimension of organizational structure that refers to the extent to which authority to make decisions is retained in top management.

Classical Design Theory. A body of literature that evolved from scientific management, classical organization, and bureaucratic theory. The theory emphasizes the design of a preplanned structure for doing work. It minimizes the importance of the social system.

Classical Organization Theory. A body of literature that developed from the writings of managers who proposed principles of organization. These principles were intended to serve as guidelines for other managers.

Coercive Power. Influence over others based on fear. A subordinate perceives that failure to comply with the wishes of a superior would lead to punishment or some other negative outcomes.

Cognition. This is basically what individuals know about themselves and their environment. Cognition implies a conscious process of acquiring knowledge.

Cognitive Dissonance. A mental state of anxiety that occurs when there is a conflict among an individual's various cognitions (for example, attitudes and beliefs) after a decision has been made.

Command Group. The group of subordinates who report to one particular manager constitutes the command group. The command group is specified by the formal organization chart.

Commitment. A sense of identification, involvement, and loyalty expressed by an employee toward the company.

Communication. The transmission of information and understanding through the use of common symbols.

Complexity. A dimension of organizational structure that refers to the number of different jobs and/or units within an organization.

Confrontation Conflict Resolution. A strategy that focuses on the conflict and attempts to resolve it through such procedures as the rotation of key group personnel, the establishment of superordinate goals, improving communications, and similar approaches.

Conscious Goals. The main goals that a person is striving toward and is aware of when directing behavior.

Consideration. Acts of the leader that show supportive concern for the followers in a group.

Content Motivation Theories. Theories that focus on the factors within a person that energize, direct, sustain, and stop behavior

Contingency Approach to Management. This approach to management believes that there is no one best way to manage in every situation but that managers must find different ways that fit different situations.

Contingency Design Theory. An approach to designing organizations that states that the effective structure depends on factors in the situation.

Continuous Reinforcement. A schedule that is designed to reinforce behavior every time the behavior exhibited is correct.

Counterpower. Leaders exert power on subordinates, and subordinates exert power on leaders. Power is a two-way flow.

Criterion. The dependent or predicted measure for appraising the effectiveness of an individual employee.

Decentralization. Basically, this entails pushing the decision-making point to the lowest managerial level possible. It involves the delegation of decision-making authority.

Decision. A means to achieve some result or to solve some problem. The outcome of a process that is influenced by many forces.

Decision Acceptance. An important criterion in the Vroom-Yetton model that refers to the degree of subordinate commitment to the decision.

Decision Quality. An important criterion in the Vroom-Yetton model that refers to the objective aspects of a decision that influence subordinates' performance aside from any direct impact on motivation.

Decoding. The mental procedure that the receiver of a message goes through to decipher the message.

Defensive Behavior. When an employee is blocked in attempts to satisfy needs to achieve goals, one or more defense mechanisms may be evoked. These defense mechanisms include withdrawal, aggression, substitution, compensation, repression, and rationalization.

Delegated Strategies. Strategies for introducing organizational change that allow active participation by subordinates.

Delegation. The process by which authority is distributed downward in an organization.

Delphi Technique. A technique used to improve group decision making that involves the solicitation and comparison of anonymous judgments on the topic of interest through a set of sequential questionnaires interspersed with summarized information and feedback of opinions from earlier responses.

Departmentalization. The manner in which an organization is structurally divided. Some of the more publicized divisions are by function, territory, product, customer, and project.

Development. A criterion of effectiveness that refers to the organization's ability to increase its responsiveness to current and future environmental demands. Equivalent or similar terms include institutionalization, stability, and integration.

Diagonal Communication. Communication that cuts across functions and levels in an organization.

Differentiation. An important concept in the Lawrence and Lorsch research that refers to the process by which subunits in an organization develop particular attributes in response to the requirements imposed by their particular subenvironments. The greater the differences among the subunits' attributes, the greater is the differentiation.

Discipline. The use of some form of sanction or punishment when employees deviate from the rules.

Dominant Competitive Strategy. A concept defined in the Lawrence and Lorsch research to refer to the subenvironment that is crucial to the organization's success. The dominant strategy may be production, marketing, or product development, depending on the industry.

Downward Communication. Communication that flows from individuals in higher levels of the organization's hierarchy to those in lower levels.

Dysfunctional Conflict. A confrontation or interaction between groups that harms the organization or hinders the achievement of organizational goals.

Dysfunctional Intergroup Conflict. Any confrontation or interaction between groups that hinders the achievement of organizational goals.

Effectiveness. In the context of organizational behavior, effectiveness refers to the optimal relationship among five components: production, efficiency, satisfaction, adaptiveness, and development.

Efficiency. A short-run criterion of effectiveness that refers to the organization's ability to produce outputs with minimum use of inputs. The measures of efficiency are always in ratio terms, such as benefit/cost, cost/output, and cost/time.

Encoding. The conversion of an idea into an understandable message by a communicator.

Environmental Certainty. A concept in the Lawrence and Lorsch research that refers to three characteristics of a subenvironment that determine the subunit's requisite differentiation. The three characteristics are the rate of change, the certainty of information, and the time span of feedback or results.

Environmental Diversity. A concept in the Lawrence and Lorsch research that refers to the differences among the three subenvironments in terms of certainty.

Environmental Forces. Forces for change beyond the control of the manager. These forces incude marketplace actions, technological changes, and social and political changes.

Equity Theory of Motivation. A theory that examines discrepancies within a person after the person has compared his or her input/output ratio to that of a reference person.

ERG Theory of Motivation. A theory developed and tested by Alderfer that categorizes needs as existence, relatedness, and growth.

Eustress. A term made popular by Dr. Hans Selye to describe good or stimulating stress.

Expectancy.   The perceived likelihood that a particular act will be followed by a particular outcome.

Expectancy Theory of Motivation.   In this theory, the employee is viewed as faced with a set of first-level outcomes. The employee will select an outcome based on how this choice is related to second-level outcomes. The preferences of the individual are based on the strength (valence) of desire to achieve a second-level state and the perception of the relationship between first- and second-level outcomes.

Experiment.   To be considered an experiment, an investigation must contain two elements—manipulation of some variable (independent variable) and observation of the results (dependent variable).

Expert Power.   Capacity to influence related to some expertise, special skill, or knowledge. Expert power is a function of the judgment of the less powerful person that the other person has ability or knowledge that exceeds his own.

Extinction.   The decline in the response rate because of nonreinforcement.

Extrinsic Rewards.   Rewards external to the job, such as pay, promotion, or fringe benefits.

Field Experiment.   In this type of experiment, the investigator attempts to manipulate and control variables in the natural setting rather than in a laboratory.

Fixed Interval Reinforcement.   A situation in which a reinforcer is applied only after a certain period of time has elapsed since the last reinforcer was applied.

Formal Group.   A group formed by management to accomplish the goals of the organization.

Formalization.   A dimension of organizational structure that refers to the extent to which rules, procedures, and other guides to action are written and enforced.

Friendship Group.   An informal group that is established in the workplace because of some common characteristic of its members and that may extend the interaction of its members to include activities outside the workplace.

Functional Conflict.   A confrontation between groups that enhances and benefits the organization's performance.

Functional Job Analysis.   A method of job analysis that focuses attention on the worker's specific job activities, methods, machines, and output. The method is widely used to analyze and classify jobs.

General Adaptation Syndrome (GAS).   A description of the three phases of the defense reaction that a person establishes when stressed. These phases are called alarm, resistance, and exhaustion.

Goal.   A specific target that an individual is trying to achieve; a goal is the target (object) of an action.

Goal Approach to Effectiveness.   A perspective on effectiveness that emphasizes the central role of goal achievement as the criterion for assessing effectiveness.

Goal Commitment. The amount of effort that is actually used to achieve a goal.

Goal Difficulty. The degree of proficiency or the level of goal performance that is being sought.

Goal Orientation. A concept that refers to the focus of attention and decision making among the members of a subunit.

Goal Participation. The amount of a person's involvement in setting task and personal development goals.

Goal Setting. The process of establishing goals. In many cases, goal setting involves a superior and subordinate working together to set the subordinate's goals for a specified period of time.

Goal Specificity. The degree of quantitative precision of the goal.

Graicunas' Model. The proposition that an arithmetic increase in the number of subordinates results in a geometric increase in the number of potential relationships under the jurisdiction of the superior. Graicunas set this up in a mathematical model:

$$C = N\left(\frac{2^N}{2} + N - 1\right)$$

Grapevine. An informal communication network that exists in organizations and short-circuits the formal channels.

Grid Training. A leadership development method proposed by Blake and Mouton that emphasizes the balance between production orientation and person orientation.

Group. Two or more employees who interact with one another in such a manner that the behavior and/or performance of one member is influenced by the behavior and/or performance of other members.

Group Cohesiveness. The strength of the members' desires to remain in the group and of their commitment to the group.

Group Norms. Standards that are shared by the members of a group.

Groupthink. The deterioration of the mental efficiency, reality testing, and moral judgment of the individual members of a group in the interest of group solidarity.

Halo Error. A positive or negative aura around a ratee that influences a rater's evaluation.

Hardiness. A personality trait that appears to buffer an individual's response to stress. The hardy person assumes that he or she is in control, is highly committed to lively activities, and treats change as a challenge.

Hawthorne Studies. A series of studies undertaken at the Chicago Hawthorne Plant of Western Electric from 1924 to 1933. The studies made major contributions to the knowledge of the importance of the social system of an organization. They provided the impetus for the human relations approach to organizations.

History. A source of error in experimental results. It consists of events other than the experimental treatment that occur between pre- and post-measurement.

Horizontal Communication. Communication that flows across functions in an organization.

Horizontal Differentiation. The number of different units existing at the same level in an organization. The greater the horizontal differentiation, the more complex is the organization.

Incentive Plan Criteria. To be effective in motivating employees, incentives should (1) be related to specific behavioral patterns (for example, better performance), (2) be received immediately after the behavior is displayed, and (3) reward the employee for consistently displaying the desired behavior.

Influence. A transaction in which a person or a group acts in such a way as to change the behavior of another person or group. Influence is the demonstrated use of power.

Informal Group. Formed by individuals and developed around common interests and friendships rather than around a deliberate design.

Information Flow Requirements. The amount of information that must be processed by an organization, group or individual to perform effectively.

Initiating Structure. Leadership acts that imply the structuring of job tasks and responsibilities for followers.

Instrumentality. The relationship between first- and second-level outcomes.

Instrumentation. A source of error in experimental results. The error changes in the measure of participants' performance that are the result of changes in the measurement instruments or the conditions under which the measuring is done (for example, wear on machinery, fatigue on the part of observers).

Integration. A concept in the Lawrence and Lorsh research that refers to the process of achieving unity of effort among the organization's various subsystems. The techniques for achieving integration range from rules and procedures, to plans, to mutual adjustment.

Interaction. Any interpersonal contact in which one individual acts and one or more other individuals respond to the action.

Interaction Effects. The confounding of results that arises when any of the sources of errors in experimental results interact with the experimental treatment. For example, results may be confounded when the types of individuals withdrawing from any experiment (mortality) may differ for the experimental group and the control group.

Interest Group. A group that forms because of some special topic of interest. Generally, when the interest declines or a goal has been achieved, the group disbands.

Intergroup Conflict. Conflict between groups, which can be functional or dysfunctional.

Internal Forces. Forces for change that occur within the organization and that can usually be traced to *process* and to *behavioral* causes.

Interpersonal Communication. Communication that flows from individual to individual in face-to-face and group settings.

Interpersonal Orientation. A concept that refers to whether a person is more concerned with achieving good social relations as opposed to achieving a task.

Interpersonal Rewards. Extrinsic rewards such as receiving recognition or being able to interact socially on the job.

Interpersonal Style. The way in which an individual prefers to relate to others.

Interrole Conflict. A type of conflict that results from facing multiple roles. It occurs because individuals simultaneously perform many roles, some of which have conflicting expectations.

Intervention. The process by which either outsiders or insiders assume the role of a change agent in the OD program.

Intrapersonal Conflict. The conflict that a person faces internally, as when an individual experiences personal frustration, anxiety, and stress.

Intrarole Conflict. A type of conflict that occurs when different individuals define a role according to different sets of expectations, making it impossible for the person occupying the role to satisfy all of the expectations. This type of conflict is more likely to occur when a given role has a complex role set.

Intrinsic Rewards. Rewards that are part of the job itself. The responsibility, challenge, and feedback characteristics of the job are intrinsic rewards.

Job Analysis. The description of how one job differs from another in terms of the demands, activities, and skills required.

Job Content. The factors that define the general nature of a job.

Job Definition. The first subproblem of the organizing decision. It involves the determination of task requirements of each job in the organization.

Job Depth. The amount of control that an individual has to alter or influence the job and the surrounding environment.

Job Description. A summary statement of what an employee actually does on the job.

Job Descriptive Index. A popular and widely used 72-item scale that measures five job satisfaction dimensions.

Job Enlargement. An administrative action that involves increasing the range of a job. Supposedly, this action results in better performance and a more satisfied work force.

Job Enrichment. An approach developed by Herzberg that seeks to improve task efficiency and human satisfaction by means of building into people's jobs greater scope for personal achievement and recognition, more challenging and responsible work, and more opportunity for individual advancement and growth.

Job Evaluation. The assignment of dollar values to a job.

Job-Order Technology. A form of production in which products are tailor-made to customer specifications.

Job Range. The number of operations that a job occupant performs to complete a task.

Job Relationships. The interpersonal relationships that are required of or made possible by a job.

Job Rotation. A form of training that involves moving an employee from one work station to another. In addition to achieving the training objective, this procedure is also designed to reduce boredom.

Job Satisfaction. An attitude that workers have about their jobs. It results from their perception of the jobs.

Laboratory Experiment. The key characteristic of laboratory experiments is that the environment in which the subject works is created by the researcher. The laboratory setting permits the researcher to control closely the experimental conditions.

Leader-Member Relations. A factor in the Fiedler contingency model that refers to the degree of confidence, trust, and respect that the leader obtains from the followers.

Learning. The process by which a relatively enduring change in behavior occurs as a result of practice.

Learning Transfer. An important learning principle that emphasizes the carry-over of learning into the workplace.

Legitimate Power. Capacity to influence derived from the position of a manager in the organizational hierarchy. Subordinates believe that they "ought" to comply.

Life Change Events. Major life changes that create stress for an individual. The work of Holmes and Rahe indicates that an excessive number of life change events in one period of time can produce major health problems in a subsequent period.

Linking-Pin Function. An element of System 4 organization that views the major role of managers to be that of representative of the group they manage to higher level groups in the organization.

Locus of Control. A personality characteristic that describes people who see the control of their lives as coming from inside themselves as *internalizers*. People who believe that their lives are controlled by external factors are *externalizers*.

MAPS Design Technology. An acronym for multivariate analysis, participation, and structure, a method for designing and implementing an organizational structure through organizational development.

Matrix Organizational Design. An organizational design that superimposes a product- or project-based design on an existing function-based design.

Maturation. A source of error in experimental studies. The error results from changes in the subject group with the passage of time that are not associated with the experimental treatment.

MBO. A process under which superiors and subordinates jointly set goals for a specified time period and then meet again to evaluate the subordinates' performance in terms of the previously established goals.

Mechanistic Model of Organizational Design. The type of organizational design that emphasizes the importance of production and efficiency. It is highly formalized, centralized, and complex.

Merit Rating. A formal rating system that is applied to hourly paid employees.

Minnesota Multiphasic Personality Inventory (MMPI). A widely used inventory for assessing personality.

Mission. The ultimate, primary purpose of an organization. An organization's mission is what society expects from the organization in exchange for its continuing survival.

Modeling. A method of administering rewards that relies on observational learning. An employee learns the behaviors that are desirable by observing how others are rewarded. It is assumed that behaviors will be imitated if the observer views a distinct link between performance and rewards.

Modified or Compressed Workweek. A shortened workweek. The form of the modified workweek that involves working four days a week, 10 hours each day, is called a 4/40. The 3/36 and 4/32 schedules are also being used.

Mortality. A source of error in experimental studies. This type of error occurs when participants drop out of the experiment before it is completed, resulting in the experimental and control groups not being comparable.

Motion Study. The process of analyzing a task to determine the preferred motions to be used in its completion.

Motivator-Hygiene Theory. The Herzberg approach that identifies conditions of the job that operate primarily to dissatisfy employees when they are not present (hygiene factors—salary, job security, work conditions, and so on). There are also job conditions that lead to high levels of motivation and job satisfaction. However, the absence of these conditions does not prove highly dissatisfying. The conditions include achievement, growth, and advancement opportunities.

Multiple Roles. The notion that most individuals play many roles simultaneously because they occupy many different positions in a variety of institutions and organizations.

Need for Power. A person's desire to have an impact on others. The impact can occur by such behaviors as action, the giving of help or advice, or concern for reputation.

Need Hierarchy Model. Maslow assumed that the needs of a person depend on what he or she already has. This in a sense means that a satisfied need is not a motivator. Human needs are organized in a hierarchy of importance. The five need classifications are: physiological, safety, belongingness, esteem, and self-actualization.

Needs. The deficiencies that an individual experiences at a particular point in time.

Noise. Interference in the flow of a message from a sender to a receiver.

Nominal Group Technique (NGT). A technique to improve group decision making that brings people together in a very structured meeting that does not allow for much verbal communication. The group decision is the mathematically pooled outcome of individual votes.

Nonprogrammed Decisions. Decisions required for unique and complex management problems.

Nonverbal Communication. Messages sent with body posture, facial expressions, and head and eye movements.

Operant. Behaviors amenable to control by altering the consequences (rewards and punishments) that follow them.

Optimal Balance. The most desirable relationship among the criteria of effectiveness. Optimal, rather than maximum, balance must be achieved in any case of more than one criterion.

Organic Model of Organization. The organizational design that emphasizes the importance of adaptability and development. It is relatively informal, decentralized, and simple.

Organizational Behavior. The study of human behavior, attitudes, and performance within an organizational setting; drawing on theory, methods, and principles from such disciplines as psychology, sociology, and cultural anthropology to learn about *individual* perceptions, values, learning capacities, and actions while working in *groups* and within the total *organization;* analyzing the external environment's effect on the organization and its human resources, missions, objectives, and strategies.

Organizational Behavior Modification. An operant approach to organizational behavior. This term is used interchangeably with the term *behavior modification.*

Organizational Climate. A set of properties of the work environment, perceived directly or indirectly by the employees, that is assumed to be a major force in influencing employee behavior.

Organizational Culture. The pervasive system of values, beliefs, and norms that exists in any organization. The organizational culture can encourage or discourage effectiveness, depending on the nature of the values, beliefs, and norms.

Organizational Development. The process of preparing for and managing change in organizational settings.

Organizational Politics. The activities that are used to acquire, develop, and use power and other resources to obtain one's preferred outcome when there is uncertainty or disagreement about choices.

Organizational Processes. The activities that breathe life into the organizational structure. Among the common organizational processes are communication, decision making, socialization, and career development.

Organizational Profile. A diagram that shows the responses of the members of an organization to the questionnaires that Likert devised to measure certain organizational characteristics.

Organizational Structure. The formal pattern of how people and jobs are grouped in an organization. The organizational structure is often illustrated by an organization chart.

Organizations. Institutions that enable society to pursue goals that could not be achieved by individuals acting alone.

Participative Management. A concept of managing that encourages employees' participation in decision making and on matters that affect their jobs.

Path-Goal Leadership Model. A theory that suggests that it is necessary for a leader to influence the followers' perception of work goals, self-development goals, and paths to goal attainment. The foundation for the model is the expectancy motivation theory.

Perception. The process by which an individual gives meaning to the environment. It involves organizing and interpreting various stimuli into a psychological experience.

Performance. The desired results of behavior.

Performance Evaluation. The systematic, formal evaluation of an employee's job performance and potential for future development.

Person-Role Conflict. A type of conflict that occurs when the requirements of a position violate the basic values, attitudes, and needs of the individual occupying the position.

Personal-Behavioral Leadership Theories. A group of leadership theories that are based primarily on the personal and behavioral characteristics of leaders. The theories focus on *what* leaders do and/or *how* they behave in carrying out the leadership function.

Personality. A stable set of characteristics and tendencies that determine commonalities and differences in the behavior of people.

Personality Test. A test used to measure the emotional, motivational, interpersonal, and attitude characteristics that make up a person's personality.

Pooled Interdependence. Interdependence that requires no interaction between groups because each group, in effect, performs separately.

Position Analysis Questionnaire. A method of job analysis that takes into account the human, task, and technological factors of job and job classes.

Position Power. A factor in the Fiedler contingency model that refers to the power inherent in the leadership position.

Power. The ability to get things done in the way that one wants them to be done.

Power Illusion. The notion that a person with little power actually has significant power. The Miligram experiments indicated that the participants were obedient to commands given by an individual who seemed to have power (wore a white coat, was addressed as "doctor," and acted quite stern).

Process. In systems theory, the process element consists of technical and administrative activities that are brought to bear on inputs in order to transform them into outputs.

Process Motivation Theories.   Theories that provide a description and analysis of the process by which behavior is energized, directed, sustained, and stopped.

Process Technology.   An advanced form of manufacturing in which a homogeneous input is converted into a relatively standardized output having a mass market.

Production.   A criterion of effectiveness that refers to the organization's ability to provide the outputs that the environment demands of it.

Programmed Decisions.   Situations in which specific procedures have been developed for repetitive and routine problems.

Progressive Discipline.   Managerial use of a sequence of penalties for rule violations, each penalty being more severe than the previous one.

Punishment.   Presenting an uncomfortable consequence for a particular behavior reponse or removing a desirable reinforcer because of a particular behavior response. Managers can punish by application or punish by removal.

Qualitative Overload.   A situation in which a person feels that he or she lacks the ability or skill to do a job or that the performance standards have been set too high.

Quantitative Overload.   A situation in which a person feels that he or she has too many things to do or insufficient time to complete a job.

Ranking Methods.   The ranking of ratees on the basis of relevant performance.

Realistic Job Previews.   A procedure used at the point of employee recruitment that provides the prospective employee with accurate and realistic information about the job.

Recency of Events Error.   The tendency of recent events to bias ratings.

Reciprocal Causation of Leadership.   The argument that follower behavior has an impact on leader behavior and that leader behavior influences follower behavior.

Reciprocal Interdependence.   Interdependence that requires the output of each group in an organization to serve as input to other groups in the organization.

Referent Power.   Power based on a subordinate's identification with a superior. The more powerful individual is admired because of certain traits, and the subordinate is influenced because of this admiration.

Reward Power.   An influence over others based on hope of reward; the opposite of coercive power. A subordinate perceives that compliance with the wishes of a superior will lead to positive rewards, either monetary or psychological.

Role.   An organized set of behaviors.

Role Ambiguity.   A person's lack of understanding about the rights, privileges, and obligations of a job.

Role Conflict.   Arises when a person receives incompatible messages regarding appropriate role behavior.

Role Management Socialization. Socialization activities undertaken or experienced during the stable career/work stage.

Role Set. Those individuals who have expectations for the behavior of an individual in a particular role. The more expectations, the more complex is the role set.

Satisfaction. A criterion of effectiveness that refers to the organization's ability to gratify the needs of its participants. Similar terms include morale and voluntarism.

Scaler Chain. The graded chain of authority that is created through the delegation process.

Scientific Management. A body of literature that emerged during the period 1890–1930 and that reports the ideas and theories of engineers concerned with such problems as job definition, incentive systems, and selection and training.

Scope. The scale on which an organizational change is implemented (e.g., throughout the entire organization, level by level, or department by department).

Selection. A source of error in experimental studies. The error occurs when participants are assigned to experimental and control groups on any basis other than random assignment. Any other selection method will cause systematic biases that will result in differences between groups that are unrelated to the effects of the experimental treatment.

Sensitivity Training. A form of educational experience that stresses the process and emotional aspects of training.

Sequential Interdependence. Interdependence that requires one group to complete its task before another group can complete its task.

Shared Approach. An OD strategy that involves managers and employees in the determination of the OD program.

Shared Strategies. Strategies for introducing organizational change that focus on the sharing of decision-making authority among managers and subordinates.

Situational Theory of Leadership. An approach to leadership that advocates that leaders understand their own behavior, the behavior of their subordinates, and the situation before utilizing a particular leadership style. This approach requires diagnostic skills in human behavior on the part of the leader.

Skills. Task-related competencies.

Social Support. The comfort, assistance, or information that an individual receives through formal or informal contacts with individuals or groups.

Socialization Processes. The activities by which an individual comes to appreciate the values, abilities, expected behaviors, and social knowledge that are essential for assuming an organizational role and for participating as an organization member.

Span of Control. The number of subordinates reporting to a superior. The span is a factor that affects the shape and height of an organizational structure.

Status. In an organizational setting status relates to positions in the formal or informal structure. Status is designated in the formal organization whereas in informal groups it is determined by the group.

Status Consensus. The agreement of group members about the relative status of members of the group.

Strategic Contingency. An event or activity that is extremely important for accomplishing organizational goals. Among the strategic contingencies of subunits are dependency, scarcity of resources, coping with uncertainty, centrality, and substitutability.

Stress. An adaptive response, mediated by individual differences and/or psychological processes, resulting from any environmental action, situation, or event that places excessive psychological and/or physical demands on a person.

Stressor. An external event or situation that is potentially harmful to a person.

Strictness or Leniency Rater Errors. The harsh rater gives ratings that are lower than the average ratings usually given. The lenient rater gives ratings higher than the average ratings usually given.

Structure. The established patterns of interacting in an organization and of coordinating the technology and human assets of the organization.

Structure (in group context). Used in the context of groups, the term *structure* refers to the standards of conduct that are applied by the group, the communication system, and the reward and sanction mechanisms of the group.

Superordinate Goals. Goals that cannot be achieved without the cooperation of the conflicting groups.

Survey. A survey usually attempts to measure one or more characteristics in many people, usually at one point in time. Basically, surveys are used to investigate current problems and events.

System 4 Organization. The universalistic theory of organization design that has been proposed by Likert. The theory is defined in terms of overlapping groups, linking-pin management, and the principle of supportiveness.

Systems Theory. An approach to the analysis of organizational behavior that emphasizes the necessity for maintaining the basic elements of input-process-output and for adapting to the larger environment that sustains the organization.

Task Group. A group of individuals who are working as a unit to complete a project or job task.

Task Structure. A factor in the Fiedler contingency model that refers to how structured a job is with regard to requirements, problem-solving alternatives, and feedback on how correctly the job has been accomplished.

Technology. An important concept that can have many definitions in specific instances but that generally refers to actions, physical and mental, that an individual performs upon some object, person, or problem in order to change it in some way.

Testing. A source of error in experimental studies. The error occurs when changes in the performance of the subject occur because previous measurement of his performance made him aware that he was part of an experiment.

Thematic Apperception Test (TAT). A projective test that uses a person's analysis of pictures to evaluate such individual differences as need for achievement, need for power, and need for affiliation.

Time Delay Error. The error made by a rater who fails to record an observation at the time it occurs. By delaying the documentation, there is a chance of forgetting or being inaccurate at the time the observation is actually recorded.

Time Orientation. A concept that refers to the time horizon of decisions. Employees may have relatively short- or long-term orientations, depending on the nature of their tasks.

Time Study. The process of determining the appropriate elapsed time for the completion of a task.

Timing. The point in time that has been selected to initiate an organizational change method.

Tolerance of Ambiguity. The tendency to perceive ambiguous situations or events as desirable. On the other hand, intolerance of ambiguity is the tendency to perceive ambiguous situations or events as sources of threat.

Trait Theory of Leadership. An attempt to identify specific characteristics (physical, mental, personality) that are associated with leadership success. The theory relies on research that relates various traits to certain success criteria.

Type A Managers. Managers who are aloof and cold toward others and are often autocratic leaders. Consequently, they are ineffective interpersonal communicators.

Type A Behavior Pattern. Associated with research conducted on coronary heart disease. The Type A person is an aggressive driver who is ambitious, competitive, task-oriented, and always on the move. Rosenman and Friedman, two medical researchers, suggest that Type As have more heart attacks than do Type Bs.

Type B Managers. Managers who seek good relationships with subordinates but are unable to express their feelings. Consequently, they are usually ineffective interpersonal communicators.

Type B Behavior Pattern. The Type B person is relaxed, patient, steady, and even-tempered. The opposite of the Type A.

Type C Managers. Managers who are more interested in their own opinions than in those of others. Consequently, they are usually ineffective interpersonal communicators.

Type D Managers. Managers who feel free to express their feelings to others and to have others express their feelings. Such managers are the most effective interpersonal communicators.

Unilateral Strategies. Strategies for introducing organizational change that do not allow for participation by subordinates.

Universal Design Theory. A point of view that states that there is "one best way" to design an organization.

Upward Communication. Upward communication flows from individuals at lower levels of the organizational structure to those at higher levels. Among the most common upward communication flows are suggestion boxes, group meetings, and appeal or grievance procedures.

Valence. The strength of a person's preference for a particular outcome.

Values. The guidelines and beliefs that a person uses when confronted with a situation in which a choice must be made.

Vertical Differentiation. The number of authority levels in an organization. The more authority levels an organization has, the more complex is the organization.

Vroom-Yetton Model. A leadership model that specifies which leadership decision-making procedures will be most effective in each of several different situations. Two of the proposed leadership styles are autocratic (AI and AII); two are consultative (CI and CII); and one is oriented toward joint decisions (decisions made by the leader and the group, GII).

Weighted Checklist. A rating system consisting of statements that describe the various types and levels of behavior for a particular job. Each of the statements is weighted according to its importance.

Whistle-Blowing. The process in which an employee, because of personal opinions, values, or ethical standards, concludes that an organization needs to change its behavior or practices and informs someone about that conclusion.

Woodward Research. A pathbreaking research project that documented the association between technology and organizational structure and stimulated a wide range of subsequent studies that contributed to the contingency design point of view.

Work Module. An important characteristic of job redesign strategies. It involves the creation of whole tasks so that the individual senses the completion of an entire job.

Company Index

Name Index

I 3

Subject Index

Red Bordeaux

1966	excellent	1970-80
1965	poor	1968-71
1964	very variable, some excellent	1968-78
1963	very weak	now, if at all
1962	very good, soft and fruity	now-1974
1961	strong, superb	1969-85
1960	weak, pleasant, some good	now-1969
1959	very good, full	now -75
1958	light, no great appeal	now
1957	still immature, getting very good	1968-80
1956	light, uneven	now
1955	good, reliable, not thrilling	now-1972
1954	inconsistent, not strong	now
1953	wonderful	now
1952	good to very good	now-1970
1950	was good, but fading	now
1949	strong, superb	now-1968
1948	very good, full	now
1947	fine but fading	now
1945	superb but still immature, Pomerol ready now	1969-80

Red Burgundy *excluding Beaujolais*

1966	excellent (best in north)	1970-78
1965	weak, thin, very poor	now -68, if at all
1964	very good	1968-76
1963	weak and light	now, if at all
1962	very fine, not very strong	now -70
1961	superb	1969-75
1960	very poor	now
1959	very fine, round and soft	now-1970
1958	poor	now
1957	very good, still improving	1968-73
1955	good, powerful	now-1968
1953	very fine	now-1970
1952	still strong	now-1968
1950	fading	now
1949	very good but fading	now
1947	very good but fading	now

Red Rhône

1966	very good	1971-80
1965	good to very good	1970-80
1964	good	1969-75
1963	poor	now
1962	fine, not great	now-1970
1961	excellent	1969-75
1960	good	now
1959	good, heavier	now-1970
1958	good, good value	now
1957	strong	1968-70
1955	very good	now-1970

Port

1963	excellent, heavy	1983 onwards
1960	very good, lighter	1977 onwards
1958	good but very light	1972-80
1955	excellent, strong	1975-85
1954	rare, fair	now-1975
1950	very good, delicate	now-1972
1948	wonderful, heavy	1969 onwards
1947	weak	now-1968
1945	excellent, still heavy	1970-1990
1942	very good, light	now-1972
1935	excellent	now-1970
1934	even better	now-1970
1931	superb, very rare	now-1980
1927	very fine	now-1975

WINE

Hugh Johnson

With line drawings by Owen Wood

Simon and Schuster · New York

Printed in Great Britain by Thomas Nelson (Printers) Ltd., London
and Edinburgh

Contents

To the many lovers of wine who have helped and instructed me, and particularly to those kind friends who read the manuscript of this book and suggested improvements, I offer my heartfelt thanks; to none more than TO MY WIFE, JUDY.

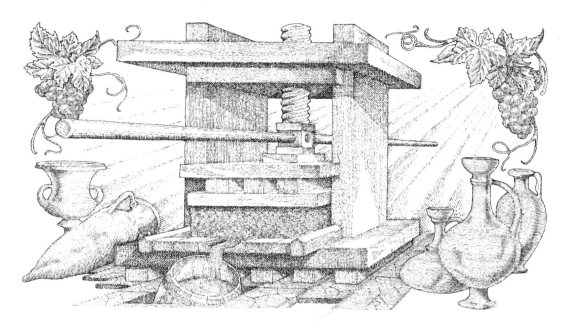

Wine

THINK, FOR A MOMENT, of an almost paper-white glass of liquid, just shot with greeny-gold, just tart on your tongue, full of wild-flower scents and spring-water freshness. And think of a burnt-umber fluid, as smooth as syrup in the glass, as fat as butter to smell and sea-deep with strange flavours. Both are wine.

Wine is grape-juice. Every drop of liquid filling so many bottles has been drawn out of the ground by the roots of a vine. All these different drinks have at one time been sap in a stick. It is the first of many strange and some—despite modern research—mysterious circumstances which go to make wine not only the most delicious, but the most fascinating, drink in the world.

It would not be so fascinating if there were not so many different kinds. Although there are people who do not care for it, and who think it no more than a nuisance that a wine-list has so many names on it, the whole reason that wine is worth study is its variety.

From crushed grapes come an infinite number of scents and flavours, to some extent predictable, to some extent controllable—to some extent neither. The kind of grapes, where they are planted, how they are pruned, when they are picked, how they are pressed and how long they are aged all bear on the eventual taste. And behind each of these factors there is a tradition or argument or set of reasons why it should be done this way rather than that, and a wonderful variety of ideas about the ideal in view.

1

Wine is the pleasantest subject in the world to discuss. All its associations are with occasions when people are at their best; with relaxation, contentment, leisurely meals and the free flow of ideas. The scope of the subject of wine is never-ending. It is its fascination to me that so many other subjects lie within its boundaries. Without geography and topography it is incomprehensible; without history it is colourless; without taste it is meaningless; without travel it remains unreal. It embraces botany, chemistry, agriculture, carpentry, economics—any number of sciences whose names I do not even know. It leads you up paths of knowledge and byways of expertise you would never glimpse without it. Best of all, it brings you into friendly contact with some of the most skilful and devoted craftsmen, most generous and entertaining hosts you will find anywhere.

Wine has the most precious quality that art has: it makes ideas, people, incidents, places, sensations seem larger than life. It is, in Bernard Berenson's awkward but irreplaceable phrase, life-enhancing.

Unfortunately, one of the things which wine can make larger than life is a bore. A wine bore is a serious menace. Worse still is a wine snob. But boredom and snobbery lurk in every calling and every subject. They are no monopoly of wine. To me a car bore is far worse than a wine bore. I find even in an old droner's reminiscences about cobwebbed bottles a possible source of illumination.

There is, as I have already said, no end to what you can learn about wine. I know perfectly well that I have only just begun. Everybody will find some hole in this book. Some will find more holes than substance. But if this is the case I hope they will at least, like the holes in lace, make a pattern.

How Wine is Made

THE DIFFERENCE BETWEEN GRAPE-JUICE, simple and sweet, and wine with all its qualities of keeping, of maturing and finally of inspiring, is the process of fermentation. In fermentation sugar is transformed into alcohol: grape-juice becomes wine.

Fermentation comes naturally to grapes. Wine did not have to wait to be invented. A grape left alone could make wine if its skin were broken. Everything needed to make wine is there already when the grape has ripened on the vine.

In the final stages of ripening, yeast cells appear from somewhere—it is not clear where—on the skin of the grape and cling to it. As soon as its skin is broken they pounce on the sugar in its juice, which is their object, and turn it into alcohol. Only a grape has enough sugar for this to happen naturally. So-called wines are made from other fruit, but all need extra sugar. Something like 30 per cent of the juice of a ripe grape is sugar, and this the yeast cells set about converting.

Pressing

The way the grapes are broken and the container they ferment in are two of the most variable things about wine. On small farms in Chianti all the grapes, black and white, are bundled together into a large opening at the top of a barrel. They still have their stalks, even the mud from the fields on them. They have only been slightly broken up, in the big tub on an ox-cart into which they were gathered, by the farmer with a knotty club. He plunges it up and down a few times to see that a fair proportion of the grapes have been smashed, relying on the heat generated in the barrel when fermentation starts to swell and burst the rest.

On other small farms in France, Portugal, Spain and some parts of Italy the grapes are still trodden by bare feet, as they have been since wine was first made.

Larger wine-properties now all have presses or mechanical crushers to break the grapes, but even these vary from old hand-operated squeezers to huge revolving horizontal drums. The latest kind have a gigantic rubber balloon inside. When it is inflated it presses the grapes against the slatted sides and forces out their juice without crushing their pips, which contain unwanted and evil-tasting substances.

The biggest presses of all are those of Champagne, in which an enormous weight descends by scarcely perceptible degrees on an enclosure containing four tons of grapes at a time.

Usually the juice and broken grapes, or for white wine the juice alone, is pumped for fermentation into vats or barrels, traditionally of oak but now more and more made of concrete, glass or stainless steel. Sometimes it is left to ferment where it has been crushed or trodden.

Fermentation

The process of fermentation, which is what is happening when the yeast cells get to work, produces turbulent eruptions in the juice. Not only alcohol is made, but carbon dioxide gas is given off in large quantities. Its bubbles keep the mass of broken grapes moving. At the same time the heat given off by the reaction makes it warm.

Fermentation goes on until the sugar supply runs out, or until the yeast cells are asphyxiated by the growing concentration of alcohol, whichever happens sooner. Usually it is the sugar which gives out first. The liquid, then, instead of being a solution of sugar and water, is a solution of alcohol in water, with the same small quantities of the acids and oils which give it its peculiar flavour and scent. On an average there will be about 10 per cent of alcohol in red wine, a little more—11 or so—in white. There is no sugar left at all and the wine is completely dry.

If, on the other hand, the grapes were so ripe that there was still more sugar to ferment when a concentration of 15 per cent alcohol was reached, it would be the yeast cells which would give out first. In a solution of alcohol this strong they grow drowsy and cease to function. They are not dead, but they are completely under the table. When this happens there is still some sugar left unconverted into alcohol and the wine is more or less sweet to the taste.

This process is the basic one for the making of all wine and, come to that, of any other alcoholic drink.

Table wine

A wine made in this way, without any diversions from the natural processes, will be what we call a table wine. It will be mild in flavour, moderate in alcoholic strength; still, not sparkling. It will be red or white or pink according to whether the juice was separated from the skins before or after it was allowed to ferment, and according to what colour of grapes it was made from.

Diversions can be put in its way during the fermentation process, however, which can make it other things. It can be made to stay sweet, by keeping its natural sugar, or it can be made to sparkle, by keeping its natural gas. These two techniques together with the first make up the three principal classes of wine; natural, sparkling and fortified.

Sparkling wine

Champagne is the greatest and best-known sparkling wine. All other makers of quality sparkling wines proceed on principles worked out in Champagne over the last three hundred years. It is a question of bottling the wine before the fermentation is quite finished, so that some of the natural carbon dioxide is trapped in the bottle. (This will be explained in the chapter on champagne in the Aperitifs section.)

Fortified wine

Port is the typical fortified wine. The object is to make it as sweet as possible. It is done by starting the fermentation in the usual way, with very ripe grapes capable of continuing to ferment until there is at least 15 per cent alcohol, and then suddenly, at the halfway point, emptying them out of the tank where they are fermenting into a barrel a quarter full of brandy. The alcohol level is immediately raised to the point where the yeast cells are stupefied and can do no more. Half the sugar from the grapes remains in the wine, which is hence very strong and very sweet at the same time.

Sherry, though a fortified wine, is made quite differently. Fermentation goes right on to the end, and no sugar whatsoever is left. Fortification comes afterwards; the brandy is used as a sort of preservative. Any sweetness which is required has to be added in a blend.

Chaptalization

In some northern wine-areas, notably in Burgundy and Germany, the sun sometimes fails to produce enough sugar in the grapes. The growers then have to resort to adding sugar—a process known as chaptalization after M. Chaptal, the French Minister for Agriculture who first authorized it—to get the fermentation going and to make the wine strong enough to keep. This only happens in poor years: it makes poor wine, but the wine would be worse without it.

Wine in the Past

IT IS NOT KNOWN who first discovered wine. *Vitis vinifera,* the species of vine which grows wine-grapes, is apparently a native of Persia. Certainly wine was drunk in ancient Persia, in ancient Egypt and in ancient Greece. It spread as our civilization spread, from the East. At each move of civilizing influence—of the Phoenicians to Spain, the Greeks to Italy and Provence, the Romans through Gaul to Germany—the vine moved too. Wine lies at the roots of our civilization. It is an integral part of both the Christian and Jewish religions.

The Romans   There is no room here to trace its progress in detail. It came to many of what are now its most prosperous regions with the Romans. The routes the Romans took, and made their lines of communication, were the river valleys. In France and Germany they are still the centres of wine-growing, for nothing has challenged their old-established position, their accessibility and the convenience of their transport. At the start there were probably two considerations. The first was to clear the forests on the river banks to make guerrilla warfare and ambushes more difficult; where the ground was cleared would be the natural place to plant vines. The second was that transport of bulky wine-barrels was impossible except by water.

In the event it was found that nothing had such a pacifying and civilizing effect on the tribes as having their own vineyards. People whose previous life had been hunting and fighting became farmers for the sake of wine. The vine is as demanding as it is rewarding to grow. It needs constant care, so it required settling down. Out of the inspiration it gave, the arts of peace grew. In a very important way you can say that wine was responsible for the establishing of a stable society, and hence of civilization, in Europe.

So it is not surprising that the vine is an age-old symbol of peace and prosperity. As James Busby, the man who inspired the beginnings of the Australian wine industry, declared: 'The man who could sit under the shade of his own vine with his wife and children about him, and the ripe clusters hanging within their reach, and not feel the highest enjoyment, is incapable of happiness and does not know what the word means.'

The Church   The decline and fall of the Roman Empire in Continental Europe left the Church in power. It was the Church which kept alive the vital skills of civilization—agriculture, letters, the law—while the new races from the East came to take over the Empire. The knowledge of wine-making and vine-growing became almost a monopoly of the Church. All the biggest and best vineyards were owned and operated by religious houses.

So it remained, by and large, for a thousand years. All over the vineyards of Europe the traces remain to this day. In France it was the Revolution which deprived the Church of her lands and auctioned them among the

5

people. In Germany many of the monasteries were secularized by Napoleon. The Church has few vineyards of note now except in Germany, but to her we owe the whole of the long wine-making tradition which is continuous from the Romans to the twentieth century.

Establishment of regional characters

Already in Roman times most of the vineyards we know in Europe today were planted and producing. The wines were different. Champagne was not sparkling; sherry was not fortified; we do not know where white wine was made and where red. None of the now familiar and long-established types of wine were known—but the ball had been set rolling. Each district would slowly discover for itself what its natural inclinations were, for white or red, for one kind of grape or another, for longer or shorter periods of ripening, of fermentation, of maturing. Nobody came to Burgundy and said, 'Here we will make a rich, savoury, ruby-red table wine'; nobody planting a vine on the Mountain of Reims ever dreamt that its wine would one day be full of glittering foam. It was Burgundy which decided what burgundy would be like, and Champagne which put the first bubbles into champagne. After generations, centuries, of experiment the character of the region began to emerge and men began to see what had to be done to perfect it. In this sense the wines of Europe are direct expressions of the country they come from: natural, not designed; emerging, not induced.

Each of the vineyards of Europe now has one kind of wine and makes no other. The result of centuries of trial and error is complete specialization. One grape-variety and one method of making the wine has always established itself as the best for the district in the end.

The New World

Wine has been a brilliantly successful transplantation from the Old World to the New. The first of the European settlements to have the vine were South America and South Africa. To South America it went with the Conquistadors. It was already well established at the Cape by the end of the seventeenth century. California and Australia, the two other chief New World vineyards, started their development simultaneously in the second quarter of the nineteenth century.

The New World settlers took over from Europe not only the vine but the ideas of what kinds of wine they wanted to make. The process of trial and error to establish the country's own kind of wine was never really allowed to happen. The principal difference between the wines of the New and Old Worlds results from this transplantation of ideas.

In California or Australia one winery often makes 'champagne', 'port', 'claret' and 'Chablis' from the grapes of one vineyard. It is only a matter, they tell you, of planting the right variety for the job and using the right techniques of vinification. Rather than give the country the chance to express itself through the wine it produces, by experimenting until a new personality emerges, wine-makers still try to get burgundy, for example, out of Australia, a task more difficult than getting blood out of a stone.

It is apparently better business for a wine-maker to be able to offer a

6

complete range of products than to be famous for one; say, his sparkling wine or his dessert wine. The difference in philosophy is basic. It should always be borne in mind when comparing the vintages of the New World with the vintages of the Old.

It is curious that wine-making in North America had to wait until the developing of California. By that time the Eastern States had been settled and civilized for two hundred years. Their climate was equally suited to the vine. Their people were good wine-drinkers. Why did Virginian wine not grow up in the seventeenth century at the same time as the wine of the Cape?

The answer lies in the terrible little beetle-like creature called the phylloxera, a native of the eastern United States. Nothing was known about him until about a hundred years ago, but he had meanwhile been preventing the growing of grapes for wine anywhere in his domain. All that the farmers knew was that the European vines they planted withered and died. There is a kind of vine which is native to North America; it grew profusely—giving really terrible wine where anybody tried to tame it— and was immune to the attacks of the phylloxera. But the imported vines of Europe were no sooner planted than their roots were eaten up and they died.

The importance of this for Europe was not realized until too late. The little beetle found its way to France in the 1860s, probably on an American vine being imported for experimental grafting purposes. Its progeny swept through the country like the plague, doing the most appalling damage. Within twenty years they had killed virtually every vine in France—in Bordeaux, Burgundy, Champagne: nowhere was spared. The rest of Europe suffered the same fate. For a while it looked like the end of European wine. But it was discovered that the roots of the American vines were immune to phylloxera. There was nothing else for it but to bring in millions of American vine-stocks and graft on to them the remaining cuttings of the old European vines. To everybody's infinite relief it worked. The roots resisted the scourge; the branches bore their old fruit. There will always be arguments about whether the wine is quite as good as it was before the disaster. But it was saved, that was the great thing. And to this day every vine in Europe, with a handful of exceptions, is grafted, before it is planted, on to an American root.

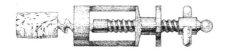

Wine in Britain and the United States

An English autumn, though it hath no vines
Blushing with Bacchant coronals along
The paths, o'er which the far festoon entwines
The red grape in the sunny lands of song,
Hath yet a purchased choice of choicest wines;
The claret light and the Madeira strong.
If Britain mourn her bleakness, we can tell her,
The very best of vineyards is the cellar.

Byron, *Don Juan,* 13, LXXVI

English vineyards

THERE IS NO REASON why wine should not be grown in England. At the present time there are only three commercial vineyards—at Beaulieu and Hambledon in Hampshire and Horam in Sussex. But there are a number of vineyards in small-scale production. The climate is no more unsuitable for the vine than it is in the northern Rhine vineyards of Germany. Indeed Britain's chief drawback as a vineyard seems to be the number of its birds which are fond of grapes.

The Middle Ages

Wine used to be grown in England on a large scale, and might easily be a normal part of British agriculture today had it not been for the marriage of King Henry II of England to Queen Eleanor of Aquitaine in 1152. The Queen's lands included the vineyards of Bordeaux. There was a plentiful supply of the best red wine in the world, grown on an estuary within easy sailing distance of England. As Edward Hyams says in *Dionysus,* his history of the vine, 'the infant English industry was overlaid at birth by its immensely vigorous Gallic mother'.

During the three hundred years that Bordeaux belonged to England its wine was the everyday English drink. The discovery of Bordeaux by the English made a tremendous difference to that quiet province. Nothing like today's vast acreage was planted with vines in those days. The whole of the Médoc, the district which is now the most important, was unplanted;

8

production was, by present-day standards, minute. But the connection with England changed things completely. The English soon proved to have an unquenchable thirst for claret, which was what they christened the pale red wine which was Bordeaux's principal produce. New vineyards sprang up everywhere—even on the corn-lands, causing a serious shortage of bread.

It is astonishing to think that in the fourteenth century more claret was being drunk in England than is today. The population was not a twentieth of today's but the total gallonage of claret shipped was as high or higher. So important was the wine trade in medieval England that the size of all ships, whatever their cargo or purpose, was measured in the number of tuns of wine that they could carry.

A tun was a cask which held about 250 gallons. In Froissart's *Chronicle* there is a reference to the wine fleet of 1372 of ships from England, Wales and Scotland at Bordeaux. There were, he said, two hundred ships. According to Sir John Clapham, in his *Concise Economic History of Britain,* 'the average tonnage of the time would be well over fifty, seeing that at Bristol rather later it was eighty-eight'. Allowing sixty tuns to the ship, the total cargo of wine in 1372 was three million gallons; perhaps something in the region of six bottles of claret per head for every man, woman and child in England, Wales and Scotland. Today, of all table wines, claret included, we drink a bottle and a half each.

That claret was considered a part of the staple diet, even of the ordinary man, is clear from the fact that, again according to Clapham, in 1282 Edward I, providing for his Welsh war, ordered six hundred tuns of wine (a hundred and fifty thousand gallons) as an ordinary commissariat operation.

England lost Bordeaux in 1453. At an action which was nonetheless heroic—though a good deal less talked about in England—because we lost it, Marshal Talbot was killed defending the last of the dwindling English interests in Aquitaine. An apple tree grows today on the spot where the last English troops are said to have held the last piece of English Bordeaux. The place is called Castillon.

From that time on, claret supplies slowly became more difficult for the English. The people of Bordeaux, who were not necessarily any too pleased by their liberation, could not afford to stop selling their wine in its best market. Precautions had to be taken, though, to prevent the English wine fleet from singeing the King of France's beard. For a time the English ships were compelled to heave to at the fortress of Blaye on the way up the Gironde and land their guns on the quay, like gunfighters going into a Dodge City saloon. They then sailed up to Bordeaux unmolested and checked out again at Blaye on the way back.

The story goes that the Scottish merchants took advantage of the friendly relations between Scotland and France to get the pick of the vintage each time. Not having to stop to surrender their guns, they managed to get the best wine at the best price. The taste for fine claret persists in Scotland to this day.

The English have never drunk so much claret as they did in the days when it was, as it were, native produce. They turned to Rhenish, the wine of the Rhine, and more and more to the sweet Mediterranean wines which the Genoese merchants brought. The best of these was sack.

Nevertheless the claret habit never completely died in England. It is at the end of the seventeenth century that we find the first mention of a château of Bordeaux by name in English. It was Pepys who mentioned it, and the wine was 'Ho Bryan [Haut-Brion]; that hath a good and most particular taste that I ever met with'. The date was 10 April 1663. Three hundred years later a dinner was held in London to drink the same wine and celebrate the anniversary of Pepys's entry.

But that was the age of Louis XIV. With the fall of the royal house of Stuart, animosity between England and France grew from dark dealings to war, and then, as now, economic sanctions were a useful weapon. The trade in French wines was sharply discouraged by the English government, and England made a treaty with Portugal (whose wine she had first met when Charles II married a Portuguese princess) to ensure herself an alternative supply, as well as a market for her manufactured goods.

That the change from claret to port was not a change of taste is shown by the famous Scottish verse:

> Firm and erect the Highland chieftain stood
> Old was his mutton and his claret good.
> 'Thou shalt drink Port' the English statesman cried.
> He drank the poison—and his spirit died.

To start with, certainly, the Portuguese wine which the English and (since the Parliamentary Union of England and Scotland in 1707) the Scots were obliged to drink instead of claret was a poor substitute. How merchants— it is interesting that some of the first were Scotsmen—went out to Portugal and invented port is another story. They made out of a bad substitute for claret one of the great, and completely different, wines of the world. During the eighteenth century it was port—and in America Madeira—which might have been called the favourite and most fashionable wine.

But during this time also the vineyards of Bordeaux were taking on a new splendour. In the eighteenth century the great invention, the cork, changed the nature of claret—and indeed of every wine. It made its long ageing in bottle (instead of its rapid consumption from the barrel) a possibility. It brought new sensations into being, and changed wine from a mere healthy, pleasant, enlivening drink to something which was capable of real character, and hence of every level of enjoyment from the purely sensual to the purely aesthetic.

Claret changed, during the century when it was least drunk in England, from being a pale, short-lived, hand-to-mouth sort of drink—indeed the wine which had earned the name of claret—to a deep, brilliant, strong and incredibly long-lived, subtle, delicate and delicious wine.

In the cellar of Château Lafite there is to this day a bin of the vintage of 1797. When they last opened a bottle, not many years ago, it was still good wine. That was the difference the cork had made.

The Golden Age

The nineteenth century is often called the Golden Age of wine. The great estates were making wine regardless of cost. It was bought by a discerning few who had time and space to lay it down for twenty or thirty years. A race of connoisseurs grew up (there had been no such things since ancient Rome, for there had not been wine worth tasting and discussing). Vintages of superb quality seemed to come with amazing regularity.

It was then that the blow of phylloxera fell. At the time, after an extraordinary run of fine vintages in Bordeaux in the 1870s, it must have seemed to wine-lovers like the end of the world. But, oddly enough, after the replanting the recovery was remarkably swift in the best vineyards. The years 1894, 1896, 1899 and 1900 were all famous vintages. The older generation who foretold that things would never be the same again were disappointed.

The return of claret as the everyday British wine, or indeed of wine as the everyday British drink, did not come quite so easily. High rates of duty were still very much against it for most of the nineteenth century. It was not until Gladstone, with understanding unique among politicians, realized that Britain was starving herself of exactly what she needed—a supply of cheap, healthy, nourishing wine—that duties on light (i.e. table) wines were lowered, and it began to be possible, after two hundred years of being forced to drink bad spirits or heavy, liverish, cheap, fortified wines, to go back to the old English habit of a glass of red wine at every meal as a matter of course.

Prohibition in the United States

In the second and third decades of this century the United States were foolish enough to keep themselves out of the market for the wonderful wine which Europe offered—or which California could grow. Prohibition let Britain have it all her own way. It was not really until after the Second World War that the American influence began to be felt in the auction rooms of Beaune and Trier, and wherever it is that prices are decided in the dignified silence of Bordeaux.

Wine as a luxury and necessity

Today the rates of duty again force us to look at wine as an exotic import. In a certain sense, therefore, it has changed its nature before it even arrives on our shores. To us it is classed and taxed as a luxury; to its own countrymen it is a necessity.

Wine means more to the French than even beer to the British. It almost plays the part of tea as well in their lives. Workmen start with wine for breakfast, and never stop drinking it until they go to bed. There has been a great deal of talk recently about how wine consumption is on the increase in Britain and the United States, but the process has hardly started yet.

Compared with the French the Anglo-Saxon countries still scarcely touch it. The following are the total wine-drinking figures for the United Kingdom and France:

Every man, woman and child in the United Kingdom—2½ bottles a year.
Every man, woman and child in France—160 bottles a year.

The figures for the United States are slightly higher than those for Britain—owing, perhaps, to the number of Italians in America—but only slightly. Nobody, at the moment, can call us wine-drinking nations.

Excise

In Britain this is mainly due to the absurd and unjust excise duties imposed on wine. A tradition of hypocritical puritanism makes it possible for the government to raise enormous revenue from wine on pseudo-moral grounds. The implications of the restrictions and high duties are that wine comes into the country heavily laden with the sin and sensuality of the South. The people, the laws imply, may just be allowed to drink wine (if they can afford it, and then only between stated hours in public), but they must expiate their naughtiness with gold.

Medicinal properties

In treating wine this way the government chooses to ignore, for its own ends, the evidence of medical science as well as the evidence of the senses of every citizen. I am told that the medical benefits of wine are many and its disadvantages few or none. It is an antiseptic, a stimulant to the appetite (which is especially valuable to old people), an aid to digestion. It can be a help in cases of diabetes, anaemia and heart trouble. On the undiscovered borders between physical and psychological disorders its morale-raising and soothing properties can literally save life. It is absorbed at a slow and steady rate by the blood, unlike spirits, which enter the bloodstream at a gallop and, for a shorter time, raise the blood alcohol to a higher level.

People of perfectly sound health are aware of how it helps to keep them so, how it helps the body and mind to relax after the strain of work and regain the fluidity and naturalness which tension destroys. Why this useful and natural drink should pay duties and, for example, soft drinks, which have no beneficial properties, none, is hard to see.

The wine-trade

Being importers, seeing wine as a luxury, England and America have developed a highly specialized and immensely skilful wine-trade. With no commitment, save in frequent times of war, to or against any wine-growing country or district we have learnt how to bring home the best from everywhere. In Bordeaux no-one has burgundy; in Germany nobody drinks Sauternes. Each district is loyal to its own produce. So the French, if they are the greatest producers and drinkers of wine, are also the most hidebound. To find a connoisseur in the English sense is almost impossible in France. Even a Parisian gourmet who knows his Bordeaux and burgundy back to front ignores the Moselle, say, and certainly knows nothing of sherry. Nor has he ever tasted vintage port. But we have a unique opportunity. The whole world's wines are offered to us. A good London or New York wine-list is a compilation of the best that is made in every corner of

A vine just before the vintage. *(Unless stated otherwise, all the photographs in this book were taken by the author)*

the globe. The Londoner has, if anything, the advantage over the New Yorker for variety. With wine from the Commonwealth, Eastern Europe and South Africa (even, now, from China), London is really the wine market of the world.

Modern increase in variety

We are lucky in time as well as in place. There is a greater variety of wine on our lists now than there has ever been before. Modern methods and knowledge are making the production of good wine possible in countless countries where it used to be out of the question. They are also making the moving of wine safe enough to be a sound business proposition. 'Small' wines have always been hamstrung in the past by the fact that even a short journey altered them radically, even if it did not spoil them altogether. With knowledge of chemistry they can be stabilized, and with stability there comes the possibility of a world market for every wine under the sun.

Decline in quality

On the debit side it may be true that Bordeaux and burgundy used to be even better than they are today, and that German wine is not what once it was. Modern conditions have skimmed off the cream of the cream. During the Golden Age in the last century and at the beginning of this, demand was comparatively low, prices of the finest wines were low, and storage of a great red wine for the twenty years or more which it takes to reach maturity presented no problem. There was no urge to keep the relatively small amount of capital involved moving. The connoisseur had a fine cellar in his own house. The wine reached its maturity slowly and a few lucky people were more than satisfied.

This is virtually impossible today. First-growth clarets come on the market at £40, or over $100, a case. The interest on the value of a good cellar of such wine over twenty years is enough to make anyone pause. Even the cheapest of fine clarets which are really worth cellaring involve tying up a fair sum of money for a long, financially unprofitable time.

Changes to come

What is happening, and is bound to happen more and more, is that the growers, knowing perfectly well that none of their wine will be allowed to reach its maturity in the old slow way, will make a quicker-maturing wine. The logical conclusion of this is that claret will become *vin rosé* again, as it once was, needing no maturing at all. Either this or the use of ray treatment to speed up maturing artificially is almost bound to come.

We are lucky, therefore, that we live at the time when Lafite is still a red wine, so that the chance is still there, for those with money and patience enough, to take advantage of its superlative qualities. No doubt it will make a good rosé, but somehow it will not be quite the same thing.

The Names of Wines

IT IS NOT HEREDITY so much as environment which shapes a wine's character. Where a vine is planted, far more than how or even what kind of vine it is, decides the kind of wine it will give. The importance of the exact spot is graphically illustrated by the classification of the wines of Bordeaux according to quality, which was done over a hundred years ago. Since that time everything in that country—the methods, the people, even the vines themselves—have changed radically, sometimes repeatedly, and yet most of the list still holds good. The same vineyards are the best today as were the best then. In fact the land, the one unchanging factor, has turned out to be the most important.

Logically enough, then, wines are named after their birthplaces. The better the wine the more specific it is about its origin. At one end of the scale there is the homeless, anonymous *vin rouge* (or even lower perhaps the bottle simply labelled Le Bon Vin, which I saw a fisherman swigging from in Brittany). At the other end there is the exceptional German growth which puts all its cards on the table, telling you the village, the vineyard, the kind of grapes, when they were picked and even the number of the barrel the particular wine comes from, where it was bottled and who is responsible for each stage of its history: the growing, the bottling and the shipping.

Even among the wines whose nature depends on blending, where more specific information about their birthplace would not be available or would be far too complicated to put on a label, the better the wine the more details we are given. Sherry, champagne and port are all blended wines; we buy them by the maker's name and not by their vineyard origins, but nonetheless the best champagne and port is the one which has specific information on the label about its vintage year, the best sherry always carries its exact description in the Spanish classification—fino, amontillado or oloroso.

As the wines of the New World come of age they follow the same pattern. From merely being 'Australian burgundy' the specifications begin to creep in. First it is the grape-variety, then the winery; possibly, before long, it will be the particular vineyard, as it is in France.

Fraud

It is no secret that the names of wines which have turned out, over the years, to be best and most popular have been borrowed, not to say stolen, by competitors. In some cases it is a borrowing, admitted and outright. 'Spanish Chablis' may be a regrettable way of describing a white wine which has nothing whatsoever to do with the famous town in France, but it can

14

scarcely be said to be making a false claim. False claims are, however, often made. The art of faking has at various times been carried further with wine than with any other commodity. There is plenty of wine about which pretends to be real Chablis from Chablis (France) and is not. In everybody's interest the French government has taken a firm—if not totally effective—line about this. The result of its defence of the unique rights of places to use their own names on their wines are the laws of *Appellation Contrôlée*, which can be taken as representative of the efforts of all wine countries to regularize and protect their growers. As such they have become an integral part of the naming of wine. If we are to understand the meaning of modern wine-labels at all we must have some idea of what *Appellation Contrôlée* means.

The laws of Appellation Contrôlée

The phylloxera disaster in the 1870s and 1880s, in which virtually every vine in France died and had to be replaced (an operation which cost France considerably more even than the disastrous Franco-Prussian War), started a wave of fraud in the wine industry. Phylloxera, more than anything else, brought the government into the affairs of the wine-grower and merchant to regulate activities. Old vineyards were in many places abandoned and new ones planted in easier, but unsuitable, places where wine was plentiful but terrible. The wrong vines were planted. In the general uproar the forgers got to work as never before.

As a result, after years of discussion, the government evolved control systems for all the important wine-areas of France. There could be no standard formula. Variation in practice, in traditions, in land-holding and every other possible aspect of wine-making meant that each system had to be evolved for the particular place. A grape which was banned in one place might be exactly right for another. In Bordeaux it was enough to protect the names of villages; in Burgundy individual plots had to have their own protection. These are the laws of *Appellation Contrôlée*. They have their counterpart in Germany, and Italy is even now initiating a similar system. In Portugal you can see the French words *Appellation d'origine contrôlée* on labels as though the French laws applied in that country—so wide has been their influence.

Quality control

The laws of *Appellation Contrôlée* have simplified the customer's life enormously. They have laid down a naming system for each wine-district which, once you have grasped it, is pretty well foolproof. It is as well to remember, though, that it is not law in England. Until Britain joins the Common Market the wine-merchant can print *Appellation Contrôlée* on any label he likes and commit no legal offence. If he is interested in this kind of dealing he finds no lack of co-operation in France.

The laws of *Appellation Contrôlée* have another object, too. Apart from laying down what a wine may be called, they do a great deal to control its quality. They only grant the right to a name to wine which is grown on the right vine of the right age, pruned in the right way, achieves the right degree of alcoholic strength and comes up to a standard of flavour which is tested by tasting. The requirements are admittedly minimal, but they prevent any serious lagging behind by the owners of fine land.

Only the best wines are dealt with under the *Appellation Contrôlée* laws. Among *vins de pays* there is always the possibility of improving enough to achieve an *Appellation*. The cadet branch, as it were, for wines which are better than *ordinaire* but not quite in the *A.C.* class, is known as *V.D.Q.S.— Vins Délimités de Qualité Supérieure*. *V.D.Q.S.* wines are often seen in France, but so far the initials have made little impact abroad.

Château-bottling

At more or less the same time as the government in France started to talk about State controls on wine-dealing, the best dealers and growers began to take their own action. The producer's or merchant's way of tackling the problem was to bottle his wine himself with his own branded cork and give his own guarantee that the wine his customer eventually drank was the wine he grew. The practice started in Bordeaux. This bottling of the wine at the château where it was grown adds to the cost, but it is the most complete guarantee of authenticity. The words *mis en bouteilles au château,* or alternatively *mise en bouteille au château,* appearing on the label, are the guarantee. Château-bottling was followed by its equivalents, estate-bottling in Germany and domaine-bottling in Burgundy, so that now the greater part of the finest wines of all these areas are bottled where they are grown and shipped abroad, with extra freight costs, in crates instead of barrels.

The German term for estate-bottled is *Originalabfüllung*, sometimes shortened to *Orig.-abf.* The term *Kellerabfüllung* or *Kellerabzug* is sometimes used. In Burgundy there is a variety of terms, of which the commonest and best is the forthright *mise au domaine, mise du domaine* or *mise en bouteille au domaine*. Alternative forms: *mis en bouteilles à la propriété,* or *mise en bouteille dans nos caves* (bottled in our cellars) are suspect. Even 'bottled by the proprietor' is no real guarantee; the same man may be proprietor of several widely different properties. His *caves,* come to that, may be anywhere and contain anything.

Despite the extra cost of shipping wine in bottle rather than bulk the practice gains ground every day. Apart from the question of authenticity there is a certain amount of snobbishness in it. Shippers hope that some of the glory of the great château-bottled clarets will rub off on the cheap wines if they can announce that these, too, were château-bottled. In places—Italy is the chief example—it also helps the grower to ship his wine in good condition; he can pasteurize it in its bottle. Again, there are some wines, like the Portuguese sparkling rosé, which can only be made to stay fizzy by shipping them in bottle. Champagne, which is made in its bottle, is another matter. It simply does not exist in bulk, so there is no question of shipping it except in bottles.

16

Anyone who has high claims for his wine, then, tends to be as specific as possible about it. He uses whatever cover the law of his country allows him—the most specific appellation he is entitled to. He often goes further and bottles it himself, adding his personal guarantee.

If these precautions seem over-elaborate, consider what danger there is in more generalized naming. It is the same with food. The statement 'Yorkshire pudding is delicious' is of very limited value. The important thing is who cooks it.

'Ordinary', 'Good', 'Fine' and 'Great' Wine

Ordinary

THE DAILY DRINK of real wine-drinking countries—not those for whom wine is a luxury—is ordinary wine. In France *vin ordinaire* has a definite connotation. It is not a vague term for anything which is not very exciting. Its price depends on its strength—nothing else. It is almost always red. In Germany it is called *Konsumwein*, in Spain *vino corriente* ('current', or running, wine), in Portugal *Consumo*. We have no real term of our own for it in English. *Ordinaire* is the word most commonly used.

Vin de pays

Vin de pays—wine of the country—is a cut above *ordinaire*. Though the wine in itself may be no better it has one added dignity; you know where it comes from. *Ordinaire* is completely anonymous. It is often a blend of the wine of France, Spain, North Africa, Italy or anywhere where the price per degree of alcohol is low at the time. *Vin de pays* at its worst is simply *ordinaire* with a birth-certificate. At its best, on the other hand, it can be one of those excellent regional specialities which are always referred to in a patronizing way as 'little'. A good hotel almost anywhere in the southern half of France should have quite a good *vin du pays* (switched from *de* to *du* because it is referring to the particular bit of *pays* in question). The *patron* gets it by knowing the grower. There is not enough to become a widespread marketable proposition, but it is none the worse for that.

Good

With 'good' wine we are on trickier ground. What does a dealer mean when he says that a picture is 'good'? What do you mean when you say that a dish is good? They are not quite the same thing. 'Good' must be allowed to cover all wine from just plain well-made upwards to the top. But at the same time it has a field of its own, between ordinary and fine. Whereas ordinary is not worth tasting with any attention, has no scent or characteristics of its own, good wine begins to be worth thinking about. It is well made and has its own character, its own variation on the general character of its region. In this class come most of the wines of Bordeaux, for example, which are not Classed Growths; the wines of Burgundy which are known by their village-names alone, not the names of their individual vineyards; the blended German wines such as Liebfraumilch; the Chiantis and Orvietos of Italy—all the wines which carry the name of their type, when that name is one of the world's great wine-regions.

Fine

There is no general agreement on what is meant by the word 'fine', often as it comes into discussions about wine. I would narrow it down to the field above Good and below Great. All the Classed Growths of France are, beyond question, fine wines. Indeed all wines which tell their full story—their vintage year, the particular vineyard and not just the village where they were grown, often the name of the owner—on their labels probably come into this class. Most—though not all—estate-bottled wines deserve to be called fine wines. In the French consumption statistics the section for fine wines includes all named growths (154 million gallons a year, as against 1,100 million for ordinary wine, are drunk in France). In fact, one to seven is probably the proportion of fine to other wine, taking fine at its broadest meaning.

Great

Great wine is a different matter. There is no vineyard in the world which always produces great wine, however great and famous its name. Great wine is the rare and exquisite result of perfect conditions in a perfect vineyard, perfectly handled by the grower and carefully matured afterwards. Where the line comes between fine and great is always a matter for debate. But the word should not be used lightly. A great wine is a work of art, capable of providing aesthetic pleasure of the highest order to anyone who will be attentive. As an everyday drink it is as fitting as *Hamlet* is for cabaret in a night-club. Only five or six districts in the whole world have shown themselves to be capable of producing wine like this with any regularity. They are Bordeaux, Burgundy, the Rhine and Moselle, Champagne, the Douro river in Portugal and Jerez in Spain. At various times great wine has been made in Hungary, in Italy, in South Africa, California, central Portugal and maybe elsewhere. But it remains rare, and grows more and more expensive as more and more people want to taste it. Even a convinced ordinary-wine drinker should taste great wine sometimes. It is easy to get into a rut with wine and to wonder what all the fuss is about when anyone mentions the glory of the best growths. I hope nobody drinks them every day, because it is partly by comparison that their superlative qualities stand out.

It is hard to put a finger on the quality of greatness in wine. To me there is always something faintly sweet, but sweet in the sense of sweet-natured rather than sugary, about one. There is a definite tendency to reach a quintessential taste of fresh grapes, as even really fine cognac does although it has been distilled. But this they all have in common, whether they are clarets, delicate fino sherries, champagne or hock or burgundy; they provoke discussion. To drink a great wine alone is almost painful. There must be somebody to share the experience with, for it is an experience, and it needs discussing, analysing and gloating over just as a great play does; or, to put it more precisely, a great picture, for it is not dramatic—it is beautiful.

Wine and Time

IT IS WRONG to assume that because a wine is older it is better. Tales of wonderful cobwebby old bottles have led to a general belief that age is in itself a good thing for wine. It is only partially true. There are wines which need a long time to mature. But there are others which are ruined by being kept for even as much as a year or two.

To make a very broad—in fact over-broad—rule, red wine needs more time to mature and reach its best; white wine needs less. The making of red wine, which involves the skins and the pips as well as the juice of the grapes, leaves extra substances dissolved; above all, tannin. This gives the wine the quality of hardness, of drying up your mouth.

These extras need time to resolve themselves, to carry out slow and obscure chemical changes which make all the difference in the world to the eventual glass of wine. The better the wine, the longer it takes.

The process of maturing

What actually happens to wine when it ages in its bottle is not known. It is assumed that it is a slowed-down version of what happens when it ages in cask. The oak staves of a cask are porous; they allow a certain amount of oxygen through to the wine and this, together with oxygen which is already absorbed in it from its previous fleeting contacts with the air, feeds the wine and causes it, in some mysterious way, to grow.

Its life-cycle is very like that of man. It develops until it reaches maturity. It stays at its peak for longer or less long; it declines and grows feeble; it finally dies. When it is dead it corrupts and grows rotten.

When a wine is bottled it has time to take, so to speak, a deep breath of oxygen from the air on its way from cask to bottle. Once in the bottle the air supply is short but it still, apparently, exists. Oxygen finds its way either through the cork or through the tiny space between cork and glass.

19

On the oxygen dissolved in it and what it can get through the cork the wine lives and grows in bottle, as it did in the cask only more slowly. But the difference in speed of development is vital. If it were left in cask its strength and nerves would be exhausted by the growing process and it would grow old before it even matured. Only in bottle can it reach maturity.

The cork   For this reason the invention of the cork is the most important event in the history of fine wine. Until the time of the cork the bottle was only a decanter. Wine was kept in barrels. When it was wanted it was poured into a bottle (which might have been made of leather, earthenware or glass) and brought to table. Some wine was shipped in bottles stoppered with twisted straw or even with a film of olive oil over the wine to protect it from the air. But no wine was stoppered up for the express purpose of improving it.

However well our ancestors may have been able to make their wine in those days, therefore, it could never have reached anything like the point of soft, sweet perfection which a claret or burgundy can, if it is given the chance, today. One vintage lasted until the next, and even by this time the wine in some of the barrels had started to turn into vinegar. Usually the safest, most stable wines were those with most sugar in them, which acted as a preservative. For this reason sweet sack, Malmsey and the muscat family of wines were the luxuries of the late Middle Ages and the Renaissance; they did not 'prick', as it was called, and need disguising with honey and herbs.

When, at the beginning of the eighteenth century, the cork arrived on the scene the perfect method of not-quite-airtight sealing was invented. From that day on, probably with port before table wine, the possibility of a wine reaching superlative maturity began to be realized. In the course of the eighteenth century the technique evolved; first with corks, then with corkscrews (without them the cork could not be rammed right home; it would never be got out again), then with the shape of the bottle changing from the old decanter shape, which could only stand up, to the modern cylindrical shape which is stored lying down.

The latter was a vital part of it. If a corked bottle is left standing up the cork eventually dries out and shrinks, air gets in and the wine turns to vinegar. The way to keep the cork from shrinking is to keep the wine touching it, and the way to do this is to keep the bottle on its side.

A few old wine 'bins' in country-houses bear the marks of an intermediate stage, when it was realized that the wine must touch the cork, but the bottle shape had not yet evolved. These bins are shelves with holes cut in them so that the necks of the bulbous bottles could go downwards.

By the middle of the eighteenth century the wine had begun to emerge which would benefit by this new kind of storage. A race of connoisseurs grew up to appreciate and discuss it. Then began the age of vintage wine which is still, after two hundred years, with us.

20

The vintage: a peasant family at Orvieto in Umbria

A good many wines are still made today in the way they were before bottle-ageing came on the scene. They are all light in colour, even when they are red. To this family belong the rosés and many white wines; those with not very much alcohol—refreshing, often slightly sharp, like ordinary Moselles, Muscadet, Portuguese *vinho verde*.

The fermentation of these wines is quick. There is not very much sugar to turn into alcohol, and not very much of the other substances which give wine flavour and body.

Pink wine is made like this on purpose, quickly, drawing only a thin veil of red from the skins in the fermenting vat. Of the red wines which are made this way the most famous is Beaujolais—at least in the form in which it is drunk in the restaurants of Lyons and Paris. It is fruity but ephemeral, purple but translucent, above all light enough to drink in full-throated swallows.

All these wines should bear as a vintage date, if they bear one at all, the latest one. In France they are called *vins de l'année*—the wine of the year. The lightest of all, which you see sometimes in cafés, is called *vin d'une nuit*—wine which only took one night to make.

By far the greater part of wine in any part of the world belongs to a middle category. It has nothing special—no lovely freshness—to lose by being kept. But it has nothing to gain either. It will be drunk, because it will be needed, within a year or two of being made. It could be stored longer, but it would get no better—so why tie up the capital in it?

But all the world's best wines, certainly all great wines, belong to the last class—those which are barely drinkable when they are new; which are drinkable but rather difficult, strong-tasting, harsh, when young; but which find balance, smoothness and the full flowering of their individual character only when they have been carefully and patiently stored.

It may take six years; it may take sixteen; it may take even twenty or forty. I have tasted a wonderful old South African wine, Constantia, which after a hundred and thirty years was still showing no sign of declining, but had been getting slowly better and better all that time.

That was a very sweet after-dinner wine. But I have had a claret of 1870, almost a hundred years old, which though it had no sugar to support it, nevertheless, light as a feather as it was, was lovely; complete, barely faded.

Most remarkable of all—indeed probably the only case of its kind there has ever been—was a bottle of Steinwein 1540 (everybody always thinks the second figure is a misprint), the wine of Wurzburg on the river Main in Germany, which Ehrmann's, the wine-merchants of Grafton Street in London, had salvaged from the cellar of King Ludwig of Bavaria. Nobody who was there when it was opened expected the contents to be wine at all. They should have been too old to drink when Shakespeare was born. Bottles of Johannisberger 1820 and Rudesheimer 1857 had been opened first, and had been far, far too old; not a trace of the taste of wine was left. But the Steinwein 1540 was still wine; Madeira-like, dark, feeble but quite definitely alive. There was a mouthful or two, still, somehow, with the smack of a German wine about it—before it turned to vinegar in the glass. The year 1540 was an utterly exceptional one. It is said that the Rhine dried up so that you could ride a horse across it. Water cost more than wine. There never were riper grapes or sweeter wine in Germany. A big tun, or cask, was built to hold the best of the vintage at Wurzburg, and there it stayed until bottles were invented to put it in two hundred years later.

If, in fact, it had been left so long it would all have evaporated—if it had not been drunk—which rather spoils the story. What really happened in all probability was that it was kept topped up with the best and sweetest of the wine from subsequent vintages. It may have been run off into smaller and smaller casks as time went on. Another German habit is to fill up the space in the cask as wine evaporates by dropping in pebbles through the bung-hole: as long as the cask is full to the top the danger of the wine going bad is minimized.

In any case the wine which was eventually bottled in the eighteenth century no doubt contained a proportion of that wonderful vintage, but rather in the way that a solera sherry is partly wine eighty or a hundred years old. Its character is handed down, as it were, to its successors in the same cask. What actual liquid is the original precious grape-juice of that far-off hot summer is anybody's guess.

What cannot be denied is that this wine, after a long time in cask, was still able to survive two hundred and more years in bottle. I doubt if it will ever have a challenger.

Red table wine

The wine which usually needs keeping most, and repays it best, is red table wine—and, of course, port. Vintage port is a subject in itself. No other wine demands laying down in such clear terms, being undrinkable until it is at least ten years old. The effects of time on port, and the comparatively tricky business of looking after it and decanting it are discussed in the After-Dinner Wines section (pp. 228–30).

Each red wine has its own optimum age for drinking. It varies from vintage to vintage of the same vineyard, and from vineyard to vineyard of the same vintage. In the vintage charts on the endpapers of this book there are comments on the age to drink each of the classes of wine from each district. The very lightest and weakest of clarets and red burgundies (the kind of wines which are made in rainy years) need eighteen months in cask before bottling; stronger wines with a longer future ahead of them will be in the wood for two and a half years or more.

This means that the newest claret you will ever find yourself drinking will be two years old, and that will be a wine with no pretensions to class. Better wines, which are made with a view to how good they can eventually become

22

rather than how quickly they can be ready to drink, are offered for sale two and a half to three years after the vintage, with the idea that people will buy them to keep until they are ready.

The system tends to break down nowadays. Everything has speeded up to such an extent; cars, jets and telephones have produced such a state of mind that it is difficult to believe it is really necessary to keep the bottle you buy for five, even ten, years before it is ready to drink. And since many of the people—and firms—who can now afford to buy the best and most expensive have no personal experience or tradition of great wines they do not know what they are missing when they drink fine clarets too young. The honest ones admit their disappointment at having to pay two or three pounds a bottle for something much less pleasant to drink than the Beaujolais of the same year that they can get for a fifth of the price. The snobs pretend they like it because the name Lafite or whatever it may be is known all over the world as a superlative wine. Certain unscrupulous firms in the wine-trade more or less encourage the drinking of wine too young because it means that their money turns round faster. I remember reading in 1964 the circular of a New York wine-merchant of high repute, which said that the finest of 1961 clarets could do with a few more years in bottle 'though they are excellent for drinking now'. The first part is a serious understatement; the first-growth 1961s will scarcely be ready for tasting at ten years old. They may not be at their best (if any of them still exist then) for twenty or thirty years. The second part is, to anyone with experience of drinking fine claret, a palpable lie. Only a snob could pretend that Lafite 1961 was, in 1964, as good a drink as an ordinary red Bordeaux which had come quickly to its prime. This matter of age is vital. There is no short cut. Great clarets are glorious only when they are mature, never before. To try to find out what Château Haut-Brion is like by drinking a bottle less than (at the very least) six years old is like trying to judge a painting by not even a photograph, but a sketch.

If this seems like flying in the face of the *status quo*, if restaurant wine-lists offer three- or four-year-old first-growth clarets for drinking now, there is only one thing to be said; it is a pity. They are throwing down the drain something excellent, of which there can never be more than a limited supply.

What, then, do you drink if there is no fine claret old enough to be mature on the list? The answer is that while you are restricted to that wine-merchant or that restaurant you drink cheap wine, which has no need to be old to be at its best. For your fine wine you go elsewhere, to a merchant who has a supply of the older vintages, for wine to drink presently. And you buy some young wine, with his good advice, to lay down and keep until it is ready to drink.

White wines There is no agreement about the maturing of white wines. Some like them all young. Some think nothing of them until they have begun to

23

deepen to gold. In general it is the French taste to drink them up without waiting, the English to give them three or four years in their bottles.

The effect of time on a white wine is not quite the same as it is on a red one. Red wines start with a great knot of flavour which slowly unravels itself, becoming smoother and more harmonious, lighter and easier to drink. White wines tend to intensify their flavours. While red wines slowly fade toward brown, white wines slowly darken in the same direction. It is sometimes difficult with a very old wine to tell whether it started red or white; it reaches the centre of the spectrum.

So a Château d'Yquem, the greatest of Sauternes, or a Montrachet, the best of white burgundies, is not exactly unready to drink at four or five years old, but it will go a long way before it starts to deteriorate at all, and many think it is getting better all the time. The same is true of champagne, and of the best wines of the Rhine and the Moselle. With age the richness and depth of flavour grows, freshness gives place to mellowness, the flavour of spring to the flavour of autumn.

Opportunities for discovering how fine old white wines can be come rarely. Personally I lay down white wine as well as red, in smaller quantities and for less long. But far more wine is drunk too soon than too late—white or red.

Vintages

NANCY MITFORD ONCE SAID 'There is even a public for yesterday's weather'. On the face of it whether or not it rained yesterday does seem the most barren of all topics. As far as most people are concerned once the clouds are gone they are gone. Only the wine-grower will have reason to reflect on it, to be glad or sad about it, two—or even ten—years later.

The weather in northern Europe is always uncertain. At any time of year it can have an effect for good or ill on the vine and its grapes. While the vine lies dormant in the winter there is the possibility of frosts, which can come, too, in the spring. If a frost comes after the vital budding time it can utterly destroy the crop before it ever even appears.

The hundred days   And in the hundred days that it takes a vine to bear ripe grapes from the time of flowering the weather is of the utmost importance. There must be sun, but not only sun. A little rain is needed—but at the right times. Some early morning mist is helpful—but not too much. Really heavy rain can be disastrous. Hail can destroy everything—even the vines themselves. There is nothing the grower can do about any of these things. He may see everything ripening to perfection with day after cloudless day of sunshine, and only rain on the days he has to stay indoors to do his accounts, or he may have to stand helpless, with tears in his eyes, as he sees hail tearing his

24

beloved vines apart. The wine-grower is a farmer, and a farmer learns patience by bitter experience. But one must not be too sorrowful. Can there be any more satisfying, natural way of life than tending vines and making wine?

The actual weather pattern of those hundred days between flowering and ripeness decides, if all has gone well up to that point, the nature and quality of the vintage. Not surprisingly, it is never the same two years running—or any two years. In Australia or California the weather follows a fairly predictable pattern. Vintages are all similar, if not identical, and the chief reason the drinker should want to know which vintage produced the wine is to tell its age. In France it is the character of the wine which changes completely from year to year. A knowledgeable wine-merchant cannot confuse 1952 and 1953, or 1957 and 1959, or 1961 and 1960 and 1962.

To anyone who is not very interested in wine it may seem just another nuisance that vintages matter. The fact is that they matter—where they matter at all—very much indeed. For example, practically all the claret of 1956 was hopeless. 1955 was a splendid year, but it was followed by a really wicked winter. So long and hard was the frost that vines whose natural resistance to cold is very high were frozen to death. Many had to be grubbed up. Not even the normal warmth of the summer of 1956 could bring the vines back to their right state of health. The wine was miserable, thin and hard. Some say that even the next year was affected; certainly the wines of 1957 that survive are only now beginning to get over a rather off-putting lack of warmth of flavour.

Exceptions And yet—to upset any calculations—there is always an exception. Someone, through some stroke of luck or genius, always manages to pull off a fine wine while everyone else is bemoaning a disaster. So it was in 1956. By some mysterious alchemy, M. Cazes, the Mayor of Pauillac and proprietor of the popular Château Lynch-Bages, made a fine, firm wine which was still good seven years later. And in Graves the Domaine de Chevalier, which, like Château Latour, seems to make a habit of being the best wine of its district in a bad year, repeated its trick. I have been told that the owner of the Domaine has large properties in the forests of the Landes to the south of Bordeaux. The theory is that he alone of the proprietors of Graves can conjure up a vintaging-party at the drop of a hat to pick all his grapes at the exact moment of ripeness, before another disaster overtakes them. Often it takes as long as three weeks to pick a large estate with the small work-force available. If a man has enough employees to get it all done in three days he obviously has a head-start, because he can leave the grapes on the vines that much longer to catch the last of the sun, or snatch them all out of the teeth of the coming bad weather. The whole Graves area, on the other hand, has the advantage of being on the very outskirts of Bordeaux, and thus having a greater labour-force available for fast picking than the more rural districts.

Such considerations as this are the life and soul of wine. They are the

25

source of its endless fascination and the reason why there are more exceptions than rules.

Micro-climates

If anyone asks whether vintage charts are helpful or a pitfall the answer lies here. Of course some years are better than others, and of course it is possible to generalize about what happened in any given district as a whole. But it can rain in Hampstead while Chelsea basks in the sun. There is a micro-climate for each locality, as well as the overall climate of the area. The tilt of a hill; the depth of the subsoil, affecting drainage; a stream, which makes morning mist, or a dip in the ground which catches frost, are all factors which can give one field the edge over its neighbour in one year, and do the reverse in another. Vintage charts, therefore, like all quick-reference works, need a pinch of salt. But this does not disqualify them completely.

On the endpapers of this book I have tried to characterize the recent vintages rather than classify them. The important thing is when the wine will be at its best. For poor years maturity comes quickly, for great years slowly. Similarly, for cheap wines age can do less than it can for good ones. Even such a chart as this is too broad a generalization to be defended in detail, but it may help.

Individuality of a vintage

Even given two vintages which everyone agrees in calling good, or even great, for a particular area, the wine, even from the same vineyard, will not be the same. The years 1949 and 1953 were great ones for Château Lafite, yet the characters of the two wines are different. Even discounting the difference in age, the fact remains that the 1949 was smooth and elegant, sleek and splendid, while the 1953 was more delicate and subtle, more feminine, more scented and possibly a shade less satisfying. Yet both were unmistakably Lafite.

National tastes

So there are not only good and not-so-good vintages (not to mention downright bad vintages), there are vintages which appeal to different tastes. The British, for example, found 1959 a superlative vintage for German wine; it was rich, strong and every wine's individuality was brought out almost to the point of caricature. It was a school for studying the districts of Germany and their distinctions in itself. The glory of hock (to the British) is the sort of clear and concentrated flavour it can only achieve in this sort of year. And yet to the Germans the 1959s were out of balance. They were alcoholically too strong. The German likes to drink his wine in draughts and refill his glass often; the 1959s were for respectful sipping. So to say that 1959 was a great vintage is only relatively true.

Personal tastes

Apart from national tastes you will find that personal tastes, even among acknowledged experts, differ on a vintage. One famous English merchant was almost alone in seeing a great future for the 1957 burgundies. Others, who were in the majority, happy with their stocks of 1952, 1953 and 1955, gave it a miss. They thought it unripe, awkward and harsh. As it happened, they were right in the short run and wrong in the long one: '57s were late in developing, but they finally found a finesse which is all too rare in

26

burgundy today. Those that still exist are superb, and will get even better.

Vintages, therefore, cannot usefully be discussed without very particular references. To prophesy about them as soon as the grapes are gathered is folly. It is good to be told of a plentiful vintage, because of the effect it may—or at any rate should—have of stabilizing prices. About the quality of the vintage you must make up your own mind when you come round to tasting it.

'Vintage'

A word must be said about champagne and port vintages. Here the word has a special meaning. In the normal way neither of these wines carries a vintage year, because the wine which is sold is a blend of those of many years, the whole being better than any of its parts. When an exceptional year comes along—which may happen perhaps three times in ten years— the shippers 'declare a vintage'. They announce that this wine is so good that there is no need to blend it; indeed that it would be a waste of its well-balanced natural character. Then you have a vintage port or champagne, which is always more expensive and usually better than the non-vintage wine of normal years.

Before we finish with vintages, it is worth mentioning the misunderstanding that has made the word come into use as a term of praise. To qualify port or champagne with the word vintage is reasonable; you are referring to the best, or one of the best. But all claret is 'vintage'. To say 'vintage claret', therefore, is not to add anything to just saying 'claret'.

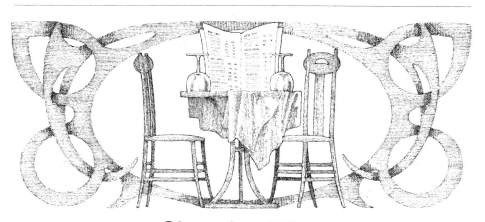

Choosing Wine

The price

THERE ARE VERY FEW PEOPLE whose choice of a wine is not guided, in the first instance, by the price. You know, when you look at a list, whether it is the bottom of the column, where the Great First-Growths grow, or the top, where the cheapest wines live, or somewhere in the middle reaches, which is your territory. I have been told time and again by restaurateurs and

27

wine-merchants that the strategic place to put a wine to sell it is number three on the list. The undecided are apparently all in agreement that number one looks downright mean, number two perhaps a bit stingy, but that number three is safe. If only they knew it, the cheapest wine was probably much better value and the third one down a drug in the market which the restaurant was trying to get rid of. But so, apparently, buyers are guided, and so, I fear, they are often disappointed.

Still, you know your price. The essential thing to do is to stick to it. If you are wondering what is the cheapest you can get a bottle of wine at all there is no sense in buying anything but the cheapest on the list. It is often very good. Restaurants usually find the carafe wine the wrong thing to save money on.

If, on the other hand, price is no object it is rash to head straight for the bottom and buy the most expensive. The most expensive white wine on many lists is the honey-sweet Château d'Yquem. It is glorious after dinner, and superb—occasionally—before. But the only-the-best-will-do technique has led people to drink it with steak, which is, to put it mildly, rather like having chocolate sauce on kippers.

There is, in short, an appropriate wine somewhere on the list for each dish, pocket and temperament. The business of finding it is very different in a wine-merchant's shop, where you have time and leisure to read and compare what he offers, and in a restaurant, where wine-waiters make some of their most (to them) satisfactory sales by using the feeling of pressure and hurry which is at their disposal. So different are the circumstances, in fact, that I will deal with them separately.

In a wine-shop   The best place to read a wine-list, to start with, is at home. Every wine-merchant has a list of what he offers, which he will willingly give to anyone who looks as though he might buy something. The first thing to do is to acquire one—or better, two or three from different merchants—and take it home. There, though you may not want a bottle at the moment at all, you can see what is available when the time comes, compare prices and values, and mark things to try for the future.

You can also look up in a reference book wines you are not sure about, so that you can approach the storeman with confidence the next day or whenever you are buying the wine. I put this plan forward humbly after having seen and felt the predicament of going into a shop whose range is unfamiliar and being quite overwhelmed by the choice. You are (I am, anyway) determined to come out with a bargain, something unspeakably delicious, and yet you do not know where to begin. Finally, the man behind the counter, who, as I suspect, knows next to nothing about what he is selling anyway, sells you the one thing he does know about, which is the wine with the biggest profit margin. All these difficulties are overcome if you ask for a list and take it home.

Are you choosing a wine to go with a particular dish or meal, or to be at

28

hand whatever dish comes along? Are you looking at the thing as an investment in future pleasure or with the immediate moment on your mind? Can you think in terms of buying a dozen bottles rather than one at a time? These are the things which will influence you. To take the last first, there is every possible reason why buying wine a little at a time, just when you want it, is a bad idea. First, you have the trouble of remembering to go and get it or order it every time. Second, you never have the right thing if someone turns up out of the blue and you cannot go shopping. Third, the wine is never at its best if you open it just after a quick flight from the corner shop, any more than any of the food which goes with it is ready without preparation (of the preparation, which is simple but nonetheless necessary, we will speak in a moment). Fourth, which is worth considering, orders of a dozen at a time are often blessed by a discount. Fifth, it is a good feeling to have a rack of assorted wine bottles in the house—but I have said enough. Avoid buying the odd bottle when you want it if you possibly can. Carrying this way of thinking a little further is starting what is so impressively called a cellar.

Really long-term buying, laying down young wines to go through their essential stages of development under your roof, is fascinating and even profitable. Wine always costs less, naturally enough, when it first comes on the market, too young to drink, than when it has been stored, paying rent and interest charges, for several years. Nowadays, I know, very few people do lay down wine in the old-fashioned way, but this does not weaken the arguments for it. The principal one against it, in most cases, is lack of space.

A cellar   Very few modern houses, even in France, are built with wine-cellars. The number of people who have the satisfaction of going down their short flight of stairs into their little vault of wine, therefore, must be declining all the time. Architects and builders who are so careful to provide utility-rooms for every other aspect of life might well consider changing this state of affairs, but I cannot see it happening. Most of us, then, must find a cellar-substitute. The cupboard under the stairs is often suggested. It is not ideal, because it is usually too small and stuffy, suffers the pounding of feet on the treads above it all day, and doubles as a broom-cupboard. But most houses and apartments have some accessible and otherwise wasted space. And cupboards can easily be fitted with racks for bottles. All that is asked of the wine-store, then, is that it never freezes, never boils, but stays at a comfortable temperature (even central-heating temperature will probably do little harm so long as it stays constant). Constancy is the most important thing. It is the reason why underground storage is traditional and best for wine. But the combination of central heating and air-conditioning in modern apartments has almost the same effect.

Light and vibration are the other things which could harm wine, but they are comparatively easy to avoid. Finally, wine must be kept lying down. All wine-bottles which are going to be kept for longer than a week or two should stay horizontal. If you put the label uppermost it helps you remember where the sediment, if any, will be in the bottle—lying along the side opposite the label. The reason for keeping bottles lying down is perfectly simple; it keeps the corks wet, which prevents them shrinking and letting the air in.

Laying down

There is more profit in laying down good red wines than any other kind. Vintage port, as we shall see in the chapter on port, demands it. It forms sediment in such a way that if it is not drunk where it has been resting, or at least decanted there, it will be stirred up and stay like mud for a long time. Almost all wines benefit by a little keeping. The improvement even in a bottle of the cheapest available red wine which I kept for a year was astonishing. Wine-merchants can save costs by bottling their cheap lines when they are called for, so that the wine you buy could have only a few days in bottle behind it. It is a well-known phenomenon that the transfer from barrel to bottle leaves wine in a shocked state for a while. It tastes as though there is something wrong with it for a month or so. The trade knows it as 'bottle sickness'. A great deal of wine is drunk in this state with no great satisfaction by people who expect it to be drinkable when it is sold. Good wine-merchants avoid it by ageing their wine before putting it on the market, but it still pays to buy and keep all your red wine for at least three months before drinking it. The one wine which I would except from this rule is new Beaujolais. It is best as young as you can get it.

I have discussed (in Wine and Time, p. 19) the laying down of fine wine to mature. Clarets are the wines which demand this treatment most. Burgundies also benefit enormously, more or less depending on the vintage. In talking about wines as they occur later in this book I have named a number which can be laid down with profit, particularly the wines of the Rhône valley, Portugal, Spain, California and Italy.

Wine for immediate drinking

The wine to choose for drinking straight away or in the near future is either wine which has, in effect, been laid down already because the merchant has had it for a long time, or wine which is better drunk quite young—or at least which would gain little with age. The second category are the cheaper wines—rosés, whites, light reds and brand-named products. Cheap, sweet white wines always come into this class because they have been treated in such a way that age can do nothing to improve them. So does any wine which has been pasteurized, but there is unfortunately no way of telling in most cases if it has or not. All too many have. Aperitif and after-dinner wines—sherry, and tawny and ruby ports, for example—are always sold ready to drink and change little, if at all, with keeping.

Wine-merchants used to be able to keep a stock of good table wines until they were really ready to drink, and list clarets at ten or fifteen years old as a matter of course. Now they feel less and less inclined to invest the money in them for so long. A quick turnover is their theme, and to this end they will assure the public that a wine is at its best long before it really is. Four-year-

30

old clarets are offered as ready for immediate drinking. They will do if there is no alternative, but it is worth finding a wine-merchant who can offer a choice of clarets at least seven or eight years old. With most other wines, in most stores, sad to say, there is rarely a choice of vintages at all: one German vintage comes on the market as the previous one is used up. To go to a specialist wine-merchant—or to buy the wines as they come on the market and keep them for yourself—is the only answer here.

The thing not to do at any price is to spend a lot of money on a bottle of a really fine wine which is not nearly old enough to drink—and drink it.

The food   The food you are going to be eating will be your main consideration when you come to choose the wine for a particular meal. I will discuss this in the chapter on Food and Wine (p. 37). But it is one of the charms of wine that there are other considerations as well.

Other considerations   Wine has a wonderfully personal and intimate character. A bottle of somebody's birth-year, or wedding-year, opened at a party specially for them is worth a tremendous amount of trouble. There is no more thoughtful way of reminding a friend of something pleasant in the past than by producing again the same wine as you drank then, or finding an association—the wine from a friend's favourite spot in Europe, for example. All these things take on a personal character and add to celebration in a way which may often be far beyond the wine's intrinsic merit. They are evidence of your foresight, thoughtfulness and imagination. Even just remembering somebody's particular favourite and making sure that you have a bottle of it when they come to see you is a compliment you can only pay with wine.

Two wines at a time   So is the very simple device (which far too many people think of as an affectation of advanced gastronomy) of serving two bottles of similar and comparable wines—or very dissimilar wines—at the same time, so that your guests can notice the difference and say which they prefer. You can serve two clarets of the same château, for example, and consecutive vintages, or different châteaux of the same vintage. Unless you occasionally do these things you may well say with some justice that all the fuss that is made about the differences between wines is unimportant, and that differences are so slight as not to be worth taking your time. As far as your memory of one wine compares with the taste of another, you may be right. But yet one can be the success you want, live up to your expectation, make the food taste delicious and make the meal: the other can be disappointing and add nothing to the evening. That is the difference between vintage and vintage which, tasting them at different times, you may not notice. But seeing them side by side it comes into focus. It becomes all the more interesting if you have friends there to help you to decide.

In a restaurant   Much as I love restaurants and the exotic experiences they offer without any effort on my part, I am uneasy about the choosing business. It is a two-edged weapon. It is fine in places you know well, or places which offer

31

well-defined and obvious specialities—in Provence, for example, what would you order but the wine of the house?—but in the commoner kind of restaurant or hotel, which offers a long list of what looks, to the optimist, like every delight of Eden, there are snags. I know what *coq au vin* should be, you say to yourself, but what will it be like here? Or, back on the wine-list, I know what Beaune should be, but where do they get theirs?

The choosing of wine is usually also complicated by the different tastes of the party. There is that tiresome old J.B., to quote one of the advertisements, with his *tournedos,* and Roscoe with his Dover sole. At home, of course, the worst that happens is that the vegetarian of the party is eating his nut cutlet; the rest are unanimously eating whatever is on offer. You choose the wine which seems a good idea with the one dish (which, for that matter, you know about beforehand). But in a restaurant you are choosing a wine to go with a gastronomic Tower of Babel. Lobster on the one hand, chicken pancake on the other, and on the third *Boeuf Strogonoff.* It is too much to ask of any wine that it should be the perfect accompaniment to all these things. If there cannot be unanimity about the food there cannot be any about the wine. Even pink wine is a poor compromise: although it is rarely nasty (if you like it) with any food, it is even more rarely an aesthetic revelation. And champagne, which some people fall back on, has the same fault. The answer—I see no other—is to order two kinds of wine. If it is a party of two, have two half-bottles. If there are three or more, order two whole bottles, or even two carafes—one of red and one of white.

I confess I even do this at home sometimes. With all kinds of informal meals there can be a division of opinion about which wine is ideal, so why not have a choice? A carafe of white wine and a carafe of red can go round together. People can have one or the other or both if they want. If there are enough people to drink it, there might be a bottle of pink as well.

Ordering in advance

The ideal host in a restaurant would go round there on the morning of the day and choose a dinner which would suit everybody, and the wine to go with it. There would be no fluttering over the menus when the party arrived. The chef would have a chance to get everything ready at the right moment. The performance would go off like clockwork. But that is a counsel of perfection, and hardly anyone ever does it. And it is true that some people feel cheated if they cannot see the menu for themselves. They feel that they are missing something, if it is only the prices.

But, as far as the wine is concerned, if the host has not done this he is foolish to order a really fine one. The conditions of keeping wine in restaurants, with very few exceptions, are anything but ideal, and the handling of wine is worse. Whether you like it or not, the best wine, the kind that any restaurant prides itself on having in its cellar, takes a little time and care to be got ready for drinking. It cannot be at its best if it is just brought up from the cellar the moment you ordered it; nor, for that matter, if the alternative has happened and they have been keeping it in readiness over the last few months in the hot dining-room.

Compromise [margin note aligned with paragraph above]

32

It is not elaborate precautions that are needed to see that a wine is at its best when you drink it (and is it not wasted if it is not at its best?) but a little gentleness and a little patience. If you realize that the wine has been cooped up in its bottle for five or perhaps ten years when suddenly, at the drop of a hat, you ask it to put on its best performance without warning, you can see that it may easily be a bit shy. And shy, despite the mockery that usually follows the use of words like this about wine, is just what it very often is. You open it, you drink it, and just as you are swallowing the last drop of what has been (at the price) a frankly disappointing bottle you suddenly get a whiff of magic: the scent has begun to come out, the wine has begun to expand and show itself, like a peacock spreading its tail. But it is too late. You have finished the bottle.

The sommelier routine

What actually happens when you order wine in the majority of restaurants makes this only too likely. The *sommelier* (the wine-waiter, in the United States as often as not in an apron, hung about with bunches of keys and a silver tasting-cup) loses all his dignity as he moves through the service door. He rushes to the wine-bin, grabs the bottle (or gets a boy to go and grab it for him), waves it around as he weaves back through the milling *commis* waiters, slams it down in a basket, recomposes himself and arrives at your table triumphant, sedate, as slow and stony as the best of butlers. With infinite gravity he condescends to let you glimpse the still palpitating bottle before going into his routine with his corkscrew.

With ordinary, carafe-type wine it obviously does not matter how much he waves it around. His worst offence is pretentiousness in serving it in a cradle as though it were liquid gold. But with the sort of wine you sometimes go to restaurants specially for, because nobody else has such old vintages or such noble growths, it is a pitiful waste.

This pantomime and its sad consequences can be avoided to some extent by asking the restaurateur beforehand to decant the wine. But this means choosing it in advance, too. In short, as a general rule, it is wiser to keep to the kind of wine which cannot suffer much harm and needs no time to take the air before it reaches its best; not to buy the best unless you know all about the restaurant.

White wine is normally an easier case than red. All it needs is long enough in an ice-bucket to be well chilled, or if it has been kept in a refrigerator, long enough to warm up to a pleasant coolness. It is worth noting, though, that the ice-bucket should be full of water with ice in it, not just ice; it is far more quickly and evenly effective. The bottle will probably need five minutes' standing on its head in the ice, for few ice-buckets are deep enough for the water to reach the wine in the neck.

Sending wine back

The wine-waiter pours half an inch of wine into your glass before he sets off round the table with the bottle. The idea is both to see if there is anything wrong with this particular bottle and also to see if you like the wine in a general way. As to the first, the chances of a bottle being corky, which

33

means smelling musty from having had a dud cork, are very slim. The corky smell is immediately obvious and very unpleasant. Any restaurant will take back a bottle afflicted with it. Occasionally, though, perfectly good bottles have an odd smell in the first minute after opening—with white wine there is often a smell of sulphur, with red sometimes a dank smell. This will go away almost at once. The trick, in fact, if you are not sure about the smell of the sample you have been given, is to swirl it round your glass for a minute and sniff it again. If it is as bad as ever you have a bad bottle; if it has gone you will not have risked a clash of opinions with the management.

Whether or not you can return a bottle which has no intrinsic faults depends, I suppose, on how certain you are that it is not what it claims to be, and also how wide of the mark it is. Some can do it with panache; others turn pale at the thought. It is, in fact, a matter of personality, which does not call for discussion here.

Serving Wine

YOU CAN PLAY stereophonic records on an ordinary record-player. Similarly with wine you can just pull the cork, pour it out and knock it back. But either is a waste of the potential you have paid for. It is worth taking the little extra trouble to see that all its qualities (neither ordinary records nor wine can be made wonderful by wonderful equipment) can be appreciated.

Wine does not even need any special equipment. You have glasses. You have a corkscrew. That's it. The refrigerator will come in useful, and the next thing you will want will be a decanter or carafe—one of the most useful and decorative pieces of glassware anyway, whether you use it for wine or not.

Wine-glasses   Your glasses must be two things—large and clear. Small glasses not only look mean, they have to be filled to the top. There is no possibility of the wine's scent collecting in the top of the glass so that when you drink it comes to you all at once, scent and flavour. A wine-glass should never be more than half full. For half a glass to be a reasonable measure the glass has to be big.

As for clarity, one of the joys of wine—a minor one, but still a joy—is its colour. There are infinite variations between petal-white and gold, and between purple and tawny. Coloured, or even slightly shaded, glass ruins the colour of the wine.

A good wine-glass, in short, is a big one, clear and uncoloured, preferably with a stem and a round or roundish bowl, cupping in towards the top to embrace the wine's bouquet. A glass like this is perfect for any wine, French or German, Californian or Chilean, red or white, still or sparkling. Different wine-glasses for different wines can be a pretty sight, but as far as the wine is concerned there is no need for them. A glass which is good for one wine is good for all wines.

Corkscrews

There are better and less good corkscrews. The best kind, without question, is the one made of boxwood with two threads which turn in opposite directions. With the top handle you drive the screw into the cork in the usual way. When it is in and the wooden body of the corkscrew is resting against the rim of the bottle you turn the other handle. The cork is drawn steadily and easily into the body of the device. I have never known a cork, however tough, to resist it. Simple corkscrews can be helpless against a really solid cork. The kind which inject air are terrifying if the cork does not come out straight away. You feel as if you are holding a bomb.

Preparing wine

The objects of preparing the wine beforehand, rather than just opening it and drinking it straight away, are three. It may have sediment; you must get this to the bottom of the bottle so that it does not get into the glasses. Its temperature probably needs adjusting. It will almost certainly be improved by contact with the air.

Sediment

It is remarkably hard to convince people, especially in the United States, that sediment in wine is harmless and natural. More than that, it is a good sign. It means that the wine is natural and untampered-with. But there is a fetish about a speck of deposit, or a single crystal appearing in a bottle. It is sometimes carried to well-meaning but absurd lengths. One of the best-known shippers of German wine to Britain and the United States told me how he once had a thousand cases of wine held up in Chicago because there was said to be broken glass in the bottles. In fact there were crystals of tartaric acid, which often form in white wine in cold weather. It was harmless, natural—indeed expected—but it caused a tremendous crisis.

If wine has been pasteurized, put through very fine filters or otherwise denatured it is possible to avoid sediment, either in the short run or the long. But it is no longer natural wine; it will no longer age properly and develop its potential. It seems too high a price to pay to avoid the chance of a speck in the bottom of the bottle.

Red wine

Red wine, especially, of any age should have a few black dregs in it. While it is lying in its rack they will lie along the bottom side of the bottle. The object of the cradle which restaurants use for serving wine which has been taken straight out of its rack is to keep them there. Once a bottle has been stood up and the sediment moved from the side there is no point in laying it down again in a cradle. I have often seen wine-waiters take bottles out of their cradles to pull the cork and then put them back on their sides again. The customer may be sure of a muddy glass of wine.

Decanting

The decanter or carafe is the answer (oddly enough, the French have no word for decanter; *carafe* is equally a water- and a wine-container). The ideal arrangement is to plan twenty-four, twelve or even six hours ahead which bottle you are going to open, and stand it up in the dining-room or the kitchen, wherever it is warm. The sediment will settle at the bottom. An hour before you are going to drink the wine you pull the cork and pour it gently and steadily into the decanter. As you reach the bottom of the bottle, hold it against a light or a white surface. You will see the first of the dregs move in arrowhead formation towards the decanter. When they reach the neck of the bottle stop pouring. The wine is as clean as a whistle.

If you now leave it for the hour before dinner in the kitchen where it is warm—not near the fire, where it is hot—it will be in perfect condition at the right time. It will be clear, at room temperature, and in the full flow of its perfume. Its contact with the air will have livened it up and given it much more vigour than it had at the moment the bottle was opened. You will, in other words, be getting your money's worth. The younger a wine is, the more it stands to gain by contact with the air. Three or four hours is even better for strong young red wines. On the other hand, very old wines can fade away altogether unless they are drunk soon after the cork is pulled. But it takes thirty or forty years for them to reach that condition.

Using a cradle   If foresight has failed, and you must open the wine the moment you take it from the rack where it has been lying, a cradle or basket is useful. It keeps the wine in the nearest position to the horizontal which allows the cork to be taken out without the wine spilling. Bring the cradle to the rack and put the bottle straight in it without moving it more than you can help. Pull the cork as it lies in the cradle. A double-action corkscrew is essential for this; you cannot hold the cradle and tug at the end of it at the same time.

Decant the wine (this is what restaurants so rarely do) from the cradle. The cradle is not a substitute for a decanter. If you pour intermittently from a bottle at all, as you must if you are filling several glasses, the wine washes back on to its dregs each time you stop pouring. There is no way of preventing it getting mixed with them. Only by pouring in one continuous movement can this be avoided. So unless you are dining alone and filling one enormous glass the decanter is the only answer.

I hasten to say that all this business takes far less effort and time to do than it does to read—let alone write.

White wines   There is no reason why white wines should not be decanted, but less reason why they should. Very old ones have a deposit, but the great majority of bottles of white wine are clear to the last drop. With white wines the only problem is the temperature—and letting them have a little air. Open all wines, red or white, beforehand if possible to let them breathe.

Temperature   I do not think that there is a right temperature for white wines. It is certain that they are better cool, but some people like them icy, some just chilled. I think they are usually served much too cold in the United States, but then so is the water, the beer and even the salad. But at least I can wait until my glass warms up a bit, whereas no amount of waiting will cool down a glass served too warm. My favourite image to give the right idea for white wine is that of well-water. Freshness is the thing, not frostiness.

36

Food and Wine

IN GENERAL IT IS TRUE that table wines are never better than when they are served with some suitable food. This much is almost a truism. But from here the schools of thought divide. One would have it that any wine goes with any food, the other that there is for each wine a dish pre-ordained by divine decree: that, for example, a Volnay Caillerets should be drunk with well-done lamb, and Volnay Clos des Chênes should be drunk with under-done lamb; that a little parsley with the potatoes brings out the individuality of the Caillerets, particularly the 1957, to perfection; that the 1959 should never be served with green peas, and so on.

There is a good deal of private amusement to be had from this sort of talk, though it is double-Dutch to most people, just as discussion of British Honduras penny reds or uncancelled triangular blue twopennies has meaning, and brings pleasure, to the initiated.

The difference with wine is that everybody thinks he ought to be one of the initiated. As somebody has said, wine is like sex; nobody will admit to not knowing all about it.

There are dinners where the whole gamut of wines is gone through. They start, as it were, at the beginning of this book and go on until they reach the end, picking and choosing, but visiting each section, and dwelling in some for more than one wine.

Formal dinners   There are dinners that begin with an aperitif glass of champagne; that have a glass of sherry with the soup; a glass of Rhine wine with the fish; a claret with the entrée. With a roast pheasant there is a glass of burgundy, and maybe another, a different one, with some cheese after it. Then there is a glass of Sauternes and a great gorgeous *bombe* of some kind or other; then port; then brandy. This is at least a dinner which I could eat, if I had room. But look at the following. This is a dinner that was really given, and by George Saintsbury, the man who was considered to be one of the

37

greatest English connoisseurs of his day, at about the turn of the century:

The wines	The food
Montilla	Consommé aux pointes d'asperges
Johannisberg Klaus Auslese 1874	John Dory, Sauce livournaise
Château Grillet 1865	Filets de saumon à la gelée
	Cotelettes à la Joncourt
Champagne, Dragonet 1874	Plovers' eggs
(a Jereboam)	
	Aspic de volaille à la reine
Romanée-Conti 1858	Haunch of mutton
Château Margaux 1868	Mayonnaise de homard
Port, 1853	Soufflé glâcé au marasquin
Pedro Ximenes	Canapés de crevettes

Tastes change. If this was the fashion in eating and drinking within the last seventy years, I have great doubts if there is anything so profound or unchanging about what we call the art of the table. If you produced a lobster mayonnaise today after a haunch of mutton and an aspic of chicken, not to mention soup, two kinds of fish, cutlets and plovers' eggs, everybody would think you were mad. At that moment the wines on the table were presumably burgundy (Romanée-Conti) and claret. The port appears to have been served with a maraschino soufflé and followed by a very sweet sherry with shrimp canapés (the fourth fishy manifestation of the meal).

We could, presumably, turn our meals inside out and very quickly believe that it was unnatural to start dinner with anything but roast meat, or end with anything but soup. We are, after all, only subject to the three-course habit because that is the way hoteliers set things up at the beginning of this century. What it boils down to is that far too much is written and said about what goes with what, what goes before or after what, or what to do and what to avoid.

The enemies of wine   Wine has certain basic enemies, at table as in barrel or bottle. Its first enemy is vinegar. A vinegary salad will turn the wine to vinegar; this is a matter of science, not taste.

Its second enemy is acid—the acid of grapefruit, orange or lemon. You cannot taste a wine with any of these fruits. There is a third enemy, but I am not sure what it is. It is something which occurs in some oily kinds of fish. It makes wine, particularly red wine, taste steely—something like the taste of tin cans.

All these things positively spoil wine, so it is a waste to serve it with them. Beyond this, though, taste is an anarchy; all anyone can hope to do is suggest combinations which have appealed to him. This is the object of the following pages.

HORS D'OEUVRE	The typical mixed hors d'oeuvre leans heavily on vinegar for its savour, and thus becomes the enemy of wine. Most of the courses we start meals with—artichokes, avocadoes, tomato salad, radishes, little dishes of carrots and cucumbers, smoked fish or sausages, eggs, pâtés, melon—are happy with the remains of the glass of sherry which was an aperitif, or another glass of the same thing. Alternatively, a first glass of whatever is to be the main wine of the meal goes well with the hors d'oeuvre. The principal exceptions to this simple arrangement are shellfish, which are always best
Oysters	with a very dry white wine. The association of oysters and Chablis is no accident; the sharpness of the wine does something essential to an oyster. It has the effect of a squeeze of lemon. Champagne is equally effective, and so—much less expensive, too—is Muscadet. Some people find that the rich
Smoked salmon	oiliness of smoked salmon or eel is too much for a light white wine. Dry sherry in this case is ideal. All meaty and savoury hors d'oeuvre are fine with an ordinary red wine or rosé. If there are enough people to drink more than one bottle with the meal it makes things more interesting to have different wines with the hors d'oeuvre and the main course.
SOUP	There is no need for a special wine to go with the soup at an ordinary meal. Wine goes *in* a number of soups—particularly Madeira, Marsala or sherry in clear soup—to great effect. The same wines are good sipped with most soups. I would never choose a wine to go specifically with a soup, however, unless the soup were the main part of the meal—as, for example, in a snack lunch of soup, bread and cheese. Then it would be a cheap, light, red wine.
PASTA, PIZZA, PAELLA, etc.	The obvious thing is to drink Italian wine with pasta, although some Italians drink water with it. It makes a difference whether pasta is the whole meal, or, as in Italy, merely the opening salvo. In any case, and whatever the sauce, I find red wine is usually best with pasta and related dishes—all those in which cereals of some kind play an important part, whether it be rice, pastry, bread-dough or noodle. There is a way out for a risotto made with prawns, of course—Soave is perfect for this—although it is worth noting that the Spanish usually drink red wine with paella, which should contain plenty of seafood. Pizza and Chianti are inseparable. *Quiche Lorraine,* on the other hand, is usually eaten with a white Alsace wine, if only for geographical reasons.
EGGS	Egg dishes are very comforting and satisfying, but they are not a good background, or foreground, for fine wines. A little egg dish at the beginning of a meal (baked egg, scrambled egg or egg in aspic) would make no difference to the wine which followed it. Allow the choice of wine, in fact, to be influenced by the other elements in the meal and treat the egg as neutral. For a simple omelette and salad a cheap red wine is perfect; say, a Côtes-du-Rhône.

39

The pleasure of a picnic is the simple joy of refreshment in the open air. It is not the time for assertive or expensive wine, but for something thirst-quenching. If there is some way of making it cold (a stream will do very well) a white Loire wine, a cheap Moselle, an Alsace wine, or virtually any rosé is ideal. If conditions hardly allow this kind of refinement, drink plain good red Bordeaux, not old enough for any sediment to have formed to cloud it when it is shaken about en route. If you are in wine-country, of course, there is no hesitation—drink the *vin du pays*.

FISH

White wine tastes better than red with most fish because its acidity helps to cut out the fishy taste which red wine somehow emphasizes. There is a peculiar metallic quality about a fish eaten with red wine which spoils every other sensation. Fish with considerable flavour, either in their flesh or in their sauce, are best matched by fairly rich-flavoured wines: the more expensive white burgundies, Rhine wines (though really good ones are wasted on fish) or any of the white wines of farther south. Very white and light-flavoured fish, unsauced, can easily be, as it were, over-wined. A young Moselle or a Loire wine is best for the delicate flaky river-fish and the subtler creatures of the sea.

More depends, usually, on the way of cooking than the fish itself. A plain grilled sole, for example, is a much more subtle-flavoured dish than a *sole Deauvillaise*, which is smothered in onions and cream. A trout *au bleu* is a more delicate one than a trout from a hot buttery pan with brown butter poured over it. Along these lines, then, you would choose a younger, fresher, more northern wine for the grilled sole or the trout *au bleu*; a warmer-flavoured, more assertive wine with the fish *Deauvillaise* or *meunière*. The fish of the Mediterranean cooked with garlic are another matter again; they are better with the rather hard-tasting, strong and mellow wines of their own countries.

Salmon

Salmon needs a word of its own. Some like claret with it when it is served hot. I always like it best with as good a white burgundy as I can afford. The earlier in the season, the better the fish, so the better the wine.

If the fish comes before a meat course, one, or at the most two, glasses of white wine is usually enough with it. A half-bottle for two people, therefore, or a whole bottle for three or four is plenty, if you are going to have a red wine afterwards.

MEAT

Pork
Veal

There is good sense in the old rune about white wine with white meat, red wine with red. Pork, veal and chicken are the principal white meats. Chicken we will come to in a minute, but both pork and veal are usually, depending on the sauce, excellent with a not-too-dry white wine. They will make a young Moselle, a Muscadet or cheap Chablis taste a bit thin, but a wine of any power or warmth of flavour—an Alsace wine, a hock, a good white burgundy, a Graves or a Hungarian wine, or virtually any white wine from southern Europe—will go well with them. Light red or rosé will

The grapes for sherry. They are cut from the vines with a short, curved knife, and carried in baskets to be pressed. *(Photo: Judy Johnson)*

go equally well, but strong red wines of real character—all the best wines of France, for example—are better matched with beef or lamb.

Beef
Lamb

With beef and lamb I personally much prefer red wine to white. Tender, expensive cuts of these meats are an ideal accompaniment to the world's best red wines—Bordeaux and burgundy. The cheaper cuts which take more cooking are best with their opposite numbers, as it were, among the wines of the same districts. If there is ever a question of opening a very fine bottle of wine it is as well to avoid any of the really pungent seasonings of meat—whether they be garlic, mint sauce or anything flavoured with herbs or onions. If the wine's flavour is overwhelmed there is little point in spending more money on specially good wine.

Ham

I would not have the very best wine with ham, either—much to my regret, as it is one of my favourite kinds of meat. But halfway between ordinary and great there are any number of good clarets and burgundies which would do a ham every kind of pleasure.

Venison

Really gamey meat, oddly enough, although the darkest of all in colour, can be as good with a rather sweet white wine as with a dark, strong red. I am thinking particularly of the venison and wild boar which is the best meat of all in Germany. The luxuriously full-flavoured white wine of the Rhineland Palatinate is perfect with it.

In meat's hinterland, as it were, the world of kidneys and sweetbreads and liver, tripe and brains, tongue and the more visceral kind of sausages, what are known as sound red wines, not fine ones, are called for. This, to me, means experimenting among the best of Italian, Spanish, Portuguese, Australian, Macedonian and Californian wines.

BIRDS

Chicken

The chicken is the most versatile of all dishes. It is a wonder to me how it has changed from being a luxury to being the cheapest of all forms of meat, and yet remained a luxury. Even roadside fried chicken has failed to give it a bad name. It remains the chef's favourite canvas for his more elegant flourishes. As far as wine is concerned everything depends, of course, on the way it is cooked. A *coq au vin* where the *vin* is Chambertin clearly calls for Chambertin in the glass beside it. A *coq au vin jaune* in the Jura, where it is cooked in the strange mellow white wine of the country, also dictates its own accompaniment. But you can cook chicken in a way to go perfectly with almost any wine under the sun. For a really good wine nothing is as good as a young bird plain roasted in butter. Whether the wine was claret or white burgundy would be a matter of whim.

Game

The guinea-fowl, the turkey and the capon are as adaptable as the chicken and are usually even better to eat. Game birds, on the other hand, even those which are eaten unhung—the partridge, the young grouse, the snipe and the quail—are all committed red-wine dishes. A simple rule is to drink (very) good red Bordeaux with unhung game, (very) good red burgundy with any game which has been hung, burgundy with game pie, and either Châteauneuf-du-Pape, strong and soft-flavoured, or rather sweet

Rhine wine with duck or goose—birds which need their fat counterbalanced.

CHEESE It is a matter of faith among wine-lovers that cheese is the perfect accompaniment to any wine. I am a dissenter from this view, but I must record it. Cheese is always served after the meat in France to give you an opportunity of finishing your red wine with it, and to tempt you to open another bottle.

All except the milder cheeses, I find, have too strong a flavour for any except the strongest-tasting red wines. Roquefort, for example, is as pungent and salty a morsel as civilized man ever put in his mouth. Many of the soft French cheeses have either a goaty or an ammoniac reek. English cheese is frequently harsh. Italian cheese, curiously enough, is milder and goes very well with Italian wine; but for Stilton and most of the other cheeses which are offered in Britain I find the best wine is port, which is sweet enough to take care of itself.

SWEET DISHES AND DESSERT You rarely find among sweet wines and sweet food the same kind of perfect match as you do among savoury things. Two different sweet tastes in the mouth at once seem to be too much of a good thing. It is hard to taste a Sauternes, for example, at all if you drink it with ice-cream or fruit salad. The more cake-like kind of sweet dishes, on the other hand, and the lovely diversions which good cooks make with strawberries or raspberries, peaches or apricots, and pastry and cream, are delicious with the heavier kind of sweet wine—Madeira, tawny port, the muscatels, Tokay.

Peaches and grapes, pears and apples do not call for any special wine, but it is worth remembering that any wine you do serve with them must be good; they show up the faults of a thin or phoney wine more than anything else.

Aperitifs

Origins

ANYTHING YOU DRINK before a meal, with the idea of getting into the right frame of mind for eating, is an aperitif. Aperitifs are a modern idea. By a significant coincidence, the word entered our language in the same year as the word motor-car. A hundred years ago it was not the custom to drink anything before sitting down at table. Our ancestors found no difficulty in setting about their food as single-mindedly as cats about milk. True, the awkward moments of meeting in the drawing-room before dinner were known as the Black Half Hour. But no-one thought of having a drink to break the ice.

Social drinking used to take place at the end of dinner. It was then that the champagne, if any, was drunk, and, of course, after dinner that the port went round. But the first glass of the evening was the Madeira with the soup. The unwinder before dinner was unknown.

In this century things have gone too far the other way. In the United States, especially, the habit is to spend an hour drinking cold hard liquor on an empty stomach, and then to go into dinner and drink nothing but water. The stomach has been primed all right—but too far. It has gone past the point of sharpened receptivity; it is numbed into insensibility. All food tastes alike. Wine is pointless because it cannot be tasted.

The word aperitif, after all, means appetizer. A small amount of the right kind of wine—sherry, any dry white wine, vermouth or champagne—can

43

put you in the right state of mind to enjoy the food, the company and the whole occasion.

Spirits

I have a bias towards wine, rather than spirits, for drinking before meals, principally, I think, because I normally drink wine with the meal itself. Wine goes well after wine, after gin or whisky not so well. This is my experience, and everyone has his own. If I were asked to explain it I should say that spirits have a way of drying up your mouth which is the opposite of appetizing. The great sign of appetite is plenty of saliva. Spirits remove it. Worse, perhaps, they leave behind a flavour which interferes with the taste of the next thing that comes along. It is what we mean when we say that things go, or do not go, together. To me, spirits do not go with wine, so I go without spirits.

The aperitif qualities

The qualities which make a wine really appetizing, and hence good to drink before a meal, are cleanness of taste, coldness, strength, dryness, tartness or bitterness.

A sweet drink taken before lunch or dinner does the opposite of stimulating the appetite. It depresses it. Sugar produces a feeling of satisfaction, which is the last thing an aperitif should do. Sweetness cloys the appetite, which needs to be pointed up, balanced, set off with a tang and a hint of a shudder.

The same is true of a warm drink: ice brings it to life. It is also true of a long drink—say, a pint of beer. It fills you up—so it cannot be appetizing. For this reason an aperitif should be reasonably strong.

Table wine as aperitif

Very often a glass of the wine you are going to drink with the meal—white wine especially—is as good an aperitif as anything. Vermouths are stronger, champagne more stimulating, sherry more soothing, but the appetite-making qualities you want are all present in a glass of dry white wine. On a hot summer day, for that matter, a bottle does not go all that far.

A Moselle, an Alsace or Loire wine, a Graves or a Yugoslav or Hungarian Riesling makes an excellent aperitif. In Portugal the white *vinho verde*, slightly sparkling and almost cidery, is the natural choice. In any wine-growing district, in fact, the ordinary café white wine, brought to table in a jug or carafe from a barrel, is the one to have before eating.

If you prefer red, or only intend to open a red wine for the meal, a glass of this can be almost as good. It should be a light one, preferably—a Beaujolais rather than a burgundy. Claret, though, seems too austerely dry without food.

Of the wines which exist simply for the pleasure of a glass before eating, sherry is the universal champion.

44

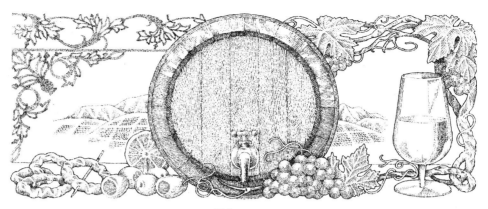

Sherry

SHERRY CAN BE as dry as a lemon or as sweet as a date. It can be almost white or almost black. It is the most appetizing wine under the sun. Sherry's place is before a meal: its strength is too high, its flavour too forceful for a table wine. It is the wine to drink with the perfume from under the kitchen door.

The name sherry

Sherry is the English name for a town in Spain. Its original Moorish name was Scheris. Its modern name is Jerez de la Frontera. The wine of Jerez belongs to a class that used to be known as sack, which was strong and sweet—a great luxury in the cold, sugarless days of the sixteenth century, when it first reached England. Falstaff drank 'an intolerable deal' of it, and composed a superb canticle in its praise.

Sack came from all over the Mediterranean. Malmsey wine from Cyprus and Greece was sack. There was sack from Sicily and Canary sack from the Canary Islands. The sack from Jerez, though, soon came to be established as the best, partly as the result of the plundering of Cadiz, when Sir Francis Drake carried off shiploads of it from the burning town.

For a while the wine was known as sherris-sack. Then the word sack was dropped, and by the early seventeenth century the drink was sherry.

Sherry clearly means the wine of Jerez. As everyone knows, it has now been borrowed to such an extent by South Africa, Australia, California, Cyprus and even Surrey, where 'British sherry' is made, that it seems unlikely that the Spanish will ever get it back. Some of these places make wine which is intended to be as near as they can get to the Spanish original, and is often very good. Others simply trade on the established name because it is less trouble than launching a new one.

Jerez de la Frontera

Jerez is the biggest of the three towns which produce sherry, and the capital of the industry. It is prosperous enough to be much less squalid than

45

the majority of Spanish towns—though it has its share of mud streets and hovels. The other two sherry towns, Sanlucar de Barrameda and Puerto de Santa Maria (Port St Mary's to the British wine-trade), remain in unrelieved medieval squalor. The three lie in a triangle twenty miles north of Cadiz and eighty south of Seville, a hundred and twenty miles from Gibraltar. Sanlucar and Puerto are on the sea, Jerez fifteen miles inland.

It was here that the Moors conquered Spain. The site of the battle, which is said to have raged for four days, on the Guadalete river, is just outside Jerez. Though it was not in this part of Spain that they held out longest against the reconquest, the Moorish influence is still strongly felt. Andalusia is the luxurious part of Spain, where every door offers a glimpse of a cool patio, green leaves and blue tiles. It is the country of flamenco dancing.

The Feria   Jerez should be seen at the time of its *Feria,* which starts each year on 8 September. It is the most spectacular, romantic and beautiful form of celebration imaginable.

The Feria begins with a ceremony for the blessing of the vintage. On the steps outside one of the great Baroque churches of the town a *lagar*—a treading press—is set up. The prettiest girls of Jerez, dressed in their Andalusian costumes, bring baskets of grapes to the press and, as the men begin to tread and the grape-juice begins to flow, a cloud of white doves is released, to rise above the belfry, wheel and soar into the dazzling sky, taking the good news of the new vintage to the neighbouring districts.

The afternoons are spent in bullfights—for the Feria goes on for four or five days—and the evenings in balls and parties. As night falls the whole town goes to the public gardens, which are closed to all traffic except horses and carriages. Flowing dresses and mantillas are everywhere, and the air is full of the music of guitars. Here and there in the crowd a girl breaks into a dance.

At intervals among the trees and side-shows in the park there are pavilions of wrought iron and soaring glass. Here the great families entertain, have supper, dance and pass the sultry evening. Many of them are sherry families, as proud of their olorosos and amontillados as they are of their horses and fighting bulls.

The vineyards The grapes of sherry, all white, are grown within the small area bordered by the three sherry towns. The land rises and falls in low hills of startlingly white earth. Under the tremendous southern sun they are quite dazzling. It is chalk, the best soil for clean-tasting white wines.

It is all the more surprising, in this heat, that the vines covering the hills are so green. Even at vintage time, when in the vineyards much farther north the leaves are beginning to turn, they are as fresh-looking as in the spring. The secret of this is the first of the secrets of making good sherry—the deep and constant cultivation of the soil.

Before ever a sherry vineyard can be planted it has to be ploughed to a depth of three feet, in virgin, hard-baked earth. This used to be done by a team of twelve mules, using a winch. Now an eighty-five horse-power tractor can do it, at crawling pace. All the moisture the vines can get in the summer, while they are fattening huge bunches of juicy grapes, is obtained from the sub-soil. There is no rain. The vines must be able to draw on the moisture below. The land has to be constantly worked and broken up all the year through to keep the moisture rising. Otherwise the vine would starve, its leaves flag and its grapes wither.

Sherry vines are not trained up on wires or on poles, but kept low on the ground. Their only support is a short stick under the grape-bearing branches. They are kept so low because of the searching wind, the *Levante*, which howls through the vineyards in winter from the east.

The vintage
By vintage time the grapes are golden, very much the colour of the finished wine. Their juice is deliciously sweet. The sun, reflected by the white chalky soil, makes them as warm as pies from an oven. The great sherry grape is the Palomino, which has the alternative name—as though there were not far too many grape varieties already—of Listan. It is used for all except the sweetest and darkest wines.

The grapes are picked by teams of men. In the most modern vineyards they are immediately put into shallow boxes, as carefully as if they were going straight to market to be sold for eating.

What is needed for sherry is a high concentration of sugar, which will make strong wine. Ripe as they are, the grapes are not quite sweet enough. The practice is to lay them out in their boxes or on esparto-grass mats in the sun. If light wine is wanted they sometimes stay there only for a few hours, until they are almost imperceptibly withered and shrunk. For heavy, sweet wines they sometimes stay on the ground in the vineyard, sun-scorched by day and by night protected from the dew by matting, for a week or more.

Pressing
The pressing of the grapes took place, until very recently, in the vineyards where the grapes were grown. It is still done like this in many cases, although the biggest firms are nearly all setting up modern pneumatic presses at their headquarters, and taking the grapes there to extract the maximum from them under ideal conditions.

Jerez is one of the very few places, in fact, where an important part of the wine is still trodden by foot. Not by bare foot, however, as port is, or was, but by feet in heavy hide boots. The boots are patterned on the sole with rows of nail-heads sticking out to catch the pips and prevent them getting crushed and adding their tannin to the juice.

The treading takes place at night, in *lagares* in long white barns among the vines. The grapes are brought in from the yard outside where they have been sunning themselves and are tipped on to the platform. As soon as the men begin to tread, the juice (which is called *mosto* from this moment until

47

months later, when it is finally declared *vino*) begins to run. It is channelled off into waiting butts.

But a large part of the juice has to be squeezed out. In the middle of each *lagar* there is a tall iron screw. The men pile the skins into a great toppling cake round the screw, and bandage it round with a long strip of esparto-grass matting. This they attach to the top of the screw and then turn it with bars like sailors round a capstan. The bandage acts as a tourniquet, squeezing the juice out without crushing the pips.

Fermentation

As soon as the *mosto* is in its butt it begins to ferment. The weather is warm and the sugar content high. The yeast cells lose no time. As fast as the butts of *mosto* are loaded on to lorries and carts and hurried into town to the cool bodegas some of them begin to ferment on the way.

Lorries rumble down the narrow streets with froth streaming from the bung-holes of the casks on top. In the bodega fountains of froth erupt as high as the ceiling in the first stages of what is graphically called the 'tumultuous fermentation'.

It is not so surprising that the sense of propriety of some of the senior shippers should make them prefer these things to happen in an orderly way under white-coated supervision. These dramas will be seen less and less in the future as the pale horizontal cylinders turn out impeccable must into unsullied casks. They are part of the wonderful variety of wine-lore which will soon only be in museums. They seem to be part of the essence of the wine itself. But no doubt sterile conditions will prove that they were not, and that they added nothing but a good anecdote.

The bodega

From this moment until the day it is shipped off to be drunk, the wine lives and grows in a *bodega*. The bodegas are the cellars and the factories of Jerez: colossal white-walled sheds, inevitably likened to cathedrals because of their long rows of tall arches. Until recently there was only one kind of building—one storey on ground level. But now the firm of Gonzales Byass has broken with even this tradition, and has built a three-storey bodega.

A bodega has a special kind of shade. It is unchanging, like the light in a painter's studio. A few windows high up near the roof throw bright shafts about far above, but the lines of butts, piled three high in avenues of endlessly fascinating perspective, remain in permanent half-light.

As long as it is fermenting violently, and later more gently, the new butt of sherry is left untasted. At this time of year, soon after the vintage, the sour smell of fermentation is inescapable in Jerez.

At the beginning of the new year the wine is ready to taste. This is the moment that decides each butt's future. The object of this tasting is to classify them.

Classification

Sherry has this peculiarity: until you taste an individual butt of wine you do not know what it will be like. Perhaps this does not sound so surprising. But knowing that a cask came from a certain vineyard in France, for example, and knowing the vintage, its maker will be able to

48

form a very good notion of the wine before he tastes it. Furthermore he will expect all the casks from one vineyard to be the same. But this is not so in Jerez. This cask and that cask were made at the same time from the same grapes from the same slope, and yet this one has delicacy, style, promise of beautiful wine in the future; that one has a flat, coarse, feeble taste, and will never be worth drinking unless something is done to liven it up.

This mystery about Jerez has been exaggerated. The shippers do know from experience to quite a large extent what style of wine each vineyard mainly produces. One area is more famous for finos, another for olorosos. But the element of chance remains. Until the wine is tasted nobody can say what its future is going to be.

The director in charge of the new wine and the *capataz* of the bodega will taste and classify as many as two hundred butts a day. They may have four or five thousand butts of the new vintage to get through. They record their findings—in a form of hieroglyphics that fascinates visitors—on the end of the butt. Wine which shows signs of being fino—the highest class—they mark with a tiny formalized palm, known as a *palma*. Wine with the recognizable oloroso character, which from the start is fuller in body, with a less fresh and fine scent, they mark with an O. Rayas, wines which lack the style to be anything much on their own account, and may even be such failures that they have to be disposed of outside the stocks or turned into vinegar, are marked with a stroke of the chalk. On the other hand many rayas make up the body of a medium-class blend of the sweeter kind. It is wonderful what a small addition of a really fine old wine will do.

Flor and finos

The distinguishing mark of a fino is its tendency to grow *flor*. *Flor* is a peculiar form of yeast which is native to Jerez and its area and practically nowhere else on earth. It is peculiar because it breaks most of the laws which govern the treatment of new—or indeed any—wine. The first thing to do to new wine is to keep the air away from it. Air carries all sorts of wild yeasts and bacteria which will inevitably, if allowed to get at the wine freely, turn it into vinegar. *Flor* is, indeed, one of the wild yeasts that the air carries, but once it has settled there is nothing to fear from the others. It grows and covers the wine in the cask with a thick white scum. To let it grow freely, the wine is left several inches below the top of the barrel.

The taste of *flor* is fresh and yeasty. It reminds one a little of new bread. This is the quality it imparts to the wine. A real fino has a delicate freshness which is extraordinary in such a strong wine.

Among the wines that grow *flor* there will always be some that are better than others, for sherry does not categorize itself as neatly as all that. Those that show all the characteristics of delicacy and finesse that make them seem almost drinkable at once, without further age, will be set aside in the *criadera,* or nursery, for finos. Those with a less perfect balance which seem to need more ageing will more probably go into the *criadera* for amontillados.

At this stage, when they are classified, put into clean casks and sorted out into their different nurseries, the wines are slightly fortified with pure alcohol. For a fino the fortification is very light; it brings the strength up from about fourteen and a half to about fifteen and a half degrees. Finos are sometimes sold as pale and dry as they naturally are. More often, though, they are slightly sweetened with sugar—which does not affect their taste and colour—or blended.

Olorosos The oloroso category is the basis of all sweet sherries. It lends itself perfectly to blending to make the sweet sherry known as cream. Olorosos are rarely—even more rarely than amontillados—drunk unsweetened. When they are, and when they are old, they can be superlative. The Spanish word *oloroso* means fragrant, although, curiously enough, the wine which is classed as fragrant is less scented than the wine which is classed as fine.

At the time of the classification it is quite easy to tell fino and oloroso apart. The fino is starting to grow *flor* freely; the oloroso shows little or no sign of it. In the sampling-glass the fino has the freshness which will still distinguish it when it is ready to be drunk; the oloroso has a rounder, flatter, less exciting smell. The clarity of scent is not there. It is almost as though it were muffled.

As oloroso ages it begins to acquire authority and definition. It seems to ripen almost like a cheese—the scent getting stronger and sharper and at the same time the body expanding into something which seems to explode in your mouth. But this is only at great age, and only in an unblended state. Olorosos like this are virtually never seen outside a bodega. They are none-theless the basis of the personality of many of the most popular and finest sherries on the market.

Palo cortado A palo cortado is a rarity—and proof of the fact that nothing is easy and predictable in wine. Sometimes a wine is excellent at the classification, and yet it is neither fino of the lightest kind, nor the kind of fino which will develop into an amontillado, nor is it an oloroso. This wine may be a palo cortado. The best way to describe it is as something between a fino and an oloroso; but not even extreme age will make it incline either way. It holds a middle course, developing along fairly predictable lines—for if this style appears at all it will be a good one—into a wine of lovely balance and distinction; dry, but soft, full-flavoured and rich. There are one or two on the market. They are probably unblended, possibly just slightly sweetened. The word Cortados will probably be part of the name. In any case they are some of the very finest sherries you can buy.

The solera system The sherry-shipper's objective is to have his own peculiar style of each category of wine always on tap, and never changing. The only way he is able to do this is, logically enough, to get it all out of one barrel. This is the basis of his way of blending, which is known as the solera system.

A solera is a group of barrels of wine, all of different ages. The only wine which is ever drawn off for bottling comes from the oldest barrel. To make good the deficit in the oldest barrel when some is drawn off it is filled from

50

the second oldest barrel, and so on down the line. Thus new wine is continually being added to the solera at one end, and old wine taken out at the other.

The new wine which is chosen to replenish the first barrel is the one from the nursery which is nearest to the rest of the solera in character. It will probably be eighteen months or two years old when it joins the line. By the time it reaches the end it may be three or four years old, perhaps ten or twelve. It depends how many stages there are in the solera.

In the course of the new wine's progress through the solera it is not only mixed with older wine, it takes on the older wine's character. An amazingly small proportion of older wine will affect an amazingly large proportion of younger. After successive drawings-off and toppings-up over a number of years the proportion of the original wine will naturally be minute—and yet its character will have been bequeathed to its successors in the same butt.

Each shipper has a large number of solera systems operating. One will be his most delicate and straw-pale fino, another a stronger fino from Chipiona or one of the outlying districts, another a gloriously pungent oloroso, another a lovely old fino becoming amontillado. There are also soleras of rayas— sound base-wines—and soleras of lesser and greater olorosos and amontillados of various ages. He has perhaps fifty of these unique essences of his own particular idea of what such a wine should be, and with these as his materials he can blend a wine for any taste under the sun.

Blending   Rarely is the final produce of the solera the exact sherry which is offered for sale. There are cases, and they are nearly always particularly expensive wines appealing to a limited public. The reason for this is that sherry is naturally completely dry. Even the dark olorosos are fermented to their natural finish, when all the sugar is turned into alcohol. Fortification does not, as it does with port, keep the wine sweet: it comes too late.

The public does not like completely dry sherry. It is an austere taste, which takes a bit of acquiring. It is an expensive taste, too, for only a first-class wine is good enough to enjoy in its natural state.

The shipper's resort, then, is blending. He follows either his own idea of what the public wants or the order of a wine-merchant who wants a brand of his own. Thus the name of an English wine-merchant can justifiably appear on a bottle of sherry, though he has no bodegas in Jerez. It is his sherry, because it is made to his specification, but in fact it comes from a shipper who also has his own ideas of what a popular sherry should be.

A blended sherry is a wine designed for a particular market. The first and easiest thing to calculate about that market is the price that it will be willing to pay. When the shipper knows that, he can see what can be done.

He is asked by a merchant to provide, say, an amontillado which will sell at a fairly low retail price. He looks at his soleras of amontillados. The best would cost far more than that. It is made of superb and long-aged finos. There is another which would almost do, except that it is also a bit expensive. It would, of course, need a good deal of sweetening to be what the English understand by amontillado. It is dry as a bone, and clear gold. It has the fine rich, nutty scent that is needed, but almost too much flavour. Let us suppose, though, that he mixed this wine with another, much younger and less splendid—a raya. It would bring the price down and at the same time soften the penetrating flavour. Then perhaps a small measure of a youngish, rather strong fino to give it more freshness. Now he has a wine at the right price, already more to the English taste than the original amontillado. It is still dry, so he sweetens it with a little Pedro Ximenez, which also gives it colour. Not quite enough, in fact, so he adds a measure of a jet-black colouring wine. He has the perfect medium wine the market requires.

If this blend, which he has made in his sample-room in sample quantities, meets with approval from the merchant who is going to launch the brand, he goes ahead and makes it up. The right number of butts of the various wines are poured into a vat and stirred. When they are thoroughly mixed they are run back into butts and left to marry and mature together. Perhaps before they are actually shipped they will be fortified a little more with alcohol, 1 per cent or so, to make sure of their stability en route.

Pedro Ximenez
Three categories of wine are kept apart for blending alone. One is for sweetening, which is made of Pedro Ximenez (P.X.) grapes. These are left out in the sun to shrivel and become raisins before they are pressed. The wine they make is almost black, treacly, undrinkably sweet on its own. Its influence in a blend is immensely powerful.

Very old sherry
The other infinitely valuable additive in making a blend which is to have the depth of flavour and some of the value of a really fine wine is very old sherry. One or two soleras are established in any of the great shippers' houses simply to provide the oldest sherry possible. The wine is used with great discretion, for its influence is immense. An oloroso that has been in the solera for forty years is so strong in taste that it is almost painful to hold a sip of it in your mouth. It is another of sherry's peculiarities that age concentrates it, in strength and flavour, until it is the very quintessence of the wine it once was. A small quantity of such a wine will go a long way in a blend.

Vino de color
Finally there is the colouring wine. This is made by boiling and reducing *mosto* until it is almost black. Its taste is a little caramelly, but almost neutral. With this the colour of the blend can be adjusted to whatever the market requires. Paxarete, a mixture of this wine and sherry, is bought by whisky-blenders and shipped to Scotland for colouring their blends in exactly the same way.

The finished wine
When the wine is ready to be shipped it is no longer necessarily described in the way it was when it was first classified. The trade in each country has its own terms, which the customers know better than the Spanish names. In English the principal terms which appear on labels are 'fino', which keeps its name, 'amontillado', whose name has come to mean something

52

different in English, 'cream', 'old full pale', 'dry', 'golden', 'brown' and other words of pure description.

The meaning of label terms

Besides these universally understood type-names there are also many blends which sell on their brand-name alone, without any description. The choice of sherry by its name is complicated by this practice more than any other. The following are some of the words which occur most often on sherry labels.

Dry

The word dry has lost most of its original meaning. It used to denote without any, or much, sugar. Thus all sherry is dry until it has been sweetened. But 'dry' is now used either to mean comparatively dry, as in Dry Sack (which justifies itself by saying, quite rightly, that for a sack—a sweet kind of wine—it is fairly dry), where it means medium; or just as part of the name, as in Dry Fly, where it does not mean dry at all. The word is also used to mean the driest of a range, as in Regency Dry or Bristol Dry, where its meaning is fairly clear, although it still does not mean without sugar, by any means. It is more certain, if you want a really dry sherry, to look for one labelled 'fino'.

Fino

All—or nearly all—finos are sweetened slightly for the British and American markets. It has been quite rightly observed that a wine which tastes perfectly dry in Spain is hard to drink without a shudder in England: the farther north you go the more a little sugar is needed to keep a balance. Finos are nonetheless the driest, palest and perhaps least blended of all sherries. They are comparatively young, and (for sherry) delicate. A brown sherry can be left in an open bottle for months without coming to harm, but a fino loses the freshness which is its principal charm after a few days. Similarly, a bottle of fino ought to be opened and drunk quite soon; six months on the shelf in a shop has often been enough to ruin it. A good fino is intensely appetizing. It is never so good as it is before a meal. It goes excellently with olives and almonds, or crumbled dry cheese. In Spain it is never drunk without *tapas*, little morsels of some kind. They range from a few shrimps to a young banquet of steak and onions or lobster claws and mayonnaise.

The perfect glass for a fino is the Spanish wine-taster's *copita*. It is slim, elegant, tall; a narrow rose-bud in shape. The wine can be swirled in it with magnificent panache without a drop going astray. There is just room for your nose at the top.

Williams & Humbert's 'Pando', Gonzales Byass's 'Tio Pepe', Valdespino's 'Inocente', Pedro Domecq's 'La Ina', Garvey's 'San Patricio', Avery's 'Elizabetha', La Riva's 'Tres Palmas', Sandeman's 'Apitif' and Harvey's 'Bristol Fino' are some of the best finos to be had.

Manzanilla

The manzanilla characteristic is something that a fino can acquire or lose. It is found in the very tart, pale finos made in the distinct area of Sanlucar de Barrameda, which starts some fifteen miles from Jerez. Sanlucar is on the sea, or rather the broad estuary of the Guadalquivir. The local fino has a style which can only be described as salty, as though the sea air somehow impregnates it. But take it to Jerez and store it there and the peculiar taste goes; it becomes just a plain, very elegant fino. Conversely, a plain fino taken from Jerez to Sanlucar and stored there takes on, after a while, the manzanilla character. The thing is a mystery.

Manzanillas are shipped abroad, but they run the risk of losing the very thing that makes them manzanillas and not just finos en route, and very often lose it they do. Moreover, this particular style of wine is light in alcohol for sherry, and always needs fortifying, which changes its character, before it can travel.

Sad to say, therefore, to taste a real manzanilla there is no alternative but to go to Sanlucar. It is no hardship, for it has one of the best fish restaurants in the world, Casa Juan, which serves its food on a wooden platform out over the beach with the fishing boats all around. If you should ever be there in bad weather the restaurant on the beach will be out of action. You can still eat just as well in the bar, but it is just a fisherman's bar, and the odd tables they set up do nothing to subdue the fishermen. There, and I believe only there, you may taste a rare and superb thing, a manzanilla amontillado— a wine which has been in cask, in the sea air, for ten or fifteen years and has acquired, with quite a dark colour, the most clean, full, salty, savoury taste it is possible to imagine. Half a bottle of this, with dishes of *langostinos* and grilled red mullet and herbs, is the finest eating and drinking in Spain.

Amontillados   Strictly speaking, an amontillado is a fino which has become, with age, heavier, stronger, darker, with more depth and intensity of scent and flavour—in fact, more like the wines of Montilla, a district to the north-east of Jerez, near Cordoba, which is famous for this type of wine. A fine amontillado is, in fact, much better than the wine it is named after, but the name came in to describe the type at the beginning of the last century, and it has remained.

The word amontillado is now used commercially to mean nothing more than a medium sherry. Real amontillado is medium in the sense that its colour and flavour lie between those of a fino and those of an oloroso. In quality it is far from medium: it has an extraordinary individuality which is, in my opinion, the very best thing Jerez produces.

Not all finos turn into amontillados as they grow old. Some just become— though it is rare—old finos: they keep their lightness and freshness even as they intensify with age. Many just lose all their qualities and become good for nothing. But others move gradually through an intermediate stage, which is known as fino-amontillado, until they reach the stature of fully fledged amontillados. Then they are dark, dry, pungent, almost tarry; as nutty as a hedgeful of hazels.

Very often wines which are called amontillados, on the other hand, are medium in the sense that they are neither one thing nor the other. They are blended to be middling-sweet, middling-brown. They are supposed to appeal to everybody and end by exciting nobody.

Full   The word full comes into such phrases as 'old full pale'. It must be construed to mean soft and sweet. The paleness mentioned in this phrase is an exception to the general rule that the darker the sherry, the sweeter it is. Bristol Cream is a pale, very sweet wine.

Milk   The word milk only occurs in sherry shipped, or which used to be shipped, to Bristol. It implies sweetness and softness, and I suppose to some extent harmlessness, though there is no particular justification for the latter. There is a story that the Ministry of Food tried to object to the word milk being used on something which did not originate in an udder. Bristol used to be so full of its famous milk that horse-drawn sledges, rather than iron-tyred wagons, were used in its cobbled streets to avoid vibrating the precious wine below.

Cream   A cream sherry is one which is older, softer and better than a milk. It is usually a fine oloroso, sweetened and tinged with a lighter gold colour.

Golden   The term golden is virtually interchangeable with cream. Where a range of sherries includes both, however, the cream is usually sweeter than the golden.

Amoroso   Amoroso also means very much the same. Although the word means amorous in Spanish, a perfectly appropriate adjective for a soft, sweet wine, it is the name of a vineyard—far removed, I imagine, from the famous Inocente vineyard which produces austere finos. Amoroso is really only another word for oloroso now.

Vino de pasto   *Vino de pasto* literally means table wine. It is used, though rarely now, on light medium sherries of no special quality.

Brown   Brown, or East India, sherry has more in common with Malmsey Madeira than with a fino. It is greatly sweetened and darkly coloured, very rich in taste and often stronger in alcohol than most sherries. To me it is most welcome after a sharp walk in a deep frost.

Serving sherry   Clearly a range of wines so wide can produce something for whenever a shortish, strongish drink is wanted. Since longer and not so strong drinks are found to be better with meals, sherry tends to be everywhere but at table. Natural dry sherries are supremely appetizing before, sweetened sherries are popular both before and after meals.

If there is any time when a drink is called for with no meal in the offing, sherry—dry, sweet or medium—is the ideal choice. There used to be a custom of having a glass with a piece of cake where now we take tea or coffee at mid-morning—but office-workers and wives in centrally heated houses find that it makes them drowsy.

But there is a place for sherry at table too. A number of the richer and oilier kinds of hors d'oeuvre, notably smoked salmon and smoked eel, have a tendency to overpower the light table wines with their oiliness, producing a taste in the mouth which is not pleasant. A dry sherry is excellent with smoked salmon, or with any of the strongly flavoured hors d'oeuvre dishes. At the beginning of a meal when you are going to have a bottle of red wine and feel like drinking something with the first course, but do not want to order a whole bottle of white, a glass of dry sherry is perfect. It is also perhaps the best wine to drink—if you want wine at all—with most kinds of soup. It is good either with or in consommé and all clear soups.

At the other end of the meal sweet sherry is quite good with cheese, though not with sweet dishes. Nuts go extremely well with sweet and medium-sweet sherries, amontillados and olorosos.

The decanter

In Britain there are so many handsome old decanters around in antique shops for so little money that there is no reason not to use a decanter for sherry. There is no mystery or difficulty about using one. You pull the cork of your bottle of sherry and pour it in. If the wine is to stay there for more than a day you need a stopper, but once the stopper is in all is well for a couple of weeks. Very dry sherry loses more by being kept than sweet sherry, but neither will show any appreciable change in the first week at least.

The only advantage of a decanter for sherry is that it looks pretty. It does not help the wine to develop its scent to be at its best for drinking as it does with red table wines, nor is there any sediment to get rid of as there is with port. A decanter is an elegant extra—and all the better for that.

Any smallish, round or bud-shaped glass is fine for sherry. It should never be more than half-filled, or the scent of the wine is lost. In summer some people like it in a bigger glass with a lump of ice, and even a splash of soda. Dry sherry definitely improves with half an hour in the refrigerator at any time of the year. It is best cold, not icy.

THE 'SHERRIES' OF OTHER COUNTRIES

The other countries of the world which make wine that they call sherry inevitably challenge Spain to a comparison. If their wine is indistinguishable from its original—for even they will not deny that they are copying Spanish sherry—it is hard to make out a case against their calling it sherry. It seems a pity from their point of view that they must admit that the best they can do is to copy someone else. But that is their business.

South Africa

There are very few people who can tell the best of South African sherry from an ordinary Spanish one of the same character. It is not entirely surprising, because the vineyards of Andalusia and the Cape have many things in common. Their latitude, on opposite sides of the equator, is almost the same. In their climate and their nearness to the sea they are very similar. Both the Spanish and South African sherry vineyards lie on low hills.

Their soil, however, is completely different. The staring white chalk of Jerez is not found in South Africa. The vineyards there are largely sandstone —which you would not expect to give the wonderful cleanness of flavour which chalk gives, whether in Jerez or Champagne. The South Africans, however, use the Palomino sherry grape, and the Pedro Ximenez, as well as a South African variety, the Steen.

They make the wine in a very similar way to the Spaniards, and see to it that *flor*, whether natural or induced, is in every barrel where it is wanted.

56

In a sherry bodega. The butts are piled in rows three or four deep. The wine is always tasted in a bud-shaped glass which funnels the scent up to the nostrils

Indeed the South Africans discovered, to their great delight, that the mysterious yeast called *flor* was as native to the Cape as it is to Andalusia. In itself this seemed to sanction their calling their wine sherry.

Finally, the best South African sherries are made by the same solera system as the Spanish. Some of the soleras have now been in operation for over twenty years, not the same matter as the century or more that the oldest and most valuable blending wines of Jerez have been in the bodegas, but still a respectable length of time, and enough to have started giving the best oloroso-type wines some of the depth of flavour they should have.

In Britain South African sherries are slightly cheaper than the Spanish wines with which they are bound to be compared. Where they are comparable, therefore, there is an advantage in buying them. But this is only in the middle, medium-to-sweet range.

There are no very dry and delicate South African sherries, nor very full, old and nutty ones. They can be as sweet as you like—and there is probably less noticeable difference between Spanish and South African in the sweet wines than among the dry—but they are not anything like as good as the best of Spanish sherry, whether sweet or dry.

I have had an old amontillado-type South African wine which would have worried a *Jerezano* seriously. But it was a special bottle from a special solera, not on the market—the old story. I am not saying what South Africa can or cannot do—let alone what she could do if the South Africans themselves were discriminating and devoted sherry-drinkers. But what she does, commercially, is to produce good-quality ordinary, unexciting wine. The only motives for drinking it in preference to Spanish can be economic, or sentimental.

The Kooperativ Wijnbouwers Vereeniging (K.W.V.), by far the largest South African wine-producer, puts out two full ranges of sherry at slightly different prices and qualities. The more expensive, the Paarlsack range, has the edge for age and smoothness, includes a more fino-like dry wine and very good cream sherry. Both are best, I think, in their medium categories —still quite light but distinctly sweet in the mouth. I find these indistinguishable from comparable Spanish wines.

Australia   The greater part of the Australian wine which is called sherry finds a totally different market from that of the Spanish wines. Australia's natural advantage is sun. The tendency for all Australian wines, with the exception of a few grown on high ground, is to have a great deal of sugar and a very low natural acidity. Sun makes grape-growing easy (so easy, in fact, that Australia has an enormous annual surplus of grapes, which are processed in whatever way comes to hand, to make raisins, alcohol or wine) but it makes wine-making difficult. A good part of the wine is strong, sweet and rough— qualities which in a well-balanced wine would develop, as port does, into excellence with age, but which in an unbalanced wine lead nowhere except into a strong public-bar drink.

Where great care is taken to imitate Spanish sherry, in bottles which cost the same as the best South African, Australia makes a pleasant, medium-dry, good-quality wine. But it still would never be mistaken for the real thing, as South African often is. Where Australian wine strives to achieve a light balance it so often goes too far, and achieves wateriness instead. Where it does not, it remains heavy and heady.

No European vineyards, of course, attempt, as Australian and Californian vineyards do, to produce several completely different types of wine from the same soil. Europe learnt long ago the value of specialization. Bordeaux does not make good wine as an all-rounder; it makes good claret. If it tried to make sherry the results would be disastrous. Conversely, any attempt at making claret at Jerez would be doomed. For some reason the Australians have failed to take this point. True, some areas specialize in one type of wine, some in another, but no-one will admit that there is a possibility that certain kinds of European wine simply will not grow in Australia, and that Australians would be far better employed in experimenting to discover a peculiarly Australian kind of wine which cannot be made in Europe.

Cyprus

The sherry-type wine of Cyprus is not the most successful of the island's wines, again for the reasons I have just been talking about. At its best it tastes like a moderate parody of sherry, at its worst the name does not fit it at all.

This is not to say that there are not excellent Cyprus wines. Table wines from Cyprus are often very good. The island's own sweet dessert wine, Commandaria, is like nothing else—and is none the worse for that. But Cyprus sherry, except in the sweetest categories where it is a good, smooth, intensely sweet drink—indeed almost more like a port than sherry—has little except extreme cheapness to recommend it. In the words of the Cyprus High Commission in London, 'The island has been successful in exploiting the gap between British sherries and South African and Australian sherries'.

British 'sherry'

One in every four bottles of wine sold in Britain is not wine at all, by any strict definition. These British wines, which the wine trade knows affectionately, and not inappropriately, as sweets, are made of preserved and concentrated grape-juice. The grapes are pressed and their juice dehydrated in the country where they were grown, which is often Cyprus or North Africa, before fermentation has a chance to begin. The solid concentrate which is shipped to England is non-alcoholic and hence immune to the preposterous duties. On this fact, and the saving of almost four shillings a bottle which it achieves, hangs the considerable prosperity of the British wine-industry.

British 'sherry' at its best, when it is still only about half the price of the cheapest Spanish, manages to conjure up a taste which reminds one of sherry. The greater part of it, however, is designed merely to be a sweet,

58

smooth, strong and consistent drink. It succeeds in being the cheapest form of alcohol, money for degrees, in Britain outside the old last resorts of methylated spirits and rubbing alcohol.

California It is a great pity that sherry is almost a dirty word in the United States. The fault for its low reputation lies with the Californian producers who have made it merely a cheap, strong wine. 'Sherry-drinkers' used to be the term for ragged layabouts borrowing rides on freight trains and drinking from the bottle. The wine, needless to say, was not sherry at all. It was cheap south Californian wine, more or less processed by cooking to give it a kind of burnt taste which was supposed to bear some resemblance to sherry.

California still produces considerably more wine which it calls sherry than the sherry area of Spain (according to Frank Schoonmaker's invaluable *Encyclopaedia of Wine*, over three times as much). I personally do not find that the 'sherry' sold in gallon jars in supermarkets in the United States has any of the aperitif qualities, or indeed anything except alcohol in common with sherry. There is a little premium *flor* sherry made in California, but its resemblance to the real thing is still very remote.

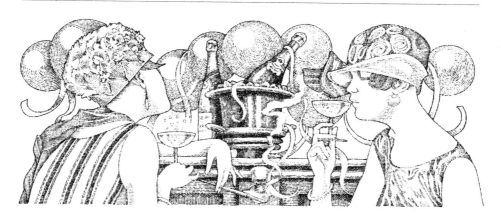

Champagne

CHAMPAGNE HAS THE STIMULATING QUALITIES of an aperitif, rather than the savoury, mouth-watering ones, in the highest degree. It owes a large part of its reputation, in fact, to its magical effect on the morale. To say that it is more often drunk for its boosting qualities than for its taste is not to belittle its taste: there is nothing else which has an even comparable stimulating power.

It was by some of the neatest and most painless public relations the world has ever seen that champagne came into power. Somehow, at the end of the last century and the beginning of this, it just seemed to fall into its ready-

59

made slot in the social pattern. What, we now have to ask ourselves, did they drink at weddings, dances, christenings, launchings, comings-out, before they had champagne?

Good champagne has an incomparably fresh and delicate taste of grapes. There is hardly any sugar in it at all, but just enough to balance a slight acidity—the perfect balance of, say, a crisp golden-green apple. It has an extraordinarily pungent smell—you can smell a bottle being opened in the next garden—and yet the scent in the top of your glass is as delicate and fresh as the wine itself. Finally it has a perfect mill-race of pin-point bubbles, slowly settling down to gently racing streamers from the bottom of the glass. The total effect of the wine is one of richness, belying the fact that it is completely dry, and never, at least in my experience, cloys.

No other wine has these qualities all together—or indeed any of them so perfectly. There are innumerable other sparkling wines, a great many of them imitating champagne, but there is no effective substitute.

The name champagne

So successful is champagne that it continually has to defend itself against the danger of becoming a notion rather than a wine. Its name is borrowed by anything that wants to sound gay, luxurious and expensive. The hint of old-fashioned elegance it carries with it has been used to sell almost anything—including, come to that, other wine.

But Champagne is a place, like Bordeaux, Alsace and the Loire. It is one of the few world-famous wines which does not have an English name. We call Bourgogne burgundy, Jerez sherry, Rhine-wine hock, red Bordeaux claret. All these names, being our inventions, have been borrowed by imitators. But Champagne is an area, a small county of French soil, and its name should only be used for wine which comes from its superlative vineyards.

The champagne country

The vineyards of Champagne are the nearest vineyards to Britain. To reach them is barely half a day's drive from the Channel ports. Reims, the capital, is familiar to anyone who has driven south from Calais on the way to Switzerland and Italy. It is not a particularly beautiful town, due to the First World War, which razed most of its fine old buildings, but its glorious Gothic cathedral, wonderfully restored after having been completely gutted, is sometimes called, with full justice, the Parthenon of France. Reims is honeycombed with cellars. Some of them are said to have once been Roman stone quarries. In many cases the galleries through the chalk under the city are three or four storeys deep—all full of champagne.

All the vineyards lie to the south of the city, above and around the valley of the Marne. It is neither majestic nor pretty country, but simply peaceful, and in autumn, when the leaves of the vines are red and gold and the smoke of bonfires rises quietly into the cool air, marvellously beautiful.

No wine region throws open its doors more readily to the visitor. The shippers are always ready to welcome people and show them round their colossal establishments. It is not uncommon for a firm to have ten or fifteen

60

The essence of serving wine is to give a feeling of plenty. Champagne in a silver mug is one of the traditional ways of producing this feeling. Some even say that the wine tastes better out of silver

miles of dank chalk cellar to show anyone who is that interested. Above ground the buildings are no beauties; most of them were built during the nadir of architecture at the end of the last century and the beginning of this. The Avenue du Champagne, though, in Epernay, the second town of Champagne, is worth seeing. For half a mile the top-heavy mansions of the shippers alternate with the huge courtyards of their *maisons* (as they call the office-cum-cellars-cum-factory where the wine is made). Never did proprietors live so near their work so pleasantly. It was one of the houses in this street, the house of the Pol Roger family, which Sir Winston Churchill once called 'the greatest address in Europe'.

At no moment of the day is champagne not being drunk somewhere in Epernay—and the visitor is sure to get his share.

The wine

Champagne, the wine, is the outcome of an ideal site for the growing of vines being so far north that the coming of cold weather influences its making. The chalk soil is perfect for a clean, dry, white wine. Its arrangement in gentle slopes, sheltered from the north and canted towards the sun, is perfect for ripening grapes, which need all the sun they can get. But being so far north the harvest is late, and the grapes are not over-full of sugar when they are picked. So they ferment slowly, and are still in the last stages of fermentation when the winter catches up with them. Cold weather temporarily stops the fermentation. The characteristic of champagne is that when the spring comes and the temperature of the wine slowly rises it begins to ferment again. This is the so-called secondary fermentation. It is used to make champagne a sparkling, rather than a still, wine.

Sparkling champagne is a wonderful example of how experience has taught the grower to bring out the best in his wine—even at great risk and expense. Still champagne is perfectly possible, in fact very good. But it has the drawbacks of delicacy. It is fine in Champagne. But bring a bottle to England and it has lost its character. There is obviously no very profitable market for such a wine—and yet there was the potential of making millions of gallons of it. The answer to the riddle is traditionally ascribed to a monk, the legendary Dom Pérignon.

Dom Pérignon

Pérignon was the cellar-master at the Abbey of Hautvillers, a lovely spot looking southwards over the wide valley of the Marne. Tradition says that he was blind. He conceived the notion of bottling the wine, in which he had discovered the tendency to ferment and become fizzy again in the spring after the vintage, while it was thus troubled. Furthermore he was the first man to use corks for the job. Previously an ineffectual stopper of rags had been used. Thick bottles were needed, and stout string to keep the corks in, but those that survived, among the many that burst with the pressure of mounting bubbles, became a most marvellous drink. The monks found, in place of the fragility and tartness of the still wine they were used to, a fine, more fragrant, more robust, more spirited wine, better than they had ever

61

been able to make. Best of all, it had lovely bright ribbons of bubbles, rising and waving endlessly in the glass. There was no instantaneous gassiness about it; the bubbles seemed to appear from nowhere at the bottom and form columns processing upwards. The gas, the by-product of fermentation, having no room to go elsewhere, had dissolved in the wine.

Champagne, however, did not just appear fully fledged from the blind master's cellar one fine spring morning. He worked on it constantly for year after year. Naturally he found, as every wine-grower finds, that one year produces fine, full-flavoured wine, another a liquid which is hardly wine at all. He discovered, in addition to this, that the vineyards of the area had qualities which separately left something to be desired, while their finest points could all be brought to the fore in a blend.

Thus the wine of the Marne valley slopes of what is called by courtesy the Mountain of Reims was as round and full-bodied as any in the area. Those of the gentle slopes to the south, on the other hand, from Avize and Cramant, had more of the qualities of finesse and brightness in the mouth. The cellar-master saw in his mind's eye the notional champagne—a perfectly balanced blend of these desirable characteristics. It could be, he thought, the finest wine on earth.

But there was a serious problem yet to be dealt with. The fermentation which brought the bubbles had other side-effects. As yeast cells multiply in the bustle of fermentation the old ones die. The fermentation itself leaves a deposit of solid particles, all of which are trapped in the bottle. Instead of a clear golden wine you have a thick unhappy-looking one full of 'fliers'. It may taste good, but it looks most unappetizing. This is the great difficulty in making champagne.

If you ever see an eighteenth-century champagne-glass—and there are not many, for the fashion had not really begun—you will see that it is frosted like a bathroom window. It will be flute-shaped, a long thin V, the classical and still the best shape for sparkling wines, but you will not be able to see the wine in it. That was before the problem had been mastered.

The cellar-masters of Champagne gradually developed ways of removing the débris from the bottle. To filter it was fatal; all the sparkle went too. Somehow it had to be done under pressure or with the pressure released only for a moment. They had, in fact, to take the cork out, remove the sediment and get the cork back in again without letting the wine, or the gas, escape.

The widow Clicquot

The credit for finding the way the whole vast industry does it now goes to another of the legendary figures of Champagne, the widow Clicquot. Her husband was, among other things, the head of a small wine-making business in Reims. As the story is told in a little book published by the widow's firm and written by the Princesse de Caraman Chimay, the wife of a present director, the young couple would drive out in their trap round the vineyards, learning about every stage in the making of wine, from winter pruning to the treading of the grapes at vintage time. Madame Clicquot became fascinated by the many skills, the patience, the naturalness of everything that went on in the farms and the cellars. But the idyll was shattered. A fever took away the young husband and the wife was left a widow.

She carried on. She built up a trade and a reputation for the wine with her husband's name. She found partners and took risks, chartering ships and following up contacts. Russia was her principal market, for the Russian army was quartered in Reims in the final campaigns before Waterloo, and had acquired a thirst for champagne which went back home with them. To Prince Serge Alexandrovitch Wolkonski, their humane and convivial commandant, Reims owes a great debt. The widow Clicquot is supposed to have pondered the problem of the bits in the bottles until she came to the logical solution. The bits must be obliged to collect on the cork, where they can be removed without affecting the rest of the wine. To do this she had a big table pierced with holes, and stuck the bottles in the holes upside-down. In some the deposit, which looks like a line of fine white sand along the lowermost side of the bottle, obediently slid to the cork. In others it stuck.

Then was devised the simple expedient of giving the bottle a gentle shake, lifting it slightly from its hole, giving it a slight clockwise turn, and knocking it against the wood as it was being put back. It had to be done discreetly, or all the accumulated deposit would be shaken back into the wine, and the whole process would have to start again. The trick was called *remuage*, or moving.

Remuage

Refinements followed. The tables were leant up at a sharp angle so that they took up less room, and the holes ovalled slightly so that the bottle could still be stood almost on end. In this form they were christened *pupitres*—desks. The *remuage* was brought to a fine art, so that an experienced *remueur* could, using both hands, shift 3,000 bottles an hour. Instead of just being upside-down from the start they were tilted more and more each day, so that the deposit rolled slowly down the hill to the cork. Even so it took three months in the *pupitres* for a bottle to be ready for the next stage.

Dégorgement

This was the disgorging *(dégorgement)*. The deposit was now resting on the cork, the bottle standing on its head. It remained to get the cork and the deposit out, and another cork in, as quickly as possible. To do this, a man took each bottle in turn, upside-down, cut the string, pulled the cork, let out the first two inches of wine holding the waste matter, topped it up with a little more and handed it to his neighbour, who rammed in another cork. Then more string to hold the new cork in against the pressure, and the job was done.

There was one more modification. The wine, at the end of its second fermentation, is always completely sugarless and dry. The Russians, in particular, liked it sweet. So the topping-up wine became a mixture of sugar, wine and—just to make sure the wine would stand up to its long journey—a drop of stabilizing brandy. And so it is today.

The sweetness of champagne is easy to adjust. It is simply a matter of
how much sugar is put in the *dosage,* the topping-up. In theory, *brut,* the
driest champagne, has none, but is topped up with wine alone; *sec* has a
little, *demi-sec* more and 'rich' a good deal. In practice even *brut* has a little.

Since the process—the whole of which is known throughout the world as
the champagne method—became established at the beginning of the nineteenth century the principle has not altered. Modern methods have been
able to speed up and simplify some things, but *remuage,* for example, still
baffles the makers. New ways of doing it by machine are continually being
invented, but none of them work as well as the patient, lonely men with
cold hands down under the chalk.

One development has helped a great deal. The neck of the bottle, containing the deposit to be removed, is now dipped into a freezing mixture
just before the disgorging, so that the wine in it becomes ice. When the cork
is removed it is a plug of frozen wine that shoots out, to be replaced by the
dose. A great deal of wine has been saved this way.

Further developments are taking place all the time. Most of the big firms
now use concrete or glass vats for fermenting the new wine instead of the
traditional barrels. It is notable, though, that two of the firms which all
connoisseurs of champagne agree in calling the best at the present day—
Krug and Bollinger—still use oak barrels.

Large firms are also changing over to crown corks from the more expensive and laborious real cork for the first fermentation. Again, some firms are
resisting it. It is these little differences, they are sure, which add up to the
big difference between the best possible champagne and a passable one.

But more important by far than the details of processing is the wine which
is processed. The deciding factor in the quality of champagne is the original
wine that goes into it. All champagne, you remember, is a blend. A shipper
may grow his own wine or he may buy it from farmers. But wherever he
gets it, if it is not good in the first place he cannot turn it into good
champagne.

The vineyards   The vineyards of Champagne have their own classification. You cannot
of Champagne   buy a first- or a second-growth champagne, because it is all blended. The
object of the classification is not to help the consumer; it is a scale of prices
for the farmer.

Each of the villages of Champagne has been given a percentage figure.
Ay, the most famous of the black-grape-growing villages, and Avize, the
most famous of the Côte des Blancs, for example, are among those classified
as 100 per cent. Some villages are 95, some 90 and so on.

At each vintage time a committee of growers, shippers and other interested parties get together and decide the price for the year. They take into
account the quality, the quantity, the stocks, the demand and anything
else that crops up. Then they announce so many francs a kilo for the grapes.
Ay and Avize get 100 per cent (the whole price), Hautvillers 80 per cent

64

and so on. It is equitable, it reflects the value of the land, and everybody is happy.

Therefore a shipper who is buying grapes to make his wine can decide to have more or less of the 100 per cent in his blend, to fill up with cheaper wines or restrict himself to what he can afford of the more expensive ones. It is here, at this stage, that the quality of champagne is really decided.

The vineyards of Champagne are roughly divided in two; those which grow black grapes and those which grow white. Both, needless to say, make white wine. The black-grape country is the valley of the Marne and the Mountain of Reims, the wide, plateau-topped hill which lies to the south of Reims, between the city and the Marne. Its slopes to the north, east, south and south-west are a solid mass of vines. The flat top is wild forest country. No vines grow there.

Over the valley of the Marne, beyond the town of Epernay is the Côte des Blancs, the white-grape country. It stretches out along a line of hills for ten miles south.

Blancs de Blancs

Classical champagne is a blend of the wines of these two regions. Each has something to offer the other. Recently, however, champagne made of the juice of white grapes alone, called *blanc de blancs*, has come on to the market, under the guise of being lighter than the traditional kind. I have not met anyone who has found the old kind of champagne too heavy, but the power of suggestion is great, and since 'lighter' Scotch has been such a success, and lighter rum and drier gin and vodka—with no taste at all— have all proved extremely popular, it seemed a reasonable assumption that the public would swallow the same thing with champagne.

It is usually sold at a higher price than classical champagne, though in what way it can be worth more it is hard to say; white grapes are no more expensive than black ones. It is, in fact, a fashion, which will eventually stand or fall on its merits. But it is a pity that anyone should be misled into thinking that no champagne is good enough unless it is *blanc de blancs*.

The vintage

At vintage time, which varies in Champagne from mid-September in a good year to mid-October in a sunless one, parties of pickers, many of them mining families from the industrial belt up near the Belgian border, descend on the vineyards. Hampers are dropped from trucks along the lanes through the vines, each marked with the name of the shipper who has bought the crop, or who owns the vineyard in question. They might be mistaken for laundry-baskets. They fill quickly, as messengers go back and forth between them and the picking parties with little wooden trug baskets, maintaining an endless chain. Before the trucks come back for their load some of the women of the party have been sorting all the grapes, sitting at trestle tables in the lanes, rejecting any that have mildew or are muddy or in any way undesirable.

The trucks or tractors go on their round again, and the baskets go straight to the pressing station. Sometimes this is close by, at a farmhouse in the fields or in the nearest village; sometimes they are taken straight into the headquarters of the firm in Ay or Epernay.

The pressing
Then the grapes are pressed. The presses are enormous: some of the biggest used anywhere: four tons of grapes go into one press at a time. They are wooden, round or square pens with slatted sides. Into the top of the enclosure descends a wooden grill with tremendous force, imperceptibly slowly, pressing all the juice out of the grapes and into the runnels, where it collects to run down to a waiting vat or cask below.

The press is used three times on each load of grapes—once for the *tête de cuvée* (the best of the wine); once, harder, for a second batch of wine which could be used for blending or sold to brokers who carry stocks of such wine in case they are needed; once, a third time, after the *marc* (the remains) have been broken up and rearranged with spades, for ordinary wine for the workmen. (In Champagne even the *marc* is used: it is distilled to make *eau de vie*.) In the casks the wine begins to ferment quickly if the weather has been good and there is plenty of sugar in the must, slowly and reluctantly if a wet summer is being followed by a chilly autumn. It goes on until most of the sugar has been converted into alcohol and the night-frosts have set in. Then the shipper throws his windows open to let the cold air circulate round the casks and vats. The fermentation dies down.

The winter
The cold weather serves many useful purposes in Champagne. Besides having originally given the idea for a sparkling wine, by interrupting the fermentation before it was complete, it helps to clarify the young wine and to reduce its acidity.

A great part of the acid content, a very necessary element in the composition of all wines, consists of tartaric acid. Champagne tends to have an acid content higher than the makers really want. Fortunately, when the weather gets very cold tartaric acid emerges from its solution in the wine in the form of crystals. These, which are called cream of tartar, are heavy enough to fall to the bottom of the barrel, so that when the wine is racked off a proportion of the acid content is left behind. A warm winter in Champagne, therefore, is far from welcome, as the spring will find the new wine as acid as the autumn left it.

Blending
The vital process of blending takes place in the spring. The directors of the firm meet in the tasting-room, sometimes day after day for weeks, to examine all the wines that have emerged from their vintage of six months previously. It is then that they discover whether they have bought well, and got what they need. For their object now is to make up the *cuvée*, the blend, which will eventually bear their name.

Most of the well-established firms follow a fairly standard buying pattern year after year. They know that the particular kind of light or not so light wine for which they are famous demands a certain proportion of grapes

66

from the village of Ay, a certain proportion from the village of Verzenay, and so on.

Needless to say, there are always opportunist firms who buy whatever they can get at a cut rate, and try to disguise the taste as best they can, but the good firms will let nothing seduce them from obtaining and blending the best possible wine, for the vintage, that their experience and ingenuity can manage.

I say 'for the vintage': if it is a fine year, with all that a great champagne needs—body, balance, bouquet—the blenders have the opportunity of modelling their very finest and most individual product, a vintage champagne.

Vintage champagne   Vintage champagnes are only made in extra-good years. In Champagne this almost always means years with more than the usual amount of sunshine. More sun produces riper grapes, and riper grapes richer wine. A vintage champagne, therefore, though not sweeter, is always a heavier, fuller and-rounder wine than the ordinary, non-vintage kind. It has more individuality; it is not made to be as similar as possible to the current wine of the same firm. On the contrary, it is planned to be unmistakable as the wine of this particular year—the year when the grapes were ripe by, say, 10 September, or the year the flowering happened before the children went back to school; the year we never thought the thunderstorms would hold off, or the year of the Anniversary celebrations.

In fact this is not quite true. To a certain extent a good shipper will cheat over a vintage wine if he feels he can make it still better by adding something he has in reserve. This was true of some of the 1959s, which were almost too rich, and lacked the balance of acidity. Several shippers provided what was lacking—and made a better wine—from the stocks of the leaner wine of the year before. The shipper can never use this as a means of stretching his vintage, because he is not allowed to sell more wine of any given year than he has made. In a certain sense, therefore, you can say that a vintage is a shipper's first-quality champagne.

Non-vintage   Most champagne is non-vintage. It does not carry a date on its label. The making of the *cuvée* is done on a different principle in the spring following an ordinary or mediocre year. The object is to maintain the constant standard of the brand by combining the new wine with stocks of the previous year or years to obtain a result as similar as possible to the wine of the current non-vintage. It is easy to see that this is one of the most skilled processes in the whole tricky field of wine-making. The tasters have to be able to foresee the future, after a further fermentation and three years in bottle, not of one wine but of a complicated combination of perhaps a dozen which they have before them. Only experience, of course, can make this possible. When the decisions have been taken and the *cuvée* made up and thoroughly mixed together, it must be bottled.

The young wine used to be bottled haphazardly, the makers knowing its tendency to ferment again in its bottle, but not knowing exactly how much it would ferment and what the resulting pressure in the bottle would be. Innumerable burst bottles were the result. It was not unknown for half the wine of a vintage to be lost in this way. When one bottle exploded, the sides of its neighbours would be stove-in, and the destruction would spread. The floors of the cellars were running with wine and crunchy with broken glass.

It is now possible, however, to add exactly the right quantity of sugar-syrup to the wine as it is being bottled, so that it will ferment a predictable amount, and the pressure in the bottle will rise to a predictable and tolerable level. Bottle-bursts are very rare now, although the champagne bottle still has to be much thicker and heavier than any other.

The wine will be at least two years in its bottle before the long and elaborate preparations for its final appearance begin. During this time it is lying in a stack in the cold, damp cellar, and the fermentation of the extra dose of sugar is imperceptibly going on. With no more oxygen than the tiny amount in the bottle and what can get through the cork, the life of the yeasts is not so energetic as it is in an oak cask. It will take them two years to convert all the sugar to alcohol. Occasionally the cellar-man will come along and rouse them up, giving each bottle a hearty shake to mix all the yeast thoroughly into the wine again and keep the fermentation going.

Only at the end of all this is it put in the *pupitres* to collect the sediment on the cork. To keep this process going all the time the shippers have to have enormous stocks of literally millions of bottles—another addition to the eventual cost of the wine. In this state, undisgorged, champagne will keep in perfect condition almost indefinitely. I have had a wine from the last century that had been kept *sur point,* standing on its head, for the last sixty years and only disgorged ten minutes before we drank it. But this pleasant habit can only be indulged by shippers and their friends, and by them only in their own houses above the cellars where the wine is kept.

Once the champagne is disgorged it is, in theory, ready to drink. In fact it improves immensely if it is kept a little longer for the dose to marry with the wine. There is a surprising amount of disagreement among experts on what should be a very easy thing to decide: whether it goes on improving after this, and whether it is, in fact, a wine which you can lay down with profit (not that there are many people who would or could) or not.

To me there is no question about it. A bottle of champagne is always worth keeping for a year or two before drinking. Vintage champagne can be worth keeping for ten years. In the course of time even non-vintage champagne seems to lose its sharpness, and broadens out in flavour. After several years it begins to lose a little of its sparkle, and become noticeably richer in flavour and colour. Eventually it will probably go almost flat and acquire what some people call a chocolate taste. It is usually avoided in this condition, and for this reason old champagne, if it ever crops up, is usually sold for less than new. In fact it can be superb. You should never pass by an opportunity of tasting it.

68

The vintage comes late in Champagne. The vineyards are red-leaved and the air is misty and chill by the time the last grapes are picked. The river Marne winds in the distance below the vines of Hautvillers

There are, broadly speaking, four classes of champagne on the market. The cheapest is that sold by a retailer under his own brand-name, which is known as his 'Buyer's Own Brand'. It is always recommended for parties, and there is rarely anything wrong with it. On the other hand, it is never the wonderful drink that champagne can be. Champagne is so expensive anyway that it seems a pity not to pay the little extra which is necessary to get a really good one.

B.O.B.s can do the champagne industry a great deal of harm by disappointing people who, tasting them, wonder what all the fuss is about. On the other hand, there are some which, in all fairness, are as good as or better than some of the shippers' marques.

The second class is non-vintage champagne with the French shipper's name. The leading dozen-odd names in the industry are household words. The biggest house, Moët & Chandon, has an astonishing turnover. The thirteen commonly thought of as the finest shippers are the following: Bollinger, Charles Heidsieck, Heidsieck Dry Monopole, Krug, Moët & Chandon, Mumm, Perrier Jouet, Piper Heidsieck, Pol Roger, Pommery & Greno, Louis Roederer, Taittinger, Veuve Clicquot.

To these might be added the names of Ayala, Besserat de Bellefon, De Castellane, Delbeck, Deutz & Geldermann, Henriot, Irroy, Lanson, Mercier, Ruinart.

Some houses raise their standards and some lower them as time goes on. No rating of these houses has any permanent value. It is nonetheless worth mentioning that if an *hors concours* class were to be made at present, the names which are likely to appear in it are among the following: Bollinger, Krug, Pol Roger, Louis Roederer, Veuve Clicquot.

Non-vintage champagnes from this class are good enough for practically anybody and practically any occasion. They are lighter than vintage wines and almost better, therefore, as aperitifs. For a party they are ideal: one could ask for nothing better.

For vintage champagne the same names apply. Normally nowadays a vintage is not put on the market until the stocks of the preceding one have been sold. This is a pity, because it deprives us, unless we have the forethought to keep some ourselves, of the pleasure of comparing two vintages side by side. Vintage champagnes are the ones to drink with food, if any are. Otherwise they are for keeping for occasions even more special than those that call out the non-vintage.

Several houses have put out a brand which is supposed to be even better than their vintage wine. In some cases it is a *blanc de blancs*, which is not necessarily better, though it may be more to your taste—lighter, more delicate, thinner in body. Some of the others, though, are what is known as *tête de cuvée*: wine made only from the first and most gentle pressing of the finest grapes, blended in the usual way but intended to be a superlative —even better than the same firm's vintage wine. Dom Pérignon, Moët's champagne named after the old monk, is the original one of these. There is always a suspicion that these •wines are made only for people who are anxious to spend as much as possible on a bottle; for whom the best is not good enough. Some *tête de cuvée* champagnes, in short, are the superlatives they are said to be, some are merely good champagne gift-wrapped. To buy one because it is more expensive is to lay yourself wide open to having your leg pulled.

Rosé
Pink champagne, made by mixing in some red wine, is very pretty. It used to be a fashion, and could, it seems to me, easily become one again. Nothing is more suggestive of pretty girls and shady lawns. What is more, with age it takes on a pale tawny colour which, lit with bubbles, is the most beautiful sight. In taste it is very similar to ordinary champagne. It is most certainly worth trying.

Crémant
Crémant means 'creaming'. Fully sparkling champagne is *mousseux*. *Crémant* has about half as much fizz. It is for some reason rarely seen, but it can be superb. The village of Cramant (in the white-grape area) is famous for it, which causes rather a confusion of names. *Crémant* should certainly be sought out by people who swizzle out the bubbles in normal champagne—a complete waste of all the long and expensive process of putting them there. It tends to be extremely light and delicate, gentle both in bubbles and taste—another drink which could easily become a craze.

Consumption
It is surprising to find that by far the greater part of the 70-odd million bottles of champagne which are sold every year stay in France. (In fact, 52 million of them, according to the 1964 figures.) The French are devoted champagne drinkers. There is hardly a café in the whole of France which cannot produce a bottle of a good make to order—and this despite the fact that it is barely cheaper in France than it is abroad.

Serving champagne
I have put champagne, you notice, among the aperitif wines. It is often said that champagne is the ideal wine right through any meal. This may help to sell more of it, but I do not think it is true. For almost any part of any given meal I could name a wine which was more exactly appropriate, and would make a better meal. To use champagne as we use *vin rosé,* to avoid making up our minds what other wines to choose, in the spirit of compromise, is to do it a great injustice.

Champagne is wonderfully, uniquely stimulating before a meal or at a party. On the other hand it has lost more potential admirers by being served when something else would have gone better than almost any other wine.

It loses friends by the dozen in cold marquees at tea-time on a rainy wedding-day, when a hot cup of tea would be far more to the point. It loses more friends when it is served with a great mound of roast beef, when the soul yearns for a fat red wine, and loathes the thin white one which is the only thing in sight.

70

One of the chief reasons why so many people say they do not like champagne is because they have it when they do not really want it—in that dripping marquee—and do not have it, because it is so expensive, when they do want it.

As an appetizer, or a party-maker, champagne is without a rival. The physiology of it—why champagne has a different effect from every other wine—seems to be something to do with the dissolved carbon dioxide in it. Although you see a good part of it escape in bubbles before you drink it there is still a good deal left dissolved when it goes down. The gas escapes, and carries the fumes to your head. Or alternatively it makes it easier for the stomach lining to absorb the alcohol. Whatever the reason, champagne produces its effect more quickly, keeps you on a pleasant level more steadily, and lets you down more gently than any other wine. It is the easiest of all drinks to serve. One of the effects of its long conditioning in the cellars of Reims or Epernay is that it is as stable as a rock. You never have to worry—as you do with other wines—about whether journeys have shaken it up, or whether a hot summer or a cold winter has spoilt it. It survives all these things.

Temperature
The only care you must take is not to shake it about too much in the hour or so before you uncork it, and see that it is reasonably cold. There is a tendency, particularly in the United States, to serve champagne as cold as a freezer can make it. This is quite a good way to serve a money-saving substitute for champagne, but it is a waste of the real thing. Neither the scent nor the taste can come out when it is icy. The temperature of a deep cellar is best: distinctly cool, perfectly refreshing, but not searingly cold in the throat like a can of lager out of the ice-box.

Glasses
Any big glass is good for champagne. There is no need for special glasses of any kind, though the beautiful flutes and tulips look very pretty. A goblet is good. A silver mug is better. André Simon, who so characteristically describes the champagne on a picnic in the country as 'a bottle of something cold', has the most perfect glasses for it I have ever seen. They are crystal half-pint mugs, each with a constellation of five stars engraved inside the bottom from which five columns of bubbles form and ascend in a steady stream.

There is one kind of glass which is no good for champagne, or any wine—the kind caterers, who have vast stocks of them they have to use, insist on calling a champagne-glass—a saucer on a stem.

Quantities
Each person has his own experience of his friends' drinking powers. Without experience it is difficult to predict how much champagne anyone will drink. Half a bottle per head is a minimum allowance for a party where champagne alone is being served. A man can usually drink a whole bottle in two hours without ill effects: there are only five or six (depending

71

on the size) glasses in a bottle. For this reason it is always worth getting champagne for a party in magnums, which hold two bottles. There are half as many corks to pull, and the sight of a magnum is a generous and cheering one. A magnum would last four people for a whole evening, or eight just for drinks before dinner.

Champagne can be bought in quarter-bottles (one good glass), half-bottles, double magnums and even bigger sizes. Anything bigger than a double magnum, however, is very hard to handle.

Other Sparkling Wines

FRANCE

THE CHAMPAGNE METHOD is now used all over France. There is hardly a wine-district which does not have a sparkling wine of one kind or another. The trouble, however, with most of them is that the process is used to make poor wine marketable, rather than—as is the case with champagne—to bring out the natural qualities of the best wine that can be made.

Vouvray

The best of the other sparkling wines comes from the Loire. If any of the districts can be said not to be following champagne, but making a first-class sparkling wine in its own right, it is Vouvray, in the ancient province of Touraine. Sparkling Vouvray tends to be a little richer and rounder than champagne, a reason why a good many people prefer it, if they would but admit it. There is more flavour of grapes about it, if a little less subtlety. It is never quite as dry as the driest champagne, but it is none the worse, in many people's opinion, for that.

The Vouvray vineyards cover a hill of chalk in the same way as those of Champagne, and, as in Champagne, the cellars are cut out of the chalk beneath. At Vouvray even the houses of the vintners are often cut straight into the rock. The wine they make is either made sparkling or left still; still white Vouvray can be a very good, rather sweet, wine.

Saumur

The Saumur area, following the Loire downstream and westwards, also produces a great deal of sparkling wine of very much the same kind as Vouvray, possibly not quite so good. The difference in price between these wines and champagne, once duty has been paid, tends to be so slight that it seems worth paying the extra for champagne. But, as I have suggested, I am sure there are a great many people who would not only be none the wiser, they would actually be happier to be given the Vouvray. The slight extra 'generosity of flavour', as they say in the trade, can be very 'comforting'.

The most famous of the sparkling wines of Saumur in Britain is Golden Guinea—a medium-sweet, gently muscat-flavoured wine. The brand has been popular for over fifty years. Oddly enough, such wines as this, brands which are well known all over the country, never excite comment nor even

72

get a mention in wine textbooks. The wine-conscious overlook them, but the public goes on buying them, which probably says more for their quality than a little passing acclaim.

Three other districts also have a long tradition of making sparkling wines (tradition is a thing worth taking into account, for it means they have not just jumped on the bandwagon to use up stocks). Their wines are St-Péray and Clairette de Die, both from a long way south down the Rhône valley, and Seyssel, from higher up the same valley, above Lyons.

St-Péray

Clairette de Die

Seyssel

St-Péray and Clairette have nothing in common with champagne except the sparkle. St-Péray is strong, golden and dry, a much heavier wine than any champagne, and to that extent better with food, if you like sparkling wine with food at all. Clairette de Die (Die is in the hills to the east of the Rhône valley, almost in Provence) is a slightly muscat-flavoured, slightly sweet and generally very well-made *méthode champenoise* wine without much delicacy. Seyssel, on the other hand, could be confused with champagne if anything could. It is not often seen, but when it is, it should be tasted. Dry, delicate and pale, it has the aperitif qualities to a high degree.

Sparkling burgundy

Sparkling burgundy is as often red as it is white. Sometimes it is made by the champagne method, sometimes not. The thing to bear in mind is that no-one would waste good burgundy by making it sparkle. To me there is something absurd and ungainly about sparkling red wine. It is like a fat old man dressed up as a fairy. Perhaps the best of the sparkling burgundies is neither the red nor the white but the pink, which glories in the name of

Oeil de Perdrix

Oeil de Perdrix—Partridge Eye. I do not remember ever having waited until I saw the pinks of a partridge's eyes, but it is expressive as a name, and the wine is good. There is excellent sparkling white burgundy to be had, too, but its recommendation is rather a negative one: it does not taste like white burgundy at all. It seems a pity for a wine to give up its native character, for it can never adopt another successfully. But good, if rather neutral, white burgundies there are, made by the champagne method.

Blanquette de Limoux

I should also mention Blanquette de Limoux, which is white—sometimes almost paper-white—and fairly delicate in taste, usually medium sweet. Limoux is near Carcassonne.

Cuve close

There are two common short-cuts in the making of sparkling wines. That of simply pumping them full of gas is only used for the very cheapest. It can never make bubbles which stay in the wine after it has been poured out. The wine froths for a moment and then is flat. The other method, perfectly respectable but still nothing like as effective as the long laborious business of the second fermentation in bottle, is known as the *cuve close*. By this method the wine is made to have a second fermentation, but in a pressurized vat rather than a bottle. The carbon dioxide is not allowed to escape, so it stays in the wine. The difficulty with the sediment is overcome completely: it is simply filtered out as the wine is bottled. Wine made like this foams well, and keeps a sparkle for a while—though not as long as the *méthode champenoise* wine. It is the sensible way to make cheap sparkling wine; the labour involved in doing it the long way would be out of all proportion to the value of the wine being treated.

Cuve close is used in Bordeaux to make very pleasant sparkling white wine. If a bottle of sparkling wine says nothing on the label about the champagne method being used you are pretty safe in assuming that this is what has been done.

Sparkling Bordeaux

ITALY

The most popular sparkling wine of Italy is Asti Spumante (*spumante* being Italian for sparkling). The characteristic taste of Asti is muscat. It is an unmistakable scent wherever the grape is used in a wine, even in small quantities, for no grape has such a strong smell. Even its skin is perfumed.

Asti Spumante

Asti Spumante is always more or less sweet—sometimes ravishingly so, the most honeyed mouthful imaginable. What makes it so drinkable is that the bubbles prevent the sweetness cloying. It is even refreshing, despite its sweetness. If there is any wine for a picnic by a stream, in long scented grass, with the sun winking in the ripples, it is Asti Spumante.

The town of Asti is in the hills south of Turin, not far from France and the Mediterranean, the country which grows several of Italy's best wines. It is a small country market-town, modest in its attractions and accommodation, but the scene of a major wine-converting industry. The local muscat wine is made there into either Spumante or vermouth. The firms of Martini, Gancia, Cinzano all make both.

It is a good idea to serve Asti Spumante very cold—much colder than champagne. When it is at all warm the taste seems to get out of hand, but when icy it is nicely balanced and slips down easily. It has a surprisingly low alcoholic strength—less than normal table wines—which makes it all the more suitable for drinking freely in warm weather.

Other Spumante

There is hardly a corner of Italy which does not make sparkling wine of some sort—but it is limited to local consumption and rarely worth seeking out. One or two have a name and reputation, and others deserve one.

Signor Ferrari of Trento, in the Italian Tyrol where German is almost as commonly heard in the streets as Italian, is typical in the scale of his operations, if not (unfortunately) in the quality of his wine. His premises are no bigger than the cellars of an old bishop's palace. (Trento was full of bishops for the twenty-odd years it took the Council of Trent to deliberate its counter-Reformation policy.) The labelling of the bottles is done by two small boys: the smaller one licks the labels and puts them on, the larger one puts them straight. The wine which is bottled under these conditions is much the best Italian sparkling wine I have had; very clean in taste, as dry as all but the driest of champagne. But it is not, I fear, typical.

GERMANY

In Germany a vast industry, as big as the champagne industry itself, has grown round the process of converting ordinary wine into sparkling wine. The product is known as *Sekt*—by tradition because an actor who was

74

famous for his Falstaff was always calling for sack when he wanted what used to be called *Schaumwein*, foaming wine.

Sekt varies from the rather nasty, cheap, chemical-tasting varieties to wines which are almost as expensive as champagne, and are therefore bound to be compared with it. I have never known one which did not suffer by the comparison, though one or two are excellent drinks of a rather different kind.

Sparkling Moselle The chief fault they have in common, to my taste, is rather too strong a flavour. The best I know is a sparkling Moselle, with many of the qualities of the still wine—but this is the best that can be said of it. The sparkle seemed to me to add nothing: perhaps it was hiding something. Wines from individual and famous estates are also, oddly enough, sometimes processed into sparkling wine. Presumably they are the wines of poor vintages. It would be a terrible waste of their successful wines.

The greater part of sekt, however, is made from wine imported in tankers to Germany from wherever it is cheapest—Italy, France, Africa or Spain. The processing of this wine is analogous to the making of vermouth rather than the making of champagne. The first object must be to remove whatever character of its own the wine has so that it can be made to taste 'German' by the addition of a little German wine or flavouring.

Such wine is immensely popular in Germany. There alone the annual sales are greater than those of champagne in the whole world. On top of this Germany is no mean market for French and other sparkling wines. One of the best things to do with sekt is to mix it with fresh orange-juice; to make, in fact, the drink which, made with champagne, is called Buck's Fizz. Sekt, in any case, should be served very cold. It is usually made dry, but a sweet type is also available.

SPAIN Catalonia, in the north-east, is the sparkling wine area of Spain. It was Perelada, one of the wines from this district, which lost a London High Court case brought by the champagne industry to prevent it being sold in England as Spanish champagne. *Xampan,* the Spanish phonetic equivalent (as *coñac* is of cognac) is still seen on labels in Spain.

Many of the Spanish sparkling wines are very good. In general they are made by the *méthode champenoise* rather than by any of the short-cut methods. Some sparkling white Rioja is made in the district near San Sebastián which is responsible for all the best Spanish table wines, but it is from Catalonia that the best *Espumoso* comes. It is never very dry, and rarely very sweet, but maintains a very pleasant drinkable middle path. The names Codorniu, Frexenet and Perelada I can vouch for personally.

California Californian sparkling wine is sold as champagne. It deeply vexes the French originators of the idea and the method, but there seems to be little they can do about it. The *champenois* can take some crumb of comfort from the thought that at least the wine which is sold under their name is one of the best made by their method in the world. Some of the *brut,* the driest, Californian sparkling wines are very fine—among California's best produce. A simplified version of the champagne method is now being used by some producers. They avoid the laborious process of *remuage* and *dégorgement* by decanting the wine, after it has re-fermented in its bottle, into a tank, and thence filtering it into another bottle. Almaden and Paul Masson are among the pioneers of this method. It results in rather shorter-lived bubbles than the original *méthode champenoise.* Adherents to the old way (Korbel is a good example) are now labelling their product 'fermented in *this* bottle', to emphasize the difference.

New York State

Moussec

None of these wines taste like champagne exactly, but they are superb aperitifs; light, delicate, as dry as can be. In Britain they are only of academic interest, because American production costs combined with high freight charges make them as expensive as champagne. In the United States, however, they are of the greatest possible interest. New York State 'champagne' is often called the best of the New York State wines. None of the wines of this state, however, are made of real wine grapes. All share a penetrating, un-winelike, scented taste.

Moussec is British sparkling 'wine', made by the *cuve close* method of second fermentation from concentrated grape juice brought from the borders of the Champagne area. The factory in Rickmansworth near London produces two kinds, sweet and dry, the sweet having, to my mind, a shade more character. Most of the firm's business is done in little one-glass bottles in bars. Only one champagne-shipper, they say, comes near the volume of their sales in England.

Madeira

SHERRY IS FIRST AND FOREMOST the drink for before a meal. Port is first and last the drink for after one. Madeira is not so simple, and not so fortunate. It seems almost to have lost its way. There was a time when Madeira was the first wine at every dinner: later it appeared as the last. The island still makes wines to fill both bills, but none of them succeed in the way port and sherry do.

Madeira's trouble was two terrible outbreaks of vine plague in the second half of the last century. Oidium was the first, phylloxera the second. It has never quite recovered from the blow. Nevertheless the wine made today is extremely good value and—unless you remember the wine they used to make—nothing to complain about. The main thing is that it has Madeira's special burnt taste, one of unforgettable character.

The island

Madeira was the first of Portugal's finds when she began sending out her explorers in the fifteenth century. The island lies five hundred miles out in

76

the Atlantic, west of Casablanca. Prince Henry the Navigator, the sponsor and inspiration of the voyages of discovery which brought to light, among other things, both the Cape of Good Hope and Cape Horn, took Madeira under his wing. When it was found the island was naturally enough uninhabited, but covered from shore to shore with trees. Prince Henry had these burnt, in a forest fire that lasted for years and covered the island with ash. On the bare and ashen remains he ordered the planting of vines.

Ageing treatment

Thus was consciously founded what later became, at one point, the greatest vineyard in the world. The wood-ash made the volcanic soil fertile, and Mediterranean sweet-wine vines were planted. The vines, ash and lava established the special sweet, sharp, smoky character of Madeira wine.

Experience showed that long exposure of the wine in its cask, after it was made, to the sun and air improved it enormously. Madeira is constitutionally strong: stronger than any other wine. Treatment which would finish off a lighter-built wine completely only brings out its finer points. Long sea voyages, which were in any case inevitable in delivering the wine to the Portuguese colonists round the Cape in the Eastern trading stations, were best of all for it. A combination of a year or two of cooking in the sun, and four or five months of rolling and pitching in the bilges of a galley or a carrack, smoothed and rounded it in an amazing way. The return voyage to the Indies, involving nearly a year of tropical heat and ship's movement, brought it to perfection. And yet the wine was still as tough as ever. It has never been known to have travelled too far or grown too old. As far as anyone knows it is immortal.

It is still possible to buy Madeira a hundred years old. Several merchants in Britain and the United States list considerable quantities of vintages from 1845 or so until about 1900, to this day. For wines of this age they are ridiculously cheap. Furthermore, unlike any other wine as old as this they are a completely safe buy: they have never been known to go off, or even fade, except in colour.

But the Madeiras we are considering as aperitifs are a slightly different matter. Modern Madeira is classified under four headings, corresponding to four different types of vine which are grown on the island. Two are dryish; the kind of thing you would want to drink before a meal. The other two you would be more inclined to drink after.

Only the very finest of the dessert wines, the Malmseys, are aged today in their casks under the sun. The rest are artificially heated in big sheds called *estufas* (stoves).

Sercial
Verdelho

The two drier types which are made in this way are called Sercial and Verdelho. What proportion of the wine actually comes from these two classical vines depends on the quality of wine you buy, but the idea is to follow their characters.

Sercial is the drier. It is a full, brown wine, with a superb perfume, but markedly sharp, which helps to make it appetizing. Verdelho is almost equally dry, but with a little fatness—a beginning of the peculiar buttery scent and soft flavour which distinguishes the dessert—and the best—Madeira wines.

A third kind, made, in theory, by blending the two above, is sold under the name of Rainwater. This unflattering, if rather pretty, name comes from the United States, which has traditionally been the island's best customer. A Mr Habisham of Savannah, Georgia, used to sell a particularly light and pleasant Madeira which was given this name, perhaps because he used to leave his casks outside, like rainwater-butts.

Madeira is a fortified wine, like port. The principle of its making is that a part of the sugar of the grapes—large for dessert wine, smaller for aperitif—is prevented from fermenting by the addition of alcohol in the form of cane-sugar spirit, a first cousin of rum. Thereafter it is stored in an *estufa* at a high temperature for at least a year. This treatment gives it its slightly burnt, caramel flavour. In California, curiously enough, a similar technique is used to make so-called sherry.

There used to be a good score of Madeira shippers, as there is of port shippers today. But lack of interest in Madeira, and the shortage of first-class wine, has led to massive amalgamation, so that, for all intents and purposes, Madeira today comes from one large enterprise, still using, however, the old companies' names, among which are Blandy, Cossart Gordon, Leacock, Henriques & Henriques, and Rutherford, Miles.

In most cases these names appear on two ranges of wines, under the grape-names Sercial, Verdelho, Bual and Malmsey, making eight wines in all—a complete scale from dry to sweet in two price-ranges.

Sercial, Verdelho and Rainwater are all equally suitable for drinking before a meal, in place of sherry. Like dry sherry, they are much better for being chilled for half an hour before they are drunk. As the rich and powerful scent is half the joy, it is important to use large glasses, in which it gets a chance to expand.

A full account of port comes later, in the After-Dinner Wines section. It occurs here, however, in its white version, which has recently been launched in England as an aperitif. Personal taste is bound to obtrude into a book about wine, and I might as well come clean. White port is not my drink.

There is no difficulty about making port with white grapes instead of red, or about making it dry instead of sweet. The difficulty comes, it seems to me, in making it taste as though it was a good idea.

It is not a new idea. Port has been made white as well as red for centuries. But the reason it has not been popular in all these years is the reason it is not particularly exciting now: it is heavy, ungraceful. It cannot stand comparison with even an indifferent sherry.

In fact tawny port (see the After-Dinner Wines section, p. 229) makes an excellent aperitif—much better than white port. Both need chilling if you are going to drink them as appetizers; either by being left in the refrigerator for half an hour or with a lump of ice in the glass—one lump, not the full 'on the rocks' treatment.

OTHER APERITIF WINES

There is no sharp dividing-line between aperitifs and table wines. Most people find that high-strength and sparkling wines are better on their own before a meal, but there are a great many wines which are neither high-strength nor sparkling which go as well as ever before a meal. One or two, in fact, have the aperitif qualities in such a degree that there seems to be no better time to drink them.

Château-Chalon

Château-Chalon is the most peculiar of these. It is most like very light sherry: yet it is not sherry. It is never fortified, yet it lives to a great age and builds up to a good strength.

It belongs to the family of *vins jaunes*—yellow wines—from the Jura mountains in eastern France. The town of Arbois nearby is famous for a number of wines; white, grey (the local name for rosé), red and yellow. Arbois yellow is unusual, and good with the dish of chicken which is cooked in it, but Château-Chalon is a different wine altogether.

Its oddity is due to the fact that, through some vinish freak, it is the only French wine to grow the *flor* which is found on the best sherry. Southern Spain has it, South Africa has it and this one village in France has it.

Flor gives Château-Chalon the ability to age for seven or eight years in cask, far longer than would be good for a normal white wine. It also gives it the strange, yeasty, soft freshness which is found in a good fino. In fact it is lower in strength than sherry, less dry and more acid. It is remarkable, perhaps, more because of its peculiarity than because of its ultimate quality. Yet—and also despite its formidable price—it is well worth trying. It is a good reminder that there are worthy things in the world of wine outside the usual circle of sherry, hock, claret and port.

The Château-Chalon bottle is unmistakable. It is short and dumpy—locally called the *clavelin*. It is worth using large glasses to enjoy the special scent. Over-chilling kills it.

Chinese dry white

Into the category of unusual wines which are really best drunk before a meal comes perhaps the greatest curiosity of all, a Chinese white wine—a red Chinese white wine, in fact. It comes from Shantung, or so I gather from its modest label. It is extremely palatable, very dry, with a reasonable scent and a distant cousinship of flavour to a light sherry. It is only available in half-litre bottles, and is by no means cheap, but its sheer curiosity value and, to some extent, its quality make it well worth trying.

Lagoa

There is a less exotic wine, similar to sherry, from the Lagoa vineyards in southern Portugal, called Afonso III. There is an excellent high-strength

Vernaccia

dry white wine called Vernaccia in Sardinia—there are, in fact, wines of this type from more places than I shall ever know about. But they are almost never shipped to be sold abroad. The wine trade has to specialize to some extent. Nobody would argue that in choosing sherry among all these strong wines to specialize in it has neglected anything which is even comparable in quality and range.

In the Frenchman's ceaseless quest for new things, and particularly new sweet things, to drink—he is the mortal enemy of his liver—he has produced countless curiosities. Fortified wine is not—may I be forgiven—France's forte. But she has a product called muted wine, which has never been allowed to ferment at all. In this case, brandy is added to fresh grape-juice before fermentation has started. The yeast is doped by the alcohol and never gets to work. The resulting drink is as sweet as the grape-juice and as strong as the brandy, without having the characteristic winey taste of anything which has ever fermented. The two most famous of these concoctions are the specialities of the Cognac and Champagne areas. They are called,

respectively, Pineau des Charentes (the two Charentes are the two *départements* of France in which cognac is made) and Ratafia. When they are old they can be good, though I think it is fair to say that they are a taste that has to be acquired. Ratafia is sometimes flavoured with almonds. It was one of the favourite cordials of Victorian England, but it is rarely seen today.

Vermouths and Patent Aperitifs

QUOIQUE CE SOIT—'whatever this may be'—was the name of a French patent aperitif in the last century. It might be the motto of all patent aperitifs to this day.

A vermouth, or a patent aperitif—and in this class go all the tribe of Byrrh, Dubonnet, Campari, Lillet, Pernod—is a conspiracy of silence. It is offered as a drink with one particular, unchanging taste. You can take it or leave it. You will never know what is in it.

Vermouths are flavoured and fortified wine. Wine is their base and gives them their character. Its strength is brought up to about the strength of sherry, or a little above, with pure alcohol. It is sweetened with sugar, and flavoured with any number of herbs and spices. Among the classical, and probably universal, flavouring agents is wormwood, whose German name, *vermuth,* gives the drink its name.

Vermouth has its origin in the medieval, and even older, practice of improving wine which had gone sour, or which was otherwise not worth drinking. Honey and herbs were the original additives. It has developed into a major industry, particularly in Italy.

The vermouth country is the foothills of the Alps on both sides of the French and Italian border. Turin is the capital city of vermouth. Broadly speaking there are two kinds, which still tend to be known as French and Italian, although both are made in Italy now more than in France. French

80

is the drier, and Italian the sweeter of the two. Italian comes in two colours, *bianco* and *rosso*. Each of the major Italian manufacturers therefore has at least three main products: dry white, sweet white and sweet red.

The dry white vermouth is the flavouring in the gin of a dry martini, the most famous of all cocktails. It is highly perfumed, with an elusive herb-and-spice scent which makes it a very good drink on its own, iced, on the rocks or with soda. *Noilly Prat* is perhaps the most famous of the French manufacturers of this style of vermouth. The vermouth of Chambéry, a small town near the Italian border, is less known, but is generally considered to be France's best. It is particularly dry, rather lighter in flavour than most, and mixes well. The firm of Dolin in Chambéry have a particularly delicious speciality of making their vermouth with the juice of wild strawberries. The pink, slightly sweeter than usual Chambéryzette, as it is called, is a wonderful spring and summer aperitif. I sometimes make a cup by mixing it with *vin rosé* which, if you are susceptible to pretty colours, is extremely agreeable.

The sweeter version of white vermouth is typified by Cinzano bianco. It seems usually to have a rather more richly coloured label than the pale green of the dry one. (Vermouth labels all follow a pattern of curious circus-poster Baroque which suits the drink so well that they could never be changed.) Bianco is perhaps less good for mixing, and better on its own, than dry vermouth. It needs icing; without ice it is rather syrupy. With an edge of lemon and a touch of soda it is excellent. Red vermouth is the essential ingredient in any number of well-known cocktails. Americanos and Manhattans depend on it. I prefer it half and half with the dry white to straight, but as a straight drink it is treated in the same way as the bianco.

Two brands of vermouth are made in England; Votrix and Duval. Both are made by the same process as British 'wine', by fermentation of preserved and concentrated grape must in Britain, followed in this case by the usual addition of sugar, herbs and spirit. The saving in duty from not importing anything which contains alcohol makes these several shillings cheaper than imported vermouths. They are perhaps the least obviously British of British wine-type products.

On the fringe of vermouth and almost overlapping into the next section, patent aperitifs, there are one or two Italian dark and sweet ones with the addition of quinine. Quinine provides a bitter element which is strangely appetizing. The finest example of this type is Carpano's famous Punt e Mes. The name means 'point and a half', and has its origin among the stockbrokers of Milan who used to order it, for some reason, with this cryptic phrase. It is at the same time extremely sweet and extremely bitter, a contradictory but compelling combination. It needs icing.

In places this craze for quinine has got quite out of hand. In Spain you will meet with Sherry Kina, sherry with quinine added, which has a certain saloon-bar public. In Italy there is a Chinato made from Barolo, the best of Piedmontese red table wines. Cynar, another curious aperitif with quinine

Noilly Prat
Chambéry

Chambéryzette

Cinzano bianco

Rosso

Votrix
Duval

Quinine aperitifs

Punt e Mes

Sherry Kina
Barolo Chinato
Cynar

81

flavour, is made from artichokes, and has a faint, rather pleasant, artichoke flavour. The most popular application of quinine in England, of course, is in tonic-water.

Patent aperitifs

Patent aperitifs are so nearly related to vermouths at one end of the scale that it is hard to distinguish them. At the other, however, they get nearer to gin. They can, in fact, be either based on wine or on spirits. The dividing-line is easy to spot by the price, if nothing else. The spirits are twice as expensive. I include them here for clarity's sake, although they have nothing to do with wine.

The enormous family of drinks which the French use before meals, or at any other time, are evidence of the nation's sweet tooth. All French aperitifs are sweet. They drink port as an aperitif; they have never heard of sherry. It is a curious contradiction that, as far as aperitifs go, the French are children: as far as everything else concerning the stomach goes, they are gods.

I cannot hope to repeat all the names of all the potions stocked by French bars. They greet you, often in truncated form, among the peeling posters at the entrance to every grey French village: Dubonnet, both red and white (which is also made under licence in California); St-Raphaël, red and white; Lillet, white (drier than most); Byrrh, red; Cap Corse from Corsica. In bars in France they are often served at bar temperature. They all taste much better iced.

Dubonnet
St-Raphaël
Lillet
Byrrh
Cap Corse

The other names you see in France, Italy and increasingly at home are those of spirit-based aperitifs, which cover an even wider range. It is perhaps useful to divide these into bitters and sweets.

Bitters are either always diluted to some extent for straightforward drinking, or are dripped into other drinks to point up the flavour. The chief drinking-bitters are Campari (the brilliant red, extremely bitter Italian champion, which is also sold in little bottles already mixed with soda), Amer Picon, Fernet Branca and Underberg. The last two are medicinal, and are claimed to be good for hangovers. Amer Picon is black and bitter; it needs the addition of orange-juice or grenadine to sweeten it. There is also a strange French drink called Suze, which is bright yellow and tastes of gentian. It is good on the rocks; too pungent for mixing.

Campari
Amer Picon
Fernet Branca
Underberg

Suze

Angostura

The bitters you drip need not keep us long. Angostura—the Worcester Sauce of the drink world—is the best known. The best use I know for it is in making what its advertisements call Pink Ice—adding it to the water in the ice-cube tray. It can easily be overdone.

Pernod
Ricard
Pastis
Ouzo

The sweet section is the monopoly of the *anis* drinks: Pernod, Ricard, Pastis from France and Ouzo in Greece. When neat, they are clear and slightly yellow. Diluted with water, which is how they must be drunk, they go cloudy like milk. There is no absinthe in them, as there once was, but they nonetheless need watching. They taste insidiously harmless and soft, although they are stronger than brandy.

82

White Table Wines

WHITE IS REALLY the wrong word for these wines. Any wine which is not distinctly red or pink is described as white, whether it is really the palest possible gold or almost brown. In fact there is a far greater variety of white wines than of red. Among the reds there are no differences as great as that between a tart, prickling Muscadet and a deep gold, syrupy Sauternes. As the companion of food white wine ranges much wider, too. There are many dishes which would lose everything by being eaten with a red wine, but hardly one which has not a perfect match somewhere in the endless list of the world's white wines.

With a few exceptions—which include some of the most wonderful wines of all—the essence of white wine is freshness. It must always have a suggestion of acidity about it—just as even the ripest of peaches does. We drink white wines cold so that the temperature adds to the sensation of freshness in the mouth. Most white wines also have a little sweetness in them—enough to balance the sharpness of fruit. Those with a great deal of sugar—so much, sometimes, that the liquid moves like oil in the glass—are kept for drinking after the meal as dessert wines.

The real difference between white and red wines lies not in the colour but in the way that they are made. Briefly, white wine is pressed, while red wine is squeezed.

Each wine-making area has its own methods, which vary in detail so much that sometimes they are hardly recognizable. Yet the underlying

83

rule is universal: to make white wine you get the juice out of the grapes as quickly as possible, separate juice from skins and let the juice ferment and become wine on its own. For red wine you merely break the grapes open to get a pulpy mass of juice, pips and skin. Fermentation starts with the complete crushed grape. Each component contributes something to the eventual wine.

Since white wines are made without the grape-skins it does not matter what colour they are. Some white wine is made from white grapes, some from black, some from both. What matters is that the juice is white. One class of grapes has not only black skins, but red juice as well. They are known as *teinturiers*—dyers—and are the only ones which cannot be used for making white wine.

Unlike red wines, white wines start life ready to drink. Their make-up is simpler. The extra flavours which red wine gets out of the skins during fermentation take time to settle down. While they are very young they are (there are exceptions to this rule, of course) hard to the taste—positively unpleasant to hold in your mouth. Most ordinary white wines, on the other hand, are drinkable the day they stop fermenting. They still have a great deal to gain by staying in barrel for a while, and some, mainly the best ones, from being kept for several years in bottle, but there is nothing inherently undrinkable about them new: they are merely not at their best.

Dryness and sweetness

The natural process of fermentation makes grape-juice into wine by converting sugar into alcohol. The amount of sugar in a normal ripe grape can all be turned to alcohol without any trouble. If the fermentation is allowed to go on until it finishes of its own accord there will—unless the grape is abnormally ripe, as it is in making Sauternes—be no sugar left. The wine will be completely dry, or very nearly so: the natural state of light white wine.

Something has to be done if the wine-maker wants to produce medium wine, as he often does. He has to stop the fermentation before all the sugar has gone. What is more difficult, he has to prevent it starting to ferment again, as it normally would, at some later stage. He does this by getting rid of the yeast, without which the fermentation cannot take place.

To stop his wine from fermenting out, and drying out, completely, the vintner either doses it at the appropriate stage, when there is a little sugar left, with sulphur dioxide, which puts the yeast to sleep, or he refrigerates it, or he seals the tank where it is and puts the liquid under high pressure. In any of these circumstances fermentation will stop.

He then has to get rid of the yeast, which he can do in various ways, of which fine filtering is one. He must then keep the wine under completely sterile conditions and finally put it, with another dose of sulphur dioxide, in sterilized bottles.

All this is extra trouble and expense to him. Wine processed in this way is therefore certain to cost more than the natural wine. It obviously has a wide appeal, or he would not trouble to do it, but it is never as good, in any real

84

analysis, as wine which has gone its own natural way and ended up dry, with scents and savours of its own.

You can be pretty sure that this denaturing process has been applied to any fairly cheap, sweet or medium-sweet, light and low-strength table wine. Very sweet wines are a different matter (see the After-Dinner Wines section).

White Burgundy

IF IT MATTERED whether or not the wines in this book were put in order of importance there would be two major rivalries: between Bordeaux and Burgundy for the first place among red table wines, and between Burgundy and Germany for the first place among white table wines.

I put Burgundy first out of personal prejudice—though I would rather call it taste—and, perhaps more important, from a very realistic consideration: it is relatively easy to find a very good bottle of white burgundy at almost any wine-merchants at a reasonable price. The equivalent excellence in German wine would cost you almost twice as much.

Having rated white burgundy as the finest white wine in the world I must immediately qualify this claim. I am not comparing it with champagne or sherry, and both Germany and Bordeaux produce equally glorious white wines of a completely different kind. But the principal glory of Sauternes and the German vineyards is wine so sweet that it leaves the ranks of table wine. Nobody would want to drink it during the course of a meal. It is for sipping with dessert, with a peach or some grapes or on its own, and belongs to the After-Dinner Wines section. So white burgundy is left as the greatest still, dry white wine grown anywhere in the world.

Its qualities are essentially savoury ones. The least among white burgundies is fresh and fair, refreshing and enticing; the greatest is rich and sappy, dry without exception, but fat with flavour. Its perfume can have a haunting fruitiness, a really peach- or apricot-like quality, without being sweet. It can be soft and succulent or hard and strong.

Burgundy is not one neat continuous wine-district, growing white wine here, red there, but an old and extensive duchy in which several separate wine districts happen to lie. In French it is *Bourgogne*. It is odd to think that the splendid name of Burgundy, with its undertones of thunder, should not be its own, but a mere anglicized version of the real name, for it is tremendously evocative of the ancient glories of France. I can never say it without seeing in my mind's eye the grand gaunt figure of the Duke of Burgundy in the film of *Henry V,* pleading for peace:

> Her vine, the merry cheerer of the heart,
> Unpruned dies; her hedges even-pleached . . .
> Put forth disordered twigs; her fallow leas
> The darnel, hemlock and rank fumitory
> Doth root upon, while that the coulter rusts . . .

His velvet cap and gown, regally red, his voice, a reverberating bass, stand for a land of country riches, of fat pastures and rich upland, of farmyards full of poultry and fields full of cattle—above all, for the long broad-backed hill of vines called the Côte d'Or.

The Côte d'Or (Hill of Gold) is Burgundy's backbone from north to south. Its eastern flank supports half of the most famous names in the whole wine-drinking world: Chambertin, Clos de Vougeot, Romanée, Nuits-St-Georges, Corton, Beaune, Pommard and Volnay for red wines; Montrachet, Meursault and Corton-Charlemagne for white.

And yet Burgundy has more. To the north, as though hurrying to get to Paris, lies Chablis; to the south, heading for Lyons, lie Mâcon, with the white wines of Pouilly-Fuissé, and the Beaujolais, the lovely high hills round Beaujeu, a cornucopia of light, sweet, succulent red wine. If you go west, over the mountains of the Morvan or the Charollais, famous for France's best beef, you come, within eighty miles, to the upper valley of the Loire, where the spice-scented white wines of Sancerre and Pouilly-Fumé grow. If you go east, across the wide plain of the river Sâone, you come to the Jura, where the wine is a rainbow of red, white, pink and yellow.

Burgundy, in short, lies in the heart of France. On one side of her the beef is, say the French, the world's best; on the other side, in Bresse, it is the chickens. It is simple farming country. Burgundy has none of the orderliness, daintiness even, the feeling that vineyards are a form of parkland or that each grey château is the manor of its particular plot, which is the characteristic of Bordeaux. There is a noticeable lack of seigneurial houses dominating the Côtes. In fact there are very few large estates.

In Burgundy most of the land belongs to small farmers. They live in the villages, make their wine in the villages, and go out to work with their own, and their families', hands among their own vines. Where, at the harvest, many of the proprietors of Bordeaux can fill two or three hundred barrels with their new wine, most Burgundian farmers are lucky if they can fill thirty or forty. The total production of fine wine in Bordeaux is often ten times that of Burgundy.

Burgundy, therefore, is a picture of small units in a small frame. The finest burgundies come from a pitifully small slope of hill. The world-demand for them is insatiable. In view of how little wine there is and how many people want it, it is quite extraordinarily cheap.

Names and the trade in Burgundy

Much as everyone would like everything about Burgundy to be as straight-forward as the rows of vines and the cherry-trees in the peaceful landscape, the situation, unfortunately, has become more and more confused over the years. Stories of faking and cooking come to be attached to Burgundy more than any other wine-district. Before looking at the wines themselves it is worth seeing how they get their names.

Like any European countryside, Burgundy consists of parishes, and within the parishes, of fields. Where in England there might be a hillside divided into fields called Acre Piece, Colman's Bank, Half-mile Bottom and Tinkerpot Shaw, in Burgundy you have Cailleret-Dessus, En Champans, Carelle-sous-la-Chapelle, En l'Ormeau, Les Mitans, Brouillards. The Burgundian name for these fields, where they are planted with vines, is *climats*.

Climats

As time goes on it becomes apparent that some of these *climats*, despite changes of ownership, always tend to make better wine than their neighbours. As these names become known the wine from the lucky plots goes to market with its own name while the rest simply goes under the name of its village. In some cases, where the village was not on a road and the local market was in another, more accessible, village, the wine might even not bother with its own village's name, but be sold, and asked for again, under the name of the market where it was bought.

Thus, for example, the red wines of the villages of Chassagne and Santenay used to go to market at the village of Pommard. Their wine was known as the wine bought at Pommard (which in any case is a good simple name to remember). In fact, it was often considerably better than the wine grown at Pommard itself.

This loose, informal trading system was adequate for simpler times. At the beginning of this century, though, it was being so much abused that action had to be taken. A law was passed, a well-meaning but misinformed attempt to regulate the use of names. Pommard, it said, must be grown in Pommard: Santenay must be sold as Santenay.

The situation now was not good, either for Pommard or for Santenay; least of all for the customer. Any wine, however poor, grown in Pommard now had the sole and exclusive use of all the reputation and goodwill built up by Pommard in conjunction with its neighbours. Santenay, on the other hand, had no market at all. No-one had heard of it.

Certain towns and villages which had always been centres of commerce and handled the wine of the whole region—Beaune, Meursault, Pommard, Volnay—were sitting pretty. Many of the others, to identify themselves, adopted the names of their best-known wines, a habit which had been growing for many years. Thus Chassagne took the name of the famous Montrachet *climat,* which lies half in the parish, and became Chassagne-Montrachet. Gevrey took the name of Chambertin. Puligny, which has the other half of Montrachet, also attached its famous name and became Puligny-Montrachet. Nuits became Nuits-St-Georges. Chambolle claimed the splendid name of Musigny. Vosne, where the Romanée vineyards lie, called itself Vosne-Romanée. Gilly, the hamlet dwarfed by the great Clos de Vougeot, was known as Gilly-les-Vougeot for a while. But now the Gilly has almost been forgotten—it is referred to simply as Vougeot.

Naturally this move had the desired effect. Chassagne had been unknown, and unsaleable. Chassagne-Montrachet was unmistakable. Of course, it had something to do with that wonderful Montrachet. There is always the possibility that someone may think it must be better, in the way that Fotheringay-Jones must be better than plain Jones.

The fact that the only connection between a Chassagne-Montrachet and a Montrachet is that they have the same parish priest and the same postman is not immediately obvious. The important thing, that they have different soil on a different slope, and that Montrachet comes from one specific, superlative vineyard, and Chassagne-Montrachet from any old patch of vines within the village boundaries, can easily be forgotten.

The vineyards are subdivided

The complications of Burgundy do not end here. Even within the illustrious *climats* whose names have been borrowed all is not as simple as it seems.

Hardly any of the vineyards belong to one man. The wine which any two men make, even of the same grapes from the same soil in the same season, will not be identical. One leaves it to ferment longer, one not so long; one picks out the unripe or overripe grapes, another leaves them in; one starts picking two or three days before the other—one, in fact, will always be better than another. When you have narrowed it down to one vineyard and one vintage, therefore, in Burgundy you will still be offered, perfectly honestly, several different wines.

And in some cases the fault is partly that of the vineyard itself. The soil of a hillside is never exactly the same from top to bottom and from side to side. Yet several vineyards spread from the valley right up the hill, from flat land to a steep tilt, through a variety of soils. The wine, therefore, although all bearing the vineyard's name, will vary enormously according to which part of the vineyard it comes from. The most notorious example of this is the famous Clos de Vougeot, whose 120 acres include everything from Burgundy's best soil to the most ordinary flat valley-land, all entitled to the same great name.

These are the internal difficulties of the trade in Burgundy. The result of it all is that the dealers in wine have to resort to blending. It is impossible to trade with goods which have so little consistency, unless they are worth the very high price which this kind of specialized business is bound to charge. In Germany there are some cases where the wines of different casks, even of

88

the same picking and pressing, are kept apart, unblended, and are eventually labelled with their cask numbers. But they cannot possibly cost less than £4 or £5 a bottle; as collector's items they cannot be the basis of a consumer trade.

Burgundy has kept both kinds of business as far as it can. On the upper level it maintains a business in individual wines from individual growers in named vineyards—a business which can only be done with wines which are intrinsically worth the extra trouble and extra costs involved. For the rest it buys in bulk from anyone who has wine to sell, and makes up what it hopes are typical and representative wines in the blending vats.

The first and most important thing, then, about Burgundy is to distinguish an individual estate wine from a merchant's blend. Unfortunately, one sometimes has to do this with less than the full co-operation of the designers of labels. But the first thing is to know which is the name of a village and which the name of a vineyard.

Classification

The official, definitive classification of the vineyards by quality has never been done in Burgundy as it has in Bordeaux, or at any rate part of Bordeaux. The Burgundian system, which is generally accepted, though not official, takes a local view of comparative excellence. The best vineyard of each *finage*, or parish, is the *tête de cuvée*, or first-growth, sometimes also called a *Grand Cru*. Where more than one are superb there are several *têtes de cuvée*; where none reach the standard suggested by the name there need not be any.

Vineyards of the second rank are known, confusingly enough, as *Premiers Crus* (first-growths); third-rank vineyards are called second-growths.

Not too much weight is placed on these rankings. Unevenness of quality from *finage* to *finage* means that the *tête de cuvée* of one may be less good than the *Premier Cru* of another. In practice, the *tête de cuvée* wines very rarely mention their rank on labels, nor do any wines below *Premier Cru*. The thing to remember, in fact, is that when you see *Premier Cru* on a label, with or without the name of the vineyard (if it is without it will probably be a blend of several) it does not mean first-growth in the Bordeaux sense. It really just means one of the good growths.

Domaine-bottling

The usual Burgundy word for an estate is *domaine*. Domaine-bottled is the equivalent of the Bordeaux château-bottled. It is harder to find domaine-bottled burgundies than it is to find château-bottled clarets, which abound on every wine-list. Very few estates in Burgundy have the facilities for bottling. One wine-merchant has even overcome the problem for the growers by having a truck fitted up with all the necessary equipment and backing it into their courtyards, bottling the wine there and then and carrying it away with him, domaine-bottled.

Although domaine-bottling is usually only carried out with good wines it is no real evidence of their quality. It could be done by anybody. Many

89

people say that some British wine-merchants are better at the cellar-work of bottling than Burgundians.

In the United States, though, it is almost assumed that a wine has been tampered with unless it was bottled at the domaine or château. Domaine-bottled wines are, therefore, much more common there than they are in Britain.

THE WHITE WINES

Less than a quarter of the wine made in Burgundy is white. All white burgundy is dry. It ranges in price from almost the cheapest French white wine to about the price of a bottle of vintage champagne. But at that you have one of the very finest wines that money can buy.

Chablis

Chablis and Sauternes are probably the best-known, and most imitated, white wines in the world. Chablis is taken to be the archetypal dry young white, very fresh, rather hard, a trifle green. The description fits the ordinary cheap wines of Chablis well enough, and they are the kind which are best known, but it comes nowhere near the extraordinarily scented and powerful great growths. It is a common mistake to think that Chablis is just Chablis and that's that. From the tiny town, in fact, comes as wide a range of quality and price as from the whole of Burgundy.

Chablis is only fifteen minutes' drive down Sussex-like lanes from the autoroute which is being built from Paris to the south. In a few years' time the autoroute is going to burst right through the Côte d'Or, flying on a bridge over the vineyards of Beaune (what effect it will have on the Marconnets vineyard underneath is anyone's guess). So far it has only got to between Auxerre and Chablis.

The little town lies in a valley, straddling the dreamy little river Serein, all ducks and reeds. It is grey, a good part of it is very old, and by eight in the evening it is dead. Round the bridge, as in so many towns of central France, the old buildings have been destroyed and ugly new concrete ones have taken their place. It was a tank battle that ruined the centre of Chablis.

But it is not the town, but the hills to the south and north-east which are important. Immediately above the town to the north they are at their steepest, and here, for a stretch of a mile and a half, the *Grands Crus*, the superlative wines, grow. The names of the *Grand Cru* vineyards are Bougros, Les Preuses, Moutonne, Vaudésir, Grenouilles, Valmur, Les Clos and Les Blanchots. In the area round them are several other bigger vineyards which are perhaps better known, since their wine has a wider circulation. They include La Fourchaume, Vaulorent and Montée de Tonnerre. There are about a score of these, which are entitled to call themselves Chablis *Premier Cru*. Below this level the wine can only be called plain Chablis, without a vineyard name. There is an appellation below that of Chablis; Petit Chablis, used for light wines from the outlying parts of the district which have less alcohol than Chablis proper. In poor, sunless years it is common for even good growths to fail to contain the necessary amount of alcohol: in this case,

The Grands Crus

Premier Cru

Petit Chablis

90

so long as they achieve 9·5 per cent alcohol, they can call themselves Petit Chablis.

In general, then, the identifying mark of the best Chablis is one of the eight names of vineyards above, plus the term *Grand Cru*. No-one is obliged to name the vineyard if he does not want to. It could just be Chablis *Grand Cru*, but it is unlikely. Chablis *Premier Cru*, on the other hand, since not all the vineyards entitled to call themselves this are well known, is much more often found without the name of the individual *climat*.

The taste of one of these great Chablis is bone-dry, but by no means thin. They have a remarkably powerful scent, and a flavour which I can only describe as slightly mineral, rather than fruity. In alcoholic degrees they can be formidable. I have heard of one wine which in 1959—admittedly a very hot year—reached an unprecedented 17 per cent alcohol. The Chablis qualities which are found all the way down the line to the Petit Chablis are the same, only less marked. It is never remotely sweet, always slightly stony in flavour. What you are paying for in one of the superior growths is greater strength—of everything, not just alcohol: strength of character, of scent, of taste, and length of rich lingering after-taste.

In poor years, which are common, none of these things are found. The best wines are cut down to size and the worst wines are not worth drinking. The greater part of the common wines of Chablis, in any case, are the restaurant-drinking of the neighbourhood and Paris.

Chablis grows something like a tenth of the wine which is sold as Chablis. It is one of the world's most imitated wines. There is very little hope, in fact, that the carafe white wine in fish restaurants which is called Chablis really is. On the other hand it is usually agreeable, and answers its purpose of washing down oysters and sole well enough.

St-Bris-le-Vineux
There are a number of white wines from the same area which might be described as sub-Chablis. The village of St-Bris-le-Vineux has evidently been noted for its contribution for some time. It makes a very light dry wine from the Sauvignon, the white grape of Bordeaux and the Loire rather than of Burgundy. The effect, here, however, is to make something a little like the familiar Muscadet of Brittany. It is not a wine which is shipped, but it is a good example of the kind of thing to look for among the local wines when you are travelling in France. Drink St-Bris in the restaurant of the Hotel de la Ville d'Auxerre at Toucy, between Auxerre and Briare, before eating the *Escalope de veau à la tante Nini*. Aunt Nini's sauce is made with sorrel, lemon-juice and cream.

The Côte de Nuits
Having started in the north of Burgundy with Chablis we will take the other white-wine vineyards in order as we go south. The first we meet are in the line of hills between Dijon and Nuits-St-Georges, the part of the Côte d'Or which is known as the Côte de Nuits.

The Côte De Nuits is in fact almost pure red. Only four of its villages make any white wine at all, and that in quantities so small that it is almost never seen. It is, however, supremely good, as good as any other white wine in France except that from just down the road. It is one of the curiosities which make wine all the more fascinating to find the name of a familiar red wine on a bottle of white. It can happen with Musigny, a superb, full, dry wine, with Morey-St-Denis, Clos de Vougeot, and with Nuits-St-Georges. The peculiarity of these wines is their similarity to their red brothers. It is perfectly possible to shut your eyes, drink an old Clos Blanc de Vougeot, and imagine that you are drinking the red wine. You can always spot the difference, but it is the similarity which is more striking.

The Côte de Beaune   The southern half of the Côte d'Or, after the town of Nuits-St-Georges, and a break in the hills where the Comblanchien free-stone quarries have turned old vineyards into an ugly scar of industry, it is the white-wine half. Beaune, the beautiful old walled town which gives this part of the Côtes its name, lies near its northern end.

Beaune   Of the wine of Beaune itself only a very small part, from the vineyard called Clos des Mouches, is white. It is very good, but Beaune means, almost exclusively, red wine.

Savigny-les-Beaune   The same is true of Savigny-les-Beaune, the little village with one of Burgundy's few châteaux which borders Beaune on the north-west, up under the hillside. Most of its wine is red; a little is white. They are not Burgundy's very best, but they are almost always worth buying, and are comparatively cheap.

There are three key white-wine names in the Côte de Beaune: Corton-Charlemagne, Meursault and Montrachet. Together with Chablis and Pouilly-Fuissé they make up the total of the great white burgundies—or rather the white burgundies which can be great, for the names of Montrachet and Meursault, in certain combinations, are as applicable to ordinary wine as they are to fine or great wines.

Corton-Charlemagne   Corton-Charlemagne is exceptional. There is only one Corton-Charlemagne. It is the vineyard at the western end of the south side of a curious round hill which juts out from the Côte north of Beaune. The eastern end, above the village of Aloxe, is a red-wine vineyard, Corton. No visible line divides the two parts, but somewhere on that hillside, perhaps by a certain tree or alongside a hut, the exposure changes from south-east to south-west—and makes all the difference between a wine for the fish and a wine for the beef.

I cannot describe the taste of Corton-Charlemagne, but I can differentiate it to some extent from the other great whites of the Côte de Beaune, Meursault and Montrachet. Of the two, it is more like Meursault, but it is not so soft. It is what is known as a bigger wine, with a mouth-filling savour which has a noticeable tendency to linger in your mouth after you have swallowed it. It has been called monotone in flavour; the first impression is very like the last (some wines, on the other hand, 'develop' in the mouth, surprising you by starting succulent and ending astringent, or vice versa). Corton-Charlemagne is very elusive: burgundians like to say that it smells of cinnamon, and yet suggests flint and steel to the taste. This is the kind of thing one is up against in trying to describe the taste of a wine.

Corton   There is a slightly less exalted white wine made in a small part of the Corton vineyard, next to Corton-Charlemagne. In this case what is usually true of Burgundy, that the wine with the shorter, unqualified name (Corton as against Corton-Charlemagne) is the better, is reversed. Corton for red wine is the supreme name; for white it is second best.

Meursault   Meursault is the biggest village of the Côte de Beaune. It is pretty, grey and not electrifyingly animated. In fact it always seems asleep. The wine of Meursault is remarkable for being very dry and at the same time soft and mellow. It is described by some people as mealy, reminding them of oatmeal, by others as being like hazelnuts. In its colour, which is very pale gold, there is a suggestion of green.

It is remarkably consistent. It is never the cheapest white burgundy, and never the most expensive. There is no single Meursault vineyard as superb and world-famous as the neighbouring Montrachet. But the best vineyards of Meursault, to the south of the village, which are called Les Perrières, Les Charmes, La Pièce-sous-le-Bois, Les Genevrières, and some slightly less exalted ones (the best-known of which are Le Poruzot and La Goutte d'Or) produce the most appealing of all white burgundies; a soft, smooth and scented wine.

A friend of mine is a typical grower of Meursault; burly, perhaps fifty, given to wearing open-necked khaki shirts. He might almost be a tea-planter. He has small parts of the Goutte d'Or, Poruzot and Charmes vineyards. He cycles from one to the other (they are quite widely spaced on the gentle slopes of this part of the Côte) on his Mobilette, working all day among the vines on his own.

His cellar, though not large, is stately and vaulted. The casks are in single file on the floor round the walls. In one corner a bin of slats holds treasured old bottles. I once asked him about the keeping qualities of Meursault. Before I could stop him he had found a bottle of his wine of 1929, unthinkably old from any commercial point of view, and started to open it. Time had done nothing but round off its formidable qualities into a beautifully polished prism of scent and taste. It had not even taken on, as white wines usually do, a darker colour with age, but had remained as light and vital as the day it was bottled.

Plain, unqualified Meursault could vary as much as any burgundy from merchant to merchant. Nevertheless in my experience it is one of the most reliable names. Production is comparatively large, and no superlative name has given the whole area a false glamour.

Auxey-Duresses   Above Meursault the steady slope of the hill falters and lets a road

93

through. In this gap stands a pretty little village, primitive and flowery, the gateway to a lovely pastoral valley of rocks, meadows, birches and a stream, the way to the fortress of La Rochepot and the main Paris road. Auxey-Duresses is not one of the famous names of Burgundy, but its white wines, neighbours and cousins of the Meursaults, are excellent and very similar to the more famous growths. In a good year they are touched with sweetness; lively, fresh and slightly green. Their biggest advantage of all is that they are not a fashion: they fetch no fancy prices. An Auxey-Duresses on a wine-list is almost certainly a sign of careful and imaginative buying, and consequently of good value.

Montrachet

Montrachet has a habit of being the one name people remember when they think of white burgundy. In the United States, where 'greatness' is at a premium, it is linked with Romanée-Conti, representing the best red burgundy, Château Lafite as the best claret and Château d'Yquem as the best white Bordeaux. Then comes Krug as the best champagne, Steinberger Cabinet or Schloss Vollrads as the best hock, Bernkasteler Doktor as the best Moselle. It is a simple and trouble-free approach to wine, and hideously expensive. For these wines, whatever their actual or relative quality from year to year, have been enthroned as the best. Sad to say, they are probably more drunk by people who drink only what they are told is good and less by people who appreciate their extraordinary qualities than any lesser growths. Their price, moreover, often bears little relation to their value. At its worst, Romanée-Conti comes down to something like twice the price of any other red burgundy. Nobody seriously claims that it is worth it, but it will fetch it.

What is it that makes Montrachet stand out from the wines of the surrounding countryside, not as a giant among pigmies, but as a colossus among giants? It is simply the power and beauty of its taste. I will never forget a long tasting of new wines in the cellars of M. Remoissenet in Beaune, standing among the casks in the half-light with Ronald Avery of Bristol, who is his agent in England. The wines were the new 1964s. We started by tasting four Meursaults—the peculiar mealy Meursault taste ran through them all. Some brought it to more fruit, more freshness, more vitality than others. Les Perrières seemed to have most to offer.

Then came Corton-Charlemagne, which tasted strong and forceful after the Meursaults. 'Suave but broad-shouldered,' I put down in my notes. (They demonstrate very clearly the difficulty of finding words for tastes; every expression you use has to be borrowed from some other sense, except the four words sweet, sour, salt and bitter. Words follow lumberingly after the clear, precise and yet indefinable impressions of the tongue.) The Corton-Charlemagne, I noticed, had less scent than the last Meursaults, and yet came and went with a marvellous evenness of power, lingering at the back of the tongue and in the throat, perfuming the breath.

Then followed the Montrachets; a clear ascent from a Puligny-Montrachet, a village wine (though a beauty, flowery and fresh), through Bâtard-Montrachet ('capped it completely; what could be more perfect? The same flowers on a sunnier day; somehow much more clean-cut; authoritative is the word'), to Le Montrachet. 'Still fermenting a little in its second fermentation,' I have down. 'Nevertheless a tremendous heady scent of peaches and apricots and an intense sweetness of character, though fully dry, in the mouth. It declares itself immediately to be something *very* special.'

That was Le Montrachet before it was even fully made, let alone bottled and ready to drink. The notes I have made on mature bottles of it—the 1953, for example—would make me blush to repeat them. What one can say is this: the character of Montrachet is that of the complete balanced white wine. It is sweet in its nature, yet there is no spare sugar; it is not syrupy, but dry and lively. It is soft to drink, but firm and clear-cut. It suggests, without imitating, all the ripest and most perfect of fruit.

(See plan of the Montrachets in map section)

The Montrachet vineyard which is responsible for such ecstasies lies in both the villages of Puligny and Chassagne, both of which have availed themselves of its name, at the southern end of the Côte de Beaune. The hill is solid with the clear green of the vineyard, but it is divided, by tracks and crumbling stone walls, into three parts across the slope. The centre part of the hill is Le Montrachet, the lower part Bâtard-Montrachet and the upper part, from Montrachet itself up to the crest, Chevalier-Montrachet. When one says that Bâtard and Chevalier are lesser vineyards it is not to belittle them. Many find them more drinkable than Le Montrachet.

Montrachet has three owners of any consequence: the Marquis de Laguiche, Baron Thénard and the firm of Bouchard Père et Fils. The rest of its area is divided in lots so small that the wine cannot be made on its own, for it will not fill a cask for its fermentation. It must be mixed with the same owners' grapes from other plots in Bâtard or Chevalier which also belong to them. It loses its identity, and also its right to the great name.

It is worth going off the high road to see the Montrachet vineyard, if only to see how Burgundians concentrate on essentials. Its dry stone wall is worse kept, if anything, than its neighbours. Its simple, wide open gate is tottering. But still at half-past eight on a summer evening the sun is flooding down the alleys of vines, painting them bright apple green and giving the brown earth a touch of auburn. Despite the fact that the hill seems to face the morning sun, the sun is still on it after the workmen have had their summer-evening supper. It is such tricks of topography as this which give a vineyard a slight advantage over its neighbours.

Bâtard-Montrachet
Chevalier-Montrachet

And what of its neighbours? Bâtard-Montrachet and Chevalier-Montrachet are still pure nectar, if they are not Jove's own selection. Bâtard is, perhaps, the more tasty and solid of the two; Chevalier the more ethereal and delicate—but we are splitting hairs. Both these wines are the glories of the village of Puligny-Montrachet, which is lucky enough to have them within its boundaries.

Bâtard-Montrachet overspills, like Montrachet itself, into the next village going south; Chassagne. Along the southern wall of Bâtard is another vineyard in the same class: Criots-Bâtard-Montrachet. Its opposite number in Puligny is called Les Bienvenues-Bâtard-Montrachet.

*Puligny-Montrachet
Chassagne-
Montrachet*

These are all superlative wines. Hardly less good are the other named vineyards of Puligny and Chassagne, with the usual kind of Burgundian names; Combettes, Les Pucelles, Cailleret. Even below named-vineyard level the plain village wines, the ones most often found on wine-lists in Britain, are as fine as any in France. Ordinary Chassagne-Montrachet is thought to just have the edge on plain Puligny-Montrachet for delicacy. Either, in any case, from a good merchant, should be a really fine wine.

Montrachet and food

It is difficult to know what to eat with a wine which has as much personality as Montrachet. I am of the school of thought which would drink it alone, if not, as Alexandre Dumas claimed was the correct procedure, kneeling, with head bared. I do not know the food that would not be completely overpowered by it.

I have enjoyed Le Montrachet immensely with a cold salmon-trout early in the summer, but that was not a wine of one of the great, powerful vintages, when ripeness makes it really full-blown in scent (it was a 1958 or a 1960). I think I would fall back on a chicken, plainly roasted or grilled or even boiled. There is no better accompaniment to any great wine, white or red.

With Le Montrachet we are discussing the food that goes with the wine; with its Montrachet cousins, for the most part, we are back in the realms where wine goes with food. Where do they fit in?

At dinners which aim to show the best of French (or indeed of any) wine against a formal menu, where fish comes before meat, white burgundy is almost always represented by a hyphenated Montrachet. The perfect menu, I have heard many good eaters say, has white burgundy for the first wine, claret for the second. White Bordeaux is never that wonderful. Red burgundy after white fails to use the amazing potential of France. Between them, white burgundy and claret represent the best of everything. In these circumstances there is no fish or shellfish which would not be a good match for a Meursault or a Puligny- or Chassagne-Montrachet. The same would be true of a meal in which fish was the main or the only dish. It is the quality of the fish, in fact, which is on trial in the presence of wines as delicious as these.

But nothing limits them to fish. Chicken, veal, ham—anything without red blood and strong savour—match them well. Whether it is habit, training or prejudice, I do not like them with lamb, beef or game.

The town of Chagny (a little wine bears its name) brings the Côte de Beaune to an end in the south. The villages immediately south-east of Chagny make good white wine. Their lovely names of Cheilly, Dézize and Sampigny-les-Maranges might be seen on the list of an enterprising merchant who found better value for money among their unknown wines than in the villages down the ·road whose names ring round the world.

*Cheilly, Dézize,
Sampigny-les-
Maranges*

White wine is most appetizing with the hors d'oeuvre or fish course. A fine trolley of shellfish, salads and cold meats is accompanied here by a white burgundy

But their yield is so small that it is not worth anyone's while building up their reputations.

Côte Chalonnaise

After Chagny the hills have nothing like the old consistent sweep. The Côte, such as it is, is broken up into puny mounds, which nevertheless bear the name of the Côte Chalonnaise, from the town of Chalon-sur-Sâone in the valley to the east. Rully, Mercurey, Givry and Montagny, the villages of the Côte Chalonnaise, all make white wine. Of these, Rully and Montagny make mainly white wine, the others only a little. But all can be good.

Rully, Mercurey, Givry, Montagny

None of these wines has the power or apparent strength of the great white burgundies, none the way of expanding in the mouth, lingering in the throat or scenting the air. They are light, pale, clean-tasting and capable of becoming more interesting with age—a test no second-rate white wine will pass. All, on the other hand, if you can find them, are almost certainly good value.

South again, between Chalon and Mâcon, the next big town as we follow the river Sâone, the hills return again, and the countryside changes character. Still the Côte faces east across the river, but behind it the ground is broken up into a much more confused formation. These are young mountains, as hard to follow in their convolutions as waves in a choppy sea.

Mâcon Blanc

The white wine of the Mâcon area, simply Mâcon Blanc, is the white-burgundy equivalent of the Beaujolais, unqualified by any village or vine-yard name, which is to be found everywhere in France, Switzerland or England. Some of it, indeed, is now sold as Beaujolais Blanc.

Mâcon Supérieur

Mâcon Blanc is usually the cheapest of the white burgundies on any list. The second cheapest may well be Mâcon Supérieur. They are not to be despised for this; the production is large, over a considerable area, and there is every chance for a shrewd wine-merchant to find something exceptional at a very reasonable price. Ordinary Mâcon Blanc is not as dry as Chablis, nor as soft as Meursault. It is a little more yellow in colour than either, firm and strongish in taste; rarely acid. In fact it is as good as any general-purpose carafe white wine, for fish or fowl or drinking in hot weather to quench your thirst.

Pouilly-Fuissé

The Mâcon area has one wine, however, which steps straight into a different class; whose equivalent can only be found among the better, if not the best, wines of Chablis or the Côte de Beaune. It is Pouilly-Fuissé—a name well enough known to be a victim, at times, of its own popularity.

Five villages sell their wine under the name of Pouilly-Fuissé: Fuissé, Pouilly, Solutré, Vergisson and Chaintré. They stand in tumbling, tender-green countryside with farmhouses which are beginning to get a look of the south about them. The light is very bright and strong violet shadows cut the stone-walled roads in half down the middle. A field here and there, fallow or pasture, stands out from the hillside vines as a flat rectangle among endless stripes of green, tilted every way.

The Château de Fuissé, the fifteenth-century manor of this tiny village, is a property better than most, producing some of the finest wines of the area. Its proprietor, Marcel Vincent, is the fourth generation of his family to make wine there. His son is being trained to follow him. In Vincent's cellar, going from cask to cask among the new wine, I first understood what makes Pouilly-Fuissé, which I had always thought of as a moderate, often dull wine, a great one. They are qualities of tenderness, gentleness, freshness and clarity.

In the courtyard of the Château de Fuissé under the apple trees is a little mossy tank of trout, looking marvellously cool in the bright dusty afternoon. The trout and the apples seem to symbolize Pouilly-Fuissé; not powerful or stimulating, but gentle and reviving.

Vincent, not Marcel but another, is the patron saint of wine. Just outside the cellar-door, which is insulated with wool and brown paper to keep it cool inside, Marcel Vincent keeps a little shrine to the saint; a wooden statue, a little table, a bowl of marigolds. He is a big proprietor for these parts, with about seventy acres of the best vineyards of the commune, from which he makes several distinct wines every year. The wine which goes out under his own label as Château de Fuissé is his best. Only in good years does he give it a vintage. The wine of indifferent years he puts out as a non-vintage under the title of *cuvée privée* (private selection)—'Like M. Krug of Champagne,' he says.

The comparison with a champagne-shipper is apt in a way. Vincent is not typical of the peasant proprietors of Fuissé, though with his working-clothes and thick pebble glasses, until you hear him talk, you might take him for one. He is educated. He sells his own wine. He has capital and bargaining power.

Solutré   A typical peasant, like Emile Renault of Solutré, the next village, is in a different boat. He has two acres of vines, from which he is perfectly capable of making good wine, but he has nowhere to keep it, and no contacts except unsolicited visits from dealers. His eight or ten *pièces* of wine, in fact, are kept in the back of the garage with the cows and the oil for the tractor, protected only, like the rest of the tumbledown farm, by the nightly closing of the old gate on to the village street. Ask to taste his wine and he will produce, as all Burgundians will, his silver or silver-plated *tastevin* from his pocket, where he keeps it wrapped in a handkerchief. The *tastevin* is used everywhere in Burgundy for tasting wine from the cask. It is like a small ashtray with a handle and a hill in the middle. The light reflected off the middle through the wine shows its colour well in a dark cellar, where a glass would hold too much wine for the poor light to give an accurate idea of its shade.

Pouilly-Loché   Two villages besides the five I have mentioned make wine of the same
Pouilly-Vinzelles kind as Pouilly-Fuissé. Their names are Pouilly-Loché and Pouilly-Vinzelles. They are rarely exported under these names.

Pouilly-Fuissé closes the list of fine white burgundies. It has all the

98

character, and—almost as important—it has the quantity, to support a world-wide reputation. For meals of sea-food, for the opening of formal dinners or the enjoying of a chicken it is one of the best-value wines of France.

White Beaujolais

Farther south, where Burgundy ends with the beautiful Beaujolais mountains, it is almost exclusively red-wine country. A little white Beaujolais is made, but there is no real reason to make white wine in country which is so justly famous for its red, and whose red, for that matter, is in chronically short supply. White Beaujolais is an adequate, dry and middling-strong wine, full of the taste of the grape and attractive, but it has none of the character and style of either Pouilly-Fuissé among white wines, or red Beaujolais among red.

Bourgogne Aligoté

The controls on the naming of the wines of Burgundy are very specific about which variety of grape will be cultivated. All the great and classical red wines of Burgundy are made from the Pinot grape, all the whites from the Chardonnay. One other white grape which is grown a great deal (for local consumption as much as anything) from end to end of Burgundy is called the Aligoté. Wine made from the Aligoté is only allowed to call itself Bourgogne Aligoté, without mentioning a place-name. If you are in Chablis you will, if you ask for Aligoté, be given Chablis Aligoté, if you are in Meursault it will be Meursault Aligoté, but if you are in England or America there is usually no evidence of where it comes from. It is never, in any case, anything very special. In the hands of a good wine-maker, on the other hand, it can be surprisingly delicate, like the shadow of his Chardonnay wine from the same district. A good wine-merchant can find a good one and list it at a very reasonable price as his burgundy *ordinaire*.

White Bordeaux

BORDEAUX STANDS APART from every other wine-growing area. It is not only supreme for quality; it produces gigantic quantities. The vineyards cover a large part of the land for about fifty miles in one direction by about seventy in the other. They have been known to produce over a hundred and thirty million gallons of wine in a good year, while the top figure for Burgundy (including Beaujolais) is about fifty million.

The best wines of Bordeaux come into other parts of this book. Best of all are the great red wines, known to forty generations of Englishmen as claret. Almost equal to them in a completely different way are the supremely luscious sweet wines of Sauternes. (There is a full description of the Bordeaux area in the Red Wines section, pp. 166–71.) However, under the heading of

99

white wines for the table, for drinking with food, we are restricted to the dry or medium-dry or medium-sweet wines which we think of under the broad heading of Graves, but which are grown in almost all districts of the wine-country of Bordeaux.

Graves

Graves is a district name. The Graves country, in which the city of Bordeaux itself lies, and which stretches away to the south among old buried sand dunes and straggling pine woods, makes better red wine than white. It makes some of the finest of all clarets. Yet, curiously enough, the name of Graves is only used on labels tó indicate the district's less important white wine.

The red wines bear the names of their distinct parishes within Graves— Pessac, Léognan, Gradignan. There is no red wine called just plain Graves. But the white wine of the area can call itself Graves if it contains 10 per cent of alcohol, or Graves Supérieures if it contains 12 per cent.

Graves Supérieures

Graves (and Graves Supérieures) is one of the most popular basic white wines in Britain. At its best it is dry but full-flavoured and mellow, somehow not quite clean-cut, having something rather like a hint of vanilla at the end of its taste. Cheap versions are just plain medium-sweet and insipid.

As it grows older both taste and colour grow stronger. Old Graves is more like Sauternes without the sweetness. Young Graves is just the average, medium, useful white wine.

Graves is the only part of Bordeaux where the red and white vineyards share the honours of the land. Several of the best estates grow both. Their red wine is almost always better than their white, but tradition seems to dictate that certain parts of the countryside are planted with the white-grape varieties, and indeed new white Graves vineyards appear from time to time.

Château Haut-Brion

Even the great Château Haut-Brion, the brightest star of Graves, and the only wine of the area to be included in the famous claret classification of 1855 as a first-growth, or at all, has a small plot of white vines, and makes a wine which few have tasted but all agree in praising. Châteaux Carbonnieux and Olivier, of the great châteaux´ which make both red and white, are more famous for their white (although the name Olivier nowadays is used for a brand of white wine rather than the actual wine of the château's vineyard). Châteaux Laville Haut-Brion, Bouscaut, Pontac-Monplaisir, Couhins and Domaine de Chevalier, on the other hand, are like Haut-Brion—more distinguished for their red wine than for their white.

The white wine of any of these châteaux is of superb quality, but it is not typical of the Graves which is listed by most wine-merchants. A few proceed as they do with other wines, seeking out growers who make a small quantity of a good, individual wine and listing it under its own name, whether the name is a well-known one or not. Much more Graves, though, is sold anonymously. It rarely has much to say for itself. A smell of sulphur hangs

100

around a lot of it, like the air round a gas-works. Graves, unqualified, is normally a thing to be avoided.

Of the thirty-odd communes or villages which are included in the Graves area the most distinguished by far are Pessac, the northernmost, on the outskirts of Bordeaux, and Léognan, a little farther south. All the châteaux I have named above lie in these two. As you move south towards the

Sauternes district, moreover, the wine grows sweeter, fuller and more like Sauternes, until the last commune of Graves, Cérons, makes a wine which could easily be mistaken for Sauternes. There is no sharp dividing line between the two. Graves tends to be dry and Sauternes should, in a good year, be very sweet. But they meet in the middle.

The showplace of Graves stands in the middle of the region. Every visitor to this rather sad, sandy country must see the Château de la Brède. It was the home of the philosopher Montesquieu and still stands as he left it two hundred years ago, inhabited by his descendants. But its history goes back long before its most illustrious owner. It is a medieval moated castle, sitting in a meadow with the trees standing back from it, for all the world like something out of an illuminated Book of Hours. The Comtesse de Chabannes, its present owner, drinks a glass of her white wine before lunch out on a little lawn by the old narrow defensive bridge, waiting to greet visitors, who have to pass under the old portcullis. It is a short walk through the meadow to where the *chai* (the Bordeaux word for where the wine is made and kept) stands by the wood, like a little farm. It is pitch-dark inside; slowly you can make out the forms of barrels resting in rows on the earth floor, with chickens scratching around among them. A glass of the cool yellow wine, smooth, dry and satisfying, is drawn out with a glass 'thief', a pipette, from one of the casks. You go outside in the sun to sip it and look back at the castle. Such a homely jumble of cottages and fortress it looks that it seems impossible that it has been standing like this for five hundred years, silently reflected in its moat.

Almost every part of Bordeaux makes a little white wine, and some parts a great deal. Graves has the best of the dry whites, but the Médoc (treated at length under Red Wines) makes a little very good dry white. Even the great first-growth Château Margaux makes some, which it calls Pavillon Blanc du Château Margaux. It is like a good dry Graves. Château Talbot at Saint-Julien in the Médoc makes Caillou Blanc du Château Talbot. Château Loudenne in the Médoc makes a very popular dry white, and Château La Dame Blanche, just north of Bordeaux, makes another.

Across the river Garonne the enormous district of Entre-Deux-Mers, between the Garonne and the Dordogne which comes to meet it from the east, is known chiefly for its medium, neither dry nor sweet, white wine. The growers of the area evidently feel that the wind is blowing in the direction of drier wine, for their produce is getting drier. They are selling it with the idea of it going with the oysters which everyone eats in Bordeaux —excellent fat ones from the Bay of Arcachon just over on the Atlantic, forty miles away. Their new motto, *Entre Deux Huîtres, Entre Deux Mers,* Between Two Oysters, Between Two Seas (the two rivers which enclose the region), though laboured in the telling, is having deserved success.

Côtes de Bordeaux Ste-Macaire

A limited area at the south end of Entre-Deux-Mers has an appellation of its own: Côtes de Bordeaux Ste-Macaire. It tends to be sweeter than the others and might equally well be included among the sweet white Bordeaux wines which follow Sauternes in the After-Dinner Wines section.

White Loire Wines

THE WINES WE CALL LOIRE wines differ so much in every way from each other that it would be better if we thought of some other way to describe them. We call them Loire because they are strung out along the length of that river and its tributaries. But the Loire is six hundred miles long, and a lot can happen to the geology and climate in six hundred miles. Both are vital factors in determining the character of a wine.

Thus at the source end of the river, only eighty miles from the famous Côtes of Burgundy, the white wines of Pouilly-Fumé and Sancerre have a near-burgundian character. A hundred and fifty miles farther west the sweet white wines of the Côteaux de la Loire and the Côteaux du Layon are more like white Bordeaux. And the westernmost wines of the Loire from the vineyards clustered round the port of Nantes are a completely different matter again; forceful dry wines, more like, if anything, Chablis than either of their namesakes.

The Loire wines are growing in popularity faster than almost any others. Everybody agrees to call them 'charming', which always seems to me a patronizing thing to say about anything. Very few people call them great wines, and then only a very small quantity of the sweet wines from curious idiosyncratic vineyards, and then only at a considerable age.

Muscadet

The seaside wines of the Loire are called Muscadet. Muscadet is not a place, but the name of the grape from which they are made. They are the *vin du pays* of Brittany. Fortunately, in view of their situation so near some of the busiest fishing ports of France, they go perfectly with almost anything that comes out of the sea. The Brittany fleets fish the Grand Banks off Newfoundland, the waters of Iceland and the Channel as well as the Bay of Biscay. Their haul includes cod, whiting, sole, skate, turbot, squid. For shellfish they have mussels, scallops, lobsters, langoustines, shrimps and excellent oysters. With all these things Muscadet is in its element.

Being a light, tart wine Muscadet has nothing to gain from being kept. It is often treated as the white equivalent to Beaujolais in Paris cafés and sold as soon as they can get it after the vintage as the *vin de l'année*. Muscadet

102

bottled in the March after the vintage is called, and often labelled, *sur lie* —on its lees. A certain amount of deposit is normal in it—though it is very hard to convince any but the initiated that this does not mean there is something wrong with it.

The vineyards of the Muscadet area, around the city of Nantes, are desultory in appearance. The vines, low on the ground in single, pale-leaved bushes, are scarcely distinguishable from the cabbages with which they share the fields.

Nobody claims greatness for Muscadet, and yet it is one of the most useful of the lesser wines of France. From a mere *vin de pays* it has recently established itself as something which no self-respecting restaurant can do without. Its price, correspondingly, has gone up recently to equal that of a minor white burgundy. It has to be a very good specimen to be worth that much, and no vineyard names help you to be selective. Half of the Muscadet vineyards are in the *département* of Sèvre-et-Maine. Often Muscadet de Sèvre-et-Maine appears on the label of slightly superior wines, which is some help. But again, a good wine-merchant, or in France a good restaurant, is the only answer.

Sancerre and Pouilly-Fumé

Odd though it seems to jump from the Atlantic coast to the centre of France to talk about the almost-burgundian wines of the upper Loire, they are, in a sense, next in order. They serve the same purpose as Muscadet at table. They are drunk young, often in their first year; are very dry and light in alcohol. Their colour, like that of Muscadet, is very pale and their whole character leans towards summer drinking and plates of oysters or shrimps.

Sancerre, Pouilly, Quincy and Reuilly are the four wine-villages of the district. The first two are the better known. Pouilly on the Loire, the one in question, is often confused with the Pouilly near Mâcon, which produces a superior wine, Pouilly-Fuissé. That one wine should be called Fuissé and the other Fumé seems to be designed to confuse. There are only eighty-odd miles between them.

Pouilly-Fumé is an appellation reserved for wine grown at Pouilly-sur-Loire from a grape called the Blanc Fumé. If the wine is made from any other grape it can call itself Pouilly-sur-Loire, but not Fumé. This grape's special contribution, in combination with the chalky soil, is to give the wine a strong scent of what is technically known as gun-flint—like the puff of smoke given off by striking two flints together.

In Pouilly-Fumé the scent is aromatic, obvious and unmistakable—too much so for my taste. In sunny years it is overwhelming, attractive for the first few sips, but growing rather dull after a while. On the other hand Sancerre, the town across the river on the western side, produces wine with just the right amount of this scent in combination with a delicate fresh taste of the grape, which I find intensely refreshing. I have heard someone say that the scent reminded him of fine old cognac—the quintessence of the grape.

Both Sancerre and Pouilly-Fumé are joining the regular list of many wine-merchants abroad as good-value alternatives to the cheap-to-medium growths of white burgundy. They may seem rather thin and unsubstantial at first, particularly in winter—their turn comes with summer food, very cold, in large glasses beaded and dewy with the chill. Château du Nozet is perhaps the best-known, certainly the most expensive Pouilly-Fumé; Chavignol the best wine of Sancerre.

Touraine

If you follow the Loire downstream, north-west at first and then almost due west, from the old dukedom of Berry where the Pouilly is Fumé, Orléans is the first of the large towns. Orléans wine used to be well-known, possibly because it is so near Paris, but now it is famous only for the vinegar it makes. After Orléans comes Blois, and after Blois, now in the middle of the château (real château, not wine-château) country, Vouvray. Vouvray is famous for its white wine.

Vouvray

It is the curious character of these wines of the middle Loire that they are neither dry nor sweet in the sense we can usually give these useful—though overworked—words. Vouvray can manage to be both dry and sweet at the same time or, if you like, neither at all, in a way of its own. In poor years it is thin and meagre, more acid than anything else, struggling to keep a hint of grape-sugar in it. In exceptional years it becomes really syrupy—and yet still not entirely sweet; there is always a sharp touch about it. It is often strong, and has the capacity to live to a great age—at a great age, indeed, it can improve; I have had a thirty-year-old Vouvray which was like glorious flower-honey. Most often, however, it is marketed as a medium wine, to appeal to everybody, and this is how it is generally known. If nature gives a light and acid wine the Vouvray merchants are not above helping it along with a drop of grape-juice which has been muted (prevented from fermenting by adding brandy or sulphur) and thus kept sweet. A great bottle of Vouvray is so rare that it virtually never makes an appearance outside the grower's own home. It may well, if you ever find it, come

Jasnières

from the diminutive vineyard of Jasnières which is in reality outside the Vouvray area, but which is said to surpass true Vouvray in good vintages.

Montlouis

Montlouis, on the other hand, which faces Vouvray across the Loire, and thus faces north, always produces lesser, though similar, wines.

Anjou

The border country of Touraine and Anjou, the next region travelling westwards down the Loire, is given, in the main, to red and rosé wines. The next white wines are from vineyards lining the north bank of the great river, and of three of its tributaries, the Loir (masculine, not to be confused with La Loire) to the north, and the Aubance and Layon to the south. Those of the Côteaux de la Loire, as the north bank of the Loire is called,

Côteaux de la Loire
Savennières

are best. Savennières is the most famous name, and at Savennières two vineyards command higher prices than any others in the whole of the Loire

La-Roche-aux Moines

valley in all its six hundred miles. They are called La-Roche-aux-Moines and Coulée de Serrant. These are essentially dessert wines—big, full of alcohol and sugar, and yet they are never, at least until they are very old, very sweet. They have a fine scent, a kind of balance of qualities which reminds you rather of the great German wines, but to someone who is used to the equivalent growths of Sauternes they lack richness.

They are virtually impossible to match with food; a peach would probably be the best thing—or, better still, nothing at all. But their place is not necessarily after a meal. I believe they are really more enjoyable quite divorced from any meal at all, when you are simply sitting at a table by the river with legs outstretched and time to think.

Quarts de Chaume from the north bank of the Layon to the south is similar to these. It is a little less highly regarded, perhaps not so delicately scented, certainly cheaper, but the third great name among sweet Loire wines. Bonnezeaux, its neighbour, is similar but rarely exported.

For the rest, the wine of Anjou tends to be firmer and more positive in character; better, in short, than the wine of Touraine. You can expect a plain Côteaux du Layon to be a light, rather sweet wine, almost apple-like in a way, easy to drink at almost any time, excellent with pork or ham.

Alsace

IF IT WERE NOT FOR GERMANY France could claim to have a royal flush of all the best table wines in the world. But Germany has mastered a style of wine to which France has no real rival; soft and gay, sweet and sour, thirst-quenching and light, wine which asks to be drunk as a long drink and yet is so aromatic that the drinker pauses, and sniffs again, and is carried back in imagination to harvest-time; low sun and leaves turning to red and gold.

The wines of Alsace are France's answer to Germany. Indeed, from the Franco-Prussian War to the end of the First World War Alsace was part of Germany. In those days nobody heard of its wine. It was sold anonymously as *vin ordinaire*. Alsace has had to make its reputation for good wine since the Second World War, when the vineyards and villages were fought over again. It has succeeded, and now stands high as one of the most consistent producers of good, reasonably-priced wine in the world.

The wines of Alsace are dry and full-flavoured. They do not flirt with sweetness as German wines do, but tend to be stronger, in taste and alcohol, less delicate and less complicated and interesting in your mouth.

They are, above all, table wines, wonderful with food, especially rich and creamy food. The special taste of Alsace is spicy and aromatic. With pig and goose, the fat creatures which are often found in Alsatian, and indeed German, cooking, they get along very well. If they were any sweeter the arrangement would be sickly, but, as they are, they act as excellent seasoning. *Pâté de foie gras* is Alsace's most famous dish. It can profit enormously from a piquant cold Traminer. There are some who like Sauternes with *foie gras*; honey, as it were, with cream. I would rather have the touch of seasoning, the mustard on the beef, which an Alsace wine provides.

The Alsace vineyard, like the bulk of the German Rhine vineyards farther north, faces east across the Rhine, but on hills set back from the river by several miles. Through these hills, never particularly steep or spectacular but always shifting and rolling in perspective, narrow stone-walled lanes twist overshadowed with vines. Here the vines are strung on poles as tall as hop-poles, emphasizing the green leafiness of the plants. It seems as if the whole world is made of vines.

Riquewihr

Colmar

Such old villages as the war spared are almost absurdly picturesque, with the painted eaves and gables, the cobbles, the wellhead, the baskets of geraniums, the archways, the clocks and bells, the leaded panes of an opera-set. Riquewihr is the one perfect survival. It looks as though it has just been built. In fact it has not changed seriously since the town-hall was built in the early eighteenth century, and under its streets long vaults are stocked, as they always have been, with the new wine of the neighbouring fields. Colmar, less involved in the making of wine itself, since it is down in the flat valley-bottom, but the scene of a great annual wine-fair, has an old area, and a big one at that, which no amount of tourist-literature can prepare you for. It is beautiful, busy, natural; the Middle Ages still seem to be in full swing.

The wines of Alsace are not known, as all German wines and most French wines are, by the names of vineyards or villages. They are identified by the grape-variety from which they are made, the name of the maker (as in Champagne) and sometimes by a qualifying phrase such as *Réserve Exceptionelle*, which leads you to expect a higher price, and indeed a better wine.

The grape-varieties are all-important. The best, beyond a doubt, is the great German grape of the Rhine and the Moselle, otherwise not grown in France, the Riesling. Riesling wine has a quickly recognizable kind of floweriness, not obvious but always true to type, and greater delicacy than almost any other. Normally it tends to sweetness, at least when the grapes have had a chance to get fully ripe, which is later in the year than most. In Alsace the wine it makes is not sweet, but it has more power than usual. Power and delicacy, floweriness and balance—this is not really describing it. Nothing can: it is a wine you must taste.

Gewürztraminer

The next grape of Alsace is the Gewürztraminer—the really spicy one. A grape called the Traminer used to be used, and the name is used still to denote a less than full-powered Gewürztraminer, but the Gewürtz (or spicy) is now the one in use almost everywhere in Alsace.

This is the most characteristic wine of Alsace. Its aroma is strong, its taste is strong; it does not just slip down, but seasons (as I have said) every morsel of food that goes with it. It is almost always fully dry, though sweeter ones from late-picked and very ripe grapes are sometimes made.

Muscat

The muscat is also grown in Alsace. Normally it is associated with very sweet, very grape-like wine, but here even this is used to make a dry, and surprisingly delicate, one. The firm of Dopff & Irion, whose headquarters is in the old Château de Riquewihr, owns a vineyard called the Clos des Amandiers (there are almond-trees in it), which is planted with muscat grapes and which produces one of the few Alsace wines sold under a vineyard name. It is light, pretty, only gently muscat-flavoured and possibly even a little bit almond-like. A good apéritif and excellent with trout.

Sylvaner
Pinot Gris

Two lesser wines are made from other grape-varieties, the Sylvaner and the Pinot Gris. Sylvaner is the local tap wine (superior taps often have Riesling) and Pinot Gris is also used to make a rosé, which is extremely good. If an Alsace wine does not state the grape it comes from you may assume that it comes from grapes like these, and is probably a blend of several. The words *Grand Vin* can only be used on a wine coming from the superior grape-varieties, and containing 11 per cent alcohol, which is the same as most white burgundies.

Alsace wines are always bottled in long thin Moselle-type bottles, either green or brown; often slightly larger and longer than the German ones. The best-known shippers are Hugel (who makes some superb special, more expensive late-gathered wines under the description *Réserve Exceptionelle,* as well as a normal range and a very popular cheaper blend called Flambeau d'Alsace), Dopff & Irion, Dopff (a separate firm, just as there are three Heidsiecks in Champagne), Schlumberger (whose wines tend, I think, to be a shade softer and sweeter than some), Trimbach, and Preiss Zimmer (lovely delicate wines). There are many others: these are the ones I know.

The Rhône Valley

WINE IS MADE IN THE VALLEY of the river Rhône all the way down from its glacial beginnings in Switzerland to its turbid dispersement into the Mediterranean. When we say Rhône wines, however, we mean those of the hundred-and-forty-mile north-south stretch from Lyons to Avignon. Châteauneuf-du-Pape, the wine of Avignon, is sometimes called a Rhône wine, sometimes a wine of Provence. Geographically it is both. In character it belongs more to the Rhône.

The white wines of the Rhône are rich and strong, full yellow-gold in colour and nine-tenths dry. The best of them has a superb scent and lingering lusciousness—is, in fact, one of France's very best white wines— the least is still strong and fine-flavoured. As value for money, all Rhône wines are above average. Their production is low and reputation limited, they are by no means listed everywhere, but a bad one is seldom found and they can cost barely more than half as much as an equivalent burgundy.

They are strong, both in alcohol and flavour; not the wine for delicate food or lunchtime on a busy day. But their richness, sharpened to a flinty edge, is a wonderful accompaniment to dishes which are themselves rich. I have had a white Hermitage with a steak of grilled salmon which seemed at the time one of the most perfect of wine-and-food combinations.

Château Grillet

The best and most famous of white Rhône wines is called Château Grillet. It comes from a tiny vineyard on the western bank of the river, producing so little wine—a mere thousand bottles or so in many years—that it can never be more than a curious rarity. It is hopeless trying to describe it, beside saying that it is fairly deep-coloured, very scented, full and suggestive of spice in your mouth, and has a long unfading soft and dry aftertaste which still remains a full minute after you have swallowed it. Many people, Germans particularly, compare it with the great German wines—usually to their advantage. It is bottled in long thin Moselle-type bottles. It is necessarily extremely expensive from sheer rarity. Sooner or later every wine-collector has to try it. Vienne, the town twenty miles south of Lyons where the Rhône vineyards start in earnest, is the place to go to have your sample. The Pyramide restaurant there has from time to time been called the best in France.

Condrieu

Beside the ultimate rarity of Château Grillet the village of Condrieu produces similar and less-serenaded wine. There is not much of this either, and it is almost never exported, but those who try it locally will find it excellent, scented, sometimes slightly sweet. Such a wine would be good with a chicken cooked in cream—the kind of rich food for which the Rhône valley is famous.

There is a gap of thirty miles after Condrieu before the next white-wine vineyards—here in country which is more famous for its red wine—at Hermitage. The hill of Hermitage on the east bank of the Rhône at Tain, opposite Tournon, is alone allowed to call its wines Hermitage, but those from several villages round about are able to label themselves Crozes-Hermitage (Crozes is a village just to the north of the sudden bleak Hermitage hill).

Hermitage

Crozes-Hermitage

White Hermitage is fat with a richness which fills your mouth, but also with a flinty edge. It is one of those white wines which you could, with your eyes shut, almost mistake for a red. Its colour, in fact, is singularly golden. Again, there is little of it, but it is exported, stores and travels perfectly, improves with age (even, I believe, with great age) and costs less than some lesser wines from better-known areas.

The Crozes-Hermitage area, too, produces similar and excellent white

108

In France's most modern vineyards—here near Arbois in the Jura—vines are being planted far enough apart for a tractor to get between them, instead of in the old measure of one metre between rows

wines. Of these the best-known is Chante-Alouette (Lark-song). There is also another called Chantemerle (Blackbird-song).

The last of the Rhône white wines, again going south, is Châteauneuf-du-Pape. Only a minute proportion of this famous growth is white. It shares the qualities for which the red is famous, principally what the wine-trade happily calls 'stuffing'. In fact it is strong, rich and not very subtle in flavour, and dry with some of the dryness of a hot wind off the desert. For the refreshing drink which is more likely to be what you would need in Provence it might be better to choose one of the lighter and altogether more thirst-quenching wines of the coast near Marseilles.

THE SOUTH OF FRANCE

It is best to take the south of France in two bites; to the east and west of Provence and the Rhône delta. The eastern bite has much less, but on the whole better wine; the western has the vast bulk of *vin ordinaire,* but one or two notably superior growths.

Haute-Savoie

The mountains of Haute-Savoie, south of Switzerland, have two or three white wines whose names are more familiar than their tastes even to devoted bottle-collectors. Crépy, Seyssel, Thonon-les-Bains and Apremont are some of the most familiar names. All are dry and none of them are very strong. There is a tendency to sparkle which is encouraged in some places, discouraged in others. They are essentially wines to study in detail on the spot, where both the food and the scenery, whose fame far outdoes that of the wine, can be taken into account.

Côtes de Provence

Cassis

The Côtes de Provence, which is the name allowed for all the wine from the eastern coastal belt which satisfies the authorities as to its strength and quality, are better known. Cassis, from the very doorstep of Marseilles, is perhaps the best-known of all. It is offered almost as a matter of course with the inevitable *bouillabaisse* in Marseilles. Indeed, it is ideal to quench the thirst which follows this highly-seasoned dish.

Vin blanc cassis

Great confusion is caused by the name Cassis. It is both a wine and a blackcurrant liqueur made in Burgundy. A *vin blanc cassis* is an aperitif made by pouring a glassful of white wine on to a spoonful of the liqueur, whereas a *vin blanc de Cassis* is a white wine from the Cassis district, on its own. The mixed aperitif does not need a wine as good as the fresh and tasty Cassis. It can be made well enough with any dry white wine.

Bandol

Bandol, only a step eastwards along the coast, is better known for red wine, but produces good white not unlike Cassis. Farther east in the Var department, round St-Tropez and Hyères, it is red and rosé wine rather than white which has a reputation. The best of the white is often described as *blanc de blancs.*

Palette

In the hills north of Marseilles, on the other hand, near Aix-en-Provence and in the valley of the Durance, good white wine is made. Château Simone has a virtual monopoly of the name of Palette and hence of the local wine section on lists at Aix-en-Provence. Its white is not quite as good as its red, which tastes of the pines and herbs of the countryside.

The Massif of the Lubéron which rises to the north of the valley of the Durance has surprisingly delicate white wines, at least one of which—that of Lourmarin—makes a good, and remarkably cheap, sparkling version. The name Côtes du Lubéron is the thing to look for.

Côtes du Lubéron

There is no need to dwell on the *départements* of Gard and Hérault west of the Rhône. A good deal of their white wine, which in any case is much less plentiful than their red, is bought to be made into vermouth. In Hérault a white wine is made from the Clairette grape, which entitles it to the name Clairette du Languedoc. When Gilbeys introduced it in England some years ago it was a great success—it was dry, sound and remarkably cheap. The supply seems to have dried up now, which is a pity.

Clairette du Languedoc

Only Limoux, in the extreme west of this area, in the Aude *département*, makes a good white table wine. The coastal area makes very sweet wines (see under Muscats in the After-Dinner Wines section). Limoux, though, makes a *blanc de blancs* of good quality, both still and sparkling.

Limoux

To the north of this region in the mountains round the lovely gorge of the river Tarn the Gaillac white wines are made. This used to be a district of sweet white wines, but modern trade has encouraged the growing of a complete range of wines—dry white, rosé and red—and some of the character, though not the quality, has been lost.

Gaillac

Farther west yet, in the Pyrenean foothills of Béarn, whose capital is Pau, a more than adequate *blanc de blancs*, not unlike that of Limoux, is made. But the most famous wine of this area is called Jurançon. It should be, and traditionally is, supremely sweet, and said to smell of carnations and taste of cloves. Tall tales are told of the high-strung vines and heavenly mouthfuls of Jurançon. Sad to say, the only one of its wines which is exported, as far as I can discover, is a dry one of no amazing distinction.

Béarn

Jurançon

THE JURA

The most characteristic and best white wines of the Jura are the *vins jaunes*, strange, strong and dark, more of an aperitif than a table wine (see under Aperitifs, p. 79) or the raisin-like *vin de paille* (see the After-Dinner Wines section, p. 252).

The Jura also makes white table wines, but they are not as good as the pink and yellow ones. Under the broad description of Côtes du Jura good *ordinaires* are found, in one case well described as a *vin de campagne*—a country wine. Rather better ones are made within the controlled area of Arbois. An Arbois *blanc* can remind you of a Pouilly-Fumé; a good dry white wine, perhaps a little strong and obvious in scent and taste, but good for country food.

Arbois

Both the ordinary Jura and more special Arbois wines have a smell of their own which I have not met elsewhere—a rather fat, nutty scent which might lead you to think that they are going to be better than they really are. One firm also makes a Blanc de Blancs du Jura from white Burgundy grapes —a lighter-weight wine with much the same character.

110

German White Wines

FRANCE, SPAIN, ITALY, Portugal, Austria and Switzerland are real wine-countries. They have wine as their national drink—it is as much a part of their diet as bread. Only as a hobby of a few and the preoccupation of vineyard proprietors does connoisseurship come into it. You might say that wine works upward from a broad base in these countries. It is assumed that everyone will drink it; it so happens that a few take a special interest in what they are drinking.

Germany, though, is more like England in her attitude to wine. Wine, for all the two thousand years it has grown on the vertiginous hillsides of the Rhine and the Moselle, does not come naturally to her. Her total production is not a tenth of that of France. In perhaps three years out of five the grapes in German vineyards never ripen properly at all but remain green and acid, giving (unless they have the help of added sugar) a thin sour wine. Making fine wine under these conditions is not just farming, it is craftsmanship, and of a particularly laborious and dogged kind. The results, when they are good, are expensive, but they are unique: they are *Wine for wine's sake* wine for wine's sake. In a good vintage a good German vineyard-owner is not making something just to quench thirst, or even to make a perfect drink with a fine meal. He is trying to give his wine all the individual flavour of his own land in its highest possible intensity. He considers his wine to be better or worse according to the clarity and strength of the taste by which it expresses its difference from all other wines. He will make as many different wines as necessary—even keeping the contents of each cask separate from all the others and thus adding immensely to his problem of selling it—to make sure that the best he has to offer is the best his land can possibly produce. Compared with this dedication to the wine itself the most perfectionist of French growers is commercial and carefree. Even an estate as famous as Romanée-Conti or Château Lafite makes all its wine of a year together, giving the poorer parts of the crop the benefit of mixture

111

with the ripest and the best. But this does not happen in Germany. A German grower thinks it a sin to level down his masterpiece, even to improve his other wine. Hence the multiplicity, and in a sense obscurity, of German wine-names.

Their obscurity, in fact, is often exaggerated. What they suffer from is an excess of clarity: they are not dark but blindingly light. They tell you, albeit in German, often in archaic gothic type and in astonishingly long words, exactly what is in the bottle in your hand. No French wine does this so conscientiously. No country, indeed, has such a logical and precise wine-law as Germany. There is a great deal that even France could learn from it if she would.

But when we describe these elaborately and accurately named wines we are speaking of the traditional, and by far the best, German product, not about the bulk of that which is made now. A vast number of small quantities of different goods is hardly a sound basis for trade. Besides, in most years most of the wine of Germany is a long way from being worth the trouble of individual bottling and labelling, let alone marketing. Logically enough, then, the wines of poorer years and more ordinary vineyards are blended together to give a good average product which can be made consistently to order, and so is susceptible to modern marketing and advertising. This is the story of most German wine today.

The taste of German wine

The immediate and most noticeable difference between German and French wines is that German wine tastes weaker. It is a matter of body, or of what wine-merchants call vinosity—the mouth-filling sensation of alcoholic strength peculiar to wine. French white wines, as a rule, have plenty of it—most German wines have much less. Their taste is somehow clear and tenuous, not reinforced by an impression of warmth and strength. This does not mean that they are sour, but rather that their fermentation does not go so far and produce so much alcohol. Their light body is the perfect vehicle for their delicate taste, in which sweetness is balanced against acidity.

The balance which good German wines achieve between sugar and acid is a lull in a perpetual struggle between the two elements. The acidity wins more often than the sweetness, in poor, cold and wet years, resulting in sour wine. On the other hand, when the sweetness predominates, the wine is hardly any better: it is flat, dull, unrefreshing. A balance of the two is essential.

The ideal, reached naturally only by fine wines in fine vintages, is a great measure of both; enough sugar to make the wine like syrup coupled with enough acidity to make it fresh and uncloying. The ideal is expressed in terms of the laboratory as 10 degrees Oechsle (the measure of sweetness) to 1 gram per thousand of acidity. In terms of the nose and mouth, it is a wine which is a sheer pleasure to smell and drink, giving you the feeling that you could go on for ever and never grow tired of it.

112

Despite their delicate flavour, German wines have a more powerful perfume than any others. None, perhaps, in the world can compete with a fine young Moselle for sheer volume of scent. As soon as the cork is out it can be smelt all over the room. It is a blossom-like, spring-flower scent with a hint—sometimes a very noticeable one—of pear-drops. If the other German wines are not quite so pungent as Moselle they are still highly, and delightfully, scented—as much so as any wine from France, except possibly champagne.

German wine and food

Wine like this—delicate in body, fresh and balanced in taste and scented like a garden of flowers—is a different matter from the savoury and appetizing white wine of, say, Burgundy which goes so well with food. Good German wine is not really table wine in the French sense at all. It is not so good with a meal as on its own. There are many exceptions to this—the wine of the Palatinate being the most important—but the rule holds for the best wines of Moselle and Rheingau, which are Germany's best. No matter what the meal, what the dish, they are wasted on it; their appeal is a matter of subtleties and food simply gets in the way.

A German, then, drinks his best wine on its own, in morning, afternoon or evening—it is not very strong, so it does not matter. At mealtimes he drinks something simple and straightforward, quite often the wine of the district, which is kept in a cask or in label-less bottles. He might drink one of the advertised national brands or, if he wants a particular type of wine—say, a light Moselle to drink with trout, or a heavy spicey Palatinate to drink with some game—he would have the less expensive wine of the appropriate region, without all the trappings and extra expense of estate-bottling.

The Rhine

The wine-country of Germany is the basin of the river Rhine and its tributaries. The Rhine cuts Germany in two from south to north on its way from the Alps to the North Sea. Wine of some kind is grown along most of its route, but by far the best of the wines of the Rhine are those grown in the fifty or so miles above and the twenty-five miles below a great bend in the river where the Main flows in from the east. The Rhine wines from this area have been known for the last century or more in England as hock. Hock is supposed to be a contraction of hockamore, which in turn is an anglicization of Hockheimer, the wine of a fine vineyard-town right on the river bend, by repute the favourite of Queen Victoria.

Rhine wine used to be called Rhenish in England. It is Rhenish, not hock, which is referred to (as a superior kind of wine, fit for courts and feasts) in Shakespeare's plays. But the Rhenish of those days seems to have been a red wine, whereas now all hock, and indeed all the German wine which is considered good enough for export, is white.

The Moselle

The other German wine which equals Rhine wine in its reputation, and

113

nowadays more and more often surpasses it in price, is Moselle. The river Moselle, coming out of France beside Luxembourg, carves its way north-east through a range of pine-covered mountains to join the Rhine at Koblenz. In its central section it has had a nightmarish time getting through the mountains; every mile to the north-east has meant a detour of six or seven miles to west, east or south. As a result, its banks may face any point of the compass. Where they face south, regardless of how inaccessible or steep they may be, they are planted with vines.

Two tributaries of the Moselle, and two more of the Rhine, also have fine vineyards on their banks. The little rivers which join the Moselle at the top of its German course are the Saar and the Ruwer. Both have some wines which are among the world's very finest. Of the Rhine's other tributaries, the Nahe, which lies between the Moselle and the great hock bend, makes wine which is always treated as Rhine wine. The Main, whose vineyards lie far to the east, round Würzburg in Franconia, has a different character, a different bottle, and a reputation of its own.

All the wines which come into the Moselle complex are shipped in slim, sloping-shouldered, green bottles; those which belong to the Rhine appear in brown ones. The Franconian bottle is like a gourd.

South Germany

These are not Germany's only wines, nor even the greater part of them. The south is more prolific than the north, and the consumption of wine is a far more everyday affair in districts whose wines have never been heard of abroad. The shores of Lake Constance, the slopes of the Baden hills which face Alsace across the Rhine, and, above all, the banks of the river Neckar

Württemberg

in Württemberg, far above where it joins the Rhine at Heidelberg, are the home of *Konsumwein*—ordinary daily wine—red, white or a mixture of the two, a pale pink known as *schillerwein*. Good growths and even great vine-yards are not unknown in these regions. The Kaiserstuhl, a hill like an

The Kaiserstuhl

island in the broad valley of the Rhine north of Freiburg, has several famous growths—Ihringer, Achkarrenner, Oberrotweiler—which are offered with pride in, for example, the Casino at Baden-Baden. But I have never seen one of them on a wine-list in any country but Germany. They are strong-flavoured, fruity wines in a good year. When young, they are fine, and they are no doubt used for blending with hock when supplies are short. Their fault is usually that they are made from a haphazard variety of grapes and not a single, classical stock like the Riesling, which gives the lovely cleanness of the great German wines.

'Commercial' wines

The wine-trade often uses the word commercial to describe the wines it can buy and sell in large quantities at a reasonable profit to earn its living, as opposed to the finer wines whose minute quantities and vast variety make them a barely economic proposition. Obviously, there is nothing pejorative in the term, unless it is applied to a wine which has pretensions to being in a higher category.

114

Commercial wines have a more important role in Germany than anywhere else, partly for the reason I have mentioned (that there is such a tangle of nomenclature that many a drinker thinks himself too busy to sort it out) but also, more pressingly, because of the weather.

It is common for three-quarters or more of the wine made in the whole of Germany in a bad year to need sugar and water added to it to make it drinkable—1965 was such a year. In some areas all the growers, even in the best vineyards in Germany, simply sold all their too-acid wine to be turned into *Sekt*. It is not that chemistry cannot make drinkable wine out of, as it were, a sow's ear, but if they add sugared water and use various processes for reducing the acidity, the wine loses its right to its full description. The grower cannot sell it as estate-bottled or use any of the precious talisman-words of quality about it, so he sells it to the merchants. They have no difficulty at all in turning it into a very palatable drink—adding, perhaps, some more successful and full-bodied wine from another part of the country, or wine of the riper vintage of the previous year. The world relies on these circumstances to keep it supplied with its regular mealtime German wine—among others, its Liebfraumilch.

Liebfraumilch

The name Liebfraumilch on its own means quite simply Rhine wine. It is not wine from a particular place or of a particular kind. In combination with one of the famous brand-names applied to it by the great shippers (of which Sichel's Blue Nun, Deinhard's Hanns Christoff Wein, Langenbach's Crown of Crowns and Hallgarten's Blackfriars are the most famous), it is a complete guarantee of a good-quality blend of medium-price, soft-flavoured, faintly sweet and eminently harmless hock. Without a good shipper's name attached it might be anything.

A Liebfraumilch offered at half the price of a good brand will not be a bargain; it will be half as good—if that.

In the city of Worms in Rheinhessen (the district which produces most of the Liebfraumilch-type wine) there is a church called the Liebfrauenkirche, surrounded by a small vineyard. This is where the original Liebfraumilch is supposed to have come from, although its wine today is known as Liebfrauenstiftswein.

Moselblümchen

An approximately equivalent wine to Liebfraumilch from the Moselle is sometimes called Moselblümchen, which means Little Moselle Flower, but the name has never achieved the popularity of Liebfraumilch. The most popular Moselle wines, on the other hand, are almost the same kind of thing—a broadly regional blend which appears under the name of the best-known town or even vineyard of the region. Bernkasteler Riesling, Zeller Schwartze Katz (named after the Black Cat vineyard at Zell) or Kröver Nacktarsch (named after the Bare Bottom vineyard at Kröv) are wines from within a radius of (officially) nine miles of the town named, and are called after it because of simplicity—in the case of Bernkastel—or the graphic, easily remembered label.

Compared with Liebfraumilch, such commercial Moselles as these typify the difference between Rhine and Moselle wines. It is a difference which is well symbolized by the colours of their respective bottles; the Rhine a warm reddish-brown, suggesting a soft, sweet, full-flavoured drink; the Moselle a cool green, the colour of sharp, refreshing fruit. To put it another way, if a hock were a peach, a Moselle would be an apple.

German wine-labels

The labelling of fine German wines—which the proprietors of successful brands must remember in their prayers every night, since it drives so many people to the short-cut of ordering Liebfraumilch—proceeds, in fact, on a simple and just principle, that to mislead customers is wrong.

In support of this principle the law decrees a long list of words which may only be used if the wine is unblended and natural—not made with the help of sugar. They are the emblems of quality, words whose English equivalents are such phrases as Special Reserve or Selected. We have come to regard them with a certain amount of cynicism as a result of their over-use, but in Germany they are firmly protected by law.

German law goes further and insists that even bottling wine at the estate implies that it is good enough to be worth the extra trouble—and that therefore it must be so in fact. Nor can the word *originalabfüllung* (estate-bottled) or its equivalent be used on 'improved' wine. Even such words as Noble and Growth, which in British or American trade practice would be regarded as empty gestures and ignored by law and customers alike, are prohibited on anything except the pure, natural wine of the estate. If no such descriptions appear on the label, embellishing the simple name of village and vineyard, you must assume that the wine makes no claim to be regarded as genuine and unsugared.

I must add here that in this matter of labelling the Germans feel themselves hardly dealt with by their Common Market partners in France. Helping out the fermentation of wine with sugar is by no means uncommon in Burgundy. It is, of course, strictly regulated, but the regulations state nothing about labelling. A Chambertin is a Chambertin, sugared or not. Why, the Germans ask, should they be compelled to reveal whether they have had to resort to sugar to make good wine when the French can keep it hidden?

One hopes that it will be the French who have to start putting an indication on their labels, rather than the Germans being allowed to stop their present practice.

Words of guarantee

The words which the law prohibits on any bottle of wine which has been *verbessert,* or improved by adding sugar before fermentation, are the following: *Natur, Rein, Naturrein* (all meaning natural), *Echt* (genuine), *Edel* (noble), *Wachstum, Crescenz, Gewächs* (all meaning growth), *Cabinet* or *Kabinett* (Special Reserve), the number of the cask (*Fuder* or *Fass* number), any of the phrases meaning estate-bottled *(original-, keller-, Schlossabfüllung* or *-abzug)* or finally any of the classifications of quality *(Spätlese, Auslese, Beerenauslese* or *Trockenbeerenauslese)*.

116

The vineyards of the Moselle in Germany are the steepest in
the world. The famous Bernkasteler Doktor looks down the
chimneys of the old town of Bernkastel and across the river far
below. It is winter, and the vines are bare. The work in hand
is tying up the branches left by the pruners

In the sometimes apparently endless description of the wine on a good German label, the first word is the name of the village, ending in -er, except in the case of a few vineyards which are so famous that the village-name is left out (for example, Schloss Vollrads, Markobrunn—sometimes also called Erbacher Markobrunn, Scharzhofberger, etc.). The second word

is the name of the vineyard (or 'site'), exactly as it is in Burgundy. Thus Oestricher Doosberg is wine from the Doosberg vineyard at Oestrich.

Thirdly, sometimes—but not always—comes the name of the grape. This will usually, for better wines, be Riesling; occasionally Scheurebe or Müller-Thurgau, Sylvaner or Traminer. On the Moselle and in the better parts of the Rheingau, however, nothing is grown but Riesling, so it is not mentioned. Lastly comes a word or phrase describing the wine's quality. If this is omitted it means that the wine is the run-of-the-mill of that vineyard, not a special selection of any kind.

The quality words refer to the state of ripeness at which the grapes were picked. Here we are back with the German grower's necessary pre-occupation with weather. To him, the riper the grapes when the wine is made, the better. He carries it further to say that if they can be made over-ripe, so that they actually shrivel on the vine, the wine is the best of all. Wines made like this move completely out of the context of table wines, for they are usually as sweet as liqueurs and are best after dinner; they are very expensive to make and fetch the highest price of any wines in the world (see After-Dinner Wines, pp. 241, 246).

Before this stage is reached, however, a good grower who has the opportunity of a good vintage classifies his wine according to sweetness. A wine made from slightly riper grapes, and thus rather fuller in body and sweeter in taste, he calls a *Spätlese,* which means late-gathered. One which goes farther in the same direction, and which is made with great care from the best and ripest bunches as they are brought in from the fields he calls *Auslese,* which means selected picking. This is the limit with wines which could possibly be regarded as anything but liqueur-wines. Thereafter he may make a cask or two of wine by picking the individual ripest grapes off the bunches, or even selecting only those which have shrivelled up completely, concentrating their juice to syrup. These wines, *Beerenauslesen* and *Trockenbeerenauslesen,* will be discussed later. In any case, these descriptive terms, if the wine qualifies for them, appear after the name of the place, the vineyard and sometimes the grape on the label.

To some extent local practice is followed in this final business of placing the wine in relation to its fellows. In the Rheingau, for example, the word *Kabinett,* implying that the wine is of the quality the owner keeps for his own special cupboard, is commonly used. On the Moselle, on the other hand, owners often classify their casks individually, giving them besides their classifications into type, the accolade of *feine* (fine), *feinste* (finest) or *hochfeinste* (best of all).

One producer in one vineyard in one year could produce seven or eight different wines. Other owners of other plots in the same vineyard, of course, could make the same number. To take one example, the famous Bernkasteler Doktor vineyard has three owners. In a good year each may have an ordinary Bernkasteler Doktor, a Bernkasteler Doktor Spätlese, a Bernkasteler Doktor Auslese (and perhaps Feine and Feinste Auslese), a Bernkasteler Doktor Beerenauslese and a Bernkasteler Doktor Trockenbeerenauslese. There would then be twenty-one completely different Bernkasteler Doktors of one year, ranging from a fine, dry, light and almost stony, though strongly perfumed, wine to a golden syrup of a wine, three times over, each with the differences due to different owners' ideas and techniques.

The rest of the contents of a German label are, in a sense, the most important part of all. They tell you the name of the grower and where the wine was bottled. With such fine wines as we are discussing it is the commonest thing for the wine to be bottled on the estate where it was made, and thus to qualify for the phrase *originalabfüllung* (often shortened to *orig.-abf.*) or one of its equivalents. Which of the proprietors of the vineyard (for the great majority of famous vineyards in Germany have several owners) it comes from is vital. Growers' names mean even more in Germany than they do in Burgundy. A few (on the Moselle several of them religious foundations, in the Rheingau most of them old noble families, and throughout Germany very prominently the Federal State) have such high reputations that any wine from them can be assumed to be completely reliable.

<table>
<tr><td>

THE MOSELLE
Luxembourg

</td><td>

The Moselle comes into Germany out of France and Luxembourg already dressed with vines. Luxembourgeois Moselle is a caricature of the kind of wine the valley will produce later in its path. It is very light, sharp, often bubbly in its bottle from the effects of unfinished fermentation, almost colourless and wonderfully refreshing to drink. It is rather like miraculously light and scented cider, or the *vinho verde* of Portugal.

</td></tr>
</table>

For most of its way through Germany the river is accompanied by the tilting green lines of vineyards on little terraces and precipitous slopes far above the valley floor. Sometimes, where a bend gives the whole bank for a mile or more a directly southern exposure, the hill of vines is continuous from the river's edge to the crest six or seven hundred feet above. The Moselle vineyards are some of the world's most beautiful, and must certainly be the world's steepest. In places, ladders laid on the ground are the only way of getting up the hill. A glance below your feet shows the river as a mere stream. A stranger on these slopes can hardly make his way about at all, but the men and women who work all year on the vines have adapted themselves to their cliff-hanging life. At harvest-time they run up and down all day with hods of grapes, weighing a good hundredweight, on their backs.

The soil of the Moselle is grey slate. It is thin, and looks poor, but the hardy Riesling vine, which is grown there to the exclusion of all lesser types, thrives on it. The light slatey soil has one great advantage: rain falls straight

118

through it. Where in the sandstone vineyards of the Rhine the surface traps the water, turns to runny mud and pours down the hill, the slate of the Moselle stays in its precarious place. If it were not for this fact, a heavy rainstorm would leave the roots of the vines bare, and the whole vineyard would slide to the bottom of the hill.

Only a small part of the Moselle, however, grows fine wine. It is a series of curves in the central part, known as the Middle Moselle, which contains all the best vineyards of the river itself. These, and a few villages in the tributary valleys of the Saar and Ruwer farther upstream comprising at most only a quarter of the whole river's wine-production, are the wines which are exported, and are known by name all over the world.

The Saar The Saar valley is the southernmost of these districts. There are five great wine-villages on the Saar, with barely a thousand acres of vineyard between them. Their names are Wiltingen, Ayl, Oberemmel, Ockfen and Kanzem. In very good vintages they produce what some consider the best of all Moselle wines: in a bad year, on the other hand, their wine is hardly drinkable at all without sugaring.

In 1965, for example, even the best estates in the valley had to sell all their wine to the *Sekt* factories, so sour and—as they say—*stahlig*, steely, was it. Yet in 1964 the best Saar wines were among the finest in Germany. Their greatest appeal to wine-lovers, in fact, is in the hint of hardness— again, this steeliness—which they keep even in warm and ripe years. Rather as a Chablis, however rich in flavour, always has a stony, austere finish, the Saar wines keep their firm, ungentle individuality.

The greatest name of the Saar is a vineyard so famous that it leaves the village-name off its labels. The wine of Scharzhofberg, although near Wiltingen, is always called just Scharzhofberger. Its neighbour, confusingly called Scharzberg, lies both in Wiltingen and Oberemmel, for which reason it, too, often is called, like Montrachet, by its own name alone. The Ayl vineyards of Kupp, Herrenberg and Neuberg, the Ockfen vineyard of Bockstein, half a dozen besides the two mentioned at Wiltingen, the Hütte and Agritiusberg vineyards in the villages of Serrig and Wawern also make great wine in great years (and bad wine in bad ones).

The most famous estate of the valley is that of the Egon-Muller family, who live at the handsome old country-house which gives its name to Scharzhofberg. Other very important holdings belong to the various religious foundations of the city of Trier, which lies on the Moselle only a short way downstream from the mouth of the Saar.

Trier At Trier, more than any other town in the wine-growing world, the endowment of charities with vineyards is a flourishing concern. The secular foundation of the famous hospital at Beaune, which operates on the proceeds of the sale of its wines, has several counterparts in Trier—some religious, some not. The Catholic cathedral itself is an important vineyard owner (it adds the word *Dom*, meaning cathedral, to the names of the wines it sells from its vineyards). The Bischöfliches Konvikt (a boarding-school), the Bischöfliches Priesterseminar (a training-college for priests), the Friedrich Wilhelm Gymnasium (the school where Karl Marx was educated) and the Vereinigte Hospitien (an almshouse) are all endowed with excellent vineyards, and belong to an association, known as the Great Ring, which sells part of its wine by annual auction, setting a very high standard and allowing none but natural wines under its rules. The labels of these foundations are some of the best-known and most reliable on the Moselle, for their estates are dotted over all the finer stretches of the river. Their prices are always high, but there is no finer German wine.

Avelsbach

Trier is the centre of the wine-growing Moselle. It is the oldest city in Germany. A completely-preserved Roman gateway still dominates it, although most of the city was destroyed in the Second World War and there are few old houses left. Near Trier in the hills the village of Avelsbach has important vineyards belonging to the cathedral and the State Domain, which owns and operates some of the finest sites in every part of Germany. Avelsbacher has most of the characteristics of a Ruwer wine, although it officially lies on the Moselle itself.

The Ruwer

The wines of the Ruwer valley are softer and lighter, more delicate and with even less alcohol than the other wines of the Moselle. Like the Saar wines they need a hot summer to ripen properly, and can be worthless in bad vintages. But in a fine year (1964 was an example) there are people who argue that they are the Moselle's, and even the world's, best white wines. The villages of Eitelsbach, Kasel and Waldrach are the only three of consequence, with only about five hundred acres between them. The most famous vineyards of the Ruwer are the estates of the von Schuberts, Maximin Grünhaus, and, just opposite it, the Karthäuser Hofberg vineyards of the Rautenstrauch family of Eitelsbach.

The Middle Moselle

From the mouth of the Ruwer downwards, the Moselle is accompanied by vineyards, but here the hills stand back and the essential combination of steep slopes and the twisting river, which seems to be a prerequisite for the best wines here, is lacking. As soon as the river plunges back into the hills, however, the vineyards come clustering round, and the names of Mehring, Trittenheim, Neumagen and Dhron, though not on the top level, are familiar from good wine-lists.

Piesport

Piesport is the first village of the Middle Moselle which grows wine in the highest category. It stands on the outside of a broad bend in the river at the foot of an amphitheatre, two miles long and five hundred feet high, of solid vines. 'All Goldtröpfchen,' a wine-merchant once said to me jokingly as we stood looking up at the hill. He meant that the name of one little vineyard, Goldtröpfchen—'little gold drop'—has been so successful that every owner in the place has started calling his wine Piesporter Goldtröpfchen, sometimes even adding after it the name of his own vineyard, so that we have, for example, Piesporter Goldtröpfchen Treppchen. It seems a pity that the law allows a vineyard name to become devalued in this way. German wine-names are quite difficult enough to remember without having to

120

The great wines of Germany—Rhine and Moselle. Their characters are reflected in their colours, and in the colours of their bottles; the Rhine full and gold, deepening almost to orange with time, the Moselle fresh and green, to be drunk young, while it still smells of the grape

worry about whether they mean what they say or not. It would be so much simpler if a vineyard-name could only mean one thing—that the wine comes from the vineyard in question.

Brauneberg
The wines from Piesport, and from the next stretch of the river down to Brauneberg, are some of the sweetest and least characteristically sharp of the Moselle. The north bank of the river here is a continuous wall of vineyard above the villages of Wintrich and Kesten, and opposite the little town of Brauneberg. Kesten is known only for the fine wine of one vineyard, Paulinshofberg, which is very like Brauneberg wine. Brauneberg has more spiciness and richness than any other Moselle. It is the most hock-like wine of the river and, perhaps for this reason, used to be considered easily the best in the last century. Brauneberger Juffer is the best-known site.

Brauneberg is one of several villages on the Moselle which are across the river from their vineyards, leaving the south-facing slopes entirely free for vines. It means that the growers have to go by boat to work, and bring their grapes to the press-house by boat at vintage-time, but they believe that it is better than giving up good vineyards to mere houses.

Bernkastel
The town of Bernkastel-Kues straddles the river round the next bend. The river at Bernkastel makes such a sharp turn that the vineyards cross over and face south from the right bank. From the bridge between Bernkastel and Kues there is one of the finest views on the whole river, looking north-west downstream at an unbroken cliff of vines six or seven miles long, with the vineyards of Bernkastel merging into the vineyards of Graach, and those of Graach into those of Wehlen. This, by common consent, is the greatest stretch of the Moselle from the point of view of wine.

Bernkastel is one of the prettiest of all wine-towns. Along its front runs the river, high above hang the vineyards and the ruined castle of Landshut, and in the centre is preserved a perfect medieval town square of brown and white timbered houses, inclining in gossiping attitudes over narrow alleys. Right over the town, gazing down its chimney-pots from a slaty slope as steep as a gable, is one of the most famous vineyards in Germany, Bernkasteler Doktor. With the sites which flank it, Graben and Badstube, it makes what many consider the best Moselle. The Doktor is only a small vineyard but it has three owners; Dr Thanisch, Deinhard & Co. and the Lauerburg estate. Dr Thanisch combines his Doktor grapes with those from his part of the Graben site to make Doktor und Graben, in bigger quantities of equal quality. Deinhards sometimes do the same with their holdings in Badstube to make Doktor und Badstube. These are considered the supreme Bernkastel wines; Schwanen, Schlossberg and Bratenhöfchen, and particularly the wine from the scattered properties of the Parish Church (Pfarrgut St Michael), are also magnificent.

The typical Bernkasteler is one of the drier of the Moselles, with something of the stony, mineral taste which occasionally reminds me of Chablis, yet no less of the fragrance of Riesling grapes than any other. Now, however, the wave of fashion which made the Doktor the best-known wine of the river has passed downstream, and higher prices are paid for the wines of Wehlen.

Graach

Bernkastel's vines merge with those of Graach. Graacher Himmelreich and Domprobst, and the von Kesselstatt's estate of Josephshof, are the best-known growths. They are very fine, but they tend to be overshadowed by the reputations of their neighbours. Exactly where on that mighty hill Graach ends and Wehlen begins I am not sure, for there is no break in the

Wehlen

vineyards, but at Wehlen we come to the Moselle's most highly-prized site, Wehlener Sonnenuhr. Sonnenuhr means sun-dial, and there is a massive one shaped out of an outcropping cliff halfway up the vineyard. The best Wehlen wines are rich and full-flavoured for the Moselle, but manage never to overbalance into heaviness. There is always an underlying delicacy about them which distinguishes them clearly from, for example, a great hock of the Rheingau. They fill your mouth and linger on your palate not out of strength, but simply out of lovely freshness, with always a suggestion of the taste of honey.

There is one great name in Wehlen; the Prüm family and its connections. Various branches of the family make all the finest Wehlen wines. They live in solid big houses down by the river's edge, gazing up at the sun-dial—for Wehlen is another of the villages which is across the river from its vineyards. You might easily pay three times as much for a bottle of their best wine as for any claret or burgundy in the world.

Wehlen does not end the great hill. Its vineyards merge in turn with those

Zeltingen

of Zeltingen, which is the biggest in area of all the Moselle parishes. Plain Zeltinger, as a result, is often one of the cheaper Moselles on any list, and often one of the best value. Zeltingen also has part of the Sonnenuhr vineyard, which is here called Zeltinger Sonnuhr, or even, by the estate of J. J. Prum which has property there, 'Wehlener-Zeltinger Sonnuhr'. No list of the properties of Germany, I think, has ever got to the bottom of such vagaries as these. Every one of Germany's tens of thousands of growers has his own ideas about what his property is called, and absurd anomalies are sometimes found on labels—which makes it all the more difficult to get the hang of them, let alone to lay down any general rules.

Zeltingen, in fact, is one of the parishes which has tried to rationalize matters recently. It has divided its vineyards into four, so that all growers may now use one of four well-known names: Himmelreich (the best), Deutschherrenberg, Schlossberg or Kirchenpfad. It has not proved as simple as this sounds, however, to get growers to abandon their old names, and most of them have not.

After Zeltingen the river bends again, and the vineyards cross over back to the left bank, which is once again the northern one. On the bend lies the

Uerzig
Erden

town of Uerzig, whose vineyards join those of Erden immediately downstream, on an even steeper slope and in even more difficult and rocky conditions than those we have just passed. Production here is small, but in good vintages the wine is excellent and full of spicy, fragrant character.

The great stretch of the Middle Moselle ends here. Farther downstream there are plenty of vineyards, and two or three with famous names, but none of the quality which the last three bends have achieved. The best-known Lower Moselle wines are Kröver Nacktarsch, Trarbacher, Enkircher and Zeller Schwartze Katz. The Kröver and Zeller wines have achieved their reputations as much by the use of a picture (of a bare bottom and a black cat, respectively) on their labels as by the taste of the wine.

THE RHEINGAU

The Taunus mountains are really no more than hills, forested with pine and beech to their crests, but they cause the Rhine to change direction and, instead of flowing north, to skirt them to the west, running along their south side for twenty-five miles between Mainz and Rudesheim. The combination of shelter from the hills to the north and the moisture and warmth of the wide river to the south is supposed to be the secret of the best of all Rhine wines, for the foothills of the Taunus coming down to the river are called the Rheingau.

The Rheingau is to the Rhine what that great cliff between Bernkastel and Zeltingen is to the Moselle; the best of many good things. The little towns along its busy riverfront, from west to east, are Rudesheim, Geisenheim, Winkel, Mittelheim, Oestrich, Hattenheim, Erbach, Eltville and Walluf. In the hills behind there are Johannisberg, Hallgarten, Kiedrich and Rauenthal. All these, except possibly Mittelheim, are or can be the names of great wines.

Rheingau wines come in great variety. It is harder to generalize about them than it is to generalize about, say, the Médoc. But of all hocks they are the best balanced, most firm (as opposed to soft) in your mouth, with most scent and the cleanest, most positive characters. They owe some of these qualities to the fact that the Riesling is grown on most of the sites, exclusively on all the best ones, of the Rheingau, whereas along the rest of the Rhine the more prolific Sylvaner and lately the Müller-Thurgau is dominant.

At the western end of the Rheingau where the river turns north the hills are cut clean through by the stream. The two high banks crowd together over a little castled island, and the water runs in rapids as though it is still only just breaking through. This is the Bingen Hole. It is as far up the river as ships from the sea used to get before the days of steam-tugs. To it the town of Bacharach downstream owed its reputation for wine—it was once thought to be the source of all good Rhine wine—although its vineyards are insignificant. It was the *entrepôt* for the whole of the upper Rhine.

Rudesheim On the Rheingau side this flurry of rock and water is overlooked by the castle of Ehrenfels on the Rudesheimer Berg. The Berg is the high hill behind and downstream of the town of Rudesheim. All the best Rudesheimer vineyards are on it, and use it as an additional name, so that, for example, the wine from above Schloss Ehrenfels is known as Rudesheimer Berg Schlossberg. Rudesheimer wines are called variously the softest wines of the Rheingau (by those who do not like them) and the most delicate (by those who do). It is agreed, though, that they have the curious habit of being better in fairly wet years than in very hot summers. The drainage of the steep hill is so effective that without rain the vines fail to grow and ripen properly, so that the lesser wines of Rudesheim are the ones to choose in a great vintage. For the last few years the Berg has been the scene of a rationalization scheme for consolidating properties, to simplify the endless subdivisions of vineyards. It is being done by the direct method: with a bulldozer. Machines have been at work levelling the tiers of old terraces into great smooth slopes on which, though they are steep, some kinds of mechanical aids will be able to work. One grower calculates that when the changes are finished the work which used to be done by twenty-five men will be done by fifteen.

Rudesheim is a resort—and in summer a place to avoid. It sums up the life of the Rhine-front, with its crowds, its ferries, the throbbing barges and the clattering trains which pass just under all the towns' windows along the river.

Geisenheim

The wines of Geisenheim, the next little town, are some of the Rheingau's least well known, but are no less excellent for that. On the far side of Geisenheim rises the most unmistakable, and perhaps the most famous, vineyard in Germany, the hill of Schloss Johannisberg with the castle on top, its vineyards falling away round it like skirts. Schloss Johannisberg really belongs to the wines of the river-front rather than the hills behind, although the village of Johannisberg and most of the other vineyards with its name lie farther back in the hills. It is the property of Prince Metternich. Schloss Johannisberger wines are distinguished from each other in quality by a series of coloured capsules on the bottles, in which it is hard to discern any logic. You would be fairly safe in assuming, though, that of any two of the wines of any given year the more expensive of them would be the sweeter. Of all the great wines of the Rheingau they are perhaps the mildest and most delicate in flavour, for among the others there are some very powerful and spicy mouthfuls.

Johannisberg

The other wines of Johannisberg are not to be despised because they are not Schloss. The vineyards of Erntebringer, Hölle and Klaus are among the best-known of a dozen good ones which are also Johannisbergers.

Winkel

At the foot of the Schloss Johannisberg hill to the east the vineyards of Winkel stretch down to the river and up into the hills behind. Their most famous site is known without the village-name, simply as Schloss Vollrads, but sandwiched between the two schlosses lie a number of really excellent sites, the best-known of which is Winkeler Hasensprung, or Hare-Leap. Schloss Vollrads lies well back from the river in a fold in the hills, with an air of great dignity and reserve, beneath its mighty square tower. It is the estate of Count Matuschka-Greiffenclau, whose family have lived there since the fourteenth century. Here again, quality is designated by a system of coloured capsules and different label markings which very few people

Schloss Vollrads

alive can know by heart. Many argue, however, that the best of Vollrads, with its extreme elegance and lovely bouquet, is the best of the Rheingau, and therefore of the Rhine.

Oestrich

Mittelheim and Oestrich continue the vineyards along the river. Oestricher Doosberg and Lenchen are the best of a dozen good vineyards, producing wine with a certain earthiness and heaviness, which is attractive in its own way but prevents them from being among the classic great wines of the river. The next town of Hattenheim, however, has it both ways; three

Hattenheim

very fine vineyards down by the river and one supreme one up in the hills a mile behind. The riverside sites are called Nussbrunnen, Wisselbrunn and Mannberg. The hill site, famous enough not to use the name Hattenheimer, is Steinberg.

Steinberg stands on a steep slope to the south-west nearer to the village of

Hallgarten

Hallgarten than to Hattenheim. Hallgarten is a dull little place, the highest in the hills of the Rheingau villages, with three very fine vineyards, Deutelsberg, Jungfer and Schönhell, which give good, strong and long-

Steinberg

lasting wine. Steinberg, however, has the advantage not only of a magnificent situation, surrounded by a wall (a cousin of the famous wall at Clos de Vougeot in Burgundy, built by the Cistercians seven hundred years ago), but of having one owner, the Federal State Domain. Not all its sixty acres are of the same quality, and only wines from the central and best part are ever marked *Kabinett,* but, generally speaking, it is the greatest single vineyard in Germany.

Kloster Eberbach

The monastery which created the Steinberg, Kloster Eberbach, still exists in perfect preservation in a little green valley behind it. It was secularized by Napoleon, and now belongs to the State, which uses it for official receptions and wine-auctions, as well as for the cellaring of Steinberger wine. It is hard to say which is the most fascinating part of this lovely place; the great empty church with its magical echoes, the cloisters, the vast dormitories or the old press-house, where the giant wooden wine-presses of the Middle Ages still stand.

Beside the State Domain the most important property-owner in Hattenheim is Count von Schönborn.

Kiedrich

The next of the hill-towns, Kiedrich, is not particularly famous, though it has three vineyards in a class not far from the top—Wasserose, Gräfenberg

Erbach

and Sandgrube—and several others not far below. Erbach, down on the Rhine, has a much higher reputation, no doubt because of its one supreme site—Markobrunn (or Marcobrunn, for different owners spell it in different ways). The river-front at Erbach is dominated by Schloss Reinhartshausen, the mansion of the late Prince Friedrich of Prussia, which he made into a hotel.

Markobrunn is perhaps the most surprising-looking of all great vineyards, for it is on almost flat land, a mere slope, down by the railway near the river. The soil and drainage must, however, be perfect, for its name is certainly among the top six, possibly among the top four, of the Rheingau.

Eltville

Eltville, which virtually joins Erbach on the east, might almost be called the Zeltingen of the Rheingau; it touches the greatest but itself produces large quantities of fine and reliable, reasonably-priced wine. In Eltville live two of the great growers of the Rheingau, Baron Langwerth von Simmern and Count Eltz, besides the headquarters of the State Domain, the biggest proprietor of all.

Rauenthal

Behind Eltville in the hills lies the final jewel—the most highly valued land in Germany, the vineyards of Rauenthal. The name of Rauenthaler Baiken is not as familiar as, for example, Schloss Johannisberg, but its wine regularly fetches a higher price, the highest price of any Rhine wine. The other great vineyards are Gehrn, Herberg, Rothenberg, Wulfen and Wieshell. Rauenthalers are big and strong, spicy and smooth, marvellously flower-scented and astonishingly delicate in the complexity of their flavours.

The Rheingau ends with the big city of Wiesbaden, the capital of the State of Hesse, at its eastern end. Nonetheless the wine of Hochheim, although outside the Rheingau property, the far side of Wiesbaden and in fact on the Main rather than the Rhine, is in the Rheingau class, and rates high even in comparison with the better Rheingau growths. Two vineyards

Hochheim

at Hochheim are considered classical and truly fine, Domdechaney and Kirchenstuck. The more famous Königin Victoria Berg, the one which was named by its owners after Queen Victoria, on hearing of her weakness for 'hock', is less well thought of.

RHEINHESSEN

Rheinhessen is the opposite bank of the Rhine to the Rheingau. Its best vineyards lie a little upstream, above the river bend at Mainz, on a long slope set a little way back from the river.

Most of Rheinhessen is devoted to quantity production of second-rate wine, using the Sylvaner and Müller-Thurgau grapes. Except under certain rare conditions, the Sylvaner gives wine with nothing like the balance and clarity of flavour, the scent or the refreshing acidity of the Riesling. Sylvaner wine, the typical Rheinhessen wine and the bulk of what is sold as Liebfraumilch, has, as its fault or virtue according to your taste, a softness of character which makes it pleasant, unobtrusive and not particularly memorable. Less than 10 per cent of the Rheinhessen vineyards are planted with Riesling, but these 10 per cent grow virtually all the best wine.

There are only half a dozen parishes in the district which make fine wine. One of them is probably the best-known of all the wine-towns of Germany abroad; not only, however, because of the quality of its best wine but because its name has become what is known as generic—in other words free to be used by any who fancy that their wine is similar enough for them to get away with it.

Nierstein

The famous name is Nierstein. It stands right on the Rhine, about ten miles above Mainz, with its great sand-red slope of hill behind it. Along the hill are ranged the sites whose famous individual names are still intact—

126

Orbel, Hipping, Auflangen, Flaschenhahl, Gluck, Olberg and, above all, Rehbach. Rehbach at the north end runs on into the parish of Nackenheim, where it is called Rothenberg and Engelsberg. These wines, both Niersteiners and Nackenheimers, are the finest of Rheinhessen, as scented as Rheingau wines, as solid, full-flavoured and individual.

The name of Niersteiner Domtal, however, which sounds as though it may well be another such wine, is no longer that of a vineyard at all, but is used by everybody for his ordinary Nierstein (and Nierstein-type) wines.

The next town upstream from Nierstein is Oppenheim, hardly less famous and only slightly less fine. Sackträger is considered the best vineyard, along with Kreuz, Goldberg, Reisekahr and Krötenbrunnen, the last of which, alas, has joined the Domtals and Schwartze Katz as a generic, or meaningless, name.

This little group of villages represents all the great wine of Rheinhessen. To the north the neighbours, Daubenheim and Bodenheim, and to the south Guntersblum and the city of Worms produce some similar wines but more of the common kind. Otherwise the only wine of Rheinhessen which deserves to be called fine comes from the far corner of the district, across on the Rhine facing Rudesheim at Bingen, where the tributary Nahe breaks the hills of the left bank to pour its contribution into the main stream.

The hill above Bingen on the east, seen from down by the Nahe, seems to ape the Rudesheimer Berg, across the Rhine, giving its vines a perfect exposure to the south and south-west. It may be the sandstone which gives the hill its name—Scharlachberg, the scarlet hill. It is said about Bingen wine that it has a slightly smoky taste from the smoke of the trains which pass the vineyards. The same thing has been said of the Bernkasteler Doktor —that it tastes of the smoke of the chimneys below it. Of the many tall stories about wine this is perhaps the tallest. Whether the change to diesel engines and central heating has given the wines a taste of oil I have not heard.

The Nahe is not a dramatic stream where it joins the Rhine. It has been flowing straight through flat country for fifteen miles. But in its upper reaches, where it winds through the lower hills of the Hunsrück—the mountains which put the loops into the course of the Moselle—it has the kind of pretty scenery which seems unfailingly productive of good wine.

Nahe wine is described as halfway between Rhine and Moselle, which is exactly true geographically, but less so gastronomically. The Nahes are like very fine and rather delicate Rheingau wines. Some Rheingau wines have a faint taste of earth under their floweriness, as though you were drinking the whole garden. This seems to me to be the taste of the Nahe: others have described it as blackcurrants or honeysuckle, but in so subjective a matter language is more likely to give the wrong impression than the right. Perhaps it is better to play safe and say that Nahe wines are comparatively light and mature quickly, but nonetheless have excellent scent and a flavour which puts them among Germany's very best.

Bad Kreuznach
Niederhausen
Schloss Böckelheim

There are three very important names to remember on the Nahe: Bad Kreuznach, Niederhausen and Schloss (which is not a Schloss, but a village) Böckelheim. Roxheim, Norheim, Munster and Mönzingen also grow fine wines.

The two most famous vineyards of the valley are Schloss Böckelheimer Kupfergrube (which means copper-mine) and Niederhäuser Hermannshöhle, which are both worked by the State Domain. The names of the Anheuser and von Plettenberg families are also connected with the very finest of Nahe wines, and are often seen on their labels. For cheap wine for everyday use, too, the Nahe is one of the most reasonable and reliable parts of Germany.

THE PALATINATE

The Palatinate (in German *Pfalz*) is not far south of Rheinhessen— Worms is indeed almost in both regions—but it seems to enjoy a completely different climate. It is more like Alsace, which is said to be the sunniest part of France. The orchards of the Palatinate, which cover the valley-floor on the left bank of the Rhine up to the base of the Haardt mountains (the range which at its French southern end is called the Vosges) are full of southern fruit—figs, peaches and almonds. The foothills of the Haardt are covered with Germany's most extensive vineyards, growing wine in easier conditions than anywhere else in the country.

Only a small part of this region, as in the case of Rheinhessen, concerns itself with fine wines. A great deal of Palatinate wine is intended for immediate drinking, and the extremely *gemütlich* little cafés, heavily timbered in the German forest manner, supply excellent open wine which is much stronger than that of the Moselle, and is best, I think, when it is rather sweet and very fresh. When it is dry it is heavy and rough. All Palatinate wines, however, have more flavour and fuller body than other German wines—and usually rather less scent. For this reason they are the ones to drink with food. With the game of the forests, which is always the best thing to eat in this part—and most parts—of Germany, they are perfect. Venison and wild boar are commonplace, I should add, and by no means the exotic luxuries they sound.

The Middle Haardt

The small stretch of vineyards which concentrate on fine wine is called the Middle-Haardt. There are only half a dozen parishes in it, but they include all the famous names of the Palatinate. Their names, from the north, are Kallstadt, Ungstein, Bad Dürkheim, Wachenheim, Forst, Deidesheim and Ruppertsberg. Of these, Wachenheim, Forst and Deidesheim are the really great names. The best vineyards are Wachenheimer Goldbächel and Gerumpel, Forster Kirchenstuck, Jesuitengarten and Ungeheuer, and Deidesheimer Grainhübel, Hohenmorgen, Leinhöhle, Kieselberg, among a dozen others of great fame. Deidesheimers are perhaps

Wachenheim
Forst
Deidesheim

128

the finest Palatinate wines, although they are less well known, at any rate in England, than Forsters. Forster Jesuitengarten, in particular, is so often seen in England that suspicions are aroused as to whether it all comes from the tiny site with that name.

Deidesheim and Forst concentrate on Rieslings more than any other Palatinate parishes. The Traminer and the Muscat, grapes which are more familiar in Alsace than in the rest of Germany, are also grown to add spiciness to the flavour of the wine. Here there is more of a concentration on selected and late-gathered sweet wines, *ausleses* and *beerenausleses*, which are magnificently rich in flavour, often deep gold in colour and almost tropical in scent.

Three producers' names, above all, mean the highest quality in the Palatinate. All three begin with B: von Bassermann-Jordan, von Bühl and Bürklin-Wolf. However, this does not mean that very fine wines are not found with other labels. The words *Winzerverein* and *Winzergenossenschaft*, which both mean a co-operative establishment of small growers, are by no means to be despised, either here or in any part of Germany.

FRANCONIA

Steinwein

Franconian wine is the only German wine which is bottled in anything but the familiar long thin flask. The Franconian bottle is the *bocksbeutel*, a flagon shaped like the kind of wineskin which would swing from the girdle of well-fed monks. It is a jealously guarded right to put wine in this kind of bottle, which establishes the individuality of Franconia's wine—usually called, generically, *Steinwein*—perhaps better than the wine, bottled normally, would do.

Steinwein, from the banks of the Main in and around Würzburg, is the most similar to French wines of the wines of Germany. You can often honestly use the word dry about it, which you cannot do with most German wines. Instead of balancing between sweet and sour, Steinwein has strength and stoniness, slight earthiness perhaps, not unlike Chablis. Both the Riesling and the Sylvaner are grown: many say that here is the only place where the Sylvaner makes really fine wine. Not all Steinwein is made dry, however—*beerenausleses* as sweet as any in Germany are made in hot years.

The best Steinwein parishes are above all Würzburg itself, the capital of Franconia, Randersacker, Iphofen and Escherndorf (whose best vineyard is called Lump, which means idiot). The finest grower is the Juliusspital, a hospital in Würzburg. The normal, not late-gathered, Steinwein of any of these villages in a normal vintage is the most suitable German wine of all for drinking with a meal, and makes a very fine match with fish. Here its comparatively non-aromatic and more substantial nature stands it in good stead. It should not be too expensive, either.

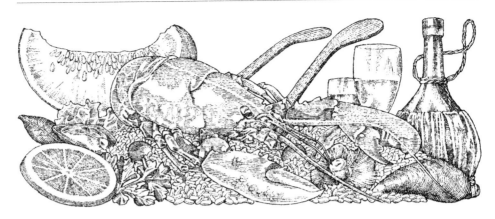

Italian White Wines

NOBODY KNOWS ALL the wines of Italy. She is the biggest wine-producer in the world, and the most disorganized. There are trends and tendencies in this region or that which can be recorded without too much trouble, but there is always the individual to be considered. In Italy he still rules the roost.

So when I say that the best of the wine in such a village is white, you are not unlikely to go there and taste a red wine which is just as good as the white wine, or perhaps better. When I say that it is still, it is very likely to be sparkling; when it is supposed to be dry it will turn out sweet. It will certainly be a mistake on my part. It may even be a mistake on the part of the grower. But Italy is like that. Its most sedate bottles are liable to explode into fountains of delicious froth; its most publicized wines to lack anything worth talking about and its unknown ones to be like nectar.

The white wines of Italy never quite achieve the distinction of some of the reds. The best that I know have good clean characters, sometimes the right balance and the right shade of acidity, sometimes a refreshing scent, sometimes a lovely greeny-gold colour. Soave, for example, can have all of these. But they tend to be dull. It has often been said that no wine can achieve dullness under certain characteristically Italian conditions—under an arbour of vines, on a terrace high above the sea, in the square facing a cathedral—but this is not a comment on the wine.

Taken out of their context, with their props, so to speak, removed, they are very often a disappointment. There is a mediumness about their characters which I long to force one way or the other. Those that do commit themselves to something definite (some Sardinian wines, for example), carry it off beautifully. But whether it is a matter of over-careful or over-careless making, or whatever it may be, the majority are not inspired.

130

The truth is that in Italy there is often no stage between the totally primitive state of affairs where the farmer's son treads the grapes in a wash-tub, hanging on to the side of an open-ended barrel—the family fermenting-vat—for support, and the new, hygienic *cantina sociale* (or co-operative), with every device for avoiding the old weaknesses of inconsistency and cloudiness and fermentation in the bottle, including sterilizing and pasteurizing plants. They are justifiably proud of producing a stable wine, as bright as a new pin. They have achieved a good deal. But they have thrown out the baby with the bath-water.

This makes you realize the tremendous achievement of the French wine-industry. Somehow in France exactly the right degree of orderliness, of regularity and cleanliness to make fine, secure, characteristic wine has been reached by peasants of no more apparent intelligence than their Italian counterparts. Yet both have been making wine for an equal length of time.

It is simply that in Italy a tradition of craftsmanship has never grown up. There has never, until just now, been the large middle-class market to urge on the grower. Where he is making wine only for his village his standards do not matter. But in producing wine for the cities he is completely out of his depth, and the *cantina sociale* has to come and do his wine-making for him.

You can never expect to find in Italian wine, then, the quality which we call greatness in a French or German one.

Italian wine-names

In Italy vineyards are almost never named on labels as they are in France and Germany. The name of an Italian wine is either that of the grape-variety involved or of the district where it was made, or, in a few cases, a simple name such as Lachryma Christi or Est Est Est, implying that it comes from the particular place which is famous for this wine, but not explicitly saying so.

Which are the grapes and which the villages is not always obvious. In Piedmont, for example, Barolo is a place, but Barbera a grape. In Alto Adige, Termeno is a village and Teroldego a grape. Certain grape-names— Nebbiolo, Trebbiano, Malvasia, Moscato, Aleatico, Sangiovese—occur again and again. Eventually one learns them, but there is no golden rule. Italian wine-labels are a law unto themselves. I have seen a modest ordinary red wine in Italy labelled Château-bottled Vintage Claret, whether out of sheer exuberance or in the hope of finding some exceptionally gullible customer it is hard to say.

New laws have recently been passed, however, to do for Italy what the laws of *Appellation Contrôlée* have done for France. They are based on the voluntary local associations which have for years been allowing their seal only to bottles of wine which pass their standards. The best-known of these is the seal of Chianti Classico; a black cock and a number. In future, wines which are *Controllato e Garantito* (the equivalent of *Appellation Contrôlée*) will all be shipped in bottle with a state seal over the cork. There is little doubt that when some of the more unscrupulous merchants are controlled the

131

general reputation of Italian wines abroad will rise, and we shall begin to see some of Italy's best wines, and not just her ordinary ones, for sale.

PIEDMONT

Cortese

Piedmont, on the French border in the north-west, is the country of Italy's best red wines. White wine, apart from the vastly popular muscat, most of which is made into Asti Spumante, is almost ignored. Cortese is the best-known white. It is a dry, light, savoury kind of wine with a peculiar scent and enough taste to linger in your mouth, without being very appealing. Some of the best Cortese is sold under the name of the village of Gavi, as Gavi Bianco.

Liguria

Cinqueterre

From Genoa and the coast of Liguria come a number of white wines; Coronata, Portofino, Vermentino, which are all middle-weight, more or less dry, and subject to the Scenic Fallacy. Look out for them there, in other words, but not here. Liguria's most famous wine is Cinqueterre, famous perhaps more for the spectacular tilt of the vineyards into the sea and the fact that in places the grapes have to be fetched off by boat than for any special qualities. In the endless debate about which is the world's most beautiful vineyard Cinqueterre and the not dissimilar Sorrento peninsula both have a good case.

Pavia

Crossing the north of Italy to the more important vineyards of the north-east you encounter little white wine with a name of its own. Brescia and Pavia have their own. Vino Pavese I have not tasted, but the Pusterla of Brescia is good, a little aromatic, dry, clean and light.

VENETO

Soave

In the Veneto, which stretches all the way from Venice to Lake Garda, down to Ferrara in the south and north to, at one point, the Austrian border, wine is everywhere. Soave, to start with, which is grown at and around the pretty old village of Soave, north-east of Verona, is often called Italy's best white wine. To me it has never really been better than satisfactory: dullness is its fault; freshness, balance, even delicacy its virtues. It is a pale, dry 'fish' wine, as they say in Italy, bottled in narrow green bottles, like Moselle. It has been known to taste and smell a little of sulphur —but it is not alone in this. Verona, the city which claims it as its own, does not lack other good wines—red Valpolicella and Bardolino, white Luzana and pink Chiaretto are all near at hand.

Bianco dei Colli Euganei

South-east of Verona in the lush, volcanic Euganean hills sweet, light-weight and very drinkable white muscat wine is made. Wine which is simply called Bianco dei Colli Euganei, on the other hand, is not sweet *moscato* but a mixture of grapes, giving a yellow wine which may be sweet or dry, good or not so good.

Prosecco

Farther east, north of Venice, Conegliano is well known for rather sweet white wine called by the name of the Prosecco grape. The Prosecco of Treviso, on the other hand, is more delicate, dry and attractive.

The same area, and the easternmost province of northern Italy, Friuli, have a grape of their own called the Tocai (there is no connection with the more famous Hungarian sweet wine) which gives an aromatic, yellow-lit dry wine which makes a good aperitif. The name Verdiso, which you will also meet in this region, is another grape-variety, making a dry wine without much strength or character.

Friuli   Friuli, to make matters worse, has another grape called the Verduzzo which gives a wine more like the Tocai—but once you start going into detail about the different varieties there is no end to it. It is hard enough to know which is the place-name and which the name of the grape in Italy. The best guide very often is a good waiter who will tell you which is the best wine, regardless of place or grape.

TRENTINO-ALTO ADIGE   Things are made rather more simple in the province north of Veneto, tucked away between the Dolomites and the Alps to the north of Lake Garda. Many of the people at Bolzano, the more northerly of the two big towns of the region, are German-speaking, and correspondingly more organized about their wine. The Trentino-Alto Adige area makes some of Italy's most attractive and reliable light wine. The Trentino is probably the area of all Italy where most is being done to standardize names and types, to raise standards and to increase sales. It accounts for nearly half of all Italy's wine exports. Austria and Germany take most of them. Names of grapes which are familiar north of the Alps—Sylvaner, Traminer, Riesling and Pinot Grigio—are common.

I have had a Pinot Grigio from northern Veneto (it was at George's Restaurant in the via Marche in Rome, which must have one of the best wine-lists in Italy) which was excellent, better than typical of this variety, which sometimes gives rather dull, unscented wine without a refreshing touch of acidity. The Pinot Grigio of the Trentino itself I do not know. Both the Sylvaner and the Traminer are very good, typical of the grapes which are most familiar to us in the wines of Alsace; the Traminer spicy and aromatic, the Sylvaner light and fruity, a little green in taste. Of purely

Terlano   local names Terlano (or Terlaner) is the best-known.

EMILIA-ROMAGNA   The little river Trebbia joins forces with the Po at Piacenza, in the west of the long province of Emilia-Romagna, which almost cuts Italy in two south of Milan and north of Florence. The Trebbia has its own grape, the

Trebbiano   Trebbiano, which makes the sweetish local wine of Piacenza. Presumably this was its first home, but now it is found throughout Italy.

As you go south-east across the province, Parma comes next, then the industrial town of Reggio. Reggio's local white wine is called Scandiano.

Scandiano

After Reggio comes Modena, famous for motor-cars and the fizzy red wine of Lambrusco, and after Modena, in this flat and tedious landscape,

Albana   Bologna. Bologna's white wine is Albana. It is middling in every way except in its strength, which can be formidable.

TUSCANY   Tuscany is overwhelmingly the country of one red wine—Chianti. There

133

is such a thing as white Chianti, but it has no special character of its own. Any white wine grown in the country between Florence and Siena (or, I suspect, anywhere else) can be sold as white Chianti. You can expect it to be quite strong, pleasantly hard, rather earthy and dry.

But in the territory of Chianti Classico, nearer Siena than Florence, a number of once-feudal estates make small quantities of wine in the patient, painstaking way of the French or the Germans, experimenting all the time and perfecting styles of their own. A small part of this wine is white.

Brolio Bianco

The Barone Ricasoli at Brolio (of whose family I shall say more) makes a Brolio Bianco of a surprising mixture of grape-varieties; classical burgundian Pinot Noir and German Riesling. Neither grape is usually grown in Tuscany at all. The results, with the first-class technique of expert wine-makers (a different matter from the traditional methods of most of Tuscany), are extremely good. Brolio Bianco is one of Italy's best white wines. It has a very marked scent and great delicacy and freshness. You would drink it very happily with a trout.

Bianco Val d'Arbia

The more traditional white wine which Ricasoli also makes, and which is made by others, too, in his immediate area, is named after the little river Arbia. Bianco Val d'Arbia, or just Arbia Bianco, is more the wine for salmon than for trout; it has a fat richness in its scent, a certain softness of flavour which is not delicate but still manages to be, in one of the wine-taster's favourite expressions, elegant.

ELBA

The island of Elba between Tuscany and Corsica produces both red and white wines. The white, though rather strong, is dry and refreshing; exactly the thing for open-air suppers of fish and shellfish. Whether it is possible for wines to take on a tang of the sea or not—it may easily just be imagination—Elba to me has something distinctly maritime about it.

UMBRIA
Orvieto

If you are driving south from Florence to Rome down the Autostrada del Sole you will see the town of Orvieto occupying the top of a table mountain a mile or two away to the right. Orvieto produces one of Italy's most famous white wines; its *abboccato*.

All Orvieto is white. It is never very dry, but always a little soft and velvety with, as it were, potential sweetness. It reminds me more than anything of a white Graves from Bordeaux. It is comparatively light in alcohol, or seems so after the Frascati of Rome, which is described by its growers as 'food as well as drink'.

In places like Orvieto, with its world-famous name, the wine-trade has reached a pitch of sophistication which is not entirely typical of Italy. The firms whose names appear on the bottles are often not growers, but shippers, like the makers of sherry. Many buy the produce of small farmers who make their own wine in the countryside, where vines have taken over completely; orchards, cabbage-patches, everything is a mass of vines. They call it 'promiscuous cultivation'. The wine is left to ferment on the farm for the winter following the vintage, and only brought to Orvieto in the spring. The best of the wine is then allowed to go on fermenting very slowly, turning more and more of its rich store of residual sugar into alcohol, for two or even three years, in casks under the earth.

After such a long time in wood it is natural for a wine to be completely dry; all the sugar will have fermented away. The *abboccato* for which Orvieto is famous has to be made by adding a little intensely sweet and scented wine made from dried grapes to the normal, nearly-dry, type. There is a modern short-cut—that of stopping the fermentation with sulphur before all the sugar has gone—but the best firms resist it.

It is interesting that even the firms which are most proud of their wine—Barberani and Cortoni is one, Petrurbani another—sterilize and pasteurize it before they sell it, so that it cannot change at all once it is in bottle. I suspect this is because nothing they can do, besides leaving it in cask for years so that all the sugar disappears and it is bone-dry, will prevent the fermentation from tending to restart after bottling. This is the basic instability which is the curse of Italian wines, and which makes even the best bottle of Orvieto nothing beside the French wine which is unpasteurized, and hence capable of continuing its normal path of development in its bottle.

THE MARCHES AND ABRUZZI

Verdicchio

The Adriatic coast opposite Umbria is the province of Marche. Inland from the port of Ancona in the Appennine foothills a small district called the Castelli di Jesi, a group of five or six villages, makes wine from the Verdicchio grape. It is a fresh and appetizing wine, without much scent or particular character, but pleasantly dry and even a little bitter in your mouth. It has, in fact, more delicacy than most white wines from so far south. It is more like Soave, for example, than Frascati. To this it owes its wide fame. It is sold, either as Verdicchio dei Castelli di Jesi or just plain Verdicchio, in fancy-shaped bottles all over Italy and is often one of the few Italian wines appearing on wine-lists abroad.

South of the Marches the Trebbiano grape crops up again. Its yellow, rather strong wine is what you are most likely to find in the high empty spaces and lost little towns of the Abruzzi.

LAZIO
Est Est Est

In the north of the province of Rome the town of Montefiascone has a reputation for a wine called Est Est Est. The story of how it got its name is the only memorable thing about it—and this only because it is impossible to repeat such an absurd name without being asked its meaning.

A bishop called Fugger was on his way to Rome. His servant went ahead of him to report on the facilities (which meant, as all beds were hard and all food tough and poor, the wine). The servant's method was to chalk on inn-doors a cryptic *Est* if the inn passed muster, *Non Est* if not. Arriving saddle-sore and thirsty in Montefiascone, and downhearted by the dismal appearance of the town, he alighted and ordered wine. By some miracle they gave him a good one, because he was moved to give the first three-star accolade in history by scrawling *Est! Est! Est!* on the inn-door. The curious thing is that Fugger went no farther, but ended his days drinking Montefiascone, and no doubt boring his boon-companions to death with the story of Est Est Est.

According to all history and tradition Est Est Est is white wine. If you ask for it at Montefiascone they will, however, offer you red as well. I think the red (which is sweet and fresh) has a slight edge on the white. Neither is particularly well made, and thick bottles are necessary to avoid bursts from unfinished fermentation. Commercially Est Est Est is normally a semi-sweet or sweet white wine.

Lazio's best wine comes from the area known as the Castelli Romani in the Alban hills just south of Rome. It is Rome's own *vin de pays*. Perhaps this surrounds it with more lovely images and memories than it deserves. *Frascati* Frascati is the most famous name of the area. The town faces Rome from the middle slopes of a high hill to the south. Patrician families have had summer villas there for two thousand years: the centre of the town is dominated to this day by the Renaissance villa Aldobrandini, which is still the summer house of Prince Aldobrandini.

As vintage-time approaches the great tubby barrels are cleaned and got ready out in the streets of Frascati. They line every street and fill the centres of the squares, their tops always gleaming with a pool of water which is put there to swell the staves. Below ground stretch cold, cavernous, musty *grottas* which no modern vintage has ever been able to fill; the wine-stores of every age of Rome's history. Today wine is only taken down into many of them for the hottest of the summer when the temperature upstairs would make it start to ferment again.

At night in Frascati every street-corner has its stall selling roast sucking-pig, which is eaten with hunks of bread and flasks of white wine at trestle-tables outside the cantinas, under the plane-trees. Frascati is strong wine. We are a long way south now, and it is difficult to avoid over-heaviness in white wine at this latitude. But Frascati is fragrant, dry and easy to drink. I imagine its grapes are easy to eat, too: I have never seen such heavily-guarded vineyards. Barbed wire and locked gates surround every patch of vines. It is presumably picnickers from Rome who make this necessary.

The villages of Marino, Grottaferrata and Monteporzio Catone all make wine which is sold as Frascati. Other places in this area make wine which is similar but bears its own name: Albano from Lake Albano, a volcanic crater-lake full of huge tough trout hidden in the hills; Castel Gandolfo, where the Pope has his magnificent summer villa overlooking Lake Albano; Velletri; and Colonna.

Falernum Of the favourite wine of ancient Rome, Falernum, a pale shadow (one must presume it used to be better) now remains. It is now a rather heavy dry yellow wine from the coast half-way between Rome and Naples.

CAMPANIA At Naples we have virtually reached the southern limit of white wine

136

The cooper who makes and mends barrels is a vital craftsman in a wine-making community. Early in the morning the cooper of Frascati, near Rome, is checking the huge barrels which will hold the new white wine

making. The ordinary wine here which would come under the heading of white—since it is not red—is brown. It has the flat, oxidized taste of over-heated fermentation and overripe grapes. If you do not treat it as white wine (above all do not ice it), it is drinkable. A splash of water often improves it.

Amalfi

Finding a good wine here is a matter of luck. At Amalfi, for example, the specimen in one of the best hotels is undrinkable, whereas in a little café in a back street the one they produce with the superb *zuppa di pesce* is extremely good. (For the record the café is called Barocca; the wine is made by a man called Girola 'up the hill'.)

'Up the hill' is the secret. Down by the coast around the lovely peninsula of Sorrento and in the Bay of Naples, as well as on the islands of Capri and Ischia, it is too hot for vines. To find the better wine you must go inland and uphill: in the case of the Bay of Naples up Vesuvius, to find the famous Lachryma Christi; in the case of the peninsula up to Ravello.

Lachryma Christi

Lachryma Christi is all things to all men. It is red or white, sweet or dry to order. The genuine article is predominantly white and medium, and should say unequivocally that it is '*del Vesuvio*'; up the mountain it is grown on soil which is merely crumbled lava.

Ravello

Ravello is made in three shades, of which the pink is the most popular. The white is heady but pale and tart enough to be refreshing—qualities it owes to the altitude of the vineyards, the sea-mists which gather in the mountains, and the fact that most of the vines are grown pergola-fashion, even in arbours forming tunnels over the twisting road.

Capri
Ischia

Very little of the wine called Capri comes from Capri. I have never had any which was any good. Ischia, on the other hand, has some excellent white wine which, whether it comes from the island or not, is worth looking out for. Two Ischian wines in particular which I have had, Forastera and Biancolella, were good.

SICILY

There are two well-organized vineyards in Sicily making table wine for export. Both make red and white wine—without much character but clean, consistent and adequate. The vineyards of Mount Etna produce and give their name to one; the hills above Palermo the other, which is called Corvo. Taormina in the east also has a good dry white wine. It is generally agreed that Etna is, apart from dessert wines, Sicily's best.

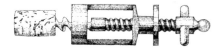

Portuguese White Wines

TO BE IN PORTUGAL at vintage-time in September is to see that the whole country north of the river Tagus—about two-thirds of the total—is kept busy by wine. On every road the ox-carts are lumbering and groaning their way to and from the vineyards. In every village street the heady smell of wine-making fills the air. Donkeys jog by with laden panniers. The fields are dotted here and there with working-parties. As you drive through the country details change: ox-harness or the shape of tumbrils for the gathered grapes or the baskets on women's heads or donkeys' backs alter in inexhaustible variety even from village to village. It is not surprising that the wine does too. Most of these country wines are good, but not many of them even have names.

I remember at a little inn at Alcobaça (under the shade of the most superb of monasteries, a palace whose kitchen was designed for Titanic feasts—a trout-stream bubbles in at one end, and the chimney is like a blast-furnace) the white wine with a savoury dish of minute clams had a distinct and delicious scent of wild strawberries. It was the local ordinary wine. It would have been welcome anywhere, but it did not even have a name. This is always happening in Portugal. To go through a list of the Portuguese wines which are at all generally available is not necessarily to name the best ones. The list, in any case, is absurdly short, because no-one has studied them properly, or exploited any except the easiest to buy and mature.

In some ways Portugal comes second only to France among the wine-countries of Europe. She not only produces a great variety of excellent wines, but seems to do it without effort. Some of the things which are true of Italy—that naming is careless, wine-making sometimes amateurish (and sometimes over-commercial), that vineyards' names are never used and vintage dates are used with gay abandon—are true of Portugal too. Organizations and supplies are unpredictable. And yet the wine always seems to reach the standard required. Furthermore it is the cheapest good wine anywhere.

It is literally impossible to pay as much for a bottle of the best Portuguese table wine in the best hotel in Portugal as a carafe of ordinary wine would cost you in England or America. Nor have I ever been given in Portugal any standard open wine which was not as good, or better, than such a wine would be in France.

All the conditions for wine-growing seem to be perfect in Portugal. It is all too easy to despise the wine merely because it is cheap. If any wine-merchant would seek good growths, make sure that they are well bottled and offer them in England or America he would be doing a public service.

138

As things are, the only wines which are offered for sale abroad are the easily handled brands which can be made in sufficient quantity to be worth advertising. They are often far from being Portugal's best. In some cases I was amazed to find when I went to Portugal that what I had taken to be the name of a village was, in fact, just a brand-name (this is the case, for example, with the very good brand of Serradayres).

The government is starting to legislate to rationalize things by approving appellations of origin not unlike those in France. But so far this is not notably successful or fair. All *vinhos verdes,* for example, are approved just because they are *vinhos verdes,* regardless of quality. But some of the best of all Portuguese white wines, being brands, are unapproved.

These problems are not our concern. I mention them because they underline, and to some extent explain, the foreign wine trade's concentration on wines which are not necessarily the best the country can offer.

Of the appellations which are approved by far the biggest (about three-quarters of the country's total) and most exploited name is *vinho verde.*

VINHO VERDE

Portugal's real speciality among white wines bears the strange name of green wine. It is green in the sense of being young and unstable. Sometimes it seems barely alcoholic: sometimes it is just like new cider. It can even be red, and still be called green.

Vinho verde comes from Portugal's northernmost province, the Minho, named after the river which washes the Spanish border to the north. The southern limit of the province is the river Douro in its lower reaches, below the mountains where port-grapes grow. Oporto, in fact, is the city both of port and of *vinho verde,* possibly the two most dissimilar wines in the world.

No countryside compares with the Minho for garden-like beauty. It is astonishing at first that what you are seeing is farmland, and not some vast pleasure-ground. It is small-scale country, where streams and hillocks rather than rivers and mountains divide up the land into a series of little amphitheatres. The eucalyptus tree with its narrow leaves and peeling trunk is the biggest object in sight. Medieval farms, sometimes a little chapel with its cloister converted into a farmyard and full of barrels, two-house hamlets and buried, leafy lanes are the landmarks. But the prettiest thing of all is the fields.

Around every field, held high on pergolas to form a maze of green arbours, vines make a border. In the centre, as irregular in shape as pieces of a jigsaw puzzle—octagons, hexagons, wedges, parallelograms—are patches of maize. There are no vineyards, no serried ranks of trimmed and sulphured little bushes. The vine grows as it grew in Eden.

The object of holding the vine high and surrounding it with green and growing things is to stop the grapes overripening in the blazing summer sun. White wines as far south as this are usually strong, not refreshing. But by preventing the heat from reflecting off the ground on to the grapes, as it does when they are trained low, and also stopping the residual warmth in the earth at night from continuing the sun's daytime work, the growers of the Minho have contrived to make just the wine they need. It is often only about 9 per cent alcohol, and carries a refreshing trace of acidity. Indeed the Minho soil is much prized for its acidity. It is great azalea and rhododendron country and even its pears and peaches are sharp. The wine needs no maturing, but is drunk while there are still traces of fermentation; tiny bubbles cling to the side of your glass. Above all, you can drink a lot of it. A bottle each is a reasonable lunchtime ration on a Portuguese summer's day.

White *vinho verde* is a marvellous drink on its own. It is often drunk with Portugal's superb fish and shellfish; a good idea when the weather is hot, though a good rich dish makes it taste very thin and watery. If it is simply a matter of quenching thirst, in fact, it is ideal.

Despite the fact that it is quickly made, quickly drunk wine there is considerable variety in the kinds that are made. The cheaper ones are sometimes no better than water with a squeeze of lemon-juice. Widely known brands such as Casal Garcia and Casal Mendes are the safest. There are a few even better ones: Vinhos de Moncao's Alvarinho (the name of the grape) Cepa Velha, which bears a vintage year and is bottled in a long green Moselle-type bottle, is perhaps the best but it is almost leaving the simple, ordinary field of *vinho verde*. It lasts well and even improves in bottle, developing a fine and delicate, almost freesia-like scent, staying fresh but turning into a full-scale table wine. This is not normally the idea. Most *vinho verde* should be drunk as young as possible.

It is so obviously the kind of wine which will appeal even to people who find most wine too strong-tasting, too dry or too heavy—some even, searching for a word, call all wine 'bitter'—that the exporting of it has become big business. There never was a wine with less chance of travelling well. Everything made it likely that it would lose all its qualities en route. But careful research has made it possible to ship a slightly sweetened, not quite so fresh version—the Casal Garcia, Casal Mendes and the rest which are gaining ground fast in Britain and the United States. It is odd that the Portuguese wine which should have most success abroad is the one which is least suited to foreign travel—and far better at home.

VINHO MADURO	Wine which is not green, but which has had a year or two in barrel to settle down and finish fermentation, is described as mature wine—*vinho maduro*. In this category come all the best wines of Portugal.

Four regions producing white *maduro* wines are 'approved' by the law. They are Colares, near Lisbon, whose crop is nearly all red; Bucelas, north of Lisbon; Dão, in the north of Portugal but south of the Douro; and the river Douro.

Bucelas Bucelas lies up the Tagus from Lisbon. Its wines are fairly hard in character and always either dry or nearly dry. The firm of Alves seems to have a large share in the business, which has one of the most respected

140

names in Portugal but is nevertheless dwindling. Vineyards in Bucelas are being sold as building-land. In Carcavelhos, nearer Lisbon to the west, the process has gone so far that there are no vineyards to be seen at all; nothing but villas as far as the eye can see (and yet the wine mysteriously arrives from somewhere—the neighbouring villages, perhaps). I never have had a Bucelas which excited me, but the name can be relied upon for regular quality.

Dão Dão is already a well-known name in Britain. It is associated principally with red and white wines as cheap as those of Rioja in Spain. Neither area does itself justice by the ordinary bottom-of-the-market wines it sends abroad.

White Dão (the red is on the whole more interesting and better) is Portugal's white burgundy. It is dry, savoury, clean. It could do with a little more of the richness, almost like a memory of sweetness, which makes burgundy so lovely. But that is a lot to ask. In every case where a very dry white wine is needed—and a soft, not a sharp one—Dão is a great stand-by. It does not age well, as the red does, but grows very flat with time. I have found that it pays to open a bottle an hour or so before drinking it if possible. There is often a smell of sulphur about it at first, but it quickly dissipates in the air.

Douro The Douro is amazing. It grows good wine of every kind. It is not commonly known that the famous Mateus Rosé has a white twin (and also a red one). The red comes from Dão, but both the pink and white are Douro wines. Vila Real, the town where Mateus is made, is in the northern part of the Douro district, near the border of the Minho, the *vinho verde* country. It is curious to think that Britain has now gone crazy about a sort of pink sparkling port.

Little white wine is sold using the Douro appellation. I believe Ermida, one of the best dry white brand-named wines, does come from the Douro, but it does not say so. Douro white wine is generally dry and has the quality of hardness and freshness which Dão sometimes lacks. It ages well. By far the greater part of it is country wine, never bottled but freely drunk with the various dishes of salt cod, the famous (or notorious) *bacalhau,* which they never stop eating in Portugal. In any part of Portugal it is not only safe but wise to ask for the wine of the house when eating in a restaurant. In the Douro you may get the most enjoyable of many pleasant surprises.

Brand-named wines come from every part of Portugal. Some of the best-known names are Almada, Arealva, Justina, Estoril, Serradayres, Allegro, Campo Grande, Solar, Serrador, Realeza or just plain Branco Seco (dry white). They are not meant to be anything more exciting than cheap blends, but they are usually good value.

Reserva For the finer wines there is nothing for it but to visit Portugal. The words
Garrafeira to look for which indicate that the wine is a special selection are *Reserva* and *Garrafeira*. Both are usually followed by a date, which is (more or less) that of the vintage year. The idea of a vintage year is not nearly so strictly

141

adhered to as it is in France or Germany, where it makes all the difference between good wine and bad. The climate of Portugal is more equable, and variations are rarely great. Where a label says *Garrafeira* 1957 it means that the wine was specially made in 1957 from the best of that year's wine—and perhaps a little good wine of the previous year or so if it helped the blend. In any case the *Reservas* and *Garrafeiras* are the best the firm in question can do (or, rather, *Reserva* is better and *Garrafeira* is best).

White *Reservas* you may find in Portugal include that of the illustrious house of José-Maria Fonseca, their Branco Seco Especial; the Ermida I have mentioned; Gaeiras; Lagoa (a rather strong dry wine from southern Portugal, in its humbler forms the ordinary wine of the Algarve); Lezirão; Planalto; Quinta d'Aguieira; Sanguinhal and Tres Cunhas. The makers of Serradayres have a wine called Caviar. There is quite a good sweet one called Grandjo.

As it is one long sea-coast, Portugal has a great deal of sea-food. Apart from the universal *bacalhau*, there are magnificent lobsters and wonderful little clams which come in many guises, either on their own or in a very good dish with pork. The dry white wines, therefore, are on every table, and constitute perhaps the most typical of Portugal's wines. It is a mistake to think that *vinho verde* is the only or even the best of them. Richer dishes call for *Reservas*. Fish restaurants in Britain and America could do worse than to find some good ones.

It would take longer than I have been able to spend in Portugal to discover where all the wines come from, or even to taste them all. I have not met anyone who has really made a study of them. But there are some really excellent wines among them. The field is wide open.

Spanish White Wines

SPAIN PRODUCES VERY LITTLE table wine which can compete in the international market by any virtue except extreme cheapness. The one important exception to this is the Rioja district in the north—and even in Rioja the red wine is better than the white.

The Spanish climate is not at all conducive to white wine. Common wines (of which vast quantities are made all over the country, except near the Atlantic coast or on very high ground) have some of the characteristics of sherry—high alcohol, strong colour, abundant flavour. But they lack the vital quality of acidity—the balancing, refreshing factor in every good white wine—and the result is flatness. Sherry is a lonely miracle. And yet sherry is not so different from other Spanish white wines as we tend to think. In fact, to the Spanish, it is simply the best of them, not separated in their minds from all table wines in the way it is in countries where it pays a different duty and fulfils a completely different function.

Given the overabundance of sun in Spain it is clear that the best wines (always excepting sherry) will be in the north. The province of Catalonia, the northern part of the Spanish Mediterranean coast, has some of them. Rioja, far away beyond Aragon and Navarre, where the Ebro breaks out from the Cantabrian Sierra to begin its long search for the Mediterranean, has most. The uplands of the north, towards the Portuguese border, have a few. And Galicia, the Atlantic province, between Portugal and Biscay, has its wild, cider-like country wine.

Alella   The districts of Alella and Panades lie on either side of Barcelona. Alella is to the north, on the coast and the coastal hills, between Barcelona and Mataro. Panades, a much bigger district, centres round the town of Vilafranca de Panades between Barcelona and Tarragona. The seaside resort of Sitges lies on its coast. Alella wine is some of Spain's best *vino corriente*, open carafe wine for cafés and restaurants. Some of the best of Barcelona's excellent fish-restaurants sell it—or rather give it with the bread as part of the cover. Superior white Alella is sometimes put into long green Moselle-type bottles. Every effort is made to give this wine some of the lightness, sharpness and agility which the associations of the bottle imply. Modern techniques have gone a long way towards ironing out the faults of the old *vino corriente*—heaviness, strength and flatness. But it is the old story of the baby and the bath-water. Special Alella costs three or four times as much and has about half the character.

Panades   Panades gives the greater part of its best white wine over to the manu-facture of *Xampan*—sparkling wine. The town of San Sadurni de Noya in the north of the district is one of the most important centres—is said, indeed, to have the biggest sparkling wine cellar in the world. Otherwise white Panades is made either dry or sweet, is always fairly strong, and at its best is rather like Alella.

RIOJA   The Cantabrian Sierra cuts off the north coast of Spain from the rest of the country. South of it the old kingdom of Castile stretches in wild open country and range upon range of bare hills. Almost on the borders of Navarre in the north-east the river Ebro comes south through the Sierra, still only a stone's throw wide. Its green valley, just below the entry of its tributary Rio Oja, which gives its name to the country, is Spain's best table-wine vineyard.

A good deal of the white wine of Rioja is sold, over-modestly, as Rioja Chablis and Rioja Sauternes, the names corresponding to the sweeter and drier types, though neither is particularly like the French wine whose name it borrows. Some of the Spanish wines which sell themselves as Spanish Chablis and Spanish Sauternes would be unsaleable without the borrowed names—they are young and horrible. But the Rioja wines would do much better to keep their own names and sell on their own considerable merit.

The wines do fall into two broad kinds, sweet and dry. There is none of the peculiar 'noble rot' which gives fine Sauternes its intense sweetness. Rioja is never normally more than weakly sweet. The dry white, though, is excellent. It is a strongly built, not a light-weight, wine, aged for two or three years in barrel, having a good gold colour, a faint but good scent and a flavour rather like a white Rhône wine; round but a little hard.

This is the general pattern. I have had a very old Brillante, one of the brand-names signifying sweet white, a 1910 from Bodegas Bilbainas, which genuinely had some of the deep honeyed sweetness of fine Sauternes. Some of the dry ones, too, are lighter and harder, stonier than I have suggested. In every case the firms of Rioja sell their best wine under several patent- or estate-names of their own, not just under the name Rioja This or That.

Vintage years are often put on these better wines. Often they seem improbably ancient to anyone who is used to French wines and their current vintages. This is largely due to the slow turnover, and the genuine need to keep Rioja wines, which are made in an old-fashioned way, for several years before they reach their best. A vintage of eight or ten years ago would be a reasonable date to see on even a white wine.

The names of some of the best Rioja bodegas (or wine-houses) will be found under Rioja on page 213.

Ribeiro

The wines of Spain's north-west are not exported. For the traveller there are the Galician wines, whose near-affinity to the Portuguese *vinho verde* is natural enough; the river Minho is in Spain too. Ribeiro is the important Galician wine-name. Between Valladolid and remote, dusty old Zamora on the upper reaches of the river Douro (in Spain the Duero) a 'delicate white' called Rueda is made.

Rueda

White wine is also made in the districts of Tarragona, Alicante and Valencia on the east coast and of La Mancha on the central plateau. Its merit is cheapness.

Swiss and Austrian White Wines

SWITZERLAND AND AUSTRIA are both real wine-countries. That is, they not only grow wine; it is their habitual drink. Germany is far more famous for her wine—and produces much better wine than either—but to a German it remains a drink for special occasions. Only in the heart of the wine-making Rhine country is it constantly on every table.

Switzerland is the biggest wine-importer in the world. More burgundy, for example, goes to Switzerland than anywhere else. Austria is one of Italy's best customers for wine. No two capitals are more in the heart of wine-country than Vienna and Geneva. Grapes grow right in the suburbs of both cities. All their best wine, in both cases, is white.

144

In Switzerland the main vineyards follow the course of the river Rhône from its headwaters in the Bernese Oberland, down the long, cliff-sided, flat-bottomed Valais and along the north shore of the Lake of Geneva. If you drive over the Simplon Pass from Italy and follow the road to Lausanne you pass almost all the best vineyards of Switzerland. Indeed at vintage-time you can hardly get along the road in some places for the carts and lorries parked on the verge, loading hideous red and yellow plastic boxes of grapes.

Visperterminen

Up near the head of the valley, where a southern side-valley leads from the ski-resort of Zermatt down to Visp in the Valais, the highest vineyards in Europe, the near-vertical Côtes of Visperterminen, face a glorious prospect of Alps and birches and snow. Lower down the Valais the rocky citadel of Sion stands out in the widening alluvial plain, providing more slopes, and more exposure to the sun, for the mellow Fendant grapes which make the Sion wine.

In the Canton of Vaud, where Lausanne follows Vevey and Vevey succeeds Montreux with hardly a break for countryside, the vines and villas, road and railway have become inextricably entangled. It is hard to see how they cultivate the little wedges of vines trapped between railway and lake.

Elsewhere in Switzerland, on the north shore of Lake Neuchâtel, round Zurich, Geneva and in Italian Switzerland, Ticino, wine is grown. Of these areas only Neuchâtel makes wine good enough for export.

THE VALAIS

Sion

The wines of the Valais are usually known by the name of the grape-stock and often by a brand-name as well. Only occasionally is the name of the place used. Wine made from the Fendant grape at Sion makes mention of the fact, but not all Fendant de Sion necessarily comes from Sion. In addition, there are two wines named after the wines of other countries —Johannisberg and Hermitage—presumably on account of fancied resemblances.

The Fendant (light, soft, good café wine), Arvine, Amigne and Humagne are all white wines, more or less dry. Malvoisie is a sweet wine used as an aperitif and after dinner. The *vin du glacier* is a peculiar speciality. It is taken when it is young from the valley vineyards to the cellars of high, cool villages to finish its fermentation very slowly, and develops a hard, almost bitter taste and more than usual strength. Of all these wines only Fendant and Johannisberg are commonly exported. Both could be described as light wines in the German—or perhaps rather Alsatian—manner.

THE VAUD

Lavaux

The Canton of Vaud, in which lies the north shore of Lake Geneva, includes all Switzerland's most reputed growths. Three districts lying on both sides of the city of Lausanne produce them. Of these the best is called, confusingly, Lavaux. It is on the steep lake-shore to the east of the city.

The best growths of Lavaux are Dézaley and St-Saphorin. Their wines are dry, not too strong and often thought to be the best in Switzerland,

145

although they are rarely exported. The Clos des Abbayes at Dézaley is sometimes called Switzerland's best vineyard.

La Côte

To the west of Lausanne the La Côte district is bigger but less distinguished. East of the lake altogether, where the Rhône widens out into a delta-shaped plain and the mountains fall back, the third district, Chablais, occupies the spectacular near-cliffs of the north side. Aigle and Yvorne are the best names here, making richer wine than Lavaux. They cannot be much more than ten miles, as the crow flies, from the border of France. All the good Vaud wines are made from the Fendant grape. All in all, it is Switzerland's best.

Chablais

Neuchâtel

The white of Neuchâtel is almost comparable with the Portuguese *vinho verde*; a wine of minimum alcoholic content, a good streak of tartness and a just perceptible bubble. It needs hot weather or a great thirst to make it appropriate.

AUSTRIA

The eastern end of Austria, the district of Vienna, produces the country's domestic supply of wine. Some of the vineyards have fine old reputations, and have even been mentioned in the same breath as the wines of the Rhine, but the same care is no longer taken with them. Wine from a particular named vineyard or estate-bottled wine is rare now. A village name is usually considered to be sufficient.

Austrian wine is linked geographically with Hungarian and Yugoslavian wines. The vineyards of the three countries are all grouped round the eastern end of the Alps: Austria's to the north, Hungary's to the east and Yugoslavia's to the south. All three produce wines in what might be described as the German manner, although they have different problems from the overriding German one of being so far north. Their wines are less delicate than German wines and less full of complicated and delicious scents and suggestions of scents—what is well called a bouquet, on the analogy of the many scents in a bouquet composed of different flowers. But they are clean, flowery, scented wines nonetheless.

Vienna is the place to see how good the best of Austrian wine can be, for practically none of the very limited supply of fine wine is exported today. Three areas—Wachau, along the Danube to the west of Vienna; the very suburbs of Vienna on the south side; and the north shore of the Neusiedlersee thirty miles south-east—produce good wine, almost all white. Krems, Durnstein and Loiben are the names of the Wachau wine-towns. They face south over the Danube just as Erbach and Oestrich in the Rheingau pick up the sun over the Rhine. Their wine tends to be quite sweet and full of flavour. Ordinary dry Wachauer wine, almost the only kind exported, is called Schluck.

Wachau

Vienna

Vienna wine is actually called Wien, and is often the *öffener* (open, i.e. carafe) wine in the city's cafés. The ordinary bulk produce is very light and drinkable. Some of the better wine is called Wiener Nussberger. Grinzing is another wine-producing suburb.

Gumpoldskirchen

Gumpoldskirchen is the one great name of the southern wine area. Several grape-varieties are grown in the area, and usually appear as the second word on the label, thus: Gumpoldskirchener Rotgipfler (an Austrian grape), Gumpoldskirchener Veltliner (another), Riesling, etc. All are fair, slightly sweet but light and pleasant.

The German principle of late-gathering is sometimes applied to make sweeter and more intense-tasting wines. They are called, as in Germany, *Auslese, Spätlese,* etc.

Eastern European White Wines

THE OPERATIONS OF A SOCIALIST RÉGIME have their effect on wine, as they do on every aspect of life. They level standards. The best may come down, but at least (in the case of wine, anyway) the worst improves. The fascination of individual growths and the exercise of the critical and comparative faculties disappear. But we are offered very sound, safe, miraculously consistent and very reasonably cheap wine in compensation. Indeed we do nothing but gain from the agricultural revolution in the countries of eastern Europe, however the farmers feel about it. It has given us a greater choice of better cheap wine than we have ever had before.

All the Communist countries concentrate on a range of standard lines, varying as little as possible even from vintage to vintage. Vintages are sometimes given, but never with the element of choice; one vintage is used up before another is offered. If a date is put on the bottle it can be used as an indication of age, but there is no question of whether or not it was a good year. The wine, they will tell you, is always good. The date is there for prestige.

Yugoslavia and Hungary are the two best wine-countries of eastern Europe. Their wine can be taken seriously, not as a cheap substitute for French or German, but as something excellent, and of great character, in its own right. Both make better white wine than red, but the red wine of Yugoslavia is not by any means to be rejected. Both also make among Europe's very best rosés.

HUNGARY

Hungary undoubtedly makes the finest wine of the Communist world, Tokay. Tokay is in the same class (see After-Dinner Wines) as Château d'Yquem or the *trockenbeerenauslesen* which are the apotheosis of German wine-making. It is honey-sweet, relatively old and necessarily expensive.

The other white wines of Hungary have nothing like the same reputation in the English-speaking world. Our sights tend to be rather narrowed to

147

France and Germany, Italy at a pinch, and Spain and Portugal for their specialities and their cheap wines. The Poles and the Scandinavians know better. They are great drinkers of the outlandish-sounding Badacsonyi Szurkebarat and Debroi Harslevelu.

Most Hungarian wine is on the heavy side and inclined to be sweet. The word the Hungarians often use for it, fiery, has all the wrong implications for us. It reminds us of rough hooch, bath-tub whisky or emery-paper Algerian wine. What I think they mean by it is that it is encouraging, warming, generous stuff. Their thin light wines they drink with soda as thirst-quenchers *(froccs)*: by serious wine-drinking they mean beakers of something rich and strong.

I find Hungarian wine delicious. Running through it all there is a thread of a special flavour, the same flavour as Tokay has *in excelsis,* something I can only describe as being rather like overripe butterscotch. There is a Hungarian scent too; a sort of floweriness which is somehow more autumnal and less spring-like than the German bouquet. In the way of lusciousness— drinkable, acceptable, not cloying lusciousness—they follow close on the heels of all but the very best of German wines.

The names are admittedly a problem. I have learnt how to pronounce them impeccably, but I promptly forgot again. If I did not think that a wine's identity was its most precious possession, and that to lose its name is to become, as Cassio said, poor indeed, I would say that they should go in for simple and memorable brand-names like the German Liebfraumilch. Happily, there are not many to remember, though, for as in all Communist countries the state is the sole exporter and no names of individual estates or merchants appear. In Britain, apart from the deservedly popular ordinary Hungarian Riesling, which is very much in the same class as the Yugoslav Riesling, there are only about half a dozen white table-wines available.

Lake Balaton Lake Balaton is the biggest and most important wine-district, leaving aside Tokay. Its shores yield district wines, in the broad sense of being no more specific than by saying, for example, Bordeaux red, of very high quality. The Riesling, as familiar as any grape to the English, takes on a new richness here, making round, golden wine with a hint of the familiar Hungarian overripeness. The other grape they use widely, the Furmint, which does not seem to appear anywhere except in Hungary but in Hungary is supreme, has the Tokay taste (it is the Tokay grape) to a marked extent— although, of course, nothing like its sweetness.

Both Balatoni Riesling and Balatoni Furmint are table wines in the sense that they would do no dish any disservice; both, on the other hand, have the strength and style to be good drinks on their own, either as aperitifs or, for example, at a party or when you are sitting reading late at night. Their touch of sweetness makes them this adaptable.

The best wine of Lake Balaton comes from a hill on the north shore—the *Badacsonyi* hill of Badacsonyi. Here are grown the Riesling again, a grape called the

148

Keknyelu and another called the Szurkebarat (which means Grey Friar). (I mention the grape-names not out of sadism but because they appear on the labels as they do with Alsace wines.) Badacsonyi wine is sweeter than plain Lake Balaton wine, stronger and more aromatic: in fact, to the Hungarian way of thinking, better. The best vintages made from the ripest grapes are purely dessert wines; the rest—including those which are exported—are for people who like these qualities in a table wine.

My Hungarian topography and much else I owe to a little book on Hungarian wine by Zoltan Halasz, published in Budapest. I cannot resist quoting him on the delights of Badacsonyi:

> One could hardly wish for a better way to relax than by taking a rest on the terrace-dotted slope of the hill, settling down on a small cask or a sawn log as a seat in front of a wine cellar. Laid out on a trestle table, an assortment of cold meat—sausages, greaves, smoke-cured bacon—soft bread and pickles lure the rover, who feels a gnawing hunger from the bracing air of the lake.

The wine he is offered with most pride by the cellarer, who goes on to invite him into his stone-and-thatch press-house, is the Keknyelu, a 'stiff, manly, fragrant wine'.

Somlo   Somlo and Debro are the other great table-wine districts of Hungary. Somloi (the name has a final 'i' in the same way as a German place-name gets an 'er' when it refers to a product) does not seem to be shipped to England. It is strong and fragrant, typical of Hungary. Its reputation is that it causes the begetting of male children. Debro in northern Hungary

Debro   grows the Harslevelu, which gives a strong-flavoured but not quite so luscious wine as those from Balaton. It would be more suitable with fish.

Mor   Finally there is Mor, from which comes Mori Ezerjo, possibly the most familiar and certainly the shortest of Hungarian wine-names. Mor lies to the north of a line from Balaton, which is in the south-west of Hungary, to Budapest. Its wine is considerably less luscious than the rest (although again, in good years, it is said to produce very sweet wine). For the ordinary table uses of white wine, and particularly with oysters or other shellfish, Mori would probably be Hungary's most suitable produce. It is a wine for the drinkers of white burgundies rather than hocks.

I find that these rather sweet and very prettily scented wines lose a great deal by being served too cold. Like all white wines, they are best decidedly cool, but anything approaching iciness kills the floweriness and lusciousness which are the whole point. They are worth big, beautiful glasses and time to ponder and discuss what the smell reminds you of.

YUGOSLAVIA   The Riesling, the vine of hock and Moselle, is responsible for most of the
Slovenia   Yugoslav wine exported. It is at its best at Lutomer in Slovenia, the north-west corner of the country near the Austrian and Hungarian border. Here there are even estate, rather than regional, wines. The Kapela estate near the town of Lutomer is famous for its Renski (Rhine) Riesling.

The wine which is shipped as simply Yugoslav Riesling, without the

Serbia

superior name of Lutomer attached, comes from Serbia, the area in the north-east where Belgrade lies, and where the Danube turns to wash the border of Rumania. To the north-west of Belgrade the Fruska Gora mountains face the wide, monotonous plain of the Sava. These are the biggest vineyards in Yugoslavia.

The northern vineyards also grow other grapes familiar in Germany and Alsace, the Sylvaner and Traminer.

Macedonia

Farther south, in Macedonia, the familiar names of Riesling and Sylvaner disappear. Native grapes take over, and the names here are wholly unfamiliar. This should not be a deterrent from buying the wines—we do not hesitate about buying Chianti because it is not made from Pinot grapes. The Zilavka of Macedonia is one of the most bewitchingly different grapes. It gives a wine with a sweetness of savour and scent, and a dryness of final taste, which are astonishing in something so cheap and unknown. It would take the place of a white burgundy at dinner perfectly well—not perhaps every day, but every now and then.

All these wines so far have been in the dry or semi-dry class; as sweet as Liebfraumilch at the sweetest. There is also a Lutomer late-picked wine, Tigermilk, or Ranina Radgona Spätlese, which is very much sweeter and more like a Hungarian wine, though not as good.

THE BLACK SEA

The vineyards of Russia and the Balkans are grouped about the Black Sea. On the east, starting from the south, there are vineyards in Bulgaria, in Rumania, in Moldavia, the Crimea, the Russian Republic, Georgia and the Caucasus (Armenia). All the wine they export is made from large co-operative vineyards working to a standardized pattern, and is pasteurized when it is bottled, so that it can neither improve nor deteriorate—nor ever be more than an ordinary, rather dull brand. For variety they look to different grapes, each being made to give a stylized consistent wine. It is rather as though we asked all our best painters to paint exactly the same picture over and over again. There is interest, for a while, in comparing artist with artist, but it is not long before we long for them to develop and paint something else.

The red wine of the Black Sea area tends to be better than the white. Rumania and Bulgaria make better wine than the Soviet Union. Rumania has, if anything, the better name of the two for white wine.

Rumania

Within this century Rumania has been the third most prolific wine-country in Europe, and there are signs that wine has a high priority in her economy. She has, however, lost Bessarabia, her chief wine-making region, to the Soviet Union (it was liberated, as they say in those parts, and re-christened Moldavia in 1940). Most of her white wine is rather sweet and not particularly good. Murfatlar and Muscat Ottonel are both in about the range of sweetness of Orvieto—too sweet, to my mind, to enjoy with most food but not quite sweet enough for after dinner. The Riesling of Tirnave is

150

Rumania's best white wine. The Riesling of Perla is a sweeter version. Both are comparable with Yugoslav or Hungarian Riesling. The Chardonnay of white burgundy is also grown in Rumania, I believe, although I have not tasted a Rumanian one. In Bulgaria it makes an excellent clean and dry white wine—one of the nearest approaches to a white burgundy which I have tasted outside France.

Bulgaria

The Black Sea coast is the chief white-wine region of Bulgaria. Some of its vineyards are beautiful, sloping right down to yellow sandy beaches between groves of oak trees like the setting for a Greek tragedy. The Dimiat and the Grozden (both apparently relations of the Riesling) and the Misket, a kind of Sylvaner, are grown on the coast and all make adequate white wine. I must confess that on my one visit to Bulgaria I was not always sure what I was drinking. The custom is to start every meal with the delicious white plum spirit, Slivova, which has a numbing effect on the palate. Despite this, the Bulgarians are wine-drinking people. There is always wine on the tables in the cafés. The vaults of the opera house of Sofia, where the youth and beauty of the capital gather late in the evening to talk, has the atmosphere of a Rhineland *weinstube,* with the addition—universal in Communist countries—of an energetic little orchestra.

The Soviet Union

I have frequently had leaflets from what is euphemistically called the Russian Information Service about enormous new tracts of the Soviet Union being turned over to vines. The production of Champanski, in particular, seems to double every year or so. Few white wines, however, appear in the West. In Britain we see Tsinandali and Gurdjani, which are both Georgian wines—the former light and harmless, the latter more courageously exotic. Both are dry. I prefer the Gurdjani because it has more taste. There is one other white wine—the one product of the Russian Republic itself which is exported—Anapa Riesling, which fails to reach the standard set by Rumania in this field.

Californian White Wines

OF ALL THE VINEYARDS of the New World California is the one which has suffered most discouragement—from 1919 to 1933 the Volstead Act prohibited wine-making altogether except for use in churches—and yet the one which makes the best wine. Of the other new lands of the vine you can say that many of their wines are good and some fine. Of California you can say that many of her wines are fine, and some great.

Broadly they are divided into two kinds—as, indeed, French wines are. The great bulk of the state's produce is ordinary and cheap, the equivalent

151

of the wine of the Midi. This, again broadly speaking, is the harvest of the great interior valley of California, with Fresno as its capital; a land of intensely hot, utterly dry summers. The smaller, but far more interesting, part, which includes all the fine table wines of the state without exception, is grown in the counties surrounding San Francisco Bay. Here the influence of the Pacific and its great land-bound extension, the Bay, moderates the climate. The nights are cool. Often heavy sea-mist rolls in over the Coast Range at night to provide moisture for the vines. These conditions make the perfect maturing of the grapes possible. It is sometimes hard to believe, as you see the strange juxtaposition of vineyards and cattle-ranches, of bare grass hills—the West of horse-opera—with Pinot Noir and Pinot Chardonnay, the delicate grapes of Champagne, that anything but a rough-and-ready drink for cowboys can come of it. And yet of all the places which have ever set out to imitate the great wines of France only California has ever succeeded. I am not using the word great loosely. There are a handful of wine-makers in the Napa and Sonoma valleys who have demonstrated that what they can make is comparable with a Chevalier-Montrachet or a Château Latour; not just a vague white burgundy or claret. They are, of course, very much in the minority—as the great wine-makers are in France—but it has been proved beyond question that certain areas of California have the potential. It only remains to be seen what commerce will make of it.

Generics and varietals Slowly but surely the wineries (an ugly but inescapable word) of California are moving from generic to varietal names for their wines. By generic they mean the name of a type (Chablis, Moselle, Sauternes—one even used to make a 'Château Yquem'), by varietal the name of a grape-variety. The names of Semillon, Sauvignon, Pinot Chardonnay and Cabernet Sauvignon have already become part of the Californian language, strange as it may seem. Frenchmen who have been drinking the juice of these grapes all their lives may well have barely heard of them, but you will hear sunburnt, slow-walking ranch hands drawl them out like the names of their home towns.

Vintages These grape-names, with the name of the winery, usually constitute the whole nomenclature of fine Californian wines. Some, but they are a minority, carry the vintage year; whether they do or not is more a matter of commercial convenience than anything else—they are up against a reluctant and slow-witted retail and restaurant trade, who are frightened and put out by the simple fact that wine is made in annual harvests, with inevitable variations, and not in a steady consistent stream.

Again, in commercial self-defence, all the larger wineries which look for wide distribution carry a full range of types of wine, even to what they call a sherry, a rather sweet drink dimly (if at all) related to the real thing, for which they buy the grapes in the hot interior valley. Without this complete armour they would apparently be edged out of the wine-lists by competitors.

The list of Californian white wines is longer than the list of reds. The white grapes of Bordeaux, Burgundy, Alsace and Germany, the Loire and

152

Château Tronquoy-Lalande at St-Estèphe in the Médoc, a typical minor claret château, classified as a *Cru Bourgeois Supérieur*. Some of the best-value wines of Bordeaux come from such estates as this. *(Photo: Guy Gravett)*

northern Italy are all grown with considerable success. One grape, above all, though, gives wine as good as any but the greatest of its native land; the Pinot Chardonnay, the white grape of Burgundy. It is almost always the most expensive Californian white wine, for the yield of grapes per vine is low and farmers have been reluctant in the past to plant the variety. In richness and freshness of scent, in savouriness and complexity of taste, and in balanced and appetizing dryness, however, it is so outstanding that vast new plantings are being made to increase the supply. It is grown in the fertile and beautiful Napa and Sonoma valleys north of San Francisco Bay, the Livermore valley east of the Bay and Santa Clara and San Benito counties to the south—all the best areas in California. It is commonly thought to reach its very best in Napa and Sonoma, in the hands of such small-scale wineries as Hanzell, Stony Hill and Heitz. But wines like these are rare and expensive. They are seriously to be compared, in value and price, with fine Meursaults and even Bâtard-Montrachets. The wines made on a more commercial scale by the best of the larger wineries—Beaulieu, Almaden, Louis Martini, Charles Krug are examples among many more—are far more widely available, and less distinguished only in the proportion that a good plain Meursault comes below, for example, a Meursault Perrières.

Three or four other white grapes besides have almost the prestige of the Chardonnay. The Sauvignon Blanc, the principal white grape of Bordeaux, makes an excellent, rather strong dry wine, particularly in the Livermore valley. The fertile, gravelly floor of this valley is, sad to say, however, in great demand for new house-building. Under a system which taxes a vineyard owner on what he could get for the land if he sold it for housing, rather than what it is worth as agricultural land, a number of these fine old vineyards are being abandoned. For the moment, however, the Wente Bros, Concannon and Cresta Blanca wineries all make fine wines in the teeth of the eastwards suburban sprawl of the Bay area.

The white Riesling, the grape of Rhine and Moselle, makes a good dry wine, too, though not one which challenges Germany to a direct comparison as the Sauvignon does the growers of Graves. The Gewürztraminer of Alsace is also thought of as one of the finest Californian whites. The aromatic and spicy quality which makes it so remarkable in Alsace is less marked in California, though. Californian Gewürztraminers tend to be rather soft in your mouth, mildly perfumed and pleasant rather than exotic.

The good Californian white table wines come as a slight surprise to one who is accustomed to French and German wines, for while they keep the characters of their grapes very clearly, they usually do so with more strength, more scent and a more positive and uncompromising dryness than their European opposite numbers. It may be because there is rarely any trouble in getting ripe grapes, so that few or none of those in the press are green, or because in California the temperature of the fermentation is always kept firmly under control—whatever the reason, the slight tenderness which

Pinot Chardonnay

Sauvignon Blanc

White Riesling

Gewürztraminer

153

stops a white burgundy from ever being as dry as, say, an unsweetened sherry is not there. The difference is most noticeable in Rieslings, where the subtle sweet-and-sour balance of German wines is replaced in California by an extra 2 per cent of alcohol, with a resulting gain in power and loss of delicate complexity.

The Sylvaner, the Green Hungarian, the Pinot Blanc, the Chenin Blanc and the Semillon Blanc are all grapes which are used to make varietal wines on, as it were, the second level. Whereas the finest varietals are supposed to be 100 per cent the grape named (legally, the words 'estate-bottled' on the label commit them to this percentage) the lesser ones may still legally be labelled as varietals if they contain 51 per cent of the grape in question. To the outsider it seems a curiously permissive piece of legislation.

Sylvaner

All the above names are commonly used with the exception of Sylvaner. For some reason Sylvaner wine is sold as Riesling. Real Riesling is distinguished by the qualification 'white' or 'Johannisberg'. 'Riesling', so called, Green Hungarian and Pinot Blanc are useful, interchangeable everyday table wines. The Chenin Blanc usually makes a slightly sweeter wine than these—one, to my mind, as good drunk before or after a meal as

Semillon

with it. The Semillon is used as a varietal on its own, making a soft, rich-flavoured wine, but also in the making of California Sauterne.

Sauterne

Sauterne, spelt in the Californian way without the final 's', is normally a dry wine. Nobody really seems to know how the name of one of the world's great sweet wines was adapted to apply to the very opposite, a rather ordinary dry one, like this. Perhaps it was originally a piece of irony. In any case in California Sauterne is dry; qualified by the word Haut it is usually medium sweet; if it is really sweet it will probably be called by a name involving the word Château. Labels which need decoding, in fact, are by no means confined to France and Germany.

In recent years the University of California's Department of Viticulture has added new varieties of purely Californian invention to the wine-maker's list. One of the best-selling of all California's white wines today is made of a grape which is unknown in Europe. This is an important step, for the new hybrids seem to be capable of doing what no old variety could do—maintaining enough acid to give a balanced table wine even in really hot conditions. It is the lack of acidity, above all, in the grapes of the central valley which makes them suitable only for fortified wines. The best known of the

Emerald Riesling

new grapes is the Emerald Riesling, which makes an unusual, refreshing, slightly sharp, light wine. Another new variety, called Gold, makes a good cheap sweet wine.

Not only are the wines of all these grapes, European and Californian, perfectly good, and sometimes excellent, everyday drinking; they are almost always infinitely better value at a dollar and a half or so a bottle than any imported wines within a dollar of the same price.

In Britain few Californian wines are obtainable, and those which are have the handicap of the usual duties and the high cost of such long-distance

154

freight on top of the comparatively high basic price. Nonetheless no-one who aspires to know what good things the world of wine offers can afford to ignore them.

Other White Wines

Although Britain is the main export market for Australian wine the British have, sad to say, little respect for what they buy. They learn from statistics that three bottles of fortified wine are drunk in Australia for every one of natural table wine, and from hearsay that the great wine-country is addicted to beer. If they buy a bottle of Australian wine the odds are ten to one it will be sweet, heavy and dull—in no way comparable with the wonderful delicate wine they are used to from just over the Channel. Looking no farther, they conclude that it is all chauvinistic talk about superb Australian vintages, or, charitably, they suppose that Australia keeps all its best wine at home. Neither notion is true. There are fine wines, and they are exported, but they are poorly distributed, and very difficult for someone who is used to European wines to understand.

All the sanctions of the French and German wine laws have to be forgotten. They only lead to misunderstanding of the wines of Australia. The thing to remember is that wine in Australia is labelled on the basis of gentlemanly understanding and confidence, rather than on what Europeans like to regard as truth.

For example, Riesling is the name of the great German grape; one of Europe's proudest viticultural possessions. Its name appears on Australian bottles. But the wine called Riesling is not Riesling, and does not taste of Riesling. It is usually made of one of the white Bordeaux grapes, the Semillon. If you want a Riesling you must ask for a Rhine Riesling.

More surprising still is the practice of some of the best wineries of splitting their crop into several denominations. On these estates each day's picking is kept apart from that of the previous day, pressed separately, fermented and stored in a separate vat. The day's work is given a bin-number. The first bin, of course, was made when the grapes were less ripe than the last, which came perhaps three weeks later. The wine in the first is dry, in the last sweet. The first they sell as Chablis, the second as hock.

Most of the confusion arises from the use of European wine-names. It has other disadvantages, too. Australians are constantly, and rightly, saying that they want their wine to be judged on its own merits. But this will only be possible when it has its own names. With however good a will one cannot help comparing a wine which is called claret with claret. And in no single case is the Australian wine good enough to benefit by the comparison.

The practice which the best California wine-makers have adopted—of naming the wine by its grape-variety and the valley of its origin—is spreading in Australia. Its usefulness is called in question if, for example, Semillon wine is to be called Riesling. But with these difficulties out of the way it will simplify the chooser's task enormously. It need not take very long, either, for the names of the best estates, Coonawarra, Tahbilk, Ewell and so on, to become known. Then Australian wines will get what they have been asking for all along—the respect, attention and the sales that they deserve.

New South Wales
South Australia
Victoria

Wine-making started in each of the three great wine-states of Australia— New South Wales, South Australia and Victoria—within ten years of the state's foundation. It can truthfully be said that it is as old as Australia, and in South Australia at least an important part of the country's way of life. As far as fine white wine is concerned, the most important regions are the Hunter River Valley north of Sydney, the vineyards almost in Adelaide and those north of Melbourne. Mount Pleasant, Lindeman's Ben Ean and Oakvale in the first area, Hamilton's Ewell vineyards and Yalumba in the second, and Château Tahbilk and Milawa in the third are some of the places which produce Australia's best white table wines. Seppelt's estate west of Melbourne at Great Western is best known for its sparkling wine, but also produces excellent still whites. You will notice that it is in general the more southern and coastal areas which are best for light wines. The Hunter Valley is something of an exception, but it has a damp climate of its own, which explains its fine wine being so far north.

Wines from all these areas are available in Britain under specific estate names, most of them bottled in Australia. Vintage years are not normally mentioned. Their prices are reasonable, perhaps a shade higher than those of French wines of similar quality. I believe they can fairly be said to represent Australia as the serious wine-country she can be, as distinct from the processor of overripe grapes into over-strong wines—the image in which she is usually presented.

SOUTH AFRICA

The climate of South Africa has more in common with Spain and Portugal, the countries of strong aperitif and dessert wines, than it does with France and Germany, the countries of fine white table wines. But Portugal, with its exposure to the west and the influence of the Atlantic, has good white wine to its credit. The western province of the Cape is in a similar position.

There is a tendency for white wines in very hot countries to be over-strong, rather dark-coloured and completely dry. They are likely to be coarse and flat to the taste. If great care is not taken the grapes become overripe, fermentation in the hot air is violent and short, what little natural acidity there was is lost and all subtlety and bouquet is dispersed. It seems that South Africa would have little hope. But cool calculation and liberal use of refrigeration have got over most of these difficulties. By counteracting each of the threats in turn (picking the grapes as they ripen, keeping the fermenting vats cool and closed so that the process can be gradual and the bouquet can be saved, never allowing the wine to have contact with the air, not even through the staves of an oak cask, but keeping it in concrete vats until the moment of bottling) the South African wine-farmers have won. They can now make light and fragrant white wines after the model which has always been in their sights—the wine of Germany.

The alcoholic content of South African wines is always fairly high; a little higher than those of Germany. A local law prevents them from ever being very sweet (with more than 2 per cent of sugar they have to be fortified with brandy, and so come into the port and sherry category). The best examples available in Britain—which are not many—are dry to medium-dry, well scented and good value, costing less than virtually any German wines, though rather more than comparable wines from Yugoslavia and Hungary. The Co-operative Wine-Farmers' (K.W.V.) Steen is one of the best of them. This, indeed, has more affinity to a Portuguese wine than to a German one. It is almost like a heavier, more wine-like version of a *vinho verde*.

A rather sweeter Late Vintage Steen comes from the same stable. A comparable pair is shipped by another firm under the name of Twee Yongegezellen—Two Young Friends. One English wine-merchant also has a dry white Constantia, which bears the least possible likeness to the Constantia wine which was, a hundred and more years ago, one of the world's very finest sweet wines. Another has the most charmingly-named La Gratitude, a dry wine which must be one of South Africa's very best.

There remains a large bulk of cheap sweet wine shipped under borrowed names—notably South African Hock, which is not in the least like hock, any more than Australian Burgundy is like burgundy. But the signs are that South African table wine has graduated from this stage and is ready to come to table under its own names, to be judged on its own considerable merit.

Paarl, Stellenbosch and Tulbagh are the centres of the best white-wine area, on the west of the Cape.

THE EASTERN MEDITER-RANEAN Although the eastern Mediterranean made wine long before France did, the hand of the Prophet was laid on it in the early years of Christendom. The Koran forbade (though not always successfully) the drinking of wine, and it died out in its own home-country, giving place to the wines of the upstart Europe.

There is no long tradition of wine-growing, therefore, in most of the eastern Mediterranean countries which are now growing wine again. Their wine comes into the category of the New World's wine—a direct transference of the grapes and the styles of wine from its most famous homes. The new Israeli wine, for example, sometimes compares itself with Alicante —unambitiously enough, for it has chosen about the worst example of any traditional wine that it could find. Even Cyprus, whose wine-growing tradition was never really stopped by the Turks, uses terms such as burgundy for its very unburgundian produce.

Greece   Greek wine, it is true, lies right outside the mainstream of wine tradition in a quiet, undrinkable backwater. The Greek taste for putting resin in the new wine makes it a struggle for anyone who is not used to it. Retsina, with its taste of turpentine, becomes a memory of Greece which it is difficult, once you have drunk it there, to forget. No country expresses itself so uncompromisingly in its wine—but wine is hardly the word for it. I have only once discovered any merits in it, and that was in a little inn in Thrace where the beans in oil, the potatoes in oil and the hard grey bread desperately needed something to take the taste away. Even the taste of turpentine was better than the musty oil and the soggy hopelessness of the food.

There are, however, a number of unresinated wines in Greece, of which the white, on the whole, are more pleasant than the red. The sweet muscat *Samos*   of Samos has the greatest reputation of these, though I have never had a very wonderful bottle. Of the others, the brand Demestica is widespread and adequate, and a number of the islands make better than average whites. *Rhodes*   That of Rhodes (which is said to be so fertile that there are three vintages in a single year) is better than most in my experience, but I would recommend conversation with one who has really drunk his way round the Aegean rather than reliance on my limited experience.

Cyprus   All the eastern Mediterranean wines suffer from the excess of sunshine so far south. They are all scaled up in strength, so to speak, so that, for example, Cyprus rosé has the sort of flavour you associate with a very stout burgundy, while Cyprus red has more of the taste of port. Ordinary white wine has most of the power of sherry. They are a race of Superwines. But to those who are used to French wine they tend to be too much of a good thing; rather than quenching thirst they set your head spinning. The kind of new techniques which South Africa is using, however, are coming into play. Refrigeration is making a great difference. No doubt there will soon be excellent Cyprus white wine (at the moment the red is better).

Israel   Israel is already making some very light dry whites with a good deal of character of their own. Some have a slight background taste of raisins, reminding one of how hot it must have been in the vineyard at vintage-time, but there is no reason why the original lands of wine should not come back to their inheritance and, with modern methods, add yet more good wines to the vast variety we have to choose from. At the moment, I should add, most of the Israeli wines are rather sickly sweet.

Rosé Wines

The word rosé has moved into the English language. Pink was too undignified a word for wine. Rosé is simply French for rose-coloured. Its similarity to *arrosé*, which means watered, is quite coincidental.

It is useful to have a wine which you can fall back on at any time, which is good as a drink on its own, or good for a glass with lunch, good for sipping as you cook or good for supper in the garden. No wine has a monopoly of these qualities; many fine German wines, for example, would be good for any of these things, or with practically any dish. But German wine is expensive, and not so very simple. Rosé is cheap, has no long pedigree, needs no special serving—is in fact, the all-purpose wine for thirsty people.

Rosé has, besides, the prettiest range of colours of any wine. Colour is not everything, by a long way, but a really glowing coral glass, a cherry-coloured one or one with a touch of tangerine about it fairly beckons you in. The wine-makers themselves have toyed with the poetic in their words for the pinkness of their wares—*oeil de perdrix*, partridge-eye, is one the lipstick people might try. *Pelure d'oignon*, onion-skin, would probably go less well.

There is no great range of tastes and scents among rosé wines. It is the connoisseur's—many, unjustly, would say snob's—argument against them. The grower making a rosé is not following, as more serious wine-makers do, the specific practice of his region to bring out the regional character and make a wine which could be recognized anywhere. Character is considered expendable for pink wine. What the maker is after is the simple taste of wine; the lowest common denominator (or, if you like, the highest common factor) of all wine. He will make it sweeter or drier, still or a little sparkling, to suit your fancy, but this art touches that of the confectioner rather than the ancient skills of making wine. The colour comes, as does the colour of red wine, from the skins of black grapes. For rosé less skins are left in the fermenting wine for less long—the length of time depending on the colour and richness of flavour the maker wants. No doubt there are those who make it by mixing red and white wine, or even putting cochineal in white, but they work by night if they do.

Whereas in buying most other kinds of wine I would counsel you to buy the best you can afford, with rosé I would say buy the cheapest you can find, for there is not very much to choose between them. Rosés from northern parts, it is true, tend to be weaker in flavour and alcohol than some from farther south. Italian rosés, which are in the main more like light reds, have more character than some French ones. Portuguese rosés are usually shocking pink with titillating little bubbles. But basically the same, essential, appealing wine is there behind the frills and frou-frou. It is the wine for lunches, picnics, kitchen-parties—but not for fine food at a good dinner.

FRANCE

Tavel

One of France's rosés takes itself, and is taken, more seriously than the others. It is Tavel, the pink cousin of Châteauneuf-du-Pape, from just across the Rhône in the same hot and stony countryside. Like its cousin it is a strong wine, leaning towards the onion-skin (imagine the colour Cézanne would have painted an onion) in colour, high-flavoured, not remarkably scented but pungent and assertive, happy with the strong-flavoured food of Provence. It goes equally well with the herb-smoky grills and the astonishingly thirst-provoking *aioli*, or with that strange Provençal concoction, the oily, creamy cod porridge known as *brandade de morue*.

But even Tavel, leader of the *vins rosés*, is not regarded as a wine of vintages or a *vin de garde*—a wine to keep. It is drunk, like all pink wines, regardless of its vintage but on the understanding that it is not more than two or three years old.

Côtes de Provence

Provence produces a great many *vins rosés* besides its most famous one. They are among the most plentiful and best of the Côtes de Provence region which stretches east from Marseilles behind all the resorts of that crowded coast. They all tend to be dry and strong rather than soft and sweet. This tendency is sometimes reversed in the cause of commerce; some of those which are shipped abroad in rather more fanciful bottles than good wine usually needs are medium-sweet, without much of the clean refreshing taste which makes them such good drinking in Provence. The Vacation Syndrome, or whatever you like to call it, works powerfully against the rosés of Provence in a foreign land; we ask them to take us back to our summertime Garden of Eden, we expect a sip to transport us, like the Caravelle, to Nice. There are wines which can give satisfaction when so much is asked of them, but Provençal rosés are not often among them.

The Loire

At the other extreme of wine-growing France, in the Loire valley, the rosé is blessed by nature with all the qualities its tender pinkness promises.

160

It is light, soft and slightly sweet. It should be the perfect thing for a kind of party I shall never be invited to—a gathering of ladies for lunch. Suppose they are going to eat a chicken salad, or some veal or even just starch-reduced rusks and cream cheese, I propose the rosé of Anjou as the wine. There are two kinds of Anjou rosé in circulation, the cheaper known as plain Anjou Rosé and the (slightly) more expensive as Anjou Rosé de Cabernet, made of the Cabernet, the black grape of Bordeaux. The Cabernet wine is usually less sweet than the other, but more scented.

Anjou Rosé

Burgundy does not waste much time with rosés. A small part of the produce of Beaujolais is made into rosé instead of red—and suffers loss of character accordingly. At the northern end of the Côte de Nuits, near Gevrey-Chambertin, the village of Marsannay specializes in rosé, and makes a very fine, very pale one which is popular in the United States but rarely seen in Britain.

Beaujolais

Marsannay

A small part of the crop in Alsace is also made into rosé, and is excellent, but is not widely circulated by the wine-trade as the white Alsace wines are.

Alsace

Bordeaux also produces good rosé with very little fuss, cheaper than most and just as good. It is comparatively dry, and light and clean to the taste. It could even be the wine which made the English call all red Bordeaux claret, which was certainly pale red—though perhaps not quite so pale as the modern rosé.

Bordeaux

Last of the big rosé-producers of France—every area produces a little—is the Jura, whose lovely unvisited hills are like a ramp up to Switzerland from what feels like the heart of France. The Jura owes its fame to some small quantities of unusual white, brown and red wines, but not less to large quantities of rosé of very high quality. The Jura word for a rosé, just to round off the spectrum, is *gris*—grey.

The Jura

Jura pink wines are, in taste, light red ones. They are made from the same two local grapes, the Poulsard and the Trousseau, as the velvety local red wines. Their quality varies more or less in proportion to the amount of Poulsard and the amount of Trousseau each wine has in it. The Poulsard is the better, although each contributes something to help the other. There is always some Trousseau, even when the finest quality is the object.

The best part of the Jura area for red wine is the neighbourhood of its chief town, Arbois. The same is true for rosés. Rosé d'Arbois is therefore a superior appellation to Rosé du Jura. Beyond this it is hard to specify, because most of the wines have brand-names. Their quality is deliberately related to their price.

Arbois

A good Arbois rosé has more scent than most pink wines, the characteristic kernel-like scent of the Poulsard. It is round, satisfying and faintly sweet—simply, as I have said, a pale red. Compared with it a Jura rosé seems a little thin but has, on the other hand, a kind of individuality, a rather stony quality, which is very attractive. There is one called Cendré de Novembre whose name alone goes a long way to persuade me. It is not difficult to imagine that you see the glow of embers in its colour, as its name suggests. November, on the other hand, is not the month I would choose to drink it. It is a carafe wine for summer, a picnic wine, a really refreshing mouthful for a hot day.

ITALY

The best of Italy's pink wines, too, is a pale red rather than a true rosé. It is Chiaretto, the wine of the calm lakeside of Garda. At the south end of the enormous lake which divides Lombardy from the Veneto the steep, misty, olive-clad hills which surround its north, east and west subside. In these faltering hills the wine is bright cherry-red. Under typical Italian holiday circumstances, in hot weather, with pasta or salads and on picnics, Chiaretto del Garda is perfect. The best Chiaretto of many good ones I know is made at a little place called Moniga in the south-western corner of the lake, by the firm of Nino Negri. Moniga is a tiny walled town, no bigger than a big farm, surrounded by vineyards. Its wine is sold as Moniga del Garda, with Chiaretto added as though as an afterthought.

Chiaretto del Garda

Lagrein Rosato

To the north of Garda in the Italian Tyrol a paler, very delicate and attractive pink wine with the name of its grape, Lagrein Rosato, is made. It is curious that these wines are hardly shipped to Britain at all. They are certainly among the world's best rosés, and there is every sign that the market for rosés is expanding. The greater part of the produce of the Tyrol at the moment goes to Austria and Germany.

Ravello

Italy's two other famous and noteworthy *rosatos* come from the other extreme, the farthest south. Of these Ravello is the better known. Of the three shades of Ravello wine which are well known, particularly in the United States, pink is the most popular, though I personally think least good. It is a bit too strong for my taste, at any rate at home. It is remarkable how the rapid evaporation from the body in hot weather makes degrees of alcohol less noticeable. The wine which seems more or less normally strong when you are by the Mediterranean can be far headier at home in cold weather simply because the pores are shut and it has no way out.

Rivera

The much less frequented Adriatic coast of Italy at Bari makes an extremely good *rosato* called Rivera. I have not yet seen it exported anywhere, but no doubt it will be, and will be as good abroad as it is at Bari—or, come to that, in Rome, where I first met it.

SWITZERLAND
GERMANY

In Switzerland the vineyards round Lake Neuchâtel produce good rosé. In Germany a small amount of rosé is made, but it is never particularly distinguished and is rarely exported. On the other hand, the very pale—it seems almost accidentally pink—Schillerwein which is made in the southern Rhine vineyards of Baden-Württemberg is a local speciality you will be pressed to try if you go there.

EASTERN EUROPE

Two of the best and cheapest rosés you can buy in Britain come from eastern Europe. They are the equivalents of the Riesling which has had

162

such success recently. Perhaps they are even more outstanding in their field.

Hungary

Yugoslavia

Hungary's rosé is a very pale tangerine colour, Yugoslavia's a deep plummy pink like a light red wine. They have as much character as rosé can—the Hungarian light and refreshing, the Yugoslav warm and fruity. The Yugoslav is always known as Ruzica, but the Hungarian might appear under any brand-name. Magyar is one current name in England.

PORTUGAL

The Portuguese have had the most astonishing success with their pink wine, considering that it costs at present twice as much as the Hungarian and Yugoslav ones. Part of the high cost is caused by its import in bottle— and very fancy bottle too. Part is due to the various processes by which the wine is made pink, slightly sweet and slightly sparkling.

In the United States, Lancers, which is described as crackling, and in Britain Mateus are the biggest selling wines of all. They are, in a sense, wines for people who do not really like wine. They form an intermediate stage between childish fizzy drinks and the adult taste for wine. As such, they do an invaluable service, for anything which leads more people to drink wine as part of their daily diet helps them towards health and happiness.

THE NEW WORLD

As you would expect, rosé wine has transplanted to the New World's vineyards better than most. There is no great difference in character between Californian and European rosés, partly because neither has a very strong character to assert. Where the grape of France's most famous rosé, Tavel, is used, which is increasingly often, results can be on a level with the French wine. The Grenache is the grape, and its name is seen on the best rosés of both California and Australia. The Beaujolais grape, the Gamay, is also used to make a good rosé.

California

Most—possibly all—of the great California wine-firms make good rosé, happy to be compared with French wines, and losing nothing by the comparison. In Maryland the Boordy vineyard makes a rosé with a high reputation, and Widmers make a Finger Lakes rosé in Upper New York State which is said to be among the better New York State wines.

Maryland

New York State

Australia

In Australia Lindeman's also use the Grenache for their rosé. Leo Buring makes a good light rosé and Angove's produce a cheaper, rather heavier wine. It is perhaps odd that rosé is not made more in Australia. In South Africa it seems to be similarly neglected. It should be the universal base-wine for countries whose table-wine consumption is very low. So much can be done, as the Portuguese know, to make it attractive.

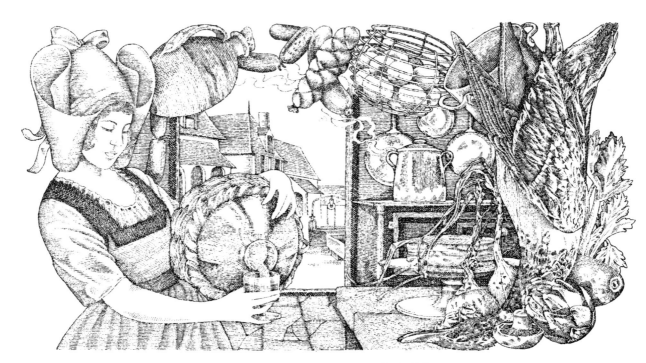

Red Table Wines

WHEREAS WHITE WINE is made from the juice of grapes alone, red wine is made from the skins as well; and whereas white wine can be made from black or white grapes, red wine can only be made from black grapes. The colouring pigment in the skin makes it red, and various other constituents of the skins alter its taste. In fact, it is white wine plus. But so great a difference do the skins make that it seems like a completely different drink.

Red wines are rarely sweet. While white ones vary from tart to luscious, red stays somewhere in the middle. Some clarets are extremely dry. Some wines from the far south are very rich. Occasionally red wines are bitter. Others have a mouth-coating property. Principally, though, they have the appetizing taste which makes them the ideal companions for savoury food.

Red wines tend to come from hotter places than white, although most of the world's vineyards grow both to some extent. In Germany, the northern-most vineyard, what little red wine is made is not very good. In the south of Italy, on the other hand, red is far more widespread than white and tends to be better. This phenomenon is not always convenient; we more often feel like a cool white wine in a hot country and a rich red one where it is cold. But white wine needs some acidity, which it loses when the grapes get very ripe under a hot sun. In red wines the balancing factor which keeps them from being flat and dull to drink is tannin.

Tannin is the substance which is used for tanning leather. It is found in the barks of trees, particularly the oak, in tea and in the skins, stalks and

164

pips of grapes. Its taste is hard and harsh, but this gives it its vital role. Without it the wine would be insipid.

The strength of a red table wine varies from about 8 to about 18 per cent alcohol. The usual figure is 10 or 11 per cent. It can be either more or less strong than a white wine, but usually it is a degree or so less. White grapes tend to contain that much more sugar.

The world's finest wines are both red and white; it is not possible to say that either is finer than the other. Most *vin ordinaire*, though, is red. The word 'wine', alone, conjures up a glass of something red rather than white. Certainly the first wine was red: separating the juice from the rest of the grape came as a later refinement.

In fact, if it had to be a one-wine world, the majority of wine-drinkers would probably settle for red. There is something satisfyingly complete about it. And there are not many things that it does not go well with.

FRENCH RED WINES

If there was some doubt about whether France leads the world for white wines, there is none about red. There is not even a remote challenger to her position as the producer of the best, and very nearly the most, red wine in the world.

She has such a strong position that there are very few red wines made in other parts of the world which can say that they owe nothing to France. A good many owe even the names under which they are sold: claret and burgundy are both English names for French wines which have been used by the whole world to designate two kinds of red wine. Those that do not owe their names very often owe their grapes to the vineyards of France.

Bordeaux and Burgundy are indisputably the world's greatest red-wine areas. Even in France there is nothing else to touch them. The Rhône valley comes next, giving wine which is at its best probably as good as any other in the world. Besides these three there are four or five excellent smaller areas and a vast sprawl of ordinary and very ordinary ones.

You have only to look at the proportion of the space taken up on any wine-list by the wines of Burgundy and Bordeaux to see that all the rest of the world's wine together cannot compare in variety and in the care with which individual vineyards are kept apart and given labels and distinctions of their own. Elsewhere—with Germany only excepted—it is enough to say which village, which county or even which country the wine comes from; in Bordeaux and Burgundy we must know which vineyard, even which part of the vineyard, who made the wine, bottled it, and when.

You have, then, the prospect of perhaps two thousand different names in Bordeaux, five-hundred-odd in Burgundy and another five hundred in the rest of the country. It is safe to say that nobody knows them all. There are perhaps three or four hundred of these which a regular wine-drinker gets to know in time—which, in fact, regularly appear on wine-lists overseas. It is at least as many names as he will need to know from the whole of the rest of the world.

I shall concentrate, in the following pages, on the wines which are best known and most shipped overseas. They include all the best ones. The specialists in the British and American wine-trades often know more about the districts of Bordeaux and Burgundy than the people who live there.

Red Bordeaux

BORDEAUX IS THE LARGEST fine-wine producing area in the world. Its red wines, which make up a shade under a half of its total production, are known in Britain as claret. Historically, they are the table wine of the ordinary Englishman. There was a long period when this was no longer true—the greater part, in fact, of the seventeenth, eighteenth and nineteenth centuries—but the British have always had a weakness for claret, even when war or taxation have prevented them getting it. Today it is once again the most commonly drunk, as well as the most highly prized, of the red wines which are described as 'table' because they are incomparably at their best with food.

The taste of claret   Red Bordeaux is among the light and dry red wines. So large an area obviously has wide divergencies of style—from year to year as well as from place to place—but the overriding hallmark of claret is to be slightly mouth-drying and at the same time to taste of fresh soft fruit. It is not what is known as 'fruity'. Very fine old clarets eventually reveal that there is still some sugar in their systems; they seem to allow themselves to smile after decades of keeping a stiff upper lip. But sweetness (except of character) is not the thing to look for in a claret. Spiciness—the kind of scent found in a cigar-box—there sometimes is, and quite frequently a slight hardness and taste of the stalks. In poor years red Bordeaux can seem thin, poor stuff—acid and watery—but it never loses its typical, refreshing, individual taste.

The country   Bordeaux lies in country which owes its nature to rivers and the sea. The Dordogne, flowing from the east, and the Garonne, running north from the

166

foothills of the Pyrenees, meet some fifty miles before they flow together into the Bay of Biscay. The country round the confluence of those rivers is the Bordeaux country.

The city of Bordeaux

The city of Bordeaux lies just above it on the wide grey Garonne. It is a grey city itself, but to anyone who admires the taste of the eighteenth century it is one of the finest in France. Its quarter of a million inhabitants live and work in streets of the period of Louis XVI. Just before the French Revolution, at a time when French taste was at its most perfect, the city was the centre of the trade with the Indies, both East and West. Its merchants and bankers set out to make it one of the finest cities in the world.

As it is today, it is a pleasure to walk along any of its serene, elegant streets. It reminds me a little of Dublin or Edinburgh. The black iron balconies against grey façades, graceful and monochrome, suggest an exquisite charcoal drawing.

The approach to the city over its one busy bridge is magnificent. It is worth walking out along it (for it is impossible to linger on it in a car). The quay, almost six miles long, stretches as far as you can see in both directions. Spires and towers rise above a lovely even line of buildings which form a low grey cliff down to the river.

The port

The quay, not surprisingly, is a mass of barrels. Huge grey and white ships with derricks like the dipping oars of a quinquereme load where centuries of merchantmen have loaded before them with claret for Bristol, Leith, Boston, Bremen, The Hook, New Orleans. Under the splendid terrace opposite the ships the shippers' cellars stretch for miles. There should be sails, furled and spread, and the dark wedges of rigging there to balance the beauty of the old city on the water.

The vineyards

The vineyards of Bordeaux are all around. Upstream, downstream, almost in the city to the south, across the Garonne in Entre-Deux-Mers, the beak of land that separates the two rivers as they flow to meet each other, and again across the far river, on the hills that overlook Bordeaux from the east. They fill the whole of the *département* of the Gironde, which is the name the two rivers take when they have become one. And they are all legally Bordeaux.

Upstream, to the south, is the country of the white wine. Graves, whose best wine is red but which is most famous for medium-dry white, and Sauternes, where virtually no red wine is made at all, lie in the valley of the Garonne above the city. Across the river the district known as the Premières Côtes de Bordeaux produces good red wine too, but not the best. It is to the north, twenty or thirty miles outside the city, and an equal distance to the east, that the finest wines are made. These are the districts of Médoc and St-Emilion.

They are very different places. The Médoc has a character which you immediately associate with the seaside. Not only is it flat, or nearly so, but the air has that feeling and the light that special luminosity. St-Emilion is a hill-town and nothing suggests than it is any nearer the sea than Burgundy. In both—indeed in all the areas of Bordeaux—the wine-growing unit, an estate of any size, is called a château.

*A château*However you translate the word château, referring to the châteaux of Bordeaux, the equivalent is not castle. Farm might almost be a better word, though there are many that are much too elegant, or pretentious, for that. It means any building that is the residence and headquarters of a wine-growing estate, and the estate itself.

A typical château consists of a six- or eight-bedroomed house, rarely lived in all the year round but the scene of splendid lunch- and dinner-parties at vintage-time, and another building, at least as big as the house again.

*The chai*The other building is the *chai*. The word *chai* is Bordelais for both winery and cellar, that is, both where the wine is made and stored. It is under the control of the *maître de chai*, who takes responsibility for the wine from the moment it is made to the moment it is sold. He is foreman of the château, sometimes responsible to a *gérant*, or agent, sometimes to the owner himself.

Many of the *maîtres de chais* of Bordeaux are famous and formidable figures in their own right. They tend to act the role of host to any casual visitors to the château; they will show their new wine, cold and hard from its cask, to any who come and ask, with a mixture of pride and suspicion.

*The vintage*At harvest-time the *chai* is a scene of ordered industry. From the vineyard the grapes are arriving in tipping-wagons like coal-scuttles, or in chest-high drum-shaped tubs of wood. A hoist of chains swings out from the building, lifts off the tub and tips the grapes into a chute. The tub goes back to the vineyard to be refilled. The grapes are drawn down into the *égrappoir,* which tears off their stalks and splits them open, and are then pumped up into tall wooden drums or vats (or cold-looking concrete ones more often nowadays) to ferment. As soon as fermentation begins the sides of the vat grow warm, and the air is full of the heady, slightly sickly smell. In hot weather great ingots of ice are standing by in case they are needed to cool the vats down to prevent the fermentation running away.

So the must, which soon becomes wine, stays for about two weeks, fermenting violently at first, then calming down. The mass of skins and pips which rose to the top and formed a cap on the vat sinks as the yeast's work draws to an end. The next job is to draw the wine off the *marc,* as the solid remnants are called. The *marc* is pressed, for it is still full of wine. This *vin de presse* can come in useful, for it is rich in tannin, and if the *vin de goutte,* the unpressed wine, is at all flabby in taste, a little can be added. But it is more likely to be used for the workmen's ordinary ration.

So the young wine is in barrels. The room where the barrels are stored is a long low barn, its floor a little below ground-level. The barrels are stretched in rows like vines from end to end; two, three or four hundred of them, the year's produce. In the bung-hole of each is a glass weight to keep out the air. Once a week this must be taken out and the barrel topped-up

168

Château Margaux in the Médoc. Bordeaux at its most elegant, in both wine and architecture. Château Margaux is one of the three First-Growths of the Médoc. *(Photo: Guy Gravett)*

with the same wine, a process known as *ouillage*. It prevents evaporation, and the absorption of wine by the new wood, from leaving a gap in the top of the barrel where air could lie and harm the wine. The word has come across into English as ullage. 'On ullage' to the English wine-trade means not topped-up, slightly less than full, as very old bottles sometimes are.

The trade

So the wine stays for about two years. *Courtiers*, who might be described as 'jobbers', *négociants* and possible customers from England and America will come, taste the wine and try to judge what its future is going to be. Some come as early as the February or March after the vintage, hoping to get the pick of the crop, while it is still so cold in the *chai* that they can barely taste the wine at all. Muffled up to the ears and wearing three pairs of socks they try to peer ahead into the future of the ungrateful, almost black liquid in their hands. Other more traditional and less frenzied merchants wait until the summer, when the wine has settled down a little, before they make up their minds about it.

Unfortunately, though, not all buying is done with the all-important object, the wine itself, as evidence. More and more it is a matter of speculation. Merchants are prepared to buy even before the grapes are ripe to make sure of their supplies. This buying *sur souche,* as it is called, which means on the vine, does not leave the merchant the alternative of not taking the wine if he cannot honestly recommend it to his customers. He can, of course, try to sell it all to another merchant if he does not like what he has bought. But so lucrative is the trade in good claret, so certain is it of a sale, that speculation is an obvious way to enter the trade, and more and more people are doing it.

The structure of the trade in Bordeaux is extremely complicated and formalized, and need not detain us here. Many an outsider has stubbed his toe against it, and I do not propose to add my name to the list. However the wine changes hands, therefore, it is eventually sold for shipping, and there are three alternative ways in which it can be shipped. The first, which is universally used by the great classed growths for at least some of their wine, is in bottle, bottled at the château. The second, which is done less and less, is in bottle, bottled by a *négociant* in Bordeaux. The third is in barrel, to be bottled in London, Amsterdam or wherever it may be.

The argument for the first is that it guarantees absolute authenticity, and against it, that it is more expensive, an argument which has no force in the United States. The second must be defended by the supposition that the French wine-merchant is more trustworthy than his foreign counterparts; it is also more expensive, but sometimes merchants who are on the spot are in a better position to find bargains. The value of the third depends on who your wine-merchant is—and nothing else.

The classification of 1855

All France's wine-districts have been divided officially into better and less good parts at one time or other, but Bordeaux is the only one where a list of the best wines, in order of quality, has ever been made. It was done

169

in 1855, on the occasion of the Great International Exhibition in Paris. How well it was done is shown by the fact that it is broadly correct to this day.

The merchants of Bordeaux agreed to accept an aggregate of the prices each wine had fetched over the previous years as the measure of its quality. The sixty-five most expensive they divided into five classes; again, natural differences of price indicated where the divisions came. The five classes are the five 'growths'.

There are several qualifications about the classification, apart from the fact that it is, of course, more than a century old.

The first is that it only includes great wines, whereas the list of good (and occasionally great) wines could have extended it considerably. There are, in fact, several hundred *bourgeois* growths (the name the merchants gave to wine which fell behind the great classic wines) and considerably more *artisan* growths, the category for small vineyards of only moderate quality.

The second objection is that it is territorially incomplete. It takes into account the Médoc area and Sauternes (in a separate sub-classification). It admits its incompleteness in making an exception for Château Haut-Brion in Graves, which lies outside its area, and including it among the first-growths, though it does not mention any other Graves wines. St-Emilion and Pomerol, equally red Bordeaux wines but from the other side of the river, it ignores completely.

The first problem was overcome to some extent in 1932, when the *bourgeois* growths were graded as *Crus Exceptionnels, Crus Bourgeois Supérieures* and *Crus Bourgeois*. There were seven of the first, about seventy of the second and hundreds of the third. Below them came the *Crus Artisans* and below them, though rarely referred to, the *Crus Paysans*. The sense of hierarchy is evidently strong in the Bordeaux trade.

Classifications of Graves, St-Emilion and Pomerol

Recently Graves, St-Emilion and Pomerol have been given separate local classifications of their own. Unfortunately, each proceeds on a completely different basis. The wines of Graves are merely listed without comment on their relative quality; the ten reds can simply put *Cru Classé* (classed growth) on their labels. The wines of St-Emilion were divided into *Premiers Grands Crus Classés, Grands Crus Classés* and *Grands Crus*. Those of Pomerol are *Premiers Grands Crus, Premiers Crus, Deuxièmes Premiers Crus* and *Deuxièmes Crus*.

So it can be seen that the words first-growth are fairly casually flung about. In the Médoc there are only three first-growths: Lafite, Latour and Margaux, whereas in Pomerol about twenty-five châteaux lay claim to the title, and a further twenty, unwilling to accept the title which the great Château Mouton-Rothschild must be content with in the Médoc, and call themselves second-growths, must be secondary first-growths. As a general rule, in fact, it is a good idea to take the phrase first-growth with a pinch of salt.

A new classification of the wines of Bordeaux is always being suggested. It would be interesting, and no doubt fairer than the present historic document and its successors, but it is hard to see what purpose it would serve.

170

It would be far better to drop the classification altogether. A wine, after all, ought to fetch its price on its quality, not its reputation.

In Bordeaux the laws of *Appellation Contrôlée* are not quite as involved as they are in Burgundy. They only really affect anyone buying a bottle of the cheaper kinds of wine. In Burgundy the great vineyards have an elaborate fabric of appellation laws of their own, but in Bordeaux there is no *Appellation Contrôlée* more restrictive than a village name. Château Lafite and the co-operative wine cellars at Pauillac, its commune, are equally *Appellation Pauillac Contrôlée*.

You can safely assume that a Bordeaux wine will always be sold under the highest (or in other words most restrictive and specific) appellation to which it is entitled. Any wine sold as plain Bordeaux, then, will be less than 10·5 per cent alcohol, for more would entitle it to the appellation Bordeaux Supérieur. If it is sold as Bordeaux Supérieur it will not come from any of the better parts of the area with restricted appellations of their own; it will come from one of the undistinguished fringes of the Bordeaux vineyards.

If a wine has any of the wide-ranging district names—Médoc, St-Emilion or Côtes de Fronsac, for example—it may come from any vineyard in that area, be a blend of the wines of that area, or be the wine of a local co-operative. If it has anything to gain by naming its origin more specifically, or by stating which vineyard in the neighbourhood it came from, presumably it would do so.

The level of appellations above districts, that of communes, is as far as they go. The commune names which are protected are Listrac, Moulis, Margaux, St-Julien, Pauillac and St-Estèphe, all within the Haut-Médoc district. The villages around St-Emilion which do not quite merit the appellation St-Emilion also have their own appellations; their own names hyphenated to the name St-Emilion.

So the levels of quality, as far as they can be read from labels, are as follows: Bordeaux, Bordeaux Supérieur, then a district name, then a commune or village name. Some districts are better than others; some communes are better than others. Haut-Médoc, for example, is better than just plain Médoc; Pauillac is better, in general, than Listrac. But it is beyond the scope of *Appellations Contrôlées* that the real interest of different growths in Bordeaux begins. There are nearly two thousand different estates which sell their wine with the intention that it shall reach the eventual drinker bearing its own name. In these wines the appellation, whatever it may be, is only in small type; the important thing is the château's name. There can hardly be anyone alive who knows them all, but it is among these that the wine-merchants pick their way, looking for value. More and more they are finding the kind of wine they want at a sensible price among the *bourgeois* growths. The name has such Marxist-Leninist undertones that it is rather unfortunate, but it should not discourage anyone. It is among them, rather than the great classified growths, that the future of the non-millionaire claret-drinker lies.

The Médoc is the eastern, or river, side of a long flat promontory caught between the Gironde and the sea. Its western half is pine forests, sand dunes and long empty beaches. Huntsmen and woodsmen are the only people who go there. Larks and pigeons have the country to themselves.

Even the line of villages along the Gironde, whose names everyone knows —Margaux, St-Julien, Pauillac, St-Estèphe—are lost and sleepy for eleven-twelfths of the year. Their stony vine-covered slopes slip down to the river in a mood of quietness that changes only with the seasons, never with the years. Where they reach the flat land at the river's edge the vines stop, and for a space nothing but coarse grass and blackberries grow. Here fishermen leave their long rods day-long, bobbing over the brown flow of the river, and plovers dip and wheel in still air.

In the Médoc more great red wine is made than anywhere else on earth.

All the finest part of the wine-growing Médoc is included in the area known to the laws of appellations as Haut-Médoc. The word Médoc is used to refer to what was once, less confusingly, called the Bas-Médoc; the north end of the promontory, where less brilliant, though still excellent, wine is made.

Bas-Médoc

Not many of the wines of the Bas-Médoc are known by name outside their immediate locality. The names of Châteaux Loudenne, Laujac, Livran and du Castera are quite often seen on English wine-lists, Loudenne particularly since it has belonged to the English firm of Gilbeys for ninety years. They bought it as a result of Gladstone's benevolent budget of 1865 in which he lowered duties on table wines, believing that they were far more beneficial than the fortified wines which everybody was then drinking. Up to that time, Gilbeys had been concentrating on selling South African wines, which enjoyed an imperial preference. This was the only way they could offer reasonable wines that ordinary people could afford. As soon as the Chancellor made it possible they became the first English firm to secure their own supply of good cheap claret.

This is the chief usefulness of the Bas-Médoc. In the finest years some of its wines will rise to the quality of the lesser growths of the Haut-Médoc in normal years. Its prices, however, always stay very reasonable. If you see a Bas-Médoc growth on a wine-list (it will say after its name simply *Appellation Médoc Contrôlée*) you can be fairly confident that the merchant has selected it for solid worth. It is almost always comparatively light, even for claret, which gives it the advantage of needing no more than three or four years of ageing before it is ready to drink.

HAUT-MEDOC

Haut-Médoc begins in the north at the village of St-Seurin-de-Cadourne. From there down to Blanquefort, almost in the northern suburbs of Bordeaux,

Claret at Christmas. The slightly brick-red tinge in the colour of a fifteen-year-old claret, a perfect partner for rich Christmas food; here, a baked ham and a game pie

is a distance of thirty or so miles as the crow flies, as extraordinary as the thirty miles of Burgundy's wonderful Côtes, a long file of good, fine and great vineyards.

There is no chance of mentioning even half of the châteaux of the Haut-Médoc by name. *Bordeaux et Ses Vins*—'The Bordeaux Bible'—by Cocks and Feret, which is reissued every few years, has over two hundred pages on this area alone. Specialized books have given it the detailed coverage it needs. Here I can mention only the greatest of the wines and some of the others which are often seen in Britain and the United States.

St-Seurin-de-Cadourne

At St-Seurin-de-Cadourne, Châteaux Coufran, Verdignan and Bel-Orme-Tronquoy-de-Lalande are all well-known *crus bourgeois*. There are no *crus classés*.

ST-ESTEPHE

The next village is St-Estèphe. Here, suddenly, we are in the middle of the famous Haut-Médoc, with superlative growths and names known all over the world on every hand. Five of the classic classified growths are in St-Estèphe. Of all the wines of the Médoc they are the strongest in flavour, perhaps the least delicate but some of the most splendid, warm and grand in character. Châteaux Montrose and Cos d'Estournel are second-growths, only one removed from the top flight of all. Each has its character—it is one of the distinguishing marks of the wines that deserve to be called great that they impress you with a personality, they become like acquaintances with characters which can inspire endless discussion.

Château Cos d'Estournel

Cos d'Estournel is a curious-looking place. The château was given an outer wall with Chinese pagodas all over it some time in the last century. The d'Estournelle family fortune was in some way tied up with Chinese trade, leaving this odd and rather ungainly mark on the Médoc. With the familiarity of old customers, English wine-merchants usually refer to Cos d'Estournel (the first 's' is silent) as Coss, like a lettuce. Its wine has more power than most Médocs, and correspondingly is one to keep for a longer, rather than shorter, time to mature. It can be rather hard and fierce in its early years, but in later life it becomes one of the finest of all clarets. This is not entirely surprising. Its neighbour to the south, just over the parish boundary, is Château Lafite.

Château Montrose

For Montrose I have a special weakness. The château belongs to Madame Charmolüe, but it is her son and his wife who are always there, and the wine today is his responsibility. The château is a small Victorian house, very mildly assuming the airs of a great proprietor. From its windows you can see the vines slope away in the distance down to the broad brown river.

Montrose always seems to me to have a touch of lovely sweetness, a trace of some very generous and kindly quality, kept back by the elegant balance of a great and classic wine. No doubt memories have coloured it in my mind, for it was here that, on my first visit, M. Charmolüe quietly put half a dozen bottles of his wine in the back of my car before I drove away. The next weekend I was on my own up in the lovely remote country of the Dordogne, staying and eating my evening meal at a *routiers* café. I drank

173

one of the bottles of Montrose with my dinner, and was so happy with it that I went out to the car to get the other five and gave them (it makes me sound mad) to the lorry-drivers who were in the café eating their stew. They evidently thought I was mad, too: they had probably never drunk a château-bottled second-growth claret before. In any case, they raised their glasses politely, and were about to empty them, when they stopped in mid-swallow. A look of immense pleasure, the expression of a true connoisseur face to face with a masterpiece, came over their faces. It was the scent of the wine, the clean, sweet, exquisite breath of autumn ripeness, which held them rapt. I do not think I exaggerate. It was a wonderful sight to see those great *onze-degrés* men, those pushers of gigantic trucks and trailers, breathing in the bouquet of a wine which spoke straight to them.

Châteaux Calon-Ségur, Rochet and Cos-Labory are third-, fourth- and fifth-growths respectively. The first is a very fine, reliable wine; the others are not so well known as one or two of the Superior Bourgeois growths below them. Châteaux Tronquoy-Lalande, Meyney, Phélan-Ségur, Pomys, Marbuzet, Beausite, Capbern, Houissant, La Haye, Fatin, Fontpetite, Le Boscq are ranked next after the classified growths. Close behind them come Châteaux Les Ormes de Pez, Beauséjour, Ladouys, MacCarthy-Moula, Morin, Andron-Blanquet, de Pez and Le Roc. Besides all these, any of which you might see on a wine-list, the co-operative at St-Estèphe makes one of the best of the co-operative wines of the Médoc.

PAUILLAC

St-Estèphe borders on Pauillac, the finest and most famous of all the communes of Bordeaux, on the south. Both communes lie beside the river. Pauillac, indeed, has a long quay, for it is more than a village, and has recently become an important oil-refinery centre, which brings in ships from all parts of the world.

Vertheuil, Cissac, St-Sauveur

In the hinterland behind Pauillac and St-Estèphe good wine is grown, although its name means little beside the superlatives of the riverside. The inland villages are Vertheuil, Cissac and St-Sauveur. Châteaux du Breuil and Larrivaux at Cissac and Fontesteau, Peyrabon and Liversan at St-Sauveur are the most important. All are *bourgeois* growths, with the exception of Liversan, which is Superior Bourgeois. Could there possibly be a less attractive description of anything? Liversan's production is large for a *bourgeois* estate, which means that it is often seen on wine-lists.

Pauillac is the only town anywhere which has three of the world's greatest red wines within its boundaries. They are Châteaux Lafite, Latour and Mouton-Rothschild. Lafite and Latour were listed first and third of all the wines of Bordeaux in the classification of 1855. Mouton was placed fifth, the first of the second-growths. Nobody today would place it anywhere except among the first-growths, and some would even give it precedence over its neighbours.

If I had to try to characterize the three wines—for they are very different —I should say that Lafite is the most beautiful of the three, Latour the most

174

stylish and Mouton-Rothschild the most tremendous. Yet all are very much Pauillacs. Pauillacs are the most typical of all clarets; strong and clean, dry and scented, incomparably subtle and delicate and yet solid and substantial in your mouth. There is often a touch of the cigar-box scent about them.

Château Lafite

Lafite stands well back from the road on a little hill at the northern end of Pauillac. It is not a very striking house, although it is nearer to a castle than most in the Médoc. Inside it is decorated in the grand late-nineteenth-century manner of the Rothschilds, for it is one of the two great vineyards of the Rothschild family—two which, they note with satisfaction, are among the best in the world. The drawing-room is red and white, the little library dark, meditative green, lit with oil-lamps and, at vintage-time, a bowl of marigolds is displayed. Through the french windows on the terrace is a constantly-sprinkled lawn, one of the few pieces of grass in Bordeaux which deserve the name.

Lafite's vineyards are large; they cover a hundred and fifty of the three-hundred-odd acres of the estate, but only the best of their wine in any year is sold as Château Lafite. The rest, or the better part of it, is sold as Les Carruades de Château Lafite. Any wine which would possibly damage the château's reputation is disposed of as *vin rouge*. The price the wine fetches in a great vintage makes one ask how it will be in a medium or poor one. The answer is that it will almost certainly be among the best wines of any vintage, and may even manage still to be a great wine when lesser growths are not worth drinking. Its extraordinary finesse remains even when the wine has less strength than it should. But, as Professor Roger says in *The Wines of Bordeaux*: 'The man who has never tasted a great bottle of Lafite cannot know the perfections of which claret is capable.'

Château Latour

Château Latour makes a somehow less sensuous, more masculine wine. It has the reputation above all châteaux for consistency. In great years it is superb; in poor years, when many fine châteaux fail to live up to their reputations, it is still superb. Many people, in fact, go as far as to prefer it in what are known as 'off-vintages': 1960, for example.

The tower which gives it its name is no more than an embattled dovecot among the vines. The château itself is a simple, four-square house in a grove of trees. The interest of Latour lies in its *chais,* which lie apart from the house in the vineyard, forming a courtyard shaded by pollarded plane-trees. They are the first of the first-growths' wine-making equipment to be modernized, and to have the old oak fermenting-vats replaced with stainless steel. The fermenting-room is a very different place now from those of its rivals, but the quiet lines of barrels holding the wine of the last three vintages are the same as ever. The scene when I first went to Latour only a few years ago, when old M. Brugière, the manager who must have been over eighty, ran it for the de Beaumont family, when the old house was like a country rectory blinking through its shutters at the sun on the vines and the river, and the sunlight fell in shafts on cobwebs in the dim *chai,* is so very different from the bustle today, with all the shutters thrown back and directors in dark suits everywhere, that it is hard to believe that the wine will be the same. And yet these vineyards have impressed their personalities on generation after generation for two hundred years. It may be more than even stainless steel and dark suits can do to change it.

Château Mouton-Rothschild

Mouton-Rothschild, the third of the great three of Pauillac, makes, as I have said, the most tremendous wine. It is strong, very long-lasting, hard at first, very full of flavour. Its labels, every one of which bears the total production of the vintage and how it was bottled into so many bottles, magnums, double-magnums, etc., with the number of the bottle in your hand, bear its motto: 'First I am not. I do not deign to be second. I am Mouton.' Mouton today is the work of one of the most remarkable men in Bordeaux, Baron Phillippe de Rothschild. He inherited the little farm with its famous vineyards when he was a young man. The wine has progressed from strength to strength under him, but at the same time he has done wonderful work in forwarding the cause of the whole of the Médoc.

Recently he opened a museum at Mouton of works of art connected with wine, ranging from ancient drinking-vessels to medieval tapestries of the vintage and some of the loveliest glass anywhere. He is also a poet, and the translator of Christopher Fry's plays into French for the stage. He has transformed Mouton from a little farm into a lovely house, and brought to it all the elegance which progress is chasing out of other parts of this quiet country.

The Pichon-Longuevilles

Pauillac has two second-growths besides Mouton: Châteaux Pichon-Longueville and Pichon-Longueville-Lalande, which flank the road like fairy castles as it enters Pauillac from the south. The first is sometimes considered to be very slightly the better of the two, but both are among the greatest of all red wines.

The classifiers must have felt at this stage that they could not go on handing out such high honours in Pauillac; twelve more châteaux were classified as fifth-growths, and one, Duhart-Milon, as fourth. The fifth-growths of Pauillac include at least two which would probably, if re-classification were ever done, move up to second:

Château Lynch-Bages

Lynch-Bages, one of the most popular of all clarets in England, and Pontet-Canet, one of the most popular in France. Lynch-Bages belongs to M. Cazes, the Mayor of Pauillac. The wine he makes is full and fruity, almost sweet at times. He has a mysterious way of maintaining his quality even in poor years.

Château Pontet-Canet

Pontet-Canet is the property of the Cruse family, one of the great merchant houses of Bordeaux. Its vineyards (the biggest of any *cru classé*) border on those of Mouton-Rothschild. They have been known to make a wine as superb as that of their neighbour: the 1929, in particular, is one of the finest clarets I have ever drunk. Oddly enough, Pontet-Canet is never château-bottled. It is seen a great deal on the French Railways.

Châteaux Grand-Puy-Ducasse, Grand-Puy-Lacoste, Mouton-Baron-Phillippe, Batailley (very good and increasingly popular), Haut-Batailley, Lynch-Moussas, Haut-Bages, Pédesclaux, Croizet-Bages and Clerc-Milon

176

are the other fifth-growths. The names of some of the *Crus Bourgeois* of Pauillac are also often seen listed. The most prominent are: Châteaux Haut-Bages-Averous and Haut-Bages-Drouillet, La Tour-Milon, La Tour-Pibran, d'Anseillan, Bellegrave, Colombier-Monpelou and Constant-Bages-Monpelou, Daubos-Haut-Bages, Duroc-Milon, Malécot-Desse, Fonbadet, Pibran and La Couronne. In this class also comes Mouton Cadet, the younger cousin of Mouton-Rothschild, though no blood relation. It is said to be the world's biggest-selling claret. It is a blended wine; not as good value as some of the unadvertised *bourgeois* growths, but more consistent from vintage to vintage; duller, and so in a sense more reliable.

Mouton Cadet

ST-JULIEN

St-Julien is the next of the great riverside communes. Pauillac has more superlative wines, which take longer to mature and eventually reach greater heights, but St-Julien has perhaps the highest average standard of any commune. Even its co-operative wines, sold simply as St-Julien, are of a high standard and fetch a comparatively high price. It has no first-growths but it has five seconds, two thirds and five fourths. Two of its fourth-growths are among the best wines of Bordeaux in many years.

The St-Julien characteristic is often described as tenderness. Its wines nonetheless improve over a very long period, and might be called the safest wines of the Médoc. The demand for them is correspondingly high.

The Léovilles

The best wines of the commune are those nearest to Pauillac, the three châteaux which share the name of Léoville: Léoville-Las-Cases, Léoville-Poyferré and Léoville-Barton. The first of the three has the best reputation, although in England Léoville-Barton is more often seen. The property, with the third-growth Langoa-Barton next door, belongs to the English Barton family, who have been merchants and growers in Bordeaux since the beginning of the last century. Ronald Barton is the present owner. Château Langoa, where he lives, is a typical eighteenth-century Bordeaux country-house. It is elegant, quite small, placed high up over its property and by its shape—all the main rooms in a row so that each room has two main outside walls—subject to all the draughts of a long winter by the sea. In a corner of the Barton *chais* is one of the enormous old kitchens which are only brought into play at vintage-time, where the soup for the vintagers is stirred in cauldrons over a wood fire in a vast chimney—a scene from some medieval calendar.

Château Langoa-Barton

Château Ducru-Beaucaillou makes a superb wine which seems to get better with each vintage. Château Gruaud-Larose, the other second-growth, is also one of those which rarely produces anything but lovely claret. Gruaud-Larose and Château Talbot, one of the fourth-growths which deserves a higher place, both belong to the big Bordeaux shipping house of Cordier. In Bordeaux the Cordiers have a beautiful eighteenth-century town-house called La Bottière. All three are among the showplaces of the countryside; their upkeep, furniture and elegance are as studied as the marvellous silky wine of their cellars.

Château Ducru-Beaucaillou
Château Gruaud-Larose
Château Talbot

The rest of the fourth-growths, St-Pierre-Bontemps, St-Pierre-Sevaistre, Branaire-Ducru and Beychevelle, are led by Beychevelle. This is one of the most magnificent of the châteaux and most distinguished of the wines of the Médoc. It is reputed to have got its name from the salute of a dipped sail which passing sailors gave to the Lord High Admiral of France, the Duc d'Epernon, who lived there. The order was '*Baisse les voiles*'. It was corrupted to Beychevelle. Now the house is the home of the Achille Fould family. Beychevelle can be a rather thin and sharp wine in poor years, but in hot summers it sometimes overtakes every other St-Julien in all the classical qualities of balance and finesse.

The leader of the *crus bourgeois* of St-Julien would undoubtedly be among the classified growths if a new list were ever made. Château Gloria, while probably the least impressive château, has one of the best vineyards in the district. It is due to Henri Martin, the owner, who is also prominent in all the organizations for promotion and teamwork among the Médoc growers. His creation of a great new vineyard from scratch is remarkable—although perhaps the phrase from scratch gives the wrong idea. His land used to be parts of the vineyards of Gruaud-Larose, Duhart-Milon and the other classified growths. His neighbour to the north, Château Glana, on the other hand, has a dwindling reputation. Châteaux Grand-St-Julien, Médoc, Moulin-de-la-Rose, des Ormes and Bontemps-Dubarry are also well-known *crus bourgeois*. The hinterland of St-Julien is the commune of St-Laurent,

which, although its only appellation is Haut-Médoc, has a good fourth-growth, Château La Tour Carnet, and a well-known fifth-growth, Château Belgrave, as well as several lesser-known *bourgeois* growths. There is also a

remarkable and little-known vineyard on the island of Patiras, out in the Gironde off St-Julien and Pauillac, called Château Valrose.

For a while south of St-Julien the best vineyards leave the river-banks and keep to the gravel ridges which here go inland. The next two villages

to have their own appellations, Moulis and Listrac, are well west of the road which leads straight up from Bordeaux along the Gironde. Neither has any classified growths, although Châteaux Chasse-Spleen and Poujeaux-Theil in Moulis and Châteaux Fourcas-Dupré and Fourcas-Hostein in Listrac would probably make it next time. Château Villegeorge in the

neighbouring commune of Avensan is also well known. These wines are all similar in a way, fairly full and strong, perhaps more like St-Estèphes than the wine of Margaux or St-Julien, their two great neighbours. Châteaux Bibian, Clarke, Duplessis, Dutruch-Grand-Poujeaux, Fonréaud, Lafon, Lestage, Maucaillou, Moulis, Gressier-Grand-Poujeaux, de Peyrelebade, Pomeys, Semeillan and du Testeron are all in this area. All are *crus bourgeois*, which are likely to be bought by British wine-merchants particularly and appear, as the classified growths all used to year after year until they became so expensive, on British wine-lists.

The villages of the river road below St-Julien (below on the map, above in terms of the stream of the river) are of less importance until we get to

Margaux and Cantenac, which, for all intents and purposes, are one.

Cussac

Cussac, Lamarque, Arcins and Soussans all have the appellation Haut-Médoc, but none of their own. At Cussac (not to be confused with Cissac near St-Estèphe) Château Lanessan is the best-known wine, followed by Châteaux La Chesnaye and Beaumont. At Lamarque, the sleepy old village whence the ferry plies over the river to Blaye, making a short-cut of about fifty miles—instead of going into Bordeaux—to the road north, the war-like old Château de Lamarque makes a good wine. At Arcins the best of the wine has traditionally been used up in various more or less underhand ways by the growers of rich Margaux, down the road.

Lamarque

Arcins

It is strange that a place like Arcins, so near Margaux, one of the richest townships in Bordeaux, and with not dissimilar soil and growing conditions, can be almost a depressed area, as it is. The root of the trouble is partly the archaic laws of inheritance, by which at every death, unless there is a well-paid family lawyer to do something about it, the land is divided among all the relations until there is hardly a grape for each of them in a small vineyard.

A young Englishman called Nicolas Barrow, who bought a small château—Château Courant—at Arcins, spent two years ferrying one relation to another trying to get a family consensus from some of his neighbours to exchange rows of vines so that they all could have continuous plots. Up to that time he had to go into his own vineyard with a chart to make sure he was not pruning someone else's vine.

Despite the great demand for fine claret there are many excellent vineyards at this moment where the proprietors are giving up the struggle and planting cabbages. They lack the means to make their own wine. They send in their grapes to the local co-operative where the wine is not necessarily very well made, where their grapes, which may well have been better than anyone else's, acquire total anonymity—indeed the only thing required of them is that they be ripe enough to give the required alcoholic strength. The growers' shares of the year's earnings come round years after the harvest—in fact, it is a disheartening business.

But the hunt for new names by the merchants who see the market for good and reasonably cheap claret expanding is a good sign. It may yet save many a good row of vines from conversion into a cabbage-patch.

Soussans

Soussans, the village which borders Margaux to the north, has three vineyards which are up to the Margaux standard: Châteaux La-Tour-de-Mons, Paveil-de-Luze and La Bégorce-Zédé. They are allowed to use the appellation Margaux.

MARGAUX
Château Margaux

Margaux is the last of the superlative, peerless communes of the Médoc, and perhaps the best known of all. Undoubtedly the fact that Château Margaux, its one first-growth, has the same name as the village has helped. Many people have confused the two and thought they were getting one of the world's greatest wines when they were only really getting a blended wine from the co-operative.

It is the same story with Chambertin and Gevrey-Chambertin in Burgundy. The difficulty is to remember which of the two similar names is the star, and which the supporting cast. In fact, the price ought to make it clear enough; Château Margaux would always cost at least four times as much as plain Margaux.

Château Margaux is the most mansion-like of the first-growth châteaux. It presents a neoclassical façade to a fine avenue, and it has a park. The wine it makes is as unmistakable as the pediment and pillars, and very much more beautiful. Of all the first-growths, Margaux has the most ravishing scent; a flowery, fascinating bouquet. The wine is light and silky, but full of the quiet power of a great wine, not pungent and transitory but slowly moving through its stages of development, from hard and fine to soft and exquisitely delicate. Some of the other châteaux of Margaux, notably Châteaux Palmer and Rausan-Ségla, and sometimes Châteaux Lascombes, Rauzan-Gassies, Kirwan, Cantenac-Brown and Boyd-Cantenac, make similar wine, though rarely as fine. Châteaux Brane-Cantenac, Malescot-St-Exupéry, d'Issan, Marquis-d'Alesme-Becker, Marquis-de-Terme, Pouget and Prieuré-Lichine are all classified growths. Of these, Lascombes and Prieuré-Lichine have American owners, with the energetic direction of Alexis Lichine, whose selections of wine are well known in the United States; Rausan-Ségla belongs to an English firm, Holts, who used to be in the African trading business; and Palmer has owners in England, Holland and France, flying all their flags from its crazy-picturesque rooftop.

Château Palmer

Palmer is perhaps the most outstanding of all. Even in poor years its wine has a lovely soft quality and a flowery scent. It is rightly popular in Britain —one of the cases where a third-growth should really be a second.

The best of the *crus bourgeois* of Margaux are Châteaux Bel-Air, Marquis-d'Aligre, Labégorce-de-Lamouroux and Angludet.

Arsac and Labarde

A number of châteaux on the south side of Margaux and Cantenac, which are united under the name of Margaux, are also allowed to use the appellation Margaux. They lie in the communes of Arsac and Labarde, which themselves only have the appellation Haut-Médoc. Château Giscours at Labarde is the best of these, followed by Château du Tertre at Arsac; both lie on (for the Médoc) a high ridge of ground. Their neighbours, Châteaux Monbrison, Dauzac, Siran and Rosemont, are also very well thought of.

Macau

Château Cantemerle

The rest of the Médoc has no other appellation than Haut-Médoc, despite the fact that it includes some superb growths and two famous communes, Ludon and Macau. Macau is the northern one of the two. It has one classified growth, a fifth which is now considered level with the seconds or thirds, Cantemerle. It is a fine great building hidden by a lovely wood, in which you can well believe that the blackbirds of the name (which means blackbirds' song) sing with all their might. Cantemerle has less polish, perhaps, than the great Margaux wines, but a fine, full softness of its own. Its second wine is sold under the brand-name 'Royal Médoc'.

180

Burgundy and a casserole. With beef cooked in burgundy, burgundy is the wine to drink

Châteaux des Trois Moulins, Constant-Trois-Moulins, Maucamps, Cambon-la-Pelouse, Priban and Larrieu-Terrefort-Graves are all Superior Bourgeois growths of Macau.

Ludon
Château La-Lagune

At Ludon there is also one classified growth, Château La-Lagune, which is sometimes known as Grand-La-Lagune. It has a very high reputation as a strong, solid and slow-maturing wine with a softness and scent which distinguish it. The château is small but fine, by tradition the work of Bordeaux's greatest architect, Louis, who designed the front of the Bordeaux theatre, one of the finest public buildings in France. The *chais* of La Lagune are also notable—modern and recently equipped. It is the nearest of the *crus classés* of the Médoc to Bordeaux, only about ten miles away, and welcomes visitors, which makes it perhaps better known than it would otherwise be without one of the magic names such as Margaux on its label. Châteaux d'Agassac, Pomiès-Agassac, Ludon-Pomiès-Agassac and Nexon-Lemoyne are Ludon's Superior Bourgeois growths.

Le Pian, Parempuyre,
Blanquefort
Le Taillan

There remain the relatively unimportant communes of Le Pian, Parempuyre and Blanquefort on the road to Bordeaux, and to the west, away from the Gironde, the commune of Le Taillan. At Le Pian, Château Sénéjac, at Parempuyre, Châteaux Parempuyre, Ségur and Ségur-Fillon, and at Le Taillan, Château du Taillan, another Cruse property, are well known. Le Taillan is a very fine house with two façades of equal grandeur. It must be the only house in the world with a different name on each side, for one façade is used for the labels of its red wine, Taillan, the other is called La Dame Blanche on the labels of its white wine.

GRAVES

Maurice Healy, an old Irish claret-lover and the author of *Stay Me with Flagons*, a book about his loves, made one of the most splendidly opaque remarks on the subject of wine when he described the difference between claret from the Médoc and from Graves. They are, he said, like matt and glossy prints of the same photograph. The matt ones are the Graves.

The name Graves only appears on bottles of white wine. It comes as a surprise to most people to know that there is such a thing as red Graves, although the red is by far the best wine of the region, and constitutes over a quarter of its production. The word Graves, unqualified, now means white wine. The reason for this is that the châteaux of Graves carry the names of their villages, rather than that of the area, on their labels.

Graves starts at the very gates of Bordeaux. In fact, it is more true to say that Bordeaux is in Graves, and so is Bordeaux's airport, Mérignac. The noblest suburb of the city is now undoubtedly Pessac, for here, even before the little villas finally end, the road out of Bordeaux passes the gates of

Château Haut-Brion

Château Haut-Brion. Although the merchants who devised the 1855 classification were not taking Graves into account, they could not ignore Haut-Brion. There was only one place for it—in the top four. Haut-Brion is a first-growth, but none of the other Graves châteaux are any kind of numbered growth at all. They are simply *crus classés*.

181

Château Haut-Brion is another American property. It belongs to Clarence Dillon, formerly the American Ambassador to France, now, as it were, France's ambassador to America. The kind of wine they make at Haut-Brion is very different from the first-growths of the Médoc. It seems more powerful and less clean-cut, full of flavour but needing a long time in bottle to bring out what eventually becomes a heavenly scent. I was once lucky enough to be at a dinner-party at the Mirabelle Restaurant in London when an Imperiale, a giant bottle holding eight and a half normal bottles, of Haut-Brion 1899 was opened. A fine plate of beef had just been put down in front of me. I forgot all about the beef: I shall never forget that wine. Its scent rose firmly to a peak like the pediment of the Parthenon. Below it were great depths of taste. It was pure delight of a kind which only the greatest of wines, or music, or poetry, or painting, can give.

Château La Mission Haut-Brion
Château Pape Clément

Immediately across the road from Haut-Brion is Château La Mission Haut-Brion, which often makes wine almost as good as its neighbour. Pessac's other great château is Pape Clément, whose vineyards were first planted by the Bishop of Bordeaux who became Pope in the fourteenth century and moved the papal headquarters (so great, one supposes, was his love of French wine) to Avignon. It is surprising that he did not move it to Bordeaux.

Château La Tour Haut-Brion lies beside La Mission; Château Fanning-La Fontaine is nearby.

However, the greater number of the best growths of Graves are in the communes of Léognan and Martillac, four miles south of Pessac in the typical sandy, pine country in which growing vines is hard, unrelenting work and the rewards small. Yield is low and the wine relatively expensive. It has to be good to sell at all. At Léognan the great growths are Châteaux

Léognan

Haut-Bailly, Domaine de Chevalier and Malartic-Lagravière, followed by Châteaux Carbonnieux, Fieuzal, La Louvière, Le Pape, Olivier, Larrivet-Haut-Brion. Many of these châteaux are equally famous for their white wine—a very rare state of affairs. Graves is the only great wine-area in France where red and white vineyards are inextricably mixed.

Martillac

Cadaujac

At Martillac, Châteaux Smith-Haut-Lafitte, La Garde, Latour-Martillac are the best growths, the first being the finest of the three. In the commune of Cadaujac next-door Château Bouscaut is very fine, and Château Couhins in Villenave-d'Ornon is well known.

Red Graves are rarely less than very special. There are no common, everyday ones. They are wines of strong character, even in their less good years (bad vintages are rare in Graves), and ask to be used well, with simple roast meat or game. To me they are dinner-party wines. If the company is interested in wine it enjoys them for being unusual: if it is not, it enjoys them all the same.

ST-EMILION

Fashion swings back and forth from one end of the Bordeaux country to another. At one time no-one would hear of any wine except red Graves.

Then it had to be Médoc. At the moment the districts of St-Emilion and Pomerol are in high favour.

St-Emilion has more representatives on most wine-lists than any other Bordeaux district today. Perhaps this is not so surprising—it is the biggest. But Pomerol, which is the smallest of all the communes, has almost as many. The reason is partly that these wines need less time to mature than the great Médocs, and are good, though not at their best, after a mere four years or so. Partly it is their warmth of flavour. They are less dry and scented than the Médocs, more powerful, and with more of the savoury appeal of a burgundy. It is so often said that St-Emilion is the burgundy of Bordeaux that you might expect St-Emilions to taste like burgundy. They do not: they taste like claret, but claret moving towards burgundy; full, savoury and strong.

The town of St-Emilion ranks after Beaune as the most interesting and attractive little wine-town in France. St-Emilion has vines in every nook and cranny. Whether you look up, down (for it is on a steep slope) or sideways, there is a vineyard in sight. The town fills the thin end of a wedge-like re-entrant in a hill of vines. Its cobbled streets and equally cobbled-looking rooftops, made of the Roman pattern of curved tiles, lead up to its astonishing old church which was cut out of the living rock of the hillside. I know of no other building like it. It has aisles, side-aisles, nave and chancel, the usual size but dug out, not built up—a church-shaped cave. Its belfry is built above it on what appears from above to be a platform of ordinary flat ground. It shares the view over the rooftops and the vines down to the Dordogne in the valley below with the town's best restaurant; one of the pleasantest terraces in France.

St-Emilion is about thirty miles east of Bordeaux, overlooking the Dordogne from the north. Its vineyards not only cover the hillside leading up to the town, but a wide plateau of high country behind. There is a distinction between the wines of the hill and those of the flat land. The hill-wines are known as Côtes-St-Emilion, the others as Graves- (meaning gravel) St-Emilion. A third area, Sables- (sand) St-Emilion at the foot of the hill by the river also makes wine, but of lesser quality. The terms are not used on labels—only in conversation.

Côtes-St-Emilion
Château Ausone

Côtes wines are the most full and generous, in the self-explanatory phrase of the wine-trade, of all clarets. Château Ausone is the most famous of them. It is reputed to have been the estate and vineyard of the Roman poet Ausonius, who celebrated wine-growing both here and on the Moselle in the fourth century. If the story be true, it is one of Bordeaux's oldest vineyards. Its position under the brow of the hill, sheltered from the north wind and canted towards the sun, is more like Corton or one of the burgundy vineyards than the usual Bordeaux site. Its neighbours, Châteaux Belair, Magdelaine, Canon and Beauséjour, Châteaux La Gaffelière-Naudes and Pavie opposite and Clos Fourtet almost in the town, with Château Trottevieille just the other side of it, are the most distinguished names of

183

the Côtes. They were all classified as *Premiers Grand Crus Classés* in 1954.

The best known of the second rank, the *Grands Crus Classés,* are Châteaux Curé-Bon-La-Madeleine, Grand-Mayne, Troplong-Mondot, Canon-La-Gaffelière, Laroze, L'Angélus, Balestard-La-Tonnelle, Cap-de-Mourlin, Tertre-Daugay—and there are a score of others.

In the country surrounding St-Emilion to the south, too, there are five villages which can use the great name. Their wines are not in the same class as the best of the Côtes wines, but are more and n.ore widely bought either as plain St-Emilion to go into a blend, or under their own names, despite their lack of reputation, because they are good value for money. The one of these châteaux which does have a well-known name is Château Monbousquet, the property of M. Daniel Querre, who is the driving force behind most of the promotional moves of St-Emilion growers. The Jurade de St-Emilion, the local equivalent of the Chevaliers du Tastevin of Burgundy, is largely his concern. Château Monbousquet is a beautiful house, standing white and shuttered beside a lake. Its fine, rich wine is one of the most popular of the lesser St-Emilions abroad.

Graves-St-Emilion
Château Cheval Blanc

The most famous name of St-Emilion, oddly enough, is only just in the district. The edge of its vineyard is the boundary of Pomerol. Château Cheval Blanc is usually mentioned in the same breath as Châteaux Lafite, Haut-Brion and Latour as one of the finest of all clarets. Occasionally it wins the distinction of being the best claret of all in a vintage, as it did in 1947. The wine of Cheval Blanc at its height—of which the 1947 was the classic example—is a wine of more power and solidity than the Médoc, even Mouton-Rothschild, ever achieves. At a dinner at Brooks's Club in London, where I first met it, I heard someone describe it as a monolithic wine, a single great upright pillar of polished stone, monumental, unyielding, perfect in proportion. He was right about the general effect but wrong, to me, about the stoniness. There is a velvet quality about it which is very different from cold stone. Above all, Cheval Blanc has more scent than most St-Emilions, almost the wonderful blossoming of perfume which we find in the first-growth Médocs.

This far corner of St-Emilion, which looks as though it should belong to Pomerol, is the Graves-St-Emilion district. It has far fewer wines than the Côtes, but some of the finest of all. After Cheval Blanc come Châteaux Figeac, Corbin and Chauvin. Châteaux Ripeau, La-Tour-du-Pin-Figeac, Corbin-Despagne, Corbin-Michotte and Grand-Barrail-Lamarzelle-Figeac are all in the class which would, in the Médoc, be classified as a fourth- or fifth-growth. All have something of the velvety quality which is characteristic of Pomerol, with the power of flavour which is pure St-Emilion. It is not the country in which you would look for superlative vineyards, for it is more or less flat, and flat land often gives flat wine. It has nothing of the grand picturesqueness of the Côtes, but a dull, prosperous look.

184

Pomerol is the continuation of the plateau above St-Emilion to the northwest. It lies on the outskirts of the town of Libourne, which even its importance as a wine-centre has not been able to save from utter dullness. It has been called France's most provincial town, which, seeing the competition, is some distinction. Libourne takes its name from Sir Roger de Leyburne, steward of Edward I of England, which gives it a sister-town, the little village of Leybourn in Kent where he had his castle.

There are many more châteaux crammed into the tiny commune of Pomerol than into any other, giving it the air of a suburb rather than the country. Everywhere you look there is a little villa, sometimes merely a big shed, proudly designated Château. Every acre of the gently undulating plateau seems to be covered with vines.

The best wines of Pomerol are those near the St-Emilion border, as the best wines of St-Emilion are those nearest Pomerol. The same patch of gravel mixed with clay which produces Château Cheval Blanc gives almost equal quality to Châteaux Petrus, La Conseillante, L'Evangile, Vieux-Certan, Petit-Village, Lafleur, Gazin, Certan and La Fleur-Petrus. All these have been classed as *Premiers Grands Crus*. Petrus is sometimes called *Premier des Grands Crus* to lift it above the herd; its wine normally fetches far more than any other Pomerol. In 1962 it fetched more than Châteaux Mouton-Rothschild, Latour and Margaux. It is perhaps the easiest to enjoy of the great clarets, the one which takes least maturing, is soft, round and yet forceful and powerfully sweet-scented.

Only one of the châteaux classed as *Premiers Grands Crus* in Pomerol, in fact, lies outside the magic strip of soil between the village of Pomerol and the St-Emilion boundary. It is Château Trotanoy, a very fine wine which is well able to look after itself among the small fry. Of the next class, the *Premiers Crus* without the *Grands,* nearly all the wines are grouped round the village and its southern edges. The best-known of these wines are Châteaux La-Croix-de-Gay, La-Grave-Trigant-de-Boisset, Clos l'Eglise and Domaine de l'Eglise, Châteaux Beauregard, Certan-Marzelle, Clinet, Nenin, La Pointe, Le Gay and Rouget. There are also about forty other châteaux whose wines might easily appear on a list in Britain or the United States.

Pomerol is very reliable, both as to the standard of its growths and the evenness of its vintages. In a poor year for most of Bordeaux the Pomerols are often good, rather light and soft wines but with enough sweetness about them and not too much tannin. Pomerols rarely even start life as the sort of wine which makes you screw your face up. Their gentle qualities are probably what is making them so popular at the moment. They are very much the taste of France today, as well as of Britain and the United States. It is not hard to guess why; no-one wants to lay down wine for years any more, and Pomerol, of all the districts of Bordeaux, makes the wines which need least laying-down. This is not to say that they are like Beaujolais, which must be drunk as soon as you can lay your hands on it, by any means. But four or five years is a respectable age for a Pomerol, even of a good year—and for a poor year three or four may easily be enough. Their lasting properties are unaffected by this; fine Pomerols live as long as almost any wine.

Bordeaux has eight other red-wine areas, each closely defined by the laws of *Appellations Contrôlées*. None of them makes wine as fine as those I have described, but in each some good wine is to be found, and wine-merchants are spending more and more of their time outside the classical areas in finding it.

Blaye

Opposite the Médoc across the Gironde the large district of Blaye, named after the pretty old fortified port in its centre, contains the smaller district of Bourg. There is a large production of white wines as well as red in these districts, but the white is less good and less well known.

Bourg

Bourgeais red wine is not unlike St-Emilion, though it is less fine; Blayais is not normally quite so good. There are far too many châteaux in both to list, and few really have names to remember. On the other hand, a wine-merchant might easily be able to recommend a very good wine he has been offered in Bordeaux. It is the Bordeaux trade's business to keep an eye out for bargains across the water.

Néac, Lalande de Pomerol
Côtes de Fronsac
Côtes de Canon-Fronsac

Pomerol is surrounded on its north and west sides—the sides away from St-Emilion—with the communes of Néac, Lalande de Pomerol and Fronsac. The first two produce what might be called sub-Pomerols, less fine than the real thing, but cheaper. Château Bel-Air in Lalande de Pomerol is well known. The Côtes de Fronsac, with their superior central area, the Côtes de Canon-Fronsac, occupy the pretty hills west of Libourne in a bend of the Dordogne. Their wine is strong-flavoured, rather like a wine from farther south, with character and scent but, for me, little appeal. Château Rouet is the best known.

Graves de Vayres

Opposite the south end of the Côtes de Fronsac is the district confusingly called Graves de Vayres, which has nothing to do with Graves, but takes its name, as the part of St-Emilion does, from its gravel soil. Its red wines are supposed to be like lesser Pomerols.

St-Emilion has its satellites, too, the villages of St-Georges, Montagne, Lussac, Puisseguin and Parsac, which cluster round its northern boundary. All add St-Emilion to their names. Their wines are good, just like lesser St-Emilions, and are often seen under château-names abroad.

Ste-Foy-Bordeaux
Premières Côtes de Bordeaux

Far up the Dordogne beyond St-Emilion and Castillon on the south bank the district of Ste-Foy-Bordeaux makes both red and white wine. Finally, the long thin strip of the Premières Côtes de Bordeaux, right up the Garonne's east bank from Bordeaux to opposite Sauternes, is an appellation for red wines as well as white. Most of the red comes from the villages of Bassens, Ste-Eulalie, Yvrac, Carbon-Blanc, Lormont, Cenon, Floirac,

Bouliac, Latresne, Camblanes, Quinsac and Cambes in the northern half of the area. A great deal of the wine is sold simply as Premières Côtes de Bordeaux. As such, it is cheap and good.

When to drink claret

Claret has always been the Englishman's everyday wine, when he has had one. The reason, apart from the convenience of Bordeaux as a port for shipping to England, is that Bordeaux is the largest producer of good ordinary wine in the world. *Vin ordinaire* as the French understand it, which comes from the Midi, is not to the English taste. It is not an inspiring drink. There is a move to sell it in England now, but I doubt if it will ever become popular. It is essentially dull, flat, and prone to penetrating, though faint, tastes of a kind which are foreign to clean, honest wine.

Even the most ordinary honest Bordeaux, on the other hand, is a clean, balanced and very straightforward wine. It is refreshing, comforting and slips down easily. It is not too strong, and whenever any particular character becomes apparent in it, it is pleasant and familiar. What is more, it is cheap. Although its bulk price is a few pennies more a bottle than *vin ordinaire,* the difference is nothing compared with the four shillings and more which is the basic price of any wine after shipping, duty and bottling costs have been paid. Some large wine-merchants believe in paying less, even a few pennies less, for the wine, and taking the difference as profit. They create a demand for the inferior wine by advertising, and add to the price to pay for the advertisements. Nobody employs this technique for the cheap red wines of Bordeaux, which therefore remain some of the best value of all in the cheapest class for, literally, everyday drinking.

As an everyday drink they go with virtually everything. Like all red wines, they are at their best with meat, vegetables, cheese (the savoury part of a meal), and less good with fish and sweets. They are good in summer, even mixed with iced lemonade or soda-water, and in winter warmed in front of the fire. They should be treated freely as a basic ingredient: like water, in fact—drunk from tumblers, poured from a jug.

When one basic Bordeaux has become familiar in this way, its slightly superior cousins fall into place for special occasions. The little differences that make the similar, but better, wine you choose for a special dinner a more agreeable drink, with more in it to think about and enjoy than your daily wine, will come to be the basis of a really sound knowledge of claret. There is nothing more satisfying.

I think it is worth making a point, if you drink claret regularly, of drinking a really great claret occasionally—even if it is only once a year. Each time it is like a fresh revelation. Each time you will ask yourself how you could have forgotten that wine can do such wonderful things. There are some clarets in the world that are simply beautiful; there is no other word for them. They offer as much to the aesthetic sense as great music or great painting. If you ever come to the point of asking what all the fuss is about, why people talk so much about wine, that is the answer. Between the ordinary, which you do not bother to taste consciously before you swallow it, and the superb, which offers and suggests so many beautiful tastes that even after you have swallowed it the perfume lingers on your tongue and your lips, and you cannot bear to let it go . . . between these two comes the whole study of wine.

Red Burgundy

I HAVE INTRODUCED BURGUNDY in the White Wine section of this book. The salient facts of its peculiar system of naming and blending wines and the difficulties in knowing exactly what you are getting are all there, and I shall not repeat them here. But it is important to read the Introduction to the section on Burgundy (p. 86) before reading about red or white burgundy.

It is the custom to talk about Bordeaux and burgundy as though they were the opposite poles of red wine. Between them, the implication is, they cover everything that a red wine can be. Burgundy is popularly supposed to be fruity, dark, full-bodied and sweet; claret is supposed to be light, dry and delicate. The rest of the world's red wines are therefore divided into claret- or burgundy-types following these theoretical characteristics.

In fact, burgundy and claret both find themselves near the middle of the spectrum of red wine. There are much darker and fuller wines than burgundy, and much drier and lighter wines than claret. Considering all the world's wines, burgundy and claret are seen to be not opposites but neighbours. They have in common the delicacy and balance that makes them the world's best red wines. Compared with the difference between them and almost any other red wines, they are twins.

When we discuss the difference between claret and burgundy, therefore, we are discussing subtleties. There is more similarity between claret and burgundy than, for example, between Australian burgundy-type wine and the real thing.

188

The village of Santenay in the Côte de Beaune of Burgundy. A summer storm is coming. The vines, freshly sprayed with sulphur to protect them from disease, look lurid against the darkening landscape. *(Photo: Guy Gravett)*

When I begin to describe a wine there is always the same difficulty. It is impossible. You must taste burgundy—real burgundy—to learn what the burgundy taste is. Remarks in a vacuum about it being sweet and yet slightly reminiscent of green sap in perfume; full but penetrating in taste; more savoury than Bordeaux and yet at the same time slightly sweeter, are of no use. The answer to the question 'What kind of wine is burgundy?' is that it is a very savoury, inviting wine, as tempting as good smells from the kitchen. When you find a good mature one, it is soft and sweet. Like a soft sweet face with a good bone structure, it is beautiful.

What burgundy is not, though it is often reputed to be, and sometimes I fear fraudulently made to be, is something like an Australian tonic wine; rich, heavy, coarse, alcoholic, full of iron to build you up and keep out the cold.

Burgundy is the northernmost good red-wine district. It gets little sun and its wine suffers from, if anything, lack of alcohol. It is delicate—very rarely rich. The great burgundies in great vintages are famous for their big-bodied richness for this very reason. The rest of Burgundy makes smooth, savoury, light and beguiling wines like nowhere else on earth.

Burgundy is more expensive than claret because there is so much less of it. Leaving aside Beaujolais, which happily is produced in very great quantities —though not enough—and stays quite cheap, the cheapest of even the blended wines of villages, which are known as commune wines (Pommard, for example), costs almost 50 per cent more than its opposite number in Bordeaux, which would be called, simply, St-Julien or Margaux. I doubt if anyone would argue that it is 50 per cent better.

However, as soon as you enter the more expensive field of classified château-wines from Bordeaux, starting at about twice the price of the commune wines, their equivalents in Burgundy, the *Premiers Crus,* begin to look much better value. Their prices continue up more or less level to the top; the Bordeaux first-growths and the Burgundian *têtes de cuvée.* The most expensive Bordeaux, in fact, can be ten times as expensive as the cheapest: the highest burgundy price only about six times as high.

The northernmost district of Burgundy, Chablis, grows no red wine. Nearby Irancy, a village a few miles to the south, near the new motorway from Paris, has a reputation for its *vin du pays,* Irancy Rouge, but it is not in the class of wine we expect to bear the great name of burgundy.

The Côte d'Or has a monopoly of the red vineyards. From the start of its central slopes south of Dijon—for it begins as some beautiful wooded hills to the north of the city—it has the great name of the Côte de Nuits. For thirty miles with only one break the narrow strip of vineyards along the middle slopes of the hill—never more than five hundred yards wide—produces what its growers, and about half the world beside, consider the finest red wine on earth. They are immediately at their very finest. As soon as you leave Dijon on the road south to Beaune, the road which follows the Côtes all the way, the names begin to have a familiar ring. The first is Fixin, famous, if not world-famous, for fine red wine. The second is Chambertin.

The name of the village, in fact, is Gevrey-Chambertin. I have explained how the old single-barrelled village-names grafted on the more illustrious names of their best-known vineyards to identify themselves in a tricky market. The village of Gevrey was distinguished above all for one vineyard. Its name was Chambertin. The next field on the same level on the hill, going north, is called the Clos de Bèze. These names have been equal in reputation and quality for centuries. Both are *têtes de cuvée*. The fact that Clos de Bèze, too, has now taken the name of Chambertin as its prefix should not be taken to mean that it has eventually given way to its great neighbour and rival. The tradition was getting so strong in the neighbourhood that it could hardly resist. All the *Premier Cru* wines here have now added the name of Chambertin to their own: Charmes-Chambertin, Chapelle-Chambertin, Griotte-Chambertin, Latricières-Chambertin, Ruchottes-Chambertin, Mazis-Chambertin, Mazoyères-Chambertin. Any names which appear on labels following that of Gevrey-Chambertin can be taken to be those of the *Deuxièmes Crus*—confusingly enough, the third-growths. The best known of these is the Clos St-Jacques. All these wines are among the best of red burgundies. Chambertin and Clos de Bèze are often called the greatest of the whole region. Even the simple parish appellation of Gevrey-Chambertin, while not very restricting to the merchant, usually means a very good wine. Oddly enough, considering that this is the farthest north of fine red wines, and that for the Côtes of Burgundy the vineyards are on fairly flat ground, the wine here is the most robust, as the terminology goes, of all burgundies. It has tremendous strength of purpose, somehow; great staying-power and an almost oak-like solidity. Chambertin is the wine for moments of great decision, or great joints of beef on the bone and other things which you know are going to have plenty of flavour, character and savour of their own. Legend has it that Napoleon never took anything else with him on campaign. There was even Chambertin sold as 'back from Moscow'.

The name of the next parish, Morey St-Denis, is not so well known. It has, indeed, added a vineyard name, that of Clos St-Denis, to its old short name of Morey. But it miscalculated. The Clos St-Denis is small, and not even the best in the parish. In short, the village is swamped by its great names. There are not many people who even know that the superlative vineyards of Clos de Tart, Clos des Lambrays, Bonnes Mares and Clos de la Roche are in Morey St-Denis at all. Of these, Bonnes Mares, I should add, has its greater part in the next parish of Chambolle-Musigny.

All these five vineyards are in Burgundy's top class. All are big strong wines, almost as big as Chambertin and as strong, though, as I think, with a little more grace and flexibility in them. Clos de Tart, particularly, which

190

has the good fortune, rare among the vineyards of Burgundy, to belong entirely to one man, Jean Mommessin, is a lovely, soft, strong and savoury wine. It is capable of long life, and yet surprisingly ready to drink when quite young. Again these are wines for great feasts—as their prices, I fear, suggest. The other wine of Morey St-Denis, bearing the village name, is not often seen abroad. If you do see it, on the other hand, you may be fairly certain that the wine-merchant has followed quality rather than fashion—for few people have heard of it.

CHAMBOLLE-
MUSIGNY
Musigny

Hard on the heels of Morey St-Denis, sharing the big vineyard of Bonnes Mares with it, comes the more famous Chambolle-Musigny. The *tête de cuvée* of Chambolle-Musigny is Musigny, sometimes called Le Musigny to underline the point, but never called anything else. The village is dominated by the biggest proprietor, Count Georges de Vogüé, whose family also own the greater part of two of the biggest and best champagne-houses. In his superb, airy cellar, like the crypt of a great cathedral, rest the finest wines which are made here—and often, some say, in the whole of Burgundy. One *Premier Cru* here, with the lovely name of Les Amoureuses, is on the *tête de cuvée* level. Another, Les Charmes, is not far off. De Vogüé goes one better and makes a *tête de cuvée* of the *tête de cuvée,* a special selection of the best of the best, which he calls Musigny Vieilles Vignes ('Old Vines'—those which give the finest fruit).

Musigny is a slightly more delicate wine than Chambertin. The soft savouriness of burgundy comes out in it more than in any other wine. It lingers and spreads in your mouth, making what French tasters call 'the peacock's tail' with its bouquet of flavours and flavours-within-flavours.

Chambolle-Musigny, the blended wine of various vineyards within the village boundaries, is often one of the best of the burgundies which are almost universally stocked by wine-merchants. It varies, of course, enormously from shipper to shipper, for it is in the blending-vats of the shipper that it takes its final shape, but it is often less built up into a heavy-weight than most village-named wines which have undergone this treatment. It remains almost tender in character.

CLOS DE
VOUGEOT

The southern border of Chambolle-Musigny is the edge of the Clos de Vougeot, an enormous vineyard walled about with one great stone wall and dominated with the Burgundian countryside's one impressive building, used by the Burgundians as their symbol. Its foundation was the work of the Cistercian order. Today it is the headquarters of the Order of the Chevaliers du Tastevin.

As a vineyard it has its faults. In fact it is not really one *climat* at all, but a whole *finage* (parish) of them. Its quality varies as much as the quality within any other parish. On the hill-slopes it is good—indeed superb. The top of the vineyard is right next to Musigny. On the flat land at the bottom of the hill it is no better than any other such vineyard. The lowest part

191

would rate perhaps as a *Deuxième Cru* if it were rated separately from the top. Thus the wine with the great name need not necessarily be great at all.

Clos de Vougeot is sometimes called the claret of Burgundy. It is markedly drier than most burgundies; the wine-merchants of the region, perhaps with tongue in cheek, call it feminine. The best of it has the most beautiful scent in Burgundy, with a faint suggestion of autumnal dankness about it which is typically burgundian.

The Chevaliers du Tastevin

The Chevaliers du Tastevin are members of a body formed by the growers and merchants of Burgundy to promote the sales of their wine. It holds frequent dinners for as many as four or five hundred guests in the great hall of the old fortress-like building in the Clos de Vougeot. Recruitment for the order is carried on at a brisk rate. Each firm of *négociants* in Burgundy has to introduce ten new members a year in order to qualify for hiring the building for a dinner of its own. Members wear medieval-type red robes for the dinners. There is singing and a good deal of fulsome praise for the wines of Burgundy in general and for those in the present glasses in particular. A good dozen of similar societies have sprung up to uphold the honour of the wines of their respective parts of France.

Flagey-Echezeaux

The name of the next village, Flagey-Echezeaux, is never used on wine-labels, although it is very much a wine-growing community. The village is in the valley, away from the best vineyards. Its common wine is sold under the name of Vosne-Romanée, its immediate neighbour on the other side.

Grands Echezeaux

Flagey has, on the other hand, in the vineyard of Grands Echezeaux on the south side of the top of the Clos de Vougeot, one of the best of all red burgundies, a wine definitely in the *tête de cuvée* class. I imagine it is only kept off wine-lists—it is not often listed in Britain or the United States—by its sneeze-like name, which has the advantage of keeping the price down. Grands Echezeaux and Bonnes Mares are probably the two least known of the world's greatest wines.

Wine of the *Premier Cru* class from the Flagey vineyards surrounding Grands Echezeaux are sold as Echezeaux without the word Grands.

VOSNE-ROMANEE
(*see plan of village in map section*)

The wine of the tiny vineyard of Romanée-Conti on the hill above the village of Vosne, marked with a crucifix and covering less than four and a half acres, fetches the highest price of any red wine. It belongs to an estate known as the Domaine de la Romanée-Conti, which also owns the vineyard of La Tache, most of Richebourg and parts of Grands Echezeaux.

Romanée-Conti

André Simon has said that Romanée-Conti has something almost oriental about its fragrance. It is certainly spicy in a way which makes it, and the other wines made by the Domaine, immediately recognizable. There is something almost oriental, too, about a visit to the dank and crowded cellar which houses it: you feel you should leave your shoes at the door.

Whether or not the Domaine does something special in the making of its wine—there are whispers about adding a touch of brandy, or concentrating a small proportion of the unfermented juice—it gives a stamp of sheer luxury which, combined with its amazing price, makes it quite irresistible to a large number of customers. The tiny courtyard and cellar, indeed, are always brimming over with American visitors, who put this with Montrachet as one of the sights of Burgundy to be seen. No doubt the whispers are the work of envious neighbours.

Vosne-Romanée has no less than five *tête de cuvée* vineyards—none of them, it must be admitted, very big. Besides La Romanée-Conti they are La Romanée-St-Vivant, the biggest, not quite such a perfumed and splendid wine; La Romanée, the smallest, perhaps a shade lighter; La Tache, which some say is better even than the most expensive; and Le Richebourg, which also has its supporters for the crown.

The second-rank wines of Vosne-Romanée must not be overlooked. They are labelled with the village-name as well as their own vineyard-names. La Grande Rue, a vineyard barely wider than a road running up the side of Romanée-Conti, Les Gaudichots, Les Suchots, Aux Malconsorts and Les Beauxmonts are all well known, often exported and of very high quality. Vosne-Romanée *tout court* is also often excellent; a middle-weight burgundy, a Sunday-lunch wine.

The town of Nuits-St-Georges brings us to the end of the Côte de Nuits, the hillside of Burgundy's best red wine. Nuits and Prémeaux next door, to the south, whose wines are sold as Nuits, are not the very greatest of burgundies, but they are typical, soft, savoury wines with plenty of meat in them. If they lack anything it is scent. Les St-Georges on the border of Prémeaux is the vineyard from which Nuits took its name. The best of the others are Aux Boudots, Aux Cras, La Richmone and Aux Murgers near Vosne-Romanée, and Les Cailles, Le Clos de la Maréchale, Les Didiers, Les Porrets, Les Pruliers and Les Vaucrains to the south. The total quantity of Nuits-St-Georges wine, partly owing to its merger with Prémeaux, is large for any one Burgundian name: its share of the hillside is almost four miles long. It is also often 'stretched' with cheaper, stronger wine.

Corton, the northernmost vineyard of the Côte de Beaune, is the one which is said to approach most nearly to the wines of the Côte de Nuits in character and in quality. In general, wines from the Côte de Beaune, the southern one of Burgundy's two wonderful hillsides, are a little less highly regarded than the wines of Chambertin, Musigny and Romanée. Corton is the only one which is mentioned in the same breath.

While this holds true for the best wines of all, no doubt, it needs qualifying straight away. In the second class the Côte de Beaune wines hold their own with ease. They have the great advantage of quantity. Beaune has about two and a half thousand acres of vines; Pommard over one and a half; Volnay over a thousand. About half of these are planted with fine grapes for first-class wine. Chambolle-Musigny, which is typical of the Côte de Nuits, has less than two hundred acres.

Beaune, Volnay and Pommard have, therefore, made their name for supplying perhaps not the most wonderful wine the world has ever seen, but plenty of really admirable wine to drink regularly and often. Their wines mature sooner, taking perhaps six or seven years on the average as against ten or more for the Côte de Nuits wines. They are lighter, though not light in the sense in which a claret is lighter than a burgundy. They are no drier or more acid. They just have less of the quality so happily known as 'stuffing'.

ALOXE-CORTON

After Nuits-St-Georges, again taking the same road south, there is a gap in the hills before the hill of Corton, rising above the village of Aloxe, which has embellished its name in the usual way. I have described how the hill is divided among white wines and red. I cannot honestly say that one is better than the other. It is probably the only great vineyard in the world of which this is true.

Corton

Corton, which, like Chambertin and Montrachet, sometimes has the word Le added to its name to stress that it is the real thing and not one of its sisters and its cousins and its aunts that you are getting, shares the honours here with Corton-Clos-du-Roi and Corton-Bressandes. One shipper of high repute, Louis Latour, has a brand-name which sounds like another Corton vineyard—Corton-Grancey. In fact it is simply the name of his house, under which he sells some of his best Corton wine.

The village name, Aloxe-Corton, is one of the best-known for shippers' blended red burgundy, partly because the villages on both sides also avail themselves of it. Of these, one, Ladoix-Serrigny, is never heard of under its own name; the other, Pernand-Vergelesses, sells the greater part of its red and white wines under the names of Aloxe-Corton and Corton-Charlemagne (part of the great Charlemagne white-wine vineyard is in the parish), but also sells very good and largely neglected wine under its own mouthful of a name. Its best vineyard is called Ile des Vergelesses.

Ladoix-Serrigny
Pernand-Vergelesses

You would look for the vineyard called Aux Vergelesses, too, in Pernand, but you would not find it. It is in the next village to the south, Savigny-les-Beaune. Savigny adjoins the vineyards of Beaune itself on the north. Its wines are very like those of Beaune; rather pale in colour, light and soft in taste but with the background suggestion of strength which is always there in good burgundy. Their scent is if anything more fruit-like and less savoury than the scents of the Côte de Nuits wines. Strength and solidity, within reason, are at a premium in the Beaune and Savigny vineyards. They appear in good vintages but sometimes stay away in poor ones.

Savigny-les-Beaune

BEAUNE

The town of Beaune, and its hospital, are the showplaces of Burgundy. Dijon is the old capital. There there are superb churches and the old Ducal palace. But Dijon has other interests; it is not in the thick of the wine-country. Beaune lives and breathes wine.

The Hospices de Beaune

The Hospices de Beaune, which is the local hospital, is the most remarkable and beautiful building in the whole world of wine. It sounds odd that

194

it should be both a hospital and so wine-minded. It was a stroke of charitable genius by a fifteenth-century statesman. Nicolas Rolin, Chancellor to Duke Philip the Good of Burgundy, and his wife Guigonne de Salins founded the Hospices in 1443. They endowed it for its income with vineyards. Others followed suit, and to this day its expenses are paid out of the income of its vineyards, which are, on the whole, some of the very best of the Côte de Beaune.

At that time, although Dijon was the capital of Burgundy, its artistic and commercial centre was in its Flemish provinces. From Brussels Rolin fetched Rogier van der Weyden, the greatest Flemish painter of his day, to do an altar-piece for his new foundation. Van der Weyden's 'Last Judgement' still hangs there, though now in an upper chamber instead of the chapel.

The Hospital today is a remarkable mixture of ancient and modern. To enter its Gothic courtyard, with steep-pitched roofs of polychrome tiles like jesters' motley, with nurses in long religious habits and wimples, with its old elaborate wellhead of wrought iron, or to go into the kitchen, where great log fires make the copper pans beam and glow and where a smell of real old Burgundian cooking puts aside all thoughts of steamed fish and sick-bed food, you would have no idea that operating theatres with all the devices of modern medicine share the same venerable walls.

Every November the courtyard of the hospital is the scene of the auctions of its wine which decide its revenue for the next year. Merchants and wine-lovers come from all over the world to this remarkable event; an opportunity to buy some of Burgundy's best wine and to subscribe to an ancient and worthy charity at the same time.

The prices set at the Hospices auction are those which guide all dealings in the wine of that vintage in Burgundy. Hospices wines themselves tend to be a little expensive, not only because they are good but for charity's sake; all other burgundies have their fixed relationships to the publicly-decided Hospices prices. The weekend of the sale, therefore, sets off a busy week of dealing throughout the Burgundy countryside, as the *négociants*, the local wholesalers, go round to replenish their stocks.

Hospices de Beaune wines carry on their labels the name of the benefactor who gave the vineyard to the Hospital. They are known by these *cuvée* names rather than the names of their vineyards. There are twenty-two red and seven white (all the white except one are Meursaults). Of the red the best known are those in Beaune given by Nicolas Rolin and his wife themselves, which bear their names, and the Corton wines given by Charlotte Dumay and the unfortunately-named Doctor Peste. Hospices wines appear on some of the best wine-lists in every country; there is every reason to buy one when you see it.

The vineyards of Beaune

The vineyards of Beaune are large and vary from moderate to excellent. The best are called Les Marconnets, Les Fèves, Les Bressandes, Les Grèves, Les Teurons, Aux Cras and Les Champs Pimont. The list can be extended many ways. Le Clos des Mouches, Clos-du-Roi, Les Cent-Vignes, Les Toussaints, Clos-de-la-Mousse, Les Avaux, Les Vignes-Franches, Les Epenottes are all fine wines which are often exported.

I have said that Beaune tends to be rather pale and light in weight except in exceptional years. In the wines I have mentioned by their vineyards' names you can expect considerable character and the true burgundian savouriness. Wine labelled simply Beaune varies widely from merchant to merchant. He can find some very good wine to sell under that name, or he can use it as a way of selling something rather ordinary. In any case, *Côte de Beaune* wine labelled Beaune is slightly better than wine labelled simply Côte de Beaune. Beaune must come from Beaune; Côte de Beaune can come from anywhere between Aloxe-Corton and Santenay, from high or low ground. The difference in appellations is the same as that between, for example, Margaux and Haut-Médoc in Bordeaux.

Appellations
Contrôlées
The appellations of Burgundy cannot be grasped without a certain bafflement at first. Two other uses of the words Côte de Beaune have different legal meanings again, and must be mentioned. One is when the words are preceded by the name of a village, which is hyphenated to them (Santenay-Côte-de-Beaune, for example). This is that village's own appellation. It indicates that although the village is not all that well known its wine is worth seeking out. The other is the label Côte de Beaune-Villages, which *Côte de Beaune-* means that the wine is a blend of the wines of two or more of the lesser-*Villages* known villages of the Côte—not Aloxe-Corton, Beaune, Pommard or Volnay.

The appellations in descending order for the Côte de Beaune are as follows. Best of all is one of the great vineyards which has its own appellation and needs no qualification; for example, Corton. Second best are the *Premiers Crus,* which can either say, for example, Beaune Les Marconnets or Beaune-Marconnets. Third best would be simply Beaune. Then comes a village which needs -Côte de Beaune to reinforce it (for example, Santenay-Côte de Beaune). Then comes just plain Côte de Beaune. Finally, Côte de Beaune-Villages. Anything which fails to qualify for any of these names may yet get in one of the lower range of appellations. The hills behind the great *Hautes-Côtes-de-* Côtes to the west have their own class, either Hautes-Côtes-de-Beaune or *Beaune* Vin Fin des Hautes-Côtes-de-Nuits (Hautes in this case meaning high in *Vin Fin des Hautes-* altitude, nothing else). Anything made anywhere in Burgundy of the right *Côtes-de-Nuits* grapes—the classical Pinot—can call itself simply Bourgogne. Anything *Bourgogne* made from a third of the classical grapes and two-thirds of the common Gamay can call itself Bourgogne Passe-Tout-Grains. There is a bottom *Passe-Tout-Grains* catch-all class; Bourgogne Grand Ordinaire, for low-strength wines which *Bourgogne Grand* were at least made in Burgundy, and indeed often taste like it. *Ordinaire*

Labels are usually obliging enough to sort out for you which part of the name is the controlled appellation and repeat it underneath. Thus we have Corton, and then underneath *Appellation Corton Contrôlée.*

None of these regulations, incredibly enough, have any legal power at all

196

In Burgundy at vintage-time pickers eat their lunches on the stone walls between the vineyards. The vineyard here is Chambertin; in the background rises the steep Côte de Nuits

in Britain. A wine-merchant is entirely on trust; he can print *Appellation Contrôlée* on anything he likes. For this reason, people who are concerned about authenticity often prefer to buy wine which was bottled and labelled in France, where there would have been trouble in store for anyone who broke the rules. This is not, however, to say that the French have a monopoly of innocence or the British of guilt.

POMMARD

At the southern limit of the vineyards of Beaune the road which has brought us past all the famous villages since Dijon turns away from the Côte. To reach the next famous parishes of Pommard and Volnay you have to fork right along a side-road. You are immediately between the stone walls which shelter two of the Pommard vineyards from the road. On the left, between the main road and the side-road, is the flat vineyard of Les Perrières, and next to it the Château de Pommard. Neither is of great note. On the right, where the hill begins to rise, are the Petits and Grands Epenots. Grands Epenots makes one of Pommard's two best wines.

The only other vineyard of Pommard which reaches a really high standard is Les Rugiens-bas, on the far side of the village where the parish of Volnay begins. Epenots and Rugiens-bas are often seen (both are *Premiers Crus*) in Britain and the United States. I have seen the Clos de la Commaraine listed, too, but few other Pommard *climats*. Pommard, the single village name, is far more common.

It is at the same time the least wonderful and the best known of the villages of Burgundy. Its best wines have a good, straightforward character, but rarely the interest and subtlety of the greatest wine. I have tasted superlative Pommard Rugiens-bas, but on the whole Pommard has a tendency to dullness which is particularly noticeable if you taste it after the wines of the surrounding villages, each of which has its own vitality.

VOLNAY

Volnay, next door, I must confess is my special favourite. It is the most delicate red burgundy. The vineyards of Caillerets, Champans and Fremiets are its *têtes de cuvée*. En Chevret, Les Angles, Le Clos des Chênes, Carelle-sous-la-Chapelle and five or six others are all excellent, and make their appearance on wine-lists from time to time.

Volnay Santenots

Volnay Santenots, which is also a very well-known name, is in fact the name under which the red wine of the neighbouring village of Meursault is sold. Meursault is famous only for white wine. It is nonetheless very like a Volnay and extremely good.

A Volnay with its vineyard name is often a wine of real beauty. It has a pronounced scent—more than Beaune, certainly more than Pommard—and a way of being exquisitely fresh and lively without losing the richness of flavour which distinguishes good burgundy. It is not a surprise, when you taste it, that it is the last great red burgundy before you come into the white-burgundy country of Meursault and the Montrachets. I would not drink Volnay with any of the very rich and tasty dishes of Burgundy—*Coq au vin* or *Boeuf Bourguignon*—but with roast young lamb or a pheasant which has not been hung too long.

Plain unqualified Volnay is often not as light as it should be; shippers tend to reinforce it with something to give it more weight and colour. Wine with the name Volnay alone, in other words, will rarely justify so much enthusiasm. It costs remarkably little more, though, to buy a specified-vineyard wine which will immediately demonstrate what is meant by character.

Monthélie
Auxey-Duresses

CHASSAGNE-
MONTRACHET

Clos St-Jean

SANTENAY

Now the red-wine vineyards of Burgundy tail off. To the west the hill above Volnay hides two little villages, Monthélie and Auxey-Duresses, whose red wine is not often listed but will be good value if you see it. To the south Meursault's red wine is sold as Volnay Santenots. Puligny-Montrachet makes virtually no red wine. Chassagne-Montrachet, on the other hand, has very important and excellent red-wine vineyards: Clos St-Jean, La Maltroie, La Boudriotte and Morgeot. It comes as a surprise to people who know the name of Montrachet only as a white wine. As in Meursault, the change from white to red comes in mid-village; south of the Montrachet vineyard there is a gap in the hill. Then red wine begins. Clos St-Jean is often seen in England and is generally very good value. It is not, however, an extremely light Volnay-type wine, as you might expect. It has, oddly enough, a similarity to the bigger wines of the Côte de Nuits. It is full of flavour and well-scented, deep red and a slow developer, a slightly sweeter wine than most—all the things which should make it very popular.

The last village of the Côte de Beaune is Santenay. It makes both red and white wines, but its red is better. Les Gravières, which goes on from the vineyard of Morgeot in Chassagne-Montrachet, is the best vineyard; Santenay-Gravières, indeed, is about the only Santenay you ever see in England. It is not so different from Chassagne-Montrachet; good and strong, with a tender softness about it. I remember having a Santenay-Gravières which made me think very differently, a thin poor wine, at a charming little restaurant called the Auberge du Camp Romain in the hills above Santenay. When I reported this to a *négociant* in Beaune he knew the wine straight away. 'Ah, that was Monsieur Untel's wine,' he said. 'No wonder. He only planted those vines five years ago. You had his first wine from that plot.' Whereupon he produced a wine to cancel out my bad impression of Santenay-Gravières—the big, tender wine that it should, and can, be.

SOUTH
BURGUNDY

There are three more famous outbreaks of vineyards in Burgundy after leaving the Côte de Beaune, the last hills of the Côte d'Or, going south. They are called the Côte Chalonnaise, Mâcon and Beaujolais.

Beaujolais is far and away the most popular and most important of the three. The demand for it is so great that all kinds of wines from near and far are used to stretch the supply. Switzerland or Paris alone would drink considerably more than the total production of the area if other wines were not called in to help.

The Côte Chalonnaise

The Côte Chalonnaise and Mâcon, though they produce wines which are often just as good, have never made it to this extent. Two Côte Chalonnaise wines are sometimes met on the kind of wine-list which looks for the best wine for the money rather than a popular name. They are called Givry and Mercurey. You might say they belong in the same class as Côte-de-Beaune-Villages but are considerably lighter and less substantial.

Mâcon

Mâcon's best wine is white: Pouilly-Fuissé. Mâcon Rouge is a good *vin du pays*, at least as good as most commercial Beaujolais, though not as good as really good Beaujolais, beside which it seems rather lifeless and dull. But then few wines are as lively and drinkable as Beaujolais.

Moulin-à-Vent

To do Mâcon justice, I should add that the best wine of Beaujolais is right on the border of the two districts, at the village with the lovely name of Romanèche-Thorins. The wine is called Moulin-à-Vent. Moulin-à-Vent is not typical of Beaujolais. Beaujolais's great attribute is that it is soon ready for drinking. Moulin-à-Vent is almost like a Côte de Beaune wine: it takes five or six years to be at its best. After that time it is well into the class of fine wine, and can almost be great. The vineyards of Rochegrès, Carquelin and Château des Jacques are the best.

BEAUJOLAIS

It was a Château des Jacques 1959 which I had at the Chapon Fin at Thoissey near Pontanevaux in Beaujolais, with a glorious dish of *Volaille de Bresse aux morilles* (Bresse, of the famous chickens, is twenty miles away), followed by the delicious potato-flour pancakes, *crêpes Parmentier*. Lunch that day was cold Cavaillon melon, crayfish *à la nage*, the chicken in its cream sauce with morels, the *crêpes Parmentier* and *tartelettes aux framboises*, the raspberries sitting on that magic custard which makes two or three tartlets easy meat after enough food to last a weekend.

I was surprised to see that they proposed to serve the Moulin-à-Vent in the enormous glasses which are reserved for very special red wines; they were perfectly right.

The other villages of Beaujolais cluster in the foothills of the Beaujolais mountains. It is some of France's least-known and loveliest country. The highlands, rising sometimes to three thousand feet, are wooded to the top. The forests of pine and chestnut tilt and tumble this way and that, following no ranges but thrusting up from meadows and brooks wherever they feel inclined. Cattle feed by the streams; otherwise there is no sign of life. There are no houses for miles. The occasional village is pure *Clochemerle*.

Beaujolais-Villages

Beaujolais Supérieur

Beaujeu is the village in the foothills which has given its name to the district and its wine. The other wine-villages which call their wine by their own names are Juliénas, St-Amour, Brouilly, Chenas, Chiroubles, Fleurie and Morgon. These and a number of other villages may call their wine Beaujolais-Villages. Beaujolais Supérieur may come from anywhere in the area but it must have a 10 per cent alcohol content. Just plain Beaujolais is 1 degree of alcohol weaker than Beaujolais Supérieur.

199

The Beaujolais which is served as carafe wine in the restaurants of Lyons and Paris is often the *vin de l'année,* the wine of the previous vintage. It is very light, translucent but purple like some kinds of cherry, smelling of fresh grapes more than wine and sometimes a little prickly on your tongue with the last traces of fermentation. It is very faintly sweet and distinctly soft in your mouth. Its most noticeable characteristic is that a bottle goes nowhere: two people need two.

Beaujolais abroad is often another matter. It has had its body built up with stronger-tasting wine. It is darker, harsher and altogether less light-hearted and drinkable. In Britain the wine-trade is fond of saying that this is the way people like it; they complain that it is watery otherwise.

Only recently have estates in Beaujolais started selling their wine under their individual names, and even bottling it themselves, although the extra cost of shipping it in bottle is high in proportion to the whole value of the wine. It is now quite common to see Domaine, Château or Clos names, some of them real, some invented, attached to Beaujolais. One or two wine-merchants have even started shipping the Beaujolais *de l'année* in the March following the vintage.

The Rhône Valley

THE RHÔNE IS USUALLY badly represented on wine-lists. Often one vaguely-named Côtes-du-Rhône, which might come from anywhere in a hundred-mile stretch of the Rhône valley, and an almost equally vague Châteauneuf-du-Pape are its only representatives. Both are expected to be strong in alcohol and taste, rather black in colour, and cheap.

A good deal of Rhône wine is like this. The Rhône leaves behind the delicacy of burgundy and Bordeaux. It is a wine of the south, where the sun fairly bakes the ground. The grapes ripen fully; the alcohol content is correspondingly high. Moreover the great grape of the Rhône, the Syrah, is one with a very dark colour, which gives the juice such a bite of bitterness that it is often mixed with a little white grape juice before the wine is made to soften it.

The result is a wine which needs a very long time to mature. If it is bottled young it will throw a deposit in the bottle almost like that of port. In the last century it was often offered as an alternative to port after dinner. Old Hermitage was reckoned, at thirty or forty years, a match for any wine on earth.

It is not made in quite this way now. Modern methods have cut down the time it takes to mature, but it still is rarely kept long enough. The oldest Rhône wine I have been able to find on any London wine-list is ten years old, and that is exceptional. No wine could so reward anyone who bought it while it was very young—and half the price of a comparable burgundy—and forgot about it for fifteen or twenty years. He would eventually have something priceless and unique, which he could send to auction or drink, or both. It would be soft, scented and so mouth-filling and warm in character that almost any other red wine would taste like red ink beside it.

There are few names to remember in the Rhône valley, despite the fact that the vineyards stretch almost from Lyons to Avignon. Like the white wines, the reds are found in three principal places on the way. The first and (at any rate, by reputation) the best, just north of the vineyards of the great white Château Grillet at Condrieu, is the Côte Rôtie—the roasted hill. Its vineyards and production are both small but its wine is excellent; dark purple when it is young, browning slightly with age, heady, full of flavour and life, scented—more and more as it gets older—like lovely soft fruit. It is like an elder brother to Beaujolais. The Côte Rôtie is divided into two parts, named, so the story goes, after the two daughters of a former proprietor, the Côte Brune and the Côte Blonde. The soil of the two parts corresponds to the description, being darker and lighter, and so, curiously enough, does the wine. I have only once, however, seen which half the wine came from specified on a wine-list. Proprietors who, like those in Burgundy, usually have several small plots, make their wine with grapes from both.

Côte Rôtie

Both sides of the river at the bend where Tain faces Tournon, thirty miles by road south of Côte Rôtie, make red wine. The west-bank appellation, St-Joseph, is an umbrella name for wine from a number of villages. It can be good, but it cannot be relied on like the Hermitage from opposite. The hill of Hermitage looks as though it was designed to give its front every minute of sunshine in the year; it faces south, rising above the river almost like the Rock of Gibraltar above the Straits.

Hermitage

Hermitage was called by Professor Saintsbury, the first man to write a book solely about the wine in his cellar, the manliest wine on earth. Dr Johnson was of the view that men should drink port (and boys claret). The juxtaposition of port with Hermitage again suggests its strength of character. But it is rarely old enough to show this character properly when it is offered to be drunk. If it were, it would be much more popular than it is.

Crozes-Hermitage

The village of Crozes-Hermitage lies just to the north of Hermitage proper. Its wine may not be sold as Hermitage, but Crozes-Hermitage is often seen. It is slightly cheaper; perhaps not quite so good but an excellent substitute.

Game is usually suggested as the food for Hermitage and the other Rhône wines. Well-hung venison and wild boar, however, rarely come my way, and I prefer briefly-hung game-birds with a lighter wine. To me the Rhône wines are for winter evenings when even the log fire and the candles leave a suspicion of chill in the dining-room. Then, whether it is liver and bacon or roast sirloin, cheese omelette or duck for dinner, they are fine.

Cornas

St-Joseph is the name used all the way down the west bank of the river to the village of Cornas, some six or seven miles. At Cornas a hill stands back from the river and the village. Its wine has not the qualities of Hermitage; it is rather dull beside the best of Rhône wines, clean but unsubtle; but it is often found as a speciality in the excellent restaurants of the area.

Châteauneuf-du-Pape

Châteauneuf-du-Pape is far and away the most famous of the wines of the Rhône valley and Provence, for it is in both regions and both claim it.

The old castle, now in ruins, which gives it its name is a little way north of Avignon. The vineyards surround it and accompany the Rhône on its way for six or seven miles, stretching inland nearly to the old Roman city of Orange. Another ten miles or so inland lie the vineyards of Gigondas.

Gigondas

These should be considered part of the same complex; the Gigondas wine is very like its more famous neighbour, though it has less guts—in short, is not quite so good.

Châteauneuf-du-Pape is unusual among French wines for being made of a large number of different kinds of grapes, some optional, some compulsory if the grower wants to keep his appellation. The wine they become is a by-word for strength, although alcoholically it is not necessarily any stronger than any other Rhône wine—it sometimes reaches 14 per cent.

What gives it its reputation more than its power to turn the head or buckle the knees is its warmth and strength of flavour. Without having the hard and almost overwhelming taste of young Hermitage it could almost hold its own with port for flavour, and yet it is not sweet.

Cheap Châteauneuf-du-Pape does not deserve this kind of praise—what cheap wine does?—but the best growths, which are becoming better and better known, can sometimes turn, in five or six years, into unbeatable flavour and unbeatable value for money. They can be almost as distinctive as a fine burgundy and considerably cheaper.

Château Fortia, 'Chante Perdrix' ('Partridge Song', if song is the word), the Domaine de la Nerthe, Château Rayas and Château Vaudieu are some of these fine ones. Again, they are often described as the wine for game, but they should be drunk more often than this implies. If they were called the wine for steak they would have more of the use they deserve.

Châteauneuf-du-Pape is usually bottled in a sloping-shouldered burgundy-shape bottle. Some of the growers get carried away and use absurd rough-glass bottles which are supposed to look handmade, and as though they had been under the cobwebs for a century or two. If the wine were as old as the bottle looks it would be far too old. It is a publicity stunt and certainly detracts from the value for money of the package, including the wine. The wine inside may be good or bad, but it would be wiser to look for an ordinary bottle.

Vins de Pays

THE MIDI

VIN DU MIDI—the wine of the south—means one thing only to a Frenchman —the lowest possible category of wine, whose price is measured (and quoted daily in the papers, like a share price) by so many francs per degree of alcohol.

Vine-growing is one of the chief industries all the way from the Italian border to the Spanish. The most notorious area on the way is the dull flat country west of the Rhône delta. There is a constant surplus of bad red wine in this area. The growers are given to striking and picketing if the government does not do something to help them get rid of it. Sometimes the government distils it to make industrial alcohol, sometimes it gets the army to drink it (at other times, when there has been a milk surplus, the long-suffering army has been switched over to milk).

The wine of the south used to be grown in the foothills of the mountains standing back from the coast, from hardy old vines which gave a wine of some character, if not great quality. It was the work of the phylloxera, the terrible beetle which destroyed every vine in France, to send the growers down to the flat land along the coast where the wine cannot possibly be better than mediocre.

In the wine shortage that followed immediately after the plague the growers abandoned their old vineyards and moved to where broad acres could be cultivated without trouble, planting varieties of grapes which grew the maximum quantities regardless of the total loss of quality.

Côtes de Provence

In this depressing area there are a few lighter patches. The position is much better east of the Rhône in the hills behind the smart coast, from Marseilles to Nice. The area is broadly called the Côtes de Provence. Most of its wine is pink and white. Two or three estates make good red. Those at

Bandol

Bandol, just east of Marseilles on the coast and at Palette, inland, just east of Aix-en-Provence, are the best known. There are two Bandol wines exported: Domaine Tempier, which is made very light for a southern wine, and Château Pradeaux, which is allowed all its southern colour, strength and power.

Palette

The wine of Palette is Château Simone. It is on every list in every restaurant in the area as the best wine of Provence. Round Aix the country is heavily wooded with pines. Where there are not pines there is a thick scrub of rosemary, thyme and savoury. All these things are reputed to be discernible in the wine of Château Simone.

Apt

In the sweeping red sandstone valleys the *vin du pays* is also good. The Château de Mille at Apt makes a very pleasant, rather thin red wine.

Lirac

West of the Rhône, still in the valley, the district of Lirac, next door to Tavel which is so famous for rosé, has broken away from its rich neighbour,

203

under whose name its wine used to go to market, and made a name for itself. Lirac is red as well as rosé. It is very much like Châteauneuf-du-Pape.

Costières du Gard   The bulk wine-area of the Costières du Gard also has one or two estates which make wine above the common run, but maintaining the strong, dark, character of the region. Of these Château Roubaud has made itself known in Britain.

THE LOIRE   The Loire valley is more a land of white wine than of red. Its red wines are easily dealt with. They have the fruitiness and distinctly grape-like taste of Beaujolais, though they are a little drier than young Beaujolais. The big difference is in the grapes from which they are made. Loire wines are made with the claret grape, the Cabernet. This gives them some of the tannin which conveys such full colour and long life to claret. They have the purple *robe* (the lovely French word for the colour of a wine) but not the bite which makes young Bordeaux sour to the taste.

Chinon, Bourgueil   Two towns, one on each side of the Loire, produce virtually identical red wine. They are Chinon and Bourgueil. Their place in life is as a change from Beaujolais, drunk cool with some simple dish—a salad or a sumptuous *croque-monsieur,* the cheese melted and bubbling, blending with the ham on a doorstep of succulent fried bread.

CHAMPAGNE   So precious is the production of the best villages of Champagne for the blends of sparkling wine that their grapes can hardly be spared for making *Bouzy Rouge*   anything else. The village of Bouzy, in the black-grape district, still makes a little red wine each year, chiefly for the families of the proprietors. Some is needed for mixing with white wine to tint pink champagne. A very little finds its way on to the market as Bouzy Rouge.

It is capable of being one of the best red wines of France. In style it is like a very light and delicate burgundy, with all the finesse of one of the really good ones, with the addition of the peculiar fresh scent of champagne.

Bouzy will never become popular or be anything but hard to find. But it is a good card to have up your sleeve. I have one bottle in my cellar. I have as much amusement wondering who I am going to open it for as I shall have in drinking it.

THE JURA   The Jura hillsides, the last gestures of the Alpine ranges in the direction of Burgundy, specialize in yellow and pink wines. Jura red has no great fame. The extraordinary enterprise of M. Henri Maire of Arbois, however, has red wine to offer as well as the other colours. M. Maire has made an industry out of the old small-time viticulture of the Jura. He has collected three-quarters of the production of the entire region into his own hands. The factory in a field which he has established near the old town of Arbois is like nothing else in France. Australians would recognize it from the great wineries of the Barossa valley. More than twenty different types of wine are

204

Chianti: a farmer's breakfast in Tuscany

processed there, from grape to despatch, complete with one of a range of gay and gaudy gifts tucked into the carton for good measure.

Maire has a way of giving his wines romantic names which makes it hard to find out exactly what they are. His range of labels is astonishing in its fertility of invention. Sub-history, sub-geography, sub-folklore are all represented. Among his red wines two of the best which have wide distribution, though they might possibly appear under different names in different parts of the world, are Tervigny, a soft, rather sweet and gentle wine (a favourite in Canada) and Frédéric Barberousse, a stronger wine, like a rather bulky burgundy. The Barberousse is evidence that the hillsides of Arbois can make fine red wine.

The black wine of Cahors St-Pourçain-sur-Sioule

There are still a good number of *vins de pays* I have not mentioned, and probably many I have never heard of, scattered among the lonely hillsides of France. France is still an empty country by European standards. There are not many more than forty million inhabitants; in England the same number fit into a country only a quarter of France's size. In many places cultivation is desultory and, for all we know, what could be a wonderful wine remains the local drinking of a few farmers and shopkeepers. There are wines which are almost legends—the Black Wine of Cahors, for example, in the upper reaches of the Lot, a tributary of the Garonne, or the famous St-Pourçain-sur-Sioule of the upper reaches of the Allier—a tributary of the Loire. You usually hear about these wines as you hear of the wines of Greece; they are the snatches of Elysium which somebody brings back from an enchanted holiday. If you ever find them anywhere but in their own land they are disappointing, and yet you cannot disbelieve the stories of their wonderful powers which generations of travellers have lovingly constructed. The Dordogne, the Basque country (Irouléguy is one of its odd, lilting names), the highlands around Vichy, the hills around Poitiers and the unvisited villages of Lorraine all have their wine-myths. Even Paris has its own wine—Suresnes—a by-word, in this case, for sourness.

In every case—except that of Paris—the answer is to ask for the *vin du pays,* or look under the entry on the wine-list, when you are in any region whose wine is not familiar from wine-lists at home. If it is unpleasant, as it sometimes is, you will not make the same mistake there again. But the chances are that you will have as good a wine as any in the house for very little money.

North Africa

Algeria, Morocco and Tunisia are all great producers of wine, but none of it that I have ever tasted has any appeal for me. I have met wine-merchants who have come back from North Africa all aglow with their new discoveries; something which will revolutionize wine-drinking, they say, so cheap and so good is it. I have known it cheap and I have known it (quite) good; but the two qualities never met in one wine. I can see no point in paying as much for a dark dull African wine as you would for an ordinary light and pleasant claret, and if you pay less it is rather unpleasant.

North African wine is chiefly used for *coupage*—for bolstering feeble French wines after bad harvests. No doubt we drink plenty of it unknowingly in brewers' burgundies.

Italian Red Wines

TWO PARTS OF ITALY can grow wine which is in the international first rank. Piedmont in the north-west is one; Chianti is the other. All their best wine is red.

Red wine in Italy is as variable as white. Virtually none of the best is exported; British wine-merchants in particular are extremely unadventurous about looking for it. Their generalized Barolos and Chiantis are never enough to convince anyone that it is worth going deeper. But splendid wines are there, which can stand comparison with everything except the finest of clarets and burgundies. Their character leads most naturally to comparison with Rhône red wine, dark, tasty and strong.

PIEDMONT Piedmont is the Rhône valley, the Burgundy and the Champagne of Italy. Its sparkling Asti is the champagne. Its Grignolino and Dolcetto are the Beaujolais. Its Barolo and Gattinara are the great growths, its Barbaresco the second-growths, its Barbera the Côtes du Rhône. Nebbiolo is the good everyday wine and Freisa the sparkling red which even Burgundy cannot do without.

It is wrong, of course, to compare these with French wines. They are not like them, nor, like some wines which borrow plumage, do they desperately need the comparison. But Piedmont plays in Italy the role of all these areas in the life of France.

Piedmont is a large province. It stretches from the French border eastwards almost to Milan, south almost to the Italian Riviera and north, past Lake Maggiore, right up to the Simplon Pass in the Alps. Turin is its capital, the city of vermouth. Everywhere south and east of Turin, from Cuneo in the foothills of the Alpes Maritimes, thirty miles from France, to Novara, just south of Lake Maggiore, in an almost north-south line ninety miles long, the wine is Italy's best.

One great grape, the Nebbiolo, is as supreme in Piedmont as the Pinot is in Burgundy. Wine called just Nebbiolo, without any place-name, is good, light, ordinary table wine. Nebbiolo from the district where the three towns of Alba, Asti and Alessandria are strung out along the river Tanaro is best. The great names here are Barolo and Barbaresco. The tendency of wine-names to begin with 'Bar' is even more marked than that of towns to begin with 'A'. We still have to deal with Barbera and, to avoid further confusion, Bardolino, though it is a stranger in these parts.

Barolo   Barolo and Barbaresco are both village-names. They are the two classic Nebbiolo wines, the Barolo the heavier and better of the two, needing more age. Old Barolo has an almost freakish amount of scent—a really rich and spicy, slightly autumnal smell, with a faint suggestion of dead leaves and mushrooms, but very far from being dead itself. Ten-year-old Barolo from one of the best estates (which include that of the Marchesi di Barolo, Franco Fiorina and the Istituto Tecnico Agrario Viticolo Enologico Statale at Alba) is almost brick-red, slightly sweet at first but intense in flavour, dry and lingering at the end. It is one of the world's great wines.

There is a vast modern wine-making establishment at the old royal hunting-box of Fontanafredda in Barolo, in beautiful hilly country, which is well worth the short drive out from Turin if you are ever there. Unfortunately, it is at Fontanafredda that they make, besides Barolo and Asti Spumante, an aperitif of old Barolo and quinine—one of the most absurd uses of good wine I have ever heard of.

Barbaresco   Barbaresco is a less heavy, scented and impressive wine than Barolo. It has not the hardness to be softened down by time before it is at its best. For this reason it is often a safer wine to choose. Both come into what the Italians call the great roast wine category, meaning that they are wines to drink with great roasts, or great wines to drink with roasts.

Barbera   Barbera is not the name of a village, although it would seem reasonable to suppose that it was a neighbour of Barbaresco. The Barbera is a grape. The wine has not the body or strength of flavour of Nebbiolo; it is good, not fine. It has a tendency to sharpness, but makes good carafe-wine. In Turin I have had it with the amazing *fonduta*, a rich puddle of melted cheese and eggs and butter over which you shave slivers of the curious dank-tasting white truffle of Piedmont. It was a more than satisfying combination.

Bardolino   Bardolino, I should add here, because it is always being confused with the similar-sounding wines of Piedmont, is a light and delicious red wine from the shore of Lake Garda near Verona.

Dolcetto   Dolcetto grapes are grown everywhere in the Langhe hills, where Barolo and Barbaresco are found. They make the Beaujolais of the area; light,

207

sometimes slightly fruity red wine to be drunk very young. There is some

Grignolino better and higher-strength wine made of the Grignolino, but it is hard to find.

The end of our line north towards Lake Maggiore is around Novara and Vercelli, in country more famous for its rice than its wine. The Nebbiolo is called the Spanna here. It produces a wine which, although I have never

Gattinara, Ghemme seen it outside Italy, is as good as Barolo. Gattinara and Ghemme are the two main producing areas which usually give the wine its name, although

Vino Spanna it is sometimes called just Vino Spanna. The firm of Antonio Vallana makes a superb Spanna wine; it has great colour even at ten years old, and the same spicy scent as Barolo.

Gattinara and Ghemme should specify that they are made from Spanna grapes. There is no regulation to say that they must be, as there is with Barolo. They are quite ordinary if they are not.

LOMBARDY The best wine of Lombardy, the next province going east, is from the extreme north, from a mere crack in the mounting Alps where the river Adda forces its way through and forms the narrow, spectacular Valtellina.

Valtellina The north wall of the Valtellina is not unlike the north wall of that other valley, the Rhône in Switzerland, where the Alps give way to the power of water and allow the growing of vines. Above it is the Swiss border and, though there is no way of getting there except on foot, St-Moritz. Opposite it the south wall is no good for anything; it is so steep that it is in almost perpetual shadow.

In vineyards which appear, from down below on the flat valley floor, to be vertical, the wines of the Valtellina are grown. The best have the delight-

Sassella, Grumello, ful names of Sassella, Grumello and Inferno. All are made from the great
Inferno Nebbiolo grape, which here has yet another name, Chiavennasca, mixed with a little of two or three other varieties. Sassella, Grumello and Inferno are different parts of the valley between Sondrio and Chiuro. I asked Nino Negri, one of the principal and best producers of the valley, what was the difference between the three. 'None,' he said. 'They're all the same.' His habit is to take the best of whichever turns out best in a good year and keep it as his reserve for as long as six or seven years in wood before bottling, which suggests that it is an immensely hard, strong wine when it is made. After this time, and after three or four years in bottle, it has become another of Italy's very finest wines. It has all the body of Barolo with, I think, even more delicacy of flavour, if not quite so much scent.

Castel Chiuro This superb wine he sells as Castel Chiuro, but there is very little of it.

The ordinary Infernos and the rest cannot be treated in this way. Even so, they are generally four years old before they come on the market. They would benefit from more time to age, which they rarely get. They are very good, rather hard and dark-coloured, strong and well-made wines.

Sfursat The Valtellina has another speciality, which I must confess is not quite to my taste; a curious strong red wine called Sfursat. The grapes are left hanging up indoors until the January after the vintage to concentrate their

208

sugar, a practice usually used for sweet wines. They are then made into wine by the usual methods for red table wine and allowed to ferment until the wine is dry and very strong. It has a curious intense flavour which I do not find appetizing, but which is highly thought of for drinking with the Sunday joint when there is time to sleep it off.

Buttafuoco, Sangue di Giuda, Frecciarossa

Southern Lombardy tries to outdo northern Lombardy in names. Memorable though Inferno may be, Buttafuoco (Spitfire), Sangue di Giuda (Judas' Blood) and Frecciarossa (Red Arrow) are evidently designed to spring to mind even more readily. The first two are traditional names of the red wines from the district of Pavese in the Po valley, the last a brand-name for a pleasant light red wine from Casteggio. Frecciarossa describes itself on its label as a Château-bottled Vintage Claret. Perhaps if it had not gone quite so far in its claims it might have caused more confusion.

Lambrusco di Sorbara

One sparkling Lombardy red wine which has made a name for itself is called Lambrusco di Sorbara. Sorbara is just north of Modena, in flat unpromising country, which looks much more suited to the production of the Maseratis and Ferraris which are built there than to the growing of any very special wine.

It is not easy to make acquaintance with Lambrusco. Even as nearby as Modena they tell you that it does not travel the dozen miles from the vineyards and keep its character. In the scruffy little café in Sorbara where I ordered it an incident happened which is all too typical of the Italian attitude to wine. The bottle they brought was labelled Lambrusco. In tiny writing underneath was a legend I did not understand until I had tasted it. The rich pink foam on it, and the extraordinarily unpleasant taste, were the work of a chemical which had been added. When I complained, the waitress whisked the bottle away without a word and came back with another, labelled Il Vero Lambrusco. The look she gave me said 'If you wanted the real thing why didn't you ask for it?' The real thing was, in fact, delicious, as I had been led to expect. It might have been young Beaujolais with a dash of blackcurrant, put through a soda syphon. The only one I have had in England tasted like nothing on earth. The moral is that it is a mistake to take Italian wine too seriously. When it happens to be good, be thankful. There is another sweet fizzy red wine from Valpolicella called Recioto, which might be good, but I would not count on it.

VENETO

Valpolicella

Valpantena

Veneto is more distinguished for white wine than for red. Bardolino we have looked at, by the lovely shore of Lake Garda, a red which is barely more than rosé, soft, gentle and pleasant. Valpolicella, its inland neighbour, has greater pretensions, more colour, scent, flavour and everything. It is still, to my mind, a light wine to be drunk rather after the manner of Beaujolais, cool rather than at room temperature, as it is often served as an open wine in Verona and Venice. It is drier than Beaujolais, though, and has a certain nuttiness which is an incentive to drink more. Valpantena is very similar wine from the same countryside.

209

The best red wines of the Trentino and the Alto Adige should be much better known in Britain and the United States than they are. Where the Adige cuts her valley southwards from Merano, leaving clean walls of granite hanging above the green valley-floor, the vine seems to have taken over everything. It laps like a tide against the cliffs and rolls in waves over the old rock-falls which give shape to the landscape. Every vine is trained up on to a lofty pergola, which makes the vineyards like endless burrowings in green earth, the roof held up by rows of props and the light filtering through a filigree of green and purple and gold—leaves and heavy, pendulous grapes.

The old road north from Rome and Florence to Germany over the Brenner Pass leads through this valley. At Bolzano, high up the valley, a magnificent Medici palace bears witness to the interests bankers had in this great trade-route over the mountains. Most of the wine of this country crosses these mountains today.

Teroldego

Teroldego is the red wine of the Trentino. It is made very light for local drinking—for it is the universal drink of Trento—but the best Teroldego, which is bottled, has considerable strength of alcohol and character.

Santa Maddalena,
Lago di Caldaro

The Alto Adige round Bolzano has two good red wines; Santa Maddalena and Lago di Caldaro. Santa Maddalena is a village. Its wine is soft and strong. Lago di Caldaro (known almost as often by its German name, Kalterersee) is more delicate, dry, more scented and interesting. The Caldaro vineyards cover the hills around a delightful lake. Low though the cultivated hills seem to be, there is always the presence of the bare rock and snow of the mountains not far behind. Even in summer the evening air is cool here.

All the rest of north-east Italy is wine-country, more or less, but the red wine I have had from the eastern Veneto and Friuli has not been exciting. Two familiar French grapes, the Cabernet and the Merlot of Bordeaux, give their names to two of the wines. Neither is particularly memorable; they taste rather thin. From Gorizia, the border of Yugoslavia, there is a pleasant wine called Colfortin Rosso, which reminded me of a light and rather sweet claret.

Colfortin Rosso

TUSCANY

Not until after the Apennines, in Tuscany, do we meet another really good red wine. But this is Chianti, the best known of all Italian wines, the symbol of them all; the round flask in the straw jacket.

Chianti

Chianti has no clearly-defined character. It is simply the red wine of the hills between Florence and Siena. It varies greatly from a light, rough, ordinary wine which is drunk before the next batch is made to a smooth and perfumed wine, not at all unlike a French one. The farmer continues to make his wine from the old, chaotic, mixed vineyards, which really means no vineyards at all, but a vine here and there among the olive-trees, cabbages, walnuts; whatever chance or fancy has given root in the fertile, sun-baked earth. The large estates clear and plough the land, roll away the great rocks which lie on the surface, drain hollows, decimate woodland and throw the ranks of vines from crest to crest. The farmer piles all his grapes, stalks, pips and skins, into a barrel to ferment, and then forgets about them. The proprietor of two valleys carefully measures proportions of this grape and that, sorts out the bad ones, strips off leaves and stalks and nurses every moment of the wine's progress. The contrast is familiar; there is no wine-country where some old farmers are not to be found doing things according to their old methods. But in Chianti it becomes pointed and plain. Both wines are equally Chianti. But they are as different as Algerian red and Chambertin.

In the middle of the last century Barone Bettino Ricasoli (a man of the nineteenth century if ever there was one, Prime Minister of Italy, a collector, an architect and a devoted drinker of his own Chianti) experimented with the traditional methods of making Tuscan wine at his own estate.

Brolio

His castle, Brolio, the last outpost of Florentine territory on the Sienese border in the centuries when the two cities were never at peace, is in the heart of Chianti. From its high battlements the walls of Siena can be clearly seen. It had to withstand siege after siege. The Ricasolis have lived there for nine hundred years or more; nonetheless Barone Bettino was moved to rebuild the living-quarters of the castle in the red brick of Siena, leaving only the old battlements and towers which even nineteenth-century workmen could not pull down.

In the castle cellars he performed the experiments which established the classical formula for making Chianti. It is a very strange one.

Four kinds of grapes go into the blend. At first they ferment in the usual way together. But as the fermentation is dying down more of the same grapes, unfermented but slightly dried in the sun, are added. The fermentation starts again and continues very slowly, giving the wine, if it is drunk while it is still young, a slight prickle of fermentation—the slightest possible fizz—in the mouth. This is the characteristic Chianti which is so popular in the restaurants of Florence.

The best Chianti, however, is not drunk so soon. It is left to age for a formidable time—even as long as seven or eight years—in oak casks. When it is bottled it is ready to drink, unlike French wines. The extra fermentation works itself right out during this long time in the wood. The result is a perfect blending of the four grapes with something extra, a slightly roasted sort of richness, from the dried ones which were added. Such wines as these

Reservas

are called Reservas. They are not found in the usual Chianti flask but in brown bottles of the narrow, high-shouldered Bordeaux shape. They are usually on the market at eight or nine years old.

A good Reserva is second to no wine in Italy; it has all the qualities of a very fine one—scent, strength, character and delicacy. Like the best Barolos, unfortunately, they are not often listed by wine-merchants. Barone Ricasoli's Brolio Reserva is probably the best-distributed. It alone is enough to vindicate the name of Chianti from all the sour thin wines which have been perpetrated under it. The estates of the Marchesi Antinori, Marmoross Sergardi, Serristori-Macchiavelli and Badia a Coltibuono produce superb Chiantis within the Chianto Classico area. There must be many others I have not tasted.

Outside the classical area there are others producing Chianti without quite the same control, and usually considered slightly inferior in quality. Six areas are recognized: the Chianti dei Colli Aretini, Chianti Rufina (not to be confused with Ruffino, a shipper), Chianti dei Colli Fiorentini (the local wine of Florence), dei Colli Pisani and dei Colli Senesi (of the Sienese hills). These wines are rarely treated as Reservas, but in their litre flasks in the restaurants of Florence and Siena they can be excellent.

At vintage-time the game to be had in Tuscany is astonishingly varied and abundant. Little birds whose names I would rather not know succeed each other in endless variety to the table. At night in a little square in Siena, with the brick walls of palaces disappearing into the dark all round, and the flicker of a faint street-lamp giving a theatrical air to the scene, you can have dinner at a lonely table; the primitive charred little bodies of birds and a fat flask of Chianti from the Sienese hills.

Brunello di Montalcino

There is one other very little-known Tuscan wine which is not entitled to be called Chianti, but which is better than any except the very best Chiantis. It is made only at the village of Montalcino, near Siena, and takes the name of its grape, the Brunello. Brunello di Montalcino has more of the power and richness of a Barolo than of a Chianti. It has the cleanness and character of a very fine wine, strong but wonderfully delicate at the end. The firm of Biondi-Santi make it, and ten years is a good age for it. It makes a magnificent match for a partridge.

SOUTHERN ITALY

Puglia

None of the wines of the south can be mentioned in the same breath as the fine wine of Chianti or Piedmont. Most south Italian wine needs blending with something lighter to make it pleasant to those who are not used to it. Puglia, the heel of Italy, is the biggest wine-maker of any of the provinces, but its wine is virtually unknown under any local name. It reaches the markets of the world as the body in a northern wine of a bad year, via the tankers which sail from Brindisi for the ports of the north.

Lachryma Christi

On the way south, though, especially in Campania, around Mount Vesuvius, adequate red wine is made. Red Lachryma Christi is made on the lava slopes of the mountain itself, or should be. Inland from Vesuvius round Avellino, an unfrequented region, Taurasi red is well spoken of.

Taurasi

Ravello Rosso

On the Sorrento peninsula red wine is not so much in demand as white because of the weather, but Ravello Rosso is, if anything, the best of the three shades of wine made up that lovely hill.

Aglianico del Vulture

South again, in the area of Potenza, the wine with the rather forbidding name of Aglianico del Vulture is typical of the more drinkable kind of southern wine. It is very strong (15 per cent alcohol, or half as strong again

212

The grapes in many parts of Italy and Portugal are piled into an open cask on an ox-cart to be taken to the press-house

as French *vin ordinaire*). Aglianico has more scent than most of these wines and a flavour more interesting than the usual black bite of the far south.

SICILY

Corvo,
Etna Rosso,
Faro, Eloro

Sicilian red wine in general has the same trouble as Puglian wine: too much of everything. The estate of the Duca di Salaparuta near Palermo, which makes Corvo, and that of the Barone di Villagrande which makes Etna Rosso are probably the best. Faro is the red wine of Messina and Eloro that of Syracuse. But do not expect anything very wonderful. Most Sicilian wine tastes as though it will stain your teeth blue, and does.

SARDINIA
Oliena, Cannonau

The red wines of Sardinia are often made heavy and sweet. Oliena and Cannonau, which are two of the best known, have this fault. They are not, curiously enough, nearly as good as the heavy, dry, rather sherry-like, white Vernaccia.

Spanish Red Wines

RIOJA

IF I WERE ASKED what I think is the best value for money of any red wine in the world today—wine, that is, which is freely available—I would say Rioja, one of the old Reservas, wine fifteen or more years old, which is no harder to obtain than sherry, but which wine-merchants persistently ignore. Why they are virtually never listed by merchants I cannot understand. The growers of Rioja are longing for someone to appreciate what they are offering, something which no-one else has to offer, and yet we pass them by to spend far more money on wine which is often far less good. There is, however, no reason why customers should not ask for them specially, or write to the shippers themselves.

The Rioja Reservas are like neither claret nor burgundy, nor any other French wine—and they do not claim to be. They have a style of their own; a very warm and smooth, velvety, very slightly roasted-tasting flavour. The lighter ones behave as a claret does after fifteen years or so—they begin to thin out a little, losing intensity and gaining delicacy. When the wine is good it grows fresher and sweeter with age.

The heavier ones stay stronger in flavour, but seem to radiate comfort and warmth like a roast chestnut. All have a subtle, fresh and somehow altogether Spanish smell.

They are certainly to be counted among the world's best red wines. Nothing except a traditional addiction to the wines of France prevents our using them as freely and as confidently as we do claret.

While the best old Reservas have little to lose by being compared with fine French wines, the cheap ordinary red Rioja has everything to gain from being compared with its opposite number in France. It is in every

213

way a better and more satisfying everyday drink than the French *ordinaire* which is being sold in Britain today at a considerably higher price. It has far more freshness and even delicacy than the dreadful thick-tasting *pinard* (the French army's name for it) which is advertised as France's favourite. The French wine has been blended so much that not even age will redeem it, while the natural, cheaply made but honest wine of Rioja gains enormously from a year or two in bottle.

The Rioja district lies in the north of the kingdom of Castile, in territory which has from time to time changed hands between Castile and Navarre. The extraordinary little town of Najera in Rioja was at various times capital of both kingdoms, and keeps to this day some of the least-known monuments of medieval Spain, where the Moors were only seen fleetingly on their sorties from the south. The Moorish-inspired Gothic of the cloisters and the rock-hewn shrine of Najera are rarely visited. Like the whole of Rioja, they belong to the Spain of the past, not of oranges and mantillas but of cold steel and mountain-passes.

Haro
Haro, the chief wine town of Rioja, is a small, dreary place. It stands on a muddy bluff over the river Ebro, gazing north at a great wall of mountain, the Sierra of Cantabria. Clouds hang, even in hot summer, on the crest of these hills like a warning.

The true, dusty, broken-down look of Spain, the pot-holes, the tattered terraces and patched walls make Haro a melancholy place. The crest of its hill, immediately behind the handsome old church, is a bald desert of dust and thistles, where a few gypsies live in holes in the ground and pick among the rubbish-heaps for fuel for their foul-smelling fires. The new hotel seems to be made of cardboard; someone shuts a door at the far end of the building and everything shakes. The food is cold and late and tasteless.

It is perhaps small wonder that few people go there. But the great bodegas at the foot of the hill present a different picture: not a scene of bright new paint, exactly, but of calm and shade and order. Big dusty gardens of alleys and oaks and box-hedges surround the shuttered houses. The wine, in casks, vats and bottles fills barn after cavernous barn—the bodegas themselves.

The vineyards come right up to the walls of the bodegas. They are not like the orderly, staked-out vineyards of France. There are no wires or hedges of green vines. Each vine is a separate little bush, making its own way in the pale, stony, parched earth.

Some of the vineyards of Rioja are beautiful. In places they slant down from under brown rock bluffs to the row of poplars along the bank of the Ebro. Sometimes they cover a whole hill, looking from a distance like a spotted coverlet on a sleeper in bed. Sometimes they fill the spaces in orchard and woodland beside roads where the giant eucalyptus stand peeling in avenues.

The Ebro and the Rio Oja bring fertility to the region, but all around the farms are brown and bare. The High Rioja and the Rioja Alavesa over the

214

river to the north are the best parts for wine. Some of the estates here sell the wine under their own names, or the names of famous vineyards which they own. Viña Pomal is one of the best-known red-wine vineyards, Viña Paceta one of the best white. However, in the main, these names are used as the brand-names of their best wines by the firms who own them, rather than as the name for a wine from that special plot.

There are about ten leading firms of Rioja which have their headquarters either at Haro or Logroño, the biggest town in the valley, but rather outside the best wine area. The Companhia Vinicola del Norte España (the North Spain Wine Company, or C.V.N.E., always referred to as Coonie) is often called the best. Their Reserva wine is called Viña Real, either Plata (silver), the lighter wine or Oro (gold), the heavier of the two. Bodegas Bilbainas, who are the biggest shippers, have two corresponding wines, Villa Paceta and Castle Pomal. The bodegas of the Marques de Murrieta name their fine wines after his castle at Ygay. The Marques de Riscal, Federico Paternina, Vega Sicilia and Bodegas Franco-Españolas, La Rioja Alta and Bodegas Palacio are all good firms, and there are several others.

The vintage year is marked on labels of Rioja wines as the Cosecha. There is no question of better or less good vintages, as they only issue vintage wine when they are happy about it. Recent vintages are rarely seen, because the wine needs a long time in wood and in bottle to mature it. It starts life black and hard, as French wines used to before economics started to interfere with them. Even the non-vintage ordinary, which unfortunately is still often sold abroad as Rioja claret or burgundy, has two or three years in wood before it can be sold.

The red wine of the rest of Spain need not keep us. Rioja is universally acknowledged to be the best. The biggest producer is the region of La Mancha, the home of Don Quixote, south-east of Madrid. The best-known

Valdepeñas wine of La Mancha is Valdepeñas, which is very often the carafe wine in restaurants, particularly in the south of Spain. It is made light and thin and drunk young, like Beaujolais, although it has none of Beaujolais's charm, perfume and taste of the grape.

Sangria The best thing to do with Valdepeñas is what everyone in Andalusia does in summer; serve it from a jug with ice and a squeeze of lemon- or orange-juice, some cut-up oranges and a handful of white sugar. The name of the drink is Sangria.

Tarragona, Alicante The sweet red wines of Tarragona and Alicante are usually shipped as Spanish burgundy. They are never properly aged, and taste coarse and rough, although not as unpleasant as some south Italian and North African wines.

Navarre Finally, the wine of Navarre, south of the Pyrenees, is the strongest and heaviest of Spain, which is rather curious, as it comes from the north. It does not appeal to most foreigners. Some of it is used for 'cutting' thin wine from elsewhere to build it up.

215

Portuguese Red Wines

THE CHEAPNESS, THE EXCELLENCE and the unusual naming arrangements of Portuguese wine have been discussed in the White-Wine section (p. 138). Portugal's white wine is good, but her red is better. It is not easy to follow or find—and the tourist, sitting in the sun, often feels far more like a bottle of white wine than of red—but at its cheapest commercial level it is the competitor of the cheapest Rioja red from Spain, both in quality and value. Appearing simply as Dão or Serradayres red wine (its commonest form in Britain), it is one of the best buys for everyday, unceremonious drinking. Like the Rioja wine, it leaves French *vin ordinaire* far behind.

All Portuguese red wines have a quality which is found in the wine of Bordeaux—which is not to say that they are like claret—the quality of hardness when they are young, the result of thick dark grape-skins full of tannin. It is thought to be the influence of the Atlantic on the climate of the western half of France and all of Portugal, a level of humidity which encourages the skins to become thick. Certainly the red wines of western France, whether of the Loire valley, Bordeaux or the western part of the Massif Central, where the Black Wine of Cahors is made, have abundance of tannin in common with the red wines of Portugal. Black wine would indeed be a good description for Colares, which has the reputation of being Portugal's best red wine.

Hardness and blackness do not sound particularly attractive qualities. Commercially they are reckoned to be a dead loss. In a way they are good signs: they mean that the wine should last for years, eventually becoming (probably, if not certainly) very much better than a softer and paler wine ever could. But commerce would be rid of them if it were possible. In Portugal they are starting to mix some white grapes with the red to soften and subdue the wine from the beginning, as they do with the wine of the Côte Rôtie on the Rhône. In this way they can make a wine ready for the market in four years—still a long time—which previously would have taken six or eight. Even at twelve years, the age at which one of the Dão companies is currently selling its Reserva, the wine is very dark, pungent and seems young, still fairly kicking with life. Twenty or twenty-five years will probably see it at its best. Since these wines cost so very little they are the obvious ones to lay down in large quantities for anyone who has the space, to see eventual results quite out of proportion to the outlay.

DAO   Dão is certainly the best known of the red-wine regions in Portugal. Its name presents a bit of a problem; 'Dow', spoken in the nose as if you had a heavy cold, is about the nearest the English can get. Dão is the name of a river in the high country not far south of the Douro and well inland from the sea. The chief town of the area which has taken the river's name is Viseu (of which 'Vishayoo' is a rough rendering).

Dão is lovely country—rather like Provence. The soil is sand, and pine woods alternate with vineyards over monster, steep-sided sand-dunes, eventually tipping down suddenly to the rocky bed of the little river. There are few large, organized vineyards. You will come across a man with two small children and a dog, picking grapes off something like a washing-line in the middle of a wood, and eating as many, apparently, as they take home to press. The big companies of Viseu buy their grapes far and wide and make the wine under very modern conditions, but there is little indication of this in the hot scented pine woods above the town.

Viseu is also provided with a cathedral and a very fine church in a style more subdued than most in Portugal, confronting each other across a magnificent square. A new and excellent hotel, named, like everything else in the town, after its most illustrious son, the painter Grão (The Great) Vasco, has very comfortable quarters, good food and the whole gamut of Dão wines. I have never come across a bad red Dão, either there or abroad.

Douro

The red wine of the Douro is very rightly turned into port. It has few virtues as table wine. The north of Portugal is remarkable only for its red

Vinho verde

'green wine' among reds, and here remarkable is the operative word—they are more of a curiosity than a pleasure. Very young, fizzy, cidery and often cloudy—though admittedly fruity—red wine always looks and tastes like some kind of mistake to me.

It is the province of Estremadura, where Lisbon lies, between the Tagus and the sea, which makes, besides the Dão, Portugal's best red wine. No capital city is quite so surrounded by vineyards as Lisbon. It shares with Vienna alone among capitals the distinction of having a wine actually carrying its name.

Lisbon

Lisbon used to be a very sweet wine, either red or white. Eighteenth-century decanter-labels often carry the name. Today it is used by at least one shipper for an excellent, cheap, strong and full-flavoured red table wine.

Colares

Colares has, as I have said, the greatest reputation of the Estremadura wines. It is grown under unusual conditions, which gives it the distinction of being one of the very few vineyards of Europe which has never had the plague of the phylloxera, and does not need to graft its vine-stock on to American roots. The vines are planted in deep sand; the only kind of earth inimical to the destructive beetle.

The vineyards of Colares are not, as they are often said to be, on the beach, but in the dune-country on top of low cliffs along the Atlantic, just west of Lisbon. Colares is the next village to Sintra, Byron's 'Glorious Eden', where palaces are grouped about the green and misty mountain which used to lead up to the king. There never was such a case of mossy verdure. Here, rather as at San Francisco, the influence of the sea is felt in enriching and softening everything. To the north, brown farms stand parched on the plain, but where the hill of Sintra rises the sea-mists form, fertilizing the land until it stands out like an emerald on an old leather coat.

Down by the sea at Colares and the row of tiny hamlets which grow its wine the vine is a strange sight. It grows in little enclosures of piled stones like sheep-pens, two or three old gnarled bushes to the pen, straggling over the sand, weighed down with blue fruit. It is picked into tall baskets which fit snugly to the side of a donkey, and covered over with sacks while the donkey picks his way over the sand and down the road to a farmyard, where the baskets are weighed and their fruit tipped into vast oak vats out in the open air to ferment.

Real Colares wine is made of one grape, the Ramisco, a small, blue, dusty-looking grape which gives it great colour. Recently, farmers have been planting others which are easier to grow and make softer wine which can be drunk younger, but the new kind of Colares has no real distinction, none of the character which made its name. The grand old Palacio Seteais hotel at Sintra still had the 1931 Colares of Tavares & Rodrigues in 1965; it was a beautiful wine, like a strong, soft claret, still very dark in colour despite its age. Such wine is still being made, and still needs a good deal of maturing—though not necessarily for thirty-four years—but it is not what you are given if you just ask for Colares without qualification.

There are other red wines from farther north in Estremadura, but they are not geographically named or officially registered as coming from any particular district. In fact, it is work for a sleuth to discover where they do *Serradayres* come from. Serradayres is one of these wines. The name is the property of the firm of Carvalho, Ribeiro and Ferreira. I believe the wine comes from Torres Vedras, where Wellesley had his famous lines. Their ordinary wine, labelled Serradayres, is very pleasant, fairly lightweight and a brilliant ruby colour. Their *Garrafeira* (the word for special vintage)—I have had one twenty-five years old—would not disgrace one of the famous vineyards of France. It is beautiful, soft, scented and alive.

Another of the best brands—in my experience a more nervous, astringent *Evel* wine—is called Evel. The name belongs to the Companhia Vinicola do Norte de Portugal, although Evel is not made particularly far north, but in the neighbourhood of the old university city of Coimbra in central Portugal.

The names of Alianca, Arealva, Fonseca, Messias, Palmela, Periquita, Quinta d'Aguieira are all known for their vintage wines—that is, Reservas or Garrafeiras, wines which bear the date of the *Colheita* or vintage. They must be thought of as the luxury versions of their ordinary wines, rather than vintages in the way French wines are known by the year they were made. There are no critical differences from year to year—the important thing is the wine's age. In my experience it is impossible to get a Portuguese red wine too old—though it is all too easy to get a white one in this condition.

218

Portugal does not make light red wines, though, as all the world knows, she makes very popular rosés. The firm, solid reds she does make—wines which give you the feeling, when they are young, that they are staining your teeth and tongue—are ideal for casseroles and smoky roasts, strong cheese and plums. In their maturity they come into the polite company of cream sauces and tender cuts of meat with little flavour—the food of the international kind of hotel. I prefer the country way. No country in western Europe except France beats Portugal at this kind of meal.

Eastern European Red Wines

HUNGARY

Egri Bikaver

THE GREATER PART OF THE WINE made in the Austria-Hungary-Yugoslavia wine-belt is white. The red wines of Austria are only of local interest. Voslauer is the best known. Those of Hungary are not nearly so good as the white. Egri Bikaver (which means Bull's Blood of Eger) has a reputation for strength—which it deserves—and a warm, smooth style which makes it a good winter wine, the very thing for a casserole meal. It is also agreeably cheap.

The red-wine grape of Hungary is the Kadarka. The best red wines of Hungary usually bear its name. It gives the wine very little colour—it is more like dark rosé—but considerable alcoholic strength, and usually more sweetness than most people want in a red wine. Bull's Blood is a mixture of grapes: the Bordeaux Cabernet gives it more colour and scent than other Hungarian reds. The Kadarka wine which Monimpex, the Hungarian state

Nemes Kadar

export monopoly, concentrates on is called Nemes Kadar. I find it less successful than a rosé made lighter and drier with the same grapes.

YUGOSLAVIA
Kavadarka

Yugoslavia also grows the Kadarka, but calls it the Kavadarka (as far as I have been able to find out, they are the same). Kavadarka is also pale red, but drier and with more substance—a very adequate, if not exciting, wine for what Victorian advertisements would call The Family Table. I am much more impressed with another Yugoslav red wine, Prokupac. It seems to be the Beaujolais of Yugoslavia; light, plum-coloured, with a trace of sweetness and the fresh smack of young wine. It could, I should think, be extremely popular. Prokupac comes from the Serbian vineyards just south of Belgrade and from Macedonia near the Greek border (if only Greece made wine like this). Kavadarka comes from Macedonia, where there is a town called Kavadarci. So perhaps Kavadarka does not mean Kadarka after all.

Prokupac

The coast of Yugoslavia grows rather sweet red wine, of which Dinjac, Plavac and Rejoska are the best-known names. They are more familiar to travellers, who tend to stick to the coast rather than penetrate the country's rather formidable interior.

There is a wider range and more interest among red wines from the Black Sea wine-area than among white. Bulgaria, Rumania and the Soviet Union export about five wines each. They are all the usual standardized product, but there is interest in their grading, more or less providing a red wine of each type by keeping to the characteristics of a different grape.

Bulgaria

In Bulgaria, for example, in order of weight and substance from almost rosé to dark and full-flavoured, the wines are Trakya, Cabernet, Gamza, Melnik and Mavrud.

Rumania

In Rumania the list is Sadova, Cabernet, Segarcia, Kadarka and Pinot Noir. No doubt there are others, too. The visitor will almost certainly be surprised to find how good and how cheap these wines are. In Britain they cost about the same as Beaujolais. For a while they make a pleasant change, but I am sure that after a few weeks of them as my daily wine I would be longing for the familiar French taste again.

THE SOVIET UNION

Georgia

Mukuzani and Saperavi are the red wines of Georgia (their producers would be furious if they heard them called Russian wines—they even use Georgian script on their labels). Mukuzani is the drier, more strongly-flavoured wine of the two; Saperavi has more of the gentleness of Beaujolais, without its charm. The red wine of Moldavia, which used to be a Rumanian wine before the political rearrangement of this vine-prolific province, is called Negri de Purkar. It gives the impression that a generous shovelful of blackcurrants was added to the brew, is slightly sweet, very scented and pleasantly light.

Moldavia

The Red Wines of the New World

CALIFORNIA

GOOD AS THE BEST of California's white table wines are, I believe that it will be for a certain kind of red wine that she will ultimately become one of the finest vineyards in the world. Already her best red wines are great wines, within a strict understanding of that difficult word. Like her best white wines, all the finest reds are made with the juice of a single variety of grape.

Traditionally it is the wine-country just north of San Francisco Bay which is the red-wine area—the lush valleys of Napa and Sonoma. Today, in fact, red and white plantings are more or less evenly distributed over all the fine vineyards, north, south and east of the Bay, but it is still in the Napa valley, above all, that the finest red wines are found. The many wineries of the Napa valley consider themselves the best in the state, and certainly the finest Californian red wines I have tasted have come from Napa and the beautiful mountains round.

The Napa Valley

Napa is an Indian word for plenty. The upper part of the Napa valley, where civilization barely seems to have penetrated, is a sort of earthly paradise, so fruitful and green, so sculpted from the hills for protection and privacy and peacefulness does it seem to be. The broad valley floor is

A Californian hillside vineyard overlooking the Napa Valley, the home of the New World's finest red wines. *(Photo: Wine Institute)*

planted for mile after mile with vines, interrupted only for a big stone winery building in a grove of gigantic oak trees, or a quiet white house with sprinklers hissing arcs of water on a green lawn. The hills on either side are covered mainly with oak, or pine, or sometimes the bushy manzanita with its blood-red limbs. Only occasionally has the high ground been cleared to make way for a ramp, or a mound, or an amphitheatre of vine plants, which stand each on its own, like trees in an orchard, not staked and wired into hedges as they are in France. There is evidence, nonetheless, that the hills may give the best wine. Certainly any European wine-grower would expect it to be so. It is only sad to think that what may drive the wine-maker to plant in the hills in California is the encroaching of housing sub-divisions on his flat land.

Cabernet Sauvignon

The great vine of Napa is the Cabernet Sauvignon, the principal red-wine grape of Bordeaux. Just as the Pinot Chardonnay is the one white grape which makes wine seriously to be compared with fine white burgundy, the Cabernet is overwhelmingly the most successful among reds. Some of the Californian Cabernets are in no way inferior to fine clarets, some of them are better than most clarets, and a few are almost as complex, subtle, scented and extraordinary as a first-growth claret of a fine vintage.

The same qualifications, however, apply to Californian red wine as to French: it is only the work of a fine and painstaking wine-maker which can ever come into this category—and his work will always be on a small scale. Furthermore, the wine needs time to mature just as French wine does. There is, therefore, a chronic shortage of the best Californian red wine in mature condition, and the greater part of it never reaches this condition at all. Only one or two wineries in the whole state keep the wine themselves' until they really consider it ready to drink; the rest sell it shortly after it is bottled, as the French do. There is a difference, though, between the French and the Californian practice. Claret is bought from a château straight after bottling in the full knowledge that it is not ready to drink, and will not be ready for several years. A merchant buys it and either keeps it himself while it matures, or sells it to a customer who will keep it. For some reason, though, the American public expects its wineries to sell everything in the condition to be drunk immediately. They blame it on the winery, therefore, when it sells its Cabernets at three or four years old, saying (quite rightly) that they are not ready to drink. The winery has neither the space nor the funds to act as cellarer to all its own produce for ten years—especially under a tax-law which makes it pay tax on its whole inventory once a year, whether the same inventory was there at the last taxation period or not. The market is therefore running on unaged wine, which has no prospect of being mature before it is drunk. Nor is there much prospect of it catching up with stocks of mature wine—for the demand is growing the whole time. The answer, I need hardly say, is for the customer to start a cellar, fill it with fine red wine and be patient. But this is not the age to expect anyone to invest, even modestly, in future pleasure.

Of the tiny quantity of well-made Californian Cabernet which does reach maturity, then, this can be said; it is one of the finest red wines in the world. It is interesting to compare it with red Bordeaux, for the grape is the same, though the conditions of growing it are very different. What is more, California uses the great, character-giving claret grape on its own, without blending, whereas red Bordeaux is all made with a quantity of Merlot and Malbec grapes to modify its extreme hardness and strength of character.

In California, therefore, you find wine which typifies the Cabernet more than claret does. It is the Cabernet which is the spiciness, the cigar-box scent, the warmth and richness of claret, as well as the astringent, grimace-making hardness of its early years. In California these qualities come triumphantly forward. The wine does start hard—though less unpleasantly so than in Bordeaux—but it finishes rich. The best of Napa valley Cabernets has wonderful warmth and fullness, through which the delicate complexity of its flavour comes with marvellous vividness.

The best examples of this kind of wine are found among the small and medium-sized wineries of the Napa valley; above all, perhaps, at Louis Martini's, where they go to extremes to keep their wines until they are mature, very wisely not trusting their customers to see to it themselves. They still have ten- and twelve-year-old wines—though no-one may buy more than a very small quantity at a time. Beaulieu's Special Reserve Cabernet is another good example which has the added merit of being available in Britain, almost alone among fine Californian wines. Some of the very small wineries have small lots which may be even better. Of Souverain Cellars' 1961 Cabernet, for example, a director of a great Bordeaux château said that it was better than his own wine of the same year.

We must remember, too, that this is only the very beginning of Californian wine. At the moment supplies of the best wines are very short, but more and more vineyards are being planted with better grapes as demand grows. It may be that the future will see the Napa valley largely devoted to growing Cabernet Sauvignon grapes, since they make its best wine.

Pinot Noir

Oddly enough the great burgundy grape, the Pinot Noir, makes a comparatively common wine in California. It is still a premium wine—indeed possibly the next best after the Cabernet—but it never approaches the quality of a fine burgundy in the way that a Cabernet draws near to Bordeaux. It makes, at best, a fairly light wine with a powerful and almost slightly fierce flavour. It is more like a light Rhône wine than a burgundy. Pinot Noirs, of course, vary from producer to producer as much as any wine —but none, I think, makes a really fine one. One, indeed, confessed to me that he thought his Burgundy, made with a blend of three or four grapes, more successful, and I agreed with him. It could be that one day California will develop a combination of grapes which will give this style of wine the interest it lacks at the moment. There is, after all, no virtue in slavishly sticking to one-variety wine-making for its own sake.

222

Zinfandel

Before all other grapes of any kind, however, in popularity and sheer quantity of production, California grows the Zinfandel, a kind unknown in Europe. Zinfandel is, as it were, California's own Beaujolais. Its price is low; it can be drunk young; it is seen everywhere. Like the best Beaujolais, too, the best Zinfandel gains distinction with age—though I personally doubt whether it improves enough to be worth the laying down.

Zinfandel has its devotees who find in it every virtue. To me it is an agreeable, light-coloured, slightly spicy wine, sometimes a little fiery, which I would never refuse; nor would I, on the other hand, ever serve it at a dinner party. As a lunch-time wine, to accompany cold meat or salad, it is perfect.

Gamay

The Gamay of Beaujolais, in comparison with the Zinfandel, is hardly grown. The wine it makes is of no great merit in California; it has none of the magic lightness of Beaujolais. Nonetheless it makes one of California's best rosés.

Barbera

Several Italian grape-varieties are grown, chiefly by the Italian families who introduced them to the country. The most successful is the Barbera of Piedmont, which makes as good a wine in California as it does in its native land; a strong wine, full of purple colour and flavour, but inclining to be sharp—ideal, in fact, for rich Italian food. Its fellow-countryman, the Grignolino, is also cultivated; though largely, it seems, for old time's sake.

Burgundy

Most of the other red-wine varieties are grown to be blended. The Grenache is grown largely for rosé—which is very good. The Petite Syrah is sometimes found as a varietal wine, but mainly for its influence in giving strength and colour in a blend to be labelled Burgundy. Burgundy, indeed, is the principal generic name used in California. Far from being fruity caricatures, as wines named after burgundy tend to be, most of the ordinary cheap Burgundies of California are simple, clean, dry red wines of at least as high a quality as *vin ordinaire* in France, and generally higher. In this field the enormous firm of Gallo produces admirable carafe wine for well under a dollar a bottle.

AUSTRALIA

There is greater variety and, on the whole, better quality among red wines in Australia than among white ones. The hard-worked terms Claret and Burgundy in general stand for the cheaper wines, which are sometimes good but never, in my experience, either very good or remotely related to the wines they are named after. Indeed, it is hard to understand what the terms mean in Australia. A Tulloch's Dry Red of 1954 was awarded prizes in both the Claret and Burgundy classes of a local show. There is evidently no very clear line between them.

The names of grape-varieties on labels (which usually indicate better quality) are, however, more common among red wines than white. The commonest and best are the Cabernet, the Bordeaux grape and the Shiraz, the grape of Hermitage in the Rhône valley. A wine called Hermitage is also widely made, but this, apparently, may or may not be made of the

Shiraz, according to the maker's whim. In any case, both the Hermitage and the Shiraz wines are generally classed as claret-type, which is not what you would expect them to be.

The areas which make the best red wines are, in general, those that make the best white—areas of comparative coolness and humidity. The Hunter River Valley in New South Wales, in which Ben Ean and Mount Pleasant, Bellevue, Oakvale, and Dalwood are some of the best-known estates, makes wine which tends to heaviness and hardness, with strong colour and flavour, but experts seem to agree that longer maturing than they (almost) ever get would bring out a latent delicacy.

In Victoria, Château Tahbilk, although it makes more white wine than red, makes fine Cabernet wine. In South Australia, to the south of the main wine area, Coonawarra specializes in what many people call Australia's best Claret. The Adelaide area and, to the north-east, the Barossa valley also make good red table wine, a different matter from the flagons of sweet Burgundy which are what most people associate with Australian wine.

SOUTH AFRICA

In South Africa very much the same range of red-wine grapes are grown as in Australia. The star performers are the Cabernet of Bordeaux and the Shiraz or Syrah of the Rhône, which is also known as the Hermitage. The Pinot of Burgundy and the Gamay of Beaujolais are also grown and often blended.

The Cabernet in South Africa does not make the light claret-type wine you would expect from its ancestry. Here, as in Australia, Cabernet wines are the strong-flavoured, dark, winter-weight ones. Most firms produce one wine like this and another, lighter, more claret-like, often their Hermitage. The best known of the lighter kind in Britain are Château Libertas from Stellenbosch and Muratie Claret, and, of the heavier, Roodeberg.

Von Carlowitz's Carlonet, Nedeberg Cabernet and Château Alphen Claret are names only known to me, unfortunately, by hearsay. These and others sound excellent, even if they do not evoke quite the enthusiasm in visitors to South Africa which the Australian red wines always seem to do in visitors to Australia.

In South Africa these wines are wonderfully cheap—the Hermitages rather cheaper than the Cabernets—and clearly should be everybody's daily drinking. Table-wine consumption is rising steadily; undoubtedly the day will come when South Africa and Australia will be real wine-countries, when wine will be their national drink as well as the best produce of their soil. This state of affairs seems to be necessary, though, for the establishing of the sort of supreme craftsmanship in which France at the moment leads the world.

CHILE

Chile, the extraordinarily long thin country down the southern half of the Pacific coast of South America, despite being so far away, is at present one of the best suppliers of cheap table wines in the world. Wine-making is

224

apparently little organized for commercial purposes, but strictly supervised by the government. Prices are very low and standards are very high—the ideal arrangement from everybody's point of view except that of the Chilean farmer.

The Aconcagua plains to the north of Santiago, the capital, which lies in the middle of the country, and the Maipo foothills of the Andes south of the capital are the best wine-areas. 'In the *caveaux* of certain wine-vaults,' according to an article I have from the firm of Wagner Stein in Chile, 'there are respectful bottles of evoking Romanée.' About the Aconcagua area it says: 'From San Felipe to Calera, along the wide course of the Aconcagua river, running from east to west, on the south banks, an echelon series of picturesque sheltered coves of slopes can be seen descending in display from the chain of hills which separates Santiago from the provinces of Valparaiso and Aconcagua. In this location, full of natural beauty, Pinot stocks produce a marvellous wine. Its colour is brilliant; its flavour unctuous and mild, having a mild fragrance of distinction which its generous vinosity hardly covers.'

Aconcagua

A similar state of affairs is found south of Santiago, where the Maipo river also runs east–west (from the Andes to the sea), offering its north-facing banks for good wine-production. The sub-soil here is gravel and the Cabernet is grown with the Merlot, as it is in Bordeaux. The wines from the Maipo apparently need most age and are considered Chile's best.

Maipo

The names of grapes are used for most of the wines which are exported, and red wines predominate. The Cabernet gives a very pleasant, full-coloured, softish and dry wine which costs about the same as ordinary red Bordeaux in Britain and is almost as pleasant for everyday drinking. Among white wines the Riesling has the highest reputation. Although at the moment the range available is so narrow that little can usefully be said about it, there are authorities who think that Chile is potentially one of the world's great wine-countries, and could one day produce wines as superlative as those of France and Germany.

ARGENTINA

The only other South American country whose wine is at all widely exported is Argentina. She is among the world's biggest wine-makers, although there is no evidence that any of her wine is of outstanding quality. Those I have tasted have been fresh and very pleasantly scented. I have a theory that the Zilavka, a grape which makes an excellent and very characteristic wine in Yugoslavia, with a freesia- or apricot-like scent, was taken over to Argentina by Yugoslav emigrés. Certainly the very same scent appears—not quite so prettily, but very pleasantly—in the Argentine wine I have tasted, both white and red.

After-Dinner Wines

IT IS NOT JUST CONVENTION that puts the sweet things last in a meal. Sugar discourages appetite: its effect is to make you feel satisfied. The after-dinner wines are those which, for one reason or another, still have a lot of grape-sugar left in them. Their lusciousness, in relatively small doses, is the best end of all to a meal.

For the same reason—that they stave off appetite—they make an ideal snack when there is no meal coming. The mid-morning glass of wine and a biscuit, much talked about in magazines but, I fear, little practised for fear of the effects of the alcohol, should be one of these sweet ones. Madeira and Madeira cake used to be the thing. I prefer tawny port or cream sherry and digestive biscuits. The sweet after-dinner wines are also good before a meal if you do not find that they spoil your appetite. The French, after all, always drink sweet aperitifs, nor do their appetites seem any the worse for it.

Spare sugar left over in wine when the fermentation has come to an end is not something which normally happens naturally. In most cases the sugar will go on fermenting until it is all converted into alcohol. But it is not difficult to discourage the yeast from going on with the fermentation process by artificially increasing either the alcohol level or the concentration of sugar. After-dinner wines are all made in one of these two ways. They vary as much as any other class of wine. Their only common factor is that they are intensely sweet. At one end of the scale you have the sweet wine of Sauternes, whose sugar is naturally concentrated by a form of rot in the overripe grapes.

226

At the other end you have port, whose sugar is held in the wine by a massive dose of brandy, which stops the fermentation.

Most of the sweet wines come from the hottest wine-countries, where very ripe grapes are more common. Yet, curiously enough, what some people consider to be the most exquisite sweet wine of all, and certainly the most expensive, comes from Germany, the coldest wine-growing country.

The German wines which come into this category, like the Sauternes, are only the best of their districts. To most people hock and Sauternes mean table wines—sweetish, but not syrupy. Only the best wine of the best vine-yards in the best years achieves this special condition in which the juice is concentrated and the sugar outlasts the process of fermentation.

The sweet course

Whether you drink a sweet wine with a sweet course or fresh fruit, or leave it until the plates have been cleared away, is a matter of taste. I like Sauternes with a peach, or even a creamy *bombe*. Fine sweet hock, on the other hand, I prefer on its own.

Madeira goes superbly well with such things as a raspberry tart or a very rich praliné confection. Chocolate, on the other hand, is one of the few things which spoils the taste of all wines.

Port does not go so well with the sweet course. Its best partner is cheese. If the port is very good an apple, particularly a Cox's Orange Pippin, is excellent with it. There is an old saying in the port trade that you should 'buy on an apple and sell on cheese'; apple, in other words, brings out any weaknesses in the wine; cheese hides them. But if you are confident in your port with apples and nuts it makes a splendid end to a very Christmassy kind of meal.

Temperature

The same serving principle applies to sweet wines as to all others; the white ones are better cold, the red at room temperature. But in after-dinner wines there enters a third class which can only be described as brown. These are the muscatels, Malagas, Marsala and Madeiras, all sweet and strong and all, to my mind, better served stone-cold. If you should happen on one of the very rare great Madeiras, a vintage wine of the last century—and they do still exist on several merchants' lists—it might be better to serve it at room temperature. But modern Madeira profits by half an hour in the refrigerator.

You will never need as much of a sweet after-dinner wine as you will of a table wine. The days are past when a noble lord could be congratulated on having consumed three bottles of port. When the nobleman in question was asked if it was true that he had drunk them all without assistance he replied, 'Not quite. I had the assistance of a bottle of Madeira'.

Port

IT WAS THE BRITISH who invented port. It was somewhere between a desperate measure and a brilliant scheme for making the wine of Portugal palatable. The invention took place at the beginning of the eighteenth century, when the wines of France were excluded from England as a wartime measure.

If port were made as any other red wine is made it would be strong, dark red, very dry and rather unpleasant. What character it had would never emerge from the strong black taste, and it would die unlamented. It would be a table wine for those who had no better. And such it was.

Origins

It was the brilliant notion of some (we imagine) British wine-shipper, who had gone out to Portugal to take advantage of the favourable trade position, to change all this. He deserves credit just as Dom Pérignon does for champagne. His scheme was to take advantage of all the rich sugar in the grapes which was fermenting away to make over-strong wine. To stop it fermenting and keep the wine sweet (for the English, he knew, have always been sweet-toothed) he added brandy. And, after a time, he had port.

The principle of the making of port is as simple as that. In the high Douro valley, among the mountains of inland Portugal, red wine is made. Great care is taken to see that it takes as much colour from the skins as possible. It starts fermenting in the usual way. But as the fermentation reaches a half-way stage, and the wine, though weak in alcohol, is still full of unfermented sugar, the grower adds brandy. The proportions are about one of brandy to four and a half of wine.

The mixture is too strong for the yeast to work in; it is asphyxiated by the concentration of alcohol. But the sugar is still there. That mixture of brandy and wine, full of alcohol and sugar, is port. It was just what the people of England wanted.

The trouble with port is that it has to be old. Wine that has been made in this unusual—to say the least—way takes a long time to settle down. A mixture of brandy and wine is just a mixture of brandy and wine for a long time. It does not marry, so to speak, overnight.

Not only is the fermentation brought to a stop by the brandy, but all the natural ageing processes of wine are slowed down and held up. If the resulting wine is treated as red wines usually are—given two years in a cask and then bottled—it takes at least fifteen or twenty years to be ready or even pleasant to drink.

Vintage port is that wine, and has that trouble. Eventually it is the best port of all; in the meanwhile there is nothing to do but wait. But most port cannot be treated like that. It would not be so wonderful in the end as to be worth it, so it is left to age in wood.

228

Vintage port, decanted and passed round the table clockwise by candle-light after dinner

Ruby

Port which has been aged in barrels and not bottled until it is judged ready to drink is called either Ruby or Tawny. Ruby is young and still full of colour, rich, a little harsh sometimes, and the cheapest port there is.

Tawny

Tawny has spent perhaps ten or fifteen years in wood, until it has faded to the colour its name suggests. Wine ages much faster in a barrel than in a bottle. The change that takes place in the taste in that time is greater than in a vintage port of the same age. It loses some of its body, dries out a little, but gains greatly in smoothness and in scent. A very old tawny is to most people the most delicious of all ports, and the most versatile. It is almost as good before dinner, especially in winter, as after it. The smoothness and nuttiness of its flavour are incomparable.

Both ruby and tawny are blended wines, which is to say that the wine is not all of one age or from one place. The port-shipper, like the sherry-shipper, is concerned with continuity in his brands. He mixes, therefore, old and newer wine, sweeter and drier, from his stocks to make the wine he requires. He will have several brands of both ruby and tawny, ranging from a wine of about the price of the cheapest Spanish sherry to a very old and fine one, often called Director's, at about twice the price.

Vintage

Only in years when everything has gone well with the vines, the weather has been perfect and the fermentation exactly right do the port-shippers 'declare a vintage'. In some years, perhaps three times in a decade, they are unanimous. In others one is luckier than his rivals and declares a vintage alone. There are no rules. It is up to the individual shipper.

When the port of a year is declared to be vintage it is kept aside from the rest. The various wines of that year are blended together and given two years' rest in Portugal. Then they are shipped over to England, almost the only country which buys vintage port, and bottled straight away, inky, purple and pungent, in very dark glass bottles sealed with wax. In the old days no label was put on the bottle. The vintage year was sometimes sten-cilled on, the shipper's name was branded on the cork, otherwise it was anonymous. It had one distinguishing mark; a splash of white paint on one shoulder. Wherever it lies in a bin or on a shelf this mark or, today, the label, must stay at the top. It shows where the heavy crust of sediment will form—on the side of the bottle opposite to it.

The wine comes on the market as soon as it is bottled, and it is one that the merchants never have any difficulty in selling. It is almost all bought at once to be laid down.

Wine-merchants keep a small stock of matured vintage port, which means wine anything from twenty to forty years old, which they will sell to custom-ers who want their port in a hurry. If you want to drink it straight away they will suggest that they decant it for you in their cellars into a clean bottle, so that you can pour it easily when you get it home.

The disadvantage in buying vintage port when it is mature is that all the sediment, which in most wines would have been the dregs in a barrel, caused by the settling down and ageing of the wine, is still in the bottle. The port

229

has thrown a crust, as it is called; a dirty-looking veil which clings tenuously to the side of the bottle as long as it is not disturbed. But if the bottle is stood in a carton, dumped into a delivery van and hauled out again at the other end, this deposit detaches itself and mixes with the wine, making it murky and unpleasant. All is not lost: you can give it time to settle down and then filter the wine through muslin. But it is a nuisance. It is much better either to have your own port laid down at home, so that you can decant it without stirring it up, or buy it when you need it and get the merchant to decant it the same day.

Laying down port

Most vintage port is sold young to be laid down by the eventual drinker. It means having a cellar, or something like it. It also means having a permanent home, which not everybody has. Clubs and restaurants therefore take a large proportion of it nowadays. If you do buy vintage port when it is first offered (two or three years after the vintage) you will get it at a very reasonable price, and one which will always rise steadily. From the point of view of pure investment, in fact, port is the only wine which makes laying down an exciting financial proposition. You may expect to double your money in about fifteen years, or even less.

The devotees of vintage port will swear that no other wine in the world compares with it for fragrance, fatness, delicacy and strength. I cannot say that it has ever given me as much pleasure as a great claret or burgundy, although, when it is old enough, it is superb.

Late-bottled vintage

Some port-shippers offer late-bottled vintage port as a compromise for people who prefer vintage to tawny but have no space for laying it down. By bottling it late, not at two years but anything from six to ten, they avoid the heavy deposit on the sides of the bottle which vintage port throws while it is still young. That part of the development takes place in the barrel, as it does with tawny. The wine is vintage in the sense that it comes from one good year and is not a blend, but its development has started as it would if it were to be a 'wood' port. It is speeded up so that it will be ready to drink at ten or fifteen years. It can safely be treated like a bottle of ordinary wine with no fear of shaking up a deposit. In taste it is always a little light for a vintage port.

The Douro

Vines like mountains. There are many claimants to being the most spectacular vineyards in the world. The vine-covered slopes are steep on the Rhine and the Moselle, steeper still in Switzerland, more beautiful where the peninsula of Sorrento tilts headlong into the sea. But no sight can compare with the first sight of the Douro.

To come on it suddenly, as you do if you approach it from Spain, through Bragança and the lovely quiet country of Tras-os-Montes, where the valleys are green and the hills and the haycocks pure gold, has something like the impact of a first sight of the Grand Canyon. Without warning the land falls away, in range after range of escarpments and re-entrants, for thousands

230

of feet. In the dim distance, far below, the river winds among rocks. On every side, like a sapper's nightmare, terraces repeat patterns of endless fortifications in endless curves and eddies of grey-brown stone.

The countryside should really be desert. For six months of the year there is not a drop of rain. The valley walls are granite; solid rock. But through some miracle what should be a dust-bowl is a market garden. The best oranges, vegetables, olives, corks and vines in the whole of Portugal grow in prodigal profusion from end to end of this majestic valley.

As you descend from the ridge the air begins to be sweet with the scent of cedar and gum, the silver olive and the green vine alternate and mingle. *Quintas,* the big white farm-houses, and dusty villages full of donkeys and children begin to thicken as the road winds down. Each bend reveals more terraces and more vines; the scene seems to be composed entirely of granite and grapes—even the props at the ends of the rows are grey stakes of slatey rock.

In the bottom of the valley it is hotter than higher up. The vintage starts earlier. Already by mid-September picking-parties are out in the fields. The river is shrunk to a grey drain among the boulders, a mere fifty yards wide instead of the three hundred yards of foam and torn trees of its winter spate.

A Quinta   The Quinta da Roeda, which belongs to the firm of Crofts, the oldest of all the English firms in the port-trade, lies near the river, on a two-hundred-foot bluff, just upstream of the village of Pinhao. It is typical of the estates of the high Douro.

Here the road up the valley ends. Henceforward the railway and the river are the only means of communication. To reach the higher villages by car you have to drive back out of the valley, along the ridge and down into it again. Thus it takes twenty-five miles to travel five as the crow flies.

The *quinta* might be the bungalow on an Indian tea estate. It is single-storied, with a high pitched red roof and a verandah all round. Sprinklers work all day to keep the garden of grass and acacia trees green. A spring in the fold of the hill under the house runs under arbours of vines and pears in a little musical water-garden.

The house is surrounded by its vineyards and olive-groves. Above and below it on the hill are the out-buildings where the wine is made. One group of white houses, on a platform of dust, is where the staff live and the pickers eat and sleep at vintage-time. There are stables, donkeys and a cow, pigs and hens and ducks all living in the shade of olive trees. There is a large dimly-lit kitchen where the thorns crackle under a pot of vintage soup, and a flower-garden where roses and dahlias grow like weeds.

On the level below the house stands the *lagar,* a long white building, taller than most in the area. This shelters the pressing and the fermentation. Terraced on a lower level, but under the same roof, are the great oak barrels to contain the new wine.

231

The vintage   The vintage is still a ceremony, a ritual and a time of rejoicing in the Douro. Life is very primitive in the high hill-villages where the workers live. It is no exaggeration to say that their superstitions extend to witch-doctors to this day. Picking-parties at vintage-time come to the Douro valley from miles around. Each band of thirty or forty peasants brings its musicians with it; always a drum, an accordion, sometimes a pipe as well. They march as many as thirty miles over the hills as vintage-time approaches, old men and young girls, old women and boys, their possessions in bundles on their heads.

Each day as they go out to work the musicians lead the way with their monotonously jaunty tune. They go everywhere in procession, and do everything to the sound of music. After nightfall, as the men work in the *lagares,* the women and girls dance together to the tunes they have heard in the fields all day.

Making the wine   This is a time of transition in the Douro, as it is in so many wine-districts. The old method of making wine is still the most common, but the biggest and best producers are rapidly going over to new techniques which radically alter the whole appearance of the vintage.

The old method consisted of bringing the grapes down to the *lagares* and tipping them into huge stone troughs, in which, late in the evening, they were trodden hour after hour by teams of bare-foot men and boys.

In the low, lantern-lit *lagares,* heady and sweet with the fumes of fermentation and loud with the choruses of traditional songs, the men linked arms and trod, thigh-deep, the purple mass. The endless pounding of feet and the warmth of the human flesh extracted every drop of colour from the skins and set the fermentation going. The wine fermented in the *lagares* until it was run off through a sluice into the waiting barrels, already a quarter full of brandy.

The new method dispenses with the treading altogether. The grapes arrive on mules' and men's backs from the fields and are fed straight into machines, which crush them and remove the stalks. From there they are pumped up into tall concrete vats, which may take as long as two days to fill. During this time the must is kept cool and the fermentation cannot begin. When the vat is full a cover is put on, and it is not long before enough heat is generated inside to start it going. The gas given off by the fermentation operates a churning system, driving the must up a pipe on to the top of the vat, from where it drops back to the bottom. The circulation of the wine under its own power by this method has the same effect as the treading: it extracts all the colour from the skins.

When the wine has reached the correct halfway stage of fermentation (which is when it is about 8 per cent alcohol), it is run off from the vats into the waiting barrels in the traditional way.

In the villages the old method is used by the farmers. Large *quintas,* the properties of the shippers, use the new technique. Any bottle of port will

232

The wild, dusty world where port is made. Vintage-time in the Douro valley. *(Photo: Tom Jago)*

contain some wine made by both these two methods. The shippers make only a small proportion of the wine they need. The rest they buy, often under long-standing contracts, from the farmers who make it for them.

Oporto

The Douro valley itself and its side-valleys high above the tributary river Corgo are the place for the best port. From here it is fifty or sixty miles down to Oporto, the city which gives the wine its name. The legal definition of port is 'wine which has been shipped over the bar of Oporto', which means that until the wine has left its own country it is not really port. This shows the influence of the export trade, for in Portugal port is hardly drunk at all.

It is not actually in Oporto, but over the bridge on the other side of the Douro, that the shippers have their lodges—the vast establishments where they age and blend their wine.

Down the river

They bring the new wine down the river in the spring to the lodge where it will stay for perhaps two years, if it is a vintage port, or twenty or thirty if it is to become tawny. The journey down the river used to be made on the beautiful boats, the *barcos rabelos*, which now swing idly at anchor by the quays; for the railway has taken their place. The journey down the Douro in the spring, when the river was running fast, was a dangerous and exciting experience. The long Viking-type ships with square sails and six oarsmen standing at long sweeps in the bows would carry a dozen great pipes of wine. In some of the gorges where the river narrows to one tumbling channel the rapids drop ten or fifteen feet in one great smooth rush of water. The boatmen had to get the *barco's* head straight on for the fall. Then it was like going down in a lift with a great fountain of spray at the bottom. There are still some of the smaller boats on the river, but the day when they were the only way of getting the wine down from the high country is past, as are the early days when the shippers had to ride over the mountains to visit the vineyards. There is still a tradition of the hard living which used to go with port, something of the feeling that 'up the Douro' is an adventure. But the railway came, and the boatmen had blotted their book by drinking the wine and topping-up the casks with river water.

The lodges

The lodges of Vilanova de Gaia, the wine-suburb over the river from Oporto, have something of the atmosphere of the sherry bodegas of Spain. There are the long, half-dark barns, in which shafts of light saunter all day across the old unshaven beams, the rows and rows of casks, the rich smell of hundreds of thousands of gallons of wine maturing in oak. And yet the bodegas are pure Spain, lofty and white-walled, slightly forbidding, while the lodges seem to have no particularly Portuguese character. They might almost be part of an English brewery. Most of the shippers' names, too, are completely British: Cockburn, Taylor, Graham, Croft, Sandeman, Dow, MacKenzie, Offley, Warre, Delaforce.

The process of tasting and blending never stops. The white-coated managers have to maintain a constant, unchanging supply of at least half a dozen different kinds and prices of port. The blender's art is to maintain quality and value, and to establish consistency and order, in all the hundreds of slightly different pipes of wine which come down from the hills.

Nearly all port is shipped overseas in pipes to be bottled in Britain, or France, or wherever it is going. (In the last few years France has been the first country ever to buy more port than Britain.)

Ritual

Port used to have its ritual place at table, at the end of dinner, when the ladies went off to discuss whatever ladies discuss in the drawing-room and the men remained behind in the dining-room. They closed their ranks, moving up to the end of the table near their host, basking—it is easy to believe—in the feeling of relief at not having to alternate the conversation to left and right any more. The host waited importantly until the butler had got everything except candles and glasses off the table, and had put the decanters down beside him. Then he poured himself a glass, and sipped, and looked smug, and handed the decanter to the man on his left.

The port went round, cigars followed it, and everybody had the comfortable feeling of being involved in a timeless rite. However, it has turned out to be less timeless than they thought.

When to drink port

Even at dinner-parties today most people get up and move into the other room together. And by the time you have left the table, shifted your ground, resettled and been given a cup of coffee, the magic moment for port seems to have gone. A glass of brandy goes better with the coffee. Somehow the decanter going round without the polished mahogany and the gleam of candlesticks seems wrong.

Perhaps my sensitivity to the nuances of appropriateness is inflated: I hope so. There is no reason why you should not enjoy a vintage port as much in a comfortable chair as beside a dining-table. And there are the wonderful tawnies, which many people enjoy more than vintage port. Their lightness and smoothness makes them excellent after coffee—a thousand times better than the gaudy, syrupy liqueurs which are so popular.

PORT-TYPE WINES

The law in Britain prevents the name of port from being used for any wine which is not grown in Portugal. It is the only wine-name which is protected by statute in Britain. Wine from Australia or South Africa which wants to give the impression that it is of a similar type is occasionally called port-type, but more often the words Ruby and Tawny are used. They have become almost a part of the name of port.

Australia

In his interesting book, *Wine in Australia*, Walter James says: 'Port joins sweet sherry and muscat to form the terrible trinity of the Australian wine trade.' The bulk of the sweet wines made in Australia are carelessly and quickly made for an indiscriminating market. To be fair, though, I must add that most of the best wineries make a superior port-type wine with great care. They never achieve the delicacy of real port. Walter James quotes Mr Tom Seabrook, himself a senior Australian wine-maker, as

234

saying that Australian port-types can never get rid of a heavy suggestion of sugar, even in old age.

South Africa   South African tawnies approach nearer to the Portuguese, although they always seem to have a raisin flavour which is totally absent from port. Some of the light tawnies are so light that it is hard to believe that, like port, they are made from red grapes—certainly the skins are not mixed with the juice during fermentation to obtain the darkest possible colour, as they are in Portugal. It is a short-cut to an old-looking wine, of course, to make it light to start with instead of making it dark (as it should be) and then giving it time to fade.

The Shiraz grape from the Rhône valley, which is also very popular in Australia, is used to make a sweet, dark, after-dinner wine called Hermitage in South Africa. It has considerable character, a slightly raisin-like taste with a suggestion of bitterness.

In 1965 André Simon brought back with him from South Africa a bottle of a 1944 vintage port-type South African wine which was astonishing; I believe very few people would have known it was not port. Admittedly, it was a rare and uncommercial case, but it indicates that wonderful wine could be made if there was a demand for the finest quality. There was a time, after all, when all Europe vied for bottles of Constantia sweet wine from the Cape. For a short while it was the most expensive and most highly-prized wine in the world. Faking soon spoilt the market for it, but it is more evidence that there is no reason why South Africa should not make superb wine.

California   Californian wine-makers have no inhibitions about calling their wine port, any more than about calling it sherry or champagne. The problems which beset Australian port apply to most Californian port, but the exceptions, where skilful wine-making makes a very fine after-dinner wine, are more marked. The wine with perhaps the most preposterous bottle I have ever seen, made of pink glass in the shape of a heart, was a very good Californian port-type from Paul Masson. Ficklin is the most highly-esteemed Californian wine-maker in this field, particularly for his varietal Tinta Madeira wine.

Madeira

HISTORICALLY MADEIRA HAS GONE back and forth across the scene from before dinner to after dinner and back again to before it. Those who are passionate about it—and they are many—will drink it joyfully at any time. To most people it is rather an unknown quantity. They think that it is going to be very sweet and then are surprised that it is not. Or they think that it is going to be dry and get a shock when they find that it is quite sweet. The truth is that there are Madeiras of all kinds.

235

The character which is common to all the wine of Madeira is, first of all, a slightly burnt, smoky and caramel taste, subtle and running deep through the wine. Second, it is a slight sharpness. It is never pure honey, but has a delicate edge of acidity which it never loses. It keeps this balance between lusciousness and austerity beautifully. There is something very satisfying in the first scent of Madeira, a scent as fat and smooth as butter, being followed by the tang of smoke. It is a wine which keeps on surprising you and calling back your attention to the variety of sensations in a single glass.

The after-dinner Madeiras—though all kinds are possible after-dinner drinks—are above all Boal (or Bual) and Malmsey, the sweeter two of the four which are offered. There used to be a fifth grape used, giving its name to a fifth kind, Terrantez, but only very old bottles bear the name now. It was a medium-sweet wine. Occasionally old bottles (they would have to be a hundred years old, but Avery's of Bristol still list some) bear the name of other grapes, notably the Tinta and the Bastardo or even, very occasionally, place-names, such as Cama de Lobos or Campanario. The Tinta and the Bastardo are still grown, and their wine still goes into the blends of Madeira, but their names no longer appear. Only the four noble varieties of Sercial, Verdelho, Bual and Malmsey are now thought good enough to have their names mentioned.

Malmsey   Malmsey was the first and most famous of Madeiras. The name of the grape comes from the town of Monemvasia in the Peloponnese in Greece, whence it came with the traditional name of Malvasia, eventually to be called Malmsey.

It is one of history's curious coincidences (Osbert Lancaster points it out in *Classical Landscape with Figures*) that the Duke of Clarence, whose title was derived from Glarentsa, was drowned in a butt of Malmsey—by courtesy, rumour has it, of Richard III. Glarentsa and Monemvasia are both towns in the same wild corner of Greece.

Malmsey has always been the rarest and most precious of Madeiras, the most difficult grape to grow and the most luscious, sweetest and most perfumed of the wines. It is usually darker in colour, more syrupy in consistency and much fuller in flavour than the other Madeiras. I can imagine anyone enjoying any other Madeira before a meal, but Malmsey is certainly an after-dinner wine. It is comparable with port and cream sherry. Although at the age when they are usually drunk the differences between these wines are very marked, it is extraordinary how age develops the qualities they have in common. I have occasionally tasted a fifty-year-old cream sherry, for example, and been sure that it was Madeira.

Boal   Boal grapes make a paler, more golden wine with a softer, more gentle quality. It has more of the smoke and less of the honey than Malmsey. Both are equally good with or after the coffee following dinner. They are also wonderful, though rarely drunk, with a creamy sweet dish, or cake or even raspberries and cream.

236

Other Strong Sweet Wines

THE AFTER-DINNER WINES DEPARTMENT seems sometimes to be a home for lost causes, for wines which have burnt themselves out with a brief blaze of glory—often as far back as Victorian England—and which now linger on the shelves of off-licences because no-one has the heart for the deathblow.

Worst of all, they are regarded as cooking-wines. We see a Madeira sauce almost as often as we see Madeira itself. Marsala is a complete stranger except in the froth of *zabaglione*. And as for poor Malaga, where do we see it at all?

Madeira is the most healthy of the three today, and has a growing number of admirers. It is not the wine it was when it preceded all others at every dinner-table in the United States, England and even France, but it is very much alive and kicking.

But Marsala, invented by the British as an alternative to sherry at the end of the eighteenth century, had its moment when Nelson ordered five hundred butts of it for the fleet, grew to extreme popularity in mid-nineteenth century, but even by the end of the century was hanging around in decanters on suburban sideboards hoping for a happy release.

As for Malaga, once proudly engraved on silver decanter-labels as Mountain, it is no longer even listed—as Marsala still is for cooking—by wine-merchants.

The wines, however, continue to be made for their reduced circulations, and are none the worse for age. There is unlikely ever to be a great renaissance of Malaga or Marsala, but they are both worth tasting and bearing in mind for some moment when you want something different. The fact that they are unfashionable makes them very good value for money. The finest Virgin Marsala costs the same, for example, as a second-rate sherry—and is as good a drink, from the point of view of quality, as a first-rate one.

Marsala

Marsala has a taste not unlike old sherry, with some of the caramel flavour of Madeira. Many things about the conditions of its making are the same. John Woodhouse, the Englishman who invented it, seems to have learnt a great deal from the makers of sherry and of Madeira. The process he adopted for making the wines of western Sicily suitable for the English market has obvious ancestors in these older wines.

The town of Marsala is no-one's idea of heaven. It lies in flat, poor country on the west coast of Sicily, in the district with a bad reputation for violence and squalor. Partinico, one of the grape-growing towns, has an old name for undesirability. In Latin its name was Pars Iniqua, which might be translated 'The Dump'.

Woodhouse, however, saw that it could be made to produce a rival to sherry. The principle he adopted for making wine was to cook some of the grape-juice, fortify another part of it to stop it fermenting and keep it sweet, and to add various proportions of these cooked or sweet wines, as the Spanish add sweetening or colouring wine to sherry, to the local rather ordinary but very strong white. While the wine was therefore naturally dry like sherry, it could be made to any degree of sweetness. Today it comes in three categories. The first is Virgin, which is the best quality, the most expensive and least sweetened (it can be like an old oloroso sherry—dry, nuttily scented and deep-flavoured). A second quality is sometimes known as Garibaldi, after the hero's landing at Marsala, and is sometimes called Colli (Hill wine). A third is Italia, which is usually kept for cooking. Colli, as it is made by the firm of Ingham Whittaker, the second of the three Marsala companies, is a much more toasted wine, with a scent which reminds me distinctly of a good beef broth. It is considerably sweeter than Virgin, but is still not very sweet. It is, incidentally, far superior to sherry as an additive to clear soups and consommé. A drop of it in clear chicken soup is marvellous. Alternatively, Virgin Marsala is a very good wine to drink with the soup—another thing for which I think Marsala is really better than the better-known sherry.

Woodhouse developed the system of making Marsala; Ingham, who settled there just after the success of selling stores of the wine to the Royal Navy, had a great influence on the farmers' ancient methods of making wine and growing grapes. Florio was the third man to set up a firm there. All three firms now belong to the same company as Cinzano, but they continue to market their brands under their own names.

They have another popular wine, *Marsala al'uovo*, a sweet Marsala mixed with eggs and bottled as a sticky yellow mixture. A similar thing used to be done, apparently, with sherry-sack in Shakespeare's day. Like Falstaff, I can do without 'pullet-sperm in my brewage'.

I should add that Marsala, despite its inclusion here among the after-dinner wines (for it is always thought of as a sweet wine), probably has its future not after but before dinner. Every time I come back to tasting it I realize what a superb aperitif it makes. It would be interesting to put a fine Virgin Marsala in a decanter and see if anyone noticed that it was not a rather unusual (and very good) sherry.

Malaga   Malaga has a similar constitution but a longer history. It is made partly with the Pedro Ximenez grape, which is used for sweetening sherry. At one time it and sherry were equally known as sack; indeed, for a time 'Malligo sack' prevailed. But it has dropped back for want of variety, delicacy and all the qualities which make sherry great.

The port of Malaga is not far from Gibraltar, going eastwards along the coast of Spain—in the opposite direction from Jerez. Its speciality today is a comparatively low-strength fortified and partly cooked wine, either sweet or semi-sweet, made of Pedro Zimenez and muscatel grapes, either dark gold or brown in colour. It is about half the price of a good port. The finest

238

Malaga, which is known as Lagrima, is not—as far as I know—shipped abroad. No Malaga is common now in the English-speaking world, though it deserves attention—very much more so than the Tarragona wine which is popular, and which tastes as though it were made from raisins.

Commandaria

Commandaria is the Marsala of Cyprus: the distinctive, original strong wine. But whereas Marsala was invented less than two hundred years ago, Commandaria takes its name from the district of Cyprus governed by the Knights of the Temple, who bought their land from Richard Coeur de Lion in 1191. It is probably at least a thousand years old, in methods if not in name. To this day in the mountain villages which are most famous for their Commandaria—Kalokhorion, Zoopiyi and Yerasa—some of the farmers use methods of such hoary antiquity for ageing their wine—burying it in earthenware jars in the ground—that little seems to have changed since the days of Homer.

Keo

This, however, is not the Commandaria which is exported. Keo, the Cyprus wine company which is said to buy half the entire wine production of the island, has very different methods. At Limassol, where they have their plant, concrete vats rather than amphorae are used. Commandaria has become, whatever it used to be in heroic times, a rather characterless dark sweet wine; Cyprus's speciality, but no longer its best product. No doubt farmers in the hills could produce a goblet of something very different, but the Commandaria which is sold in Britain has cheapness as its main recommendation.

Cream Sherry

The sweetest kinds of sherry, the creams and browns, are not often used as after-dinner drinks. Advertisements in *The New Yorker* have been trying to persuade Americans to drink cream sherry with coffee. To me it is a case of not having the sherry with the coffee but after—or before—it. The two tastes do not go together.

Lingerers over the nuts following a meal would find sweet sherry, or old unsweetened olorosos if they can find them, good alternatives to port. They are much more often drunk, however, despite the advice of the wine-trade, as aperitifs by people who do not like, or have not tried, dry sherry.

Empire Wines

I will not take up the cudgel again here about non-Spanish sherries, but merely note that there are more sweet than dry among them, that Cyprus produces a lot of sherry in this category, and that it is in this category that all the British 'wines' come, if they come anywhere in this book. They are principally drunk, like the sweet whites, rubies and tawnies of Australia and South Africa, to keep out the cold, rather than for their taste.

British 'wines'

I have been glad of one, too, as the wind sent a chisel of sleet down Market Street in Manchester and the door of a wine-bar stood open beside me. The ruby from the wood in a 'dock' ('samples' are half the size and half the price) went perfectly with the Hogarthian scene; the whole of the centre of the room was taken up with crates and cartons, the walls were lined with small milds and sample rubies in clump-hats and caps, the atmosphere was like moving house as the door kept opening and the sleet kept adding to the puddles on the floor. The fiery strength of the wine made sense. And I realized, then, that this is what wine means to half the inhabitants of tax-ridden Britain; the strongest, warmest drink for the least money. No wonder the government sees it as fair game for duty. And what a different thing it is to the real wine of the wine-growing world.

Light Sweet Wines

ONE WAY OR ANOTHER, to produce a sweet wine, the wine-maker has to make the sheer quantity of sugar in the juice overcome the ferments which want to change it into alcohol. With fortified wine the sugar is retained by dosing the ferments with brandy. But there is another method which concentrates the juice in the grape, lowering the proportion of water in the sugar-and-water mixture of grape-juice. The ferments will then be overpowered because there is so much sugar, just as they are in jam.

In hot countries the concentrating is often done by hanging the grapes up to dry or spreading them out in the sun. Whether in sun or in shadow, they start to turn into raisins. When they have reached the right state of dryness they are pressed and fermented.

In humid countries and the north this cannot be done. The grapes will not dry properly off the vines. But there is a kind of rot which afflicts them under certain conditions which has something like the same effect.

Pourriture noble The unpleasant-looking fungus which is so useful to the wine-grower is called 'the noble rot'. In German it is *edelfaul,* in French *pourriture noble,* in Hungarian such berries are called *aszu.* It happens in good years in Sauternes, in Germany and in Hungary. If the grapes are left late on the vines until they are overripe a sinister-looking growth begins to appear on

240

their skins. It cracks them open and lives on the juice, while the sugar content of the grape gets higher and higher. By the time they are picked they are as sweet as honey, with all their elements, all the traces of acids and oils and minerals which give them their flavour and scent, concentrated into a quintessence of ripe grape-juice. From these shrivelled berries the wine is made.

Such wine is intensely sweet and extremely aromatic. All its qualities have been intensified. The work of making it is very laborious, because the grapes do not shrivel conveniently at the same time. Pickers have to go round the vineyard again and again, taking only the grapes which have reached the right stage of apparent dereliction. Fritz Hallgarten, in *Rhineland Wineland,* reports a case where it took a hundred workers two weeks to gather enough fruit from seven and a half acres of vineyard to make three hundred litres of juice. The record sweetness ever attained by a wine like this in Germany was in the 1920 Steinberger from the Rheingau, which contained well over a pound of sugar in every bottle.

The German word for wine made like this is *trockenbeerenauslese,* which means a selection of dried *(trocken)* berries *(beeren).* A less extreme use of the same technique, picking the grapes individually off the bunches but not waiting until they have reached quite the same shrivelled stage makes wine called *beerenauslese.*

The French wines in this category are the best growths, known by château names, in Sauternes and the next-door commune of Barsac.

The Hungarian wine is Tokay.

SAUTERNES

Oddly enough, no wine which is sold simply as Sauternes or Haut Sauternes, however many Special Selections and Monopoles are attached to it, is made in this laborious way. It is only the great growths, known by the names of their châteaux in just the same way as clarets, which can afford to take so much trouble. They are some of the best value for money in the whole list of wines. Whereas this kind of wine from Germany never costs less than several pounds a bottle, a superb Sauternes from one of the best châteaux only costs about twice as much as an ordinary wine briefly labelled Sauternes. The differential in price between the plain Johannisberger from the Rheingau, for example, and a Schloss Johannisberger Trockenbeerenauslese would be more like ten to one. Château d'Yquem alone stands out above the very reasonable prices of its near-peers. It usually costs twice as much as its nearest rival: whether it is always twice as good is open to debate.

The other growths of Sauternes, meanwhile, remain some of the least known of the world's greatest wines. The reason, I believe, is that Sauternes is a popular, not a fashionable, drink at the moment. There is a great sale for ordinary Sauternes—indeed, it and the wines named after it are the biggest-selling category of table wines in Britain—but very little for the best growths, although they only cost twice as much.

There is far more difference between, say, Château d'Yquem and plain Sauternes than there is between Château Lafite and plain Pauillac. Château Lafite is the same sort of wine as Pauillac, only much better. Château d'Yquem is a completely different thing from plain Sauternes. The ordinary grower of Sauternes cannot afford continually to send his pickers round the vineyard: he has to gather all his grapes at once. He waits until they are very ripe, with, he hopes, a certain amount of *pourriture noble*, then he picks and presses everything together. The wine will be sweetish, but not sweet enough. It will not arrive naturally at the point where alcohol and sugar together prevent the fermentation from going any further. It has to be stopped artificially with sulphur, which stuns the yeasts. So it has neither the strength nor the sweetness of the great growths. It is hardly, in fact, an after-dinner wine at all but a table wine, a sweet alternative to white Graves. As such, it is very popular. But this wine and the superb châteaux which cluster round Yquem, like planets round the sun, should not be confused.

Sauternes is the southernmost of the areas which make up the vast complex of Bordeaux. For Bordeaux it is hilly. Compared with the Graves district it is tiny. It reaches down from its low hills to the Garonne just where the river, flowing westwards from the mountains towards the sea, takes a turn to the north and heads up towards Bordeaux. If it has any centre it is the sleepy town of Langon, which lies just outside it. Langon has quite a respectable square, where plane-trees have been thickly planted to keep the sun off, but it barely winks at you as you go through.

Château d' Yquem

The universal place of pilgrimage in Sauternes is Château Yquem, whose labels, for some reason, call it Château d'Yquem. The château is perhaps the most impressive in all Bordeaux. It is what everyone hopes a château will be like, for it is one of the few which is a castle. The Middle Ages planted it soberly on its hilltop. The seventeenth century made it habitable —though by no means luxurious—and the twentieth century has perfected the symmetry of the rows of vines which march up the hill to it in an unbroken procession.

The entrance to Yquem is guarded by a kennel of the most ferocious-looking Great Danes, who are as used to being photographed as the guards at Buckingham Palace. The *maître de chai* is not entirely unused to photographers, either (see the jacket of this book).

At Yquem every stage of wine-making is carried out with elaborate pains; with the sort of attention that is very expensive. The wine is made with the loving care that goes into the manufacture of a Rolls-Royce. It is said to be the only place where all the wine-making machinery, without exception, is made of wood—even the intricate moving parts of presses—so that no metal ever comes in contact with the wine, in case it should affect its taste. They make what they firmly believe to be the best sweet drink in the world, and there are very few who would deny their claim. No trouble is too much for it. As a result even in poor years—though not in disastrous ones, when no

242

wine is sold under the château's name—the wine they make is an astonishing mixture of richness and freshness. It is so rich as to feel almost like cream in your mouth, but strangely uncloying—its scent and flavour are so intense that they call you back to sniff and sip again.

The Marquis de Lur Saluces, the proprietor of Yquem and one of the most distinguished figures of Bordeaux, holds that his wine is good with several kinds of food. One feels like a foolish flatterer telling him—he is over eighty, a scholar and gourmet of standing for two generations past—that his wine is too good to be a part of any meal, but should be drunk on its own. He drinks it with *foie gras*. He has made me drink it with lobster. I am obviously not in a position to say that he is wrong. To me, though, it is still the wine to sip after—or indeed before—all others, quite by itself, not even with a peach or some grapes, as many people suggest. Its balance is perfect: why add the acidity which even a perfect peach cannot avoid? A wine like this is so much better than any mere fruit.

Barsac

Château Climens
Château Coutet

Yquem is certainly the summit of Sauternes, but it is no reason to ignore the flanks of the mountain. At times the neighbouring châteaux draw near to it in every quality of richness. The names of Châteaux Climens and Coutet are the most familiar in Britain of the rest of Sauternes, although strictly speaking they are Barsacs—that is, wine of the commune of Barsac next door to Sauternes to the north. Barsac wines have the right to call themselves either Barsac or Sauternes as they see fit. The difference between the two is almost imperceptible. Perhaps Barsac is just a little less rich and sweet, with a little less of the softness of texture brought about by the glycerine which is a component of Sauternes in good years. But a Sauternes of a poor year is certainly drier than a Barsac of a good one.

Climens is often a slightly more delicate and racy, as they say in France, wine than Coutet, but both maintain standards which are second only to Yquem—and yet they fetch only half the price. Châteaux Doisy-Védrines, Doisy-Daëne, Doisy-Dubroca, Caillou, Nairac and Broustet are all important Barsacs of the second rank.

Sauternes itself is a district of four villages, which are all equally entitled to the name Sauternes, just as Barsac is. These are the village of Sauternes itself, Bommes, Fargues and Preignac. One cannot say that any of these is better than the others, except in so far as it is in Sauternes itself that Château Yquem stands.

Sauternes

Besides Yquem in Sauternes there are Châteaux Guiraud and Filhot, Château d'Arche, Château Lamothe and Château Raymond-Lafon. Filhot is remarkable at the moment for attempting, as is Yquem itself, the experiment of making a dry Sauternes in poor years. The Yquem dry wine is called Ygrec, the French for the letter Y. They are very fine, very full flavoured wines with a great deal of the velvety smoothness of the real Sauternes, but they cannot be compared with the sweet wine for interest and delicacy: they leave an impression of heaviness.

Bommes

The best growths of Bommes are Châteaux Rayne-Vigneau, Lafaurie-

Peyraguey (another very impressive castle), Rabaud-Promis, Rabaud-Sigalas and La Tour Blanche. An extraordinary thing happened in 1925 at Château Rayne-Vigneau. According to Professor J. R. Roger's *The Wines of Bordeaux*:

> The fortunate owner, the Vicomte de Roton, who had already made his name as a man of letters and a talented artist, announced to the learned world his discovery of a great quantity of gems in his vineyard. Before long more than twelve thousand stones had been gathered, some of them quite beautiful enough to stand comparison with the best of their kind from Brazil, Peru, Madagascar and Arizona. There were agates, opals, sapphires, amethysts; chalcedony, jasper, onyx, sardonyx, cornelian. More than two thousand of these jewels have been cut and are to be seen in M. de Roton's collection. 'Cornelians in melting colours side by side with Hungarian opals, their iridescent fire flickering in the moonlight beam of white sapphires. After the boreal brilliance of cold chalcedony, deep amethyst and sardonyx, the tawny flame of topaz and the flickering brightness of uncut stones reflect the sunset sky.'

Nobody has been able to explain how the stones came to be in the soil of Rayne-Vigneau and only there.

The wines of Preignac tend to be the least sweet of the Sauternes. Château Suduiraut is the one really great name. The Château de Malle at Preignac is perhaps the most beautiful building of the countryside. For centuries it has been in a branch of the Lur-Saluces family, the Bournazels. It is one of the prettiest of the small châteaux of France; a low, quiet building with two wings ended by round towers, the wings enclosing a court. Its garden and its rooms seem to stand as the seventeenth century left them. I cannot imagine that it is ever anything but autumn at Malle. Everything is the colour of walnuts; the shutters, the furniture, the leaves and the moss on the statues.

Château Bastor-la-Montagne is also seen occasionally on wine-lists in England.

Fargues, again, has one name which is equal to anything except Yquem: Château Rieussec, which is sometimes the most powerful of all the Sauternes. Château Romer and Château de Fargues are also well known.

The area producing Sauternes-type wines does not end here. Immediately opposite Sauternes on the other side of the river the districts of Ste-Croix-du-Mont and, next door to it, Loupiac produce magnificent sweet wines in good years. Named growths from these districts are not often seen, but they are usually amazing value. I once found in an auction some bottles of old Ste-Croix-du-Mont which were indistinguishable from a fine Sauternes. On the other hand there are few good châteaux which can be relied on, or names which you can expect to see on lists, so it is always rather a matter of buying a pig in a poke.

Loupiac is in a similar position, also having its own *Appellation Contrôlée* but not often being seen abroad; both lie within the larger area of Premières Côtes de Bordeaux, which stretches all the way along the eastern bank of the Garonne from the bend by Sauternes to opposite the city of Bordeaux

Château Rayne-Vigneau

Preignac

Fargues

Ste-Croix-du-Mont

Loupiac

244

itself. The names of one or two of the Premières Côtes villages are occasionally mentioned on lists, although they have no appellations of their own. Capian, Cadillac, Langoiran are sometimes seen. But Premières Côtes white wines are more comparable with Graves than with Sauternes.

Cérons

Finally, north of Sauternes and Barsac lies the district of Cérons, which comes between Sauternes and Graves in character, never being as sweet as a good Sauternes, but always being among the sweetest of Graves. In any case, only in exceptional years does it become an after-dinner wine. The communes of Podensac and Illats are included in the name of Cérons, though I have seen both listed under their own names. All three—Cérons, Podensac and Illats—have the right to call themselves Graves, just as Barsac, Bommes and the rest have the right to call themselves Sauternes. As their names are seldom seen on wine-labels, I imagine that they often take advantage of this.

Monbazillac

Although it is outside the Bordeaux area altogether, the sweet golden wine of Monbazillac, near Bergerac, fifty miles up the valley of the Dordogne from Bordeaux, has a close affinity to Sauternes. In it the flavour of muscat, which in Sauternes is entirely subdued (although a form of muscat grape, the Muscadelle, is used in small quantities) comes forward a little more. Monbazillac is by no means a muscat wine, but it is enriched by a hint of the musky scent and flavour. It is rarely aged, which is a pity. The famous hotel Le Cromagnon at Les Eyzies, in the higher Dordogne where the cliffs are honeycombed with the cave lodgings of prehistoric man, has (or had a few years ago) a collection of old Monbazillacs going back some thirty or forty years. Some were dark gold, some almost brown, but nearly all showed that the wine which is merely agreeable when it is young can become very fine with time.

When to drink Sauternes

Sauternes has this much in common with red Bordeaux; the better it is, the longer it will last and even improve in bottle, and the more there is to gain by keeping it. Château d'Yquem is kept for three years in wood anyway, because the fermentation takes such a long time to finish, so it never appears on the market until the fourth or fifth year after the vintage. At this time it is ready to drink—in a sense. It is superb, but it will get better. It is a lovely straw-gold at this age, very strong and vital, intense and penetrating in flavour. With age the gold will deepen, eventually it will be tinged with brown, but, long before this happens and before there is a hint of brown, it will change to the gold of a rich old ring. The scent will seem to embrace even more flowers and spices. It is, in short, well worth keeping good Sauternes for anything up to twenty years—indeed you can hardly keep it too long. If two alternative good vintages are offered to you, take the older one.

Temperature

The greatest pundits of Bordeaux are in favour of serving Sauternes very cold—the better and sweeter, the colder. Château d'Yquem they serve at a couple of degrees below the others. I hate to take issue with those who have far more experience in these matters than me, but I hold the opposite view.

The better your white wine, the less you need to chill it. I would drink Château d'Yquem at the same temperature as its peer, Montrachet—very cool. If it is so cold as to mist the glass it mists its own majesty. This is simple to test. Put a bottle in the refrigerator until it is really cold. Pour out a glass. Smell the scent of the wine; taste it. Then wait and warm it a little with your hand. As it comes back to cellar-temperature its intensity and balance return. All its qualities emerge. To me to ice Yquem is to waste it. If you have a poor or ordinary Sauternes, on the other hand, the way to disguise the fact is to serve it at Martini-temperature.

Imitations
The name of Sauternes is taken in vain everywhere. It is often misspelt by its borrowers 'Sauterne', which has the advantage that it helps to identify the imitation from the real thing. In general usage in Australia, Spain and many other places it can simply be taken to mean the sweeter of the local white wines, the drier being called Chablis. There is no justification for this. The product rarely bears the remotest resemblance to Sauternes. It may have merits of its own, in which case its makers are most illogical in claiming for it the merits of something else.

SWEET GERMAN WINES

The most expensive wines which ever come onto the market in the ordinary way of business, not counting auctions of old cellars and great rarities, are the sweet German wines. They often reach twice the price of Château Lafite or Romanée-Conti, or three or four times the price of Château d'Yquem. I have seen one listed in London at £14 ($40) a bottle.

The reason for this is partly their rarity, for they can only ever be made in very small quantities, and partly the fantastic cost of the sort of operation I have described, where a hundred workers are engaged for two weeks to gather enough grapes for three hundred litres.

Wines are made like this only on the very best estates, where the owner knows that the result will be well worth the trouble, and only in good years. It is a common practice for the grapes from the different parts of the vineyard, picked on different days, to be kept apart, if there are enough of them, right through every stage of the making process, so that the buyer can choose from which cask, made at which stage of the picking, he wants his wine. Normally the price rises with the cask-numbers, as the grapes become riper and riper.

As a general rule, it is safe to say that the sweeter a German wine is, the better it is, always supposing that the sweetness is natural. The struggle is always towards riper grapes and sweeter wine. Thus the best of all Germany's wines are made by this method which lifts them clear into another range of sweetness altogether, and makes them after-dinner, rather than table, wines.

Wines as precious as these, I need hardly say, are never drunk with food, but sipped and sniffed with hushed reverence—at any time, not necessarily after dinner at all. The ideal occasion would be a sunny morning or warm evening on one of those legendary terraces overlooking the Rhine or Moselle vineyards, with a vine-trellis overhead, or, as some very eighteenth-century

246

gentleman remarked, out of a golden goblet in one's gazebo. In any case, they are strictly wine for wine's sake. They are not even strong in alcohol. The very sweetest often have half the usual percentage. But the intensity of flavour in each sip makes them slow and serious drinking, all the same.

I will not go round the hills and valleys of Germany again telling of the wonderful late-gathered wines which are made on the Moselle and its tributaries, the Saar and the Ruwer, in the Rheingau (perhaps best of all), Rheinhessen and the Palatinate. It is nearly always the best and most famous growers in their best vineyards who make them (see the section on German white wines, pp. 111–29).

In good years any fine wines from the *spätlese* (just plain late-gathered) category onward, including *auslese* (selected), *beerenauslese* (selected grapes) and *trockenbeerenauslese* (selected shrivelled grapes) wines will be so sweet as to be better on their own than with food. One final category exists, more as a curiosity—for the German wine-growers love showing off—than as a *Eiswein* commercial proposition. It is called Eiswein (Ice-wine), which is wine made from grapes in which the juice has been frozen by the night-frost on the vines. They have to be picked very early in the morning and taken to the press-house while they are still frozen. The harvest for wine like this has been as late as the beginning of January. St-Nikolaus wine is made on or about St-Nikolaus' Day (6 December), Sylvester wine on New Year's Eve. These wines have been made more often recently than they used to be, notably in 1961, 1962 and 1965, when the winters were hard. They have great intensity of flavour, but not the lovely velvety quality of a *trocken-beerenauslese*, at least in my experience. Perhaps the ones I have tasted have been far too young.

Such wines as these cannot be kept too long. Age cannot harm them. Very old ones are, of course, extreme rarities because the cost of laying them down makes everyone except a German steel magnate recoil. The 1949s which still exist are superlatively good now. No wine comes so near honey and flowers, without honey's fierceness.

TOKAY

For a while it looked as though Tokay was going to join the company of legendary great wines which no longer exist. The name is vaguely familiar to everyone. Perhaps most people can link it with the old Austro-Hungarian Empire, and from there deduce that it comes from Hungary. Its reputation as an aphrodisiac and for practically raising people from the dead has certainly helped to keep its name alive.

The danger of its falling by the wayside came with the sad fate of Hungary after the war. There is no room for the superlative in a Communist régime, and the superlative was what Tokay most emphatically was. Of all wines it was the one which was most elaborately prepared to be as wonderful as any effort could make it. Tokay Essenz, wine made from the juice which the grapes squeezed out of each other with their own weight alone— the ultimate *tête de cuvée*—was, even more than the *trockenbeerenauslesen* of

247

Germany, the quintessence of ripeness and sweetness in wine. Its price was always fabulous.

Essenz

Today Essenz is no longer available at any price. It goes into the blend. The extraordinary peak has been levelled, but the other wines of Tokay are made as well as ever as a prestige product. They are expensive—the best is as expensive as old vintage port or the best champagne.

The Tokay area covers the slopes of old volcanic hills rising from the plain a hundred miles north of Budapest, near the Czech border of Hungary. Tokay is its chief town (the Hungarian spelling is Tokaji).

The principal grape of Tokay is the Furmint. It grows in several places in Hungary, and makes superb strong white table wine, but no other country has it. Its flavour is unmistakable and its scent extraordinarily penetrating. It has been said to combine the scents of meadowsweet, acacia-blossom and the lime-tree in flower. I am not sure that I can distinguish the individual flowers of the bouquet, but to me there is a taste of celestial butterscotch about Tokay.

Szamarodni

The best Tokay is the sweetest. The cheapest, about half the price of the best, is dry. The dry wine is called Tokay Szamarodni. Szamarodni is the Polish (the Poles are the greatest connoisseurs of Tokay) for 'as it comes'. It is wine, in fact, made without special precautions and careful picking of the rotten grapes, but the whole crop of the vineyard picked and pressed at once—which only happens in poor years. The special Furmint scent and taste is there, but the wine is rather sharp. It makes a good aperitif.

There is also a sweet Szamarodni—sweet in comparison with the dry, but dry compared with the best Tokay, which is known as Aszu, or occasionally by its German name, *ausbruch*.

Aszu

Aszu is the equivalent of the great Sauternes. The same laborious repeated pickings have to be done to collect only 'nobly rotten' grapes. Tokay, however, has a system unlike any other for actually making the wine. Grapes in a normal state of ripeness are pressed in the usual way and the juice run off into small casks, called *gonci;* but the *aszu* grapes are kept apart in wide open tubs called *puttonyos.* At the end of the vintage, which is often not until the beginning of December—it is common to see pickers trudging through the snow on the Tokaji hills—the juice which has collected at the bottom of the *puttonyos* simply from the grapes pressing each other is drawn off. This is the fabulous Essenz. The *aszu* grapes are then trodden in the tub where they are until there is a uniform pulp of skins, juice and pips. In grapes which have been left on the vine until the noble rot has attacked them the skin practically disappears when it is trodden, giving a total effect of a sort of paste. The *puttonyos* full of *aszu* pulp are then added to the *gonci* full of ordinary juice. The wine is sweeter or less sweet, better or more ordinary, according to how many are added. Thus after the name on a bottle of Tokay you will always see three, four or five *putts* (short for *puttonyos*). The price goes up in relation to the number of *putts,* too. More than five are rarely added now. Five *putts* Tokay, in fact, is officially

Puttonyos

248

A glass of rich, sweet, smoky Madeira with the sweet course;
after lunch at the Palacio Seteais at Sintra, near Lisbon

the best Tokay made at the moment, though no doubt the Kremlin has a supply of six *putts* or even of Essenz.

It is not just simple sweetness which is added in the *aszu* grapes, but all the essences of flavour in a greater concentration. The breaking down of the grape's skin and pulp by rot results in a high content of the acids, oils and glycerine which give wine a soft, creamy texture. This texture is prized as well as the taste in all the wines—Tokay, Sauternes and *trockenbeerenauslesen* —which are made by this method.

Aszu wines are not made every year, by any means. It is hard to know exactly what is happening nowadays. Probably, following a practice quite common in almost all wine-countries except France and Germany, they build up stocks from several vintages, blending them together, before launching a new vintage—almost like a new brand.

Old Tokay

As far as ageing is concerned Tokay is a slow starter. The extreme sweetness makes fermentation a long and slow business. It continues to ferment sporadically in cask, but particularly in the spring (when they used to say it started to work in sympathy with the sap rising in the vines from which it came), when the warm weather affects the cellar-temperature and humidity. In the famous wine-merchant's house of Fukier in Warsaw, which even in this century had Tokay of the vintage of 1606, followed by dozens of vintages of the seventeenth and eighteenth centuries, they found that very old wine, even after years in bottle, used to ferment again very slightly in the spring. It was a curious custom of the house of Fukier, after centuries of experience, to store their Tokay not lying down, as all other wine is stored so that the cork does not dry out, but standing up. They changed the cork of every bottle in the cellar every six years to prevent the shrinkage harming the wine.

Tokay has such a fascinating history as the great wine of Eastern Europe that it is tempting to relate how the Czar kept a permanent buying-agent there, and how the Emperors gave it as their most special present. Franz-Joseph used to send some to Queen Victoria every Christmas.

Temperature

It is a mistake, I think, to chill Tokay too much before serving it. There are some who like their Sauternes to make the glass fairly sweat with cold. They would presumably do the same to Tokay. Both, I think, lose some of their scent and flavour if they are really cold. Cool, the temperature of a deep well, is best. They should not be anything of a shock to your mouth, but come into it as easily and refreshingly as spring water. Then you should slowly chew Tokay while the flavour of a Hungarian autumn, of long golden days drawing into night-frosts, of the first snow on the hills, seeps into you.

The Muscat Family

OF ALL THE VARIETIES OF GRAPES which are made into wine there is one family which stands apart as unmistakable to everybody. It is the muscat. As a grape it is familiar as the tastiest of hot-house varieties. It is used for wine all over the Mediterranean—in Spain, Italy, Africa, Greece and all the islands—and in Portugal, Russia and California.

The muscat apparently gets its name from the Italian *moscato*, which means smelling of musk. Musk is the scent with which deer attract their mates, a secretion which is collected and used in making perfume. It occurs in many aromatic melons, apples and pears, and even roses, besides grapes. They all have the same haunting, sweet quality which is called musky.

Muscat wine is called Moscato, Muscatel, Muscadel or Muscadine. I suppose it changes as much as any other wine from place to place, though the scent they all have in common is so overpowering that it is difficult to say more than whether it is sweeter or drier, stronger or less strong, more or less delicate, better or worse. The best muscats come from Portugal, the south of France, the islands round Sicily and the Crimea.

Setúbal   Portugal makes what is probably the best of all; a fortified one, dark and strong, called Setúbal.

Setúbal is just south of Lisbon. To reach it from Lisbon you now go across the Tagus by a suspension bridge, one of the longest in the world, whereas previously it was an all-too-short trip in a little steamer among the big-sailed fishing boats, with the hills and churches of Lisbon growing smaller over the water. Another twenty miles, up and over the Arrabida mountains, brings you to Setúbal. It is largely a manufacturing town now. Its vineyards lie along the Lisbon road and the road west to the fishing port of Sesimbra.

Setúbal's reputation rests on its sweet, heavy wine, the port of the muscat world—an extraordinary concentration of grape flavour, the very essence of aromatic hot-house grapes.

It is golden brown wine, presented in very fine rather stumpy bottles with brilliant blue labels. It is not difficult to find it ten or fifteen years old—the older the better. As far as I know, it never stops improving. Like Madeira, Setúbal was sometimes sent as ballast in ships for the sake of the improvement which movement and tropical heat would cause. *Torneviagem* ('back from a journey') Setúbal is rare now, but a few very ancient bottles do exist, and are exquisitely fine. Age stops the wine from being so syrupy as it is in youth, and develops amazingly subtle, almost geranium-like scents under the ever-present raisin scent of muscat.

Setúbal is a fortified wine. The sugar is retained in it by the same method

250

as it is in port. Extra scent is derived from the skins of the grapes after the pressing—for in the muscat grape even the skin is scented—by soaking skins in the wine for a while after it has been made. Certainly no other wine captures so much of that magic aroma so clearly.

Setúbal is at its best with a plain rather sweet cake. It is probably one of the very best wines to be almost totally unknown in Britain. It is considerably less expensive than the best cream sherries. Both the quality and the character which could make it immensely popular are there.

Frontignan

The most famous of France's many muscats is that of Frontignan, from the Mediterranean coast not far north of the Pyrenees. It is usually sold under the name of Frontignac.

There is a special variety of the muscat grown at Frontignan, which gives the wine more delicacy than most, but it is intensely sweet; one glass is as much as most people can drink. It is slightly fortified, enough to bring it up to 15 per cent alcohol, which puts it into the official category of *vins de liqueur* —the same as port. In fact, it is considerably less strong than port.

Lunel
Rivesaltes

Beaumes-de-Venise

Lunel and Rivesaltes also make very similar wines, but famous as these are, none of them can compare in delicacy with an almost unknown muscat made just north of Châteauneuf-du-Pape, at the curiously-named little town of Beaumes-de-Venise. Muscat de Beaumes-de-Venise is unfortified, and hence far less strong and less sweet. It brings something of the balance of a Loire wine, gentle and tentative, between sweet and dry, to the muscat flavour. Its aroma is much less blatant and more intriguing, but, sad to say, it is very rare.

Pantelleria

The Sicilian and island muscats are very raisin-like. They are all made from more or less sun-dried grapes in which the sugar is concentrated to the power of treacle. Perhaps the most famous of all comes from the tiny island of Pantelleria.

Syracuse

Syracuse and Noto in Sicily are also both famous for Moscatos. That of Syracuse is the oldest of which there is any record. It was first made in 700 B.C., when Rome was still a group of tiny villages. Syracuse is like that. No place I know so gives me the feeling of having been there since the beginning of time. In spirit it is still a metropolis, the greatest city of the Greek world, although it has long since shrunk to the size of a small port. It once had ten inhabitants for every one there is today. And the wine they drank—one of the few wines we can be fairly sure has not changed out of all recognition since ancient times, was moscato.

Noto

Noto could not be more different from Syracuse, although it is only a few miles away. It is a strange little miniature Rome, a city composed entirely of a few enormous, forbidding, Baroque buildings, whose high embattled walls break only for a gesticulating frontispiece—the end of the church, for they are convents and monasteries. But Noto's moscato is indistinguishable from that of Syracuse. Paganism and Christianity evidently found common ground in the wine to drink after dinner.

The Crimea is a strange place to find another really fine muscat—but not so strange as it seems. According to Edward Hyams, in *Dionysus*, his fascinating history of the vine, it was in the sixth century B.C. that the Greeks established the first vineyards in the Crimea. What is more likely than that they took cuttings of the same vine, their favourite, which is supposed to have come from Byblia in Thrace, to their colony in Syracuse and their trading post in the Crimea? That vine appears to have been the moscato.

I have only tasted one Crimean muscat, that of Massandra, which is sold in England. It is certainly one of the smoothest, most delicate and best—very sweet, rather like a Frontignac, but, I think, better.

The other manifestations of the muscat as a grape for fine wine come into other parts of this book. It makes the excellent sparkling wine of Asti in Italy, and—I think its only performance in a really dry wine—the delicate muscat of Alsace. It plays a minor role in the making of Sauternes, and is found all over Italy under the *nom de guerre* of Aleatico. In Spain it is an ingredient of Malaga.

Elsewhere it is widely used for more or less undistinguished sweet wines, those made of it in California being less distinguished than any.

Passiti

THE THIRD METHOD OF MAKING the wine sweet, which involves neither adding brandy nor long drawn-out late harvesting, is used in Italy, Switzerland, and to some extent in France and Spain. The general word for the wine it makes in Italy is *vino passito*, or sometimes *vino santo*. The method is to pick the grapes when they are ripe and hang them up in bunches in a dry place to shrivel and become raisins before pressing them.

Almost every part of Italy uses this method for some wine. Many of the moscatos, and their close relation the Aleaticos (a red muscat grape) are made like this. Caluso in Piedmont, Sfursat in Lombardy and the best known of them, the *vinsanti* of Tuscany, are *passiti*.

All are sweet and have the natural flavour of the grape intensified and slightly overladen with the rather different taste of the raisin. As the local after-dinner wine they are worth trying when you are in Italy. They are usually much better than the local liqueurs.

Vins de paille   In Switzerland similar wines are found under the generic name of *vin flétri*; in France they are called *vins de paille* (*paille* means straw). The grapes are traditionally laid out on straw mats either in the sun or indoors over the winter to dry out.

The best-known *vin de paille* is made in the Jura. Grange aux Ceps is the

252

brand-name of the most widely distributed one. Again, it is the thing to drink after dinner if you are in the neighbourhood; each wine-district has some speciality which it keeps to itself. It is always worth enquiring for novelties.

Sparkling Wines after Dinner

Sweet champagne

CHAMPAGNE NEVER USED TO BE DRUNK at any time other than after dinner. It became known, as soon as the industry of Reims and Epernay began to expand at the beginning of the nineteenth century, as the drink for balls, for supper-parties, for everything that started late and went on all night. It was never thought of as an aperitif, for the idea of drinking before the meal or of meeting just for drinks had not arrived.

The champagne which, in Dickens' words, took its place 'amongst feathers, gauze, lace, embroidery, ribbons, white satin shoes and eau de cologne' as 'one of the elegant extras of life', 'which a cavalier might appropriately offer at propitious intervals to his danceress', was a sweet wine. It was heavily sugared in the final stages of its manufacture. The Russians, particularly, who were one of the first really big markets for champagne, liked it syrupy. It is said that they even laced it with Chartreuse —as I suspect, not because they liked the mixture but to make the slipper so sticky that their mistress could not get it off again.

Sweet champagne went right out of favour at the beginning of this century. It was not snobbishness, as many people think, which made dry champagne fashionable—indeed one British statesman is reputed to have said that anyone who claimed to like dry champagne was an unmitigated liar—but the discovery that all the best qualities of the wine, its scent and freshness, its liveliness and its way of making the drinker lively, are much more marked when it has not been sugared. Sweet champagne is still made, and has its proper place. It is a common form of celebration to end dinner with a high note, with a bottle of champagne with the ices, *bombe*, gâteau, fruit-salad, baked Alaska or *soufflé surprise*. Dry champagne tastes pitifully thin and sour with a sweet rich dish. But sweet champagne is perfect.

No champagne is labelled sweet. One or two brands call their sweet version Rich, others call it *demi-sec* (half-dry) or even *sec* (dry). Even *sec* is sweet compared with the usual dry champagne, which is labelled *brut*.

Asti Spumante

The end of dinner is also a very good moment for Asti Spumante, the Italian equivalent of champagne which is always more or less sweet. Its honeyed, musky quality is perhaps better with fruit or ices than with any other dish. I would go further and say that if you are having Asti (or any sweet sparkling wine) for a drinking-party at any time the biscuits to serve with it are not the usual cocktail canapés, cheese-straws and olives, but little macaroons, sweet wafers, dates and almonds.

Index

Figures in bold type indicate where the main information on the subject will be found
(*All château-names appear under Châteaux*)

255

256

257

264

MAPS

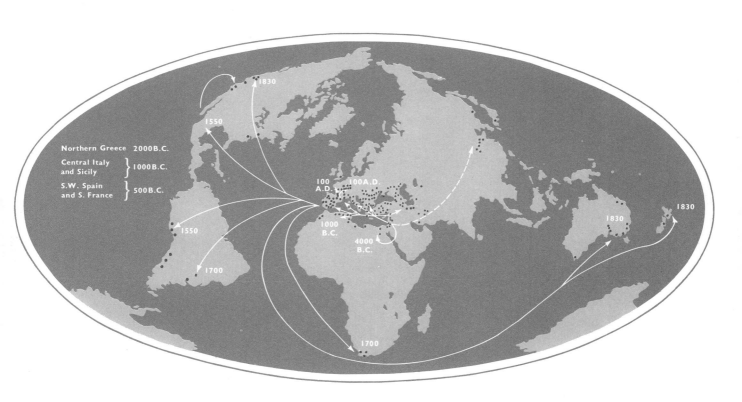

Northern Greece   2000B.C.

Central Italy
and Sicily   } 1000B.C.

S.W. Spain
and S. France   } 500B.C.

100
A.D.

100A.D.

1000
B.C.

4000
B.C.

1830

1550

1550

1700

1700

1830

1830

THE SPREAD OF WINE-GROWING

THE WINES OF EUROPE

	Red Wines
	White Wines
	Red and White (and Rosé) Wines
	Aperitifs
	Sweet Wines

© THOMAS NELSON AND SONS LTD L005

Great Britain

London •

• Amiens

Seine

Paris •

CHAMP.

France

MUSCADET   Angers •

ANJOU   VOUVRAY

Loire   CHAB

POUILLY FUMÉ

MÉDOC

Bordeaux •

POMEROL

ST. EMILION

GRAVES   *Dordogne*

SAUTERNES

Garonne

TAVEL

CHATEAU

DU PA

LANGUEDOC

FRONTIGNAC

RIBEIRO

RUEDA

RIOJA   NAVARRE

Oporto • VINHO VERDE   *Douro*

DOURO   PORT

JURANÇON

Ebro

Saragossa •

ALELLA

PANADES

DÃO

Barcelona •

TARRAGONA

Portugal

S p a i n

Tagus   Madrid •

BUCELAS

COLARES LISBON

Lisbon •   *Guadiana*

SETUBAL

VALDEPENAS

• Valencia

LAGOA

Guadalquivir

MONTILLA   ALICANTE

• Seville

MANZANILLA

SHERRY   • Granada

SHERRY

MALAGA

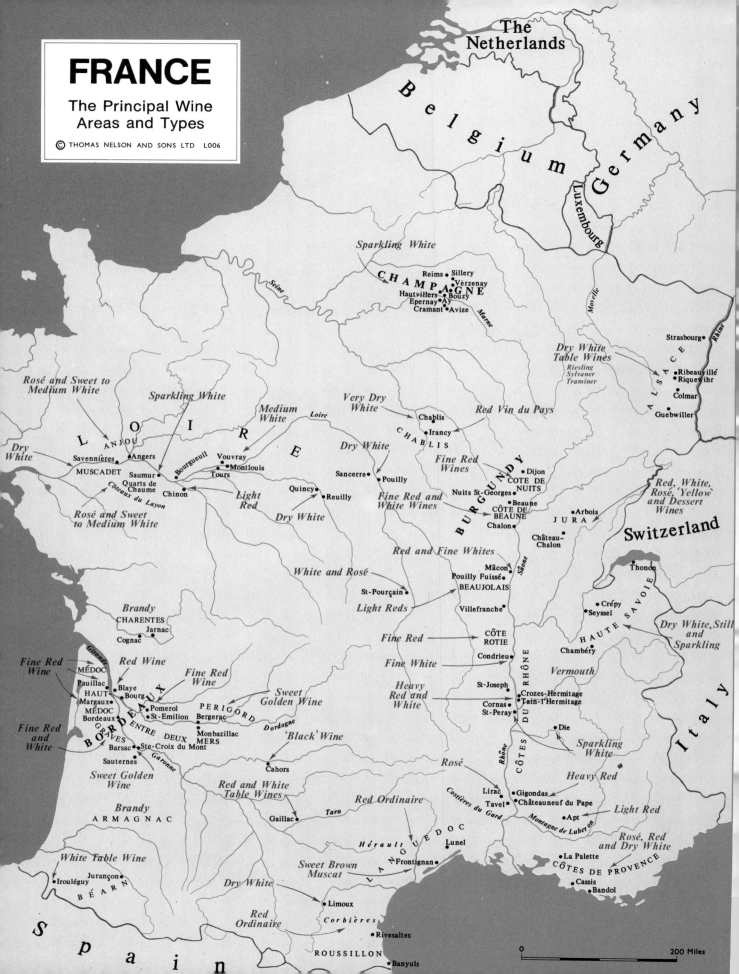

FRANCE
The Principal Wine Areas and Types

© THOMAS NELSON AND SONS LTD L006

The Netherlands

Belgium

Germany

Luxembourg

Sparkling White

CHAMPAGNE

Reims • Sillery
• Verzenay
Hautvillers • Bouzy
Epernay • Aÿ
Cramant • Avize

Seine

Marne

Moselle

Rhine

Dry White Table Wines
Riesling Sylvaner Traminer

Strasbourg

ALSACE

• Ribeauvillé
• Riquewihr

• Colmar

• Guebwiller

Rosé and Sweet to Medium White

Sparkling White

Medium White

Loire

Very Dry White

Chablis

Red Vin du Pays

L O I R E

ANJOU

Dry White

Savennières • Angers

MUSCADET

Saumur

Quarts de Chaume

Coteaux du Layon

Chinon

Bourgueil

Vouvray
Montlouis
Tours

Light Red

• Irancy

CHABLIS

Sancerre •

• Pouilly

Quincy •

• Reuilly

Dry White

Fine Red and White Wines

Fine Red Wines

BURGUNDY

• Dijon
CÔTE DE NUITS

Nuits St-Georges •

• Beaune
CÔTE DE BEAUNE

Chalon •

JURA

• Arbois

Château-Chalon

Switzerland

Red, White, Rosé, 'Yellow' and Dessert Wines

Rosé and Sweet to Medium White

Red and Fine Whites

White and Rosé

St-Pourçain •

Light Reds

Mâcon •
Pouilly Fuissé •
BEAUJOLAIS

Villefranche •

Saône

• Thonon

• Crépy
• Seyssel

HAUTE SAVOIE

Dry White, Still and Sparkling

Brandy
CHARENTES

• Jarnac

Cognac •

Fine Red Wine

MÉDOC

Pauillac •

HAUT

Margaux •
MÉDOC
Bordeaux •

GRAVES

BORDEAUX

Barsac •

Sauternes •

Fine Red and White

Red Wine

Blaye •
Bourg •

Fine Red Wine

Pomerol •
St-Emilion •

ENTRE DEUX

Bergerac •

Monbazillac •
MERS

Ste-Croix du Mont •

PERIGORD

Sweet Golden Wine

Dordogne

'Black' Wine

Cahors •

Red and White Table Wines

Garonne

Sweet Golden Wine

Brandy
ARMAGNAC

Gaillac •

Tarn

Red Ordinaire

Fine Red

CÔTE ROTIE

Condrieu •

Fine White

Heavy Red and White

St-Joseph •

Crozes-Hermitage
Tain-l'Hermitage

Cornas •
St-Peray •

CÔTES DU RHÔNE

Rhône

• Die

Vermouth

Chambéry •

Italy

Sparkling White

Heavy Red

Rosé

Lirac •
Tavel •

• Gigondas
• Châteauneuf du Pape

• Apt

Light Red

Montagne de Luberon

Costières du Gard

Rosé, Red and Dry White

• La Palette

CÔTES DE PROVENCE

• Cassis
• Bandol

White Table Wine

• Irouléguy

Jurançon

BÉARN

Dry White

Sweet Brown Muscat

Hérault

LANGUEDOC

Frontignan •

Lunel •

• Limoux

Red Ordinaire

Corbières

Rivesaltes •

ROUSSILLON

Banyuls •

Spain

0 _____ 200 Miles

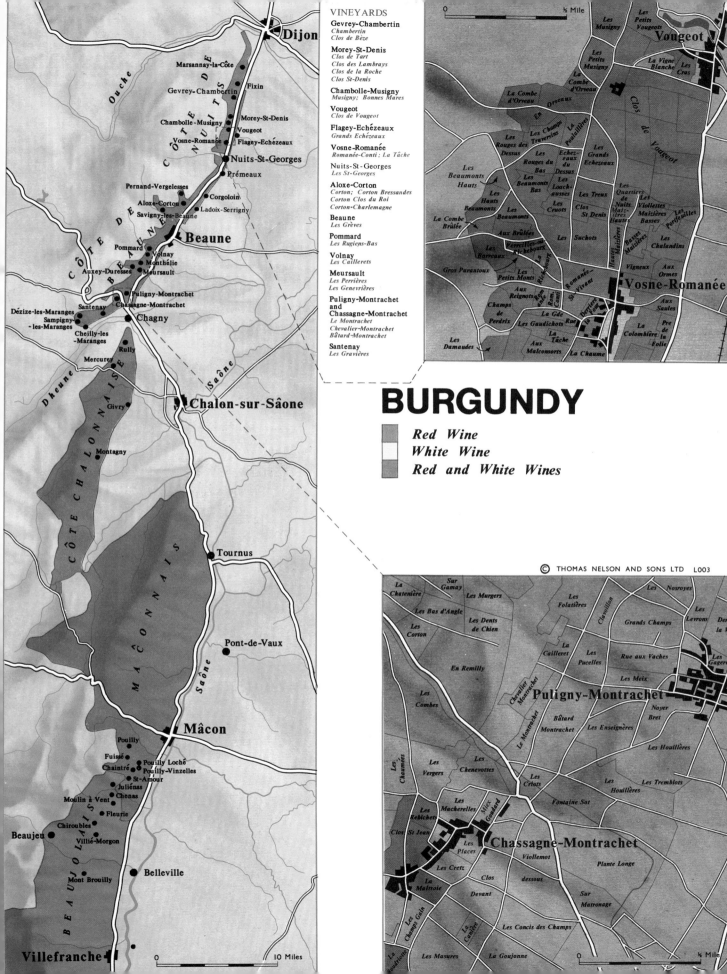

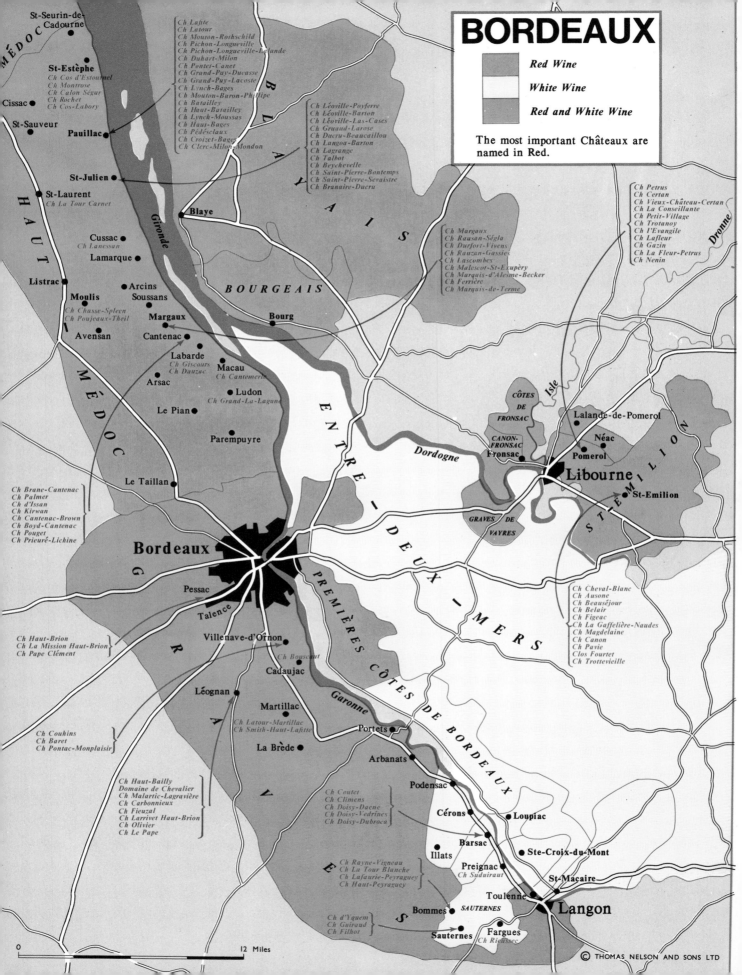

BORDEAUX

Red Wine

White Wine

Red and White Wine

The most important Châteaux are named in Red.

MÉDOC

St-Seurin-de-Cadourne

St-Estèphe
Ch Cos d'Estournel
Ch Montrose
Ch Calon Ségur
Ch Rochet
Ch Cos-Labory

Cissac

St-Sauveur

Pauillac

St-Julien

St-Laurent
Ch La Tour Carnet

Cussac
Ch Lanessan

Lamarque

Listrac

Moulis
Ch Chasse-Spleen
Ch Poujeaux-Theil

Avensan

Arcins
Soussans

Margaux

Cantenac

Labarde
Ch Giscours
Ch Dauzac

Macau
Ch Cantemerle

Arsac

Ludon
Ch Grand-La-Lagune

Le Pian

Parempuyre

Le Taillan

Ch Brane-Cantenac
Ch Palmer
Ch d'Issan
Ch Kirwan
Ch Cantenac-Brown
Ch Boyd-Cantenac
Ch Pouget
Ch Prieuré-Lichine

HAUT

**Ch Lafite
Ch Latour
Ch Mouton-Rothschild
Ch Pichon-Longueville
Ch Pichon-Longueville-Lalande
Ch Duhart-Milon
Ch Pontet-Canet
Ch Grand-Puy-Ducasse
Ch Grand-Puy-Lacoste
Ch Lynch-Bages
Ch Mouton-Baron-Philippe
Ch Batailley
Ch Haut-Batailley
Ch Lynch-Moussas
Ch Haut-Bages
Ch Pédésclaux
Ch Croizet-Bages
Ch Clerc-Milon-Mondon**

**Ch Léoville-Poyferré
Ch Léoville-Barton
Ch Léoville-Las-Cases
Ch Gruaud-Larose
Ch Ducru-Beaucaillou
Ch Langoa-Barton
Ch Lagrange
Ch Talbot
Ch Beychevelle
Ch Saint-Pierre-Bontemps
Ch Saint-Pierre-Seraistre
Ch Branaire-Ducru**

BLAYAIS

Blaye

Gironde

BOURGEAIS

Bourg

**Ch Margaux
Ch Rausan-Ségla
Ch Durfort-Vivens
Ch Rauzan-Gassies
Ch Lascombes
Ch Malescot-St-Exupéry
Ch Marquis-d'Alesme-Becker
Ch Ferrière
Ch Marquis-de-Terme**

**Ch Petrus
Ch Certan
Ch Vieux-Château-Certan
Ch La Conseillante
Ch Petit-Village
Ch Trotanoy
Ch l'Evangile
Ch Lafleur
Ch Gazin
Ch La Fleur-Petrus
Ch Nenin**

Dronne

Isle

CÔTES DE FRONSAC

Lalande-de-Pomerol

Néac

CANON-FRONSAC

Fronsac

Pomerol

Libourne

St-Emilion

ENTRE-DEUX-MERS

Dordogne

GRAVES DE VAYRES

ST-EMILION

**Ch Cheval-Blanc
Ch Ausone
Ch Beauséjour
Ch Belair
Ch Figeac
Ch La Gaffelière-Naudes
Ch Magdelaine
Ch Canon
Ch Pavie
Clos Fourtet
Ch Trottevieille**

Bordeaux

G R A V E S

Pessac

Talence

Villenave-d'Ornon
Ch Bouscaut

Cadaujac

Léognan

Martillac
Ch Latour-Martillac
Ch Smith-Haut-Lafitte

La Brède

Ch Haut-Brion
Ch La Mission Haut-Brion
Ch Pape Clément

Ch Couhins
Ch Baret
Ch Pontac-Monplaisir

Ch Haut-Bailly
Domaine de Chevalier
Ch Malartic-Lagravière
Ch Carbonnieux
Ch Fieuzal
Ch Larrivet Haut-Brion
Ch Olivier
Ch Le Pape

PREMIÈRES CÔTES DE BORDEAUX

Garonne

Portets

Arbanats

Podensac

Cérons

Loupiac

Barsac

Illats

Ste-Croix-du-Mont

Preignac
Ch Suduiraut

St-Macaire

Toulenne

Langon

Ch Coutet
Ch Climens
Ch Doisy-Dacne
Ch Doisy-Vedrines
Ch Doisy-Dubroca

Ch Rayne-Vigneau
Ch La Tour Blanche
Ch Lafaurie-Peyraguey
Ch Haut-Peyraguey

Ch d'Yquem
Ch Guiraud
Ch Filhot

Bommes

SAUTERNES

Sauternes

Fargues
Ch Rieussec

0   12 Miles

© THOMAS NELSON AND SONS LTD

THE RHINE-MOSELLE AREA

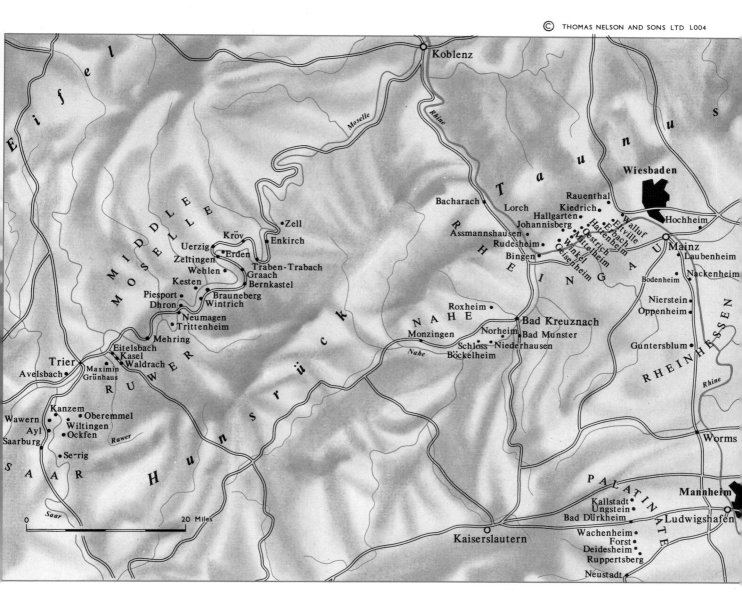

The most important vineyards of the Rhine-Moselle area are named in red after their respective village names.

SAAR

Wiltingen
Scharzhofberg
Scharzberg
Braune Kupp

Oberemmel
Hütte
Agritiusberg

Ayl
Kupp
Herrenberg

Ockfen
Bockstein

RUWER

Eitelsbach
Karthauser Hofberg

NAHE

Neiderhausen
Hermannshöhle

Schloss-Böckelheim
Kupfergrube

MIDDLE MOSELLE

Trittenheim
Laurentiusburg
Apotheke

Dhron
Hofberg

Piesport
Goldtröpfchen
Gunterslay

Brauneberg
Juffer

Wintrich
Ohligsberg
Geierslay

Kesten
Paulinshofberg

Bernkastel
Doktor
Graben
Badstube
Lay
Schwanen
Bratenhöfchen
Schlossberg

Graach
Himmelreich
Josephshof
Abtsberg
Domprobst

Wehlen
Sonnenuhr
Lay

Zeltingen
Himmelreich
Deutschherrenberg
Schlossberg
Kirchpfad

Uerzig
Würgarten

Erden
Treppchen

RHEINGAU

Bingen
Scharlachberg

Rüdesheim
Berg Bronnen
Berg Burgweg
Berg Roseneck
Berg Schlossberg
Berg Rottland
Berg Lay
Klosterkiesel

Johannisberg
Erntebringer
Schloss Johannisberg
Hölle, Klaus

Winkel
Hasensprung
Schloss Vollrads

Oestrich
Doosberg
Lenchen

Hattenheim
Steinberg
Wisselbrunn
Nussbrunnen
Mannberg

Hallgarten
Deutelsberg
Jungfer
Schönhell

Kiedrich
Wasserose
Sandgrube
Grafenberg

Erbach
Markobrunn

Rauenthal
Baiken
Gehrn
Herberg
Rotherberg
Wulfen
Wieshell

Hochheim
Domdechaney
Kirchenstuck
Königin Victoria Berg

RHEINHESSEN

Nackenheim
Rothenberg
Engelsberg

Nierstein
Rehbach
Orbel
Hipping
Auflangen
Fläschenhahl
Gluck
Olberg

Oppenheim
Sackträger
Kreuz
Goldberg
Reisekahr

PALATINATE

Wachenheim
Goldbächel
Gerumpel

Forst
Kirchenstuck
Jesuitengarten
Ungeheuer

Deidesheim
Grainhübel
Hohenmorgen
Leinhöhle
Kieselberg

NORTHERN
CALIFORNIA

Coast Range

Russian River

Healdsburg

Korbel *Stony Hill* *Hanns Kornell*
Heitz *Souverain*
St Helena *Charles Krug*
Louis Martini
Santa
Rosa *Inglenook* *Beaulieu*

Sacramento

Sacramento

Mayacamas
Christian Bros.
Sebastiani
Sonoma Napa
Buena Vista

Vallejo

San Pablo Bay

Richmond

Berkeley

Oakland

San Francisco Bay

San Francisco

Livermore *Concannon*
Wente Bros.
Cresta Blanca

Weibel

San
Mateo

San Jose

Wineries ∴

*Some of the finest
Wineries are named
in Red*

Paul Masson
SANTA
CLARA
COUNTY *Los
Gatos* *Almaden*

SAN BENITO
COUN

0   20 Miles

SOUTH-EAST
AUSTRALIA

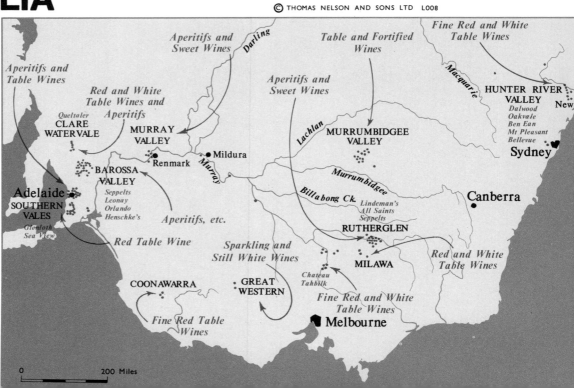

*Aperitifs and
Sweet Wines* Darling

*Table and Fortified
Wines*

*Fine Red and White
Table Wines*

*Aperitifs and
Table Wines*

*Red and White
Table Wines and
Aperitifs*

*Aperitifs and
Sweet Wines*

Macquarie

HUNTER RIVER
VALLEY New

Queltaler
CLARE
WATERVALE

MURRAY
VALLEY

Lachlan

MURRUMBIDGEE
VALLEY

*Dalwood
Oakvale
Ben Ean
Mt Pleasant
Bellevue*

Sydney

Mildura

Renmark

Murray

Murrumbidgee

Canberra

Adelaide
SOUTHERN
VALES BAROSSA
VALLEY
*Seppelts
Leonay
Orlando
Henschke's*

*Glenloth
Sea View*

Aperitifs, etc.

Billabong Ck. *Lindeman's
All Saints
Seppelts*
RUTHERGLEN

*Red and White
Table Wines*

Red Table Wine

*Sparkling and
Still White Wines*

MILAWA

COONAWARRA GREAT
WESTERN *Chateau
Tahbilk*

*Fine Red and White
Table Wines*

*Fine Red Table
Wines*

Melbourne

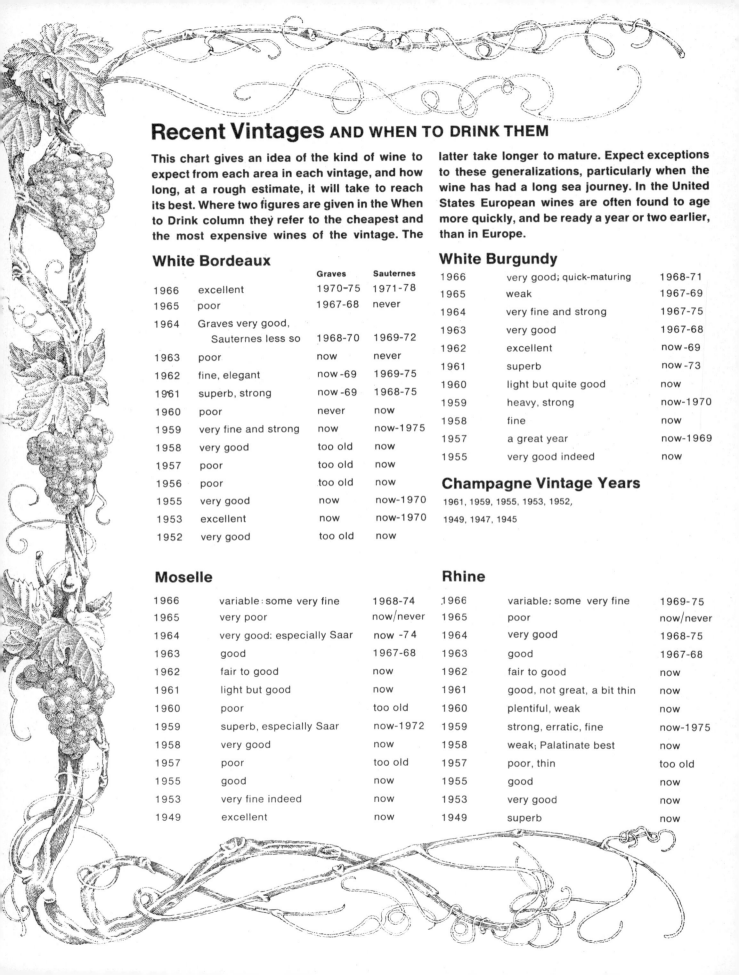

Recent Vintages AND WHEN TO DRINK THEM

This chart gives an idea of the kind of wine to expect from each area in each vintage, and how long, at a rough estimate, it will take to reach its best. Where two figures are given in the When to Drink column they refer to the cheapest and the most expensive wines of the vintage. The latter take longer to mature. Expect exceptions to these generalizations, particularly when the wine has had a long sea journey. In the United States European wines are often found to age more quickly, and be ready a year or two earlier, than in Europe.

White Bordeaux

		Graves	Sauternes
1966	excellent	1970-75	1971-78
1965	poor	1967-68	never
1964	Graves very good, Sauternes less so	1968-70	1969-72
1963	poor	now	never
1962	fine, elegant	now-69	1969-75
1961	superb, strong	now-69	1968-75
1960	poor	never	now
1959	very fine and strong	now	now-1975
1958	very good	too old	now
1957	poor	too old	now
1956	poor	too old	now
1955	very good	now	now-1970
1953	excellent	now	now-1970
1952	very good	too old	now

White Burgundy

1966	very good; quick-maturing	1968-71
1965	weak	1967-69
1964	very fine and strong	1967-75
1963	very good	1967-68
1962	excellent	now-69
1961	superb	now-73
1960	light but quite good	now
1959	heavy, strong	now-1970
1958	fine	now
1957	a great year	now-1969
1955	very good indeed	now

Champagne Vintage Years

1961, 1959, 1955, 1953, 1952,

1949, 1947, 1945

Moselle

1966	variable: some very fine	1968-74
1965	very poor	now/never
1964	very good: especially Saar	now-74
1963	good	1967-68
1962	fair to good	now
1961	light but good	now
1960	poor	too old
1959	superb, especially Saar	now-1972
1958	very good	now
1957	poor	too old
1955	good	now
1953	very fine indeed	now
1949	excellent	now

Rhine

1966	variable: some very fine	1969-75
1965	poor	now/never
1964	very good	1968-75
1963	good	1967-68
1962	fair to good	now
1961	good, not great, a bit thin	now
1960	plentiful, weak	now
1959	strong, erratic, fine	now-1975
1958	weak; Palatinate best	now
1957	poor, thin	too old
1955	good	now
1953	very good	now
1949	superb	now